ISLAMIZATION
AND
NATIVE RELIGION
IN THE
GOLDEN HORDE

HERMENEUTICS: STUDIES IN THE HISTORY OF RELIGIONS

Kees W. Bolle, Editor

Richard Marks, The Image of Bar Kokhba in Traditional Jewish Literature: False Messiah and National Hero

Joanne Punzo Waghorne, The Raja's Magic Clothes: Re-Visioning Kingship and Divinity in England's India

Devin DeWeese, Islamization and Native Religion in the Golden Horde: Baba Tükles and Conversion to Islam in Historical and Epic Tradition

Devin DeWeese

ISLAMIZATION AND NATIVE RELIGION IN THE GOLDEN HORDE

Baba Tükles and Conversion to Islam in Historical and Epic Tradition

The Pennsylvania State University Press
University Park, Pennsylvania

This publication has been supported by the National Endowment for the Humanities, a federal agency which supports the study of such fields as history, philosophy, literature, and languages.

Library of Congress Cataloging-in-Publication Data

DeWeese, Devin A., 1956–
Islamization and native religion in the Golden Horde: Baba Tükles and conversion to Islam in historical and epic tradition / Devin DeWeese.

p. cm.—(Hermeneutics, studies in the history of religions)
Includes bibliographical references (p.) and index.
ISBN 0-271-01072-X (alk. paper).—ISBN 0-271-01073-8 (pbk.)
1. Islam—Soviet Central Asia—History. 2. Mongols—Religion—History.
I.Title. II. Series: Hermeneutics, studies in the history of religions (1980–)
BP63.A4S6644 1994
297'.0958'0902—dc20

93-18488
CIP

Printed in the United States of America

Published by The Pennsylvania State University Press,
University Park, PA 16802-1003

It is the policy of The Pennsylvania State University Press to use acid-free paper for the first printing of all clothbound books. Publications on uncoated stock satisfy the minimum requirements of American National Standard for Information Sciences—Permanence of Paper for Printed Library Materials, ANSI Z39.48–1984.

For Sandy

Et miror quis diabolus portavit illuc legem Machometi...

—William of Rubruck, 1255

...and so those [Tatar] infidels have taken possession of the Northern Country. And since they have taken control of it they have not forced change upon the Community of this [final] Prophet, nor do they order the people to alter their religion; for there is no religion among them that requires this. Thus the people of this Community remain in their country as they were, except that dominion alone has departed from them. So there is benefit in those infidels for the Community of this Prophet (may God bless and keep him); and this is so because *they have no religion that is incompatible with the religion of this Community*, and their intermingling with this Community is what is inducing [those infidels] to enter into it. And so, after all, they are reckoned among its people, and lands of other infidels are being added to those countries they have already conquered. Therefore, in the end, the lands of this Community have expanded. . .

—Ibn an–Nafīs, 1270

Among the instruments of Muhammadan propaganda at the present time, it is interesting to note the large place taken by the folk-songs of the Kirghiz, in which, interwoven with tale and legend, the main truths of Islam make their way into the hearts of the common people.

—T. W. Arnold, *The Preaching of Islam*, 1896

Contents

List of Tables ix
Acknowledgments xi
Abbreviations xv
Introduction 3

1 The Religious Environment: Worldview, Ritual, and Communal Status 17
Islam and Conversion 17
Indigenous Religion in Traditional Inner Asia 27
Islamization in Inner Asia 51

2 The Historical Setting: Baba Tükles and the Conversion of Özbek Khan 67
Islamic Antecedents in Western Inner Asia 72
The Conversion of Özbek Khan 90
The Conversion of Özbek Khan in the Account of Ötemish Ḥājjī 142

3 Conversion Narrative and Religious Meaning, I: The Setting 159
Story, History, and Religious Meaning in Conversion Narrative 160
Debate and Contest 167
Ritual Intrusion and Displacement 179

4 Conversion Narrative and Religious Meaning, II: The Drama 231
Baba Tükles and Shamanic Narrative 232
The Oven-Pit: Ordeal, Sacrifice, and Sacred Enclosure in Forging a Community 243
Displacement and Assimilation 290

5 Baba Tükles in History and Genealogy 321
The Hero of the Conversion Narrative: Baba Tükles 323
Edigü and the Noghay Horde 336
Reworking the Account of Ötemish Ḥājjī: ʿAbd al-Ghaffār Qïrïmī in the Eighteenth Century 352
Making Sense of Diverse Traditions: A New Account from Khorezm in the Eighteenth Century 366
Baba Tükles and the Full Genealogy of Edigü: Tatar Historiography, Bukharan Hagiography, and Russian Heraldry 381

6 Baba Tükles in Epic Tradition and Folklore 409
The Epic Tale of *Idige* 411
Baba Tükles' Role in the Tale of *Idige* 420
Baba Tükles and the "Noghay Epic" 435
Baba Tükles as a "Nativized" Bringer of Islam 442

7 Baba Tükles and the Uses of Sacred Origins 491
Baba Tükles and Legends of Origin: Parallel Structures and Themes 492
The Mythic and Narrative Development of Baba Tükles: Reconstructions and Parallels 506
Religion and the Articulation of Communal Identity in Islamic Inner Asia 516

Appendix 1 Ötemish Ḥājjī's Account of the Conversion of Özbek Khan: Text 533

Appendix 2 Ötemish Ḥājjī's Account: Translation and Commentary 541

Appendix 3 An Eighteenth-Century Khorezmian Account of the Conversion of Özbek Khan: Text 567

Bibliography 575

Index 617

List of Tables

5.1. The Genealogy of Edigü and Baba Tükles According to Historical and Epic Accounts 386

5.2. Some Russian and Central Asian Genealogies Stemming from Edigü 388

Key to Map (page 425) and Table 6.1. Versions of the Idige Tale Featuring Baba Tükles 424

6.1. Narrative Elements in Versions of the Idige Tale Featuring Baba Tükles 426

7.1. Recurrent Motifs in Historical Legends of Origin and Tales of Baba Tükles 508

Acknowledgments

My work on this book in a sense dates back to the final weeks of 1983, when I first examined the lone accessible manuscript of Ötemish Ḥājjī's work in Tashkent and read and transcribed the conversion narrative; I returned to the narrative only in late 1987, for a conference paper, and since then a series of revisions, frequently interrupted by other projects, has produced the present study. As my thinking about this narrative and its implications developed, a number of friends and colleagues, too numerous to mention, helped and contributed to the final product, whether by reading earlier drafts, by answering specific inquiries, or by suggesting new directions to consider, in the course of wide-ranging discussions whose connection with the present work became evident only much later. My appreciation of how much I have profited from their insights removes any pretense that this study might be regarded as the product of my efforts exclusively.

I am especially indebted to Yuri Bregel, not only for his longstanding guidance and support, but for his interest in this particular project and his helpfulness in reading through several preliminary versions; many thanks are due also Larry Clark, who also read parts of several drafts and offered much-needed encouragement and guidance. Through conversations or correspondence, several colleagues have enriched my work on this study in important and substantive ways, whether in specific difficulties or in sharpening my research and analysis; my thanks go to Oleg Akimushkin, Gustav Bayerle, Peter Golden, Jo-Ann Gross, György Kara, Robert McChesney, Jürgen Paul, Nazif Shahrani, Denis Sinor, Maria Subtelny, Timur Beisembiev, and Uli Schamiloglu. Among my students, I am particularly grateful to Allen Frank, David Tyson, and Bill Wood, who aided me enormously in bibliographical matters and also raised or reinforced important elements of the arguments developed here. Needless to add, I alone am responsible for all errors and omissions in the book, and for the views and arguments sustained in it.

I am also greatly indebted to the friends and colleagues who have helped me so unstintingly during my research trips abroad to Central Asia and India. Special thanks are due my colleagues who made my work at the Institute of Oriental Studies in Tashkent so fruitful during my two visits, in particular Dr. Buri Akhmedov, Dr. Dilorom Iusupova, Dr. Muzaffar Khairullaev, Dr. Qivamutdin Munirov, Dr. Asom Urunbaev, Dr. Orif Usmon, and the late Dr. Elena Poliakova; the Institute also kindly provided me with a microfilm of Ötemish Ḥājjī's work, which greatly facilitated my research. I am also grateful to Dr. Botirbek Hasanov for his aid during my work at the Institute of Manuscripts in Tashkent, and to Dr. Bakhtiyar Nazarov for his considerable help in arranging my second trip to Central Asia. My work in India, to some extent less relevant to the present study, nevertheless contributed in important ways: special thanks go to Mr. N. B. Inamdar at Osmania University in Hyderabad; Dr. A. R. Bidar and Mr. Atiqur Rahman at the Khuda Bakhsh library in Patna; Mr. Akbar Ali Khan Arshizadah of the Raza Library in Rampur; and Dr. Awsaf Ali of the Indian Institute of Islamic Studies in New Delhi.

My initial trip to Tashkent in 1983–84 was made possible by a grant from the International Research and Exchanges Board; a second trip in 1991 was funded by grants from IREX and the American Philosophical Society. For materials uncovered in Indian collections I am grateful to the Indo-American Fellowship Program of the Council for International Exchange of Scholars, which funded my work in India during the summer of 1988. Fellowship support from the National Endowment for the Humanities facilitated completion of this work as well as the preparation of further studies devoted to other conversion narratives not explored in depth here.

Finally, I wish to thank the Staatsbibliothek zu Berlin-Preussischer Kulturbesitz, Orientabteilung, which provided a microfilm of the manuscript that turned out to include the important account of Nūrullāh Khorezmī.

As this book was well into production, I received in April 1993 a copy of the publication, announced in 1990 (see Chapter 2, note 185), of the Tashkent manuscript of Ötemish Ḥājjī's work, prepared by the late V. P. Iudin (*Utemish-khadzhi: Chingiz-name. Faksimile, perevod, transkriptsiia, tekstologicheskie primechaniia, issledovanie V. P. Iudina; Podgotovila k izdaniiu Iu. G. Baranova; Kommentarii i ukazateli M. Kh. Abuseitovoi* [Alma-Ata: Gylym, 1992]). The work contains Iudin's Russian translation and transcription (into the Cyrillic script as adapted for the modern Qazaq literary language in Soviet times) of the entire text, facsimiles of the manuscript, textological notes, and indexes prepared by M. Kh. Abuseitova; it includes also a reprint of Iudin's article, "Ordy: belaia, siniaia, seraia, zolotaia . . ." (cited in Chapter 2), as well as three previously unpublished studies by Iudin based on Ötemish Ḥājjī's work, a brief introduction by Iudin's wife, Iu. G. Baranova, and a foreword by the editor-in-chief, B. A. Akhmedov.

Iudin devoted no special attention to the conversion narrative that is our central focus here; his understanding of the text is for the most part in accord with my own interpretation, with two substantive exceptions: (1) he treats the term I have taken as representing the word "*qoruq*" differently, but unfortunately gives no explanation for his reading; and (2) he offers a somewhat different understanding of the drinking ceremony described in the narrative, one that is entirely plausible and perhaps preferable to my own. However, Iudin's textological notes, as published, are far from complete, dealing for the most part only with textual emendations rather than lexico-semantic questions, and it appears that the materials he left at his death may likewise offer few clues as to his understanding of particular terms; Baranova's introduction mentions a lexicon prepared for the text by Iudin, apparently with attention to syntax and usage, but this remains unpublished, and in any case it is usually only from his translation that we may judge how he interpreted a given term. In all fairness, however, Iudin has dealt with the entire text, and not merely the small part of it discussed here.

I have sought, for the present work, to incorporate Iudin's interpretation of these two problematic issues, and of other textual points he raises, in my notes to the text and full translation of the conversion narrative (Appendixes 1 and 2), but with few exceptions I have not added further notes in Chapter 2 regarding his analysis of the work as a whole or his use of the work as a historical source; of special interest in this regard is his discussion of the tradition of "steppe oral historiography" (pp. 57–75), which includes a discussion of several names that figure in Ötemish Ḥājjī's account of Özbek Khan's rise to power.

Iudin worked, of course, as have most researchers, without access to the Istanbul manuscript of Ötemish Ḥājjī's work; unfortunately he was also unable to consult two published works useful in analyzing the text (ʿAbd al-Ghaffār Qïrïmī's history, based in part on Ötemish Ḥājjī's work, and the study of Mustafa Kafalı, who was able to consult the Istanbul manuscript), and both the philological analysis included in the published work, and the historical commentary as well, are far from exhaustive and in general are disappointing. This new publication is thus by no means the final word on Ötemish Ḥājjī's work. Nevertheless, Iudin's efforts, and those of his colleagues who prepared his work for publication, promise to make Ötemish Ḥājjī's work widely accessible to scholars for the first time and, as such, mark a significant step forward in the study and appreciation of this remarkable source.

Abbreviations

AEH	*Acta Ethnographica Academiae Scientiarum Hungaricae*
AEMA	*Archivum Eurasiae Medii Aevi*
AN	Akademiia Nauk
BSO(A)S	*Bulletin of the School of Oriental (and African) Studies*
CAJ	*Central Asiatic Journal*
CHIr	*Cambridge History of Iran*
ED	(Clauson, see Bibliography)
EI[1], *EI*[2]	*Encyclopaedia of Islam*, 1st & 2nd eds.
EIr	*Encyclopaedia Iranica*
ERE	*Encyclopedia of Religion and Ethics*
GAL(S)	Carl Brockelmann, *Geschichte der arabischen Litteratur (& Supplement)* (Leiden: E. J. Brill, 1937–42 [Suppl.], 1943–49 [revised editions of vols. 1–2])

GRVL	Glavnaia Redaktsiia Vostochnoi Literatury (Moscow)
HJAS	*Harvard Journal of Asiatic Studies*
HUS	*Harvard Ukrainian Studies*
İA	*İslam Ansiklopedisi*
IOAIÈ	*Izvestiia Obshchestva arkheologii, istorii, i ètnografii pri Imperatorskom Kazanskom universitete*
IVAN Uz	Institut vostokovedeniia Akademii nauk Uzbekistana (formerly IVAN Uzbekskoi SSR)
Izd-vo	Izdatel'stvo [Publisher]
JA	*Journal asiatique*
JAH	*Journal of Asian History*
JAOS	*Journal of the American Oriental Society*
JRAS	*Journal of the Royal Asiatic Society*
KCsA	*Kőrösi Csoma Archivum*
KSz	*Keleti Szemle*
LOIVAN	Leningradskoe otdelenie Instituta vostokovedeniia AN SSSR (Now Peterburgskii filial Instituta vostokovedeniia Rossiiskoi Akadamii nauk)
PIA	*Papers on Inner Asia*
PIAC	Permanent International Altaistic Conference
Storey, *PL*	C. A. Storey, *Persian Literature; A Bio-bibliographical Survey* (London: Luzac, 1927–)

Storey-Bregel', *PL*	Ch. A. Stori, *Persidskaia literatura; Bio-bibliograficheskii obzor*, ed. & tr. Iu. È. Bregel'; 3 vols. (Moscow: GRVL, 1972)
PSRL	*Polnoe sobranie russkikh letopisei*
REI	*Revue des études islamiques*
RHR	*Revue de l'histoire des religions*
SAA	*Soviet Anthropology and Archeology*
SÈ	*Sovetskaia ètnografiia*
Sochineniia	(Bartol'd, see Bibliography)
SPb	*St. Petersburg*
SVR	*Sobranie vostochnykh rukopisei Instituta vostokovedeniia AN UzSSR*
Tiz	(Tizengauzen, see Bibliography)
TMEN	(Doerfer, see Bibliography)
TVOIRAO	*Trudy vostochnago otdeleniia Imperatorskago Russkago Arkheologicheskago Obshchestva*
UAJ	*Ural-Altaische Jahrbücher*
WZKM	*Wiener Zeitschrift für die Kunde des Morgenlandes*
ZVOIRAO	*Zapiski vostochnago otdeleniia Imperatorskago Russkago Arkheologicheskago Obshchestva*
ZDMG	*Zeitschrift der Deutsche Morgenländische Gesellschaft*
ZAS	*Zentralasiatische Studien*

ISLAMIZATION
AND
NATIVE RELIGION
IN THE
GOLDEN HORDE

Introduction

In 1253, the Franciscan friar William of Rubruck encountered Muslims where he may well not have expected, and certainly did not wish, to find any. Rubruck was acquainted with the Islamic world, having spent considerable time in the Middle East in the course of the French king Louis IX's crusade in Egypt and Palestine; but in 1253 he was traveling, at Louis' behest, through the lands of the Mongol khan Batu in what was to become known as the Golden Horde, on his way to the court of the Mongol Great Khan, Möngke. It is possible that even before his departure, the friar had heard reports of "Saracens" in Batu's realms from earlier travelers, but much of the world through which he journeyed was virtually unknown to his contemporaries. In any case, in his report to King Louis, completed most likely in 1255, Rubruck noted the presence of Islam and Muslims in the lands of the Golden Horde, including three noteworthy comments that at once evince his dismay at finding his own faith's chief rival there, and at the same time nicely encapsulate for us sentiments that have dominated popular and scholarly attitudes toward Islam in the Inner Asian world down to our times.

Of Berke, Batu's brother, whose accession to the throne in 1257 was to mark the first official "establishment" of Islam in a Mongol state, Rubruck wrote, "he makes himself out to be a Saracen";[1] and like Rubruck, a host of

1. Peter Jackson, tr., *The Mission of Friar William of Rubruck: His Journey to the Court of the Great Khan Möngke, 1253–1255* (London: The Hakluyt Society, 1990), p. 127 and n. 2; cf. the translation "by a nun of Stanbrook Abbey" in Christopher Dawson, ed., *The Mongol Mission* (London: Sheed and Ward, 1955), p. 124: ". . . he pretends to be a Saracen." For the text, see Anastasius Van den Wyngaert, ed., *Sinica Franciscana*, I: *Itinera et relationes fratrum minorum saeculi XIII et XIV* (Quaracchi-Florence, 1929), p. 209: *Est alius qui dicitur Berca, frater Baatu . . . et ille facit se sarracenum, et non permittit in curia sua comedi carnes porcinas.*

Western travelers, observers, and scholars, doubting the "seriousness" of Muslims in this "exotic" world, have made an assumption of "light" or "nominal" Islamization a cardinal feature of most approaches to Islam in Inner Asia.

Of the Bulghars of the Volga, whose Inner Asian state had adopted Islam already in the tenth century but was a victim of the Mongol advance in 1237, Rubruck complained that they "are the very worst kind of Saracens, clinging more firmly to the law of Mohammed than any others";[2] and like Rubruck a similar host of Western observers, when the error of dismissing Islam there as merely superficial became clear, has resorted to dismissing the "quality" of Islam in Inner Asia, falling back on the all-too-familiar Western motif of fanatical Islam.

And regarding the same Bulghars, whose land was held to be not far from the fabled "Land of Darkness" and lay, as Rubruck noted, another five days' journey north of Batu's encampment, the friar gave voice to an underlying bewilderment that unfortunately has not been much improved upon in more recent treatments of the *spread* of Islam in Inner Asia: "I wonder," he wrote, "what devil carried the law of Machomet there."[3]

Much could be written, and ought to be, about the misconceptions and inappropriate assumptions about Islam among Inner Asian peoples, both in history and at present. In a sense a persistent fear and hostility toward Islam that color both scholarly and popular attitudes in the West, combined with general unfamiliarity with the Inner Asian world, have rendered Islam in Inner Asia the focus of Western hopes (that Inner Asian peoples are not *very* Muslim) and fears (that they are as fanatical as all Muslims, after all), both resting on the same general bewilderment about the origins, history, and significance of Islam in Inner Asia, as reflected in Friar William's comments.[4]

Our aim here, however, is not to discuss the ways in which specialists on Inner Asia, or on Islam, have continued to show their essential surprise

2. Dawson, *The Mongol Mission* , p. 126; tr. Jackson, p. 131; Wyngaert, p. 212: *Et illi Bulgari sunt pessimi sarraceni, fortius tenentes legem Machometi quam aliqui alii.*

3. Cf. Dawson, *The Mongol Mission* , p. 126; tr. Jackson, p. 131; Wyngaert, p. 212: *et miror quis diabolus portavit illuc legem Machometi.*

4. Here it is only worth noting that hostility toward Islam is more often the "culprit" in these misconceptions than is hostility toward Inner Asian peoples, and that such misconceptions are all too frequent among specialists on Inner Asia or on particular Inner Asian peoples who are, for quite valid reasons, eager to highlight the distinctive Inner Asian components of the civilization of Inner Asia, but in so doing downplay or dismiss or complain about the role of Islam; naturally, the "debate" about the relative roles of Islamic and indigenous Inner Asian cultural elements has taken on a substantial load of extraneous baggage in successive campaigns by Soviets and nationalists to claim and co-opt the "national heritage" of Inner Asian peoples.

and bewilderment upon finding Muslims in Inner Asia, through their contradictory dismissals of Islam there as either ungenuine or uncivilized; suffice it to say that such characterizations still dominate even contemporary press accounts of present-day Muslim peoples of the former Soviet Union. Rather, I would like to consider "what devils" brought Islam to Inner Asia, by paying attention to accounts of Islam's introduction and spread among Inner Asian peoples as far removed from the sympathies evident in Rubruck's remark (and most scholarly accounts today as well) as possible: accounts created and transmitted and adjusted among the Muslim peoples of Inner Asia themselves—that is, among communities for whom those who brought Islam are not devils, but saints. More precisely, the present work is a study of one conversion narrative and its many echoes, in the context of the religious issues it was evidently designed to address, and above all in the context of one central character in the conversion drama and the ways this character resonated for subsequent generations.

Elements of the narrative in question must have developed already during or soon after the reign of the Mongol ruler whose conversion it recounted, Özbek Khan of the Golden Horde (r. 1313–1341). It is not until the middle of the sixteenth century, however, that we find a well-developed version of the narrative set down in a written form that survives to this day, in a rare and little-studied work from Central Asia known as the *Tārīkh-i Dūst Sulṭān*, written by a certain Ötemish Ḥājjī; and it is this version—the earliest to which we can have access—that we must adopt as our basis both for envisioning the religious import of the narrative in the two centuries between the "events" it recounts and its reduction to written form, and for evaluating later developments of the tale or its elements in written and oral venues.

That this conversion narrative survived, with much of the content reflected in our earliest written form intact, at least down to the early twentieth century is confirmed by scanty, but convincing, evidence, thus attesting to the continuing power of the story as a whole. More important, perhaps, the central character in the conversion narrative—an enigmatic figure called Baba Tükles—was the object of a truly remarkable range of narrative elaboration, popular devotion, genealogical appropriation, and saintly and shamanic invocation, among the peoples of the western half of the Inner Asian world.

In particular, the account in question casts new light on the origins of this "Baba Tükles," whose name is well known from semi-historical and epic narratives produced among the peoples of the Golden Horde. Those narratives suggest, and the new account confirms, that Baba Tükles was known first as a bearer of Islam who brought the new religion to the Golden Horde, but that his "Islamizing" role was assimilated in popular memory with the roles of royal ancestor and mythic progenitor. This assimilation itself, and in particular the *direction* of assimilation, argues for a much closer link between Islamization and "ethnic" identity than has previously been acknowledged for Inner Asian peoples; the account in question helps to reveal the essential equivalence of conversion narratives and legends of origin, both recounting the essentially sacred act of "founding" a community and defining it in fundamentally religious terms. For what emerges in considering the various stages of Baba Tükles' development from "Islamizer" to "nation former" to "mythic ancestor" is a clear pattern linking Islam with indigenous Inner Asian values—most important, with Inner Asian conceptions and formulations whereby the origin and legitimacy of human communities are sacralized.

The strange and powerful figure of Baba Tükles was hailed as the bringer of Islam to the fourteenth-century Golden Horde; he was recalled as an Islamizing ruler among the twentieth-century Noghays of the North Caucasus; he was credited with "creating," in effect, a number of Inner Asian peoples ranging from the Uzbeks to the Qalmïqs; he was claimed as an ancestor by a startling array of "Inner Asian" nobility ranging from the sixteenth-century rulers of the Noghay horde, to Sufi shaykhs in seventeenth-century Bukhārā, to Russian aristocrats in twentieth-century America; he was turned into a mythic ancestor and patron spirit in an oral epic cherished among perhaps more Turkic-speaking peoples than any other, including Noghays, Tatars, Bashkirs, Qaraqalpaqs, Qazaqs, and Uzbeks; he was revered as a saint nearly as widely, with shrines created for him from Astrakhan to Bashkiria to southern Kazakhstan; and as late as the 1980s, he was invoked as a tutelary ancestral spirit by Qazaq shamans, as one of the leading Muslim saints incorporated into Inner Asian shamanic performance.

The conversion narrative focused on Baba Tükles' activity reflects oral accounts produced from the fourteenth century to the twentieth and popular among the Muslim peoples of Central and Inner Asia—that is, among peoples who in creating and transmitting such narratives appear to have been consciously or unconsciously asserting the centrality of Islam in their own conceptions of communal origin, identity, and solidarity. Perhaps more important, the extant forms of these popular tales, dependant finally upon the conversion narrative that is the centerpiece of the present study, were clearly significant markers of both popular and learned attitudes. They formed a store of common "historical" knowledge tapped by popular bards, tribal and village elders, and court historians; they were not only "preserved" as inherited tradition, but were "kept alive" in a real sense by being altered and updated to reflect changing communal concerns and aspirations.

In this way, the conversion narrative that provides the basis for the present study, like other conversion narratives from Inner Asia whose analysis must await a later setting, offers invaluable insights into the dynamics of Inner Asian peoples' encounters with Islam, and, what is perhaps more significant, adds to the sources at our disposal for understanding those encounters a hitherto ignored or undervalued dimension: the voices of Inner Asian peoples themselves. Such an effort to listen to indigenous voices not only gives us insight into "what devils" brought Islam to Inner Asia and into why and how those bearers of Islam became saints revered among Inner Asian peoples; it also serves, ultimately, to undermine those larger misconceptions about Islam in Inner Asia.

A Note on "Inner Asia"

It may be appropriate to clarify what is meant by "Inner Asia" here in the context of Islamization, since the cultural and historical referents of the term "Inner Asia" remain unfamiliar even to many specialists in the civilizations that border the Inner Asian world. As a geographical term "Inner Asia" refers to the interior "heartland" of the Eurasian landmass, corresponding to the present-day political units of Mongolia, Tibet and Xinjiang in the People's Republic of China, what until recently were the "Soviet" republics of Central Asia, and substantial portions of Siberia, as well as of European Russia, within the Russian Federation. Today it hardly needs to be mentioned that in considering the Islamization of Inner Asia, we are in effect seeking to understand one element, and, I would argue, an often decisive one, among the distinctive historical processes and cultural traditions that gave the so-called Muslim republics of the former Soviet Union their "independence" from Moscow long before this was reflected politically.

The region comprises in the main the three ecological zones, from north to south, of forest, steppe, and desert; its primary cultural referents are the pastoral nomadic civilizations of the steppe regions, and the mutual interactions of those civilizations with the commercial and agricultural centers of the southern desert zone, and with the peoples of the vast forest belt to the north. When defined in such cultural terms Inner Asia's borders have expanded and contracted through history.

Inner Asia includes a number of ethno-cultural regions, which have enough in common to belong clearly to "Inner Asia," but are characterized by distinctive political, ethnic, and cultural features (often the result of specific patterns of interaction with outlying peoples) that set them apart from one another within the Inner Asian sphere; the "borders" of these regions too have shifted historically, but among the constants may be mentioned eastern Mongolia and Manchuria on the Chinese frontiers, the Mongol steppe and Jungharia, Tibet, Islamic Central Asia (including the steppes of present-day Kazakhstan, with East Turkistan added as a distinctive component in the fifteenth century), and the Volga-Ural basin. Islamization has "happened" in all three "ecological" regions of the Inner Asian world, and in several of these cultural regions, but only in the western half of Inner Asia, with Islam's chief "competitor," Buddhism, prevailing in the east.

In political terms, Inner Asia's history is dominated by the periodic steppe-based nomadic empires, but includes also the local polities of hunting and trading communities in the forest zone, and small-scale city-states or regional "kingdoms" of the desert region. Islamization has "happened" in each of these contexts as well, and the history of the spread of Islam in Inner Asia thus comprises the Arab conquest of the city-states of sedentary Central Asia and the subsequent transformation of the entire region into a major center of Islamic civilization, as well as the penetration of Islam into the Inner Asian steppe north of sedentary Central Asia; it includes the assimilation of Inner Asian Turks through the Islamic system of military slaves, through "tribal conversion" (e.g., the Seljüks), and through "imperial" conversion (e.g., the Qarakhanids); it includes the key era of the establishment of Islam among the western successor states of the Mongol empire from the thirteenth century to the fifteenth, a period often decisive for the emergence of ethnic groupings (or at least ethnonyms) more recognizable in contemporary terms; and it includes the spread of Islam among peoples of the steppe and forest zones, both in Siberia and in the Volga-Ural region, even during Russian imperial rule, a process continuing down to the early twentieth century and involving not only Turkic peoples, but Finno-Ugric groups as well.

The conversion narrative explored here represents one of the three broad areal spheres of Islamic culture in Inner Asia (Central Asia proper, the Volga-Ural region, and East Turkistan); its impact, however, was even more widespread, through its echoes in popular tales circulated for centuries throughout western Inner Asia, from the Crimea to Siberia and from Kazan to Khorezm.

Aims, Assumptions, and Approaches

The motivation for examining this narrative and its echoes stems in part from the misconceptions alluded to above regarding the character of Islam in this Inner Asian world. In particular, I would highlight two issues underlying our explorations in this study:

First, the lack of any substantial and serious study of Islamization in Inner Asia, combined with the relative neglect of the problem of conversion in Islamic studies in general, has produced in those scholarly books and articles that cannot avoid at least touching upon the impact of Islam in Inner Asia a litany of uncritically accepted pronouncements on Islamization, with a standard theme: Islam "sat lightly" upon the Inner Asian nomad, whose "conversion" was in name only and failed to have any serious impact on his daily life or consciousness. Such a view, that Islamization in effect did not matter, is not only clearly flawed by a remarkable misunderstanding both of the nature of Islam and of the indigenous religious conceptions that preceded Islamization, but is at the same time patently uninformed by any of the conceptual tools developed over the last century for the humanities and social sciences by the field of *Religionswissenschaft*. A more balanced consideration of the issue allows us to counter both the prevailing view and the prevailing "approach" by suggesting that Islamization *did* matter, and in a fundamental way that was both transformative and at the same time characteristically attuned to pre-Islamic traditions. With this basic assumption we may examine the conversion tale and its echoes as examples of fundamentally religious discourse that illustrate the reinforcement and recasting of deeply held values through the encounter with Islam and evince a native understanding of sacred communal origins as well as a conscious, "assertive" evocation of communal solidarity.

Second, the interplay of religious and national/ethnic identities among the traditionally Muslim peoples of the former Soviet Union—the heirs of the "Islamized" peoples of Inner Asia—has long been discussed by students of contemporary Soviet and Central Asian affairs, and has taken on even more compelling interest in the era of *glasnost'*, resurgent nationalism, and now independence, as these peoples reassert their right to define their own historical identities. This same issue, however, has never been seriously examined in its historical context, as the outgrowth of traditional conceptions among the peoples of Central Asia regarding how, when, where, and by whose influence they became Muslims and thereby took on a new communal identity; rather, "explanations" of the varying degrees of "Islamic consciousness" embedded in national feeling have rarely looked further than nineteenth-century descriptions, and, more important, have never "listened" to indigenous accounts of intertwining religious and ethnic identities.

It is the critical value of such indigenous accounts of conversion that must be stressed here, for I would argue that our *only* access to the *meaning* of conversion for those peoples lies in such narrative responses. "Conversion" is inevitably a process of such considerable psychological and social complexity that even a thorough reconstruction of the historical setting and events that occurred, and even a precise description of "what happened" could not convey the *significance* of the conversion understood and felt, religiously, by the adherents of the new faith and their communal heirs. The "conversion" happened, and had historical antecedents and consequences, but in and of itself was at the same time beyond the ken of historical reconstructions, and yet important and central enough for those who felt themselves intimately connected with it that it had to be talked about and recounted and related; in those recountings we find clues to what was regarded as important and socially meaningful in the conversion.

Beyond the general aims and assumptions regarding what may be learned from listening to these native voices, the specific hypotheses of the present study, based in part upon the preliminary analysis of a number of other conversion narratives in addition to the one that serves as the point of departure here, are as follows:

1. Conversion narratives are themselves central elements in the process of Islamization, as the community *articulates* its Islamicness and either stresses its break with the past or finds common ground with pre-Islamic traditions or values.

2. Conversion narratives are assimilable, in structure, content, and function, with the "legends of origin" reasonably well known among Inner Asian peoples telling of the creation of the world and/or of the "first man": in structure because they follow similar narrative patterns as employed in legends of origin; in content because they frequently employ specific symbols and narrative elements strikingly similar to those found in legends of origin; and in function because, like legends of origin, they appear to have been asserted and "rehearsed" as a means of declaring the sacral integrity of a particular collectivity on the basis of identity in origin.
3. For this reason we often find development of these narratives in two apparently opposite directions: the "Islamization" of indigenous mythic creation narratives, and the assimilation of figures and events associated with Islamization to sacred figures and events in pre-Islamic traditions (as we will see, it is the later epic reworkings of elements in the "original" conversion narrative that most closely parallel communal legends of origin, but echoes of the themes evoked in such legends may be found also in our earliest version of the conversion narrative itself).
4. The conversion narratives' capacity to provide a vision of communal integrity prompts us in turn to ask for what further specific ends these articulations of Muslim status were used beyond the essential assertion of sacred values and communal self-conception. In this instance we find at least two of particular interest: they are used (a) to support claims of political legitimacy through religious charisma, and (b) to lend prestige and authority to religiously defined subcommunities that could claim credit for the conversion recounted in a given narrative (certain conversion narratives clearly originated among Sufi groups who came to be regarded as the principal forces in Islamization).
5. As the equivalent of "legends of origin" articulating a community's understanding of its identity, conversion narratives express the centrality of conversion to Islam in the formation of a particular tribal, ethnic, or "national" community.
6. Narratives of Islamization, as well as conversion narratives recounting the establishment of other religions, are further illustrative of the patterns of interaction between other "world religions" and indigenous Inner Asian traditions, and among those world religions in the Inner Asian setting.

Our purpose in the present work is thus to analyze the varied complex of religious meaning conveyed by the narratives about Baba Tükles, as well as the further uses of elements from that complex, from the perspective of Islam and from that of pre-Islamic religious values, with special attention to the frequent assimilation of the two. Our interest in the narrative and its echoes is as a source not for history per se, but for religious values in general, and more to the point, *religious ways of comprehending and imagining the significance of conversion and its meaning for communal identity*. We will necessarily discuss sources that properly belong to the realms of history, literature, and folklore, but our approach is not limited to one or all of these specific disciplines; rather, our aim is to focus on the *religious meaning* conveyed in or illustrated by the sources, in order to understand how Islamization was understood and articulated in terms of both native and "Islamizing" conceptions of what is sacred in human life and community.

In particular, this study will intentionally fall short of an exhaustive history of Islam and Islamization in Inner Asia; our concern here is not "what happened," but "what people say happened," in particular, the people who consider themselves intimately connected in some way with the "reality," as they asserted it, of the conversion in question, and who repeatedly rehearsed and adapted the account of the conversion. We will *not* restrict or even concentrate our focus on any "historical facts" contained in the conversion narrative or in its later echoes; indeed, it is central to our working assumption that we would miss the point entirely were we to approach the narratives exclusively as "historical" sources to be mined for historical details. We will naturally attempt to discuss the historical settings in which the various stages, or styles, of the narrative transformations developed; but our focus is on the religious meaning revealed by the relationships between successive narrative developments, *not* the relationship between "historical reality" and the narrative tradition in part inspired by it.[5]

The argument advanced here with regard to the specific conversion narrative of immediate concern is quite simple; but inasmuch as presenting it depends upon discussing the conversion account itself (which, since it has not been studied before, requires full philological analysis) and upon introducing a wide array of material from relatively poorly

5. While it may be possible to reconstruct with some degree of accuracy the historical context and the actual "events" that accompanied the conversion of Özbek Khan to Islam, the limited value of such an approach must be acknowledged. If we were to see only the events (if even that were possible) but miss the "self-described" significance, we would have possibly missed something of historical importance; but we would have unquestionably missed something of critical value for understanding the development of narrative responses to the conversion and the way those responses reflect and influence conceptions of individual and communal identity.

known historical and epic traditions of Inner Asia, it may be useful to summarize it here as follows. The figure (Baba Tükles) to whom is ascribed, in an early narrative, the pivotal role in converting Özbek Khan to Islam became also a pivotal figure in the genealogical "myth" that lent political legitimacy and religious sanction to the Noghay horde, one of the major tribal confederations that emerged from the disintegration of the Golden Horde; as such this figure's role was preserved in the historical tradition of the Golden Horde's successor states and, what is for us more significant, in the epic and folkloric tradition preserved among the peoples of the former Jöchid *ulus*. In that epic tradition, reflecting both formulaic transmission and creative innovation among generations of bards in western Inner Asia, are found clear signs of the implicit equivalence, among the bards as well as their audiences, of the roles of "Islamizer" and "ancestor," each serving as the "founder" of a given community. And this equivalence serves to provide important, though hitherto unappreciated, insights into the subtle but unmistakable process whereby Islam was able to "fit into" and reinforce (rather than oppose) the basic Inner Asian religious values associated with community and with the centrality of human life in the communal context. Such insights, finally, suggest in turn not only a potentially fruitful perspective to adopt in attempting to understand the historical process of Islamization in Inner Asia; they suggest also the need for a reevaluation of the role of Islam, and of religious values and identifications in general, in providing unity and definition to particular Inner Asian communities even today.

Specifically, the identification of the "Islamizer" who becomes "Ancestor" is based upon the sixteenth-century account mentioned above, which offers us a clear picture of the earliest stage of the narrative traditions surrounding Baba Tükles, as well as confirmation of the initial focus of these traditions upon Islamization. We can in fact distinguish three stages, or rather styles, in the narratives about Baba Tükles produced from the fifteenth century to the twentieth: first, the story of his miraculous role in converting Özbek Khan to Islam, as preserved in Ötemish Ḥājjī's account but echoed in popular tales recorded as late as the 1920s; second, literary accounts in the Tatar historiographical tradition from the seventeenth and eighteenth centuries, which attempt to "historicize" Baba Tükles but retain his "Islamizing" role while stressing his ancestry of Edigü, regarded as the "founder" of the Noghay confederation; and third, oral tradition in the epic accounts of the hero Idige (a figure inspired by the historical Edigü), which recount Baba Tükles' ancestry of the hero and often reflect his association with Islamization, but in many cases also surround Baba Tükles with mythic themes drawn from indigenous, pre-Islamic Inner Asian religious traditions.

Herein we find the importance of Islamization, and of narratives recounting it, in the reshuffling of communal identities that has characterized much of Inner Asian history, in which political and social currents that appear as mass migrations and extinctions often mask a change in allegiances accompanied by the creation of a "national mythology" to explain and justify the newly formed group. Precisely such a reshuffling is the stuff of contemporary headlines as the peoples of the former Soviet Union reevaluate their identities, and understanding Islamization is critical for understanding that process: however much the impact and role of Islamization may have been attenuated during the past seventy-odd years, as a distinctly un-Islamic "confederative myth" was imposed upon the Muslim peoples of western Inner Asia, both the "substance" of Islamization's effects in Inner Asia, and the patterns of its evocation in national mythology-building are likely to continue to be instructive as we observe the emergence of new nations, and as these nations continue the process of defining themselves.

The Plan of This Study

With these goals and assumptions in mind we will consider the central conversion narrative and its resonance in its own time, and the later reworkings of its central character, within the following general plan. First, in an introductory essay, we will consider the general questions of what Islamization means or might mean and, on the assumption that Islam as a religious system is generally better known than the indigenous religious traditions of Inner Asian peoples, we will consider in broad outline the common, shared features of those traditions particularly relevant to the issue of Islamization, in order to set the stage for the religious "counterpoints" that follow through the rest of our discussion.

Next, we will focus more closely on the particular time and place that form the setting for our central conversion narrative, namely, the Mongol successor state of the Golden Horde in the early fourteenth century, noting the range of issues of relevance to the historical process of Islamization in this polity but considering in particular the available "historical" accounts on the "event" that is the subject of our conversion narrative, the "winning" of the ruler Özbek Khan to Islam. We will then discuss the "new" source that provides our conversion narrative, and present the narrative itself; an edition of the original Chaghatay Turkic text and a full translation of the narrative are provided in Appendixes 1 and 2, since considerable philological discussion, not all of which is directly relevant to the religious issues at hand, is unavoidable in dealing with this source.

Following this discussion of the central conversion narrative, we will begin the task of trying to understand and evaluate how this narrative spoke to and conveyed religious meaning to its audience. The popularity and longevity of at least some elements in the narrative—most important, of the central figure ascribed the pivotal role in "converting" Özbek Khan—suggest that the narrative was religiously and socially meaningful in at least certain communities for more than six centuries. Indeed, the rest of the book is devoted to outlining the forms the narrative and its "spinoffs" took, and to making an attempt—necessarily imperfect and tentative in view of the nature of our sources—to discover why this tale and its central character retained such a strong and persistent hold on the religious imagination of Inner Asian peoples from the fourteenth century to the twentieth, from the Crimea to the Altay, and from the Volga basin to Bukhara.

More precisely, we will first consider the wide range of religious counterpoints in the primary conversion narrative itself, suggesting the ways in which specific elements (and even individual words of particular resonance) in the narrative's content and structure may have "packaged" religious messages for an indigenous audience in the context of Islam, or in the context of real or imagined features of pre-Islamic religion, or in the context of both. This discussion will be accompanied by a more general treatment of a central feature, both structural and semantic, evident both in the narrative as a whole and in many of its distinctive components: the theme of "displacement" and its variations. Here we will draw upon comparative material from other Inner Asian conversion narratives that may parallel and illuminate this theme, and suggest some conclusions regarding the use of "oppositional" and "assimilative" displacement in such narratives.

Next, we will trace the central figure in our conversion narrative, known as "Baba Tükles," and his narrative transformations, first in a variety of "historical" sources and genealogical traditions, and then in a wide range of oral epic and folkloric traditions. In effect, in our preceding discussion of the religious messages implicit in the *original* conversion narrative, we will have examined how the figure of Baba Tükles came to be surrounded with an intense sacred and mythic aura; in the subsequent discussions of Baba Tükles' appearance in historical/genealogical and epic tradition, we will explore what was made of this sacred aura in subsequent generations of his story's Inner Asian "audience." This audience appears to have lost interest in many of the tensions and counterpoints that infused that *original* narrative, which gave Baba Tükles his sacred status, with religious meaning, but nevertheless seems to have clung to the figure of Baba Tükles as the repository of an impressive variety of sacral functions vital to communal integrity and solidarity.

In particular, we will explore the ways in which the figure of Baba Tükles confirms our hypothesis that Inner Asian Islamic conversion narratives are structurally and functionally equivalent to communal legends of origin, highlighting both his role in the legitimation of the Noghay horde and his transformation into a mythic ancestor who is at the same time both Culture Hero and First Man. This will lead us to consider again the implications of the wide variety of religious meaning attached to Baba Tükles for the broader issues of Islamization, and the role of Islam, in the Inner Asian world. And finally, we will discuss some conclusions suggested by the case of Baba Tükles with regard to what such conversion narratives may tell us about Inner Asian "responses" to Islam in the important areas of political legitimacy and communal self-conception.

1

The Religious Environment: Worldview, Ritual, and Communal Status

Islam and Conversion

The process of conversion to Islam remains on the whole poorly studied in either its social and historical, or affective and personal/psychological, aspects. Despite the relatively recent and signal contributions of Nehemiah Levtzion[1] and Richard Bulliet[2] who have advanced innovative classificatory, methodological, and analytical strategies in the framework of comparative and more localized approaches toward Islamization, the complex of problems associated with conversion to Islam still has not drawn sufficient attention from specialists on all "fronts" of Islamization to allow a synthetic treatment of conversion to Islam from either a theoretical or historical perspective.[3] If old notions of forced conversion and the choice of "Islam or the sword" have been abandoned, at least in scholarly literature, little serious analytical work

1. See above all the volume *Conversion to Islam*, ed. Nehemia Levtzion (New York/London: Holmes & Meier Publishers, 1979), and Levtzion's contributions therein, "Toward a Comparative Study of Islamization" (pp. 1–23) and "Patterns of Islamization in West Africa" (pp. 207–216), as well as his bibliography (pp. 247–265), in which Central and Inner Asia are predictably poorly represented; cf. also his "Conversion under Muslim Domination: A Comparative Study," in *Religious Change and Cultural Domination*, ed. D. N. Lorenzen (Mexico City: El Colegio de México, 1981), pp. 19–38.

2. See his seminal work, *Conversion to Islam in the Medieval Period: An Essay in Quantitative History* (Cambridge: Harvard University Press, 1979), and more recently his "Process and Status in Conversion and Continuity," introducing *Conversion and Continuity: Indigenous Christian Communities in Islamic Lands Eighth to Eighteenth Centuries*, ed. Michael Gervers and Ramzi Jibran Bikhazi (Toronto: Pontifical Institute of Mediaeval Studies, 1990), pp. 1–12, and his "Conversion Stories in Early Islam" in the same volume (pp. 123–133).

3. For important theoretical considerations on conversion to Islam in historical surveys see, for example, Marshall Hodgson's *The Venture of Islam*, vol. 2 (*The Expansion of Islam in the*

has been done as a means of replacing older models and assumptions of how Islam was adopted and appropriated in specific contexts; nor, in general, have primary sources been tapped or reevaluated with an eye to the particular issue of Islamization.

In the case of Inner Asia we are remarkably ill-served with regard to studies of conversion to Islam; specialists on Islam in sub-Saharan Africa and on South Asian Islam[4] for instance, have recognized the importance of cônversion as a historical and religious issue in their respective regions, and their studies are often models for approaches to Islamization in Central and Inner Asia. But to date the study of conversion to Islam in the Inner Asian world has hardly begun, either from a historical or historicist perspective, or from the perspective of Islam's religious and social interaction with indigenous traditions.

The primitive state of studies of Islamization in Inner Asia is suggested already by the meager bibliographical talley; the small quantity alone is revealing, not to mention quality. To this day the only extended narrative account of Islam's spread in the Inner Asian world is found in the quite dated work of T. W. Arnold[5] and there remains no comprehensive survey

Middle Periods) (Chicago: University of Chicago Press, 1974), esp. pp. 532–574 (with a distinctive slighting of Inner Asian Islam, however), and Ira M. Lapidus, *A History of Islamic Societies* (Cambridge: Cambridge University Press, 1988), pp. 242–252 (as well as his more extensive treatment of Inner Asia, with attention to conversion issues, pp. 413–436). See also the study of John Wansbrough, *The Sectarian Milieu: Content and Composition of Islamic Salvation History* (Oxford: Oxford University Press, 1978), and the insightful remarks of R. Stephen Humphreys, *Islamic History: A Framework for Inquiry* (revised ed., Princeton: Princeton University Press, 1991), pp. 273–283.

4. For Islamization in Africa see Levtzion's bibliography noted above. On Islamization in South Asia, see especially Bruce B. Lawrence, "Early Indo-Muslim Saints and Conversion," in *Islam in Asia*, vol. I, South Asia, ed. Yohanan Friedmann (Boulder, Colorado: Westview Press, 1984), pp. 109–145, and his "Islam in India: The Function of Institutional Sufism in the Islamization of Rajasthan, Gujarat and Kashmir," in *Islam in Local Contexts*, ed. Richard C. Martin (Leiden: E. J. Brill, 1982; Contributions to Asian Studies, vol. 17), pp. 27–43; cf. also Carl W. Ernst, *Eternal Garden: Mysticism, History, and Politics at a South Asian Sufi Center* (Albany: State University of New York Press, 1992), esp. pp. 155–168; Richard M. Eaton, "Approaches to the Study of Conversion to Islam in India," in *Approaches to Islam in Religious Studies*, ed. Richard C. Martin (Tucson: University of Arizona Press, 1985), pp. 106–123, and his "Sufi Folk Literature and the Expansion of Indian Islam," *History of Religions*, 14/2 (November 1974), pp. 117–127; P. Hardy, "Modern European and Muslim Explanations of Conversion to Islam in South Asia: A Preliminary Survey of the Literature," in *Conversion to Islam*, ed. Levtzion (1979), pp. 68–99; Zawwar Hussain Zaidi, "Conversion to Islam in South Asia: Problems in Analysis," *American Journal of Islamic Social Sciences*, 6/1 (1989), pp. 93–117; and, closer to our region, Georg Buddrus, "Spiegelungen der Islamisierung Kafiristans in der mündlichen Überlieferung," in *Ethnologie und Geschichte: Festschrift für Karl Jettmar*, ed. Peter Snoy (Wiesbaden: Franz Steiner Verlag, 1983), pp. 73–88.

5. T. W. Arnold, *The Preaching of Islam: A History of the Propagation of the Muslim Faith*

of the history of Islamization in Inner Asia.[6] For the Islamization of Central Asia proper, general histories of pre-Mongol Central Asia note the "fact" of Islamization, but to date most treatments skirt the real issues involved in understanding it;[7] similarly, the historical, documentary, and numismatic evidence on the important Islamizing dynasty of the Qarakhanids has drawn considerable attention, but its history remains obscure, as does

(Aligarh, 1896; repr. Lahore: Shirkat-i-Qualam, 1956); chapters 7 and 8 (pp. 206–253) treat Islam's spread in Central Asia and "among the Mongols and Tatars." Thoroughly obsolete on nearly all counts, Arnold's work is still the only extended discussion of Islamization in Inner Asia as a religious phenomenon; its date is indicative of the deplorable inattention to this issue in twentieth century scholarship.

6. In lieu of such a study, brief overviews are available in general historical surveys, such as Lapidus's work cited above, and in a few other works: cf. Clifford Edmund Bosworth, "Islamic frontiers in Africa and Asia: (B) Central Asia," in *The Legacy of Islam* , ed. Joseph Schacht and C. E. Bosworth (2nd ed., Oxford: Oxford University Press, 1974), pp. 116–130; Alexandre Bennigsen and Fanny E. Bryan, "Islam in the Caucasus and the Middle Volga," and "Islam in Central Asia," *Encyclopedia of Religion*, ed. Mircea Eliade (New York: Macmillan, 1987), vol. 7, pp. 357–377 ; Valeria Fiorani Piacentini, *Turchizzazione ed islamizzazione dell'Asia Centrale (VI–XVI secolo d. Cr.)* (Milan: Società Editrice Dante Alighieri, 1974), which gives primarily a political and ethnic history of Central Asia rather than a study of Islamization as such; and M. F. Köprülü, *L'Influence du chamanisme turco-mongole sur les ordres mystiques musulmans* (Istanbul, 1929). Additional studies of aspects of Islamization in particular periods or regions are cited below; here may be noted my preliminary analysis of a conversion narrative from Central Asia, "Yasavian Legends on the Islamization of Turkistan," in *Aspects of Altaic Civilization II* (= PIAC XXX), ed. Denis Sinor (Bloomington: Indiana University, Research Institute for Inner Asian Studies, 1990), pp. 1–19, which briefly treats some of the conceptual issues treated also in the present study.

7. For reliable historical surveys, see Bartol'd, *Turkestan Down to the Mongol Invasion*, tr. V. and T. Minorsky, ed. C. E. Bosworth (4th ed., London: Luzac & Co., 1977), but see also the important work of Wilferd Madelung, "The spread of Māturidism and the Turks," in *Actas do IV Congresso des Estudos Arabes et Islâmicos, Coimbra-Lisboa* (Leiden: E. J. Brill, 1971), pp. 109–68; reprinted in the author's *Religious Schools and Sects in Medieval Islam* (London: Variorum Reprints, 1985), No. II. Madelung's study, with its prosopographical approach to the problem of early Islam in Central Asia and among the Turks, draws attention to important issues too often clouded by assumptions derived from studies of Islam among the Turks of Anatolia, uncritically transferred to Central Asia. The overemphasis on a supposed Shīʿite and "heterodox" role in Central Asian Islam, dealt with for the pre-Mongol Islamization of the Turks by Madelung, is the focus of an excellent, reasoned discussion by R. D. McChesney for the Timurid era (and after) in his *Waqf in Central Asia: Four Hundred Years in the History of a Muslim Shrine, 1480–1889* (Princeton: Princeton University Press, 1991), pp. 33–36. See also Yuri Bregel, "The Role of Central Asia in the History of the Muslim East," Afghanistan Council Occasional Paper #20 (February 1980); R. N. Frye, "Comparative Observations on Conversion to Islam in Iran and Central Asia," *Jerusalem Studies in Arabic and Islam*, 4 (1984), pp. 81–88; C. E. Bosworth, "Barbarian Incursions: The Coming of the Turks into the Islamic World," in *Islamic Civilisation 950–1150*, ed. D. S. Richards (Oxford: Oxford University Press, 1973), pp. 1–16; Bernard Lewis, "The Mongols, the Turks and the Muslim Polity," *Transactions of the Royal Historical Society*, 5th series, 18 (1968), pp. 49–68; M. A. Usmanov, "Rasprostranenie islama i ego rol' v istorii Srednei Azii," in *Iz istorii obshchestvenno-filosofskoi mysli i vol'nodumiia v Srednei Azii*, ed. M. M. Khairullaev (Tashkent: Fan, 1991), pp. 10–26.

the course of its Islamization.[8] Still less is known of the actual condition of Islam among the Bulghars, a question taken up at least briefly below. Beyond these examples from the "classical" age of Islamic expansion, moreover, the situation is worse still. The process of Islamization in East Turkistan remains poorly studied and poorly known,[9] while even the establishment of Islam in the three western successor states of the much-studied Mongol empire has drawn scant attention; the "re-Islamization" of Central Asia in the late Mongol and early Timurid era remains essentially unstudied, and the spread of Islam into southern Siberia has been left virtually untouched as well.[10]

Soviet scholarship has added to this picture its own range of misinterpretations, and not only from the standpoint of rigid Soviet ideology; "nationalist" scholarship in each of the Çentral Asian republics has contributed its own slant to the history of Islam in Inner Asia, and indeed at

8. For the Qarakhanids in particular, see Peter B. Golden, "The Karakhanids and Early Islam," in *The Cambridge History of Early Inner Asia*, ed. Denis Sinor (Cambridge: Cambridge University Press, 1990), pp. 343–370; cf. Robert Dankoff's introduction to his translation of the *Qutadghu Bilig, Wisdom of Royal Glory (Kutadgu Bilig), a Turko-Islamic Mirror for Princes* (Chicago: University of Chicago Press, 1983); Robert Dankoff, "Three Turkic Verse Cycles Relating to Inner Asian Warfare," *HUS*, 3–4/1 (1979–80), pp. 151–165; Marcel Erdal, "Early Turkish Names for the Muslim God, and the Title *Çelebi*," *Asian and African Studies* (Jerusalem), 16 (1982, = PIAC XXIV), pp. 407–416; M. [*sic*] Barthold, "The Bughra Khan Mentioned in the Qudatqu Bilik," BSOS, 3 (1923), pp. 151–158; and several studies of documentary material that provides important linguistic and onomastic evidence to analyze for the course of Islamization: Marcel Erdal, "The Turkish Yārkand Documents," *BSOAS*, 47 (1984), pp. 260–301; Monika Gronke, "The Arabic Yārkand Documents," *BSOAS*, 49 (1986), pp. 454–507; Şinasi Tekin, "A Qaraḫānid Document of A.D. 1121 (A.H. 515) from Yārkand," *HUS*, 3–4 (1979–80), pp. 868–883; plus older studies of Cl. Huart, "Trois actes notariés de Yarkend," *JA*, 1914, 4, pp. 607–627, and Mohamed Khadr and Claude Cahen, "Deux actes de *waqf* d'un Qaraḫānide d'Asie Centrale," *JA*, 255 (1967), pp. 305–334 (and see the remarks by C. E. Bosworth, *JA*, 256 (1968), pp. 449–453). See also the historical studies of Omeljan Pritsak, "Die Karachaniden," *Der Islam*, 31 (1953–54), pp. 17–68; "Karachanidische Streitfragen, 1–4," Oriens, 3 (1950), pp. 209–228; "Von den Karluk zu den Karachaniden," *ZDMG*, 101 (1951), pp. 270–300.

9. For the distinctive, though still obscure, patterns of Islamization and cultural interaction in East Turkistan, from Qarakhanid times down to the post-Mongol era, cf. Haneda Akira, "Introduction (ch. 1, Problems of the Turkicization; ch. 2, Problems of the Islamization)," *Acta Asiatica*, 34 (1978) [Special Issue: Historical Studies on Central Asia in Japan], pp. 1–21; Mano Eiji, "Moghūlistān," and Oda Juten, "Uighuristan," in the same volume, pp. 46–60 and pp. 22–45, respectively; William Samolin, *East Turkistan to the Twelfth Century: A Brief Political Survey* (The Hague: Mouton, 1964); and N. N. Pantusov, "Gorod Almalyk i Mazar Tugluk-Timur-khana" and "Legenda o Tugluk-Timur-khane," in *Kaufmanskii sbornik, izdannyi v pamiat' 25 let, istekshikh so dnia smerti pokoritelia i ustroitelia Turkestanskogo kraia, general-ad'iutanta K. P. fon-Kaufmana* (Moscow, 1910), pp. 161–202.

10. The Mongol era is discussed more fully below; for the general issue of "re-Islamization" in the Mongol era, the "onomastic" approach suggested by Bulliet's work has been taken up

least two generations of the educated and modernized Central Asian elite have ignored or dismissed or underestimated the Islamic component of their "national" culture in an effort to highlight the specifically "Turkic" or, for example, Qïrghïz, component of the civilization of which they are the current bearers.[11] It is thus uncertain whether our explorations in the centrality of Islam and conversion to communal self-consciousness in pre-modern times may still "speak" to the contemporary "heirs" of the Golden Horde. But in any case, we find in narratives such as those examined in this study an opportunity to approach these issues from the indigenous perspective, and from one established prior to the Soviet-era Communist and/or nationalist transformation of (or constraints upon) the communal lenses through which Islamization is viewed.

In any case, most treatments of conversion to Islam, both in general and in Inner Asia in particular, have been concerned with "how it happened" and with imagining the conditions for and implications of extensive Islamization, as historical questions. Far fewer are studies that approach the question of Islamization from perspectives similar to that adopted for

---

briefly for the Chaghatay *ulus* in John E. Woods, "The Timurid Dynasty," *Papers on Inner Asia*, No. 14 (Bloomington, 1990), pp. 9–12. For the spread of Islam in Siberia in the post-Mongol era, cf. Abdülkadir İnan, "Sibirya'da islâmiyetin yayılışı," in *Necati Lugal Armağanı* (Ankara: Türk Tarih Kurumu Basımevi, 1968), pp. 331–338; and the interesting legendary material discussed by N. F. Katanov, "O religioznykh voinakh uchenikov sheikha Bagauddina protiv inorodtsev Zapadnoi Sibiri," *Ezhegodnik Tobol'skogo Gubernskogo Muzeia*, 14 (1904), pp. 3–28, and "Predaniia tobol'skikh tatar o pribytii v 1572 g. mukhammedanskikh propovednikov v g. Isker," in the same *Ezhegodnik*, 7 (1897), pp. 51–61.

11. This process began much earlier in some cases, with the fascination for things Russian and European and "modern" found among westernized intellectuals in pre-Soviet Central Asia under Russian rule. For an extreme example of a Europeanized Qazaq opponent of Islam, see the short tract by the celebrated ethnographer Chokan Chingisovich Valikhanov (d. 1865) entitled "O musul 'manstve v stepi" (published in his *Sobranie sochinenii v piati tomakh*, I [Alma-Ata: Izd-vo AN KazSSR, 1961], pp. 524–529); Valikhanov's hostility toward Islam (and its "fanaticism") is accompanied by an insistence (or perhaps wish) that Islam was never strong among the steppe nomads, but he is at least open in his hope that Russian education will prevent the emergence of a Shamil (the leader of anti-Russian Muslim resistance in the North Caucasus down to 1859) among the Qazaqs, and he speaks admiringly of the American example, where, he says, the Indian wars had virtually ended "since the government of the United States began to civilize the Iroquois, Creeks, Choctaws, and other redskins." For contemporary reflections of similar attitudes, but with the nationalist and anti-Russian element highlighted and adopted by a western observer, cf. Guy Imart, "The Islamic Impact on Traditional Kirghiz Ethnicity," *Nationalities Papers*, 14/1–2 (Spring–Fall 1986), pp. 65–88; by contrast, for an appreciation of traditional Islamic adaptations, cf. Edward Lazzerini, "The Revival of Islamic Culture in Pre-Revolutionary Russia: Or, Why a Prosopography of the Tatar Ulema?" in *Passé turco-tatar, présent soviétique: Études offertes à Alexandre Bennigsen*, ed. Ch. Lemercier-Quelquejay, G. Veinstein, and S. E. Wimbush (Louvain/Paris: Éditions Peeters/Éditions de l'École des Hautes Études, 1986), pp. 367–372.

the present study:[12] our theme is not "how it happened," but "how it was understood to have happened" among the peoples most directly affected. In the end, of course, our objectives do not depart so much from those that have informed most earlier studies of conversion to Islam, insofar as we hope finally to add what may be learned from listening to "how the story was told" to our understanding of conversion as a historical phenomenon; first, however, we must pay attention to the story rather than the "history," as this latter term tends to be used by specialists today.

To this end it may be worthwhile to consider some more theoretical aspects of Islam that inform religious practice and religious narrative and are important for the issue of conversion. This is hardly the place for a survey of "ideal" Islamic notions of conversion or of the proper relations between Muslims and the unconverted; neither can we take up the theoretical or historical referents of the terminology of *daʿwah* (the "summons" to adopt Islam) or *tawbah* ("repentance," "*metanoia*," and hence "conversion" in the personal sense of turning from evil to good). Rather, we will note several points of special relevance for conversion narratives and for conversion in Inner Asia, informed by other narratives not presented here.

First, the "terminology" of Islamization in Inner Asian conversion narratives is relatively limited. The term *tawbah* is virtually never used, while *daʿwah* (with its Turkic equivalent in the verb *ünde-*, "to summon"), a term that has come to mean active missionary-style proselytization in the modern world, plays primarily a formal and structural role in the conversion narratives. That is, the narratives record the "call" to adopt Islam issued by the figure who brings Islam, but the call itself is rarely the focus of discursive elaboration, while the "bearer" of Islam is not first and foremost a *dāʿī*; the summons is issued more as a narrative device to set up the decisive conversion contest or struggle than as a significant addition to the story's content.

Similarly, in many conversion narratives the motivating factor that brings a "bearer" of Islam to an infidel land or community is not *daʿwah* in the sense of "missionary propaganda" (although the summons is still issued, formulaically), but a desire to "open" territories to Islam; here the significant term is the Arabic *fataḥa,* with its connotations ranging from

12. Among these may be noted two studies in the volume edited by Levtzion referred to above, namely Russell Jones's "Ten Conversion Myths from Indonesia" (pp. 129–158) and, less directly (though in line with our concern for understanding the interplay of indigenous and Islamic religious concerns), Humphrey J. Fisher's "Dreams and Conversion in Black Africa" (pp. 217–235); cf. also David Owusu-Ansah, "Islamization Reconsidered: An Examination of Asante Responses to Muslim Influence in the Nineteenth Century," *Asian and African Studies* (Jerusalem), 21 (1987), pp. 145–163.

"conquest" to "revelation." The term is mirrored in Turkic contexts by the use of the verb *ač-*, "to open," as in the phrase "*islām ača keldiler,*" "they came to 'spread' Islam."

More commonly, the terms used to refer to conversion to Islam reflect the meaning of "*islām*" itself: a person or community will simply be said to have "submitted" (*aslama*), or to have "become Muslim" (in Persian or Turkic accounts), or to have "been ennobled with the acceptance of Islam" (using a derivative of *sharufa*), or, finally, to "have entered the faith of Islam." In the narrative of Ötemish Ḥājjī, for instance, the motivation of the bearers of Islam is both to "summon" Özbek Khan to Islam, and, more pointedly, *to make him a Muslim*. What must be noted here in connection with this terminology is what is implied in all these cases: it is not a change of heart, as might be conveyed by the use of *tawbah* or its derivatives, or of mind, as in the "intellectual" process implied by *daʿwah* or its derivatives, but a change of *status*. This change in status is evident even in the use of the Arabic *aslama*, insofar as it conveys an act of will and implies the well-known distinction between "faith" (*īmān*) and "submission" to the divine will (*islām*), thereby signaling a change of an individual's status before God; it is still clearer in the terminology, which involves "becoming" something different or "acquiring" a status that is deemed ennobling.

Most telling are the frequent instances in which conversion is spoken of as an "entering" into the religion (*dīn*) of Islam, using both the Arabic-based terminology with derivatives of *dakhala*, and Turkic *kir-*; this "entering" is clearly understood as referring to the central socioreligious concept of Islam, the *ummah*, "community." This leads us to our second point regarding the Islamic understanding of conversion to Islam, namely, the inherent links between religious identity and communal identity. The Islamic *ummah* defines itself, and other communities, on religious grounds, and hence the adherents of other *adyān* constitute distinct social groupings or communities (as is further evident from the social and religious meanings of *millah*, for instance). Conversely, this often means that distinctive communal groups are expected to be marked by a particular religious orientation; to change one's religion is to change one's communal identity, and vice versa.

In this understanding of "conversion" are two important implications for our subject of Islamization in Inner Asia. First, Islamic ideals of community in effect sanction the intimate bonds between religious and communal identity that in turn make "communal" conversion not only acceptable, but in some cases normative. Second, in its emphasis upon the religious basis of communal identity, and conversely the communal basis of religious identity, the Islamic tradition is paralleled quite closely, and with important consequences, by attitudes toward community and religious life prevalent in Inner Asian tradition, as we will discuss shortly.

In the Islamic context, the normative character of such communal conversion should not be overstated, of course, but it is present nonetheless. If the Qurʾān idealizes "prophets without honor" in their own communities and individuals (e.g. Ibrāhīm) who break with family, even, in devotion to God's will, both the social and theoretical development of the Islamic *ummah* reinforce the equation of religious and communal identities in such a way as to widen the expectation that people will come to Islam not as individuals, but as communities. This is especially pronounced in dealing with peoples well beyond the borders of the *Dār al-Islām* at a given time: if Muslim religious and political policy toward non-Islamic communities *within* Muslim-ruled territory aimed at fragmentation of communal bonds through "piecemeal" conversion to Islam, hopes and expectations with regard to peoples beyond the frontiers of Islam tended to envision their conversion *en masse* and as communities.

There is also a specifically Islamic paradigm for such "communal conversion" in the "conversion-to-community" of the first century of Islam's spread, whereby adoption of the "religion" of Islam amounted to joining the "community" not of Muslims, but of Arabs, specifically in acquiring "client" status in affiliation with a particular Arab tribe. While both the understanding of Islam implied by such a practice, and the practice itself, seem to have disappeared quite early (in part, no doubt, to resentment among the growing block of "converts" toward their subordinate status *in the community*), the paradigm remained as an understanding of conversion with important latent potential.

Indeed, in Inner Asia itself (and in Inner Asian conversion narratives) we often find a complementary divergence between paradigms of conversion stressing Islamization of territory, on the one hand, and Islamization of communities, on the other. In the first case we find that the vocabulary of "opening" the land to Islam is employed, while the terminology conveying a change of *status* predominates in the latter. The "territorial" model, of course, as evident in the division of the world into *Dār al-Islām* and *Dār al-Ḥarb*, is more familiar to students of the Islamic world, but is at once less "sociologically" sophisticated, and less practically relevant in the Inner Asian context; and for this reason the "communal" model is worth emphasizing here.

It is particularly noteworthy that a variety of "mechanisms" emerged in popular and learned Islamic religious thought to explain and articulate such "communal" conversion among distant or simply alien peoples, the Turks of Inner Asia among them; most of these mechanisms would appear to be outgrowths of Islamic discourse itself, but were quickly appropriated by the Islamizing community concerned as part and parcel of their Islamization. Links with Islamized genealogies provided one obvious mechanism, as in the case of the discovery of "Turk b. Yāfith"; another was the "seeding" of particular holy people through the world (as in the discovery of ʿĀdites in distant places, or in stories of the Prophet's companions appearing in various localities), while more mystically oriented strategies include stories placing particularly prominent converts among the Prophet's interlocutors during his *miʿrāj*, or the theory of "Uvaysī" Sufis (who could provide not only conversion, but mystical initiation, for noteworthy converts). Occasionally, indigenous models of sanctification are adapted with a thin veneer of Islamization, as in stories of a "convert" supernaturally conceived or of an infant who refuses his infidel mother's breast; but still more often the "mechanism" used to explain communal conversion is the one with which we are most directly concerned here: legendary and hagiographical conversion narratives evoking both Islamic paradigms and indigenous religious themes.

A final and fundamental feature of the Islamic understanding of conversion is suggested already by both the communal paradigm of conversion, and by the change of status (rather than change of heart) signaled by "conversion." It is also one of the most difficult to appreciate for those rooted in Christian conceptions of religious conversion, or in modernist iconoclasm and anti-ritualism, which insist upon the "heart" as more important than "the law," emphasize "content" over "form," and consider "religion" first and foremost as a matter of "personal belief"; they would be more comfortable if "conversion" in Islam were indeed spoken of in terms of *tawbah* and understood primarily as a "change of heart." This feature springs from the distinctly Islamic approach to the formal and external, an approach already clear in the divinely and prophetically sanctioned designation of Muhammad's religion as *islām*: to overstate the case, we may suggest that the Islamic tradition regards even *purely* formal and "external" adoption of Islamic practices and patterns as religiously meaningful, since those patterns, *even in their formal aspects*, are conveyors of divine grace, *barakah*.

That is, as much as a true change of the inner man is demanded by

Islam, a purely formal, and even minimal, change of the external man is not to be dismissed as easily in the Islamic experience as it often is in the Christian tradition, or for that matter among irreligious critics of religious "hypocrisy"; inherent in the Islamic outlook is the conviction that the formal and external manifestations of Muslim religious obligations, as ordained by God and exemplified by the Prophet, may themselves transmit the divine grace which alone can "turn" the soul toward God and lead to a "change of heart." In effect, it is laudable if a person truly "repents" of evil and unbelief and in this spirit performs his obligatory prayers. But even if he does not repent, his community should see to it that he performs those prayers nevertheless, for if he does so, the divine grace inherent in those external forms may eventually succeed in its transformative work; and as he prostrates his body in prayer, his heart and mind may follow.

What this understanding of religiosity may mean or imply in other contexts need not detain us here; what it means in the case of conversion, however, is that *from an Islamic perspective* there is no such thing as the purely formal or nominal or external adoption of Islam that is so often noted with disdain by students of Inner Asia. Even a conversion—of an individual or of a community—that is "imperfect" from the standpoint of either full ritual attentiveness or inner spirituality is nevertheless a first step toward deeper religiosity, and in any case should not be dismissed or belittled inasmuch as it is, in however rudimentary a form, a token of God's grace and solicitude toward his creature. To come full circle to our emphasis upon communal status, what that "imperfect" conversion signals, above all, is indeed God's greatest gift from the Islamic perspective: the conferral of membership in a salvific community.

Such an approach is already sanctioned within Islamic tradition, with specific Inner Asian relevance, as noted in an important article by Wilferd Madelung with regard to a statement attributed to Abū Ḥanīfah. Asked about "the status of a Muslim in the territory of polytheism who affirms Islam as a whole but does not know or affirm the Koran or any of the religious duties of Islam,"[13] Abū Ḥanīfah affirmed that such a person could still be counted as a "believer"; and, as Madelung observed, the dominant theological school in Central Asia at the time of the conversion of the Turks no doubt intentionally "misread" part of this passage, turning "in the territory of polytheism" (*fī arḍ ash-shirk*) into "in the territory of the Turks" (*fī arḍ at-turk*). The response of Abū Ḥanīfah was thus "appropriated" in Central Asian tradition, and through a slight orthographic

13. Madelung, "The Spread of Māturīdism," pp. 122–123.

change an express statement of his leniency in matters of doctrine and ritual was assigned to the specific context of deciding what made a Central Asian Turk a member of the Muslim community.

We will return to these issues shortly. For now, it is hoped that this brief consideration of the value of "external" Islamization as understood within the Islamic tradition may already suggest alternatives to the tired chorus of views on the "nominally" Muslim peoples of Inner Asia that effectively dismisses the importance and effectiveness of Islamization. To appreciate these alternatives from the Inner Asian perspective, as well as from an Islamic one, however, we must turn to a consideration of the religious traditions of the Inner Asian world.

Indigenous Religion in Traditional Inner Asia

The traditional indigenous religion of Inner Asian peoples prior to their entry into Islamic or Christian or Buddhist cultural and religious "spheres of influence" (as well as many traditions retained after their entry into these originally foreign traditions) belongs to a realm of religious life, common and even normative throughout the world and throughout history, for which scholarship in the humanities and social sciences has still failed to devise a suitable and "comfortable" terminology. Labels ranging from "primitive religion" and "animism" to "natural" or "archaic" or "tribal" religion have been proposed or suggested or simply used, but in the end found wanting; each conveys a set of assumptions or implications objectionable in some way, whether as excessively pejorative or as historically romanticizing, and none has been widely accepted as more "scientific" or illuminating or useful, in any particular way, than older labels such as "paganism."

In part this lack of suitable labels stems from the nature of the traditions themselves; they are, in the final analysis, not something separable from the course of life itself, from the human experience as a whole, as organized and classified by the communities in which these traditions prevail, and as such in most cases are not marked by special terminology native to these communities. We are thus ordinarily unable to find a "native" designation among peoples marked by such traditions, either for "religion" in general or for "our religion" in particular, unless and until it is recognized as distinctive by being opposed to some "religion" from outside. This absence of indigenous terminology is, however, hardly a sign that conceptions and practices immediately recognizable as "religious" are unimportant or poorly developed among such peoples; on the contrary, it is most often a sign that these "religious" conceptions and practices are so intimately linked with all aspects of life—that is, with all aspects of what being human is considered by those peoples to mean—that life is inconceivable without them, leaving no rationale for a separate taxonomy devoted to "religion" as such.

For our purposes we will not belabor the terminological difficulties presented by these "primitive" or "archaic" traditions, nor seek by using a particular set of terms to suggest any special suitability beyond mere convenience. Rather, we will speak of "indigenous" or "native" Inner Asian religious traditions, only as a convenient way of referring to the "systems" of belief and practices evident among Inner Asian peoples before those peoples' contacts with and/or adoption of the religions of peoples beyond the Inner Asian world. In settling upon this rather prosaic and colorless (and misleadingly all-encompassing!) terminology we should not lose sight of the rich diversity and conceptual depth of the mythic and religious world created by Inner Asian peoples; nor at the same time should we forget the real and often decisive distinctions of "ethnic" and linguistic affiliation, geographical distribution, and economic and environmental adaptation that characterize the diverse communities lumped together in the phrase "Inner Asian peoples."

Moreover, by speaking of "native" or "indigenous" traditions among these communities, we should not understand these traditions as somehow hermetically sealed from "outside" religious influence down to the time when we first find descriptions or other reflections of their religious life in our sources; the heritage of contacts between the inhabitants of the Inner Asian world and the civilizations of China, Iran, the Near East, and Europe long predates our earliest historical records for Inner Asian peoples, and it would be foolish to suggest a rigid body of hallowed traditions tenaciously held by "Inner Asian peoples" from their earliest appearance in our sources down to the time of their adoption of a particular "outside" missionary religion. What we find instead is a dynamic and fluid "tradition-in-development" among Inner Asian peoples, shaped by "indigenous" responses to economic, social, political, and spiritual life, but also by interaction with "outsiders"—and such interaction unquestionably involved early and regular exposure to such "world religions" as Buddhism and Zoroastrianism, and later Christianity, Manicheism, Judaism, and Islam. What we are concerned with is not to argue what was "indigenous" and what reflects "outside" influence or "borrowing" in Inner Asian tradition in some historically absolutist fashion, but to explore a pattern of indigenous religious concepts, values, and practices that appear to have shaped not only the "native" tradition as distinct from imported faiths, but the response to, and modes of assimilation of, those imported faiths as well.

By the "indigenous Inner Asian tradition," then, we mean only the adaptations of home-grown and "imported" religious concepts and patterns that had been assimilated and appropriated *as its own* by a particular community at a particular time, regardless of its "origin" as a cultural historian might insist upon; and it is indeed a central theme of our discussion that Islam itself eventually became part of that "indigenous" tradition just as earlier "foreign" elements had. Our aim here, then, is to highlight the features of conceptualization (rather than "belief") and practice that may be considered central and fundamental to the Inner Asian peoples who encountered Islam, at the time of that initial encounter, and to trace the echoes of those features in the ongoing interaction between the Inner Asian worldview and the religious ideals and communal expectations of the Islamic tradition.

Problems in Interpreting Inner Asian Religion

In identifying these central features, we are hampered by a number of purely practical considerations surrounding the scholarly study of Inner Asian religion. The most obvious is the relative scarcity of indigenous sources prior to the recordings of oral tradition undertaken by ethnographers in the nineteenth and twentieth centuries; for earlier periods we must rely, in most cases, upon accounts of Inner Asian religious practices left by travelers, historians, geographers, or missionaries, from the outlying civilizations of China, Iran and the Near East, and Europe, with their inevitable mixture of hostility and misunderstanding and, in some cases, idealization. As for the indigenous sources themselves, they do exist, and many have been studied, but arguably the richest repository of indigenous Inner Asian religious lore—the enormous body of oral tradition, especially epic narrative—has only recently begun to attract analysis, and moreover appears to have suffered significant abuse in recent times in the name of various modern ideologies.

Similarly, we are obliged not only to view Inner Asian religious life through the eyes of outsiders, but also to look through the prism of adopted foreign traditions; and these, precisely because of their adoption and assimilation and nativization, are often more obscuring of earlier ways than the obviously distorted outside accounts. This means, among other things, that we must look to more recent ethnographic descriptions of religious life among peoples less subject to Islamic, or Buddhist or Christian, influence, since we rarely have comparable descriptions for the peoples who adopted Islam or Buddhism or Christianity *prior to their conversion*. In other words, we are compelled to rely upon nineteenth and twentieth century accounts of religious life among relatively un-Islamized peoples such as the Tuvans or Altays, for example, since we have few accounts (and none comparable to ethnographic descriptions) of religious life among the still un-Islamized "Uzbeks" of the fourteenth century (leaving aside the obvious questions of ethnic identity and continuity). We are obliged to assume some similarity between the religious concepts and practices of these peoples, and as justified as such an assumption may be in most cases, we must not lose sight of its essentially conjectural nature.

Moreover, the traditional religious beliefs and practices and values of Inner Asian peoples have not enjoyed the same level or quality of scholarly attention as has been devoted to other "aboriginal" peoples, whether those of North America, pre-Christian Europe, or sub-Saharan Africa. This is due in no small measure to the historical fact of the incorporation of most of Inner Asia into the Soviet state, where for the better part of a century the academic study of religion was markedly stunted by official dogma and academic predilections shaped by the state. While Soviet scholars produced usable and in many cases quite admirable ethnographic studies including extensive data on religious life, Soviet ideology precluded the development of a serious interpretative framework for understanding religious life as such. Even in the more "purely" academic works—not to mention the frequent cooperation of academics in producing tracts belonging to the genre of antireligious literature—the essential hostility and contempt for religious "belief" and practice, as well as an uncritical adoption of *a priori* categories and ideologically sanctioned evolutionary historical patterns offered by Soviet Marxist orthodoxy, are often evident, both in outright dismissals and categorizations of elements of religious life as "survivals," "superstitions," and signs of backwardness and primitiveness to be abandoned by progressive thinkers, and more insidiously in the analytical frameworks imposed upon the data.

Finally, it must be remembered that the most recently nativized—how deeply or successfully remains to be seen—foreign "faith" for many Inner Asian peoples is precisely that Marxist-Leninist ideology, which has shaped not only the way the Soviet academic establishment has presented Inner Asian religion, but the way native but Soviet-trained Inner Asian scholars and the Soviet-educated Inner Asian public view their heritage. It is unfortunately the case that scholarship among many of the newly independent, or at least newly self-assertive, peoples of the former Soviet Union is often not the best source for an "indigenous" understanding of pre-modern Inner Asian religious life; all too often native Inner Asian scholars brought up in the Soviet system have adopted the same Soviet-style approaches noted above, or more recently have traded Soviet ideological constraints for scholarship in the service of "national pride." In either case the link between native elites and native tradition has been significantly weakened. This in itself is not so remarkable if understood as simply the current stage of the reworking of communal identities among Inner Asian peoples, but we must remember that at each stage of such reworkings in the past, something of the original flavor and intent of indigenous traditions was lost in the rush to find in them a basis for a native response to new political or social challenges; we must expect something to be lost at this stage as well.

We thus cannot point to any adequate attempt at a synthesis of "religion in Inner Asia," either for Inner Asian peoples as a whole (presuming that such a grouping would be meaningful), or for individual Inner Asian peoples or subgroups (whether historically defined or viewed, as has been the unfortunate practice in most Soviet literature, from the perspective of modern ethnic or national groupings). The scholarly edifice of the study of traditional, indigenous Inner Asian religion remains to be built, and the same holds true for the various parts of the Inner Asian whole (with the exception of the substantial scholarship on Tibetan religion). This means that the "structure" that might serve as the backdrop for understanding religious change and conversion in Inner Asia is not available, and unfortunately we cannot presume to construct it here, either for "Inner Asia" as a whole[14] or for the Mongol and Turkic worlds of direct rele-

14. Among surveys of some aspects of religious life in Inner Asia may be cited the works of the prolific Jean-Paul Roux, of which we may note his recent summary (with extensive bibliography of his earlier publications), *La religion des Turcs et des Mongols* (Paris: Payot, 1984); *Faune et flore sacrées dans les sociétés altaïques* (Paris: Librairie d'Amérique et d'Orient Adrien-Maisonneuve, 1966); and *La mort chez les peuples altaïques anciens et médiévaux d'après les documents écrits* (Paris: Librairie d'Amérique et d'Orient Adrien-Maisonneuve, 1963); Uno Harva [né Holmberg], *Die religiösen Vorstellungen der altaischen Völker* (Helsinki: Werner Söderström

vance for us.[15] In the absence of such a survey we may sketch here a number of issues central to the indigenous pre-Islamic religious worldview, and, at the risk of overgeneralization, note those features, in "synthetic" and interpretative fashion, may help us to understand the issue at hand: Islamization in the Jöchid *ulus*.

Inner Asian Religion: "Shamanism" and Beyond

If we examine the essential features of the ways in which the nature of man and the cosmos is commonly conceptualized among Inner Asian peoples, as evident in both indigenous sources (above all, oral tradition of

---

Osakeyhtiö, 1938; Folklore Fellows Communications, vol. 125), which provides a detailed survey of concepts of the structure and origin of the world, souls and death, hunting rites, shamanism, etc., remains an essential work, of which an "abbreviated" English version is available: Uno Holmberg, *The Mythology of all Races*, vol. 4, *Finno-Ugric, Siberian* (New York: Cooper Square, 1964 [originally published 1927]). Perhaps the most comprehensive survey of religious beliefs and practices among Inner Asian peoples appears in Wilhelm Schmidt's *magnum opus, Der Ursprung der Gottesidee* (Münster: Aschendorff; 1926–1955), of which vols. 9–12 cover the indigenous religious traditions of Inner Asia; Schmidt's work is marred by an interpretative framework based on his assumption of "original monotheism," and despite the wealth of data collected must be used as cautiously as much Soviet scholarship.

15. A concise and readable introduction to Mongol religion is provided by Walther Heissig, *The Religions of Mongolia*, tr. Geoffrey Samuel (London: Routledge & Kegan Paul, 1980). On religion among Turkic peoples see, in addition to the works of Roux and Schmidt mentioned above, Annemarie von Gabain, "Inhalt und magische Bedeutung der alttürkischen Inschriften," *Anthropos*, 48 (1953), pp. 537–556; the excellent philological discussion of Alessio Bombaci, "'Qutluγ bolzun!' A Contribution to the History of the Concept of 'Fortune' among the Turks," *UAJ*, 36 (1964), pp. 284–291, and 38 (1966), pp. 13–43; Hans-Joachim Klimkeit, "Qut: Ein Grundbegriff in der zentralasiatischen Religionsbegegnung," in *Humanitas Religiosa: Festschrift für Haralds Biezais* (Stockholm, 1979), pp. 252–260; and Robert Dankoff, "Kashgari on the Beliefs and Superstitions of the Turks," *JAOS*, 95 (1975), pp. 68–80. Of Soviet surveys, we may cite (with the caveats in place regarding Soviet religious studies in general) two of N. A. Alekseev's works, *Rannie formy religii tiurkoiazychnykh narodov Sibiri* (Novosibirsk: Nauka, Sibirskoe otdelenie, 1980), and *Shamanizm tiurkoiazychnykh narodov Sibiri* (Novosibirsk, 1984), the latter with a full German translation, *Schamanismus der Türken Sibiriens: Versuch einer vergleichenden arealen Untersuchung*, tr. Reinhold Schletzer (Hamburg: Reinhold Schletzer, 1987), and a partial English translation, "Shamanism among the Turkic peoples of Siberia," *SAA*, 28/1 (Summer 1989), pp. 56–107; promising recent exceptions to the primitive Soviet treatment of religion include the collective series produced by E. L. L'vova, I. V. Oktiabr'skaia, A. M. Sagalaev, and M. S. Usmanova, entitled *Traditsionnoe mirovozzrenie tiurkov Iuzhnoi Sibiri*; the three volumes (bearing the subtitles *Prostranstvo i vremia; veshchnyi mir* [Novosibirsk: Nauka, Sibirskoe otdelenie, 1988], *Chelovek; obshchestvo* [1989], and *Znak i ritual* [1990]) provide an excellent thematic survey of elements of religious conceptions among the Turkic peoples of southern Siberia, based on ethnographic material. Of similar quality, with a wider ethnographic scope, is the insightful work of E. S. Novik, *Obriad i fol'klor v sibirskom shamanizme: opyt sopostavleniia*

epic and shamanic narratives) and in "solicited" descriptions of native conceptual systems recorded by ethnographers, we note immediately that the Inner Asian religious worldview is marked by an elaborate and quite complex spiritual morphology of human beings, with systems of multiple souls representing the rich spiritual and psychic capabilities of human life,[16] as well as an equally richly developed cosmological structure for the world and its spiritual underpinnings; the elaborate cosmologies customarily involve an axial center that at once separates, and provides for passage between, the tripartite cosmos of underworld, earth, and heaven, multiple layers in the heavens and underworld, and a host of spirits enlivening natural objects and formations and inhabiting the entire mythic universe.[17]

These systems, however, are reflected in "practical" religious life almost exclusively in connection with the individual spiritual experiences and communally oriented ecstatic and ritual functions of the chief religious specialist of the Inner Asian world, the *shaman*.[18] Now in much of the scholarship dealing with Inner Asian religion, and indeed in most incidental surveys of Inner Asian religion by nonspecialists, the role of the shaman has been emphasized to such an extent that it has become commonplace to refer to the religious life of Inner Asian peoples prior to their adoption of, say, Buddhism or Islam (and even after their "conversion" as well) as "shamanism," as if the term could designate something akin to the other religious "-isms" that entered Inner Asia. Without raising here the conceptual issues involved in "defining" what is called shamanism, and without raising the historical problems involved in equating the

struktur (Moscow: Nauka, GRVL, 1984), of which a partial English translation appeared in *SAA*, 28/2 (Fall 1989), pp. 20–84, entitled "Ritual and Folklore in Siberian Shamanism: Experiment in a Comparison of Structures."

16. On conceptions of the soul see, for example, in addition to general works noted above, Ivar Paulson, *Die primitiven Seelenvorstellungen der nordeurasischen Völker: Eine religionsethnographische und religionsphänomenologische Untersuchung* (Stockholm: Ethnographical Museum of Sweden, 1958); S. M. Shirokogoroff, *The Psychomental Complex of the Tungus* (London: Kegan Paul, Trench, Trubner, 1935); and Ivan A. Lopatin, *The Cult of the Dead among the Natives of the Amur Basin* ('s-Gravenhage: Mouton & Co., 1960).

17. In addition to the general treatments noted above, see A. F. Anisimov, "Cosmological Concepts of the Peoples of the North," in *Studies in Siberian Shamanism*, ed. Henry N. Michael (Toronto: Arctic Institute of North America, 1963), pp. 157–229; cf. the Russian original, *Kosmologicheskie predstavleniia narodov Severa* (Moscow/Leningrad: Izd-vo AN SSSR, 1959).

18. Mircea Eliade, *Shamanism: Archaic Techniques of Ecstasy*, tr. Willard R. Trask (Princeton: Princeton University Press, 1972), is the standard introduction to the subject; often factually unreliable for Inner Asian shamanism, it remains the signal reference point from which other studies (by supporters or, now more commonly, critics, of Eliade's approach) begin. For Inner Asian shamanism in particular, the literature is now quite extensive; for summaries and/or use-

modern "ethnographic shaman" with the religious specialists noted among historical Inner Asian peoples, we must object to this tendency on other grounds, above all on the grounds that the emphasis upon the spiritual career of the shaman often obscures the more normative domestic and communal focuses of Inner Asian religious life. These *domestic* and *communal* focuses are vital, as we will consider shortly, for understanding the appeal of Islam (or rather the way in which Islam was appropriated with a communal focus) in the Inner Asian setting; they are often lost sight of, however, due to the frequent overemphasis upon the role of the shaman.

That role is, to be sure, of profound interest, both because the shaman is the central religious specialist charged with the deepest knowledge in the community of both "practical" and "theoretical" religion, and because the shaman fulfils vital social functions beyond his ecstatic expertise;[19] moreover, as we shall see, the "heroic" shaman's ecstatic journey provides an important model for our understanding of several aspects of

---

ful bibliographical guides, see the work of Alekseev, *Shamanizm tiurkoiazychnykh narodov Sibiri*; Vilmos Voigt, "Shamanism in Siberia (A Sketch and a Bibliography)," *Acta Ethnographica Academiae Scientiarum Hungaricae*, 26 (1977), pp. 385–395; Mihály Hoppál, "Shamanism: An Archaic and/or Recent System of Beliefs," *UAJ* [Bloomington], 57 (1985), pp. 121–140; T. M. Mikhailov, *Buriatskii shamanizm: istoriia, struktura i sotsial'nye funktsii* (Novosibirsk: Nauka, Sibirskoe Otdelenie, 1987). See also Abdülkadir İnan, *Tarihte ve bugün şamanizm: materyaller ve araştırmalar* (3rd ed., Ankara: Türk Tarih Kurumu Basımevi, 1986). Among the most useful and detailed ethnographic studies of shamanism among Inner Asian peoples are the works of Vilmos Diószegi, including his "Pre-Islamic shamanism of the Baraba Turks and some ethnogenetic conclusions," in *Shamanism in Siberia*, ed. V. Diószegi and M. Hoppál (Budapest: Akadémiai Kiadó, 1978), pp. 83–167, and "The Problem of the Ethnic Homogeneity of Tofa (Karagas) Shamanism," in *Popular Beliefs and Folklore Tradition in Siberia*, ed. V. Diószegi (Bloomington, Indiana/The Hague: Indiana University/Mouton, 1968), pp. 239–329. One of the first analyses of the religious meaning conveyed by various components of the shaman's costume (a subject emphasized by Eliade, Diószegi, and indeed most students of shamanism) remains standard: Uno Harva [né Holmberg], "The Shaman Costume and Its Significance," *Annales Universitatis Fennicae Aboensis*, ser. B, 1 (2) (1923), pp. 1–36. For a more recent examination of the social functions and "ritual" methods of the shaman based on Siberian material, see Anna-Leena Siikala, *The Rite Technique of the Siberian Shaman* (Helsinki: Suomalainen Tiedeakatemia, 1978; Folklore Fellows Communications, v. 220). Accounts of shamanic practices among the Turks and Mongols down to the fourteenth century have been collected by John Andrew Boyle, "Turkish and Mongol Shamanism in the Middle Ages," *Folklore*, 83 (1972), pp. 177–93; see also Jean–Paul Roux, "Le nom du chaman dans les textes turco-mongols," *Anthropos*, 53 (1958), pp. 133–142, and his "Le chaman gengiskhanide," *Anthropos*, 54 (1959), pp. 401–432.

19. See in particular on the social roles of the shaman the work of Siikala cited above, and the interesting article of I. R. Kortt, "The Shaman as Social Representative in the World Beyond," in *Shamanism in Eurasia*, ed. M. Hoppál (Göttingen: Edition Herodot, 1984), vol. 2, pp. 289–306.

the conversion narrative of central concern here. But it is usually the individual elements of the shaman's life that receive attention, whether his initial "sickness" and alienation from his community or his initiation and ecstatic performances; and the shaman, in turn, despite his important social roles, is often cast as a kind of spiritual "loner," set apart from his community and serving it almost grudgingly. In any case it is often overlooked that the shaman's specialist services are called upon primarily in times of individual crisis or communal imbalance, leaving the vast realm of everyday religious life, of sacralized norms of living in a human community, outside the purview of "shamanism"; with minimal exaggeration it is safe to say that the ordinary, workaday religious life of everyone *but* the shaman is all too often ignored or neglected, as if it were less interesting—or less central in the Inner Asian religious tradition—because it is less dramatic than the shaman's spiritual *tour de force*.

Inner Asian religious life is much richer and more diverse than the label "shamanism" suggests. However extensive a role the shaman may play in explaining elements of this domestic cult, or in officiating at communal versions of ancestral rites, or in "mobilizing" a community to observe certain norms, the fact remains that the ancestral and communal focuses of Inner Asian religion were customarily more directly linked with the daily lives of most people—affecting their conceptions of individual and communal "health" and soundness, affecting their life-supporting economic activities, from hunting to animal husbandry to agriculture, which ancestral spirits were believed to protect, and affecting their individual status as members of a family and their conceptions of belonging to a particular tribe or "nation"—than were the ecstatic performances or personal religious journeys of the shamans.

For the ordinary individual who is not a shaman, neither the wealth of souls nor the elaborate cosmological structures are experienced directly (aside from exceptional cases of visionary experience); he of course knows of them, for they fill and inform the entire spectrum of the shaman's dealings with both the individual and with the entire community, and as such the shamanic cosmology and "soul-culture" shape even the ordinary individual's religious expectations. But as a rule the ordinary person does not come face to face with them except through the shaman's mediation, nor does he manipulate them or interact with them ritually.

Both the macrocosmic and microcosmic worlds of the Inner Asian spiritual universe, then, are well developed conceptually, but the religious "practice" associated with them—the "handling" of human souls and the "navigation" of the vast spiritual worlds as a guide or seeker of souls—is reserved for religious specialists. Little of the elaborate cosmology evident in shamanic narratives or even epic tales is ritually significant for most people at most times: we find virtually no examples in Inner Asia, for instance, of publicly reenacted creation myths of a type well known from ancient Chinese, Indian, or Mesopotamian religion, wherein the creation of those macrocosmic structures is ritually repeated to celebrate, and ensure the preservation of, cosmic order and, thereby, human life. Nor do we find significant evidence of an abstract or speculative inquiry into the nature of the multiple human souls that might have both reflected and encouraged aspects of "practical" religion at an individual level ranging from asceticism to alchemy, as evidenced in Indian or Chinese thought-systems.

If we seek instead the sphere of religious activity that *directly and regularly* affects and involves the ordinary individual in Inner Asian societies, what we *do* find is an emphasis not upon the origin of the cosmos as such, but upon the origin of the human being, and, more important, of man as a social creature. Inner Asian traditions clearly belong to the normative class of "aboriginal" religions in which *life* and *health* are the chief values, with ritual action focused on "life-sustaining" activities; these naturally involve "crisis intervention" on the part of religious specialists, the shamans, at times of sickness and death. But the distinctive Inner Asian focus on what makes *life* possible is *communal* and *ancestral.* That is, with its central religious focus, broadly speaking, directed toward the maintenance of human life, Inner Asian tradition outside the occasionally "individualistic" spiritual career of the shaman knows only one setting within which such life is deemed religiously meaningful and thus conceivable and even possible: community.

This focus on the maintenance of human life in a communal setting infuses virtually all religious activity in traditional Inner Asia, including but not limited to the individual and social healing performances of the shaman, from life-cycle rites and the concern for healing, to the system of taboos and ethical norms, and from household offerings to ancestral spirits at the hearth to other domestic rites linked with enhancing economic success in animal husbandry, agriculture, hunting, or craft production. The same focus infuses the very sense of community and social belonging: to be accepted into a community is the equivalent of birth, often ritually celebrated as such, while to be deprived of one's community is to die, and the same principle is evidenced in the frequent occurrence in Inner Asia, as elsewhere, of communal ethnonyms denoting simply "people," "human beings." In both cases such conceptions have not only to do with the living community, but with the souls of deceased members in the afterlife, and, with notions of the "cycling" of souls within the bounds of a given community (i.e., through common beliefs that a newborn child is inhabited by the soul of a deceased ancestor), with the future of the community, those yet unborn, as well.

One of the central features of indigenous Inner Asian religious life may thus be found in its steady and persistent focus on the centrality of *community* as the setting for human life, and naturally for religious life as well. Here we find a key to Inner Asian religion deeper and more revealing than is suggested by calling that religion "shamanism." And in any event, the unifying concern that ties the domestic ancestral cult with the activity of the "specialist" shaman is the essential recognition that "religious" life consists—like economic life and political life—of ways of understanding and manipulating the world in order to maintain the central sacred value of (communal) life and (communal) well-being.

A natural and vital focus of such religious life, designed to maintain and promote life and well-being, falls naturally upon the Ancestors, who are the key to the community's health and well-being as protectors not only of the family's stock and lineage, but of its economic foundations as well. The ancestor spirits are customarily assimilated to the spirits of the earth and soil in agricultural communities, are regarded as protective patrons of the herds' fertility in pastoral nomadic communities, and are the recipients of offerings and appeals for thevsuccess of a hunt, alongside the master spirits of nature and of the intended victim, among hunting communities; they are likewise assimilated to the patron spirits of craft production, and play a vital role as the tutelary spirits of shamans. More important, the ancestral spirits, as the "numinous" embodiment of the social structures of family and community, are a central focus of the most common and most sacred religious *practice* among Inner Asian peoples; for the vast majority of individuals and communities, religious life lies primarily not in recourse to a shaman or "worship" of some deity, but in the periodic offerings to the ancestral spirits in their various forms, intended to preserve the health and continuity of the family and community.

Herein we find already an important clue to the centrality of communal self-identity for religious practice (and religious conversion!), and vice versa. The most sacred and fundamental religious rites are those focused on spirits regarded as the ancestors of the family and community. Consequently, the ways in which the family and community are defined, through contemporary relationships and mutual obligations as well as through assertions of genealogical ties, have direct and profound cultic significance, and hence a profound religious component; conversely, that religious component, both in its "affective" and ritual aspects, provides many of the symbolic structures employed in the process of asserting the definition of a given community. Communal identity shapes the form and content of the central rites and "sentiments" that belong to the sphere of "religion," rites and sentiments that "conversion" directly affects; and at the same time, the religious worldview, thus infused with specific communal content, in turn provides the discursive paradigms, and their ritual "reification," whereby the legitimacy and sacrality of familial and communal groupings are asserted.

Accordingly, it is the origin of, and ritual celebration of, the familial and communal group that is the religious focus of Inner Asian domestic cults, and the origin of the communal group, immediately assimilable to the origin of humankind, is one of the central elements of Inner Asian religious life in which both "myth" and "ritual" elements were of ongoing vitality and importance.[20]

Before considering these domestic myths and rites more carefully, however, we may note here, in connection with the reflection of social organization in the Inner Asian religious worldview, yet another common feature of the prevailing scholarly approaches to Inner Asian religion that, alongside the fixation on the shaman, has tended to skew our understanding of the foundations of that worldview. This is the attention, at times inordinate, devoted to the sacral foundations of, or religious legitimation of, political rule at the broadest levels of social organization in Inner Asia. One of the most prolific writers on Inner Asian religion, Jean-Paul Roux, has gone so far as to speak of an "imperial cult" in Inner Asian history, as an apparent constant that is called up at times of political unification and is expressly opposed to the shamanic religion (which Roux

20. The mythic focus on the origin of human community does not seem to have produced in Inner Asia an abstraction explaining the origin of the cosmos as such in human and/or social terms; we find no Inner Asian equivalent to the Vedic Purusha-hymn, in which the world is formed through the ritual dismemberment of the Cosmic Man, nor do we find either the ritual development reflected in such an abstraction, or the speculative and mystical thought such an abstraction might fuel. Rather, in Inner Asia the origin of the local community is more often equated with the origin of the world, or at least of the world that matters—the social world—with little attention to the formation of the elements of the cosmos; whatever "mythic abstracting" may have occurred (and examples may be found in some Inner Asian myths), the important point is that these never were taken as the basis for ritual practice, which remained focused on the origin of human community, at the family, clan-tribal, and state level.

casts as nonimperial). A full evaluation of this view, and others that assume a structural bifurcation between "imperial" and "domestic" religion in Inner Asia, lies beyond the scope of this study; but it must be noted here that the present exploration of Islamization, and especially of the "nativization" of Islam, suggests quite different approaches to the relationship between what may be more properly regarded not as two competing "levels" of religious thought and ritual, but as "imperial" and "domestic" *styles of evoking* essentially the same system of religious values and practices.

These issues will be taken up later in connection with the legitimizing functions of narratives relating communal origin and/or conversion, but for now we must reemphasize the central importance of domestic rites in the ordinary, "everyday" religious life of *most* people at *most* times.[21] In general the "ancestor-cult" among Inner Asian peoples, and the closely linked and pervasive offerings to familial and household spirits, have not received the attention they deserve, but it is difficult to escape the conclusion that this domestic religious practice is the focus of *meaningful* and *ongoing* religious life for the majority of people. It is precisely the meaningfulness of the religious complex at this most basic level of social organization in Inner Asia that on the one hand impels indigenous "imperial" state-formers to appeal to it, and on the other hand makes the nativization of a "foreign" religion within the familiar structures of that same complex such a potentially potent weapon both for "imperial" reformers and for groups and individuals hostile to the status quo and in need of an affective basis to unite people in *anti*-imperial structures. It is in this light that we may understand the use of the central conversion narrative under consideration here both by Chingisid representatives of imperial prerogatives and by their opponents.

The Domestic Rites and Their Universalizing Role: An Inner Asian Mythic Complex

It is precisely in the domestic cult that we find the only recognizable ritual evocation of cosmological principles in Inner Asia, through the mythic assimilation of the focus of domestic rites with the central structures of the cos-

21. Even Roux, who has so strongly emphasized the role of the shaman and of what he sees as an "imperial tradition" in Inner Asian religion, seems to grudgingly acknowledge the centrality of the household ancestral offerings, writing, "Il n'est pas exclu, même, que pour le bas peuple. . . , cette religion intime soit la religion essentielle" (*La mort*, p. 131).

mos; this in turn helps us to appreciate why appeals to sacred communal origins as articulated within the framework of a mythic complex embodying those cosmological principles have such powerful resonance not only with khans and ruling dynasties at the imperial level, but with the ordinary tribal population as well. To understand this more clearly, we must explore the domestic ritual and the mythic complex associated with it more closely.

The system of domestic rites is typically focused within individual households, in the offerings made to ancestral spirits most often conceived of as dwelling at or near the hearth, and within communities, in the often seasonal (fall and spring) communal rites involving offerings to protective clan spirits;[22] the latter in particular are, as noted, often clearly "economic" in focus, involving appeals to the protective and engendering capacities of the ancestors to fructify herds, to help make hunts successful, or to make croplands fertile and productive, with household rites likewise involving appeals for successful hunts as well as for blessings on various types of craft production, but more often linked to more direct human and familial concerns of health, protection of children and aid in childbearing, and fertility.

The household rites are usually quite simple in form, involving offerings of food and drink to the ancestral spirits, both by smearing fat or grease on the mouth of wooden or felt figures ("idols") representing the ancestors or household spirits, and through offerings of meat or fat directly in the hearth fire as burnt offerings, accompanied by libations of kumiss (fermented mare's milk) or other drinks (either sprinkling the liquid into the fire, or casting it into the air). Even when the figurines are used, however, the connection with the hearth is maintained by keeping the "idols" either wrapped up or enclosed in a small chest near the hearth.[23]

Such offerings are noted first in the thirteenth century among travelers to the Mongols, including Rubruck and Marco Polo, but appear also in descriptions of religious customs among many Inner Asian peoples from travelers and ethnographers down to the present century; they are among the chief constants in daily life that not only affirm the temporal continu-

22. See Harva, *Die religiösen Vorstellungen der altaischen Völker*, pp. 570–577 on seasonal offerings to clan protectors.

23. Cf. Harva, *Die religiösen Vorstellungen*, pp. 230–238; Roux, *La mort*, pp. 117–131. See also the excellent account of domestic rites among the Tuvans in Erika Taube, "Die Widerspiegelung religiöser Vorstellungen im Alltagsbrauchtum der Tuwiner der Westmongolei," in *Traditions religieuses et para-religieuses des peuples altaïques* (Paris: Presses universitaires de France, 1972; = PIAC XIII), pp. 119–138, esp. pp. 128–131 on libations and burnt offerings to ancestral figurines kept near the hearth. For illustrations of such wooden and felt images, cf. S. V. Ivanov, *Skul'ptura altaitsev, khakasov i Sibirskikh tatar, XVIII-pervaia chetvert' XX v.* (Leningrad: Nauka, 1979).

ity and "solidarity" of individual households and families and communities, but provide the foundations upon which sentiments of inclusion in communal structures of larger scale must be built. Although accounts of such images predominate among peoples not yet "converted" to Islam or Buddhism or Christianity, a steady series of Western travel accounts affirms their ongoing significance in the domestic rites of Inner Asian peoples even after their adoption of other religions; in particular, ancestral offerings focused upon the hearth and involving the use of such jarringly un-Islamic "idols" are repeatedly mentioned by outside observers as a continuing presence in the homes of nomadic Muslim peoples of Inner Asia (i.e., in places rarely, if ever, mentioned in indigenous sources) in the post-Mongol period,[24] suggesting not so much the inferior quality of the Islam adopted there as the enormous strength of the specifically ancestral rites that survived, often with "Islamized" form, from the old pre-Islamic ways. It is precisely this ancestral complex (including related funeral customs) that inevitably persisted most strongly after the adoption of Islam, seamlessly integrated, in both ritual practice and in conceptualization, into the sacralized daily lives of peoples now considered (by themselves and others) as Muslims; this survival in turn provides the rationale for the prominence attached to "Islamized" ancestral spirits not only in domestic rites, but in the mythic articulation of sacred origins that is most relevant for our focus in the present study.

The central role of the hearth in such offerings, both as the seat of the fire, honored in its own right and as a conveyor of sustenance to the ancestors, and as the ritual and "orientational" center of the household, is evidenced even earlier in Inner Asia; it was Herodotus, after all, who af-

24. Cf. Roux, *La religion des Turcs et des Mongols*, pp. 231–234. Giles Fletcher, describing the Tatars of the Crimea in the latter sixteenth century, writes: "Herein they differ from the Turkish religion, for that they have certeine idole puppets, made of silke or like stuffe, of the fashion of a man, which they fasten to the doore of their walking houses, to be as Janusses or keepers of their house. And these idols are made not by all, but by certeine religious women, which they have among them for that and like uses" (Edward A. Bond, ed., *Russia at the Close of the Sixteenth Century, comprising The Treatise "Of the Russe Common Wealth," by Dr. Giles Fletcher; and The Travels of Sir Jerome Horsey* [London: Hakluyt Society, Series I, No. 20, 1856], p. 90; cf. Giles Fletcher, *Of the Rus Commonwealth*, ed. Albert J. Schmidt [Ithaca, New York: Cornell University Press / Folger Shakespeare Library, 1966], p. 96). Captain John Smith (better known for his adventures in Virginia) describes similar felt "puppets," and their feeding, among the Crimean Tatars, though he cribs from Rubruck (cf. *The Complete Works of Captain John Smith (1580–1631)*, ed. Philip L. Barbour (Chapel Hill: University of North Carolina Press/ Williamsburg, Virginia: Institute of Early American History and Culture, 1986), vol. 3, pp. 192–193. For the use of such "idols" among the Islamized Baraba Tatars of southern Siberia, cf. Diószegi, "Pre-Islamic Shamanism of the Baraba Turks," pp. 88–95, 152–153.

firmed that no oath was more sacred among the Scythians than one sworn by the royal hearth fire. This in itself suggests the close links between the hearth and the seat of sacred human identities, but the explicit "seating" of communal life and identity in the hearth is especially well evidenced among peoples of Inner Asia. The Altay and Teleut, for instance, regard the hearth fire as the preserver of the life of each family and clan, and refer to the "stone hearth (*ochoq*) dug out by the mother;" the hearth fire is not to be taken outside the home, except in the ritually controlled context of family ceremonies (e.g., when brothers establish new homes), and the extinguishing of the hearth fire is typically regarded as the symbolic equivalent of a clan's extinction.[25] From Herodotus through accounts of the medieval Turks and Mongols to modern ethnographic descriptions, we find the recurrent observation that Inner Asian peoples regard fire as among the most sacred things, and in most instances this is to be understood not as referring to "fire" in the abstract, but to the particular hearth fire in each household;[26] and the ritual use of the domestic hearth is, as noted, one of the central familial and communal religious practices of the "old" religion to survive among Islamic Inner Asian communities.[27]

The sacrality of the hearth and hearth fire in the domestic cult is of particular importance, for the hearth and its symbolic significance convey religious meaning both in ritual and in spatial or "orientational" contexts, in both cases linked to the Ancestors. In the first regard, the hearth is clearly the locus of ancestral spirits (and of the figures that represent them and "receive" offerings to them), as noted; but the spatial orientation of the hearth as the "center" of the household also links it to a larger cosmological symbolism that both solidifies the hearth's familial, ancestral links

25. Cf. N. P. Dyrenkova, "Kul't ognia u altaitsev i teleut," *Sbornik Muzeia antropologii i ètnografii*, t. 6 (Leningrad, 1927), pp. 63–78 [esp. pp. 63, 66–67, 74–77].

26. Cf. Taube, "Wiederspiegelung," pp. 122–123; Dyrenkova, "Kul't ognia," p. 63; L'vova et al., *Traditsionnoe mirovozzrenie* (1988), pp. 136–147; and in general on the sacredness of fire, cf. Jean-Paul Roux, "Fonctions chamaniques et valeurs du feu chez les peuples altaïques," *RHR*, 189 (1976), pp. 67–101, and N. Poppe, "Zum Feuerkultus bei den Mongolen," *Asia Major*, 2 (1925), pp. 130–145.

27. We have, for example, a revealing description for a people who will be of importance for us, the Noghays, in the observations of a nineteenth century observer who notes the importance of the hearth in the daily life of the people. Asserting that Islam had weakened the "cult of fire" and thereby deprived the hearth of spiritual significance, the writer nevertheless notes one "survival" of "the cult of fire linked with the cult of ancestors": he describes a festival in which all family members eat a meal around the hearth while remembering deceased relatives, believing that the spirits of the dead return to the homes of their living relatives and join in the revelries at the hearth (G. Maliavkin, "Karanogaitsy," *Terskii sbornik*, vyp. 3, kn. 2 (1893), pp. 133–173 [pp. 150–151, note]).

and ties it to a larger system of beliefs and conceptions vital to an appreciation of communal identity in Inner Asia. It is through the hearth as a gateway to the world of the Ancestors, both ritually (in the domestic offerings) and conceptually (in the symbolic equivalences known through cosmological assumptions and shamanic report), that we find the keys to the "universalization" of domestic ritual experience in the mythic assimilation between the center of the dwelling and the center of the world.

This assimilation, which lies at the heart of the evocative power of the legends of origin and conversion narratives we will be considering, in effect equates the individual domestic hearth at the center of the household with the center of the universe (that is, of the religiously and humanly significant world), a sacred center marked by a number of recurrent and virtually universal images evoked also in cosmogonic myth, heroic epic, shamanic narrative, and straightforward, ethnographically solicited "descriptions" of the spiritual cosmos that Inner Asian peoples inhabit.

The images most often associated with the sacred cosmic center, and thus assimilated domestically to the hearth, are the axial and chthonic symbols of a Mountain, a Tree, a Stream or Lake or Pool, a "Goddess" (i.e., a feminine spirit), and a Cavern (or hollow or other subterranean enclosure): the Mountain and Tree are immediately implied in the microcosmic, domestic context by the axis linking the hearth with the smoke-hole of the dwelling; the Goddess is mythically reduplicated in the ancestral female spirits (the "grandmothers") who dwell by the hearth in each family's household (and she herself implies the nourishing "water of life" that fills the Stream or Lake at the macrocosmic level, for she offers the sustaining liquid to the First Man born there either from the pool itself or from her own breasts); and the Cavern finds its mythic equivalent in the hearth itself, since both are passageways to the chthonic world of the Ancestors (the hearth being "dug" into or "hollowed out" of the earth, and at the same time being the seat of the ancestral spirits who in macrocosmic conception are believed to dwell in the underworld).

These images are usually found together, occasionally associated with other mythic motifs and at times, perhaps, with one or another image missing from the set (though no doubt mythically *implied* by the others' presence); their recurrent reflection in legends of origin from throughout the Inner Asian world is an important indication that these images together amount to a potent mythic complex intimately connected with sacred origins at both the universal and particular level, and hence repeatedly evoked in the religious, economic, social, and political circumstances in which such sacred origins take on special significance.

At the universal level, this mythic complex is marked above all by the World Mountain and World Tree, familiar axial images usually combined with a Cave that serves as the First Man's birthplace; this universal and communal center is inhabited by a feminine spirit who, regardless of the form she takes in the varied evocations of this myth, is none other than the mother of humanity, and she serves variously to give birth to the First Man and/or to nourish him with the water of the sacred Lake or Stream that completes the basic mythic complex. Reflected in an enormous range of Inner Asian traditions, this mythic complex of Mountain/Tree/Cave/Water/Goddess is one of the primary religious conceptions central to traditional Inner Asian life, belief, and ritual. It is a standard feature of shamanic narratives, and is frequently depicted on the shaman's drum and costume; linking the heavens and the underworld, the Mountain and Tree form the orientational centers for the shaman's ecstatic journeys in either direction, and shamanic narratives thus repeatedly affirm their axial nature. Among the Altai-kizhi, for instance, shamanic descriptions tell of a mountain in the center of the earth, with the Milk Sea at its peak and the "holy golden poplar" (*bay terek*) rising from its top as well, at the "navel of earth and heaven."[28]

But this mythic conceptualization does not by any means belong to a purely "shamanic cosmology." Rather, it appears consistently in popular songs and epic tales among Inner Asian peoples; it appears in Inner Asian "iconography," as well, and, is clearly reflected in the domestic religion that occupies most people at most times, i.e., when the shaman is not needed.

In popular songs praising the World Tree collected among the Turks of Minusinsk in south-central Siberia, for instance, nearly all elements of the mythic complex are evoked: "Piercing the twelve heavens / On the summit of a mountain / A birch in the misty depths of air. / Golden are the birch's leaves, / Golden its bark, / In the ground at its foot a basin / Full of the water of life, / In the basin a golden ladle . . ."[29] Similarly, the complex appears in hero-tales that clearly combine in one figure the traits proper to both shaman and First Man. In the Altay epic tale of *Maday Qara*, for instance, the hero dwells in the Altay mountains in a stone yurt where seventy rivers flow together and the "eternal poplar with a hundred boughs," the Bay Terek, stands reaching up to heaven. When his people

28. Cf. Alekseev, *Schamanismus*, p. 98.

29. Tr. Holmberg / Harva, *Mythology*, p. 350, citing Anton Schiefner, *Heldensagen der minusinskischen Tataren* (SPb., 1859), p. 62.

are nearing destruction, he leaves his son, the future hunter-hero Kögüdäy Märgän, atop a high black mountain beneath a birch tree, whose juice will sustain the boy; through his protective abandonment—a familiar theme in legends of origin—he hopes to ensure the child's survival, and indeed, as the hero's people is defeated and enclosed in an iron prison, the boy is found and cared for by an old woman, "the mistress of the Altay," under whose tutelage he grows up to eventually free his people.[30]

The structuring of this mythic world is remarkably similar throughout Inner Asia, and one of its most frequently invoked, and ritually significant, elements is the sacred Tree.[31] Its symbolism may well be in evidence already in the archaic motifs of the so-called animal-style art of Scytho-Siberian civilization in Inner Asia,[32] and as the "Tree of Life" it is an essential feature of most Inner Asian worldviews. This Tree, on the cosmic Mountain, is typically the dwelling place, and often the birthplace, of the First Man, and the tree itself is frequently identified with, or simply houses, the "goddess" who nourishes him. The tree's spirit is customarily feminine, appearing as a woman to the First Man—himself born from the tree—and nourishing him from her breasts; and this intimation of the tree-spirit's close association with a clan's life and continuity is quite normative. Among the Evenki (Tungus) of northeastern Inner Asia, for instance, the female clan spirit is believed to reside among the roots

30. See Ugo Marazzi, tr., *Maday Qara: An Altay Epic Poem* (Naples: Istituto Universitario Orientale, 1986), pp. 30–32, 46, 58 ff., and the synopsis, pp. 9–10.

31. See, on the Tree of Life, Roux, *Faune et flore sacrées*, pp. 357–380, and his *La religion des Turcs et des Mongols*, pp. 148–154, and, more generally, E. A. S. Butterworth, *The Tree at the Navel of the Earth* (Berlin: De Gruyter, 1970). On the Terek or Bay Terek ("mighty poplar") as the sacred clan tree, see also the material collected in the valuable work of R. G. Akhmet'ianov, *Obshchaia leksika dukhovnoi kul'tury narodov srednego Povolzh'ia* (Moscow: Nauka, 1981), pp. 94–96; on echoes of the notion of the world tree in the Volga-Ural region, cf. G. M. Davletshin, "O kosmogonicheskikh vozzreniiakh Volzhskikh bulgar domongol'skogo perioda," in *Iz istorii tatarskoi obshchestvennoi mysli* (Kazan, 1979), pp. 44–55 [pp. 50–54]. Of some interest for the contemporary resonance of such images may be noted the evocations of such elements in modern Central Asian literature, as in the case of the Uzbek writer Mamadali Mahmudov's *Ölmäs qayälär* (1981), in which a sacred tree at the edge of a high cliff figures repeatedly in the story; the tree is the object of pilgrimages, and the hero appeals to it before battle, addresses it as his "mother," and is restored to health in a cavern at its base (cf. William Fierman, "Cultural Nationalism in Soviet Uzbekistan: A Case Study of *The Immortal Cliffs* , *Soviet Union / Union soviétique*, 12/1 [1985], pp. 1–41 [pp. 9–10]).

32. On the tree symbolism of the stylized cervine antlers so prominent in the animal-style art, see Esther Jacobson, "The Stag with Bird-Headed Antler Tines: A Study in Image Transformation and Meaning," *Bulletin of the Museum of Far Eastern Antiquities*, 56 (1984), pp. 113–180; essentially the same view is advanced, apparently independently (but less well developed) in Anatoly I. Martynov, *The Ancient Art of Northern Asia*, tr. Demitri B. Shimkin and Edith M. Shimkin (Urbana: University of Illinois Press, 1991), pp. 99–111.

of a sacred clan tree that is symbolically identified with the World Tree.[33]

The connection between this cosmological conception and individual life and domestic rites is well illustrated in conceptions of the Turkic peoples of the Altai: the Milk Sea is found in the third heaven, where Paradise is located, atop a high mountain in the midst of a great forest containing the Tree of Life; from the base of the Tree of Life flows the same substance as that which fills the Milk Sea, and this same Milk Sea is the source of the life-force placed by the birth spirit (*yayuchï*) into each child as it comes into the world.[34] This life-force is *qut*, a term with a wide range of numinous connotations among the Turkic peoples of Inner Asia, from this humble use to refer to the "embryonal force" that enlivens children, to its use in designating the "fortune" that ensures a household's health and physical well-being when it falls through the smoke-hole (i.e., above the hearth) in the tent, and finally to more exalted uses signaling the power and prosperity that divine favor grants to a monarch; in each case, however, the term's association with the sacred power that underlies the security of a family's or community's health, economic foundations, and reproductive continuity is evident at each level of its use, and in each case should remind us of its conceptual association with the mythic complex under consideration.

The mythic complex and the cosmic structure it signifies are thus well represented in ethnographic accounts and epic literature for a wide range of Inner Asian peoples; most important for our purposes, the complex provides the mythic framework for many Inner Asian legends of origin and for a number of Inner Asian "nativizations" of conversion narratives, as discussed below, although the appearance of this mythic complex in such tales has not always been recognized as such. But what makes the features of this mythic complex so compelling as elements in hero tales and shamanic narratives, and as a basis for legends of origin, is their symbolic assimilation of the universal and particular focuses of Inner Asian religious conceptions and practices.

As suggested, this assimilation works in both ancestral and cosmological directions. First, the hearth is closely associated with the feminine ancestral spirits who are the preservers and transmitters of the veritable "substance" of the family and clan, both as the "dwelling-place" of these

33. Cf. A. F. Anisimov, "Cosmological Concepts," p. 176.

34. Cf. Harva, *Die religiösen Vorstellungen*, pp. 85–89, 170; on this use of *qut* see Bombaci, "Qutluγ bolzun!" p. 32.

spirits and as the point of intimate ritual contact with them; these feminine spirits, represented in the wooden or felt figures and offered food and drink in this form, are more often than not assigned the telling appellation of "the grandmothers" (i.e., the *emegender*[35]). Second, the hearth, as center of the dwelling, is spatially associated with the axis joining the upper world through the smoke-hole of the *yurt*, for instance, with the chthonic world of the Ancestors reached spiritually through the hearth itself (which is conceived as an opening into the earth, whether it is actually a pit or enclosed oven in form, or is merely marked by three stones, etc.); as such the hearth is "orientationally" equivalent to the center of the earth where the Axis of the world, conceived as the World Mountain and/or World Tree, meets the earth and joins the three realms of Heaven, Earth, and Underworld, and it is ritually equivalent as well. And both conceptions are joined in the mythic assimilation of the "grandmother" spirits to the feminine spirit who dwells at the base of the World Tree and nourishes shamans and heroes either with her own breasts or with the Water of Life.[36]

The hearth is thus the symbolic equivalent of the center of the earth, ritually reiterated in each household; and the feminine spirits who inhabit the domestic hearth correspond to the feminine figure, appearing alternately in the form of a beautiful maiden, a maternal nourisher, and a grandmotherly protector, as well as in other forms (including animal consorts and guides), who inhabits the base of the World Tree at the site where a spring wells up or a stream flows. Through this mythic identification of the microcosmic individual hearth with the macrocosmic center of the world, the system of universal sacred symbols is localized in each Inner Asian dwelling, and the individual ritual center is universalized, allowing the individual family group to participate in a symbolic cosmos

35. Cf. Harva, *Die religiösen Vorstellungen*, pp. 173–174; see also E. Lot-Falck, "A propos d'Ätügän, Déesse mongole de la terre," *RHR*, 149 (1956), pp. 157–196 [pp. 186–190 on "the grandmothers"]. On the Turkic feminine spirit *Umay* and her conceptual development, cf. L. P. Potapov, "Umai—bozhestvo drevnikh tiurkov v svete ètnograficheskikh dannykh," in *Tiurkologicheskii sbornik 1972* (Moscow: Nauka, GRVL, 1973), pp. 265–286, and Denis Sinor, "'Umay,' a Mongol Spirit Honored by the Türks," in *Proceedings of the International Conference on China Border Area Studies* (Taipei: National Chengchi University, 1984), pp. 1771–1781.

36. The Water of Life, of which heroes and shamans partake, is mythically associated with the body of water situated at the base of the world tree on the world mountain; it is no doubt this water that is symbolized, for example, in stone carvings of medieval Turkic warriors holding cups at their chests, and the mythic bestowal of the water of life to the hero/ancestor beneath the World Tree most likely found pictorial expression in the famous Scythian goldwork and the Pazyryk felt hangings.

whose essential structures are known not only throughout a particular community, but throughout the entire Inner Asian world.

Our point here is not to further explore the rich symbolism of this mythic complex or to analyze its origins from any particular perspective; rather, the importance of this mythic complex—which will be taken up later in specific connection with legends of origin—lies in its being the meeting-place of household domestic rites preserved at the local level throughout Inner Asia even after conversion to other religions, and a widespread cosmogonic myth common among Inner Asian peoples through at least two and a half millennia. In the elements of this mythic complex that recur among so many communities over such a long time we find reflected one of the simplest and most powerful religious values of Inner Asian peoples, namely, the assumption that *significant* (i.e., *ritually relevant*) cosmogony consists of the origin of human beings, and not of human beings in the abstract or as individuals but as familial and communal groupings. In effect, the creation of the world and its structures may be recounted, but it no longer has ritual significance—only human origins are reflected in the domestic cult.

Yet what the domestic cult celebrates in its "universalized" aspect is not merely the origin of Humanity in the abstract or in the whole; rather, it is only when the framework for human origins, provided by this mythic complex of Mountain/Tree/Cave/Water/Feminine Spirit, is given particular social content that it becomes ritually significant in the domestic and communal context. At its basic level this social content is obviously the family and clan, and some religious meaning is potentially quite sustainable at this level; for social and political meaning, however, the social content infused into the traditional mythic context must be located somewhere between the individual family and the abstraction of all humanity.

In effect the very ubiquity of this mythic complex suggests that simply recounting the birth of the Hero or First Man at the World Tree on the World Mountain by the World Stream, and his nourishment and guidance to personhood by the feminine spirit there, might become as ritually irrelevant as the story of the earth's creation; the same motifs may recur in such recountings, but they become a cosmogonic, or rather ethnogonic, myth only when infused with particular names and identities that bear social and communal significance. And this consideration in turn tells us that a cosmogony that is both *relevant* and religiously *meaningful* must recount a particular collectivity's origins within the structural framework, which is to say within the social expectations, indicated by the recurrent motifs of the familiar mythic complex. Those motifs offer the structural means of universalizing and sanctifying the collectivity's origins, of linking it with the normative and holy structure of the cosmos, and thus of asserting its legitimacy and sacrality. When those universalizing motifs are linked with the "personnel"—i.e., "ancestral" names—"believed" or asserted to link an assemblage of households and communities (which already signal their acceptance of those universal motifs in their domestic ritual practice) into a larger confederative or imperial structure, the stage is set for a politically significant ritual affirmation, alongside the politically significant narrative affirmation of what amounts to a communal charter.

The present study will be less concerned with the ritual affirmation of social cohesion than with the social and political implications of the "charter," as evidenced in our central conversion narrative and its permutations; this issue will be considered later, after looking at the recurrence, in the conversion narrative and the tales rooted in it, of the mythic framework on which legends of origin are repeatedly hung. Here it is appropriate, however, to note briefly the political implications of this mythic assimilation of the universal and domestic, for in the ancestral focus of the latter as well as in the "creational" focus of the former lies an enormously potent symbolic basis for the conceptualization of communal integrity and identity, and for the legitimation of political inclusion and organization. That mythic complex links the universal and domestic, and so naturally we find it evoked in legends of origin seeking to mobilize people for whom the domestic rites are sacred and valid, into accepting the social, political, and ultimately sacral validity of a larger-scale collectivity.

When ancestral spirits are honored and fed in a particular household, the members of the household express their membership in a community that includes not only the household and its deceased and unborn members, but other descendants of those ancestral spirits as well, as far afield as may be actually or assertively "remembered," all in a ritual setting immediately and universally recognized as the local reflection of sacred cosmic structures. When an entire community (e.g., a tribal encampment or a village) celebrates a memorial feast for the departed "communal" ancestors (i.e., those not specifically commemorated), it likewise asserts its communal identity and solidarity in a way that sacralizes the community's origins and ancestry in the context of that same cosmology. At this level we find clearly evoked communally based myths of the First Man/Ancestor with the assemblage of mythic elements associated with such figures in Inner Asia; that is, we do not expect to find the universalization of particular household ancestors into First Man, but we do find communal ancestors so universalized, and at levels ranging from individual clans or villages up to tribal confederations and groupings as inchoate (retroactively, at least) as, for example, the "Oghuz." At this level, already, we must no doubt appreciate the "assertive" character of such universalizations of communal ancestors, since the social grouping "imagined" by them is already not "natural" and inevitable; rather, it is held together in part by the affective appeals, communally endorsed and rehearsed, to a common ancestral figure who is surrounded with the mythic accoutrements appropriate to First Man and Founder of "a people." The conscious discursive act—which we witness above all in oral tradition—of attaching those mythic accoutrements to an ancestral figure accepted by or asserted for a community is itself a political statement on the ultimate legitimacy of that community, essentially marking an assertion that the community's origins are equivalent to the origins of the universe, or at least of the universe's significant and relevant component, that of human beings.

It is thus not surprising to find stock features of legends of origin present in what amount to "confederative charters," giving us confederative legends of origin in which a common ancestor is "discovered" or "asserted" and sacralized as founding a *legitimate* community in a number of ways that most commonly involve (1) the universalization of the ancestor as First Man (for the community in question at least) through surrounding him with the mythic symbols appropriate to First Man, and/or (2) the legitimizing power of a "new religion" that the ancestor is regarded as introducing through conversion.

We will discuss the potential political functions of such confederative legends of origin at the conclusion of our study, but here we may note that the power of "rehearsing" the communal "charter" clearly rests upon the religious and magical/ritual functions of narrative recitation, and indeed of speech itself, in Inner Asian tradition; the impact of religious modes of language beyond specifically religious contexts has been noted, especially in the case of shamanic narratives,[37] but has wider implications for social and political organization in Inner Asia, as we will see.

37. On the relationships between religious language (in shamanic narrative or in ritual and magical contexts) and heroic epic and folklore, cf. Arthur Hatto, "Shamanism and Epic Poetry in Northern Asia," in his *Essays on Medieval German and Other Poetry* (Cambridge: Cambridge University Press, 1980), pp. 117–138; Novik, *Obriad i fol'klor;* D. K. Zelenin, "Religiozno-magicheskaia funktsiia fol'klornykh skazok," in *Sergeiu Fedorovichu Ol'denburgu k piatidesiatiletiiu nauchno-obshchestvennoi deiatel'nosti 1882–1932: Sbornik statei* (Leningrad: Izd-vo AN SSSR, 1934), pp. 215–240; E. Taube, "South Siberian and Central Asian Hero Tales and Shamanistic Rituals," in *Shamanism in Eurasia*, ed. Hoppál, vol. 2, pp. 344–352; and P. A.

Islamization in Inner Asia

In view of these considerations on Islam and conversion and on the nature of indigenous Inner Asian religious conceptions, how are we to understand the encounter of these two traditions? This, or at least some pieces of the puzzle, is essentially what we will hope to learn from exploring the conversion narrative and its echoes in the following pages; but a few further general considerations on the integration and assimilation that occur in the meeting of Inner Asian and Islamic worldviews may now be in order, as a means of underscoring the assumptions adopted here regarding what "Islamization" may mean.

We must acknowledge first off that the process signified by the unfortunately inelegant term "Islamization" is in reality a dual process that necessarily works in two different directions: on the one hand the introduction of Islamic patterns into Inner Asia involves the "imposition" of Islamic norms in a new setting, an alien environment; on the other hand, the nativization of Islamic patterns involves their incorporation and assimilation into indigenous modes of thought and action. That this process of integration and assimilation—which after all would be expected naturally on the basis of other local adaptations of Islam—requires comment at all in the case of Islam in Inner Asia is indicative of the imposing array of primarily modern voices that, for quite diverse motives, have ignored or rejected outright this normal and ordinary integration, often seeking in the process to fragment or destroy the integrity of traditional religious life among Inner Asian peoples who considered themselves Muslims.

The diversity of such voices is as remarkable as the extent to which they have virtually silenced other views. They range from Tsarist Russian missionaries and educators eager to weaken Islam but often willing to make a Christian accommodation with, for instance, the cherished ancestral veneration, to largely westernized (in this case Russianized) intellectuals from among particular Inner Asian peoples who viewed their communities' inherited mythic and ritual patterns with embarrassment or only thinly veiled contempt. They range from homegrown Muslim purists who with reasonable legitimacy, from the internal logic of Islamic discourse (which, after all, was implicitly and potentially endorsed by their communities by virtue of their adoption, even if "only nominal," of Islam), sought to rid

Troiakov, "Promyslovaia i magicheskaia funktsiia skazyvaniia skazok u khakasov," *SÈ* 1969, No. 2, pp. 24–34, with an English translation, "Economic and Magical Functions of Taletelling among the Khakasy," *SAA*, 14/1–2 (Summer-Fall 1975), pp. 146–167.

their communities of non-Qur'ānic practices, classed as either remnants of paganism or as *bid'ah*, and to move closer to an ideal defined in strictly Islamic terms, to modern nationalists seeking to evoke pre- or non-Islamic elements of "national culture" as a means of asserting yet another vision of communal identity along lines of modern (and essentially European) notions of the nation. They range from moderately westernized and modernized Muslim "reformers" eager to root out "backward" and "irrational" or "unscientific" elements of both strictly Islamic, and pre- or non-Islamic, origin, more or less equally hostile to backward elements of both origins but simply inclined, analytically, to distinguish the two, to Soviet academics, both Russian and "native," who by training and by institutional orientation learned to analyze religious life and practice into bits and fragments whose "origins" could be assigned to various Marxist-ly conceived eras of history or pre-history (since by demonstrating such "origins" they supported the central governmental and academic goal, whether unspoken or openly avowed in a particular context, of showing the essential irrationality and incoherence of "religion"). In all cases the approach is essentially modern and western and "scientific," and often proudly committed to ignoring or belittling the voices of the simple, "primitive," "uneducated," "ignorant," and "backward" peoples of Inner Asia; in the end these approaches are more or less equally divorced from the realities of ordinary life and religion, as it touched most communities, in the traditional Inner Asian world.

By and large this array of voices intent upon minimizing the historical role of Islam in Inner Asia have successfully reinforced the standard assumptions of "light" Islamization in this region. In some measure these assumptions stem from the general lack of serious analysis of Islam in Inner Asia, and from ideological motivations suggested earlier; more insidiously, they stem from two more basic, and in some ways contradictory, assumptions, both of which I believe are seriously off the mark, though ingrained in much traditional scholarship on Islam. First is an assumption that Islam in local settings relatively isolated from the urban intellectual centers of "Islamic civilization" is essentially ignorant, substandard, and uninformed by the richness of intellectual life and social relations thought to be limited to urban settings; in part this assumption rests on an understandable, though still pernicious, tendency in academic settings to admire what is most compatible with one's own outlook and experience, namely "intellectual" and "cultural" life in urban environments. Second, there is an assumption, touched upon above, which is more difficult to dismiss: that Islam is not Islam—or, more generally, that religion is not religion—if it is "only external" or "merely nominal." This assumption stems from a similar academic emphasis upon intellectual systems whose internalization is supposed to be the mark of "genuine" adherence to a religion, and from a neglect of the patterns of daily living that are the focus of most traditional religion.

The first issue has been targeted in recent decades through the social sciences, as anthropologists, especially, have shown the richness and, more important, the meaningfulness of Islam outside the urban environment (or outside the intellectual elite even in cities). Recently, for instance, assumptions of the "ignorant" or "primitive" nature of Islam in Afghanistan have been targeted, with arguments that the knowledge of Islam that reaches rural villages and nomad camps is not defective or significantly different in qualitative terms from the "high" Islamic tradition; to the contrary, extensive "textual" bases may be found for the literary and oral transmission of the material needed to develop knowledge of Islamic-style discourse, including handbooks, verse summaries of the essentials of the faith, hagiographies, poetic *dīvāns* and prayer collections, and heroic and romantic tales enunciating Islamic themes, but including as well the individuals able to communicate those literary sources to an even wider audience.[38] In this context the role of epic narratives with "Islamized" heroes may be added as well, as will be discussed further below.

At the same time, however, we may widen our consideration of what the local and "popular" understanding of Islam amounts to. If on the basis of textual sources widely known among supposedly ignorant and unlettered Muslims we can stress the solidity of Islamic values and the role of such texts as internalizers of these values, we are coming close once again to the assumption that *if* the beliefs and practices of local rural "unlettered" Muslims were to be regarded as "mere forms and externals," they would be somehow less important behaviorally, culturally, and socially. That is, it is undoubtedly important to show the relative sophistication of local knowledge of Islamic ideals and practices, but we should not lose sight of the depth of the transformation already effected *outside* those textual bases if a community has adopted forms—even if only forms—from Islamic models, within a traditional religious environment (1) which is already well-supplied with formal behavioral and ritual expec-

38. Cf. M. Nazif Shahrani, "Local Knowledge of Islam and Social Discourse in Afghanistan and Turkistan in the Modern Period," in *Turko-Persia in Historical Perspective*, ed. Robert L. Canfield (Cambridge: Cambridge University Press, 1991), pp. 161–188.

tations addressing the same spheres of life as the "new" Islamic rites (since these rites were not entering a vacuum), and (2) in which individuals and groups do not ordinarily do something *new* and without precedent among the Ancestors without a specific reason and without an accompanying "assertive" assimilation of the new to past precedent. The strength and depth of the change is all the more remarkable if we note that in adopting new behavioral and ritual forms, the community is acknowledging those new forms as more efficacious—and implicitly more *meaningful* religiously—than inherited traditional norms.

Here we must again avoid the "idealist" insistence that "meaning" be always or primarily in "intellectual" terms; to turn prevailing attitudes upside down, we may argue that if Islam offered a nomad or peasant *only* intellectual and discursively articulated religious "meaning," we might well question the depth of Islamization. But when Islamic norms of behavior, Islamic patterns of social discourse, and even external Islamic ritual forms offer the nomad or peasant greater "meaning" than indigenous ways in the practical economic and social spheres that are the focus of traditional religious life—as is assumable on the basis of their adoption—we should recognize the profound and intimate sphere they have touched. Even in the case of "old" ways not entirely displaced by Islamic ones—the usual situation, after all, with some ritual patterns retained and others more consciously adapted to Islamic patterns[39]—we should keep in mind the extent of what has been "let in" through "nominal" Islamization, recalling that these old pre-Islamic ways have survived alongside the deep and intimate aspects of life affected by Islamization (self-designation on personal and communal levels, ritual performance, in many cases conceptions of purity linked with the performance of ablution and methods of slaughtering animals, etc.). For what has been "let in" is the potential for more-than-nominal Islamization, with the introduction of new discursive reference points and new values and figures to evoke in social dialectic.

39. It should be stressed that finding such clear examples of pre-Islamic thought and practice in the lives of Muslims—a favorite analytical approach in the Soviet ethnography of *perezhitki*—should not mislead us into expecting that such "survivals" would be regarded by the people who cherish them as anything other than normative religious practices in a community whose self-understanding as "Muslim" immediately "Islamizes" those "survivals." In other words, if we look at the religious behavior of people who consider themselves Muslim, instead of only at an abstraction of "Islam," we are compelled to acknowledge that the ancestral focus of pre-Islamic Inner Asian religious traditions has not simply "survived," but has found reaffirmation, integration, and assimilation, among Muslims following Islamization; and in that reaffirmation, which implicitly and quite simply removes any onus of "un-Islamic" links, lies much of the strength of Islamization's hold on Inner Asian communities.

Understood in this way, Islamization is perhaps less "dramatic," and its immediate impact on traditional ways of life less pronounced, than upholders of a strictly Islamic ideal would like; it is also less of a "historical watershed," insofar as taking on Islamic identity was "simply" another stage in the "reshuffling" of communal and confederative identities and designations with which Inner Asian history abounds. But for precisely this reason the centrality of Islamization in communal self-designation is underscored.

It may be objected that in focusing on the adoption of the *name* or *status* of "Muslim," or of a name linked to or defined in terms of Islamization, we are in effect acquiescing in the purely "nominal" and superficial character of Islam among Inner Asian peoples; in this objection we find the "affective" counterpart of the argument that the nomads, and Inner Asian peoples in general, adopted Islam only "formally," taking only some external signs and ritual forms.

This objection is, I would argue, fundamentally misdirected, from two perspectives. First, from the indigenous Inner Asian perspective, to downplay or underestimate the depth and importance of adopting the self-designation "Muslim," or of an awareness of bearing a communal self-designation rooted in or *explained by* Islamization, is to seriously misunderstand the signal importance of the name and the spoken word in traditional Inner Asian society. The name and its utterance have a sacred character; utterance has power, and the correspondence of a thing's name and its essence or reality is assumed, not in some abstract or metaphysical sense as argued in Chinese or Indian philosophy, but in terms of a virtually physical and magical link between the name and the named. To call oneself "Muslim" or by a name whose mention evokes recollection of an Islamizer, or of an entire "sacred history" or genealogy linked to Islamization, is no trivial matter. To adopt a name is to change one's reality, and in this sense there is hardly a *deeper* "conversion" than a *nominal* one; in any case such a nominal conversion, reflecting a change of status, is particularly well-suited for expression through the discursive patterns of conversion narratives modeled upon legends of communal origin.

Similarly, ritual forms or spoken ritual formulas (as well as central elements of language itself, especially those vital to social decorum and etiquette) are not to be trifled with: old ones are not lightly given up without a corresponding *conscious* change, and, in later generations, recurrent affirmations of the "choice" made by the community and the pain it entailed (as indicative of its seriousness). In particular, the "ritual" formulas involved in "genealogical" constructions of identity, through the acknowledgment of ancestors, are central to the entire scope of religious life in Inner Asia; the acknowledgment of, for example, a Muslim saint as one's individual or communal ancestor marks a singularly vital assimilation of Inner Asian and Islamic values: the centrality of the Ancestor in Inner Asian tradition ensures that he is not "renamed" lightly, while his Islamic character (even when evoked in popular lore quite succinctly, through simple external symbols indicative of Muslim status) conveys the religious and indeed communal status of his "descendants."

Second, from the Islamic perspective, the "name" and "form," are also similarly linked with sacred power; they are understood to be rooted in reality, and so are not to be taken lightly. With the name, in particular, we find a clear and profound conception of the correspondence of the name, at the fundamental level of utterance and the word's oral "shape," with reality, tied to the notion of the sacred origin of names in the speech of God.[40] It is in this light, for instance, that we should understand the famous "Islamization" of the ethnonym "Türk" through Arabic semantic analysis of its "root," whereby it is properly situated, potentially and implicitly, in the Qur'ān.

Beyond this, the Islamic assumptions regarding the sacred power of the external to affect the internal, of the form to shape the spirit, and of religious ritual and "ritualized" and sacralized social interaction to serve as a channel for divine grace, all shape an Islamic approach to "conversion" wherein adoption of the *name* and basic ritual forms are the *crucial* first step. From a deeper Islamic perspective as well, then, "nominal" and "external" conversion is not regarded as inherently superficial or without meaning. Rather, such "conversion" amounts to, as implied in the typical Muslim term for the spread of Islam, an *opening*: Islamic rule (and identity) is established, and the observance of external forms is facilitated, thus "opening the way" for the Islamization of hearts.

Finally, the adoption of the name and form, moreover, amounts to an implicit and potential communal endorsement of "Islam" as an ideal, thereby opening the way, through new, Islamically defined latent possibilities, to new sets of transformative forces that are both "Islamic" and "native" at the same time. Islamization not only brings the reaffirmation and integration of certain "assimilable" native traditions; it also brings the

40. See the discussion of orality in Islamic religious conceptions in William A. Graham, *Beyond the Written Word: Oral Aspects of Scripture in the History of Religion* (Cambridge: Cambridge University Press, 1987), pp. 96–115.

potential for more socially and politically transformative action, for even the "purely nominal" adoption of Islam allows into the community, potentially, the entire "cast of characters" of Islamically defined religious and political figures, who would renew or reform or purify or strengthen or defend "Islam" as they imagine it. What is important here is not simply that we find such figures and movements, but that it is the "original" adoption of Islam, however "nominal" or superficial it may have been, that makes these figures "native" rather than alien forces—more to the point, that the original Islamization is often at least tacitly evoked by these figures to justify their program. At the same time, that "original" Islamization may hand indigenous "reformers" a potentially powerful tool to use, in combination with native mythic patterns, in challenging an existing social and political order.

We must also consider here, finally, another objection to the depth or quality of Islamic "conversion" in Inner Asia, for these are doubted not only on the grounds of conversion's nominal or superficial character, but on the grounds of "impure" or "nonreligious" motives as well. We often read, that is, that such and such a community or ruler "converted" to Islam only for the somehow implicitly base motive of seeking thereby diplomatic or economic or political benefits; such portrayals amount to a dismissal of the "quality" of the underlying "sentiment" upon which the "conversion," inappropriately regarded as a "change of heart," is based, since in this way of thinking "religion" ought to be primarily a matter of belief rather than of practice or status.

If we adopt such a view, however, we are clearly letting modernist and Christian-based and idealist sensibilities intrude too far into our consideration of Islamization and its conditions and implications. From the Muslim perspective, again, there is nothing inherently base in conversion to Islam for economic or even political benefit; such conversion offers the same potential for effecting an "opening" of hearts as does the "purely nominal" conversion, and from the early days of Islam the promise of participating in the material benefits enjoyed by and ensured by the Muslim community *by joining it* was recognized as a legitimate and in no way disreputable inducement to the change of status involved in "conversion" to Islam. If the change of status led to a change of heart, so much the better; but Islam promises blessings of various kinds in this life, above all the blessings, tangible and intangible, derived from normal participation in a human community sacralized by divine forms. We should not belittle the open and avowed Islamically defined acceptance of "conversion" for less than "spiritual" motives, since the material or social benefits brought by conversion form part of the "material" wedge that may provide the "opening" needed to effect changes in the spirit as well as in the form. These considerations must be kept in mind as we consider the important ways in which Islam, and narratives of Islamization, were "used" politically in Inner Asia; we have become accustomed to dismissing the political "use" of religion as inevitably cynical and deceptive (and ultimately injurious to religion itself), but the political use of religion is much of what Islam is about in social terms.

In attempting to understand Islam in Inner Asia from an Islamic perspective, then, we would do well to recall the famous *ḥadīth* affirming that Islam was not meant to be a burden on humanity; rather, Islam is, from an Islamic perspective, an avenue for divine grace, and encompasses a wide spectrum of behaviors and attitudes, some set as ideals, some enjoined, and some merely accepted or tolerated. Islam entails for individuals and communities alike an aspiration to the best and highest in spiritual, moral, social, and ritual life; an enjoining of a set of formal and minimal obligations (of faith, ritual, and morality) expected of all serious Muslims; and an acceptance of even quite substandard "performance" of those obligations so long as the divine grace of membership in a sacralized (and salvific) *community* is not blatantly rejected through an act of apostasy. As would be expected, Islam in Inner Asia offers examples of individual and communal religious life at all three of these levels; but all too often the vitality of Islam in Inner Asia is judged solely on the basis of the first two, missing the profound significance—again, from the Islamic perspective itself—of the retention of a self-identity signaling membership in that salvific community.

But even if the quality of some person's or some community's conversion to, or knowledge of, Islam in the Dasht-i Qïpchaq, for instance, would not satisfy a jurist at al-Azhar—and *why*, after all, would we adopt him as a standard by which to judge the Islam of Inner Asia?—it seems reasonable to pay more attention to what the *change* (in status, in name, in patterns of social and religious ritual) amounts to *from the perspective of the person or community that underwent the change*.

If we keep this standard in mind, we must first recall that in traditional Inner Asian religion, one of the chief, if not the preeminent, purposes of the sphere of activity that we would label "religious" is precisely to promote "life": that is, to protect health and the survival of the community, to ensure material well-being and prosperity, to fructify herds and fields, to render "manufactured" craft objects effective and productive, etc. Alongside these economic aims are the political purposes of sanctioning rule and organizational principles in order to ensure the community's life and prosperity in relation to other peoples, that is, through warfare, diplomacy, and trade. In all cases one does not—in Inner Asian religious tradition, as in "normative" Islam—employ "religious" concepts or practices to escape or downplay these fundamentally human aims, but to negotiate them.

So to find that a particular individual or ruler or community has decided that the value system and complex of rites which the society in question has long recognized as efficacious for upholding life—trusting in it and investing it with individually affirmed credence, socially enforced expectations, and ritually (and ecstatically) evoked numinous power—is after all no more useful or effective than "the way of the Muslims," or is even less powerful, is to admit a transformation of enormous import, precisely because of its "banality." To acknowledge that elements of one's communal tradition are less efficacious in securing the things that "religious life" is intended to secure in traditional society is perhaps somewhat staid and undramatic from our customary perspective, because in this case what Islam is sought for, or adopted for, is the same thing sought from the "old" tradition. However, it is just because of this banality, because of the enormous psychological and social shift signaled by seeking the same ends but through what had been an "alien" system of worldview and rites, that the shift is all the more remarkable and noteworthy *from the indigenous perspective.*

The Example of Almambet

In order to illustrate the type of reevaluation we are suggesting regarding Islam in Inner Asia, we may consider briefly the lessons of a conversion narrative of a type quite different from those primarily "literary" accounts with which we will be concerned in the balance of this study. The account in question comes, by contrast, from Inner Asian oral tradition, from the Qïrghïz epic cycle of *Manas*,[41] and provides an excellent illus-

41. See now the new edition and English translation of the major accessible mid-nineteenth-century recording of the epic, by Arthur T. Hatto, *The Manas of Wilhelm Radloff* (Wiesbaden: Otto Harrassowitz, 1990), based upon Radlov's publication, *Proben der Volkslitteratur der nördlichen türkischen Stämme* (Russian title: *Obraztsy narodnoi literatury severnykh tiurkskikh*

tration of the narrative displacement so prominent in the originally oral tale preserved by Ötemish Ḥājjī. In this massive Qïrghïz epic corpus the theme of the Muslim struggle with the infidel Qalmaqs may well represent simply the latest "cultural overlay" on more archaic structures of heroic and shamanic struggles and journeys; but in one substantial section the theme of conversion to Islam is especially well developed, and is clearly highlighted as in tension with ancestral and communal identities. The section in question[42] recounts the early career of Almambet, a hero who becomes Manas's most trusted friend and ally, though born a Qalmaq; the account also clearly signals the tension between Chingisid khan and "commoner," with the latter "justified" by Islam, for Almambet is a khan's son but rejects his patrimony for the sake of Islam.

The account of Almambet begins by posing an essential and primeval distinction between the infidels (*kapïr*) and Muslims (*busurman*), a distinction assumed, in a natural "universalization" of communal experience, to be as basic as the elemental dichotomies of creation: "When land became land, and water water, there were the infidels, Sons of six Fathers, and the Muslims, Sons of Three." This distinction can be overcome, however, through "heroic" choice, and this is perhaps the central message of the story. Among the infidels was born Almambet, the son of the Oyrat [i.e., infidel Qalmaq] khan; but Almambet's destiny was evident already before his birth, for in the epic account he is said to have been conceived through the intercession of the "saints" (*ōliya*; i.e., *awliyā*) and the Muslim God (*azrät Alda*). That Almambet's Muslim destiny was evident even before his birth is further emphasized in one variant, in which Almambet is born already circumcised, while in a theme

plemen) (SPb., 1866–1907) [hereafter "Radlov, *Proben*"], ch. 5, "Narechie dikokamennykh kirgizov" (SPb., 1885), with the *Manas* cycle on pp. 1–368; cf. Hatto's "Kirghiz, Mid-Nineteenth Century," in *Traditions of Heroic and Epic Poetry*, vol. I, *The Traditions*, ed. A. T. Hatto (London: Modern Humanities Research Association, 1980), pp. 300–327. For an extensive survey of the variants of the Manas cycle and its episodes, see A. S. Mirbadaleva, N. V. Kidaish-Pokrovskaia, and S. M. Musaev, "Obzor zapisei variantov èposa 'Manas,'" in *Manas: Kirgizskii geroicheskii èpos*, kn. 1 (Moscow: GRVL, 1984), pp. 443–491. As Hatto has stressed (as an antidote to the modern Soviet Qïrghïz "nationalist" appropriation of *Manas*), the heroes of *Manas* are called Noghays, suggesting the borrowing of epic narratives and personages from Qazaq tradition (see his *Manas*, introduction, pp. xiv–xvi, with further pertinent comments on twentieth-century "intellectualizations" of the epic, and his *The Memorial Feast for Kökötöy-Khan (Kökötöydün Ašï): A Kirghiz Epic Poem* [Oxford: Oxford University Press, 1977], pp. 90–91, 272); the various themes found in the Manas epic are thus potentially more closely relevant to a discussion of "the Noghay epic" than is suggested by labeling it strictly "Qïrghïz."

42. Hatto, *Manas*, pp. 14–27; Radlov's edition, pp. 6–61; cf. *Manas: kirgizskii geroicheskii èpos*, kn. 2 (Moscow: GRVL, 1988), pp. 188ff. (text), 511ff. (tr.).

quite common in the context of Islamization—well known from the legend of Oghuz Khan and applied also to the Jöchid khan Berke—another variant has Almambet suckled by a Dungan (Chinese Muslim) woman upon his birth, whereupon he refuses to return to his infidel mother.[43]

In view of the intimate association, which both nature and tradition strengthen, between the complex of womb, birth, and childhood-nurturing on the one hand, and the spiritual and physical continuity of the family and community on the other, such a displacement is of no small consequence—that is, we see (1) the displacement of the ancestral spirits who oversee the conception, birth, and protection of the child by Muslim saints and Allāh; (2) the implicit displacement of traditional "infidel" rites performed for newborn children by the "rite" of miraculous prenatal circumcision;[44] and (3) the displacement of the birth mother from the infidel community by a Muslim mother. In each case, we should not expect exposition of the meaning: the evocation of these powerful images and their juxtaposition with their Muslim replacements makes the point quite clearly for an audience familiar with current traditions and familiar enough with notions of what traditions preceded the current ones to

43. Hatto, *Manas*, p. 408, note to I, 2, lines 99ff. The close parallel in narrative structure between this part of *Manas* and the story of Berke's Muslim upbringing and subsequent conversion (see the following chapter) should probably not be taken as establishing the story of Berke as a prototype for Muslim conversions, which the *Manas* bards mimicked; rather, the parallels probably point to "narrative imperatives," suggesting, as we would expect, that the indigenous accounts of Berke's conversion reflect developed oral narratives featuring such a sequence of Muslim inclination through miraculous Islamic intervention at birth (the Muslim mother's milk) and then the "choice" of conversion in adulthood, just like Almambet.

44. The treatment of circumcision here invites comparison with that in the tale of Er Töshtük, often included as part of the *Manas* cycle (discussed more fully below), in an early episode in which the shaman-hero comes upon the dwelling of a hideous woman, Bek Toro, while searching for his father's lost herds (a theme recalled in Herodotus's telling of a Scythian legend of origin, as discussed below). The woman promises to aid the hero in his search if he will spend the night; he eats and drinks and falls asleep, waking at midnight to find the hut resplendent with light, and the woman beautiful and alluring. But as he begins to caress her hair and undo her blouse, Bek Toro stops him, revealing that she knows his identity and origin, and that indeed it was she whose prayers ensured his birth; she is thus his spiritual mother, but what she tells him to allay his amorous intentions suddenly takes on a distinctly Islamic cast: "Do not touch me, Töshtük! You are still impure of body, you have not yet been circumcised, you remain unlawful." She laments that she would have taken him for her own, "but this lower world is full of blemishes," and so she resolves to "reclaim" him on the Day of Judgment; eventually she makes a deal with the intended bride of Er Töshtük whereby the bride will have him in this world, but Bek Toro in the next (cf. Pertev Boratav and Louis Bazin, ed. and tr., *Aventures merveilleuses sous terre et ailleurs de Er-Töshtük le géant des steppes* [Paris: Gallimard/Unesco, 1965], pp. 38–40; see also Nora K. Chadwick and Victor Zhirmunsky, *Oral Epics of Central Asia* [Cambridge: Cambridge University Press, 1969], pp. 101–102).

understand that "what we do now" and "who we are now" were determined by just such a sacred displacement.

Despite the early signs of his Muslim destiny, it is still the mature Almambet who must be "converted" and make the fateful choice that pits him against his family and community.[45] The agent of his conversion is the Muslim Kökchö, who befriends Almambet and awakens his desire to become a Muslim; it is to Kökchö that Almambet declares his wish to cast off the signs of his Qalmaq heritage, and it is in his presence that Almambet opens the Qurʿān and reads (naturally, without instruction or assistance) and announces, "I will become a Muslim!" (*men busurman bolom*). But following this lone allusion to Almambet's conversion as his individual act, the communal focus comes plainly back into view: he at once announces his intention to make his people Muslims, and to break with them if they do not heed him, and his words clearly reflect the notion that his people, as a community, should enter "the Muslim tribe" (*busurman qomï*, i.e., the *qawm* of Muslims).

Almambet then journeys back to his people, and at every step we find a challenge to Qalmaq tradition: he enters his father's house and greets him, in the Qïrghïz version of the Muslim greeting, "*Asalau malikim, atam*," but receives no answer; he stands "at the head of the hearth," the sacred center of the yurt (*öy*), where the fire-pit dug in the earth to join the underworld with this world meets the celestial world, beneath the opening in the yurt through which good fortune is portrayed as descending, and there challenges his father and his people to become Muslims. In the refrain, the elements of the conversion he demands from them are made clear: let us, says Almambet, learn the Qurʿānic words "*Kulkuldabat kualdat*;"[46] let us "seek a place between Mecca and Paradise;" let us become Muslims; and, in a tellingly sophisticated encapsulation of

45. In the hero's Muslim birth followed by decisive contest-induced conversion we see a parallel to a common structure in other conversion narratives, wherein an initial inclination is followed by a conversion provoked by some threat or crisis and effected through a dramatic "contest"; the initial inclination, in turn, may be presented "theologically" by evoking the primeval *fiṭrah* of humankind, "miraculously" through intercession for the hero in the womb or at birth, or "historically" through the hero's affiliation with a previously Muslim people (the latter strategy is common in accounts of the Turks and Mongols cast as "historical" traditions, with their latter-day descendants depicted as having fallen away from a primeval Islam adopted by legendary ancestors, e.g. Oghuz Khan; it is not at work in the case of Almambet inasmuch as the Muslim/Kafir distinction is itself primeval, disallowing both a primeval conversion and the *fiṭrah*, and highlighting the *choice* entailed in changing religious communities).

46. Hatto, *Manas*, p. 411, note to I, 2, line 217, identifies this as the words of *sūrah* 112 affirming monotheism, *qul huwa'llāhu aḥad[un]*.

what Islam had to offer his people, let us "seek" or "learn" "the goodness of this world with That World."[47] Almambet tells his people to discuss the issue in council (*kengäsh*), thus appealing for a communal decision, and promises to return in the morning to learn the choice.

Almambet's father, however, not only refuses to adopt Islam, but effectively disowns his son, wondering how Almambet could speak such words and ordering his people to keep his son from his sight and to kill him when he returned in the morning; he refers to Almambet as his "spent arrow" and his "hard excreted turd," expressions that may be said to "amount to a formula of unclanning or disinheritance."[48] Almambet manages to reach his father the next morning and again repeats his summons, urging his people, "Rather than be khans of the Infidel, let us be Muslim slaves";[49] here, the frequently encountered opposition between khan (implicitly Chingisid) and "commoner" is clearly invoked and linked to the legitimacy accorded to the latter by conversion to Islam. His father, however, flatly refuses to become a Muslim, and departs. Almambet next goes to his mother, reporting his father's rejection and appealing to her not to abandon her child, but the mother sides with the father, and Almambet resolves, in effect, to renounce his patrimony, his family, and his community; recalling his unheeded appeal to his people, he declares again his individual choice to prefer being a "Muslim slave" over being an infidel khan.

As he prepares to do battle with his infidel kinsmen, then, Almambet first invokes the aid of the Muslim hero Koshoy, whose success he ascribes to the protection of his ancestor-spirits (*arbak*) and angels (*berishtä*). Koshoy's Muslim status is affirmed as Almambet praises his turban, calls him "my Khoja," and compares his voice to the prayer-summons (*azan*), and the new convert asks that his ancestral spirits and angels support him as well.[50] It is thus made clear, in another instance of displacement, that Almambet has cut himself off from the protective ancestral spirits of his own people and must seek protection from Muslim spirits.

He next appeals to his Muslim friend Kökchö, or rather to the protective spirits who support Kökchö; in a foreshadowing of Almambet's disappointment with Kökchö—as a result of which he will leave him and take up with Manas—we are told that Kökchö's "angels" (*berishtä*) could not

47. *a dünö minän bu dünö jakšılık surap ketäli, a dünö minän bu dünö jakšılık jayın bilälik.*

48. Hatto, *Manas*, pp. 411–412, note to I, 2, lines 247ff.

49. *Kapirdin kanı bolğončo, busurman kulu bololu*, p. 22, I, 2, lines 293–294.

50. Hatto, *Manas*, pp. 24–25; cf. pp. 413–414, notes to I, 2, lines 394ff.

help Almambet, but Manas' ancestral spirits (*arbak*; i.e., *arvāḥ*) did come to his aid without even being invoked (and without Almambet ever having met Manas), clearly demonstrating their solicitude for the new Muslim convert.[51] Thus supported, Almambet slays myriad Oyrat infidels and then departs. His falling-out with Kökchö still in the future, Almambet in effect seals his conversion to Islam and his new membership in the Muslim community as he again meets his friend and the instigator of his conversion: he has returned to his true community, for his greeting, *asalau malīkim*, left unrequited by his own father and his own people, is returned by his friend Kökchö.

Incidentally, the story of Almambet is also instructive with regard to the role of the narrative itself: in recounting the hero's adoption of Islam and his struggles in defending it against the challenge from his own family, the bard and audience effectively relive the dramatic tension vividly enough to appreciate the fact that "we" are not forced to face it again; the reason "we" need not face the disruption of family, way of life, etc., is that we are now part of a Muslim community (and must take care not to fall away from Islam), thanks to the early heroes whose difficult choice we need only reaffirm.

A final element in the "Islamization" of Almambet and his physical and "familial" integration into the Muslim community occurs after his disenchantment with Kökchö (who remained only his "friend") and his coming to Manas (who becomes his "brother"). To be sure, the figure of Manas may appear less explicitly Muslim than Kökchö, in large part because he is more richly developed than Kökchö, and because of the latter's specific role in Almambet's conversion. But a prominent, if not paramount, theme of the epic is the nobility and superiority of Almambet, a convert to Islam, contrasted with the venality and outright betrayal exhibited by characters born Muslim, and this superiority is highlighted most effectively in Almambet's valor in defense of Manas.[52]

51. Hatto (*Manas*, p. 415, note to I, 2, lines 426ff.) sees in this "an effort to bridge the contradictions between new and old in the outlook of the superficially Islamized Kirghiz;" see below on this supposed superficiality.

52. Cf. Hatto, *Manas*, p. 227; the contrast is most clear in the case of Köz-kaman, whose life is the reverse of Almambet's: he was a "Noghay," born a Muslim, but was abducted as a child by the Qalmaqs, and although he himself retained some signs of his origin, his offspring are the worst of infidels, who submit to circumcision as a formal sign of accepting Islam (pp. 262–263) but whose "Qalmaqized" nature is revealed in their treacherous poisoning of Manas. See also Hatto's "Mongols in Mid-Nineteenth-Century Kirghiz Epic," in *Gedanke und Wirkung: Festschrift zum 90. Geburtstag von Nikolaus Poppe*, ed. Walther Heissig and Klaus Sagaster (Wiesbaden: Otto Harrassowitz, 1989), pp. 139–145, where in connection with this episode he

In any event, Manas's Muslim status is never in doubt in the epic. Although Manas's army includes both Muslims and infidels, the dialogues among Manas and his companions are repeatedly punctuated with Muslim greetings, and together Manas and Almambet lead holy wars against the infidel Qalmaqs, Russians, and Chinese; Manas likewise is restored to health, after being poisoned, through the intercession of "Kan Kojo" of Mecca, and he himself travels to Mecca to revive his Forty Companions.[53] The bond between the two heroes is likewise portrayed in a telling mix of Islamic and pre-Islamic elements: when Almambet is first spotted on the way to Manas's camp, Manas is drawn to him as he observes him from a distance, noting that although his form resembles that of an infidel, the "golden traits" of his countenance "resemble a Muslim's;"[54] and later, when they have become the closest of companions, Manas praises Almambet's conversion to Islam, when "Rather than be a Kalmak khan, you said 'I shall become a Muslim slave!'" as the event that brought them together.[55]

The most dramatic element in forging their bond, however, comes when Almambet, alienated from his own mother through his conversion to Islam and his effort to extend that conversion to his people, in effect takes Manas' mother as his own: as, miraculously, the withered breasts of Manas's mother again flow with milk, Manas and Almambet each suck one breast, thereby becoming brothers and affirming Almambet's inclusion in a new family and community.[56]

The archaic mythic and "shamanic" themes of the *Manas* epic are often cited as evidence of the "superficial" Islamization of the Qïrghïz, and it is possible to find quite little of a certain type of Islam even in the account of Almambet's conversion, if that is what one is looking for. Nevertheless, although it is true that "Islam" as a doctrinal structure or developed literary tradition or urban-style cultural system was noticeably less prevalent among the nomadic Qïrghïz than, say, among sedentary communities of Mawarannahr, to call Qïrghïz Islam superficial is to ignore the historical devotion of the Qïrghïz, from the Farghana valley to East Turkistan, to Sufi shaykhs; it ignores the incorporation of Muslim

observes: "What the Kirghiz valued was not race, but a way of life. Their own stock could deteriorate under Kalmak influences: an Oirot [*sic*] prince converted to Islam could be the Khan's trusted bosom friend!" (p. 140).

53. Hatto, *Manas*, pp. 298–301; cf. p. 228.

54. Hatto, *Manas*, pp. 62–65.

55. Hatto, *Manas*, pp. 272–273.

56. Hatto, *Manas*, pp. 70–71; cf. p. 49.

patterns in life-cycle rites among the Qïrghïz; it ignores the Islamic-style sacralization of Qïrghïz territory through the proliferation of saints' shrines; it ignores the Islamization of Qïrghïz genealogies; it ignores Qïrghïz communal identification with the Islamic world; and it ignores the assimilative acts evident in the epic accounts themselves. Whether the Islamic features in the Manas cycle reflect the adoption of Qazaq and Noghay epic heroes with already established Islamic elements, or the addition of Islamic elements after the adoption, we find a remarkable inclusion that belies "superficiality."

The argument that Qïrghïz Islam was superficial ignores also the *depth* of the Islamic element adduced in the epic: it is hardly conceivable that the focus on the familial and communal break in the story of Almambet was considered meaningless or trivial by the epic's audience. To be sure, the "reformist" Muslims who sought to strengthen *their* style of Islam among the Qïrghïz would have found Qïrghïz Islam superficial; but we should not judge the level or depth of Islamization solely or even primarily from the standpoint of a particular group's ideals of Islamic doctrine or practice—to do so concedes the validity of that group's vision of Islam, which may or may not be suitable in a given instance, but beyond this it involves us in a fruitless academic pursuit for an abstracted and ideal Islam instead of a more appropriate examination of Islam as self-defined Muslims live it. Rather, the depth of Islam and of the *change* that Islam entailed should be judged on the basis of their relationship with values and self-conceptions native to the Qïrghïz, not in relation to the values of some "normative" Islamic standard from an entirely different environment.

The story of Almambet, then, offers insight into the indigenous appropriation of Islam and the often decisive impact of this appropriation. Despite its "heroic" rather than "historical" character, it also includes a number of more specific parallels to the conversion narrative with which we are most directly concerned. To appreciate these, however, we must consider that narrative in its historical context and in the religious meaning—at times shared with the tale of Almambet—that it conveyed to its audience.

2

The Historical Setting: Baba Tükles and the Conversion of Özbek Khan

Within a century of its emergence as a distinctive political and administrative unit, the westernmost division of the Mongol empire, the *ulus* of Chingis Khan's eldest son Jöchi, commonly known as the Golden Horde, became firmly and self-consciously a part of the *Dār al-Islām*.[1] Its Islamic character, of course, never manifested itself in a complete or even large-scale rejection of the typically Inner Asian political structures and traditions inherited from the Mongol empire; rather, the Golden Horde was marked by the coexistence, assimilation, or even fusion of Inner Asian and

1. There is as of yet no serious study, from any perspective, of the Islamization of the Jöchid *ulus* or, for that matter, of any of the Mongol successor states; the lack of attention to the spread of Islam is all the more glaring when compared with the considerable body of literature on Christianity in the Mongol empire, which for all its interest lacked the ongoing impact which Islamization had. For a brief overview, see the recent summary article by M. A. Usmanov, "Ètapy islamizatsii dzhuchieva ulusa i musul'manskoe dukhovenstvo v tatarskhikh khanstvakh XIII–XVI vekov," in *Dukhovenstvo i politicheskaia zhizn' na Blizhnem i Srednem Vostoke v period feodalizma* (Moscow: Nauka, GRVL, 1985), pp. 177–185. A good treatment of one period, with a thorough consideration of virtually all available sources and a refreshing skepticism toward the old distinction between "real" history and legend, is the recent article of István Vásáry, " 'History and Legend' in Berke Khan's Conversion to Islam," *Aspects of Altaic Civilization III* (=PIAC XXX), ed. Denis Sinor (Bloomington: Indiana University, Research Institute for Inner Asian Studies, 1990), pp. 230–252. Aside from this the subject has not fared well. From the standpoint of source analysis, Jean Richard's "La conversion de Berke et les débuts de l'islamisation de la Horde d'Or" (*REI*, 35 [1967], pp. 173–184) is incomplete and by now outdated even for the limited period covered, while from the theoretical standpoint of understanding conversion as a social and religious process, the brief remarks of the late Joseph Fletcher published recently ("The Mongols: Ecological and Social Perspectives," *HJAS*, 46 [1986], pp. 11–50; of relevance here, pp. 43–45, under the heading, "Why did the Mongols Convert to Islam but not to Other Religions?"), full of allusions to "nomadic religions" and the like, can hardly be said to have broken new conceptual ground; likewise, Jean-Paul Roux's

Islamic elements in politics, society, and culture, with its Islamic character evidenced in the avowed Muslim faith of its leadership, in the leadership's patronage of Islamic institutions, in the state's identification with the Muslim world in the religious rivalry between Christendom and Islam, and finally, though of all these issues this is the least understood, in the spread of the Islamic religion—or more appropriately, of a consciousness of Islamic affiliation—among the population of the Jöchid *ulus*.

As for the consequences of the Golden Horde's Islamization, these are sufficiently evident even today so as to require little comment; though the "process" of the Golden Horde's Islamization is known primarily through accounts focused on the khan's court and administration, it is clear that the emergence of a consensus on Islamic affiliation among the Turkic population of western Inner Asia dates to this pivotal period. From the Tatars, in a sense the direct heirs of the Islamic polity of the Golden Horde, to the Uzbeks who entered and came to dominate sedentary Central Asia, a significant majority of the peoples and nationalities of Muslim heritage that until recently belonged to the Soviet Union can trace their Islamic roots to the Golden Horde; at the same time, the Islamization of the Jöchid *ulus* added an important religious dimension to the later struggle between the Muscovite princes and other successor states of the dismembered Golden Horde, thereby setting the tone for centuries of Russian interaction with the Muslim world.

A comprehensive study of the process of Islamization in the Jöchid

attempt to analyse religious "pluralism" in Inner Asian societies ("Les religions dans les sociétés turco-mongoles," *RHR*, 201 [1984], pp. 393–420) remains colored by outmoded assumptions of "Mongol tolerance" and other anachronistic categories; and the brief remarks on Islamization in the Golden Horde in Charles J. Halperin, "Russia in the Mongol Empire in Comparative Perspective," *HJAS*, 43 (1983), pp. 239–261 (cf. pp. 255–256) likewise refer to "vestigial Mongol religious tolerance from the shamanist Chinggisid era." In the absence of more appropriate treatments of a process of such profound significance, the standard surveys must suffice: for the Jöchid *ulus*, cf. Bertold Spuler, *Die Goldene Horde: Die Mongolen in Russland 1223–1502* (Wiesbaden: Otto Harrassowitz, 1965), pp. 85–87, 213–220; G. A. Fedorov-Davydov, *Obshchestvennyi stroi Zolotoi Ordy* (Moscow: Izd-vo Moskovskogo Universiteta, 1973), esp. pp. 100–107; M. G. Safargaliev, *Raspad Zolotoi Ordy* (Saransk: Mordovskoe Knizhnoe Izd-vo, 1960), pp. 64–71; B. D. Grekov and A. Iu. Iakubovskii, *Zolotaia Orda i ee padenie* (Moscow and Leningrad, 1950), pp. 166–169; the older study of Joseph von Hammer-Purgstall, *Geschichte der Goldenen Horde in Kiptschak* (Pesth, 1840), pp. 281–283; and a new study of the Golden Horde by Uli Schamiloglu, forthcoming. For the place of the Jöchid *ulus* in the larger Mongol world, and especially its relations with Ilkhanid Iran, see P. Jackson, "The Dissolution of the Mongol Empire," *CAJ*, 22 (1978), pp. 186–244. See also Mustafa Kafalı, *Altın Orda hanlığının kuruluş ve yükseliş devirleri* (Istanbul, 1976); George Vernadsky, *The Mongols and Russia* (New Haven: Yale University Press, 1953); Henry H. Howorth, *History of the Mongols from the 9th to the 19th*

ulus, or for that matter in any particular area within the long history of Islam in the Inner Asian world, would necessarily entail a much more extensive work than the present contribution. Such a thorough investigation of Islamization in the Golden Horde would require consideration of the development of Islamic institutions of state, based on a careful reexamination of the full range of written sources (from contemporary Arabic, Persian, and Russian chronicles to later historical works, from as far afield as India, which may preserve relevant material from the Jöchid *ulus*, as well as diplomatic and numismatic material), to identify the sequence of the appearance, coexistence, and/or displacement of pre-Islamic steppe institutions and Islamic ones. It would require acquaintance with the abundant archeological research produced especially in the Soviet era, as clues to the adoption not only of Islamic architectural styles or burial methods, but in general of patterns of spatial organization reflecting sacred Islamic models;[2] it would take account of the epigraphic evidence, above all in the extensive "Bulghar" grave inscriptions, as sources on patterns of naming, places of origin, and the distribution of Muslim communities, for instance;[3] and it would be informed by a thorough analysis of literary production in the Golden Horde, both as a clue to the adoption of Arabic and Persian and Islamized Turkic linguistic features and of adaptations of indigenous Turkic or Mongol terminology in the religious lexicon, and as evidence of the development of patronage relationships between khans and princes of the Golden Horde and Muslim literati and

---

Century, Part II, "The So-Called Tartars of Russia and Central Asia," Division 1 (London: Longmans, Green, 1880); Charles J. Halperin, *Russia and the Golden Horde* (Bloomington: Indiana University Press, 1985); René Grousset, *The Empire of the Steppes: A History of Central Asia*, tr. Naomi Walford (New Brunswick: Rutgers University Press, 1970), pp. 392–408; and much more briefly David Morgan, *The Mongols*, (Oxford: Basil Blackwell, 1986), pp. 136–145.

2. Cf. for example the *Arkheologicheskaia karta Tatarskoi ASSR; Predkam'e* (Moscow: Nauka, 1981); see esp. E. A. Khalikova, *Musul'manskie nekropoli Volzhskoi Bulgarii X-nachala XIII v.* (Kazan: Izd-vo Kazanskogo universiteta, 1986).

3. The best introduction remains G. V. Iusupov, *Vvedenie v bulgaro-tatarskuiu èpigrafiku* (Moscow/Leningrad: Izd-vo AN SSSR, 1960), which covers also much later times. On the thirteenth and fourteenth centuries in particular see now András Róna-Tas and S. Fodor, *Epigraphica Bulgarica: A volgai bolgár-török feliratok* (Szeged, 1973; Studia uralo-altaica, 1), which provides a useful tabulation (p. 174) of dates on the monuments studied (ranging from the 1280s to 1357); Talât Tekin, *Volga Bulgar kitabeleri ve Volga Bulgarcası* (Ankara: Türk Tarih Kurumu Basımevi, 1988); the survey of O. Pritsak, "Bolgaro-Tschuwaschica," *UAJ*, 31 (1959), pp. 274–314; the old studies of J. Klaproth, "Notice et explication des inscriptions de Bolghari," *JA*, 2nd ser. 8 (1831), pp. 483–503 and N. I. Ashmarin, "Bolgary i chuvashi," *IOAIÈ*, 18/1–3 (1902), pp. 1–132; and the works of F. S. Khakimzianov: "Èpigraficheskie pamiatniki g. Bulgara," in *Istochnikovedenie i istoriia tiurkskikh iazykov* (Kazan', 1978), pp. 21–36; "New Volga Bulgarian

religious figures.[4] In addition, the rich body of "folkloric" and epic oral literature among the peoples whose communal roots go back to the Golden Horde includes much material that, used prudently, may illuminate the integration of Islamic religious terminology and personages into the fabric of the traditional pre-Islamic worldview.

In each case, however, the groundwork remains to be done, and the present study is much more limited. The goal here is not to analyze historical accounts of the "spread" of Islam or the Islamization of institutions or even of the personal or political or economic or social motives that might have spurred adoption of Islam by common people or by sovereigns; rather, it is to consider narrative accounts that relate the course or "event" of royal conversion, and to approach them not as sources of "facts" about the conversion itself, but as sources of popular conceptions of the conversion and, more important, of the conversion's significance to a given community that repeatedly rehearsed and adapted the account of the conversion.

Here we must acknowledge that the actual human, historical process covered by the term "Islamization" is extremely problematical to define and understand; such a process itself is not easily susceptible to the tidy but superficial "terminological" analysis implied by a careless and summary appeal to "Islamization," a word that hides a vastly more complex range of essentially discrete historical, cultural, communal, personal, and psychological events than historians unaccustomed to grappling with (or simply insensitive to) the structures and categories of religious life have appreciated. This is true in general for virtually every region that underwent this process, with the situation in the Golden Horde further complicated by the relative scarcity of sources. For the sources counted as reliable by most historians tell us of events at court, of administrative and fiscal developments, of international relations, and of life in the cities; they inevitably lend themselves to a focus on the social and political leadership of the Golden Horde (in particular the Chingisid royal family and urban mercantile interests) and on the implicit diplomatic and commercial motivations within the leadership for a "policy" of Islamization. They tell us little, in general, about the nomadic population of the Golden Horde, and, in particular, virtually

Inscriptions," *AOH*, 40/1 (1986), pp. 173–177; and especially his two philological studies of two corpuses of, respectively, forty–three and forty–five inscriptions, *Iazyk èpitafii Volzhskikh Bulgar* (Moscow: Nauka, 1978), and *Èpigraficheskie pamiatniki Volzhskoi Bulgarii i ikh iazyk* (Moscow: Nauka, 1987).

4. On the development of Turkic Islamic literature in the Golden Horde, see the survey of J. Eckmann, "Die kiptschakische Literatur," *Philologiae Turcicae Fundamenta*, II (Wiesbaden: Otto Harrassowitz, 1964), pp. 275–304.

nothing about what Islamization meant to this population and how "Islam" was understood and received at the communal or individual level.

In the face of this situation we may despair of our sources and surrender all hope of understanding the process of Islamization at any level below that of the khan and his administration; or we may widen the range of available sources that may speak to us by including materials usually dismissed as "legendary" and therefore irrelevant to "real" history. If we adopt the latter course, I believe, we will find that we are not so ill-served by the sources as has been assumed. In particular, we may often find, scattered in sources judged to be of questionable "reliability" in conventional historiography, traces of quite instructive narratives about the conversion to Islam of an individual ruler of the Golden Horde. These narratives are instructive not because they tell us "what happened" when a particular khan adopted Islam, but because they show us how conversion to Islam was understood among the people who looked to that khan's adoption of the new religion to explain their own adherence to Islam; these narratives show us "how the story was told," and in so doing can provide important clues for understanding how Islam was fit into the traditional worldview of Inner Asian peoples and made suitable for appropriation by them. In short, if we ask of such sources the questions they were intended to answer, we may find them more illuminating, in previously unexplored directions, than the tendency to dismiss them as "fantastic" would suggest.

The assumptions underlying the historical approach adopted in the present chapter, then, are that new approaches to the religious "history" of the Golden Horde, beyond the narrow confines of traditional historiography and beyond even the more recent fashions in political, social, and economic history, are necessary in order to begin to define a conceptual framework for understanding the process of Islamization at the popular level and in general, and that a search for religious meaning in the "legendary" native accounts of Islamization may provide one such approach that is both particularly apt (since we are dealing with a transformation defined in fundamentally *religious* terms) and potentially fruitful.

Islamic Antecedents in Western Inner Asia

Islam and Narrative Tradition in the Volga Basin before the Mongol Conquest

The broad outlines of the Golden Horde's Islamization and its implications are generally appreciated, at least in the context of its political development and international position. The process of Islamization was favored by commercial, cultural, and political patterns, some surviving the Mongol conquest from earlier periods and others emerging as a result of it; commercial ties in particular linked the Volga valley with the Islamic world through Central Asia along the great north-south axis of international trade which at the time rivaled the better-known east-west routes of the old Silk Road.[5] Drawing upon the local Muslim tradition of the Volga Bulghars, where Islam was implanted in the tenth century; upon the established centers of Islamic civilization that fell within or near the sphere of influence of the Jöchid *ulus*, such as Khorezm and the Caucasus; and upon the close ties with Egypt and the Near East that developed from the second half of the thirteenth century, the Golden Horde was to a large degree predisposed to become part of the Islamic world, and historians have often highlighted the political, diplomatic, and commercial advantages of Islamization for the rulers of the Jöchid *ulus*.

The influence of Muslim figures from Central Asia and the Caucasus in the Golden Horde was inevitably heightened by the general commercial and diplomatic consequences of Mongol political domination, and especially by the incorporation of the north Caucasus and part of Khorezm into the administrative structure of the Golden Horde itself. At the same time the Islamic heritage in the heartlands of the Jöchid *ulus*, in the Volga valley from Bulghar southward and in the steppes north of the Caspian and Black Seas, is of particular importance for us, both because the peoples inhabiting those regions at the time of the Mongol conquest were already, in many cases, acquainted with Islam, and because those peoples, who naturally constituted the bulk of the Golden Horde's population base (and thus the foundations of later "ethnic" communities that formed

5. On these commercial ties and the role of the Volga Bulghars, cf. Thomas S. Noonan, "Suzdalia's Eastern Trade in the Century before the Mongol Conquest," *Cahiers du monde russe et soviétique*, 19 (1978), pp. 371–384, and the article immediately following by Élisabeth Bennigsen, "Contribution a l'étude du commerce des fourrures russes: La route de la Volga avant l'invasion mongole et le royaume des Bulghars," pp. 385–399.

in the Jöchid *ulus*), had evidently already been active in the creation of narratives recounting their conversion to Islam and the centrality of that conversion in their communal lives.

With this in mind it is worth reviewing the history of Islam in the western part of Inner Asia, a region marked, before its organization as the Jöchid *ulus* in the Mongol era, by large-scale imperial structures such as the Khazar state, by less centralized nomadic confederations of Turkic peoples bearing such names as Pechenegs, Oghuz, and Qumans, and by principalities of the forest belt with Turkic, Slavic, and Finno-Ugric populations. If the heritage of Bulghar Islam, as noted, goes back to the tenth century, in the larger sphere of western Inner Asia, Islam makes its first appearance already in the seventh-century Arab raids across the Caucasus frontier, where the Arabs faced the Khazar empire. It seems likely that military operations against the Khazars were accompanied by the conversion of some groups within the Khazar state to Islam; already from the year 737 we find a defeated Khazar *khāqān* reportedly receiving, upon his request, two jurists who taught him the principles of Islam, whereupon he duly acknowledged himself a Muslim.[6]

Although the Khazar ruling class eventually adopted Judaism, there is no doubt that a strong Muslim presence remained in the Khazar state even before the celebrated conversion of the Bulghars in the early tenth century. This is clear from the accounts in the Arabic geographical works of Ibn Rustah, al-Iṣṭakhrī and al-Masʿūdī all writing in the first half of the tenth century, as well as from the travel account of Ibn Faḍlān, who visited the Bulghars in 922; all describe the sizable Muslim population, numbering more than 10,000 according to al-Iṣṭakhrī, of the Khazar capital on the Volga, and mention the mosques and schools that served the Muslim inhabitants.[7] Even allowing for exaggeration or wishful thinking, the evidence points to the existence of a substantial Muslim community, with a quite respectable institutional base, in the Khazar state that dominated western Inner Asia from the seventh to the tenth centuries; we cannot point to clear evidence of continuity in Muslim traditions from this

6. Cf. D. M. Dunlop, *The History of the Jewish Khazars* (Princeton: Princeton University Press, 1954), p. 84; cf. Peter B. Golden, *Khazar Studies: An Historico-Philological Inquiry into the Origins of the Khazars* (Budapest: Akadémiai Kiadó, 1980), vol. 1, p. 64.

7. Cf. Dunlop, *History of the Jewish Khazars*, pp. 92–93 (for al-Iṣṭakhrī's account), 105 (Ibn Rustah), 113 (Ibn Faḍlān), and 205–207 (al-Masʿūdī). Incidentally, the envoy sent to the ʿAbbāsid Caliph by the Bulghar ruler conveying the request that prompted Ibn Faḍlān's journey is identified by the *nisbah* assigned him as a Khazar (cf. A. Zeki Validi Togan, *Ibn Faḍlān's Reisebericht* [Leipzig, 1939; Abhandlungen für die Kunde des Morgenlandes, XXIV/3], p.3).

early period, but at the same time it is not unlikely that Islam and its social, cultural, and linguistic impact upon the indigenous population appeared in the region that later became part of the Golden Horde at least by the middle of the ninth century.[8]

The legacy of Bulghar Islam[9] is of particular interest because of its evident strength and stability as well as its early establishment. We cannot here explore this legacy in full, but the adoption of Islam among the Bulghars points to two particular issues of direct relevance for our study:

First, Islam was adopted, by all accounts, when the Bulghar state was subject to the Khazar *qaghan*, by a ruler with a title indicating his subordinate status,[10] a title borne also by an earlier vassal of the Khazars in the North Caucasus whose conversion to Christianity was the subject of legendary narratives, as discussed in Chapter 4; this suggests clear political motivations for conversion to Islam, not in the crass sense of irreligious opportunism (the hope, mentioned by Ibn Faḍlān, for relations with the Caliph notwithstanding), but in the sense of a search for a potential source of communal solidarity and political legitimation outside the discursive

8. See further Dunlop, *History*, pp. 108–109 on the antiquity of Islam within the Khazar state.

9. The *locus classicus* on the establishment of Islam among the Bulghars is the travel account of Ibn Faḍlān, who went as the Caliph al-Muqtadir's envoy to the Bulghar king in 310/922; see Togan, *Ibn Faḍlān's Reisebericht*; A. P. Kovalevskii, *Kniga Akhmeda Ibn Fadlana o ego puteshestvii na Volgu v 921–922 gg.* (Khar'kov, 1956); and an unpublished English translation by James E. McKeithen, "The Risālah of Ibn Faḍlān: An Annotated Translation with Introduction," Ph.D. dissertation, Indiana University, 1979. The status of Bulghar Islam is also well described in medieval Arabic geographical literature, especially in the works noted above and cited extensively in Dunlop's study of the Khazars. On Bulghar Islam, see further Peter Golden, "The Peoples of the Russian Forest Belt," in *The Cambridge History of Early Inner Asia*, ed. Denis Sinor (Cambridge: Cambridge University Press, 1990), pp. 229–255 [pp. 237–242]; idem, *Khazar Studies*, pp. 42–49, 86–88; I. Hrbek, "Bulghār," EI^2, I, pp. 1304–1308; V. V. Bartol'd, "Bolgary," *Sochineniia*, II/1, pp. 509–520 (from EI^1, I, pp. 819–825); and on the archeological remains of Bulghar Islam, cf. Khalikova, *Musul'manskie nekropoli*; V. F. Gening and A. Kh. Khalikov, *Rannie bolgary na Volge* (Moscow, 1964); A. P. Smirnov, *Volzhskie bulgary* (Moscow, 1951; Trudy Gosudarstvennogo istoricheskogo muzeia, vyp. 19), esp. pp. 35–52; B. D. Grekov, "Volzhskie Bolgary v IX–X vekakh: predvaritel'nye zamechaniia," *Istoricheskie zapiski*, 14 (1945), pp. 3–37, repr. in his *Izbrannye trudy* (Moscow, 1959), vol. 2, pp. 519–553; A. Iu. Iakubovskii, "K voprosu ob istoricheskoi topografii Itilia i Bolgar v IX i X vekakh," *Sovetskaia arkheologiia*, 10 (1948), pp. 255–270; and more recently A. Kh. Khalikov, "Kul'tura narodov Srednego Povolzh'ia v X–XIII vekakh," *Voprosy istorii*, 1976, No. 4, pp. 102–119, of which an English translation (marred by unchecked transcriptions of Arabic-script names based entirely on the Cyrillic) was published in *SAA*, 16/1 (Summer 1977), pp. 49–86. Still of value is the old survey of I. Berezin, "Bulgar na Volge," *Uchenye zapiski Kazanskogo universiteta*, vyp. 3 (1852), pp. 74–160, with archeological and epigraphic material as well as attention to indigenous sources on Bulghar Islam.

10. Ibn Rustah, writing nearly twenty years before Ibn Faḍlān's visit to Bulghar, gives the name of the Bulghar "king" (*malik*), whom he says "professes (*yantaḥilu*) Islām," as "Almush" (cf. the text, ed. M. J. de Goeje, *Kitâb al-aʿlâk an-nafîsa* [Leiden: E. J. Brill, 1892; Bibliotheca

framework of the political symbolism that legitimized the Khazar imperial system. The use of Islamization, and above all of narratives recounting Islamization, in political legitimation will be a recurring theme when we turn to the stories of Baba Tükles, and it is worth noting here our sources' intimations of this pattern's precedents already in pre-Mongol times.

Second, the Bulghar conversion itself inspired legendary conversion narratives, that are clearly attested as early as the twelfth century but are most richly developed in popular literary accounts of the late eighteenth and nineteenth centuries. The contemporary "eyewitness" account of Ibn Faḍlān gives no hint of the legendary conversion narrative that had developed by the twelfth century; here the adoption of Islam by the Bulghar king entails his appeal to the Caliph for someone to instruct him in the principles and laws of Islam and construct a mosque and *minbar* for him, as well as a fortress for defense against hostile kings. This account itself is attractive for its sober and straightforward approach to the adoption of Islam, as distinct from the "miraculous" elements, which so trouble historians, in the legendary conversion narrative; nevertheless it should not be accepted at face value, since it is already at variance, for instance, with the account of Ibn Rustah, which has the same king professing Islam already twenty years earlier. In any event, as is most often the case in the "historical" and "legendary" accounts of later conversions, there is virtually no common ground between Ibn Faḍlān's depiction and the atmosphere and details of the conversion legend (except for the mention in both of military and political tension with the Khazars).

The fact that the Bulghar conversion inspired narratives of the sort with which we are concerned for a later period highlights the antiquity of this kind of communal response to Islamization; indeed, we can trace in pre-Mongol times *three* apparent reflections of the kind of oral conversion narrative with which we will be concerned.

The early echoes of the Bulghar conversion legend are preserved in the Arabic account of the twelfth-century Andalusian traveler, Abū

Geographorum Arabicorum VII], p. 141; tr. Gaston Wiet, *Les atours précieux* [Cairo: Publications de la Société de Géographie d'Egypte, 1955), p. 159); this name is certainly to be identified with the "Almish ibn Shilkī Yilṭawār" who wrote to the Caliph and who, upon Ibn Faḍlān's urging, adopted the name Jaʿfar b. ʿAbdullāh (thereby posthumously "Islamizing" his father, for whose paganism he expressed his regret) for use in the *khuṭbah* (cf. Togan, *Reisebericht*, pp. 1–2, 45–46). On the title *yiltavar*/Common Turkic *elteber*, cf. Golden, *Khazar Studies*, pp. 147–150, Togan, *Reisebericht*, pp. 105–107, and the comments of V. Minorsky, *Ḥudūd al-ʿĀlam, 'The Regions of the World,' A Persian Geography* 372 A.H.–982 A.D. (2nd ed., ed. C. E. Bosworth; London: Luzac & Co., 1970), p. 461.

Ḥāmid al-Gharnāṭī (d. 565/1169–1170), who visited Bulghār and Saqsīn in the Volga valley in the early 1130s.[11] He cites as his source for this story a *Tārīkh Bulghār*, which he ascribes to "*al-qāḍī' l-bulghārī*" whom al-Gharnāṭī identifies as among the pupils (*aṣḥāb*) of Abū'l-Maᶜālī al-Juwaynī;[12] this *qāḍī* al-Bulghārī is in turn most probably to be identified with the *qāḍī* Yaᶜqūb b. an-Nuᶜmān, whom al-Gharnāṭī says he met in Bulghār.[13]

The account in al-Gharnāṭī's work begins with the note that the name "Bulghār" means "wise man," and the story in effect explains why this appellation came to be applied to this country. The etymology is incorrect, of course, but evidently reflects an attempt to link the name to the Turkic verb *bil-*, "to know"; it is not clear whether we should assume an "authentic" folk etymology here, or a (semi)-learned interpretation, although the latter seems more likely.

In any event, the story runs thus: A Muslim merchant who was also a *faqīh* and well versed in medicine came for commercial reasons to this land, where the "king" (*malik*) and his wife were suffering from a grave illness; "they treated them with such remedies as they knew," but their illness worsened. The Muslim asked them if they would enter his religion if he treated them and restored them to health; they agreed, he cured them, they became Muslims, and the people of the country became Muslims too. Then the king of the Khazars came against them with an enormous army and made war upon them, angry that they had entered this religion without his command. The Muslim told the new converts not to fear, but rather to glorify God; and the people, crying out "*Allāhu akbar*" and praising God and blessing the Prophet and his family, fought with the king and routed his army to the point that he was compelled to make peace with them. The king likewise entered their newfound religion, and told

11. The account of al-Gharnāṭī survives in his own work entitled *al-Muᶜrib ᶜan baᶜḍ ᶜajā'ib al-buldān al-maghrib* [Brockelmann (*GAL* I 477–478, *GALS* I 878) cites the work as *al-Mughrib ᶜan baᶜḍ ᶜajā'ib al-buldān*], and in a slightly different form in an apparent citation from this work (or from an intermediary work) by Zakariyā al-Qazvīnī (d. 682/1283); the latter citations are published also with Gabriel Ferrand's edition of al-Gharnāṭī's other famous work, "Le *Tuḥfat al-albāb* de Abū Ḥāmid al-Andalusī al-Ġarnāṭī édité d'après les Mss. 2167, 2168, 2170 de la Bibliothèque Nationale et le Ms. d'Alger," *JA*, 207 (July–December. 1925), pp. 1–148, 193–303 [p. 237], while the *Muᶜrib* itself was published with translation and commentary by César E. Dubler, *Abū Ḥāmid el Granadino y su relación de viaje por tierras eurasiáticas* (Madrid: Imprenta y Editorial Maestre, 1953), pp. 11–12 (text), 54–55 (tr.).

12. I.e., the eminent Shāfiᶜī jurist Abū'l-Maᶜālī ᶜAbd al-Malik al-Juwaynī, d. 478/1085, on whom cf. *GAL* I, p. 388, *GALS* I, p. 671.

13. Ed. Ferrand, p. 132; their meeting evidently came in 530/1135–36.

the Muslim merchant-*faqīh* that, during the battle, he had seen enormous men mounted upon whitish horses battling his troops and putting them to flight; the Muslim explained to him that these were the army of God (*jundu'llāh*). The account concludes with the explanation that a wise man (*ʿālim*) is called among those people "*b.lār*" (intended, evidently, to reflect the participial form "*bilär*"), and so they called that country "*b.lār*" implicitly in honor of that wise Muslim who had brought Islam to them;[14] the name "Bulghār," concludes al-Gharnāṭī, reflects an Arabized form of this native term for "wise man."

The narrative al-Gharnāṭī relates thus comes complete with the arrival of a Muslim in Bulghār, the conversion of the ruler in return for this Muslim's prompt cure of the ruler and his wife, the ensuing conversion of the entire country, a challenge from a hostile king, the victory of the newly converted Muslims over this king through reliance upon God, the report of a miraculous intervention on the Muslims' side, and finally an etymology linking the name of the new Muslim people with the name or status of the Muslim who brought the new religion. In short, many of the standard features and structures of conversion narratives appear here; but, as in many cases, the fact that we have this narrative preserved only in an "external" retelling means in this case that any appeals, in the "original" oral narrative, to elements of the pre-Islamic tradition have been attenuated to the point of virtual disappearance (with only a faint echo of a probable "contest" with native healers in the story of the curing of the ruler and his wife).

This latter element—a "contest" involving Muslims healing, in this case, not the king and his wife, but the king's daughter—appears as the pivotal event in a late (eighteenth-century) conversion narrative recounting the establishment of Islam in Bulghār. This narrative, found in a curious Turkic "history" of this region[15] produced at a time when Bulghār had become an important religious and "national" focal point for Muslims of the Volga valley under Russian rule, is of enormous interest, showing as it does a much clearer appeal to *both* Islamic and Inner Asian religious

14. Qazvīnī's account, evidently owing to the ambiguity of al-Gharnāṭī's words (*wa'l-ʿālim ʿindahum yusammī b.lār*), says that "B.lār" was the *name* of the Muslim who brought Islam.

15. The work in question bears the title *Tavārīkh-i Bulghārīyah*, and exists in numerous nineteenth–century manuscripts; several sections have been published in transcription or translation, but the work as a whole has not been edited or thoroughly analyzed. The best description remains that of M. A. Usmanov, in his *Tatarskie istoricheskie istochniki XVII–XVIII vv.* (Kazan': Izd-vo Kazanskogo Universiteta, 1972), pp. 134–158; on the conversion narrative, see pp. 142–143. The conversion narrative itself was translated in part, from a single manuscript, by Berezin in his "Bulgar na Volge," pp. 146–149, and a fuller translation (into Latin, of a slightly different

values than is evident in the narrative preserved in al-Gharnāṭī's work. In this late narrative the Bulghars are converted by companions of the Prophet, sent with an inkstand, a staff, and a turban given them by the Prophet himself; the decisive cure is effected when the khan's daughter is scrubbed in a steambath with branches of a birch tree that had grown miraculously, in midwinter, from the Prophet's staff, placed in the inkstand as one of the companions donned the turban and prayed. As our purpose here is to demonstrate the currency of narratives of Islamization in the lands that became part of the Golden Horde in pre-Mongol times, we must defer full consideration of this later account to a subsequent study. It is nevertheless worth noting here that conversion narratives regarding the Bulghars cannot be traced in sources between the thirteenth and eighteenth centuries, although they must have survived; they appear to have found literary elaboration only when Tatar Muslims under Russian rule began to appeal to the heritage of Bulghar Islam as a unifying (and communally sanctifying) force.

Islam was not only a force among the Bulghars in the forest belt of western Inner Asia; it was clearly of some importance in the steppe between the North Caucasus and the Black Sea and the middle Volga basin where Bulghār lay. It was established to some degree among the Khazars, as noted, and survived them as well, although we have only minimal information on Islam among the Turkic nomads, from Pechenegs to Oghuz to Qumans, who inhabited this region in the centuries between the Khazars and the Mongols. Nevertheless, in one instance we find echoes from this region as well of a legendary conversion narrative worth noting here.

version) was published together with the text by Kh. D. Fren (C. M. Fraehn), *De numorum bulgaricorum forte antiquissimo*, libri duo (Casani [i.e., Kazan], 1816), pp. 75–86; the latter work was probably the basis for the brief retelling of the tale found in the work of an English visitor to Kazan published in the mid-nineteenth century (Edward Tracy Turnerelli, *Russia on the Borders of Asia: Kazan, the Ancient Capital of the Tartar Khans* [London: Richard Bentley, 1854), vol. II, pp. 244–245). Berezin's account was in turn the basis for the notes by Ch. Ch. Valikhanov published in his *Sobranie sochinenii v piati tomakh* (Alma-Ata, 1964), t. 3, pp. 181–185, 566–567. For the text, see MS LOIV B749, ff. 18a–19a [cf. *Opisanie tiurkskikh rukopisei Instituta narodov Azii*, ed. L. V. Dmitrieva, A. M. Muginov, S. N. Muratov, t. I (Moscow: Nauka, GRVL, 1965), pp. 56–58, No. 36]; MS LOIV B3492, ff. 5b–6b [cf. *Opisanie*, I, pp. 63–64, No. 46]. Berezin published extensive excerpts from one manuscript of the work in his *Turetskaia khrestomatiia*, t. II (Kazan', 1862), with the conversion narrative on pp. 126–128; the conversion narrative is given in transcription into modern Cyrillic-script Tatar, according to a single manuscript, in *Borïngï Tatar Ädäbiyatï* (Kazan: Tatarstan Kitap Näshriyatï, 1963), pp. 452–453, and, with accompanying Russian translation, according to yet another manuscript, by A. N. Khairullin, "O novom spiske 'Tavarikhe Bulgariia' Muslimi," in *Istoriko-lingvisticheskii analiz staropis'mennykh pamiatnikov* (Kazan', 1983), pp. 132–139.

For the Pechenegs of the Pontic steppe we have the interesting report of the geographer al-Bakrī (d. 1094), in whose account we most likely find echoes of indigenous oral narratives about the Pechenegs' communal conversion. According to al-Bakrī, who cites reports from Muslims captive for a time in Constantinople, it was after the year 400/1009–1010 that a Muslim prisoner who was a *faqīh* arrived among the Pechenegs, who had formerly practiced what al-Bakrī calls the "Magian" religion; this man taught many of them the doctrines of Islam, and these Pechenegs embraced the religion sincerely. The "call" (*daʿwah*) to Islam spread among the Pechenegs, but those who remained uncoverted grew hostile, and the tension between these and the new Muslim Pechenegs ended in war between the two groups; God gave victory to the new Muslims, even though they numbered around 12,000 as against twice that number of infidels. The converts killed the non-Muslims, and the remnants embraced Islam; and al-Bakrī's account closes declaring that the entire nation is presently Muslim, and includes scholars, jurists, and Qurʾān-reciters.[16]

However "reliable" or unreliable the account may be historically as an attestation to a genuine Muslim presence among the Pechenegs, we find in this brief report a series of elements that seem to clearly echo the style and themes of an indigenous conversion narrative in oral circulation: the coming of a "teacher" of Islam; the internal dissension produced by his success in converting some Pechenegs; the warfare between the Muslim and infidel members of the community; the victory of the Muslims against daunting odds; and the elimination of Islam's opponents through death or through the submission and conversion of the remainder of infidel Pechenegs. The report is thus of interest here as a possible indication of the antecedents of Islam in the lands of the Golden Horde; but its real interest, as in the case of the Bulghar story reported by al-Gharnāṭī, lies in the currency, and evident popularity, it suggests for oral narratives recounting communal Islamization in those same lands.

Finally, we may also find echoes of an oral conversion narrative, with less clear historical referents, in a curious interpolation, regarding a

16. C. Defrémery, tr., "Fragments de géographes et d'historiens arabes et persans inédits, relatifs aux anciens peuples du Caucase et de la Russie méridionale," *JA*, 4th ser. 13 (1849), pp. 457–522 (tr. pp. 467–468; text p. 461). The report of al-Bakrī is noted by Golden, "The Peoples of the South Russian Steppes," in the *Cambridge History of Early Inner Asia*, p. 275; cf. O. Pritsak, "The Pečenegs: A Case of Social and Economic Transformation," AEMA, 1 (1975), pp. 211–235 (p. 230); and Edward Tryjarski, "Les religions des petchenègues," in *Traditions religieuses et para-religieuses des peuples altaïques* (PIAC XIII, 1970) (Paris: Presses Universitaires de France, 1972), pp. 139–148 (p. 146).

northerly outpost of Islam, in the famous account of "Sallām the Interpreter" and his journey to the Wall of Gog and Magog in the time of the ʿAbbāsid Caliph al-Wāthiq (r. 227–232/842–847). First cited in the ninth-century geography of Ibn Khurdādhbih,[17] the account describes Sallām's journey north through the Caucasus, through the realms of the Armenians and Alans, to the king of the Khazars and further north where his party reached the mountains in which the Wall was located; there he found people speaking Arabic and Persian, who were Muslims, able to read the Qurʾān and possessing schools and mosques. The passage in Ibn Khurdādhbih's work recounts beyond this only the report of these Muslims' astonishment upon hearing of the Caliph in ʿIrāq, but the geographical work of al-Idrīsī, completed in 548/1154 for the Norman king Roger II of Sicily, provides a slightly different version of Sallām's account, omitting mention of the Khazars but naming the "Basjirt" between the Alans and his destination; more importantly, al-Idrīsī identifies the Muslims encountered by Sallām as subjects of the "*khāqān* of the Adhkash,"[18] and recounts the story of their adoption of Islam as purportedly told to Sallām. Sallām, writes al-Idrīsī, asked them about their Islam, whence it had come and who had taught them the Qurʾān. They replied that Islam had come to them long ago, brought by a man riding on an animal which they described in such a way that Sallām understood it to have been a camel. The man "settled among us and spoke to us with words we could understand; then he taught us the laws and obligations of Islam, and we accepted them, and he taught us also the Qurʾān and its meanings, and we learned it and memorized it from him."[19]

Sallām's account of these Muslims was designed to portray them as the guardians of the Wall of Gog and Magog, whose vigilance was vital to ward off the forces of barbarity and unbelief; nevertheless, the addition of al-Idrīsī has the ring of a popular tale of communal Islamization, and its

17. M. J. de Goeje, ed., *Kitâb al-masâlik wa'l-mamâlik (Liber viarum et regnorum) auctore Abu'l-Kâsim Obaidallah ibn Abdallah Ibn Khordâdhbeh et excerpta e Kitâb al-Kharâdj auctore Kodâma ibn Djaʿfar* (2nd ed., Leiden: E. J. Brill, 1967; Bibliotheca Geographorum Arabicorum, VI), pp. 125–126 (tr.), 163–164 (text). Cf. C. Barbier de Meynard, tr., "Le Livre des Routes et des Provinces par Ibn Khordadbeh," *JA*, 6th ser. no. 5 (1865), pp. 490–496; and Étienne Zichy, "Le voyage de Sallâm, l'interprète, à la muraille de Gog et de Magog," *KCsA*, 1 (1921–1925), pp. 190–204. The same account is given by Ibn Rustah; cf. Wiet, tr., *Les atours*, pp. 167–172.

18. This name is listed already by Ibn Khurdādhbih (ed. de Goeje, p. 31) among the Turkic peoples, in the sequence Tughuzghuz, Kīmāk, Ghuzz, "j.f.r" (= Chigil?), Bajānāk, Turkash, Adhk.sh, Khifshākh, Khirkhīz, Kharlukh, Khalaj; Kāshgharī also identifies it as the name of a Turkic tribe.

19. For the text see the new edition of al-Idrīsī, *Opus geographicum*, ed. A. Bombaci, U.

most likely explanation is that al-Idrīsī knew of such stories associated with "northern" peoples, independently of Sallām's account, and added the account to elucidate and "confirm" Sallām's description of the Muslim guards at the Wall. The misguided "historicization" of narratives originally circulated for quite different reasons is a common feature of the treatment of originally oral conversion narratives (and other legends of origin) by later "literary" interpreters, as we will see.

Islam and the Jöchid Ulus

The political structure in which the social and religious changes entailed in the "re-Islamization" of western Inner Asia were played out was the *ulus* of Jöchi,[20] which emerged, at least in name, with Chingis Khan's assignment of territories conquered by the Mongols to his sons, already in 1218, but which actually took shape following the campaign of 1236–1241 into western Inner Asia; this campaign, led by Jöchi's son Batu, saw the conquest of the Bulghar state and the Russian principalities, as well as the subjugation of the Qïpchaq nomads and thrusts deep into central Europe. The actual organization of the Golden Horde is usually assigned to the years following this campaign, with Batu ruling until his death in 653/1255.

As was the case in other parts of the Islamic world that came under Mongol domination in the thirteenth century, the Mongol conquest at first

---

Rizzitano, et al. (Leiden: E. J. Brill / Naples-Rome: Istituto Universitario Orientale de Napoli–Istituto Italiano per il Medio ed Estremo Oriente, 1978), fasc. 8, pp. 935–936; cf. *La Géographie d'Édrisi*, tr. Pierre-Amédée Jaubert (1836–1840; repr., 2 vols. in one, Amsterdam: Philo Press, 1975), II, pp. 417–418.

20. The major sources on the history of the Golden Horde are Arabic chronicles of Mamlūk Egyptian, and less often Syrian, provenance, as well as Persian historical works from the Ilkhanid realm; for a discussion of the relative biases of these groups of works, see Jackson, "Dissolution," pp. 188–190. The sections of most of these sources relevant to the Golden Horde have been assembled, usually with both texts and translations, in the standard works of V. Tizengauzen, ed. & tr., *Sbornik materialov, otnosiashchikhsia k istorii Zolotoi Ordy*, t. 1, *Izvlecheniia iz sochinenii arabskikh* (SPb., 1884), hereafter "Tiz I"; the Persian sources assembled by Tizengauzen were published in 1941 under the same title, t. 2, *Izvlecheniia iz persidskikh sochinenii sobrannye V. G. Tizengauzenom i obrabotannye A. A. Romaskevichem i S. L. Volinym* (Moscow/Leningrad: Izd-vo AN SSSR, 1941), hereafter "Tiz II." Cf. also the Turkish translation of Tizengauzen's Arabic volume, *Altınordu devleti tarihine ait metinler*, tr: İsmail Hakkı İzmirli (Istanbul: Maarif Matbaası 1941). For further and more up-to-date discussion of many of the Arabic sources used by Tizengauzen, cf. Donald Presgrave Little, *An Introduction to Mamlūk Historiography: An Analysis of Arabic Annalistic and Biographical Sources for the Reign of al-Malik an-Nāṣir Muḥammad ibn Qalāʾūn* (Wiesbaden: Franz Steiner Verlag, 1970); and Ulrich Haarmann, *Quellenstudien zur frühen Mamlukenzeit* (Freiburg im Breisgau: K. Schwarz, 1970), esp. pp. 85–118.

dealt a number of blows to the position of Islam in western Inner Asia. The Bulghar state was destroyed, if its cultural legacy endured, and the destruction of the Khorezmshāh's empire—which had furthered the extensive commercial and political links, as well as the growing cultural and religious ties, between the Turkic nomads of the Dasht-i Qïpchaq and the urban Islamic civilization of Central Asia—removed, albeit temporarily, an important source of "Islamizing" momentum for the western steppe. The internal life of the Turkic nomads was itself disrupted, their ethnic identities often reshaped in the administrative assignments of peoples and territories among Mongol princes of the blood and important commanders and early supporters; precisely this disruption, however, may have actually furthered the social conditions in which Islam might be adopted or appealed to as a potential focus for communal identity and political legitimacy.

The absence of state patronage for Islamic institutions was likewise not so damaging to the position of Islam in the lands of the Golden Horde as it was in Iran and Central Asia, perhaps because such patronage had never been so extensive or deep. At the same time, however, the Mongols of western Inner Asia were avidly courted by European powers eager for an ally against the Muslims, and the Jöchid *ulus* became the scene of extensive Christian missionary activity that lasted well into the fourteenth century.[21] There is substantially less evidence for the Golden Horde of a significant Buddhist presence; Buddhism was a serious rival of Islam, at court at least, in Ilkhanid Iran, but it is not clear that the presence of Buddhists in the Jöchid *ulus*, as implied by the well-attested Uyghur presence there, posed any specifically religious challenge to Islam in the way that Christianity did.[22]

21. Cf. the sources assembled in Girolamo Golubovich, *Biblioteca Bio-bibliografica della Terra Santa e dell' Oriente Francescano*, II–III (Florence: Collegio de S. Bonaventura, 1913, 1919); and see further the study of Jean Richard, *La papauté et les missions d'Orient au Moyen Age (XIIIe–XVe siècles)* (Rome: École Française de Rome, 1977 (esp. pp. 86–98, 156–163, 230–246), and his surveys, "Le christianisme dans l'Asie centrale," *Journal of Asian History*, 16 (1982), pp. 101–124, and "Les missions chez les Mongols aux XIIIe et XIVe siècles," in *Histoire universelle des missions catholiques*, I: "Les missions des origines au XVIe siècle" (Paris, 1956), pp. 173–195. Cf. also Mefküre Mollova, "Traces des querelles religieuses dans le Codex Cumanicus," *AOH*, 39 (1985), pp. 339–351; István Vásáry, "Orthodox Christian Qumans and Tatars of the Crimea in the 13th–14th centuries," *CAJ*, 32 (1988), pp. 260–271. Batu's immediate (and short-lived) successor, Sartaq, probably adopted Christianity, and Franciscan missionaries claimed important converts well into the fourteenth century, as noted below.

22. As elsewhere in the Mongol-ruled world, the principal bearers of Buddhism in the Golden Horde were most likely Uyghur *bakhshīs*, whose religious role was accompanied by their more general political and cultural contribution as scribes at the Mongol courts; the term *bakhshī* was thus subject to wide-ranging semantic development (see on the term Doerfer, *TMEN*, II,

Nevertheless, the weight of cultural and commercial links between the Golden Horde and parts of the Islamic world—from Khorezm to the Caucasus to the Near East—helped to bring about an earlier "royal conversion" there than in any other Mongol dynasty, with the accession of Berke in 1257. From then on in coinage and diplomacy, the Golden Horde belongs to the Muslim world, despite the "unconverted" status of most of Berke's successors down to the time of Özbek Khan.

The conversion of Berke has drawn relatively more attention than that of Özbek Khan, most likely because the former was the first Chingisid of consequence known to adopt Islam, and certainly the earliest Mongol khan to rule also as a Muslim monarch. We need not enter into the question of when or how Berke became Muslim;[23] we may note only the nearly unanimous opinion that the Bukharan Sufi shaykh Sayf ad-Dīn

---

pp. 271–277), at times clearly meaning a Buddhist monk, at times meaning only a scribe literate in the Uyghur script, and in some cases referring to religious "specialists" not of Buddhism, but of the indigenous tradition. It is difficult to judge how soon the latter use of the term developed. The word *bakhshï* became, in Central Asia, the standard term both for "shamans" and for the "bards" who combined elements of shamanic performance and epic recitation, and the mention of *bakhshīs* as the religious figures whom Toqtogha honored but Özbek killed (see below), combined with the minimal evidence of extensive Buddhist activity or presence in the Jöchid *ulus*, suggests that this semantic development began quite early; it may be, however, that the term *bakhshī* was used by the Arab writers imprecisely, merely as a generic designation for Islam's opponents. In any case, the Uyghur script was certainly in wide use in the Jöchid *ulus*, and in itself attests to the presence of individuals most likely linked by origin and culture with the Buddhist Uyghur world; the designation "Uyghur" itself seems to have carried, in the Golden Horde as well, a more specifically "Buddhist" connotation than even the term *bakhshī*. It is thus not impossible that Buddhist elements survived in the Jöchid *ulus*, as suggested by the early fifteenth-century report of Schiltberger apparently referring to "Uyghur" Buddhists active there (cf. *Hans Schiltbergers Reisebuch nach der nürnberger Handschrift herausgegeben*, ed. Valentin Langmantel [Tübingen, 1885], p. 40, where he ascribes to these "Uygiur," whom he claims to have seen in "Siberia" while with the Chingisid khan Chegre ["Tzeggra"], the worship of an image of the infant Jesus; Telfer's English translation of the work published by the Hakluyt Society [cited below] gives the name as "Ugine"), and by Barbaro's remark on the effective Islamization of the region only under Edigü (see Chapter 5 on these sources); but our information is too scanty to allow a proper evaluation of Buddhism's role in the Golden Horde. On the continuation of the use of the Uyghur script in the Jöchid *ulus*, see now István Vásáry, "Bemerkungen zum uigurischen Schrifttum in der Goldenen Horde und bei den Timuriden," *UAJ*, Neue Folge, 7 (1987), pp. 115–126, published also in *Beşinci Milletler Arası Türkoloji Kongresi, İstanbul, 23–28 Eylül 1985; Tebliğler*, I, Türk dili, cilt 2 (Istanbul: Edebiyat Fakültesi Basımevi, 1987), pp. 235–247. On the dual meaning of the term *bakhshï* in the Jöchid *ulus*, both religious "cult figure" and scribe, cf. M. A. Usmanov, *Zhalovannye akty Dzhuchieva ulusa XIV–XVI vv.* (Kazan: Izd-vo Kazanskogo universiteta, 1979), pp. 125–128.

23. See on these issues the articles of Jean Richard and István Vásáry noted above; a full analysis of the sources on Berke's conversion remains to be undertaken. See further on Berke's reign Bartol'd's treatment, "Berkai," *Sochineniia*, II/1, pp. 503–507 (from *EI*[1], I, pp. 737–739, reworked by J. A. Boyle in *EI*[2], I, pp. 1187–1188).

Bākharzī played a crucial role in his religious development,[24] and the early testimony, from Berke's contemporary, the historian Jūzjānī, that Berke's religious training had begun already in his early youth. The remark by William of Rubruck noted at the outset is often cited as evidence that Berke's "conversion" certainly predated his accession to the throne, as against the Mamlūk sources, which seem to suggest, at least, that Berke's conversion accompanied his accession. There is most likely no real discrepancy here, since the letters Berke dispatched to Egypt had, no doubt, the dual purpose of announcing his accession and proclaiming his fidelity to Islam, with the political and diplomatic shifts implied thereby.

The impact of Berke's adopted religion upon his rule seems quite substantial. Without overemphasizing the religious bases of his quarrel with Hülegü, which led to chronic warfare between the Jöchid and Ilkhanid states over the Caucasus, it is hardly deniable that Hülegü's sack of Baghdād served to provoke Berke's resentment and sharpen the growing tensions between the two Mongol successor states. The extent of "genuine" adoption of Islam is difficult to judge, of course, but Arabic sources speak of "most of his people" and "most of his army" as becoming Muslims at the same time as Berke did,[25] and the important account of al-Mufaḍḍal reports that the *amīrs* of Berke had converted to Islam, each maintaining a *muʾadhdhin* and *imām* in his service.[26] The detailed account of Rukn ad-Dīn Baybars cites a letter from the new khan listing the "Tatar" households in which Islam had been adopted, and actually gives several of the names of Berke's relatives and *amīrs* who became Muslims.[27] A well-known story first related by an-Nuwayrī mentions that Berke's wife, Jijak-khātūn [i.e., Chichek] also converted to Islam and had a portable tent-mosque built to accompany her retinue;[28] and a well-known Ḥanafī

24. Their relationship is affirmed already in Jūzjānī's work (c. 1260) and by Jamāl Qarshī (early fourteenth century), in addition to the fourteenth-century Arabic sources from the West; see also my "The Eclipse of the Kubravīyah in Central Asia," *Iranian Studies*, 21/1–2 (1988), pp. 45–83 [pp. 47–50].

25. Cf. the accounts of an-Nuwayrī and adh-Dhahabī in Tiz I, pp. 130–131 (text), 151 (tr.), and pp. 202 (text), 205 (tr.), respectively.

26. Tiz I, pp. 183 (text), 194 (tr.); cf. Moufazzal ibn Abil-Fazaïl, *Histoire des sultans mamlouks*, ed. and tr. E. Blochet, pt. 1, in *Patrologia Orientalis*, t. 12, fasc. 3 (Paris, 1919), pp. 454–462.

27. Tiz I, pp. 77 (text), 98–99 (tr.).

28. Tiz I, pp. 130–131 (text), 151 (tr.); cf. al-ʿAynī's account, pp. 478, 507. See also the new edition of an-Nuwayrī, *Nihāyat al-arab fī funūn al-adab*, ed. Saʿīd ʿĀshūr, M. Muṣṭafā Ziyādah, Fuʾād ʿAbd al-Muʿṭī aṣ-Ṣayyād (Cairo: Dār al-Kutub al-Miṣrīyah, 1405/1985), vol. 27, pp. 358–359 on Berke's Islam.

faqīh is said to have dedicated a treatise to Berke Khan.[29] Berke's Islam continued to play a role in his diplomatic exchanges with the Mamlūk court; the report of one embassy's further mission to go on to Mecca and Madīnah to pray for Berke there is no doubt instructive in this regard.[30]

Of greater interest for us in connection with Berke is the fact that legendary narratives based upon his conversion were evidently in circulation quite soon after his accession to the throne. The earliest echo of this appears in the tales surrounding Berke's Islam cited in Jūzjānī's *Ṭabaqat-i Nāṣirī* (c. 1260),[31] including the report that the newborn Berke was nursed, on his father's instructions, by a Muslim midwife, in order to make him a genuine Muslim.[32] By the time of the sixteenth-century *Shajarat al-atrāk*, in which much of the information dates to the mid-fifteenth century, the story has changed somewhat, with the infant Berke supposedly refusing his own mother's milk and eating nothing until nursed by a Muslim woman; the same story appears in the sixteenth-century work of Ötemish Ḥājjī, which contains the conversion story of primary concern to us.[33] As has been observed,[34] this motif of refusing the milk of a non-Muslim mother bears striking resemblance to the account in the "Islamized" *Oghuz-nāmah* known from Rashīd ad-Dīn and Abū' l-Ghāzī and other historical works (discussed more fully below), in which the infant Oghuz Khan refuses his mother's milk until she consents

29. The late sixteenth-century Arabic chronicle of al-Jannābī (d. 999/1590–91) mentions a *risālah* entitled "*an-Nāṣirīyah*" composed in Berke's honor by Mukhtār b. Maḥmūd az-Zāhidī (d. 658/1260), a well-known Khorezmian jurist (see on him Brockelmann, *GAL*, I, p. 382, *GALS*, I, p. 656); the work has apparently not survived. This information is cited by al-Jannābī from "the history of al-Malik al-Muʾayyad," ruler of Ḥamā, apparently referring to the Syrian historian of the early fourteenth century, Abū'l-Fidā; the passage is not found, however, in the extant version of Abū'l-Fidā's work (on similar citations by other historians, cf. Little, *Introduction*, pp. 40–41). The section of al-Jannābī's work cited here is not given in Tizengauzen's collection; I have consulted a fragment of the work appearing in MS British Museum Or. 1761, ff. 295b–309a [f. 298a on this *faqīh*], which Rieu (III, 1023b) describes as an anonymous Arabic history of the Dasht-i Qïpchaq.

30. Tiz I, pp. 420 (text), 431–432 (tr.) (al-Maqrīzī); cf. pp. 52, 61–62 (Ibn ʿAbd aẓ-Ẓāhir).

31. Cf. *Ṭabaḳāt-i-Nāṣirī A General History of the Muhammadan Dynasties of Asia . . . by Maulānā, Minhāj-ud-Dīn, Abū-ʿUmar-i-ʿUsmān*, tr. H. G. Raverty (Calcutta, 1881; repr. New Delhi: Oriental Books Reprint Corporation, 1970), vol. II, pp. 1283–1293.

32. Tr. Raverty, II, p. 1283; the account is discussed by Richard, "La conversion de Berke," pp. 178–183. A possible echo of this element of the story, that Berke's father Jöchi wished him to become a Muslim, may be found even earlier, in an-Nasawī's history of the last Khorezmshāh's son, Jalāl ad-Dīn; an-Nasawī reports that a sister of Jalāl ad-Dīn, taken captive by the Mongols, succeeded in getting word to her brother that the *khāqān* (it is not clear who is meant by this designation) had assigned her to teach the Qurʾān to his children.

33. Ötemish Ḥājjī's work (discussed below), Tashkent MS, ff. 41a–b.

34. Cf. Vásáry, " 'History and Legend,' " p. 239.

to convert to Islam. We thus find stories associated with legendary heroes such as Oghuz Khan already attached to Berke as the "first convert" to Islam among the Mongol rulers.[35]

Similarly, among the "legendary" narratives that sprang up around Berke's conversion are reports of his association with the Sufi shaykh Sayf ad-Dīn Bākharzī; in particular, Bākharzī figures in an elaborate legendary account of Berke's conversion and accession in Ötemish Ḥājjī's work,[36] and his role is also highlighted, with appropriate hagiographical dialogues and motifs, in the Arabic histories of Ibn Khaldūn and al-ʿAynī.[37] The narrative reflections of Berke's conversion are thus important examples of the persistent paradigm for royal conversion from the post-Mongol era on, which assigns the central role in the ruler's conversion to a Sufi shaykh; however important Bākharzī's influence may have been, the religious figures whose presence is noted at the court of the Golden Horde are more often jurists and theologians than dervishes, and it may be that the role of Sufis in "royal" conversion as recounted in later sources is somewhat exaggerated, reflecting the social position of Sufis in the age of the sources rather than the age of the conversion. Nevertheless, it appears likely that Sufi shaykhs did in fact play an increasingly important role in the Islamization of Mongol-ruled western Inner Asia, and the case of Berke's conversion provides our earliest illustration both of the likely actual role of Sufis, and of the literary elaboration of that role.

Less often noted than Berke's adoption of Islam is the report of conversion to Islam by Berke's second successor, Töde Mengü (Mongol form Töde Möngke, r. 1280–1287), included in several historical works which already noted the conversion of Berke. In the *Tashrīf al-ayyām wa'l-ʿuṣūr fī sīrat al-Malik al-Manṣūr*, a biography of the Mamlūk Sulṭān Qalāwun ascribed to the historian Ibn ʿAbd aẓ-Ẓāhir (d.692/1292–1293), we find the earliest mention of Töde Mengü's conversion,[38] and the report is expanded in the universal history, entitled *Zubdat al-fikrah fī tārīkh al-hijrah*, of Rukn ad-Dīn Baybars al-Manṣūrī (d.725/1325–1325), a high official under al-Malik an-Nāṣir, and an authoritative writer on affairs of

35. Berke's renown as a Muslim Mongol khan is further echoed in a fifteenth–century Ottoman work, reflecting popular tradition, linking Berke Khan to the "Islamizing" career of the saint Sarï Saltïq (on whom see Chapters 4 and 5); cf. Paul Wittek, "Yazijioghlu ʿAlī on the Christian Turks of the Dobruja," *BSOAS*, 14 (1952), pp. 639–668, esp. pp. 648–649.

36. Vásáry surveys this account (" 'History and Legend,' " pp. 246–247; cf. Tashkent MS ff. 41a–43a.

37. Cf. Vásáry, " 'History and Legend,' " p. 241.

38. Tiz I, pp. 68 (tr.), 66 (text).

the Golden Horde;[39] on that basis the story is repeated in the encyclopedic work of an-Nuwayrī (d.732 or 733/1331–1333),[40] and the history of Ibn al-Furāt (d. 807/1404–1405).[41] The account reports the arrival in 682/1283–1284 of an embassy announcing the adoption of Islam by Töde Mengü, who had acceded to the "throne of Berke"; the embassy consisted of two men from among the "*fuqahā al-Qifjāq*," whose names are given as Majd ad-Dīn Aṭā (a clear reflection of the Turkic honorific *ata*, "father") and Nūr ad-Dīn, and they brought a letter written in "Mongol." When the letter was translated, it was seen to contain a report on the khan's accession and "entrance" (*dukhūl*) into the religion of Islam; it declared further that the khan had established the laws of Islam, and included his request that the Mamlūk Sulṭān facilitate his performance of the pilgrimage to Mecca. The envoys further conveyed the khan's request that the Sulṭān supply him with banners appropriate to a Caliph and a Sulṭān, under which he might fight against the enemies of religion.

Nothing more is known of the consequences of this announcement of conversion, which clearly seems to involve an official "establishment" of Islam as well. Töde Mengü did not become popularly associated with Islamization so far as we know, perhaps due less to the relative brevity of his reign (seven years) than to the succession struggles that followed it. Appeals to Islam may well have played a role in those struggles, and in any case the request conveyed by the Qïpchaq *faqīhs* for Islamic religiopolitical symbols to use in the struggle against the "enemies of religion" suggests that religious issues, and in general the tension between proponents of Islamization and those hostile to it, were already a factor in mobilizing opponents and supporters of Töde Mengü.

The reports of this khan's conversion thus attest to the still unresolved tensions within the Jöchid *ulus* resulting from Berke's initial decision to declare himself on the side of Islamization, whatever that may have entailed. For what Berke's conversion appears to have ushered in was a period of tension between growing forces favoring "official" Islamization on the one hand, and those in favor of preserving indigenous traditions; these tensions

39. On the work, see further E. Ashtor, "Some Unpublished Sources for the Baḥrī Period," in *Studies in Islamic History and Civilization*, ed. Uriel Heyd; "Scripta Hierosolymitana," vol. 9 (Jerusalem: Hebrew University, 1961), pp. 11–30 [pp. 12–13 on Baybars]. The passage appears in Tiz I, pp. 105 (tr.), 82–83 (text); a briefer account is included in Baybars's other work, *at-Tuḥfat al-mulūkīyah fī'd-dawlat at-turkīyah*; cf. Tiz I, pp. 122 (tr.), 97 (text).

40. Tiz I, pp. 165 (tr.), 143–144 (text); ed. ʿĀshūr et al., vol. 27, p. 365.

41. See on this work Ashtor, "Some Unpublished Sources," pp. 13–24; Little, pp. 73–75; the passage appears in Tiz I, pp. 362 (tr.), 355–356 (text).

were often used, undoubtedly, in the political struggles between vying contenders for the throne and between those contenders and the leading tribal chieftains and "commanders." We are no doubt justified in assuming that adoption of Islam was often inspired or influenced by the hope for advantages (in external relations perhaps, but with an internal constituency as well) in such political struggles; this is clearly the situation, after all, portrayed in most of the accounts surrounding the "decisive" adoption of Islam in the Golden Horde by Özbek Khan, as we shall see.

The case of the famous Noghay, the powerful figure who served as Berke's chief military commander and whose support was vital in engineering the succession of most subsequent khans down to Özbek's predecessor Toqtogha, is instructive with regard to these tensions and their political implications: already Rashīd ad-Dīn, writing before this khan's death, portrays the enmity between Toqtogha and his former mentor Noghay as having been fueled by religious resentments. Noghay's own family may indeed illustrate the religious confrontations frequent in the Jöchid *ulus* at that time. A Franciscan source reports the baptism, in 1286 or 1287, of a certain "Yaylaq," identified as a wife of Noghay, in the Crimea; she had been converted to Christianity after visiting a Franciscan convent at Solkhat.[42] Noghay himself, however, was evidently a convert to Islam; shortly after Berke's death, Noghay dispatched a letter, in 669/1270–1271, to the Mamlūk Sulṭān al-Malik aẓ-Ẓāhir, proclaiming his sincerity in his new faith and quite transparently seeking the support of the Egyptian ruler.[43] We should no doubt understand here an indirect appeal by Noghay to the "Islamizing" party within the Jöchid *ulus*, a party no doubt actively courted by Berke but a potentially powerful force still in the second half of the thirteenth century. According to Rashīd ad-Dīn's account of Noghay's fall, Toqtogha's father-in-law, the Qonghrat tribal chief Saljïday Güregen, whose realm was near Khorezm, had sought the hand of a daughter of Noghay for his son,[44] but after the marriage was consummated, Noghay's daughter became a Muslim; her new husband, however, was an "Uyghur," a term here most likely indicating Buddhist incli-

42. Golubovich, *Biblioteca*, II, pp. 443–445; cf. Richard, *La papauté*, pp. 89–91, noting the growing Islamic presence reflected in the letter reporting the event, which was dated 10 April 1287, in Kaffa.

43. The letter is included in the *Zubdat al-fikrah* of Rukn ad-Dīn Baybars (d. 725/1325); cf. Tiz I, pp. 101–102 (tr.), 80–81 (text). It is mentioned also in al-Maqrīzī's history with the date specified as Muḥarram, 669/August–September 1270 (Tiz I, pp. 422, 434).

44. The son's name was Yaylaq, according to Rashīd ad-Dīn, recalling the "Yaylaq" mentioned above, named as a wife of Noghay and a Christian convert. Yaylaq Khatun is named as Noghay's

nations (since his *tribe* was already identified as Qonghrat), and mistreated Noghay's daughter, prompting Noghay to complain to Toqtogha. The khan refused Noghay's demands for satisfaction against Saljïday and his son, and the tensions culminated in the open warfare that ended with Noghay's defeat and death in 1299.[45]

This explanation of the enmity between Noghay and his former protégé naturally veils other political and military calculations as well as tensions resulting from familial, tribal, and regional rivalries; nevertheless, Rashīd ad-Dīn's account points to the likelihood that expressions of political resentment might already be enhanced and legitimized for certain audiences if couched in terms of religious differences.

If tensions persisted after Berke's reign between Muslims at court and in the ruling dynasty, and upholders of Mongol, Inner Asian traditions, there seems to have been at least some appreciation of the meaning of Berke's conversion for the Golden Horde. Later Muslim historians often refer to the Jöchid *ulus* as the realm of Berke, writing, for instance, about the holders of "Berke's" throne long after his death; more revealingly, the geographical term "Dasht-i Qïpchaq" (i.e., the Qïpchaq steppe), commonly used by Muslim historians and geographers as a synonym for the Jöchid *ulus*, was sometimes replaced by the term "Dasht-i Berke," evoking a play on words that equated the Mongol name "Berke" with the Arabic *barakah* ("spiritual grace," "blessing") spelled the same way.

It is not certain, however, to what extent this appellation reflects only learned views of external observers rather than internal evaluations of Berke's significance; certainly in the dominant "internal" tradition, such as we know it, Berke's role paled next to that of Özbek, and indeed the source that provides our central conversion narrative, the work of Ötemish Ḥājjī, is unique among sources that reflect indigenous traditions in portraying a

wife by Rukn ad-Dīn Baybars and an-Nuwayrī, as well (Tiz I, pp. 86, 108–109, and pp. 136, 157–158, with the form "Baylaq"; an-Nuwayrī, ed. ʿĀshūr et al., vol. 27, pp. 368–369), and is portrayed as playing a prominent role in his relations with Toqtogha early in the latter's reign; it is possible the names, relationships, and roles in the story have been confused in one of the sources, but it is difficult to judge which is more correct. In support of Rashīd ad-Dīn's version, one fragmentary manuscript of the Turkic *Muḥabbat-nāmah* (composed by the poet Khorezmī in the mid-fourteenth century) identifies the poet's patron, the Qonghrat Muḥammad Khoja Bek, as the son of "Yaylagh Qutlugh;" cf. the discussion in H. F. Hofman, *Turkish Literature: A Bio-Bibliographical Survey*; Section III (Chaghatai), Part I (Authors) (Utrecht, 1969), III, pp. 262–265.

45. Cf. *The Successors of Genghis Khan*, tr. John Andrew Boyle (New York: Columbia University Press, 1971), pp. 126–127; essentially the same account appears in the slightly later work of Banākatī, *Tārīkh-i Banākatī, Rawżat ūlī'l-albāb fī maʿrifat at-tavārīkh va'l-ansāb*, ed. Jaʿfar Shiʿār (Tehran, 1348/1969), pp. 396–397.

general "apostasy" following Berke's conversion, necessitating Özbek's conversion as the decisive event in the Islamization of the Golden Horde.

The Conversion of Özbek Khan

As noted, although Islam found its initial royal sponsor in the Golden Horde in the khan Berke (r. 1257–1266), it was not until the first quarter of the fourteenth century that Islam was effectively and definitively established at court. The decisive Islamization of the Golden Horde is ascribed in native tradition among the peoples of the Jöchid *ulus* and in Islamic historiography to the reign of Özbek Khan (1313–1341); the Noghay saying "*din özbekten qaldï*" ("religion has remained since Özbek")[46] reflects an awareness among the peoples formerly part of the Golden Horde that the firm establishment of Islam among them dates from his reign, and historical sources from the Muslim world are in agreement on Özbek Khan's active support and patronage of Islamic institutions.[47] It is to Özbek Khan's reign, and in particular to the circumstances of his accession and the nature of his "conversion," that we must turn in order to set the stage for evaluating this previously unknown version.

46. Cf. Usmanov, "Ètapy islamizatsii," p. 179; cited also in his *Tatarskie istoricheskie istochniki*, p. 84. Usmanov cites the late nineteenth-century *Mustafād al-akhbār fī aḥvāl Qazān va Bulghār* of Shihāb ad-Dīn Marjānī, printed in Kazan (I have consulted the second edition of vol. 1, issued in 1897, pp. 101–102, for Özbek Khan); the abridged edition recently published in Cyrillic-script Tatar (Shihabetdin Märjani, *Möstäfadel-äkhbar fi äkhvali Kazan vä Bolgar*, ed. Ä. N. Khäyrullin [Kazan: Tatarstan Kitap Näshriyatï, 1989]) does not include the relevant section. Marjānī's report of this Noghay aphorism is somewhat out of character, insofar as his work generally reflects a quite "modernized" approach to "historical scholarship" that left Marjānī hostile to "legendary" and "fantastic" elements within popular traditions; on his work as a historian, see Uli Schamiloglu, "The Formation of a Tatar Historical Consciousness: Şihabäddin Märcani and the Image of the Golden Horde," *Central Asian Survey*, 9/2 (1990), pp. 39–49.

47. See in general on Özbek Khan's reign and his conversion Spuler, *Die Goldene Horde*, pp. 85–99, cf. pp. 212–220; Safargaliev, *Raspad*, pp. 64–71; Grekov and Iakubovskii, *Zolotaia Orda*, pp. 90–94; Hammer-Purgstall, *Geschichte der Goldenen Horde*, pp. 281–304; Kafalı, *Altın Orda*, pp. 73–82; Howorth, *History of the Mongols*, II/1, pp. 148 ff. We may note here, recalling the remarks in the introduction, that modern "historical" evaluations of Özbek Khan's Islam have been of two basic types: we find dismissals of the significance of his conversion, portrayed as a move inspired by "mere" political considerations and argued on the basis of Özbek's continued adherence to Mongol customs and on the basis of the absence of "genuine" Islamic sentiment in his dealings with the Ilkhans and with the Byzantines (by which standards the significance of many Muslim rulers' Islam might be dismissed); and, conversely, we find regrets over Özbek's turn from the "tolerance" of his Mongol predecessors to Muslim "fanaticism." In the

The Reign of Özbek Khan and the Establishment of Islam

Özbek became khan early in 1313 through the death of his uncle Toqtogha (r. 1291–1312) and the succession struggle that ensued, and ruled without evident internal challenge for nearly thirty years until his death in 1341. His reign, the longest of any khan of the Golden Horde, and exceeded only by that of Qubilay among effective khans of the Mongol successor states, is almost universally regarded as the highest point in the political development of the Jöchid *ulus*, an era of relative stability and solid centralized control. This image is enhanced by the stark contrast it offers with the internecine struggles that preceded his reign, including the struggle between the commander Noghay and a series of khans unable at first to assert their power, and with the virtual disintegration of the Golden Horde in the succession struggles that followed the death of Özbek's son Jānī Bek (r.1341–1357). The picture of stability evident in the sources may itself be somewhat misleading, of course, and the near unanimous applause for Özbek's successful assertion of the khan's prerogatives against the "centrifugal forces" represented by the interests of the tribal chieftains may reflect more a taste for centralized administration among historians than a balanced evaluation of the political situation under Özbek. As is clear from the accounts discussed below in connection with his conversion, Özbek's accession to the throne was hard-won and involved not only a veritable coup d'état by his supporters but widespread reprisals against his opponents in which by minimal count at least a hundred Chingisid princes and members of the tribal "aristocracy" were killed;[48] this in itself may account for the respite from internal struggles among Chingisids and betwen the khan and tribal chieftains that seems to characterize Özbek Khan's reign.

In any event, the era of Özbek was indeed marked by a heightened profile for the Golden Horde in its international relations and by important internal political and cultural developments. He initiated or maintained diplomatic contacts with the Byzantine state and with Mamlūk Egypt, in both cases cementing relations through political marriages; he fostered commercial relations with the Mediterranean world through the Genoese

latter regard a good indicator of the attitudes underlying such portrayals is Grousset's citation of an edict of Özbek Khan in 1320, forbidding the ringing of bells at Sudaq in the Crimea, as a sign that the Golden Horde was increasingly abandoning Mongol tolerance in favor of " 'totalitarian' Muslim fanaticism" (*Empire of the Steppes*, pp. 405, 617).

48. On the implications of Özbek's seizure of power for succession in the Jöchid *ulus*, cf. Fedorov-Davydov, *Obshchestvennyi stroi*, pp. 103–107.

and Venetian trading colonies on the Black Sea coast; and he continued the struggle, by his time more than a half-century old, between the Jöchid *ulus* and the Ilkhanid state over Azerbaijan and the Caucasus.

In the latter case Özbek's efforts were markedly unsuccessful. He managed through threats of invasion to gain small concessions from Öljeytü in 1315, when the latter agreed to execute a renegade Jöchid prince who had taken refuge with the Ilkhanids following an attack against Khorezm (an attack that Özbek's forces were unable to punish without help from a Chaghatayid prince), but in general Özbek's policies toward the Ilkhanids failed to secure any advantage. He suffered setbacks in several early campaigns into the Caucasus and Khurāsān from 718–723/1318–1323, in which he appears to have cooperated with princes of the house of Chaghatay,[49] while his peace with Abū Saʿīd in 1323 seems to have been prompted more by military necessity brought on in part by a cooling of relations with the Mamlūks than by the avowed reason of Abū Saʿīd's Islam.[50] In any event, the death of Abū Saʿīd brought a renewed offensive by Özbek's troops, which nevertheless failed despite the growing fragmentation of the Ilkhanid state.

Similarly, though we are relatively poorly informed about Özbek's relations with the other Mongol successor states, we find occasional evidence of hostility toward his succession, or dissatisfaction with his reliability as an ally, both among the Great Khans in the east and among the rulers of the Chaghatay *ulus*.[51] Internally the course of Özbek's reign is less well known, due largely to a lack of sources interested in internal events in the Golden Horde beyond issues of succession. We know of his "administrative" shift in moving his "capital" from the older center, referred to as Saray Batu, further up the Volga to Saray Berke, known also as Saray al-Jadīd, "New Saray"; in general the growth of urban life in the Golden Horde is linked to his reign, fostered in part by the extensive construction of, in effect, monuments to Özbek's adoption of Islam.[52] From the standpoint of internal politics, however, we can only conjecture, on the basis of available sources, about the administrative implications of the apparent "dismissal" or "retirement" and subsequent recall of a central figure in Özbek's reign, the *amīr* Qutlugh

49. Cf. the accounts of Ibn Duqmāq, Tiz I, pp. 319, 321 (text), 326, 328 (tr.); of Ibn Khaldūn, pp. 372 (text), 387–388 (tr.); and of al-ʿAynī, pp. 491 (text), 521 (tr.).

50. Cf. al-ʿAynī, in Tiz I, pp. 494 (text), 524–525 (tr.).

51. Cf. Tiz II, pp. 139–141 (tr.), 243–244 (text).

52. Of the buildings erected under Özbek Khan, none of those built in Saray Berke have sur-

Temür;[53] similarly we can do little more than speculate on the administrative developments suggested by the various divisions of the Jöchid *ulus*, developments complicated by the joining or coexistence of administrative structures for the urban areas (Khorezm, the Crimea, etc.) and for the nomadic population. And we have only the vaguest information, still not thoroughly analyzed, on the domestic interrelationships between Özbek Khan's power as supreme ruler of the Golden Horde and the nominally autonomous rulers of the eastern wing of the Jöchid *ulus*.[54]

A relatively minor "internal" event of Özbek Khan's reign, which is nevertheless widely known because of its impact in Russian sources, came in 1327 with the suppression of an uprising in Tver', formerly the premier Russian principality and the chief rival to Moscow. Both through his suppression of the revolt itself, which effectively eliminated Tver' as the chief rival to the more loyal Moscow, and in the free hand he gave to Muscovite troops in dealing with the rebels in Tver', Özbek Khan in effect boosted Moscow to the position of primacy among the Russian cities that it enjoyed ever after. It is ironic to find the khan credited with establishing Islam in the Golden Horde also responsible, in large measure, for raising Moscow to the status that enabled it to absorb the remnants of the Golden Horde some two centuries after Özbek's death.

Özbek Khan's conversion is also registered in the Russian chronicles, but without any particulars; the standard entry notes only that in the year 6821/1313 the khan "Tokhta" died and the new khan, Özbek, took the throne and "became a Muslim" *(obesermenilsia)*.[55] Russian chronicles and hagiographies recalled Özbek's Muslim status as part of the hos-

vived, while the structures surviving in Urgench dating from his reign are linked with the name of his governor in Khorezm, Qutlugh Temür. The only surviving structure dating to Özbek's reign is the mosque-*madrasah* complex built in 1314 in Solkhat, in the Crimea, the site of the old city called "Qïrïm;" cf. A. L. Iakobson, *Srednevekovyi Krym: Ocherki istorii i istorii material'noi kul'tury* (Moscow/Leningrad: Izd-vo "Nauka," 1964), pp. 106–108, and photographs in plates XXV–XXVI.

53. Cf. Ibn Duqmāq, in Tiz I, pp. 321 (text), 328 (tr.); Ibn Khaldūn, pp. 372 (text), 387–388 (tr.); and al-ʿAynī, pp. 492 (text), 522 (tr.).

54. Cf. Th. T. Allsen, "The Princes of the Left Hand: An Introduction to the History of the *Ulus* of Orda in the Thirteenth and Early Fourteenth Centuries," *AEMA*, 5 (1985 [1987]), pp. 5–40, esp. pp. 24–26. The chronology adopted by Allsen for the rulers of this eastern wing is open to considerable question, however, due to his reliance upon the work of Muʿīn ad-Dīn Naṭanzī, whose chronology for the Jöchid *ulus* is hopelessly confused: he inserts Özbek Khan's father as his predecessor on the throne, assigning him a reign from 720/1320 to 737/1337, with Özbek himself ascribed a reign from 737 to 767; figures from the eastern wing called contemporaries of Özbek Khan thus cannot be dated with certainty on this basis.

55. Cf. the chronicle of Nikifor Simeonov, ed. in *PSRL*, t. 18 (SPb., 1913), p. 88; the Nikonian

tile image they presented of him, and that hostility remained in popular memory even in the absence of his identification with Islam;[56] but without question the growing identification of Mongol rule with Islam that so shaped Russian attitudes toward the Muslim world may be said to have begun in Özbek Khan's reign.

It is, finally, that definitive Islamization of the Golden Horde for which, as noted earlier, Özbek's reign is best known. This should not necessarily be understood in "official" terms of "proclaiming" Islam the "state religion," although announcements that could be construed in such a sense were evidently sent with embassies to Muslim courts, as reported in the historical sources of Mamlūk and Ilkhanid provenance discussed below. These should no doubt be understood as declarations intended to formally remove any grounds, at the Mamlūk court in partic-

---

chronicle, *PSRL*, t. 10 (SPb., 1885), p. 178, cf. *The Nikonian Chronicle*, tr. Serge A. Zenkovsky and Betty Jean Zenkovsky, vol. 3 (1241–1381) (Princeton: Kingston Press, 1986), p. 97. The other standard setting for reference to Özbek Khan's conversion is in the accounts of the execution of Prince Mikhail of Tver' at the khan's camp in 6826 or 6827/1318 or 1319 (see *The Nikonian Chronicle*, vol. 3, pp. 104–111, in which, however, the element of the khan's conversion is not worked into the account); in several versions of this account, Özbek Khan's entry into "the Saracen faith" (*voide v bogemerskuiu veru srachin'skuiu/ sratsynskuiu*) and his consequent mercilessness toward Christians are mentioned as prelude to Mikhail's "martyrdom" (cf. the late fifteenth-century "Muscovite Chronicle," *PSRL*, 25 (Moscow/Leningrad, 1949), p. 161; the Piskarevskii chronicle, *PSRL*, 34 (Moscow, 1978), p. 105; the "Tipografskaia" chronicle, *PSRL*, 24 (Petrograd, 1921), p. 108).

56. For an analysis of the treatment of Özbek Khan's status as a Muslim in medieval Russian chronicles and hagiographies, with further references, see Charles J. Halperin, *The Tatar Yoke* (Columbus, Ohio: Slavica Publishers, 1986), pp. 81–93; not noted by Halperin are echoes of the hostility evoked later by the Muslim status of "Özbek the son of Toghrïlcha," which may be found in the epic tale of the hero Sukhan, put in written form as early as the mid-seventeenth century, wherein "Tsar Azbuk Tovruevich" is made the leader of a pagan Tatar host threatening the Russian land and the Christian faith (cf. V. I. Malyshev, *Povest' o Sukhane: Iz istorii russkoi povesti XVII veka* [Moscow/Leningrad: Izd-vo AN SSSR, 1956], pp. 63–64, and text pp. 135–139, 139–143; cf. pp. 217–219); tr. in Serge A. Zenkovsky, tr., *Medieval Russia's Epics, Chronicles, and Tales* [2nd ed., New York: E. P. Dutton, 1974], pp. 505–510). As Malyshev notes, the same "*tsar*," called variously "Azviak Tavruevich," "Vozviak Tavrol'evich," "Vezviak Vez'iakovich," or "Zviaga Tavrol'evich," figures as the Tatar ruler in the much older song of Shelkan Dudent'evich, which is regarded as echoing the events of the Tver' uprising in 1327 (for the chronicles' version of the uprising, cf. *PSRL*, t. 15 (Petrograd, 1922), cols. 42–43, and the translation in Basil Dmytryshyn, *Medieval Russia: A Source Book, 900–1700*, 2nd ed. [Hinsdale, Illinois: Dryden Press, 1973], pp. 151–152). Here again "Vozviak" is not specifically Muslim, but a bloodthirsty Tatar who demands that Shelkan drink blood before he will be granted the city of Tver' as his "prize; cf. the versions in A. F. Gil'ferding, *Onezhskie byliny*, III (Moscow / Leningrad: Izd-vo AN SSSR, 1951), pp. 273–275, 341–342, 404–405, 451–453; *Drevnie rossiiskie stikhotvoreniia sobrannye Kirsheiu Danilovym*, ed. A. P. Evgen'eva and V. N. Putilov (Moscow/Leningrad: Izd-vo AN SSSR, 1958), pp. 28–32, 595–597; and V. N. Putilov, "Pesnia o Shchelkane," in *Russkii fol'klor: Materialy i issledovaniia*, t. 3 (Moscow/Leningrad: Izd-vo AN SSSR, 1958), pp. 46–68. Curiously, each of

ular, for religiously motivated (or religiously rationalized) hesitation regarding relations with the Golden Horde. To suppose on this basis a proclamation of Islam as an "official state religion" would be both anachronistic in general, and contrary to the specific traditions of rule and administration current in the Mongol-ruled world.

Özbek's association with Islamization should rather be understood as a reflection both of the khan's genuine and avowed status as a Muslim and of the heightened profile of Islamic figures and institutions in his reign; in the final analysis it undoubtedly rests as well in the popular narratives about his Muslim status that dramatized the effects of his conversion, narratives that are the focus of the present study. In any event, it goes without saying that Özbek Khan's status as a Muslim hardly entailed an overnight transformation of the Golden Horde or the instant elimination or repression of "rivals" to Islam, however much the popular narratives we will examine may portray his "conversion" in such stark terms. Rather, in the first regard, the "work" of Islamization at the institutional and social levels continued well after Özbek's time; his son Jānī Bek is especially closely linked with even stronger support for Islam than his father,[57] and important personages in the history of the Golden Horde continue to be honored for particularly close ties with Islamization well into the fifteenth century, as we will note in the case of Edigü.

As for Özbek's treatment of rivals to Islam, the verdict is mixed. On the one hand Muslim sources consistently link his elimination of Mongol princes and *amīrs* who opposed his accession to their stubborn refusal to abandon their religion for Islam; their religion would appear to have

---

these specialists suggests an explanation for the patronymic "Tovruevich" or "Tavrul'evich," without recognizing in it the name of Özbek Khan's father Toghrul[cha].

57. The history of Muʿīn ad-Dīn Naṭanzī, from the early fifteenth century, credits Jānī Bek with having "brought the entire *ulūs-i ūzbak* to Islam," and with the destruction of idol temples and the construction of mosques and *madrasahs* (*Muntakhab at-tavārīkh-i Muʿīnī*, ed. Jean Aubin [Tehran: Kitābfurūshī-i Khayyām, 1336/1957], p. 83. While he mentions Özbek's conversion (as noted below), Naṭanzī devotes considerably more space to Jānī Bek's solicitude for Islam. In the late fifteenth century, the Timurid historian Mīrkhwānd ignored Özbek altogether, highlighting Berke's Islam and Jānī Bek's justice and respect for the *ʿulamā* (*Rawżat aṣ-ṣafā*, vol. 5 [Tehran: Khayyām, 1339/1960, p. 222). Jānī Bek figures prominently in several Central Asian legends of Islamization that we cannot take up here; he is also credited with military and administrative changes evidently marked by Islamic influence, such as in the report that he instituted elements not only of Islamic, but of specifically Sufi, garb as standard military dress. This is mentioned by the chronicler ash-Shujāʿī, who records (twice, under consecutive years) that upon his consolidation of power (after killing his brother Khiżr Bek), Jānī Bek ordered the Tatar troops to wear the turban (*ʿimāmah*) and "mantel" (*farajah*); cf. Tizengauzen, I, pp. 254–255 (text), 263–264 (tr.), and the new edition and translation by Barbara Schäfer, ed., *Die Chronik*

been the indigenous traditions of the Mongols and Turks, but it is not impossible that some of them were Buddhists, as may be suggested by the term *bakhshī* applied to many of Özbek's victims. On the other hand, despite complaints about his persecution of Christians and reports of monks martyred during his reign,[58] Özbek continued to extend favors to

aš-Šuğāʿīs, erster Teil, arabischer Text (Wiesbaden: Franz Steiner, 1977), pp. 214, 234; and Šams ad-Dīn aš-Šuğāʿī, *Tārīḫ al-Malik an-Nāṣir Muḥammad b. Qalāwūn aṣ-Ṣāliḥī wa-aulādihī* [*sic*], tr. Barbara Schäfer, zweiter Teil, Übersetzung (Wiesbaden: Franz Steiner, 1985), pp. 249, 267–268. Schäfer reads for the latter term "*farajīyāt*," and gives without comment two readings for which the version of Tizengauzen (who used the same unique manuscript) is to be preferred: Schäfer reads consistently "Jāy" Bek, and in the second occurrence, where the detail is added that the *amīrs* killed Tinī Bek in Saraychïq [as in Tizengauzen's reading, *bi-bilād Ṣ.rāy-j.q*], Schäfer reads in text *bi-bilād ṣarāy ḥ.q.*, and translates only that they killed him "im Gebiet von Ṣarāy" (neither of these lapses are noted in the review of the translation by Karl-Heinz Golzio, *CAJ*, 31 (1987), pp. 150–152; and he does not note Tizengauzen's earlier edition and translation of the sections from this chronicle relevant to the Golden Horde). See also on this issue the remarks of al-ʿUmarī from the mid-fourteenth century (cf. Klaus Lech, *Das mongolische Weltreiche: Al-ʿUmarī's Darstellung der mongolischen Reiche in seinem Werk Masālik al-abṣār fī mamālik al-amṣār* [Wiesbaden: Otto Harrassowitz, 1968], pp. 147 [tr.], 320 [n. 165], text p. 84). With regard to Jānī Bek's Islamizing role may also be noted the change in diplomatics suggested by the Latin and Italian translations of the treaties concluded between the Venetian republic and the khans of the Golden Horde: the pact with "Husbecho" from 1333 begins with a formula that is clearly the equivalent of that found in old Mongol decrees beginning "By the power of the eternal Heaven . . ." ("*In uirtute eterni Dei . . .*"; cf. *Diplomatarium Veneto-Levantinum*, ed. George Martin Thomas [Venice, 1880; repr. New York: Burt Franklin, n.d.], I, p. 243, and see also A. P. Grigor'ev, V. P. Grigor'ev, "Iarlyk Uzbeka venetsianskim kuptsam Azova: Rekonstruktsiia soderzhaniia," in *Istoriografiia i istochnikovedenie istorii stran Azii i Afriki*, vyp. 13 [Leningrad: Izd-vo Leningradskogo universiteta, 1990], pp. 74–107, esp. pp. 81–82); the same holds true of the treaty with his successor "Zanibecho" in 1342 (*Diplomatarium*, I, p. 261), but the 1347 pact with Jānī Bek begins "*In nomine Domini et Maomethi, profete Tartarorum*" (I, p. 311).

58. On his reported persecution of Christians, see the account of William Adam discussed below. For reports of Franciscan friars martyred or persecuted in the Golden Horde under Özbek, see Golubovich, *Biblioteca*, III, pp. 181–182, 223–224, 424. Among the more celebrated cases was the martyrdom of the Hungarian friar Stephen in 1334, which is mentioned also in a letter dated 1338 by the Spanish Franciscan Pascal of Vittoria, who traveled through the Golden Horde, spending a year in Saray learning the "Chamanian" [i.e. Quman] language and the Uyghur script; he notes, apparently as a contrast with his own well-being in the Golden Horde (Pascal himself was martyred in Almalïq, in the Chaghatayid *ulus*, about a year after he wrote this letter), that only three years earlier this friar Stephen had been martyred by the "Saracens" in Saray, which he calls "a city of the Saracens of the Tartar empire" (cf. Henry Yule, *Cathay and the Way Thither, Being a Collection of Medieval Notices on China*, new ed., revised . . . by Henri Cordier, III [London: Hakluyt Society (2nd ser., No. 37), 1914], pp. 81–88 for Pascal's letter). Pascal's martyrdom, in turn, is reported in the memoirs of the Florentine Franciscan John de Marignolli, who traveled through the Golden Horde on his way to Khanbalïq as part of a papal legation to the Great Khan; Marignolli notes his own good treatment in Saray by Özbek Khan, who provided his party with horses and supplies, lodging them through the winter of 1339–1340. Of Pascal, Marignolli wrote, "this one was a prophet and saw the heavens open, and foretold the martyrdom which should befall him and his brethren, and the overthrow of the

Christian communities in his realm, both with regard to apparent mercantile and diplomatic advantages,[59] and in connection with specifically ecclesiastical matters. In particular, his *yarlïqs* to the Russian Orthodox clergy are well known,[60] and Franciscan sources also preserve his confirmation, in 1314, of an earlier *yarlïq* (apparently from Möngke Temür) granting privileges to the Friars Minor, exempting them from military service and acknowledging the khan's protection of their churches and convents.[61] Catholic bishoprics and Franciscan monasteries are registered in cities of the Jöchid *ulus* from the Crimea to Saray and even Urgench, and possibly Bulghar,[62] while the Christian presence in Özbek Khan's realm had among its most interesting consequences the compilation of the famous *Codex Cumanicus*, a language manual for Qïpchaq Turkic complete with translated versions of Christian prayers and hymns.[63]

Tartars of Saray by a flood, and the destruction of Armalec in vengeance for their martyrdom, and that the Emperor would be slain on the third day after their martyrdom, and many other glorious things" (Yule/Cordier, *Cathay*, III, p. 212).

59. Özbek's good relations with the Genoese and Venetian mercantile centers in the Crimea are in marked contrast to the hostile measures adopted by both his predecessor, the non-Muslim Toqtogha, in 1308, and at least temporarily by his successor, the Muslim Jānī Bek, whose expulsion of the Italians from Tana in 1343 and siege of Kaffa in 1345–1346 (the occasion of the transmission of the Black Death to Europe via Genoese ships) are well known.

60. Cf. M. D. Priselkov, *Khanskie iarlyki russkim mitropolitam* (Petrograd, 1916); Pl. Sokolov, "Podlozhnyi iarlyk Uzbeka mitropolitu Petru," *Russkii istoricheskii zhurnal*, kn. 5 (Petrograd, 1918), pp. 70–85; A. K. Borovkov, "Opyt filologicheskogo analiza tarkhannykh iarlykov, vydannykh khanami Zolotoi Ordy russkim mitropolitam," *Izvestiia Akademii nauk SSSR*, seriia literatury i iazyka, t. 25 (1966), vyp. 1, pp. 13–24; V. Grigor'ev, *O dostovernosti iarlykov, dannykh khanami Zolotoi Ordy russkomu dukhovenstvu* (Moscow, 1842), esp. pp. 112–118.

61. Cf. the Latin translation published by M. Bihl and A. C. Moule, in "Tria nova documenta de missionibus Fr. Min. Tartariae Aquilonaris annorum 1314–1322," *Archivum franciscanum historicum*, 17 (1924), pp. 55–71 [p. 65]. The decree is in the name of "Vsbek," and confirms privileges granted by "*Culuk progenitor noster*" and his successor, "our elder brother;" on these designations as references to Möngke Temür and Toqtogha, see Paul Pelliot, *Notes sur l'histoire de la Horde d'Or* (Paris, 1949), pp. 58–62, and Richard, *La papauté*, p. 93. See also Denis Sinor, "Some Latin Sources on the Khanate of Uzbek," in *Essays on Uzbek History, Culture and Language*, ed. Denis Sinor and Bakhtiyar A. Nazarov (Bloomington: RIFIAS, 1993; Uralic and Altaic Series, vol. 156, pp. 110–119.

62. Cf. Richard, *La papauté*, pp. 157–163; Golubovich, *Biblioteca*, II, pp. 266–268, III, pp. 197, 205; cf. Yule/Cordier, *Cathay*, III, p. 84, n. 2 to p. 83, citing a list of ten convents in the custodia of Saray (he mentions without naming them four more in the custodia of Gazaria, i.e., the Crimea); one of the ten is Organae/Orgune, but on p. 82 n. 2, Yule/Cordier doubt that this is Urgench because of the "bigoted Islamism" of that city's people.

63. For descriptions and discussions of the work's origins, see A. von Gabain, "Die komanische Literatur," *Philologiae Turcicae Fundamenta*, II (Wiesbaden, 1964), pp. 243–251; Peter B. Golden, "The *Codex Cumanicus*," in *Central Asian Monuments*, ed. Hasan B. Paksoy (Istanbul: Isis Press, 1992), pp. 33–63; and especially Louis Ligeti, "Prolegomena to the Codex Cumanicus," *AOH*, 35/1 (1981), pp. 1–54.

It is not unlikely, however, that the Franciscans, at least, who no doubt were dismayed by Özbek's overtures to Constantinople and Mamlūk Egypt, did indeed enjoy greater prestige under Toqtogha than under Özbek. This is suggested by the reports of numerous baptisms, by Franciscan friars, reported among court figures and the imperial family, as well as among military commanders and "barons," evidently from the time of Toqtogha's reign,[64] and by the reported conversion of the "emperor" himself, called "Coktoganus," with his mother "Thodothelia," his wife "Kerley," and his three sons, "Georgio," "Curamas," and "Abusta,"[65] the latter mentioned also independently, as "Abuscan" the son of "Cosogan" or "Cotogan," as a convert.[66] The identity of this "Coktoganus" remains unclear,[67] as do his relationships with (1) the "Cathogonti," buried in Saray, mentioned as the *brother* of the Tartar emperor,[68] (2) the "emperor of the Tartars" called "Iohannes," described as having been converted, with his mother, by Franciscans and as having been moved from his grave thirty (or thirty-five) years after his death to another burial place,[69] and (3) the unnamed emperor described as "recently deceased," who died a Christian and left three Christian sons, two of whom apostatized in an ultimately vain attempt to appease the Tartar lords and

64. Cf. Golubovich, *Biblioteca*, II, p. 73, III, p. 182, citing a collection of Franciscan material relating to the Orient compiled in 1329 or before. The baptisms include three "princes" of the emperor's court, whose names are given as "Tholethemur," "Gassur," and "Petra the son of Caramus" (the latter figure perhaps to be identified with "Curamas," one of the three baptised sons of "Coktoganus," on whom see the following note); a prince, five or six years old, named "Petrus," whose father was a "Saracen baron" named "Dolossa" of "Sarray;" many commanders of a thousand and of a hundred, with their sons; a certain "Tharmagar," son of a commander, baptized by Henry the German; and "Estokis," lord of "Baschardia," with his wife and sons.

65. Cf. Golubovich, *Biblioteca*, II, p. 73, III, p. 170, citing the same Franciscan collection mentioned in the preceding note. In his *Shuʿab-i panjgānah*, the genealogical supplement to the *Jāmiʿ at-tavārīkh* preserved in a single manuscript at the Topkapı Sarayı Müzesi in Istanbul (MS Ahmet III, No. 2937, f. 43a), Rashīd ad-Dīn gives the names of four sons of "Qūtūqān," a brother of Toqtogha, as "Nāymtāy" (?), "Āb.šqah," "Kūnkīz, also called Kūrkīz," and "Kūr.mās." The latter three correspond well with the three sons of the converted "emperor" (with "Kūrkīz" the Turkic/Mongol equivalent of "Giorgio"), rendering it less likely that "Coktoganus" should be identified with Toqtogha, but it is possible that either the Franciscans or Rashīd ad-Dīn (or their copyists) have confused the relationships involved.

66. Cf. Golubovich, III, pp. 210–211, citing letters addressed to "Abuscan" in 1321 and 1322 from Pope John XXII.

67. For discussions, cf. Pelliot, *Notes*, p. 71; Richard, *La papauté*, p. 157; Golubovich, *Biblioteca*, III, pp. 170–177).

68. Golubovich, II, p. 272, III, p. 171, citing a Franciscan source of the latter fourteenth century.

69. Golubovich, III, p. 170, citing a chronicle of the Franciscan order compiled between 1360 and 1374 (*Chronica XXIV Generalium Ordinis Minorum*, in *Analecta Franciscana*, III [Quaracchi: Tipographia Collegii S. Bonaventurae, 1897], p. 456), and another Franciscan history from

thereby win succession to the throne.[70]

The most likely explanation seems to be that "Coktoganus" (reflecting a common scribal error for "Toktoganus") is indeed Toqtogha, who is reported in several Islamic sources as having had three sons (though the names do not correspond with those reported in the Franciscan source); Toqtogha would thus have received baptism and adopted the name "Iohannes," and this emperor's brother, "Cathogonti," also a convert, is perhaps to be identified with the "Qoduqai" or "Qoduqan" named by Rashīd ad-Dīn as a brother or half-brother of Toqtogha (or, assuming a similar *t/c* scribal error, with his half-brother "Tödeken").[71] "Coktoganus" is said to have been buried in a Franciscan center called "St. Johns," the burial place ascribed also to "Iohannes," who was later moved from that site as noted; one of the accounts of Iohannes's removal specifically mentions that he was transferred along with his (unnamed) brother, whose grave was taken by a "demonic Saracen," and a similar story is told of the tomb of the "Cathogonti" who is called the emperor's brother; and the three converted sons of the unnamed Christian emperor mentioned in the letter of 1323 from the Franciscan friars in Kaffa seem to correspond to the three sons of "Coktoganus."

Moreover, the same letter, which mentions the unnamed emperor who died a Christian, also describes the circumstances of the succession to this emperor in such a way that they seem to reflect the events surrounding the accession of Özbek Khan. As noted, the Christian emperor had three sons who had adopted Christianity, two of whom abandoned the faith "out of ambition for imperial honors"; the individual who *did* become emperor killed these two on account of their conspiracy against him, and although the new emperor confirmed the privileges accorded to the Franciscans, the friars complained of new impediments hampering their work under this ruler, who is portrayed as dealing evenhand-

c. 1385; both refer to the period of tenure of a particular Franciscan general, from 1304 to 1313, the first noting that "Iohannes" was buried in accordance with solemn imperial custom in a place called "Sanctus Iohannes," some three miles from Saray, and lay beneath the earth for thirty-five years [thirty, according to the second source] before being transferred by the friars, "on account of wars," to Saray itself. Both sources note that when he was transferred, he was found whole and uncorrupted, provoking even the Saracens to amazement; the second source reports that he was moved together with his brother, "to whose sepulchre a demonic Saracen was delivered."

70. These events are described in a letter from Franciscan "*fratres peregrini*" in the Golden Horde, dated 15 May 1323, at Kaffa, published by M. Bihl and A. C. Moule, "De duabus epistolis Fratrum Minorum Tartariae Aquilonaris an. 1323," *Archivum franciscanum historicum*, 16 (1923), pp. 89–112 [pp. 106–112 for this letter, p. 111 for the discussion of the succession].

71. Cf. Boyle, tr. *Successors*, p. 109.

edly with "all sects and laws" and allowing the "infidels" to adhere to the "sect" to which their parents belonged.[72] In this account's mention of a conspiracy against the eventual successor, of the death of members of the previous khan's family, of the confirmation of privileges, and of the less hospitable environment for the Franciscans, we are justified in finding clear echoes of the accession of Özbek Khan as described in the Muslim sources discussed below, further suggesting the identity of "Coktoganus" and Toqtogha. There can be little doubt that the emperor whose succession is noted in this letter is Özbek Khan, in view of its date; and if indeed the Franciscans had gained special status through their role in converting Toqtogha and his family, the loss of distinctive imperial favor accompanying Özbek's succession may well have entailed an overall setback in the friars' ambitions.

What may be suggested in any case is that Özbek's Islam and his treatment of other religions should be considered outside the rather hackneyed framework of assuming "religious tolerance" on the part of the Mongols, a tolerance that Özbek is usually blamed (along with other converts to Islam among the Mongols) for abandoning. What is at work is not a break with "tolerance," but a shift from one policy to another, both based upon assumptions of the *communal* basis and implications of religious affiliation.[73]

It is not so much the actual historical and competitive position of Islam under Özbek that is of primary concern for us, however, but rather the popular memory of his Muslim status and its significance among the Muslim community, as known from narrative accounts of his conversion. To come to terms with these narratives—and in particular, with the "new" narrative that is our chief focus here—we must nevertheless consider the treatment of Özbek Khan's Islam in the available historical sources, many of which bear signs of reflecting "legendarized" oral reports, and all of which may help us to understand the elements of the literary tradition surrounding Özbek that appear also in the oral narratives concerning him.

72. Cf. Bihl and Moule, "De duabus epistolis," p. 111.

73. As avowedly hostile as they were toward each other and toward Inner Asian "paganism," medieval Christian and Muslim observers were no doubt better positioned than moderns to understand the close link between religious affiliation and communal identity; and that link was assumed by the medieval Mongols as well, as suggested by the well-known comment of William of Rubruck in connection with Sartaq, brother of Batu and convert to Christian *belief*: "Before we took our leave of Sartach . . . [they] said to us, 'Do not say that our master is a Christian, for he is not a Christian but a Mongol.' This is because the word Christianity appears to them to be the name of a race, and they are proud to such a degree that although perhaps they believe something of Christ, nevertheless they are unwilling to be called Christians, wanting their own name, that is, Mongol, to be exalted above every other name" (*Mongol Mission*, p. 121). In attributing the Mongols' rejection of the Christian label to their "pride," Rubruck is perhaps closer to the

The Conversion of Özbek Khan in Islamic Sources

In narrative historical and biographical sources for the era of the Mongol successor states, the standard paradigm for the establishment of Islam in a particular region is that of "royal conversion" at the hands of a saint, usually a Sufi shaykh. As indicated above, the preliminary Islamization of the Golden Horde under the khan Berke (r. 1257–1266) is ascribed to his conversion and training by the Kubravī shaykh Sayf ad-Dīn Bākharzī, and other Sufis are credited with the conversion of the Chaghatayid Tughluq Temür and even of the Ilkhanid Ghāzān. Most of the available accounts of Özbek Khan's conversion produced *within* the context of his political legacy—that is, among constituent elements of the Golden Horde—follow the same pattern.

In literary sources of Central Asian provenance, the conversion of Özbek Khan is ascribed to a saint of Yasavī lineage of the early fourteenth century known as Sayyid Ata. This figure is known from the famous Central Asian Naqshbandī hagiography, the *Rashaḥāt-i ʿayn al-ḥayāt,* completed at the very beginning of the sixteenth century as a biography of Khoja Aḥrār and his predecessors, as one of four disciples of the Sufi shaykh known as Zangī Ata, a disciple of Ḥakīm Ata, who was in turn a disciple of Khoja Aḥmad Yasavī. According to the *Rashaḥāt,* Sayyid Ata was a contemporary of the eminent shaykh of the "proto-Naqshbandī" *silsilah* of the "Khojagān," Shaykh ʿAlī ʿAzīzān Rāmitanī (d. 736/1336); Sayyid Ata and his companions—Uzun Ḥasan Ata, Ṣadr Ata, and Badr Ata—entered the service of Zangī Ata in Tashkent after their period of study in a Bukharan *madrasah.*[74]

The *Rashaḥāt* tells nothing of Sayyid Ata's role in converting the Dasht-i Qïpchaq to Islam, but a roughly contemporary source does make this connection. The anonymous *Shajarat al-atrāk,* evidently based upon materials collected under the patronage of the Timurid ruler Ulugh Beg (d. 1449) but certainly edited into its extant form only in the early sixteenth century,[75] recounts Sayyid Ata's story along the lines of the *Rashaḥāt,* but

mark than the vast majority of twentieth-century students of the Mongols (the view actually goes back at least as far as Gibbon) who ascribe to the thirteenth-century Mongols the anachronistic trait of religious "tolerance" (a quality much vaunted by moderns who equate it with religious *indifference*); what is at work in Mongol attitudes toward religions such as Christianity and Islam is hardly "tolerance" or ecumenism, and certainly not religious indifference, but an assumption that religion is above all a matter of practice and communal affiliation, not of "belief."

74. Cf. *Rashaḥāt-i ʿayn al-ḥayāt,* ed. ʿAlī Aṣghar Muʿīnīyān (Tehran, 2536/1356/1977), I, pp. 25–29; On Sayyid Ata, see further my brief article, "Atāʾīya Order," *Encyclopaedia Iranica,* II, pp. 904–905.

75. On this work in general, in addition to the studies cited in the following note, see Storey-

adds that he was sent from Tashkent by Zangī Ata to spread Islam in the Dasht-i Qïpchaq. The account in the *Shajarat al-atrāk* is not heavily dramatized; in it we learn simply that Sayyid Ata converted Özbek Khan, renamed him Muḥammad Özbek Khan, and led those among the peoples of the Dasht-i Qïpchaq who joined their khan in embracing Islam toward Turkistan. Those who accompanied Sayyid Ata, the story affirms, took the name Özbek, and this account was the basis for the most widespread popular understanding of the origin of the ethnonym "Özbek."[76] This latter feature of the account of Sayyid Ata already points to an important Inner Asian adaptation in understanding the process of Islamization, namely, the assimilation of the role of religious "founder" to that of ethnic or

---

Bregel', *PL*, II, pp. 777–779, and V. V. Bartol'd, "Ulugbek i ego vremia," *Sochineniia*, II/2, pp. 141–142, and the English translation by V. and T. Minorsky, *Four Studies on the History of Central Asia*, vol. II, "Ulugh-Beg" (Leiden: E. J. Brill, 1958), pp. 136–138. The *Shajarat al-atrāk* has been curiously neglected in studies of Mongol history, and to date there is no thorough historiographical analysis of the work and its relationship to the so-called "*Tārīkh-i arbaʿah ulūs*" ascribed to Ulugh Beg. The likelihood that the material presented in the *Shajarat al-atrāk* was indeed gathered at Ulugh Beg's court is of some relevance for our purpose, since at his court were no doubt several people with important insight into the traditions about Özbek Khan's conversion. More precisely, two of Ulugh Beg's wives were apparently lineal descendants of Özbek Khan through the *amīr* named "Nanghïday" or "Nïghday," who was prominent at Özbek's court and who figures in traditions about Sayyid Ata. One wife, Bakhtī Bī Khātūn (see Woods, "The Timurid Dynasty," pp. 43–44), was a daughter of Aq Ṣūfī of the Qonghrat tribe, while another wife, Akā Bekī [or as Bartol'd transcribes it, Öge Beki; cf. Woods, pp. 29–30] was a daughter of Muḥammad Sulṭān, who was in turn born to Temür's son Jahāngīr and his bride Sevin Beg; and Sevin Beg was a daughter of the same Aq Ṣūfī. Aq Ṣūfī's brother, Yūsuf Ṣūfī, had arranged this marriage in 775/1374, following Temür's punitive expedition against Khorezm; Yūsuf Ṣūfī had become ruler of Khorezm when his brother Ḥusayn Ṣūfī died during Temür's siege of the city, and sought to restore peace with Temür. It is possible, incidentally, that there were only two brothers, since the work of Ötemish Ḥājjī (Tashkent MS, ff. 53b–54a) refers to "Aq Ḥusayn, the son of the Qonghrat Nāghādāy," as ruler of Khorezm; it is not clear whether the earlier sources have divided one person into two, or the later source has combined two persons into one. In any event, the two or three "Ṣūfī" brothers were sons of Nanghïdāy, according to two sources from the early fifteenth century, the works of Muʿīn ad-Dīn Naṭanzī (*Muntakhab*, ed. Aubin, pp. 411, 427; cf. Tiz II p. 155, n. 2) and Sharaf ad-Dīn ʿAlī Yazdī (cf. the facsimile edition published by A. Urunbaev, *Sharafuddin Ali Yazdiy, Zafarnoma* [Tashkent, 1972], ff. 148a–b; cf. 146a, where Ḥusayn Ṣūfī's father is called "Tanghadāy"); Yazdī writes that Sevin Beg was Aq Ṣūfī's daughter by a "daughter of Khān Özbek," and such a relationship is quite reasonable in view of Ibn Baṭṭūṭah's testimony that the *amīr* "Naghaṭay," whom he met in the khan's encampment, was the father of Özbek Khan's second *khatun*, Kebek. The links between Ulugh Beg and the family of the Khorezmian "Qonghrat Sufi" dynasty are clear; and these links in turn not only tie his court to the lineage of Özbek Khan, but do so through precisely the figure who in later tradition (see below) is said to accompany Sayyid Ata to Khorezm following Özbek Khan's conversion, a figure who is at the same time probably identifiable with a close courtier of Özbek Khan known from Ibn Baṭṭūṭah's eyewitness report, as discussed further below.

76. For the account of the *Shajarat al-atrāk*, cf. Tiz II, pp. 206–207 (tr.), 266 (text); MS India

national "founder" or ancestor; we will later return to this theme.

Elements of this basic story, first encountered in the *Shajarat al-atrāk*, appear frequently in Central Asian sources. The explanation of the ethnonym "Özbek" appears in the seventeenth-century Chaghatay Turkic history, entitled *Shajarah-i Turk va Moghūl*, by the Chingisid khan of Khorezm, Abū'l-Ghāzī, who reports that Özbek brought the "people and realm" (*el va ulus*) into the religion of Islam and that it was through him that the entire people were ennobled by the honor of Islam; he adds that thenceforth the entire "people" (*el*) of Jöchi began to be called "Özbek," and would be called thus until the Day of Resurrection. Abū'l-Ghāzī omits the role of Sayyid Ata, however, perhaps because of the khan's distrust of the political ambitions of the saint's descendants.[77] The nineteenth-century Khivan history of Muʾnis, also written in Chaghatay Turkic, closely follows Abū'l-Ghāzī in recounting Özbek Khan's reign, noting that he adopted Islam, summoned his people to Islam, and *commanded* that all those who became Muslims under him should be called by his name; "and after that they called the people (*el*) of Jöchi the people of Özbek."[78] Elsewhere in the same work, however, Muʾnis gives an account, known from no other source, probably taken from oral tradition among the Qonghrat tribes of Khorezm, in which the role of Sayyid Ata in converting Özbek Khan to Islam and naming the Jöchid *el* "Özbek" is explicitly highlighted, in the course of recounting the history of "Naghdāy," a Qonghrat *amīr* who accompanied Sayyid Ata to Khorezm following his missionary endeavors;[79] this *amīr* is no doubt to be identified with a figure whom Ibn Baṭṭūṭah met at Özbek Khan's court, as discussed below.

Office, Ethé 172, ff. 153a–154a. The obsolete English translation by Col. Miles, *The Shajrat ul Atrak, or Genealogical Tree of the Turks and Tatars* (London, 1838), obscures all personal, ethnic, and geographical names, but at least conveys the essentials of the narrative (pp. 231–232). The work is discussed, with reference to the account of Sayyid Ata's role in the conversion of Özbek Khan, by B. A. Akhmedov, "Ulugbek i ego istoricheskii trud 'Tarikh-i Arba'ulus,'" *Iz istorii nauki èpokhi Ulugbeka* (Tashkent: Fan, 1979), pp. 29–36, and by A. A. Semenov, "K voprosu o proiskhozhdenii i sostave uzbekov Sheibani-khana," *Materialy po istorii tadzhikov i uzbekov Srednei Azii*, I (Trudy Instituta istorii, arkheologii i ètnografii AN TadzhSSR, t. XII, Stalinabad, 1954), pp. 3–37 (pp. 14–17 on this account).

77. Cf. *Histoire des Mongols et des Tatares par Aboul-Ghâzî Béhâdour Khan*, ed. and tr. P. I. Desmaisons (St. Petersburg, 1871–1872), I (text), pp. 174–175, II (tr.), pp. 183–184. Abū'l-Ghāzī notes approvingly that an earlier Sayyid Atāʾī descendant declined political power (I [text], pp. 196–197, II [tr.], pp. 211–212), but is critical of a later descendant who meddled in political affairs (I, pp. 288–289, II, pp. 309–310); cf. "Atāʾīya Order," p. 904.

78. Shīr Muḥammad Mīrāb Mūnis and Muḥammad Riżā Mīrāb Āgahī, *Firdaws al-Iqbāl: History of Khorezm*, ed. Yuri Bregel (Leiden: E. J. Brill, 1988), p. 99.

79. *Firdaws al-Iqbāl*, pp. 204–205, and the translation in Yuri Bregel, "Tribal Tradition and

Most interesting, Sayyid Ata's role in Islamization is described independently in a seventeenth-century work that clearly preserves traditions passed down orally within a family that claimed descent from Sayyid Ata.[80] This work also reflects the Sufi tradition about Sayyid Ata and his three companions and their service to Zangī Ata, but tells more of Sayyid Ata's activity in the Jöchid *ulus*, where he was sent by Zangī Ata. He went to the Dasht-i Qïpchaq and to "the farthest reaches of the Manghït and Tatar," and there, through wonders and miracles, he led "most of the Uzbek khans" *(akthar az khānān-i uzbakīyah)*,[81] who were still infidels, to the felicity of Islam. "Many groups," we are told, "among the *ulūsāt-i uzbak va tātār*" accepted Islam through his efforts, and day by day the religion of Islam grew stronger, until "in the steppes of those regions the sound of prayer and the summons to prayer replaced the voice of the *ozan*."[82]

The figure called "Sayyid Ata" is himself the focus of an extensive legendary elaboration in Central Asian "historical" sources that we can trace from the seventeenth century to the twentieth; these cannot be taken up here, but I intend to devote a separate study to them. The name of Sayyid Ata, however, is virtually unknown in the historical and hagiographical literature produced in the Golden Horde itself or in its successor states.[83]

Dynastic History: The Early Rulers of the Qongrats according to Munis," *Asian and African Studies* (*Journal of the Israel Oriental Society*), 16 (1982), pp. 357–398 [pp. 369–371]; cf. my "Atā'īya Order," and notes on "Naghdāy" above and below. Interestingly, Mu'nis' account makes Özbek Khan "Islamize" the Turkic title *bīy* by assigning it to Naghday in place of its Mongol equivalent *noyon*, "to distinguish this from the custom of the infidels" (tr. Bregel, "Tribal Tradition," p. 370). Both *bīy* (equivalent to *bek*) and *noyon*, of course, were used among the pre-Islamic Mongols and Turks to refer to tribal chieftains, and were both rendered by the Arabic *amīr* (whence, through Persian *amīr-zādah*, the additional equivalent *mīrzā*); it is a small but telling example of the "Islamization" of native Inner Asian terminology to find Mu'nis appealing not to the Arabic *amīr*, but to the Turkic *bīy*, as the title that would effectively distance its bearer from infidel ways.

80. The *Manāqib al-akhyār*, known from the description of the only manuscript registered in published catalogues as "*Maqāmāt-i Sayyid Atā'ī*," is preserved in two manuscripts: one in the India Office Library in London (Hermann Ethé, *Catalogue of the Persian Manuscripts in the Library of the India Office*, I [Oxford, 1903], cols. 268–270, No. 644; ff. 16a–b for the conversion account), and a second, complete copy that I discovered in the Raza Library in Rampur (*Tadhkirah* No. 2378; ff. 20a–b). The work is discussed further in Chapter 3; see also my "A Neglected Source on Central Asian History: the 17th-Century Yasavī Hagiography *Manāqib al-akhyār*," in *Essays on Uzbek History, Culture and Language*, ed. Sinor and Nazarov (Bloomington, 1993), pp. 38–50.

81. This phrase may reflect an earlier tradition, ascribing the conversion of "Özbek Khan" to Sayyid Ata, "modernized" on the basis of the later understanding of the "khans of the Özbeks."

82. *be-jā-yi āvāz-i ōzān bāng-i namāz-u-azān baland kardīd*; the term *ozan* refers to the singers of popular narratives among the nomadic Turks, usually identified with or associated with shamans.

83. The one exception is the mention of a descendant of Sayyid Ata among the chief organizers of the defense of Kazan against a Russian attack in 1550, as described in the contemporary eyewitness report by Sharīf Ḥājjī-tarkhānī published by Zeki Velidi Togan, "Kazan Hanlığında

As we shall see, the historical material on Özbek Khan's reign provides substantial information on the Muslim jurists, poets, theologians, physicians, and shaykhs active in the Jöchid *ulus* during Özbek Khan's reign, but with one possible exception none of these is suitable for an identification with "Sayyid Ata"; and the other material from this region known before now—late historical works and oral literature—speaks rather vaguely of Özbek Khan's acceptance of Islam upon the arrival in his realm of "Baba Tükles." This Baba Tükles figures most prominently, as noted, in the historical legends produced in the Tatar khanates that emerged from the Golden Horde's breakup not primarily as a religious "founder" or "bearer" of Islam, but as an ancestor of the famous Manghït chieftain Edigü Bek, as is discussed in Chapter 5. The same Baba Tükles, cloaked in archaic mythic garb as a quasi-supernatural progenitor, also plays a prominent role in a series of epic tales based on the figure of Edigü. For confirmation of this Baba Tükles' role in popular memory as a "bearer" of Islam, we must look outside the better-known historical and epic tradition of the Golden Horde, to the poorly known source that provides us with our central conversion narrative.

Before we can do that, however, we must consider the earlier historical sources available for Özbek Khan's conversion to Islam, both as a basis for comparing the account of Ötemish Ḥājjī with earlier and more sober sources, and as confirmation of the early and nearly unanimous depiction of Özbek's role in Islamization. In considering the historical material on Özbek Khan's conversion, we will first examine the earliest accounts that mention his status as a Muslim, and note the elements of the historical tradition about his conversion that remained standard features in histories down to the fifteenth century; we will then explore the available evidence on the religious figures active at Özbek Khan's court as known from such outside sources, including several explicitly or implicitly credited with converting him to Islam, and consider the more general issue of the circles responsible for promoting Islam in the Golden Horde.

We may note here again, however, that all of these earlier, and yet "external," sources are at variance with both the tale of Ötemish Ḥājjī and with the developed Central Asian tradition about Özbek Khan's

İslâm Türk Kültürü (Kanunî zamanında 1550 de Kazandan gönderilen bir rapor)," *İslâm Tetkikleri Enstitüsü Dergisi*, 3/3–4 (1959–60), pp. 179–204 (text, p. 189; cf. p. 196; the text and translation are reprinted in part in A. N. Kurat's *IV–XVIII. yüzyıllarda Karadeniz kuzeyindeki Türk kavimleri ve devletleri* [Ankara: Türk Tarih Kurumu Basımevi, 1972 ed., pp. 181, 370]). The account explicitly mentions that the defenders invoked the spirit of Sayyid Ata as they went into battle.

conversion on several counts. All of them place his conversion at or implicitly prior to his accession to the throne; none of the religious figures mentioned in these sources (except one man met by Ibn Baṭṭūṭah, discussed below) as prominent at Özbek Khan's court bears any resemblance to Sayyid Ata or Baba Tükles; and none of these sources mentions what is usually the underlying reason for recounting the conversion of Özbek Khan in the Central Asian tradition, namely, the understanding that his conversion to Islam was the reason for the adoption of his name as a communal designation.

A final point worth noting before examining the accounts is the considerable lag between the reign of Özbek Khan and the appearance of new elements in the historiographical tradition surrounding him. New information not reflected in other extant sources appears for the first time in works compiled between fifty and one hundred years after Özbek Khan's death, and if we are not to assume pure fabrication on the part of the compilers, as seems unlikely, we must consider these new elements as signs of narrative traditions accessible to the compilers and possibly reflecting "authentic" information (i.e., reflecting both "real" events and indigenous narrative responses to such events).

ÖZBEK KHAN AND ISLAM IN MUSLIM HISTORICAL TRADITION: THE EARLY SOURCES

The fact that Özbek Khan was a Muslim is mentioned already in the Persian work of the Ilkhanid historian Banākatī, writing in 717/1317,[84] who describes "Özbek the son of Toghr[il] Bek the son of Mengü Timür," the ruler of the Jöchid *ulus* "at present," as a just and Muslim ruler. More vividly, his contemporary Vaṣṣāf, writing around 728/1328, describes Özbek Khan as a pious Muslim in the course of recounting his campaign into Arrān in 718/1319; the historian notes that Özbek dispatched several close companions to make a pilgrimage to the tomb and *khānqāh* of Pīr Ḥusayn,[85] and describes the khan's harsh punishment of two of his soldiers who had stolen property belonging to the tomb's *waqf*

84. *Tārīkh-i Banākatī*, ed. Shiʿār, p. 397; the work was not included in Tizengauzen's collection.

85. On this famous site and the shaykh buried there (Pīr Ḥusayn Shirvānān, d. 467/1074–75), see V. A. Krachkovskaia, *Izraztsy mavzoleia Pir-Khuseina* (Tbilisi: Izd-vo AN Gruzinskoi SSR, 1946); A. A. Seid-zadè, "Pir-Khusein Shirvani (Shirvanan)," *Doklady Akademii nauk Azerbaidzhanskoi SSR*, 16/12 (1960), pp. 1265–1268; L. T. Giuzal'ian, "Chetyre dvustishiia na iranskom izraztse XIII v.," in *Kul'turnoe nasledie Vostoka: Problemy, poiski, suzhdeniia* (Leningrad: Nauka, 1985), pp. 297–306; S. B. Ashurbeili, "Khanaka na reke Pirsagat i Shirvanshakhi," in *Dukhovenstvo i politicheskaia zhizn' na Blizhnem i Srednem Vostoke v period*

and had otherwise harrassed the Sufis there.[86]

Our earliest extended account of Özbek Khan's rise to power, however, makes his support for Islam a central element in the struggle prior to his accession. This is the Persian *Tārīkh-i Ūljāytū-Sulṭān* of Jamāl ad-Dīn ʿAbdullāh b. ʿAlī Qāshānī,[87] written most probably soon after the death of the Ilkhanid ruler Öljeytü in 716/1316 (the author was evidently still alive in 724/1324).[88] This account became the standard version of Özbek's accession in most later Persian historical sources that deal with the event; it was later repeated, with minor variations, by Ḥāfiẓ-i Abrū in the early fifteenth century and, possibly independently of Ḥāfiẓ-i Abrū, by Ḥaydar Rāzī in the early seventeenth century.[89] Qāshānī's account is of special interest not only because of its early date, but because of its dramatic structure, in which Özbek Khan's support for Islam engenders hostility among the tribal *amīrs*, whom he must overcome; the decisive confrontation involves a feast, and in this and some other particulars the narrative echoes the style of Ötemish Ḥājjī's account of Özbek Khan's accession (though not his account of the khan's conversion).

Qāshānī's account appears in the context of his report on the arrival, on Sunday, 10 Dhū'l-ḥijjah 712/8 April 1313, of ambassadors from the new ruler of the Jöchid *ulus*, led by figures he calls Kök-Timūr Güregän,

---

feodalizma (Moscow: Nauka, GRVL, 1985; "Bartol'dovskie chteniia," 1982), pp. 32–36; M. S. Neimatova, "Nadpisi kak istochnik dlia izucheniia istoriia khanaki Pir Khusaina," in *Vostochnoe istoricheskoe istochnikovedenie i spetsial'nye istoricheskie distsipliny*, vyp. 1 (Moscow: Nauka, GRVL, 1989; "Bartol'dovskie chteniia," 1984), pp. 292–298.

86. Cf. Tiz II, pp. 86–87, citing the Bombay lithograph edition, pp. 635–636; the same edition underlies the paraphrase of Vaṣṣāf's history, *Taḥrīr-i Tārīkh-i Vaṣṣāf*, ed. ʿAbd al-Muḥammad Āyatī (Tehran: Intishārāt-i Bunyād-i Farhang-i Īrān, 1346/1967), pp. 364–365, where, however, the name "Özbek" has been transformed into the word "*awrang*." In Persian historiography, between Vaṣṣāf's work and the *Tārīkh-i Shaykh Uvays* (discussed below), we find only a brief mention in Ḥamdullāh Mustawfī Qazvīnī's *Tārīkh-i guzīdah*, from 730/1330, that Özbek Khan had become ruler in the realm of Jöchi and "spread Islam" there (ed. ʿAbd al-Ḥusayn Navāʾī, Tehan, 1339/1960, repr. 1362/1983, p. 585).

87. His *nisbah* is given in the form "Qāshānī" in his history of Öljeytü, but is known also in the form "Kāshānī;" both forms of the place-name are common in the fourteenth century.

88. On him, see Storey-Bregel', *PL*, I, pp. 320–322; II, p. 768; III, pp. 1395–1396. This important work, which Tizengauzen did not use, survives in only two manuscripts, in Paris and Istanbul; excerpts from the latter copy (Aya Sofya 3019/3, dated 752/1351) were published in notes to Najīb ʿĀṣim's edition of ʿAbd al-Ghaffār Qïrïmī's work (see Chapter 5), pp. 33–34. More recently the entire work has been edited: Abū'l-Qāsim ʿAbdullāh b. Muḥammad al-Qāshānī, *Tārīkh-i Ūljāytū*, ed. Mahīn Hambly (Tehran: Bungāh-i Tarjimah va Nashr-i Kitāb, 1348/1969; Persian Texts Series, No. 40), pp. 144–145 on Özbek Khan's accession.

89. On Ḥaydar Rāzī, cf. Storey-Bregel', I, pp. 427–428. The editors of Tizengauzen's Persian volume state that Ḥaydar Rāzī's account is based mostly on Naṭanzī, with the addition of details from some other source, but it is clear that he used Qāshānī, either directly or via Ḥāfiẓ-i Abrū.

Bāynāl,[90] and Bāy-Būqā; these ambassadors were presumably the source of the author's information, although this is not explicitly stated. Qāshānī first recounts events toward the end of the reign of Özbek's predecessor, whose name he gives in the form Tūqtā (i.e., Toqtogha). The latter had two sons, Bāyān and Mūm.k.qiyāy [*sic*];[91] the elder had been designated as his father's successor, the younger had attacked him, the elder had appealed to his father for aid, and, faced with his father's forces, the younger son had fled, with the elder confirmed as Toqtogha's successor. The khan had then placed his nephew Özbek the son of Toghr[ïl] Bek at the head of his army; but shortly thereafter, on his way back to his own "capital," Toqtogha fell ill and died near Sarāy, on a boat carrying him across the river Itīl (the Volga), on Wednesday 4 Rabīʿ II 712/9 August 1312.

Upon Toqtogha's death, the *amīrs* and *noyons* of the *ulus* assembled to choose the khan's successor. The "*amīr* of Sarāy," Qutlugh-timūr, spoke at the assembly and supported the rights of Toqtogha's son to be made khan; but he insisted that it was essential to deal with Özbek first, whom he called an enemy of the kingdom, and only then raise Toqtogha's son to the throne. Those assembled agreed. When Özbek heard the news of Toqtogha's death, he left his army and set out at once, evidently to claim the throne; someone had warned him of the *amīrs*' treacherous intentions, says the account, which further explains the reasons for the hostility toward Özbek among the *amīrs*: he constantly demanded "*islām va īmān*" from them. The chief of the *amīrs* had refused, giving Özbek a veiled warning: "O *pādshāh*, you demand Islam (*musulmānī*) from us, but how can we obey and comply with this demand? What complaint have we with the *yāsā* and *yosūn* of Chingiz Khan that you summon us to the old *sharīʿah* of the Arabs?"[92] According to Qāshānī, Özbek killed this recalcitrant *amīr* on the spot, whereupon the other *amīrs* and *noyons*, repelled by such a deed, conspired to kill Özbek.

They took counsel (*kīngāč*, that is, *kengesh*) with one another and resolved to invite him to a feast and finish him off there. Özbek came to the feast (*ṭūy*), and after he had drunk two or three cups of "wine" (*arghuvānī*),

90. "Bānyāl" in the edited text.

91. The only other sources of comparable antiquity to name Toqtogha's sons ascribe him three: Banākatī lists Tükel Būqā [*t.w.k.l yūqā*], Il-Basār [*yasār* in the printed edition], and "Bīrūs" (?), while Rashīd ad-Dīn (in the *Shuʿab-i panjgānah*, MS Topkapı, Ahmet III, No. 2937, f. 43a) names Tūkāl Būqā, Īl-Bāsār, and "Tūkīl Būqā" (?); the middle son is an important figure in the story of the succession to Toqtogha as given in later sources, as discussed below.

92. Ḥāfiẓ-i Abrū's version (Tiz II, pp. 141 [tr.], 244–245 [text]) has the *amīrs* address Özbek thus: "You are hoping for our submission and obedience; what business of yours is our religion and faith?

as singers performed, one of the *amīrs* gave him a surreptitious signal of the impending attack; Özbek understood, and on the pretext of needing to relieve himself he got up and went outside. The *amīr* who had given the signal came out after him and confirmed the plot, whereupon Özbek fled at once on a fast horse; he gathered several thousand men, and returned in strength to attack the duplicitous *amīrs*, seizing and killing all of them together with more than a hundred princes and sons of Tūqtā. The *amīr* who had warned him, however, enjoyed the care and favor of the new khan, becoming Özbek's adviser and confidant; and the account closes noting that Özbek sent out envoys announcing the good news of his accession.[93]

A number of problematical issues raised by this account are unfortunately unresolvable on the basis of available information. The most curious is the role of Qutlugh Temür, here evidently cast as an opponent of Özbek, although his prominent role in the new khan's reign is a standard feature of most later accounts of Özbek Khan and is confirmed already by Vaṣṣāf's mention of him, along with ʿĪsā Güregän, as the chief *amīrs* of the *ulus* of Jöchi under Özbek.[94] In other accounts that mention Qutlugh Temür, he is portrayed as the central figure in Özbek's accession, whose crucial support is in some versions of the story exacted at the price of Özbek's conversion to Islam. It is clear that Qāshānī's account disturbed the later historians who clearly must have consulted the *Tārīkh-i Ūljāytū*: the early seventeenth-century *Tārīkh-i Ḥaydarī* gives the same account of Özbek's rise but omits all mention of Qutlugh Temür,[95] while Ḥāfiẓ-i Abrū[96] meets the problem head-on: he mentions the *amīr* Qutlugh Temür who spoke against Özbek at the initial assembly, and then notes that another *amīr*, also named Qutlugh Temür, warned Özbek of the plot against him, stating pointedly after repeating Qāshānī's comment on Özbek's favor and solicitude for this *amīr* that "this was the Qutlugh Temür who for a long time served as *amīr* in the countries of the Dasht-i Qïpchāq and Khorezm."

It seems likely that Qāshānī's account is already garbled or abbreviated, or evidences a conflation of two or more accounts. In particular, the initial reference to the assembly of *amīrs* and princes and the hostility toward Özbek confirmed there, appears to reflect a separate story joined to the more complete account of hostility bred by Özbek's efforts to impose

---

And why would we abandon the *tūrah* and *yāsāq* of Chingīz Khān to enter the Arab religion?"

93. Ḥaydar Rāzī adds here that following Özbek Khan's reign, the *ulus* of Jöchi Khan became known as the *ulūs-i ūzbak* (Tiz II, pp. 213 [tr.], 272 [text]).

94. Vaṣṣāf, in Tiz II, pp. 87, 89 (Bombay ed., pp. 636, 638); paraphrase, ed. Āyatī, p. 366.

95. Tiz II, pp. 213 (tr.), 272 (text).

96. Tiz II, pp. 141 (tr.), 244–245 (text).

Islam on the *amīrs*; as a whole the account is somewhat disjointed, and it seems clear that Ḥāfiẓ-i Abrū has made the narrative noticeably "smoother" in adapting Qāshānī's original version. In any case we may choose to distrust Qāshānī's account as it stands and either follow Ḥāfiẓ-i Abrū's "improvement" or assume that Qutlugh Temür's role at the assembly was confused with that of another *amīr* (possible candidates are suggested by later sources discussed below); otherwise, we must envision a historical rapprochement between the powerful Qutlugh Temür and the khan whose elevation he forcefully opposed. We have little basis for deciding between these interpretations, but it seems more prudent to assume errors or omissions in Qāshānī's narrative (produced before Qutlugh Temür's prominence under Özbek might have induced him to correct his account) than to explain away the nearly unanimous later verdict on the relationship between Özbek and Qutlugh Temür.

The combination of the feast and the "signals" appears also in Ötemish Ḥājjī's account of Özbek Khan's accession, but otherwise Qāshānī's account includes several of the common elements found in later Persian and Arabic histories from outside the Golden Horde, in particular the hostility toward Islam among opponents of Özbek Khan, and the killing of the most vocal of those opponents of Islam. His account—again, the earliest one extant—thus portrays a virtual coup d'état against the house of Toqtogha, with the latter implicitly associated with opposition to Islam; Toqtogha's religious status becomes a common element in later sources about Özbek's accession, and is often portrayed in quite positive light, but it is difficult to judge whether Qāshānī's account, as an Ilkhanid work produced in a political environment governed by the hostility between the Jöchid khans and the Ilkhanid rulers (hostility that Özbek Khan himself furthered on several occasions), has portrayed Özbek's accession as more of a wrongful usurpation than it was.

It seems likely that Özbek Khan and his supporters indeed regarded his accession as a return to direct lineal succession, "restoring" his father's line.[97] If such is the case, we may see support for Islam as a genuine political

97. In support of this may be cited a note by Rashīd ad-Dīn (*Shuʿab-i panjgānah*, MS Topkapı, Ahmet III, No. 2937, f. 43a; cf. Boyle, *Successors*, pp. 124–126); in the *Shuʿab's* concise account, he lists ten sons of "Mūnkkā Timūr" (the manuscript's orthography appears to reflect the Uyghur-script versions of the name given alongside those in Arabic-script), and next to the name of one of them is found this remark: "This Alghūy, his brother Ṭūghrīlchah, Tūlā Būqā, and Kūnchāk together seized the kingdom from Tūdā Munkkā, and for five years they ruled jointly; after that, Tūqtā, with the aid of Tūqāy [*sic*, for "Nūqāy"], seized the kingdom from them and became ruler." That Özbek's accession may be regarded as an "overthrow" of

strategy important to Özbek's success, especially since Toqtogha was famous as the vanquisher of the *amīr* Noghay, who may also have used support for Islam as a strategy in his struggle with his former protégé, as noted earlier. What is clearly assumed in Qāshānī's account, however, is that Özbek was already a Muslim even before his accession. This clearly contradicts, as do most early sources, the account of the *Shajarat al-atrāk* as well as that of Ötemish Ḥājjī, according to which Özbek reigned for several years before the conversion. What is at work in the later sources, it may be suggested, is a narrative adjustment designed to break up the story of the khan's accession from the account of his conversion, a split quite clear in Ötemish Ḥājjī's work, as discussed below; where earlier the element of Özbek's Islam may have served to legitimize his seizure of power for an audience supportive of Islamizing policies, by the time of the developed conversion narrative evident in Ötemish Ḥājjī's work (and in the *Shajarat al-atrāk*), the same element had taken on larger communal significance, legitimizing not merely one khan's accession, but a community's formation.

In any case, we next hear of Özbek Khan's accession and simultaneous "establishment" of Islam in the Golden Horde in the encyclopedic work of Shihāb ad-Dīn Aḥmad an-Nuwayrī (d. 732 or 733/1331–1333) the *Nihāyat al-arab fī funūn al-adab*; in this work an-Nuwayrī mentions—in both the section on the history of the Mongols, and in his history of the Mamlūks—that an embassy arrived at the court of al-Malik an-Nāṣir, on Saturday 26 Dhū'l-ḥijjah 713/13 April 1314,[98] announcing the accession of the "king" Özbek on the throne in Ṣarāy as ruler of the "country of the house of Berke," and bearing extraordinary gifts; and through the embassy, Özbek Khan

> presented our lord the Sulṭān al-Malik an-Nāṣir with the good tidings of the spread of Islām from China (*aṣ-Ṣīn*) to the most distant lands of the west; and he said that there had remained in his realm a party adhering to a religion other than Islām, but that the king had offered them the choice between entry into the religion of Islām, or war;

Toqtogha's illegitimate lineage is suggested by documentary evidence as well; when the Russian metropolitan Petr (d. 1326) sought to have his privileges confirmed upon the new khan's accession, Özbek evidently repeated the terms and language of a *yarlïq* of Möngke Temür rather than those of a more recent *yarlïq*, given in 1308, from Toqtogha. Cf. M. D. Priselkov, *Khanskie iarlyki*, p. 47.

98. The precise date is given only in the history of the Mamlūks, cf. Tiz I, p. 145 (text), p. 166 (tr.), Turkish ed. pp. 298–299.

> and further that they had refused and had fought, and that he had attacked them and annihilated them, slaying or capturing them; and he provided our lord the Sulṭān with a number of the captives.[99]

After Nuwayrī's account the next work, chronologically, to refer to Özbek Khan's conversion is an important chronicle not included in Tizengauzen's collection of sources on the history of the Golden Horde, namely the universal history of Ibn ad-Dawādārī, completed in 736/1335–1336, still in the lifetime of the khan. He reports the arrival at his sovereign's court, on 25 Rabīᶜ I 720/5 May 1320, of an embassy "from the country of Berke," escorting Özbek's niece, who was to be given in marriage to the Mamlūk sulṭān; in the embassy, says Ibn ad-Dawādārī, was "a *qāżī* named Nūr, and they say that it was this *qāżī* who guided the king Özbek to Islām."[100] This *qāżī* is named also by al-Mufaḍḍal, but neither source gives any further information allowing us to identify him, nor do any other sources expand upon his role.

Of greater importance, in terms of its echoes in subsequent sources, is the work of al-Birzālī (d. 739/1338–1339), *al-Muqtafā li-tārīkh ash-Shaykh Shihāb ad-Dīn Abī Shāmah*, written as a continuation of the thirteenth-century chronicle of Abū Shāmah;[101] al-Birzālī reports that Toqtogha died in Rabīᶜ I 712/August 1312, as Qāshānī confirms, but includes an evaluation of Özbek's predecessor that became a standard feature of many later Arabic accounts. Toqtogha, writes al-Birzālī, was an infidel in the "school" of idol worshippers, and loved the "Uyghūrīyah," who were *bakhshī*s and sorcerers, and paid them great honor; but he was just and inclined toward worthy people of all religious communities (*millah*), preferring Muslims above the others and loving wise men and physicians. Furthermore, the account affirms that Toqtogha had a son who had converted to Islam and loved to hear the Qurʾān recited,

99. Cf. Tiz I, p. 141 (text), p. 163 (tr.); and the new edition of the *Nihāyat al-arab*, ed. ᶜĀshūr et al., vol. 27, p. 375. The account of the Mongols in an-Nuwayrī's work is drawn largely from Rukn ad-Dīn Baybars' slightly earlier *Zubdat al-fikrah*, but the sections of the latter work containing the account in question are no longer extant.

100. *Kanz ad-durar wa jāmiᶜ al-ghurar*, a universal history, of which the ninth part, separately entitled *ad-Durr al-fākhir fī sīrat al-Malik an-Nāṣir*, covers 698–736/1298–1336; cf. H. R. Roemer, ed., *Die Chronik des Ibn ad-Dawādārī*, neunter Teil, Der Bericht über den Sultan al-Malik an-Nāṣir Muḥammad ibn Qalaʾun (Cairo, 1960; Deutsches Archäologisches Institut Kairo; In Kommission bei Sami al-Khandji), p. 302. On Ibn ad-Dawādārī see further Haarmann, *Quellenstudien*, pp. 61–84, and the discussion in Chapter 4.

101. Tiz I, pp. 172–175, text and tr.; cf. Little, pp. 46–53.

"even though he did not understand it," and planned upon his accession to the throne to allow only Islām in his realm; but this son died before Toqtogha, who had then designated this son's son as his successor.[102] But Özbek Khān, the son of Toqtogha's brother and a good Muslim, succeeded in establishing himself: "He killed a number of the *amīrs* and notables and killed a sizable group of the Uyghurs and the *bakhshīs* and the sorcerers; and he spread the word of Islām, and ascended the throne of the kingdom at the end of Ramażān in the year 712/late January 1313." Al-Birzālī also reports an important source of his information on the size of Özbek Khan's realm, a source who must have also supplied much of the information about the succession and conversion; we will return to this figure later.

The account of al-Birzālī thus echoes the report of opposition toward Islam (and toward Özbek) and the deaths of many opponents of Islam (including, evidently, both *amīrs* and religious figures), but adds important elements to the tradition surrounding Özbek Khan's accession and his establishment of Islam: first the mention of his predecessor's justice and inclination toward Islam despite his infidel status; and second, the mention of Toqtogha's son (though not by name) and intended successor, who is here said to have been a Muslim and to have predeceased his father. The two accounts of al-Birzālī and an-Nuwayrī provided the foundation for mention of Özbek Khan's conversion by most subsequent Arab chroniclers. After al-Birzālī's account,[103] from the mid-1330s, it is nearly seventy years before significant extended narratives of Özbek Khan's accession and "conversion" appear in Arabic historical sources from Egypt and Syria; instead we find only brief acknowledgements that Özbek was a Muslim, recorded most often under the year of his accession or the year of his death, all based upon the accounts of an-Nuwayrī and al-Birzālī.[104]

102. The mention of this Muslim son is often omitted from later histories that base their accounts of Toqtogha and Özbek on al-Birzālī.

103. It is possible that important information on Özbek Khan appears in the chronicle of al-Yūsufī, which survives in a fragment covering 733–738 A.H., identified in Donald P. Little, "The Recovery of a Lost Source for Baḥrī Mamlūk History: al-Yūsufī's *Nuzhat al-nāẓir fī sīrat al-Malik al-Nāṣir*," *JAOS*, 94 (1974), pp. 42–54. The work is especially valuable for Mamlūk-Mongol relations, according to Little; see further his "Notes on Aitamiš, a Mongol Mamlūk," in *Die islamische Welt zwischen Mittelalter und Neuzeit: Festschrift für Hans Robert Roemer zum 65. Geburtstag*, ed. Ulrich Haarmann and Peter Bachmann (Beirut: In Kommmission bei Franz Steiner Verlag, Wiesbaden, 1979), pp. 387–401. The source unfortunately remains inaccessible.

104. Even al-ʿUmarī (d. 749/1348–49), who elsewhere discusses the status of Islam in the Golden Horde as noted below, makes only the briefest mention of his contemporary Özbek Khan's Islam: on one occasion he names Özbek, ruler of the house of Berke in Saray, Khorezm,

Meanwhile, we find an important independent treatment of the events surrounding Özbek Khan's accession in a "post-Ilkhanid" Persian source. The *Tārīkh-i Shaykh Uvays,*[105] completed in the 1360s by Abū Bakr al-

Qïrïm, and the Dasht-i Qïpchāq, as among Muslim khans of Tūrān (Tiz I, p. 228 [text], p. 250 [tr.]), while elsewhere he notes that Özbek Khan is a sincere Muslim, "observant of religion and firm in the *sharīʿah,*" who keeps to his prayers and is persistent in fasting (cf. Klaus Lech's partial edition and translation, *Das mongolische Weltreiche*, p. 68 [text], p. 137 [tr.]). The enormous historical work of adh-Dhahabī (d. 748/1347–48), the *Tārīkh al-Islām,* remains largely unavailable. The excerpt given by Tizengauzen (I, pp. 202–203 [text], 206 [tr.]; cf. Little, pp. 61–66) cites some particulars about the Jöchid *ulus* taken from al-ʿUmarī, but follows al-Birzālī's account of Toqtogha's devotion to "sorcery" and admiration for Muslims, as well as his son's love of Qurʾān recitation, and Özbek's accession and sincere Islam; adh-Dhahabī gives much the same account in the continuation which he himself added to his work *al-ʿIbar fī khabar man ghabar* (cf. Muḥammad Rashād ʿAbd al-Muṭṭalib, ed., *Min dhuyūl al-ʿIbar li'dh-Dhahabī wa'l-Ḥusaynī* [Kuwait: Maṭbaʿah Ḥukūmat al-Kuwayt, n.d.], pp. 72–73). A contemporary of al-ʿUmarī and Dhahabī, Ibn al-Wardī (d. 749/1348–49; cf. Little, pp. 66–67), appears to have based his account (which is not included in Tizengauzen's collection) entirely on that of al-Birzālī: under the year 712 he notes that in it died "Ṭaqṭaqāy, king of Qifjāq," who died an infidel who worshiped idols, but loved worthy people from all nations and preferred Muslims; the account also mentions his son who planned to establish Islam in the realm when he acceded to the throne, but died, and concludes noting that the king after him was Özbek, the son of his brother, who was a Muslim (*Tatimmat al-mukhtaṣar fī akhbār al-bashar,* known also simply as *Tārīkh Ibn al-Wardī*, ed. Aḥmad Rifʿat al-Badrāwī [Beirut, 1389/1970], vol. 2, p. 373). The historian al-Mufaḍḍal, writing around 759/1358, likewise records the accession of "King Yūzbak Khān" in the last decade of Ramażān 712/late January 1313; the new khan was a sincere Muslim, who "killed a number of the *amīrs* and notables, and killed a party among the *bakhshīs* and sorcerers" (Tiz I, p. 186 [text], p. 197 [tr.]; Moufazzal ibn Abil-Fazaïl, *Histoire des sultans mamlouks*, ed. and tr. E. Blochet, pt. 3, in *Patrologia Orientalis*, t. 20, fasc. 1 [Paris, 1928], pp. 228–229). The universal history of Ibn Kathīr (d. 774 or 775/1373–74; cf. Little, pp. 69–73) reports similarly that "Ṭughṭāy Khān" had been firm in the religion of the Tatars, worshiping idols and the stars, but that he honored physicians and wise men, and especially honored Muslims; he died in Ramażān 712, and after him ruled Özbek Khān, son of his brother; "he was a Muslim and spread the religion of Islām in his country, and killed people among the infidel *amīrs*, and raised the Muḥammadan laws above other laws . . ." (Tizengauzen, I, pp. 274 [text], 277 [tr.]; *al-Bidāyah wa'n-nihāyah fi't–tārīkh*, ed. Cairo, 1932–1939, 14 vols., here vol. 14, pp. 67–68). This pattern of brief references continues even after the new elements found in fifteenth-century works noted below; for example, al-Qalqashandī (d. 821/1418–19), drawing upon al-ʿUmarī, notes Özbek's conversion and his sincerity but gives no details (Tiz I, pp. 397 [text], 406 [tr]; *Ṣubḥ al-aʿshā fī ṣināʿat al-inshā* [14 vols., Cairo: al-Maṭbaʿah al-Amīrīyah, 1913–1919], vol. 4, p. 474), while the account of al-Maqrīzī (d. 845/1441–42; Tiz, I, pp. 417–442, esp. 425, 427 [text], 437, 441 [tr.]; cf. Little, pp. 76–80, F. Rosenthal, *EI*², VI, pp. 193–194) combines al-Birzālī's mention of Toqtogha's devotion to the idol-worshiping *bakhshīs* with an-Nuwayrī's account of the khan's sending the Chingisid princess to Egypt, and otherwise mentions Özbek Khan's conversion only when reporting his death. The account of al-Qalqashandī is, however, of some interest for highlighting the "falling away" from Islam between Berke and Özbek, an issue also addressed in the account of Ötemish Ḥājjī.

105. The work was described, with a translation and facsimile of its "original" part, by J. B. Van Loon *Taʾrīkh-i Shaikh Uwais (History of Shaikh Uwais), An Important Source for the History of Ādharbaijān in the Fourteenth Century* ('s-Gravenhage, 1954); cf. Storey-Bregel, *PL*,

Quṭbī al-Aharī, speaks of a conspiracy between Özbek and Qutlugh Temür to ensure the former's accession; here Qutlugh Temür is not hostile to Özbek as in Qāshānī's account, but cooperates with him in a synchronized assault on his rivals that in part echoes the description of Özbek's accession in the account of Ötemish Ḥājjī, as discussed below. Although the account in al-Aharī's work is quite problematical,[106] the passage is worth noting precisely because it does *not* say anything about Özbek's conversion:

> And in the Dasht-i Qifchāq, Ṭūghtā'[107] died in the same year. He had a son named Īlbāṣmīsh.[108] And Qādāq was grand-emir and wished to install Īlbāṣmīsh on the throne after Ghazān.[109] Ūzbek, the son of Ṭūlījah, conspired in Khwārizm with Qutlugh Timūr, and pretending to pay their obsequies to the king, they entered the camp ("urdū") and Uzbek stabbed Īlbāṣmīsh, and Qutlugh Timūr stabbed Qadāq at the same moment and they killed them both. And the reign passed into the hands of Uzbek and he ascended the seat of government.

The passage thus accounts only for his accession to the throne, and in this it mirrors Ötemish Ḥājjī's account, where Özbek's accession is the subject of a narrative altogether distinct from the story of his conversion. Together the two accounts suggest the circulation of narratives that per-

---

I, pp. 337–338. For the account in question cf. p. 49 (text facsimile, pp. 146–147). See also Tiz II, pp. 100 (tr.), 229 (text); he too cites the Leiden manuscript.

106. The evident problems in the account most likely reflect a garbled transmission at some point. In its extant form, to begin with, al-Aharī's work appears to recount Özbek's accession under the year 703 instead of 712, suggesting a lacuna in the available early manuscript; the account mentions Toqtogha's son "Ilbasmïsh" (on which form see below) as the candidate of the senior *amīr*, Qādāq (not known from any other source), for the throne, but names the Ilkhanid *Ghāzān* (whose death in 703 is correctly reported just before the account of Toqtogha's death in the Dasht–i Qïpchaq) as the ruler whom this "Ilbasmïsh" was to succeed (Tizengauzen treats this as a simple error and emends to Tokhta).

107. The form "Ṭūghtā'" probably reflects this author's source's "Ṭūghtāgha," the final *ghayn-hā* ligature taken by a copyist as a final *hamzah*; likewise, Özbek's father's name, given here in the form "Ṭūlījah," probably masks an original "Ṭ.ġ.r.l.jah," the original *ghayn-rā* ligature becoming a *vāv*.

108. The form "Īlbaṣmīsh" given here instead of the name "Īl-baṣār," etc., found in other sources, may have been suggested by the mention of one of the Ilkhanid Ghāzān's *amīrs* named "Īlbāsmīsh" shortly before this passage.

109. The name of the ruler whom Īlbaṣmīsh was to succeed is written here "Ghazān," while the author everywhere else writes "Ghāzān" when referring to the Ilkhanid ruler; this may be a further sign of the text's corruption at this point.

haps purposefully separated the circumstances of Özbek's usurpation of power from those of his adoption of Islam.

This source also marks the "reappearance" of Qutlugh Temür in the account of Özbek Khan's accession; the problem of this figure's role in Özbek's accession as portrayed in our earliest source on these events, the *Tārīkh-i Ūljāytū Sulṭān*, was noted above, but aside from his prominence in Ibn Baṭṭūṭah's travel account as the governor of Khorezm, Qutlugh Temür is not mentioned in connection with Özbek Khan's rise in Arabic sources until the beginning of the fifteenth century. Also curious is the appearance here, in garbled form, of Toqtogha's son Il-Basar, who is mentioned already by Banākatī and appears in Arabic sources from the fourteenth century as well; there, however, Il-Basar is said to have died in 709/1309–1310,[110] precluding his actual installation on the throne as portrayed in this Persian source. Finally, al-Aharī's work is distinctive in explicitly situating the events surrounding Özbek's accession in Khorezm, rather than in the more westerly heart of the Golden Horde as is at least implied in other sources.[111]

After the *Tārīkh-i Shaykh Uvays*, we find no further information on Özbek Khan in Persian historical sources until the emergence of the Timurid historiographical tradition in the early fifteenth century, but here again the narrative treatment is minimal. In the *Muntakhab at-tavārīkh* of Muʿīn ad-Dīn Naṭanzī, dating from 817/1414 and, for the Golden Horde in particular, evidently dependent upon oral tradition, we nevertheless find only a summary account of the effects of Özbek Khan's reign: in his reign, writes Naṭanzī, the Dasht-i Qïpchaq, "which had always been a place of unbelief and heresy and a site of rebelliousness and sedition, became an abode of worship, and buildings for pious endeav-

110. Cf. Baybars, in Tiz I, pp. 98 (text), 123 (tr.), and al-ʿAynī, pp. 484 (text), 513 (tr.); in Tizengauzen's version (pp. 140 [text], 162 [tr.]), an-Nuwayrī dates his death to 707, but the edition of ʿĀshūr et al.(vol. 27, p. 375) gives 709. As noted below, Toqtogha's son "Il-basar" is also mentioned as having predeceased his father in Ötemish Ḥājjī's work. In any case his death before that of Toqtogha suggests his identity with the convert to Islam designated as Toqtogha's successor according to al-Birzālī, who does not give his name; al-Birzālī is the only original source to specify that Toqtogha's son had converted to Islam. We may note here in connection with the name assigned to the son in these early sources and in Ötemish Ḥājjī's work (and echoed, at least, in the *Tārīkh-i Shaykh Uvays*), it is possible that we do not in fact have the son's *name* as such, but a reflection of a general designation of the son as "heir-apparent," as "usurper," or as "oppressor," all plausible meanings for the term *il-basar*.

111. I have briefly discussed al-Aharī's account, with reference to events in Khorezm as alluded to in yet another source, in "Bābā Kamāl Jandī and the Kubravī Tradition among the Turks of Central Asia," *Der Islam* (forthcoming).

ors (*biqāʿ-i khayr*) and places for devotional practices (*mawāżiʿ-i ʿibādāt*) were revived."[112] Naṭanzī's reliance upon oral material, no doubt similar to the accounts collected by Ötemish Ḥājjī, in many cases makes his work an important record of oral tradition (however dimly reflected), but has also rendered its chronological and genealogical details quite confused, and such is clearly the case in the account of Özbek Khan.

Similarly, of the Timurid historians who might have made mention of Özbek Khan's conversion, the two principal chroniclers, Niẓām ad-Dīn Shāmī and Sharaf ad-Dīn ʿAlī Yazdī, offer nothing at all on his conversion or accession; only Ḥāfiẓ-i Abrū discusses Özbek's accession, and his account is dependent upon Qāshānī's. Otherwise after this we come to the time of the *Shajarat al-atrāk*, which, as noted earlier, combines material drawn from oral tradition and recorded under Ulugh Beg but probably reflects a sixteenth-century Shïbanid redaction of the material. In general we may infer from the Timurid-era material that the importance of Özbek Khan's status as the first Muslim ruler of the Jöchid *ulus* was well known,[113] but bore no particular dynastic significance to warrant special historiographical treatment.

It is at the beginning of the fifteenth century that we next find new details reported about the events surrounding Özbek Khan's accession, in two important Arabic sources. Perhaps the richest of these is the universal history of Ibn Duqmāq, entitled *Nuzhat al-anām fī tārīkh al-islām*, which remains relatively little studied.[114] Ibn Duqmāq includes two references to Özbek Khan's Muslim status, one obliquely under the year 720/1320–1321 when he records the arrival in Egypt of the Jöchid princess supplied to the Mamlūk Sulṭān by Özbek, noting that among the members of

112. Naṭanzī, *Muntakhab*, ed. Aubin, pp. 82–83; Tiz II, pp 128 (tr.), 232 (text).

113. In his famous letter to "Dāy Ming," the *pādshāh* of China, Temür's son Shāhrukh summarized the signal events in the spread of Islam to the Chingisid dynasties of Iran and the Golden Horde; in the latter realm ("Sarāy and Qïrïm and the Dasht-i Qïpchāq"), "some rulers, such as Özbek and Jānī Khān, accepted the religion of Islam and adhered to Islam and the Muslim way, and acted in accordance with the *sharīʿat* of Muḥammad, the Prophet of God, and of his people" (cf. the text in ʿAbd al-Ḥusayn Navāʾī, ed., *Asnād va mukātabat-i tārīkhī-i Īrān az Tīmūr tā Shāh Ismāʿīl* [Tehran: Bungāh-i Tarjimah va Nashr-i Kitāb, 1341/1962], p. 134).

114. Cf. Tiz I, pp. 315–330; Little, pp. 84, 94, mentions his works but has not analyzed them. On the importance of his *Nuzhat al-anām*, see the discussion of Ashtor, "Some Unpublished Sources," pp. 27–30; Ashtor lauds Ibn Duqmāq's work as comprehensive, detailed, and objective, noting that "above all he reports on the events in the two Mongol states in Western Asia and Southern Russia: the first, that of the Persian Ilkhans, the second that of the Golden Horde. The history of these two states is followed with particular interest, the author not contenting himself with merely registering the dynastic changes as usual."

the delegation was the *imām* of Özbek, a certain Shaykh Burhān ad-Dīn;[115] similarly, he reports Özbek Khan's death under the year 743/1342–1343, noting of him that he was a pious ruler who honored *shaykhs* and *faqīrs*.[116] The most important account, however, appears earlier, in the description of Özbek's accession. Under the year 713/1313–1314,[117] Ibn Duqmāq reports the death of "Ṭuqṭāy," without an heir, and notes that "Quṭluq-timür," who had governed the realm during Ṭuqṭāy's reign, sought aid in arranging the succession from the senior *khātūn* of the late khan; the name of this queen is given later in the account, but Ibn Duqmāq specifies here that she had formerly been the wife of Ṭughrīljā, the father of Özbek.[118] Quṭluq-timür and the senior *khātūn* agreed on installing Özbek as successor, and Ibn Duqmāq adds the important element that Quṭluq-timür had obtained Özbek's promise to become a Muslim and support Islam upon his accession; and indeed, when Özbek took the throne after his uncle's death, "he entered the religion of God in all earnestness, and had a mosque built for himself in which he performed the five prayers at their appropriate times."[119] Some of the Tatar *amīrs* opposed Özbek, however, and conspired to destroy him; of these Ibn Duqmāq names "Ṭunghūr" and "Ṭāz b. Münjük."[120] But when Özbek Khan's rule was consolidated, he killed both of these as well as a party among the Tatar notables, aided in this by the jurist ʿImād ad-Dīn b. al-Maskīrī. The same figure allowed

115. Tiz I, pp. 320 (text), 327 (tr.).; this is reported also by al-ʿAynī (Tiz I, pp. 489 (text), 519 (tr.).

116. Tiz I, pp. 322 (text), 329 (tr.).

117. Tiz I, p. 316 (text), 323 (tr.).

118. This corroborates one part of what Ötemish Ḥājjī's account says of Bayālïn, namely that Toqtogha had taken Bayālïn, the wife of "Tughrul," for himself after Tughrul's death. Ötemish Ḥājjī's other major claim about Bayālïn—that she was Özbek's mother—is contradicted by all other early sources, which if they provide any details note that Özbek Khan took her as his wife, an act that required special juridical dispensation and could be approved because her former husband, though Özbek Khan's father, had been a *kāfir*, a point added for the first time by Ibn Duqmāq.

119. This element was adopted from Ibn Duqmāq's account by Ibn Shuhbah al-Asadī (d. 850–851/1446–1448; cf. Tizengauzen, I, pp. 443–448) in his *al-Iʿlān bi-tārīkh ahl al-Islām*, in which most of the account follows al-Birzālī (through Ibn Kathīr, evidently) on Toqtogha's idol-worship and Özbek's Islam.

120. The first of these names is no doubt to be emended to "Ṭunghūz" (cf. Tizengauzen), i.e., the Turkic *tonguz*, "pig" perhaps suggesting a narrative that pointedly mentioned the term in order to emphasize an implication of hostility toward Islam. These two *amīrs* figure prominently in the account of Noghay's fall, earlier in Toqtogha's reign, given by Rukn ad-Dīn Baybars and an-Nuwayrī (cf. Tiz I, pp. 86–93, 108–117 [Baybars], pp. 137–140, 158–161 [an-Nuwayrī], and the latter source, ed. ʿĀshūr et al., vol. 27, pp. 369–372 [reading *ṭ.n.ġ.r*]): Ṭāz b. Münjük married Noghay's daughter and was among the *amīrs* who sought refuge from Toqtogha with Noghay as their relations worsened, while "Ṭunguz" is named as a *nāʾib* of Noghay's son "J.kā"

Özbek Khan to marry Bayālūn, his father's wife, says Ibn Duqmāq, on the grounds that his father had been a *kāfir*.

Ibn Duqmāq's account thus echoes the succession crisis, the role of Qutlugh Temür, a link between support for Islam and support for Özbek, and the violent end of Özbek's opponents, all known from the *Tārīkh-i Ūljāytū Sulṭān* and, in the case of the killing of the hostile *amīrs*, from most of the Arabic sources as well. But Ibn Duqmāq adds several important elements: the names of Bayalun, wife first of Özbek's father and then of the khan Toqtogha; of two of the hostile *amīrs*; and of a *faqīh* who both "aided" Özbek in destroying his opponents and pronounced his marriage to Bayalun lawful.

Ibn Duqmāq's account is also of particular interest for its portrayal of Qutlugh Temür. In Ibn Duqmāq's work we find the first explicit assertion that Qutlugh Temür's support for Özbek was (1) confirmed in collusion with Bayalun Khatun and (2) dependent upon Özbek's consent to convert to Islam. Qutlugh Temür's role during Özbek Khan's reign is further clarified by Ibn Duqmāq, who twice portrays him as the khan's chief adviser and follows his later career.

The better known of the two early fifteenth-century Arabic historians is the famous Ibn Khaldūn (d. 808/1406),[121] whose *Kitāb al-ʿibar* likewise provides the names of several figures instrumental in engineering Özbek's seizure of power. Ibn Khaldūn reports the death of Ṭuqṭāy's son Īl-baṣār in 709/1309–1310 and of Ṭuqṭāy himself in 712/1312–1313, noting of Il-basar only that he had been given the domains formerly accorded a brother of Ṭuqṭāy after that brother conspired against the khan with a son of Noghay,[122] a sequence somewhat resembling the situation reported for Toqtogha's sons by Qāshānī. Of Özbek's accession Ibn Khaldūn tells the same story as Ibn Duqmāq, except for identifying Bayālūn only as the wife of Ṭughrïljāy, Özbek's father, and omitting mention of the names of the chief *amīrs* who opposed Özbek and of ʿImād ad-Dīn al-Maskīrī; following the reference to Özbek's marriage of his father's wife, however, Ibn Khaldūn adds an element expanded in al-ʿAynī's work a half-century later, remarking that Özbek Khan made "Quṭluq-timür" governor of Khwārazm and Urgench after removing

after Noghay's death. The two *amīrs* are paired in both accounts, which relate their reconciliation with Togtogha as they turned against Noghay's son.

121. Tiz I, pp. 365–394; cf. Little, pp. 75–76.

122. Tiz I, pp. 371 (text), 384 (tr.); Il-basar's death in 709 is also noted by Baybars and al-ʿAynī, with an-Nuwayrī giving 707 or 709 (see note 110).

their previous governor, who was the brother of the *khātūn* Bayālūn.

It is the *ʿIqd al-jumān fī tārīkh ahl az-zamān* of the Egyptian historian al-ʿAynī (d. 855/1451) that marks the culmination of the historical tradition surrounding Özbek Khan in Arabic historiography: al-ʿAynī combines several of the earlier reports, but adds still new details, evidently from sources that have not survived. Under the year 713/1313–1314,[123] al-ʿAynī reports the death of Ṭuqṭāy, who had been an idol-worshiper, devoted to the *bakhshī*s, but honored the Muslims above all, following the standard account given first by al-Birzālī. Then al-ʿAynī notes that Özbek Khan was aided in his accession by "Quṭluq-timür," adding that the latter's two brothers, Ṣarāy-timür,[124] and Muḥammad-Khwājā [*sic*], conducted affairs for him; it is not clear what role, if any, in the accession of Özbek Khan is ascribed to these two brothers by their mention here. As in the accounts of Ibn Duqmāq and Ibn Khaldūn, Quṭluq-timür is said to have sought aid from Bayālūn, the wife of Özbek's father, and to have secured Özbek's promise to convert to Islam upon his accession, and al-ʿAynī repeats Ibn Duqmāq's report on his fulfilment of this promise virtually word for word. Similarly, he records the names of the *amīrs* who opposed Özbek, given in Tizengauzen's text as "Ṭayfūr,"[125] "Ṭāz," and "Münjükī," making two persons out of Ibn Duqmāq's "Ṭāz b. Münjük." Like Ibn Khaldūn, al-ʿAynī omits the name of the "scholar" who approved Özbek's marriage to Bayālūn, but adds two details in recounting Özbek Khan's dismissal of Bayālūn's brother from the governorship of Khorezm and Urgench and his conferral of this post upon Quṭluq-timür: first, he gives the brother's name as Bay-timür (*b.y.d.m.r.*), and second, he recounts Bayālūn's anger over this, Özbek's apology following her strong rebuke, and their reconciliation (although there is no mention of the khan's having undone his replacement of Bay-timür).

Altogether, the above sources display essential agreement on several points, beyond the often unreconcilable divergences in details; many of these points are found also in Ötemish Ḥājjī's account of Özbek's accession. They suggest a succession crisis due to the death of Toqtogha's son and designated successor, as Ötemish Ḥājjī confirms; they suggest

123. Tiz I, pp. 485–486 (text), 514–515 (tr.); this passage from al-ʿAynī's work (for most of which there is still no edition; cf. Little, pp. 80–87) is also published in notes to Najīb ʿĀṣim's edition of ʿAbd al-Ghaffār al-Qïrïmī's history of the Jöchid *ulus* (see Chapter 5), pp. 35–36.

124. Vaṣṣāf, in the account noted earlier, mentions a brother of Qutlugh Temür named "Sarāy Qutlugh."

125. I.e., for Ibn Duqmāq's "Ṭunghūr," reflecting "Tonghuz" (see note 120), all three orthographically similar.

the role of religious affiliation and support in the crisis, whether through asserting the planned support for Islam on the part of the intended successor, through discussing Toqtogha's own religious leanings, or through highlighting the anti-Islamic character of opposition to Özbek (absent in Ötemish Ḥājjī); they attest to the turmoil entailed by Özbek's accession, both in the form of the hostile infidels he killed and in the curious stories of tension between Özbek and Bayalun over appointments (Ötemish Ḥājjī names Bayalun but omits the issue of appointments, and reports the turmoil entailed by Toqtogha's death but limits the bloodshed to a single usurper); and they perhaps suggest opposition to Özbek's usurpation even among Muslims, through mention of a jurist willing to sanction a questionable marriage (absent from Ötemish Ḥājjī).

Finally, from as late as the second half of the fifteenth century, we find a new element involved in Özbek Khan's conversion alongside material adopted from other extant sources, in the history of Ibn Taghrībirdī, *an-Nujūm az-zāhirah fī mulūk Miṣr wa'l-Qāhirah*. Ibn Taghrībirdī follows al-Birzālī's account under the year 713 A.H., on the death of "Ṭuqṭāy," but adds that "the one who aided Özbek Khān in attaining the throne was one of their *amīrs*, from among the Muslims, called 'Quṭluqtamur,' who administered the country";[126] it is not certain from which earlier source this addition was drawn. Of greater interest, however, under the year 742 A.H. Ibn Taghrībirdī reports the death of Özbek after a rule of about thirty years; he applauds his justice and summarizes the religious consequences of his reign as follows: "He had become a Muslim, and his Islam was sincere; he urged his subjects toward conversion to Islam, and some of them converted. After he became a Muslim Özbek Khan did not wear the *sarāqūjāt*, but wore instead a girdle of steel, for it is said, "wearing of gold is forbidden to men." He was inclined toward religion and goodness, and frequented the company of *faqīrs*."[127]

The term given as an Arabic plural, *sarāqūjāt*, reflects the term *sarāqūj*,[128] a Turkic designation for a type of headgear the Mongol rulers

126. *an-Nujūm az-zāhirah fī mulūk Miṣr wa'l-Qāhirah*, vol. 9 (Cairo: Maṭbuʿah Dār al-Kutub al-Miṣrīyah, 1361/1942; repr. 1963–1972), p. 226 (year 713).

127. *Nujūm*, vol. 10 (Cairo, 1368/1949; repr.1963–1972), p. 74; this account is also mentioned in a note by Tiz I, pp. 528–529, as appearing both in *Nujūm* and in Ibn Taghrībirdī's biographical dictionary, *al-Manhal aṣ-ṣāfī* [citing MS Paris, Bibliothèque Nationale, Anc. Fonds Ar., No. 747, f. 166v, and MS Vienna No. 1173, f. 106v], as well as in Abū'l-ʿAbbās Aḥmad al-Qaramānī's early seventeenth-century work *Akhbār ad-duwal wa āthār al-awwal* (on which see *GAL*, II, p. 301, *GALS*, II, p. 412).

128. Cf. Sir Gerard Clauson, *An Etymological Dictionary of Pre-Thirteenth-Century Turkish*

were famous for wearing. It is not clear whence Ibn Taghrībirdī derived this brief allusion to a religiously inspired change in Özbek Khan's imperial insignia, but it is of interest as an echo of the changes in dress associated with Jānī Bek's policies of Islamization; in both cases the mention of a change in dress offers yet another indication of the external symbolism, and its communal significance, entailed by the adoption of Islam. At the same time, however, we may note that the wearing of the Mongol headgear, in this case called *sarūqūj*, as well as of a jewel-encrusted golden girdle or belt (*ḥiyāṣah*) is attested for the Muslim Berke, with no unfavorable comments, in the description given by al-Mufaḍḍal.[129]

Such are the sources on Özbek Khan's accession and adoption of Islam. Beyond these accounts we have further information, worth considering, on various individuals assigned important roles in both the accession and conversion of Özbek; the information is of interest not only for illustrating the religious "personnel" who shaped the environment in which, at least at court, Islam was established, but also because one or more of these individuals may have served as the prototype, either historical or narrative (or both), for the figure of "Baba Tükles" as the bearer of Islam to Özbek Khan.

THE ISLAMIC PRESENCE IN ÖZBEK KHAN'S REALM

We are generally poorly served when it comes to biographical information on Islamic religious figures of the Golden Horde, owing to the lack of indigenous sources.[130] Mamlūk sources give some details, and in the growing body of Turkic literary production from the Golden Horde we find some allusions to patronage relations between Muslim religious figures and poets and the khans; but the earliest biographical compendium on jurists, for instance, to pay close attention to the lands of the Jöchid *ulus* does not appear until the latter sixteenth century in the still unpublished work of al-Kaffawī. Sufi biographical literature likewise covers the Jöchid *ulus* quite sparsely until long after the demise of the Golden Horde. We are left only with scattered information on several figures who may be linked to Özbek Khan and deserve attention here.

(Oxford, 1972) [hereafter "Clauson, *ED*"], p. 849, s.v. "saraǧuç," which form he explains as a metathesis from *saruġač*, from *saru-*, "to wind, wrap," and thus a a woman's hood or head dress; see further G. Doerfer, *Türkische und mongolische Elemente im Neupersischen* (Wiesbaden, 1963–1975, 4 vols.) [hereafter "Doerfer, *TMEN*"), III, pp. 242–243, *sarāġūc* (cf. pp. 221–222, *sārūqčï*, "turban").

129. Ed. Blochet, pt. 1 (*Patrologia Orientalis*, 12/3 [Paris, 1919], p. 460.

130. See the brief discussion of such figures in Fedorov-Davydov, *Obshchestvennyi stroi*, pp. 100–103.

To begin with, among the figures specifically linked to Özbek Khan's conversion or support for Islam may be mentioned the *amīr* Qutlugh Temür, a figure of unknown tribal origins whose high rank under both Toqtogha and Özbek is confirmed by a number of sources; Ibn Duqmāq is the earliest source to specifically ascribe Özbek Khan's conversion to Islam to Qutlugh Timūr's promise of support, however, and it is not impossible that such a scenario is modeled on the widely known stories in which the *amīr* Nawrūz is portrayed as having demanded the conversion to Islam of the Ilkhanid ruler Ghāzān in return for his pivotal support. Ibn Duqmāq and Ibn Khaldūn, as well as al-ᶜAynī, suggest also the *khatun* Bayalun's support for Islam in reporting her collusion with Qutlugh Temür, but nowhere is she depicted as an important player in the religious aspect of Özbek's accession.

Whatever Qutlugh Temür's role may have been, he evidently continued to serve Özbek for the rest of his life; he is portrayed as counseling the khan against accepting an offer from the *amīr* Chūbān, made following Öljeytü's death, to assume power in the Ilkhanid realm,[131] and led campaigns against Abū Saᶜīd's armies before being "dismissed" to the governorship of Khorezm;[132] his continuing importance is signaled by reports of the disarray that struck Özbek's army, sent against Iran after Abū Saᶜīd's death, upon word of Qutlugh Temür's death.[133]

As for specifically "religious" figures—jurists, Sufis, and literary figures who produced works with a mystical or religious coloring—we find relatively few who can be directly linked to Özbek Khan's court. We know of no Islamic religious work explicitly dedicated to or commissioned by Özbek Khan, with the possible exception of the *Qalandar-nāmah*, a Persian Sufi work comprising five "books," and written in imitation of Rūmī's *Mathnavī* by a certain Abū Bakr Qalandar, who lived in the Crimea but calls himself "Qalandar-i Rūmī." The work includes many stories about famous Sufi shaykhs, but these are apparently all or mostly the "classical" saints (although figures as late as ᶜAṭṭār and Rūmī are mentioned). The work was begun in 720/1320–1321 in the Crimea, and took more than twenty years to complete; the first four of the books were written under Özbek Khan, with the fifth under his son "Jānī Bek

131. Cf. the account of Ibn Duqmāq in Tiz I, pp. 317 (text), 324 (tr.).

132. Tiz I, pp. 321 (text), 328 (tr.).

133. Noted already by Ḥamdullāh Mustawfī Qazvīnī in the continuation of his *Tārīkh-i guzīdah*, cf. Tiz II, p. 93; cf. the fifteenth-century *Mujmal-i Faṣīḥī* of Faṣīḥ Khwāfī (ed. Maḥmūd Farrukh [Mashhad, 1339–1341/1960–1962], III, p. 46, and the Russian translation,

Maḥmūd."[134] In any case the Crimean provenance of Sufi literary activity suggested by this work coincides well with the impression conveyed by Ibn Baṭṭūṭah, as discussed below.

The jurist named by Ibn Duqmāq as having blessed Özbek's "unconventional" marriage is otherwise unidentifiable from available biographical sources, and the same holds true for most other figures ascribed a role in Özbek's conversion by external sources: for example, the otherwise unidentifiable "*qāżī* named Nūr" mentioned by Ibn ad-Dawādārī as a member of the delegation that escorted Özbek's niece to Egypt in 720/1320, noting that "they say that it was this *qāżī* who guided the king Özbek to Islām." As suggested, this figure is probably to be identified with the "Shaykh Nūr ad-Dīn" whose recent death was reported, according to al-Mufaḍḍal, by an embassy from the Golden Horde which arrived in Cairo in Jumādā II 724/late April–May 1324;[135] al-Mufaḍḍal specifically identifies him as the person who had accompanied Özbek's niece in 720/1320. In the same context, however—that is, as a prominent member of the escorting delegation—Ibn Duqmāq (and after him al-ʿAynī) mention instead a Shaykh Burhān ad-Dīn, named as the *imām* of Özbek Khan.[136]

Mudzhmal-i Fasikhi (Fasikhov svod), tr. D. Iu. Iusupova [Tashkent: Fan, 1980], p. 59).

134. *SVR* IX (Tashkent: Fan, 1971), pp. 471–474, cat. no. 6705, inv. no. 11668; according to the description, the author affirms that the third book was finished in 740. This substantial work (400ff.) is preserved in a unique manuscript copied in Shaʿbān 761/June–July 1360 by Shaykh Bāyazīd al-ʿUshshāqī as-Samarīnī [*s.m.r.b/n/y/.nī*] (the *nisbah* may be connected with a town named Samar in the Golden Horde, possibly on the site of the town of Samara, later Kuibyshev, on the middle Volga; cf. V. L. Egorov, *Istoricheskaia geografiia Zolotoi Ordy v XIII–XIV vv.* [Moscow: Nauka, 1985], pp. 132, 139). Incidentally, one ʿAlī b. Muḥammad b. Dihqān [ʿAlī an-Nasafī] al-Baykandī (i.e., from Paykand near Bukhārā) wrote a commentary on the third section of the famous grammarian Sirāj ad-Dīn Yūsuf as-Sakkākī's *Miftaḥ al-ʿulūm*, completing it in Khorezm in 718/1318 (*GAL*, I, p. 294, where the commentator's *nisbah* is given as "Kabindī"); evidentally on the basis of a copy of this commentary no longer extant (or at least not registered in a published catalogue), Shihāb ad-Dīn Marjānī (*Mustafād al-akhbār*, I, p. 102) says that the work was finished in Shaʿbān 719/September–October 1319 and presented to Özbek Khan, and it is not unlikely that other works produced in Khorezm in this era may bear dedications to or benedictions upon Özbek Khan. Literary patronage seems to have expanded considerably under Jānī Bek, to whom a number of Arabic and Persian works were dedicated; the Turkic *Muḥabbat-nāmah* was evidently produced during his reign, and even his short-lived predecessor Tïnï Bek was the dedicatee of the Turkic version of *Khusraw va Shīrīn* by the poet "Quṭb."

135. Cf. Samira Kortantamer, *Ägypten und Syrien zwischen 1317 und 1341 in der Chronik des Mufaḍḍal b. Abī l-Faḍāʾil* (Freiburg im Breisgau: Klaus Schwarz Verlag, 1973), p. 93. Tiz I, p. 187 (text), p. 199 (tr.), gives the year as 732, but this is certainly an error, no doubt ascribable to the incorrect ordering of the pages in the unique manuscript; the incorrect pagination was noted by Kortantamer (p. 92, n. 3), but without reference to Tizengauzen's work.

136. Tiz I, pp. 320 (text), 327 (tr.).; for al–ʿAynī, pp. 489 (text), 519 (tr.).

One of the most interesting figures linked with Özbek's conversion *and* accession is mentioned first by al-Birzālī, writing in the late 1330s. As an important source of his information on the size of Özbek Khan's realm, a source who must have also supplied much of his information about the succession struggle and conversion, al-Birzālī names the worthy Shaykh ʿAlāʾ ad-Dīn an-Nuʿmān b. Dawlatshāh b. ʿAlī al-Khwārazmī al-Ḥanafī, who came to Damascus in Ramażān 718/November 1318, remained there several days, and then traveled on to the Mamlūk court in Cairo, where he stayed for a year before making the pilgrimage and returning to "his master" Özbek Khān. It was then, apparently, that al-Birzālī met him personally.[137] This remarkable man, al-Birzālī writes, had left his homeland at the age of twenty-one, had traveled to numerous lands, studied logic, dialectics, and medicine, and had returned to his own country in 701/1301–1302, attaching himself to its "king," Malik-Temür (i.e., *Malik-d.m.r*); he served him as physician and became the chief physician of the hospital (*māristān*) in Khorezm. Later in his account al-Birzālī states that this Nuʿmān was born in Khorezm in the middle of Ramażān 657/early September 1259, allowing us to suppose that he left his native land in 678/1279–1280 and spent twenty-three years "abroad" before returning to Khorezm in 701/1301–1302.

From his service to "Malik Temür" in Khorezm, Shaykh ʿAlāʾ ad-Dīn an-Nuʿmān had been sent to the king Tokhtay (whom al-Birzālī here calls the son of Berke!), king of the country of the Dasht al-Qibjāq; when this king died, Özbek Khān, a Muslim, ruled after him, evidently making use of Shaykh Nuʿmān's services. The new khan furnished the shaykh with money to donate to several *khānkāh* [*sic*] in al-Quds [Jerusalem] and to bestow upon the *mujāvurs* at the noble sanctuaries [Mecca and Madīnah]; the latter element is not further explained in the extant portions of al-Birzālī's *Muqtafā*, but is considerably elaborated in later sources that may have used fuller versions of al-Birzālī's work, as we will note below.

This Khorezmian shaykh is also cited in the encyclopedic work of Ibn Faḍlullāh al-ʿUmarī (d. 749/1348–1349), the *Masālik al-abṣār*. Here, however, he is usually referred to as ʿAlāʾ ad-Dīn *ibn* Nuʿmān al-Khorezmī, although he is occasionally cited with the words "*qāla'n-nuʿmān*," implying that Nuʿmān was indeed his *ism*; it is not certain whether al-ʿUmarī met him personally or merely cites him from a fuller version of al-Birzālī's

137. The excerpts from al-Birzālī's work cited by Tizengauzen also refer to this figure's visit to Damascus in 710, when he recounted the extent of Özbek's realm, but it seems likely that the date as given reflects the omission of an "8" in the manuscript or printed text.

work.[138] The considerable confusion over the proper form of his name is only worsened by Ibn Baṭṭūṭah, who remembered him as "Nuᶜmān ad-Dīn al-Khwārazmī"; but more important, Ibn Baṭṭūṭah confirms his prominent position at the court of Özbek Khan as indicated by al-Birzālī. In Saray Berke, Ibn Baṭṭūṭah notes, he visited the *zāwīyah* of this "Nuᶜmān ad-Dīn," whom he calls *faqīh*, *imām*, and *ᶜālim*; this man was one of the distinguished shaykhs, "of good qualities and generous soul," and was both full of humility and "exceedingly harsh toward the people of the world." In illustration of this he notes that Sulṭān Özbek would visit the shaykh every Friday, but that the shaykh would not come out to meet the khan or even rise before him; rather, the Sulṭān would sit opposite the shaykh, speaking "sweetly" to him and showing the utmost humility while in his presence. The shaykh's behavior was in stark contrast to the khan's deference, although, Ibn Baṭṭūṭah affirms, the shaykh was exceedingly kind toward the poor and unfortunate, and toward strangers.[139]

There can be little doubt that the same figure is intended in all these accounts. Moreover, it is worth noting that this Nuᶜmān al-Khorezmī was clearly a scholar of some eminence, and was also a Sufi renowned for his understanding of the mystical works of Ibn ᶜArabī. In the first regard, Nuᶜmān al-Khorezmī is named as the author of a commentary on an important work by the famous Ḥanafī jurist Burhān ad-Dīn Nasafī; the likelihood that this particular Nuᶜmān Khorezmī is the author in question is suggested, if not confirmed, by the dates of Nasafī's death (687/1288) and the (apparently unique) manuscript's date (900/1494).[140]

138. Cf. al-ᶜUmarī/Lech, p. 31; Lech notes that al-ᶜUmarī might have met Khorezmī in Damascus or Cairo, but that he never cites this source using phrases indicating direct contact between them; what is clear is that al-ᶜUmarī cites Shaykh Nuᶜmān for information not found in the extant sections of al-Birzālī. Both include the shaykh's report on size of country, but al-ᶜUmarī (Lech, pp. 79–80 [text], 144–145 [tr.]) has him report also (1) on the size of the army of the Golden Horde, for which Khorezmī relates figures from the war between Toqtogha and the Chaghatayid khan Esen Bugha; (2) again on the extent of the country, but with expanded information on lands to the north, including Alexander's Iron Gate and his journey to the Land of Darkness, and mention of the land of Yūghra, and the Land of Darkness; and (3) on the population of the Golden Horde, where he relates that the Turks of the Dasht-i Qïpchāq include both Muslim tribes and infidel tribes.

139. *Voyages d'Ibn Battûta*, ed. and tr. C. Defrémery and B. R. Sanguinetti (Paris, 1854; repr. Éditions Anthropos Paris, 1969), II, p. 449; cf. the English translation by H. A. R. Gibb, *The Travels of Ibn Baṭṭūṭa* A.D. *1325–1354*, II (Cambridge: Cambridge University Press, 1962), p. 516 (since Gibb's translation is keyed to the text published by Defrémery and Sanguinetti, future references will be given only to that edition).

140. *GAL* I, p. 615 mentions a commentary by him on Nasafī's work entitled *Muqaddimah*

More striking is this Nuʿmān's reputation as a student of Ibn ʿArabī's mysticism.[141] One of the earliest Persian commentaries on the latter's *Fuṣūṣ al-ḥikam* was written in 743/1343 by a member of the Kāshānī/Qayṣarī circle in Iṣfahān, named Rukn ad-Dīn Shīrāzī. In his introduction to this work Shīrāzī notes that he also consulted Nuʿmān al-Khorezmī[142] in studying the *Fuṣūṣ*; their meeting came, he specifies, in 739/1338–1339 in Sarāy Berke. He does not indicate what business took him to the Golden Horde, saying only that he sought from Nuʿmān Khorezmī an explication of some difficulties in the *Fuṣūṣ*, for in ascertaining the meanings of this work this shaykh was "singular in his age." Nuʿmān told Rukn ad-Dīn that he had heard that part of the commentary was already written, and insisted upon seeing it; Rukn ad-Dīn let him examine it, and Nuʿmān, he says, urged him to complete it and showed great solicitude for his work, so that Rukn ad-Dīn's text was finished still during "the days of his blessed life." This latter indication confirms that Shaykh Nuʿmān's death must have come between 739 and 743, near the time of Özbek Khan's death, and indeed, a fifteenth-century source records the death of Nuʿmān ad-Dīn Khorezmī on 25 Muḥarram 740/2 August 1339.[143]

Further details on Nuʿmān Khorezmī's close relationship with Özbek Khan appear in two works of the mid-fifteenth century, one the famous

---

fī 'l-jadal wa'l-khilāf wa'n-naẓar; see also Wilferd Madelung, *EIr*, IV, p. 371, s.v. "Borhān-al-Dīn Nasafī," where he mentions the commentary on this work by "an otherwise unknown" Nuʿmān Khorezmī. Both Brockelmann and Madelung cite only one manuscript, W. Ahlwardt, *Verzeichnis der arabischen Handschriften der königlichen Bibliothek zu Berlin* [Berlin, 1887–1899], vol. IV, pp. 468–469, No. 5167, MS Mq.55, 95ff., copied 900/1494, a commentary on an-Nasafī's *Fuṣūl* by Nuʿmān al-Khwārazmī, entitled *Wuṣūl an–nuʿmānī fī sharḥ fuṣūl al–burhānī*.

141. We may note in this regard that an "ʿAlāʾ ad-Dīn Khorezmī" is named by Jāmī as a Sufi teacher of al-Yāfiʿī; cf. his *Nafaḥāt al-uns*, ed. Mahdī Tawḥīdīpūr (Tehran, 1337/1958), p. 585.

142. One manuscript variant cited in the recent partial edition of Shīrāzī's work confirms this Nuʿmān al-Khorezmī's *laqab* as ʿAlaʾ ad-Dīn. Cf. *Nuṣūṣ al-khuṣūṣ fī tarjamat al-fuṣūṣ, sharḥ-i Fuṣūṣ al-ḥikam-i Muḥyī'd-Dīn Ibn ʿArabī, az Rukn ad-Dīn Masʿūd b. ʿAbdullāh Shīrāzī*, ed. Rajab-ʿAlī Maẓlūmī (Tehran: McGill University / Tehran University, Insitute of Islamic Studies, 1359/1980), text, pp. 5–6 (cf. the introduction by Jalāl ad-Dīn Humaʾī, pp. "10," "15"); cf. *Abstracta Iranica*, 5 (1982), p. 168, No. 562. We may note here that a figure who is surely to be identified as Rukn ad-Dīn Shīrāzī's son was a disciple of the Kubravī shaykh Sayyid ʿAlī Hamadānī, to whom he related one of his father's anecdotes about a certain Shaykh Muḥammad Tamīmī, whom he had met in Khorezm (cf. J. K. Teufel, *Eine Lebensbeschreibung des Scheichs ʿAlī-i Hamadānī (gestorben 1385): Die Xulāṣat ul-Manāqib des Maulānā Nūr ud-Dīn Caʿfar Badaxšī* [Leiden: E. J. Brill, 1962], pp. 106, 118); Shīrāzī himself mentions in his work (p. 40) that he met this Shaykh Tamīmī (who had earlier been in Shīrāzī's native city) in Sarāy Berke, no doubt at the same time that Nuʿmān was there. Hamadānī disapproved of this shaykh's "yogic" style practices, further attesting to the wide range of figures drawn to Özbek Khan's realm.

143. *Mujmal-i Faṣīḥi*, III, p. 58; Russian tr., p. 65.

"centennial" biographical compendium of Ibn Ḥajar al-ʿAsqalānī, *ad-Durar al-kāminah*, and the other the history of al-ʿAynī cited above. The published text of *ad-Durar al-kāminah* assigns two biographical entries to this figure, evidently signalling two separate sources. In one[144] he is called "an-Nuʿmān b. Dūlāt-shāh [*sic*] b. ʿAlī al-Khwārazmī"; he is said to have been born in the year [6]47 (but two manuscripts give this date as 657 as in Birzālī), and in the mention of serving "Ṭuqṭāy b. Berke" and the "Qān Özbek" as a physician, this entry shows its reliance upon al-Birzālī, directly or indirectly. The date of his death is missing in this entry, further suggesting as its source a work compiled before the shaykh's death.

In the other,[145] much of his name is omitted, with a blank space left in manuscripts; he appears as "an-Nuʿmān b. . . . al-Uzbakī," and the entry states that "the king Özbek, the Mongol, ruler of Rūm[!], was devoted to him and honored him," since he had been with Ṭuqṭāy earlier and had been kind to Özbek. In this and in the entry's rather garbled account of Shaykh Nuʿmān's unsuccessful efforts to build a *madrasah* in Jerusalem we see the echoes of a more complete account given in the work of Ibn Ḥajar's contemporary al-ʿAynī (d. 855/1451), who gives an extended and revealing anecdote illustrating the close relationship between Nuʿmān and Özbek Khan. It is not certain where this account originated; most probably it was found in a part of al-Birzālī's work no longer extant, and was adapted independently by both Ibn Ḥajar and al-ʿAynī, whose more detailed version may thus reflect much earlier information than his own fifteenth-century date would suggest.

Under the year 722/1322 al-ʿAynī records the return to the Mamlūk court of Sulṭān Nāṣir's ambassador to the Golden Horde, complaining of his treatment by Özbek Khan. The origin of his complaints, writes al-ʿAynī,[146] lay in Özbek Khan's displeasure over the treatment of "a man named Shaykh Nuʿmān" when the latter had accompanied the Chingisid princess delivered to the Mamlūk Sulṭān (i.e., in 720/1320). When Shaykh Nuʿmān had described his mistreatment to Özbek Khan, the khan had been angered to the point of allowing his *amīrs* to kill a merchant favored by the Mamlūk Sulṭān and plunder his goods; this act had in turn prompted the dispatch of the Mamlūk ambassador to complain to Özbek Khan, but the khan had ignored his appeal and harrassed him, and had sent

144. Ibn Ḥajar al-ʿAsqalānī, *ad-Duraru'l-kāmina fī aʿyāni'l-miʾatith-thāmina*, vol. VI (Hyderabad: Daʾiratu'l-maʿarifi'l-Osmania, 1396/1976), pp. 161–162, No. 2429.

145. Hyderabad ed., VI, p. 162, No. 2430.

146. *ʿIqd al-jumān*, Tiz I, pp. 492–493 (text), 523–524 (tr.).

his own envoy with a letter complaining that Shaykh Nuʿmān had not been allowed to build a place for worship in Jerusalem with funds provided by the khan for that purpose. The khan's letter specifically contrasted the Sulṭān's refusal in Shaykh Nuʿmān's case with the permission he had granted to the king of Georgia to build a church in Jerusalem.

According to al-ʿAynī, the Sulṭān ignored the message and sent the khan's envoy away without dispatching a return embassy; and in reporting these events al-ʿAynī appears intent upon explaining the cooling of relations between Mamlūk Egypt and the Golden Horde following 722/1322. The change in relations may more likely reflect the failure of the khan's efforts to enlist Mamlūk support in the struggle with the Ilkhanid ruler Abū Saʿīd, a struggle marked by several reversals for Özbek Khan between 718 and 721, noted above; in particular, Ibn Duqmāq records, under the year 722, the heightened tension between the Mamlūk Sulṭān and Özbek Khan over the former's conclusion of peace with Abū Saʿīd, which he justified in a message to the khan by invoking the Ilkhanid's Islam and his entry into the true faith.[147]

In any event al-ʿAynī's account is of further interest for its explanation of the tremendous esteem with which Özbek Khan regarded Shaykh Nuʿmān. The latter had been at Ṭuqṭāy's court and had treated Özbek kindly before his accession; when Özbek would come to Ṭuqṭāy's court, writes al-ʿAynī, "Shaykh Nuʿmān would say to him in secret, 'The kingdom will fall to you, and you will be ruler after Ṭuqṭāy.' "

We thus have in Nuʿmān Khorezmī a Muslim scholar and Sufi of considerable reputation established in Özbek Khan's capital, with direct and powerful influence over the khan himself; in al-ʿAynī's account the same figure is ascribed a role in inciting Özbek to seek the throne. As a historical figure Nuʿmān Khorezmī would appear to be eminently suitable for identification as a "bearer" of Islam to Özbek Khan. But in fact we have no basis for identifying him with either of the figures who in actual conversion narratives are ascribed the pivotal role in the khan's conversion—Sayyid Ata and our Baba Tükles—nor can we identify any of the other figures (i.e., the *qāżī* Shaykh Nūr ad-Dīn, Shaykh Burhān ad-Dīn) suggested as prominent players in the Islamization of Özbek Khan with these two names. In short, there is virtually no case—with one possible exception among the figures met by Ibn Baṭṭūṭah—in which we can link well-defined historical personages with the "legendary" figures linked to Özbek

147. Tiz I, pp. 321 (text), 329 (tr.).

Khan's conversion. This means, on the one hand, that we are working with truly "legendary" figures, that is, figures for whom a "historical" basis is essentially impossible to uncover beyond the simple assumption that there may have been one; and on the other hand it suggests that none of the historical figures found at Özbek Khan's court was sufficiently charismatic to project his personality or even his identity into popular tradition about the Islamization of the Golden Horde.

We must turn, at last, to one of our best sources on the religious environment of Özbek Khan's court, the travel account of Ibn Baṭṭūṭah, already noted in connection with his visit to Nuʿmān Khorezmī's "convent" in Sarāy Berke. Ibn Baṭṭūṭah visited Özbek Khan's court in 1334, first at his camp near Beshdagh in the steppe north of the Caucasus, and then again at the capital of Sarāy; he also traveled extensively in the Golden Horde, visiting the Crimea, Ḥājjī Tarkhān, Sarāychïq, and Khorezm as well.[148] His account provides extensive information on the "presence" of Islam in the Jöchid *ulus* and on the links between Islamic figures and institutions in the Golden Horde with both Central Asia and the more westerly Islamic lands. In particular, Ibn Baṭṭūṭah's observations attest to the prominence at Özbek Khan's court and in his realm of Islamic religious figures whose origins seem to lie primarily in Central Asia, with some from ʿIrāq and Rūm and the Caucasus.[149]

148. On the dates and itineraries of Ibn Baṭṭūṭah's travels in Özbek's domains, see Ivan Hrbek, "The Chronology of Ibn Baṭṭūṭah's Travels," *Archiv Orientální*, 30 (1962), pp. 409–486 [pp. 469–473, 482–483].

149. In this connection may be noted that the places of origin of foreign Muslims suggested by the *nisbahs* preserved on thirteenth- and fourteenth-century Bulghar tombstones strengthen an impression of the Caucasian and Central Asian role in the Islamic presence in the Golden Horde; most names appear without *nisbahs*, and most individuals were no doubt native to the region, but on the basis of the lists provided by Khakimzianov (*Iazyk*, pp. 188–191, and p. 89; *Èpigraficheskie pamiatniki*, pp. 180–181) we may tabulate the *nisbahs* by region: in addition to 8 from Bulghār (and several others from the Volga basin), we find four from Central Asia (one each from Samarqand, Kardar [in Khorezm], Jand, and "Qūrāsān"), and three from the Caucasus region (one "Shirvanī" [*sic*] and two Shamākhīs). As a clue to the wider contacts of Muslims in this region, we may note that there are evidently seventeen individuals bearing the title *ḥājjī* indicating that they had made the pilgrimage to Mecca. See further Berezin, "Bulgar na Volge," and Iusupov, *Vvedenie*, pp. 48–50; and on the role played by Khorezmians in particular in religious developments in the Jöchid *ulus*, see A. Iakubovskii's deceptively entitled "K voprosu o proiskhozhdenii remeslennnoi promyshlennosti Saraia Berke," *Izvestiia Gosudarstvennoi Akademii istorii material'noi kultury*, 8/2–3 (1931), pp. 1–48 (esp. pp. 22–25). I have not discussed here the many religious figures Ibn Baṭṭūṭah met in Khorezm, although many of these no doubt also spent time at the khan's court; one, for instance, Rażī ad-Dīn Yaḥyā b. Fakhr ad-Dīn al-Qaṣṣārī al-Barchïnlïqī (Ibn Baṭṭūṭah, III, pp. 7–8), was in Sarāy al-Jadīd at the time of his death in 740/1339 (*Mujmal-i Faṣīḥī*, III, pp. 57–58; Russian tr., p. 65; cf. my "Bābā Kamāl Jandī").

In the Crimea, where he notes that the cathedral mosque of the city had been built by order of the Mamlūk Sulṭān al-Malik an-Nāṣir, Ibn Baṭṭūṭah stayed in a *zāwīyah* run by a shaykh from Khurāsān; there also he met a certain *faqīh* ʿAlāʾ ad-Dīn al-Aṣī (i.e., "the Ossetian"), as well as Shaykh Muẓaffar ad-Dīn, a Greek convert to Islām from Rūm (Anatolia).[150] From there Ibn Baṭṭūṭah moved on to Azāq (Azov), governed by a native of Khorezm, where he made the acquaintance of an eminent man who provided food and lodging to travelers, Akhī Bichaqchī; he does not indicate this person's origin, but he specifically identifies him as a member of a *futūwwah* organization (II, p. 368; cf. II, p. 290). In Azāq Ibn Baṭṭūṭah was also entertained at the *zāwīyah* of a shaykh of ʿIrāq called Rajab an-Nahrmalikī, and lodged outside the city near a *rābiṭah* named for Khiḍr and Ilyās (II, p. 369).

In the town of Mājar (north of the Caucasus) Ibn Baṭṭūṭah lodged in yet another *zāwīyah*, this one belonging to Shaykh Muḥammad al-Baṭāʾiḥī, also from ʿIrāq, whom he identifies as a successor (*khalīfah*) of the famous Sufi shaykh Aḥmad ar-Rifāʿī. This *zāwīyah* housed about 70 *faqīrs*, notes Ibn Baṭṭūṭah, including Arabs, Persians, Turks, and Greeks, with some married and others celibate, all subsisting on alms; the people of this country, explains Ibn Baṭṭūṭah, have a high regard for *faqīrs*, and bring horses, cattle, and sheep to the *zāwīyah*. This shaykh and his *zāwīyah* were also patronized by "the Sulṭān (i.e., Özbek Khan) and his wives (*al-khawātīn*), who frequently visited the shaykh to receive his blessing and bestowed many gifts upon him, "especially the women," who gave alms (*ṣadaqah*) in great amounts (II, p. 375). The "preacher" (*wāʿiẓ*) in that city's mosque, whom Ibn Baṭṭūṭah calls ʿIzz ad-Dīn, was a *faqīh* from Bukhārā,[151] while a certain Ḥusām ad-Dīn al-Bukhārī was an *imām* and Qurʾān-reciter in Özbek Khan's retinue whom Ibn Baṭṭūṭah met at Beshdagh in the North Caucasus (II, p. 398).

In discussing the peoples represented in the population of Özbek Khan's "capital" of Sarāy Berke, Ibn Baṭṭūṭah notes that some of the Mongols (*mughul*) are Muslims, but he groups the Qïpchaqs together with the Cherkess, Russians, and Greeks as Christians (II, p. 448); among the eminent figures of Sarāy Berke he names a Lezgī, Ṣadr ad-Dīn Sulaymān al-Lakzī, as the Shāfiʿī *faqīh*, and an Egyptian, Shams ad-Dīn al-Miṣrī, as the Mālikī *faqīh*.[152] In the same city he notes the *zāwīyah* of a pious *ḥājjī*,

150. *Voyages d'Ibn Battûta*, ed. Defrémery and Sanguinetti, II, pp. 359–360. Subsequent volume and page references in the text are to this edition.

151. II, p. 376; another manuscript (noted II, p. 458) gives the *laqab* as Majd ad-Dīn.

152. II, p. 449; we should no doubt find evidence of Mamlūk influence in Özbek Khan's

Niẓām ad-Dīn, as well as the *zāwīyah* of Nuʿmān ad-Dīn al-Khorezmī, noted above. And yet another *zāwīyah*, run by a pious and aged Turk whom Ibn Baṭṭūṭah identifies only as "Aṭā," provided the traveller's lodging in Sarāychïq as he made his way toward Khorezm (III, pp. 1–2).

Beyond these figures in various parts of Özbek Khan's domains (omitting Khorezm here), Ibn Baṭṭūṭah provides important information on the environment within the khan's immediate retinue, including remarks on the religious figures prominent there. His information is unfortunately limited, however. Of Özbek Khan's conversion Ibn Baṭṭūṭah tells us nothing. Rather, he attests to his status as a Muslim by referring to him—on only one occasion—as "the great Sulṭān Muḥammad Özbek Khān," whom he styles "the conqueror of the enemies of God, the people of Constantinople"(II, pp. 381–382), thus going halfway in linking him with a feat not to be accomplished and turned into a royal epithet for another 120 years. Beyond this Ibn Baṭṭūṭah notes on two occasions the permissive attitude toward fermented liquor (*nabīdh*) in Özbek Khan's domains, which he ascribes to the prevailing Ḥanafī *madhhab*, once in the case of *būzah* offered at the *zāwīyah* of Amīr Tülük Temür,[153] on their way between Qïrïm and Azāq,[154] and once in the case of the honey-wine offered at the feast marking the end of Ramażān, discussed below. Similarly, he notes with evident irony the large meals brought during Ramażān to Özbek Khan, who nevertheless in keeping with what Ibn Baṭṭūṭah regarded as Mongol custom would not touch the plate of sweets that the traveler had had prepared as a gift for the khan (II, p. 365).

Ibn Baṭṭūṭah also refers, if obliquely, to Özbek Khan's Islam in noting his deference to Nuʿmān ad-Dīn Khorezmī in Sarāy Berke, as noted above, and in mentioning his treatment of the Islamic religious figures who evidently formed part of his retinue, traveling with the khan. Of these Ibn Baṭṭūṭah names altogether five, who must have been of particular prominence among the many unnamed shaykhs, *qāżīs*, jurists, *sharīfs*, and *faqīrs* noted as in attendance at two feasts arranged by Özbek Khan (II, pp. 386 ff., 403 ff.). These five are the *qāżī* Ḥamzah, (II, pp. 386, 398, 403), the *imām* Badr ad-Dīn Qivāmī, (II, pp. 398, 403), the *imām* and Qurʾān-reciter Ḥusām ad-Dīn al-Bukhārī noted above (II, p.

---

apparent attempt to have the four orthodox juridical schools represented in his realm.

153. He was governor of the Crimea under Özbek Khan, and aided Ibn Baṭṭūṭah in his journey; apparently a grandson of his (ʿAlī-Bek b. ʿĪsā b. Tülük Temür) was also governor of the Crimea sometime after 750 A.H. (cf. al-Muḥibbī in Tiz I, pp. 401 [text], 413 [tr.]).

154. II, pp. 366–367; the *zāwīyah* was at a place which Ibn Baṭṭūṭah calls "S.j.jān."

398), the chief *qāżī* (*qāżī'l-qūżāt*) Shihāb ad-Dīn as-Sāʾilī,[155] and the figure usually referred to *as-Sayyid ash-sharīf*, identified only as Ibn ʿAbd al-Ḥamīd (II, pp. 386, 396, 398, 403, 409, 410).

None of these figures can be conclusively identified from other sources, but it is the latter figure who is of special interest for our purposes. He is mentioned more often than any of the other religious figures in Özbek Khan's retinue noted by name, and seems to have been of special importance. He is identified, when first mentioned, not only as a descendant of the Prophet, but as the chief of the *sayyids*, using a term of considerable later importance in this context, namely *naqīb ash-shurafā*; beyond this explicit appellation, it is clear that he is *the* descendant of the Prophet of signal importance in Özbek Khan's retinue, since he could be referred to, as he is in two instances (II, pp. 409, 410), by that designation alone (i.e., *as-sayyid ash-sharīf*), without adding his name. This figure spoke with the khan on Ibn Baṭṭūṭah's behalf; he is the only individual specifically named among the many *faqīhs*, *qāżīs*, *ṭālibs*, shaykhs, and *faqīrs* summoned by the khan's daughter It Küchük (who figures prominently in Ibn Baṭṭūṭah's account and was married to an *amīr* named ʿĪsā, who must be identified with the ʿĪsā Güregen paired by Vaṣṣāf with Qutlugh Temür as Özbek Khan's chief *amīrs*); he is reported, quite significantly, as having been entrusted with the education (*tarbīyah*) of Özbek Khan's second son (and later khan) Jānī Bek, whom he, along with other named religious figures, recommended to Ibn Baṭṭūṭah; and he was prominent among the honored guests at the feast arranged by the khan to celebrate the end of Ramażān.

The latter occasion is of special significance, for it is here that Ibn Baṭṭūṭah implies a special relationship between Özbek Khan and this Sayyid. As Ibn Baṭṭūṭah describes, the khan was somewhat late in arriving for Friday prayer at the mosque opposite the enormous tent that had been set up to accommodate the guests at the feast. When the khan came, still staggering from the effects of the drinking at the feast, "he greeted the noble Sayyid [Ibn ʿAbd al-Ḥamīd] and smiled at him," and here Ibn Baṭṭūṭah adds that the khan "used to address him as 'Āṭā,' which is 'father' in the Turkic language." We thus have Ibn Baṭṭūṭah's eyewitness testimony on the presence at Özbek Khan's court, among the many religious dignitaries there, of a Sayyid of particular prominence, who had been entrusted with the education of the khan's second son, who was regarded as *naqīb*, and who was addressed by the khan as "Ata;" it is difficult *not* to

155. II, p. 403; he is presumably not the same as the Shams ad-Dīn as-Saʾīlī named as the Ḥanafī *qāżī* of Qïrïm (II, p. 360).

see in this figure—whose *ism* is never given—the inspiration for the figure of Sayyid Ata. Despite the available genealogies of this saint, in which Sayyid Ata's father is called variously Abū Bakr and ʿAbdullāh, but never "ʿAbd al-Ḥamīd," it seems likely that Ibn Baṭṭūṭah's Sayyid Ibn ʿAbd al-Ḥamīd is as close to the "historical" Sayyid Ata as we are likely to come.

In this connection it is worth stressing that this Sayyid Ibn ʿAbd al-Ḥamīd, addressed as "Ata" by Özbek Khan, was among the religious figures who evidently preferred the khan's younger son Jānī Bek to his elder brother, the designated heir Tïnï Bek, because the former was "better and more virtuous" than his elder brother. The Sayyid and his associates urged Ibn Baṭṭūṭah to stay in the camp of Jānī Bek "because of his excellence," and Ibn Baṭṭūṭah's account, set down already well after Özbek Khan's death in 1341, includes mention of these two brothers' eventual fate: the younger son became khan after Tïnï Bek had reigned only a short time as his father's successor and "then was killed on account of the shameful matters for which he was responsible."[156] The specific statement that this Sayyid was charged with Jānī Bek's education, together with the clear preference for the younger son evidently imparted by the Sayyid and others to Ibn Baṭṭūṭah, are important to note in considering the later role of "Jānī Bek" in the legends of Sayyid Ata, as well as in interpreting the variety of accounts about the figures responsible for Özbek Khan's conversion and the establishment and strengthening of Islam in the Golden Horde; for it may be suggested that Sayyid Ata's prominence was emphasized in accounts passed down within court circles allied to the partisans of Jānī Bek, while the narrative built around "Baba Tükles" reflects traditions of different provenance. In support of this may be noted further the reports that Jānī Bek implemented Islamically inspired military reforms,[157] and the Central Asian tradition ascribing an important military function to the descendants of Sayyid Ata, as discussed in Chapter 3.

It is also worth noting that in the same place where Ibn Baṭṭūṭah met all these figures, including the Sayyid addressed by the khan as "Ata," the traveler also met the *amīr* Naghaṭay, father of Özbek Khan's second *khātūn*, Käbäk.[158] This figure is surely to be identified with the *amīr*

156. On the succession struggle after Özbek's death, which ended with Jānī Bek's victory, see the account of ash-Shujāʿī cited in note 57. The heir-apparent Tïnï Bek had been dispatched on a campaign against the Chaghatayids, and Jānī Bek conspired with his mother and supportive *amīrs*; a group of the latter met the returning Tïnï Bek in Saraychïq and killed him, and the new khan's younger brother Khiżr Bek was soon murdered as well.

157. See note 57.

158. II, pp. 392–393, 397. Ibn Baṭṭūṭah notes that this Naghaṭay was suffering from gout,

"Nanghïday" who, as noted above, is named in fifteenth-century sources in connection with the Qonghrat Sufi dynasty of Khorezm and linked in the nineteenth-century Khivan work of Muʾnis with the subsequent move of Sayyid Ata to Khorezm following Özbek Khan's conversion.

THE HISTORICAL "BEARERS" OF ISLAM IN THE GOLDEN HORDE: GENERAL CONSIDERATIONS

We may ask, after all, a more general question: who, or what types of people, were responsible for the Islamization of the Golden Horde? We will examine the "popular" Muslim answer to the question in the remainder of this book, but here we may suggest the likelihood of some degree of correspondence between the popular accounts and "actual" history. To begin with, it is clear that the popular accounts inevitably "popularized" the figures ascribed the central role in Islamization: our early sources show us Islamic jurists and scholars surrounding the khans, while the popular accounts portray dervishes as instrumental in conversion. The two types of sources are not necessarily incompatible, since jurists, physicians, and merchants alike were often Sufis as well, but the difference in tone is instructive. Where the later hagiographical accounts are most likely in error is not so much in assigning Sufi shaykhs important roles in converting Mongol khans to Islam, but in linking those shaykhs with the kind of Sufi activity, and the kind of Sufi organizations, characteristic of the later ages in which those hagiographies were produced.

It is worth recalling in this regard the absence of any evidence for an organized, state-supported, Islamic missionary endeavor among the Mongols, of the type clearly and purposefully undertaken by Franciscan and, to a lesser extent Dominican, friars during the thirteenth and fourteenth centuries. The hope of converting the Mongols to western Christianity, fueled by general missionary impulses further strengthened at the time by doctrinal and practical developments as symbolized by the two new orders, but also clearly oriented toward making the Mongols allies in the struggle against Islam (or at least preventing their alliance with Muslim states), was an issue of genuine concern in Europe, especially in the latter thirteenth century as Franciscan and Dominican "the-

---

which he notes as a common malady among the Mongols; Muʿīn ad-Dīn Naṭanzī, who mentions the *amīr* "Nānghïdāy" (or "Nāngghïdāy") among the powerful figures killed in the turmoil following Berdi Bek's murder (ed. Aubin, pp. 85–86; Tiz II, pp. 129 [tr.], 234 [text]), notes elsewhere that this Nānghïdāy was remembered "in the lands of the Uzbeks" for the stoutness of his body (*żakhāmat-i juththah*) (Naṭanzī, *Muntakhab*, ed. Aubin, pp. 98–99; Tiz II, pp. 133, 238).

orists" argued methods and justifications for missions to the "Tartars," with several popes and monarchs actively engaged in the debates. In the Islamic world of the time, however, we find nothing of the sort; as much as Sufi circles and *futūwwah* organizations may have engaged in proselytizing activities comparable to those of the friars, and as popular as dervish shaykhs appear to have been among the Mongol and Turkic nomadic groups in the western Mongol successor states in the thirteenth and fourteenth centuries, we find no clear evidence in the Islamic world either of a concerted or organized effort to convert the Mongols to Islam, or of a clear articulation of the importance of their conversion, whether in spiritual or religio-political terms. The *effects* of the Mongol conquests in Islamic lands were, of course, discussed in religious terms, and those effects no doubt included a considerable rise in social and religious self-examination regarding the nature and meaning of the Islamic *ummah*; similarly, the conversion of Mongol rulers and their realms was noted and applauded, with appropriate congratulations on the enlargement of the Dār al-Islām.[159] But we find no written sources arguing the importance of converting the Mongols to Islam, nor any urging Sufis or *akhī*s to carry Islam to the infidels.

In large measure this absence of organized and articulated Islamic missionary activity reflects the fundamentally different paradigms of the spread of religion in the Christian and Islamic traditions; if the paradigm of carrying the Gospel throughout the world sets the expectations to be met in recounting "conversion" in the Christian environment, it is rather the paradigm of holy war that informs most accounts of Islamic conversion. The "organized" Muslim counterpart to Christian "mission" is thus "holy war," and here of course we find concerted, state-supported endeavors that also spurred theoretical argument; and in narrative terms, as well, the paradigm of holy war was so strong that accounts of the spread of Islam in regions where little or no military activity was involved in establishing the faith almost invariably assign holy war a prominent place in

159. Ibn an-Nafīs's discussion of the Mongols' conversion in the Golden Horde, for instance, cited in part at the outset of this study, welcomes their adoption of Islam and the spread of Islam's borders entailed thereby; but he ascribes their conversion only to the intermingling of the Mongols with Muslims native to the northern regions they had conquered. Cf. the edition and (mostly summary) translation by Max Meyerhof and Joseph Schacht, *The Theologus Autodidactus of Ibn al-Nafīs* (Oxford: Clarendon Press, 1968), pp. 66–67 (tr.), 41–43 (text); and a later (poorer) edition by ʿAbd al-Munʿim Muḥammad ʿUmar, *ar-Risālat al-kāmilīyah fī's-sīrat an-nabawīyah taʾlīf al-faqīh al-mutaṭabbib ʿAlī ʿAlāʾ ad-Dīn b. Abī'l-Ḥazm al-Qurashī al-maʿrūf bi-Ibn an-Nafīs* (Cairo, 1985), pp. 158–159.

the story (this is especially pronounced when Islamization is described in territorial, rather than communal, terms).

What emerges in the Mongol era, however, alongside the paradigm of holy warfare, is a new style of recounting conversion to Islam, one that emphasizes neither *mujāhids* nor *dāʿīs* as such, but rather highlights the role of Sufi shaykhs of various types. Because of the prevalence of narratives ascribing royal conversion to Sufi shaykhs, most of which date from the post-Mongol centuries, it is often difficult to judge to what extent the narrative paradigm reflected the actual emergence of Sufis as "bearers" of Islam to infidel courts, rather than a mere narrative convention based in, say, sixteenth-century realities and imposed upon thirteenth-century events through hindsight. To a degree the alternatives are overstated here; clearly the strong political and social roles of Sufis in the sixteenth century, even if they led to the reshaping of conversion narratives set in the Mongol era to stress the role of Sufi shaykhs, were themselves more than literary devices, and it is likely that those roles were already emerging in the thirteenth century. But the question is worth pondering in the stark terms suggested by the alternatives as stated, both because we know so little of the actual role of Sufis in Islamization, and because our image of the Sufis themselves has been shaped by later sources.

What seems clear is that conversion by Sufi shaykhs becomes the typical "historical" paradigm[160] for recounting conversion to Islam in the Inner Asian world from the Mongol era on; while this may reflect a "literary" development, the literary development itself reflects a new *religious* development in which Sufis are linked with conversion in popular consciousness, which in turn must reflect to some degree a historical reality of an increased Sufi role in serving as the "bearers" of Islam in infidel environments. And, as noted, the clear social and political prominence of Sufi shaykhs in post-Mongol times presupposes historical developments for which often the only sources are hagiographies already infused, in many cases, with the social and religious atmosphere of post-Mongol times. What this means is that we must be prudent in utilizing those sources, taking care not to impose features of sixteenth-century Sufism onto thirteenth-century Sufis, nor automatically to read those features into sources produced between the thirteenth and sixteenth centuries. If we do so, I believe we will find that the Mongol era does indeed witness a

160. By "historical" I am referring to accounts that are at least somewhat concerned with chronology, enough at least to speak of conversion in historical rather than mythic terms, and to ascribe conversion to figures other than the Prophet, etc.

distinctive and quite important new phase in the "missionary" activity of Sufi shaykhs, but that this activity was not yet coordinated or organized within a framework of Sufi "orders"; rather, it was in many cases narrative reports about the "heroic deeds" and "wonders" displayed by individual Sufi shaykhs in the work of spreading Islam in the Mongol-ruled world that lent prestige and authority, at court and among the people, to familial and spiritual lineages linked to those bearers of Islam, thus providing the "currency" with which Sufi "orders" developed into large-scale organizations. That is, the prestige of conversion, as articulated by particular Sufi communities, provided a basis for (or at least a model for) social and political authority and influence that could best be exploited through the organizational structures of the developed *ṭarīqah*; and we should thus appreciate the impact of the Mongol era on the emergence of actual Sufi "orders," as Sufi communities responded organizationally and intellectually to the challenges posed by Mongol rule.

Without here exploring the issue in full, I will outline an argument I hope to develop further in other settings,[161] inasmuch as it is relevant, at least in part, to the specific questions of Islamization considered in the present work. I would suggest that the narrative tradition presenting Sufi shaykhs as Islamizers in the Mongol era indeed reflects an important new development within the Sufi tradition in general during the thirteenth century, but not the development often supposed. It is often assumed that Sufi *orders* were well established as such by the thirteenth century, and that those orders were instrumental in spreading Islam among the Turkic and Mongol tribes brought face to face with the Muslim world following the Mongol conquest. My contention is, rather, that the narrative traditions about Sufi Islamizers do indeed rest upon historical foundations, but were extensively elaborated and codified during the era that saw the real crystallization of Sufi orders—an era that should be understood to have come at least a century later than is ordinarily assumed. More specifically, I suggest (1) that, in Central Asia at least, the Sufi orders emerged with the standard, definitive features of the orders as known in the sixteenth and seventeenth centuries no earlier than the end of the fourteenth century (and most likely well after that); (2) that hagiographical literature underwent a significant shift in style and orientation at the same time, reflecting the political and social strategies of the orders as they competed

161. These remarks are informed by examination of sources on the early Kubravī, Yasavī, Naqshbandī, and, to a lesser extent, Khalvatī, Shaṭṭārī, ʿIshqī, and Ṣafavī lineages, most of these reflecting "orders" supposed to have taken shape as early as the thirteenth century; I suspect that the same conclusions may be drawn from a reexamination of Mawlavī and Suhravardī literature.

with one another for political patronage and popular support; and (3) that conversion stories often played an important role in the "new" hagiography, ascribing to the "founder" of the order or some other significant figure the prestige garnered by winning an infidel ruler to Islam.[162]

In suggesting the later formation of actual "orders" than is usually supposed, there is no denying the existence and growing social importance of organized Sufi communities in the thirteenth and fourteenth centuries; rather, I want to distinguish such communities, marked in those centuries by organizational patterns based on local and regional traditions and shrines, on hereditary lineages of shaykhs, or on the individual charisma of particular teachers or wonder-workers (of varying degrees of "orthodoxy"), from the actual Sufi *ṭarīqahs* organized around specific *silsilahs* and conscious of themselves as distinct spiritual communities based upon a particular "way" of doctrine and practice that lent charisma to the "order" itself, and not just to an individual shaykh. The emergence of the orders naturally rested in part upon the cultivation of political patronage in the centuries following the Mongol conquest, and that cultivation itself in many cases presupposes a pattern of actual, historical influence wielded by Sufi shaykhs among the khans and *amīrs* of the western Mongol successor states. But I believe that that influence belonged originally to shaykhs who, although they may have established local communities of their followers and enjoyed considerable esteem among particular villages and/or tribal groups, nevertheless did not understand themselves as representing an "order;" such shaykhs were suitable for "adoption" several generations later, however, by individuals and "orders"—who may in fact have had familial or *silsilah* links with those shaykhs, or on the other hand may have shared only the earlier shaykh's prominence in a particular locality—eager to show to a sixteenth-century ruler both the importance of paying attention to Sufi shaykhs, as the ruler's thirteenth-century predecessor would be portrayed as observing, and the traditional ties between the "order," now "founded" by that earlier shaykh, and the heritage of rulership that linked the thirteenth- and sixteenth-century sovereigns.

Evidence in support of the actual, and not merely literary, importance of Sufis in bringing Islam to the peoples of the Golden Horde is found in

162. I have developed some of these suggestions, in a specific context, in "Sayyid ʿAlī Hamadānī and Kubrawī Hagiographical Traditions," in *The Legacy of Mediaeval Persian Sufism*, ed. Leonard Lewisohn (London: Khaniqahi Nimatullahi Publications / SOAS Centre of Near and Middle Eastern Studies, 1992), pp. 121–158. See also my "An Uvaysī Sufi in Timurid Mawarannahr: Notes on Hagiography and the Taxonomy of Sanctity in the Religious History of Central Asia," *PIA*, No. 22 (1993).

somewhat unexpected sources: Catholic missionary writings of the early fourteenth century, contemporary with Özbek Khan. In a letter written in "a Tartar camp in Bascardia" (that is, the land of the people then called Bashkirs, near the juncture of the Volga and Kama rivers) in 1320, a Hungarian Franciscan who calls himself Brother Iohanca describes to his superior the missionary activities that he and his companions (two Hungarians and an Englishman) undertook in the Golden Horde;[163] noting that the four friars, "wandering for the honor of God," had found the life of accompanying the Tartar encampments more productive in souls than the life of the cloister, the writer says that they journeyed to "Baschardia, a great nation subject to the Tartars," and describes the monks' encounters with Mongol officials there. The account provides a vivid illustration of the extent of religious competition in the Golden Horde, well beyond the urban centers of Sarāy or the Crimea: in "Bascardia" the Franciscans encountered not only many Muslims, but also Mongol leaders familiar with Nestorian Christianity, and the letter affirms that while the friars were in "Bascardia," envoys arrived from the Tartar governor of "Sibur" (i.e., Siberia) requesting that Latin monks be dispatched there and describing the missionary activity of a schismatic "Ruthenian" (i.e., Russian) cleric, who had baptized many people in those parts. Of particular importance, however, is the description of the friars' "competitors" among the "Saracens": these, he says, have a "sect" especially known for piety, whose "brethren" are called *faqīrs*.[164]

More striking, and more directly linked with Özbek Khan, are the words written (perhaps as early as 1317) by the Dominican William Adam, who in the early 1320s was named archbishop of Sulṭānīyah, the Ilkhanid capital. William's remarks appear in his treatise *De modo sarracenos extirpandi*,[165] in which he calls for increased missionary work among the "Tartars" in order to counter "Saracen" influence and to further the century-old dream of an anti-Muslim alliance between Christian Europe and the Mongols. His account is already of value as independent confirmation, apart from Muslim sources, of Özbek Khan's conversion to

163. Cf. Bihl and Moule, "Tria nova documenta," pp. 65–70; cf. Richard, *La papauté*, p. 96.

164. *Saraceni autem qui propriam legem makometi habent, sectam quamdam habent religiosam reputatam, cuius fratres falsarios vocant* (Bihl and Moule, p. 66); the editor notes that the term *falsarios* ought to be read *falcharios*, representing the term *faqīr*.

165. Guillelmus Adae, "De modo sarracenos extirpandi," ed. Ch. Kohler, in *Recueil des historiens des Croisades, Documents Arméniens*, t. II (Paris: Imprimerie Nationale, 1906), pp. 521–555 [pp. 530–531 for the account of interest here]; cf. Richard, *La Papauté*, pp. 170ff.; Golubovich, *Biblioteca*, III, p. 180.

Islam; William does not mention the khan by name, but from the time in which he wrote, and from his description of the four "empires" of the "Tartars,"[166] there is little doubt whom he has in mind. But beyond this, the account explicitly ascribes the conversion of this emperor of the "northern Tartars" to the influence of the same *faqīrs* mentioned by Friar Iohanca, described by William as "Saracen monks" sent to the khan of the Golden Horde by his Mamlūk ally.

William's remarks follow his enumeration of the four Tartar empires. He laments that the emperor of the "northern" Tartars has recently become a close ally of the *soldanus* of "Babylonia," by which designation he clearly refers to the Mamlūk *sulṭān* as the leading ruler of the Muslim world; their alliance and cooperation, writes William, were specifically targeted against the two rulers' mutual enemy, the Tartar emperor of Persia (i.e., the Ilkhanids). The emperor of the northern Tartars, writes William, sends ambassadors and gifts to the *soldanus*, as well as slaves, and receives from the Mamlūk *sulṭān* "Saracen *facarii*, that is, monks," and others of various kinds, in his realm; moreover, he writes, on account of these *facarii* sent by the *sulṭān*, the Tartar emperor "has lately, along with many other Tartars, become a most evil Saracen, an enemy and persecutor of Christians."[167]

The identification of the Muslims responsible for the conversion of Özbek Khan and the "perversion" of his people as "*faqīrs*" is repeated shortly after this, in a passage in which William complains bitterly about the Genoese merchants who out of greed, contrary to God and the Church, facilitate the contacts between the Tartar emperor and the Mamlūk *sulṭān*. Were it not for the skill and cooperation of the Genoese, he writes, the two rulers could not maintain their ties: the *sulṭān* would be unable to send "to the Tartar emperor the *facarii*, that is Saracen monks, and other envoys, in order to pervert him and his people," while the Tartar could not supply the *sulṭān* with slaves; "for indeed whatever these two, the Tartar and the *sulṭān*, want to send each other, the Genoese transport it in their ships and galleys."[168]

The two writers thus agree in asserting the important role played by

166. William describes these as the "first and greatest" in the east called "Catay;" the second in the north, called "Gazaria" (i.e., "Khazaria," the *ulus* of Jöchi); the third in the south, comprising Persia; and the fourth in between the southern and the first, called "Doa vel Caydo" (i.e., the Chaghatay *ulus*, assigned the names of the renowned rulers Duwa and Qaydu).

167. "*Sarracenos ejus facarios, id est monachos, et alios quoscumque in suo dominio recepit, promovet et tuetur, per quos tandem ipsemet, cum multis aliis Tartaris, Sarracenus pessimus et Christianorum inimicus et persecutor est effectus*" (p. 530).

168. "*Has vero societates predicti duo imperatores per se tractant et firmant, scientibus et cooper-*

these "Saracen monks," figures who must be understood as Sufis or dervishes, in spreading Islam in the Golden Horde. It is of course possible that each writer may have overemphasized the role of the *faqīrs* in spreading Islam both at court and among the people in the Jöchid *ulus*, perhaps regarding the dervishes as the counterparts of their own orders, Dominican or Franciscan, and thereby implicitly elevating their own communities' contributions as well. William, in particular, must have been thoroughly familiar with Sufi shaykhs and their followers through his extended residence in Iran and Anatolia; Sulṭānīyah, in particular, was near a number of Sufi centers of the late thirteenth and early fourteenth centuries, from Suhravard and Sujās to Gīlān and Qazvīn, as well as Ardabīl, and it is not implausible to suggest that he overstated the strength of such *faqīrs* in the Golden Horde on the basis of their growing power in precisely the region in which he was posted. But it seems more likely that these accounts indeed reflect an awareness, in circles directly involved with proselytization among the Mongols and their subjects, that "Saracen monks" were among the primary bearers of Islam to the peoples of the Jöchid *ulus*.

The Conversion of Özbek Khan in the Account of Ötemish Ḥājjī

In the treatments of Özbek Khan's accession and establishment of Islam considered above, we find a number of elements and themes echoed also in Ötemish Ḥājjī's work; what is most important to note about these sources, however, is that every one of them was produced outside the world directly affected by Özbek Khan's inclination to Islam. As "reliable" as they may be as historical sources, and as much as they reflect information and narratives stemming from the Jöchid *ulus* itself, these accounts remain external sources; whether able, as "Islamic" sources, to applaud the extension of the Islamic *ummah* to the Golden Horde, or inclined, as some

antibus Januensibus, sine quibus has colligaciones inter se minime facere possent, nec soldanus ille Tartaro imperatori facarios, id est monachos sarracenos, et alios nuncios, ad pervertendum eum et suum populum, nec Tartarus soldano posset mittere pueros et hujusmodi encenia pravitatis. Quicquid enim isti duo, videlicet Tartarus et soldanus, sibi mutuo volunt mittere, hoc Januenses transvehunt in suis navibus et galeis; et talis iniquitatis ministri et cooperatores effecti, exardescentes ad lucrum et ad pecunias iniantes, ad omne quod contra Deum et Ecclesiam est, et ad omnium Sarracenorum et Tartarorum crimina fautores et promotores se exhibent et actores" (p. 531).

Ilkhanid Persian sources, to highlight the savagery and treachery involved in the accession of a khan whose realm remained an enemy of the Ilkhanid dynasty down to its collapse, the accounts were nonetheless produced outside the Inner Asian Mongol world and give an essentially external view.

For an "internal" view we are in a far less fortunate position with regard to sources, for no written history of the Golden Horde reflecting an internal perspective appears until the fifteenth century at the earliest; and when such "internal" sources are produced, they come not from the centers of the Golden Horde itself, but from Central Asia, where they emerge first from Timurid, and later from Shībanid Uzbek, patronage of Islamic historiographical endeavors. There is thus no indigenous historiographical tradition in the Jöchid *ulus*; if something existed along these lines, no remnant or record of it has survived. What did exist in the way of "historical" production was the body of oral tradition reflected in the historical works produced in Central Asia and Iran. These sources thus often provide only dim reflections of the "historical" traditions preserved among the peoples of the Jöchid *ulus*, but for an indigenous perspective they are all we have; moreover, for our particular focus on Islamization they are of signal importance, for they provide insight into the way "conversion" to Islam was portrayed and understood among the peoples and communities who owed their affiliation with the community of Islam to their (or their ancestors') status as constituents of the Golden Horde.

Of the sources that provide important material, evidently based in part on oral tradition preserved among the peoples of the Jöchid *ulus* (including those who moved into Central Asia beginning from the late fifteenth century), the most directly reflective of this oral material is the work of Ötemish Ḥājjī, which we shall discuss below. At the same time, the Central Asian historiographical tradition of the Uzbek era clearly includes works (such as the seventeenth-century *Baḥr al-asrār* or the slightly later works of the Khīvan khan Abū'l-Ghāzī) which transmit reliable and authentic fragments of oral tradition from among peoples formerly part of the Golden Horde; unfortunately for our purposes, there is only minimal treatment in these works of the reign of Özbek Khan or the process of Islamization.[169]

From an earlier period, other examples of such sources include the

169. Abū'l-Ghāzī's account was noted above. The *Baḥr al-asrār* (see Storey-Bregel', *PL*, II, pp. 1135–1138) is distinctive in making no mention of Özbek Khan's conversion to Islam; on the contrary, it attributes his elevation to the throne to the fact that "he was distinguished above all other princes in the *ulus* of Jöchi Khan" in justice and in "observance of the *yāsā and yōsūn* of the Lord of the World (*kayhān-khidīv*)" [i.e., Chingis Khan] (MS Tashkent, IVAN Uz, Inv. No. 1385, f. 111b).

early Timurid "history" of Muʿīn ad-Dīn Naṭanzī, the *Muntakhab at-tavārīkh*, which almost certainly reflects oral tradition from the Jöchid *ulus* (and often in garbled form, the garbling as likely due to Naṭanzī's efforts to "historicize" his sources as to the oral sources themselves), and the more problematical *Shajarāt al-atrāk*, both discussed above. From the same era comes the Turkic *Tavārīkh-i guzīdah-i nuṣrat-nāmah*, which, however, contains nothing on the conversion of Özbek Khan in its extant form. Between these works and the age of Abū'l-Ghāzī, however, we find an important though rarely utilized Turkic source on the history of the Jöchid *ulus* that gives an elaborate legendary account of the conversion of Özbek Khan; though this work, like that which ascribes Özbek Khan's conversion to Sayyid Ata, is also of Central Asian provenance, its author traveled widely in the lands of the Jöchid *ulus* and collected oral anecdotes and tribal lore from among its inhabitants. The work thus provides a useful glimpse of early oral tradition about the Islamization of the Golden Horde, and its account of Özbek Khan's conversion may serve as a convenient focus for exploring the figure of Baba Tükles and the important assimilation of his roles as "bearer" of Islam, genealogical ancestor, and mythic progenitor.

The Work of Ötemish Ḥājjī

The work in question is the *Tārīkh-i Dūst Sulṭān*, written by Ötemish Ḥājjī b. Mawlānā Dūstī in Khorezm in the 1550s and dedicated to Dūst Muḥammad Khān[170] (d. 965/1557–1558) of the Khorezmian Uzbek "ʿArabshāhid" dynasty. The work's chief value, as well as its major limitation, as a historical source, stems from its author's reliance upon oral tradition; he writes, "The words and stories written in this work are not found in any *daftar* or chronicle; I have written all of them from what I have heard. And it is well known that most of the talk that one hears is a lie."[171]

That the work of Ötemish Ḥājjī has not drawn more attention as a historical source, or as a valuable record of historical legends transmitted

170. See on him Abū'l-Ghāzī, ed. Desmaisons, pp. 234–236 (text), 251–253 (tr.); he was a son of Buchugha Khan, whose father was Amīnak, who with his brothers Berke (or "Burge") and Abūlak (all sons of Yādgār) headed the Jöchid lineages which ruled in Khorezm after the Ṣafavid occupation of 1510–1511.

171. MS IVAN Uz 1552, ff. 37a–b; this introductory section of the text was published by Bartol'd in his "Otchet o komandirovke v Turkestan," *Sochineniia*, VIII, p. 165 (see below).

orally among the peoples of the Jöchid *ulus*, has been due largely to the inaccessibility of the two known manuscript copies;[172] in the absence of either manuscript, Ötemish Ḥājjī's work has been utilized primarily through the usually incomplete and often misunderstood paraphrases of the original work included in ʿAbd al-Ghaffār Qïrïmī's eighteenth-century Ottoman Turkish historical work, the *ʿUmdat al-akhbār*, as further edited in the partial edition published by Najīb ʿĀṣim.[173] The only complete copy of Ötemish Ḥājjī's work was owned by Zeki Velidi Togan,[174] and evidently still remains in his private library; Togan apparently planned to publish the text,[175] and at least two Turkish scholars have been able to consult the manuscript,[176] but this copy remains, regrettably, essentially unavailable.

172. The work of Ötemish Ḥājjī is discussed, with full references, in Hofman, *Turkish Literature*, vol. VI, pp. 72–74.

173. This redaction was published as a separately paginated supplement to the *Türk Tarih Encümeni Mecmuası*, 15–16 (1925–26); it includes only the sections of the work (a universal history) dealing with the Golden Horde and the Crimean khanate. It was apparently through Najīb ʿĀṣim's publication that the *Tārīkh-i Dūst Sulṭān* was known to M. F. Köprülü; cf. his *Türk edebiyatı tarihi* (Istanbul, 1926), pp. 384–385. The unique manuscript of the *ʿUmdat al-akhbār* is preserved in Istanbul at the Süleymaniye Library, in the Esad Efendi collection, No. 2331; a print of a portion of the work from microfilm was kindly supplied to me by my colleague Uli Schamiloglu. In the case of the account of Özbek Khan's conversion, the manuscript's text shows virtually no divergences from the text published by Najīb ʿĀṣim. ʿAbd al-Ghaffār's work, and in particular his version of the conversion narrative, are discussed more fully in Chapter 5.

174. Cf. his "Vostochnyia rukopisi v Ferganskoi oblasti," *ZVOIRAO*, 22 (1915), pp. 303–320, where (p. 320) he provides the fullest-known description of the manuscript in question: it was dated 1019/1610–11, and comprised 75 folios, of which ff. 15b–46b correspond to the text preserved in the Tashkent copy. See also his *Tarihde usûl* (Istanbul: İbrahim Horoz Basımevi, 1950), p. 241, and his *Bugünkü Türkili (Türkistan) ve yakın tarihi*, Cilt I, Batı ve kuzey Türkistan (Istanbul: Arkadaş İbrahim Horoz ve Güven Basımevleri, 1942–1947), pp. 41–42, n. 19, pp. 147–149; curiously, while noting elsewhere (p. 197) the appearance of "Baba Tüklas" (*sic*) in the genealogies of Manghït *mīrzās* and his mention in a now-lost Yasavī hagiography (see Chapter 6, note 171), Togan apparently nowhere alludes to Baba Tükles' role in Ötemish Ḥājjī's work.

175. Cf. Çağatay Uluçay and Martin B. Dickson, "Unpublished Works of Prof. Z. V. Togan," *Zeki Velidi Togan'a Armağan* (Istanbul, 1950–1955), pp. xlvii–xlviii; cf. Nazmiye Togan, İsenbike Arıcanlı, and Tuncer Baykara, "A. Zeki Velidi Togan'ın Kendi Tasnifine Göre Mesai Evrakı," in *Fen-Edebiyat Fakültesi Araştırma Dergisi; Ord. Prof. Dr. Ahmed Zeki Velidi Togan Özel Sayısı*, fasükül 1, sayı 13 (Erzurum: Atatürk Üniversitesi Basımevi, 1985), pp. 40, 50.

176. Mustafa Kafalı used the manuscript in an article, "Cuci sülâlesi ve şu'beleri," *Tarih Enstitüsü Dergisi*, 1 (1970), pp. 103–120, and in his study of the Golden Horde mentioned above (*Altın Orda hanlığının kuruluş ve yükseliş devirleri*); cf. p. 82, where he refers to the passage on Özbek Khan's conversion by "Baba Tökles," citing ff. 32a–34a of the Togan manuscript. Much earlier Abdülkadir İnan cited a portion of the same passage ("ff. 31–32" of the "unique, old manuscript in the hands of Ahmet Zeki Velidi Bey") as evidence of the presence of "Dede Korkut" at the court of Özbek Khan (see below, note no. [10] in the commentary to the translation in Appendix 2, on this question), in ""Kitab-ı Dede Korkut" hakkında," *Türkiyat Mecmuası*, 1

As Togan noted,[177] he acquired this copy in Orenburg from "Rizauddin Fakhruddinov," the famous Tatar writer, historian, and religious figure who died in 1936. Fakhrutdinov, who later served as the head of the Muslim Religious Board based in Ufa during the time of the most intense Soviet anti-religious campaign, was editor of a Tatar newspaper and journal published in Orenburg when Togan obtained the manuscript of Ötemish Ḥājjī's work from him; he himself produced a number of important historical and biographical works, and investigation of these may reveal how extensively, if at all, Fakhrutdinov may have cited or described the copy in question, but his works remain largely unpublished and inaccessible.[178]

The other copy of Ötemish Ḥājjī's work is preserved in the Institute of Oriental Studies in Tashkent, as part of a manuscript that also contains the oldest and best text of Abū'l-Ghāzī's *Shajarah-i tarākimah*;[179] the manuscript also includes extensive genealogical and hagiographical

(1925), pp. 213–219 (p. 215 on this passage), reprinted in his *Makaleler ve İncelemeler* (Ankara: Türk Tarih Kurumu Basımevi, 1968), pp. 165–172 (p. 167 on this passage).

177. Cf. "Vostochnyia rukopisi," p. 320.

178. On this figure see the brief article of Mahmud Tahir, "Rizaeddin Fahreddin," *Central Asian Survey*, 8/1 (1989), pp. 111–115, and Mirkasïym Gosmanov [M. A. Usmanov], "Rizaetdin Fäkhretdinev mirasï," in his *Utkännän-kilächäkkä* (Kazan: Tatarstan Kitap Näshriyatï, 1990), pp. 51–70, and the same author's "Katlaulï chornïng karshïlïklï väkile," *Kazan utlarï*, 1984, No. 1, pp. 142–157 (with the following article, by Änver Khäyrullin, "Galimneng kul'yazma mirasï," pp. 157–164); the importance of Fakhruddinov's biographical compendium, entitled *Athar*, was highlighted by Edward Lazzerini, "The Revival of Islamic Culture," pp. 371–372, and the work was recently used by Hamid Algar, "Shaykh Zaynullah Rasulev, the Last Great Naqshbandi Shaykh of the Volga-Urals Region," in *Muslims in Central Asia: Expressions of Identity and Change*, ed. Jo-ann Gross (Durham: Duke University Press, 1992), pp. 112–133.

179. Abū'l-Ghāzī's work appears on ff. 65a–106a, and was adopted as the basis for the text edition; cf. A. N. Kononov, *Rodoslovnaia turkmen: sochinenie Abu-l-Gazi Khana Khivinskogo* (Moscow/Leningrad: Izd-vo AN SSSR, 1958), pp. 25–26. The manuscript was examined also by George Larry Penrose for his 1975 Ph.D. dissertation, "The Politics of Genealogy: An Historical Analysis of Abu'l-Gazi's *Shejere-i Terakima*" (Indiana University; June 1975); cf. pp. 7, 60–62. As Penrose noted, Kononov and other students of Abū'l-Ghāzī's work have neglected the passage that follows the text of the *Shajarah-i tarākimah* in this manuscript, giving a genealogy that stems from Oghuz Khan and concluding with the statement that the work—presumably not only the genealogy but Abū'l-Ghāzī's work as well, which is in the same hand—was copied "in 1079, the year of the dog, on a Monday in the month of Rabīᶜ I, in Māngqïshlāq *yurt*" [i.e., on the 5th, 12th, 19th, or 26th of Rabīᶜ I, corresponding to 13, 20, 27 August or 3 September 1668; this date is problematical, however, inasmuch as by the standard conversion, the year of the dog did not begin until a year and a half later, in Shawwāl 1080/March 1670]. Penrose concludes from this that a copy of Abū'l-Ghāzī's work was made in 1079/1668 in Mangïshlaq, with a "personal" genealogy appended to it, and that the extant MS IVAN Uz Inv. No. 1552 probably represents an eighteenth-century copy made from that 1079/1668 copy; Penrose was not concerned with Ötemish Ḥājjī's history, but it is possible that this work was also included in the conjectured seventeenth-century manuscript.

material on Yasavī Sufi saints,[180] and all of these works appear to be written in the same hand.[181] The text of Ötemish Ḥājjī's work in this manuscript is incomplete at the end, breaking off in the account of Tokhtamïsh, but it nevertheless provides important material on the Jöchid *ulus* down to the late fourteenth century—including naturally the period of Özbek Khan. First described in 1889,[182] this copy was studied, and excerpts from it were published, by Bartol'd,[183] but aside from the brief catalogue description[184] from 1952 and a recent article by V. P. Iudin citing its account of the structure of the Golden Horde,[185] the Tashkent copy has lain virtually unstudied for decades. I was able to transcribe portions of this manuscript during my trip to Tashkent in 1983–1984; I examined the manuscript again in 1991, and a microfilm of the entire text of Ötemish Ḥājjī's work, obtained following my initial trip,

180. This material includes: ff. 24a–b, a *nasab-nāmah* listing ancestors and descendants of Khoja Aḥmad Yasavī; ff. 25b–35b (immediately preceding the text of Ötemish Ḥājjī's work), a collection of tales about the Yasavī saint Ḥakīm Ata (quite similar to those published by K. G. Zaleman, "Legenda pro Khakim-Ata," *Izvestiia Imperatorskoi Akademii nauk,* 9/2 [SPb., 1898], pp. 105–150); f. 60a, a genealogy of Sayyid Ata; and ff. 63b–64b and 110a–114b, further stories and prayers of Ḥakīm Ata.

181. Pending the promised publication of facsimiles, it may be noted here that the hand of the Tashkent manuscript of Ötemish Ḥājjī's work bears a close resemblance to the style of handwriting common in manuscripts provening from the Volga valley region in the eighteenth century, which remain little studied. These include, for instance, several copies of the *Tavārīkh-i Bulghārīyah,* noted above, and a quite similar hand is found in the Turkic manuscript(s) discovered in Bashkiria and published by È. I. Fazylov (cf. "Un texte inédit en proto-Çagatay," *Turcica* 4 [1972], pp. 43–77 [facsimiles pp. 47–54], and the manuscript published, but without indication of where it was found, in Fazylov's *Fragmenty neizvestnogo starotiurkskogo pamiatnika* [Tashkent: "Fan," 1970], facsimiles pp. 59–69); remarkably close, likewise, is the handwriting in the Messerschmidt manuscript of Abū'l-Ghāzī's *Shajarah-i Turk* (now preserved in the Niedersächsische Staats- und Universitätsbibliothek in Göttingen, cf. *Die Handschriften in Göttingen* [Berlin: A. Bath, 1894; *Verzeichnis der Handschriften im Preussischen Staate,* I, Hannover, 3: Göttingen], pp. 481–482, MS Turc. 22), copied in 1129/1717 in Tobol'sk in western Siberia.

182. E. Kal', *Persidskiia, arabskiia i tiurkskiia rukopisi Turkestanskoi Publichnoi Biblioteki* (Tashkent: Tipografiia Okruzhnago Shtaba, 1889), pp. 51–54, No. 80; Kal' included in his description a brief excerpt from the text dealing with the composition of the work and its author. As noted in the later catalogue description (see below, note 184), Kal' wrongly concluded that the manuscript was copied in 1071/1660–1661, which date is in fact noted as the date of *composition* of Abū'l-Ghāzī's *Shajarah-i tarākimah.*

183. In his "Otchet o komandirovke v Turkestan," published originally in *ZVOIRAO,* 15 (1904), pp. 226–232, and reprinted in his *Sochineniia,* VIII, pp. 164–169.

184. A. A. Semenov, ed., *SVR,* I (Tashkent, 1952), p. 65, No. 148 (Inv. No. 1552/III).

185. V. P. Iudin, "Ordy: Belaia, siniaia, seraia, zolotaia . . .," in *Kazakhstan, Sredniaia i Tsentral'naia Aziia v XVI–XVIII vv.* (Alma-Ata, 1983), pp. 106–165; more recently Ötemish Ḥājjī's work was utilized, through Iudin's article and Bartol'd's excerpts, by Thomas T. Allsen in "The Princes of the Left Hand," and the Tashkent manuscript itself was consulted by Vásáry for his study of Berke's conversion (see note 1). Publication of a facsimile and translation of this man-

is available in the Central Asian Archives at Indiana University.

Ötemish Ḥājjī's work is, as noted, structured as a history of the Jöchid *ulus*, but his treatment, especially of the origins of the Golden Horde, is naturally shaped by the interests of his patron, whose Shïbanid lineage is especially (and anachronistically) glorified in the account. According to his account,[186] Shïban himself was one of three sons of Jöchi distinguished by special honors from Chingis Khan shortly before their grandfather's death: Chingis established three great territorial and tribal divisions within Jöchi's realm, the account goes, comprising (1) the *altïn bosaghalï aq orda* ("the White Horde of the Golden Threshold"), assigned to Sayïn Khan (i.e., Batu); (2) the *kümüš bosaghalï kök orda* ("the Blue Horde of the Silver Threshold"), assigned to Ichen (i.e., Orda); and (3) the *bulat bosaghalï boz orda* ("the Grey Horde of the Steel Threshold"), assigned to Shïban. Ötemish Ḥājjī notes further that the descendants of Shïban, based on this early division, used to boast of their preeminence to the descendants of Toqay Temür, a later (thirteenth) son of Jöchi who was not thus distinguished by Chingis Khan, but who rivaled and generally excelled the Shïbanids in actual status and influence during the disturbances in the Golden Horde which followed Jānī Bek's murder.

Aside from its Shïbanid bias, Ötemish Ḥājjī's work is also marked by a more obvious feature worth noting here, inasmuch as it bears on our evaluation of the work's silence on a key aspect of later elaborated narratives of Özbek Khan's conversion, namely, the ancestral ties between the figure who converted Özbek Khan—Baba Tükles—and the Manghït *bek* Edigü. The feature in question is the work's clear pro-Chingisid tone, and although such a tone is hardly distinctive in Central and Inner Asian historiography—since, after all, with the exception of the Timurid historical tradition, most histories were commissioned by Chingisid khans—it stands in contrast to the often anti-Chingisid flavor of the later elaborations of Baba Tükles' story. Despite its Chingisid bias, however, it appears that the history of Ötemish Ḥājjī had only minimal circulation in Central Asia; it seems to have been better known in the Volga basin, as attested by ʿAbd al-Ghaffār Qïrïmī's use of it, but a century after Ötemish Ḥājjī wrote in Khorezm, Abū'l-Ghāzī was evidently unaware of the work (he never mentions it) and lamented the lack of such historical literature.

---

uscript, prepared by Iudin, was announced by the Kazakh Academy of Sciences, in late 1990, as planned for the fourth quarter of 1991; this work has not yet appeared. [See the postscript to the Acknowledgments, pp. xii–xiv.]

186. Tashkent MS, ff. 38a–b.

Ötemish Ḥājjī's account thus follows the familiar sequence of the khans of the Golden Horde, distinguished only by the originally oral character of its information. The work treats the rule of Batu and Berke, providing, as noted, an interesting conversion narrative for the latter khan. It follows the succession through Möngke Temür and Töde Mengü, reversing the proper sequence of their reigns, but devotes only a few lines to the former; the account of Töde Mengü, meanwhile, is taken up entirely by anecdotes, one a wonderfully comical story illustrating the khan's idiocy.[187] Ötemish Ḥājjī then provides only a summary treatment of Toqtogha's reign before dealing with Özbek's accession and conversion. Özbek is clearly a major figure for Ötemish Ḥājjī, with more than eight pages[188] devoted to his accession and conversion, out of a total of forty-seven pages constituting the Tashkent manuscript whose account breaks off in the reign of Toqtamïsh; although it is not our focus here, we may add that the remainder of the accessible portion of the work, covering the latter half of the fourteenth century, is especially deserving of study, since it contains oral traditions of particular importance for the obscure years between Jānī Bek's death and the rise of Toqtamïsh.

The account of Özbek Khan's conversion in Ötemish Ḥājjī's work follows his account of the khan's rise to power (MS, ff. 45b–47b), set during the end of his predecessor Toqtogha's reign.[189] This account is of special interest in judging the authority of the narratives preserved in Ötemish Ḥājjī's work: in several instances his account clearly reflects stories known otherwise only from the most reliable Mamlūk and Iranian sources. Among the most striking cases is in the mention of Toqtogha's intention to have his son Il-basar succeed him, a plan thwarted by the son's death; this is known from Ibn Khaldūn and Ibn Duqmāq, but is implied already by the earlier accounts of al-Birzālī (who does not name the son) and the *Tārīkh-i Shaykh Uvays*. That Toqtogha had a son named Il-basar[190] is mentioned already by Banākatī and other early sources—sources that Ötemish Ḥājjī quite plainly did not consult. Likewise, in the setting for the final drama in which Özbek seizes the throne, Ötemish Ḥājjī's account echoes the independent versions of Qāshānī and the *Tārīkh-i Shaykh Uvays*.

187. Tashkent MS, ff. 43b–44b.

188. Not counting the additional page (ff. 53a–b) discussing the fate of the golden tent-palace handed down from Özbek and Jānī Bek.

189. The account of Özbek's accession in Ötemish Ḥājjī's work is summarized in Kafalı, "Cuci sülâlesi," pp. 106–107, 110, citing ff. 27b–31b of Togan's manuscript.

190. See on him Pelliot, *Notes sur l'histoire*, pp. 71–72; Spuler, *Die Goldene Horde*, p. 79, nn. 7–8; Golubovich, *Biblioteca*, III, pp. 170–171.

It is remarkable to find these narrative elements preserved in the oral tradition upon which Ötemish Ḥājjī drew for his account. In fact, his version is much more "complete," which would seem to suggest that the Mamlūk and Ilkhanid sources knew only abbreviated echoes of similar narratives, or else heavily "edited" fuller versions available to them; in any case, it seems unlikely that the richer detail of Ötemish Ḥājjī's account should be attributed to his own invention or elaboration, rather than to the richness of his oral sources, since for this to be so we would have to assume that Ötemish Ḥājjī consulted some of these Mamlūk chronicles or Iranian histories—which though not impossible is certainly more unlikely than the conclusion that he is recording authentic oral tradition about these events. This conclusion, in turn, reinforces the notion that the conversion narrative that Ötemish Ḥājjī reports also reflects authentic oral tradition from the Jöchid *ulus* that was preserved and transmitted virtually from the time of the events they were intended to reflect. The Mamlūk and Persian sources thus attest to the circulation, in the early fourteenth century, of narrative accounts about Özbek's accession, while Ötemish Ḥājjī's account confirms that quite similar accounts must have been circulating in oral form still in the mid-sixteenth century; with this in mind we are justified in assuming that Ötemish Ḥājjī's conversion narrative reflects traditions of comparable antiquity.

Despite the striking convergence of some elements in Ötemish Ḥājjī's narrative with accounts of earlier but more distant sources, one glaring discrepancy must be noted. Nowhere in Ötemish Ḥājjī's account does the name of the figure ascribed in earlier sources the central role in Özbek Khan's succession, and often in his conversion as well, appear: Qutlugh Temür does not figure in the narrative in any way, not even at junctures where his role was, according to the earlier sources, pivotal (e.g., seeking support through Bayalïn, the struggle with the *amīrs*). Instead we find the names of two chief supporters of Özbek Khan among the *beks*, and the most likely conclusion to draw from this is that the narratives preserved in Ötemish Ḥājjī's work represent traditions passed down within the tribal groups, or families, who celebrated these two *amīrs*' support for Özbek Khan well after Qutlugh Temür was forgotten. Indeed, Qutlugh Temür—so prominent in many earlier accounts and likewise so prominent in his own time as governor of Khorezm (where Ötemish Ḥājjī's work was produced)—ceases to play any part in the histories of Özbek Khan transmitted within the oral and written historical tradition of Central Asia.

At any rate, Ötemish Ḥājjī's account runs as follows. The khan Toqtogha

("Tūqtāghah") had killed off all his relatives, seeking to ensure that his son Il-basār[191] would succeed him; but as he neared the end of his life and his son died before him, the khan came to regret bitterly his annihilation of his relatives. Then his wife Bayālīn,[192] who had been the wife of Toqtogha's brother Tūghrūl [*sic*], revealed to him that she had secretly sent off her son Özbek to the mountain of the Cherkes[193] to ensure his survival. The dying khan was overjoyed, and sent a large force with two of his trusted *beks*, Astāy of the Qïyāt tribe,[194] and Alātāy of the Sījūt tribe, to bring Özbek back to assume the throne.

After these *amīrs* had gone to fetch Özbek Khan, however, Toqtogha died, and his counselor (*atalïq*) Bājir Tūq Būghā[195] proclaimed himself khan and succeeded in winning support from many princes and *beks* and *nökers*. Ötemish Ḥājjī ascribes his assumption of the throne, despite his

191. In the MS, *īl b.syār*, the same form appearing in ʿAbd al-Ghaffār's Ottoman version; the latter work also specifies (p. 32), without indicating a source, that this "Īl-bisyār" was Toqtogha's son by "a daughter of the khan of Khitāy," but Ötemish Ḥājjī makes no mention of this.

192. Ötemish Ḥājjī always refers to her as "Kelīn Bayālīn"; i.e., "the bride Bayalïn"; here again ʿAbd al-Ghaffār (p. 32) "supplements" Ötemish Ḥājjī's account from an unidentified source, noting that Bayālīn was among the daughters of the "*salāṭīn-i Chaghatāy*."

193. There may be an echo here of a hero's "protective abandonment" by his mother, often on a mountain; the theme, as discussed in Chapters 6 and 7, recurs in many legends of origin, including the epic cycle in which Baba Tükles figures. Interestingly, the nineteenth-century history of Muʾnis identifies the *amīr* "Naghday" as Toqtogha's governor of the Cherkes before he befriended Özbek (cf. Bregel, "Tribal Tradition," p. 369).

194. Bartol'd ("Otchet," in *Sochineniia*, VIII, p. 168) transcribed this figure's name as "Kat-Astai," on the basis of the same manuscript, but the reading "Qïyāt" is clear; he is named also in the Turkic work of Qādir ʿAlī Bek Jalāyirī, from the early seventeenth century, as discussed below (note 203). A descendant of "Qïyāt Astāy Bek" is named in the Turkic *Tavārīkh-i guzīdah-i nuṣrat-nāmah*, written in Mawarannahr at the beginning of the sixteenth century for (or by) Muḥammad Shïbānī Khan, among the supporters of the latter's grandfather Abū'l-Khayr Khan during his rise to power around 1430; cf. the facsimile of the British Museum manuscript (Or. 3222) published by A. M. Akramov, *Tavarikh-i guzīda-Nuṣrat-nāme* [*sic*] (Tashkent: Fan, 1967), p. 266 (f. 119a), where the descendant's name appears as "Būdānjār Bek," and the Russian translation (by V. P. Iudin) of portions of this work published in *Materialy po istorii kazakhskikh khanstv XV–XVIII vekov (Izvlecheniia iz persidskikh i tiurkskikh sochinenii)* (Alma-Ata: Nauka, 1969), p. 16 (based on another manuscript, with the form "Buzanjar Bek;" Iudin transcribes the ancestor's name as "Isatay"). The same passage (giving the forms "Turan Dzhar Bek" [an understandable misreading] and "Gkiiat Asstai") appears in I. Berezin, tr., *Sheibaniada, istoriia mongolo-tiurkov* (Kazan', 1849; Biblioteka vostochnykh istorikov, t. I), p. liv. Ḥāfiẓ-i Abrū (Tiz II, pp. 140 [tr.], 244 [text]) mentions a certain "Aq Buqa" of the Qïyat "bone" as Özbek's envoy sent to Öljeytü in 715/1315 to handle the affair of the fugitive Chaghatayid prince Baba Oghul's raids in Khorezm; the Qïyat envoy is portrayed as reprimanding one of Öljeytü's vassals on his lax observance of the *yasaq* and *yosun*.

195. This figure also appears in the work of Qādir ʿAlī Bek Jalāyirī from the early seventeenth century, as discussed below (note 203); the form of his name as preserved in that later source

status as a "commoner" (*qara kishi*), to the "suggestion" (*vasvasah*) of Satan, and indeed makes much of the indignity of such a *qara kishi* becoming khan (and taking Bayālīn and the late khan's other women as well), but in fact his account may suggest another reason for the evident hostility toward Bājir Tūq Būghā in the narrative tradition Ötemish Ḥājjī transmits, by noting that this usurper was of the Uyghur "clan" (*ūyghūr ūmāqlï*). Although Ötemish Ḥājjī treats the designation "Uyghur" as a sign of tribal affiliation,[196] as it certainly was by his time, the identification of this figure as an Uyghur may well reflect narratives in which the designation "Uyghur" implied "Buddhist"[197] and in which, as the previous khan's "infidel" counselor, Bājir Tūq Būghā served as a convenient villain for an account of Özbek Khan's rise to power—a rise that by most other accounts looks itself like a wrongful usurpation. We may thus see personified in the figure of Bājir Tūq Būghā the strong opposition to Özbek among powerful *amīrs* in the Jöchid *ulus*, and the inevitable narrative portrayal of this opposition as rooted in religious antagonisms; by Ötemish Ḥājjī's day, of course, emphasizing the "Uyghur" nature of Özbek Khan's opposition would hardly have conveyed any sense of religious antagonism or the Uyghur's identification with Buddhism, and it was thus only natural for Ötemish Ḥājjī, writing for a Chingisid audience, to stress the usurper's non-Chingisid character.

In any event, Özbek had the support of the two *beks* whom Toqtogha had sent to fetch him, and presumably their army as well, thus setting the stage for the climactic confrontation. Here, as Ötemish Ḥājjī tells the tale, we find clear echoes of the accounts in Persian sources in which some kind of feast or celebration or assembly is the setting for the decisive blow whereby Özbek Khan seizes power, as well as a possible exculpatory tale in which accounts of Özbek Khan's assassination of a rival are justified by the rival's plot to do the same to Özbek. In Ötemish Ḥājjī's account, the setting appears to be the funeral feast for the deceased khan

("Bāchqïr-Tūqbūghā") suggests an echo of Bashkir "ethnic" affiliation, but Ötemish Ḥājjī's work carries no such implication.

196. In addition to using the term *ūmāq*, he stresses that Bājir Tūq Būghā's "tribe" was "a mighty people" (*qawmū-qabilasï [sic] köp-küčlük el erdi*).

197. Such may still have been the case in the early fifteenth century, a century and a half before Ötemish Ḥājjī wrote, when Muʿīn ad-Dīn Naṭanzī produced his history, for he largely repeats Rashīd ad-Dīn's account of the enmity between Toqtogha and Noghay as rooted in the mistreatment of Noghay's Muslim daughter by the "Uyghur" son of a Qonghrat *amīr* favored by Toqtogha (Naṭanzī, *Muntakhab*, ed. Aubin, p. 77); he evidently did not feel compelled to explain what "Uyghur" meant in this context.

Toqtogha; he describes what he calls a "Qalmaq" custom, noting that "when one of their rulers or great men died, they would come in groups with their tribes and conduct the mourning (*yās*, for Arabic *ya'ʾs*), crying out '*jaw jaw*' three times; in the Ulugh Tagh,[198] that same custom still existed among them." For this funeral, however, Bājir Tūq Būghā had arranged with his *beks* to destroy Özbek and his supporters when he gave the signal, by waving his hand, after only two cries of mourning.

One morning before dawn, the story goes, Özbek and his *beks* were on the move when a man wielding a lasso (*ūqrūq*) rode up from behind his party and passed it; when he shouted out, "Say *jaw* and say *je*!"[199] the first time, no one paid attention, but when he did it again, the Qïyāt Astāy became curious and rode after him. The man[200] told him,

> Bājir Tūq Būghā has joined with his *beks* and agreed that when you come to the gate of the *orda*, after saying "*jaw jaw*" twice in mourning, he will wave his hand for you to be destroyed. If you do not wave your hand and move against him after saying "*jaw*" one time, you would all perish; this was the point of what I said to you.

Astay conveyed this warning, and Özbek's party agreed to act:

> The next morning they arrived at the place where the *orda* was; Bājir Tūq Būghā was in the *orda* seated upon the throne, and his

198. Evidently the place name, for the mountains in central Kazakhstan between the Aral Sea and the Irtysh, is intended here, rather than a generic "great mountains." As noted below, oral tradition from the Dasht-i Qïpchaq recorded in the sixteenth century places the tomb of Jöchi in the Ulugh Tagh.

199. The latter form is spelled simply *jīm-hā*.

200. He gives his name as "Sānggsūn," telling Astay "You will understand it as 'Sūnggūsūn';" there is apparently a play on words here, perhaps signaled by the optative ending *-sun* attached to two hypothetical verb stems *sang-* and *sungu-* , but the forms as implied by the spelling in the text yield no suitable explanation. Iudin (*Chingiz-name*, p. 104) translates the passage as "My name is Sangusun [he writes the name thus, without comment], you will understand the rest, "but the text's "*sūnggūsūn*" is orthographically peculiar if indeed a possessive version of "*song*" (i.e., "the end of it") is intended. Curiously, ʿAbd al-Ghaffār Qïrïmī (printed version, pp. 33–34) gives his name as "Ṣānggūysīn," and says that he was a Qonghrat *bahādur* who served the Chingisid dynasty; his source for this addition to Ötemish Ḥājjī's account is unclear, but despite ʿAbd al-Ghaffār's evident misunderstanding of much terminology in the text, it is of course not impossible that he had access to a copy of Ötemish Ḥājjī's work fuller than the text in the Tashkent manuscript. In any case, the form he gives for this figure's name recalls the form of "Sānqūy" cited by Rashīd ad-Dīn as the name of one of three important *amīrs* who deserted Noghay in his final battle with Toqtogha (cf. Boyle, *Successors*, p. 127).

> *beks* and *nökers* had surrounded the gate. These [supporters of Özbek] came and stopped at the gate; and after they had performed the mourning by saying "*jaw jaw*" one time, they shouted "*je*" and rushed upon Bājir Tūq Būghā. Before he could rise from the throne, Astāy reached him and struck at his neck; and his head fell one step away.

Özbek's supporter "Ālāṭāy" [*sic*] "speared it with a dagger[201] and raised it high," and warned those present not to move from their places; and indeed "everyone became still and remained seated, and after that they took the head off to the *qoruq*,"[202] proclaiming that by this act no "commoner" should ever be made khan again (*qarā kishī khān bolmaq mundïn kesilsün*). Having thus slain Bājir Tūq Būghā, the *beks* raised Özbek Khan to the throne; and there follows a brief account (ff. 47b–48a) of how Özbek Khan, angered by the support given to the "commoner" Bājir Tūq Būghā, summoned "the princes [descended from] the 17 sons of Yūjī (i.e., Jöchi) Khān born from another mother" and angrily rebuked them for supporting a *qarā kishī*; in retribution Özbek Khan gave them and their peoples over to his chief supporters in the struggle with Bājir Tūq Būghā, namely, the Qïyāt Astāy and the Sījūt Alātāy.[203]

201. The term here, *būydah*, is explained in ʿAbd al-Ghaffār's version only as "a knife called *būydah*," as is deducible from the context; I have not found the term in standard dictionaries for Chaghatay Turkic, but Radlov (*Opyt slovaria tiurkskikh narechii* [SPb. 1893–1911; repr. Moscow, 1963] IV, col. 1801) lists the term *buida* as Qazaq and cites the phrase "*buida p(ï)shaq*" (i.e., "*buida*-knife") with the meaning "Qoqandian knife."

202. The phrase here is unfortunately unclear, and seems again to indicate that the copyist did not understand the passage; ʿAbd al-Ghaffār's Ottoman version is of little help here (publ., pp. 33–35, esp. 34 on this passage), for it is heavily abbreviated, and the author appears not to have understood the passage in question either, for at this point his version says only that Alatay "speared the head and threw it outside"! The passage in Ötemish Ḥājjī's work appears to read "*bū bāšnï qūrqūr / qūdqūr / qūrqūd-ġa kedhdūrūp*." The latter term I have understood as a peculiar spelling for the verb *kezdür-*, a causative form meaning "to convey," rather than as a causative formed from the archaic form of the stem *kiy-*, "to wear," since such a reading allows no plausible interpretation. As to the term spelled *q.w.r/d.q.w.r/d*, the place to which the usurper's head was taken, there appears to be no reasonable reading outside of assuming, yet again, that the spelling masks the word *qoruq*, a term discussed more fully below, which the copyist was not certain how to interpret. A possible emendation in the present context would be *quduq*, "well," but it is difficult to imagine that the copyist and ʿAbd al-Ghaffār would have found such a common term incomprehensible. Reading the term as *qoruq* presents the difficulty of having the head of the "commoner" portrayed as having usurped the throne taken to the sacred royal burial ground; but Bājir Tūq Būghā *had* taken the throne as khan, according to the account, and so may have been regarded, in the logic of the original narrative, as entitled to burial there. Iudin's interpretation is discussed in Appendix 2.

203. Aside from the parallel account in ʿAbd al-Ghaffār Qïrïmī's history, clearly derived from

The Conversion Narrative

The account of special interest here, dealing with the conversion of Özbek Khan, begins immediately after this story of this khan's rise to power and the consolidation of his rule; the account,[204] summarized below, portrays the "interruption" of a court ceremony enjoyed by Özbek Khan, occasioned by the arrival of four Muslims—Baba Tükles among them—as the setting for a dramatic contest proving the superiority of Islam over the prevailing "pagan" religion of the Jöchid *ulus*. The text, from the Tashkent manuscript, and a full translation, with philological notes, are provided in Appendixes 1 and 2. It should be noted here that a number of uncertainties remain in the reading and interpretation of the text, and these are analyzed in the notes to the translation, together with my arguments on how I have understood the narrative.

The account begins thus: "The cause of Özbek Khan's conversion to Islam was [that] inspiration came from God most high to four saints [*valī*] from among the saints of that age: 'Go and summon Özbek to Islam.' And by the command of God most high they came to the door of Özbek Khan and sat outside his royal reserve" [*qoru*]. The arrival of these Muslim holy men at Özbek Khan's court was blamed for spoiling a ceremony conducted by the khan's religious counselors. The ceremony is described in such a way as to leave little doubt that the "historical core"

Ötemish Ḥājjī's, these three central characters in the story of Özbek Khan's accession—Qïyat Astay, Sījūt Alatay, and the villain Bājir Tūq Būghā—appear in the same role only in the work of Qādir ʿAlī Bek Jalāyirī from the beginning of the seventeenth century (see Chapter 5). In discussing the descendant of Qïyat "Isatay" named in the *Tavārīkh-i guzīdah-i nuṣrat-nāmah*, Iudin notes (*Materialy po istorii kazakhskikh khanstv*, p. 493, n. 8) that Qādir ʿAlī Bek's work identifies "Isatay"/Astay as the figure who installed Özbek Khan on the throne. Iudin cites ff. 60a–b of a manuscript of the latter source, but provides no information on the copy he consulted; and the text of Jalāyirī's work published by Berezin (*Sbornik letopisei. Tatarskii tekst* [Kazan, 1854; Biblioteka vostochnykh istorikov, t. II, ch. 1) does not include such a passage (the text is clearly corrupt, however, at the place where Özbek's accession should be recounted, p. 155 of Berezin's edition, although "Bāchqïr Tūq-būghā" does appear here just before the evident break in the text). A recent transcription of Jalāyirī's work, based upon both Berezin's text and the "Barudin" manuscript discovered in 1922, clarifies the situation, confirming that this early seventeenth-century source in effect summarizes the account of Özbek Khan's accession known from Ötemish Ḥājjī's work (R. G. Syzdykova, *Iazyk "Zhami'at-tauārikh" Zhalairi* [Alma-Ata: Nauka, 1989], p. 228): according to this version (which omits the plotting and the dramatic confrontation), "Qïyat Istay" and "*čin iut* [*sic*] Alatay" went to Iran[!], brought back Özbek the son of "Tağrilčï" [*sic*], and made him khan, killing the usurper "Bačqïr Toqbuğa." It is difficult to judge whether this reflects actual use of Ötemish Ḥājjī's work by Jalāyirī , or simply the latter writer's access to a similar stock of oral tradition.

204. MS IVAN Uz 1552, ff. 48a–49b; the text is given in Appendix 1.

of this part of the narrative must have described a ritual conducted by the khan's shamans and reasonably well attested from accounts at other Mongol courts; the setting for the ceremony allows us to specify further that what is echoed in the description may have been a libation ritual in honor of the khan's royal ancestors, for the setting appears to be a sacred royal burial ground, also well attested as a feature of Mongol royal practice. The esteem of the khan for his shamans is affirmed in the account: he "considered all his sorcerers and diviners as his *shaykhs*, and, seating them at his side, he paid them great respect and honor."

When the ceremony is spoiled, however, the stage is set for the religious confrontation. When the khan asked why the ceremony had failed,

> His *shaykhs* said, "Probably a Muḥammadan has come near, and this is his sign." The Khan commanded, "Go and look beyond the royal reserve, and if there is a Muḥammadan there, bring him." When the servants went out and investigated beyond the royal reserve, they saw that outside the royal reserve four persons of a different appearance were seated with their heads cast down. The servants said, "What kind of people are you?" They said, "Take us into the Khan's presence;" and they brought them there. The Khan's gaze settled upon them; and because God most high illuminated the Khan's heart with the light of guidance, an attraction and affection appeared in his heart toward these whom he saw. He asked, "What kind of people are you, and on what business have you come?" They said, "We are Muḥammadans, and we have come by the command of God most high in order to make you a Muslim."
>
> At this moment the Khan's *shaykhs* cried out saying, "These are bad people; one should kill them rather than speak with them." The Khan said, "Why would I kill them? I am a *pādshāh*; I have no cause for alarm from any of you. Whoever's religion may be true, I will be with him; if their religion is not true, why was your work today confounded and left without effect? So debate with one another; whoever among you has the religion that is true, I will follow him."
>
> These two parties fell into discussion with one another, and together made much turmoil and contention. At last they gave him their decision: they would dig two oven-pits (*tanūr*) and fire up each

> one with ten cartloads of tamarisk (*süksük*) wood; one person from among the sorcerers would enter one oven, and one person from among these saints would enter the other oven. "Whoever emerges without being burned, his religion will be true," they resolved.

They prepared the ovens on the following morning, and the four Muslim saints discussed among themselves which of them should enter the fire.

> These saints [*ʿazīzlär*] were solicitous for one another, saying "Which of us shall go in?" One of them was called Baba Tükles, because all of his limbs were covered with body hair [*tük*]. He said, "Give me permission; let me go in. You fix your attention on me." The other saints recited the *fātiḥah* on his behalf. Then that Baba said, "Prepare armor [*jība*] for me;" and when they had prepared the armor, he put it on over his bare flesh.

Thus donning what was evidently a chain-mail cuirass, Baba Tükles began to walk toward the oven-pit, reciting the Sufi *dhikr* and exhibiting one clear sign of his spiritual fervor: "They say that the Baba's body hair stood straight up and came out through the eyelets of the armor; everyone saw this phenomenon."

Baba Tükles then entered the oven; "and they brought the flesh of a sheep and hung it over the oven, and fastened its opening." At this point the narrative shifts its focus briefly to the "pagan sorcerers," who grabbed one of their fellows and cast him into the oven assigned to them; when the khan and the assembled people saw that this unfortunate sorcerer was immediately consumed, "their hearts turned away from the infidel religion and inclined to the Muslim way." Meanwhile, Baba Tükles' voice could be heard, still reciting the *dhikr*:

> And the voice of the Baba uttering his recitation came uninterruptedly out of the other oven. When it was presumed that the sheep's flesh was fully cooked, they opened the mouth of the oven; and the Baba, wiping the sweat from his blessed face, came out of the oven, saying "Why did you hurry? If you had held off for a time, my business would have been finished." They saw that the armor was glowing red hot, but by the power of God most high not a hair of the Baba's body was burned. When all the people, beginning with the Khan, saw this situation, they at once

> grasped hold of the hems of the *shaykhs'* garments and became Muslims; praise be to God for the religion of Islam!

The account then closes with, in effect, a summary of the Golden Horde's religious history:

> The Özbek nation[205] had become Muslim in the time of Berke Khan, but after him they apostatized and became infidels. But the great Özbek Khan became a Muslim, and since then the Islam of the Özbek nation has not wavered.

The account of Ötemish Ḥājjī is quite rich, and offers a number of important religious counterpoints that, by highlighting the religious tension of the narrative, underscore the pivotal role and sacral function of Baba Tükles, whose "career" in later tradition must be understood as rooted in the richness of this "original" account. The setting of the account and its structure require further consideration of several aspects of the pre-Islamic religious practice characteristic of the Mongol courts in the thirteenth and fourteenth centuries; these aspects appear often in the account only in evocations that in effect mark a "code" signaling a complex of pre-Islamic religious conceptions and practices. It is to these that we turn in Chapters 3 and 4.

205. The phrase rendered here as "Özbek nation" is "*Özbek ṭāʾifa-sï*," which may also be understood as "the people of Özbek"; while the term "nation" cannot be understood in a modern sense, of course, the distinction between the "appellative" construction in "Özbek nation" and the "possessive" construction in "people of Özbek" is artificial, violating not only the significant linguistic ambiguity, but conceptions of communal identity proper to the context as well.

3

Conversion Narrative and Religious Meaning, I: The Setting

To understand the widespread currency and evident popularity of tales about Baba Tükles and his role in Islamization and/or "nation-forming" in subsequent centuries, we must understand why and how he, as a narrative figure, and the narratives about him, captured the imagination of earlier generations: if we assume that the status of Baba Tükles from the sixteenth century on, when we begin to find his story and his personality evoked in various historical, genealogical, and eventually mythic venues, was naturally dependent upon the currency and popularity of an earlier stratum of narratives focused on his activity in the Jöchid *ulus*, how then are we to account for the particular resonance he and his story held during the fourteenth and fifteenth centuries, when his reputation and image must have begun to coalesce? To a degree the answer is simple, and its obviousness is indeed part of our argument: Baba Tükles was important because he was credited with bringing Islam. But it was the *way* he brought Islam, or more precisely the *way* his bringing of Islam was *recounted* in narrative tradition, that ultimately must explain the special resonance of Baba Tükles for later generations; this is why we must consider carefully the earliest form we have of the narrative tradition surrounding him, and the wealth of religious themes conflated in it.

Our consideration will necessarily lead us far afield as we seek parallels to the themes and fragments of themes evoked, often by only a single word or phrase, in Ötemish Ḥājjī's account; but these themes—some of which survived, some of which fell into obscurity—provided the essential narrative affirmations of Baba Tükles' sanctity and sacred power in bringing Islam to the Golden Horde without which his survival as a dynamic and "productive" character would have been unlikely. This, at least, is the assumption underlying the explorations here and in Chapter 4; for we must try to understand what it was about Baba Tükles and the way his story was told that ensured his enduring significance in Islamic Inner Asia through six centuries. To do so we must begin with all the riches, some more evident than others, to be mined from Ötemish Ḥājjī's narrative.

Story, History, and Religious Meaning in Conversion Narrative

In light of the echoes, in Ötemish Ḥājjī's account of Özbek Khan's accession to the throne, of historical events known from much earlier sources, it would not be entirely inappropriate to seek some "historical core" in his account of Özbek Khan's conversion; it is, however, less relevant for our purposes, since what we are concerned with is not the extent to which certain narratives reflect "historical reality," but the way in which those narratives were constructed and transmitted, building upon earlier accounts and inspiring later narrative transformations. In general, as noted above, the accounts of Özbek Khan's conversion found in Ötemish Ḥājjī's work and those preserved in Central Asian narratives of Sayyid Ata—which place his conversion several years after his accession to the throne—are at variance with the weight of historical evidence from near-contemporary sources, which in one way or another link Özbek Khan's acceptance of Islam with his seizure of power in the Jöchid *ulus*. But this divergence from more historically reliable sources—all of which were produced *outside* the world directly affected by Özbek Khan's conversion—should not deter us from appreciating the value of later accounts such as those of Ötemish Ḥājjī, which reflect indigenous oral traditions circulated among communities more immediately concerned with the impact of that conversion on their own lives.

It would be easy to deride the account of Ötemish Ḥājjī as fantastic and ahistorical, and on that basis to decide that it should be disregarded in attempting to understand Islamization in the Jöchid *ulus*. This approach, however, not only ignores the enormous popularity, for more than six centuries, of the traditions first reflected in Ötemish Ḥājjī's narrative, but fundamentally misses the mark with regard to the meaning of those traditions.

Underlying the supposition that some "historical core" underlies a "legendary" account such as that of Ötemish Ḥājjī is the assumption that individuals and communities are inclined to organize and remember their experience first and foremost as *history*. It would then be natural to suppose that an early, "reliable" narrative account was produced by "eyewitnesses," only to be distorted by later generations. The assumption here is quite the opposite: namely, that *important* events in communal and individual life were more likely to be structured in memory and in narrative with essentially religious language, suitable to "sacred" values, and that the religious language in question naturally included a wide range of latent styles of discourse, from the mythic to the dogmatic; the narratives usually developed within several of these styles, but often tended to become less multivalent in the course of their development (as we will see in Chapter 5).

Far from representing a "distortion" of the sober eyewitness narratives that historians might like individuals to produce and communities to preserve, the later narratives, at least in the literary forms in which we gain access to them, often show signs of an attempt to "historicize" them. That is, the historians and writers who made use of oral material were often uncomfortable with its multivalent character, and often with the essentially religious nature of its language, and so sought to "demythologize" it in the hopes of distilling a kernel of "historical" truth; such an approach, after all, has predominated in most modern scholarly treatments of the later narrative traditions that echo Ötemish Ḥājjī's account, as we will consider below. It is our assumption here, however, that the hearers and transmitters of the oral narratives that underlay our sources were rarely interested in what passes today for "historical" truth, but sought to express their vision of human and communal truths with the religiously charged language at their disposal. We ought to analyze these sources with this in mind.

In this case we must simply accept that, as in similar circumstances in other communities, in constructing narratives expressive of the religious and political meaning of Özbek Khan's conversion to Islam both in his time and among his subjects' descendants, the raw materials for such narratives were not "historical events" as conceived by historians, but rather other, earlier narratives, widely circulated and adapted as circumstances required. In particular, such narratives or narrative themes as we will consider below had been applied to earlier social and religious tensions evident to communities that were more or less acquainted with the chief "foreign"—Muslim or Inner Asian, as the case may be—tradition that confronted them, and were therefore suitable for adaptation to express not "what happened," but "what must have happened." In other words, whoever may have put together the narrative reflected in Ötemish Ḥājjī's "history" was working not with chronicles or accounts recorded for "historical" purposes as in the Islamic historiographical tradition that prevailed in Ilkhanid Iran, but with narratives that, though developed *in response* to historical events, were designed to make those events meaningful to a quite different audience; they thus adapted or evoked stories, episodic narratives, and "floating" themes that were well known to their audience—and therefore accessible and *meaningful* to them—precisely because they were not "original" tales descriptive of "new" events, but were rather reflective and evocative of fundamental verities or of conditions deemed normative or universal, conditions that provided the basis for *making sense* out of the Islamization of the Golden Horde under Özbek Khan.

We are thus not so much concerned with the extent to which the narrative elements in Ötemish Ḥājjī's conversion narrative "accurately" reflect historical events or practices; in some cases they may, but this is not the point, nor, certainly, is it the chief contribution our narrative has to offer. Rather, we will assume that the themes evoked in the narrative reflect religious counterpoints in the meeting of Islam and indigenous traditions, not "as they were," but *as they were imagined* among later generations. It is in light of this assumption that we may fully explore the religious meaning provided by the conversion narrative for Islamic, or Islamizing, communities in Inner Asia, without being inordinately troubled by the lack of *historical* evidence on the links between themes that are clearly conflated in the narrative; the *narrative* evidence is in most cases quite decisive. In the final analysis, even though we may find signs of the "practical" encounter of Islam and indigenous traditions, our chief concern is with the narrative *response* to that encounter. We want to know how the communities most directly affected by the simultaneous confrontation and assimilation of the two traditions talked about the process and made sense out of it, using discursive patterns drawn from both traditions; this, after all, was a substantial, though too little appreciated, aspect of the "practical" encounter of Islamic and Inner Asian traditions, with quite real historical consequences.

In seeking the narrative elements (rather than the "historical facts") that underlay Ötemish Ḥājjī's account, we are hampered, to be sure, by the virtually total absence of any identifiable record of oral tradition, as such, that may have provided the raw material for producing the narrative he transmits; that is, Ötemish Ḥājjī's work is in general our earliest record of what is clearly oral tradition in the Jöchid *ulus*, and we are not better served by the historical traditions of Mongol-ruled Iran or China, not to mention regions left outside Mongol domination.

Nevertheless, we can identify a number of themes in the account of Özbek Khan's conversion that appear to echo elements of pre-Islamic religious practice attested at various Mongol courts in the thirteenth and fourteenth centuries; these echoes, often faint and more often distorted, not only reflect popular knowledge of—or imaginings of—Mongol religious practice, but also, and more important, they reflect popular awareness of—or, as is more likely, efforts to shape popular awareness of—the contrast, tension, and opposition between those stereotypical Mongol religious practices and the Muslim norms whose fostering was no doubt a primary purpose of the narratives themselves as they evolved.

They tell us not so much that Ötemish Ḥājjī or his informants knew of these practices and sought consciously to evoke them in their accounts of Özbek Khan's conversion; rather, they suggest that narratives originally inspired by these practices—or, more properly, by a stereotyped conceptualization of these practices' opposition to or tension with normative Muslim usage—must have circulated in the world where Mongol and Muslim ways confronted one another from the thirteenth to sixteenth centuries, to be attached to events, such as the conversion of Özbek Khan, that sharply and dramatically expressed that confrontation. That this is the case is further suggested by the apparent conflation of narrative motifs known from other contexts to produce the multivalent version of the tale as found in Ötemish Ḥājjī's work.

The motifs we find evoked in the narrative account of Özbek Khan's conversion as preserved by Ötemish Ḥājjī thus provide us with at least some evidence of the way in which those earlier tales and stories, out of which Ötemish Ḥājjī's account must have been built at some stage in its development, must have "spoken to" and conveyed religious and human and communal meaning to their earlier audiences. Taken individually, each of these motifs is only thinly reflected in the "final" version we have in Ötemish Ḥājjī's work, and in view of the absence of earlier records of oral tradition, and of the absence of clear written sources consulted by Ötemish Ḥājjī, there is no case in which we can actually trace a narrative development as such. Taken together, however, these motifs provide a substantial basis, I believe, for arguing that at some unfortunately indeterminable stage in its development, the narrative complex reflected in Ötemish Ḥājjī's account of Özbek Khan's conversion evoked a number of themes reflecting primarily "oppositional," but also "assimilative," displacement, intended to highlight the tension between Mongol and Muslim ways and to applaud, and reassert, the "right choice" made by the khan and his people—who were, of course, understood as the "forebears" of that narrative complex's audience.

In this regard it is probably more, rather than less, supportive of this argument, that the "motifs" are reflected in Ötemish Ḥājjī's account often *without* elaboration or explanation; as obscure as this lack of exposition renders the extant account for us today, it suggests that the mere mention of or allusion to the litany of "oppositional" themes was enough to evoke the desired atmosphere, in which that "choice" would be reaffirmed by the tale's audience. In short, in having only Ötemish Ḥājjī's work at hand, we are most likely dealing with an account that reflects not so much complete narrative expansions of the full range of earlier motifs, but a series of encoded, "shorthand" allusions to themes whose particulars were either immediately familiar to at least early generations of the tales' audience, or could be quickly expanded upon by the tale-tellers, or both.

The "oppositional" nature of these motifs is worth stressing here, because it is precisely this element that soon disappears in many of the echoes of the narrative of Özbek Khan's conversion produced in later centuries. As we will see, the one element of the narrative not only to survive, but to be developed in remarkably productive ways—the figure of Baba Tükles—becomes a figure whose evocation usually reflects not opposition, but the assimilation of Islamization to indigenous, pre-Islamic ways of conceptualizing communal origins and identity. It is certainly instructive, in seeking to understand the process of Islamization from an "inside" perspective, to note that the tension between Islam and pre-Islamic ways seems to be stressed more at the beginning of a community's relationship with and entry into the Dār al-Islām—when the "choice" was a clear memory and a clearer metaphor—but is increasingly forgotten or ignored as the now-Islamic community, in typical Inner Asian fashion, "universalizes" its communal history and assumes, or asserts, that it was always, inherently and essentially, Islamic, and that its essentially Islamic character is to be understood in language familiar to the Inner Asian traditions of the community (now regarded as not incompatible—for how could an Islamic community's traditions be incompatible?—with the norms of Islam).

We may also note that while the narrative themes and structures to be discussed are of primary importance in illustrating how Baba Tükles' sanctity and religious power were evoked and asserted in the earliest account to which we have access, they also, in one case of pivotal importance, suggest that already in Ötemish Ḥājjī's narrative sources, mythic and symbolic motifs employed to identify the *founder* of a religiously defined community had been attached to Baba Tükles. We are thus considering not only the ways in which Baba Tükles was "made" holy, but the specific element of that holiness—its power to forge communal bonds—which becomes especially important in the "historical" and epic elaborations of Baba Tükles' character.

In any event, we will concentrate for now on the ways in which this earliest available form of the Özbek Khan conversion narrative may have spoken to recently Islamized, and more properly *Islamizing*, communities in the Jöchid *ulus*. These "oppositional" themes, which, again, reflect not the "real" historical tensions or oppositions but rather ways of articulating the import of the *change* from and break with the old traditions, are evoked in the narrative through a series of elements that may be classified and analyzed within the following framework (which will provide the structure for this chapter and Chapter 4):

1. The doctrinal and ritual setting, involving:
 (a) The theme of the "contest" and/or "debate" among representatives of various religious communities;
 (b) The theme of ritual intrusion and displacement, involving first the motif of the *qoruq* or royal burial ground, the setting for the conversion, and the "intrusion" into it by the Muslim saints; and second, the theme of the drinking ceremonial "spoiled" by the Muslim saints' appearance, a theme whose form in Ötemish Ḥājjī's narrative reflects most likely a conflation of several related ritual or celebratory practices from the Mongol courts, linked with the role of the shamans.

2. The structure and meaning of the decisive drama, involving:
 (a) The shamanic structure of the narrative, explored through parallel accounts;
 (b) The theme of the oven-pit wherein the chief Muslim saint is tested and proves his faith's power, a theme that again reflects the conflation of a wide range of Islamic and Inner Asian elements; this is the most dramatic and pivotal of themes, and the one in which the "nation-forging" motif is most clearly evident at this stage of the narrative;
 (c) The thematic and structural role of assimilation and displace-

ment, likewise explored through comparison with other conversion narratives;

(d) The figure of Baba Tükles himself, explored in the remaining chapters.

In each case, but especially in the ritual displacement and the drama of the oven-pit, we are suggesting the likelihood that in mentioning a practice or even a single term, or even in only obliquely evoking some aspect of pre-Islamic religious tradition, the narrator was in effect using a "code" signaling an entire complex of associated terminology and activities belonging to the old tradition. Early on in the narrative development those elements of the pre-Islamic tradition suggested by these "codes" might be more fully elaborated by a narrator for a particular audience, or might more often be left without commentary, since they would be immediately recognized by and meaningful to the audience; later, when the traditions were in many cases forgotten, the code words remained in the narrative, with explanations imagined or contrived for them, or without further elaboration.

With regard, finally, to the comparative material adduced in the fourth chapter it is worth noting that we will consider structural elements in the narrative that add to its religious "meaningfulness," though in apparently disparate directions, highlighting two especially striking features in particular: first the echoes of shamanic narrative in Ötemish Ḥājjī's account of Baba Tükles, and second the centrality of oppositional and assimilative displacement in other, comparable conversion narratives. In the first regard, we can point to specific thematic and general structural parallels between Ötemish Ḥājjī's account of Baba Tükles on the one hand, and narratives of shamanic journeys and initiations on the other. These parallels let us understand yet another element in the religious resonance of the tale of Baba Tükles, namely, that the account of his confrontation and ordeal at the court of Özbek Khan is assimilable to the type of shamanic journey, confrontation, and ordeal recounted in an abundance of narratives known to have been widespread in eighteenth-, nineteenth-, and early twentieth-century Inner Asia and assumed to have been well known earlier as well. Second, we will consider the consistent appearance of the structural narrative device of "displacement" in a number of other conversion narratives, strengthening thereby our understanding of how such displacement was used, and what it may have meant, in the narrative tradition whose traces remain in Ötemish Ḥājjī's account.

Debate and Contest

According to Ötemish Ḥājjī's account, the decisive test of faiths in the fire-pits was arrived at by the representatives of the two sides, Muslims and infidels, as the most suitable method for judging the truth of the competing religions; they settled on this method after what is described as an appropriately tumultuous debate, as the two parties "fell into discussion with one another, and together made much turmoil and contention." This preliminary "debate" is, in turn, identified as the result of Özbek Khan's own directive, and is thus portrayed as the royally sanctioned method for discerning the true religion, suggested by the khan himself. Ötemish Ḥājjī's account thus belongs to the circle of narratives that, even if they do not assign the "court debate" a pivotal role in conversion, at least include the motif alongside others in setting a scene of religious confrontation.

This element of Ötemish Ḥājjī's narrative, as incidental as it appears in the extant account, falls clearly within the literary and/or historical tradition of the royally sponsored formal debate among representatives of major religious communities, held at court and convened with the express purpose of comparing the claims of competing religions against one another and, in cases where the debate is aimed explicitly at the conversion of the "presiding" monarch, against an indigenous tradition. Within this motif of "debate" must be included both staged discussions among religious figures and individual interrogations of "holy men" by rulers; the image of the "hero" confronting a ruler at his court had epic resonance as well, as we will see. The motif of debate, moreover, itself belongs structurally in the larger framework of religious "contests" that range from the calm and rational debates depicted in historical, hagiographical, and doctrinal works, to the heated argument alluded to in Ötemish Ḥājjī's account, to the raw and dramatic duel between wielders of holy power of distinctly nondiscursive type.

Examples of such dramatic contests will be considered later. They often fit the pattern of "intrusion and displacement," since they involve the victory of the new religion's representatives, over those of the native tradition, in manipulating signs of sacred power; in particular, those signs most often reflect modes of sacrality cherished by the indigenous community—or more precisely, modes of sacrality *imputed* to those communities by their converted "descendants"[1]—and as such serve the theme of

1. As is most evident, in our case, in the reworking of the Baba Tükles narrative in ʿAbd

displacement when the bearer of the new religion proves more adept, or more powerful, than an upholder of the indigenous tradition, in controlling the very signs of sacred power proper to that indigenous tradition, or in undoing the "pagan" holy man's use of that power.

However, this "displacement" is qualitatively different from that discussed below, where specific ritual is involved: in those cases, the new religion's rites are intruded into a setting of ritual significance in the old tradition and thereby displace the old cultic complex. In the "contest" motif, it is one individual or group that displaces another, and the confrontation is more personal than ritual, pitting holy men against one another, rather than holy rites.

In any case, the very drama of the contests suggests their lack of historicity. With the motif of debate, however, the situation is less clear. It is difficult to judge whether and when the numerous accounts of such debates reflect actual practice or reflect only dramatized confrontations or even literary conceits; certainly in the case of debates or interrogations held to aid a monarch in choosing a new religion there is less historical basis, but actual cases are not unknown. In any event, the very fact that the accounts of such debates or interrogations involve royal figures is indicative of a traditional paradigm evidenced also in Ötemish Ḥājjī's narrative; the image of the holy man confronting a sovereign and being "tested" by him is of virtually universal resonance.

At least as literary conventions, the associated complexes of court debate and royal interrogation were well known throughout the ancient and medieval Eurasian world. On the one hand the motif of the court debate or dialogue between representives of two or more religions was a common format for the presentation of theological arguments going back at least as far as early Christian/Muslim polemics in the West and Taoist/Buddhist disputes in the East; on the other hand the motif of a holy man's royal questioning often serves as the impetus for doctrinal exposition preserved in specific treatises, and underlies a wide range of hagiographical episodes, from the meeting of Zoroaster and Vishtaspa and the Buddhist *Questions of King Milinda*, to the trials of eminent Sufis[2] and the interrogations of figures such as Jesus and Mani.

---

al-Ghaffār Qïrïmī's work, in which the Mongols affirm their worship of fire, and their belief in fire as the strongest and holiest thing is made the reason for the form of the "contest" between the Muslim saints and the infidel sorcerers (see Chapter 5).

2. For a discussion of the hagiography of Sufi trials, see Carl W. Ernst, *Words of Ecstasy in Sufism* (Albany: State University of New York Press, 1985), pp. 97–115.

Such themes were clearly evident in the Inner Asian world of more direct relevance to us, as well, both in indigenous tradition and in accounts by Chinese, Muslim, or European observers. The paradigm of royal interview and patronage is implicit in the reports of Chinese sources on the residence of Buddhist monks at the courts of *qaghans* and princes of the first Türk empire, and in a Soghdian inscription from c. 581 confirming patronage of the Buddhist *sangha*;[3] similarily, the Uyghur conversion to Manichaeanism is reflected in the Chinese inscription of Qarabalghasun, from c. 820, which describes the *qaghan* bringing four Manichaean teachers to his realm to teach the Uyghur people, presupposing his instruction by them in the course of the "conversion" he underwent during a military campaign in China,[4] while an Uyghur Turkic text recounts the counsel and discussion between the Manichaean clergy and Bögü Qaghan, the first royal convert in the Uyghur state.[5] What is worth noting here is the standard assumption that "conversion" and the establishment of a "new" religion are first and foremost matters of state concern; this assumption, combined with the "heroic" character of the holy man tested before a monarch, made tales of "royal conversion" such as that in Ötemish Ḥājjī's work *the* typical paradigm for articulating a vision of the spread of Islam and other religions in Inner Asia.

Closer to the region of concern to us, we find some of the most vivid Inner Asian examples of the "court debate" in the pre-Mongol period. The celebrated story of Vladimir's search for the best religion for the Rus' state in 987–988 allows representatives of Christian, Muslim, and Jewish communities to make their case in royal audience; in this well-known account,[6] Bulghars, Jews, Germans, and Greeks first come to the Kievan court and present their doctrine, whereupon Vladimir sends his emis-

3. On Buddhism in the first Türk empire, cf. Annemarie von Gabain, "Buddhistische Türkenmission," in *Asiatica: Festschrift Friedrich Weller*, ed. Johannes Schubert and Ulrich Schneider (Leipzig: Otto Harrassowitz, 1954), pp. 161–173; Louis Bazin, "Turcs et Sogdiens: les enseignements de l'inscription de Bugut (Mongolie)," in *Mélanges linguistiques offerts à Emile Benveniste* (Louvain: Éditions Peeters / Société de linguistique de Paris, 1975), pp. 37–45; Sergej G. Kljaštornyj and Vladimir A. Livšic [*sic*], "The Sogdian Inscription of Bugut Revised," *AOH*, 26/1 (1972), pp. 69–102.

4. Tr. Éd. Chavannes and Paul Pelliot, "Un traité manichéen retrouvé en Chine," Pt. 2, *JA*, sér. 11, 1 (January–June 1913), pp. 99–199, 261–394 [on Manichaeanism, esp. pp. 190–196].

5. Cf. the discussion in Jes P. Asmussen, *Xuāstvānīft: Studies in Manichaeism* (Copenhagen: Munksgaard, 1965), pp. 147–148, and further references below in Chapter 4.

6. *Povest' vremennykh let*, I (Moscow-Leningrad, 1950), pp. 74–80; cf. Zenkovsky, ed., *Medieval Russia's Epics, Chronicles, and Tales*, pp. 66–71; and Dmytryshyn, ed., *Medieval Russia*, pp. 39–43.

saries to report on the ritual practice of each religion in its "home." The consensus is clearly in favor of Greek Christianity, but Vladimir's baptism awaits the need for a miraculous cure of blindness, while the mass baptism of his subjects awaits the ritual humiliation of pagan idols. The composite nature of the extant account in the *Russian Primary Chronicle* is evident from the variety of themes evoked and the multiple "climaxes," and in this, as in other composite conversion narratives, we find a parallel to the account of Ötemish Ḥājjī. The same pattern of conflated motifs and fused narrative traditions—with a court debate among them—appears especially clearly in the case of the Khazar conversion to Judaism and the vivid account of the conversion of a group of "Huns" in the North Caucasus in the late seventh century, both discussed in Chapter 4. For now we may note that the historicity of Vladimir's court debates has recently found defenders, in the age of *glasnost'* and *perestroika*, in Soviet scholarship inspired by the millennium of Christianity in Russia;[7] it would appear that an insistence on the historicity of Vladimir's "choosing of faiths" is perhaps one reflection, in the Soviet academic world, of the recent humiliation of ideological idols.

After the conversion of the Russians, perhaps the most widely reported case of a court debate staged to facilitate the right choice of faiths in an Inner Asian state is that of the Khazar conversion to Judaism in the eighth century.[8] The best-known account of this debate is also the latest: a styl-

7. Cf. I. Ia. Froianov, A. Iu. Dvornichenko, and Iu. V. Krivosheev, "Vvedenie khristianstva na Rusi i iazycheskie traditsii," *Sovetskaia ètnografiia*, 1988, No. 6, pp. 25–34; English translation, "The Introduction of Christianity in Russia and the Pagan Traditions," *SAA*, 29/3 (Winter 1990–1991), pp. 12–24. The authors insist that the element of "faith choosing" in the narrative "is not a popular folklore plot, but a historical reality" (English tr., p. 23, n. 24); the editor of the journal issue, Marjorie Mandelstam Balzer, adds a note (pp. 21–22, n. b) essentially rejecting the authors' acceptance of this theme's historicity, but perhaps we should rather recognize it as yet another example of reevaluating a body of "historical" tradition with an eye to changing ideological parameters and the need for a new "charter" in an age of political uncertainty. Part (over-)reaction to Marxist-Leninist dismissals of the conversion legend, part reflection (by asserting *historical* reality instead of merely narrative function) of the historicist and materialist assumptions encouraged by Soviet dogma, and part affirmation of the ties between Christianization and Christianity (fought by the Soviet regime) and "pagan" Russian folk traditions (often glorified, at least by contrast, by that regime)—an affirmation intended perhaps to fit into and advance a view of Christianity's role in Russian history suitable for the era of *glasnost'* and beyond—the article is itself a document of relevance to our theme of the reworking of conversion narratives as a process with important political and communal implications.

8. The standard account remains Dunlop, *History of the Jewish Khazars*, with the available accounts of the conversion analyzed pp. 89–170. For more recent surveys see Omeljan Pritsak, "The Khazar Kingdom's Conversion to Judaism," *HUS*, 2–3 (1978), pp. 261–281; P. B. Golden, "Khazaria and Judaism," *AEMA*, 3 (1983), pp. 127–156; and the discussions of Norman Golb

ized dialogue between Christian, Muslim, and Jew was used by the illustrious theologian Judah Halevi in the twelfth century both as a purportedly historical account of the eighth-century Khazar conversion to Judaism and as a literary device to structure his defense of his faith, the *Kitāb al-Khazarī*.[9] Despite its clear adoption as a literary device in this particular work, the motif of a religious debate among Christians, Jews, and Muslims, staged by the Khazar ruler as a method for choosing a faith, appears in accounts of Khazar Judaism in two Hebrew accounts written well before Halevi's work,[10] as well as in one eleventh-century Arabic account.[11] These widespread and evidently independent attestations would seem to support the historicity of some kind of court debate,[12] but, more important, clearly suggest the currency of tales recounting the conversion and originating among the Khazar Jewish community itself.[13]

Here it is certainly of interest, for comparative purposes, that such accounts made their way, through travelers' reports and correspondence (and in this case the "authenticity" of the Khazar correspondence is hardly relevant), to Jewish communities outside the Khazar state and to the Muslim world as well. What is of interest in the present discussion, however, is not only the transmission of an original narrative into various sources and in

---

and Omeljan Pritsak in their *Khazarian Hebrew Documents of the Tenth Century* (Ithaca: Cornell University Press, 1982). As Dunlop discusses (pp. 84–86), Muslim sources record the conversion of the Khazar "*khāqān*" to Islam in 737 (i.e., prior to the adoption of Judaism), following his defeat by Arab armies, noting religious discussions between the Khazar ruler and two *faqīhs* sent to instruct him; it is difficult to judge whether this account obliquely attests to a "historical core" in the story of religious debates at the Khazar court, a suggestion Dunlop finds attractive, or merely reflects the theme of "royal interview" used by Muslim authors.

9. Halevi's work (the Hebrew translation bears the title *Sefer ha-Kuzari*) is available in English translations by Hartwig Hirschfeld, *The Book of Kuzari by Judah Hallevi* (New York: Pardes, 1946), and Henry Slonimsky, *The Kuzari (Kitab al-Khazari) of Judah Halevi (12th Century)* (New York: Schocken Books, 1964).

10. These are the correspondence of Ḥasdai b. Shaprut and the Khazar "King Joseph," and the fragmentary text found in the Cairo Geniza and known variously as the "Cambridge document" (from its present location) and the "Schechter text" (from its first editor); cf. Dunlop, *History of the Jewish Khazars*, pp. 125–155, 155–169; Pritsak, "The Khazar Kingdom's Conversion to Judaism," pp. 272–276; and see the reedition and translation of the Schechter text in Golb and Pritsak, *Khazarian Hebrew Documents*.

11. That of al-Bakrī (d. 487/1094), which probably goes back to a lost work of al-Masʿūdī written at least a century and a half earlier; cf. Dunlop, *History of the Jewish Khazars*, p. 90.

12. The latest specialist to evaluate the multiple issues involved in the question of Khazar Judaism, Peter Golden, appears to accept the historicity of such debates as part of a slow and gradual "process" of conversion, writing of "this gradual and unspectacular spread of Judaism, apparently highlighted by formal religious debates at the Qağanal court" ("Khazaria and Judaism," p. 135).

13. Pritsak ("The Khazar Kingdom's Conversion to Judaism," p. 276) highlights the value of

several forms (some garbled, some purposely adapted, as is clear in al-Bakrī's account of the Jew having the Muslim poisoned to prevent the latter's otherwise inevitable victory), but, again, the incorporation of the element of court debate or religious contest within a larger narrative that evokes also other themes (e.g., the cave theme discussed below); it is this situation that mirrors the narrative of Ötemish Ḥājjī in its brief and "coded" evocation of a series of pregnant themes. Other conversion narratives discussed below likewise parallel Ötemish Ḥājjī's account in joining a number of themes, suggesting both the conflation of multiple narrative traditions, and the capacity of brief allusions to signal a host of narrative associations.

Of primary importance among Inner Asian conversion narratives is one set in the eighth century, but recorded only in the thirteenth century (thus perhaps reflecting motifs drawn from Mongol tradition); we will discuss its larger significance below. This is Juvaynī's account of the conversion of the Uyghur ruler Būqū Khan: as problematic as his account may be,[14] Juvaynī affirms the topos of contest and conversion, noting that the khan staged a debate between Buddhist monks he invited from China and the native shamans (*qam*) with the aim of adopting the religion of the victorious party; the monks recited certain religious texts (*nom* is the term used, a Turkic equivalent of the Buddhist term *dharma* used as a designation for sacred texts), whereupon "the *qam* were completely dumbfounded" and the Uyghurs "adopted idolatry as their religion."[15] Juvaynī's account is also of interest for implying a foreshadowing of the conversion in the khan's dream of an old man dressed in white,[16] and for providing evidence, in his account of the maiden who visited the khan by night through the smoke-hole in his tent and took him to the mountain called Aq-Tagh,[17] of the attachment of indigenous Inner Asian signs of sacredness to the figure—Būqū Khān—revered for his conversion to a foreign

the Cambridge document as "an indigenously Jewish account, rather than a proselytic one."

14. Juvaynī portrays this as a conversion to Buddhism (i.e., to the religion of the *toyins*, Buddhist monks, invited from China), which is historically mistaken (since the ruler with whom "Būqū Khan" is certainly to be identified, the eighth-century Uyghur *qaghan* called Bögü, converted in fact to Manichaeanism), although quite sound from the tendentious perspective that by rights characterizes conversion narratives (since it reflects the Buddhist status of the Uyghurs in Juvaynī's day); see further on this account J. Marquart, "Čuwainī's Bericht über die Bekehrung der Uiguren," *Sitzungsberichte der Königlich Preussischen Akademie der Wissenschaften* (Berlin), 27 (1912), pp. 486–502.

15. Juvaynī, tr. Boyle, I, pp. 59–60.

16. Juvaynī/Boyle, I, p. 58.

17. Juvaynī/Boyle, I, p. 57. The account, which has the khan converse with the maiden every night until dawn for over seven years and receive from her a promise of great power on the last

faith, a pattern evident also in the case of Baba Tükles, as we shall see.

The Mongol era produced an abundance of accounts of court debates and royal interrogations: best known, and of quite likely historicity, are Rubruck's accounts of his audiences with the great khan Möngke and of the debates arranged for the khan pitting Rubruck against Nestorian Christians, Buddhist monks, and Muslims.[18] Also celebrated, but of questionable historicity, are the Buddhist-Taoist debates supposedly convened by Qubilay in 1258, before his accession to the throne, to choose a "winner" for the benefits of state patronage.[19] Similar accounts in Muslim literature of the Mongol era are less well known, but they do exist; the historian Rashīd ad-Dīn left an account of his religious discussions with the Ilkhanid ruler Öljeytü, and we have also a brief personal account of the "interview" by Öljeytü's brother Ghāzān of the Sufi shaykh Ṣadr ad-Dīn Ibrāhīm Ḥammūyī. Both royal interrogation and court debates are recorded in the case of the famous Sufi ʿAlāʾ ad-Dawlah Simnānī, who left descriptions of his doctrinal debates with Buddhist monks, encounters arranged by Simnānī's patron Arghun.

In these latter cases there is little reason to doubt the historicity of the debate or interview; the Mongol era also inspired numerous accounts, however, especially in Christian literature, in which it is just as clear that the debate or interview was no more than a literary device, as in several works of the Catalan mystic Ramón Lull (who used a pagan but earnest "Tartar" seeking the true religion—now as a foil, now as a participant—in narrating a theological dialogue among a Christian, a Jew, and a "Saracen," a device aimed both at demonstrating the victory of Lull's own faith and at inspiring his coreligionists to missionary work among the Mongols).[20]

Both the actual religious debates in the presence of Inner Asian rulers,

---

night when they say farewell, is uncannily reminiscent of one of the legends of origin of the Türks known from Chinese sources, as discussed in Chapter 7; only the site of the meeting (a mountain instead of an underwater cave—which are assimilable, after all) differs, and the story of human sacrifice following the Türk legend is omitted in this account.

18. For reflections on these audiences and debates, and of Qubilay's religious discussions with the Polos (with, however, the familiar assumptions of "Mongol tolerance"), see Leonardo Olschki, *Marco Polo's Asia: An Introduction to his "Description of the World" called "Il Milione"* (Berkeley and Los Angeles: University of California Press, 1960), pp. 178–189.

19. On the Buddhist-Taoist debates at the Mongol court of China, see E. Chavannes, "Inscriptions et pièces de chancellerie chinoises de l'époque mongole," *T'oung pao*, sér. II, 5 (1904), pp. 357–447, esp. pp. 366–404; and now Morris Rossabi, *Khubilai Khan: His Life and Times* (Berkeley and Los Angeles: University of California Press, 1988), pp. 37–43, with further references.

20. Lull wrote a "Book of the Gentile and the Three Wise Men," in 1272 or 1273, and later a

and their fictional counterparts narrated for didactic purposes, attest to the currency of expectations that the conversion of monarchs would entail debate and argument over religious dogma. To an extent the inclusion of this element in conversion narratives stands as an advertisement for scholastic theology, but we should not lose sight of how often the simpler and more dramatic "arguments" for the faith far outshine any religious disputation; such is certainly the case in Ötemish Ḥājjī's narrative.

These simpler arguments are the religious contests with which so many Inner Asian conversion narratives reach their climax. The specific contest of Ötemish Ḥājjī's narrative—the episode of the fire-pit—is discussed more fully below, together with other conversion narratives employing that same motif. Here we may simply call attention to a number of other conversion narratives, of Inner Asian provenance, employing the religious "contest" as the decisive event of the story.

These include the following already well-known cases:

1. the account of the Chaghatayid khan Tughluq Temür's conversion to Islam in the mid-fourteenth century, preserved in Mīrzā Muḥammad Ḥaydar Dūghlāt's sixteenth-century *Tārīkh-i Rashīdī*, involving a wrestling match between the Sufi Islamizer and a Mongol hero;[21]

2. implicit contests, resulting in mass conversion, between Sufi

---

"Book of the Tartar and the Christian," in 1285 or 1286, both cast as debates among representatives of the three major Western traditions in the presence of an outsider whose character is clearly inspired by the appearance of the non-Christian, non-Muslim, non-Jewish Mongols; cf. E. Allison Peers, *Ramon Lull: A Biography* (London: Society for Promoting Christian Knowledge, 1929), pp. 83–97, 197–200; Raymundus Lullus, *Liber Tartari et Christiani*, in his *Opera* (Frankfurt am Main: Minerva, 1965; reprint of the Mainz edition of 1737), IV, pp. 347–376; and see my "The Influence of the Mongols on the Religious Consciousness of Thirteenth Century Europe," *Mongolian Studies*, 5 (1978–79), pp. 41–78 [pp. 60–70]. A later example of a similar literary device is found in the *De Pace Fidei* of Nicholas of Cusa (d. 1464), where representatives of a wider range of peoples—French, Spanish, Italians, Germans, Greeks, Arabs, Indians, "Chaldeans," Jews, Syrians, Persians, Turks, and "Tartars"—discuss the unity and diversity of the world's religions; cf. Etienne Gilson, *Les métamorphoses de la Cité de Dieu* (Paris: Librairie Philosophique J. Vrin, 1952), pp. 154–181.

21. Cf. N. Elias and E. Denison Ross, *A History of the Moghuls of Central Asia, being the Tarikh-i-Rashidi of Mirza Muhammad Haidar, Dughlát* (2nd ed., London, 1898; repr. London: Curzon Press / New York: Barnes and Noble, 1972), pp. 10–15 for the conversion story; this account follows the pattern discussed below, of an initial acceptance of Islam, a subsequent challenge, and a decisive demonstration of the new faith's power in the dramatic contest. We may note here that L. I. Alishanina and F. B. Inoiatova, "Toponim Uzbekistan," in *Onomastika Srednei Azii*, 2 (Frunze: Ilim, 1980), pp. 226–230, describe a similar wrestling contest as the decisive event in the conversion of an unnamed khan of the Golden Horde, citing the Russian translation of Jean-François de La Harpe's *Abrégé de l'Histoire générale des voyages* (Paris, 1780–1801), itself based upon Antoine

shaykhs and Qïrghïz infidels, recorded in the seventeenth-century Naqshbandī hagiography *Żiyāʾ al-qulūb*, involving in one case the Sufi's calm fearlessness before a warrior who is about to slay him but instead falls from his horse and dies, and in another the Sufi's cure, through prayer, of a sick Qïrghïz chief whose people had been unable to cure him by offerings of food to a silver idol hanging from a tree;[22]

3. the "contest" between a missionary bishop and "pagan sorcerers" in an account of the conversion to Christianity of a group of "Huns" in the North Caucasus in 682 (discussed below in connection with the theme of "assimilative displacement");

4. the "healing competition" in an account of the conversion of the Bulghars to Islam reported in a twelfth-century travel account and echoed with further developments in a late eighteenth-century Turkic "history" of Bulghār, referred to earlier.[23]

The theme of the contest is perhaps starker, appearing in tandem with the theme of "displacement," in the brief report on the adoption of Christianity by an unspecified Turkic people in 644, preserved in an anonymous Syriac chronicle of the late seventh century; in this account, a Turkic ruler's "priests" conjured up a violent storm with clouds, winds, thunder, and lightning, a clear case of the activities of the shamanlike *yadachï* who wielded the fabled "rain-stone" to produce storms;[24] when

---

François Prévost d'Exiles' *Histoire générale des voyages* (Paris, 1746–1789); this work is clearly based, however, upon the account known from the *Tārīkh-i Rashīdī*, as confirmed by the name assigned to the Chingisid khan who converts ("Togalak"), and the story has nothing to do with the Golden Horde (cf. *Istoriia o stranstviiakh voobshche po vsem kraiam zemnago kruga* [Moscow, 1782–1787], "book 5," in vol. 8, pp. 602–603).

22. Cf. Joseph Fletcher, "Confrontations between Muslim Missionaries and Nomad Unbelievers in the Late Sixteenth Century: Notes on Four Passages from the 'Ḍiyāʾ al-Qulūb,'" in *Tractata Altaica: Denis Sinor sexagenario optime de rebus altaicis merito dedicata* (Wiesbaden: Otto Harrassowitz, 1976), pp. 167–174, esp. episodes 2 and 3, pp. 171–172; episode 4, p. 172, involving a fire "contest," is discussed in Chapter 4.

23. The motif of the miraculous healing of a ruler (or a ruler's daughter or son, etc.), which implies a "healing contest" insofar as the representatives of the indigenous religion are unable to effect a cure, also appears in the eighteenth-century legends about Sayyid Ata and his conversion of Özbek Khan, alluded to in Chapter 2; in the account of Russia's adoption of Christianity under Vladimir, noted above; and in the legend of a Mongol prince converted to Russian Christianity following a bishop's miraculous healing of the khan Berke's son (on the latter tale, see the discussion in Jaroslaw Pelenski, *Russia and Kazan: Conquest and Imperial Ideology (1438–1560s)* (The Hague/Paris: Mouton, 1974), pp. 256–259, and a fuller treatment by Charles J. Halperin, "A Chingissid Saint of the Russian Orthodox Church: 'The Life of Peter, *Tsarevich* of the Horde,'" *Canadian-American Slavic Studies*, 9/3 (1975), pp. 324–335.

24. On the "rain-stone" in Inner Asia, which still awaits a thorough study, see the note by

the Nestorian metropolitan was able to disperse the storm by making the sign of the cross, however, the ruler understood the power of the "new" religion and became a Christian.

> . . . the king said to him, "If thou showest to me a sign similar to those shown by the priests of my gods, I shall believe in thy God." And the king ordered the priests of the demons who were accompanying him, and they invoked the demons whom they were worshipping, and immediately the sky was covered with clouds, and a hurricane of wind, thunder, and lightning followed. Elijah was then moved by divine power, and he made the sign of the heavenly cross, and rebuked the unreal thing that the rebellious demons had set up, and it forthwith disappeared completely. When the king saw what Saint Elijah did, he fell down and worshipped him, and he was converted with all his army. The saint took them to a stream, baptised all of them, ordained for them priests and deacons, and returned to this country.[25]

Here a raw demonstration of sacred power—couched in this case as mastery of the weather rather than power over fire as in the Baba Tükles legend, or physical strength as in the *Tārīkh-i Rashīdī*—seals the establishment of the new religion, and although the theme of "contest" predominates, the links between communal identification and "mastery of the wind and rain"[26] among the Türks of the sixth and seventh centuries may

---

Quatremère in his *Histoire des Mongols de la Perse* (Paris, 1836; repr. Amsterdam: Oriental Press, 1968), pp. 428–440, and M. F. Köprülü ["Keuprulu Zadé Mehmed Fuad Bey"], "Une institution magique chez les anciens Turcs: Yat," in *Actes du Congrès International d'Histoire des Religions* (Paris, 1923), t. 2 (Paris: Librairie ancienne Honoré Champion, 1925), pp. 440–451; cf. also Boyle, "Turkish and Mongol Shamanism," pp. 187–193, S. E. Malov, "Shamanskii kamen' "iada" u tiurkov zapadnogo Kitaia," *Sovetskaia ètnografiia*, 1947, No. 1, pp. 151–160, and the recent review of Adam Molnár, "Qām, Yātčï and Bügü: Notes on Old Turkic Shamanism," in *Beşinci Milletler Arası Türkoloji Kongresi* (İstanbul, 1985), *Tebliğler*, I. Türk Dili, cilt 1 (Istanbul: Edebiyat Fakültesi Basımevi, 1985), pp. 197–204.

25. Tr. A. Mingana in his survery, "The Early Spread of Christianity in Central Asia and the Far East: A New Document," *Bulletin of the John Rylands Library*, 9 (1925), pp. 297–371 [pp. 305–306]; cf. Nöldeke's somewhat more sober translation, "Die von Guidi herausgegebene syrische Chronik, übersetzt und kommentiert," *Sitzungsberichte der Wiener Akademie der Wissenschaften*, 128 (1893), No. 9, pp. 1–48 [p. 40], as well as Erica C. D. Hunter, "The Conversion of the Kerait to Christianity in A.D. 1007," *ZAS*, 22 (1989–1991), pp. 143–163 [p. 160], and, on the source, K. Czeglédy, "Monographs on Syriac and Muhammadan Sources in the Literary Remains of M. Kmoskó," *AOH*, 4 (1955), pp. 19–90 [pp. 44–45, 58].

26. Medieval Islamic accounts of the rain-stone assign "proprietary" rights to this magic to

be recalled as well, to lend this contest and displacement some communal ritual signficance.

As a final example of Inner Asian evocations of both the "debate" and "contest" motifs we may note a late popular legend of origin among the Dungans.[27] In the legend,[28] the Dungans are portrayed as descendants of a group of Arabs, led by a figure identifiable with Saʿd b. Waqqāṣ (whose name appears as Vankhas or Seid al-Vakhas), who were invited to China by the T'ang emperor T'ai-tsung following a frightening dream: he saw himself chased by a dragon[29] or hideous monster in his palace, and res-

particular Turkic peoples, most often the Oghuz; similarly, the theme of "power over wind and rain" figures in a legend of origin reported for the sixth-century Türks, as discussed in Chapter 7.

27. The Dungans are Chinese-speaking Muslims of Central Asia, dwelling primarily in the former Soviet republics of Kyrgyzstan and Kazakhstan and adjacent areas of the People's Republic of China.

28. The versions of the Dungan legend are discussed in Svetlana Rimsky-Korsakoff Dyer, "T'ang T'ai-tsung's Dream: A Soviet Dungan Version of a Legend on the Origin of the Chinese Muslims," *Monumenta Serica*, 35 (1981–1983), pp. 545–570; in addition to the version of this legend which she gives in full (pp. 552–560), she describes two others recorded in the early 1940s among Soviet Dungans in the Kazakh, Kirgiz, and Uzbek republics (p. 551), and another version recorded in Kazakhstan a decade earlier (pp. 564–565). The legend also appears in Chinese versions known to early students of Islam in China (cf. p. 554, n. 24), which Dyer discusses only for comparison with the Soviet Dungan versions. Her treatment tends to focus on the "historicity" of the legends, but she observes that these tales, which "the Dungan people seem to treasure" (p. 565), can "provide us with insights about the people who have created them and about the needs they satisfy" (p. 547); she also highlights the rhetorical excesses of Soviet specialists intent upon portraying the legend as the creation of "Muslim reactionary clergy and Dungan feudal lords," designed to strengthen "ideas of pan-Islamism, religious fanaticism and nationalism" (pp. 565–566, citing M. Sushanlo, *Dungane (istoriko-ètnograficheskii ocherk* [Frunze: Ilim, 1971], pp. 46–49). Here it may be added that, as silly as such scripted Soviet evaluations may sound, they in fact support the argument made here, attesting to the centrality of tales of Islamization in the (pre-Soviet) communal self-consciousness of Muslim peoples in Inner Asia; the very vehemence with which the Soviet academic establishment sought to discredit such legends (and to replace them with tales of Sovietization) may be regarded as an additional measure of how closely Islamic identity was interwoven with communal self-definition.

29. At the beginning of the full version presented by Dyer (cf. pp. 552–553), the monster who torments the emperor is identified as the "King of the Dragons of the Eastern Seas," whom the emperor had angered by failing to protect him as promised from the "sage and fortuneteller" who would eventually interpret T'ai-tsung's dream as signifying the need for assistance from the Muslims. The sage, seeking a remedy for the empress's illness, had made a deal with a talking fish that he was about to prescribe as medicine; the fish turned out to be the dragon king's son, and the sage agreed to set him free in return for the real medicinal fish. Upon learning of this, the dragon king, skeptical of the sage's talents, challenged his ability to predict the weather: the sage predicted rain, the dragon king replied that none would fall, and the two argued for awhile, agreeing finally that whoever was right would cut off the loser's head. When the sage "won" the weather-contest, the dragon king succeeded in winning the emperor's promise of protection, and the emperor arranged to ensure that the sage would fall asleep and be unable to fight the

cued by a young man wearing a turban and green robe and carrying a rosary.[30] A debate staged at court between "Vankhas" and a Buddhist "priest" follows, interestingly involving not only doctrine, but practice as well; the emperor, impressed by both the dogma and ritual of the religion of Muḥammad ("especially with the rites of the worship of the ancestors and the dead"), declares his adoption of Islam. Then follows the effective fulfillment of his dream: the northern nomads[31] attack China, and Vankhas and his Arabs come to the rescue. The struggle is decided by a contest of weather-control between the Buddhist *lama* of the nomads, who sends a hailstorm upon the Arabs, and Vankhas, who sends a windstorm to turn the hail back upon the nomads.[32]

---

dragon king; as the sage slept, however, he began sweating profusely "as if he were battling with someone," and soon awoke with the announcement that he had cut off the dragon king's head. The soul of the dragon king then became the monster of the emperor's dream. This part of the legend, as Dyer observes (p. 553, n. 24, p. 561), is found only in the Soviet Dungan version; it includes a number of motifs—the sage at the sea, the serpent, the control of the weather, the zealous struggle with the dragon—that appear in the legends of origin discussed below, including a number of versions of the mythic tale of Baba Tükles. It is also structured in such a way as to suggest an entirely separate mythical "commmunal origin-by-contest" tale grafted onto a more explicitly Islamic legend of origin through the device of "reviving" the slain dragon king and inserting him in the emperor's dream. We thus see the sage involved with the dragon through his efforts to heal the empress, a challenge to the sage and his "contest" with the dragon, and his final victory over the dragon, all constituting a coherent tale that on the one hand would seem to reflect a generic legend of origin-by-contest complete with a number of the themes characteristic of such legends as discussed below, and on the other hand is infused with Islamic significance by preceding the explicitly Islamic tale of the emperor's dream, whereby that tale's identifications may be projected back upon it: the sage will become in effect the "bringer" of Islam, while in the emperor's initial protection of the dragon we find reflected the dramatic device of the ruler's devotion to the opponents of Islam, a devotion not undone until the dragon turns on the emperor in his dream and must be countered by the sage calling in the Muslim forces.

30. In one version, the emperor is menaced by "a big snake" in his dream (Dyer, "T'ang T'ai-tsung's Dream," p. 565); in another, the emperor appears not to be threatened himself, his dream instead pitting a green lion symbolizing Islam against a white elephant representing Buddhism (Dyer, p. 551).

31. Dyer notes that a Chinese version of the legend has the Muslim army assist in the defeat not of northern nomads, but of the An Lu-shan rebellion (756–762) against the T'ang (pp. 558–559, n. 39).

32. Two elements found in this Dungan story—the infidel northern nomads symbolized as a dragon in a dream, and rival attempts at weather-sorcery waged by a Muslim saint and a non-Muslim holy man during a pivotal battle between new converts and infidels—figure in tales associated with the Islamizing figure of Sayyid Ata produced in early-eighteenth-century Central Asia, alluded to earlier. These more dramatic elements are absent in yet another version of the Dungan conversion tale, preserved in a Turkic "history" of East Turkistan from the late nineteenth century, the *Tārīkh-i jarīdah-i jadīdah* of Qārī Qurbān-ʿAlī b. Khālid Ḥājjī Ayākūzī (MS LOIV C578, ff. 62b–68a; the work, published in Kazan in 1889, is described in Dmitrieva

Here we find several stock motifs common to other conversion narratives in Inner Asia: the assertion of genealogical links to Muslim saints from the centers of Islam; a dream impelling the monarch to seek assistance from the soon-to-be-adopted religion (implied also in Juvaynī's account of the Uyghur conversion); a court debate; and a weather-contest between holy men. Once again, as is likely the case in Ötemish Ḥājjī's narrative, we find the debate motif included almost incidentally, as a minor but nevertheless obligatory element in the complex of dramatic tensions evoked in the story as a whole.

In the final analysis Ötemish Ḥājjī's inclusion of the "debate" pales in dramatic decisiveness beside the pivotal contest in the fire-pits; but its appearance nevertheless points to a narrative tradition recounting a court debate, a stock feature of Inner Asian conversion narratives, and undoubtedly identifying the Muslim participants in the debate as Sufis. We will encounter further elaborations of the tale of Baba Tükles in which his Sufi character is especially pronounced; in Ötemish Ḥājjī's account, this element is decidedly muted, evoked only through Baba Tükles' identification as a "saint," through his Sufi-style recitation inside the fire-pit, and here, perhaps, in the debate with the infidels, a challenge typically assigned to Sufi shaykhs.

Ritual Intrusion and Displacement

The Qoruq *and Ancestral Tombs*

The setting for the initial confrontation between the Muslim saints led by Baba Tükles and Özbek Khan with his retinue of infidel "sorcerers" is a place designated in Ötemish Ḥājjī's work by a term whose most likely reading is as a variant of the Turkic word *qoruq* or *qorïq*. The saints sit outside it when they arrive at Özbek Khan's court, and the khan sends his servants outside it when the "ceremony" is spoiled, indicating that the ceremony itself, as well as the subsequent interrogation of the Muslim saints, are to be understood as occurring inside this "place." As noted, the reading of this term is problematical; it evidently occurs four times in Ötemish

---

et al., *Opisanie tiurkskikh rukopisei*, I, p. 143, No. 137), where, however, a man in a white turban and green robe with a rosary in one hand and a staff in another appears in the emperor's dream that induces his conversion.

Ḥājjī's account (plus one possible occurrence outside the conversion narrative), and the specific textual, paleographical, and philological issues connected with the reading of the term[33] are taken up in the notes to the complete translation in Appendix 2. But here we must keep the term's problematical reading in mind in suggesting what it may have meant to the hypothetical audience of "earlier" versions of the Baba Tükles tale.

In the first place, the uncertainty with which the term appears to have been written, further discussed in Appendix 2, in itself suggests that the appropriateness of the *qoruq* as a site for the events described was unclear to the copyists of the two known manuscripts. It is likewise clear that ʿAbd al-Ghaffār Qïrïmī, writing in the eighteenth century, did not understand the term, evidently interpreting it in the form *qūr* and glossing it as *jamāʿat*, i.e., "gathering place."[34] Our manuscripts and our external sources thus fail us on this issue, and we are left to rely on somewhat circular reasoning: the probable semantic and religious implications of the term are themselves important elements in arguing for the form "*qoruq*" as the most likely reading (and indeed the only one that can make sense), while my argument, in turn, that it is specifically the religiously charged meaning, among two or three possible meanings for the word *qoruq*, that is most likely in the present context naturally depends upon assuming that *qoruq* is the most likely reading. This assumption is adopted here, however, on the basis of (1) the way the term is written in the manuscript(s) and (2) the fact that there is no other satisfactory explanation for the term as used in Ötemish Ḥājjī's work.

Inasmuch as this assumption adds such important dimensions to the "original" religious message of the Baba Tükles narrative, we must consider the meaning of *qoruq* in the context of the time and place in which the term was included—with pointed religious significance, I believe—in the narrative that eventually found its way into Ötemish Ḥājjī's work, and I will argue that it means precisely what the term meant most often in the

33. The problems evidently appear in both manuscripts, although I have been able to examine only one directly; see the discussion in Appendix 1.

34. In his version the four saints wait "outside the *qūr-lar*, that is, the place of assembly (*jamāʿat*), which was outside the *dīvān-i khānī*," glossing the term read as *qūr*—the need to explain it in itself attests to its unfamiliarity—as a place for "assembly"; the various Turkic words of the form *qur*, however, appear to have no suitable meanings either in this context or with the meaning "*jamāʿat*" (*qur* is noted with meanings such as "belt," "girdle," "rank," and "stage," and is used for a row or tier, as in a course of masonry, cf. Clauson, *ED*, p. 642, and Sir James W. Redhouse, *A Turkish and English Lexicon* [1890; repr. Istanbul: Çağrı Yayınları, 1978], p. 1482). ʿAbd al-Ghaffār renders subsequent occurrences of the term appearing in Ötemish Ḥājjī's text as *qoru* or *qorï* as *ʿaskar*, i.e., "army," without further comment.

extensive thirteenth- and fourteenth-century attestations of the term: the sacred and inviolable burial places of the khans in the Mongol empire.

THE TOMB-*QORUQ* AND SACRED INVIOLABILITY

The term *qoruq* as used for inviolable royal burial grounds has not drawn the attention it deserves in studies of Inner Asian religion.[35] To be sure, although we find many customs associated with the *qoruq* described among Inner Asian peoples such as the Huns, Türks, Khazars, and Qumans, it is not until the Mongol era that we can decisively (if still not exclusively) link the practices with the term; but the centrality of the term in the burial and funerary customs of the Mongol age is so clear that its neglect is surprising.

The best accounts of the term *qoruq* and its cognates in the Mongol era appear in an article by Bartol'd[36] and in the extensive discussion by Paul Pelliot in his notes on the publication of Marco Polo's travel account,[37] with important material on the term's use in the Ilkhanid domains adduced by Quatremère[38] (curiously ignored by Bartol'd) and more recently by Doerfer.[39] The term is surely of Turkic origin, being derived from the verb *qorï-*, meaning "to fence in," "to protect," "to enclose." Attested in Old Turkic in the form *qorïgh*,[40] it implies a "reserved," forbidden area set aside for private (usually royal) use in capaci-

35. It is not mentioned at all, for instance, in Harva, *Die religiöse Vorstellungen*, or in Roux's *La mort* (or in his other works), even though both writers discuss some practices associated with the *qoruq*; nor does it appear in N. F. Katanov, "O pogrebal'nykh obriadakh u tiurkskikh plemen s drevneishikh vremen do nashikh dnei," *IOAIÈ*, t. 12, vyp. 2 (1894), pp.109–142.

36. "K voprosu o pogrebal'nykh obriadakh turkov i mongolov" (*Sochineniia*, IV, pp. 377–396; cf. J. M. Rogers's translation, "The Burial Rites of the Turks and Mongols," *CAJ*, 14 (1970), pp. 195–227; cf. also Abdülkadir İnan's Turkish translation in *Belleten*, No. 43 (1947), reprinted in his *Makaleler ve İncelemeler*, pp. 362–386).

37. Paul Pelliot, *Notes on Marco Polo* (Paris, 1959), I, pp. 335ff.

38. E. Quatremère, "Notice de l'ouvrage persan qui a pour titre: Matla-assaadeïn ou-Madjma-albahreïn et qui contient l'histoire des deux sultans Schah-Rokh et Abou-Saïd," *Notices et extraits des manuscrits de la Bibliothèque du Roi et autres bibliothèques*, 14/1 (1843), pp. 65–66.

39. Doerfer, *TMEN*, III, pp. 444–450.

40. Cf. Clauson, *ED*, p. 652, noting among the more common forms a "Qïpchaq" form *qoru* given in a fourteenth-century Arabic-Turkic glossary; cf. p. 43 [s.v. "ataç"], where *qorïgh* is cited in a context linking it with the *yogh* ("funeral feast"). See further on the term Doerfer, cited above, and L. Budagov, *Sravnitel'nyi slovar' turetsko-tatarskikh narechii* (St. Petersburg, 1869; repr. Moscow, 1960), II, pp. 52–53, cf. pp. 78–79; Redhouse, *Turkish and English Lexicon*, citing the form *qoru* (spelled *qūrī*) as "a piece of meadow or forest land kept for private use" (p. 1486); Radlov, *Opyt*, II, cols. 555–559, citing *koru* in Ottoman, meaning a park or forest preserve for private hunting, *koruk* in "Uyghur" and Chaghatay, meaning a place protected by a fence or wall, *korugh* in Chaghatay, meaning a fortified place, a preserve, or pastures reserved

ties ranging from that of a hunting preserve to that of a burial site. It thus refers to a place, or less often a thing, characterized as being "reserved," "protected," "inviolate," "taboo," or "sacrosanct." As such it was used to refer to a wide range of places and things, the most frequently encountered of which are two: a special, often fenced-off "preserve" enclosing an expanse of pastureland (or of forest, or of hunting grounds) reserved for the exclusive use of the ruler, *or* the sacred royal burial grounds, the forbidden precincts of the imperial cemetery.

Now in Central Asian usage from the sixteenth century on, the former use predominates, and indeed the term *qoruq* became a standard term for royal hunting reserves in the Central Asian khanates down to the nineteenth century.[41] Similarly, as Bartol'd noted,[42] the only use of the term known to him from pre-Mongol times, in Narshakhī's history, referred to a royal reserve of pastureland enclosed by a palisade. Earlier occurrences not known to Bartol'd do occur, as noted above, in Old Turkic sources; some appear to reflect only the sense of lands "reserved" for royal or other private use, while one clearly implies that the term was associated with death and burial: in the eighth-century Ongin inscription, a son addresses his father, saying, evidently, that he has duly celebrated "your funeral feast" (*yoġ*) and established "your *qorïġ*."[43] Both uses clearly survived into the Mongol era; but it seems likely that the term *qoruq* was used in the Mongol era *primarily* to refer to something sacred and forbidden connected with death and burial, most often the sacred

for the ruler, and an interesting meaning for the Teleut form *korū*: "a place on the body which must be protected, which is easily injured, for example the temple." The term is also in use in modern Uzbek, Qazaq, and Qïrghïz, with "preserve" the only attested meaning in each case; the modern Uzbek term *qoriqkhanä* (with *khanä*, "room," "house," "abode"), meaning a state-protected nature preserve in which hunting is prohibited, may be noted here, as well as the term's use, recalling its sacred connotations as discussed below, in a recent environmental slogan proclaiming that the *anä säyyarä* ("mother planet") is a *qoriqkhanä*.

41. Cf. the chapter on "*khanskii kuruk*" in R. N. Nabiev, *Iz istorii Kokandskogo khanstva (feodal'noe khoziaistvo Khudoiar-khana)* (Tashkent: Fan, 1973), pp. 133–162; Ivanov, *Khoziaistvo*, p. 73, n. 1; and A. L. Troitskaia, "Zapovedniki kuruk kokandskogo khana Khudaiara," in *Sbornik Gosudarstevennoi Publichnoi Biblioteki im. M. E. Saltykova-Shchedrina* (Leningrad), vyp. 3 (1955), pp. 122–156, as well as her *Katalog arkhiva Kokandskikh khanov XIX veka* (Moscow: Nauka, GRVL, 1968), p. 550. This meaning appears to have been standard already by the early sixteenth century, as suggested by its use in Babur's memoirs, cf. *The Bābur-nāma in English*, tr. A. S. Beveridge (London: Luzac & Co., 1922, repr. 1969), pp. 81ff.

42. "Burial Rites," tr. Rogers, pp. 204–205.

43. Cited in Clauson, *ED*, p. 43; for a review of differing intepretations of this passage, however, see Bruno Öhrig, *Bestattungsriten alttürkischer Aristokratie im Lichte der Inschriften* (Munich: Minerva, 1988), pp. 162–165.

royal burial grounds of the Chingisid khans.[44]

To be sure, as Pelliot observed,[45] a *qoruq* was not necessarily an actual tomb-site in the Mongol age; the term could refer to any forbidden precinct, and as Bartol'd observed, the term was not restricted to "topography" in its application: the *name* of a deceased khan, which was not to be used or spoken for three generations, is spoken of as *qoruq*, i.e., "taboo," by Rashīd ad-Dīn, and the term *qoruġčï* applied to the guardians of the royal tombsites was also used for guardians of the royal harem.[46] More commonly, though, the term *qoruq* was used for plots of land, especially forest or pastureland; while he does not use the term, the Franciscan traveler Plano Carpini is certainly describing a grove of trees, intended "to grow for his soul," set aside as *qoruq* by the Great Khan Ögödei: "he ordered that no one was to cut there, and anyone who cuts a twig there, as we ourselves saw, is beaten, stripped and maltreated. And when we were in great need of something with which to whip our horse, we did not dare to cut a switch from there."[47] Here it is not impossible, however, that we should understand the "forbidden" nature of the trees in this inviolate grove to derive from the locality's status as, or designation as, a royal burial site; that is, it is not altogether clear that the "inviolate" nature of trees, or of game, etc., found in the territory of a *qoruq* is the primary motive for a region's designation as a *qoruq*: rather, they may be off-limits "secondarily," as things that happen to be on a site declared *qoruq* as a proposed or actual burial site.

The "Great *Qoruq*" of the Mongol era, spoken of by the Persian historian Rashīd ad-Dīn as *ġorūq-i buzurg* and by the Mongol designation *yeke qoruq*, was the burial place of Chingis Khan himself; we need not take up the question of its exact location,[48] especially since it was only natural for a number of localized cult sites to be claimed, in time, as the *real* burial place of the heroic ancestor. Of more interest than its actual location is the tradition reported by Rashīd ad-Dīn concerning the selection of the site: Chingis Khan had come to the spot, near the sacred

44. Rashīd ad-Dīn also refers to a *qoruq* of Chingis Khan's enemy, the Kereyt Wang-khan, as having been plundered; cf. Bartol'd/Rogers, p. 206. Bartol'd noted the uncertainty left regarding whether this *qoruq* was the ruler's pastures or sacred groves or ancestral cemeteries.

45. *Notes on Marco Polo*, I, p. 338.

46. Bartol'd/Rogers, "Burial Rites," pp. 205–206.

47. *Mongol Mission*, p. 13; cf. Pelliot, *Notes on Marco Polo*, I, p. 338.

48. See Pelliot's discussion, *Notes on Marco Polo*, I, pp. 339–353; Bartol'd/Rogers, "Burial Rites," pp. 209–210, 215–216; and Paul Ratchnevsky, *Genghis Khan: His Life and Legacy*, tr. and ed. Thomas Nivison Haining (Oxford: Basil Blackwell, 1991), pp. 142–144.

mountain Burqan Qaldun, where he found "an exceptionally verdant tree" by itself on the steppe, and after resting beneath it for a time he had declared that he should be buried beneath that tree; the place thus became the Great *Qoruq*, and soon so many trees grew up that the original lone tree could no longer be identified.[49] This story seems to reflect conceptions of the World Tree at the center of the cosmos as discussed earlier, and may reinforce the idea that the "inviolate" nature of sacred groves was often a secondary outgrowth of a place's status as a burial site or as a ritual center of some kind established in the context of the cosmogonic complex discussed above.[50]

For the practice of establishing tomb-*qoruqs* in the Mongol world of the thirteenth and fourteenth centuries[51] we have virtually no information from the Chaghatayid *ulus*, but considerably more from the realm of the Great Khan in Chinese sources, and from the Ilkhanid state, assembled by Bartol'd, Pelliot, and Quatremère. All these sources and descriptions show the preponderance of thirteenth- and fourteenth-century evidence on the use of the term *qoruq* to refer to royal burial grounds, and in view of the evident appearance of the term in Ötemish Ḥājjī's conversion narrative, such an understanding is indeed the only one that makes sense. While it might be reasonable for the narrative to place the khan in his "royal hunting reserve," the ceremony described (however obscurely) in the account clearly does not belong in the hunting grounds. And although we cannot be certain that such a ceremony was actually, in historical terms, performed in the royal burial grounds, the evidence points in that direction; the ceremony, portrayed after the fashion of a drinking ceremony and/or libation ritual, will be discussed below, but it seems likely that such ceremonies may indeed have been associated with ancestral rites tied to the royal burial grounds. And in any case, it is at least rea-

49. Cf. Pelliot, *Notes on Marco Polo*, I, p. 336; Bartol'd/Rogers, "Burial Rites," pp. 209–210.

50. Citing Rashīd ad-Dīn's story, Bartol'd ("Burial Rites," tr. Rogers, p. 210) suggests that the royal cemeteries "seem to have been established in the context of a cult of forests or groves of trees," but it would appear that such cults in themselves ought to be understood in the context of the larger mythic complex of the World Tree and associated imagery.

51. See in addition to Bartol'd, Pelliot, and Quatremère as cited above, I. Berezin, "Ocherk vnutrenniago ustroistva ulusa Dzhuchieva," *TVOIRAO*, 8 (1864), p. 447; J. A. Boyle, "The Thirteenth-Century Mongols' Conception of the After Life: The Evidence of their Funerary Practices," *Mongolian Studies*, 1 (1974), pp. 5–14 (pp. 8ff. on the *qoruq*); Boyle, "The Burial Place of the Great Khan Ögedei," *Acta Orientalia*, 32 (1970; = PIAC XI), pp. 45–50; [Boyle translates the term as "inviolable sanctuary"]; B. Vladimirtsov, *Le régime social des Mongols*, tr. Michel Carsow (Paris, 1948), p. 146; and Henry Serruys, "Mongol '*Qoriγ*': Reservation," *Mongolian Studies*, 1 (1974), pp. 76–91.

sonable to suggest that, whatever the "actual" historical practice in such ceremonies, it would have been quite natural to link the elements of ancestral libations and ancestral burial grounds in *narrative*.

The weight of the evidence thus shows the predominance of the funerary associations of the *qoruq* in the era that inspired the conversion narrative in Ötemish Ḥājjī's work; and it is certain that the use of the term *qoruq* to mean a sacrosanct royal cemetery continued in a number of contexts. Even in Central Asia, where we find the term used mostly to refer to hunting reserves or other lands privy to the khan, we find a possible survival of the use of the term *qoruq* to refer to a sacred tomb in a very telling case: the term is apparently used, in an early nineteenth-century work, to refer to the burial place of the Naqshbandī Sufi saint Khoja Bahāʾ ad-Dīn Naqshband. One manuscript of the work in question, a universal history in Persian entitled *Gulshan al-mulūk* and completed around 1246/1830 by Muḥammad-Yaʿqūb b. Muḥammad Dāniyāl-bīy (the youngest son of the Manghït *amīr* Dāniyāl Bīy, the actual ruler of the Bukharan khanate from 1758 to 1785), includes a marginal note apparently by the author mentioning the burial of the Ashtarkhanid ruler Subḥān-Qulī Khan at the "*qoruq* of the illuminated grave" in Bukhārā in 1114/1702.[52] More widespread, certainly, is the survival of the term *qoruq* to refer to putative graves of Chingis Khan himself among the Mongols down to the present. A site in the Ordos in Inner Mongolia where the cult of Chingis Khan still flourishes is centered at the putative shrine of Chingis, called Ejen Qoruġ-a.[53]

Finally, in arguing the probability that it is the *qoruq*-cemetery that is intended in Ötemish Ḥājjī's narrative, we may note its suitability for the theme of displacement, as a sacred site into which the Muslim saints intrude after spoiling a ceremony being performed there. That the *qoruq*

52. The passage is noted by McChesney, *Waqf in Central Asia*, p. 161, n. 33; McChesney suggests the reading *furaq*, noting *quruq* as an alternative, without indicating the voweling of the text; the khan is said to have been buried Monday 25 Jumādā I 1114/17 October 1702; the manuscript McChesney cites (MS IVAN UzSSR Inv. No. 1507, f. 132a [descr. *SVR*, I, p. 83, No. 208]) confirms the probable form *qūr.q* (or *fūr.q*), only the former making sense, i.e., *dar qūruq-i mazār-i fayż-an[v]ār*; on the *Gulshan al-mulūk*, cf. Storey-Bregel', *PL*, II, pp. 1160–1162.

53. Cf. Elisabetta Chiodo, " "The Book of the Offerings to the Holy Činggis Qaγan:" A Mongolian Ritual Text," *ZAS*, 22 (1989–1991), pp. 190–220 [pp. 214–215 on the shrine, which was built in 1956 and restored several times by 1987]. See also Klaus Sagaster, "Die Verehrung Činggis Khans bei den Mongolen," *XXIV. Deutscher Orientalistentag*, ed. Werner Diem and Abdoldjavad Falaturi (Stuttgart: Franz Steiner Verlag, 1990; *ZDMG*, Supplement VIII), pp. 365–371, and S. D. Dylykov, "Èdzhen-Khoro," in *Filologiia i istoriia mongol'skikh narodov: Pamiati akademika Borisa Iakovlevicha Vladimirtsova* (Moscow: Izd-vo Vostochnoi Literatury, 1958), pp. 228–234.

into which the Muslim saints were led was a place regarded as "off-limits" to outsiders is suggested by the sorcerers' call to have them killed; this element clearly heightens the dramatic effect (and establishes both the khan's independence from the sorcerers and the seminal presence of God's guidance in the khan), but its specific evocation may reflect knowledge of the tradition of inviolability adhering to the *qoruq*. At the Ordos site claimed as Chingis Khan's burial place, for instance, the principles of secrecy and inviolability are maintained in the ceremonies at which offerings to Chingis are made; a "special" language is used (recalling Chinese accounts of using a "secret" name of the deceased and speaking only the native language), and those who were on their way to perform the ceremony would beat those whom they happened to meet on their way;[54] this no doubt ritually stylized practice reflects the tradition of slaying those encountered on the way to a khan's burial site, as well as the sorcerers' appeal, in Ötemish Ḥājjī's account, to have Baba Tükles and his companions killed as intruders.

The latter point highlights two particular themes regarding the *qoruq* that appear consistently in European, Islamic, and Chinese sources as evidence of the sacrosanct nature of the burial ground; these themes are no doubt more reflective of what seemed most striking to outside observers, than of the real significance of the *qoruq* in native tradition, but they are nevertheless based upon authentic elements in the establishment and maintenance of *qoruq*s. First is the theme of secrecy: this is affirmed through anecdotes about the process of burial (sod is carefully removed over the gravesite in order to be replaced later, and horses are ridden over the site to ensure that it blends in with the rest of the terrain and cannot be distinguished) and about the killing of anyone who might be so unlucky as to meet the burial party or otherwise discover the site. Anecdotes of both kinds are well represented not only for the Mongols, but for earlier Inner Asian peoples as well.[55] The second, related theme is that of inviolability: the precincts are marked in some way, and guards are posted to keep "unauthorized" people away from the site, with heavy penalties exacted from those who even unwittingly violate the taboo.

54. Chiodo, "Book of the Offerings," pp. 218–219.

55. E.g., the killing of those who buried Attila as reported by Priscus (cf. Otto J. Maenchen-Helfen, *The World of the Huns: Studies in their History and Culture*, ed. Max Knight [Berkeley and Los Angeles: University of California Press, 1973], pp. 276–278); the "flooding" of the Khazar royal burial site, as well as the killing of those who buried the *qaghan*, reported by Ibn Faḍlān (cf. Dunlop, *History*, pp. 111–112).

These themes of secrecy and inviolability are noted in Chinese sources dating already soon after the death of Chingis Khan, with a Chinese envoy describing the practices of trampling the burial site, and of marking the sacred precinct by setting up arrows stuck in the ground and posting guards;[56] no terminology is given in this early account, however. Pelliot cites similar accounts from later Chinese sources that emphasize the "restoration" of the gravesite to an undisturbed appearance in order to ensure its secrecy.[57] Similarly, the European travelers Plano Carpini and Rubruck noted these practices, again without terminology. The strong taboos against violating the burial grounds are mentioned by Plano Carpini; speaking of the two cemeteries in the Mongol lands, he writes, "No one dare go near these cemeteries except the keepers who have been put there to look after them. If anyone does approach them, he is seized, stripped, beaten and severely maltreated. We ourselves unwittingly entered the bounds of the cemetery of the men who were killed in Hungary, and they bore down upon us and would have shot at us with arrows, but, since we were envoys and did not know the customs of the land, they let us go free."[58] Carpini also describes the secrecy involved in Mongol burial practices,[59] noting that one among the "less important" men would be buried "in secret in the open country," seated inside one of his dwellings and furnished with meat and a goblet of mare's milk for nourishment in the next world, as well as with horses for shelter and transportation. For their "chief men," however, "they go in secret into the open country and there they remove the grass, roots and all;" after digging a pit and completing the interment, "they put the grass over it as it was before so that no one may be able to discover the spot afterwards. The other things already described they also do, but his tent they leave above ground in the open." Rubruck, similarly, remarks: "Near the grave of a dead man they always leave a dwelling, if he is of the nobility, that is of the family of Chingis, who was their first father and lord. The burial place of him who dies is not known; and always around those places where they

56. Cf. Pelliot, *Notes on Marco Polo*, I, p. 333, and now Peter Olbricht and Elisabeth Pinks, *Meng-ta Pei-lu und Hei-ta Shih-lüeh: Chinesische Gesandtenberichte über die frühen Mongolen 1221 und 1237; nach Vorarbeiten von Erich Haenisch und Yao Ts'ung-wu übersetzt und kommentiert* (Wiesbaden: Otto Harrassowitz, 1980; Asiatische Forschungen, Bd. 56), pp. 224–225.

57. Cf. Pelliot, *Notes on Marco Polo*, I, pp. 333–334; see also Paul Ratchnevsky, "Über den mongolischen Kult am Hofe der Grosskhane in China," in *Mongolian Studies*, ed. Louis Ligeti (Amsterdam: Verlag B. R. Grüner, 1970), pp. 417–443 [pp. 437–442].

58. *The Mongol Mission*, p. 14.

59. *The Mongol Mission*, pp. 12–13.

bury their nobles there is a camp of men who guard the tombs."[60]

Marco Polo likewise noted the secrecy and inviolability of the Mongol tombs:

> And you may know truly that such a custom is observed; for all the great Kaan and the great lords of the Tartars who are descended from the line of their first lord Cinghis Kan are carried for burial when they are dead to a very great mountain which is called Altai. And wherever the great lords of the Tartars die, if they die a good hundred days marches away from that mountain, they must be carried there to the said mountain for burial with the others, nor are they willing to be buried in another place. Moreover I tell you another great wonder, that they have this custom that when the bodies of these great Kaan of the Tartars are carried to that mountain to bury, though they may be distant forty days marches or more or less, all the people whom they met by the way by which the bodies are carried are put to the edge of the sword by those who conduct the said body. And they say thus to them when they kill them, Go serve your lord in the other world. For they have come to such foolishness and the devil has so blinded them and surrounded them with such madness that they believe truly that all those whom they kill for this cause must go to accompany & to serve the great lord in the other world. And they do the same with the horses which they find on the road, & say that he has so many horses in the other world. For when the lord dies they kill all the best horses, camels, & mules that are left that the lord had. They have them killed believing that the lord may have them in the other world; & so they all believe. And you may know that when Mongu the fifth Kan died more than twenty thousand men were killed on the way, as I have told you, all those who met the body when it was being carried by the horsemen, who held this wicked and firm belief, to that mountain to burial.[61]

60. *The Mongol Mission*, p. 105; Rubruck further describes burial practices he ascribes specifically to the Comans, involving building mounds over the tomb, erecting a statue of a man facing the east and holding a cup in front of his navel, setting up horse-skins on poles facing the cardinal directions, and providing kumiss and meat for the deceased—despite the fact, notes Rubruck, that he had been baptized.

61. Marco Polo, *The Description of the World*, ed. and tr. A. C. Moule and Paul Pelliot

And the Catalan friar Jordanus of Sévérac, in his brief description of the "Great Khan" of the Tartars (written around 1330), affirms that: "When the emperor dies, he is carried by certain men with a very great treasure to a certain place, where they place the body, and run away as if the devil were after them, and others are ready incontinently to snatch up the body and bear it in like manner to another place, and so on to the place of burial; and they thus do that the place may not be found, and consequently that no one may be able to steal the treasure."[62]

One of the best descriptions of the establishment of the *qoruq*, and one curiously neglected by both Bartol'd and Pelliot,[63] is of particular interest insofar as it comes from an Islamic source and deals with the death of Batu, the real founder of the Golden Horde. This relatively early account, from Jūzjānī's *Ṭabaqāt-i Nāṣirī* (c. 1260), includes other important elements discussed further below; here we may note that it describes Batu's burial in an underground chamber seated on a throne and supplied with weapons and various vessels; it includes the notice that, in Raverty's translation, "In the night-time the place is covered up, and horses are driven over it, in such a manner that not a trace of it remains."[64]

Although the two themes of secrecy and inviolability are mutually contradictory in their most extreme formulations (i.e., why post guards if the tomb sites are genuinely and completely unknown?), they thus recur regularly in thirteenth- and fourteenth-century sources, and reduce to a common foundation of the tombs' status as taboo. This in turn makes intrusion into the *qoruq* an important violation of both Chingisid legitimacy and indigenous notions of sacred power, and hence a potentially powerful image in stories of Islamization.

(London: George Routledge & Sons, 1938), I (tr.), pp. 167–168; cf. the popular translation by Ronald Latham, *The Travels of Marco Polo* [Harmondsworth: Penguin Books, 1958], p. 97. The emphasis here upon burial on a great mountain not only recalls the mythic complex of Mountain and Tree, but is reflected as well in Rashīd ad-Dīn's comment that the body of the khan Baraq of the house of Chaghatay was sent to a mountain for burial (tr. Boyle, *Successors*, p. 141, cf. p. 153); and Ötemish Ḥājjī, of course, affirms the same tradition in his account of Toqtogha's obsequies as noted in Chapter 2. See further Magdalena Tatár, "Two Mongol Texts Concerning the Cult of the Mountains," *AOH*, 30 (1976), pp. 1–58 (esp. pp. 5–7).

62. *Mirabilia Descripta. The Wonders of the East, by Friar Jordanus, of the Order of Preachers and Bishop of Columbum in India the Greater (circa 1330)*, tr. Col. Henry Yule (London: Hakluyt Series No. 31, 1863), p. 48.

63. Boyle, however, does cite it in "A Form of Horse Sacrifice amongst the 13th and 14th Century Mongols," *CAJ*, 10 (1965), pp. 145–150 [p. 145], and after him, Ratchnevsky, "Über den mongolischen Kult," p. 439.

64. Jūzjānī, tr. Raverty, II, p. 1173.

THE *QORUQ* AND ISLAMIZATION

Bartol'd insisted that the tradition of the *qoruq* was forgotten early on in areas that Islam came to dominate.[65] To an extent we must agree, since the obscurity of the term, as well as of the practices it signaled, during the sixteenth century and after, is here assumed to be the cause of the uncertainties arising from the extant versions of Ötemish Ḥājjī's text. Bartol'd missed, however, not only Jūzjānī's description of Batu's burial, but indeed most of the available material on the *qoruq* in the Ilkhanid realm, as well as some on the Golden Horde; and Pelliot, for his part, acknowledged that "I have no information on the tombs of the members of the branch of Jöči . . ."[66] Since the role of the *qoruq* in these eventually Islamized parts of the Mongol-ruled world is of primary importance for our concerns, it is worth examining in more detail.

In the Ilkhanid context,[67] the sense of the term *qoruq* is difficult to trace precisely because of its common use in designating places of considerable diversity. The common denominator in places designated *qoruq* is the fact that ordinary people are forbidden to enter them, but the reasons for this are not always clear. Rashīd ad-Dīn uses the term to refer to such "inviolate" places, noting that a particular site was "made *qoruq*;" this use does not necessarily imply any association with tombs, but there are some indications that each khan was provided with a new *qoruq*, so that the number of places called by this name proliferated; we have frequent reference to the visitation of the several *qoruq*s by subsequent khans. In particular, the movements of Öljeytü (r. 703–716/1304–1316) show repeated visits to various sites designated as *qoruq*s, and to the tomb of his brother and predecessor Ghāzān near Tabrīz; but it is not clear if any of the *qoruq*s he visited were primarily tomb-sites.[68] It may be that this proliferation reflects already the growing shift from "tomb-*qoruq*s" to *qoruq*s as hunting or recreational preserves.

On the other hand, specific places of particular importance to the rul-

65. Bartol'd/Rogers, "Burial Rites," p. 221; he notes the rapid disappearance of all memory of these royal burial preserves in areas which came under Islamic influence. Bartol'd makes no mention of the use of this term in the present account, despite his earlier study of Ötemish Ḥājjī's work.

66. Pelliot, *Notes on Marco Polo*, I, p. 339.

67. As noted above, the best assemblage of data on the *qoruq* in Ilkhanid sources is given by Quatremère, "Notice."

68. Cf. Charles Melville, "The Itineraries of Sultan Öljeitü, 1304–16," *Iran*, 28 (1990), pp. 55–70. Melville notes (p. 57) Öljeytü's frequent visits during the early years (from 704–708/1304–1309) of his reign to Ghāzān's tomb; he understands Qāshānī's *qur.n.ġ* as an error for *qurīġ*, but interprets this always as "hunting grounds."

ing dynasty as imperial centers and/or burial sites are also prominent among the *qoruqs* named by Rashīd ad-Dīn and other Ilkhanid-era writers. The new city completed during Öljeytü's reign to serve as the Ilkhanid "capital," Sulṭānīyah, is frequently called a *qoruq*, and is linked with important state ceremonial occasions—such as enthronements—in several contexts. Rashīd ad-Dīn speaks of a *qurīltay* (assembly of Mongol princes) held in the *qoruq* of Sulṭānīyah, and its role in enthronements is suggested in Banākatī's history, in which the last event recorded is the Ilkhanid Abu Saᶜīd's enthronement in 717/1317 "in the *qoruq* of Sulṭānīyah" (possibly associated with the well-known grave of his predecessor Öljeytü in that city).[69] Likewise, the Persian *Baḥr al-asrār*, a history completed c. 1640 by Maḥmūd b. Amīr Valī of Balkh, mentions the *ghorūq-i aᶜẓam* of Abaqa (r. 663–680/1265–1282), already during his life, as the site where the khan received an embassy from the Jöchid *ulus*;[70] the place also served as the site of Abaqa's second, ceremonial enthronement (reflecting his confirmation by the Great Khan), according to earlier sources.[71]

Unfortunately our only information on the Ilkhanid *qoruqs* comes exclusively from Islamic sources dating from after Ghāzān's conversion to Islam, and again aside from the regular visits and the occasional linking of a new khan's enthronement with a particular *qoruq* (as in the case of Abū Saᶜīd), we find no mention in the Muslim sources of any ritual performance at the *qoruq*. Nevertheless, the preponderance of evidence suggests that the "older" meaning of this term, and its association with imperial burial, remained current certainly in Öljeytü's day, since it was still known in the mid-fourteenth century.

This is confirmed by the only use of the term *qoruq* in the Ilkhanid realm which is clearly and explicitly linked to a royal burial site, in connection with the place near Sajās [or Sujās] where Arghun (r. 683–690/1284–1291) was buried. The designation "*qoruq-i Arghūn*" became, to be sure, a simple place name noted in sources down to Timurid times at least,[72] but there can be little doubt that the site of Arghun's tomb was originally designated as a *qoruq* with precisely the same meaning implied by that term when attached to the burial place of Chingis Khan or other

69. Banākatī, ed. Shiᶜār, p. 478; the event is also noted in the mid-fifteenth-century compilation of Faṣīḥ Khwāfī, the *Mujmal-i Faṣīḥī*, ed. Farrukh, III, p. 26, tr. Iusupova, p. 46.

70. MS IVAN Uz, Inv. No. 1385, f. 108a; here the place is apparently spelled *jīġ.tūbād*, no doubt reflecting the familiar place-name "Jaghātū."

71. Cf. the notes in ᶜUmarī/Lech, *Das mongolische Weltreich*, p. 323, citing Rashīd ad-Dīn and Mustawfī's *Nuzhat al-qulūb*.

72. Cf. Quatremère, "Notice," p. 65.

khans. The best evidence of this appears in a well-known source whose important mention of this *qoruq* appears to have been overlooked by Quatremère, Pelliot, and Bartol'd; the passage, from Ḥamdullāh Mustawfī Qazvīnī's *Nuzhat al-qulūb* (completed in 740/1340),[73] is doubly significant for our purposes, because it also suggests the importance of intruding Islamic institutions and Muslim "holy men" into the sacred *qoruq* of Mongol tradition.

In describing the region of Sajās and Suhravard, Qazvīnī writes, "The grave of Arghūn Khān is in the mountain of Sajās, and as was the Mongol custom, they had concealed it; they made that mountain a *qūrugh*,[74] and affliction would come to people who crossed its borders;[75] but (Arghūn's) daughter, Öljey Khātūn, making her father's grave public, established a Sufi hostel at the site and settled people there."[76]

The passage provides a clear example of the "violation" of the *qoruq* by a Muslim convert, Arghun's daughter, involving not only the indignity of the "secret" place's exposure, but the specific intrusion into that inviolate site of the bearers of Islamic-style sanctity. This in turn supports the supposition that such an intrusion is suggested already in the narrative of Ötemish Ḥājjī, as one of several instances of "displacement" consciously intended to reinforce the religious meaning of the account.

A further sign of the tension between the maintenance of the sepulchral *qoruq* and conversion to Islam is indicated without specific reference to the term "*qoruq*," in the Timurid historian Sharaf ad-Dīn ʿAlī Yazdī's note on the burial of the Ilkhanid khan Ghāzān, famous for his conversion to Islam; Yazdī writes that Ghāzān was buried near Tabrīz within a domed tomb (*gunbadh*) that he himself had built, as is well-known from other sources, but adds that "before him the graves of the Mongol sovereigns were not public (*āškārā*)."[77]

73. G. Le Strange, ed. and tr., *The Geographical Part of the Nuzhat-al-Qulūb composed by Ḥamd-allāh Mustawfī of Qazwīn in 740 (1340)* (London: Luzac & Co., 1915 [part I, text], 1919 [part II, tr.]), text, p. 64, transl., p. 69.

74. I, text, p. 64: a variant is *qūrīgh*;

75. *va mardum-rā az ḥudūd gudhashtan zaḥmat rasīdī*.

76. *dukhtarish ūljāy khātūn qabr-i padar-rā ashkār karde ānjā khānqāh sākht va mardum benishānīd*; cf. Le Strange's translation: "The sepulchre of Arghūn Khān was made in the mountain of Sujās, and according to Mongol custom, they concealed the place, making the whole mountain an inviolable Sanctuary [*Qūrugh*], so that people could not without difficulty pass that way. Arghūn's daughter, Ūljāy Khātūn, however, made manifest her father's grave, founding a Darvīsh-house, and settling a community here." Arghun's burial in Sajās is noted also in Banākatī (ed. Shiʿār, p. 446), but without mention of the site's designation as a *qoruq*.

77. Yazdī, *Ẓafar-nāmah*, Tashkent facsimile ed., f. 70b.

What is clear for the Ilkhanid domains is (1) the frequent link between the named *qoruq*s and enthronement sites named at the accession of new khans, suggesting dynastic ancestral symbolism, (2) an implicit tension between the adoption of Islam and the maintenance of inviolate imperial tombs, and (3) the explicit account from Mustawfī of an "intrusion" of a Sufi community into the *qoruq* in which an infidel khan was buried, a theme implicit in Ötemish Ḥājjī's account of Baba Tükles and his companions. The association of the *qoruq* with royal enthronement and the example of Muslim intrusion into the *qoruq* as a sign of conversion both allow us to suggest the likely existence among the Muslim community of narratives linking the notion of the *qoruq* with the khan's death and burial, the enthronement of his successor, Mongol ancestral rites, and the intrusion of Muslim holy men as a sign of Islamization.

The *qoruq* of the khans of the Golden Horde was probably near Saraychïq, on the lower Yayïq/Ural river; this was Bartol'd's conclusion,[78] and although other burial sites are recorded for various Jöchid khans,[79] Saraychïq is indeed the site most commonly noted as the burial place (and enthronement site) for the khans of the Golden Horde. The seventeenth-century *Baḥr al-asrār* affirms that Özbek Khan's predecessor "Tūqtāy" was buried in "Sarāy-jūq,"[80] while somewhat later the seventeenth-century Khivan khan Abū'l-Ghāzī specifies that Özbek's predecessor "Toqtaghu" was buried there, as was Özbek's son and eventual successor Jānī Bek, and the report that Jānī Bek assumed the throne in Saraychïq (as did Jānī Bek's successor Berdi Bek) probably implies that Özbek Khan himself was buried there as well—or rather was expected to have been buried there.[81]

78. Cf. Bartol'd/Rogers, "Burial Rites," p. 221; on Saraychïq, see Egorov, *Istoricheskaia geografiia Zolotoi Ordy*, pp. 124–125, where, however, there is no mention of its status as the Jöchid *qoruq*. It may also be noted here that with the diminutive suffix *-čïq*, the very name of the royal burial site ("the little palace") recalls the practice of constructing a courtlike sepulcher for a ruler's burial, as attested at least as early as Ibn Faḍlān's account of the Khazars, and the "tent" or dwelling left atop the grave as reported by Plano Carpini and Rubruck.

79. Bartol'd ("Burial Rites," tr. Rogers, pp. 221–222) cites the sixteenth-century Central Asian history of ʿAbdullāh Khān, the *Sharaf-nāmah-i shāhī* (MS LOIV D88, f. 334b, a portion not yet published in facsimile), as mentioning the *mazār* of Jöchi Khan himself in the region between Sarï Su and Ulutau (i.e., Ötemish Ḥājjī's "Ulugh Tagh"); the text is published in V. V. Vel'iaminov-Zernov, *Izsledovanie o kasimovskikh tsariakh i tsarevichakh*, II (SPb., 1864; *TVOIRAO*, 10), pp. 307, 316–317.

80. MS Tashkent, IVAN UzSSR, Inv. No. 1385, f. 111b.

81. Ed. Desmaisons, I (text), pp. 174–176, II (tr.), pp. 183–185. Golubovich (*Biblioteca bio-bibliografica*, III, p. 176), cites a *Storia Universale* published in Amsterdam in 1771 as affirming that "Toktai" was buried, according to his instructions, near the city of "Shari Sarayjik"; this was probably based upon Abū'l-Ghāzī's work. He also notes (II, p. 565) that "Saraicik" was men-

If Abū'l-Ghāzī's report on Jānī Bek's burial site is correct, Saraychïq evidently maintained its status as the site of the royal burial ground after the Islamization of the Golden Horde; but the city, later the most important center of the Noghay horde in the fifteenth and sixteenth centuries, may have also maintained its sacral and ancestral associations for the Noghay horde. According to Ibn ʿArabshāh's history of Timur, the historical Edigü, regarded as a descendant of Baba Tükles and as the founder of the Noghay confederation,[82] may have been buried there;[83] an eighteenth-century source has Edigü's son Nūr ad-Dīn buried there as well,[84] and the city appears to have retained associations with sepulchral inviolability well after Edigü's time. In discussing the Jöchid *qoruq*, Bartol'd noted the complaint of a Noghay prince, recorded in diplomatic correspondence, that that during the destruction of Saraychïq by the Cossacks in 1581, the attackers did not stop with the living, but "pulled the dead as well from the ground and destroyed their graves";[85] Bartol'd did not draw attention

tioned as the place of *sepoltura de' Kan e loro zecca,* (i.e., the tomb and mint of the khan), and assigns the same description to the city on the map in that volume, but his source for this is not clear.

82. As we will see below, Edigü's charisma rested, in genealogical ascription and in epic "advertising," upon Islamic bases of sanctity often contrasted with Inner Asian notions of Chingisid legitimacy, including one case of a mocking derision of the "inviolable" graves of the Chingisid khans; nevertheless, Edigü's burial there (or stories about it) may reflect an appropriation of the *qoruq*'s symbolism rather than an outright rejection of it.

83. For Ibn ʿArabshāh's problematical account, which appears to have Edigü drown in the "Sayḥūn" (the Syr Darya or the Yayïq in this context?) but pulled out at (or more likely carried for burial to) Saraychïq, see Tiz I, p. 473; cf. Saadet Çağatay, "Die Ädigä-Sage," *UAJ*, 25/3–4 (1953), pp. 243–282 [p. 271, citing the 1718 Ottoman translation]; the reference to Saraychïq (often spelled as *Sarāyjūq*) disappears in J. H. Sanders' English translation (*Tamerlane, or Timur the Great Amir* [London, 1936], p. 87), where we read, "they drew him out of the river Jaxartes on to the dry land of Huq"! Togan called attention to this error and suggested that the "Sayḥūn" refers here to the Ural/Yayïq River in "Timur's Campaign of 1395 in the Ukraine and North Caucasus," *Annals of the Ukrainian Academy of Arts and Sciences in the U.S.*, 6 (1958), pp. 1358–1371 [cf. pp. 1370–1371, n. 29]). A tradition of Edigü's burial at Sarāychïq may be reflected in a late (nineteenth-century) anonymous work preserved in MS 1388T at Kazan University; the work bears no title, is appended to a copy of the genealogical "history" of "Bulghār" by the Bashkir Tāj ad-Dīn b. Yalchïghul from the beginning of the nineteenth century, and is clearly based in part upon the late seventeenth-century *Daftar-i Chingīz-nāmah* (discussed in Chapter 5), although it otherwise reflects local oral tradition. In a list of saints cast as successors of the "Followers" of the Prophet's Companions, it names "Īdūkah Khūjah" as being buried in Sarāychïq (I am indebted for this reference to Allen Frank, who photographed the manuscript in 1992).

84. According to the *ʿUmdat al-akhbār* of ʿAbd al-Ghaffār Qïrïmī (mentioned above and discussed more fully in Chapter 5), Nūr ad-Dīn died in "Ṭūrā" and was taken to Sarāychïq for burial (MS Esad Efendi No. 2331, f. 323a [Latin]/326a [Arabic]).

85. Bartol'd/Rogers, "Burial Rites," p. 221; Bartol'd cites the history of Karamzin (whence it is

to this as an evident allusion to a heightened sense of outrage connected with the inviolable burial ground, but this complaint would seem to support the association of the region of Saraychïq with the sacrosanct *qoruq* of the Golden Horde. To this may be added another report, from 1577, that a Noghay prince had complained to a Russian envoy that a band of people in state service had come to Saraychïq and desecrated the body of his deceased father; other accounts as well confirm the reports that the 1581 destruction of Saraychïq, when the city was plundered and burned, was accompanied by the evidently purposeful destruction of the Noghay cemeteries.[86]

Pelliot, as noted, professed ignorance on the *qoruq* of the Jöchid khans, but assumed that "they must have been buried in the basin of the Volga." He suggests, however, that the burial place of the Mongols killed in Hungary, mentioned by Plano Carpini, "must have lain somewhere between Kiev and the Volga;" Plano Carpini himself gives no details of this cemetery's location, but it seems possible that in claiming that the Mongols have *two* cemeteries—one "where the Emperors, chiefs and all the nobles are interred" and "one where lie buried those who were killed in Hungary"[87]—Plano Carpini is unwittingly attesting to the existence of separate *qoruqs* in the two Mongol realms in which he spent the most time and in which we may presume he received his information: one in the realm of the Great Khan, and one in the *ulus* of Jöchi. The latter, which he accidentally violated, may well have been described to him as the place where those killed in Hungary were carried for burial, since it was the Jöchid princes who were, after all, responsible for the Hungarian campaign.

Further material on the burial place of the Jöchid khans not cited by Bartol'd was mentioned by Joseph von Hammer-Purgstall in his history of the Golden Horde;[88] here and more fully in an earlier review of literature on the Black Sea littoral[89] he notes that the Venetian map of Francesco

---

noted also by Howorth, *History of the Mongols*, II/2 [1880], p. 1039), who in turn cites the archival documents on Russian dealings with the Noghays, the so-called "*Nogaiskie dela*," specifically No. 10 for the year 1581, f. 140 (N. M. Karamzin, *Istoriia gosudarstva rossiiskago* [St. Petersburg: Izdanie Evg. Evdokimova, 1892), IX, p. 145, n. 666).

86. Both reports are cited in G. I. Peretiatkovich, *Povolzh'e v XV i XVI vekakh (ocherki iz istorii kraia i ego kolonizatsii)* (Moscow, 1877), pp. 305–306.

87. *The Mongol Mission*, pp. 13–14.

88. *Geschichte der Goldenen Horde in Kiptschak*, p. 11, and p. 280, n. 3; Saraychïq is also said to be frequently mentioned as the burial place of the khans in W. Heyd, *Histoire du commerce du Levant au Moyen-Âge*, tr. and ed. F. Raynaud (Leipzig, 1885; repr. Amsterdam: A. M. Hakkert, 1959), II, p. 229, citing von Hammer.

89. In *Jahrbücher der Literatur* (Vienna), 65 (January-March, 1834), pp. 1–31, esp. pp. 17–20.

Pizzigani, dated 1367, labels a point on the Yayïq/Ural river *"Torcel, i.e. Sepulchrum Imperatorum, qui decedunt circa flumen de Sera,"* that is, "Torcel,[90] the tomb of the emperors who die near the river of Saray," a clear reference to the khans of the Jöchid *ulus*. The map referred to by Hammer-Purgstall is one of two well-known maps done by Francesco and Marco Pizzigani in Venice, one a large chart dating from 1367 and the other a "portolano" or set of nautical maps produced in 1373; the latter has been more extensively described,[91] and contains a detailed chart of the Black Sea, but does not appear to include the north coast of the Caspian Sea. It is thus the production of 1367 to which Hammer-Purgstall must have referred, but in any case, it seems reasonable to assume that both cartographic productions of the Pizzigani brothers reflect the same sources of information, and in view of the well-known Venetian role in the Black Sea commerce with the Golden Horde, and of the map's early date,[92] the Pizzigani map is of considerable importance in establishing the early currency of the notion that the Jöchid tombs were near Saraychïq.[93]

90. Von Hammer suggests a reading reflecting the term *turbe*, which seems unlikely; it is of course difficult to judge without access to the chart itself, but it may be suggested that reading the initial *t* as a *c* would give an original form that might reflect the term *qoruq*.

91. See its description in Theobald Fischer, *Sammlung mittelalterlicher Welt- und Seekarten italienischen Ursprungs* (Venice: F. Ongania, 1886; repr. Amsterdam: Meridian, 1961), pp. 148–150; see also Visconde de Santarem (Manuel Francisco de Barros), *Estudos de Cartographia Antiga*, I (Lisbon, 1919), pp. 60–66, and A. E. Nordenskiöld, *Periplus: An Essay on the Early History of Charts and Sailing Directions*, tr. Frances A. Bather (Stockholm: P. A. Norstedt & Söner, 1897), p. 58.

92. The age of the information reflected in the map is suggested on p. 188 of Fischer's *Sammlung*, where he refers to the Pizzigani map's depiction of two castles in the Caucasus region, the border between the Jöchid and Ilkhanid realms: one is marked *"hic est custodia Husbeci"* (i.e., Özbek Khan), while the other is *"custodia Bunsa"* (i.e., the Ilkhanid Abū Saʿīd, d. 1335). Fischer's remarks on the two castles are noted, and a photograph of the Pizzigani map is reproduced (but so reduced in size as to be illegible) in Edward Luther Stevenson, *Genoese World Map, 1457: Facsimile and Critical Text Incorporating in Free Translation the Studies of Professor Theobald Fischer revised with the Addition of Copious Notes* (New York: American Geographical Society / Hispanic Society of America, 1912), pp. 30–31. The passage was noted already by von Hammer, *Jahrbücher*, p. 17.

93. An even earlier attestation may be found in an anonymous atlas, called the "Portolano Laurenziano Gaddiano," dating from 1351, which contains an especially detailed depiction of the Caspian Sea; near the mouth of the "Jancho" (i.e., the Yayïq or Ural river), roughly halfway between "Organichy" (Urgench) and "Agitarcham" (Astrakhan) along the Caspian littoral, it places a "City of Monuments," which may allude to the notion that the khans' burial monuments were located there (this atlas is briefly described in Nordenskiöld, *Periplus* [p. 58], where the relevant portion, showing the Caspian, is reproduced as Plate X). The world map of Fra Mauro, dating from 1459, likewise depicts the burial place of the rulers of Saray in the same region; along the lower "Iaincho" river, the *"Sepultura Imperial"* is shown, but without mention

Von Hammer also called attention to the account in the Jahān-numā, the geographical work of Ḥājjī Khalīfah or Kātib Chelebī (d. 1067/1657), which includes a description of the cities along the shore of the "Sea of Bākū" (i.e., the Caspian).[94] The author mentions the river he calls "Yāyqū,"[95] which rises in Sībīr, evidently the Yayïq/Ural; then he notes, "Near the mouth of the aforenamed river there is a city (*shahr*) called Qāmīnāzār,[96] in which the khāns of the trans-Volga (*zāvulq*) Tātārs used to be buried." This city had been destroyed, however, by the "Perekop" (i.e, Crimean) Tatars. He next mentions the city of Qanābūrī,[97] and then the "Jānqū" river (i.e., the Iaincho of many European maps), near the mouth of which is found the city whose name is given in a form that clearly conceals the name "Sarāychïq";[98] Ḥājjī Khalīfah notes that this city was formerly the capital of the Qumans, but had been restored by the Noghay Tatars, whose "khans" now dwell there.

As von Hammer showed,[99] Ḥājjī Khalīfah's account is drawn primarily

---

of the city Saraychïq (cf. L. S. Bagrov, *Materialy k istoricheskomu obzoru kart Kaspiiskago moria* [SPb.: Tipografiia Morskogo Ministerstva, v Glavnom Admiralteistve, 1912], pp. 26–28, 82–89; the relevant features as depicted on the Fra Mauro map are not described by Bagrov, but the relevant portion of the map itself is reproduced as Plate 16). It seems likely that Fra Mauro's map depended upon earlier charts for some information on the Volga-Ural region, but the mid-fifteenth-century production also reflects the campaign of "Tamberlan" in the Golden Horde and may attest to more current information on the tombs of the khans of the Jöchid *ulus*. Less clear is the brief caption on the world map of Andrea Bianco, dated 1436, identifying a "temple of the emperors" near the northeastern coast of the Caspian Sea (cf. *Periplus*, p. 19; the map is also reproduced in the work of Vincenzio Formaleoni, *Saggio sulla nautica antica de' Veneziani, con una illustrazione d'alcune carte idrografiche antiche della Biblioteca di S. Marco* [Venice: Presso l'Autore, 1783], between pp. 34 and 35). Of comparable vagueness, unfortunately, is a large tomb depicted to the north of the Caspian Sea on a fifteenth-century Catalan world map and described as the former burial place of the great khans; this may indicate knowledge of the Jöchid *qoruq* near Saraychïq, but just as well may reflect traditions about the burial place of Chingis Khan and his immediate successors further east (cf. the description by Konrad Kretschmer, "Die Katalanische Weltkarte der Biblioteca Estense zu Modena," *Zeitschrift der Gesellschaft für Erdkunde zu Berlin*, 32 (1897), pp. 65–111, 191–218 [pp. 209–210 on this caption]).

94. I have consulted the printed edition published in Istanbul at the Müteferrika press in 1145/1732, p. 373, and a manuscript (Paris, Bibliothèque Nationale, Suppl. Turc 215 (Blochet, Turc, I, p. 265), a copy in 243ff., dated 1142/1729, f. 218b.

95. The printed edition has "*bāyqū*;" the manuscript could be read as either "*bāyqū*" or "*bābqū*."

96. In the printed ed., *qāmīnah-zār*.

97. In the printed edition, *q.tābūzī*, said to be near the *K.s.l* river.

98. In the manuscript, "*s.vān.j*" or "*s.vāy.kh*;" in the printed edition, "*s.vāykh*." The form clearly conceals the name "Sarāychïq," as confirmed by the Italian source.

99. The full discussion appears in *Jahrbücher*, pp. 17–20; cf. *Geschichte*, p. 280, n. 3: "In der

from an Italian geography from the latter sixteenth century, in which the relevant passage refers to "*Caminazar, dove si sepellivano gli Imperatori dei Tartari Zavolghensi*"; the Italian account makes it clear that it is indeed Saraychïq ("Saraich") that is mentioned as nearby the burial site, and adds nearly a century to the antiquity of the information.

Against Abū'l-Ghāzī's report on Toqtogha's burial place is the evidence of Franciscan sources, discussed earlier, about the burial of a Christian "emperor" whom it may be possible to identify as Toqtogha. One source speaks of the emperor's initial burial, with full imperial solemnities, at a place three miles from Saray, and of his body's transfer to Saray itself thirty-five years later, while another speaks of his removal after thirty years together with his brother, with the curious addition that a "demonic Saracen" was then delivered into this brother's tomb; yet another source mentions the grave of an emperor's brother, linking it with a similar "wonder": a Saracen was carried into the brother's tomb "by a devil."[100] These accounts of a "Christian" Mongol prince or ruler removed from his grave and "replaced" by a Muslim are difficult to interpret, but it may be that we should find therein echoes of stories similar to that reported by Ḥamdullāh Mustawfī, namely, an account of a Muslim "intrusion" into the sacred royal *qoruq*; if this is indeed the case, and if the "emperor" in these accounts is indeed Toqtogha, we may suppose that the original account referred to "Saraychïq" as the "initial" burial place, but that this was later "corrected" to the more familiar Saray. The timing of the transfer may also be of significance, again if Toqtogha is the emperor in question. His death in 1312 would place his disinterment and transfer in either 1342 or 1347, the former date corresponding to the death of Özbek and the accession of Jānī Bek, a time of possibly heightened religious tension due to the latter khan's more overt support for "Islamizing" policies.[101]

aus der fabrica del mondo Lorenzo Agnani's ubersetzten Stelle des Dschihannuma wird *Kaminezar*, in der Nähe von Seraidschik . . ., als die Grabstätte der zawolhensischen Chane, d.i. derer von Serai, angegeben, und auf der Pizziganischen Karte steht am Jaik: *Torcel* (vielleicht *Turbe*), *Torcel, i.e. Sepulchrum Imperatorum, qui decedunt circa flumen de Sera*"; cf. p. 11, where he mentions Sarāychïq as the chief city of the Noghay horde, and then notes, "In der Nähe desselben erwähnt die Pizziganische Karte *Torcel's*, als des Begräbnissortes der Chane, und die beste italienische Erdbeschreibung des Mittelalters nennt *Caminazar* als den Begräbnissort der Chane jenseits der Wolga."

100. Golubovich, *Biblioteca*, III, pp. 170–171, II, p. 272; cf. Fr. Bartholomaeo de Pisa, *De conformitate vitae beati Francisci vitam Domini Iesu* (written between 1385 and 1390), in *Analecta Franciscana*, IV (Quaracchi: Ex Typographia Collegii S. Bonaventurae, 1906), p. 557.

101. These considerations suggest the plausibility of a historical reconciliation of Ötemish Ḥājjī's account, placing Özbek Khan at the royal *qoruq* at the time of his dramatic conversion,

In any event, Saraychïq's status as a pre-Muslim cult center would have lent it potentially great symbolic importance in stories of Islamization, as may in fact be the case in the account of Ötemish Ḥājjī, if we may assume Özbek Khan's *qoruq* as mentioned in the tale to be the ancestral burial place in Saraychïq. Here we may recall that Abū'l-Ghāzī specifies Saraychïq, established by Batu, as the site of Berke's conversion to Islam,[102] and that a later account of Özbek Khan's conversion by Baba Tükles, which (as discussed below in Chapter 5) was recently discovered and is independent of Ötemish Ḥājjī's work, explicitly identifies Saraychïq as the site of the conversion.

Regardless of where the Jöchid *qoruq* may have been, it seems likely that Ötemish Ḥājjī's narrative preserves an echo not so much of the historical practice of maintaining a *qoruq*-cemetery, but of the potent symbolism of intruding upon that inviolate sacred center in the course of introducing Islam. The potency of the symbolism derives, as we might expect, both from Islamic and Inner Asian conceptions. From the Islamic perspective the *qoruq* resembles, and would certainly have reminded Muslims of, the Islamic notion of the sacred and inviolate, *ḥaram*,[103] and its displacement

with other information on his reign, informed also by the association of the *qoruq* with ancestral veneration as discussed further below. With this in mind, and in view of the evidence suggesting Özbek Khan's hostility toward his predecessor Toqtogha (as in the apparent removal of his designated successor, and in Özbek's apparent confirmation of his grandfather's *yarlïq* without regard for Toqtogha's earlier confirmation), as well as the Franciscan report of the khan who converted to Christianity (probably identifiable with Toqtogha) being removed from his grave to make way for a Saracen, a rationalization of disparate sources might suggest that we imagine the khan at the *qoruq*, ritually (and as a pointed political assertion) removing from the sacred site those linked to Toqtogha and regarded by Özbek as illegitimate, and perhaps posthumously "restoring" his father's rights by giving him Toqtogha's place in the imperial tombs; here the erroneous later tradition, reported by Naṭanzī, that Özbek's father indeed ruled as khan may reflect such a posthumous restoration through altered history, as the discursive counterpart to the ritual act in the *qoruq*. In any case such a reconstruction must remain purely speculative, and its historical plausibility is not our central focus here.

102. Ed. Desmaisons, I (text), pp. 172–173, II (tr.), p. 181).

103. Bartol'd noted this equivalence (Bartol'd/Rogers, "Burial Rites," pp. 205–206); and the similarity of the Muslim notion of *ḥaram* (particularly in connection with prohibitions on the cutting of trees and on hunting in the sacred environs of Mecca) with popular Turkic customs associated with tomb—sanctuaries and the cult of the dead was noted (without reference to the term *qoruq*, however) in F. W. Hasluck, *Christianity and Islam under the Sultans* (Oxford, 1929; repr. New York: Octagon Books, 1973), I, pp. 237–240, and in general his discussion (pp. 226–277) of tomb-sanctuaries is instructive with regard to the focuses of assimilation between Muslim and pre-Muslim rites and conceptions. It must be noted, however, that Kāshgharī and other Muslim lexicographers do not appear to have explained *qoruq* in terms of the Arabic *ḥaram*, perhaps precisely because of the latter term's sacred associations (or because of the other meanings of *qoruq*); rather, the element of "protection" (*al-ḥimā*) is emphasized (cf. Clauson, *ED*, p. 652).

by figures claimed in later accounts to have come from *the* Islamic sanctuaries marks a displacement of local sanctuaries by the new faith's inviolate sacred center. From the Inner Asian perspective, we find an emphasis upon the sacrosanct nature of the graves of royal ancestors as far back as Herodotus's report on the Scythians; and the sacredness and inviolability of the *qoruq* is in keeping with common Inner Asian notions of the key role played by ancestral spirits in the health and survival of the family/community/nation, both "physically" (through care for and protection of pregnant women and children, reflected in the functions of the "grandmothers" at the hearth and in the nourishing function of the feminine spirit at the cosmic Mountain/Tree/Lake) and "economically," through their protection, ensured by offerings and other guarantees of their satisfaction with the living, of the herds or the fields or the hunters' game.

Such inviolability is thus rooted in the complex of ancestral links to the community, and was a feature of communal cemeteries that survived in Inner Asia, long after the terminology of the *qoruq* and the "royal" associations of *the* sacred burial ground were forgotten, in clan or communal cemeteries that reflect assumptions that the community encompasses the dead as well as the living, and that communal intimacy and the concomitant suspicion of outsiders prevail in death as in life.[104]

Lest the *qoruq*-cemetery appear of minor importance among the themes evoked in Ötemish Ḥājjī's conversion narrative, we may also recall the evident appearance of the *qoruq* elsewhere in Ötemish Ḥājjī's work, as the place to which the severed head of a usurper-khan was taken, as well as the theme, in one of the versions of the Idige tale discussed below, of a non-Chingisid figure's disdain for the Chingisid burial ground, as he speaks of having taken a Chingisid's head and left it in Saraychïq. The theme of the severed head of a khan being taken to the *qoruq* may well have formed a powerful image lending itself to various uses in narratives, since it evokes a severe violation of sacred norms: its use in Ötemish Ḥājjī's account of the usurper Bājīr Tūq Būghā not only reinforces the Chingisid right to supreme power, but also, by according a non-Chingisid usurper at least a nominal burial according to a soon-to-be-outmoded royal ritual—and thus showing that although Chingisid legitimacy still mattered for political power, at least one old ritual expres-

104. On Qazaq clan cemeteries, for instance, cf. S. N. Akataev, "Kul't predkov u kazakhov v proshlom i Zoroastrizm," *Izvestiia AN KazSSR*, seriia obshchestvennaia, 1973, No. 2, pp. 43–49 [pp. 44–45]; on Baraba clan shrines, their location known only to clan members and forbidden to outsiders, cf. Diószegi, "Pre-Islamic Shamanism of the Baraba Turks," pp. 147–149.

sion of that legitimacy was no longer meaningful and could be trifled with—it implies a rupture between the pre-Islamic sacralization of that power and the new Islamic style of legitimation signaled by Özbek Khan's reign; similarly, by Mongol custom a Chingisid khan's blood was not to be shed, and leaving a Chingisid's severed head in the *qoruq* symbolized disdain both for Chingisid inviolability and for the *qoruq*, as is clear in the Idige tale. And in both cases the murder of a khan—in which old Mongol norms of avoiding the shedding of his blood were no longer observed—itself signaled the general social disorders understood as accompanying the breakdown of older value systems.

As a final example of the narrative motif of Sufi shaykhs "intruding" into the burial grounds of Inner Asian nomads may be cited a brief account from a sixteenth-century Central Asian hagiographical work, the *Jāddat al-ʿāshiqīn*, written in 966/1573 on the life of the Kubravī Shaykh Kamāl ad-Dīn Ḥusayn Khorezmī.[105] This work relates the shaykh's travels, on the *ḥajj*, from Khorezm to Sarāychïq, Ḥājjī Tarkhān, and "Āżāw" [i.e., Āżāq, Tana], on to the Crimea and finally Istanbul and beyond, but the passage relevant here appears in a different context, in the account of the shaykh's chief successors. One of these, Shaykh Artūq Manqïshlāqī, personally recounted to the author—Ḥusayn Khorezmī's son—his experience when he traveled once from Manghïshlaq (on the eastern shore of the Caspian) to "Ūzbakistān," which here clearly refers to the realm of the people elsewhere in the work called "*ūzbakān-i manghitī*," that is, the Noghay horde. A group of *amīrs* among that people had been acquainted with Shaykh Artūq, and told their *pādshāh*s of his mystical achievements and virtues and wonders. "A shaykh from among the successors of the holy master Shaykh Ḥusayn Khorezmī has come," they reported; "he has wondrous power over hearts, and tells the status of the people of the grave."

The shaykh was naturally taken, to be put to the test, to the graves of these "Özbeks'" ancestors, and when he looked upon them their inhabitants were at once revealed to him "in their original forms," so that he was able to address his royal examiners, saying, "this is your father's grave, and this is your mothers' grave," and so on. The people were impressed by his accuracy, and brought him horses and sheep in abundance, leading the author to conclude that "the good fortune which resulted from the blessing of serving his holiness [Shaykh Ḥusayn

105. On the work see my "Eclipse of the Kubravīyah," p. 66, n. 61, and p. 71, n. 83 for references to known manuscripts.

Khorezmī] gave assistance also in this world."[106]

The "unveiling of graves" is of course a theme not uncommon in Sufi literature, in which contemplation of death is one of the central justifications of the pious visitation of saints' tombs;[107] it is curious to see this motif evoked, however, with regard to the tombs of the royal house of the "Manghït Uzbeks," wherein the issue is made the focus of a "test" with the clear implication that the saint's power to "look into" their ancestral graves was crucial to his acceptance and prestige among them. The narrative here is of course not linked in any evident way to any account of Baba Tükles, nor is it explicitly tied to the *conversion* of the community that "tested" Shaykh Artūq, although the "reconfirmation" of this saint's power and what he represented is certainly implied. But the narrative unquestionably *does* attest to the currency, still in the late sixteenth century, of tales pitting Muslim saints against native religious traditions among the peoples of the Dasht-i Qïpchaq, traditions "encoded" in terms of these communities' devotion to ancestral burial grounds. And this narrative milieu—in which a saint is tested in the heart of the community's cemetery and demonstrates the strength of the Islamically encoded power to "uncover" the graves—helps us to understand the way in which the motif of the *qoruq* in Ötemish Ḥājjī's account conveyed similar meaning to a similar audience.

The *qoruq* thus serves as a focus for ritual intrusion and displacement in its various roles: (1) as a sacred inviolate *center* of royal and political importance (and, with the assimilation of Ruler = First Man, of religious importance for the community the khan represents), its violation by Baba Tükles threatens communal order and in this narrative restructures it with Islam as the focus; (2) as a specifically *royal* reserve, its violation raises the specter of non-Chingisid political legitimation, an issue resolved in Ötemish Ḥājjī's narrative as Baba Tükles lends the Chingisid Özbek Khan legitimacy by converting him to Islam, but given quite different resolution in the later tradition surrounding Baba Tükles and Edigü; and (3) as a place inviolate and sacrosanct, its violation implies that Mongol notions of the sacred have given way to Islamic conceptions

106. MS Aligarh Subhanullah No. 297.71/1, ff. 204a–b; MS India Office Ethé 1877, ff. 112a–b; MS Hyderabad (Andhra Pradesh Government Oriental Manuscripts Library), Persian MSS, *Tadhkirah* No. 168, pp. 254–255.

107. Cf. al-Ghazālī's discussion in *The Remembrance of Death and the Afterlife, Kitāb dhikr al-mawt wa-mā baʿdahu; Book XL of The Revival of the Religious Sciences, Iḥyāʾ ʿulūm al-dīn*, tr. T. J. Winter (Cambridge: Islamic Texts Society, 1989), pp. 149–169.

of inviolability and sacred centers, and in this regard it is worth noting the explicit links asserted for Baba Tükles, in his later narrative transformations, with those Islamic sacred centers of Mecca and the Kaʿbah.

In summary we must acknowledge of the *qoruq* in Ötemish Ḥājjī's narrative that it is not the basis of a well-developed theme, nor is its significance *explicitly* emphasized (beyond the curious repetition of the term) as the setting of the decisive religious confrontation; nevertheless, the strong association of the term with the royal burial sites, and the clear religious meaning of such burial sites as inviolate sanctuaries reserved to the royal clan that "embodies" the state and people, are suggestive of the potential resonance of the religious complex associated with the *qoruq* to an "Islamizing" audience of the fourteenth and fifteenth centuries. When we recall the implicit "intrusion" of Muslim holiness into the *qoruq* of Arghun, as noted in the *Nuzhat al-qulūb*, as well as the more explicit "intrusion" of a Sufi saint into the burial sites of the sixteenth-century Noghays, in the *Jāddat al-ʿāshiqīn*, we are further inclined to accept that the repeated mention of the term *qoruq* in Ötemish Ḥājjī's account is not coincidental; rather, however much it may have lost its meaning by the time Ötemish Ḥājjī recorded his narrative, the mention of the *qoruq* was most likely quite pointedly included in earlier stages of the narrative as a means of evoking the religiously charged "intrusion" of Islamic sanctity into the setting of an "infidel" sanctuary whose importance and inviolability would have been well known to earlier audiences if obscure in later times.

For now we will leave this issue by merely suggesting the probability that this is what the *qoruq* must have meant in the hypothetical "original" narrative about Baba Tükles; the likelihood of this interpretation will become clearer when we consider the rich conflation of themes evident in the account of the fire-pit, especially the theme of interment that immediately recalls the *qoruq*, and when we review narrative structures paralleling the symbolism of "intrusion" and displacement in other conversion narratives from the Inner Asian world. Finally, as we will see later on (in Chapter 6), the sacred inviolability of the Jöchid *qoruq* is pointedly mocked in one of the many outgrowths of the tale of Baba Tükles, involving the assertion by one of his "descendants" that Islamic legitimacy should take precedence over Chingisid legitimacy.

The Drinking Ceremony: Ancestral Libations and Court Protocol

Ötemish Ḥājjī's description of the ceremony conducted, by all appearances, in the *qoruq* and spoiled by the appearance of Baba Tükles and his companions is perhaps the most problematical passage in the entire conversion narrative. It is obscure because of uncertain readings of the crucial terminology; because of uncertain meanings for the terms; because the procedure apparently described is not exactly paralleled in other accounts, at least insofar as the unresolved terminological problems allow us to presume; and, no doubt, because what appears in Ötemish Ḥājjī's account most probably is the result of a conflation of several strands of tradition, each reflecting (however dimly) memories of distinctive ritual or ceremonial practices known from the Mongol courts of the thirteenth and fourteenth centuries. At the same time, the obscurity of the passage in Ötemish Ḥājjī's account is balanced by the wealth of accounts from European, Islamic, and Chinese sources describing ceremonies that must have underlain the account in Ötemish Ḥājjī's work, involving ceremonial libations and drinking rites; our problem is that we cannot with any certainty or precision match the terminology found in our narrative with the specific practices described in thirteenth- and fourteenth-century sources. Consequently, as clear as it is that accounts of similar ceremonies are echoed, the earlier sources do not resolve the terminological problems in Ötemish Ḥājjī's account. As in the case of the *qoruq*, the textological and philological difficulties involved in understanding Ötemish Ḥājjī's description have been relegated to the notes to the full text and translation in the appendixes; here we will focus on those several strands that appear to be reflected in the description, with the goal of understanding the religious meaning conveyed by recounting the Muslim saints' disruption of the ceremony.

To this end we may note the principal structural elements in this description that are not beset by uncertainties. First, the ceremony is clearly portrayed as being conducted by figures ("sorcerers and diviners") in whom we must recognize the shamans active at the Mongol courts; their role at court is attested in European, Chinese, and Muslim accounts, and there is little doubt that "shamanic" figures indeed officiated at rites such as the one described in Ötemish Ḥājjī's narrative; but we are less concerned with the actual practices than with the likelihood that narratives reflecting those practices, no matter how imperfectly, provided a basis for conveying religious meaning to an Islamizing audience.

Second, the ceremony or ritual is expressly characterized as a "wonder" (*karāmat*), and we are to understand that just as the effective production of this "miraculous" event was the foundation of the khan's devotion to his shamans, the equally wondrous disruption of the ceremony constituted the initial undermining of his devotion to infidel ways and thus made possible the khan's conversion.

Third, and less "clear" in the particulars but still certain, the ceremony involves the manipulation of liquids and containers for liquids—of which honey is the only one explicitly named—in such a way that we are justified in interpreting the passage as echoing descriptions of a libation ritual or of a court drinking ceremony, or as conflating both kinds of practices (a "conflation" that may have occurred in reality as well as in narrative). In either case, the ceremony was likely associated with both ancestral and "economic" concerns of communal importance, aimed at sustaining the viability and productivity of the herds but also signaling the stability and well-being of the state; it thus had important court associations, but wider and more popular currency as well, and here its disruption marks the direct usurpation of native ritual intimately linked to communal integrity.

Fourth, the ceremony may also echo a court drinking rite in which submission to the khan as well as status and rank were ritually demonstrated in an elaborate pattern involving expressions of obeisance through kneeling and repeatedly presenting cups while praising or congratulating the khan; its disruption thus potentially challenges not only the place of the shamans at the ceremony, "replaced," as they were, at the khan's side by the Muslim saints, as we will see, but also the entire ritualized structure of obeisance to the khan, thus providing another seed for casting Baba Tükles in opposition to Chingisid legitimacy in later tradition. At the same time, this court drinking ceremony appears to involve an "orientational" component, as suggested by the specific allusion to the "seating arrangement" in which the "sorcerers" sit close by the khan's side; this "orientational" component is one of the clearest indications that the ceremony in question involves the kind of court protocol widely described for the Mongol courts, and in this component we find a clear case of the "displacement" at work in this and other conversion narratives.

HONEY AND ITS NUMINOUS ASSOCIATIONS

The philological and historical questions regarding the beverages apparently employed in the drinking ceremony described by Ötemish Ḥājjī are discussed in the commentary to the translation in Appendix 2; it may suffice to note here that the narrative seems to suggest the use of kumiss, the standard beverage used in Inner Asian ceremony and ritual, mixed with honey. It is honey, however, that is specifically mentioned in the narrative, and the recurrence of this element in contexts of Islamization merits some consideration.

To begin with, the use of honey-based drinks as part of Mongol court ceremony is widely attested in the thirteenth and fourteenth centuries, and it would not be surprising to find it mentioned in accounts of court life; what is more curious, however, is the recurrent appearance of honey in stories of Islamization, and in reports reflecting the "interface" between Islam and Mongol custom. Of particular relevance in the latter regard are Ibn Baṭṭūṭah's descriptions from the court of Özbek Khan, in which he mentions the use of *fermented* honey (*nabīdh al-ᶜasal*) in the Muslim context of *ᶜĪd al-fiṭr*, the festival of breaking the fast of Ramaḍān, a practice he explains through the adherence of Özbek's people to the Ḥanafī *madhhab*, supposedly allowing them to consider fermented liquor to be licit.[108] Similarly, the historian al-Mufaḍḍal notes that in his audience with the Mamlūk ambassadors in 1262, Berke provided them with *qïmïz* and "boiled" honey (*al-ᶜasal al-maṭbūkh*).[109]

At the same time, honey and honey-based drinks (both are covered by the Turkic term *bal*) were products closely associated with the lands of the Golden Horde, with the Crimea in particular renowned for its honey;[110] it was perhaps the combination of the fame of the region's honey, of the borderline legality of honey-based drinks in the Islamic practice of the region, and of an awareness of the use of such drinks at the Mongol courts that shaped the curious inclusion of honey in a number of conversion stories, including that of Ötemish Ḥājjī. In this regard we may note the survival of the element of honey in stories circulated about Baba Tükles as late as the early twentieth century, as discussed in

108. Cf. Ibn Baṭṭūṭah, ed. and tr. Defrémery and Sanguinetti, II, pp. 378, 386, 392–393, 408.

109. Cf. E. Blochet, ed. and tr., *Histoire des sultans mamlouks*, pt. 1, in *Patrologia Orientalis*, 12/3 (Paris, 1919), p. 461.

110. Cf. A. Samojlovič [*sic*], "Beiträge zur Bienenzucht in der Krim im 14.–17. Jahrhundert," in *Festschrift Georg Jacob*, ed. Theodor Menzel (Leipzig: Otto Harrassowitz, 1932), pp. 270–275.

Chapter 6; but the role of honey in other conversion stories is also worth reviewing.

In the first place, we find a curious echo of the numinous associations of honey combined with kumiss (as well as of other elements of the epic tales discussed below) in the seventeenth-century Ottoman work *Tavārīkh-i Dasht-i Qipchāq* by ʿAbdullāh b. Rizvān. In this work is preserved an account of the divinely ordained destruction of the "city" of Qïrïm (the Crimea) as retribution for its inhabitants' miserliness and their scornful rebuke of a certain shaykh Kamāl Ata's attempts to collect *zakāt* from them. Seven districts were spared, however, because of a saintly *khatun* who met the shaykh respectfully, offering him through her two sons *bal* and *qaymaq* (cream or curdled milk); and the author remarks that those seven districts are still flourishing and are famous for their *bal* and *qaymaq*.[111]

We find similar echoes in a conversion legend reported in connection with the Crimea in the well-known assemblage of tales about the Turkish saint Sarï Saltïq; this figure, whose legends bear other parallels with the tales of Baba Tükles, is discussed more fully in Chapter 4. Of interest here is again the figure of Kamāl Ata, this time cast as a *murīd* of Sarï Saltïq, who is responsible for the conversion, not of the Crimea as such, but of a group of *kāfirs* there; the incongruities in the story suggest that independent stories of Kamāl Ata and his activities in the Crimea were grafted onto the legendary cycle of Sarï Saltïq through the familiar mechanism of making Kamāl Ata a young follower of the cycle's principal hero. The story is found in the fifteenth-century *Ṣaltūq-nāmah* (which may have undergone further editing before the late sixteenth-century date of its earliest extant manuscript);[112] the work includes a longer series of tales about Sarï Saltïq's own sojourn in the Crimea, together with companions such as Kamāl Ata, etc., but the present tale is found separately.[113]

111. *La chronique des steppes kiptchak, Tevārīḫ-i Dešt-i Qipčaq du XVIIe siècle*, ed. Ananiasz Zajączkowski (Warsaw: Państwowe wydawnictwo naukowe, 1966), pp. 29–30 (text), 80 (abridged eighteenth-century French translation).

112. This work and its legends are discussed more fully, in connection with the figure of Sarï Saltïq himself, below in Chapter 4.

113. Kamāl Ata does appear earlier in this work among the companions of Sarï Saltïq during his sojourn in the Crimea and Kaffa, where he is one of the leaders of an army of *ghāzīs* who joins the khan of the Crimea in fighting the Russians (MS, ff. 96a–109a: cf. Fahir İz, ed., *Ṣaltuḳ-nāme: Ebū'l-Ḫayr Rūmī'nin sözlü rivayetlerden topladığı Ṣarı Ṣaltuḳ menakibi* [7 parts; Cambridge: Harvard University, 1974–1984; Sources of Oriental Languages and Literatures, ed. Şinasi Tekin and Gönül Alpay Tekin, Turkic Sources, 4], pt. 2, pp. 191–217; cf. Ebü'l-Hayr-ı

The story runs as follows. Sarï Saltïq, we are told, had a young *murīd* named Kamāl, from Qïrïm, who was said to be second in esteem there only to Sarï Saltïq himself. His reputation for saintliness was so great that *kāfirs* feared him and would not come to Qïrïm. One day, however, a ship of the infidels was on the verge of sinking, and the infidels declared that if they were saved from this danger, they would give two casks of wine they had to Kamāl Ata as a votive offering (*nadhr*), noting that he could sell it to the infidels since he would not drink it himself. Within the hour God gave them agreeable weather, and the ship landed safely. The leader of the infidels aboard the ship, though, told his fellows that it would be a sin to give the wine to Kamāl Ata; they should instead sell it, buy oil (*yāġ*) and honey (*bāl*), and give *that* to him in fulfilment of their vow. The *kāfirs* tried to do just that; but during the night Kamāl Ata entered their dreams and told them, "bring those two casks to me; I will not accept anything else." The infidels thus went to Kamāl Ata's *zāwiyah* in Qïrïm, with the two casks, and presented them to him; he ordered them to open the casks, revealing that one was full of oil and one full of honey. The infidels were amazed and became Muslims in Kamāl Ata's presence; they made their homes near his *tekke* and became his *murīds*. In an echo of the account in the *Tavārīkh-i Dasht-i Qipchāq*, the story concludes by noting that Qïrïm was at that time quite prosperous (*ma^cmūr*), with 12,000 homes, and that Sarï Saltïq had a mosque built, funded by its *kharāj*, and had a *zāwiyah* built as well, in which Kamāl Ata resided; and in a "prescriptive" ending common to many such hagiographic tales, we are reminded that Kamāl Ata was still famous in Qïrïm, where the people recognized his sanctity and brought him many votive offerings and sacrifices.[114]

The honey in Ötemish Ḥājjī's narrative, to be sure, plays a quite different role, but here again we should keep in mind the likelihood that the tale of Özbek Khan's conversion already reflects a number of independent stories, combined and "rationalized" by the mid-sixteenth century; it may be that this rationalization was necessitated by the very diversity of tales in circulation and focused on Islamization, of which fragments survive in scattered narratives such as those considered here.

Rumî, *Saltuk-nâme*, ed. Şükrü Halûk Akalın, I [Ankara: Kültür ve Turizm Bakanlığı, 1987], pp. 156–178), suggesting a close identification between Kamāl Ata and Crimean Islam.

114. İz, ed., *Ṣaltuḳ-nāme*, pt. 4, pp. 654–656 (ff. 327b–328b).

THE "WONDER" OF THE CEREMONY

A curious element in Ötemish Ḥājjī's description of the drinking/libation ceremony may also find echoes in earlier sources. Ötemish Ḥājjī notes in passing that the ceremonial process conducted by the "sorcerers" amounted to a "wonder" or "miracle" (*karāmat*); why this was so might naturally be clearer if we had a better understanding of the process itself than the narrative provides, but in any case we may note that descriptions of "mechanical" and "magical" wonders connected with drinking ceremonies were not uncommon in thirteenth- and fourteenth-century accounts of the Mongol courts. The idea that a "wonder" is involved in the dispensation of beverages is reminiscent of the "marvel" of Guillaume Buchier's silver drink-dispensing tree noted by Rubruck at Möngke's court;[115] more to the point, we find in Marco Polo's book an account of a drinking ceremony at Qubilay's court quite clearly reminiscent of the tenor of Ötemish Ḥājjī's description. As he describes, it is the *bacsi*[116] who officiate at this ceremony, working a "marvel" that, if not precisely matching the "wonder" described in Ötemish Ḥājjī's account, at least reflects the currency of stories to the effect that such ceremonial occasions were the setting for strange "shows" involving the beverages to be consumed, conducted by the khan's religious advisers:[117]

> And again you may know quite truly that these bacsi of whom I tell you above, who know so many enchantments, do among the rest so great marvel past all belief as I shall tell you. For I tell you that when the great Kaan sits at dinner or at supper in his chief hall in his capital city, at his great table, which table set apart for the eating of the lord is more than eight cubits high, as will be said in the next book, and the golden drinking cups are after their manner on a table in the middle of the pavement on the other side of the hall quite ten paces away from the table and are full of wine and of milk and of other good drinks for the lord, then these wise charmers of whom I have told you above, who are named bacsi, they do so much by their enchantments and by

115. Cf. *The Mongol Mission*, p. 176; see, for further examples of such devices, Quatremère in *Histoire des Mongols de la Perse*, p. 358, in n. 155, citing examples from Marco Polo's account at Qubilay's court; from Vaṣṣāf at Sulṭānīyah; and from Clavijo in Temür's Samarqand.

116. I.e., the *bakhshīs* of Muslim accounts, by which it appears that Marco Polo too means Buddhist monks, although the term was applied to shamans early on.

117. Tr. Moule/Pelliot, I, p. 189.

> their arts that those full cups are lifted of themselves from the pavement where they were and go away by themselves alone through the air to be presented before the great Kaan when he shall wish to drink, without anyone touching them. And when he has drunk, the said cups go back to the place from which they set out. And they do this sometimes while ten thousand men look on, and in the presence of whomsoever the lord wishes to see it; and this is most true & trustworthy with no lie, for it is done at the table of the lord every day. And indeed we shall tell you the wise men of our land who know necromancy say that it can well be done.

In the role of the "charmers," in the manipulation of vessels for the khan's benefit, and in the *daily* character of the wondrous performance we well may find traces of narrative fragments associated with Mongol court ritual that also found their way into Ötemish Ḥājjī's conversion narrative.

LIBATION RITUALS AND ANCESTRAL VENERATION

In light of the substantial evidence available on the role of kumiss libations in Inner Asian ritual, it is not unreasonable to see in Ötemish Ḥājjī's account a description of an apparent kumiss ceremony directed by the shamans and conducted, if the "royal reserve" (*qoruq*) indeed refers to the sacred burial ground, with undoubted links to the cult of royal (and implicitly "national") ancestors. There is no doubt that the Muslim saints' disruption of this ceremony marks a crucial point in the narrative and the religiously meaningful displacement of the pagan tradition; but the specific displacement of an ancestrally focused shamanic rite involving kumiss libation is obviously not noted explicitly in Ötemish Ḥājjī's account. To suggest that it is nonetheless present implicitly, or that such a specific displacement was implicit in the already conflated narratives that provided Ötemish Ḥājjī with the source for his account, requires some further discussion.

The ritual use of kumiss libations in Inner Asian religion is well known from both historical accounts and ethnographic descriptions.[118]

118. For a discussion of the role of kumiss in Inner Asian and especially Mongol religion, see the introduction to Henry Serruys, tr., *Kumiss Ceremonies and Horse Races: Three Mongolian Texts* (Wiesbaden: Otto Harrassowitz, 1970), pp. 1–17, and see further V. Diószegi, "Libation Songs of the Altaic Turks," *AEH*, 19 (1970), pp. 95–106, and W. Jochelson, "Kumiss Festivals of the Yakut and the Decoration of Kumiss Vessels," *Boas Anlniversary Volume* (New York, 1906),

Such libations, the central practice of the Mongol *julagh*-ceremonies, for instance, were a standard mode of "offerings" made to spirits for a wide range of religious purposes; they were above all a means of "honoring" the spirits who could exert control over the life and health of individuals and the community, and of "including" them in the enjoyment of the community's prosperity so that they might participate in and take a benign interest in communal life. From these motives we find kumiss sprinkled in the air for the spirits of the earth and sky prior to virtually all serious undertakings; we find it daubed on the mouths of ancestral figurines in domestic ritual; we find special "first fruits" rites marked by kumiss libations and intended both to celebrate a new season's kumiss and to gain further protection of the herd's health and productivity by giving the spirits a stake in the celebration; we find a container of kumiss supplied to the dead in the course of burial rites, and depicted iconographically in representations of dead heroes; and we find a particularly close connection between kumiss libations and ancestral veneration and memorial feasts.

Already in the thirteenth century, libations of kumiss were a key feature both in seasonal "first fruits" rituals designed to guarantee the well-being of the herds and in royal ancestral rituals centered upon the cult of Chingis Khan; such libations have remained a central element in Inner Asian religious ritual,[119] and the ritual use of kumiss libations is especially well described for the thirteenth- and fourteenth-century Mongols of most direct relevance to the setting of our conversion narrative. The Franciscan William of Rubruck reports a ritual consecration of the white mares who are to produce the new year's kumiss, conducted by the "soothsayers" and held in the spring; the first new kumiss was sprinkled on the ground, and Rubruck recognized the rite as similar in purpose to the "first fruits" offerings known to him from Christianized European

pp. 257–271. The Yakut kumiss festival (*ysyakh*) is briefly described, with references to later descriptions than reflected in Jochelson's article, in G. U. Èrgis, *Istoricheskie predaniia i rasskazy iakutov*, ch. 1 (Moscow/Leningrad: Izd-vo Akademii nauk SSSR, 1960), p. 279, n. 18, where a telling, typically Soviet, remark suggests the continuing importance of assimilating still newer "religious" or ideological values to an important old communal ceremony: "At present collective farm workers also organize the *ysyakh*, but its content has been altered, and no rituals are now celebrated. The *ysyakh* has become a holiday for demonstrating the economic and cultural achievements of the collective farms, with displays of amateur artistic talents."

119. Cf. Klaus Sagaster, *Die Weisse Geschichte: Eine mongolische Quelle zur Lehre von den beiden Ordnungen und Staat in Tibet und der Mongolie* (Wiesbaden: Otto Harrassowitz, 1976), pp. 207–208, 230–232, 354–356); Serruys, *Kumiss Ceremonies*, pp. 1–7.

usage.[120] What was more important for the use of kumiss in ancestral rites, he noted, was the ritual use of felt "idols" among the Mongols. These idols were images of deceased ancestors venerated in the ordinary domestic cult; they were sprinkled with kumiss before others drank, while libations were made to the air and earth as well.[121]

Perhaps the best description of the seasonal "first fruits" libations is provided by Marco Polo, speaking of Qubilay's court; the account suggests the association of the libation rites with the prestige and sacral aura of the imperial family:

> And when he comes to the twenty-eighth day of the moon of the said month of August the great Kaan leaves this city of Ciandu and this palace each year on this day, & I will immediately tell you why. It is true that for the greater part of the food of this lord he has a breed of white horses and of mares white as snow without any other colour, and they are a vast number, that is that there are more than ten thousand white mares. And besides he has a great number of very white cows. And the milk of these white cows and mares no one else in the world dares drink of it on that day except only the great Kaan and his descendants, that is those who are of the lineage of the empire, that is of the lineage of the great Kaan. Yet it is true that another race of people of that region that are called Horiat can indeed drink of it. And Cinghis the great Kaan gives them this honour and this privilege as reward for a very great victory which they won with him to his honour long ago, and they have this preeminence. He wished that they and all their descendants should live and should be fed on the same food on which the great Kaan and those of his blood were fed. And so only these two families live on the said white animals, that is on the milk which is milked from them. Moreover I tell you that when these white animals go grazing through the meadows and through the forests and pass by some road where a man wishes to pass, one does them so great reverence that if, I do not mean only the ordinary people but, a great lord and baron were to see them passing there he would not dare for anything in the world to pass through the middle of these animals, but would wait till they were all past or would go so far for-

120. *The Mongol Mission*, p. 198.
121. *The Mongol Mission*, pp. 96, 184; cf. Serruys, *Kumiss Ceremonies*, p.1.

> ward in another direction, quite half a days journey, that he would have passed them. All give way to them and all do what is possible to please them, and as I have said they are respected by all with no less honour and reverence than would be done to their own master. And the astrologers and the idolaters[122] have told the great Kaan that he must sprinkle some of this milk of these white mares through the air and on the land on the twenty-eighth day of the moon of August each year so that all the spirits which go by the air and by land may have some of it to drink if they please, and the earth and the air and the idols which they worship, so that for this charity done to the spirits they may save him all his things, & that all his things may prosper, both men and women, and beasts, and birds, and corn, and all other things which grow on the land. And from there the great Kaan departs in the month of August from the aforesaid park for this reason and goes to another place, as I have told you, to make with his own hand that sacrifice of milk to his gods. And on the day of the festival mares' milk is prepared in vast quantity in honourable vessels, and the king himself with his own hands pours much of the milk hither and thither to the honour of his gods. And the astrologers say that the gods drink the milk poured out. After the unspeakable sacrifice the king drinks of the milk of the white mares. So this rite is solemnly observed on the 28th day of August for ever.[123]

The celebration of such seasonal "first fruits" offerings was clearly connected with the ruler's ritual responsibility to ensure the prosperity and well-being of his realm; at the same time, that responsibility was dynastic as well, and the general assimilation of ancestral spirits to the spirits who protect and fructify herds or fields is undoubtedly at work here on an imperial scale. The close link between kumiss libations and ancestral veneration, as suggested by Rubruck's account of the felt idols sprinkled with kumiss, was clearly felt both at the domestic level and at the level of the khan's court.

The ancestral focus of kumiss libations is already suggested by the

122. One version of the text reads "*incantatores*," recalling the terminology of Ötemish Ḥājjī's account.

123. Ed. and tr. Moule and Pelliot, I (tr.), pp. 187–188; cf. p. 234; cf. Pelliot, *Notes on Marco Polo*, I, p. 240.

offerings to "idols" and the supply of kumiss to the dead for use in the next world. In general the use of kumiss offerings and libations in funeral and ancestral rites is widely known in Inner Asia, from the burial of a goblet of mare's milk with the deceased to provide nourishment in the next world, as attested for the Oghuz by Ibn Faḍlān, for the Qumans by Joinville, and for the Mongols by Plano Carpini,[124] to the iconographic reflection of the goblet in the famous carved stone statues of Inner Asian "warriors" holding cups before themselves at waist-level; we also, however, find extensive evidence on the central role of kumiss libations in ceremonies surrounding the cult of imperial ancestors among the thirteenth- and fourteenth-century Mongols.

These ceremonies are best described in the case of the court of the Great Khan in China, for which the Chinese dynastic history, the *Yüan-shih*, provides extensive accounts of Mongol ceremonies. Chapter 77 includes a description of the ceremony of "aspersion with mare's milk," which parallels Marco Polo's description but also implies the ceremony's ancestral connections:

> Every year the Emperor visited Shang-tu and on the 24th of the sixth[125] (lunar) month he performed a sacrifice called "Aspersion with mare's milk;" one horse and eight castrated rams, and nine bolts each of varicolored satin and softened coarse silk, and nine ears (of corn) wrapped in white sheep's wool, and three sable skins were needed. A Mongol shaman, and four Mongol and Chinese "intelligent officials" with the rank of *hsiu-ts'ai* were ordered to conduct the ceremony: they made two reverences and announcements to Heaven and invoked the august name of the Great Ancestor Činggis and pronounced a wish (*chu*): "Relying upon Heaven and upon the Fortune of the Emperor we shall sacrifice and hold (horse) races every year." Once the ceremony [was] completed, the officials in charge were each given one inner and outer garment of sacrificial silk; the remaining silks and the sacrificial objects were equally divided among all the participants.[126]

124. *The Mongol Mission*, pp. 12–13.

125. Or eighth; see Serruys' note.

126. Tr. Serruys, *Kumiss Ceremonies*, p. 3; cf. Ratchnevsky, "Über den mongolischen Kult," in particular pp. 426–429 on the aspersion ceremony. For the account of Chinese envoys in the

It is worth noting that the *Yüan-shih* presents this "aspersion" ritual as distinct from the "ancestral rite" described in the same chapter.[127] While the occasions described may indeed have been distinct, the classification of these rites may owe more to Chinese systematization than to a real distinction in the religious content of the rites; the "ancestral rite" includes kumiss libations along with the invocation of the "secret names" of the deceased emperor in the native Mongol language, while the rite of "aspersion with mare's milk," despite its seasonal character, likewise involves kumiss libations and invocations of the "personal name" of the imperial ancestor, Chingis Khan.[128] There are further indications in Chinese accounts (confirming Marco Polo's description as well) that attendance at such libation ceremonies was restricted to members of the imperial family, likewise suggesting ancestral and dynastic associations.[129]

It is one thing, however, to note the role of kumiss libations in the ancestral offerings to the spirits of deceased khans, and on this basis to suggest that Ötemish Ḥājjī's account reflects a somewhat garbled description of a drinking ceremony involving libations to ancestral spirits; it is quite another to suggest that such a ceremony was actually associated, in practice as well as in narrative development, with the setting in which Ötemish Ḥājjī seems to portray it as being performed: the *qoruq*. The latter interpretation is not entirely without foundation, however. On the one hand we have scant basis for assigning the *qoruq* itself a specific ritual role in connection with memorial feasts or ancestral offerings; on the contrary, descriptions of the *qoruq* often depict it as such a secret and "unre-

first half of the thirteenth century, see Olbricht and Pinks, *Meng-ta Pei-lu und Hei-ta Shih-lüeh*, pp. 77–78, 82ff.

127. Cf. Ratchnevsky, "Über den mongolischen Kult," pp. 418–421.

128. Ratchnevsky, "Über den mongolischen Kult," pp. 418–421, 426–427; see also Frederick W. Mote, "Yüan and Ming," in *Food in Chinese Culture: Anthropological and Historical Perspectives*, ed. K. C. Chang (New Haven: Yale University Press, 1977), pp. 195–257. Mote cites the *Yüan-shih*, chapter 77, as revealing that "when the Mongols engaged in their traditional sacrifices to their clan ancestors, employing their own shamans as masters of ritual and using the Mongol tongue, they stressed such typical steppe cultural elements as sprinkling the sacrificial ground with mare's milk, making offerings of mare's milk or koumiss, and of meat dried in the steppe fashion, and the sacrificing of horses" (p. 205); his words on the distance maintained between Chinese and Mongol ritual are likewise relevant, no doubt, to the experience of Muslims at the Mongol courts, and ultimately to the obscurity of Ötemish Ḥājjī's account of Özbek Khan's court libation ritual: "The Chinese recognized that there was a ritualized pattern of procedures at a state feast, yet even the learned Chinese associates of the Mongol rulers appear to have remained apart from and somewhat ignorant of those Mongol rituals" (p. 209).

129. Cf. Serruys, *Kumiss Ceremonies*, pp. 3–4.

coverable" site that it would seem unlikely to have enjoyed a significant ritual role.[130] On the other hand, we do have some suggestions that the *qoruq*, as the imperial cemetery, might have been the site of certain religiously charged ceremonial functions. Ötemish Ḥājjī, after all, in his account of Özbek's accession during the funeral rites for Toqtogha, portrays this occasion as a ceremonial gathering of clear political, and implicitly religio-political, importance, combining feasting and drinking with acknowledgment of the new khan's ritual and political prerogatives; this much is clear even if our interpretation of the *qoruq*'s appearance in this part of the narrative remains conjectural, and it is this combination, of a royal ritual involving ceremonial drinking and libation offerings, conducted in the sacred *qoruq*, which seems to be evoked also in Ötemish Ḥājjī's account of Özbek Khan's conversion. Here we may stress again that regardless of the "historicity" of the *qoruq*'s ritual role, the association of all three elements—ancestral libations plus ceremonial drinking conducted in or near the *qoruq*—is not only natural, but is attested to in some early sources.

In particular, there are some indications that libations to the ancestral spirits were often made *within* the sacred precincts of the *qoruq*; as noted above, there are indications that *qoruq*s of some type were the sites of the enthronement of new khans, in the Ilkhanid and Jöchid domains, while similarly, the seasonal character of visits to the Ilkhanid *qoruq*s as recorded in Öljeytü's case may mask a ritual purpose similar to the seasonal libation rites noted for the court of the Great Khan.[131] And the celebrated secrecy of the *qoruq*s was most probably the object of considerable exaggeration.[132]

130. Likewise, the "restricted" character of court libation rites clashes with the "public" character of court feasts, including even the presence of "foreigners;" such contradictions have not prevented the two themes from being conflated in Ötemish Ḥājjī's account.

131. On the seasonal nature of these rites, cf. Serruys, *Kumiss Ceremonies*, p. 4.

132. The consensus of descriptions of the sacred, forbidden burial precinct is that its very location was generally unknown, and such extreme inviolability would seem to be in conflict with the notion that khans visited the *qoruq* and conducted ceremonies there. In fact, however, this conflict should not disturb us greatly, for the *qoruq*s were probably never so secret as certain accounts would have us believe (cf. on this point Bartol'd/Rogers, "Burial Rites," p. 208, n. 56). As noted above, some accounts go so far as to emphasize (with horses trampling the ground, or those who conveyed an imperial body to the *qoruq* being slaughtered) that the very location was unknown, but it seems likely that such stories reflect a degree of hyperbole, no doubt purposefully engendered, regarding precisely the "forbidden-ness" and "unknowability" and inviolability of the *qoruq*; in other words, such stories heightened the sacredness of the burial grounds, and the assurances of secrecy were no doubt magnified both by popular imagination and with at least the tacit approval, if not active encouragement, of the Mongol leadership. At the same time, these accounts may reflect a topos long associated with Inner Asian royal burials. In any

More to the point, there is some more direct evidence of a ritual role for the *qoruq*, again in the case of the realm of the Great Khan where we find the clearest indications of the close association between libation ceremonies, involving the ritual drinking of kumiss, and the veneration of royal ancestors. In chapter 100 of the *Yüan-shih*, there is yet another description of a ceremony entailing offerings of milk to the deceased Mongol rulers, specifically called the "Golden Tombs' Mare-Milking" rite.[133] Discussions of this passage have focused on its descriptions of the gradations in the quality or refinement of the kumiss supplied, and on the figures responsible for caring for the mares and preparing the drinks; but the description of the "scene" at the ceremony is startlingly reminiscent of the accounts from Marco Polo, the *Yüan-shih*, and Ibn Baṭṭūṭah describing the ceremonial protocol at court feasts (we shall consider Ibn Baṭṭūṭah's account of the feast he attended at the court of Özbek Khan more fully below). Beyond the linking of ancestral veneration and kumiss libations evident in this rite's appelation as the "Golden Tombs' Mare-Milking" rite, it is clearly described as a kumiss ceremony at which the khan, princes, and officials assembled in an enormous tent, while large numbers of carts laden with containers of kumiss were brought and apportioned to the assembled guests.

Of further interest in this regard is an interesting Mongolian text that has recently come to light, describing the rituals associated with the cult of Chingis Khan; the text evidently dates to the latter sixteenth or early seventeenth century, and despite its Buddhist overlay gives a detailed description of the offerings to the spirit of Chingis Khan characteristic of indigenous Mongol tradition.[134] His cult itself, which has survived into

---

event, the notion that the *qoruq's* location was secret or even entirely forgotten should not be taken literally; even for the Mongol era, most of our accounts come, it may be recalled, from individuals who only heard about a *qoruq*; when someone *did* come upon a *qoruq*, he found "keepers" there to protect it from trespassers, and the very currency of the term *qoruqčï* for the "custodian" of the sacred burial precinct attests to the fact that the site of the *qoruq* was known at least to a few, as explicitly indicated in Rashīd ad-Dīn's account of the people assigned to the guardianship of Chingis Khan's burial place. And if keepers were assigned to the precincts, it seems a small step from their role as custodians to the assumption of a ritual role for the *qoruqs*.

133. The relevant section in the *Yüan-shih* (chapter 100, on the administration of the imperial horse pastures) is recounted by Serruys, *Kumiss Ceremonies*, pp. 4–5; he does not indicate the name of the ceremony, which is, however, noted by Ruth Meserve, "The *Yüan Shih* and Middle Mongolian," *Mongolian Studies*, 13 (1990), pp. 117–131, esp. p. 119; see both for references to further studies, all of which are limited to philological considerations.

134. Only the first portion of the text has been translated as of the time of writing; Chiodo, "'The Book of the Offerings,'" *ZAS*, 22 (1989–1991), pp. 190–220.

this century especially among the Mongols of the Ordos region (where one tradition places his tomb), features the performance of kumiss libations and other ancestral rites at the site of the "sacred precinct" still referred to as *qorugh*.[135] But the description in this newly discovered text is of particular importance for us, for it includes what would appear to be striking parallels (again without clarifying terminology) to the ceremony described in such garbled fashion in Ötemish Ḥājjī's work.

The elaborate ceremony in honor of Chingis Khan described in this text[136] involves (1) ceremonial processions of participants according to a clearly delineated hierarchy, into the khan's enormous pavilion; (2) the ritual presentation of vessels filled with several kinds of drinks, and of other sacrificial offerings; (3) the sprinkling of libations and the drinking of kumiss and other beverages according to a strict and elaborate hierarchical protocol; (4) the participation of a wide range of officiants, including a "master of the tents" in charge of the ceremony and other ritual actors; (5) the performance of ritual obeisance in the form of bowings and offerings (reminiscent of Ibn Baṭṭūṭah's description). Most intriguing, the account describes complicated sequences of pourings from certain vessels into others, in the course of which the officiants present vessels to the khan for him to offer in libation or to drink; the terminology, again, does not match that of Ötemish Ḥājjī's account (and after all, the text is in Mongol), but the parallel between the process described there and the sequence of pourings and offerings in our conversion narrative is quite striking.[137]

In any event, this newly found text makes clear what is evident from other sources as well, that court ceremony involving libation and drinking rites comparable to the pattern echoed in Ötemish Ḥājjī's narrative was intimately linked to the ancestral cult, with clear political implications in each case (both in the ritual homage to the emperor and in the affirmation of dynastic legitimacy); it is thus likely that this link was not entirely forgotten or meaningless by the time the narrative antecedents of Ötemish Ḥājjī's account took shape. All told, the evidence is not so extensive as we

135. Cf. Chiodo, pp. 214–215; on the use of kumiss libations in royal ancestral rituals centered upon the cult of Chingis Khan, see also Sagaster, *Die Weisse Geschichte*, pp. 207–208, 230–232, 354–356.

136. Cf. Chiodo's translation, esp. pp. 202–208.

137. On kumiss offerings in connection with ancestral rites, see further Henry Serruys, "The Cult of Čінggis-Qan: A Mongol Manuscript from Ordos," *ZAS*, 17 (1984), pp. 82–117, esp. the rite described on pp. 46–47, in which the ceremonial distribution of the kumiss portions from a goblet follows a prescribed hierarchy and is accompanied by sequences of kneelings and bowings.

might wish, but in relative terms it is not insignificant either. It suggests that kumiss libations were closely linked to the ancestral cult of royal ancestors, the observance of which was naturally restricted to the royal family and may have involved the ritual use of the inviolate royal burial grounds; it suggests also the specific element of the manipulation of vessels, used in successive pourings and aspersions and in drinking, as a component of the ancestral libation ritual, and this feature strongly suggests that it was just such an elaborate manipulation of ceremonial utensils that Ötemish Ḥājjī's account reflects, however poorly.

Here it is not of great consequence that the ancestral libations are not *consistently* described as having been conducted at or in the sacred royal burial grounds; at the same time, of course, other kumiss ceremonies existed without direct connections to the cult of royal ancestors. What is significant is that both the ancestral libations and the practice of reserving royal burial grounds were known among Muslims as features of pre-Islamic Mongol religious and court ceremony, and their *narrative* association is entirely reasonable even if their actual association is less frequently recorded.

It thus seems likely that one of the narrative threads found in Ötemish Ḥājjī's account reflects a memory (already "stylized") of a libation ceremony in honor of the khan's royal ancestors (but with the inevitable economic benefits sought thereby), conducted by the shamans and restricted to the khan's family; even if such ceremonies did not take place within the inviolate precincts of the *qoruq*, their restricted nature may have contributed to the conflation of the two elements (since both are also tied to ancestral veneration). In Ötemish Ḥājjī's account we are left with only an *implicit* portrayal of the kumiss ceremony being conducted inside the sacred royal reserve, but the conflation heightens the impact of the displacement entailed when the Muslim saints spoil the rite and intrude upon the *qoruq*. The *qoruq* itself was naturally tied to the cult of royal ancestors, and ritual practice associated with this cult clearly involved elements typical of kumiss libation ceremonies;[138] to find both the kumiss rites and the *qoruq* portrayed together in Ötemish Ḥājjī's narrative, then, even if only in allusion, would seem to reinforce the idea that the ancestral focus of both these elements, as a key feature of "pagan" religion at the Mongol court, was the "target" of earlier versions of the narrative we know from Ötemish Ḥājjī's sixteenth-century version.

138. Serruys, *Kumiss Ceremonies*, p. 13.

It may be suggested, moreover, that it is not only the formal elements of similar ritual practice that link the general kumiss ceremonies, with their "first fruits" and fructifying associations, with the specific kumiss ceremony performed in connection with the veneration of the imperial ancestors. As Marco Polo's account suggests, the royal responsibility to ensure the realm's prosperity was both explicitly stated by the "astrologers and idolaters," and was implicitly stressed by the restriction of participation in this festival to the royal family. From this and other descriptions we may conclude that the imperial ancestral lineage is directly responsible for the entire realm's well-being; in effect the khan and his deceased ancestors' spirits, whether addressed at the royal burial ground or in some other sanctified reserve, come to represent the whole people, thereby further underscoring the vital communal and political imperatives requiring the veneration of imperial ancestors.

Finally, we may note that the very term *qoruq*, as well as its specific association not only with burials but with funeral feasts, appears to have survived in Qazaq usage[139] at least through the nineteenth century. An article published in 1895 recounts a Qazaq *as* (funeral feast) in Sarytav *volost'* of Karkaralinsk *uezd*, celebrated for a wealthy Qazaq named Jamanbala Kurmanov, with over 10,000 guests and enormous amounts of meat, kumiss, and tea; the account mentions the selection of a "reserve" (*urochishche*), by a river and well supplied with vegetation and water, as the site for the funeral repast, assigning the place the designation *Koryk* as a proper name.[140] Such funeral feasts are described often in local news-

139. In modern (Soviet "Kazakh") dictionaries the term is defined only in terms of an enclosed and restricted "preserve," without any explicit tie to burial rites.

140. The account itself has not been available to me; it is summarized in the bibliography of literature on the Qazaqs compiled late in the last century by A. E. Alektorov, *Ukazatel' knig, zhurnal'nykh i gazetnykh statei i zametok o kirgizakh* (Kazan: Tipo-litografiia Imperatorskago Universiteta, 1900), p. 665, citing an evidently unsigned article, entitled "Iz nashei zhizni: Kirgizskiia pominki," in the journal *Perevodchik*, 1895, No. 19. Other such accounts may also include the terminology of interest here; this is the only one which for which Alektorov's abstract clearly shows that it does. See further on Qazaq funeral feasts N. Zh. Zhakhanova, "Pishcha v pogrebal'no-pominal'nom komplekse kazakhov (XIX–nachalo XX v.)," in *Kratkoe soderzhanie dokladov sredneaziatsko-kavkazskikh chtenii: Voprosy ètnosotsial'noi i kul'turnoi istorii Srednei Azii i Kavkaza* (Leningrad: Nauka, November 1983), pp. 21–22; and the description, with further references, in A. V. Konovalov, *Kazakhi iuzhnogo Altaia (Problemy formirovaniia ètnicheskoi gruppy)* (Alma-Ata: Nauka, 1986), pp. 112–124. The contemporary resonance of such burial customs is evidenced in the popular novel of the Qïrghïz writer Chingiz Aitmatov, available in English translation as *The Day Lasts More than a Hundred Years*, tr. John French (Bloomington: Indiana University Press, 1983), in which the hero's "quest" is to bury a friend according to Islamized Qazaq rites in his hereditary clan cemetery, whose site has been

papers and journals, of difficult access today, from prerevolutionary Kazakhstan, but in this case at least we find a clear indication that the *qoruq* held also ritual implications as the site of funeral feasts in Inner Asia, down to quite recent times.

COURT CEREMONIAL AND RITUAL PROTOCOL

If the parallels between Ötemish Ḥājjī's account and descriptions of actual libation rituals remain somewhat tenuous, the protocol linked with drinking ceremonies at the Mongol courts is echoed with considerably greater strength. The scene described by Ötemish Ḥājjī would appear to involve a special setting and a ceremony conducted in the presence of, and possibly with the participation of, a substantial crowd; it clearly involves the manipulation of drinks and drinking utensils by the khan's shamans, culminating in the offering of the beverage to the khan; and it suggests an element of hierarchical protocol through mention of the honored position accorded the "sorcerers" by the khan, who honored "these shaykhs" and seated them beside himself. In each case we find parallels to descriptions of court drinking ceremonies well known from the Mongol-ruled world of the thirteenth and fourteenth centuries.

We may note to begin with that such drinking ceremonies themselves most likely included the ritual libations of kumiss noted above; these libations were standard features of a number of festivals celebrated in connection with ancestral veneration, enthronements and funerals, the khan's birthday, and "first fruits" rites, and there is little doubt that they accompanied virtually all court celebrations involving feasting and drinking, for whatever purpose. This concurrence of rites is evident of funeral and memorial feasts, with their ancestral focus, already in Juvaynī's description of the enthronement of Ögödey, when the celebration involved not only the customary drinking ceremony (those present kneel three times with their cups, wishing the new khan well), but the games and entertainments characteristic of libation rites as well as a three-day

incorporated into the forbidden zone of the Soviet space center; the novel is even structured as a shamanic journey to guide the soul to the land of the dead, complete with the celebration, journey, tests, and bargaining (i.e., with the "keeper" of the land of the dead), typical of such shamanic narratives (as when the hero—who, incidentally, is named Yedigei—must confront the guards at the cosmodrome). This underlying shamanic structure is not noted in Irena Jeziorska, "Religious Themes in the Novels of Chingiz Aitmatov," in *Cultural Change and Continuity in Central Asia*, ed. Shirin Akiner (London: Kegan Paul International/Central Asian Research Forum, SOAS, 1991), pp. 45–70, where, however, reference is made to other aspects of "Kirghiz" religion.

memorial feast for Chingis Khan (including the sacrifice of forty maidens and many horses "to join his spirit").[141] The association of court ceremony and libation ritual is likewise suggested in the Armenian account of Kirakos: "And when drinking *γmuz* and wine one of them took it into his hands in a large vessel and having drawn some out in a small cup scattered it skywards and then to the east and west and south and north; and then he that scattered it having drunk a little of it offered it to the most senior person."[142]

It is thus not clear that we should make a sharp distinction between the features of Ötemish Ḥājjī's narrative that recall libation rituals and those that recall court ceremonial, because the two were combined in actual practice, and their combination in narrative would be only natural.

In the case of court ceremonial, however, we have more extensive descriptions that allow us to note the parallels with Ötemish Ḥājjī's account: in particular the element of "orientation" in the seating arrangement assumes special importance.

The ceremonial aspects of kumiss drinking and court feasts in Inner Asia have attracted considerable scholarly attention,[143] and the Mongol-

141. Juvaynī/Boyle, I, pp. 187–189; on the "salutatory" portion of the ceremony, with the kneelings, cf. Marco Polo's description (Moule/Pelliot, p. 224) and that of Ibn Baṭṭūṭah, discussed below. The seventeenth-century *Baḥr al-asrār* mentions a "feast" (*ʿīd*) that was "a custom of the Mongol sovereigns" that coincided with an assembly of Mongol princes and *amīrs* under the Muslim Ghāzān, noting that the khan ordered preparations for the rites (MS IVAN Uz Inv. No. 1385, f. 110b).

142. Tr. J. A. Boyle, "Kirakos of Ganjak on the Mongols," *CAJ*, 8 (1963), pp. 199–214 [p. 201].

143. The best review of Inner Asian court ceremonial, discussing both the use of kumiss in drinking rites and issues of seating and "orientational" protocol, is that of Robert Bleichsteiner, "Zeremonielle Trinksitten und Raumordnung bei den turko-mongolischen Nomaden," *Archiv für Völkerkunde*, 6–7 (1952), pp. 181–208, prompted in part by L. P. Potapov, "Drevnii obychai otrazhaiushchii pervobytno-obshchinnyi byt kochevnikov," *Tiurkologicheskii sbornik*, 1 (1951) (= *Sbornik S. E. Malovu*), pp. 164–175, which in turn commented in part on Bartol'd's study of Uzbek court ceremonial as described in the seventeenth-century *Baḥr al-asrār* ("Tseremonial pri dvore uzbetskikh khanov v XVII veke," *Sbornik v chest' . . . Potanina* [*ZIRGO po otd. ètn.*, 34 (1909)], pp. 293–308; repr. *Sochineniia*, II/2, pp. 388–399); see further Togan, *Reisebericht*, pp. 159–160; Doerfer, *TMEN*, I, pp. 163–166, s.v. "*ōrān*;" Lech/ʿUmarī, *Das mongolische Weltreich*, pp. 107, 245, n. 177; and on the social and ritual facets of court drinking ceremonies, see also the interesting remarks of Leonardo Olschki, *Guillaume Boucher, A French Artist at the Court of the Khans* (Baltimore: Johns Hopkins University Press, 1946), pp. 52–58. For descriptions and reproductions of miniatures depicting such ceremonies, cf. M. Ş. İpşiroğlu, *Saray-Alben: Diez'sche Klebebände aus den Berliner Sammlungen* (Wiesbaden: Franz Steiner Verlag, 1964; Verzeichnis der orientalischen Handschriften in Deutschland, Bd. VIII), pp. 22–23 (and Plate VII), 91.

era accounts, from Rubruck,[144] Marco Polo,[145] Ibn Baṭṭūṭah,[146] and the *Yüan-shih*,[147] are well-known. The descriptions found in these European, Islamic, and Chinese accounts are remarkably similar: they describe the details of protocol in terms of the seating arrangement, the sequence of drinking, and the risings and kneelings and prostrations of the guests in honor of the khan; the enormous quantities of kumiss and other beverages; and the function of the "lords" or "barons" who serve the guests and supervise etiquette. The religious cast of the ceremony is suggested in one of the feasts Marco Polo describes, which features "a great prelate" who commands those present to prostrate themselves before the khan and supervises the veneration of an "altar" bearing the khan's name.[148]

As the account of a visitor to the same court that is reflected, in stylized fashion, in Ötemish Ḥājjī's narrative, Ibn Baṭṭūṭah's description is of special interest here. Its interest lies in its confirmation of the type of ceremonial otherwise known most thoroughly from the court of the Great Khan in China, but also in the divergence of Ibn Baṭṭūṭah's account, in one noteworthy particular, from the situation portrayed in the narrative of Ötemish Ḥājjī. In the latter account, a court ceremony evidently marked by ritual drinking is the setting for a religious confrontation that in effect ends with the displacement of the old infidel ways by Islamic customs, and with the displacement of the pagan "sorcerers" by the Muslim saints. Ibn Baṭṭūṭah's account describes a drinking ceremony of a type that must have inspired the narrative preserved by Ötemish Ḥājjī; yet in his account, although Ibn Baṭṭūṭah does not explicitly make the point, the celebration is the setting not for confrontation, but for a remarkable integration of the holy people and holy customs of the two traditions, Mongol and Muslim, still in the process of being assimilated one to another.

It is indeed the fact that Ibn Baṭṭūṭah describes the events without com-

144. He mentions only briefly the use of *cosmos* (Jackson emends the reading of this term to *comos*) during a ceremonial drinking festival at Batu's court (*The Mongol Mission*, pp. 127–128) and in a major "drinking festival" sponsored by Möngke (p. 202).

145. Cf. Moule/Pelliot, I, pp. 217–225; included are a general description of the seating arrangement for feasting, and the array of drinks and vessels, as well as specific descriptions of the khan's birthday feast and a new year's feast.

146. Ed. Defrémery and Sanguinetti, II, pp. 403–410, discussed more fully below.

147. Cf. the translation of the relevant passage in the notes to M. G. Pauthier's translation of Marco Polo, *Le livre de Marco Polo, citoyen de Venise, conseiller privé et commissaire impériale de Khoubilaï-Khaân* (Paris: Librairie de Firmin Didot Frères, Fils, 1865), I, pp. 291–296.

148. Moule/Pelliot, I, p. 224.

ment, and without insisting upon the point, that highlights, through their almost inadvertent juxtaposition, the linking of Mongol and Muslim features in the celebration. Ibn Baṭṭūṭah begins by noting that the occasion was the end of Ramażān and then describes the appearance of the khan, his wives, and several bodies of troops, naming the Muslim dignitaries participating as well. He then recounts the protocol observed by the Mongol *amīrs* in approaching the khan, describing the huge tent erected to serve as an audience- and banquet-hall for the *amīrs* as well as the ritual and hierarchy observed as the royal family and *amīrs* partook of the drink of fermented honey. The khan's daughter first presented a cup to the khan, then gave another cup first to the senior *khātūn* and then to the other wives according to their rank, with each presentation accompanied by greetings; then the heir-apparent (i.e., Tïnï Bek) took the cup and offered it, in order, to the khan, to the *khātūns*, and to his sister; next the khan's second son (i.e., Jānī Bek) took the cup and offered it to his brother, after which the great *amīrs* rose and each offered the drink to the heir-apparent, followed by the *abnāʾ al-mulūk* (evidently the princes of the blood, Chingisids) doing the same to the second son (Jānī Bek); finally the lower-ranked *amīrs* presented the drink to the "sons of the kings."

This detailed description of Mongol court protocol is followed by mention of the grand tent set up opposite the mosque for the Muslim dignitaries, Ibn Baṭṭūṭah among them, which included the *qāżī*, the *khaṭīb*, the Sayyid Ibn ʿAbd al-Ḥamīd, and other *faqīhs* and shaykhs; these were served, he says, by "the nobles of the Turks."[149] Some among the *faqīhs* present ate, he reports, while others abstained rather than eat from tables made of gold and silver; Ibn Baṭṭūṭah notes that as far as he could see there were carts laden with skins of *qïmïz*, which the khan ordered distributed among the people present. The festivities ended, insofar as Ibn Baṭṭūṭah describes them, with the Friday prayer in the mosque; as he notes, before the khan's delayed arrival (and his inebriated greeting of the Sayyid Ata), those assembled at the mosque discussed whether the khan would come or not: some said he would not, because he was overcome by drunkenness, while others said that he would not neglect the Friday prayer.

149. Cf. Marco Polo's "barons" who serve at the feasts (Moule/Pelliot, pp. 219–220). Both terms may refer to the offices of the *bavurchï*, the royal cook (cf. Doerfer, *TMEN*, I, pp. 202–205) or the *bökävül*, a more powerful figure with extensive responsibilities for supply and organization with respect to both court and military protocol (cf. *TMEN*, II, pp. 301–307); the latter figure is described as a kind of "master of ceremonies" at the court of the Golden Horde, cf. G. S. Sablukov, "Ocherk vnutrenniago sostoianiia kipchakskago tsarstva," *IOAIÈ*, t. 13, vyp. 2 (1896), pp. 89–146 [p.123]

The net effect of this narrative juxtaposition of Mongol and Muslim usage, with descriptions of Mongol drinking ritual interspersed with remarks on examples, evidently not universal, of Muslim abstemiousness, and with the well-made point of the integration of both worlds in the person of the khan himself—confirming in part the expectations of both parties at the mosque by attending to his prayers but doing so while still drunk and ritually impure—is the portrayal of a community learning, slowly, to be Muslim and in no way willing to jettison even those features of cherished communal custom that lent themselves to such vivid contrasts with Islamic values as are implicit, for a more seasoned Muslim audience, in Ibn Baṭṭūṭah's narrative. The picture presented is not one of a once-and-for-all choice made in response to the "summons" to Islam, but of an integration, a two-way assimilation in which Mongol/Inner Asian values and customs make way for Muslim counterparts, while Muslim religious figures make way for infidel habits in celebrating at least non-Qurʾānic Islamic rites.[150]

This assimilative image in Ibn Baṭṭūṭah's account is a further indication that the narrative expectations entailed by the Islamic paradigm for "conversion" required a *heightening* of the tension presumably necessitated by the "choice" exercised in adopting Islam, and thus required the transformation of what appears in Ibn Baṭṭūṭah's account as a joint celebration of a Muslim holiday and a Mongol feast, held by the Muslim calendar and with Muslim figures "officiating," but observing significant aspects of Mongol/Inner Asian protocol and food ways, into a confrontation between two traditions presented as unalterably and uncompromisingly opposed. If Ibn Baṭṭūṭah's "assimilative" portrayal undoubtedly reflects the actual situation at an early phase of Islamization, the narrative highlighting the oppositional displacement of the old tradition by Islam should be understood as reflecting a subsequent phase, in which Islam was being posed as an alternative basis for political organization and legitimacy, and "oppositional" Islamization as a paradigm for mobilizing support. At the same time, however, we should no doubt refrain from attaching a strict chronological sequence to the emergence

150. It may be noted here that what is missing from Ibn Baṭṭūṭah's account is any mention of shamans or *bakhshīs* or any indigenous Mongol religious figures among the khan's retinue; it is impossible to judge whether he simply chose not to mention such inconvenient figures, or whether there were indeed no longer such figures with Özbek Khan, in which case we might point to the Mamlūk sources' testimony on the khan's extermination of the supporters of infidel ways as having had real effect outside the specifically court-related customs described by Ibn Baṭṭūṭah as still flourishing.

of "oppositional" narratives, since groups and factions inclined to make use of such narratives may well have emerged quite early on, possibly in the most preliminary stages of Islamization.

Finally, we may consider a central element in the ceremonial aspects of the "drinking" ritual echoed in Ötemish Ḥājjī's account, one that particularly highlights the role of "displacement" in the conversion narrative. This is the element of orientation and seating, an issue that figures prominently in descriptions of Mongol protocol from the thirteenth and fourteenth centuries. What is most remarkable about this issue is the clear echo of a particular theme, which must have been significant in the "original" conversion narrative, in two independent traditions for which elements of that narrative must have served as sources. That is, we find Baba Tükles and his companions implicitly displacing the "sorcerers" of Özbek Khan, whose place of honor at his side was earned through their role in the ceremony that the Muslim saints magically spoiled; quite independently we find a similar displacement implied in the case of the *other* figure credited with the conversion of Özbek Khan, the "Sayyid Ata" of Central Asian tradition. In the latter case the displacement is implied by the curious report, known from a number of Central Asian sources, that the place of honor at the khan's side among the Islamized "spiritual" descendants of Özbek Khan was reserved to holders of the rank of *naqīb*, and that this rank and the accompanying place of honor had been vouchsafed to the descendants of Sayyid Ata on account of his role in the conversion of Özbek Khan.[151]

The best-known report on the *naqīb*'s position appears in the important seventeenth-century Central Asian historical work of Maḥmūd b. Amīr Valī, the *Baḥr al-asrār*; written around 1640, this work includes the author's account of the customs and etiquette observed during a drinking ceremony at the court of the Ashtarkhanid ruler of Balkh, an account noted some eighty years ago by Bartol'd.[152] The author ascribed these customs to the *yasa* and *yosun* of the "Mongols," and it is clear that much of the ceremonial described reflects pre-Islamic steppe customs preserved among the Uzbeks. The place of highest honor in such ceremonial gatherings, according to the *Baḥr al-asrār*, was assigned to the *naqīb*: the Uzbeks honor the left side above the right because the heart is on the left side of the body, and the most honored place, to the immediate left of the

151. I have dealt with this issue at length in "The Descendants of Sayyid Ata and the Rank of *Naqīb* in Central Asia," to appear in a forthcoming issue of *JAOS*.

152. Cf. Bartol'd, "Tseremonial;" Potapov, "Drevnii obychai;" Bleichsteiner, "Zeremonielle."

Khan, is the place of the *naqībs* (*orun-i nuqabā*); and the regard shown to them, the account continues, is so great that all the princes, including the heir to the throne, sit below the *naqībs*.

This passage makes no mention of the hereditary holders of the rank of *naqīb*, an element confirmed, however, by another important discussion of the *naqīb* in the *Baḥr al-asrār* that Bartol'd did not mention. In this passage,[153] following a biographical account of a particular *naqīb* who was a descendant of Sayyid Ata, the author notes that for about 200 years this post "had been attached hereditarily to the descendants of Sayyid Ata," on the basis of some unspecified, but, we are told, widely known, oral tradition; Nadr Muḥammad Khan, however, the ruler of Balkh in the author's time, had recently transferred the title to a natural and spiritual descendant of Bahāʾ ad-Dīn Naqshband.

Less well known, but some fifteen years earlier, than the *Baḥr al-asrār*, is a rare hagiographical work (noted above in connection with its account of Sayyid Ata's missionary work in the Dasht-i Qïpchaq) that confirms this exclusive reservation of the post of *naqīb* to the descendants of Sayyid Ata; the work is of particular importance in that it explicitly links, as *Baḥr al-asrār* does not, the hereditary right to the post of *naqīb* with Sayyid Ata's role in the conversion of the tribes of the Dasht-i Qïpchaq to Islam. The work in question is the *Manāqib al-akhyār*, completed in 1036/1626 by a certain Muḥammad Qāsim, known by the *takhalluṣ* "Rizvān," a descendant of Sayyid Ata, and recounts the life and sayings of the author's father, Sayyid Jamāl ad-Dīn, known as "Khoja Dīvānah Sayyid Atāʾī" (d. 1016/1607).[154]

After noting Sayyid Ata's central role in the conversion of the "Özbek and Manghït and Tatar" tribes to Islam (see above), the author goes on to stress the close relationship established between the khans of the Uzbeks and Sayyid Ata's family; the description of the *naqīb*'s status is quite close to that of the *Baḥr al-asrār*. He notes the establishment of kinship ties through marriage, and states that Sayyid Ata's descendants were admitted to councils of the *pādshāhs* and princes and were seated to their left; this place, he says, was called the "*orun-i niqābat*" (the seat of the *naqīb*), and "in the customary law [*töre*] there is no higher place than the *orun* of the

153. MS India Office, Ethé 575, f. 286b–287b, esp. 287a; noted by Buri Akhmedov, *Istoriia Balkha* (Tashkent, 1982), pp. 148–149.

154. See now on this work my "Neglected Source," and the manuscript references given above in Chapter 2; the account of interest here appears in the India Office MS, ff. 17a–b, Rampur MS, ff. 21a–b.

left hand, for as that people says, the heart is on the left." He goes on to note the participation of the Sayyids in the *kengeshs* (councils) and *toys* (feasts) of the Uzbeks, observing that the brothers and sons of the *pādshāh* would be seated "below" the seat of the *naqīb* occupied by the Sayyid. As a result, the author writes, "this *ṭarīqah* has been strong from the time of the holy Sayyid Ata down to the present." He notes, however, that the position of Sayyid Ata's descendants had recently been threatened by another group that had gained the khans' favor; this statement appears to allude to the growing political power of Naqshbandī shaykhs in Central Asia, suggested also by the passage cited earlier from the *Baḥr al-asrār*, reflecting yet another "displacement," not of shamans by Sufis in this case, but of one Sufi "dynasty" by another.[155]

Now the rank of *naqīb* has a long history in the Islamic world, and is linked above all with notions of the hereditary sacrality reserved to the Prophet's descendants; the *naqīb* appears most often, indeed, as the head of the ʿAlids or *sayyids* of a particular city, although the title was later applied to the heads of various religiously tinged groups such as craft guilds and *futuwwah* organizations. In Central Asia during the Uzbek period (sixteenth–nineteenth centuries), however, the post of *naqīb* is universally described in a military context: the bearer of the title is entrusted with the ordering of ranks and units and with the matters of military supply, and is usually portrayed as one of the most important figures in the khan's administration, often as a figure with unparalleled access to and intimacy with the khan himself. The reservation of this apparently important post to the Sayyid Atāʾī family reflects, according to the testimony of the seventeenth-century hagiography, as well as of the late legendary history, the prestige associated with the descendants of the person who brought Islam to the Dasht-i Qïpchaq.

It is also possible that there is a clue to the native understanding of Islamization in the assignment of this post to the descendants of the Islamizer. It suggests that the post was not merely a prize handed out as a result of respect for that Islamizing role, but that the functions associ-

155. Yet another source affirms the hereditary *niqābat* of Sayyid Ata's descendants, a legendary history of Central Asia compiled in the early eighteenth century and full of legendary and folkloric material on the Mongol and Timurid eras; entitled *Kunūz al-aʿẓam* (for a brief description of this work, cf. Storey-Bregel', *PL*, II, pp. 812–815), the work notes that Sayyid Ata served in the army of the newly converted Özbek Khan in the military post of *naqīb*, prompting the khan to promise Sayyid Ata's descendants the *niqābat* for as long as their descendants lived. This account makes no mention of the Sayyid Atāʾī *naqīb*'s ceremonial status, nor does it refer to the loss of the title to the Naqshbandīyah.

ated with the *niqābat* as well—namely organizing and leading the army, especially an army portrayed as one involved in war against unbelievers—were considered appropriate to those linked with the process of Islamization. It is therefore interesting to note, in view of the military implications of the rank reserved to one tradition's "bearer" of Islam in the Dasht-i Qïpchaq, the likely association of Sayyid Ata with Özbek Khan's son Jānī Bek, and the latter's association with military innovations in the Golden Horde. The close ties between the figure, mentioned by Ibn Baṭṭūṭah, whom it may be possible to identify with "Sayyid Ata," and Özbek Khan's son Jānī Bek, are noted by Ibn Baṭṭūṭah, but the persistent appearance of Jānī Bek in the later conversion stories focused on Sayyid Ata suggests a popular memory of their ties as well. And, as noted earlier, Jānī Bek is specifically named, by sources contemporary with his reign, as having instituted a requirement that his troops wear clothing identified not only with Islam, but with Sufism: he introduced the wearing of turbans and of the *farajīyah*, the latter a designation for a shirtlike tunic closely associated with the garb of dervishes.

The theme of the Islamizer's intrusion into pre-Islamic court protocol associated with drinking ceremonies is thus clearly evoked in the Central Asian tradition surrounding Sayyid Ata, whose esteem in the Jöchid *ulus* is implicitly linked with that intrusion. The Central Asian tradition itself may have further ramifications for Islamization and the role of Sufis in that process that may be relegated to a separate discussion;[156] for present purposes what it offers is additional evidence of the likelihood that such intrusion and displacement are to be found in Ötemish Ḥājjī's narrative as well.

We may recapitulate: The central point in this ceremonial component of the narrative is the Muslim saints' disruption of a ritual that involves multiple, in some ways conflicting, elements of indigenous Mongol tradition posed against the sanctifying power of the Muslims; the conflation of themes evident in Ötemish Ḥājjī's version, as in the case of the *qoruq*, no doubt added to the multivalence and flexibility of the narrative. The Muslim saints intrude into a sacred, reserved setting properly restricted to the khan and his religious advisers, and there they disrupt a ceremony whose description evokes the sacred ancestral and political associations of ancestral libation rites and of ritual affirmations of sovereignty. Here we may

156. I.e., in my "Descendants of Sayyid Ata," and planned studies of the Central Asian legends on the life of Sayyid Ata.

emphasize, in anticipation of the centrality of Baba Tükles in the narrative as sealed in the decisive "ordeal" in the fire-pit and as elaborated in later tradition, that the ceremony is directed by the shamans: its disruption challenges their power at court, and sets the stage—if we keep the "shamanic" character of Baba Tükles' activities, discussed below, in mind—for the usurpation of the role of shaman by the Muslim saints; in this case the central focus of these shamans' displacement is Baba Tükles himself, whose religious meaning is further explored in subsequent chapters.

The themes of the *qoruq* and the drinking ceremony, finally, offer an additional lesson with regard to our understanding of Ötemish Ḥājjī's conversion narrative. In each case we must be certain to appreciate the specifically *narrative* purpose involved and not fall into the trap of presuming to find "historical fact" underlying the dramatic structure of the conversion narrative. To be sure, some historical, factual core obviously does underlie the creation and circulation of the narrative. Naturally, we must consider more historically based descriptions of Mongol-era religious practices in order to understand both the significance of the religious counterpoints highlighted by the narrative, and the currency of the practices themselves as likely focuses for such religious counterpoints. But it is not the "historicity" of the practices *as described and combined* in Ötemish Ḥājjī's narrative that is of concern here, much less the historicity of the specific "events" recounted in the story of Özbek Khan's conversion. Rather, our task is only to show the "historicity" of the narrative conventions and perceived religious tensions that together lent potential religious significance to the conflation of motifs used in the narrative construction that underlies Ötemish Ḥājjī's account.

4

Conversion Narrative and Religious Meaning, II: The Drama

In the foregoing discussion we have considered some particular elements in Ötemish Ḥājjī's account of Baba Tükles and the variety of religious themes, both Inner Asian and Islamic, that they evoke. We may turn now to a consideration of the dramatic structure of the account, and the parallels between this structure and other types of religious narratives. We will first consider the shamanic character of several features in the narrative, features that together allow us to find elements of a structural parallel between the narrative about Baba Tükles and accounts of shamanic journeys and, especially, initiatic experiences; next we will examine the wider range of religious meanings evoked in the climactic episode of the oven-pit, in which we find reflections of both Islamic and Inner Asian religious symbolism and narrative paradigms; finally, we will consider the examples of several other conversion narratives that offer thematic and structural parallels to the conversion narrative focused on Baba Tükles, as a basis for exploring the themes of oppositional and assimilative displacement in such narratives. We will then turn briefly in Chapter 5 to several issues connected with the name of Baba Tükles himself, before turning to the later developments of his tale in historical and epic traditions.

Baba Tükles and Shamanic Narrative

In at least three moments in Ötemish Ḥājjī's narrative, all tied directly to the oven-pit episode, we find actions and elements that may be regarded as echoes of shamanic performance and, especially, initiation. It may be objected that these elements are too general and the parallels too contrived to provide a sufficient basis for arguing that we find a clear shamanic element among the features that add religious meaning to the narrative. I believe a case can be made, however, when these elements are considered together, and indeed, the shamanic character of at least part of the narrative is confirmed most convincingly by the parallels between Ötemish Ḥājjī's account and a narrative of unquestionably shamanic origin, as we will see shortly.

Baba Tükles himself is, of course, a rather "shamanic" character in his approach to the task of converting Özbek Khan, but we will consider his persona later. The three signal moments in the narrative all appear in the context of Baba Tükles' decision to enter the fiery oven-pit; the oven-pit's various associations (with fire, sacrifice, and tomb) are likewise discussed later in this chapter, but here we may note another, less obvious one. As Baba Tükles enters the fire, evidently to be consumed there (as is in fact described in the case of the infidel sorcerer), we see a parallel to the symbolic dismemberment of the shaman, often involving fire and the "cooking" of the shaman in a cauldron, which is a virtually universal feature of narratives recounting shamanic initiation.[1] The three moments are then (1) the act of putting on the protective "armor,"[2] which amounts to Baba Tükles' donning of a shamanic costume; (2) the act of entering the fire-pit, which parallels a prospective shaman's submission to the initiatic ritual (often regarded as occurring within a cave or cauldron), as is further signaled by the "ecstatic" fervor implied when his body hair stands on end; and (3) the commission to Baba Tükles' three companions to pray for him and fix their attention upon him, which amounts to the shaman's appeal to his protective and guiding spirits.

From this perspective we may regard Baba Tükles' entry into and safe emergence from the oven-pit—a narrative element whose links to the legends of origin based on "emergence" from a formative "enclosure" are also discussed later in this chapter—as an echo of the shamanic initiation

1. Cf. Eliade, *Shamanism*, pp. 33–45.

2. The iron ringlets that evidently make up the *jiba* that Baba Tükles put on already recall the

of ritual death and rebirth. Here we may add the role of shaman to the mythic complex attached to Baba Tükles, for he is Hero and Ancestor and First Man and Nation-Founder and Shaman, all subsumed in one numinous figure. That it is not excessively contrived to regard these features as specifically "shamanic" will be argued below on the basis of comparative material; for now, however, we must point out the links between Baba Tükles' shamanic character and his community-forming role.

In most treatments of shamanism, the shaman is approached as an individual figure, a loner beset by spiritual experiences he must learn to control; as noted above, his social roles are less often emphasized. From such a perspective we might be content to view Baba Tükles' "shamanic initiation" in the oven pit as the climax in his "legitimation" as a Hero and Ancestor, viewing it as an individual experience of importance in shaping the mythic persona of Baba Tükles. But there is probably much more at work here; indeed, the shaman's social role should not be understood solely in terms of the various practical functions he provides as healer, arbiter, ritual celebrant, and counselor. It has been suggested recently,[3] in arguing against the excessively "individualistic" approach to shamanism adopted by Eliade, that the shaman's initiatic dismemberment and reconstitution themselves involve vital *communal* aspects, and that the completed initiation experience amounts to an important reconstitution, or reaffirmation, of communal integrity. The shaman thus "stands in" for the community as a whole, establishing his identification with the group when he dons his costume (an act that allows his helping spirits to "recognize" him) and undergoing symbolically the breaking down of the body politic and its reestablishment as a functioning whole. Such an interpretation may go too far in assuming the ritual and/or magical identification of the shaman and his community, but it opens fruitful new perspectives from which to consider the meaning of *narrating* the shamanic experience, if not the content of the experience itself.

From this perspective, a narrative of the initiatic experience, in which the shaman's bones are pulled apart and then put back together, should be understood as a discursive reaffirmation of the integrity and solidarity of the community which the new shaman is to serve; the shaman *embodies* the community, his bones representing the constituent elements of the larger group (as indeed the clan-based kinship groups that form the con-

bits of iron often found on shamans' costumes.

3. See the insightful analysis of Kortt, "The Shaman as Social Representative."

stituent parts of Inner Asian communities are often termed "bones"). As the shaman himself recounts the experience, those communal bonds are accepted and affirmed by his audience, and, as a narrative recounting the experience is appropriated by the community, to be abstracted from a particular shaman and to become part of the communal picture of the world, the symbolism is reinforced of a composite whole tested and forged before emerging into the world as a community.

In the specific context of Baba Tükles, then, the element of *conversion* adds a new twist: Baba Tükles brings his helping spirits, agrees to submit to an initiatic "test," and by surviving it accomplishes nothing less than the reconstitution of the community into which he came *as a Muslim community*, with him as its spiritual guardian. He took on the role of representative of the Islamic community—soon to include the "Özbek" community—when he claimed the right to undergo the test and donned his "armor"; in the acceptance of Islam following his emergence from the fire-pit we see a parallel to the ceremonial communal acceptance of a new shaman following his successful completion of the initiatic "ordeal."

In addition to the structural ways in which the narrative of Baba Tükles parallels shamanic narratives, as well as the shamanic-style imagery of Baba Tükles' own sanctity, we may note here that the element of fire is itself evocative of the shamanic character of Baba Tükles insofar as mastery over fire is a common motif in accounts of shamans' lives, and demonstrations of imperviousness to fire often figure in shamanic performances.[4] Further resonance is added to the fire motif when the specific element of the oven or furnace is added, for now additional, potent religious symbolism is evoked as well. On the one hand the oven/furnace is an enclosure, as explored below. But insofar as it serves as a furnace in itself, we should recall both the significance of the cauldron or furnace as the place where the future shaman undergoes his symbolic dismemberment and reconstitution, with its important social implications, and the role of "metallurgical" and alchemical symbolism in religious dialectic, as analyzed by Eliade in *The Forge and the Crucible*.[5]

In the latter connection, we find a curiously suggestive parallel to the Baba Tükles narrative in Eliade's discussion of an Indian story that sets a group of smiths and their furnaces against a heavenly divinity offended by

4. Cf. Eliade, *Shamanism*, pp. 412–413, 472–477; Roux, "Fonctions chamaniques," virtually ignores this feature of shamanic initiation and performance.

5. Mircea Eliade, *The Forge and the Crucible*, tr. Stephen Corrin, 2nd ed. (Chicago: University of Chicago Press, 1978), esp. pp. 65–70.

their smoke; the god comes down to earth in the form of a weak old man whose presence spoils the functioning of the furnaces. The smiths seek his advice on how to repair them, and the old man advises them to offer a human sacrifice, for which he duly offers himself as the victim; he enters the furnace, spends three days within its flames, and emerges bearing gold and jewels. With this example the smiths themselves are eager to enter the fire, but they are quickly burned alive.[6] Eliade discusses this tale as an expression of antipathy toward smithing and its associations, but even if this interpretation is correct the tale's potential as a paradigm for religious change in more general terms is remarkable: the holy man on the side of heaven overcomes the practitioners of the offending customs by entering the fire and surviving it while the local smiths/shamans are consumed in their own furnace.

The parallels with the structure suggested by the narrative of Baba Tükles are striking; there is no basis for a direct comparison, insofar as parallel stories are not known from an Inner Asian setting, where the history of metallurgy and smithing is relatively poorly known, and in any case there is no specifically metallurgical element in the tale of Baba Tükles. What may be noted here, however, is the currency of specific metallurgical symbolism in Inner Asia, in the close association of the functions of shamans and smiths, making them potentially assimilable as opponents of Islamization,[7] and the frequent appearance of metallurgical symbolism in legends of origin (i.e., the Türks as blacksmith slaves, the widespread tales making Chingis Khan a smith, the legend of Ergene Qun), discussed further below.

The shamanic interpretation of this portion of the Baba Tükles story thus suggests a rich new approach to the conversion narrative, one that also feeds the theme of displacement to be discussed shortly. But of special interest here is one implication of regarding Baba Tükles as a shamanic figure and the establishment of Islam as the communal acceptance and appropriation of a new shamanic protector/healer/etc. Looking at him this way highlights the pivotal point in the narrative at which Baba Tükles actually "constructs" a new and Islamic community: it is, in effect, the moment when he emerges from the fire-pit, safe and whole and soon to be acknowledged by the entire community. This identification of the

6. Eliade, *Forge*, pp. 65–66.

7. Cf. A. Popov, "Consecration Ritual for a Blacksmith Novice among the Yakuts," *Journal of American Folklore*, 46 (1933), pp. 257–271; the symbolism of blacksmithing is occasionally developed in the literature of Central Asian Turkic Sufism.

nation-forming moment as the emergence from the fiery enclosure allows us, further, to understand the particular elaboration of this moment, as a nation-forming act, found in the eighteenth-century work of ʿAbd al-Ghaffār Qïrïmī, based on Ötemish Ḥājjī's account but with interesting additions, as discussed in Chapter 5. It also allows us to suggest with less hesitation that the "nation–forming" role of Baba Tükles is already present in Ötemish Ḥājjī's narrative, and in particular is present in an implied evocation of the theme of "enclosure" and "emergence" that figures as a familiar ethnogonic motif in many Inner Asian legends of origin, as explored later in this chapter.

For confirmation of the essentially shamanic character of Baba Tükles' role in converting Özbek Khan we may look to epic literature for comparative material of clearly shamanic inspiration. Among the most striking parallels, both structurally and thematically, with Ötemish Ḥājjī's account of Baba Tükles are those appearing in the oral narrative of *Er Töshtük*, a hero of distinctly shamanic cast whose epic feats are set primarily in the underworld. The tale of Er Töshtük is perhaps best known in its Qïrghïz versions, especially the one published by Radlov.[8] In its Qïrghïz environment the tale was often, but not always, incorporated into the epic cycle of *Manas*, but *Er Töshtük*, in its themes and structure, clearly reflects an independent narrative development; it was also popular among the Qazaqs,[9] and one version was recorded among the "Tatars" of Tiumen' in western Siberia.[10] *Er Töshtük* is, moreover, one of the relatively few Inner Asian Turkic epics with a substantial history of scholarly attention even in the West, and has been admirably presented in translation from a Qïrghïz version by Pertev Boratav.[11] All of the recorded versions date, naturally, from only the mid-nineteenth century on, but the tale is generally considered one of the most archaic of the Turkic epic cycles.

The tale of Er Töshtük is lavishly replete with shamanic imagery, and may be regarded as a "heroicized" narrative of a shamanic journey; this in itself (together with the signs of the incorporation of Islamic ritual and

8. Radlov, *Proben*, ch. 5 (1885), pp. 526–589.

9. Versions were recorded by Divaev and Potanin; cf. Boratav and Bazin (cited below), pp. 13–19.

10. Radlov, *Proben*, ch. 4, tr., pp. 443–476.

11. *Aventures merveilleuses . . . de Er-Töshtük*, tr. Boratav; the translation is based primarily upon the Qïrghïz version of Sayakbay Karalaev, published in Frunze (now Bishkek) in 1956, while the introduction provides synopses of the various published versions. A synopsis based on the Radlov text is provided by Chadwick in Chadwick and Zhirmunsky, *Oral Epics of Central Asia*, pp. 100–104; this summary unfortunately omits all details of the hero's adventures and ordeals in the underworld!

conceptual elements into the tale at significant junctures) makes it a rich source on the integration of Inner Asian and Islamic worldviews, but it also features a number of remarkable and specific parallels not only with other epic tales (and legends of origin), but with the conversion narrative centered upon Baba Tükles. What is perhaps most significant for our purposes is that the tale of Er Töshtük combines narrative structures and motifs paralleled in Ötemish Ḥājjī's narrative of Baba Tükles with motifs found explicitly only in the mythic and epic elaborations of Baba Tükles' persona, in particular in evocations of the same mythic cosmogonic complex discussed earlier; we thus have a parallel to the development of Baba Tükles, a parallel that *combines*, in a single narrative, elements found separately in the various "stages" or styles of the Baba Tükles narratives.

The central events of the tale of Er Töshtük, following accounts of the hero's birth and early spiritual encounters (including one with his "spiritual mother"), begin in fine shamanic fashion with the loss of his soul. More specifically, Er Töshtük's father is forced to hand over the steel file that contains his son's soul, which is said to be kept under the hearthstone, to an evil, monstrous sorceress. The circumstances of this encounter are noteworthy: the father meets the sorceress when, camped by a river near a giant poplar—in a Qazaq version it is the Bay Terek, the World Tree—he spies a lung floating on the water; when he pulls it out with his lasso, the lung turns into the monstrous woman.[12] The theme of pulling from the water something that turns out to be a woman (whether a wife, or a demon as in this sinister turn on the motif, or both) appears frequently in Inner Asian legends of origin, and is frequently linked with the figure of Baba Tükles, as we shall see.

Er Töshtük soon succeeds in retrieving his soul from the sorceress, but when she pursues him to steal it back, Er Töshtük falls through a hole into the underworld. There begins a series of ordeals and quests that eventually end successfully, and the subterranean exploits conclude when Er Töshtük goes to the center of the world and finds a dragon coiled around the base of a tree (which is again identified as the Bay Terek in the same Qazaq version); he kills the dragon, thus saving two eaglets it was about to devour. In gratitude the mother eagle swallows Er Töshtük and then disgorges him, transformed and rendered invulnerable, his bones put back together strong as steel, and flies him up to the surface of the earth.[13] In these features as well we find parallels to mythic developments in Baba

12. Cf. *Aventures*, p. 88, and the synopses of the other versions, pp. 14–18.
13. Cf. *Aventures*, pp. 162–168, and the synopses in the introduction.

Tükles' character discussed in Chapter 6 (in the mythical bird upon whose back the hero rides), as well as clear evocations of the cosmogonic complex of the world tree with the serpent at its base.

It is in the ordeals and quests in the underworld that we find the clearest structural and thematic parallels with that part of the Baba Tükles tradition preserved in Ötemish Ḥājjī's narrative. For the setting in which these ordeals and quests unfold is the encounter of Er Töshtük and three or four companions (sometimes more) with a khan at the latter's palace, and one of the "tests"—one, too, that appears in all versions of *Er Töshtük* except the Qïrghïz—involves the enclosure of one or all of the companions in an "iron house" heated up by fire on all sides.

The structural parallel with Ötemish Ḥājjī's narrative is clear in the case of the companions and in the element of the contests or ordeals. Er Töshtük meets the companions before reaching the khan, and the number of companions varies; in Divaev's Qazaq version there are six altogether, as in the Siberian Tatar version, while of Potanin's Qazaq variants one has three, another four, companions. The Qïrghïz version has four companions, referred to as "the four Mamïts," since each is named *Mamït* (i.e., Muḥammad).[14] More important, they are invariably assigned specific talents or abilities, which are usually called upon in meeting the tests set by the khan. The six companions include a man who hunts a stag with millstones tied to his feet; a man who overturns mountains; a man who listens to the earth; one who drinks all the waters of a lake or sea; one who cuts trees with a wooden axe; and one who sees everything from a great distance. In other Qazaq versions, the "constants" among the companions are the lake-drinker and mountain-destroyer; the talents of others include divining the future and running swiftly. In any event, Er Töshtük is "armed" with these helpers when he faces the khan and is put to the test.

The tests themselves also vary from version to version, as do the motives for them, but all the versions are structurally consistent in including both the companions and the tests; herein we find reflections of the shamanic character of the tale, with the companions assimilable to the shaman's tutelary spirits, and the tests to the obstacles encountered in his ecstatic journey. Most often Er Töshtük asks for the daugh-

14. Cf. *Aventures*, pp. 122–128; their Islamized character is suggested also, with what may be even more specific referents than noted by Boratav and Bazin, in their exclamation following one of their successes (cf. p. 208): they cry out "Bâbedin," which Boratav and Bazin suggest reflects *bāb-i dīn* (gate of religion), an unlikely phrase in any case, but which probably reflects an appeal to the figure whose name is more often pronounced "Bāvadīn" throughout Central Asia, namely "Bahā' ad-Dīn" [Naqshband].

ter of the khan, who sets the tests as conditions, but in one Qazaq version[15] the daughter is merely a pretext; Er Töshtük is required to bring the golden hair of the khan to the band of eighty old women whom he met upon his descent into the Underworld, and after finally winning this khan's daughter, the hero kills her father, leaves the maiden to his companions, and takes the golden-haired head to the eighty hags. Each test is, as noted, usually tailored to the special prowess of one of the companions; they include races on horseback and on foot and individual combat with the khan's champions, and in several versions a final feat is to retrieve a giant cauldron from the bottom of a well (or a lake, in one version, and in yet another the item to be retrieved is a set of precious bones).

Most relevant, as suggested, is the test or ordeal found in all the Qazaq and Siberian Tatar versions. In most of these accounts this episode is indeed cast as a test, but in one of Potanin's Qazaq versions (the same one whose departure from the others was noted above), the khan imposes this particular ordeal in anger, as punishment for Er Töshtük's effrontery in asking for his daughter. In any case, the description is the same: Er Töshtük, usually with his companions, is shut up inside a "house of iron" that is heated up by a fire kindled on all sides; in the same distinctive Qazaq version, it is even *saksavïl* wood that is used for the fire. This obvious parallel to the narrative of Baba Tükles is followed by a natural departure, since it is not the hero's steadfastness in *dhikr*, nor his protective body-hair or armor, that saves him, but the "intercession" of one of his companions: the lake–swallower spits out the water he has drunk in and extinguishes the fire. The Qazaq version adds, in connection with this motif of enclosure in an iron house, a subsequent feat for the companion who lifts or overturns mountains; when the fire is put out, the khan's people heap still more iron on top of the companions' enclosure, but this mountain-lifting helper is able to cast it off and open a way out of the iron house.

The pattern of the shamanic-style hero meeting several companions, traveling with them to confront a powerful ruler, and undergoing various tests imposed by him, appears also in the Altay tale of *Māday Qara*, where the hunter Kögüdey Mergen appears as the central character. The epic of *Māday Qara* belongs to the Altay oral tradition, generally regarded as one of the most archaic among Inner Asian peoples; a full version of the tale was recorded in 1964 and published in 1973.[16] The "quest" in

15. Potanin's first, cf. *Aventures*, pp. 16–17.

16. *Maadai-Kara. Altaiskii geroicheskii èpos*, ed. and tr. S. S. Surazakov (Moscow: Nauka, 1973); this was the basis for Marazzi's English translation cited earlier.

this case is a search for the hero's bride-to-be, and occurs not in the underworld, but in a distant land. Nevertheless, the essentially shamanic character of Kögüdey Mergen is clear throughout the narrative.[17]

The hero-companions in this tale, seven in all, include figures clearly recognizable from the tale of Er Töshtük: one moves mountains, one listens to the earth, one leaps across mountain tops, and one drinks up lakes; they are expressly described as identical in appearance with Kögüdey Mergen.[18] Upon their arrival the companions vie with one another, each claiming to be the eldest hero, recalling in an atmosphere of heroic competition the solicitous concern of the Muslim saints when faced with the ordeal in Ötemish Ḥājjī's tale. Each of the heroes is eventually called upon for his particular expertise during the tests, but all the heroes initially face together the first ordeal of being enclosed in a "seven-layered iron prison" that, as in the parallel tales, is heated up to become red hot.[19]

An enormous amount of coal is placed beneath the "oven" and lit, and the flames beneath the iron prison are fanned with bellows; the pit becomes white hot, but after seven days the lake-swallower releases one of the lakes within him and cools down their enclosure. The heroes inside begin to sing and dance for joy; the ruler's agents and those operating the bellows, however, begin to curse their failure, saying that "the spirit-master of the Altay" must have entered the oven together with them. They thus redouble their efforts, adding more coal and fanning the flames to make the iron prison red-hot a second time. But the lake-swallower again cools down the heroes' enclosure, and the process is repeated a third time. This time the fire-pit episode ends decisively when the cold water of the third lake released cracks the iron prison into seven parts.

The subsequent tests closely parallel, in many cases, those found in versions of the tale of Er Töshtük, but are less relevant for us here. What is noteworthy about the appearance of the fire-pit episode in this tale from the Altay region is the apparently independent preservation of this shamanic motif in an environment virtually untouched by Islamization. It is of course possible that the episode reflects the narrative influence of the Abrahamic paradigm from the Islamic world, but its appearance among the

17. Cf. Marazzi, *Māday Qara*, p. 8, citing the study of B. Chichlo, "L'ours chamane," *Études mongoles . . . et sibériennes*, 12 (1981), pp. 35–112 [pp. 42–43].

18. Cf. Marazzi, pp. 115–119, for the encounter with the companions.

19. Marazzi, pp. 123–124 on the fire-pit episode; cf. pp. 82–84 on the enclosure of Kögüdey Mergen's *people*, awaiting deliverance by the hero, in an iron prison. The same motif, of a hero and four companions enclosed in an iron house that is heated up, appears without evident links to a well-known epic tradition in a Turkic tale recorded in Srinagar in 1935 from a Khotanese merchant; see Gunnar Jarring, *Materials to the Knowledge of Eastern Turki: Tales, Poetry, Proverbs, Riddles, Ethnological and Historical Texts from the Southern Parts of Eastern Turkestan, I,*

Altay makes such a view much less appealing than it might be were the episode known only among the Qïrghïz or Qazaqs or in the story of Baba Tükles. In any case it supports the argument that in Ötemish Ḥājjī's narrative the theme of enclosure in the fire-pit would have appealed not only to Islamic models, but to indigenous Inner Asian religious symbols as well.

This specific thematic parallel to the enclosure of Baba Tükles in the fire-pit not only suggests the justice of interpreting Ötemish Ḥājjī's narrative on the basis of Inner Asian religious symbolism, however attenuated; it also suggests that certain elements of evident shamanic provenance appearing in the tales of Er Töshtük and Kögüdey Mergen had already been attached to a figure celebrated for his role in Islamization in Inner Asia at least three centuries before the stories of Er Töshtük and Kögüdey Mergen were recorded. This in turn suggests that the attachment to Baba Tükles of motifs reflective of shamanic contests is not unique, but occurs in the case of other heroic figures as well, leading to the conclusion that the cases of Baba Tükles, Er Töshtük, and Kögüdey Mergen stand as evidence of a larger symbolic pattern in which a hero is "defined" and his character signaled by appeals to themes of shamanic and cosmogonic origin.

In other words, we should not suppose either that the Baba Tükles narrative *as such* was drawn upon by the bards who transmitted the tales of Er Töshtük or Kögüdey Mergen, nor that these tales existed as such in, say, the fourteenth century, and provided Ötemish Ḥājjī or his informants with several components for the tale of Baba Tükles. Rather, what we appear to have here is an indication of Baba Tükles' typological status as Hero *already in the earliest narrative in which he appears*, suggesting that even by the sixteenth century he was the object of the kind of mythic elaboration proper to such a status. This in turn attests, from a particular perspective, to the "nativizing" equation of Islamizer = Inner Asian Hero; the same equation is evidenced even more widely from a perspective to which we shall come below, not in the ascription of motifs that can be clearly identified as *shamanic*, through their parallels in the tales of Er Töshtük and Kögüdey Mergen, as in the present case, but in the attachment to Baba Tükles of motifs and symbols proper to the realm of ancestral and cosmogonic imagery.

To be sure, the theme of enclosure is in itself an important part of cosmogonic imagery in Inner Asia, and the specific echoes, in the tales of Er Töshtük and Kögüdey Mergen, of Inner Asian legends of origin that involve "breaking out" or simply "emerging" from behind or within mountains—and especially the elements of iron and fire that appear in

---

Texts from Khotan and Yarkand (Lund: C. W. K. Gleerup, 1946; *Lunds Universitets Årsskrift*, N. F., Avd. 1, Bd. 43, No. 4), pp. 35–53 (see esp. pp. 39–46).

legends of Turkic and Mongol origins—suggest (1) the further extension of our "nativizing" equation, which when all the components are included will make it clear that Islamizer = Hero = Ancestor = First Man; and (2) that it is not so farfetched as might first appear to find echoes of the *cosmogonic* associations of enclosure in and emergence from the fire-pit already in Ötemish Ḥājjī's narrative of Baba Tükles.

We will leave a discussion of the further cosmogonic motifs in legends of origin until Chapter 7, however. For now we would emphasize what we may draw from the tales of Er Töshtük and Kögüdey Mergen to illuminate the conversion narrative involving Baba Tükles. We see herein both a narrative pattern and specific thematic elements found both in a sixteenth-century "recording" of a narrative of Islamization in the Jöchid *ulus*, and in a popular "shamanic" epic, one associated with Qïpchaq peoples (with which Er Töshtük is often identified) and recorded in the nineteenth and twentieth centuries. If we add to this the parallels, alluded to above, between episodes in *Er Töshtük* and in the tale of Kögüdey Mergen and elements of the mythic elaboration of the figure of Baba Tükles, as discussed below, we are rightfully struck by the larger pattern of the incorporation of Islamic elements in narratives built around Inner Asian shamanic and/or cosmogonic symbolism. And as suggested, it is pointless to speculate on some "influence" of one narrative upon another; were we to do so we would be compelled by chronology to find the narrative in which Islamization is most explicit (that of Ötemish Ḥājjī) influencing narratives in which the Islamic component is still quite thin, but the lessons to be drawn from these parallels lie elsewhere.

What they suggest is that a narrative structure involving a hero and his companions confronting a khan and engaging in a series of "contests" in the ruler's presence, as well as the specific thematic element of enclosure in a fiery pit and deliverance therefrom, belonged to a body of indigenous Inner Asian concepts linked both to shamanic experience and to ethnogonic myth, and that that body of native tradition was readily drawn upon to provide the narrative framework and symbolic development for heroic figures, whether they be "standard" epic heroes, shamanic journeyers, or bringers of Islam. That the evocation of this narrative framework, and especially of the specific motif of enclosure in the fire-pit, either "continued" or recurred not only in a distinctly un-Islamic context, as in the case of the Altay tale, but also in an Islamizing part of the Inner Asian world, is clearly evidenced in the tale of Er Töshtük in its nineteenth- and twentieth-century versions; this in turn supports an interpretation of Ötemish Ḥājjī's account of Baba Tükles that supposes that the narrative was intended, in structure and themes, to present an Islamizer in terms both familiar and religiously meaningful to a much earlier audience.

The Oven-Pit: Ordeal, Sacrifice, and Sacred Enclosure in Forging a Community

The climactic moment of the tale of Baba Tükles in Ötemish Ḥājjī's account comes when the holy man emerges unharmed from the fiery "oven" after the pagan "sorcerer" had been instantly consumed. This episode, despite its stark and simple drama, is one of the most complex elements in the narrative, for an extraordinarily wide range of motifs and themes, of Inner Asian and Islamic resonance, are detectable in it. The "composite" nature of the central element in this episode—the oven-pit—attests at once, as in the case of the conflation of themes in the *qoruq* and drinking ceremony, to the impossibility (and irrelevance) of searching for an exact historical counterpart to the description in Ötemish Ḥājjī's account; but we must remember, as in the other cases of such conflation, that it is precisely the multivalent character of the incident, yielded by its "composite" character, that makes the narrative so rich and so potent and so "developable." At the same time we may recall that it is precisely this dramatic event, so replete with symbolism of ordeal and deliverance, that consitutes the "formative" moment for the new community created by the conversion of Özbek Khan, and it is thus not surprising that several themes frequently employed in narratives of other types of origins in Inner Asia are at least alluded to here.

The separate elements evident in this episode may be summarized as follows. First, Baba Tükles enters a fire that is at once symbolic of

- the fire-ordeal described for other Islamic saints, based on the Qur'ānic paradigm of Ibrāhīm;
- the tormenting fire of Islamic eschatology, surrounded by images of sweating in inverse proportion to the sweating induced by exertions for religion;
- the fire of testing and ordeal, for proof of faith or truth;
- the fires of purification in Inner Asian tradition;
- the fire of the hearth, in the home's central and most sacred place, where burnt offerings are made (recalled here by the sheep's flesh);

- the "reconstitutive" fires in which shamanic figures are "cooked" and transformed (thereby transforming their communities);

Second, the fire which Baba Tükles enters is not only a fire; it is distinctly described as an *oven*, thus an enclosed fire, and as something "dug" into the ground; the *pit* is thus at once symbolic of

- the Islamic grave, from which Baba Tükles emerges "reborn," ransomed in Abrahamic paradigm by the offering of the sheep whose flesh is consumed;
- the Islamic "protective enclosure," linked with notions of communal religious integrity;
- the Inner Asian grave, in which Baba Tükles is interred alive as in stories of human sacrifice in Inner Asia, and miraculously emerges in a display of Islam's greater power;
- the hearth pit as a place of sacrificial offering;
- the subterranean enclosure/cave wherein shamans are tested and nations formed in Inner Asian lore (whereby we again see that his emergence from the pit marks the constitutive moment of a new, Islamized community).

We will examine these themes evoked by the incident of the oven-pit, looking first at Qurʾānic and hagiographical models implicit in its Islamic symbolism, then examining narrative evocations of Mongol-era religious practices echoed in Ötemish Ḥājjī's composite account, and finally exploring the specifically communal significance of the central structural motif in the narrative, involving the enclosure and emergence of the saint on behalf of his community.

Islamic Resonances in the Fire-Pit: The Abrahamic Paradigm and Hagiographical Parallels

The element of the fire-pit in the tale of Baba Tükles includes several images heavily laden with Islamic themes and conveys a specifically Islamic resonance. In this regard the specific element of fire recalls both the punishing fires of hell, from which deliverance is sought (and in which unrepentant unbelievers perish), and the fires of "testing" to which the Qurʾānic Ibrāhīm was subjected.

In the first case, it is not the fires of hell as such that are evoked in the narrative of Baba Tükles, for he is of course a saint, but rather the deliverance from them assured to the faithful. Here we have a quite specifically

Islamic allusion, for Baba Tükles' deliverance from the fire is symbolic of the deliverance that will be necessary for all mankind in accordance with a distinctive Qur'ānic teaching: *everyone* will be brought to hell, with only the virtuous rescued from it.[20] Conversion to Baba Tükles' faith thus amounts to joining the community that may escape the flames, as he does, while the rest are left in torment, as symbolized by the infidel sorcerer, left to perish and consumed outright.

There is also in Ötemish Ḥājjī's narrative, undoubtedly, an allusion to the Islamic teaching of "proactive suffering", i.e., the expectation that suffering and exertion on behalf of the faith in this world will diminish the punitive torments to be suffered beyond the grave. Interestingly, the element of "sweating" in holy exertion plays an important role in this complex, recalling Baba Tükles' state as he emerged from the oven. The tradition is not Qur'ānic in this case; but a number of *ḥadīths* form the basis for the belief that on the Day of Judgment, "the sun shall draw nigh to the earth so that mankind shall perspire."[21] In al-Ghazālī's discussion of death and the resurrection, he devotes a section to "The Perspiration" (*al-ʿaraq*), when, as he describes, "perspiration pours forth from the root of every hair."[22] This affliction, he stresses, comes before judgment and will be so intense that some will seek deliverance from it even to Hell; he adds that the depth to which people will be engulfed by their own sweat will be determined by their zealousness for Islam:

> You should know that all the sweat which you did not shed through some effort in God's way, such as the Pilgrimage, the Holy War, the Fast, standing [in night prayer], regularly fulfilling the needs of a Muslim, and sustaining hardships in enjoining what is good and forbidding the wrong, will be driven forth by shame and fear on the plain of the Arising, thereby prolonging your suffering. . . . to perspire through undertaking difficult works of obedience is easier to bear and less enduring than to perspire at the Arising in distress and misgiving.[23]

20. "There is not one of you but shall approach it. That is a fixed ordinance of thy Lord. Then We shall rescue those who kept from evil, and leave the evil-doers crouching there" (XIX.71–72); cf. al-Ghazālī, *The Remembrance of Death*, pp. 219–220.

21. A *ḥadīth* reported by ʿUqba b. ʿĀmir, cited in al-Ghazālī, *Remembrance of Death*, p. 181. For a survey of the religious associations of sweat, cf. H. J. T. Johnson, "Sweat, Sweat-House," in *ERE*, 12, pp. 127–129.

22. *Remembrance of Death*, p. 180.

23. *Remembrance of Death*, p. 181.

Presumably Baba Tükles' trial in the oven-pit served as an example of such holy exertions to the newly converted—or, more to the point, to those who heard of their conversion as it was recounted and elaborated.

It is the fires of "testing" and "ordeal" that most clearly echo specifically Islamic motifs but at the same time evoke Inner Asian paradigms of holiness as well; all these motifs are evident in Baba Tükles' "survival" of the fire he entered as a test, and his emergence from it unscathed. These themes are, of course, not in themselves specifically "Islamic," for they recall notions of purification and ordeal common in ancient Indo-Iranian religion and in other traditions;[24] but they received Islamic sanction early on, and appear in the tale of Baba Tükles and comparable narratives in ways that allow us to see the specifically Islamic themes evoked alongside indigenous traditions, of Inner Asian origin. The Islamic character of these themes is further supported by their appearance in a wide range of Islamic narratives wherein the Islamic models are more explicitly evident than in the account of Ötemish Ḥājjī, including many with a specifically Inner Asian setting and with the specific issue of conversion at work, as we will see shortly.

The most immediate parallel to the story of Baba Tükles' sojourn in the oven-pit is the biblical tale of Daniel's companions who enter the fire for refusing to worship a golden image, but survive unharmed, without even the hair of their heads singed.[25] This narrative does not seem to have been further developed in Islamic tradition, but it is not impossible that the theme of saints cast into a furnace was known in the Jöchid *ulus* through influence from Christian or Jewish circles. In view of the extensive Christian missionary activity undertaken by Franciscan and Dominican monks in the Golden Horde during the early fourteenth century, we might expect a Christian medium for the Daniel tale;[26] but the legacy of Khazar Judaism should not be overlooked.

Similarly, the fire-ordeal by which Siyāvush is tested in the *Shāh-*

24. For a survey, see Carl-Martin Edsman, "Fire," in the *Encyclopedia of Religion*, ed. Eliade, vol. 5, pp. 340–346.

25. *Daniel* 3:8–30.

26. The currency of the motif of fire as a means of testing in religious confrontation is evidenced by Christian stories from the Golden Horde, above all in the account of the martyrdom of the Hungarian Franciscan friar Stephen; this young monk wearied of "some severe discipline" and renounced his faith, publicly proclaiming his adoption of Islam; he then regretted his rash act and, again publicly, "recanted his apostasy," angering the Muslims, who "hacked him in pieces *in sight of the fire that was to have burnt him*" (cf. Yule and Cordier, *Cathay and the Way Thither*, III, pp. 83–84, n. 2).

nāmah[27] (an episode made the subject of countless miniatures) comes to mind as a suitable parallel, and possible inspiration, for Baba Tükles' oven-pit; although the fire in this case is lit in an open plain, not in an enclosure or pit, Siyāvush nevertheless proves his veracity before a king by passing unscathed through the fire, recalling Ötemish Ḥājjī's narrative thematically and structurally. Here again, however, it is difficult to assert any direct evocation of the "Islamized" model of Siyāvush beyond the appearance of the "generic" hero's feats and qualities; and such heroic fire-ordeals are featured prominently in epic narratives closer to Baba Tükles' Inner Asian provenance, as noted above.

More clearly relevant in the present case, the issue of entering a fiery furnace has a strictly Islamic resonance as well, in the Qur'ānic allusions to the story of Ibrāhīm.[28] The number of motifs associated with the story of Ibrāhīm and the fire that are also evoked in the tale of Baba Tükles renders it highly unlikely that Ötemish Ḥājjī's narrative was constructed without consciously evoking these Qur'ānic allusions. Ibrāhīm is portrayed as opposing his father and people on account of their worship of idols, a tension of clear significance in the context of a conversion narrative, where the new faith is implicitly (and often explicitly) set in opposition to religious traditions defended by their adherents as ancestral;[29] Ibrāhīm is solicitous for his own father and community,[30] but the choice between Islam and ancestral ways is ultimately decided when the community itself tires of Ibrāhīm's preaching and seeks to destroy him. In addition to this general setting and its suitability for evocation in conversion

27. Cf. Abu'l-Qasem Ferdowsi, *The Shahnameh (The Book of Kings)*, ed. Djalal Khaleghi-Motlagh, vol. 2 (Costa Mesa, Calif.: Mazda Publishers, 1990), pp. 233–239, lines 470–558 for this episode.

28. Allusions to the story of Ibrāhīm appear in several more or less extensive passages; cf. XIX.41–48; XXI.51–70; XXVI.70–104; XXIX.24–25; XXXVII.83–98.

29. Ibrāhīm's people worship idols not because they help or threaten, but because that is what their forefathers did (XXVI.74).

30. Ibrāhīm attempts to intercede for his father by praying to God (IX.114; XIX.47; XXVI.86; LXX.4), but only until "it became clear to him that he was an enemy to God," since "It is not fitting for the Prophet and those who believe, that they should pray for forgiveness for Pagans, even though they be of kin, after it is clear to them that they are companions of the Fire (*aṣḥāb al-jaḥīm*) (IX.113–114). The particular resonance, for an Inner Asian audience, of a choice between the Islamic *ummah* and one's parents (and implicitly one's ancestral community) is suggested by the Chaghatay Turkic tale of the Prophet Muḥammad and his son Ibrāhīm published by A. J. E. Bodrogligeti, *Ḫāliṣ's Story of Ibrāhīm: A Central Asian Islamic Work in Late Chagatay Turkic* (Leiden: E. J. Brill, 1975), cf. pp. 4 (synopsis), 22–23 (text), 35 (tr.); in the tale, the Prophet notes that he had ceased his attempts to intercede for his parents, whom he saw in the fires of hell, when the angel Jibrā'īl forced him to choose between them and his *ummah*, and then makes a similar choice: he sacrifices his son as well, and it is this choice that earns him the

narratives, we then find specific themes recalled in the tale of Baba Tükles: the "hero's" entry into the fire, his protection there by God and his safe emergence, and the idolaters' own sufferings in the fire, complete with the mutual bickering and discord ascribed to the pagan sorcerers in Ötemish Ḥājjī's account.

Specifically, his father's people decide to cast Ibrāhīm into the fire, but God protects him: "Slay him or burn him," "But God did save him from the Fire" (XXIX.24); "Build him a furnace, and throw him into the blazing fire" (XXXVII.97); they cry "burn him!" after he smashes their idols, but God says, "O Fire! Be thou cool, and (a means of) safety for Abraham!" (XXI.69). He is thus delivered from the fire unharmed, itself a proof to the unbelievers; and it is the idolaters who will perish in the fire, along with their idols, where they will bicker among themselves (XXVI.94–96), as Ibrāhīm warns his tormentors: "But on the Day of Judgment ye shall disown each other and curse each other: and your abode will be the Fire, and ye shall have none to help" (XXIX.25).

The story of Ibrāhīm itself enjoyed considerable elaboration in Islamic tradition, with three particularly noteworthy motifs appearing regularly: the gathering of wood for the fire, the enclosure of Ibrāhīm before the fire is kindled, and the sweat being wiped from his face (in this case by a figure seen with Ibrāhīm in the fire, identified as the "angel of shade").[31] It is no doubt this Abrahamic paradigm that accounts for the widespread occurrence of tales of Muslim saints involving tests or ordeals by fire; that such tales are so common in Inner Asia suggests a particular Inner

---

well-known right to intercede for his community, the Islamic *ummah*, on the Day of Judgment. The Qur'ānic story of Ibrāhīm thus also provides an example, sealed by the Prophet Muḥammad, of "fighting one's own people," a model echoed in the Golden Horde when Berke affirms with pride his enmity with the infidel Hülegü, his own "flesh and blood"; this was noted already in D. Ayalon, "The European-Asiatic Steppe: A Major Reservoir of Power for the Islamic World," in *Trudy XXV Mezhdunarodnogo Kongressa Vostokovedov* (Moscow, 1960), t. II (Moscow: Izd-vo Vostochnoi Literatury, 1963), pp. 47–52 [pp. 50, 52]. In this case the Inner Asian counterpart to this paradigm might be provided by the system of feuds, which were likewise amenable to extensive "assertive" elaboration in oral tradition; cf. Larry V. Clark, "The Theme of Revenge in the *Secret History of the Mongols*," in *Aspects of Altaic Civilization II* (= PIAC XVIII; Bloomington: Indiana University Uralic and Altaic Series, vol. 134, 1978), pp. 33–57.

31. For the traditional elaboration of the tale of Ibrāhīm cast into the fire in the *qiṣaṣ al-anbiyā* genre, cf. the twelfth-century work of al-Kisā'ī, tr. W. M. Thackston, Jr., *The Tales of the Prophets of al-Kisā'ī* (Boston: Twayne Publishers, G. K. Hall, 1978), pp. 147–148; here Ibrāhīm is first cast into an iron furnace, and then, when he survives this, into a great pit filled with so much wood that four years were needed to gather it. Earlier traditions are included in the well-known history of aṭ-Ṭabarī; cf. *The History of al-Ṭabarī*, vol. 2, "Prophets and Patriarchs," tr. William M. Brinner (Albany: State University of New York Press, 1987), pp. 58–60.

Asian resonance as well, but the Qur'ānic model is never far below the surface in most of these tales. Such is certainly the case in Ötemish Ḥājjī's narrative, and in the further development of his narrative in the work of ʿAbd al-Ghaffār Qïrïmī, but there are other instructive examples of Inner Asian provenance.

First, the motif of the fire-ordeal appears, but with a particular twist, in at least two of the several hagiographical works devoted to the renowned Naqshbandī shaykh Khoja Aḥrār;[32] both works must date from the very end of the fifteenth century, and thus amount to our earliest attestation of the fire-ordeal motif in connection with the Golden Horde. The story, given in slightly different form in the two works, is set in Sarāy, where a figure called in both texts "Kamāl Khujandī" exposes a local "saint," who claims the ability to walk unharmed into a fire, as a charlatan. The story is related in much the same form in both the *Masmūʿāt*[33] compiled by Mīr ʿAbd al-Avval Nīshābūrī, a son-in-law of Khoja Aḥrār, and the *Silsilat al-ʿārifīn*[34] of Mawlānā Muḥammad Qāżī, another direct disciple; in both cases it is Khoja Aḥrār himself who relates the story, which runs as follows.

Shaykh Kamāl Khujandī[35] was once in Sarāy, where the populace was devoted to him; while he was there a man appeared claiming the status of a shaykh and inciting "factional rivalry" (*taʿaṣṣub*), declaring that he could perform the wonder of entering fire without being burned. People

32. I am indebted for these references to Dr. Jürgen Paul, who kindly supplied me with photocopies of the relevant sections of the Tashkent manuscripts of the two works; he has outlined the story in his doctoral dissertation, now published as *Die politische und soziale Bedeutung der Naqšbandiyya in Mittelasien im 15. Jahrhundert* (Berlin/New York: Walter de Gruyter, 1991), p. 61. As Paul notes, the motif may have been a common "floating narrative," a similar story appearing in the interesting hagiographical work, devoted to a fourteenth-century "Khalvatī" shaykh, analyzed by Jean Aubin in "Un santon quhistani de l'époque timouride," *REI*, 35 (1967), pp. 185–216 [p. 205]; here the story is set in Baghdād, where the shaykh was renowned for entering a heated oven naked, until his method of rubbing his body with oil was exposed.

33. Known also as the *Malfūẓāt*, the work bears no special title beyond these generic designations; MS Tashkent, IVAN UzSSR, Inv. No. 3735 (SVR, VIII, No. 5977), ff. 192b–193a; MS India Office, Delhi Pers. 890, ff. 140a–141a; MS Lucknow, Shiblī Nuʿmānī Library, Nadwat al-ʿUlamā Madrasah, Taṣavvuf Fārsī 172/2457, ff. 123a–b.

34. MS Tashkent, IVAN UzSSR, Inv. No. 4452 (uncatalogued), ff. 125b–126a; MS Aligarh, Maulana Azad Library, Subhanullah Collection, No. 297.7/72, ff. 122a–b.

35. His title is "Khoja" in the *Silsilat al-ʿārifīn*. It is not certain who is intended here. The name appears to be that of the famous poet Kamāl Khujandī, who died most likely in 803/1400–1401, and who was well known to have lived in Sarāy for four years after being taken there by Toqtamïsh following his raid on Tabrīz in 787/1385–1386; on the other hand, the poet Kamāl Khujandī, though a Sufi, is not a common "hagiographical" figure in Central Asia, and his name is often mistakenly assigned to the earlier figure of Bābā Kamāl Jandī, a disciple of Najm ad-Dīn Kubrā, since this shaykh's unfamiliar *nisbah* was often "corrected" to "Khujandī."

were drawn to him, although Shaykh Kamāl realized that he was devoid of the marks of genuine masters. On the advice of a certain Sayyid Qāsim,[36] Shaykh Kamāl proposed that the claimant be tested: suspecting that he had rubbed himself with some medicament (*dārū*)[37] that thwarted the effects of the fire, Shaykh Kamāl proposed to take him to a *ḥammām* for several days and induce him to sweat so much that the ointment would wear off; then if he could enter the fire unharmed, Shaykh Kamāl would believe in him. They did so, making the *ḥammām* very hot, and the man sweat profusely. When they emerged from the bath, they prepared a great fire. The false shaykh himself was afraid to enter the fire, knowing his protection was gone, but his *murīds* insisted that he must go in lest they be exposed as liars, and finally they seized him and cast him into the flames to perish; the account of Mawlānā Muḥammad Qāżī specifies that it was an "oven" (*tanūr*) into which he was thrown, whereupon he burned up at once. In the *Masmūʿāt* alone the story ends with a comment by Khoja Aḥrār that gives the tale yet another turn in Sufi dialectic: the master used to say, as a joke, writes the author, that he no longer had the strength to involve himself in people's affairs as before, due to his old age and frailty; but the people would not accept this, refusing to allow him to give up his work with such an excuse, leading Khoja Aḥrār to conclude that he was in the same predicament as that shaykh, who, having formerly been in the habit of entering the fire, was compelled to do so even when he no longer wished to.

The motif of Muslim saints being cast into the fire appears also in an Inner Asian context in the seventeenth-century Persian hagiography referred to above, the *Żiyāʾ al-qulūb*; in one passage[38] this work describes

---

This Baba Kamāl was active in the towns of the middle and lower Syr Darya, which belonged to the Golden Horde, and although we have no clear indication of this, it is not unlikely that he visited more westerly regions of the Jöchid *ulus*; elsewhere I have suggested that he might be the inspiration for the figure of "Kamāl Ata" who is associated with Islamization in the Crimea (see my "Bābā Kamāl Jandī") and appears also in the legendary cycles surrounding Sarï Saltïq (see Chapter 3). It is thus possible that the story was circulated in connection with Bābā Kamāl Jandī, but was already conflated with the tradition of Kamāl Khujandī's stay in Sarāy by the time it became known to Khoja Aḥrār.

36. He is called "Mīr Qāsim" in the *Silsilat al-ʿārifīn*. His identity is also unclear; the Ṣafavid *dāʿī* Sayyid Qāsim al-Anvār (757/1356–837/1433) comes immediately to mind, and fits chronologically with Kamāl Khujandī, but another Qāsim figures in very late (eighteenth-century) legendary material about Sayyid Ata's career in the Dasht–i Qïpchaq. On Qāsim al-Anvār, see R. M. Savory, "A 15th Century Ṣafavid Propagandist at Harāt," in *American Oriental Society, Middle West Branch: Semi-Centennial Volume*, ed. Denis Sinor (Bloomington: Indiana University Press, 1969), pp. 189–197.

37. In Muḥammad Qāżī's account, he rubbed himself with oil.

38. The description here follows that of Joseph Fletcher, "Confrontations," p. 172.

the confrontation between four disciples of the Naqshbandī shaykh Khoja Isḥāq and a group of Qalmaqs (i.e., Buddhist Oyrats, but in narrative terms simply pagan Mongols). Khoja Isḥāq had sent the four disciples to these Qalmaqs, who were worshiping a fire they had built when the Muslims arrived; the four summoned the Qalmaqs to Khoja Isḥāq, but the infidels mocked them and cast them into their fire, saying that if what their Khoja Isḥāq taught was true, they would not be burned, but would come forth unharmed. Just then Khoja Isḥāq arrived and cried out, invoking divine aid to bring a strong wind and drive the fire toward the Qalmaqs; "and it burned many people of those Qalmaqs, and some 1,000 families . . . became Muslims." By contrast, the account specifies, "not so much as a thread of the four disciples' clothes was yellowed by the fire."

Perhaps the most striking parallel to the motif of the holy man's ordeal in the fire is found in the legendary cycle of Sarï Saltïq, a prominent figure in Sufi and popular lore of Anatolia and the wider domains of the former Ottoman empire, especially in southeastern Europe; his specific connection with the Crimea and other lands of the Golden Horde makes him of special interest for us as well. Stories of Sarï Saltïq[39] appear in the fifteenth-century history of Yazıcıoğlu ʿAlī, where he leads many clans of Turkish nomads to claim the region of Dobrudja between the Danube and the Black Sea coast; in fifteenth- and sixteenth-century Bektashi hagiographies, where he appears as a wonder-working saint who miraculously converts kings and peoples to Islam; in the mid-seventeenth-century travel account of Evliya Çelebi, who describes his miracles and extensive travels and makes him a disciple of Aḥmad Yasavī and companion of Ḥājjī Bektash; and, most important, in an enormous hagiographical compendium entitled *Ṣaltuq-nāmah* compiled by a certain Abū'l Khayr Rūmī in the 1480s.

It is the latter two sources that are of particular interest here, since both connect Sarï Saltïq with the lands of the Golden Horde and both describe his "ordeal" by fire. In the first regard, Sarï Saltïq's links with the Golden Horde are already attested in the fourteenth-century travelogue of Ibn Baṭṭūṭah, which is indeed the earliest source to mention him. Ibn Baṭṭūṭah passed through the village of "Bābā Saltūq" as he traveled from Ḥājjī Tarkhān (Astrakhan) to Constantinople in the company of Özbek Khan's wife, daughter of the Byzantine emperor; he men-

39. A good summary of the sources on Sarï Saltïq, with a survey of tombs ascribed to him, is provided by Grace M. Smith, "Some *Türbes/Maqāms* of Sarı Saltuq, an Early Anatolian Turkish Ġāzı-Saint," *Turcica*, 14 (1982), pp. 216–225.

tions only that this Saltūq was an ecstatic (*mukāshif*) figure of questionable orthodoxy.[40] Evliya Çelebi is more explicit in describing Sarï Saltïq's "missionary" travels to the lands of the former Golden Horde, having him visit the Crimea and Moscow in addition to his "feats" of conversion in Poland and Dobrudja;[41] he relates these exploits on the authority of Bektashī dervishes he met at the site of one of several putative tombs of Sarï Saltïq in the Dobrudja region. More significant, Evliya says elsewhere, in recounting his travels among the Noghays and Tatars of the Volga basin, that the "Hashdak" [i.e., "Istak"] tribes, by which term he refers to the Bashkirs inhabiting the region of Astrakhan, were converted to Islam by "Muḥammad Bukhārī Saltïq-bāy," known also as Sarï Saltïq Sulṭān.[42]

The *Ṣaltuq-nāmah*[43] reflects narratives similar to those recorded by Evliya, but much more extensively. This work was compiled on the basis of oral material collected by Abū'l-Khayr Rūmī in extensive travels inspired by the commission of his patron, Cem Sulṭān, who in turn became interested in the legends of Sarï Saltïq upon hearing of him from the saint's followers in Dobrudja. Here "Sayyid Ṣārū Ṣālṭīkh," as he is called, travels literally throughout the world, including Hindustan and Turkistan, but several important episodes are set specifically in the Crimea ("*Qïrïm shahri*") and Kaffa (the Genoese port of the Crimea), where he fights against the Russians.

Interestingly, as noted above, one of the tales linked to the Crimea recounts the miraculous conversion feats of one of Sarï Saltïq's *murīds*

40. Ibn Baṭṭūṭah, ed. and tr. Defrémery and Sanguinetti, II, pp. 416–417, 445.

41. For Evliya Çelebi's account of the legends of Sarï Saltïq, and further material on his tombs, see Hasluck, *Christianity and Islam under the Sultans*, vol. 2, pp. 429–439, and the "poorer version" of this section in his "Studies in Turkish History and Folk-Legend," *Annual of the British School at Athens*, No. 19 (1912–1913), pp. 198–220 (II, "The Story of Sari Saltik," pp. 203–208). See also Smith, "Some *Türbes*," p. 218.

42. See the Russian translation, prepared by A. D. Zheltiakov and A. P. Grigor'ev, *Èvliia Chelebi: Kniga puteshestviia (Izvlecheniia iz sochineniia turetskogo puteshestvennika XVII veka), perevod i kommentarii*; vyp. 2, *Zemli Severnogo Kavkaza, Povolzh'ia i Podon'ia* (Moscow: Nauka, GRVL, 1979), p. 133.

43. A facsimile of the entire Topkapı manuscript, comprising 619 folios, has been published in facsimile by İz, *Ṣaltuḳ-nāme*, cited earlier; of a planned three-volume "edition" (in a transcription based on modern Turkish) prepared by Şükrü Halûk Akalın (Ebü'l-Hayr-ı Rumî, *Saltuk-nâme*), I have seen only the first volume (Ankara: Kültür ve Turizm Bakanlığı, 1987), covering the Topkapı manuscript down to f. 226b (thus breaking off before the narrative of the ordeal by fire). See also, on manuscript copies of the *Ṣaltuq-nāmah*, Smith, "Some *Türbes*," p. 217, n. 4, and in general the fine study of the work, and of the figure of Sarï Saltïq, by Kemal Yüce, *Saltuk-nâme'de Tarihî, Dinî ve Efsanevî Unsurlar* (Ankara: Kültür ve Turizm Bakanlığı, 1987).

named Kamāl Ata, recalling the proselytizing activity of the Kamāl Ata named in the *Tavārīkh-i Dasht-i Qïpchāq* as well as the possible model for the Kamāl "Khujandī" who also undergoes an ordeal by fire in the Aḥrār biographies; there is no fire ordeal for Kamāl Ata in the Sarï Saltïq cycle, however. Kamāl Ata does appear earlier in this work among the companions of Sarï Saltïq during his sojourn in the Crimea and Kaffa, where he is one of the leaders of an army of *ghāzīs* who joins the khan of the Crimea in fighting the Russians,[44] further suggesting a close identification between Kamāl Ata and Crimean Islam.

The links between the Sarï Saltïq tradition and the lands of the Golden Horde suggest the currency of legends recounting religious confrontation and conversion in precisely the region that produced our narrative of Baba Tükles. It is thus the occurrence of the motif of the "test" in the fire that is naturally of greatest interest. The story is related by Evliya Çelebi and the *Ṣaltuq-nāmah*[45] and both place the event in Dobrudja, where Sarï Saltïq saved the kingdom, and especially the king's daughter, from a terrorizing dragon; a Christian monk (*rāhib*) tried to claim credit for the miracle, however, dismissing Sarï Saltïq as a "sorcerer" (*sāḥir*). The Muslim saint protested that his deed was no sorcery, but evidence of sanctity (*vilāyat*) and "a miracle of our Prophet." The monk thus challenged Sarï Saltïq to the decisive test; and the ordeal is described with language that recalls that used in Ötemish Ḥājjī's account. They agreed to be enclosed within a cauldron that would be heated up, resolving that "whichever of us does not burn is the [genuine] saint" (*qangïmūz yānmazsa ol valī dur*).

They each thus entered a separate cauldron (*qazān*), each of which was filled with water and covered with an iron lid (*qapāq*); their companions (as in the case of Baba Tükles, Sarï Saltïq has three) fastened the lid shut (*berkitdiler*) and set a fire beneath the cauldron. The text reports that infidels came from every country to witness the scene. Finally, the monk began to cry out, begging to be taken from the cauldron, saying that he was, in effect, "cooked to death" (*pišdim öldüm*); but Sarï Saltïq called out from inside his cauldron and warned the infidels not to take the monk out, and "out of fear of the noble [sayyid] (*sharīf*), they ignored him until the monk's voice stopped coming out as he died, and his cries ceased."

"When morning came," the account continues, "they opened the cauldrons. The *sharīf* came out from inside that cauldron, safe and sound,

44. Cf. ff. 96a–109a: İz, pt. 2, pp. 191–217; Akalın, pp. 156–178.
45. The account here follows the Topkapı manuscript, ff. 251a–252a, İz, pt. 4, pp. 501–503.

and not a single hair was out of place."[46] The monk, however, was "cooked" almost beyond recognition, and this was shown to each of the *kāfirs* present; at once they fell at the feet of the *sayyid* Sarï Saltïq, and the account closes with the interesting responses of the infidels: "Some of them became Muslims, and some of the unfortunate ones agreed to pay the *kharāj*; they showed affection to the *sharīf*, and, acknowledging that he was indeed a saint, brought gifts and offerings to his *tekke*. And the sanctity of the *sayyid* spread throughout the world."

The vivid example of Sarï Saltïq's ordeal in the fiery cauldron thus provides a close parallel not only to the fire-pit in Ötemish Ḥājjī's account, but to the use of the ordeal by fire in what amounts to a conversion narrative.[47] The possibility of direct "influence," that is, of a narrative developed around one figure and then borrowed and attached to another, is naturally suggested by the close similarity between the accounts of Baba Tükles and Sarï Saltïq, both in the *occasion* of the ordeal and in its particulars, as well as by Sarï Saltïq's clear and frequent association with the Crimea and the Golden Horde. Unfortunately we cannot be certain of such influence, nor can we say with any conviction which narrative must have developed earlier. Baba Tükles is naturally linked with a historical environment of the early fourteenth century, and Sarï Saltïq with a somewhat earlier age, but this is hardly a basis for judging the relative antiquity of particular *legends* around either figure. We find the Baba Tükles narrative in a mid-sixteenth-century work preserved in a late eighteenth-century manuscript, while Sarï Saltïq's legend is recounted first in an apparently fifteenth-century work preserved in a late sixteenth-century manuscript. A possible argument for the earlier provenance of such a tale, at least in Anatolia, is suggested by the parallel account in a fifteenth-century treatise by a Hungarian captive among the Ottomans, entitled *Tractatus de moribus condictionibus et nequicia Turcorum*; the account was translated by Hasluck:[48]

> But another marvel also must I tell for its manifest truth, and this is told by men who were themselves at that time living.
>
> Now there were on a time certain religious men of that place which was near to us, and these were slandered that they had

46. The latter phrase, *bir qïlïna khaṭā kelmemiš*, is precisely the same phrase used in ʿAbd al-Ghaffār Qïrïmī's version of the Baba Tükles tale, discussed below in chapter 5 (cf. Najīb ʿĀṣim's edition, p. 37).

47. In Evliya Çelebi's version the king of Dobrudja converts to Islam.

48. Hasluck, *Christianity and Islam under the Sultans*, vol. 2, p. 498; the author is known variously as George of Hungary and George von Mühlenbach and was a slave in Anatolia c. 1436–1458.

> made a complot against the king. Who, being exceeding wroth thereat, gave order that they should all be burnt alive. But he that was chief among them, after that he had essayed vainly to excuse or justify himself and his fellows, did publicly protest his innocence and theirs, and himself before the king entered first into the furnace to be burned. And for that the fire fled back before him, he went unscathed and abated the rage of the king and saved himself from imminent peril of death, leaving unto his descendants and to all people of that persuasion this solemn example. And the shoes that with him went unscathed in the furnace are conserved to this day in those parts.

This version of the tale gives no names, however, and undoubtedly reflects, as do *both* the Baba Tükles narrative and the episode in the cycle of Sarï Saltïq, a floating narrative combining the motifs of ordeal by fire and test of faith. In the end we most likely have in these accounts independent evocations of a common mythic theme of religious legends, and it is no doubt fruitless to conjecture about hypothetical "borrowing" of accounts or themes of this type. What is most instructive is not the possible borrowing of such a theme, but the parallels in its *use* in separate settings to make similar points. In both cases the usefulness of the theme is tied to its distinctive ability to convey religious meaning in the context of an Islamizing community, by speaking to both Islamic and pre-Islamic traditions, and evoking symbols common to both, as the Islamic resonances of the fire-pit join with its Inner Asian shamanic and ethnogonic symbolism.

In the first regard, the cauldron or furnace serves as the venue for the shaman's spiritual death and regeneration, a process that not only affects the shaman himself, but may be regarded as amounting to a ritual regeneration of his community as well, as discussed above. As such the process is already not unlike the "ordeal" suggested by the Abrahamic model, which the "saint" undergoes for the sake of his *faith*, with the Qur'ānic Ibrāhīm portrayed as unwillingly delivered to the fire by his hostile community; here the "oppositional" contrast is emphasized, between ancestral community and community of faith. But in the Inner Asian context there is only one community, the ancestral one, which is nonetheless in need of periodic regeneration and reaffirmation through the shaman's ordeal. In this context we would naturally expect the holy man to submit to the ordeal on behalf of his community, whose integrity and wholeness is affirmed by his survival and emergence from the ordeal.

It is in both senses that we should understand the underlying logic of Baba Tükles' enclosure in the fire pit. That is, his entry into the fire-pit amounts to his submission to an ordeal whose successful survival will not only result in benefits to his religion, by demonstrating its truth, but will in effect create and sanctify a new community, symbolically forged in the furnace along with the holy man. Here in the melding of these *specific* aspects of the religious vision of the two traditions that meet in Baba Tükles—the Islamic paradigm of the saint or prophet in effect forging a community of faith more holy than an ancestral community, and the Inner Asian paradigm of the shaman forging a reconstituted community through his holy ordeal—we find one of the keys to the capacity of the narrative tradition surrounding Baba Tükles to "speak to" Inner Asian peoples; here as well we find, more generally, a key to the capacity of the Islamic tradition to speak to Inner Asian tradition, and, more important, to do so *on the latter tradition's own terms* but without being untrue to its Islamic character.

Narrative Responses to Mongol Rule: Sacrifice, Purification, and Entombment

A number of Inner Asian resonances linked with the fire-pit in the narrative of Baba Tükles reflect religious practices of the thirteenth- and fourteenth-century Mongols as known to or imagined by peoples subject to them. In part these reflect the general sacredness of fire, a theme taken up in a "caricature" of Mongol religion in an eighteenth-century elaboration of Ötemish Ḥājjī's account discussed below; a number of specific elements, however, that appear to be evoked by the account may be clarified by reference to Mongol-era religious practices and especially their evocation in religious narrative.

BURNT OFFERING

To begin with, the element of the sheep's flesh placed over the mouth of the "oven" dug into the ground immediately suggests a sacrificial offering of animal flesh in a fire-pit, and precisely such a rite is described for the Mongols in China by the *Yüan-shih*, and is probably referred to in the Mongol *Secret History* as well. In the latter source, dating most probably from between 1227 and 1251, Hö'elün, the widowed mother of the future

Chingis Khan, is challenged by her relatives and effectively ostracized when she is excluded from "the sacrifice to the ancestors consisting of offerings of food burned in the ground."[49] The phrase describing this sacrifice is problematical, and the translation is based upon the Chinese gloss on the transcribed Mongol text; its ancestral character is clear, however, and the probable accuracy of the Chinese explanation is suggested not only by the *Yüan-shih*'s description but by the survival of a similar memorial rite in the Ordos featuring the burning of meat in three pits hollowed out of the ground.[50] The ancestral focus of the rite is of particular interest in view of its utilization in the *Secret History*'s narrative as the occasion for Hö'elün's break with her people, setting the stage for her son's later revenge upon those who had thus deprived her of her rightful place in her clan.

The *Yüan-shih*'s description is brief and does not explicitly link the food offering with ancestral veneration, but the invocation of the deceased ruler's "personal" or "secret" name mentioned as part of the rite suggests an ancestral focus as well. According to this description, Mongol male and female shamans would dig out a pit in the earth in which to burn the sacrificial offering, which consisted of part of the flesh from a horse and three sheep, sprinkled with kumiss; the rest of the flesh, of course, would be consumed, although this is not specified in the *Yüan-shih*'s account (it is clear from the *Secret History*), and the offerings were accompanied by both male and female shamans calling the personal name of the deceased ruler, in the "national language."[51] The latter element suggests the exclusively Mongol character of this rite, again supporting its ancestral character but highlighting also its *restrictive* nature, a feature that recalls the principle, if not specifically the terminology, of the *qoruq*; and,

49. Igor De Rachewiltz, tr., "The Secret History of the Mongols," *Papers on Far Eastern History* (Canberra), 4 (September, 1971), p. 133, §70; chapters 1–2 appear in this vol., pp. 115–163, the rest of work in later volumes. Cf. Francis Woodman Cleaves, tr., *The Secret History of the Mongols* (Cambridge: Harvard University Press, 1982), p. 19; Cleaves translates, "they offered to the ancestors the sacrifice called *γajaru inerü*," noting that the latter phrase is glossed as "to burn food in the earth and offer [it] in sacrifice."

50. See the discussion of Antoine Mostaert, "Sur quelques passages de l'*Histoire Secrète des Mongols*," *HJAS*, 13 (1950), pp. 285–361, esp. pp. 298–308; the modern rite is noted on p. 302 with reference to an article of Mostaert's that has not been accessible to me. See also De Rachewiltz' note to his translation, p. 158, §70, where he observes that the Mongol term used in the text is obscure, and that his translation was based on the Chinese gloss; cf. Cleaves' translation and note also, as well as Paul Pelliot and Louis Hambis, tr., *Histoire des campagnes de Gengis Khan: Cheng-wou ts'in-tcheng lou* (Leiden: E. J. Brill, 1951), p. 323.

51. Ratchnevsky, "Über den mongolischen Kult," p. 429; cited also in Boyle, "The Thirteenth-Century Mongols' Conception of the After Life," pp. 12–13, n. 7.

as distinct from most other Mongol rites discussed in the *Yüan-shih*'s account of "National Customs and Old Rites," this ritual of burnt food offerings was exclusively Mongol: no Chinese officials are named among those participating, from which we may conclude that it was a rite substantially less open to, or at least less conducive to, assimilation with Chinese ritual practice.[52]

Here we may add, however, that the role of the sheep also has an important Islamic resonance; in the theme of the sheep's flesh cooked in the oven while Baba Tükles remains unharmed there is, in addition to a reflection of Inner Asian sacrificial practice, an undoubted allusion to or evocation of the Qurʾānic story of Ibrāhīm preparing to sacrifice his son (Ismāʿīl), when the boy was "ransomed" (XXXVII.107) at the last moment, as, according to tradition, a sheep was sacrificed in his place.[53] Baba Tükles thus proves his faith and submission to the divine will and is saved; and the Abrahamic paradigm is of further potency since through his ransomed son Ismāʿīl, after all, Ibrāhīm is the founder of the Islamic *ummah* just as Baba Tükles would become the founder of the new Islamic community in the Golden Horde.

PURIFICATORY FIRES

The two fires, one for the Muslim and one for the infidel, may reflect stories current in both the Muslim and Christian worlds about the Mongol requirement that visitors and ambassadors purify themselves and their belongings by passing between two fires before being presented to the khan; observance of this requirement, which is well evidenced in earlier Inner Asian practice,[54] was, as a sign of submission to the custom of infidels, immediately assimilable to submission to an impious rite, and in both Islamic and Christian contexts was portrayed as a violation of one's faith. This purification rite is attested in Inner Asia as early as the sixth century, in the celebrated account of Menander Protector concerning the Byzantine ambassador Zemarchus's reception at the court of the Western Türk ruler Ishtemi: the delegation was met by "conjurors away of evil omens," who took the party's baggage for purification by fire.

52. Ratchnevsky, "Über den mongolischen Kult," p. 430.

53. Cf. al-Kisāʾī, tr. Thackston, *Tales of the Prophets*, pp. 161–162; *The History of al-Ṭabarī*, vol. 2, tr. Brinner, pp. 92–96.

54. Cf. Roux's discussion in "Fonctions chamaniques," pp. 77–81, and the examples gathered by Boyle, "Turkish and Mongol Shamanism," p. 183.

The Mongol era produced numerous accounts of such purificatory rites,[55] in most cases explicitly involving a passage between *two* fires: Plano Carpini himself, as well as the gifts he brought, had to pass between two "sacred fires" for purification; Rubruck records the same requirement in his case; and the custom was mentioned as a point of contention in diplomatic relations between the Ilkhanid Arghun and the French court in 1289.

There can be little doubt that such ritual purifications were performed, and must have been experienced by Muslim travelers among the Mongols as well; the practice appears to be only rarely attested in Islamic sources, however. The major Muslim historians of the Mongol era (i.e., Juvaynī, Jūzjānī, Rashīd ad-Dīn) make no mention of the custom, but a remarkable parallel to the European accounts has recently been brought to light. It appears in a geographical-historical work compiled around 679/1280–1281 by the historian ʿIzz ad-Dīn Muḥammad b. ʿAlī b. Shaddād al-Ḥalabī, known as Ibn Shaddād (d. 684/1285), better known for his history of the Mamlūk Sulṭān Baybars; the third volume of the former work, entitled *al-Aʿlāq al-khaṭīrah fī dhikr umarāʾ ash-shām wa'l-jazīrah*, was recently edited, and includes an account of the author's participation in a mission to the Mongol army besieging the city of Mayyāfāriqīn in 657/1259, shortly after the destruction of Baghdād. Using the Turkic term (*qam*) for "shaman," Ibn Shaddād describes an encounter with a group of Mongols who were to convey the delegation to their ruler, noting the treatment of the men, animals, and gifts borne by the party: "A group of Mongols came upon us, and with them were shamans (*qāmāt*). They inspected all of our people, and the beasts with us. Then they set up fires on two sides and passed through them with us, while beating us with sticks. From the examination of the cloth, they took a piece of gilded Khiṭāʾī cloth, and cut off from it a cubit-long . . . section. From this, they cut smaller pieces, tossed them down and burnt them in the fire."[56]

More remarkably, we have one example of an account in which submission to such a purificatory fire is proposed as an "antidote" to the error of converting to Islam, all in the context of what amounts to a conversion narrative; the occasion is the Ilkhanid ruler Öljeytü's adoption of Shīʿite Islam, as recounted by his chronicler, Qāshānī, in his *Tārīkh-i*

55. These are assembled in Boyle, "Turkish and Mongol Shamanism," pp. 183–184.

56. Tr. Reuven Amitai-Preiss, "Evidence for the Early Use of the Title *īlkhān* among the Mongols," *JRAS*, 1991, pp. 353–361 [tr. pp. 355–356]; see the edition of the third volume of *al-Aʿlāq* by Yaḥyā ʿAbbārah (Damascus, 1978), vol. 2, pp. 492–493.

Ūljāytū Sulṭān. The full account[57] is in many ways reminiscent of a typical Mongol–era conversion story. It includes the arrival of a religious figure, who provokes debates and discussions (involving Ḥanafī and Shāfiʿī jurists as well as Shīʿites) in the khan's presence, as well as Mongol *amīr*s and *bakhshī*s urging adherence to the rites and laws of Chingis Khan. It even includes a pointed exposition of the fundamental difference between Sunnī and Shīʿī Islam, explained in Mongol terms that in effect equate the charisma of Prophetic descent with that of Chingisid descent; the passage is worth recalling when we consider the political potential of Islam in undermining Chingisid ideology, for one of Öljeytü's loyal *amīr*s tells the khan, "In the religion of Islam, a person is a Shīʿite who, in the Mongol *yāsāq*, would consider the descendants (*ūruq*) of Chingīz Khān to be his rightful successors after him; the school of the *Sunnah* is the one that regards an *amīr* as worthy of his place."[58]

More to the point, however, is this account's description of Mongol shamans, hostile to Islam, calling upon the khan to renounce the new religion, an act to be sealed by his passage through fire (presumably between two fires); the parallel with Ötemish Ḥājjī's account is striking. The account as given by Qāshānī follows the debate between Shāfiʿī and Ḥanafī jurists, an encounter so acrimonious that one Mongol *amīr* was moved to ask his fellows, "What have we done, turning from the *yāsāq* and *yosun* of Chingiz Khān and entering the old religion of the Arabs, with its seventy-odd sects?" With sentiment among the *amīr*s leaning toward a return to the Chingisid code, and the khan himself wavering, Öljeytü's entourage moved from its winter pastures, most probably in the spring of 1308;[59] at one stop a violent thunderstorm developed, and lighting struck and killed several servants, frightening the khan and his entire entourage. "The *amīr*s appealed to him, saying 'In accordance with the former rites and the *yāsāq* of Chingīz Khān, you must pass through fire.' " They brought the *bakhshī*s, who would conduct the ceremony, and they declared that the lightning strike was a result of misfortune brought by Islam and the Muslims; if Öljeytü "would abandon the five-fold prayer and the sequence of *adhān* and *ṣalāt*, his repentance and recanting will

57. Ed. Hambly, pp. 90–108; it may be recalled that Qāshānī's account of Özbek Khan's accession is in many ways similar to that given by Ötemish Ḥājjī.

58. Ed. Hambly, p. 99.

59. Ed. Hambly, pp. 98–99; cf. Melville, "The Itineraries of Sultan Öljeitü," p. 65. This incident is mentioned by Boyle (*CHIr*, V, p. 402; "Turkish and Mongol Shamanism," p. 184), but he does not cite the *Tārīkh-i Ūljāytū Sulṭān*; Roux, "Fonctions chamaniques," p. 81, mentions the episode (citing Boyle) but wrongly identifies the khan in the story as Arghun.

be rendered efficacious and acceptable by passing through fire."

Evidently Öljeytü did not submit to this rite; at least, if he did, the chronicler did not register it, turning instead to the further discussion that led to the khan's adoption of Shīʿism. The account is important as evidence that the juxtaposition of Islam and Muslim ritual with the specific Mongol ceremony of "entering" fire was probably an actual occurrence, but unquestionably a well-known narrative theme, one not only current in the early fourteenth-century, but religiously charged as well, with explicit connection to a Mongol khan's religious dilemma and eventual conversion.

In any case, the well-attested practice of purification by passing between two fires in itself provides the basis for the transformation of the two fires, as symbolic of infidel rites, into a narrative motif of resonance in conversion stories. It is no doubt this transformation that is at work in the stories cited above of Muslim saints forced to enter fire, an interpretation of the Inner Asian practice in line with the Abrahamic paradigm.

The rich potential adaptability of the practice, and of stories describing it, for use in narratives of religious confrontation, is best illustrated in the case of a Russian narrative reflecting events in the Golden Horde. In a well-known account from the fifteenth-century Novgorod chronicle,[60] the practice of passing between fires is assimilated to pagan tree- and fire-worship and idolatry, and submitting to the rite turned into a test of Christian faith. The occasion for the account is the "martyrdom" of Prince Mikhail of Kiev at the court of Batu (in Russian sources, *Baty*) on 18 September 1245. The prince had been summoned to the khan's court, where Batu had the following custom: "If any one came to do obeisance, he would not order him to be brought before him, but wizards used to be ordered to bring them through fire and make them bow to a bush and to fire; and whatever anyone brought with him for the *Tsar*, the wizards used to take some of everything and throw it into the fire, and bowed to the bush, their idols, for the glory of this world." Prince Mikhail, however, resolved not to submit to this custom, which he regarded as a cowardly compromise of the Christian refusal to bow to anything but Christ. His spiritual father, too, warned him of the pressures to observe the custom, which had led many Christians astray when they "went through the fire and bowed to the sun and to the bush, and destroyed their souls and bodies"; he counseled the prince, "go not through the fire, bow not to their idols, nor eat their food, nor take their drink between thy lips."

60. Robert Michell and Nevill Forbes, tr., *The Chronicle of Novgorod, 1016–1471* (London: Camden Society, 1914; 3rd series, vol. 25), pp. 88–92.

Recognizing that refusal would mean martyrdom, Mikhail and his commander Fedor set off for Batu's camp, and when they arrived the khan ordered his "wizards" to have the two men observe the customary rite. The Russians were led to a place "where fire was laid on both sides," and saw that "many pagans were going through the fire, and were bowing to the sun and to the idols. And the wizards led Mikhail and his *Voyevoda* Fedor through the fire." At this point the prince voiced his objections to bowing to the "idols," whereupon the wizards reported to Batu that Mikhail "does not listen to thy command, does not go through the fire and does not bow to thy gods." The khan became angry and ordered them to bow or be killed; a number of other Russian notables at Batu's court urged Mikhail to submit and save his life, but both the prince and Fedor steadfastly refused. As the executioners came, the two began to sing and then took communion, and once again affirmed their choice of martyrdom; then both were killed, and although Mikhail was first beaten by the Mongols, it was a Christian apostate who cut off his head. The martyrs' bodies were miraculously preserved, with a pillar of fire appearing where they lay and reaching to heaven, "for the confirmation of Christians and for the conviction of the faithless who leave God and bow to things, and for the terrifying of the pagans."

The story echoes several specific features of the narrative of Baba Tükles, in the two fires of the "ordeal," the singing and communion (paralleling the blessings recited by the companions and Baba Tükles' own "singing" in the pit), and the "confirmatory" fire above the holy bodies; more important, it provides an illustration of a narrative adaptation of Inner Asian practices in the context of a dramatic religious confrontation, an adaptation that, although of Christian provenance, is set at the court of the Golden Horde. It is just such narrative adaptations that appear throughout the tale of Baba Tükles, adding successive and complementary layers to his sacralization.

THE TOMB PIT AND MUSLIM CAPTIVES: ENTOMBMENT AND DELIVERANCE

The "enclosure" of Baba Tükles in the pit, finally, recalls the accounts, widely known in the thirteenth and fourteenth centuries in both the Christian and Islamic worlds, about the interment of living slaves—inevitably understood as non-Mongols, and hence, in our context, Muslims—in the graves of Mongol khans or lords. The practice itself, in which the servants, much like food, drink, and other objects placed in the grave, were buried with their master in order to serve him in the next world, is well attested throughout Inner Asia down to the Mongol era,[61] and several accounts of Mongol burials describe similar customs.[62]

As a fine example of the appeal of such narratives from the Mongol era, and from among a people inhabiting the lands of the future Golden Horde, may be cited the famous account of a Quman burial from Joinville's *Life of St. Louis*, completed in 1309:

> Philippe de Toucy also told us of a most amazing spectacle he had witnessed while in the Comans' camp. A knight of very high rank among them having died, they had dug a grave, very deep and wide, in the earth. In it they had placed the knight, very richly attired and seated in a chair; they had also lowered the best horse he had, and his best sergeant, into the grave alive. Before, however, the sergeant had been put into the grave he had taken leave of the King of the Comans and the other great lords. While he was bidding them farewell, each of these lords had put a great quantity of gold and silver into his scarf, saying to him: "When I come into the other world you shall give me back what I now put into your care." "That I will most gladly do," the sergeant had replied.
>
> Next the great King of the Comans had given the sergeant a letter addressed to the first of their kings, telling him that this worthy man, having lived a good life and served his master well, deserved to be duly rewarded. After this the sergeant had been lowered into the grave with his lord, and with the live horse. Then the mouth of the grave had been covered by throwing closely fitting boards across it. Meanwhile all the men in the army had run to get stones and earth, and before going to sleep that night they had raised a great mound above the tomb in memory of those they had thus buried.[63]

61. For discussions see Ildikó Ecsedy, "Ancient Turk (T'u-chüeh) Burial Customs," *AOH*, 38 (1984), pp. 263–287; J. Jaworski, "Quelques remarques sur les coutumes funéraires turques d'après les sources chinoises," *Rocznik Orientalistyczny*, 4 (1926), pp. 255–261, and W. Kotwicz's "Remarques complémentaires" to this, pp. 261–266; Ecsedy, "A Note on "Slavery" in the Turk Rulers' Burial Customs (Around 649 A.D.)," *AOH*, 42 (1988), pp. 3–16 (esp. pp. 8–9).

62. Cf. Ratchnevsky, "Über den mongolischen Kult," pp. 439–441.

63. Joinville's "Life of St. Louis," tr. M. R. B. Shaw, *Joinville and Villehardouin, Chronicles of the Crusades* (Harmondsworth, Middlesex: Penguin Books, 1963), p. 290.

For the Mongol era the practice—or more important for our concern the currency of tales reporting the practice—of live burials of slaves with their masters is attested also by Jordanus (c. 1330), who writes, "The great lords, when they die, are buried with a horse, and with one or two of their best beloved slaves alive";[64] somewhat earlier is the remark by Ricoldo of Monte Croce that twenty living slaves are buried along with a deceased "Tartar" emperor to serve him.[65] Likewise, the Armenian historian Kirakos of Ganjak notes of the Mongols that when one of their great men is buried, "they laid some of his men-servants and maid-servants with him in the tomb, because, they said, they might wait on him."[66] Plano Carpini's account of Mongol burial practices,[67] noted above in connection with the *qoruq*, also includes an element suggestive of stories about live burials. Describing the burial of the Mongols' "chief men," he notes:

> They go in secret into the open country and there they remove the grass, roots and all, and they dig a large pit and in the side of this pit they hollow out a grave under the earth; and they put his favorite slave under him. He lies there under the body until he is almost at the point of death, then they drag him out to let him breathe, and this they do three times. If the slave escapes with his life, he is afterwards a free man and can do whatever he pleases and is an important man in his master's camp and among his relations.

In Islamic sources a similar practice is noted by Juvaynī in the case of Ögödey,[68] and by Vaṣṣāf in the case of Hülegü;[69] both of these accounts, however, describe an actual "sacrifice" of maidens to serve the deceased khan, rather than the live interment of a favorite servant. More in line with the latter theme is Ibn Baṭṭūṭah's description of a Mongol burial in Khanbalïq in China; he recounts the interment of four slave girls and six private *mamlūks*, each holding a cup full of some beverage, noting that after they entered the large subterranean chamber prepared for the

64. Jordanus, *Mirabilia Descripta*, tr. Yule, p. 47.

65. J. C. M. Laurent, ed., *Peregrinatores Medii Aevi Quatuor* (Leipzig: J. C. Hinrichs, 1864), pp. 102–141, "Fratris Ricoldi de Monte Crucis Ordinis Predicatorum Liber Peregrinacionis," p. 117.

66. Tr. Boyle, "Kirakos of Ganjak on the Mongols," p. 204.

67. *The Mongol Mission*, pp. 12–13.

68. Cf. Juvaynī/Boyle, I, p. 189, a passage noted above with regard to the drinking ceremony that accompanied a three-day memorial feast for Chingis Khan.

69. Cited in Juvaynī/Boyle, I, p. 189, n. 30; Vaṣṣāf, tr. Hammer-Purgstall, p. 97, and Āyatī's paraphrase, *Taḥrīr-i Tārīkh-i Vaṣṣāf*, p. 30 [reflecting p. 52 of the Bombay edition's first volume].

dead lord, the "door" was shut and earth heaped over the pit.[70] Similarly, Jūzjānī reports such a live burial in the case of Batu, the founder of the Golden Horde; more important, however, Jūzjānī's account illustrates the narrative possibilities of the theme, in a story that in several regards evokes the atmosphere of the tale of Baba Tükles and the fire-pit, and is strikingly reminiscent of Plano Carpini's account. Describing Batu's grave as mentioned above, Jūzjānī notes, in Raverty's translation: "They furnish it with a throne and covering for the ground, and they place there vessels and numerous effects, together with his arms and weapons, and whatever may have been his own private property, and some of his wives, and slaves, male or female, and the person he loved most above all others. When they have placed that accursed one upon the throne, they bury his most beloved right along with him in that place."[71]

Of still greater interest is the curious narrative that follows this description. Its appearance in the mid-thirteenth-century work of Jūzjānī attests to its early currency; while its later currency cannot be confirmed by its repetition or clear adaptation in other sources, the narrative is of unquestionable interest for understanding features in the account of Baba Tükles because it combines the elements of the pit and the fire, in the context of a burial site that recalls the *qoruq*, all in the name of defending a faithful Muslim against the threats of Mongol infidels. The account was related to Jūzjānī by a certain Khoja Rashīd ad-Dīn, a native of Balkh, when he came to India from Khurāsān in 648/1250–1251 for commerce and accompanied the author from Delhi to Multān; it is presented as an "astonishing anecdote":

> One of the Mughal lords, in the territory of Qarā-Quram, who possessed numerous followers and servants of great wealth, [died and] went to hell. They accordingly caused a place to be prepared, with the utmost ceremony, for the interment of that accursed one, and placed with him arms and other effects, and furniture and utensils in great quantity. A couch also, adorned and decorated, they had prepared; and desired to bury, along with him, the most loved of his people. They consulted together as to

70. Ed. Defrémery and Sanguinetti, IV, pp. 300–301.

71. Raverty, tr., II, p. 1173. The passage is cited by Boyle, "Kirakos of Ganjak," pp. 204–207, n. 32, and from him in Ratchnevsky, "Über den mongolischen Kult," p. 439; but evidently no one has drawn attention to the subsequent passage.

whom among his servants they should inter who would be the one to whom he was most attached.

There was a youth of the confines of Tirmid of Khurāsān, who, in his childhood, had fallen captive into the hands of this Mughal *gabr* in the beginning of the misfortunes of Khurāsān; and, when he reached puberty, and grew into youth and virility, and attained unto man's estate, he turned out exceedingly active, intelligent, expert, and frugal, in such wise, that everything belonging to that accursed one, in whole and in part, came under the youth's disposal; and, as this Mughal had called him son, on this account, the whole of the property and effects, and cattle, and whatever else belonged to him, the youth had taken under his control. All the servants and followers of that Mughal were under his orders, so that not one of them, without the permission of that youth, used to have the power of making use of anything belonging to that accursed one. At this time, all of them [the Mughals], with one accord, girded up their loins to despatch this youth, saying: "The deceased [Mughal] used not to regard any one more than this youth: it is necessary to inter him along with him." Their object was to destroy this youth, and take vengeance on him for the sway he had exercised; and, in this proceeding, all agreed. The Musalmān youth, in this state of affliction, was astounded, and resigned his heart to death, seeing that he had no asylum and no succour, save in the Lord, the Helper of the Helpless. He stretched out the hand of supplication to the promise of Him, "who hears the distressed when they pray unto Him,"[72] and performed the ablution of purification, donned clean clothes, and placed his foot within that subterranean [chamber].

When they had covered it up, in a corner of this chamber, that poor creature turned his face towards the *qiblah*, repeated a prayer of two genuflexions, and then occupied himself in repeating the Muslim creed. Suddenly, a side of the chamber opened, and two persons, so majestic and awe-striking that the bile of a hundred thousand lions, at their aspect, would turn to water, entered. Each of them bore a fiery javelin, out of which issued flames of fire, and the flames encircled the couch of the [dead] Mughal all round; and a small spark from the fiery sparks [issuing from the

72. Qur'ān XXVII.63.

> flames], about the size of a needle's point, fell upon the cheek of that youth, burnt it, and made it smart. One of these two persons said: "There appears to be a Musalmān here"; and the other turned his face on the youth and asked: "Who art thou?" The youth states that he answered: "I am a poor and miserable captive, captured by the hands of that Mughal." They demanded: "From whence art thou?" and I replied: "From Tirmid." They then struck one side of the chamber with the heads of their javelins, and it rent asunder to the extent of about [the size of] a doorway, and they said: "Go out!" and I placed my foot without, and I found myself in the Tirmid country.
>
> From that place, namely, Qarā-Quram of the Mughals to Tirmid, is a distance of six months' journey and more; and, up to this time, that youth is dwelling upon his own property and possessions, on the confines of Tirmid; and whatever salve he continues to apply to the hurt occasioned by that spark of fire, it is ineffectual to heal it, and it continues open to the size of a needle's point, and to discharge as before. Glory to Him who contrives what He pleases![73]

We have no clear indication of this narrative's "influence" on the account of Baba Tükles, beyond the shared elements of the pit, the fire, and the implicit "contest" of faiths; in addition, we find in Jūzjānī's story the same intrusion of Muslim saints into the Mongol tomb as is suggested in the narrative evocations of the *qoruq*. Nonetheless, the account in Jūzjānī's work illustrates the kind of narratives inspired by the same confrontation of symbol-laden cultures that inspired the narrative of Ötemish Ḥājjī. We cannot but be struck by the recurrence of several elements and their use to make similar points.[74]

73. Jūzjānī, tr. Raverty, tr., pp. 1173–1176; cf. *Ṭabaqāt-i Nāṣirī*, ed. ʿAbd al-Ḥayy Ḥabībī, vol. 2 (Lahore: Maṭbaʿah-i Kūh-i Nūr, 1954), pp. 695–696.

74. This motif of "visionary disappearance" and miraculous transference from a place of distant jeopardy to his home—both in an Inner Asian context and in the context of a conversion narrative—is suggested in the account, discussed below, of the conversion to Nestorian Christianity by a "king" of a Turkic people in the year 1007; the people is identified as the Kereyts in the early fourteenth-century works of Bar Hebraeus, but the miraculous transporting of the king is recounted only in a twelfth-century source, the Arabic *Kitāb al-mijdāl* of Mārī b. Sulaymān. According to this account, the king became lost in the wilderness (assimilable to the death that awaited the subject of Jūzjānī's story) and was saved by the appearance of the saintly Mar Sergius, who instructed the king to accept Christianity and close his eyes; when the king opened his eyes again, he found himself back in his own encampment (cited in Hunter, "The Conversion of the Kerait," p. 155; cf. L. E. Browne, *The Eclipse of Christianity in Asia* [Cambridge: Cambridge University Press,

Entombment, Enclosure, and Emergence: Magic and Metaphor in Communal Sanctification

The "enclosure" and "deliverance" of Baba Tükles in the oven-pit recalls a complex of associated themes involving the protective and/or sacrificial and/or punitive enclosure of a hero or holy man whose emergence from the enclosure confirms his faith or creates a new community. The fact that Baba Tükles' emergence from the fire-pit proves the truth of Islam, in Ötemish Ḥājjī's narrative, is explicitly stated, and would be quite obvious even if it were not. But the elements of the narrative that link Baba Tükles with the roles of shaman and culture-hero are not so transparent, and it may be useful to explore this issue at greater length. It must be noted to begin with that in view of the later transformations of the role of Baba Tükles, which we have yet to examine, it does not seem at all surprising to find echoes of shamanic and heroic and ancestral traits in Baba Tükles even at this earliest accessible stage of his story; but the following arguments may appear inconclusive until the combined weight of these later developments, and the already multivalent character of Ötemish Ḥājjī's tale in its entirety, are kept in mind.

The central point to keep in mind here is that in emerging from the oven-pit to "consitute" the new Muslim community, Baba Tükles participates in a richly multivalent symbolism evocative of both Muslim and Inner Asian ways of recounting how a community is formed and defined. In Islamic terms the narrative shows him winning or confirming a community of faith; in shamanic terms it shows him surviving his initiatory ordeal on behalf of his community; and in more generally resonant Inner Asian terms (beyond the specifically shamanic paradigms discussed above),

1933], p. 102, and D. M. Dunlop, "The Karaits of Eastern Asia," *BSOAS*, 11 [1943–1946], pp. 276–289 [p. 278]); the ritual "sealing" of the king's conversion that follows his miraculous deliverance is discussed later in this chapter. The currency of tales linking conversion or fidelity to one's faith with "visionary disappearance" or "miraculous transport" in the twelfth and thirteenth centuries, attested in these stories from Jūzjānī and Mārī, is suggested also by the parallel story in the French history of St. Louis by Joinville. The tale involves the three-month disappearance of a certain prince, who reported that he had ascended a mountain and there encountered a splendid monarch in his court; the monarch had told him of a miraculous victory for the Mongols, contingent upon their adoption of Christianity. This report is analyzed in Lionel J. Friedman, "Joinville's Tartar Visionary," *Medium Aevum*, 27/1 (1958), pp. 1–7; Friedman notes the similarity of Joinville's tale to a story in a work of the same era by Thomas of Cantimpré, both focused on the Mongols, and to Bar Hebraeus's account (he appears not to know the more fully miraculous account of Mārī b. Sulaymān), but despite his acknowledgment that these and other accounts reflect "floating narratives" current in that era, he concentrates on historical correlation of the figure in Joinville's tale with the Mongol shaman Teb Tengri.

it shows him being "enclosed," surviving, and "emerging" whole and strong, in what amounts to his own "birth" and that of his newly formed community. Baba Tükles, in Ötemish Ḥājjī's narrative, is thus "like" other nation-formers when he emerges from his ordeal of enclosure, and is "like" a shamanic communal protector in his fiery "initiation"; the narrative is not merely metaphorical, however, for underlying it are assumptions not only of the magical efficacy of these acts to "create" a new community, but also of the quasi-magical efficacy of *recounting* the creative force of these feats to define a community. We will thus consider in greater depth the themes discussed in the preceding section in connection with their echoes in other Mongol-era narratives; here our concern will be the use of these themes to articulate notions of communal origin and sanctification, keeping in mind the "shamanic" parallels to Ötemish Ḥājjī's account of Baba Tükles as noted above.

SACRIFICIAL ENTOMBMENT AND SANCTIFYING A COMMUNITY

The theme of enclosure in the earth, with its creative and community-forming power, recalls the general and widely observed sacrificial practice of entombment to sanctify and "vivify" structures of various types, such as the burial of a child in the foundation of a building. Such a practice is explicitly linked with fire and furnaces in rites discussed by Eliade in *The Forge and the Crucible*, where he notes the use of human fetuses in the consecration of smiths' furnaces; the furnace would be built above a hollow in the ground in which a fetus, aborted through magical means, was burned.[75] Eliade's examples are from Africa and ancient Babylon, but if these appear too distant or of questionable relevance for use in interpreting our narrative, we may note the same motif much closer to our setting. In a tale recorded late in the last century among the so-called "Kundrov Tatars" who nomadized in the steppes north of the Caucasus and belonged originally to the Little Noghay horde, we find not only a clear reference to this practice (or at least an example of its evocation in narrative), but also the sanctifying and "community-forming" roles of a sacrificial enclosure in a pit. The tale[76] is focused on a Noghay hero, called the holy "Ḥażrat Khamat," a powerful warrior with a fabulous steed. He built a certain mosque in Astrakhan that at the time the tale was recorded had been

75. Eliade, *The Forge and the Crucible*, pp. 67–68, 71–72.

76. Recorded by V. Moshkov in his "Materialy dlia kharakteristiki muzykal'nago tvorchestva inorodtsev Volzhsko-kamskago kraia; II, Melodii nogaiskikh i orenburgskikh tatar," *IOAIÈ*, t. 12, vyp. 1 (1894), pp. 1–67 [pp. 63–64 for this tale].

turned into an orthodox cathedral; the point of the narrative is to explain the origins of the Muslims' "misfortune" in having their mosque turned into a church (and implicitly in their subjugation by the Russians).

According to the tale, Ḥażrat Khamat ordered the builders of the mosque to seize the first young boy who came by the site and bury him in the ground; "whoever the boy is, whoever's son he is, take him and bury him," said the saintly hero. It happened that the holy man's own son came to the site first; but the builders took pity on him and would not seize him, taking instead a Russian boy and burying him in the ground. Ḥażrat Khamat came and asked the builders if they had buried the boy. They told him what had happened, and he reproached them for not having fulfilled his command, predicting that because of this their work would be in vain; and so it happened.

It may be that such a tale reflects a memory of actual practice involving such sacrificial burials; examples are not uncommon elsewhere in the world. What is more revealing for our concerns is the understanding that the enclosure or burial of the Muslim boy would have sanctified the mosque and ensured that it served a Muslim community, in this case the Noghays of Astrakhan, thereby affirming religious and communal integrity; when a Russian boy was buried instead, it was rather the political and religious victory of the Russians over the Noghays that was presaged (and here we have not only an omen of the future, but an occurrence made inevitable by the error in "ritual" performance).

In this connection we are reminded of the Bashkir genealogical legend linked with Baba Tükles and discussed in Chapter 6, in which a particular tribe delineates its territory and takes its identity upon the discovery and opening of a Muslim saint's burial place; stories of such discoveries, which in effect "found" (or at least sanctify) a community and establish its link with a particular homeland, are not uncommon. More broadly we may recall also the general sanctifying presence of tombs of holy figures, a virtually universal feature of "spiritual geography" at the local, communal level. Here the specific "sacrificial" aspect of the entombment is absent, unless the person entombed is clearly a martyr, but in general a saint's tomb nevertheless provides a powerful "centering" presence for communities in which the saint's story bears religious meaning. We cannot take up here the enormously complex issue of the role of holy tombs in communal sanctification; even to survey the subject in either an Islamic or Inner Asian context would require a separate monograph. But alongside the few earlier remarks in connection with the *qoruq* and the Islamic resonance of "seeing" into graves, it is worth at least observing, to suggest the issue's relevance for our concerns here, that the religious meaning of saintly persons' entombment in a given community is not limited to the individual (or even communal) benefits derived from pious visitation to the site, nor to the social, economic, and political impact of pilgrimage centers and shrine patronage. Rather, such shrines often form the sacred center that provides religious and "orientational" meaning (and territorial "protection") to the community, a center assimilable to the hearth and the "cave" at the center of the world in Inner Asian terms, and reflecting in Islamic terms a localization of the sacred power that is more properly restricted, at least for orthodox sensibilities, to Mecca. The Inner Asian resonance of a "founder's" sacred tomb is evident in the inviolability of the *qoruq*, as discussed earlier, but is also clearly evoked in a fourteenth-century account, noted below, in which the cave that served as both birthplace and tomb for the ancestor of the Turks is said to be a focus of worship; although it is naturally both capacities that are celebrated in the veneration of this "ancestral" cave, it is specifically the presence of one ancestor's "image" erected in the cave that further sacralizes the site. And with the "ancestral" hero enclosed in a pit and venerated by his people, we find clear parallels with the story of Baba Tükles and the oven-pit, and in general with the motif of an "entombed" saint adopted as ancestor.

Here in the notion that a holy person's death (whether as sacrifice or martyr or neither) and interment may sanctify a particular site and/or community, we find further a curious and suggestive variation on the two often distinct and contrasting paradigms of "territorial" and "communal" conversion to Islam noted earlier. In effect we find the "communal" paradigm evoked by the *shamanic* resonance of the story of Baba Tükles, with his sojourn in the fiery pit understood as a shamanic initiation undertaken for his community's restoration or reformation, as suggested by Kortt's interpretation; here the initiatic ordeal of the fire is the crucial factor, and the element of the pit in the narrative likewise evokes a "communal" paradigm, in the theme of enclosure and emergence, as we will see below.

For the "territorial" paradigm, however, the element of the pit may represent not merely an enclosure, but a tomb as well, as suggested by the parallel of the entombed child and/or saint (in this connection we may note that even though Baba Tükles clearly does not die in our narrative, he does so symbolically when he is sealed up in the oven-pit). And this equation, wherein the pit is the equivalent of the potentially sanctifying tomb, recalls a provocative interpretation suggested by a recent study by a specialist on Mongol religion, Magdalena Tatár.[77] Noting that "human beings have the right to use a territory" because "they are related to the master spirits of the place and because they give gifts of sacrifices to them," Tatár suggests that one means whereby foreign or alien individuals may be integrated into Inner Asian communities lies in their "adoption" of the territorial spirits regarded as of "alien" origin in a particular community, that is, spirits of foreigners who died in the community's territory.

In other words, a given community would continue to recognize the foreignness of those spirits residing in its territory, spirits that came to inhabit that territory through the death there of some foreign traveler; the fact that those spirits now resided in the community's territory, however, perhaps assimilated to the indigenous "master" spirits of natural features,[78] would make them "native," while the fact that their foreignness was recalled would make them suitable for adoption as "ancestral" spirits by outsiders seeking "admission" to the community. In effect, communal and territorial identity merge, and the social and religious integration of "immigrants" is made possible, all through the original outsider's death (and by extension interment) in the community's territory.

To gain "territorial" rights thus requires the "death" and "burial" of a figure suitable to serve as an "ancestor" for the foreigners; or, more likely, it requires the narrative assertion of such a death and burial. It is only a small jump from this point to suggest that this is what Baba Tükles supplies for the Muslims (who are "foreigners" in Inner Asian communal terms) through his symbolic death and burial in the ordeal and enclosure in the pit. Tatár discusses examples of communal memory of actual foreigners who supplied their spirits, through their deaths, for such integrating functions; but of equal significance, we would suggest, is the "invention" of stories by an incoming "foreign" group (e.g., Muslims) recounting the arrival and "death" and "interment" of the figure adopted as the new group's "ancestral" spirit.

It is thus not unlikely that the narrative form in which the tale of Baba Tükles reached Ötemish Ḥājjī reflected a number of mythic and symbolic

77. Magdalena Tatár, "Tragic and Stranger Ongons among the Altaic Peoples," in *Altaistic Studies* (PIAC XXV, 1982), ed. Gunnar Jarring and Staffan Rosén (Stockholm: Almqvist & Wiksell International, 1985), pp. 165–171.

78. As Tatár notes, the "master spirits" of nature are often "recruited" among ancestors associated with these sites in their lifetimes or through their burial place, and were likewise assimilated to the "nonspecific" ancestors, i.e., those whose individual lives were lost to living memory but were still celebrated communally.

themes typically evoked in recounting origins, especially communal origins, and that among them appeared both the theme of "sacrificial" burial to sanctify a community, and that of emergence from enclosure as a nation-forming event (the theme to which we now turn); it is also likely that already in Ötemish Ḥājjī's time these indigenous Inner Asian themes had been closely interwoven with religiously resonant themes evoking Islamic paradigms, through the medium of Muslim hagiolatry.

ENCLOSURE AND EMERGENCE IN LEGENDS OF ORIGIN

Less explicitly evident, though detectable, in Ötemish Ḥājjī's narrative, are echoes of the theme of "enclosure" and "emergence" as the pivotal features of legends of origin and conversion myths. In the case of Baba Tükles it is his emergence from the fire-pit that marks the climactic point of the narrative and in effect signals the beginning of a new, convinced, converted Islamic community; the element of fire appears central, but the digging of the pit for the fire, and the closing of its opening, allow us to add to the mix of themes conflated in the extant narrative not only the complex of religious associations of fire and burnt sacrifice, as discussed earlier, but also the themes of enclosure and emergence. This association appears in the story from Jūzjānī discussed above, where the enclosure becomes the grave; more important, the themes of enclosure and emergence are central elements in many Inner Asian legends of origin, wherein they are most often closely linked to the mythic complex noted in Chapter 1, involving a Mountain, a Tree, a Cave, Water, and a Female Spirit.

ERGENE QŪN Perhaps the best-known example of the function of enclosure and emergence in ethnogonic tales is the legend of Ergene Qūn, as preserved in accounts by Rashīd ad-Dīn from the early fourteenth century, and by later works not always wholly dependant upon his account, of which the best known is the work of Abū'l-Ghāzī from the mid-seventeenth century.[79] According to the tale, the Mongols were

79. Cf. Rashīd ad-Dīn, *Dzhāmiʿ at-tavārīkh*, t. I, ch. 1, ed. A. A. Romaskevich, L. A. Khetagurov, A. A. Ali-zade (Moscow: Nauka, GRVL, 1965), pp. 358–362, and the Russian translation, *Sbornik letopisei*, t. 1, kn. 1, tr. L. A. Khetagurov, ed. A. A. Semenov (Moscow/Leningrad: Izd-vo AN SSSR, 1952), pp. 153–154; Abū'l-Ghāzī, ed. and tr. Desmaisons, text, pp. 31-35, tr., pp. 31–33. Between these two accounts we find the story of Ergene Qūn in, for instance, the Persian *Shajarat al-atrāk* (fifteenth to sixteenth centuries) and the Turkic *Zubdat al-āthār* (mid-sixteenth century), and, among published sources, in the Turkic *Tavārīkh-i guzīdah-i nuṣrat-nāmah* from the early sixteenth century (MS British Museum, Or. 3222, ff. 5a–b; cf. the facsimile published with annotations by Akramov), and the Persian "*ʿAbdullāh-nāmah*" from the end of the same century (cf. Khafiz-i Tanysh ibn Mir Mukhammad Bukhari, *Sharaf–nama–ii*

once all but wiped out in a war with their Turkic enemies, and only two men, named Qïyan and Nüküz, with their families, survived; they took refuge in a place described as a well-watered and fertile valley shut off from the outside world by high mountains and dense forests. The place was called Ergene Qūn, a name explained as meaning "steep slope"; of more interest is the explanation of the name of Qïyan, which is said to mean "a torrent which comes down from a mountain swiftly and forcefully," recalling the "torrent" that plays a central role in yet another echo of the same mythic complex, namely the account of Ibn ad-Dawādārī, discussed below. When the descendants of these two families became too numerous to fit inside the mountainous enclosure, the people assembled, recalled their ancestors' homeland outside, and

---

Shakhi (Kniga shakshkoi slavy), facs. and tr. M. A. Salakhetdinova, ch. 1 [Moscow: Nauka, GRVL, 1983], pp. 65ff.). See also the comparison of Rashīd ad-Dīn's account with that of Aḥmad Tabrīzī's *Shāhanshāh-nāmah* from the late 1330s (cf. Storey-Bregel', *PL*, II, P. 775), in J. A. Boyle, "Some Thoughts on the Sources for the Il-Khanid Period of Persian History," *Iran*, 12 (1974), pp. 185–188. A further echo of the story of Mongol origins in the "emergence" from a mountainous enclosure is no doubt to be found in the late thirteenth-century history of the Armenian monk Hayton, in which we find "Changuis" leading his people out of the mountains; the story he gives even involves a parting of waters, as God responds to Changuis's prayers and opens a way through the sea (cf. "La Flor des estoires de la Terre d'Orient," in *Recueil des historiens des Croisades, Documents arméniens*, t. 2 (Paris: Imprimerie Nationale, 1906), pp. 111–363; for this account, pp. 153 [the old French text], 288 [Latin text]). From Hayton's account the story entered the popular travels of John Mandeville, cf. Malcolm Letts, *Mandeville's Travels: Texts and Translations*, I (London: Hakluyt Society, 1953), pp. 155–158. The legend of Ergene Qūn was also discussed in Denis Sinor, "A propos de la biographie ouigoure de Hiuan-tsang," *JA*, 231 (1939), pp. 543–590 [pp. 552–553], and "The Legendary Origin of the Türks," in *Folklorica: Festschrift for Felix J. Oinas*, ed. Egle Victoria Žygas and Peter Voorheis (Bloomington: Research Institute for Inner Asian Studies, 1982), pp. 223–257 [pp. 246–248]. See also the summaries of the tale, in the context of its striking parallels with the Christian and Qur'ānic legend of Alexander, in J. A. Boyle, "The Alexander Romance in Central Asia," *ZAS*, 9 (1975), pp. 265–273 [p. 269], and more thoroughly in his "The Alexander Legend in Central Asia," *Folklore*, 85 (Winter, 1974), pp. 217–228 [p. 223]; the legend of Ergene Qūn is also discussed, with attention to its parallels in the Alexander romance and to its early twentieth-century evocations in "Pan-Turkism," in Richard Hartmann, "Ergeneqon," in *Festschrift Georg Jacob*, ed. Theodor Menzel (Leipzig: Otto Harrassowitz, 1932), pp. 68–79. In view of the parallels, if inverse, between such Inner Asian legends of enclosure and emergence, and the well-known stories from Europe and the Middle East about the "Enclosed Peoples," especially as linked with the Alexander romance, Boyle argues that the Inner Asian versions reflect borrowing from Nestorian Christian versions of the Alexander romance that spread into Inner Asia; the Türk legend of "emergence" from a mountain-ringed plain (see below) would seem to predate any such influence, so it may be more appropriate to speak of archaic Inner Asian tales being incorporated into legends of Alexander. In any case, the "ultimate" origin of the tale is not so important for us as the fact that it was quite readily and widely assimilated into an indigenous mythic structure.

resolved to look for a way out; they were unable to find a path until a blacksmith[80] recalled an exposed bed of iron in the mountains and showed the people, who gathered firewood and coal and made bellows out of seventy skins. They set fire to the wood and blew with the bellows, and the fire grew hot enough to open a small hole in the iron face of the mountain. The people thus went out, and the descendants of Q̱ïyan included one, named Būrtah Chīnah (the "Blue-Grey Wolf" of the Mongol *Secret History*), an ancestor of Chingis Khan, who was chosen as ruler. Abū'l-Ghāzī adds that the Mongols marked the time of their emergence by observing the sun and moon, and have celebrated that day ever since as a festival (*ʿīd*), with a "metallurgical" rite recalling their origins: each year the khan, followed by the *beks*, heats a piece of iron, holds it with tongs, places it atop an anvil, and strikes it with a hammer; and the *beks* honor that day, regarding it as the day they went out from their "enclosure" (*qabāl*) and entered their "ancestral homeland" (*ātā yūrtï*). The "formation" of the Mongols thus described was even accompanied by the dispatch of envoys by the khan Burtah Chinah to announce their emergence.[81]

The story of Ergene Q̱ūn thus exhibits several features that parallel themes in the story of Baba Tükles, and in the epic tale of Er Töshtük as well: the enclosure; the gathering of fuel; the fire itself; and the victorious and "revivified" emergence from the enclosure.[82] If we consider ethnogonic narratives in which *only* the motif of the cave and/or enclosure is evoked, the number of parallels grows substantially: we find echoes of such a motif in legends of origin focused on the Türks of Mongolia in the sixth century, on the Oghuz of the twelfth century, on the "Turks" and Mongols from the fourteenth century, and, with a quite interesting variation, on the Uyghurs from the thirteenth century.

THE SIXTH-CENTURY TURKS In the first case, it was Pelliot, so far as I know, who first noted the parallels between the Türk legend of origin involving enclosure in and emergence from a "cavern" or mountain valley, with the story of Ergene Q̱ūn.[83] The Türk legend in question, one of

80. The blacksmith appears only in Abū'l-Ghāzī's account; in Rashīd ad-Dīn, the people themselves eventually find the iron seam.

81. Sinor, "Legendary Origin," p. 247, wrongly ascribes the account of the ritual commemoration to Rashīd ad-Dīn, but cites Abū'l-Ghāzī in "La biographie ouigoure," p. 553.

82. The same combination is echoed in Jūzjānī's story, discussed above, of the Muslim buried with his Mongol master, and with quite different intentions in the Qur'ānic account of Dhū'l-Qarnayn and the enclosure of Gog and Magog, as noted below.

83. Paul Pelliot, "Neuf notes sur des questions d'Asie Centrale," *TP*, 26 (1929), pp. 201–266 [p. 214, n. 2]. Denis Sinor seeks to "historicize" the Türk legend and thus deny its connection

three such stories that are all known only from Chinese sources, recounts the Türk ancestor's protective enclosure within a mountain-ringed meadow that was itself inside a cave in a certain mountain; the ancestor was carried there by a nurturing she-wolf that fed him and became his mate, and their descendants later emerged from their enclosure, led by a particular heroic figure whose memory was evidently preserved.[84] As noted earlier (and discussed more fully below), "ancestral caves" of the Turks are mentioned relatively often, and appear as part of the general Mountain/Tree/Cave/Water/Goddess complex outlined earlier; in this case, we find ritual echoes of this myth in the rites reportedly performed by the *qaghan* and leading dignitaries inside the "ancestral cavern" of the Türks. This ritual role of the cave among the Türks is mentioned in Chinese annals contemporary with the first Türk empire, and is directly linked there with ancestral rites; this allows us to suggest the religious meaning of the cave rite as evocative of the Türks' sacred origins (or those of their ruling dynasty, inasmuch as the two are mythically and religiously equivalent), thus giving us the full complement of a "mythic" legend of origin rooted in the familiar Inner Asian complex of sacred ethnogonic symbols, and a "ritual" reenactment (or at least celebration) of that myth. The Chinese account itself is brief and specifies only that "each year the *qaghan* [of the Türks] leads the nobles for sacrificial rites to the ancestral cavern";[85] for a more detailed exposition of the mythic and ritual components we must have recourse to an Islamic source from the fourteenth century, discussed shortly, that attests quite vividly to the ancestral associations of caves among Turkic peoples in western Inner Asia.

More suggestively, however, the earlier Chinese account affirms that the "ancestral cavern" still ritually employed by the Turks was located in the famous "sacred *refugium*" of the Türks in Mongolia, the high mountain valley called "Ötüken" and reflected not only in Chinese sources, but in the native Turkic inscriptions from the period of the second Türk empire (681–744), as well as in later Uyghur texts.[86] With the Ötüken—a

---

with the Ergene Qūn tale, insisting that the latter lacks any "truly historical character"; the cave in the Türk legend of origin and ancestral rite reflects for Sinor a memory among the Türks of their ancient cave dwellings and metallurgical labor ("A propos de la biographie ouigoure," pp. 552–553).

84. Cf. the translation in Denis Sinor, "The Legendary Origin of the Türks," pp. 223–225; cf. a somewhat different translation by Christopher I. Beckwith, *The Tibetan Empire in Central Asia: A History of the Struggle for Great Power among Tibetans, Turks, Arabs, and Chinese during the Early Middle Ages* (Princeton: Princeton University Press, 1987), pp. 206–207.

85. Pelliot, "Neuf notes," p. 214.

86. For further references on the Ötüken, cf. J. Schubert, "Zum Begriff und zur Lage des

well-watered forested plain near high mountains that evidently featured a cave suitable for ritual use—understood as a sacred territorial center and cultic site for celebrations of ancestral, and thereby communal, origins, we would appear to have a concrete manifestation of the religious symbolism expressed also in the fragments and echoes of the various Inner Asian legends of origin discussed below. As such, it not only attests to the antiquity of the mythic complex evident in later reworkings of the tales of Baba Tükles, but also reinforces the sacred associations of caves and "enclosures" to aid our understanding of the religious significance of incorporating these elements into conversion narratives and legends of origin. While it appears that the appeal of the "Ötüken" as a sacred center was evoked and transformed in the "nativistic" ideology so distinctively articulated in the eighth-century Turkic inscriptions (where we find its sacrality concretized in an insistence that the Ötüken serve as the political center of the Türk state), it is clear that the use of the Ötüken's "image" then in defining and mobilizing the "Türk people/nation" must rest upon its sacred associations with the ancestral myth of the Türks, involving the themes of protective ancestral enclosure and communal emergence, of at least two centuries earlier.[87]

The period of the Türk empires thus affords us an excellent illustration not only of the mythic *and* ritual importance of "enclosure and emergence" in ethnogonic legends, but of those legends' political potential as well, as a focus for assertions of communal identity and solidarity.

'Ötükän'," *UAJ*, 35 (1963), pp. 213–218; see also the comments of Hilda Ecsedy, "Tribe and Tribal Society in the 6th Century Turk Empire," *AOH*, 25 (1972), pp. 245–262 [p. 254] and of Jean-Paul Roux, "La religion des Turcs de l'Orkhon des VIIe et VIIIe siècles," *RHR*, 161 (1962), pp. 1–24 [pp. 16–18], where he notes the Ötüken's role as the center of the world within the cosmological framework of the World Mountain.

87. What we may be witnessing in the Old Turkic inscriptions is the "nationalization" of the more "generic" legend of origin implicit in the Ötüken's initial status as a place of ancestral ritual: when the Ötüken venerated as the site for the ritual remembrance of the mythic setting of the "first man's" birth, for a community naturally equating itself with all of humanity (i.e., first human = first Türk, and thus both ascribed mythic origins in the context of the mountain/etc. complex), becomes the Ötüken hailed as the "place of national origin" and thus a center for national rule, we see a familiar pattern of indigenous mythic universalization clothed in imperial ideology for purposes of political legitimation. As might be expected, the inevitable "concretization" of mythic symbols (or of elements in sacred narratives) that accompanies their appropriation for political legitimization at the imperial level entails a diminution of their original mythic and religious multivalence—not in terms of their ongoing potential, but in terms of discursive formulation, since religious language is in general richer than political language.

THE OGHUZ An echo of the themes of enclosure and emergence, linked with the theme of guidance by an animal spirit (as found in the Türk legend), is reflected also in the twelfth-century Syriac chronicle of Michael the Syrian (1126–1199), who gives an extended account of the Turks—above all the Oghuz tribes who had moved into Anatolia. Michael notes that the Turks used to live within mountains called "the breasts of the earth," from which they could emerge through only two gates; in their most recent migration, when they emerged from their mountain enclosure and spread throughout the earth, they were guided by an animal, "resembling a dog," that had guided earlier generations in their emergence and migrations. The creature in effect indicated when the people should move,[88] and where they should halt. Its supernatural character is clear, for "it walked before them, but they could not approach it," and after having led them for a long time, it disappeared. Its sacred character was acknowledged by the writer as well; he sees it as a sign that God guides each nation, through what is familiar to it, to what is useful, and compares the guiding creature to the means by which God guided the Hebrews in the wilderness and the Magi to Bethlehem.[89] Michael's account undoubtedly reflects oral tradition among the Turks, refracted through an uncertain number of intermediaries and Michael's own theological views.

IBN AD-DAWĀDĀRĪ Further attestation of the central role of caves and enclosures in ethnogonic myth and ritual among the Turks and Mongols is found in the remarkable but still little-known[90] account of

88. It did so by raising its voice and saying "*gūš*," says Michael, a clear allusion to the Turkic verb *göč- or köč-*, meaning to "migrate" or "move" an encampment. Precisely the same point is made by Juvaynī in connection with the Uyghurs, when at the end of his account of Būqū Khan he relates that "The tribes and peoples of the Uighur, when they listened to the neighing of horses, the screaming of camels, the barking and howling of dogs and beasts of prey, the lowing of cattle, the bleating of sheep, the twittering of birds and the whimpering of children, in all this heard the cry of '*köch, köch!*' and would move on from their halting-place. And wherever they halted the cry of '*köch, köch!*' would reach their ears. Finally they came to the plain where they afterwards built Besh-Baligh, and here that cry was silenced" (Juvaynī, tr. Boyle, I, p. 61). It is thus likely that Juvaynī also knew of legends recounting the miraculous guidance of the Uyghurs by some supernatural animal.

89. *Chronique de Michel le Syrien, Patriarche Jacobite d'Antioche (1166–1199)*, ed. and tr. J.-B. Chabot (Paris: Ernest Leroux, Éditeur, 1899–1910), vol. 3, pp. 152 (on the mountain enclosure), 155 (on the doglike guide); cf. Rauf Husseinov, "Les sources syriaques sur les croyances et les moeurs des Oghuz du VIIe au XIIe siècle," *Turcica*, 8/1 (1976), pp. 21–27.

90. Its importance as a Turkic cosmogonic myth was noted already in a report by Pertev Naili Boratav, "Le myth turc du Premier Homme d'après Abū Bekr b. ʿAbd-Allah (XIVe siècle)," in *Proceedings of the Twenty-Third International Congress of Orientalists* (Cambridge, 1954), ed. Denis Sinor (London: Royal Asiatic Society, 1954), pp. 198–199; from Boratav's brief discussion

Turkic traditions preserved in the work of the Mamlūk historian Ibn ad-Dawādārī, completed in 736/1336.[91] This rich account is purportedly based upon a book with which Ibn ad-Dawādārī became acquainted in 710/1310, a book he says was highly respected among the Qïpchaqs and Mongols. He gives its title in various forms that appear to reflect the Turkic *Ulū Khān Aṭā Bitigi*, which he explains in Arabic as "The Book of the Great Father King"; this book was itself based (insofar as the material Ibn ad-Dawādārī cites from it is concerned) on an Arabic translation, dated 211/826 and ascribed to the Christian Jibrīl b. Bukhtīshūᶜ, physician at the ᶜAbbāsid court,[92] who in turn drew upon a Persian translation, ascribed to Abū Muslim, from a Turkic original that belonged to the Sasanid royal counselor Buzurjmihr, here cast as Abū Muslim's ancestor.

The general reliability of Ibn ad-Dawādārī strongly supports the authenticity of the book, popular among the Qïpchaqs and Mongols, which he claims to cite; it must have been in existence by the beginning of the fourteenth century, and in view of the close links between the Mamlūk and Jöchid realms it is not unreasonable to assume the stories it contains were well known in the Golden Horde of Özbek Khan's era. As for its earlier history as related by Ibn ad-Dawādārī, we have virtually no basis for judging the actual age of the traditions it preserves; the Christian physician is perhaps an unlikely figure to insert in the "book's" pedigree, but in fact legendary stories of his family's medical practice were current in the Mongol era,[93] while with Abū Muslim and Buzurjmihr we have

the account was noted by Roux (*La religion*, p. 107; *Faune*, pp. 286–287), while İnan's mention of the account appears to have been independent (*Tarihte ve bugün şamanizm*, p. 21). The most complete discussion appears in Ulrich Haarmann, "Alṭun Ḫān und Čingiz Ḫān bei den ägyptischen Mamluken," *Der Islam*, 51 (1974), pp. 1–36 [pp. 16–21]; cf. Akhmed B. Ėrdzhiliasun [Ahmet B. Ercilasun], "Nekotorye soobrazheniia o dastane "Oguz Kagan"," tr. Iu. V. Sheki, *Sovetskaia tiurkologiia*, 1987, No. 6, pp. 28–31, in which the attempt to interpret "Bukhtīshūᶜ" as an error for *bakhshī* may be discounted.

91. His universal history is entitled *Kanz ad-durar wa jāmiᶜ al-ghurar*; the account of Turkic ethnogonic legends appears in the seventh volume, separately entitled *ad-Durr al-maṭlūb fī akhbār mulūk banī Ayyūb*, ed. Saᶜīd ᶜAbd al-Fattāḥ ᶜĀšūr, *Die Chronik des Ibn ad-Dawādārī*, siebter Teil, Der Bericht über die Ayyubiden (Cairo: Deutsches Archäologisches Institut Kairo, 1972), pp. 219–227, and is followed by an account of Mongol origins and the rise of Chingis Khan that evokes the same mythic complex.

92. Cf. D. Sourdel, *EI*², I, p. 1298, s.v. "Bukhtīshūᶜ," and Lutz Richter-Bernburg, *EIr*, IV, pp. 333–336, s.v. "Bok̲tīšūᶜ"; three members of the family, father, son, and grandson, served the Caliphs from Hārūn to al-Mutawakkil, and in view of the date of the translation, the name as given by Ibn Dawādārī might conceivably reflect that of either the son or grandson (i.e., Jibrīl b. Bukhtīshūᶜ [d. 212/827] and Bukhtīshūᶜ b. Jibrīl b. Bukhtīshūᶜ [d. 256/870].

93. Cf. the *Tansūkh-nāmah-i Īlkhānī* of Naṣīr ad-Dīn Ṭūsī, a favorite of Hülegü and his suc-

figures mythologized already quite early in the Islamic era (although their connection with Turks may belie a particular development of the Saljūq era in Central Asia and Iran). In any case the age of the traditions is not so crucial for our purposes as their authenticity, and in most cases the additions and interpretations made by Ibn ad-Dawādārī (or by his sources?) are plainly distinguishable from the core of the myth.

The account first describes a mythic topography that reflects quite well the Inner Asian mythic complex outlined earlier, and then recounts the origin of the First Man and Ancestor. In the first regard, the focal point is the great mountain, east of the frontiers of China (*aṣ-Ṣīn*), called in Turkic "Qarā Ṭāgh," the "Black Mountain." Springs that rise on the mountain's west side fill a lake, from which a river runs, and along the river are two great cities that were built, we learn later, by the son of the First Man; beyond them the river divides into many branches, which water a land of abundance and plenty, described as a veritable paradise in which no disease is known, but only joy and long life.[94]

As for the origin myth itself, it is naturally set at the sacred center, the mountain called Qarā Ṭāgh. In the mountain, we are told, was a cave, which now bears a golden gate at its entrance and is worshiped by the people of that land. At the beginning of time, however, a torrent[95] of rainwater passed through the cave, and its force was such that it left a rut in the earth floor of the cave, in the shape of a human being. The account specifically compares this rut to a womb, and it was here that the four elements combined to form the First Man: the water from the torrent was mixed with the earth; the element of fire was added when the mixture was warmed by the sun; and breezes blew upon it for nine months, until the human being thus formed "came out" of the depression and emerged from the cave.[96] This, the account says, was the figure the Turks call "Ay Aṭam," explained as "Moon Father"; he lived forty years alone until another person was created in the same way (but imperfectly), to become his wife, and together they lived eighty years, producing forty children. The man died at the age of 120, and his eldest

cessors, where a story connected with the use of a particular depilatory stone, able to remove thick body hair when rubbed on the arms, is ascribed to Bukhtīshūʿ (ed. Sayyid Muḥammad Taqī Mudarris Rižavī [2nd ed., Tehran: Intishārāt-i Iṭṭilāʿāt, 1363/1984], pp. 135–136; cf. pp. 286–287).

94. Ibn ad-Dawādārī, text, pp. 219–221.

95. This element in the account is reminiscent of the meaning ascribed by Rashīd ad-Dīn and Abū'l-Ghāzī to the name of one of the Mongol "refugees" enclosed within Ergene Qūn.

96. A remarkable parallel to this story of "spontaneous generation" is used, with quite different

son laid his body in the same rut inside the cave, "hoping that he would come to life again." When, instead, the body was found decayed upon the mother's death forty years later, the son buried them both in the cave and placed the golden gate at its mouth, posting custodians to guard it.[97] It is that cave, the account affirms elsewhere, that is worshiped by the people of that country; servants and guards are still found there, and when the people swear oaths by the Qarā Ṭāgh, they are referring to that ancestral cave.[98]

The son of the First Man succeeded his father as ruler of their progeny, whose number had increased considerably; he built the two cities noted above, and ruled for forty years. His son, in turn, succeeded him, but this time the royal father's body was treated differently: his body was placed within a hollow human likeness made of gold, and seated upon a throne in a "house" erected as a "temple," with golden candles kept burning constantly inside and custodians posted for service. The site was thus a place of pilgrimage, where the people would gather on the anniversary of this king's death to perform prostrations and prayers and to bring offerings; the account closes with the explanation that subsequent rulers of this king's lineage bore the title "Alṭun Khān" because of this golden sarcophagus.[99]

Following this description of the ancestral "temple" set up for the Turkic dynasty whose members are called "Alṭun Khān," the narrative turns to Chingis Khan and his struggle with the "Alṭun Khān" of his day, first reporting from a different source an account of Mongol origins that reflects the same mythic complex. In this account, a woman from Tibet went, though pregnant, to gather firewood, and gave birth to a boy who was quickly seized by an eagle and carried to the wild forest at the foot of the Qarā Ṭāgh; the boy grew and came to rule over the beasts there, and he himself took on the appearance and behavior of a wild animal.

---

aim, in the treatise entitled *ar-Risālat al-kāmilīyah* by the physician-theologian Ibn an-Nafīs (d. 687/1288) of Cairo (mentioned in Chapter 2); his purpose was to develop the "natural" origin of knowledge of the Creator, of man's social nature, and of the need for a law delivered by a prophet, through observation and rational thought on the part of the "Perfect Man" (*al-Kāmil*) born in the cave from clay and herbs mixed by a spring torrent (see Meyerhof and Schacht, ed. and tr., *Theologus Autodidactus*, p. 39 [tr.], p. 4 [text]). As indicated by the passage from this treatise cited at the outset, Ibn an-Nafīs was quite interested in the Mongols and in the conversion of Berke, and it is not unlikely that this striking parallel reflects the currency in Mamlūk Egypt, already some fifty years before Ibn ad-Dawādārī wrote, of quite similar accounts of Qïpchaq or Mongol legends of origin.

97. Text, pp. 222–224.

98. Text, p. 222. For further discussion of the cave, as refuge/prison/tomb/birthplace, see Hasluck, *Christianity and Islam under the Sultans*, I, pp. 220–225.

99. Text, p. 227.

Eventually a band of seven people, fleeing their nation's destruction, went astray in the forest, and the wild boy, after saving their lives, took a maiden from among them as his wife; the people are identified as "Tatārs," and the son born to the refugee girl and the wild boy was the ancestor of the Mongols, called "Tatār Khān," whose lineage led to Chingis Khan (who is said to have learned the art of the blacksmith at one of the cities near Qarā Ṭāgh named in the Turkic legend of origin).[100]

Ibn ad-Dawādārī's account stops short of narrating an actual "emergence" from the Mongols' protective "enclosure"; he portrays Chingis Khan as consulting a blacksmith for aid not in breaching impassable mountains, but in conquering a fortified city. Nevertheless, enough of the account remains for us to surmise the essence of the story or stories that Ibn ad-Dawādārī must have used in constructing his narrative; fragments of similar tales were known to Rashīd ad-Dīn, as noted below. Ibn ad-Dawādārī's account of the Turks thus highlights their "ancestral cave" in both its mythic and ritual aspects, while for the Mongols his account at least implies the protective transport and concealment of the ancestor and his later contacts with refugees who come to his remote and wild home. The latter elements are of particular interest: the story of the refugees echoes an element in legends of origin reported for the Kimeks and for a Bashkir tribe, while the "wild" condition of the Mongol ancestor recalls a similar description associated with a figure later cast as Baba Tükles' descendant, as we shall see.

THE UYGHURS Finally, the themes of enclosure and emergence appear alongside several other elements of the larger mythic complex in the Uyghur legends of origin noted in Persian and Chinese sources of the Mongol era, best known through the rich version given by Juvaynī. The origin of the account is unclear; Juvaynī cites it as a tale of the Uyghurs themselves, and he was certainly in a position to have access to such tales. The fact that much of it appears also in a somewhat later Chinese account also suggests its authenticity as an Uyghur tradition, and the story was evidently known to Marco Polo as well. Juvaynī's account is of particular value for situating the story within a larger mythic and historical framework of Uyghur origins involving striking parallels with other legends of origin discussed more fully below in Chapter 7;[101] for now we will consider only the particular narrative of the "enclosed" ancestors, for

100. Text, pp. 227–231; cf. Haarmann, "Alṭun Ḫān," pp. 21–31.

101. His account of the conversion of Būqū Khan (to Buddhism!) was noted above, in con-

which Juvaynī gives by far the most complete version. Juvaynī begins by noting that the Uyghurs placed "the beginning of their generation and increase" "on the banks of the river Orqon [i.e., the Orkhon in Mongolia], whose source flows from a mountain which they call Qara-Qorum"; in all, thirty rivers have their sources there, with a different people dwelling along each river, and the Uyghurs constituted two of the groups. Despite the relative geographical reliability of this account, there is little doubt that it also evokes the Mountain/Water symbolism noted earlier; the symbolism is clearer still in the subsequent account of the origins of Būqū Khan, a sacred ruler said to have arisen among the Uyghurs some five hundred years after their "origin" along the Orkhon:

> In that age two of the rivers of Qara-Qorum, one called the Tughla [Tula] and the other the Selenge, flowed together in a place called Qamlanchu; and close together between these two rivers there stood two trees. . . .[102] Between the two trees there arose a great mound, and a light descended on it from the sky; and day by day the mound grew greater. On seeing this strange sight, the Uighur tribes were filled with astonishment; and respectfully and humbly they approached the mound: they heard sweet and pleasant sounds like singing. And every night a light shone to a distance of thirty paces around that mound, until just as with pregnant women at the time of their delivery, a door opened and inside there were five separate tent-like cells in each of which sat a man-child: opposite the mouth of each child hung a tube which furnished milk as required; while above the tent was extended a net of silver. The chiefs of the tribe came to view this marvel and in reverence bowed the knee of fealty. When the wind blew upon the children they gathered strength and began to move about. At length they came forth from the cells and were confided to nurses, while the people performed all the ceremonies of service and honour. As soon as they were weaned and were able to speak they inquired concerning their parents, and the people pointed to those two trees. They approached the trees and made much obeisance as dutiful children make to their parents; they also showed respect and honour to the ground in which

nection with the themes of debate and contest.

102. I have omitted the names and descriptions of the trees.

> the trees grew. The trees then broke into speech and said: "Good children, adorned with the noblest virtues, have ever trodden this path, observing their duty to their parents. May your lives be long, and your names endure forever!" All the tribes of that region came to view the children and showed them the honours due to the sons of kings; and as they left they gave each boy a name: the eldest they called Sonqur Tegin, the second Qotur Tegin, the third Tükel Tegin, the fourth Or Tegin and the fifth Buqu Tegin.
>
> After considering these strange matters the people agreed that they must make one of the children their leader and their king; for they were, they said, sent by God Almighty. They found Buqu Khan to be superior to the other children in beauty of features and strength of mind and judgement; moreover he knew all the tongues and writings of the different peoples. Therefore all were of one accord that he should be made Khan; and so they gathered together, held a feast and placed him on the throne of the Khanate.[103]

Juvaynī's rich account strikes a number of evocative elements worth noting, from the luminary impregnation (recalling a story told of Chingis Khan's ancestor as well as of the Qarakhanid dynasty) to the specific injunction of parental and ancestral veneration and its importance for future communal blessings. Following this account Juvaynī goes on to narrate several other religiously charged stories about Būqū Khan, including his nightly trysts with a supernatural maiden,[104] his visitation by an old man in a dream, and his conversion from the old religion of the shamans (*qam*) to "idolatry"; interspersed among these stories are brief accounts of his rule and his conquests, allowing us to recognize here a narrative pattern found also in the roughly contemporary legend of Oghuz Qaghan, in which mythic and supernatural symbolism accompanies a catalogue of campaigns and conquests as far as the ends of the earth (only the element of "naming" the subject peoples, with a series of contrived folk etymologies, is missing from Juvaynī's account). In any

103. Juvaynī, tr. Boyle, I, pp. 55–57. Juvaynī himself, as a good historian, found the tale incredible, and after dismissing it as a lie provides what appears to be his rationalistic explanation (p. 60): "A friend has told us that he read in a book how there was a man, who made a hollow in the space between two trees, and placed his own children in it, and lighted candles in the middle of it. Then he brought people to see this wonder, and worshipped it, and commanded them to do likewise. And so he deceived them until he had dug up the ground and fetched out the children."

104. This feature of the Uyghur legend recalls another version of the Türk legend of origin,

event, his version of the Uyghur legend is of additional interest for us, inasmuch as its treatment of the figure of Būqū Khan offers perhaps the closest parallel to the process of development we find for Baba Tükles; this too will be taken up later.

The Chinese version of the tale known to Juvaynī appears in the *Yüan-shih*, the official dynastic history of the Mongols compiled soon after the fall of the dynasty in 1368. In chapter 122, in the biography of Barchuq Art Tegin, the ruler[105] of the Uyghur kingdom of the Tarim basin who submitted to Chingis Khan in 1211, the early "history" of the Uyghurs is recounted; the first part of the account, in Bretschneider's translation and with his transcriptions intact, runs thus:

> *I-du-hu* [i.e. *idiqut*] is the title of the kings of *Kao ch'ang*, who in former times dwelt in the country called *Wei-wu-rh* [Uyghur]. There was in that country (where the Uigurs originally lived) a mountain called *Ho-lin* [the Chinese name for Qara-qorum], from which two rivers took their rise, the *T'u-hu-la* and the *Sie-ling-k'o* [the Tula and the Selenga]. It happened once in the night-time that a stream of light fell from heaven upon a tree standing between the two rivers; whereupon the tree began to swell like a pregnant woman, and after nine months and ten days gave birth to five boys. The youngest received the name *Bu-k'o han*. He was afterwards elected king and subdued the neighboring countries.[106]

Here the role of the tree is stressed to the exclusion of the "mound of earth," but the luminary impregnation and swelling clearly reflect the same tradition. The tree is likewise emphasized in Rashīd ad-Dīn's remark that the Uyghurs described Bügü Khan as having been born from a tree, and in the same story's echo in Marco Polo, who notes of the Uyghurs that "they say that the king who originally ruled over them was not born of human stock, but arose from a sort of tuber generated by the sap of trees."[107] Yet another echo of the same story, applied, however, to another people, is found in two versions of a narrative of Mongol origins preserved in Rashīd ad-Dīn's account of Indian history; his informant for

involving liaisons between the ancestor and a feminine spirit in her underwater home (cf. Sinor, "Legendary Origin," pp. 230–231).

105. He bore the title *idiqut* < *ïdhuq-qut*, "sacred fortune."

106. Tr. E. Bretschneider, *Mediaeval Researches from Eastern Asiatic Sources* (London: Kegan Paul, Trench, Trübner, 1910), vol. 1, p. 247.

107. Tr. Latham [Penguin], p. 89; cf. Boyle in Juvaynī tr., I, p. 56, n. 16.

these tales was Kamalashri, a Kashmīrī Buddhist hermit. Each version links Mongol origins to an ancient Indian dynasty, and in this way reflects an effort to situate Mongol origins within Buddhist sacred history (an effort that was extensively developed in later Mongol and Tibetan historiography); but the elements of a common Inner Asian tradition are clear, as are echoes of Ibn ad-Dawādārī's account of Mongol origins: in each version a man and woman take refuge in a forest beneath a great tree, which in one account is hollow and provides both a protective enclosure for the woman and a birthplace for their children; and both versions include specific affirmation that the children were said to be the offspring of the tree.[108]

The account of the Uyghurs should thus be understood as a reflection of a tale widespread in the Mongol era, and one that included a clear evocation of the Inner Asian ethnogonic myth, in the "impregnation" and swelling of the land at the juncture of two rivers where a great tree grows; but the ancestors thus conceived grow and are protected inside the earth, symbolically equivalent to the cave or mountain-enclosed meadow, and eventually emerge. In this motif we find the important parallel with the story of Baba Tükles. In his case it is not until later elaborated versions of his legend, which we have yet to analyze, that we find parallel evocations of the Mountain/Tree/Water symbolism; but already in Ötemish Ḥājjī's account the theme of enclosure and emergence is clear enough to allow us to speculate that the entire complex was *suggested* by the inclusion of a few of the motifs combined in the larger mythic association. That such an approach is reasonable is further supported by the theme of the "sweet and pleasant sounds like singing" heard from inside the enclosures in Juvaynī's account: while the miraculously conceived boys, the future Uyghur rulers, are inside their "chambers" in the earth, the people outside hear singing from within, just as Baba Tükles' voice is heard from inside the pit. The motif of murmuring voices heard from inside a pit/enclosure is also a common feature of the well-known tales of the Enclosed Peoples of

108. These two accounts are translated in Karl Jahn, "An Indian Legend on the Descent of the Mongols," in *Charisteria Orientalia praecipue ad Persiam pertinentia*, ed. Felix Tauer, Věra Kubíčková, and Ivan Hrbek (Prague: Československé Akademie Věd, 1956), pp. 120–127. Curiously, Jahn (p. 125) insists that these tales recount Mongol origins in a way "entirely at variance with the Turko-Mongol genealogical sagas as they are known to us," and sees in them purely Indian and Buddhist patterns. What seems altogether striking, rather, is the way an indigenous Inner Asian tradition of "communal" origins within an arboreal "enclosure" is woven into a Buddhist structure of "sacred history"; similar patterns are at work in stories of Islamization, as is discussed below.

Gog and Magog; in Muslim tradition this element appears at least as early as the ninth-century story of Sallām the Interpreter's voyage to the Wall of Gog and Magog, in which Sallām himself put his ear to the gate of the Wall and heard the noise made by the people shut up behind it.[109]

ISLAMIC ECHOES OF ENCLOSURE AND COMMUNAL SACRALIZATION

The theme of "protective enclosure" is thus a standard feature of several Inner Asian legends of origin; a number of specific features included in narratives based on this theme are paralleled, moreover, in Ötemish Ḥājjī's account of Baba Tükles, most noticeably the element of fire and that of the sounds heard from within the enclosure. Were only these two elements evident in the story of Baba Tükles, we might not think to look for signs of more extensive thematic parallels with Inner Asian legends of origin in Ötemish Ḥājjī's narrative; but, as we will explore shortly, Baba Tükles came to be surrounded by such a wide range of mythic motifs associated with legends of origin that it does not seem unreasonable to find those further echoes already among the narrative themes and structures preserved, at least in allusions, in Ötemish Ḥājjī's work. The further resonance of these legends of origin, and the full range of motifs explicitly linked with Baba Tükles outside the story given by Ötemish Ḥājjī, are discussed in subsequent chapters; before leaving the theme of enclosure and emergence, however, it is worth considering a number of elements in its more specifically Islamic understanding, to complete the circle of Inner Asian and Muslim assimilation.

The theme of "protective enclosure" appears frequently in Islamic lore, of course, in connection with "both sides" of the enclosure but in each case closely associated with notions of communal and religious integrity. The element of the cave itself has an important Islamic resonance, not only as the place of revelation, in the cave of Ḥirā, but as a specifically protective enclosure as well; Muḥammad and Abū Bakr are kept safe in a cave during the *hijrah*, while according to Islamic tradition[110] the ancestral figure of Ibrāhīm was born in a cave, and was kept enclosed within it by his mother as well, to protect him from harm, mirroring the accounts of heroic birth and "protective abandonment" in Inner Asian hero tales.

The best-known case of "protective enclosure," however, is the Qurʾānic

109. Ibn Khurdādhbih (tr. Barbier de Meynard, pp. 490–496; ed. De Goeje, pp. 125–126 (tr.), 163–164 (text); Ibn Rustah, tr. Wiet, pp. 67–72; Idrīsī, tr. Jaubert, II, pp. 416–420; Mustawfī, tr. Le Strange, pp. 236–237.

110. Cf *The History of al-Ṭabarī*, vol. 2, tr. Brinner, p. 51.

account (with its elaborations in later tradition) of Dhū'l-Qarnayn (i.e., the Islamic Alexander) and the Wall of Yājūj and Mājūj (i.e., "Gog and Magog"), the evil and unbelieving people shut up behind a wall in high mountains for the protection of the "civilized" (and believing) world. The account of the Wall's construction (XVIII.93–99) recalls already important motifs evident in the legend of Ergene Qūn, most notably the "blocks of iron" and the blowing, with bellows, to fan the flames; the difference lies in the Mongol legend celebrating the use of these elements to break through the mountainous "walls" and emerge as a nation, an emergence that in the Qur'ānic account, as in other lore associated with Gog and Magog in both Christian and Islamic traditions, is promised at the end of history.

Perhaps more significant, however, than this specific parallel in the story of Gog and Magog, is the communal responsibility borne by the Islamic *ummah* to maintain the Wall of Gog and Magog in good repair, and the curious "inversion" of the theme of protective enclosure often linked with that responsibility. The responsibility itself is evoked in a Prophetic *ḥadīth* prescribing righteousness as a counter to the openings in the Wall of Gog and Magog,[111] as well as in the famous account of Sallām the Interpreter referred to above; Sallām describes the special duty of the Muslim community "posted" near the Wall to strike the gate three times each Friday (i.e., the day of communal prayer), in order to warn the people of Gog and Magog of the Islamic *ummah*'s continuing vigilance.

But a significant element in the "vigilance" of the Muslim community is expressed in the liturgical recitation, each Friday, before the assembled community, of the eighteenth *sūrah* of the Qur'ān, entitled *sūrat al-kahf*, the *sūrah* of the Cave.[112] This *sūrah* includes also the tale of Dhū'l-Qarnayn and the Wall of Gog and Magog, but the title refers, of course, to the widespread story of the *ahl al-kahf* or *aṣḥāb al-kahf*, the "People" or "Companions" of the Cave, a group of youths whom God, upon their appeals, enclosed in a cave to preserve them from the wickedness and idolatry of the world; the story is modeled on the Christian legend of the "Seven Sleepers of Ephesus," and has enjoyed enormous popularity

111. Cf. A. J. Wensinck in *EI*[1], IV, p. 1142, s.v. "Yādjūdj wa-Mādjūdj."

112. Louis Massignon noted the "unparalleled" position of this *sūrah* in Muslim liturgy, assembling the traditions regarding its obligatory recitation, and the purpose of its recitation, at the Friday noon prayer; cf. "Les 'Sept Dormants' apocalypse de l'Islam," in his *Opera minora*, ed. Y. Moubarac (Beirut: Dar al-Maarif Liban, 1963), vol. 3, pp. 104–118, and a study assembled by Moubarac from several of Massignon's articles, "Le culte liturgique et populaire des VII Dormants Martyrs d'Ephese (Ahl al-Kahf): Trait d'union orient-occident entre l'Islam et la Chrétienté," *Opera minora*, vol. 3, pp. 119–180.

throughout the Islamic world.[113] The story itself evokes the theme of protective enclosure in a "pit" where "saints" are preserved by God, and has lent itself to a wide range of popular and mystical interpretations; the Companions of the Cave are invoked in inscriptions and amulets for protection against fire and other dangers,[114] while their "sleep" in the cave is taken by Sufis as a symbol of withdrawal from this world. For our purposes what is worth noting is the recitation of the Qur'ānic version of the story as a communal undertaking intended for a quite clear and specific purpose: tradition ascribes to its recitation the function of maintaining and preserving the integrity of the Islamic community, for the weekly recitation of the *sūrah* of the Cave repairs the breaches made in the Wall of Gog and Magog by those infidel barbarians whose irruption from behind that barrier will herald the end of the world.

Just as the Muslims mentioned in Sallām's account strike the wall each Friday to announce the *ummah*'s vigilance, so also does the community of ordinary Muslims declare its vigilance each Friday by reciting this *sūrah* that recounts the stories both of the holy people enclosed by God to preserve their sanctity and of the unclean peoples enclosed to protect the faithful from their depredations. Here then lies the Muslim paradigm for finding in the enclosure of holy persons, in sealing them up in a pit, a sign of God's solicitude for his community, and of that community's integrity. The communal bulwark is threatened from outside by the infidel barbarians, and from within by the sinful and negligent: it is thus not surprising that a conversion narrative appealing to Muslim communal integrity would address both threats, the former through the conversion itself (and the defeat of the most obstinate infidels), the latter through Baba Tükles' saintly example of endurance and self-sacrifice.

In this way we may understand that Baba Tükles' enclosure in and emergence from the oven-pit reflect both Inner Asian and Islamic notions of communal formation and preservation. On the one hand he is the shaman tested in the flames to effectively "reconstitute" his community; he is "buried" and enclosed in the pit in the same way as ancestors and communal culture heroes are, and his emergence marks the formation of a new people. On the other hand, he is the ancestral figure modeled on

113. Massignon, "Le culte liturgique," provides a catalogue of localized caves ascribed to the *ahl al-kahf* from Spain to Turfan.

114. In addition to Massignon's discussion, see Hasluck, *Christianity and Islam under the Sultans*, I, pp. 309–319 on popular veneration of the "Seven Sleepers."

Ibrāhīm, suffering for his devotion to the true faith and setting an example of steadfastness and vigilance, like the Companions of the Cave, to preserve communal integrity. The fire-pit is at once a place of punishment from which he is delivered; a place of testing in which his survival proves the power of a new faith; a place of enclosure where his faith protects him; a place of entombment, wherein his "death" sanctifies a locale and a community; and a place of birth or rebirth, in which he is heroically and shamanically reconstituted. In each case motifs are evoked that typically accompany tales of communal "founders" and heroes; to find these motifs implicit in the tale making Baba Tükles the bearer of Islam—already, that is, at the earliest stage we know in the development of Baba Tükles' persona—helps us understand the later mythic elaborations of Baba Tükles well beyond the sixteenth-century work of Ötemish Ḥājjī.

Displacement and Assimilation

Virtually all of the specific themes considered above as religious "counterpoints" in the narrative of Ötemish Ḥājjī have in common a structural device used to convey the religious meaning that lies at the heart of "conversion." In the intrusion of the Muslim saints into the *qoruq*; in their disruption of the ritual ceremony conducted there; in the argument and "contest" with the khan's "sorcerers;" and in the rich complex of themes—mastery over fire, deliverance from interment/imprisonment and "rebirth" from sacred enclosure—evoked in the dramatic climax of the religious confrontation, in the fire-pit, we find a pointed *intrusion* of the new religion into the old, and the *displacement* of elements or figures associated with "pagan" ways by rites or persons representing the new faith of Islam.

This structural paradigm of intrusion and displacement is sometimes cast as a clear and vivid uprooting of some element of the old ways, as when the drinking ceremony is spoiled or the pagan sorcerer is consumed in the fire. In other cases we find a less clearly delineated relationship between the features representing the two traditions, as when the saints are brought into the *qoruq*, thereby intruding a Muslim presence into something whose sanctity depends upon the native tradition. And in still other cases, most vividly in the conflation of motifs evident in the episode of the fire-pit, the two religious traditions are even more strongly assimilated: there is no question that the Muslim saints emerge victorious, but their victory is sealed not only when they halt a pagan ceremony, or when the pagan sorcerer is destroyed in the fire, but when one of them submits to a "test" whose character is determined by conceptions and practices proper to the native tradition, and not only meets the test to the satisfaction of that native tradition, but infuses it with religious significance sanctioned by Islamic paradigms as well.

This theme of displacement is thus not always expressed in entirely hostile, "oppositional" terms; in some cases it is, but we see also what may be termed an "assimilative" displacement. The two are naturally closely connected, for we rarely find a narrative highlighting a purely oppositional displacement; old ways may be rooted out, but the vacuum left by their abandonment is most often quickly filled (in the narrative, that is) by some element of the new religion, and what we may take note of is the extent to which that element is in some way related to (again in narrative terms) the displaced feature of the old tradition. "Oppositional" and "assimilative" displacement are thus relative terms and should not be taken as absolute and unrelated processes; the fact of filling a void, in "oppositional" displacement, is itself indicative of an assimilative process, evoking as it does the importance of some particular aspect of indigenous, pre-Islamic tradition requiring replacement or alteration.

Examples of what we are calling "oppositional" displacement would be the frequent accounts of the destruction of idols in other narratives, or in our case the disruption of the libation ceremony. Oppositional displacement is likewise at work in the "modified" tale of Baba Tükles found in ʿAbd al-Ghaffār Q̣ïrïmī's reworking of Ötemish Ḥājjī's narrative, discussed in Chapter 5, when fire is cast as something worshiped outright by the Mongols; Baba Tükles' emergence from the fire is thus not merely an ordeal (and ʿAbd al-Ghaffār's version omits many of the more "archaic" elements of the fire-pit episode), but an actual victory over something revered by the Mongols.

Under assimilative displacement must be classed the intrusion of the Muslim holy men into the "pagan" holy site of the *qoruq*: here the sanctuary's holiness is not directly attacked; it is not destroyed as in the case of similar sanctuaries that figure in a conversion narrative focused on the North Caucasian Huns in the seventh century, discussed below, but is instead infused with renewed and transformed sacrality not only by the presence of the Muslim saints, but by the implicit occurrence there of the decisive "test" that confirms Islam's superiority and in effect "forges" the new, Islamized community. This assimilation is clearer still when we note that Ötemish Ḥājjī's narrative reflects pro-Chingisid sentiments, in which even largely forgotten symbols of the khans' inviolate lineage such as the *qoruq* might still be honored enough to spare them from outright destruction or mockery; such mockery is precisely what we find, however, when we see Baba Tükles' legitimizing reputation put to work in an anti-Chingisid context, as we will see in Chapter 6.

The themes of intrusion and displacement are evident in other Inner Asian conversion tales that highlight the religious importance of situating the central act that "seals" the conversion in a setting of ritual significance within the indigenous, "pagan" tradition being displaced—either a cultic site itself, or at least a setting marked by the ritual appurtenances of the "old" religion; [115] a consideration of some examples of this theme of displacement as found in other Inner Asian conversion narratives may serve to clarify what the narratives that formed the basis for Ötemish Ḥājjī's account may have signified for their earliest audience, and may lend weight to our assumption that the motifs of intrusion and displacement are indeed present in that account. Similar complexes of intrusion and displacement are implicit in well-known conversion narratives focused on the conversion to Armenian Christianity of an unidentified Inner Asian people termed "Huns" in 682; on the conversion of the Khazars to Judaism; and on the adoption by an unspecified Turkic people (perhaps the Kereyt) to Nestorian Christianity in 1007.

The Conversion of Alp' Ilit'uēr and His People, c. 682, to Armenian Christianity

One of the most vivid and revealing medieval conversion narratives connected with Inner Asian peoples is a long account of the Armenian bishop Israyēl's mission to a group of "Huns" north of the Caucasus around 682.[116] The identity of these "Huns," whose appellation may

115. It is worth noting that those elements "displaced" often reflect the "high" tradition of Inner Asian courts, while the "assimilated" and/or "unmentioned" elements of the "old" religion, which continued in use and were not considered significant in contrasting the new and old ways, were elements of domestic and family-ancestral ritual that survived in Islamized or Christianized or Buddhisticized environments.

116. On these North Caucasian Huns, cf. Golden, *Khazar Studies*, I, pp. 90–93, 244–246, 259–261; see also his "Khazaria and Judaism," pp. 128–129; Dunlop, *History of the Jewish*

reflect the generic use of the term to refer to Inner Asian nomads and not necessarily their connection with the Huns of the fourth and fifth centuries, remains uncertain; the description makes it clear that they worshiped "T'angri Khan" and that their religious practices and conceptions were quite similar to those known from Turkic and other Inner Asian peoples of the time,[117] while it is also clear that their leader, called "Alp' Ilit'uēr," was in the service of the Khazar *qaghan* (whose realm was then still centered in the steppes north of the Caucasus) and bore a title indicating his subordinate status with respect to the *qaghan*. In any case they belonged to the Khazar state politically, and to the Inner Asian (and probably Turkic) world culturally, and are thus relevant for our attention.

The account is preserved in the history ascribed to Movsēs Dasχuranci, generally regarded as a tenth century compilation but probably put in final form as late as the early twelfth century. The narrative is of value for the insights into the "pagan" religion of these "Huns," but, more important for us, in recounting their conversion it stresses explicitly and repeatedly the displacement and transformation of those "pagan" ways by Christian rites and symbols.

The account[118] describes the bishop Israyēl's journey to the "Huns" during Lent and his hospitable reception by their "prince," then turning to the conversion narrative itself. First the pagan ways of the people are outlined:[119] they consider a person or thing killed by lightning a sacrifice to the god "K'uar";[120] they sacrifice horses to a "gigantic savage monster" invoked as "T'angri Khan"; they celebrate funeral rites by "beating drums and whistling" over the body, "weeping and wailing" and lacerating their faces and limbs, and engaging in staged combat, horse races, games, and dances; and they sacrifice to "fire and water and to certain gods of the

---

Khazars, p. 59. Golden mentions their conversion, and recounts the bishop's description of their religion, but neither he nor Dunlop discusses the conversion narrative in detail; cf. the brief discussion of the account in Ia. A. Fedorov and G. S. Fedorov, *Rannie tiurki na Severnom Kavkaze (Istoriko-ètnograficheskie ocherki)* (Moscow: Izd-vo Moskovskogo universiteta, 1978), pp. 187–188.

117. It is not impossible that the description of these "Huns' " religion reflects notions of what such peoples *ought* to have believed and practiced current much later than the seventh century; whatever this might entail as to the "facts" of their ethnic affiliation or religious practices, however, it is the narrative tradition surrounding their conversion, which assigned them an array of beliefs and practices wholly in keeping with the mythic and ritual structures known more clearly for other, less obscure Inner Asian peoples, that is of concern to us.

118. C. J. F. Dowsett, tr., *The History of the Caucasian Albanians by Movsēs Dasχuranci* (London: Oxford University Press, 1961), pp. 155–166.

119. Dowsett, p. 156.

120. On this name cf. Golden, *Khazar Studies*, I, p. 259, suggesting Turkic etymologies.

roads, and to the moon and to all creatures considered in their eyes to be in some way remarkable." This description sets the stage for Israyēl's long address to the people on the error of their ways and on Christian doctrine, in which we first hear of the "spell-binding sorcerers and geomancing wizards" who are the chief villains of the narrative; only later do we learn of the feature of their religion that will become central to the key displacement/assimilation in the narrative: their worship of trees.

Following the bishop's discourse, the prince Alp' Ilit'uēr and his entire army accept his words and declare themselves Christians; the account then summarizes the prince's efforts in establishing Christianity, building churches and destroying pagan altars and "considering the religion of his fathers abominable and unclean." In the narrative as we have it this sets the stage for a conflict with the "sorcerers, wizards, and chief pagan priests," but in view of the thoroughness of the new faith's establishment as recounted following the bishop's "sermon," it seems likely that two originally independent accounts have been fused here, the first a sober and didactic version, the next a more dramatic narrative marked by a challenge and contest;[121] what may well have been a third narrative tradition, in which a "court debate" is the central event, is incorporated somewhat more smoothly near the end of the entire account,[122] but the incongruity of a debate following the dramatic demonstration of Christian power would again seem to signal that a third tradition was indeed accommodated by the compiler of the history.

In any event, the probable independence of this next section of the narrative is also suggested by a new cultic focus: the pagan sorcerers challenge the prince's conversion when the bishop Israyēl commands that a particular tree be cut down from among those dedicated to "Tengri" and used for horse sacrifices.[123] The tree in question is further described as "the one which was the chief and mother of all the tall trees dedicated in the name of the vain gods and which many of the land of the Huns worshipped, the prince and the nobles included, for they held it of all the idols to be the saviour and life-giver and be-

121. Dowsett, pp. 161–165.

122. Dowsett, pp. 165–166.

123. It is worth noting that in the first section of the narrative, the horse sacrifice is described as a burnt offering; here the sacrifice of horses involves "pouring their blood over the trees and throwing their heads and skins over the branches," the latter element in particular recalling well-known descriptions of Inner Asian horse sacrifices (cf. J. A. Boyle, "A Form of Horse Sacrifice amongst the 13th- and 14th-Century Mongols," *CAJ*, 10 [1965], pp. 145–150).

stower of all good things."[124] The pagan sorcerers rebuke the prince for abandoning "the native gods whom you and your forefathers worshipped" and for threatening "the fair-blossomed tree, the guardian and saviour of our land"; the emphasis on tree-worship naturally sets the stage for the central assimilative displacement wherein the tree becomes the cross, but the narrative retains enough of the native "defense" of the tree to suggest its clear links with the mythic complex of the "cosmic tree" so widespread in Inner Asia.

In response, the prince sets the terms of the "contest" that follows, challenging the "wizards and sorcerers and magicians" to use their wiles against the bishop: if they can frighten him or afflict him with illness or death, says the prince, he will return to the old ways; otherwise he will destroy them "with the trees and temples."

The pagan sorcerers then begin their "frenzied aphrodisiac witchery," performing "incantations and false geomancy"; their usual success in such efforts is described, as is their ability to "conjure up fantastic visions and make heavy rains appear," thus including their skill at weather control[125] as in other conversion narratives. This time, however, they failed, and the bishop went to the sacred grove and made the sign of the cross as the priests accompanying him cut down the great tree; what follows is worth citing in full, as an illustration of the assimilative displacement at work:

> The bishop ordered it to be taken into the town of *Varačan*, and summoning skilled carpenters he ordered them to transform it into a beautifully balanced well-finished cross with painted ornaments; and he made various images and glued them to it, covering it with accurately painted pictures, embellishing it from top to bottom with similar beautiful things. He likewise fastened shining crosses to it, arranging them beautifully in a row from one end to the other along the right side with strong nails, and at the base he made a little square door which could be opened from both sides and upon which a lily was carved; inside this there was a silver cross containing a relic of the Lord's cross.
>
> Having thus arranged and decorated the tree with many wonderful ornaments, *he erected it as a place of pilgrimage and prayers in the royal court facing the east*, and he said: "Before this symbol

124. Dowsett, p. 161.

125. Prior to the conversion narrative proper, during the account of his journey to the north, the bishop Israyēl had already displayed *his* ability to calm a furious snowstorm (Dowsett, p. 154).

> which brings salvation to all, worship the Lord your God, *that you who were accustomed to worship your tree in the error of your minds might still in accordance with your habit and custom worship this cross* and the invisible image of the Divinity. Since you eat and drink the flesh and blood of your animal sacrifices offered to the demons before the trees, He has erected His cross in the midst of your land and in place of the blood of the sacrifices He has given His blood for the redemption of us all."[126]

The ritual "assimilative displacement" is completed when, after the prince orders the "diabolically deluded, demoniac tribe of sorcerers and wizards and the principal chief priests" to be handed over to the bishop, the "pagan golden images" worn by some of the pagans are taken from them and crushed into the shape of a cross by the bishop, with his own hands. The pagan sorcerers themselves, or at least some of them, were ordered cast into a fire; with this we should probably see the ending of the second section of the narrative, for despite the failure of the sorcerers' magic and the decisive victory of the Christian bishop, the narrative turns to yet another, superfluous, "contest," held on Easter morning.

In this final section, we find "many of the chief pagan priests and principal magic sorcerers" brought, "still in painful fetters," for a public disputation:

> . . . all the citizens were assembled and a court and tribunal constituted. When each side was disputing before the crowded assembly, the bishop began to preach from the holy scriptures, and sternly refuted them and put them to shame. The wretched priests of the false religion were put to shame by the Lord's cross which the bishop held constantly in his hand, and were discouraged and disheartened, and accusing themselves, they confessed their sins and were converted to the true faith. They gave their destructive dice of witchcraft into the hands of the bishop, who burned them, and they themselves were made worthy of rebirth in the holy font.[127]

With even the pagan priests now prepared for baptism, the prince and his people, the account says, were "still more strengthened in the love of the Christian faith and estranged from the vain worship of abomina-

126. Dowsett, pp. 163–164; italics mine.
127. Dowsett, p. 165.

tions." A final and potent symbol of the abandonment of the old ways remained, however. On the day when the cross carved from the sacred tree was to be consecrated, the bishop challenged the prince and the newly converted pagan priests to participate in the destruction of the "royal graves,"[128] declaring this to be the Holy Spirit's "test" for them:

> When the pious prince of the Huns heard this, he immediately authorized him to destroy the sanctuaries. Then the bishop and the prince sent Movsēs, a man skilled in the arts, and other priests to demolish and burn down the sanctuaries with the cooperation of the ranks of pagan chief priests, and together they burned down the filthy temples of the hero-idols.

Thus ends this extremely rich account; it is instructive both as a likely example of the pattern of narrative compilation and thematic conflation that is evident in other conversion narratives, including that of Ötemish Ḥājjī, and as an example of several of the specific themes and motifs that appear in those other narratives. In the latter regard may be noted the inclusion of burnt offerings and pagan priests cast into fire; the final focus on the royal tombs as a communal symbol into which the new faith must intrude; the combination, even more incongruously than in Ötemish Ḥājjī's account, of both "contest" and "debate" motifs; and the evocation of a central ritual focus of the old religion—in this case the sacred tree—as the setting for the climactic contest and assimilative displacement.

The account thus provides fine examples of "oppositional" displacement in the burning of the grave sanctuaries and of the skins preserved from blood sacrifices, and of "assimilative" displacement in the idols and the sacred tree fashioned into crosses, and in transformation of a sacrificial meal into the Eucharist. The narrative is especially explicit in opposing, and at the same time appropriating, the pagan symbolism of the sacred tree and the pagan rite of a sacrificial meal on the one hand, and the central Christian symbol and rite on the other; in so doing it asserts not only the centrality of those former beliefs and practices in the communal life of the "Huns," but also the power of the Christian holy man to infuse and transform pagan belief and practice with new meaning that is intended to serve the similar function of sacralizing the newly converted people as a Christian community.

128. The term given in the text is *čop'ay* and is explained as the royal burial mounds; cf. Dowsett, p. 156, and Golden, *Khazar Studies*, I, p. 259.

It may be objected, of course, that the narrative as preserved in the Armenian chronicle reflects only literary embellishment of a legend of Christianization, rather than an indigenous narrative development among the "heirs" of the conversion for whom the "events" retained some decisive and definitive meaning; indeed, we have virtually no evidence of any long-lasting effect of such a conversion, nor any clear picture of precisely what people or community is meant, let alone any direct evidence of an oral narrative tradition underlying the extant account. Nevertheless, if we link the "Huns" of the narrative with the Khazars, as seems justified, and consider the half-century (or more) between the conversion described in this source and the initial stages of the Khazar conversion to Judaism, it appears quite reasonable to assume that ample time was available for a Christianizing community in the North Caucasus to develop a respectable array of narrative traditions—and after all, three are probably reflected in the extant account—of their adoption of the new faith. Even if this particular Christianizing community left no traces outside these narratives,[129] it is not unreasonable to understand the extant account as reflective of earlier written descriptions based in turn upon the oral or written reports of the proselytizers (especially the "didactic" first section) or of the converts themselves.

In the latter case it is not altogether certain, however, which direction the narrative development of the converts' own oral versions, prior to their fixation in written form, should be understood as taking. In light of what we find in the case of the Baba Tükles narrative, we might suppose, for example, that the narrative reworkings by a more solidly Christianized community would have played down the "oppositional" elements expected to predominate in early versions, by noting the bishop's "Christianizing" interpretation of their community's former, and hence stylized, indigenous religious symbols and practices (tree = cross, sacrificial repast = Eucharist); the "original" oppositional emphasis, from this perspective, would have featured only the cutting down of the tree and the destruction of the sanctuaries, etc., and the adaptation would signal a shift in communal religious needs, from asserting the greater power of the new faith in contrast to the old way's impotence, to asserting the essentially sacred antecedents of a sacralized community's pre-Christian religion (there is more than a hint in this account of a claim that the "Huns' "

129. As told in the chronicle, the newly converted community repeatedly asked for Israyēl to be appointed its bishop, but no such appointment is mentioned, and the "Huns" appear to have been left without a patriarchal see (Dowsett, pp. 166–171).

native religion would not in itself have been so evil had it not been for the deceit and wickedness of the "sorcerers"); that is, the bishop's "reinterpretation" of the sacred tree and sacrifices may conceal the notion that the indigenous tradition already bore signs of affinity to Christian doctrine and practice, an affinity evoked also in the Nestorian conversion of 1007. Here we may find echoes of an effort, evident as well in narratives of the Khazar conversion to Judaism, discussed below, to assert that these "Huns" were originally or primordially members of the "new" faith's religious communities, in this case Christians, or at least close to Christianity, but had gone astray, only to be hindered on the road to recovering their lost tradition by the evil sorcerers.

Alternatively, we might assume that one or more "original" accounts reflected an "accommodationist" perspective, in which the bishop was portrayed as quite freely making use of the indigenous tradition's symbols and rites and asserting their compatibility with Christian teachings; such accounts might then have been reworked by a more "orthodox" Christianized community intent upon superimposing more suitable or orthodox approaches to a narrative deemed insufficiently hostile to pagan ways. Thus, a narrative of the bishop's skillful appeal to the religious heritage of a pagan community—a community portrayed throughout the account as essentially open to Christianity and downright worshipful of Israyēl—would have been overlaid with the bishop's denunciation of the pagan priests and his violent destruction of the community's sacred symbols.

There is, finally, no way for us to know which direction the narrative development took, nor indeed any sure sign that the extant narrative was not itself "original" as it stands; assuming some narrative compilation and conflation, both alternatives have their attractions, but I believe the first of the two is more likely, largely on the model—of questionable applicability, to be sure—of developments in other conversion narratives.

In any event, we should not discount the likelihood that the conversion narrative(s) preserved in the Armenian history indeed reflect, at least in part, originally oral accounts passed down within the community affected by the adoption of Christianity dramatized in those narratives; in view of the other conversion narratives considered here, we are at least safe in assuming that remarkably little time is needed for wide-ranging narrative elaborations of such events to emerge and develop independently, before being compiled and "fit together" to form a more "learned" literary account.

The Khazar Conversion to Judaism

Three accounts of the Khazar adoption of Judaism in the eighth century situate the pivotal event in a cave. Despite the explicitly and implicitly Jewish associations of the cave in these accounts—on which see below—it is difficult *not* to recall in this context the "ancestral cavern" of the Türks, spoken of by a Chinese source as the site of annual rituals performed by the Qaghan and the Türk aristocracy. The Khazar state is usually regarded as the political heir, in the Kuban and the Pontic steppe, of the western Türk empire, and evidence on Khazar religion shows clear parallels with what is known of religious, and religio-political, belief and practice among the eastern Türks in Mongolia.[130] While there appears to be no direct evidence describing the use of caves or a cave for ritual purposes among the pre-conversion Khazars—aside from the religious associations of the cave, masked in Jewish terms but transparently ascribable to indigenous traditions—the general political, religious, and cultural commonalities between the Khazars and the Türks would seem to justify the assumption that caves bore numinous and ritual associations for the Khazars as well, associations of a type amenable to assimilation and transformation in conversion narratives.

As discussed above, the role of the cave in communal ancestral ritual among the Turks is attested in Chinese sources contemporary with the first Türk empire and in Ibn ad-Dawādārī's fourteenth-century description; that this rite was also maintained among the western Türks in the seventh century, of more direct relevance for the Khazars, is confirmed in the dynastic history of the Sui, which notes that each year the western Türks "send a high functionary to the cavern where their ancestors lived in order to offer a sacrifice there."[131] In each case we have a full "myth-

130. On the political continuities between the eastern and western Türk empires and the Khazar state, cf. Golden, *Khazar Studies*, I, pp. 37–42, 100–102, and his "Khazaria and Judaism," p. 127, and Pritsak, "The Khazar Kingdom's Conversion," p. 261; Golden, "Khazaria and Judaism," pp. 128–129, discusses the parallels between what is known of Khazar religion (based largely on the account of bishop Israyēl's mission) and the religion of the Türk empires. Particularly suggestive of the close political and religious ties between the Khazar polity and the Türk imperial tradition are the startlingly similar independent accounts, from tenth-century Arabic and seventh-century Chinese sources, of the practice of throttling the newly installed *qaghan* nearly to death, described among the Khazars and the eastern Türks (see Golden, *Khazar Studies*, I, p. 42, and his "Khazaria and Judaism," pp. 149–150, n. 67 for a description in the context of a discussion of the institution of dual kingship, including references to al-Iṣṭakhrī's account and, for the Chinese account of the eastern Türks, to Liu Mau-tsai, *Die chinesischen Nachrichten zur Geschichte der Ost-Türken* [Wiesbaden: Otto Harrassowitz, 1958], I, p. 8); and see further J. G. Frazer, "The Killing of the Khazar Kings," *Folklore*, 28 (1917), pp. 382–407.

131. Edouard Chavannes, tr., *Documents sur les Tou-kiue (Turcs) Occidentaux* (St. Pétersbourg,

and-ritual" complex attested, linking the ritual role of the cave to an ethnogonic myth; and in the case of the Second Türk empire, as noted, we find what is no doubt a high-level politicization of this ethnogonic myth and ritual, in the political and "ideological" importance attached to the Ötükän in the Old Turkic inscriptions. It would thus be surprising *not* to find echoes of this complex among the Khazars, even if those echoes appear already in the context of conversion tales.

It is not unreasonable, then, to see, in the conversion narratives relating the adoption of Judaism among the Khazars, reflections not only of themes drawn from Jewish lore, but of themes that would have conveyed religious meaning to the Khazars as well. We thus see not only the new religion intruding into an old cultic center, but the symbolic "co-opting" of that ancestral cavern, the sacred "womb" of the people, as the site of the "rebirth" of a transformed religious community.

The case of the Khazar conversion to Judaism is particularly instructive in part because the specifically religious aspects of the conversion and the narratives describing it have been examined recently, with admirable regard for both the Jewish and indigenous traditions. Of immediate interest here, the "epic" character of the indigenous narratives regarding the conversion has been noted.[132] Of further interest are the illustration of the persistence of indigenous tribal symbols and practices even after the "reform" of Khazar Judaism, and the suggestion that the indigenous Khazar shamans (*qams*) "assumed the office of Jewish priests" in the early stages of the Khazar adoption of Judaism;[133] here we find specific examples and well-argued speculation regarding the assimilation or coexistence of indigenous traditions with the newly adopted religion, and not merely the unsubstantiated assertions of such processes as are often met with in accounts of religion in Inner Asia, assertions usually intended, as suggested earlier, to minimize

1903; repr. with additional notes, Paris: Librairie d'Amérique et d'Orient, 1941; repr. Taipei: Ch'eng Wen Publishing, 1969), p. 15; cited also by Pelliot, "Neuf notes," p. 214, n. 2.

132. Cf. Golb and Pritsak, *Khazarian Hebrew Documents*, pp. 28–29 (Golb, noting among the religious phenomena characterizing the development of Khazar Judaism "the construction or gradual evolution of a mythic substratum justifying and explaining the conversion"), 130–132 (Pritsak, recounting "The Epic Tale of the Khazarian Conversion to Judaism and the Establishment of the 'Kingdom'); and Pritsak, "The Khazar Kingdom's Conversion," p. 272 (noting of the account preserved in al-Bakrī and of the two Hebrew accounts besides Halevi's that "they are best characterized as epic narratives"). Nowhere is the epic character of the surviving narratives, or of their substrata, further analyzed, but so far as I know these discussions of the Khazar conversion are the first to call attention to the parallels between conversion narratives and epic-style legends of origin in Inner Asia.

133. Golb, in *Khazarian Hebrew Documents*, p. 27.

the impact of the "new" religion or to deny its significance beyond small circles within an Inner Asian state or people.

Similarly, the case of the restructuring of Jewish practice among the Khazars and its reform along lines of rabbinical Judaism provides an important example of how "nominal" religious conversion—even in Inner Asia!—need not remain nominal and without effect; rather, however crude or primitive the forms of an adopted faith may seem among a proselytized people at the time of conversion, as judged by standards of long-standing and/or pure/orthodox members of that faith's community, conversion naturally marks an entrance into a religious community with modes of religious action and discourse of its own, which may then take on independent life in the newly, perhaps only nominally, converted community.[134] In other words, adopting a new faith makes a community "liable" to the entire spectrum of religious action and discourse that had developed within the adopted religion's "home" community prior to the conversion, and subsequent religious developments within the newly converted community may range from syncretic creations of new and distinctly indigenous varieties of the adopted religion, to "purist" or "fundamentalist" movements, including in between these extremes, more normatively, the kind of gradualist influence that could win "reforms" of Judaism among the Khazars or a strengthening of the specifically "Islamic" content in the life and religion of Inner Asian Muslims.

The accounts citing the role of the cave in the Khazar conversion appear in the sources referred to in Chapter 3 in connection with examples of the theme of the court debate among representatives of competing religions. In one account, from Judah Halevi's book, the king of the Khazars, after two dreams in which an angel exhorted him to find the true religion to practice ("Thy way of thinking is pleasing to God, but not thy way of acting"), traveled with his minister "to the deserted mountains on the seashore, and arrived one night at the cave in which some Jews used to celebrate the Sabbath. They disclosed their identity to them, embraced their religion, were circumcised in the cave, and then returned to their country, eager to learn the Jewish law."[135] The mythic elements evoked here (regardless of however dimly this account may reflect even

134. See, for example, the discussion in Golb and Pritsak, *Khazarian Hebrew Documents*, pp. 24–32.

135. *Book of Kuzari*, tr. Hartwig Hirschfeld, p. 82; cf. Pritsak, "The Khazar Kingdom's Conversion," pp. 270–271, and Dunlop's somewhat different translation, *History of the Jewish Khazars*, pp. 117–118; cf. Golden, "Khazaria and Judaism," p. 139, for a historicist interpretation of the cave story, which Dunlop offers as well.

the written "history of the Khazars" that Halevi cites as his source, not to mention the oral sources of that lost work) thus include the complex of mountain, sea, and cave, a common association in Inner Asian legends of origin. Nevertheless, the site is presented as of religious importance to those who are to convert the Khazar king and his minister to Judaism; indeed, the definitive ritual marking the conversion (and the joining of a community) takes place in this setting. And this setting is particularly suitable for such a ritual recognition of conversion because of its dual symbolism: it is implicitly sacred in the context of indigenous Khazar religious symbols, and is explicitly pronounced to be sacred for the Jewish community that the Khazars are to join. The nature of the audience for whom the original narrative was intended may perhaps be judged by noting which of the two traditions, native Khazar or Jewish, is assumed to be familiar, and which requires a specific narrative assertion.

More interesting from the structural perspective is the echo of the cave theme in the so-called Schechter-text, known also as the "Cambridge document." Here the decisive moment in the victory of Judaism over the "Greek" and "Arab" participants in the religious disputation comes when, in the midst of the arguments, the "officers" of the Khazars—that is, the military commanders—declared that there was a cave in a certain plain (*TYZWL*), a place considered to have been the site of the old Khazar capital;

> " . . . bring forth to us the books which are there and expound them before us." They did so. They went into the midst of the cave: behold, books of the Torah of Moses were there, and the sages of Israel explained them according to the previous words which they had spoken. Then returned Israel, with the people of Qazaria, (to Judaism) completely . . .[136]

The theme of sacred books concealed or preserved in caves has a long history in Jewish lore,[137] and the Inner Asian elements of the cave's sacrality

136. Tr. Golb, in Golb and Pritsak, *Khazarian Hebrew Documents*, p. 111, and see the synopsis p. 103; cf. Pritsak, "The Khazar Kingdom's Conversion," p. 276.

137. Cf. N. Golb, "Who Were the Maġārīyah?," *JAOS*, 80 (1960), pp. 347–359; in addition to the two accounts of the Khazar conversion with the cave motif, he discusses three other medieval traditions of books hidden in caves (pp. 350–352). Golb does not mention it, but there would seem to be an early prototype for the theme of sacred books preserved in caves, in a passage from the apocryphal Second Book of the Maccabees: according to this tradition, the prophet Jeremiah took the tabernacle and the ark of the covenant (with the written tablets of the

are less evident in this passage—from a text that Pritsak judges, by the way, to stem not from Khazar proselytes, but from among Jewish inhabitants of the Khazar state of non-Khazar origin.[138] Nevertheless, the inclusion of the theme of the cave may have evoked not only traditions of Jewish lore, but sacred associations of caves for the Khazars as well; and structurally, too, we find parallels even to Ötemish Ḥājjī's account, wherein the truth of the new religion is confirmed when a sacred man (rather than sacred books) emerge from a pit (which in both examples evokes sacred images from both the indigenous tradition and the new religion).

Paralleling this story is an account from the "Khazar correspondence" between the Cordovan Jewish courtier Ḥasday b. Shaprut (915–990) and the Khazar "King Joseph;" the account of the religious disputation found in the letters ascribed to King Joseph has been noted earlier, but the cave motif appears in the letter ascribed to Ḥasday himself in which he seeks answers to questions about Khazar Judaism. In one question Ḥasday asks for confirmation of traditions current among Spanish Jews (but certainly of Khazar origin) regarding "how Israel came to be in that place." Citing stories of "the old men of the former generations who can be relied upon," Ḥasday gives the gist of the tradition about the flight of persecuted Jews to the land of the Khazars, where they evidently forgot their tradition:

> . . . on account of their faithlessness a persecution was decreed, and an army of Chaldaeans rose up in anger and wrath. They hid the books of the Law and the Holy Scriptures in a cave, and for this reason they prayed in the cave. On account of the books they taught their sons to pray in the cave morning and evening, till the times were lengthened and they forgot and no longer knew about the cave, why they were accustomed to pray therein. But they practiced the custom of their fathers without knowing why. After a long time there arose a man of Israel who was eager to know why. He entered the cave, found it full of

law inside, naturally) to "the mountain where Moses had gone up and had seen the inheritance of God," and sealed up these sacred objects inside a cave, declaring that "the place shall be unknown until God gathers his people together again and shows his mercy" (II Maccabees 2:4–8; *The New Oxford Annotated Bible with the Apocrypha: Revised Standard Version*, Oxford, 1973). Here we find further parallels to the Inner Asian motif of enclosure and deliverance in connection with communal integrity.

138. Cf. Golb and Pritsak, *Khazarian Hebrew Documents*, p. 132.

books and brought them out from there. From that day they set themselves to learn the Law. Thus have our fathers told us, as the earlier generations heard, the one from the other. The whole matter is ancient.[139]

The wider issue of the "authenticity" of the "Khazar correspondence," and of the significance of this tale's parallels with the equally controversial Cambridge document/Schechter text, has been discussed extensively in the literature on Khazar Judaism; much of the debate loses significance if, as Pritsak has recently suggested, the accounts are approached as "epic" narratives rather than evaluated from the standpoint of their "historicity." In any case what is important for our concerns is these accounts' preservation, however abbreviated or altered, of originally oral narratives that in all probability originated among those directly affected by the Khazar adoption of Judaism.

It is of course more difficult to judge whether the tales should be ascribed to the "bringers" of Judaism or to native Khazar converts: in the first place, we should expect that distinction to have gradually been blurred, and we should expect, in any case, the two groups to have used a common narrative language that would speak to the converts' traditions, the "bringers" to reach them and the native converts to express the religious significance of the conversion with terms and symbols that would still resonate for them—terms and symbols that, in this case, were of double value insofar as they derived from the "old ways" but could be understood, in light of the new faith, as reflecting an earlier adherence to that new faith and therefore a "return" rather than a conversion.

To be sure, Pritsak is certainly right in seeing signs of two narrative traditions in the divergences of the Cambridge document and the Khazar correspondence;[140] it is not so clear, however, that the ascription of Khazar Judaism's origins to "refugee" Jews on the one hand or to native Khazar converts on the other should necessarily be taken as a sign of the tradition's provenance in the way Pritsak suggests; Khazar converts might be just as likely to assert their ancient ancestral links with Jewish tribes as immigrant Jews would have been to assert their primacy in bringing the religion to the Khazars.

In any case, this passage from the "Khazar correspondence" is striking for the way it rationalizes what was most likely a memory of "pagan"

139. Tr. Dunlop, *History of the Jewish Khazars*, p. 167.
140. Golb and Pritsak, *Khazarian Hebrew Documents*, p. 132.

Khazar religious practice associated with caves as a degenerate survival of original Judaism; the account thus melds the motifs from Jewish lore regarding books concealed in caves with an evocation of the ritual significance of caves in Khazar tradition (and not, of course, of the practice itself, but of the memory or imagination of the practice), at once "revealing" to the native Khazar community the true character of its religious traditions, and appealing as well to a more orthodox Judaic community with a familiar pattern of "primal" rectitude, a "falling away," and redemption.

As in the case of the Hun conversion discussed above, however, it is difficult to judge the direction of narrative development. We may nevertheless suggest that the clear reflection of an attempt to *assimilate* Jewish and Khazar traditions in the extant versions of the tale should not obscure the central element of displacement that must have been present in "original" versions of the Khazar conversion story, an element reflected in the "intrusion" of the fundamental communal rite of admission to the Judaic covenant into a ritual center sacred to the indigenous tradition.

Such attempts to assimilate Jewish and Khazar traditions would have been natural as the Judaic and/or specifically rabbinic content of Khazar Judaism grew in proportion to affinities for the old indigenous Khazar tradition (at least in circles that developed, transmitted, and, we presume, "rehearsed" the conversion stories), and as the chief purveyors of the proselytic tradition became uncomfortable, or unfamiliar, with the very features of the old ritual structures whose displacement had conveyed profound meaning to their communal ancestors. That is, the central ritual "confrontation" that we may understand to have been evoked in earlier tales relating the intrusion of Jewish rite into Khazar sacred center may well have provided the pivotal "message" of those tales; the "success" of the conversion, however, fostered at one and the same time (1) a dwindling familiarity with the former importance of the indigenous Khazar cultic center, thus rendering the dramatic impact of the intrusion and displacement less meaningful, and eventually turning that element into a fossilized piece of the narrative awaiting reinterpretation in line with the successful "new" system, and (2) an inclination among proselytes and "converters" alike to "nativize" the new faith by discovering that certain features of preconversion Khazar life were in fact nothing other than more or less degenerate forms of a prior Judaic tradition present among the Khazars.

That most of the later, extant versions of the tale appeal to the device of the flight of persecuted Jews to Khazaria several (i.e., an unspecified number of) generations before the conversion, and their intermarriage with Khazars—thus implicitly establishing genealogical links with non-Khazar centers of Judaism among the Khazars of the generation by whom and for whom the conversion tales were developed—should not seem particularly surprising in light of the parallel we see in the case of Islamization, as exemplified in the development of the Baba Tükles tradition. For here we find, already in the relatively old version of the conversion tale given by Ötemish Ḥājjī, only dim reflections of the former cultic significance of the various elements preserved in the narrative, so dim in fact that we are inclined to assume the melding of several distinct traditions, each emphasizing certain features echoed in the narrative as the focus of the intrusion and displacement, such as the *qoruq*, the libation ceremony, and the complex of the oven-pit. In the first case, whatever religious meaning implied by the intrusion of the Muslim saints into the *qoruq* has been lost almost entirely in Ötemish Ḥājjī's narrative, while the libation ceremony has been retained as a "wonder" whereby the upholders of the native religion maintained their influence with the khan, with the impact of the Muslim's "intrusion" left as a pivotal point in the narrative (i.e., the failure of the rite). The fire motif, on the other hand, also remains a pivotal point, and it is not certain whether the occurrence of so many explicit or implicit pivotal points (including, beyond these two, the khan's decision to bring the saints inside the *qoruq*, and the argument between the two camps) suggests several separate narratives, focused on distinct dramatic moments, combined into one, or simply a well-developed original narrative (if the latter were the case, we might surmise that the only echoes of its original religious meanings—and several are implied—would seem to be the presence of *two* fires, the fact that the fires are in *pits*, and the detail of the sheep's flesh). Instead, what we find is an implication of an Islamized understanding of a point originally fraught with dramatic tension through the intrusion of the Muslim saint into a Mongol ritual setting; that is, the story is told with implicit reference to the Qur'ānic model of Ibrāhīm being cast into the fire and emerging unharmed.

Moreover, as explored in Chapter 5, the Baba Tükles narratives quickly developed in the context of a genealogical elaboration that reveals the same thing about the emergence of Islam in the Jöchid *ulus* as the stories of Jewish refugees reveal about the emergence of Judaism among the Khazars: the new faith was brought by figures with long genealogical ties to the traditional centers of the respective religious communities, an affirmation that at once legitimizes the bearers of the new religion (as authentic Jews or as legitimate Muslims), and nativizes them as they settle in the new land and bear children (a theme always mentioned in the "genealogical" accounts of Baba Tükles discussed below). With the final stage in that nativization, however, we find divergent approaches in the two examples, reflecting no doubt the milieu in which we find the respective narratives preserved. In the Khazar case, the rabbinic preservers of the only extant tradition in effect Judaize a Khazar tradition, assimilating the cave to elements from Jewish lore, while in the case of the Baba Tükles traditions, the most thorough nativization comes in epic accounts examined below, in which Baba Tükles is made into a typical Inner Asian mythic ancestor.

The Nestorian Conversion, 1007

As a final example, the account of the conversion of 1007 from the *Kitāb al-mijdāl* of the twelfth-century Nestorian writer Mārī b. Sulaymān, based upon a letter of Mar ʿAbd Īshūʿ, the Nestorian Metropolitan of Marv, involves the intrusion of the new faith into a central feature of ritual practice in the old tradition, with a corresponding assimilative displacement. In this case it is again an apparent libation ceremony, as in Ötemish Ḥājjī's account, that is the setting for the intrusion of Christian symbols and for the use of practices from the "pagan" tradition to consecrate and validate the new symbols. Here there is no mention of any "contest" or debate, nor any explicit reference to the "old religion" at all, and the incorporation of the drinking ceremony in the conversion tale is perhaps smoother in the Christian example in view of such a ritual's formal affinities with the Eucharist. Nonetheless, the simultaneous tension and resolution is all the more striking precisely because of this affinity: "The king had made a tent to serve as an altar, with a cross and a Gospel therein. . . . He had tethered mares whose milk he took and placed before the Gospel and the cross. Saying such prayers as he knew over it, he signed it with the cross, then took a draught, as did the rest of the congregation."[141] From the "pavilion" to the milking of the tethered mares and the use of the milk in a ceremony that appears half-Eucharist, half-

141. Tr. Dunlop, "The Karaits," pp. 278–279; cf. Mingana, "Early Spread," pp. 308–311, and Hunter, "Conversion of the Kerait," p. 154, as well as the discussion by Browne, *Eclipse of Christianity in Asia*, pp. 101–103. See further on the source Czeglédy, "Monographs," pp. 47–48, 60. This conversion is recounted, without specific allusion to the use of kumiss in

libation ritual, the passage implies the intrusion of Christian symbols into the "pagan" ritual setting, as well as, ultimately, the greater power of the new religion to incorporate and give new meaning to the forms of practice in the old religion. As brief as it is, this portion of an Inner Asian conversion narrative conveys, in a more synthetic manner than we find in most other tales, the important themes of intrusion and displacement linked almost seamlessly with the theme of assimilation: a central Christian rite is performed in an Inner Asian cultic setting, and as ritual materials of the native tradition are used to celebrate the Eucharist, the Eucharist suddenly infuses a new style of sacrality into an age-old feature of the native tradition.

The mutual assimilation evoked in this account may well bear the marks of later reflection that sought to "Christianize" the ritual setting, paralleling the examples we have considered of "Judaizing" elements of native ritual echoed in the Khazar conversion stories, and of "Islamizing" certain corresponding elements in the stories of Baba Tükles; that is, the implicit equation (kumiss ceremony=Eucharist) may indicate the "reflective" interpretation, by a more thoroughly "Christianized" generation, of a received tradition recalling an imperfectly performed Eucharist, or the mechanical overlay of a native celebration with the Christian rite. If the implication of mutual assimilation were added by "outside" interpreters of the story (i.e., Mārī b. Sulaymān), it would perhaps be less instructive for us. If, however, that assimilation was already evident in the "original" account or in the tradition as reworked among those directly involved with the newly converted community (whether as proselytes or "missionaries"), as seems likely in view of its report through the Metropolitan of Marv in Central Asia, we have a powerful example of a conversion narrative structured to emphasize both displacement and assimilation.

In this connection we have interesting comparative material in the Russian conversion narrative referred to in Chapter 3, more precisely in the narrative's description of the humiliating treatment accorded to the pagan Russian idols. The account may be approached from a purely "Christian" perspective, as evoking biblical models of casting down idols, or it may be considered as a description of a pagan rite "misunderstood" by a later Christian writer; a recent reevaluation comes closer to the mark,

---

the Eucharist or the miraculous transporting of the lost king, in the ecclesiastical history of Bar Hebraeus (d. 1286), and more briefly in his general chronicle; cf. Czeglédy, "Monographs," pp. 49–50, 62–63, and Hunter, "Conversion of the Kerait." For the "prologue" to this ritual assimilation, see above, n. 74.

I believe, by stressing that the early Russian Christian writers knew quite well the meanings of the "pagan" symbols and practices alluded to in the narratives, but falls short by insisting that this demonstrates how Christianity "was accepted in Russia in a kind of pagan wrapping," thus imputing a less-than-subtle historicity to the narrative tradition.[142]

More reasonable, I suggest, is to acknowledge that we cannot know from the available record whether those who introduced Christianity or Islam or Judaism among a "pagan" people stressed the new faith's similarities with the people's cherished traditions, or instead emphasized the new faith's exclusiveness and the need for a decisive choice; a case can be made for either alternative both on principle and on narrative evidence (and as extreme alternatives neither is likely true). What we can come closer to properly evaluating, however, is the narrative development, since in many cases we have two or more "generations" of the narrative tradition.

In the case of the Russian idols' treatment, it is naturally important to acknowledge that the narrative not only appealed to Christian, biblical models, but evoked aspects of the indigenous "pagan" tradition as well; a similar conclusion is also at the heart of our discussion of Ötemish Ḥājjī's narrative. But such an evocation of "pagan" symbols and practices may be either hostile or sympathetic, and these alternatives must first be evaluated on the basis of the narrative developments, where possible, that express these attitudes. To infer, from the evocation of "pagan" symbols and practices in the extant accounts, that those pagan elements were actually incorporated into the "missionary" activities of those who brought the new faith seems excessively "historicist" and essentially misleading. Rather, we should consider first the likelihood that the framers of the narrative traditions that eventually made their way into the extant accounts were both committed upholders of the new faith and either "natives" or "immigrants" reasonably familiar with the features of the "pagan" tradition that the new faith displaced (assimilatively, of course), or at least with the memory of those pagan features as preserved differentially among various segments of the community still in the process of Christianizing or Islamizing. Our task is then to trace the attitudes toward the pagan ways evinced by the various framers of the narrative traditions as they evolved.

142. These approaches are discussed in Froianov et al., "The Introduction of Christianity in Russia," esp. pp. 19–21. The authors are intent upon deriving a historical melding of Christian and pagan features from the available narrative; such in fact may well have been the case, but the question of the use of these features' "melding" as a narrative device—and of the possible motivations for employing this device—is hardly addressed in the article.

Here again it is not always clear, as we have already discussed, that the accounts will insist upon greater "breaks with the past" as distance from the time of conversion increases. Rather, we can more clearly see in the case of the Baba Tükles tradition an opposite development, with greater hostility toward the old ways reflected in chronologically earlier accounts, and more extensive incorporation of pre-Islamic religious elements in the later versions; at the same time, the earlier version does repeatedly evoke elements of the "pagan" tradition, but with hostility and opposition. The same development may be supposed in the case of Khazar Judaism, although we lack the hypothetical earlier, explicitly hostile evocations of indigenous Khazar tradition; likewise, with the "Huns" of the North Caucasus, we find clear signs of the hostile or oppositional evocation of pre-Christian rites and beliefs, but they are found alongside assertions of the assimilation of native rites with Christian ones, and the probable composite nature of the chronicle robs us of any external chronological basis for positing a sequence of development.

Perhaps the most reasonable solution would be to suggest not a chronological evolution of the narrative treatments of the "old" religion, but to ascribe hostile evocations of native tradition to parties more concerned with orthodoxy, and more assimilative evocations to "popular" circles. This approach fails, however, in the case of Khazar Judaism, where it would seem to be rabbinic circles that assimilated the Turkic cave rite into a Jewish practice, and Khazar Jewry itself into refugees from other Jewish centers. In the final analysis our data is too sketchy to allow us to go further even with the considerable comparative material available; what we can insist upon, in any case, is that the narratives be approached first from the standpoint of their development *as narratives*, before conclusions are drawn about the "historical facts" they illustrate.

It is important to note that in each example, Jewish, Christian, and Islamic, we find not only the vehicle of a sacred person (Baba Tükles, Mar Sergius or Bishop Israyēl, a group of Jews as a sacred community) involved in the conversion, but an actual ritual intrusion, as a sacred rite representative of the new religion is "inserted" into the ritual center of the indigenous tradition: the circumcision occurs in the cave, the cross is carved from a sacred tree, the Eucharist is performed, in the setting of a libation ceremony, with mare's milk, and Baba Tükles recites his *dhikr* within the fire in the *qoruq*.

But here we must reemphasize, because of the "historicist" inclinations of most specialists concerned with these accounts, that neither the extant narratives nor whatever form we may speculate that their antecedents must have taken should be approached as sources of a "real" intrusion of a figure or ritual representative of the new religion into a ritual center of the indigenous tradition, in a narrow historical sense. It is, finally, unproductive to ask whether the narratives should be regarded as "accurate" accounts of events leading up to a dramatic "conversion"; on the one hand, we usually have no independent sources conclusively confirming or refuting the available conversion narratives, precisely because such narratives are the product of religious language with a religious purpose, not the product of chroniclers or archivists (even if chroniclers may incorporate conversion narratives, or their sanitized, "historicized" core, into their accounts). It would therefore be imprudent to insist on even the *fact* of a dramatic conversion, let alone the specific cirumstances recounted in conversion narratives.

On the other hand, "conversion" as a paradigm itself suggests the drama and suddenness of a turning point, and as such should not be discounted, since, indeed, individuals undergo the experience of conversion; more important, undergoing such an experience, with a definable pivotal point, is *expected*—in life and in biography—of members of certain religious communities who were not raised in a tradition (and even of those who were raised in a tradition in sectarian settings). It is thus pointless to protest that such drama is unlikely or overdone, because the fact of conversion (if not the specific circumstances cited in the narratives) is no more unlikely than other human experience ascribed to the rulers who take center stage in conversion narratives.

We may naturally cringe, though perhaps less vehemently or smugly than our positivist predecessors of a century ago, at the "fantastic" and miraculous elements in conversion stories, but I would argue that we go further astray if we attempt to extract a "historical" core from these accounts, by "de-mythologizing" them, than if we accept them wholesale as they stand. My point is not that we should regard the particulars of any conversion narrative as "historical" fact, but rather that we should accept the accounts for what they are—and that we should accept, in the process, that the traditional "popular" understanding of these accounts might have been much more multivalent and much less simplistic than the assumptions of many specialists would imply; even the "unsophisticated" audiences for whom these tales were rehearsed were no doubt more sensitive to the richness of religious language than many scholars of positivist bent. In any case, our effort should not be aimed at reduplicating the errors of Muslim or Christian or Jewish scholars and historians who rationalized and historicized the traditions they collected and in the process distorted the original integrity of the accounts, weeding out the impossible and fantastic. Rather, we should focus on understanding why these traditions, as imperfectly as they have been preserved, were constructed and transmitted as they were: we will be led into absurdities if we hunt for a "historical" core, but this does not mean we should not search for the "narrative" core. We should not ask, "What happened?" but "What did they say happened, and what did it mean to them?"

What these conversion narratives tell us is not "how it happened," but "what was accomplished," and the conventions of religious language require expressing the effects of what "happened"—which historians may choose to understand as a gradual process—in dramatic terms signaling the overcoming of native practices and their displacement by the new faith's ordinances, a displacement that from the religious perspective marked *the* pivotal event without which any subsequent "gradual process" would not have occurred. Telling the story of that gradual process is not the job of religious language or religious narrative.

Because of the paucity of early indigenous *written* accounts in general clearly provening from among Inner Asian peoples, we are of course on somewhat shaky ground in assuming that the accounts taken as examples here reflect narratives constructed among and/or on behalf of the particular Inner Asian peoples who adopted the new faith in question (or their rulers, which is usually as far as we can go—*cuius regio, eius religio*). In part it is the element of displacement itself that supports this contention, since evoking ritual associations of the "old" religion would seem to make sense only for an audience familiar with those former ways; beyond this, however, we often have no direct evidence on the provenance of the stories, aside from the assumption that some kind of oral narrative must have been the ultimate source of each account. Nonetheless, it is altogether likely, I would argue, that the brief accounts of these three instances of conversion in Inner Asia reflect tales originally generated and transmitted among the people converted, or at least among those who claimed credit for the conversion and who must have known the given community's traditions and ways firsthand and in some depth; in view of examples from later Inner Asian peoples—especially the Islamized communities we are focusing on—for whom the frequent narrative "rehearsal" of their (ancestors') conversion was an important element in oral literature and in assertions of communal solidarity, it is not unreasonable to assume that recitations of conversion narratives formed an important part of ("nativized") religious and social ritual in earlier contexts as well.[143]

Yet another theme evoked structurally in the narratives of "intrusion and displacement" likewise reflects an understanding of "conversion" clearly drawn from the "foreign" traditions that entered Inner Asia; it involves a two-stage interaction with the "new" religion and suggests an initial conversion, a falling away, and a decisive commitment to the new faith. This theme is common to several Inner Asian conversion narratives, whether the details of the initial conversion are narrated or not. The Turkic account of the Uyghur ruler Bögü Khan's conversion to Manichaeanism noted in Chapter 3 presupposes an earlier, preliminary acceptance of the new faith, a conversion that was not solid enough to prevent the grievous lapse alluded to in the account, but that *was* serious enough to leave the ruler open to the exhortations and threats of the Manichaean clergy; their counsel finally led to the khan's repentance and decisive conversion. This sequence appears in the Armenian account of the "Hun" conversion of 682 as well, where we find in fact several events, possibly reflecting two or more traditions about the conversion, but no doubt mirroring in their compilation a sequence *expected* in conversion.

Likewise, the "epic" Hebrew accounts of the Khazar adoption of Judaism suggest a conversion in at least two stages. One recounts an initial conversion prompted by an angelic apparition to a Khazar king, whereupon his people adopt the religion, he leads them in victorious military campaigns, and he produces various elements of the new faith's ritual apparatus; next comes the account of religious disputation, ending in the

143. Such a celebratory "recounting" of a conversion may be implied in the famous "Bögü Khan" text inspired by the Uyghur *qaghan*'s adoption of Manichaeanism in 762–763. Following the definitive repentance of the ruler under the guidance of his Manichaean preceptors, the account says, his people rejoiced and enjoyed games and entertainments in a festive celebration that lasted until dawn, and the activities in this celebration seem to have included the retelling of the events of the "conversion," if the phrase *bir ikintikä sawlašïp ištrüšüp ögrünčülänti* ("they rejoiced, speaking and recounting to one another") may be understood as implying that what they related among themselves was an account of the preceding solemnities; such, at least, was the understanding of the text's editors and translators ("erzählten sie sich wieder und wieder [das Vorgefallene] und freuten sich") (cf. W. Bang and A. von Gabain, "Türkische Turfan-Texte. II. Manichaica," repr. in *Sprachwissenschaftliche Ergebnisse der deutschen Turfan-Forschung*, Bd. 2 [Leipzig: Zentralantiquariat der Deutschen Demokratischen Republik, 1972], pp. 31–50 [pp. 411–430 according to the original pagination]; for the passage in question [lines 55–56], pp. 36 [416] (text), 37 [417] (tr.)).

adoption of Judaism, which is followed by a description of what Pritsak refers to as the "rabbinical reform" of Khazar Judaism several generations later.[144] The other account speaks of Jewish refugees fleeing to the Khazars and intermarrying with them, becoming "one people"; this implication of an initial Jewish presence is followed by an account wherein a Jew rises to military prominence among the Khazars and is made "chief officer" over the Khazar army, evidently straying from his faith in the process until won back through the example and appeals of his wife and father-in-law. At this point the narrative turns to yet another threat to the religion, in the form of Byzantine and Arab indignation over the adoption of Judaism; this provides the basis for recounting the religious disputation, which is resolved dramatically by the discovery of the sacred books in the cave, as noted above, and the decisive repentance of "Israel with the people of Khazaria."[145] In its original form this multiple sequence of the establishment of and threat to the religion may indicate two or more original narratives, one of which was already marked by the "nativization" of Judaism through the device of Jewish refugees, as noted earlier; in any case, whether indicative of multiple narratives or a single complex one, the extant account becomes subsumed into a narrative structure of Judaism's prior endorsement among the Khazars (by the acceptance of Jewish refugees and by their descendant's success) followed by a threat against, and decisive affirmation of, the new religion.

What is at work here is a standard religious and hagiographical narrative structure rooted in paradigms of "conversion" itself, involving a sequence of summons, consent, test, and decisive affirmation. In Ötemish Ḥājjī's narrative as a whole this structure is only implicit, since all we see in the account is the test and affirmation; at the end of his account, however, when, alluding to the earlier narrative of Berke's conversion, he notes that the "Özbek people" had previously converted but had fallen away, we may understand that despite the intervening accounts of khans between Berke and Özbek, the sequence of initial adoption of the new faith, lapse, and decisive conversion is present here as well.

A final and vital point may be noted here in connection with the other conversion narratives discussed for comparative purposes. In each case, the narratives considered above, though preserved only in nonindigenous accounts, most likely reflect narratives created and circulated by com-

144. Pritsak, "The Khazar Kingdom's Conversion," pp. 272–275.
145. Pritsak, "The Khazar Kingdom's Conversion," pp. 275–276.

munities or factions within the societies in question that were actively promoting the new religion in those societies. In other words, we should no doubt imagine, for example, the account of the Bishop Israyel's conversion activities as a reflection, in an external literary source, of narratives (no doubt several were known to the compiler, as discussed above) created by a "Christianizing" community, within the larger society of the North Caucasian Huns, that was eager to foster the religion it had adopted as suitable for that larger society. The same pattern might be expected in the other cases as well; in particular, that pattern is most likely evident in the narrative of Özbek Khan's conversion reflected in Ötemish Ḥājjī's account, in which we should no doubt find traces of narrative elements devised, at a time when the Islamization of the Golden Horde was not well advanced, by groups that sought to strengthen Islam and, in effect, "sell" it to the larger society of which they were a part.

There is one crucial difference, however, between the account of Islamization reflected in Ötemish Ḥājjī's work and the earlier accounts of conversion to Christianity or Judaism. In view of the similar purposes of all these narratives, and their likely similar origins among small devoted subgroups aiming at the strengthening of their religious "platform," we might reasonably regard them all equally not as popular creations evidencing a strong popular assimilation of the new faith with the old traditions, but as essentially "ideological" products of small "assimilationist" parties within their societies. Indeed, they may have been so; but in the case of the Islamization narrative, the story, and the religion it supported, *found wide popular acceptance.*

In the case of the other three conversion narratives, we know little of the actual historical impact of the religions whose place in a particular community the respective narratives, according to this view, were designed to reinforce. If the Nestorian conversion story was indeed focused on Kereyt society, and not merely attached to them when Kereyt Christianity became more widely known in the thirteenth century, *and* if we assume the dating of the conversion to 1007 to be accurate, then we could assume an approximately three-century period, at most, in which a Christianizing party might have "sold" its platform with the aid of the narrative discussed above. In any case we cannot trace a lasting survival of Kereyt Christianity for more than two centuries, nor do we have evidence of how widely a Christianizing "policy" was accepted. Similarly, in the case of the Khazars, we can trace the echoes of the conversion legend for approximately two centuries of Khazar history, although the story itself had greater longevity outside the community directly concerned by it; the extent and legacy of Khazar Judaism remains a hotly debated issue, but we are certainly justified in assuming that the narrative of the Khazar conversion did not "speak to" an active Jewish community that adopted that conversion story as the defining moment in its history for more than four centuries at the very most. As for the North Caucasian Huns, the legacy of the conversion recounted in the Armenian narrative, and of the indigenous resonance of the original narrative elements, was evidently quite short-lived, and its conscious traces had certainly vanished within a century or two at most after the events reflected in the narrative; the "Christianizing" community among them must have remained small and ineffective.

In the case of the conversion reflected, supported, and rehearsed in the narrative elements Ötemish Ḥājjī recorded, however, we are dealing with a much more persistent legacy. Not only do we have at *least* a six-century history of Islam among the peoples formed out of the Golden Horde; and not only do we also have nearly the same longevity for the specific story recounting the original conversion; but in addition we have a five- or six-century period in which the central character in the Islamization narrative captured the imagination of peoples and communities throughout western Inner Asia. He retained his links with Islamization and thus reinforced, in quite specific fashion, the "message" conveyed by the earliest stories told about him. At the same time he was important and "sacred" enough to be suitable for a remarkable degree of elaboration and a wide range of religious and social and political uses.

The original narrative surrounding Baba Tükles may thus be better understood with the aid of its parallels in themes and structures with other conversion narratives. In the end, however, it was more successful by far than any of those considered here, and its success may be measured above all by the longevity of its central character—a longevity not only as a fossilized name in an old story, but as a dynamic and living presence in the political and religious life of much of Islamic Inner Asia. It is this dynamic presence that will be the focus of the remainder of this book.

It may be useful here, before turning our attention to Baba Tükles and his extraordinary development in Islamic Inner Asia, to summarize the thematic and structural elements of Ötemish Ḥājjī's narrative that we must assume conveyed sufficient religious resonance in the Jöchid *ulus* to surround the figure of Baba Tükles with his intense sacred aura. To begin with, he is cast among the Muslim saints commissioned to convert Özbek Khan to Islam, to which end he goes to the khan's court, magically undoes the sorcerers' "miracle" in conducting the ceremony, and is brought into the inviolable sanctuary of the Chingisid tradition. He and his fellows debate with the infidels, and in the narrative of the test we see Baba Tükles marked by signs and actions that are symbolically suggestive of a number of religiously charged roles from both Inner Asian and Islamic perspectives: (1) he dons armor, displays his ecstatic fervor (through the symbols of hair and sweat), and submits to an ordeal like a communal shaman, while at the same time he enters the fire like Ibrāhīm after asking for the *fātiḥah* from his fellow Muslims, and sweats in religious exertion like a genuine *mujāhid*; (2) his voice is heard from within the pit, just as voices are heard from within the enclosures of communal ancestors, while at the same time what he utters is the divine remembrance in true Sufi fashion; (3) a sheep is "sacrificed" at the pit he enters, in an echo of a Mongol ancestral ritual, while at the same time a sheep's flesh is consumed by the fire but he is spared, evoking the Islamic theme of substitution; (4) he enters the pit and emerges from it, evoking a pattern familiar from both individual heroic/shamanic narratives and legends of communal origin in which the pit is at once the underworld, a protective enclosure, and ancestral cave, while at the same time he is "tried" as a Muslim by being shut up inside a pit, at once symbolic of a general theme of burial and rebirth, and evocative of the specific narrative tradition of a Muslim buried in the Mongol *qoruq* but miraculously delivered; and (5) he does all this within the context of a ritual intrusion into "pagan" Mongol religious rites, as signaled by the setting of the *qoruq* and by the Muslim saints' disruption of the drinking rite.

As noted at the outset, the importance of these motifs in the "original" narrative must be inferred in most cases from (1) echoes of the motifs themselves in narratives of comparable date or comparable aim or comparable style, (2) parallels in structure, and less often in motifs, from comparable conversion narratives, (3) evidence on the importance of the motifs in Inner Asian religious tradition of the Mongol era, and (4) the fact of the enormous religious resonance of the figure of Baba Tükles. The motifs are, furthermore, evident in our extant narrative only in fragmentary and/or conflated form. More important, only a few of them appear to have survived intact into later versions of the tales of Baba Tükles; specifically, only his entry into the fire, his hairiness, and his link with honey as in the drinking rite, are evidenced in twentieth-century echoes of his saintly reputation, outside the general association of his name with Islamization and "nation-forming." We must thus leave our often conjectural interpretation of how the themes and structures that surrounded Baba Tükles in the earliest extant version of his story conveyed religious meaning in the formative period of his legendary persona, and turn to the most productive and long-lived element of the early conversion narrative: the figure of Baba Tükles himself.

5

Baba Tükles in History and Genealogy

It may be somewhat misleading to consider the treatment of Baba Tükles in "historical" (or more properly "historicizing") works and genealogical traditions, before examining his treatment in oral epic tales. The order here is adopted primarily for convenience, and should not be construed as intended to posit either a chronological evolution, with sober "historical" accounts emerging first and forming the basis for later elaboration, corruption, or "fantasization," or an intellectual devolution (with an assumption that the epic tales and mythic elaboration of Baba Tükles' character are somehow more "primitive" or unsophisticated than the accounts in "historical" sources). On the contrary, it seems quite likely that oral tales of a kind closer to those extant in epic accounts involving Baba Tükles must have been created quite soon after the time of Edigü's career, and these oral traditions were in turn, no doubt, the "sources" the "historians" incorporated or adapted for their accounts.

The assumption that the epic accounts to be considered later amount to a "distortion" of history underlies much of the scholarship on the epic cycle surrounding Edigü, and seems to reflect a more general assumption, perhaps dear to historians, that individuals and communities tend to organize and articulate their experience first and foremost as "history," or at least in ways amenable to historical analysis. We will adopt a different assumption, namely, that people more often cast and recast their experience in ways reflective of their fundamental values, and thereby more suitable to other types of inquiry.

It is, rather, precisely the *arrested* narrative development of the accounts I am referring to as "historical," as well as their earlier reduction to written form—a form less resonant for the societies we are dealing with—that argues for their consideration first, for they tell us the least (though they do tell us something) about how the story of Baba Tükles and the conversion of Özbek Khan "spoke to" communities that identified with Edigü and Baba Tükles. They are less revealing, for they rarely venture beyond the historian's all-too typical approach to myth: glean genealogy from it, explain away the more "fantastic elements," and set it in real time. And it is clearly the case here that, especially in view of the religiously charged theme of the tale of Baba Tükles, the *myth* emerged soon after the "event," and that the myth lived on outside the constraints the historians sought to impose upon it.

To be sure, some of the "historical" sources offer important new developments with the tale of Baba Tükles, especially the work of ʿAbd al-Ghaffār Qïrïmī; there we find "historicizing" approaches to the myth of Baba Tükles that closely parallel the Central Asian developments of the myth of Sayyid Ata, with Baba Tükles highlighted as a bearer of Islam who "creates" peoples. Similarly, a newly discovered text discussed below provides a synthetic reconciliation of various traditions on Baba Tükles' Sufi status. But on the whole, as in the case of the Tatar historical tradition, the chief contribution of the historical and genealogical sources is to fix the early form of the genealogy of Baba Tükles. In short, the historians lacked (or surpressed) the specifically mythic imagination and creativity and sought to do what historians customarily do, seeking a rational interpretation of legends and myths that were developed not to provide people with a "history" in the contemporary sense, but to assist them in imagining themselves and their origins. We will thus deal first with these treatments of Baba Tükles—which make him a mystical interlocutor with Özbek Khan, the founder of the Uzbek people (and by a peculiar omission, of the non-Muslim Qalmïqs), and an ancestor to Noghay *mīrzā*s, Bukharan shaykhs, and Russian princes.

These accounts will be dealt with here not in the chronological order of their appearance in written form, but in a sequence based on their increasing "distance" from the account of Ötemish Ḥājjī. Before we can examine these narrative reflections of Baba Tükles, however, we must explore first some problems connected with the name of this saintly hero and what it may tell us of his numinous persona, and then consider the historical setting in which the historical and genealogical traditions to be discussed here emerged.

The Hero of the Conversion Narrative: Baba Tükles

To begin with, nothing is problematical about the saint's designation as "Baba." This is a common Turkic honorific applied to Sufi saints and other holy personages, meaning "grandfather" or "old man" and equivalent to *ata* (father) and *dede* (grandfather), the former more standard in Central Asia, the latter in Anatolia; indeed, *baba* often alternates with these equivalent terms in connection with the same figures, and in the case of Baba Tükles we find occasional reference to him as "Tükles Ata," in epic and folkloric contexts. In this regard it is worth noting that the Turkic appellation "Ata" as applied to Muslim saints is explicitly likened to pre-Muslim Mongol practice by Abū'l-Ghāzī. In his *Shajarah-i Turk,* he twice explains the Mongol title *ečige* (father) applied to Chingis Khan's protector Mönglik by noting that the Turks call "saintly persons" (*ʿazīz kišiler*) "Ata," citing the examples of Ḥakīm Ata and Sayyid Ata; Mönglik, he says in the first passage, likewise earned the honorific *ečige* because he was the *ʿazīz kiši* of the Mongols, or, as he says in the second passage, more clearly evocative of Muslim conceptions, because he "served as shaykh" (*shaykhlïq qïlur erdi*) and "was the spiritual master of all the Mongols" (*barča moġūl-nïng pīri erdi*).[1] Mönglik, of course, an intimate of Chingis Khan's father, was himself the father of the shaman Kököchü, known as Teb Tengri, the holy man who according to Mongol tradition echoed in Muslim and European sources declared Chingis Khan (a title Kököchü bestowed) to be divinely favored, thereby "proclaiming" him khan; the shaman in effect initiated the Chingisid principle of imperial charisma and legitimacy, and with his death following a failed challenge against the khan whom he had blessed, Kököchü likewise sealed that principle with autonomous religious authority independent of further shamanic sanction.

The second element of Baba Tükles' name is more problematical. The term "*tükläs*" (indicated by a spelling *t.w.k.lās*) eludes all attempts to provide a satisfying etymology; it seems to appear *only* as a proper name, and this (together with its obscure morphology) suggests that it might even be of non–Turkic origin. The possible origins of the name include a plausible, if problematical, interpretation as a Turkic word with a meaning that fits our saint's story, but it cannot be excluded that the form "*tükläs*" is, in whole or in part, of some other origin and meaning.

To begin with, the name of Baba Tükles is explained already in

1. Ed. Desmaisons, pp. 53, 72 (text), 55, 77 (tr.).

Ötemish Ḥājjī's account itself, as based on a physical characteristic, and this explanation is implicit in the forms of the saint's name (based on the form "*tükli*") preserved in the epic accounts discussed below. The explanation is simple: the saint's limbs were covered with thick "body hair," the latter phrase translating the term *tük* used in the account. Here the name is implicitly analyzed as *tük* plus a suffix +*läs*, and both these elements require comment. The former term is somewhat problematical in Ötemish Ḥājjī's text, appearing once clearly as *tük* but in another instance in a form suggestive of the word *tülüg*; the latter term is a suffixed version of the older form of the word for "body hair," *tü*, which appears to have been superseded by the form *tük* (at least in unsuffixed environments) in texts dating after the thirteenth century.[2] The textual problem is discussed further in the notes to the full translation in Appendix 2, but is worth mentioning here insofar as we must clearly presume the form *tük*, evidently a more recent, post-thirteenth-century form, as underlying the suffixed form *tükläs* that appears in our text, if we accept the explanation of the name "Tükläs" as given by Ötemish Ḥājjī. That is, if Baba Tükles' name indeed alludes to his hairiness, as Ötemish Ḥājjī tells us, and is not instead of some other origin and meaning, we might reasonably expect his name to have appeared in that form only after the thirteenth-century, a situation consistent with the "historical" setting of Baba Tükles' earliest appearance.

The "other half" of an interpretation of the type supplied by Ötemish Ḥājjī is naturally the suffix +*läs* attached, presumably, to the Turkic word *tük*, and signifying "possessing," "endowed with." Unfortunately for this interpretation, we would expect here the standard Turkic suffix, +*li* / +*lï* (or older forms in +*lig*, +*luġ*, etc.), used to create adjectives with the sense of "having" or "possessing" the thing signified by the unsuffixed noun, to

2. The material gathered by Clauson (*ED*, p. 433 [s.v. "*tü:*"] and p. 498 [s.v. "*tü:lüg*"]) suggests that the simple form *tü*, attested since the eighth century, disappears everywhere (with the possible exception of Anatolia) after the thirteenth century, with *tük* or *tüg* (forms that do not appear *before* the thirteenth century) replacing it in all texts later than the thirteenth century; only in the fossilized, suffixed form *tülüg*, "hairy," did the earlier form survive (alongside *tüklüg* , *tüylüg*), but even in this case something is awry: Clauson cites one example of the adjectival form *tülüg*, from a late fourteenth-century Chinese-Uyghur glossary (see L. Ligeti, "Un vocabulaire sino-ouigour des Ming," *AOH*, 19 [1966], pp. 117–199, 257–316 [p. 271]), but cites both the adjectival forms *tük-tülüklüg*, "hairy," and *kök-tülüklüg*, "grey-haired" (both from the Uyghur-script legend of Oghuz Qaghan, on which see below) and the nominal form *tük-tülük* (from the same Chinese-Uyghur glossary), which suggest that the suffixed form *tülük* itself came to be used as a substantive. For later forms cf. Radlov, *Opyt*, III, cols. 1528–1529 (*tüi, tüilü*), 1530 (*tük*), 1533–1534 (suffixed verbal and adjectival forms, e.g. *tüklän-*, *tüklü*, *tüktü*, *tüksüs* , etc.).

give us, perhaps, the form *tüklü*; and indeed this very form, with the meaning "hairy," is attested both in an Arabic-Turkic vocabulary of the early fourteenth century,[3] and in the *Codex Cumanicus*,[4] in both cases reflecting the Qïpchaq Turkic language most widespread in precisely the place and time—the southern steppe lands of the Golden Horde in the first quarter of the fourteenth century—in which Baba Tükles' Islamizing activity is supposed to have occurred. The appearance of the suffix *+läs* instead of *+li* or *+lü*, etc., thus suggests either (1) that the analysis of the name "*tükläs*" as *tük*, "body hair" plus *+läs* is incorrect, with the entire word reflecting some entirely different origin, or with one or more of the elements to be interpreted differently; (2) that while the analysis is correct, the suffix *+läs* reflects a non-Turkic element added to the term *tük*; or (3) that the suffix *+läs* is indeed Turkic (the unfamiliar form perhaps masking some common Turkic suffix through phonological changes) and conveys a meaning similar to that of *+li*, but is simply rare.

It is of course not impossible that a Turkic suffix *+läs/+las* existed with the same essential meaning as *+li*, but no such suffix is evidenced down to the period in which Baba Tükles' name must have appeared.[5] In view of the political and social environment of the Golden Horde in which Baba Tükles' story took shape, we might reasonably expect to find in such a figure's designation a name or suffix of Mongol, Finno-Ugric, Slavic, Iranian, or even Caucasian origin, but there appears to be no clearly suitable candidate.

In this regard we may recall immediately the appearance of the ending *-läs/-las* in Mongol and Inner Asian tribal names of the thirteenth and fourteenth centuries, as known from the *Secret History*[6] of the Mongols

3. Cf. A. Caferoğlu, ed., *Abû-Hayyân, Kitâb al-Idrâk li-lisân al-Atrâk* (İstanbul: Evkaf Matbaası, 1931), pp. 109 (index), 39 (text): he gives the phrase "*tüklū almā*," i.e., "fuzzy apple," explaining it as the "Qïpchaq" word for "quince" (*as-safarjal*). A similar formation, but from the older form of the word, is found in the terms *tülüg* and *tülüg erük* applied to various fruits (plums, peaches, apricots) deemed "hairy;" cf. Ligeti, "Un vocabulaire sino-ouigour," p. 271.

4. Cf. K. Grønbech, ed., *Komanisches Wörterbuch: Türkischer Wortindex zu Codex Cumanicus* (Copenhagen: Einar Munksgaard, 1942), p. 259; cited by Clauson, *ED*, p. 498: the editor gives the form *tüklü* on the basis of the original's *tuclu*, explained as "hairy," *pilossus* in the original, and also gives *tüksüz* on the basis of original's *tucsus*.

5. As an independent word, the form "*lās*" is attested in Chaghatay and modern Uzbek, meaning "the coarse part of silk" that is combed out, or "lint" (cf. Budagov, II, p. 185; Radlov, III, 736); the initial *l-* makes this term's non-Turkic origin clear, and it is found in Persian dictionaries as well. In view of its meaning, it would not seem unreasonable to find it combined with *tük*, but *tūklās* is a quite unlikely form for their combination to take.

6. See N. P. Shastina, "Mongol and Turkic Ethnonyms in the Secret History of the Mongols," in *Researches in Altaic Languages*, ed. Louis Ligeti (Budapest: Akadémiai Kiadó, 1975, = PIAC XIV), pp. 231–244.

and from Rashīd ad-Dīn. Here we find the tribal names spelled "Qūrūlās"/"Qūrlās"[7] and "Barūlās"[8] (the latter famous, in the form Barlas, as the name of Temür's tribe), while less often cited is the tribal name spelled variously "Tūlās," "Tū'ālās," and even "Tūkālās" and "Tūklās";[9] the latter two forms are near and exact graphic equivalents of our name "Tükläs," but as tempting as it might be to find such an ethnonym figuring in the saint's designation, the form "Tögeles" yielded by the form with *kāf* appears to reflect only an orthographic imitation of the Uyghur-script spelling of "Tö'äläs," a tribal name found also in the *Secret History* and perhaps identifiable with the "Töläsh" of the eighth-century Turkic inscriptions.[10] In any case, these tribal names are themselves of uncertain origin, and there is no Mongol suffix *+las* that would justify even the analysis of these ethnonyms as parallels to the name "*tükläs*"; moreover, even if there were a basis for suggesting that "Tükläs" was an ethnic designation of uncertain origin but paralleled by the "Mongol" tribal names, we find no other examples of the combination of ethnic designations with popular religious honorifics such as "Baba."

A suffix that may be suitable for identification with the *+läs* suggested by the "folk etymology" that Ötemish Ḥājjī gives appears in modern Bashkir, where among "less productive suffixes" is noted the ending *-les*: examples given are *birläs*, "single" (from *bir*, "one"); *kirtläs*, "toothed" or "jagged" (from *kirt-*/common Turkic *kert-*, "to notch");[11] *itläs*/*itläth*, "meaty" (from *it*/common Turkic *et*, "flesh"); *ürläs*, "elevated" (from *ür*/common Turkic *ör*, "height," "high ground"); *yönläs*, "shaggy", "hairy" (from *yön*/common Turkic *yung*/*yun*/*yün*, "wool"); and *qartlas*, "old man" (from *qart*, "old man").[12] These examples highlight what is also men-

7. The name Qūrlās is found frequently in Rashīd ad-Dīn; cf. his account of Mongol and Turkic tribal divisions, Rashīd ad-Dīn, *Dzhāmiʿ at-tavārīkh*, t. I, ch. 1, ed. A. A. Romaskevich, L. A. Khetagurov, A. A. Ali-zade (Moscow: Nauka, GRVL, 1965), pp. 388, 404, 407, 495, etc., and the Russian translation, *Sbornik letopisei*, t. 1, kn. 1, tr. L. A. Khetagurov, ed. A. A. Semenov (Moscow/Leningrad: Izd-vo AN SSSR, 1952), pp. 78, 160, 164–165, 183, and t. 1, kn. 2 (tr. O. I. Smirnova, Moscow, 1952), p. 10 (where Alan Qo'a is said to have been from the Qūrulās tribe). The tribal name appearing usually as Īkīrās or Inkirās appears once in a single manuscript variant as "Īkīrās" (text I p. 76; tr I/1, p. 75); the usual form is confirmed by the *Secret History*, but the manuscript variant may suggest that such a suffix was plausible for a tribal name.

8. Text I pp. 87, 530; tr. I/1, pp. 78, 189: "B.rūlās."

9. Text, I, p. 82; tr., I/1, p. 77 (but MS variant is "B.rlās"); text, I, pp. 233, 236; tr. I/1, pp. 121–122: Tūlās, var. Tū'ālās, a branch of the Burqūt/Barghūt. The form "Tūklās" is cited from Blochet's text in Rashīd ad-Dīn, *Sbornik letopisei*, t. II, tr. Iu. P. Verkhovskii (Moscow/ Leningrad: Izd-vo AN SSSR, 1960), p. 77, n. 86; cf. Boyle, *Successors*, p. 115.

10. Pelliot, *Notes sur l'histoire de la Horde d'Or*, p. 142; cf. Boyle, *Successors*, p. 115, n. 82.

11. These two are cited, with the description of the suffix's use as noted below, in *Grammatika sovremennogo bashkirskogo literaturnogo iazyka* (Moscow: Nauka, 1981), p. 181.

tioned in the description of this suffix: it forms "intensifying" adjectives when added to *both* nominal and verbal stems, a highly unusual feature for native Turkic suffixes, which are by rights exclusively verbal or nominal, not both. Now three of these suffixed forms are clearly paralleled in Kazan Tatar by the forms *qartlač*, *yonlač*, and *itläč*,[13] with the same meanings as their Bashkir counterparts, and the Bashkir term *kirtles* is likewise paralleled by the Kazan Tatar form *kirdlač*, meaning "cliff" (i.e., a "jagged" landform).[14] An additional Tatar example with the suffix +*lač*, though not paralleled by an attested Bashkir form, is of interest: *yertlač*,[15] derived from the common Turkic verb *yïrt-*, "to rend," "to tear apart"; the latter term is attested in several forms with a number of meanings, i.e., *yïrtlaš*, "rut," "fissure in the earth," cited as "Chaghatay"[16] (as well as the forms *yïrtmaš* and *yïrtmač* with the same meaning), and, further suggestive of an equivalence between the suffixes +*lač* and +*las*, the "Chaghatay" form *yïrtlas*, meaning (1) "torn asunder," "broken to pieces," and (2) "shameless," "impudent."[17]

These forms may thus suggest a suffix +*lač* as a candidate for the form underlying the name of Baba Tükles; indeed, such a suffix has been suggested as existing in pre-thirteenth-century Turkic, in which it usually appears in names of likely foreign origin for birds or flying creatures or in

12. The latter four are cited as bearing this unproductive suffix in T. M. Garipov, *Bashkirskoe imennoe slovoobrazovanie* (Ufa: AN SSSR, Bashkirskii Filial, 1959), p. 135. The standard Bashkir-Russian dictionary lists *qartlas* and *itläth* (plus *qïrlas*, "ridge"); S. F. Mirzhanova, *Iuzhnyi dialekt bashkirskogo iazyka* (Moscow: Nauka, 1979), p. 128, lists three examples from the southern Bashkir dialect of the use of the adjectival suffix +*läs* (of which she assumes +*näs* to be an assimilated form): *ürläs*, *billäs*, "concave," "having a waist" (from *bil*/common Turkic *bel*, "waist"), and *tübännäs*, "low place" (from *tübän*, "low"). The suffix also appears, evidently, in the Shor form *turtles*, meaning "noise-maker," noted as a term assigned to a rifle in the "evasive" language of hunters, used so as not to forewarn their prey by using the actual name; cf. Alekseev, *Rannie formy religii*, p. 261.

13. These three are cited in *Tatar tele grammatikasï (morfologiya häm sintaksis)* (Kazan: Tatarstan Kitap Näshriyatï, 1959), p. 97; cf. Radlov, *Opyt*, I, 1505 (*itläč*), II, 202 (*qartlač*). Of relevance for the possible equivalence of the Bashkir suffix +*las* and the Tatar +*lač* is the material assembled by the Tatar linguist R. G. Akhmet'ianov from Bashkir, Tatar, and several Finno-Ugric languages native to the Volga-Ural region. He cites the Bashkir word *tökläs* as meaning "wizard" or "saint," and compares it with Tatar and Finno-Ugric forms such as *tökläči*, *tuglatsï*, with meanings linked to the quasi-religious function of the "matchmaker" (*Obshchaia leksika dukhovnoi kul'tury narodov Srednego Povolzh'ia* [Moscow: Nauka, 1981], pp. 97–98). The meaning he cites for the Bashkir form, however, might itself be derived from the narrative persona of Baba Tükles, and here again there is nothing decisive.

14. Budagov, II, p. 174.

15. *Tatar tele grammatikasï*, p. 97.

16. Cf. Budagov, II, p. 354; Radlov, *Opyt*, III, 517.

17. Radlov, *Opyt*, III, 517.

words otherwise suggestive of flight or "wingedness."[18] In view of Baba Tükles' shamanic character, as well as his hairiness as clearly *described* without dependence upon the meaning of his name, it would not be surprising to find in his appellation an element indicative of ornithological features and flight, or of animal symbolism typical of shamanic spirits and shamans themselves. Inasmuch as *tük* refers not only to human body hair, but to the "fur," "down," and/or "feathers" appropriate to creatures fraught with shamanic symbolism, we might content ourselves with understanding "Tükles" to mean "furry" or "feathery," in allusion to a shamanic costume or at least to a shamanic epithet. Ötemish Ḥājjī's explanation would then stand as a more "domesticated" version of the pre-Islamic associations of the wild, hairy man.

We might thus suppose that the term "*tükläs*" is a development from an earlier form **tükläč*, both indeed meaning "hair-covered" as suggested by Ötemish Ḥājjī. The sound change (*-č* > *-s*) implied in the *attested* form of the name is indeed characteristic of Bashkir, and it would not be surprising to find the bringer of Islam to the Volga-Ural basin bearing a Bashkir form of a name; and the presence, albeit sporadic, of the suffix +*las* in modern Bashkir, equivalent to the form +*lač* in Tatar, may further support this analysis. Unfortunately, we have no basis for maintaining that the sound change in question appeared as early as the fourteenth century, nor indeed is there any clear basis for equating the modern Tatar and Bashkir suffixes with the Old Turkic suffix +*lač*—if indeed such a suffix existed at all.[19]

The situation with the suffix is thus by no means clear; the indigenous analysis of *tükläs* = *tükli* might reflect knowledge of the tale of Baba Tükles and the role of *tük* in it, in which case we might suppose an incorrect popular interpretation and simplification of a name with an originally

18. Cf. Clauson's list, *ED*, p. xlviii, grouping forms with +*lač* and +*lïč*: *ïqïlač*, "a swift horse" (p. 86, from Kāshgharī); *inglič*, a plant of the mountains resembling garlic (p. 185, from Kāshgharī); *todhlïč*, a bird named together with the swan, pelican, crane, and bustard (p. 456, from the *Qutadghu Bilig*); *qarğïlač*, "swallow" (p. 657, known, says Clauson, in this "original" form only from Kāshgharī, but common in the metathesized form *qarlïğač* and its derivatives; on the latter form as "original," however, cf. the discussion in D. Kh. Bazarova, "K ètimologii nekotorykh drevnetiurkskikh nazvanii ptits," *Sovetskaia tiurkologiia*, 1975, No. 4, pp. 11–22 [p. 17]); *soqarlač*, used descriptively in describing a tall cap or hat (p. 816, from Kāshgharī); and *sondïlač*, a small bird (p. 837, from Kāshgharī, but attested also in a fourteenth-century source and in the eighteenth-century *Sanglakh*).

19. Although Clauson lists the forms cited in the previous note as occurrences of a suffix, it seems more likely that these are foreign terms adopted in whole into Turkic, and it is by no means certain that the element +*las* should be analyzed as an integral suffix. The only exception appears to be the form *üčläč* (*ED*, p. 26, cf. p. xli), which is attested only once and is explained by Kāshgharī as a name for an apparently trident-shaped arrow (i.e., from Turkic *üč*, "three").

quite different meaning. In particular, the prevalence of forms such as *tükli* or the equivalent *tükti* in the epic tradition led some scholars familiar with the saint's epic persona to seek other explanations of his name.

The conjecture that comes most readily to mind would interpret part of the name as concealing a form based on Arabic *tawakkul*; this was indeed suggested by Saadet Çağatay in her survey of the Idige epic, where the form *tükli* suggested for her the *takhalluṣ* of the famous author of the fourteenth-century Ṣafavid hagiography, the *Ṣafwat aṣ-ṣafā*, "Tawakkulī."[20] This is rendered less likely by the earlier attestation of the form *tükläs* rather than *tükli*, not only in the sixteenth-century work of Ötemish Ḥājjī (of which the manuscripts are later), but in seventeenth-century Central Asian, Russian, and "Tatar" sources as well; nevertheless, a connection with an Arabic form is not entirely unreasonable. The form *tawakkul* is not uncommon as a name, of course, and was open to "assimilation" with the Turkic term "Tükel," meaning "complete" or "perfect,"[21] typically spelled the same way as Arabic *tawakkul*, and attested as a name or as an element of a name among Mongol princes in the thirteenth and fourteenth centuries;[22] we may note, additionally, the name of *T.w.k.l* b. Mawlā Sayyid Aḥmad, who died in 897/1491 at age twenty-three, on a gravestone from Tatarstan, where the name is said to be quite common on early Muslim gravestones.[23] None of these forms, however,

20. Çağatay, "Die Ädigä-Sage," p. 276, n. 4. Çağatay does not mention it, but at least one relatively early manuscript of the *Ṣafwat aṣ-ṣafā* evidently includes a marginal note explicitly vowelling the author's name as "Tūklī," as noted by E. G. Browne in his *A Literary History of Persia*, vol. 4, *Modern Times (1500–1924)* (Cambridge: Cambridge University Pres, 1930), p. 34, n. 3, citing the Ellis MS dated 1030/1620; on the hagiographical work see now Heidi Zirke, *Ein hagiographisches Zeugnis zur persischen Geschichte aus der Mitte des 14. Jahrhunderts: Das achte Kapitel des Ṣafwat aṣ-ṣafā in kritischer Bearbeitung* (Berlin: Klaus Schwarz Verlag, 1987; Islamkundliche Untersuchungen, Bd. 120), where the author, however, receives little attention.

21. Cf. Clauson, *ED*, p. 480; alternatively the name "Tülük," as in the Tülük Temür mentioned by Ibn Baṭṭūṭah as Özbek Khan's governor in the Crimea, comes to mind, but again we can make no clear connection.

22. E.g., a great-grandson of Jöchi named by Rashīd ad-Dīn (tr. Boyle, *Successors*, p. 115; cf. p. 312, another bearer of the same name, and p. 110, two first cousins of Özbek Khan named Babuch and Tükel-Buqa, and see also Pelliot, *Notes sur l'histoire*, pp. 52–53, n. 3); cf. also the name "Tükel Qutlugh Senggün Bay" appearing in one of the Turkic-language (Uyghur-script) birch-bark fragments from the Golden Horde discovered in 1930 (cf. N. N. Poppe, "Zolotoordynskaia rukopis' na bereste," *Sovetskoe vostokovedenie*, 2 [1941], pp. 81–134 + XXIV Pl. [p. 82]); and the *amīr* Tükäl, governor of Kāt and Khīva during Timur's early career (cf. Naṭanzī, *Muntakhab*, ed. Aubin, pp. 119–120, 210–211; Niẓām ad-Dīn Shāmī, *Ẓafar-nāmah*, ed. Felix Tauer, *Histoire des conquêtes de Tamerlan* (Prague: Orientalní ústav, 1937), I, p. 19.

23. Cf. G. V. Iusupov, *Vvedenie*, p. 145; idem, "Tatarskie èpigraficheskie pamiatniki XV v. (K voprosu o proiskhozhdenii kazanskikh tatar)," *Èpigrafika Vostoka*, 5 (1951), pp. 78–94 [p. 84].

comes close to providing a convincing explanation for either the form "Tüklâs" or the meaning attested in Ötemish Ḥājjī's account.[24]

After all, despite the rarity of the suffix +*läs* and the uncertainty of its origin or essential meaning, a case can be made for the basic soundness of the interpretation implied by Ötemish Ḥājjī: that *tükläs* must have been understood to mean "covered with body hair," an interpretation that may already have masked earlier shamanic evocations. To begin with, the element of body hair plays a central role in the story; as a sign of the saint's fear and fervor, it stands on end,[25] and the declaration that his body hair was not singed in the fire stands as the climactic moment in the narrative. That declaration survives even in ʿAbd al-Ghaffār Qïrïmī's version of the account, in which the rest of Ötemish Ḥājjī's description of the saint's body hair—the explanation of his name and the account of his body hair standing up straight and protruding out throught the eyelets of his armor—has been omitted; its omission is perhaps a sign that both the morphology through which *tükläs* meant "covered with body hair," and the shamanic nuances of the saint's hairiness, were lost on ʿAbd al-Ghaffār, in the later linguistic environment in which he lived, and in the more refined and more thoroughly Islamized religious atmosphere that his version of the narrative reflects.

Body hair, of course, had strong numinous associations. As noted, the use of the term *tük* to refer to "down" or "feathers" as well recalls the "ornithological" symbolism frequently encountered in shamanic costumes and performances, while "hairiness" itself links the shaman both to the symbolism of his tutelary and protective spirits conceived in animal form, and to traditions of ancestral figures who lived in the wild like animals, as noted earlier from the account of Ibn ad-Dawādārī. More strikingly, in connection with Baba Tükles' body hair, it may be recalled that precisely the same element appears in the famous Turkic "Legend of Oghuz Qaghan"

24. A final conjecture seems to do even more violence to the shape of the word, but the term *tägälä*, spelled without *wāw* or *alif* or *sīn* (i.e., *t.k.lah*, cf. Budagov, I, p. 562), meaning a short tunic, might have been adapted to refer to a particular type of clothing appropriate to dervishes; this remains most improbable, but appellations for Sufis drawn from articles of clothing or from fabric are not unknown (cf. the twelfth-century Tabrīzī saint Baba Faraj). The currency of the term in the relevant era is affirmed by its appearance (voweled "*tegle*") in a Mongol-Persian glossary from the middle of the fourteenth century; cf. N. Poppe, "Das mongolische Sprachmaterial einer Leidener Handschrift," *Izvestiia AN SSSR*, 1927, Nos. 12–14, pp. 1009–1040; Nos. 15–17, pp. 1251–1274; 1928, pp. 55–80 [pp. 1039, 1270].

25. The same image appears in an Uyghur Buddhist text from pre-Mongol times, in connection with a "terrified" man: *tü tübleri yoqaru turup*, "the roots of his body hair stood up" (cited by Clauson, *ED*, p. 433).

preserved in an Uyghur-script redaction dating most probably from the latter thirteenth century; in its epic style and in its content, clearly drawn from oral tradition, this text is often reminiscent of parts of Ötemish Ḥājjī's work. Alongside the various animal evocations in the physical description of the young hero Oghuz Qaghan, an additional numinous feature is noted, namely that "his entire body was covered with thick hair" (*bädäni-nüng qamağï tük tülüklüg erdi*).[26] In this regard it is worth noting that Baba Tükles' body hair remained part of the tradition about his saintly status down to the twentieth century, as discussed in Chapter 6, though with a slightly different function (*protecting* him from the fire rather than proving his imperviousness to it); and outside the narrative settings in which his Islamizing role was emphasized, as well, Baba Tükles himself was often portrayed in oral tradition as a "wild" man of the wilderness, even when the specific element of his body hair was not explicitly mentioned.

As will be evident from the discussion of Baba Tükles in epic tradition, his name was only exceptionally preserved in that presumably original form in the oral tales; rather, the element *tükläs* appears in various forms such as *tükli* or *tökti*, in which the common Turkic suffix *+li* has been added to *tük* to mean "having body hair," "covered with *tük*," and this in turn suggests that the form "*tükläs*" was immediately analyzed in oral tradition as having the same meaning as *tükli*; despite the possibility, noted above, that this analysis was already affected by traditions about Baba Tükles, it seems on balance more likely that his name was indeed originally intended to highlight his most distinguishing physical, and numinous, feature.

Finally, and still in the realm of conjecture, a possible attestation of the name "Tükläs" itself, from the Jöchid *ulus* in the mid-fourteenth century, appears on coins struck in the Golden Horde in the year

26. Cf. the edition of W. Bang and G. R. Rachmati, "Die Legende von Oγuz Qaγan," *SPAW*, Phil.-Hist. Klasse, XXV, 1932, pp. 683–724 (text p. 686, tr. p. 687); that of A. M. Shcherbak, *Oguz-nāme. Muḥabbat-nāme. Pamiatniki drevneuigurskoi i starouzbekskoi pis'mennosti* (Moscow: Izd-vo vostochnoi literatury, 1959), pp. 23 and 67; the presentations of the text by I. V. Stebleva, "Poèticheskaia struktura 'Oguz-name,' " *Pis'mennye Pamiatniki Vostoka*, 1969, pp. 289–309 (p. 299); and the publication of Geng Shimin and Tursun Ayup, *Qadïmqï uyghurlarnïng tarikhiy dastanï Oghuznama* (Beijing: Millatlar Nashriyati, 1980), p. 25. On the work in general see Paul Pelliot, "Sur la légende d'Uγuz-khan en écriture ouigoure," *T'oung Pao*, 27 (1930), pp. 247–358 (cf. pp. 261–263 on the phrase *tük tülüklüg*), Denis Sinor, "Oğuz Kağan destanı üzerinde bazı mülâhazalar," *Türk Dili ve Edebiyatı Dergisi*, 4/1-2 (1950), pp. 1–14 (tr. Ahmed Ateş), and Sir Gerard Clauson, "Turks and Wolves," *Studia Orientalia*, 28 (1964), No. 2, pp. 16–20. On the numinous associations of hairiness in the Turkic world, see also Robert Dankoff, "Baraq and Burāq," *CAJ*, 15 (1971), pp. 102–117.

768/1366–1367. The coins themselves are decidedly anomalous; contrary to the conventions of Islamic coinage observed in the Jöchid *ulus*, they bear the name of a *deceased* khan, in this case Özbek Khan's son Jānī Bek, who is specifically referred to on the coin as "the late" (*marḥūm*), although his name is followed by a standard formula invoking God's preservation of his rule. More curiously, on the other side of these coins is found an inscription that appears to read "Būlād Timūr ibn Tūklās," with the year 768, but without any title such as "khan" or "sulṭān" ascribed to this "Būlād Timūr." Now the element in his name that is of interest to us is evidently not clearly legible in most specimens of this coin; there is apparently no doubt about the reading of "Būlād Timūr" or about the *fact* that the name of this figure's father appears (itself a numismatic rarity), but the first student of these coins, the Russian numismatist P. S. Savel'ev, read the father's name as "Nugan," and his reading has made its way into historical surveys of the Golden Horde.[27] In 1954, however, a coin hoard was found in Tatarstan which included seven of Būlād Timūr's coins from 768 A.H.; these were studied by A. G. Mukhamadiev of what was then the Kazan branch of the Soviet Academy of Sciences, who concluded that the name of the father on these coins should be read "Tūklā Bī," a name Mukhamadiev sought to identify with the figure called "Tovlubii" in the Russian Nikonian chronicle.[28] Now this Tovlubii was a powerful "prince" in the era of Jānī Bek and his son Berdi Bek; but Mukhamadiev's suggestion already begins to founder on this Tovlubii's portrayal in the Russian source as the figure responsible for Berdi Bek's assassination of his father and for Berdi Bek's own murder soon thereafter.[29] Indeed the figure called "Tovlubii" in the Russian chronicle is surely to be identified with the "Ṭughlū Bāy" named by Naṭanzī as among the conspirators against Jānī Bek responsible for his death, and most likely for Berdi Bek's as well.[30] It would seem odd for the son of the man responsible for Jānī Bek's death to include his father's name when having a coin struck that commemorated the murdered khan; and the form of the name in both Russian and Islamic

27. Cf. Safargaliev, *Raspad*, pp. 118–119.

28. A. G. Mukhamadiev, *Bulgaro-Tatarskaia monetnaia sistema XII–XV vv.* (Moscow: Nauka, 1983), pp. 93–95.

29. Cf. *PSRL* X (SPb., 1885; repr. Moscow, 1965), pp. 229–230; tr. Zenkovsky, *The Nikonian Chronicle*, vol. 3 (1986), pp. 180–183. Mukhamadiev mentions this account without discussing the specific deeds of "Tovlubii."

30. Tiz II, pp. 128–129 (tr.), 211 (text); cf. *Muntakhab*, ed. Aubin, pp. 84–85. See also Safargaliev, *Raspad*, pp. 108–110; Fedorov-Davydov, *Obshchestvennyi stroi*, pp. 146–147.

sources argues against its representation on the coin with a *kāf*.[31]

Beyond this, however, and most important, Mukhamadiev himself provides the most convincing evidence that the graph he interprets as the title *bī* is instead to be read as the letter *sīn*: he notes that on one of the coins he studied from the hoard found in 1954, "it is distinctly visible that the letter written separately at the end of the name has three 'teeth' and can in no way be read as *nūn*." His aim was to improve upon Savel'ev's reading, which assumed a final *nūn*, but what he is clearly describing is a final *sīn* that combines with the form *t.w.k.lā*-or *t.w.k.l.*- to give "Tükläs" as the name of Būlād Timūr's father. Mukhamadiev's eagerness to find the powerful "Tovlubii" echoed on the coin evidently led him to ignore the clearly written *sīn* at the end of the name and interpret it as an element in the titulature of "Tovlubii."

What this suggests is the currency of the name "Tükläs" in the middle of the fourteenth century in the Jöchid *ulus*; it was evidently borne by someone whom it would not be unreasonable to connect with Jānī Bek in view of the curious inclusion of the late khan's name on the coin. What is more interesting, as Mukhamadiev observes,[32] Russian chronicles report under the year 6869/1361 that "Bulat Temir," "prince of the horde," seized Bulghār and all the cities along the Volga,[33] a move suggesting his intent to carve out a realm for himself or for a patron as the turmoil that followed Berdi Bek's murder deepened; this "Bulat Temir" appears in Russian chronicles as late as 1367, corresponding to the time of the coins issued in his name, but in that same year, apparently, he was defeated in an engagement with Russian forces during a campaign against Nizhnii Novgorod and fled to the Khan ʿAzīz—who, however, according to the Russian sources, put him to death.[34]

31. The Russian form "Tovlubii" most likely masks a Turkic name that would be written in Arabic script with a *ghayn* in the place of the Russian *–v–*, as in the case of Naṭanzī's "Ṭughlū;" even if these names from the Russian and Persian sources did not refer to the same person, the Russian form with which Mukhamadiev seeks to identify "Tūklā Bī" would require a back vowel, rather than a front vowel as would be implied by the spelling of the name with a *kāf* on the coins. In addition, it would be unlikely to find the title *bek* written on a coin of this era with a final *yā*, so as to reflect the pronunciation *bīy* (which may well have been already current, however), instead of with the spelling *b.k* or *bīk* most favored by orthographic convention.

32. Mukhamadiev, pp. 94–95, cf. pp. 90–91. Cf. Safargaliev, *Raspad*, pp. 118–119, and A. P. Grigor'ev, "Zolotoordynskie khany 60-70-kh godov XIV v.: khronologiia pravlenii," in *Istoriografiia i istochnikovedenie istorii stran Azii i Afriki*, vyp. 7 (Leningrad: Izd-vo Leningradskogo Universiteta, 1983), pp. 9–54 [pp. 39–41]; Grigor'ev's chronological reconstructions for this extremely obscure and difficult period unfortunately do not convincingly address the issues raised by Būlād Timūr's coins.

33. Cf. the Nikonian chronicle, *PSRL*, X, p. 233; tr. Zenkovsky, vol. 3, p. 189.

34. *PSRL*, XI, p. 9; tr. Zenkovsky, vol. 3, p. 201; *PSRL*, XV/1, col. 85; cf. Mukhamadiev, p. 94.

Now our sources for this period are extremely sparse (Būlād Timūr, for instance, is evidently not mentioned in Muslim sources), and it is difficult to trace the no-doubt-shifting alliances among the players, Chingisids and non-Chingisids, in the struggles within the Jöchid *ulus* during the 1360s, but it seems clear that Būlād Timūr attempted to hold on to the left bank of the upper Volga around Bulghār, perhaps opposing the growing power of the *amīr* Mamay, or the Chingisid opponents of Mamay, or both. It is also clear that during the years in which we may assume Būlād Timūr to have been active (i.e., between his seizure of Bulghār in 1361 and his coinage of 768/1366–1367), reasonably consistent lines may be drawn between, on the one hand, Mamay and his puppet khans (chief among them ʿAbdullāh), based near the Crimea, and, on the other hand, a series of khans who ruled (and minted coins) from Sarāy al-Jadīd and Gulistān,[35] among whom Murīd (coins from 762–764/1360–1363) and ʿAzīz Shaykh (coins from 766–767/1364–1366) were most prominent among the enemies of Mamay and ʿAbdullāh.

What remains unclear is what role Būlād Timūr may have played in these struggles. In the first place, it is not certain where Būlād Timūr's coins mentioning Jānī Bek were issued; Mukhamadiev cites one exemplar indicating Gulistān as the mint-site, but as he notes, this coin lacks the name of the ruler who issued it. If his coins were indeed issued there, we might suppose either that he was hostile to the khans such as Murīd and ʿAzīz Shaykh and in 768/1366–1367 succeeded in ousting the latter, or that he was allied with them and moved in that year to defend their interests, perhaps against Mamay. The former supposition fits somewhat the reconstruction of Safargaliev,[36] who assumes the ongoing independence of Būlād Timūr in his territory centered on Bulghār, and his hostility toward the khans based in Gulistān and Sarāy al-Jadīd; it also accords with the Russian source that ascribes Būlād Timūr's death to the khan ʿAzīz Shaykh (whose coins, incidentally, date no later than 768, when his "victim" Būlād Timūr also issued coins). The latter supposition, of Būlād Timūr's alliance with ʿAzīz Shaykh, fits Mukhamadiev's reconstruction, despite the apparent incongruity of the khan's "execution" of the "prince" as the Russian source suggests; in support of this reconstruction, Mukhamadiev notes several Russian princes' disregard of a *yarlïq* issued by ʿAzīz Shaykh

35. The location of this important town remains uncertain; it is usually placed near Sarāy al-Jadīd (cf. Egorov, *Istoricheskaia geografiia*, p. 114), but Mukhamadiev, pp. 21–23, argues that it was farther north, near Bulghār.

36. *Raspad*, p. 125.

in 1365, and suggests that Būlād Timūr's failed campaign against Nizhnii Novgorod in 1367 was a punitive expedition on behalf of ʿAzīz Shaykh.

If, on the other hand, Būlād Timūr's coins were issued elsewhere—perhaps in the region of Bulghār, which he seized in 1361—we may more freely imagine him either (1) as hostile to both ʿAzīz Shaykh and Mamay (in which case his coins in the name of the deceased Jānī Bek may have been intended to assert his independence from both sides and/or to project a particular religio-political orientation which Jānī Bek's name may have evoked); (2) as an ally of the khans Murīd and ʿAzīz Shaykh in their struggles with Mamay (with his odd coins issued in 768/1367 as a continuation of their challenge to the growing power of Mamay and the khans under his patronage); or (3) as an ally of Mamay, positioned to the north of the latter's base as a counter to ʿAzīz Shaykh, for instance (with his coins intended to counter the Chingisid holders of power in the old centers of the Golden Horde). In any case, the Russian chronicle's account of Būlād Timūr's death by ʿAzīz Shaykh's order, which would seem to support the first or third of these alternatives, does not *necessarily* rule out at least a temporary alliance between the two, given the complex and shifting patterns of allegiance in this obscure period of the Golden Horde's history.

We unfortunately have no firm basis for resolving the relationships among these figures. Nor, after all, do we know anything of who this Būlād Timūr's father was; if indeed he bore the name "Tükläs," we have no solid grounds for assuming that he bears any connection with the Baba Tükles ascribed the conversion of Özbek Khan. It is interesting, however, to see the son of a man who bore this name, with the etymological problems it poses, active in the northerly region of Bulghār and in campaigns against Nizhnii Novgorod, further west along the Volga upriver from the region of Bulghār; it adds at least some small weight to the supposition that the origin of the name "Tükläs" might be sought outside an exclusively Turkic environment.

More interesting connections are suggested by the possibility, which Mukhamadiev assumes, that Būlād Timūr was in effect allied with Murīd and ʿAzīz Shaykh. Little is known of these khans; the work of Muʿīn ad-Dīn Naṭanzī portrays both as Chingisids of the eastern half of the Jöchid *ulus*, the Kök Orda (which Naṭanzī wrongly calls the Aq Orda), but this source is notoriously unreliable for the Jöchid *ulus*.The second of these Chingisids, however, whom Naṭanzī calls ʿAzīz Khan, is evidently linked with the lineage of Sayyid Ata: he is said to have repented (but only temporarily) from some unspecified evil habits at the hand of "a descendant of the Sulṭān al-ʿĀrifīn Sayyid Muḥammad[37] al-Yasavī, known as Sayyid Ata," to whom the khan gave his daughter in marriage. The reference to the saint is somewhat obscure,[38] but if Naṭanzī is correct in this detail we may see here the son of a man named Tükläs serving a khan who also honored a descendant of Sayyid Ata.

We will explore further the parallels between the figures of Baba Tükles and Sayyid Ata in Chapter 6; for now, we may avoid going deeper into hypothetical conjectures and leave the questions tied to our central character's name unresolved, turning instead to the transformations of his personality and functions in historical and folkloric material.

Edigü and the Noghay Horde

In all of the treatments of the tale of Baba Tükles considered here as "historicizing" developments, one common thread is the saint's identification as an ancestor of Edigü,[39] the powerful *amīr* in the Golden Horde during the latter fourteenth and early fifteenth centuries who came to be regarded as the "founder" of the Noghay horde following the fragmentation of the Jöchid *ulus*. While Edigü has enjoyed some attention in historical studies of the Golden Horde, the history of the Noghay horde has been seriously neglected, and even Edigü himself has been approached primarily from

37. In one MS, "Maḥmūd."

38. Cf. *Muntakhab* ed. Aubin, p. 91; the translation in Tiz II, p. 130, is clearly in error identifying the man who guided the khan and received his daughter in marriage as "Sayyid Ata," but the apparent identification of Sayyid Ata with the "Sulṭān al-ʿārifīn" [the standard designation of Khoja Aḥmad Yasavī], as well as both the title "sayyid" and the name "Muḥammad" (or Maḥmūd) point to a garbled transmission.

39. I have used this form throughout when referring to the historical personage, arbitrarily using the form Idige when referring to the epic hero, despite the artificiality of distinguishing the two so completely. The name itself appears in the earliest sources as "*Ädūkū*," "*Äd.kū*," the former in the Uyghur script *yarlïq* of Toqtamïsh to the Lithuanian Grand Prince Jagello (dated 8 Rajab 795, year of the hen = 20 May 1393), where Toqtamïsh identifies Edigü as the envoy sent to Timur by several princes and *bek*s hostile to him (i.e., to Toqtamïsh; cf. I. Berezin, "Tarkhannye iarlyki Tokhtamysha, Timur-Kutluka i Saadet-Gireia," [Kazan: Tipografiia Universiteta, 1851], cf. pp. 47–49, 61–62, facsimile facing p. 12), the latter in the *yarlïq* of Temür Qutlugh, dated 6 Shaʿbān 800, year of the tiger=24 April 1398; here Edigü is named as the chief *bek* (cf. Berezin, "Khanskie iarlyki, II: Tarkhannye iarlyki Tokhtamysha, Timur-Kutluga i Saadet-Gireia" [Kazan', 1851], pp. 3,24, and A. N. Samoilovich, "Neskol'ko popravok k iarlyku Timur-Kutluga," *Izvestiia Rossiiskoi Akademii Nauk*, 1918, pp. 1109–1124 [pp. 1112–1122]). Sharaf ad-Dīn ʿAlī Yazdī gives the form "Īd.kū" (cf. *Zafarnoma*, facs. ed. Urunbaev, ff. 208b, 210a: *īd.kū-yi ūzbak, īd.kūʾ-i ūzbak*), the same form that appears in Ibn ʿArabshāh's history.

the standpoint of his impact in Russian history; his role, and that of his descendants, has rarely been placed within its Inner Asian context. We cannot take up here a detailed examination of either Edigü's career or Noghay history, but because neither is widely familiar a few general remarks are in order by way of orientation; as we will see, it is precisely the Noghay confederation led by Edigü's descendants that provides the historical setting for the elaboration of Baba Tükles' genealogical and mythic persona.

Edigü's career[40] encompassed virtually all of western Inner Asia and spanned more than thirty years, a period divided roughly in half by the deaths of the figures whose ambitions he managed to exploit in the first phase of his political and military activity. He first appears in our sources as one of the chief *amīrs* of Toqtamïsh, khan of the Golden Horde, and the first half of his career was dominated by his intrigues, with other *amīrs* and rival Chingisid princes, against the khan; in these efforts he inevitably sought the support of Temür, as the khan of the Jöchid *ulus* and the master of the Chaghatayid and Ilkhanid legacy in Central Asia and Iran vied for power. The clash of these two figures was obviously based upon more than Edigü's intrigues, but he succeeded in exploiting their rivalry to maintain and enhance his position; and the "flight" of Edigü from Toqtamïsh to Temür, celebrated in the epic tale based on Edigü's career, which we will consider later, was clearly based in his actual mission to Temür, of which Toqtamïsh complained in a famous *yarlïq*.

The culmination of the struggle between Toqtamïsh and Temür came with the latter's final campaign into the Golden Horde in the spring of 1395 and his crushing defeat of Toqtamïsh. Toqtamïsh survived to annoy Edigü and subsequent Chingisid khans for another ten years, during which Temür's attentions turned to Iran, Syria, Anatolia, and India, leaving the Jöchid *ulus* to Edigü and his rivals. From then on until his death, Edigü was among the most powerful figures in the Jöchid *ulus*, and its vir-

40. On Edigü's historical role, see Spuler, *Die Goldene Horde*, pp. 136–154; Grekov and Iakubovskii, *Zolotaia Orda i ee padenie*, pp. 374–405; Howorth, *History of the Mongols*, II/1, pp. 225–272; Hammer-Purgstall, *Geschichte der Goldenen Horde in Kiptschak*, pp. 364–377; Vernadsky, *The Mongols and Russia*, pp. 277–288; Safargaliev, *Raspad*, pp. 225–231; A. P. Grigor'ev, "'Iarlyk Edigeia': analiz teksta i rekonstruktsiia soderzhaniia," *Istoriografiia i istochnikovedenie istorii stran Azii i Afriki*, vyp. 11 (Leningrad: Izd-vo Leningradskogo Universiteta, 1988), pp. 55–93; and especially Bartol'd's article, "Otets Edigeia," *Sochineniia*, II/1, pp. 792–804 (see also his article on "Toktamysh," *Sochineniia*, V, pp. 564–567, from *EI*[1]). For the earliest primary sources to devote special attention to Edigü (beyond his ties to Temür), cf. Naṭanzī, *Muntakhab*, ed. Aubin, pp. 97–101; Ibn ᶜArabshāh, tr. Sanders, pp. 75–76, 82–87, 258–259, and Tiz I, pp. 457–459, 467–474 (translation only); and al-ᶜAynī, in Tiz I, pp. 499–501 (text), 531–533 (tr.).

tual ruler for much of that time; he was challenged only by occasional Chingisid princes and their supporters, and by renewed attempts by the fugitive Toqtamïsh to assert his power. The most serious challenge was met in 1399, as Toqtamïsh and his ally, the Lithuanian prince Vitovt, were badly defeated at the Vorskla river by Edigü and the khan Temür Qutlugh, but even then Toqtamïsh's efforts did not cease. According to Sharaf ad-Dīn ʿAlī Yazdī, Temür received envoys from Toqtamïsh in Otrar, within a month before the *amīr*'s death there; Temür, now concerned with checking Edigü's power, agreed to support Toqtamïsh against Edigü with another campaign into the Golden Horde after he returned from his planned expedition to "Khiṭāy." With Temür's death neither campaign took place, and Toqtamïsh himself appears to have died shortly thereafter.

The years immediately following the death of Temür saw the high point of Edigü's power. He maintained authority in the Golden Horde, and effectively, albeit briefly, reinforced the Jöchid *ulus*' control in Russia with his siege of Moscow late in 1408; and he even seized part of Temür's domains during the succession struggles among the Timurid princes, holding Khorezm from late 1405 until 1412. Within five years, however, his fortunes faded. A Chingisid khan installed with his blessing turned against him, forcing him to take refuge in the power base he had established on the periphery of the Golden Horde, in Khorezm; and although his stay there appears to have allowed him to recover and reenter the struggles in the more westerly centers of the Jöchid *ulus*, his power was never so secure as it had briefly been following the departure from the political scene of Temür and Toqtamïsh. At any rate, he himself left Khorezm, and his lieutenants there were forced out by troops of Shāhrukh, who thereby added Khorezm to the parts of his father's domains in which he was able to consolidate his power, though not before one Timurid army withdrew from Khorezm upon rumors of Edigü's return.

The last years of Edigü are rather obscure. We know nothing more of his relations with Shāhrukh,[41] whose sons and commanders had to contend with other forces from the Dasht-i Qïpchaq, led by Chingisids and tribal chiefs alike. Following his departure from Khorezm, Edigü's activity seems to have been concentrated in the west, where he raided Kiev and sought an alliance with the Lithuanian Vitovt against the sons of

41. According to the Timurid *Muʿizz al-ansāb* (see Woods, "The Timurid Dynasty," p. 45), Shāhrukh's son Muḥammad Jūkī (804/1402–848/1444) married a daughter of "Idīgū Manqut"; from the prince's birthdate it seems likely that this arrangement was made after Edigü's withdrawal from Khorezm.

Toqtamïsh; at the same time, however, he is said to have undertaken a campaign to western Siberia, perhaps to the *ulus* of Shïban, and it appears that he retained the ability to maneuver with some success throughout the territory of the Jöchid *ulus* until his death. It was finally his enmity with Toqtamïsh and his family that ended Edigü's remarkable career: the most reliable version of Edigü's death dates it to 822/1419 and ascribes it to Qādir-berdi, son of his antagonist Toqtamïsh.[42]

Edigü's life became the focus of a substantial body of popular tales, perhaps already in his lifetime; these are discussed further in the following chapter, but certain features of his historical career that seem to have heightened his "legendary" appeal are worth noting here. To begin with, Edigü's power seems to have involved a strong element of "popular" appeal. It is of course likely that his "popular" image was carefully cultivated by his descendants as a strategy to appeal for political and military support from the tribal power base, and his "independence" from the Chingisid khans may have been greater in later reputation (developed at a time when asserting such independence served new political needs) than in fact; but it is doubtful that Edigü's reputation and popular appeal could have rested entirely on an exaggerated or distorted portrayal by his heirs. Rather, Edigü, as a tribal *amīr* or *bek*, may indeed have cultivated tribal support in ways that set him apart from the Chingisid political tradition and lent him genuine support among the ordinary tribal population.

The latter is suggested by the report of the Egyptian historian al-Maqrīzī identifying Edigü as the ruler who "forbade the Ṭaṭars to sell their children," thus greatly reducing the number of slaves supplied to Egypt and Syria from the Jöchid *ulus*;[43] if the slave trade enriched the urban mercantile centers of the Golden Horde and thereby benefited the khans, this action may have been motivated by Edigü's efforts to undermine his Chingisid rivals economically, but it is also likely that Edigü's halting the export of "Tatar" slaves reflects a growing consciousness of the assimilation and common identity among the nomadic population of the Jöchid *ulus*, no longer easily divisible into "Mongol" conquerors and "Qïpchaq" subjects. Such a consciousness would most likely reach (both affectively and practically) tribal commanders such as Edigü before it would reach the Chingisid nobility,[44] and it is probably not too anachronistic to sup-

42. Tiz I, pp. 500–501 (text), 532 (tr.), from al-ʿAynī.

43. Cited in Tiz I, p. 474, n. 1.

44. The halting of slave exports from the Jöchid *ulus* is also ascribed to the khan Jānī Bek in

pose that Edigü's attitude toward the slave trade brought him enhanced loyalty from the tribal population upon which military power still rested.

Beyond such specific measures, however, the very opposition between the *amīr* Edigü and the Chingisid khans may have ensured his positive reception in popular memory, whatever his actual policies; and many more modern examples should relieve us of the need to look for evidence of just or humane rule on his part (rather than "mere" strength and effectiveness) as an explanation for his popular appeal. We may also note in this regard, by way of comparison, the remarkable persistence and widespread popularity of tales and legends about Edigü's *amīr*id counterpart in Central Asia, Temür. What the two figures share is not a reputation for justice or humanity, but a status as tribal leaders who successfully challenged the power of the khans (however much they may have acquiesced in, and exploited, the khans' symbolic prerogatives); this status may well have been decisive in producing the enormous body of popular legends about both Temür and Edigü, that continued to dwarf any popular literature devoted to Chingisid khans even as (or perhaps precisely because) the Chingisid dispensation was reasserted both in Shībanid Central Asia and in the successor states to the Golden Horde.[45]

Edigü's non-Chingisid status was considerably elaborated in the epic narratives based upon his life, as we will see, and his descent from Baba Tükles and implicit links to Islamization provide the important counterweight to Chingisid prestige. Edigü's association with Islam, however, may also have been a feature of his historical career, and not merely an "ideological" strategy of his descendants in undermining Chingisid charisma. Ibn ʿArabshāh speaks of Edigü's devotion to the *sharīʿah* and intimacy with *faqīr*s, noting his observance of the precepts of the Qurʾān and the Prophetic *sunnah*,[46] while the celebrated pilgrimage of Edigü's wife

connection with other "Islamizing" reforms, suggesting, as with Edigü, a specifically Islamic component in the emerging communal identity presumed here; cf. the chronicler ash-Shujāʿī (Tiz I, pp. 254 [text], 263 [tr.], Schäfer, ed., p. 214, tr., p. 249).

45. "Edigü Bīy" is mentioned, incidentally, in the work of Ötemish Ḥājjī, who does not, however (at least in the portion of the extant text preserved in the Tashkent manuscript), link him with Baba Tükles. Ötemish Ḥājjī makes no mention of any tensions with Chingisid power—he was, after all, writing for khans—but rather reports a "saying" of Edigü, further suggesting his popular status as a source of aphoristic wisdom. The passage (Tashkent MS, ff. 43b–44a) reports that Edigü used to say, "If you seek to wish evil upon your enemy, make your appeal thus: 'O One God, make my enemy ignorant (*biligsiz*), and make him pay no heed to the speech of those who are knowledgeable.' If a person does not know by himself, but will heed the words of those who know, this is still wisdom, and nothing else."

46. Tiz I, pp. 473–474.

and her retinue in 819/1416[47] may well have been intended as a pointed political statement of adherence to Islam, as much for internal as external consumption.

From a somewhat later time we find a much clearer indication not only that Edigü was the focus of popular tales, but that he was specifically associated with Islamization in popular memory already within a generation after his death.[48] The Venetian ambassador Iosaphath Barbaro (d. 1494) was based in Tana (Azāq=Azov, at the mouth of the Don near the Crimea) from 1436 to 1452, and his account of his "Voyage to Tana," written around 1490, includes these remarks on Islam among the "Tartars":[49]

> The faith of Machometo began to become customary among the Tartars around 110 years ago. In truth some of them were *machometani* earlier, but everyone was at liberty to adhere to whatever faith pleased him, so that some worshipped statues of wood or of rags, which they carried on their carts.
>
> Constraint to adhere to Machometan faith came in the time of Hedighi, military commander [*capitano dela gente*] of the Tartar emperor called Sidahameth Khan.[50] This Hedigi was the father of Naurus, of whom we shall speak now . . .

Barbaro goes on to relate the events of 1438, when Edigü's son Nawrūz, who was likewise the "*capitano*" under Ulugh Muḥammad Khan, quarreled with the khan and switched his support to Kichik Muḥammad, aid-

47. Cf. Tiz I, pp. 428 (text), 442 (tr.) [al-Maqrīzī], and pp. 451, 454 (Ibn Ḥajar al-ʿAsqalānī); both writers, from the second quarter of the fifteenth century, report of the arrival, in Shawwāl 819/November–December 1416, of "Khātūn," the wife of "Amīr Īdikī," ruler of the Dasht, accompanied by 300 retainers, to continue on the *ḥajj* from Damascus.

48. Edigü inspired "epic" style treatments in Russian tradition as well, where he is perhaps even more clearly associated with Islam than is Özbek Khan; in the tale inspired by his attack on Moscow in 6917/1408, preserved in the *Rogozhskii letopis'* (*PSRL*, XV/1 [Petrograd, 1922; repr. Moscow, 1965], cols. 177–186), "Edegei" is a Tatar, to be sure, but more often the identification of the "Tatar" with Islam is sealed when he is repeatedly styled an "Ishmaelite" and "Hagarene."

49. *Travels to Tana and Persia by Barbaro and Contarini* (London: Hakluyt Society, Series I, No. 49, 1873), pp. 8–9; unfortunately the English version published here is "the quaint old translation" by William Thomas, done in the sixteenth century for Edward VI. Cf. the Italian text and Russian translation published by E. Ch. Skrzhinskaia, *Barbaro i Kontarini o Rossii: K istorii italo-russkikh sviazei v XV v.* (Leningrad: Nauka, 1971), pp. 117 (text), 140 (tr.), §13.

50. This apparently refers to Sayyid Aḥmad Khan (r. 1433–1465), a clear anachronism; Skrzhinskaia suggests that Shādī Bek Khan would be appropriate as the khan whom Edigü "served" as "commander," but several other khans would be appropriate as well, and it appears more likely that Barbaro's memory simply telescoped matters, linking two prominent figures.

ing the latter in his seizure of power; in this passage he once again identifies Nawrūz as a son of Edigü, "under whom Tartariȧ was constrained into the Machometan faith."[51]

It seems likely that Barbaro's reference to the strengthening of Islam "110 years ago" should be understood relative to the time when he wrote,[52] and thus may refer generally to the latter fourteenth century. In any case, the avowedly vague chronology is certainly less important than Barbaro's insistence upon Edigü's association with the firm Islamization of the Jöchid *ulus*, a theme that can hardly reflect anything other than Barbaro's familiarity with oral accounts, already circulating perhaps as early as the 1430s, that linked Edigü's career, and his era, with the establishment of Islam in the Golden Horde.[53]

Barbaro's account may thus attest to the quite early ascription to Edigü of the "prestige" appropriate to an Islamizer; this in turn may be an indication of a remarkably early date for the linking of Edigü with the Islamizing figure of Baba Tükles. It is all the more interesting, then, to find even sporadic evidence that the Islamizing role ascribed both to Edigü—either through his genealogical ties with Baba Tükles or independently—and to Özbek Khan—again, whether through the agency of Baba Tükles or otherwise—may have been so strong and of such importance that in popular historical memory, the roles of Edigü and Özbek were conflated. We find reference, for instance, to Noghay legends noted in the second half of the nineteenth century, which maintained that the ancestor of the Noghays was Özbek, and that it was under Jānī Bek that the Noghays moved to their lands along the Volga.[54] Here the roles cus-

51. Hakluyt ed., p. 9; Skrzhinskaia, Russian tr. p. 141, Italian text p. 117, §14.

52. Skrzhinskaia (p. 167, n. 36), eager to link the 110 years to the Islamization of the Golden Horde under Özbek Khan, suggests that this period should be figured not from the time *when* he wrote, but from the time *about which* he wrote, i.e. the 1430s; Barbaro, however, seems to have had no intention of linking the region's Islamization to Özbek Khan or his times, and it seems unnecessary to invoke the historical Islamization of the Golden Horde in interpreting information clearly received by Barbaro from oral informants. In any case, Barbaro would hardly have sought to imply that Edigü, whose son he met personally, was responsible for strengthening Islam 110 years before the 1430s.

53. It cannot be discounted that Barbaro's report may indeed reflect the conscious assertion of Edigü's key role in Islamization by his son Nawrūz; Barbaro met both Nawrūz and the khan Kichik Muḥammad, in "an old mosque" outside the city, when he delivered the gifts dispatched for them by the Venetian consul as their army neared Tana (cf. Hakluyt ed., p. 10; Skrzhinskaia, Russian tr., p. 142, Italian text, p. 118, §17).

54. Cited in Peretiatkovich, *Povolzh'e v XV i XVI vekakh*, p. 134, note; no doubt the same legend is echoed, but with explicit mention only of the move under Jānī Bek, in the travel account of Xavier Hommaire de Hell, *Travels in the Steppes of the Caspian Sea, the Crimea, the Caucasus,*

tomarily assigned to Edigü and his sons have been transferred to Özbek and his son, respectively. Similarly, Evliya Çelebi relates a story in his account of Sarāy about that city's destruction by Temür. It is not clear whether Evliya is inventing wholesale, exercising his penchant for the fantastic, or recording a popular tale current in the seventeenth century; in any event, the story he gives here is a respectable reflection of the conflict between Temür and Toqtamïsh, except that the name of the figure who plays the historically recognizable role of Edigü (i.e,. his conflict with Toqtamïsh, his flight to Temür, and his return with Temür's army in the campaign against Toqtamïsh) is given as "*Özbek Khan*," who is specifically identified as having converted to Islam.[55] The conflation here suggests, again, the real possibility that the strong popular association of both these figures with Islamization—an association that may have involved Baba Tükles in each case—led to their confusion in oral tradition still in circulation in the seventeenth century.

A final element in Edigü's career worthy of consideration here is his relationship with his native tribe, the Manghïts.[56] The Manghït tribal group emerged as such following the Mongol conquest and the "reorganization" of much of the Inner Asian tribal population; its homeland was to the north and east of the Caspian Sea, along the lower Yayïq (Ural) and Itil (Volga) rivers, and it formed the basis of the tribal confederation that emerged there, later to move westwards, which was known in Western sources (including Russian, Polish, Crimean, and Ottoman histories and documents) as the Noghay horde,[57] but in Central Asian sources always as the "Manghït" *ulus*. The status of the Manghït tribe is obscure through much of the fourteenth century, but its leaders, Edigü among them, appear in Timurid histories on several sides of the conflicts within the Golden Horde. Edigü himself, indeed, first appears around 778/1376–1377, before his split with Toqtamïsh, as a Manghït *amīr* fleeing to Temür from Urus

& c. (London: Chapman and Hall, 1847), citing "traditions I collected among the Nogais themselves."

55. *Kniga puteshestviia*, vyp. 2 (Moscow, 1979), pp. 142–143.

56. On this ethnonym and tribal group see Yuri Bregel, "Mangit," *EI*², VI, pp. 417–418, as well as the following article by Bregel on the Manghït dynasty of Bukhara (pp. 418–419).

57. The origin of the designation "Noghay" remains obscure; efforts to connect it with the name of the *amīr* Noghay prominent in the Golden Horde in the latter thirteenth century have remained inconclusive, although the possible significance of Noghay's conversion to Islam, as discussed in Chapter 2, has generally been overlooked in seeking a rationale for the application of his name to a particular people. In any event, no better alternative has been successfully argued, leaving us with the likelihood of some connection between the *amīr* and the ethnonym, but one that remains unexplained.

Khan, Toqtamïsh's enemy; Edigü came to warn Temür that Urus Khan was preparing to pursue Toqtamïsh, who was then under Temür's protection. Nevertheless, one of the envoys sent by Urus Khan to demand that Temür hand over Toqtamïsh was likewise a Manghït, and both Sharaf ad-Dīn ᶜAlī Yazdī and Niẓām ad-Dīn Shāmī blame the later enmity between Toqtamïsh and Temür on a group of "Manghït idiots," who led Toqtamïsh astray from friendship with his erstwhile patron.[58]

Although Edigü's Manghït origins are clear,[59] it is difficult to assess the actual dependence of Edigü upon his tribe, which seems to have been particularly prone to rebellion against not only Toqtamïsh, but any Chingisid ruler. Certainly other Manghït tribal leaders made and broke alliances independently of Edigü, and the latter's political and military activity in the Golden Horde exceeded the bounds of the Manghït tribal domains; it is likewise difficult to judge to what extent Edigü's core of loyal supporters was drawn from the Manghïts once he rose to the height of his power. It is thus not clear whether Edigü should be regarded as the historical founder of the "Noghay horde" or "Manghït *ulus*," nor is it clear precisely when such a confederation can be said to have taken shape. What is clear, however, is that Edigü's descendants played a paramount role in the emergence of the Noghay horde and provided its leaders by the latter fifteenth century, and certainly exerted strong influence well before that. It was clearly Edigü's sons and grandsons who continued his legacy; he had, according to Ibn ᶜArabshāh, "around 20 sons, each a mighty king," and several lineages stemming from Edigü eventually emerged as leading forces in the consolidation of the Noghay confederation. Unfortunately the emergence of that confederation and the roles of Edigü himself and his descendants remain obscure; the decisive period seems to have been the middle quarters of the fifteenth century, a time for which our sources are extremely sparse. What also appears evident, however, is that the emergence of the Noghay horde, with its leadership

58. Cf. Tiz II, pp. 107, 109 (Shāmī), 148, 152 (Yazdī); Tizengauzen (and/or the editors of his assemblage of Persian sources) claims not to know the meaning of the term that precedes "Manghït" in both sources, in the forms "*tālbā*" and "*t.lbah,*" but this is clearly the Turkic *telbe*, "idiot."

59. The Timurid historians confirm this, as does later tradition, but Ibn ᶜArabshāh, ironically, calls his tribe Qonghrat; cf. Tiz I, p. 457. Sanders, tr., p. 75, transcribes "Qomkomat"; the text of Ibn ᶜArabshāh's work remains unavailable in critical edition, and Tizengauzen did not publish the corresponding sections of the original text for this work, but one manuscript I have been able to consult (Cambridge University Library, MS Add. 3237 [described in E. G. Browne, *A Handlist of the Muḥammadan Manuscripts* (Cambridge, 1900), No. 679, undated but probably fifteenth-century], f. 25b) clearly gives the form *q.w.n.k.rāt*.

drawn from the house of Edigü, was linked closely, but in ways which remain obscure, with the nearly simultaneous emergence of the tribal confederation that came to be called "Uzbek."

The latter point deserves further comment here, because it is often neglected in discussions of the roles of Edigü and the Manghïts in the Golden Horde; it also may explain the divergence of the two bodies of popular tradition about the Islamization of the Jöchid *ulus*, one focused on Baba Tükles and the other on Sayyid Ata. The Uzbek confederation took shape as such under the leadership of a Chingisid ruler from the lineage of Jöchi's fifth son Shïban, Abū'l-Khayr Khan, who had consolidated his power in the eastern portion of the Jöchid *ulus* by 1430. Despite his emergence from the so-called *ulus* of Shïban, in the region of western Siberia centered east of the Urals in the vicinity of Tiumen and Tura, a region then called "Ïbïr-Sïbïr," however, Abū'l-Khayr's key support in the consolidation of his rule appears to have come from within the Manghït confederation, with a particularly vital role played by one of Edigü's grandsons, Vaqqāṣ Bīy. The support of the Manghïts followed their temporary submission to a rival Shïbanid prince, Jumaduq, and it appears that Abū'l-Khayr may have been an attractive prospect to some of the Manghït *bīys* because of his youth and the likelihood that he might be a reasonably pliant figure for use in rivalries with other *bīys* or with Chingisid contenders.[60] In any case, with Manghït support Abū'l-Khayr was able to assert his authority in the Shïbanid *ulus*, thereby setting the stage for his short-lived but powerful Uzbek confederation, which successfully challenged Shāhrukh, meddled in Timurid affairs, and prepared the way for the conquest of Mawarannahr under Abū'l-Khayr Khan's grandson, Muḥammad Shïbānī Khan.

The participation of Edigü's grandson Vaqqāṣ Bīy in Abū'l-Khayr Khan's confederation is of particular interest. He joined the new khan shortly before his campaign against Khorezm in 834/1430, suggesting an interest among the Manghït followers of Vaqqāṣ Bīy in reviving the claim on Khorezm established by Edigü's rule there from 1405 to 1412. Although his temporary defection from Abū'l-Khayr is recorded, Vaqqāṣ Bīy seems to have been closely linked with the khan in popular memory as well: he was recalled, in the Shïbanid *Tavārīkh-i guzīdah-i nuṣrat-nāmah* from the early sixteenth century, as having twice been "the reason that the khan obtained the throne of Ṣāyïn [Khan]" (i.e., Batu),[61] while

60. Cf. B. A. Akhmedov, *Gosudarstvo kochevykh uzbekov* (Moscow: Nauka, GRVL, 1965), pp. 43 ff.

61. MS British Museum, Or. 3222, f. 119a; cf. Akramov's publication, p. 266, Iudin's translation in *Materialy po istorii kazakhskikh khanstv*, pp. 16–17, and Berezin, *Sheibaniada*, p. liv.

he is portrayed as Abū'l-Khayr's close confidant and virtual co-ruler in one of the later Tatar histories, from the seventeenth century, discussed below.[62] At the same time, however, Vaqqāṣ Bīy's support evidently did not entail the unanimous support of the Manghït̄s, or even of the descendants of Edigü. The famous Timurid poet and official Mīr ʿAlī-shīr Navāʾī, for instance, mentions the death of a certain Kubravī Sufi shaykh, Mawlānā Ḥusayn Khorezmī—who had been honored by Abū'l-Khayr Khan during his occupation of Khorezm—in the course of "disturbances" in Khorezm caused by a certain "Tan Ṣūfī,"[63] who is surely to be identified with the "Tan Ṣūfī" who was yet another grandson of Edigü.[64] Similarly, Abū'l-Khayr's grandson Muḥammad Shïbānī Khan had to contend with the shifting loyalties of Vaqqāṣ Bīy's son Mūsā, who at different times supported the Abū'l-Khayrid Shïbānī Khan and the rival Shïbānid prince Berke [or "Bürge"] Sulṭān b. Yādgār;[65] other Manghït descendants of Edigü figure on both sides of the frequent conflicts between the two "Uzbek" dynasties established in Khorezm and in Mawarannahr, respectively, in the sixteenth century.

Abū'l-Khayr Khan's "Uzbek" confederation thus included many, but not all, of the Manghït tribal groups, and at least some prominent descendants of Edigü; the same was true of the political and tribal alliances forged under Abū'l-Khayr's "Uzbek" descendants and under their Shïbanid rivals based in Khorezm, well into the sixteenth century. What is not certain, however, is the extent to which "Manghït" and "Uzbek" were practically synonymous in the fifteenth and sixteenth centuries. There are indications that the terms were indeed used almost interchangeably to refer to the same groups. Navāʾī specifically blames the shaykh's "martyrdom" referred to above on the "Uzbeks," while Edigü himself, associated with the "*ulus-i ūzbakī* " already in the work of Muʿīn ad-Dīn Naṭanzī,[66] is specifically called "Edigü the Uzbek" both in fifteenth-century Timurid

62. Berezin, ed., *Sbornik letopisei. Tatarskii tekst,* p. 157.

63. *Majolisun Nafois: ilmiy-tanqidiy tekst,* ed. Suyima Ghanieva (Tashkent: Fan, 1961), text pp. 9–10.

64. Cf. Alexandre Bennigsen, Pertev Naili Boratav et al., *Le khanat de Crimée dans les Archives du Musée du Palais de Topkapı* (Paris: Mouton Éditeur/École des Hautes Études en Sciences Sociales, 1978), p. 74, and Vel'iaminov-Zernov, *Izsledovanie,* II, p. 243.

65. Cf. Abū'l-Ghāzī, ed. Desmaisons, pp. 189–190 (text), 201–202 (tr.). The nineteenth-century Khivan historian Muʾnis makes this Mūsā Bīy into a Qonghrat *amīr* and a descendant of the "Naghdāy" who was prominent at Özbek Khan's court, as discussed in Chapter 2; as noted, Muʾnis makes "Naghdāy" a devotee of Sayyid Ata (cf. Bregel, "Tribal Tradition," pp. 373–374, 391–392, and n. 141 for further historical references to Mūsā).

66. Cf. Tiz II, pp. 133 (tr.), 238 (text).

sources[67] and in later Central Asian sources.[68] As late as the second half of the sixteenth century, the lands of the Noghay horde were referred to as "Uzbekistān" in the hagiographical work mentioned earlier, the *Jāddat al-ʿāshiqīn*, where the designation "Manghït Uzbeks" occurs often.

Altogether the close connection between the Manghïts, the house of Edigü, and the "Uzbeks" (both those loyal to Abū'l-Khayr and others called by that name), as well as the specific association of all three designations with the region of Khorezm, suggest that the Noghay horde should be understood as emerging as a separate political entity, centered north and west of Khorezm, only after the collapse of Abū'l-Khayr Khan's confederation upon his death in 1468, or perhaps as early as the severe shock to his rule brought on by his defeat at the hands of the Mongol Oyrats (i.e., the "Qalmaqs" as they were known in Central Asia) in 1457. By the time of Muḥammad Shïbānī Khan's efforts to revive the Uzbek confederation late in the fifteenth century, the Noghay horde already appears as a distinct, though loose, confederation, with chieftains and tribal groups free to act independently in connection with the states and alliances forming on the fringes of the Manghït world. As noted, various Manghït tribal groups and descendants of Edigü appear both among the emergent Qazaq groups and among Shïbānī Khan's rivals and supporters;[69] we must thus understand the "fragmenting" of the Noghay confederation—which left Manghït and Noghay elements among the tribal components established in Central Asia and among the Qazaqs, for instance—as an ongoing process virtually contemporary with its "consolidation."

In any event, it appears that by this time the elements constituting the Noghay horde came to be drawn increasingly into the network of political relationships that were emerging in the more westerly portions of the Jöchid *ulus* from the mid-fifteenth century on, as the independent khanates of Kazan, Astrakhan, and the Crimea emerged, their fate played out between the competing ambitions of the Russian *tsar'* and the Ottoman *sulṭān*; the subsequent history of the Noghay horde thus departs ever more

67. Cf. Yazdī's *Ẓafar-nāmah*, facsimile ed. Urunbaev, ff. 208b, 210a.

68. E.g., the seventeenth-century *Baḥr al-asrār*, MS India Office Ethé 575, ff. 33a–35b.

69. Some of his Manghït supporters may have established themselves in the Qashqa Darya valley, which became the chief Manghït tribal domain in Mawarannahr, and from which the Manghït tribal chieftains came to dominate the khanate of Bukhara by the mid-eighteenth century, producing the ruling dynasty of Bukhara that survived in power to 1920. It is also possible, however, that despite the presence of Manghït forces in Shïbānī Khan's armies, the Manghïts of Mawarannahr were later immigrants, as is most likely the case with the Manghït groups in Khorezm; cf. Bregel, "Tribal Tradition," pp. 389–390.

sharply from the history of the "Uzbek" states established in Mawarannahr and Khorezm at the beginning of the sixteenth century. This, at least, is the picture conveyed by the available sources, which themselves split along similar lines, as the Central Asian historiographical tradition increasingly turns away from any interest in the affairs of the Volga valley, which after all was dominated by the Russians, and not Chingisids, after the middle of the sixteenth century. The same historical divergence of the "Uzbek" and "Noghay" states may also be reflected in the two traditions about the Islamization of the Jöchid *ulus*, one tradition identifying the bearer of Islam as Sayyid Ata, the other as Baba Tükles; we will return to this issue.

The Noghay horde itself may thus be said to have coalesced under the leadership of Edigü's sons and grandsons, beginning in the mid-fifteenth century, with an especially prominent role played by the lineage of his son Nūr ad-Dīn; the figure of Nūr ad-Dīn came to gain popularity comparable to that of Edigü himself in oral tradition, and his name became the title for the heir-apparent in the Noghay horde, whence it was adopted also into the titulature of the Crimean khanate.[70] Even Nūr ad-Dīn's son Vaqqāṣ, mentioned above as Abū'l-Khayr Khan's ally, occasionally eclipsed his father and grandfather in popular memory. In the early sixteenth century, for instance, it was Vaqqāṣ ("Occass") who was regarded as the "founder" of the Noghay ("Nahaienses") Tatars according to the Latin "Treatise on the Two Sarmatias" by the Polish historian Matthias of Miechow (d. 1523). This account specifies that the sons of "Occass," who is called "servant and officer" to the khan of the principal "Zawolhensian" [i.e., "Trans-Volga"] Tatar horde, split from that horde following their father's death; this split is dated by Matthias to some sev-

70. On the post of "Nuradin" in the Crimean khanate, cf. N. N. Pimenov, tr., "Opisanie Chernago moria i Tatarii, sostavil dominikanets Èmiddio Dortelli d'Askoli, prefekt Kaffy, Tatarii i proch. 1634," *Zapiski Odesskago Obshchestva istorii i drevnostei*, 24 (1902), pp. 89–180 [p. 114]; *Mémoires du Baron de Tott sur les Turcs et les Tartares* (Maestricht: J. E. Dufour & Ph. Roux, 1785), II, pp. 110–111; and see Carl Max Kortepeter, *Ottoman Imperialism during the Reformation: Europe and the Caucasus* (New York: New York University Press, 1972), passim, with extensive references to appointments of *nūr ad-dīn*. On this rank and its origin among the Noghays, [after Edigü's son] whence it was adopted in the Crimean khanate, see Vel'iaminov-Zernov, *Izsledovanie o kasimovskikh tsariakh i tsarevichakh*, ch. 2 (*TVOIRAO*, ch. 10, SPb., 1864), pp. 416–419. Cf. Alexandre Bennigsen and Chantal Lemercier-Quelquejay, "La Moscovie, l'Empire Ottoman et la crise successorale de 1577–1588 dans le Khanat de Crimée: La tradition nomade contre le modèle des monarchies sédentaires," *Cahiers du monde russe et soviétique*, 14 (1973), pp. 453–487, esp. pp. 455–457 on the title *nūr ad-dīn*; on the Noghay origin of the title and its connection with the name of Edigü's son, not discussed in this article, see the same authors' "La Grande Horde Nogay et le problème des communications entre l'Empire Ottoman et l'Asie Centrale en 1552–1556," *Turcica*, 8/2 (1976), pp. 203–236 [p. 209, n. 9].

enty years before he was writing (1517, hence the late 1440s), and Matthias, noting that the *horda* they thus founded (which he calls "*recens et nova*" and the last to emerge from the Trans-Volga horde) had by his time become the largest among the Tatars, affirms that it was still ruled by the sons and grandsons of Occass.[71]

Matthias appears to have relied upon oral accounts, perhaps from travelers, merchants, or captives familiar with the region of interest to him, for his information on the various "Tatar" groups in his day,[72] and thus is of interest here insofar as his account reflects (however dimly) oral tradition among and/or about the Noghays. It is of course difficult, in view of his distance from his subject, to draw conclusions from Matthias's silence on Edigü, but it is not impossible that, already by the beginning of the sixteenth century, certain groups among the Noghays found it useful—for purposes that must remain obscure but that may have included an assertion of the primacy of one lineage descended from Edigü over members of rival lineages—to emphasize Vaqqāṣ Bīy and downplay Edigü;[73] and it may be that this process is reflected in Matthias' account. To be sure, Vaqqāṣ Bīy's prominence stems also from the pivotal role of his son Mūsā

71. Matvei Mekhovskii, *Traktat o dvukh Sarmatiiakh*, ed. and tr. S. A. Anninskii (Moscow/Leningrad: Izd-vo Akademii nauk SSSR, 1936), pp. 92–93 (Russian translation), 170–171 (Latin text).

72. Cf. Anninskii's introduction, pp. 18–20. Matthias divides the "Tatars" into "Zauolhenses" (i.e., beyond the Volga), "Przecopenses" (i.e., Perekop=Crimean), "Cosanenses" (i.e., Kazan), and "Nohacenses" (i.e., Noghay) (cf. p. 63 [tr.], p. 144 [text]); these four *hordae* have "emperors," while a fifth, which he says lacks an emperor, is called "Kazacka" (i.e., Qazaq). He notes that the "Zauolhensian" horde is called the "Great Horde," but confuses it with the Chaghatay *ulus* (the "Czahadai" Tatars), and elsewhere (pp. 85–93 [tr.], 164–171 [text]) explicitly portrays the Perekop, Kazan, and Noghay Tatars—along with the Ottoman dynasty—as essentially "branches" of the Trans-Volga Tatars. He knows virtually nothing of the Kazan khanate, and does not mention the Qazaqs again; but his treatment of the Perekop/Crimean "horde"—which he further identifies as the "Vlan" (i.e., *oghlan*, "prince," indicative of the dynasty's Chingisid status)—is by far the most complete, suggesting that his sources were most familiar with Crimean affairs. Indeed, the nature of his inaccuracies in recounting the history of the "Tatars," from "Cingos" or "Cingkis" on, further suggests his dependence upon oral sources of Crimean provenance: he inserts Temür into his treatment of the Chingisid lineage down to "Sziachmet" (i.e., Shaykh Aḥmad, a central figure in accounts of the formation of the Crimean khanate), by wrongly identifying him with the Chingisid Temür-Qutlugh and thus creating "Aksak Kutlu" (cf. pp. 63–66 [tr.], 144–146 [text]), and elsewhere (pp. 89–92 [tr.], 168–170 [text]) refers to the struggle between Temür and "Tachtamis" (i.e., Toqtamïsh) specificially in the course of recounting the Crimean khanate's history.

73. This possibility is further suggested by the account in Qādir ʿAlī Bek Jalāyirī's work (see below), where the close links between Vaqqāṣ Bīy and Abū'l-Khayr Khan, leader of the nomadic Uzbek confederation in the mid-fifteenth century, are stressed (cf. Berezin, ed., *Sbornik letopisei. Tatarskii tekst*, p. 157).

and the latter's many sons, most of whom were powerful figures in the three-way relations among the Noghays, the Chingisid khanates, and Moscow during the first half of the sixteenth century. It is these lineages, through Vaqqāṣ, that are best known through Russian sources, at a time when other Noghay lines are poorly represented in Central Asian historical sources.

In any event, from the mid-fifteenth century down to the middle of the sixteenth century, the political concerns of the Noghay horde, and of its princes or *mīrzās* from among Edigü's descendants, were focused on resisting Chingisid domination by the khans of the Crimea and Astrakhan, leading the Noghay chiefs into cooperation now with Moscow, now with the Ottomans, and into involvement with the internal succession struggles of the Crimean khanate. The competing interests aroused and addressed by such involvements served to heighten internal tensions among the Noghays, resulting, by the first half of the sixteenth century, in their division into Great and Little Noghay hordes, the former often cooperating with Moscow and the latter drawn into the Ottoman/Crimean sphere of influence. From the middle of the sixteenth century, as Russian pressure increased, culminating in the destruction of the khanates of Kazan and Astrakhan—a success facilitated by the cooperation of the Great Noghay horde and by the disarray in the Crimean khanate stemming from struggles between the khan and tribal chiefs—the two Noghay hordes were led increasingly in these separate directions, with the Little Noghay Horde seeking support from the Crimean khans and their Ottoman patrons, and the Great Noghay Horde pulled into the Russian orbit. The Little Horde managed to remain under Ottoman/Crimean patronage, serving as an ally against Moscow; elements of the Great Horde joined in this status in the seventeenth century in the face of Qalmïq pressure. In the Great Horde, however, internal dissension tended to work in Moscow's favor, and by the end of the sixteenth century Russian domination was secure;[74] we thus find leaders of the Great Noghay Horde effectively in collusion with Moscow against the Chingisids of the Crimea (as earlier, against the Chingisids of Kazan and Astrakhan).

74. On later history of the Noghay hordes and their relations with the Crimean khanate, the Ottomans, and the Russian state, see the useful recent study by B.-A. B. Kochekaev, *Nogaisko-russkie otnosheniia v XV-XVIII vv.* (Alma-Ata, 1988), and the first section of the same author's *Sotsial'no-ėkonomicheskoe i politicheskoe razvitie nogaiskogo obshchestva v XIX-nachale XX veka* (Alma-Ata: Karachaevo-Cherkesskoe Otdelenie Stavropol'skogo Knizhnogo Izdatel'stva, 1973); cf. Kortepeter, *Ottoman Imperialism*, esp. pp. 13–18, 88–91, 97–103, Halil Inalcık, "The Khan and the Tribal Aristocracy: The Crimean Khanate under Sahib Giray I," *HUS*, 3–4/1 (1979–1980), pp. 445–466 (esp. pp. 456–458), and the old survey by Howorth, *History of the Mongols*, II/2

Even after their submission to the Russian tsar, the Noghays of the Great Horde managed to maintain their territories north of the Caspian Sea and in the Volga valley, where their pastoral economy was joined with the urban mercantile centers of Sarāychïq and Astrakhan; Noghay links with the latter city were spurred by the Russian conquest of the Chingisid khanate of Astrakhan and the failure of the Ottoman attempt to drive out the Russians. Astrakhan thus became an important Noghay center, its status strengthened upon the cossack destruction of Sarāychïq toward the end of the sixteenth century; its own position suffered shortly thereafter, however, with the Qalmïq advance.

In the east, tribal groups that had belonged to the Noghay confederation must have begun their assimilation into the Qazaq hordes, as well as among Bashkir and Qaraqalpaq groups, at this time; the process is poorly understood, but the presence of Noghay groups among all these peoples is clear from ethnographic data and epic survivals. In the west, the Noghay hordes survived under Russian control, undergoing further fragmentation and migration due to renewed pressure from the Mongol Qalmïqs throughout the seventeenth century; Noghay domination in the lower Volga valley was effectively shattered in the 1620s, with the advance of the Qalmïqs, who drove the Noghays of the Great Horde westwards and settled in the vicinity of Astrakhan, and the Noghay-Qalmïq rivalry persisted, to shape the Noghay heroic epics, even after the "return" of the larger body of Qalmïqs to the east beginning in 1771. The Noghays were increasingly pushed to the south and west, into the Kuban and the steppes north of the Caucasus, but recognizable "Noghay" hordes continued to exist above and beyond the individual designations of the constituent tribes. The ethnonym "Noghay" survived as well, and although several groups were eventually assimilated among the "Tatar" population of the Crimean khanate, still others remained in the vicinity of Astrakhan or moved into the steppelands of the North Caucasus, where the "Noghay" nationality numbered more than 75,000 in the 1989 Soviet census; the modern Noghays are still divided into the Qara-Noghay and Aq-Noghay groups, reflecting the former division of the Greater and

(1880), pp. 1011–1068. On the Noghay role in the Ottoman project of 1569 to drive the Russians from Astrakhan, see Alexandre Bennigsen, "L'Expédition turque contre Astrakhan en 1569 d'après les Registres des 'Affaires importantes' des Archives ottomanes," *Cahiers du monde russe et soviétique*, 8 (1967), pp. 427–446 (with a survey of sources and earlier studies); Kortepeter, *Ottoman Imperialism*, pp. 27–32; and the later article of Bennigsen and Mihnea Berindei, "Astrakhan et la politique des steppes nord pontiques (1587–1588)," *HUS*, 3–4/1 (1979–1980), pp. 71–91.

Lesser Noghay hordes, respectively, and despite their sedentarization and collectivization appear to retain a consciousness of tribal affiliation (e.g., to tribes such as the Yedisan, Jambuyluq, Yedishkul, Mansur, etc.).[75]

The history of Edigü and the Noghay hordes provides the backdrop for the further development of the tales about Baba Tükles, as noted; but in fact these developments are known from "historical" literature only through sources produced outside the Noghay environment, which unfortunately, but characteristically, produced no written literature. As we will see in Chapter 6, the Noghay hordes produced a rich oral epic tradition crucial for our understanding of Baba Tükles. But for his development in historical and genealogical tradition, we must turn to literary sources produced in each of the three major cultural centers bordering on the Noghay realm: the Ottoman world and the Crimea, Central Asia, and Russia.

Reworking the Account of Ötemish Ḥājjī: ʿAbd al-Ghaffār Qïrïmī in the Eighteenth Century

The historical treatment of Baba Tükles most closely resembling that of Ötemish Ḥājjī is found in an eighteenth-century Ottoman universal history, the *ʿUmdat al-akhbār*, written in the Crimea in 1157/1744 by ʿAbd

75. On the modern Noghays and their status in the former Soviet Union, cf. Alexandre Bennigsen and S. Enders Wimbush, *Muslims of the Soviet Empire: A Guide* (Bloomington: Indiana University Press, 1986), pp. 170–171. See also, for ethnographic and historical studies of the Noghays of the North Caucasus, Kochekaev, *Sotsial'no-èkonomicheskoe i politicheskoe razvitie*, S. Sh. Gadzhieva, *Material'naia kul'tura nogaitsev v XIX-nachale XX v.* (Moscow: Nauka, 1976), and earlier (pre-Soviet) descriptive accounts, e.g.: "Kratkii obzor polozheniia nogaiskikh tatar, vodvorennykh v Melitopol'skom uezde Tavricheskoi gubernii," *Teleskop*, 1833, ch. 33, pp. 3–23, 210–230, 269–297; A. Arkhipov, "Ètnograficheskii ocherk Nogaitsev i Turkmen," *Kavkazskii kalendar' 1859* (Tiflis, 1858, year 14) pp. 347–355; I. Kornilov, "Zametki ob Astrakhanskoi gubernii," *Vestnik Imperatorskago Russkago Geograficheskago Obshchestva*, ch. 27 (1859), otd. 2, pp. 1–48; Hermann Vámbéry, *Das Türkenvolk in seinen ethnologischen und ethnographischen Beziehungen* (1885; repr. Osnabrück: Biblio Verlag, 1970), pp. 543–566; S. V. Farfarovskii, "Narodnoe obrazovanie u nogaitsev Severnago Kavkaza v sviazi s ikh sovremennym bytom," *Zhurnal Ministerstva narodnago prosveshcheniia*, 1909, ch. 24, No. 12, pp. 179–212; and especially I. L. Shcheglov, *Trukhmeny i Nogaitsy Stavropol'skoi gubernii: Svedeniia o khoziaistve osedlykh i kochuiushchikh inorodtsev, russkikh krest'ian i khutorian-ovtsevodov v Trukhmenskoi i Achikulakskoi stepi Stavropol'skoi gubernii* (Stavropol': Tipografiia Gubernskago Pravleniia, 1910).

al-Ghaffār b. Ḥasan b. Maḥmūd b. ʿAbd al-Vahhāb al-Qïrïmī;[76] the work, dedicated in its original form to the Crimean ruler Girey Khan b. Qaplān Girey, is of value as an independent historical source on the Crimean khanate and its Chingisid antecedents. It survives in a single manuscript, in Istanbul,[77] and has remained relatively little studied despite its availability in published form.[78]

For our purposes the importance of ʿAbd al-Ghaffār's work lies in its use of Ötemish Ḥājjī's account for the earlier history of the Jöchid *ulus* from the time of Chingis Khan. In his introduction, ʿAbd al-Ghaffār mentions Ötemish Ḥājjī's history among his sources, referring to it as the

76. Cf. Bursalı Mehmed Tâhir Bey, *Osmanlı müellifleri,* ed. İsmail Özen (İstanbul: Yaylacık Matbaası, 1975), vol. 3, p. 23, referring to ʿAbd al-Ghaffār b. Ḥasan Qïrïmī's "esteemed *ʿUmdat al-akhbār;*" see also F. Babinger, *Die Geschichtschreiber der Osmanen und ihre Werke* (Leipzig, 1927), p. 280; and the Turkish ed., tr. Coşkun Üçok, *Osmanlı tarih yazarları ve eserleri* (Ankara: Kültür ve Turizm Bakanlığı, 1982), pp. 306–307. The author indicates the date and his full name in his introduction, Najīb ʿĀṣim ed., pp. 5–6.

77. MS Esad Efendi MS No. 2331, 329 ff.; described in *İstanbul kütüpaneleri* [*sic*] *tarih-coğrafya yazmaları katalogları,* I: *Türkçe tarih yazmaları,* 1. fasikül, *Umumi tarihler* (Istanbul: Maarif Matbaası, 1943), pp. 13–14, Cat. No. 3. The manuscript is paginated with two series of folio numbers, one with "Latin" numerals and the other with Arabic-script numerals. The Arabic-script series runs two behind the Latin series until f. 317 [Latin]/315 [Arabic], but thereafter runs three ahead until the end of the manuscript (f. 318 [Latin] /321 [Arabic] through the final folio, f. 326 [Latin] /329 [Arabic]; assuming the Arabic series to be the earlier of the two, it would appear that five folios have been lost, as further suggested by the discrepancy in the catchwords between Arabic folios 315b and 321a. The section on the descendants of Chingis Khan, of which Prof. Schamiloglu provided me with a copy, begins on f. 243 [Latin] /241 [Arabic]; the main body of the text ends on f. 324a [Latin] /327a [Arabic], but the following section (on the wise counsel of Buzurjmihr, ff. 324b–326a [Latin] /327b–329a [Arabic] is evidently also by ʿAbd al-Ghaffār.

78. The printed edition of Najīb ʿĀṣim, which includes only the introduction and the sections on the Jöchid *ulus* and the Crimean khanate, was noted earlier. The work was consulted by Spuler, and since his work's appearance it has been used or noted in Barbara Kellner-Heinkele, *Aus den Aufzeichnungen des Saʿīd Giray Sulṭān: eine zeitgenössische Quelle zur Geschichte des Chanats der Krim um die Mitte des 18. Jahrhunderts* (Freiburg im Breisgau: Klaus Schwarz Verlag, 1975), in İnalcık, "The Khan and the Tribal Aristocracy," again by İnalcık in his "Power Relationships between Russia, the Crimea and the Ottoman Empire as Reflected in Titulature," in *Passé turco-tatar, présent soviétique: Études offertes à Alexandre Bennigsen,* ed. Ch. Lemercier-Quelquejay, G. Veinstein, and S. E. Wimbush (Louvain/Paris: Éditions Peeters/ Éditions de l'École des Hautes Études en Sciences Sociales, 1986), pp. 175–211, and in U. Schamiloglu, "The *Qaraçı* Beys of the Later Golden Horde: Notes on the Organization of the Mongol World Empire," *AEMA,* 4 (1984), pp. 283–297 [pp. 284–285]; the latter writer has now published a separate survey of the source, "The *Umdet ül-Ahbar* and the Turkic Narrative Sources for the Golden Horde and the Later Golden Horde," in *Central Asian Monuments,* ed. Hasan B. Paksoy (Istanbul: Isis Press, 1992), pp. 81–93. Curiously, ʿAbd al-Ghaffār's work is not mentioned in Bennigsen et al., *Le khanat de Crimée.* So far as I know only Çağatay, "Die Ädigä-Sage," notes the inclusion of the tale of Baba Tükles in the work (cf. p. 276).

"*Tārīkh-i Dūst Sulṭān-i Ūzbakī*";[79] and it is clear that ʿAbd al-Ghaffār has relied upon this work heavily for his treatment of the early khans of the Jöchid *ulus*. In most cases he did not, however, simply copy Ötemish Ḥājjī's account, but instead omitted or altered what he found there, or sought to introduce material from other sources when available. Although he names several other works as among his sources,[80] ʿAbd al-Ghaffār rarely indicates his source for specific narratives, and rarely makes explicit any critical evaluation of the traditions to which he had access.

In the case of his account of Özbek Khan's conversion, however, ʿAbd al-Ghaffār's version unquestionably depends upon Ötemish Ḥājjī's work, either directly or through some unknown intermediate source; in view of his mention of Ötemish Ḥājjī's work, the former is most likely, but ʿAbd al-Ghaffār has extensively reworked the narrative, expanding some sections for stylistic or explanatory purposes (in the latter case usually obscuring the intent of the "original"), omitting some elements entirely, and making a few substantive additions or interpretations. The features omitted are often important elements in Ötemish Ḥājjī's narrative, and it is not clear whether ʿAbd al-Ghaffār chose to leave them out because he did not understand them, because he did not consider them important, or because he did not believe them; the latter seems unlikely, inasmuch as it implies that he "believed" the rest. In other cases it seems clear that either ʿAbd al-Ghaffār, or the copyist or intermediate author who produced the copy or adaptation of Ötemish Ḥājjī's work which ʿAbd al-Ghaffār had at hand, found the original account incomprehensible; in such instances ʿAbd al-Ghaffār's version gives the impression that the narrative, or merely specific terminology, has been "adjusted" in order to make sense out of it, and it appears likely that much of the problematical terminology in Ötemish Ḥājjī's account was already unfamiliar to ʿAbd al-Ghaffār or his source.

These terminological issues are noted in the commentary on the trans-

79. Najīb ʿĀṣim ed., p. 7.

80. These range from an abridgment of aṭ-Ṭabarī's history to a number of Ottoman and Arabic chronicles, as well as the Persian histories of al-Bayżāvī and "ʿAlī al-Yazdī" (i.e., Sharaf ad-Dīn ʿAlī Yazdī's history of Timur, the *Ẓafar-nāmah*, which ʿAbd al-Ghaffār however calls the "*Tārīkh-i Jahān-gushāy*"). Most of the sources he names could only have provided him with material for the earlier sections of his work, which he casts as a universal history leading up to a focus on the Chingisids of the Dasht-i Qïpchaq and the Crimea; the only sources he names of clear relevance for Chingisid history are the *Kunh al-akhbār*, which was not the source of the supplementary material on Özbek Khan's conversion, and an otherwise unknown "*Tārīkh-i Āpūshqā-yi Chingīzī*" (*abušqa* here apparently implying "ancestor").

lation of Ötemish Ḥājjī's account in Appendix 2; here we may mention a few interesting variations on themes already present in Ötemish Ḥājjī's account, before turning to the more substantive additions found in ʿAbd al-Ghaffār's work. To begin with, his Ottoman version provides a stylized rationale for the choice of "tests" by evoking the Islamic topos of infidel (in this case Mongol) "fire-worship"; the account ascribes the ordeal of entering the ovens to the khan's command, since in his words, "Nothing is stronger than fire, and so we worship it." This appeal to a stereotyped version of the religious rival to Islam appears well within a tradition of constructing conversion narratives around "contests" with "infidels" imagined in such a way that only dim reflections of actual Inner Asian religious practice remain.

ʿAbd al-Ghaffār's treatment of the drinking ceremony[81] is discussed in the notes to the complete translation in Appendix 2, but we may note here that his version makes the four saints consciously and purposefully set about reciting the *dhikr* and invoking blessings upon Muḥammad in order to disrupt the event, adding a Qurʾānic reference for the confounding of the Mongols' "sorcery."[82] He also adds here the pagan sorcerers' derision of the Muslim community as they explain why the ceremony was spoiled: they blame the presence of men from among "the deluded people (*āzġūn ṭāʾifah*) called Muḥammadī."

In the account of the ordeal itself, the two ovens (and in this case the *süksegül* wood), as well as the forced "entry" of one of the "sorcerers" into the oven are noted as in Ötemish Ḥājjī's account; ʿAbd al-Ghaffār adds the judgment that the unfortunate sorcerer was indeed cast into hell. ʿAbd al-Ghaffār makes no mention, however, of several important elements connected with the oven-pit as told in Ötemish Ḥājjī's version of the tale. Baba Tükles' armor is not mentioned, nor is his body hair, either in connection with "explaining" Baba Tükles' name or with regard to the vivid image of the saint's body hair standing on end and protruding out through his armor. The only allusion to the element of the saint's body hair is in fact more reminiscent of the tale of Sarï Saltïq noted earlier; ʿAbd al-Ghaffār remarks that when Baba Tükles entered the oven, "trusting in eternal life," "he attained to the [state of] intimacy with and proximity to the Creator of Possibilities, and through the inviolability of those beloved by God, not a single hair of his was harmed." There is likewise no mention in the

81. Ed. Najīb ʿĀṣim, p. 36.

82. XVII.81: "Say: 'Truth has arrived, and Falsehood has perished, for Falsehood is ever bound to perish.' "

Ottoman account of the sheep's flesh hung over the oven; and although this "updated" version inserts an especially remarkable interpretation at the point in the narrative when Baba Tükles emerges from the fire-pit, as discussed below, the drama of Ötemish Ḥājjī's account is somewhat lost in ʿAbd al-Ghaffār's telling, which concludes by noting that when the people opened the oven, the saint emerged sweating "as if in a *ḥammām*."

More significant for present purposes are the occasional additions in this eighteenth-century work, or at least those that amount to substantive insertions rather than stylistic or explanatory expansions of the account known from Ötemish Ḥājjī's work. To begin with we may note two additions ʿAbd al-Ghaffār makes outside the specific narrative of Özbek Khan's conversion. One appears near the end of the work, where he gives a brief account of the descendants of Edigü and their role in the Crimean khanate; before turning to Edigü's descendants, however, he traces his ancestry, providing a genealogy, quite similar to those known from a variety of works discussed below, which makes Baba Tükles a sixth-generation ancestor of Edigü. Remarkably, though, ʿAbd al-Ghaffār presents this genealogy virtually without comment; although at this point in his work he had already recounted Baba Tükles' role in Özbek Khan's conversion, here he simply lists the genealogical links, citing as his source unspecified "histories of the Uzbeks."[83]

What is more interesting, in his introduction to the *ʿUmdat al-akhbār*, ʿAbd al-Ghaffār highlights the conversion of Özbek Khan as a signal event in the history of the Jöchid *ulus*, and, summarizing the account he gives more fully later, speaks of the time when "four saints possessed of discernment came to Özbek Khan from the holy presence of Najm ad-Dīn Kubrā, and, summoning him to Islām and manifesting miracles, brought him to the path of Islām."[84] In this concise statement ʿAbd al-Ghaffār alludes to what must have been already a well-known feature of narratives about Özbek Khan's conversion, namely, the four saints referred to in Ötemish Ḥājjī's account, in the Central Asian stories ascribing the conversion to Sayyid Ata, and in the accounts drawn from the Tatar histories discussed below; ʿAbd al-Ghaffār goes further, as we will see, giving names to all four of the saints.

In mentioning Najm ad-Dīn Kubrā, however, the eighteenth-century

83. MS f. 322b [Latin] /325b [Arabic]; Najīb ʿĀṣim ed., pp. 203–204. We will return to ʿAbd al-Ghaffār's version of this genealogy below, in connection with accounts in which Edigü's descent from Baba Tükles is a central element in the narrative, rather than an afterthought.

84. Najīb ʿĀṣim ed., p. 8.

author is adding an element known from no other source dealing with Özbek Khan's conversion. Now it is well known that the disciples of Najm ad-Dīn Kubrā, the renowned Sufi shaykh killed in 618/1221 during the Mongol assault on Khorezm, played an active role in promoting Islam among the Mongols in the thirteenth and fourteenth centuries; in the best-known examples, Sayf ad-Dīn Bākharzī's relationship with Berke was noted above, and Saʿd ad-Dīn Muḥammad Ḥammūyī and his son Ṣadr ad-Dīn Ibrāhīm were both active among the Mongols of Iran, the latter's efforts culminating, by most accounts, in the conversion of the Ilkhanid ruler Ghāzān Khan in 1295. Other followers also played important roles in the Islamization of the Turkified Mongol tribes in the three western Mongol successor states—the Golden Horde, the Chaghatay *ulus*, and Ilkhanid Iran—and in the establishment of state support for Islam at the Mongol courts; the irony of Najm ad-Dīn Kubrā's death at the hands of the Mongols, followed by his disciple's success in winning over the Mongols to Islam, was not lost on later writers.[85]

It is in all likelihood in appreciation of this irony—which, however, he does not mention, omitting any mention of the shaykh customarily ascribed responsibility for Ghāzān's conversion in his account of this khan[86]—or by extrapolation from the role of Sayf ad-Dīn Bākharzī, whose relationship with Berke he *does* discuss extensively, following Ötemish Ḥājjī's account,[87] that ʿAbd al-Ghaffār, in his introduction, links Najm ad-Dīn Kubrā with the four saints who converted Özbek Khan; there is no reference at all to Kubrā in the actual narrative account of the conversion, nor even in ʿAbd al-Ghaffār's additions to the account.

Nevertheless, it is not impossible that some reference to the activity of Najm ad-Dīn Kubrā's disciples in the Jöchid *ulus* may have been found in sources at ʿAbd al-Ghaffār's disposal that have not survived. As I have noted elsewhere,[88] Kubrā's disciple known as Bābā Kamāl Jandī was active among the Turkic nomads of the region along the lower Syr

85. Cf. Ḥusayn Karbalāʾī Tabrīzī, *Rawżāt al-jinān va jannāt al-janān*, ed. Jaʿfar Sulṭān al-Qurrāʾī, vol. 2 (Tehran: Bungāh-i Tarjimah va Nashr-i Kitāb, 1349/1970), p. 327; here Kubrā, before his death at Mongol hands, is made to prophesy his successor's role in the conversion of Ghāzān.

86. MS f. 252a [Latin] / 250a [Arabic].

87. See MS, ff. 259b [Latin] / 257b [Arabic]–260b [Latin] / 258b [Arabic]; Najīb ʿĀṣim ed., pp. 21–24. ʿAbd al-Ghaffār erroneously calls the shaykh who figures in the story of Berke "Sayf ad-Dīn Khorezmī"; Ötemish Ḥājjī's version of the story (Tashkent MS, f. 41b) gives no *nisbah* for this Shaykh Sayf ad-Dīn, but the shaykh's identity is clear from Ötemish Ḥājjī's mention of his appellation "Shaykh al-ʿĀlam" and from his identification as a successor of Najm ad-Dīn Kubrā.

88. "Eclipse of the Kubravīyah," pp. 50–51; cf. my "Bābā Kamāl Jandī."

Darya that belonged to the Golden Horde, and echoes of his activity may have inspired stories of the "Kamāl Ata" discussed above.

In any event, we at present have no way of judging the inspiration of ʿAbd al-Ghaffār's mention of Kubrā in this context, and no other known account provides any basis for linking the four saints mentioned in connection with Özbek Khan's conversion with Kubrā; the most likely explanation is that ʿAbd al-Ghaffār did indeed have access to narratives mentioning the activity of Kubrā's disciples among the Chingisids, perhaps even echoes of Baba Kamāl, and combined his sources in a way he quite clearly did in other instances (see below) to discover that the four saints *must have been* successors of Kubrā. Otherwise, it is possible that he had access to literary works in which Sayf ad-Dīn Bākharzī's role in converting Berke to Islam was displaced by the mention of Bākharzī's master, Kubrā; such displacement occurs in some later Arabic histories, but again we cannot be sure of ʿAbd al-Ghaffār's dependence upon them.

The other substantive additions provided by ʿAbd al-Ghaffār appear at the beginning and end of the actual account of Özbek Khan's conversion, and it unfortunately remains unclear whether he might have derived these additions from other, perhaps no longer extant, written sources or adapted them from oral tradition known to him. At the beginning of the account,[89] beyond the supplementary detail that the four Muslim saints came to the khan's "capital," Sarāy, ʿAbd al-Ghaffār's account provides the names of all four of these saints, with an interesting departure from Ötemish Ḥājjī's version: for Ötemish Ḥājjī and presumably for his source in compiling his work from oral narratives, Baba Tükles is the *only* one of the four saints whose name is recorded, but for ʿAbd al-Ghaffār, Baba Tükles is not even the *senior* saint among the four. According to ʿAbd al-Ghaffār, "the greatest among these saints" (*ušbū ʿazīzlerin büyükleri*) was Shaykh Majd ad-Dīn Shirvānī, "the grandfather [or simply "ancestor," *jadd*] of the famous scholar, the holy Sayyid Yaḥyā, who was among the descendants of the holy ʿAlī and a *sayyid* of sound pedigree;" one of them was a descendant of Muḥammad b. Abū Bakr aṣ-Ṣiddīq (i.e., the son of the Caliph Abū Bakr), "Bābā Tükläs Shaykh Najīb ad-Dīn;" another was Shaykh Aḥmad, a descendant of "Muḥammad-i Ḥanafīyah-i ʿAlavīyah" (i.e., a descendant of the son of ʿAlī known as Muḥammad b. al-Ḥanafīyah, born by another wife [from the Ḥanafī tribe] of ʿAlī, and thus an ʿAlid but not a *sayyid*); and the last was Shaykh

89. Najīb ʿĀṣim ed., pp. 35–36; MS f. 263a [Latin] / 261a [Arabic].

Ḥasan Kūrkānī/Gūrgānī, of whose lineage nothing is said.

This list is of interest in a number of regards. First, it is the only known source to assign a standard *laqab* to Baba Tükles, indicating that ʿAbd al-Ghaffār, if he did not, as seems unlikely, simply invent it, had access to some other written or oral source identifying Baba Tükles as a "Najīb ad-Dīn." In addition, ʿAbd al-Ghaffār's mention of Baba Tükles' descent from the Caliph Abū Bakr echoes this element of the accounts of Baba Tükles in the other Tatar histories noted below, in the Central Asian hagiography where his genealogy appears, in Russian aristocratic traditions, and in several of the epic tales discussed below. There is no mention in Ötemish Ḥājjī's work of Baba Tükles having been a descendant of Abū Bakr, and it is clear that ʿAbd al-Ghaffār must have taken this from some other source; the frequent and evidently independent citation of this descent in these varied sources attests to the currency of narratives about Baba Tükles asserting his link to such a lineage. We may note here that Baba Tükles, although listed second among the four saints after the senior figure named, is still the hero of the narrative in ʿAbd al-Ghaffār's account; it is still Baba Tükles who enters the fire and provides the decisive proof of Islam's superiority. And, following the list of the four shaykhs, ʿAbd al-Ghaffār inserts the note—taken up more extensively at the end of his account of the conversion—that "the aforementioned Baba Tükles" is said to be the *jadd-i aʿlā* [again, "great-grandfather," or "illustrious ancestor"] of Edigü [spelled in this work *adīgū*] Beg.

ʿAbd al-Ghaffār's mention of Shaykh Aḥmad should most probably be taken as a sign of the Ottoman author's familiarity with narratives of Central Asian origin ascribing a role in Özbek Khan's conversion to Sayyid Ata, whose name was Aḥmad; at the same time, mention of this Shaykh Aḥmad's descent from Muḥammad b. al-Ḥanafīyah may reflect the existence of a tradition ascribing such a role to Khoja Aḥmad Yasavī, whose descent from Muḥammad b. al-Ḥanafīyah was a standard biographical element noted in Central Asian hagiographies dealing with Yasavī, or, as seems more likely, a simple confusion between Khoja Aḥmad Yasavī and Sayyid Aḥmad, known as Sayyid Ata, who was by all accounts a spiritual descendant of Aḥmad Yasavī. As noted, there is reliable and early testimony supporting the historicity of a figure known as Sayyid Ata having contributed to Özbek Khan's conversion; more important, narratives explicitly ascribing this figure such a role were recorded relatively early as well, and both factors would appear to strengthen the likelihood that allusions to, or explicit assertions of, Khoja Aḥmad Yasavī's role in Özbek Khan's conversion reflect a confusion or corrupt transmission of tales assigning this role to Yasavī's spiritual descendant, Sayyid Ata, rather than to any "original" or independently transmitted narrative actually claiming such a role for Aḥmad Yasavī. Such confusion is, finally, quite understandable in view of the greater prominence of Aḥmad Yasavī, whose name was known much more widely than that of Sayyid Ata. Indeed, the fact that ʿAbd al-Ghaffār does not identify this "Shaykh Aḥmad" as Aḥmad Yasavī probably attests further to the confusion already present in the sources available to the eighteenth-century author. ʿAbd al-Ghaffār would surely have known of Aḥmad Yasavī, a figure of considerable prominence in traditions known among Anatolian, as well as Central and Inner Asian, Sufi circles; he may also have known enough about Yasavī to be aware of his dates and of his reputed genealogy, and his failure to identify "Shaykh Aḥmad" as Aḥmad Yasavī may with equal likelihood indicate either that his source was silent on this question, or that as a critical historian concerned with precisely those issues—such as dates—that mattered less to the transmitters of the type of narratives in which Sayyid Ata could be easily displaced by Aḥmad Yasavī, ʿAbd al-Ghaffār recognized the confusion in his source and chose not to believe it, retaining from that source only the name and the lineage.

Here we should stress that in naming these four saints, ʿAbd al-Ghaffār was no doubt attempting to make "historical" sense out of traditions to which he had access, just as in dealing with Ötemish Ḥājjī's narrative he tried to make linguistic sense out of unfamiliar terminology, and religious sense out of descriptions of practices that were no longer familiar. In each case he may well have been approaching narratives based on oral tradition with a historian's interest in comparing and utilizing the sources available to him, and in each case his historian's motivation served to obscure and distort rather than illuminate or clarify; in the process he failed even to preserve the integrity of his sources.

In any event, it is worth noting that the identification of one of the four saints—whose number was known to ʿAbd al-Ghaffār from Ötemish Ḥājjī's account, ultimately—as "Shaykh Aḥmad" represents a somewhat artificial reconstruction based on the Ottoman author's learned consideration of other accounts. Less artificial—and, thankfully, less "learned"—though of no greater or lesser "authenticity," may be the epic accounts in which Baba Tükles *himself* is identified as a saint named "Aḥmad," as discussed below; and we will see yet another example of a "learned" effort to make sense out of the multiple traditions surrounding the name and identity of the figure or figures instrumental in the conversion of Özbek Khan.

Of "Shaykh Ḥasan Gūrgānī" nothing more is known or suggested. His *nisbah* might appear to make him a native of Gurgān near the southeastern shore of the Caspian Sea, but I have not yet found any reference to a shaykh of this name in any other source. On the other hand the spelling of his *nisbah*, "*kūr.kān*," recalls the Mongol title "*güregän*," "son-in-law," borne, for instance, by Temür, as a sign of marital bonds with a Chingisid khan; but such a supposition is no more helpful in identifying the figure ʿAbd al-Ghaffār had in mind.

With the first, and senior, saint, however, we have an interesting innovation on ʿAbd al-Ghaffār's part, for here he links the conversion of Özbek Khan with a prominent figure in the lineage of the Khalvatī Sufi order, Sayyid Yahyā Shirvānī. The Khalvatī order, active throughout the Ottoman world, was established in the Crimea as well,[90] and ʿAbd al-Ghaffār's insertion of a shaykh associated with it into this adaptation of Ötemish Ḥājjī's narrative no doubt marks an effort (by ʿAbd al-Ghaffār himself, or as is more likely, by Khalvatī shaykhs resident in the Crimea to whose traditions ʿAbd al-Ghaffār had access) to link a Sufi order newly active in a part of the former Golden Horde with the establishment of Islam there. Whatever ʿAbd al-Ghaffār's own relationship may have been with the Khalvatīyah, the high status he assigns to Majd ad-Dīn Shirvānī ought to be borne in mind when considering other conversion narratives shaped within Sufi circles, and further supports the contention that "conversion" work brought considerable prestige.

The primacy assigned to this Majd ad-Dīn Shirvānī in ʿAbd al-Ghaffār's account thus seems clearly designed to highlight the prestige of the natural descendants, and perhaps spiritual as well, of his "grandson" Sayyid Yaḥyā Shirvānī, still known in ʿAbd al-Ghaffār's day. As to the "accuracy" of ʿAbd al-Ghaffār's information, it is difficult to judge. Little is known of the natural genealogy of Sayyid Yaḥyā Shirvānī, who died in 868 or 869/1463–1465 and is customarily regarded as the "founder" of the Khalvatī Sufi order—or, more properly, of the longest-surviving branches of this order that flourished in the Ottoman lands and Egypt down to the present century;[91] our sources on him give only his Sufi

90. Evliya Çelebi, in the mid-seventeenth century, mentions Khalvatī lodges in Kaffa; cf. *Evliyā Çelebī sayāḥat-nāmesi*, vol. 7 (Istanbul: Devlet Maṭbuʿası, 1928), p. 677.

91. See, on Sayyid Yaḥyā Shirvānī and the Khalvatīyah, Hans Joachim Kissling, "Aus der Geschichte des Chalvetijje-Ordens," *ZDMG*, 103 (1953), pp. 233–289, and B. G. Martin, "A

silsilah,[92] which does not include any figure explicitly called "Majd ad-Dīn Shirvānī." As for this Majd ad-Dīn, we have one mention of a figure by this name in the early fourteenth-century Arabic biographical compendium of Ibn al-Fuwaṭī. He gives a short reference to "Majd ad-Dīn Abū'l-Majd b. Sanjar b. Muḥammad, who settled in Tabrīz, ash-Shirwānī," who he says was a *qāżī* in Shirwān; Ibn al-Fuwaṭī affirms that "I saw him in Tabrīz in the year 673; he was a learned shaykh and *faqīh* and gnostic . . . he was *qāżī* in Shirwān and a *mudarris* there."[93] We have no basis on which to insist on the identity of these figures, however, nor any indication of ʿAbd al-Ghaffār's source for these names. It is nevertheless possible that his account reflects internal traditions among Khalvatī groups (or *sayyids* descended from Yaḥyā Shirvānī) about their "ancestor's" role in the Islamization of the Golden Horde; and as noted earlier, the Bulghar tombstones attest to a substantial Shirvānī presence in the region.

ʿAbd al-Ghaffār's other substantive additions, and the most revealing, come near the end of the account of Özbek Khan's conversion as adapted from Ötemish Ḥājjī's work. After recounting Baba Tükles' protest that he was in no hurry to come out of the oven, the author adds a remarkable interpretation evidently unique to ʿAbd al-Ghaffār's account: because Baba Tükles did not finish his appeal and prayer, by God's will, he declared, "a certain number of tribes from among this Mongol and Tatar people had to remain without the benefit of Islām; and in fact, the group from among the Tatars whom they call Qalmaq, which is to be understood as the Ṭūrghāʾūt, was left without becoming Muslim."[94] This explanation, whether it reflects ʿAbd al-Ghaffār's own originality or the currency in his

Short History of the Khalwati Order of Dervishes," in *Scholars, Saints, and Sufis: Muslim Religious Institutions since 1500*, ed. Nikki R. Keddie (Berkeley and Los Angeles: University of California Press, 1972), pp. 275–305; there is still no adequate treatment of the earliest phases of the Khalvatī lineages, however, and the era of Yaḥyā Shirvānī as well remains to be explored.

92. See Kissling's table, p. 283; the *silsilah*, known only from sixteenth-century sources, links Sayyid Yaḥyā through five generations (mostly Shirvānīs, and two listed without *laqabs* and hence potentially identifiable with Majd ad-Dīn) to Shaykh Ibrāhīm Zāhid, who also heads the *silsilah* adopted by the Ṣafavīyah.

93. Portions of Ibn al-Fuwaṭī's *Talkhīṣ Majmaʿ al-adab* were edited and serialized in *Oriental College Magazine* (Lahore) from 1939 to 1947, with separate pagination; cf. the *lām-mīm* volume, p. 217, No. 441 for this Majd ad-Dīn, and p. 161, No. 318 for yet another: Majd ad-Dīn Abū Muḥammad ʿAbd ar-Raḥīm b. ʿAbd al-ʿAzīz b. al-Ḥusayn ash-Shirwānī aṣ-Ṣūfī, of whom little is noted except that he reported a saying, through one intermediary, from a figure who died in the early thirteenth century (Bahāʾ ad-Dīn ʿAlī b. Muḥammad b. as-Sāʿātī, d. 604/1207, cf. *GAL* I, p. 256, *GALS* I, p. 456).

94. *ušbū qavm-i muġūl va tātār-dan bir miqdār qavm islām-dan bī-bahra qalmaq kerek dedi; va nafs al-amr-da ṭūrġāūt taʿbīr olunan tātār-dan qalmaq dedikleri ṭāʾifah musulmān olmayup qaldï.*

time of popular tales asserting this etymological interpretation, provides a striking example of imagining both self and other in terms of a holy founder's action (or lack of it), and we will return to it shortly.

Next ʿAbd al-Ghaffār summarizes that when Baba Tükles came out of the oven, Özbek Khan and his commanders and troops accepted Islam, and those shaykhs taught them the statutes of religion and "from east to west provided guidance (*irshād*) to Tātārstān." Then, once again on a genealogical note, he adds that in his time there were still descendants of Sayyid Yaḥyā Shirvānī living, and that "the descendants of Baba Tükles followed the path of *beglik*," that is, served as *beks*;[95] and, adds ʿAbd al-Ghaffār, "The statement to the effect that the illustrious and intrepid [man] they call Edigü Bek was of his lineage is sound, and is declared in the histories of the Uzbeks."[96] Finally, the account concludes by noting that "it is for this reason that these Tatars who became an Islamic people are called 'the people of Özbek'."[97]

ʿAbd al-Ghaffār thus joins a wide variety of authors in interpreting the ethnonym Uzbek as rooted in Özbek Khan's conversion to Islam. More intriguing, however, is what he adds to this interpretation in his account of Baba Tükles' incomplete prayers inside the oven: some of Özbek Khan's "Tatars" did not become Muslims and adopt his name, presumably *because Baba Tükles did not get to them in the course of his appeals to God to convert them to Islam*. ʿAbd al-Ghaffār's explanation implies a fine combination of two popular etymologies. First we find the familiar etymology of the ethnonym "Qalmïq" (or "Qalmaq" as in universal usage among the Turks of Muslim Inner Asia), referring to the western Mongol tribes known also by the collective designations Oyrat and Junghar; these western Mongol tribes, primarily in times of confederation but separately as well, repeatedly posed a substantial threat both to the Uzbek states of sedentary Central Asia and to the Qazaq, Qïrghïz, Türkmen, Bashkir, Noghay and Tatar nomads of the western Inner Asian steppe, from the mid-fifteenth century to the late eighteenth century, and their adoption of Buddhism through the medium of Tibetan lamas cast a religious coloring to their long-standing hostilities with the at least nominally Muslim Turks. The etymology thus derived their collective designation from the Turkic verb *qalmaq*, "to remain," as appropriate for

95. *va baba tükläs avlādï beklik ṭarīqina sulūk étdi* (in the Najīb ʿĀṣim edition *ṭarīqata*).

96. *ädīgü bek dedikleri ṣajīʿ-i nāmdār anïn nasli édüki qavl ṣaḥīḥ va tavārīkh-i ūzbakiyān-da taṣrīḥ-dir.*

97. *ušbū islām ahli olan tātāra ūzbak khalqï démesine bāʾith ušbū sabab-den-dir.*

the name of a people who "remained" outside Islām.[98] In addition, in identifying the particular Qalmïq tribe most troublesome to the Muslim Turks of western Inner Asia in the eighteenth century—the Torghuts, established near the mouth of the Volga from the mid-seventeenth century down to 1771 and often allied with the Russians in subduing the Bashkirs, Noghays, and Tatars—ʿAbd al-Ghaffār at least implicitly suggests their ethnonym's derivation from the verb *turmaq*, "to stand," that is, "to stand still" and thus remain unconverted.

More remarkable than his appeal to these etymologies, however, is the reinforcement of the principle of religiously defined communal designations encountered here: not only does Uzbek ethnic history begin with the adoption of Islam by the khan who gave them their name, guided by Baba Tükles and his companions, but the ethnic history of those who did *not* convert likewise begins at the same time, through their accidental exclusion from Baba Tükles' prayers. As noted earlier, the earliest narrative of the conversion of Özbek Khan by Sayyid Ata likewise explains the ethnonym "Qalmaq" in nearly the same terms, but with a spatial or territorial focus: it is applied to those who "remained behind" when those

98. As such, the Qalmïqs are often contrasted with the Dungans or Tungans, Chinese converts to Islam, whose ethnonym was popularly understood as derived from the verb *tönmek*, "to return," to mean "those who returned" to the primordial and original faith of Islam. The notion that Qalmïq ethnogenesis lay among those who "remained" in unbelief when the "Uzbeks" became Muslims appears already in the *Shajarat al-atrāk*'s account of Sayyid Ata, referred to in Chapter 2. A still more remarkable account of Qalmïq origins among those "left out" of Islam (in this case willfully) is recorded in the Persian *Majmūʿ at-tavārīkh*, compiled in the late sixteenth century in the Farghānah valley, evidently on the basis of originally oral material preserved among Uzbek, Qazaq, and Qïrghïz tribal groups (see the partial facsimile edition of the manuscript preserved at St. Petersburg University, prepared by A. T. Tagirdzhanov, *"Sobranie istorii"-Madzhmūʿ at-tavārīkh* [Leningrad: Izd-vo Leningradskogo Universiteta, 1960], text pp. 23–25 [MS ff. 12a–13a]; cf. MS B667 at the St. Petersburg Branch of the Institute of Oriental Studies of the Russian Academy of Sciences, ff. 18a–19b). In this acount, the Qalmïqs originated from the younger, impious sons of "Qalmāq," who was one of ninety-two "Uzbek" tribal ancestors converted to Islam in the Prophet's time. After his death, "Qalmāq" had appeared to his faithful eldest son in a dream beseeching him to bury his father's body atop a mountain in the midst of the "sea" (*tengiz*). The eldest son did so, but was martyred by his angry brothers upon his return, whereupon the brothers began digging in search of their father's grave. Finally, Satan assumed the form of an old man and offered to find the body for them if they would do as he commanded; they agreed, and Satan provided an image of "Qalmāq" to which he commanded prostration, at the same time enjoining the now infidel Qalmïqs to eat pork. The story not only seems to echo the tension between Islam and Inner Asian burial rites, as the Muslim "Qalmāq" seeks to thwart his pagan sons' plans for his body, it also provides a vivid inversion of the principle whereby an "ancestor's" sacred remains sanctify a people's homeland, for instead of "our" people discovering a buried "ancestor" (as, for instance, in the Bashkir genealogical legend discussed in Chapter 6), here the alien infidels are deprived of the real grave and thus led astray by a Satanic forgery.

who *did* convert moved south toward Turkistān. In ʿAbd al-Ghaffār's version, the decisive "nation-forming" activity—in both positive and negative senses—is even more directly focused on the saint, since in the story of Sayyid Ata the "Qalmaqs" clearly *choose* to remain unconverted, and indeed each group, converts and nonconverts, had a hand in its own definition as a group. In ʿAbd al-Ghaffār's account, however, we find echoes of the kind of "magical" and tutelary connection between the saint and the peoples who are created by his action: both the conversion of those who *by virtue of their conversion* became known as Uzbeks, and the exclusion of those destined to remain "Qalmaqs" and "Torghuts" were ordained through the saint's prayers. In this account, the non-Muslim Qalmïqs did not simply "stay behind"; they were quite literally "left out." And what they were left out of was the tutelary and appellative connection linking the new converts/new people with their patron saint Baba Tükles and with their "royal" and "paternal" namesake Özbek Khan. We thus find an intriguing example in ʿAbd al-Ghaffār's work of a community imagining itself in terms of what its founder "left out" in the case of those alien to it.

As for Edigü, it is of no small significance that ʿAbd al-Ghaffār mentions the genealogical link between Edigü and Baba Tükles. It confirms that he had access to traditions asserting such a link; and indeed, ʿAbd al-Ghaffār's work is the only account we have linking (1) the specific narrative of Baba Tükles' role in Özbek Khan's conversion given by Ötemish Ḥājjī—beyond the fact of that role affirmed in the Tatar histories discussed below—with (2) the identification of Baba Tükles as Edigü's ancestor *and* with (3) the assertion of the "ethnogenetic" aspect of the conversion. Here in particular it would be helpful to know whether his knowledge of accounts affirming Edigü's descent from Baba Tükles came through the Central Asian literary tradition, through the Tatar historical works discussed above, or through oral tradition preserved among the Noghays or in the Crimea; the first of these possibilities is favored by his mention of "the histories of the Uzbeks," which certainly in ʿAbd al-Ghaffār's day could have meant only written histories produced in Uzbek-ruled Central Asia. In this case we might take ʿAbd al-Ghaffār's remark as testimony to the wider currency of stories about Baba Tükles or genealogies of Edigü in the Central Asian historical corpus than is evident from extant works. In any case, however, Edigü is of relatively little interest to ʿAbd al-Ghaffār, either in historical terms or in "ethnic" terms. Although he does devote a small section of his work to listing the descendants of Edigü, ʿAbd al-Ghaffār is more concerned with the Crimean khans, with their Chingisid descent, than with Edigü and the Noghays who looked to him for their origins as a people, and there is no hint in ʿAbd al-Ghaffār's account of any sanctifying or nation-forming role that Baba Tükles might play for Edigü's descendants or for the Noghays. In confirming that Baba Tükles' descendants were *begs*, ʿAbd al-Ghaffār implicitly limits their status, and the only sanctifying or nation-forming service that ʿAbd al-Ghaffār ascribes to Baba Tükles appears in the case of the Uzbeks (and negatively, of the Qalmïqs), not the Noghays.

Making Sense of Diverse Traditions: A New Account from Khorezm in the Eighteenth Century

Among the "historical" or "historicized" treatments of Baba Tükles may be counted a brief but revealing text, from the early eighteenth century, which so far as I know has never drawn the attention of specialists; it exists in an apparently unique copy, and has remained entirely unknown, perhaps due to its incomplete description in the only published reference to it of which I am aware. I discovered it quite by accident, while examining microfilms obtained for the Central Asian Archives at Indiana University; at the time, I was already working on Baba Tükles and Ötemish Ḥājjī's conversion narrative, and this text's mention of Edigü and Baba Tükles naturally caught my eye, but it was pure chance that I paid attention to the part of the manuscript that includes this brief but remarkable account.

This previously unknown text appears on three folios bound in a manuscript volume preserved now in the Staatsbibliothek zu Berlin-Preussischer Kulturbesitz, Orientabteilung. It was described in Wilhelm Pertsch's 1889 catalogue of the Turkish manuscripts in the royal library of Berlin,[99] and bears the designation *Diez A. Quart. 14*. The entire volume runs to 238 folios, of which the vast majority (ff. 12a–232a) constitute a copy, defective at the beginning,[100] of Abū'l-Ghāzī's famous *Shajarah-i Turk*; this manuscript was used by Desmaisons in his edition of the work, and it

99. W. Pertsch, *Verzeichniss der türkische Handschriften der Königlichen Bibliothek zu Berlin* (Berlin, 1889; *Die Handschriften-Verzeichnisse der Königlichen Bibliothek zu Berlin*, Bd. VI), pp. 228–230, Cat. No. 204.

100. The missing first page has been replaced with a transcription supplied, says Pertsch, by Desmaisons.

is to this least interesting part of the manuscript that Pertsch devoted most of his attention. The copy is written in a poor *nastaʿlīq*, and was copied by a certain Muḥammad Ḥusayn[101] b. Ḥājjī Aqā-yi Ṣūfī of the village of *T.r.k.kī* (Terek?); he completed it in Saint Petersburg (*b.t.r.būr.k qalʿa-sïnda*) on Thursday, 15 Safar [*sic*] 1150; the date corresponds to 14 June 1737 (3 June according to the Julian calendar of relevance for Saint Petersburg), which was a Friday, but differences of one day in figuring day-and-date correspondences are not uncommon due to different methods of calculating the beginning of the month. The copyist affirms that he completed the work "during the blessed time of Her Grand Imperial Highness, the glorious and just Anna Ivanovna, and in the shade of this world-succouring sovereign,"[102] suggesting that the Tsarina (r. 1730–1740) was the copyist's patron and that she actually commissioned the transcription.

These particulars may be of importance in assessing the environment in which the rest of the material in the volume was produced, but we cannot be sure of this, since the other short texts are mostly by other hands. Although it is difficult to judge from the microfilm, the paper appears uniform throughout the volume, suggesting a common origin, but in any case it is impossible to determine conclusively where and when the other sections were produced. In addition to the different handwriting, other dates appear elsewhere in the volume as well—most clearly in the brief text of interest to us—and there is a correspondingly wide variety of orthographic systems (all the texts are in Turkic, but some, such as Abū'l-Ghāzī's work, retain a more or less standard "Chaghatay" or eastern Turkic orthography, while others are more heavily "Ottomanized").

The other texts in the volume were described cursorily or not at all by Pertsch, who dismisses them as "unimportant." The first eleven folios comprise a collection of legends and stories, described by Pertsch as of "historical content," but in fact primarily devoted to stories of the Prophets and of the pre-Islamic Iranian kings; each entry begins with a phrase such as "*ammā rāvī rivāyat eder kim . . .*" or "*ammā ṣāḥib-i rivāyat der kim . . .*," but there seem to be no tales of more "recent" setting included here. The text is copied in a fine *naskh*, and the orthography in these tales is the most "Ottomanized" of all the short texts in the volume.

The final folio of the *Shajarah-i Turk* (232a) includes miscellaneous notes and verse, but ff. 232b–234a, as Pertsch noted, constitute a separate

101. The element "Ḥusayn" is omitted in Pertsch's description.

102. *šawkatlū ʿadālatlū annā īvānūnā īmpirāṭūr-i ʿaẓīmī ḥażratleri-ning mubārak vaqt-i ʿaṣr-da va pādšāh-i ʿālam-panāh-nïng sāya-sïnda* (f. 231b).

text giving a genealogy and brief history of the Crimean khans, beginning with Chingis Khan and ending with mention of Qaplān Girey I's third accession in 1143/1730. The text is less "Ottomanized,"[103] and Pertsch judged the handwriting to be most likely the same as that in Abū'l-Ghāzī's history; this is not impossible, but the "Crimean history" appears in fact to be much less "hastily" copied, in a smaller *nastaᶜlīq*, than the text of Abū'l-Ghāzī, and moreover seems to be "signed" with a name that remains partly illegible in the microfilm due to the smearing of the ink.[104]

Following this text comes the short piece of primary concern to us, on ff. 234b–236a; it is in yet another hand, different from all the others, and we will discuss its peculiarities below. Pertsch left this text, and indeed the rest of the volume, undescribed, remarking only that "on the remaining folios, written by various hands, are brief notes of mixed content, including some on the history of the Tatars."

The contents are indeed mixed. The text of primary concern here—the conversion narrative—ends on f. 236a, and the rest of that page has been filled with a separate and unrelated historical note that appears to be of some potential interest; its heading promises an account of the "state" of Qaṣāy Bek and his *oghlāns*, and the text relates the deeds of various *mīrzas* and *nökers* whose names belie Cherkes, Tatar, or Noghay provenance, but their identification would lead us too far astray. This note is written, however, in a hand close to that of the conversion narrative; the orthography of this note also shows approximately the same degree of "Ottomanization" as the conversion narrative, but the separateness of these two texts is still supported insofar as the conversion narrative

103. E.g. the form *boldï* is used throughout, though "1000" is *bing*.

104. The name, parts of which appear to be written as many as three times on f. 234a and once on f. 236a (suggesting calligraphic "practice" and thus possibly unrelated to the text), appears to read "Kalmat bin Valī ibn . . . āj," which makes little sense; specifically, the name appears as (1) *k.l.m.t b.n* followed by a deliberately crossed-out word apparently written as *w.w.lī*; (2) an initial *kā* intended as the start of a *kāf-lām* ligature but abandoned, followed by *kalmat b.n w.lī* (the first element of which is clearly vowelled with *ḥarakāt*), followed by nearly illegible characters interpretable as *a.b.n* or *a.y.d*, after which comes a clearly legible *alif* and final *jīm*; (3) the word *k.l.m.t*, again possibly vowelled as in (2), followed by characters interpretable as *b.n* or *b.s.l*, followed by a clearly written *w.lī a.b.n*, this time followed by nearly illegible characters similar to those in (2) and interpretable as *a.y.n* or *a.b.n* or *a.n.d*, followed by *aj* again; (4) on f. 236a, the initial *kā* as in (2) followed by what appears to be *k.l.m.t.n*. The first element might be "Gülmat," but is specifically vowelled as "Kälmät," in which the element *-mat* is a typical abbreviation (but relatively rarely represented orthographically, though common in pronunciation) of "Muḥammad," but the first element appears quite unusual; he is clearly "the son of Valī," but the rest of the name has so far defied explanation.

is distinguished by the Qïpchaq form *ūš* (three) instead of the form *üč* that appears in the historical note.[105]

Finally, from f. 236b to the end of the manuscript, on f. 238b, the handwriting may well be the same, and appears close to that in the text of Abū'l-Ghazī, and closer still to the hand evident in the "Crimean history," but again unrelated to the conversion narrative; the brief texts here include one short collection of historical notes of the type reflected in the "Crimean history" mentioned above.[106]

The conversion narrative itself, on ff. 234b–236a, appears without separate heading and takes up three full pages of 17, 14, and 17 lines, respectively, followed by 11 short lines written diagonally, with a good top margin later filled, on f. 236a. It is written in a small *naskh*, not so fine as that in the first section of the manuscript but quite legible; the hand in fact bears some similarities with that found in the Tashkent manuscript of Ötemish Ḥājjī's work, and resembles that found in many texts copied in Khorezm and in the Volga valley in the eighteenth century.[107] Orthographically the text recalls the "mixed" texts common in the Volga valley, in which some features characteristic of Ottoman language and orthography appear side by side with features proper to the more easterly Chaghatay tradition.[108] As noted above, one surprising orthographic feature is the graphic representation of the Qïpchaq pronunciation (*üš*)[109] of the Turkic word for "three," which according to Chaghatay orthographical "conventions" was virtually always written *ūč*, even in Qazaq and Qïrghïz environments in which the Qïpchaq pronunciation

105. This note seems to be continued on the *facing* page, f. 235b, where it is added in the margin. The marginal note on f. 235b (small parts of which have been lost due to the trimming of the page) ends with a date, 1148/1735–1736, designated as that of the accession of Nādir Shāh in the Mughān steppe; but none of this appears related to the conversion narrative, and the same is true for other miscellaneous notes at the top of f. 236a.

106. On f. 236b are two sets of notes, the first prescribing the appropriate frequency of sexual intercourse for each decade of life from age twenty to seventy, and the second on the distance between Istanbul and Mecca. On f. 237 begins a series of mathematical riddles introducing a story about ʿAlī that continues on through the top of f. 238b; this final page is filled with further historical notes on the Crimean khans and Ottoman sulṭān, bearing dates from 880/1475-76 to 993/1585.

107. E.g., manuscripts of the legendary histories of Bulghār referred to above in Chapter 2, notes 15 and 181.

108. For example, the final *-ng* of the genitive ending is represented, in Ottoman fashion, by the single letter *kāf*, as is often the case in the manuscript of Ötemish Ḥājjī; the form *édi* appears alongside the more common *érdi*; both *bol-* and *ol-* are used; and the dative suffix appears both as a simple vowel indicated by final *hā*, and as *-ġa* and *-kä*.

109. By contrast the final *-č* of the gerund suffix, as in the form *olġāč* that occurs once, is not altered to *-š*.

was current, well into the nineteenth century. The author of the text was evidently a native of Khorezm, but this orthographic peculiarity suggests that he may well have been of Qazaq, or more likely Qaraqalpaq, origin.

The short text, translated below, is given in Appendix 3. The text stands as a remarkable attempt, by a man evidently well acquainted both with hagiographical literature and with tribal lore among the Noghays, to come to terms with conflicting traditions about the conversion of Özbek Khan; beyond the above comments and the "internal" evidence of the text itself, we have no further evidence on where the author obtained his information, but in view of his preliminary "disclaimer" and in his frequent reference to Noghay lore, it seems likely that most of his information reflects oral, rather than written, sources. Written sources, to be sure, clearly inspired his "reconciliation" of accounts, but in this case his sources are obvious; similarly, it is not impossible that the author actually knew and used the work of Ötemish Ḥājjī, although if he did, its influence must have been primarily negative, inasmuch as his account of Özbek Khan's conversion is quite different, both in its setting and in its dramatic confrontation, from that of Ötemish Ḥājjī. It is also possible that the author of this conversion narrative had access to the "Tatar" historical works discussed below, which alone among written accounts of Baba Tükles' role in Özbek Khan's conversion predate the brief text discussed here;[110] but in this case as well, there is little similarity between this text and the accounts in the "Tatar" histories, beyond the fact of Baba Tükles' role in converting the Khan, and the name of one son of Baba Tükles. Rather, we find that although the Khorezmian author of the present text knows of the ascription of Bakrid lineage to Baba Tükles, he does not give the full Bakrid genealogy, or any part of it, as known from the Tatar histories and other sources; at the same time, his narrative of the conversion itself is much richer than the spare account in those earlier "historical" works.

Most likely the author did not have access to any written versions of the tale of Baba Tükles and Özbek Khan, beyond possible written registries of tribal genealogy similar to the *shajarah*s preserved among many Inner Asian Muslim peoples down to the present century. Rather, for the material specifically dealing with Baba Tükles and the conversion of Özbek Khan we are clearly in the presence of an eighteenth-century recording of oral traditions about Baba Tükles collected among the

110. ʿAbd al-Ghaffār Qïrïmī's reworking of Ötemish Ḥājjī's narrative was still nearly thirty years in the future, if the date given in the text is correct.

Noghays of the Black Sea steppe a full two centuries after Ötemish Ḥājjī. He presents those traditions as common knowledge in those regions, and however much he may have "clarified" those traditions himself, at the very least his account confirms the continued currency and vitality of popular lore linking Baba Tükles *both* to the conversion of Özbek Khan *and* to the ancestry of Edigü and the Noghay *mīrzās*.

Of the author himself, Nūrullāh b. ᶜUbaydullāh aṣ-Ṣiddīq al-Khorezmī, nothing is known beyond his Khorezmian origin. As noted, he was possibly a Qaraqalpaq, although we do not know whether the text as we have it was actually transcribed by him; if the text was written independently and later bound with the copy of Abū'l-Ghāzī's work, it may indeed be in the author's hand and copied in 1131/1719, but if it was added to blank pages included with the *Shajarah-i Turk* we must assume that it was copied no earlier than 1150/1737, and certainly not in Khorezm. It is possible that this figure might turn up in the rather meager historical or hagiographical literature of eighteenth-century Khorezm; he is in any case not mentioned by this name in Muʾnis' *Firdaws al-iqbāl*, the only substantial work to cover the period in which he must have lived, nor does he appear in the eighteenth-century hagiographical compendium of Khorezmian provenance, the *Tadhkirah-i Ṭāhir Īshān*.[111]

TRANSLATION

Let it not remain hidden from men of perception and discernment and masters of wisdom and sagacity, [that] although the words of historians and genealogists are not free from the imputation of falsehood and invention, nevertheless, their predilection for words is built upon widespread renown, and the reliability of a genealogy too depends upon a foundation in repeated oral transmission [*tasāmuᶜ*]. Historians and genealogists require a narrative transmission; and the responsibility lies with the first narrator.

Among the Nōghāys and Mīrzās who dwell on the banks of the Īdīl and Qūbān, it is well known that Ädīgī Bīy is a descendant of Bābā Tükles,[112] and that Özbek Khan and the people (*el*) subject to him were ennobled with the honor of [converting to] Islam through the summons (*daᶜvat*) of that saint (*ᶜazīz*). Evidently his name must have been Ṣadr ad-Dīn Aḥmad, who is known in

111. On this Persian work, completed in 1157/1744, cf. *SVR*, III (Tashkent, 1955), pp. 364–365, Nos. 2692–2695; I have consulted MS IVANUz Inv. No. 855.

112. Spelled *t.k.l.s*.

the countries of Khorezm and Mawarannahr by the *laqab* "Ṣadr Ata;" because he was covered with hair (*shaʿrānī*) and had a great deal of body hair [*badanlari-ning tūkī köp*], they call him Bābā Tükles among the Noghays. And in some genealogies (*nasab-nāmah*), they call him Ḥājjī Ākhī as well, because he was apparently a foster brother (*ākh-i rażāʿī*) to the holy Sayyid Ata.[113]

And the holy Sayyid Ata and Ṣadr Ata and Badr Ata and Ūzūn Ḥasan Ata—these four saints—were companions together in the same place since childhood; and when they were engaged in studying the exoteric sciences in Mawarannahr, a desire to travel the mystical path of the shaykhs arose within them. Searching for a Perfect Master *(pīr-i kāmil)*, they paid pious visitation to all the shaykhs of Khorezm and Mawarannahr: the instruction [given] to them by all the shaykhs was that they should go to the country of Turkistān and seek their goal there.

And so these four saints, with the guidance of the shaykhs, went to Turkistān and achieved their aims through Zangī Ata; and Zangī Ata was licensed by Ḥakīm Ata, and Ḥakīm Ata was licensed by Sulṭān Khoja Aḥmad Yasavī, may God's mercy be upon them. Then Zangī Ata gave first to Ṣadr Ata the permission [to certify disciples, *rukhṣat*]; for this reason they call him the chief successor (*bāš khalīfah*). Later those [other] three saints were licensed as well.

And then the holy Zangī Ata commanded Sayyid Ata and Ṣadr Ata, "Go to the Dasht-i Qïpchāq and Sarāychïq, and summon the infidels and people there to Islam!" At that time the ruler (*pādšāh*) in Sarāychïq was Özbek Khan, who was a descendant of Shïbān Khan, the fifth son of Chingīz Khān's eldest son Jöchī Khan. At that time, among the descendants of Chingīz Khan there had still not appeared a ruler who had become a Muslim. And the holy Sayyid Ata and Ṣadr Ata went to Sarāychïq by their master's command, and summoned Özbek Khan to Islam;

113. I have not encountered this designation elsewhere for either Baba Tükles or Ṣadr Ata, although the author implies that he found it in written sources. The explanation given here for this designation seems quite improbable in view of the common appellation *ākhī* borne by members of *futuwwah* organizations and Sufi orders; the title (which incidentally is probably *not* derived from Arabic *ākh*, "brother," but from a Turkic term, cf. Clauson, *ED*, p. 78, s.v. "akı") was quite common in Anatolia and Iran in the fourteenth century, and it seems likely that the author had access to hagiographical material ascribing "missionary" activity to a figure linked with such organizations and thus made another of his learned identifications.

[235a] and they manifested many wonders and miracles.

Özbek Khan was intelligent and discerning, and knew well the tales and histories of past kings. He said to these saints: "I know the truth of your religion; let me set a condition. My condition is this: at the time when Pharaoh's sorcerers (*sāḥir-lar*), confronting the holy Mūsā (peace be upon him), did their conjuring (*siḥr*), it had no effect on Mūsā (peace be upon him); [rather], a miracle (*muʿjizah*) of Mūsā (peace be upon him) spoiled (*bāṭil qïldï*) their conjurings, for his staff became a serpent and swallowed up and destroyed all that they had conjured.[114] At that time all the sorcerers acknowledged their faith to Mūsā (peace be upon him); and at once, through the good fortune of faith, the seven layers of the earth and the seven layers of the heavens and the Throne and the Seat (*ʿaršī va kūrsī* [*sic*]) were revealed to those sorcerers. If [these] are revealed in this way to me as well when I too have become a Muslim, I will know that your religion is true."

Then the holy Sayyid Ata directed Ṣadr Ata [saying], "You are the chief successor; this matter is consigned to you." And so the holy Ṣadr Ata taught Özbek Khan the profession of faith (*kalimah-i shahādat*), and instructed him in the pillars of faith and the conditions and principles of Islam and in ablution and prayer. When it came time for the ritual prayer,[115] they turned toward the *qiblah*; then Özbek Khan said, "If I do not see the Kaʿbah, why should I perform the prayer?" When he had said this, Ṣadr Ata raised his hand and pointed, and said, "That which you see is the Kaʿbah"; and the veils were lifted from the vision of Özbek Khan and all the people standing there, [235b] and the holy Blessed Kaʿbah became clearly and plainly manifest. This was the first unveiling (*kashf*) which became manifest to Özbek Khan; and it is well known that Özbek Khan used to say, "Throughout my life, whenever I set about performing the ritual

114. For the story of Moses' staff and the confounding of Pharaoh's sorcerers, see the Qurʾān, X:80–81, XX:65–70; cf. Exodus 7:9–12. See also *The Tales of the Prophets of al-Kisāʾī*, tr. Thackston, p. 229, and further references in A. Fodor, "The Rod of Moses in Arabic Magic," *AOH*, 32/1 (1978), pp. 1–21. The initial Qurʾānic reference (X:81) provides the model for the account's language of sorcery and its "confounding": Moses tells the sorcerers, "What you have done is sorcery; God will surely render it of no effect" (*mā jiʾtum bihi's-siḥru inna'llāha sayubṭiluhu*).

115. Written "*beš vaqtī namāz boldï érsä*"; most likely the common phrase "*beš vaqt-i namāz*," "the five times for prayer," induced the writer or copyist to write *b.š* instead of *b.s* for the introductory word *bas*.

prayer (*namāz*), I would not even utter the opening words[116] until I had seen the Kaʿbah." In sum, on that day 70,000 persons were ennobled with the honor of [converting to] Islam: "Praise be to God, who has guided us to this: never could we have found guidance, had it not been for the guidance of God."[117]

There are contradictory views on the genealogies of Ṣadr Ata. Some say that Ṣadr Ata is of the lineage of Imām Muḥammad Ḥanafī,[118] and some say [that he belongs to] the lineage of Abū Bakr-i Ṣiddīq (may God be pleased with him). It is possible that in these two traditions there is a basis for reconciliation, for one version may be according to the father's side, and one version may be according to the mother's side. However, among the Noghays he is known for belonging to the lineage of the holy [Abū Bakr-i] Ṣiddīq; and God knows best.

Ṣadr Ata's father was Darvīsh Adham, who was the youngest son of Sulṭān Ibrāhīm b. Adham. Now Sulṭān Ibrāhīm was the ruler in the country of Balkh. One night he was engaged in worship upon his throne; someone walked on top of his palace. Ibrāhīm asked, "Who is it on top of my palace?" The answer came, "I am an Arab; I am searching for a camel." Ibrāhīm said, "What a strange thing to say! How is it possible for a camel be on top of this palace?" The answer came, "How is it possible to live the life of a Sufi, and seek Almighty God, on top of a throne?"[119] These words affected Ibrāhīm, and he abandoned his rule,

116. Literally, "I did not say the *takbīr-i taḥrīmah*" (i.e., the holy glorification of God that initiates the prayer). Intriguingly, precisely the same statement—that he would not begin to utter the *takbīr-i taḥrīmah* until he had had a vision of the Kaʿbah—is recorded by the nineteenth-century Khivan historian Muʾnis as having been popularly transmitted about "Naghdāy," the *amīr* of Özbek Khan whom Ibn Baṭṭūṭah met and who appears in Timurid-era sources as the father of the brothers who founded the "Qonghrat Sufi" dynasty of Khorezm; Muʾnis, as noted above, portrays this "Naghdāy" as a devotee of Sayyid Ata who followed the Sufi shaykh to Khorezm after the conversion of Özbek Khan. See the text in Muʾnis, *Firdaws al-iqbāl*, ed. Bregel, p. 206, and the translation in Bregel, "Tribal Tradition," pp. 370–371.

117. Qurʾān VII.43.

118. I.e., of Muḥammad b. al-Ḥanafīyah, the son of ʿAlī by a wife other than the Prophet's daughter; Khoja Aḥmad Yasavī is regarded as a descendant of Muḥammad b. al-Ḥanafīyah.

119. This story of Ibrāhīm b. Adham's repentance, a common theme in Sufi literature, appears to be based upon the account in Rūmī's *Mathnavī* (cf. R. A. Nicholson, tr., *The Mathnawí of Jalálu'ddín Rúmí* [London: Luzac & Co., 1930, repr. 1977], translation, vol. 2, p. 318 [Book IV, lines 829–835]); the only significant difference is Rūmī's account of several people atop the palace, as against this account's single "Arab." It is not clear whether the account was adapted from the *Mathnavī* itself, in view of its popularity, or from any number of Sufi works to repeat the story.

donned the habit of a dervish, and departed from Balkh, heading for the Kaʿbah. His wife and son went in search of Ibrāhīm; they went to the Kaʿbah and attained God's mercy there. And the young[est] son Adham chose the life of a dervish and left Balkh. However, Sulṭān Jalāl ad-Dīn Rūmī was not Sulṭān Ibrāhīm's father; rather, he was a cousin of Sulṭān Ibrāhīm.

And the story is well known that Ṣadr Ata, who is at present known by the *laqab* "Bābā Tükles," took [in marriage] a fairy-girl [*parī qïzīn alūb-dūr*]. Even if this story were confirmable, it would be possible, because in the *sharīʿat* it is appropriate for a man to marry a female-*jinn*.[120]

All told, the Bābā had three sons. The name of his eldest son was Islām Bābā; [f. 236a] he was versed in theoretical and practical sciences, and the appellations "Shaykh" and "Ata" were left to him. He settled in the country of Khorezm; and one son settled in Turkistān, and one of them was orphaned. And the Manghïts looked after him; the name by which he is famous is Terme, who is the ancestor of all the *mīrzā*s among the Noghays. And God knows best the truth of the matter, and unto Him is the return and the power.

The poor wretch needful of God, Nūrullāh b. ʿUbaydullāh aṣ-Ṣiddīq al-Khwārazmī, produced this, [in] the year 1131 [24 November 1718–13 November 1719].

Commentary

Beyond the evident basis in oral tradition of this account's central point, as noted above, a number of other features are worthy of comment. Above all, this text evidences a much stronger Sufi "flavor" than the account of Ötemish Ḥājjī; this is suggested not only by the author's evident familiarity with the hagiographical tradition surrounding Zangī Ata's disciples, but also (1) in the allusions to the famous Sufis Ibrāhīm b. Adham and Jalāl ad-Dīn Rūmī, (2) in the mystical visions of the Kaʿbah portrayed as pivotal in the conversion, and (3) in the affirmation that one of Baba Tükles' sons "inherited" his father's Sufi appellations of "shaykh" and "*ata*."

In the first regard, Nūrullāh Khorezmī was clearly acquainted with the

120. For further references on the question of the admissibility of marriages with the *jinn*, see Ignaz Goldziher, *Introduction to Islamic Theology and Law*, tr. Andras and Ruth Hamori (Princeton: Princeton University Press, 1981), p. 64, n. 88.

story of Zangī Ata's four disciples, as mentioned above, first recorded in the well-known early sixteenth-century hagiography, the *Rashaḥāt-i ʿayn al-ḥayāt*. The *Rashaḥāt* is, of course, only the earliest hagiographical source to include the story of the four disciples of Zangī Ata, a story it shares with the *Shajarat al-atrāk*, in which is found the specific element of Zangī Ata's instructions to his disciples to summon the peoples of the Dasht-i Qïpchāq to Islam; as noted earlier, an account similar to that of the *Shajarat al-atrāk* is found in a seventeenth-century Khorezmian hagiography devoted to the life of one of Sayyid Ata's descendants, and the *Rashaḥāt's* account of the four saints made its way into many hagiographical compendia produced in Central Asia and India from the sixteenth century to the nineteenth, especially in the relatively few hagiographies devoted to shaykhs of Yasavī lineage. We cannot say for certain which of these works, if any, was the direct inspiration for Nūrullāh Khorezmī's identification of Baba Tükles as one of those four; nor can we do more than speculate, without a thorough study of the entire Central Asian hagiographical corpus, on whether other extant works may contain a similar identification, upon which Nūrullāh might have drawn for his account.

In the absence of any other attestation of the identification of Baba Tükles with Ṣadr Ata, then, we must assign it tentatively to Nūrullāh Khorezmī himself. But what is curious about our author's identification, whether his original contribution or a borrowing from some unknown source, is the choice of Ṣadr Ata as the saint to be identified with Baba Tükles. Of the four saints, only Sayyid Ata clearly remained a strong focus of legendary tales and genealogical ascriptions in Central Asia; his putative descendants may be traced at least down to the nineteenth century, and legends about his Islamizing role were circulated nearly as long. By contrast, we know almost nothing of any literary, spiritual, or familial legacy from the figure called Uzun Ḥasan Ata, while the other two companions are only slightly better represented in later sources: descendants of Badr Ata living in Khorezm are mentioned in the early sixteenth century by a Kubravī Sufi native to the region, while descendants of Ṣadr Ata are mentioned in the vicinity of Shāhrukhīyah, near Tashkent, in a hagiographical work from the latter fifteenth century.[121] Ṣadr Ata was also claimed as a seventh-generation ancestor by the sixteenth-century writer Ḥasan Nithārī Bukhārī, who notes also that most of the tribes of "the *ūlūs* of Ṣāʾin Khān"—he uses the usual Turkic designation of Batu, and

121. *Hasht ḥadīqah*, MS IVAN Uz, Inv. No. 1477 (*SVR*, III, p. 271, Cat. No. 2441), f. 29b.

means the Jöchid *ulus*—had been *murīds* of his forefathers in that lineage;[122] Nithārī does not explicitly mention Ṣadr Ata in this connection, but his "family history" may add further support to the tradition of Ṣadr Ata's "missionary" activity in the Dasht-i Qïpchāq.

In any case, Ṣadr Ata's relative obscurity would seem on the one hand to render him a less likely candidate for an entirely spurious identification, one invented by Nūrullāh Khorezmī or his source, but on the other hand would appear to reduce the likelihood of such an identification being widely recognized as contrived. We are thus left without decisive evidence by which to judge the plausibility of Nūrullāh's equation of Baba Tükles with Ṣadr Ata. Most likely the tradition of Ṣadr Ata's involvement, together with Sayyid Ata, in the conversion of Özbek Khan, or at least with the spread of Islam in the Jöchid *ulus*, was an early and authentic tradition, and was known to Nūrullāh, probably through literary sources; similarly, the traditions about Baba Tükles linking him both to Özbek Khan's conversion and to Edigü's genealogy were also known to Nūrullāh, undoubtedly through reports he heard either from Qaraqalpaq or Qazaq groups near Khorezm, or from Noghays he may have encountered during travels he may have undertaken. His account should thus be understood as an effort to reconcile the two traditions about the figure(s) responsible for the conversion of Özbek Khan.

In his allusions to Ibrāhīm b. Adham and Rūmī, our author is most likely betraying his familiarity with legendary genealogies, of the type preserved in

122. *Mudhakkir-i-Aḥbāb ("Remembrancer of Friends") of Khwāja Bahā al-Dīn Ḥasan Nithārī Bukhārī*, ed. Syed Muhammad Fazlullah (Hyderabad: Osmania University, Da'iratu'l-Maᶜarif Press, 1969), pp. 493–494, 505–506; cf. pp. 56–57. Nithārī's genealogy makes Ṣadr Ata the natural, as well as spiritual, son of Zangī Ata; see also Hofman, *Turkish Literature*, II, pp. 103–106 (on Nithārī's grandfather ᶜAbd al-Vahhāb, known by the *takhalluṣ* "ᶜĀrif"), IV, pp. 273–275 (on Nithārī himself), and V, pp. 1–4 (on his father Pādshāh Khoja). Pādshāh Khoja is famous as the author of Turkic verse and of two Turkic prose works, one entitled *Gulzār* (written in honor of the Shïbānid Jānī-beg in 945/1538–1539; excerpts were published in a work that has remained unavailable to me, *Uzbek ädäbiyati tärikhi khrestomätiyäsi* [Tashkent, 1945], pp. 90–99), and the other *Miftāḥ al-ᶜadl* (excerpts published in an anthology of Uzbek literature prepared by the famous Äbdurrauf Fiträt, *Özbek ädäbiyati nämunäläri*, Tashkent-Samarkand, 1928, pp. 112–124; the work has not been available to me). The two works of Pādshāh Khoja (referred to now only as "Khoja") are discussed in the collective volume *Özbek näsri tärikhidän*, ed. I. Sultanov and Ä. Häyitmetov (Tashkent: Fän, 1982), pp. 75–87, where further references are given to works also unavailable to me: V. Zakhidov, "O 'Miftokhul-adle,'" *Uchenye zapiski Tashkentskogo Gosudarstvennogo Pedagogicheskogo Instituta*, vyp. 4 (filologiia) (1957); V. Zahidov, "'Miftahul-ädl' va 'Gulzar' häqidä," in the collective volume *Özbek ädäbiyati tärikhidän* (Tashkent, 1961); and M. Mirzäähmedova, *Khojä (häyati vä ijadi)* (Tashkent, 1975). The life and works of Pādshāh Khoja are also discussed at length by N. M. Mälläev in his *Uzbek ädäbiyati tärikhi*, vol. I (Tashkent: "Uqituvchi" Näshriyati, 1965), pp. 718–734.

the Tatar historical works discussed below, which include "Sulṭān Jalāl ad-Dīn" and "Adham" in the lineage of Baba Tükles and Edigü. But at the same time Nūrullāh Khorezmī's intellectual milieu is illustrated by his extended discussion of Ibrāhīm b. Adham—a minor, and often unidentified, figure in the full genealogies of Baba Tükles— complete with the story of his renunciation drawn ultimately from Rūmī's *Mathnavī*. We may note here, however, that our author, if he was indeed acquainted with genealogical narratives of the type preserved in the Tatar histories, certainly "adjusted" them, since the more complete genealogies reverse the relative positions implied for Rūmī and Ibrāhīm in Nūrullāh's work: "Jalāl ad-Dīn" is cast as Baba Tükles' father in the genealogies, with "Adham" a distant ancestor, while Nūrullāh makes "Adham" the father and indicates his familiarity with tales making "Jalāl ad-Dīn" the father of Adham's father Ibrāhīm by rejecting this sequence. To be sure, Nūrullāh ascribes this lineage specifically to Ṣadr Ata rather than to Baba Tükles, and despite his identification of the two it is not impossible that in this case the allusions to Ibrāhīm and Rūmī (linked originally, no doubt, through their common ties to Balkh) reflect the author's familiarity with Central Asian traditions about Ṣadr Ata rather than with Noghay tales about Baba Tükles.

In any event, it is worth noting that in affirming such ancestry, Nūrullāh again shows his Sufi intellectual environment, for he is clearly affirming the sanctity of Baba Tükles/Ṣadr Ata by emphasizing the saint's descent from the archetypal renouncer in Islamic tradition. Ibrāhīm b. Adham is above all a ruler who gives up the throne, of course, setting Nūrullāh Khorezmī's portrayal of Baba Tükles in quite noteworthy contrast to the clear political intent of the better-known genealogies, in which Edigü's ancestors, including Baba Tükles, are all Muslim *rulers*.

The Sufi coloring of Nūrullāh's narrative is perhaps most clearly manifested in his account of the conversion "contest," in which the demonstration of sacred power begins not with a heated argument, but with the khan's own calm recounting of the story of Moses; it ends, likewise, not with an ordeal in the fiery furnace, but with the khan and his people experiencing a mystical *ḥāl* before their prayers. Aside from the saint's role in *inducing* that experience, the magical elements so vivid in Ötemish Ḥājjī's narrative have been entirely replaced in this account by the mystical.

Moreover, Nūrullāh's Sufi environment is no doubt reflected in the "division" of titles reported in the case of Baba Tükles' sons. One "inherited" the titles of "shaykh" and "*ata*," settling in Khorezm as a typical

Sufi shaykh clearly regarded by Nūrullāh as the legitimate "heir" to his father's most important functions. The other, the orphan Terme who was raised by the Manghïts, became the ancestor of the Noghay *mīrzās*, and we thus see again Nūrullāh's relative disregard for the heritage of rulership that was so central to the other treatments of Edigü's lineage as discussed below.

In addition to these instances of Sufi interpretation in Nūrullāh's account, we may note also other features of structure and content of particular interest for appreciating our author's approach. To begin with, the central narrative of the conversion of Özbek Khan is itself a hybrid; it begins with echoes of the account in Ötemish Ḥājjī's work, noting Baba Tükles' "summons" to accept Islam, then identifies Baba Tükles with Ṣadr Ata and turns to the account of the latter figure as given in the *Rashaḥāt*, departing from it after the directive to go to "the Dasht-i Qïpchāq and Sarāychïq." Here we find a further conflation of "Noghay" and "Central Asian" elements, as the emphasis upon Sarāychïq seems to reflect Noghay traditions, while the "genealogy" ascribed to Özbek Khan—wrongly assigning him to the lineage of Shïbān, whose descendants *did* rule in Central Asia—reflects the persistence of this error in Central Asian sources of the Uzbek era. Finally the account returns to echoes of Ötemish Ḥājjī's narrative, in the miracles at Özbek Khan's court and the mention of the "sorcerers"; here, however, the sorcerers have been "sanitized," and the "contest" intellectualized, or rather spiritualized: convincing the khan requires not only an exposition of the principles of the faith, but the inducement of a vision or "revelation" (the ability to induce such visionary experiences at will is, of course, a standard mark of an especially accomplished shaykh in Sufi hagiographical lore). That the author has "edited" the traditions he received about the conversion of Özbek Khan, and not too well, is suggested by the inconsistencies in the account: the khan acknowledges the truth of Islam but requires several more proofs, promising to acknowledge its truth if he experiences the same vision vouchsafed to Pharaoh's sorcerers.

Further evidence of the author's vain attempt to reconcile disparate accounts appears in his treatment of Ṣadr Ata's more distant ancestors, that is, those prior to the figure (Ibrāhīm b. Adham's son) he has anachronistically cast as the saint's father. It is curious to find Imām Muḥammad b. al-Ḥanafīyah alluded to as an ancestor of Ṣadr Ata; ʿAbd al-Ghaffār Qïrïmī also refers to him, but distinguishes Baba Tükles from the "Sayyid Aḥmad" whom he casts as the descendant of Muḥammad b. al-Ḥanafīyah. The latter figure is usually linked with Aḥmad Yasavī (who as the descendant of Muḥammad b. al-Ḥanafīyah is indeed an ʿAlid, but *not* a *sayyid*) rather than with Ṣadr Ata, and it is not clear that the two ancestries cited by Nūrullāh Khorezmī reflect distinct traditions about the pedigree of Baba Tükles and/or Ṣadr Ata; rather, they may reflect a popular conflation, known to the author, of Baba Tükles with Aḥmad Yasavī himself. The Abū Bakrid lineage is of course well known from the Noghay tradition about Edigü's lineage, and it is in keeping with the approach and tenor of this text's author that he suggests a reconciliation of the two conflicting traditions. Although he does not say so explicitly in the case of the entire account, this is essentially what he is attempting to do with the conflicting narratives of Özbek Khan's conversion familiar to him.

The final passages of the account are of special interest because they attest not only to elements of the historical and hagiographical traditions about Baba Tükles current in the late seventeenth and early eighteenth centuries, but also the existence in that era of stories ascribing to Baba Tükles the kind of dalliance with a "fairy-maiden" that we find in several of the epic tales of Idige. True to form, our author seeks to justify these stories in juridical terms, but the fact that he was aware of such tales already in 1719 pushes back our attestation of the thoroughly "mythologized" Baba Tükles by about a century (since the earliest epic recordings date from the very end of the eighteenth century and the beginning of the nineteenth).

Lastly, in addition to the "division" of the functions of "shaykh" and "*mīrzā*" noted above, we find an echo of traditions also implicit in the Tatar histories discussed more fully below, in the several "destinations" of Baba Tükles' sons. Here in Nūrullāh's account they end up in Khorezm, Turkistān, and among the Noghays, respectively; in the Tatar histories conflicting traditions seem to be included, some making all of his sons except "Terme" "return" to Mecca, and others more closely paralleling Nūrullāh's version by placing Baba Tükles' sons in "Urgench" (i.e., Khorezm), in the Crimea, and in the Volga-Ural valley. It is also instructive, perhaps, that Nūrullāh knew the names of only two of Baba Tükles' sons: "Islām Bābā" is said to have settled in Khorezm, suggesting that Nūrullāh knew of traditions in his native country perhaps ascribing such lineage to a local saint, while the prominence of "Terme" among the Manghïts (his name, as noted below, survived in Bashkir tradition while other descendants of Baba Tükles were forgotten) ensured his mention as the ancestor of the Noghay *mīrzā*s. In any case, the element of the saint's sons moving to various regions no doubt reflects a common hagiographical response to an awareness of Baba Tükles' veneration in such widely scattered locales, attesting once again both to the widespread currency of tales about him, and to our author's penchant for reconciling those tales, which had long since diverged in many particulars in their independent, local developments.

Baba Tükles and the Full Genealogy of Edigü: Tatar Historiography, Bukharan Hagiography, and Russian Heraldry

Both the reworking of Ötemish Ḥājjī's account of Baba Tükles by ʿAbd al-Ghaffār Qïrïmī and the independent attempt at "reconciling" disparate traditions by Nūrullāh Khorezmī date from the eighteenth century, 200 years after our earliest record of Baba Tükles' story. For the earliest historical treatment of Baba Tükles and his genealogical ties with Edigü we must turn to a different historiographical tradition reflected in several quite diverse sources, all of which assign minimal importance, if any, to Baba Tükles' role in the conversion of Özbek Khan, but stress the genealogical connections whereby Baba Tükles legitimized Edigü and his descendants. While ʿAbd al-Ghaffār's account reflects Ötemish Ḥājjī's narrative and adds a brief mention of Baba Tükles' ancestry of Edigü (with only passing attention to genealogical elaboration), Nūrullāh Khorezmī stresses Baba Tükles' conversion of Özbek Khan but also acknowledges his ancestry of Edigü, demonstrating a clear familiarity with genealogical traditions linking Baba Tükles to Abū Bakr and to "Ibrāhīm b. Adham"; the Khorezmian author also provides a rationale for the "adoption" of one of Baba Tükles' sons by the Manghïts, whence the saint's ancestry of the Noghay *mīrzās*. But in the accounts discussed below, little remains of Baba Tükles' Islamizing activity; it is rather the full lineage of Baba Tükles, back to Abū Bakr and down to Edigü, that all these accounts have in common.

Baba Tükles in Tatar Historiography: The Work of Jalāyirī and the Daftar-i Chingīz-nāmah

This genealogical elaboration is known primarily from two works in the Tatar historiographical tradition, in which Baba Tükles figures as an important link in the genealogy of Edigü. The existence of other, relatively early versions of the same genealogy (discussed below) probably indicates that accounts, possibly written, of Edigü's lineage were in wide circulation (especially among his descendants) and were simply incorporated by the authors of these two "Tatar" works. Such a conclusion is reinforced by the apparent conflict between the Chingisid focus of at least one of these works and the likely motives of the genealogy in question: the two works preserve little of Baba Tükles' role in the conversion of Özbek Khan as told by Ötemish Ḥājjī (and the derivative work of ʿAbd al-Ghaffār Qïrïmī), but instead portray Baba Tükles as a sixth-generation ancestor of Edigü, and as a fourteenth-generation descendant of the Caliph Abū Bakr; the probable motive of this genealogy is suggested by the affirmation that Abū Bakr's descendants were rulers of various lands of Islam in each generation down to Edigü, who as a non-Chingisid is thereby supplied with both religious and political legitimacy.

The earliest of the two histories is the work known as the *Jāmiʿ at-tavārīkh* of Qādir ʿAlī Bek Jalāyirī,[123] written in 1602 in the "khanate" of Kasimov, where for a century and a half Chingisid dynasts had ruled

123. On this work, the best description remains that of Usmanov, *Tatarskie istoricheskie istochniki*, pp. 33–96 (pp. 82–84 on the genealogy of Edigu); cf. Z. A. Khisamieva. "Nekotorye tekstologicheskie problemy dastanov Kadyir-Gali Bika," in *Istochnikovedenie i istoriia tiurkskikh iazykov* (Kazan', 1978), pp. 63–69, and Schamilogu, "The *Umdet ül-Ahbar*," pp. 85–86. The work was also discussed and excerpted in Vel'iaminov-Zernov's *Izsledovanie o kasimovskikh tsariakh i tsarevichakh*, ch. 2. The text of one defective manuscript of the work was published, as noted, by I. Berezin in his series "Biblioteka vostochnykh istorikov," t. 2, ch. 1: *Sbornik letopisei. Tatarskii tekst, s russkim predisloviem* (Kazan, 1854). Berezin's text (with supplementary material from another manuscript of the work, however) has now been published in a modifed Cyrillic transcription with accompanying linguistic (but not historical) analysis (aimed at placing the work within a Qazaq, rather than Tatar, historiographical tradition) by Syzdykova, *Iazyk "Zhamiʿ at-tawārikh" Zhalairi* [sic] (Alma-Ata, 1989). Neither Usmanov nor Syzdykova notes the existence in Paris of an extensive (276ff.) manuscript of a translation (into "Noghay Tatar") of Rashīd ad-Dīn ascribed to Qādir ʿAlī Bek in Blochet's catalogue (E. Blochet, ed., *Catalogue des manuscrits turcs* [Paris: Bibliothèque Nationale, 1932–1933], II, pp. 57–58, Suppl. Turc 758; this copy is noted by Hofman (*Turkish Literature*, V, pp. 114–115); Blochet gives the date of the work's completion as 1005/1596–1597, rather than 1011/1602 as given in the less extensive copies known to Soviet researchers. It is worth further investigation to determine whether the Paris copy represents an earlier redaction of the translation—and one to which, in any case, the translator's supplements were not added.

under Russian suzerainty; the author, indeed, dedicates his work, in a florid encomium, to "Bārīş Fīdrāvich Khān" (i.e., the *tsar'* Boris Godunov). The work consists of a Turkic translation of portions of Rashīd ad-Dīn's history (hence the title customarily assigned to it) and Qādir ʿAlī Bek's own additions, in the form of nine *dāstāns* or "tales," on later figures from the history of the Golden Horde; eight of the *dāstāns* are devoted to Chingisid khans, and one to Edigü Bek. Less well known, and of less clear provenance, is the *Daftar-i Chingīz-nāmah*,[124] an anonymous compilation apparently produced toward the end of the seventeenth century somewhere in the lands of the former Golden Horde. It consists of six epic-style *dāstāns*, most of a decidedly more "legendary" character than those employed by Jalāyirī, and non-Chingisids (including Temür, with whom two of the *dāstāns* are concerned, and Edigü) figure much more prominently in the anonymous work.

In the account of Qādir ʿAlī Bek[125] (essentially repeated in the *Daftar-i Chingīz-nāmah*[126]), the lineage of Abū Bakr down to Baba Tükles is

124. This work, one version of which was published long ago by I. Khal'fin (*Zhizn' Dzhingiz-khana i Aksak-Timura*, Kazan, 1822) is discussed by Usmanov, *Tatarskie istoricheskie istochniki*, pp. 97–133; cf. Köprülü, *Türk edebiyatı tarihi*, pp. 278–280; and Abdülkadir İnan, "Destân-i nesl-i Çengiz Han kitabı hakkında," *Azerbaycan Yurt Bilgisi*, 3 (1934), pp. 9–14, 131–135 (reprinted in his *Makaleler ve İncelemeler* (Ankara, 1968), pp. 198–206). It is mentioned (as is the Idige epic cycle) with a brief discussion in Ahmet Temir, "Die alten Quellen der Kazan- und nord-türkischen Literatur (bis zum XIX. Jahrhundert," in *Studies in General and Oriental Linguistics prtesented to Shirô Hattori on the Occasion of his Sixtieth Birthday*, ed. Roman Jakobson and Shigeo Kawamoto (Tokyo: TEC Company, 1970), pp. 612–626 (p. 618, 619–620). Further copies of the work are noted in I. G.Galiautdinov, "Paleograficheskie osobennosti spiskov pamiatnika 'Daftar-i Chingiz-name,' " in *Bartol'dovskie chteniia 1981 (god piatyi): Tezisy dokladov i soobshchenii* (Moscow: Nauka, GRVL, 1981), pp. 27–28.

125. *Sbornik letopisei*, ed. Berezin, p. 161; cf. Valikhanov's notes on this text as published in Ch. Ch. Valikhanov, *Sobranie sochinenii v piati tomakh* (Alma–Ata, 1961), I, p. 152. The printed text, based on a defective manuscript, lacks the generations from Abū Bakr down to Baba Tükles; their presence in fuller copies of the work is confirmed by Usmanov, *Tatarskie istoricheskie istochniki*, p. 82, and the text from one copy is transcribed by Syzdykova, *Iazyk*, pp. 234–235.

126. Usmanov (*Tatarskie istoricheskie istochniki*, p. 116) implies the similarity of the accounts, but gives few particulars on the section of the work bearing the heading "Dāstān-i Edige [*īdīkah*] Bīy" (which does not appear in all copies). Khal'fin's publication of the text has not been available to me, but Valikhanov's translation of the account of Edige from Khal'fin's text (*Sochineniia Chokana Chingisovicha Valikhanova*, ed. N. I. Veselovskii [St. Petersburg, 1904; *Zapiski Imperatorskago Russkago Geograficheskago Obshchestva po otdeleniiu ètnografii*, t. 29], pp. 228–229), despite several divergences in the forms of proper names and in two problematical passages, shows the essential identity of the content. I have been able to consult only one manuscript of the *Daftar-i Chingīz-nāmah* that contains the section on Edige (the Paris, Berlin, and British Museum copies do not)—one, incidentally, not mentioned at all in Usmanov's survey of

recorded,[127] along with the dwelling- (and ruling-) places of each figure in the genealogy (e.g., Syria, Egypt, Madīnah and/or Madā'in, Antioch, Constantinople) (see Tables 5.1 and 5.2). Then the lineage of Baba Tükles, who is said to have "ruled" in Mecca, is given through his son Terme down to Edigü: this Terme ("*t.r.mah*") came to "Idil-Jayïq" (that is, the Volga-Ural region), and his son Qarapchï (or "Qïzïjï or "Qarïjï")[128] lived there also, as did *his* son Islām-Qïyā[129] and the latter's son Qādir-Qïyā; Qādir-Qïyā's son, however, named Qūtlū-Qïyā, lived in "Qumkent," and it was this Qūtlū-Qïyā (who was killed, says the account, by Urus Khan), who was the father of Edigü.[130]

Following this genealogy from Abū Bakr to Edigü, the account returns to Baba Tükles, attesting at once to his central role in Edigü's lineage and to the wide variety of accounts already in existence regarding his sons and his (or his son's) move to the Volga-Ural region:

---

manuscripts, p. 102—preserved in Edinburgh University Library, MS No. Or. (Turk) 7, copied in 1240/1825 (on this copy see John R. Walsh, "The Turkish Manuscripts in New College, Edinburgh," *Oriens*, 12 (1959), pp. 178–179); the account of Edige here (ff. 64b–65b) corresponds well with Valikhanov's translation and is nearly identical to the available portion of Qādir ʿAlī Bek's account in Berezin's publication.

127. The lineage is as follows: Abū Bakr > Muḥammad ["Maḥmūd" in Syzdykova] > Sulṭān Kaʿb > Sulṭān Hurmuz > Sulṭān Khālid > Sulṭān Valīd > Sulṭān Qaydah ["Qaydur" in Syzdykova] > Sulṭān Mavlūd > Sulṭān Abū'l-ʿĀṣ ["Abu Algha" (!) in Syzdykova] > Sulṭān Salīm > Sulṭān Ṣadāq > Abū'l-Ḥaqq > Sulṭān ʿUthmān ["ʿUshmān" (!) in Syzdykova] > Sulṭān Jalāl ad-Dīn; the latter had two sons, one named Ibrāhīm (or "Adham"), the other Baba Tükles. The "historical" and epic versions of the Edigü/Baba Tükles genealogy are summarized in Table 5.1, and simplified genealogies reconstructed from Russian and Central Asian pedigrees discussed below are presented in Table 5.2.

128. The spelling of this name varies widely, with forms interpretable as *q.r.jī* or *q.rījī* or *q.r.b.jī* most common; the form *q.z.jī* also appears, which, with "orthographic license," recalls the name of Qazanchi Bahādur, named by Muʿīn ad-Dīn Naṭanzī as a commander under Toqtamïsh's rival Urus Khan who, after the latter's death, deserted his second successor Temür Bek Khan and entered Toqtamïsh's service (*Muntakhab*, ed. Aubin, pp. 94, 363, 422). Neither form, however, is otherwise attested or easily interpretable. Syzdykova adopts the reading "Qarïjï," but early epic versions of the genealogy (discussed in the following chapter) give the name in forms reducible to "Qarapchï," a form reflected also in ʿAbd al-Ghaffār Qïrïmī's version and in early Russian adaptations, both discussed below.

129. The element *qïya* in the names of these figures is spelled *q.yā* in Arabic-script texts, and is often interpreted as "Qaya"—a vocalization suggested also by transcription texts of the epic versions discussed below. As an element in personal names, however, the term is certainly to be understood as the Mongol word *qiya*, meaning "page," "aide-de-camp," "bodyguard" (cf. Doerfer, *TMEN*, I, pp. 445–446, No. 315); the form *k.yā* in some Arabic-script texts reflects the same term.

130. Abū'l-Ghāzī also names as Edigü's father one "Qutluq Qïya" of the Aq Manghït tribe (ed. Desmaisons, I (tr.), p. 171, II (text), p. 162). On the historical accounts of Edigü's father, see Bartol'd, "Otets Edigeia," *Sochineniia*, II/1, pp. 797–804 (where he notes the error in Desmaison's translation).

> But Baba Tükles had four sons: one of them was the ruler (*pādshāh*) at the Kaʿbah, one of them lies [buried] beside the Kaʿbah, one of them lies in Urgench, and one of them lies in the Crimea, in Üch-Ütlük.[131] According to [another] account, Baba Tükles had three known sons: one of them, named ʿAbbās, lies at the right side of the Kaʿbah; one of them, named ʿAbd ar-Raḥmān Khoja, also lies at the Kaʿbah; and one of them, named Terme, came to Idil-Jayïq.

Then follows an obscure passage, unclear both in itself and in its connection with the preceding accounts. It begins abruptly:

> From the holy grave of the Prophet (God bless him and keep him) a voice came to Sayyid Nāqib [*sic*]; the second was ʿĀlam–Murtażā Sayyid; the third was the saintly miracle-worker Baba Tükles Ata.[132] When Özbek Khan became a Muslim, he sent Örek-chura [or "Üzek–chura"] to the holy Kaʿbah; he brought these three men and [the khan] became a Muslim.[133]

Such is the account in the Tatar histories. The genealogical sections are clear enough, while the second portion of the passage, dealing with Baba Tükles and his sons, evidently points to the wide disparity of traditions surrounding Baba Tükles and to the somewhat garbled transmission of the traditions themselves (unless the obscurity in the narrative may be attributed to the author's attempt to reconcile, or at least make sense out of, the

131. Valikhanov's notes on Berezin's text (*Sobranie sochinenii*, I, p. 152) give the same account, but his translation from Khal'fin's text (*Sochineniia*, p. 229) has the first son (the ruler at the Kaʿbah), buried there, and the other three sons buried respectively in Urgench, "Keriman," and Üch-Ütlük; this interpretation is clearly ruled out by both Berezin's text and the Edinburgh manuscript of the *Daftar-i Chingīz-nāmah*.

132. The text (text appearing in the Edinburgh MS given in {}, text only in Berezin given in [], variant readings in < >): *payğambar (ṣallā'llāhu ʿalayhi va sallama)-ning {mubārak} qabr-larïdïn sayyid nāqib-qa <MS: nāqibāğa> āvāz berip-dur; ikinči ʿālam murtażā sayyid; üčünči[si] ʿazīz karāmat{i} baba tükles ata turur.* For the last four words Syzdykova (p. 235) emends to *baba tükles ata[sï] turur*, but there seems to be no compelling reason to do so.

133. Valikhanov's translation from Khal'fin's text (*Sochineniia*, p. 229) interprets the most obscure part of this passage differently, rendering *āvāz berip-dur* as "one honors" rather than as "a voice came" (as he himself translated the same words in his notes on Berezin's text, *Sobranie sochinenii*, I, p. 152); he thus understands the passage to mean that the grave of the Prophet is honored above all others, but that the grave of "ʿĀlam-murtażā" (i.e., ʿAlī) is second in esteem and the grave of Baba Tükles third. While it is tempting to find such a meaning in an otherwise obscure passage, both the context and the wording of the passage would seem to argue against it.

Table 5.1. The Genealogy of Edigü and Baba Tükles According to Historical and Epic Accounts

Osmanov	Jalāyirī/Daftar	Iusupov genealogy, 1654 list	Iusupov genealogy, 1686 list	Maṭlab aṭ-ṭālibīn	Qara-Noghay epic account, Anan'ev	Chodzko	ʿAbd al-Ghaffār Qïrïmī	Ming Bashkir Shajarah (see Ch. 6)
Abū Bakr	Abū Bakr	Abubekkir	Ababuk/Babekir	Abū Bakr	Ababakiar	Abubekr-Saudyk	Abū Bakr aṣ-Ṣiddīq	Abū Bakr Ṣiddīq
Muḥammad	Muḥammad ["Maḥmūd" in Syzdykova], Shām	Magamet Damascus	Magomet	Sulṭān Muḥammad	[missing]	sultan Mahmud	Muḥammad	Muḥammad Sulṭān, Miṣr
Sulṭān Kaʿb	Sulṭān Kaʿb Shām	soltan Kegap Damascus	Sultan Kegab	Sulṭān Kaʿb	Soltan-Kiab	sultan Ibrahim	Shaykh Kaʿb	Sulṭān Kaʿb Shām
Sulṭān Hurmuz	Sulṭān Hurmuz Miṣr	soltan Girmez Egypt	Sultan Girmis	[missing]	Soltan-Irmiz	sultan Abbas	Shaykh Murād	Sulṭān Hurmuz Miṣr
Sulṭān Khalīd	Sulṭān Khālid Ṣarṣar	soltan Khaleb Sarsar	Sultan Khalid	Sulṭān Valad	Soltan-Khanit	sultan Hamza	Shaykh Khālid	Sulṭān Ḥālīd Ṣarṣar
Sulṭān Valīd	Sulṭān Valīd Ṣarṣar	soltan Zalid Sarsa	[missing]	Sulṭān Khāldār	Soltan-Valit	Khalid	[missing]	Sulṭān [ ] Ṣarṣar
Sulṭān Qaydah	Sulṭān Qaydah ["Qaydur" in Syzdykova] Ṣarṣar	soltan Kyiaye Sarsar	[missing]	Sulṭān Mavlūd	Soltan-Kaida	Walid	Shaykh Q.ydār	Sulṭān Qayd [ ] Ṣarṣar
Sulṭān Mavlūd	Sulṭān Mavlūd ["Mulud" in Syzdykova] Ṣarṣar	soltan Kuled Sarsar	Sultan Kuliud	Sulṭān Qāydār	Soltan-Mavlut	Osman	[missing]	Sulṭān Mavlūd Ṣarṣar
Sulṭān Abū'l-ʿĀṣ	Sulṭān Abū'l-ʿĀṣ ["Abu Algha" (!) in Syzdykova] Anṭākīyah	soltan Abulgazy Antioch	Sultan Abulgazi	Sulṭān Abū'l-ʿĀṣ	Soltan-Abul-Az	Jalal-ed-Dyn	Shaykh Khāṣṣ	Sulṭān Abu'l-[ ] [?]
Sulṭān Salīm	Sulṭān Salīm Anṭākīyah	soltan Selim Antioch	Selim	Sulṭān Salīm	Soltan-Selim	Abul-Kalipheh	[missing]	Sulṭān Salīm Anṭākīyah

Sulṭān Ṣadāq	Sulṭān Ṣadāq ["Sadik" in Syzdykova] Anṭākīyah	soltan Syddyk Antioch	Sultan Syddyk	Sulṭān Ṣafā	Soltan-Sydak	Salim	Shaykh Ṣafā	Sulṭān Ṣadāq [?]
Abū'l-Ḥaqq	Abū'l-Ḥaqq Madā'in	soltan Abdiulkhak Medoin	Sultan Abdel'khak	[missing]	Abdulkhak	[missing]	[missing]	Sulṭān ʿUthmān Madīnah
Sulṭān ʿUthmān	Sulṭān ʿUthmān ["ʿUshmān" (!) in Syzdykova] Madā'in	soltan Usmanor Medoin	Sultan Osman	[missing]	Soltan-Osman	[transposed]	[missing]	Sulṭān ʿAlā' ad-Dīn "Quṣṭanṭah"
Sulṭān Jalāl ad-Dīn	Sulṭān Jalāl ad-Dīn Qusṭanṭīyah two sons: Ibrāhīm (or "Adham") &	soltan Dzhalialiaddin Konstiantin grad	Sultan Dzhalialeddin	Sulṭān Jalāl ad-Dīn *Rūmī*	Soltan Dzhalalèddin	[transposed]	Jalāl ad-Dīn Sulṭān al-ʿUlamā Shaykh Bahā' ad-Dīn Valad (adds:) Shaykh Ibrāhīm	Sulṭān Jalāl ad-Dīn "Quṣṭanṭah"
Tūklās Bābā	Bābā Tūklās Kaʿbah	Babatiuklias Kegai	Babatiuklias Kekhba	Tūklās Bābā	Babatukles	Bābā Tūklās	Bābā ʿĀlam-Shaykh ʿĀrif bi'llāh Tūklās	Sulṭān Bābā Tūklās, Kaʿbah
Terme [T.r.mah]	Terme [T.r.mah] Idil-Jayïq	Termes Volga/Yayïq	Termia	Tūr.m Bīy	Turma [Turme]	Túrbay-Kurabchi	Tūrah-mah [*sic*] Bek	Tīrmah Khān
Qïzīchī	Qarapchï / Qïzïjï	Karapchi	Karapchi	[missing]	Kzychi [Kzyche]		Qarāpchī Bek	Qazanchī Bīy
Islām Qïyā	Islām Qïyā	Islamkaia	Slamkai	Islām Qïyā Bīy	Islam-Kaya [Islan-kaya]	Islam-Kaya	Islām Qïyā Bek	Islām Qïyā
Qādir Qïyā	Qādir Qïyā	Kadylkaia/ Kydylkaia	Kaddyrkai	[missing]	Kadyrkaya	Kaddyr-Kaya	Qādir Qïyā Bek	Qādir Qïyā
Qūtlū Qïyā Bīy	Qūtlū Qïyā Qumkent	Kutlukaia, to Kumkent	Kadlukai Kunkent	Qūtmūq [*sic*] Qïyā Bīy	Kutlukaya	Kúlly-Kaya	Qūtlū Qïyā Bek	Qūtlū Qïyā
Idige	Idige	Èdigi	Iddigei	Edigī Bīy	Adige	Adiga	Mīr-i Kabīr Ädīgü Bek	Idige Bīy

Table 5.2. Some Russian and Central Asian Genealogies Stemming from Edigü

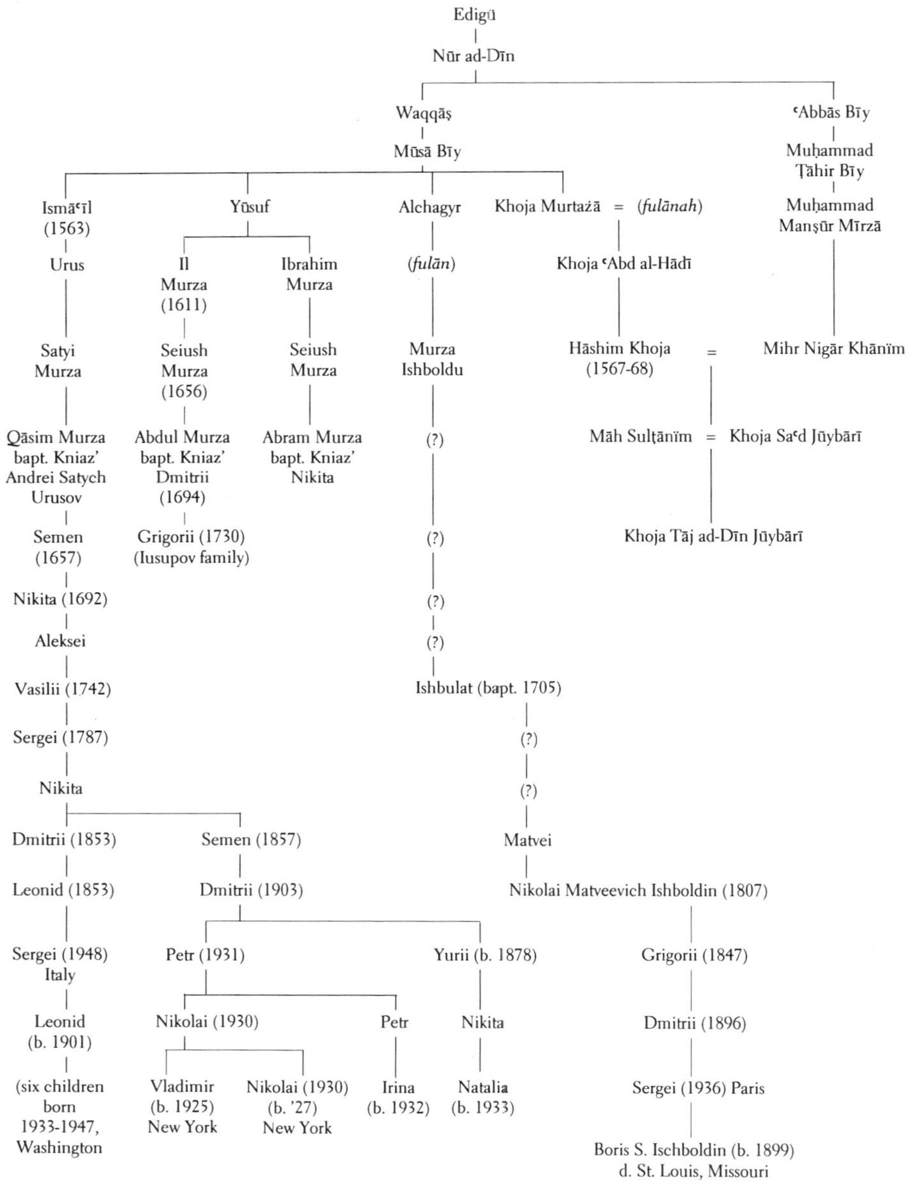

various accounts). In fact at least three traditions appear to be reflected in the second part of the account: one ascribes four unnamed sons to Baba Tükles and links one with Urgench in Khorezm and another with the Crimea; the second lists three sons of Baba Tükles by name and emphasizes the move of one of them to the Volga-Ural region; and the third, as obscure as it is, was probably focused in its original form on the conversion of Özbek Khan, mentioning the prophetic "summons" that brought Baba Tükles himself—rather than one or two of his sons, who seem not to have figured in this tradition—to the lands of the Golden Horde.

Of the three traditions condensed in the second part of the account, it is most likely the second, in which Baba Tükles' son Terme appears as the first of his lineage to move to the Volga-Ural region, that formed a continuous narrative together with the genealogical section. This is suggested not only by the appearance of Terme and the focus on the "Idil-Jayïq" region within the account, but also by the striking similarity of the genealogical section to accounts from several versions of the epic cycle based on the career of Edigü, to be discussed in Chapter 6, in which Terme appears as well; on this basis we can surmise that Q̱ādir ʿAlī Bek made use of oral genealogical accounts about Edigü, similar to those included in the "Idige" epic, that must therefore have reached a more or less stable form by the end of the sixteenth century.

In the account of Q̱ādir ʿAlī Bek and those who followed him, however, the genealogy and the three traditions are, if not fully reconciled, at least understood and presented as an integral narrative without explicit internal contradictions; even the "three-son" account is made flexible and nonexclusive when the author specifies that Baba Tükles' *known* sons numbered three. What may be derived from the entire passage, despite its obscurities, as the common core of the account that made its way into the Tatar historiographical tradition, is that the ancestors of Edigü in the lineage of Abū Bakr made their appearance in the Volga valley during the time when Özbek Khan accepted Islam, through the arrival of Baba Tükles, who came from the sacred centers of the Muslim world together with two companions, as well as, presumably, his son Terme; this Terme settled in the Volga-Ural valley, where his descendants also lived until the time of his great-grandson, Q̱ūtlū-Q̱ïyā, the father of Edigü, who is said to have dwelled in the town of Q̱umkent. If in fact the four-son and three-son accounts represented separate traditions in need of reconciliation, it would follow that the Terme in the three-son account should be identified with the son buried in the Crimea in the four-son account; but in fact it seems most likely that the two versions of the number of Baba Tükles' sons, as well as the garbled account of his two companions (or three, including his son), may represent different interpretations of the tradition—encountered also in the work of Ötemish Ḥājjī—that Baba Tükles came to Özbek Khan as one of a group of four saints. Similarly, the key figures in the genealogy are Edigü and Baba Tükles, and to a lesser extent Terme, Qūtlū-Qïyā, and of course Abū Bakr. The other links are no more than mere names, and as such are more susceptible to both fragmentation and recombination as the various epithets and elements in single names were split into separate generations, or as distinct appellations from two separate generations were combined in single names; these processes seem to explain both the variations in the forms found in "historical" and epic versions of the genealogy, and the relative stability of the accounts in terms of the elements of names included in the lineage.[134]

The town of Qumkent mentioned in the account is significant: as we will see, it plays an important role in several "mythologized" versions of the epic tradition based on Edigü's career. The town is certainly to be identified with the "Qūmkent" mentioned by Abū'l-Ghāzī as a flourishing town near the larger Khorezmian city of Vazīr; Vazīr, however, appears to have been established only in the 1450s under Muṣṭafā, the Shïbānid rival of Abū'l-Khayr Khan,[135] while Qumkent appears as the name of a Khorezmian town already in the works of Niẓām ad-Dīn Shāmī (806/1404) and Muʿīn ad-Dīn Naṭanzī (817/1414)—that is, in the

134. For a discussion of the signs and motives of alterations in oral genealogies, see David P. Henige, *The Chronology of Oral Tradition: Quest for a Chimera* (Oxford: Clarendon Press, 1974), pp. 27–38 (on shortening or "telescoping"), pp. 38–64 (on lengthening). Both processes are evident in the case of the Baba Tükles/Edigü genealogies, as will be clearer in the case of versions given in the epic accounts, but it is difficult (and ultimately of little consequence) to argue which extant version reflects the tradition closest to an "original" genealogy: the chronology of the accounts themselves is not always clear, and it is impossible to insist upon a normative sequence for the two complementary processes of alteration (as Henige notes [p. 6], lengthening "often represents a belated effort to compensate for earlier telescoping"). Here it is worth noting that in one of the earliest versions we have of the story of Chingis Khan's genealogical links to a woman miraculously impregnated by a ray of light, it is Chingis himself who is thus conceived (Boyle, "Kirakos of Ganjak," p. 202); other versions adopt this theme in recounting Chingis's distant sacral ancestor Alan Qoa, and in this we have a parallel to the wide range in genealogical distance reported in various accounts of the links between Edigü/Idige and Baba Tükles.

135. Such is Khwāndamīr's account, cf. Akhmedov, *Gosudarstvo*, p. 64; Muṣṭafā, incidentally, occasionally enjoyed the support of the Manghït Vaqqāṣ Bīy, a grandson of Edigü. Vazīr was evidently already a prominent town by the time of Muḥammad Shïbānī Khan's campaign in Khorezm in 1505; cf. *Materialy po istorii kazakhskikh khanstv*, pp. 24–27 (from the *Tavārīkh-i guzīdah–i nuṣrat–nāmah*).

lifetime of the historical Edigü.[136] Abū 'l-Ghāzī portrays Qumkent as rich and populous as late as the mid-sixteenth century,[137] and, of special interest, links the nearby Vazīr with the descendants of Sayyid Ata; we will consider the implications of this in Chapter 6.

Little more may be learned from the genealogical and "historical" material included in the works of Qādir ʿAlī Bek and his successors. Here Baba Tükles is an ancestor of Edigü, linking him with an Islamic heritage and, more specifically, with a tradition of Islamic rulership; he is also associated, though somewhat vaguely, with the general spread of Islam in the Golden Horde. It must be noted that the form of the genealogy given in the Tatar historiographical tradition is immediately suspect, since Edigü can hardly have been separated from the time of Özbek Khan by six generations, but in any event, it is not the "historicity" of the account, already discussed extensively,[138] that is our chief concern; rather, what we must bear in mind is the transformation of the figure of Baba Tükles—whose role in the Islamization of the Golden Horde is nevertheless still echoed in these works—into a genealogical link in Edigü's "Islamized" pedigree, as well as the recurrence of various elements (of detail and of tone), known from other sources on Baba Tükles, in the cultured, educated literary tradition of the Tatar khanates.

Here we may note that ʿAbd al-Ghaffār Qïrïmī's presentation of Edigü's genealogy in the *ʿUmdat al-akhbār*,[139] referred to earlier, differs from that of Qādir ʿAlī Bek and his successors in several noteworthy respects that highlight the probable motives underlying the traditions preserved by Qādir ʿAlī Bek. First, in ʿAbd al-Ghaffār's work there is only minimal connection between Baba Tükles' Islamizing activity and his ancestry of Edigü: indeed, when the latter's full genealogy is recounted, Baba

136. The Khorezmian Qumkent was evidently of some significance by the latter fourteenth century, for it figures as a geographical landmark in these historians' accounts of Temür's final campaign against Khorezm (i.e., Urgench) in 790/1388, intended to punish the city for its support of his enemy Toqtamïsh (Shāmī, *Ẓafar-nāmah*, ed. Tauer, I, pp. 107–108; Naṭanzī, *Muntakhab*, ed. Aubin, p. 340; cf. Yazdī, *Zafarnoma*, facs. ed. Urunbaev, f. 194b).

137. Abū'l-Ghāzī, ed. Desmaisons, pp. 220–222 (text), 236–237 (tr.); cf. Bartol'd, "Svedeniia ob Aral'skom more," *Sochineniia*, III, pp. 63, 67, 88.

138. Bartol'd, "Otets Edigeia;" cf. the researches of V. M. Zhirmunskii in connection with the epic tale based on Edigü's career, cited below, and see also Pelliot, *Notes sur l'histoire de l'Horde d'Or*, pp. 105–107.

139. MS, f. 322b [Latin] /325b [Arabic]; Najīb ʿĀṣim ed., pp. 203–204. The lineage runs as follows: Mīr-i Kabīr Ädīgü Bek < Qūtlū Qïyā Bek < Qādir Qïyā Bek < Islām Qïyā Bek < Qarāpchī Bek < Tūrah-mah [*sic*] Bek < Bābā ʿĀlam-Shaykh [or *ʿālim?*] *ʿārif bi'llāh* Tūklās < Shaykh Ibrāhīm < Jalāl ad-Dīn *sulṭān al-ʿulamā* ash-Shaykh Bahāʾ ad-Dīn Valad [*sic*] < ash-Shaykh Ṣafā < ash-Shaykh Khāṣṣ < ash-Shaykh Q.ydār < ash-Shaykh Khālid < ash-Shaykh

Tükles appears in it but with no mention of his role in Özbek Khan's conversion. Second, ʿAbd al-Ghaffār offers no narrative "expansion" for any of the links in Edigü's genealogy: there is no mention of where his ancestors lived or at what point they moved to the Volga valley. More important, perhaps, there is no hint, in ʿAbd al-Ghaffār's version, of the tradition of rulership associated with Edigü's ancestors in Qādir ʿAlī Bek's account, where that tradition is both explicitly stated, as noted, and implied through the title of *sulṭān* assigned to nearly every link in the genealogy. For ʿAbd al-Ghaffār, Edigü's ancestors as far back as Baba Tükles are simply *beks*; and from Baba Tükles back to Abū Bakr, they are *shaykhs*.

As noted, ʿAbd al-Ghaffār cites "histories of the Uzbeks" for his account of Edigü's genealogy, and it is entirely possible that his account reflects, quite independently, traditions that differed from those recorded in Qādir ʿAlī Bek's work and the *Daftar-i Chingīz-nāmah*. On the other hand, it seems unlikely that ʿAbd al-Ghaffār would have been entirely unfamiliar with the earlier Tatar historiographical tradition as represented by Qādir ʿAlī Bek's work; if he was indeed aware of the presentation of Edigü's genealogy in that tradition, both his brevity and his divergent emphases may reflect a conscious decision to downplay the heritage and role of the non-Chingisid Edigü. Qādir ʿAlī Bek, of course, also wrote for Chingisids, but in his case their submission to Russian power may have rendered the assertion of Chingisid rights less of an ongoing concern than in the case of the Crimean khans still compelled, in ʿAbd al-Ghaffār's time, to wrestle with the prerogatives of the tribal aristocracy.

Baba Tükles and the Naqshbandī Shaykhs of Bukhārā: The Jūybārī Khojas and Their Sacred Lineages

The relative stability of the genealogy attested in the accounts discussed above is suggested further by its appearance, in a quite similar form, in a Central Asian source produced far from the milieu of the

---

Murād < ash-Shaykh Kaʿb < Muḥammad < Abū Bakr aṣ-Ṣiddīq. This version has clearly telescoped the generations between Abū Bakr and Baba Tükles; the latter's designation seems to echo the names found in the account of Qādir ʿAlī Bek, but only vaguely; the "Ibrāhīm" who appeared as Baba Tükles' brother in Qādir ʿAlī Bek's account is here cast as his father, while a "*bin*" has probably been omitted that would have made "Jalāl ad-Dīn" [*not* explicitly Rūmī here] the son of "Bahāʾ ad-Dīn Valad"; and the title of *sulṭān* assigned to most links in Qādir ʿAlī Bek's version has been retained only for one, and transformed into a juridical honorific.

Tatar histories, namely a mid-seventeenth-century hagiographical work, entitled *Maṭlab aṭ-ṭālibīn*, devoted to the famous Jūybārī *khojas* of Bukhārā;[140] this work's author was the son of Khoja Tāj ad-Dīn Ḥasan (d. 1056/1646), who was in turn a grandson of the real founder of Jūybārī power, Khoja Muḥammad Islām (d. 971/1563), and the work includes extensive genealogical material on the various lineages of the major Jūybārī *shaykhs*.[141] These Naqshbandī leaders, who played such a prominent role in Central Asian political and economic affairs in the sixteenth and seventeenth centuries, were well positioned to add to their Islamic pedigree sacred lineages of Inner Asian origin; by the time the *Maṭlab aṭ-ṭālibīn* was written, the leading Jūybārī shaykh's ancestors included Abū Bakr and, through ʿAlī, the Prophet, as well as Chingis Khan and Edigü.

The Jūybārī lineage as outlined in the *Maṭlab aṭ-ṭālibīn* (see Table 5.2) in fact includes two links to Edigü, both through Khoja Tāj ad-Dīn's mother, Māh Sulṭānïm; but only one is explicitly traced so as to include Baba Tükles. Māh Sulṭānïm's mother, we are told, was Mihr Nigār Khānïm, who was descended from Shïbān b. Jöchi on her mother's side and from Abū Bakr—through Edigü—on her father's side; her father, more precisely, was Muḥammad Manṣūr Mīrzā, *his* father was Muḥammad Ṭāhir Bīy, and *his* father was ʿAbbās, whose father was in turn the famous Nūr ad-Dīn, Edigü's son. Khoja Tāj ad-Dīn's maternal grandmother was thus a great-great-great granddaughter of Edigü, whose lineage is given thus: Edigī Biy < Qūtmūq [*sic*] Qïyā Biy < Islām Qïyā Biy < Tūr.m Biy < Tūklās Bābā. The names are clearly recognizable,

140. The Jūybārī shaykhs remain little studied in the West, and in general. The only substantial treatment remains that of P. P. Ivanov, *Khoziaistvo dzhuibarskikh sheikhov; k istorii feodal'nogo zemlevladeniia v Srednei Azii v XVI-XVII vv.* (Moscow/Leningrad: Izd-vo Akademii nauk SSSR, 1954); though focused on the family's economic history, the work includes the most extensive survey available of the hagiographical corpus produced by and about the Jūybārī shaykhs. See also the more recent article of B. A. Akhmedov, "Rol' dzhuibarskikh khodzhei v obshchestvenno-politicheskoi zhizni Srednei Azii XVI-XVII vekov," in *Dukhovenstvo i politicheskaia zhizn' na Blizhnem i Srednem Vostoke v period feodalizma* (Moscow: Nauka, GRVL, 1985), pp. 16–31.

141. The fact that the Jūybārī *khojas* were ascribed genealogical links with Edigü was noted by Ivanov in his *Khoziaistvo dzhuibarskikh sheikhov*, p. 48, n. 2, citing the *Maṭlab aṭ-ṭālibīn*. Ivanov noted as "curious" the fact that Edigü's "clearly fantastic genealogy" is there traced back to Abū Bakr, but did not mention Baba Tükles; he did, however, note elsewhere that Edigü's descent from Abū Bakr is asserted in the text (of the *Daftar-i Chingīz-nāmah*) published by Khal'fin ("Ocherk istorii karakalpakov," in *Materialy po istorii karakalpakov; sbornik* [Moscow/ Leningrad: Izd-vo Akademii nauk SSSR, 1935; *Trudy Instituta vostokovedeniia*, t. 7], p. 25, n. 3). I have consulted the Berlin manuscript of the *Maṭlab aṭ-ṭālibīn* (Staatsbibliothek zu Berlin-Preussischer Kulturbesitz, Orientabteilung, MS Or. oct. 1540 [cf. *Verzeichnis der orientalischen Handschriften in Deutschland*, XIV/1, No. 158]), where the genealogy in question appears on f. 38a.

although two links (Qādir Qïyā and Qarapchï) are omitted, reducing the generational difference between Edigü and Baba Tükles to a more reasonable four instead of six as in Qādir ʿAlī Bek's version. Baba Tükles' lineage back to Abū Bakr is also given,[142] with some omissions and several discrepancies when compared with the versions known from the Tatar histories and the epics (see Table 5.1), but the identical forms of the majority of names are more striking than the inevitable differences; they attest not to any "real" genealogical links, but to an established tradition of asserting the fact, and even the details, of these links. Interestingly, the genealogy given here in the *Maṭlab aṭ-ṭālibīn* adds to the name of Baba Tükles' father, called "Sulṭān Jalāl ad-Dīn" in the Tatar histories, the *nisbah* "Rūmī," recalling the account of Nūrullāh Khorezmī as well as epic versions of the lineage as noted below.

The other link to Edigü[143] proceeds through the paternal line of Khoja Tāj ad-Dīn's mother Māh Sulṭānïm; her father was Sayyid Hāshim Khoja (912/1506–1507–975/1567–1568), a descendant of Ḥusayn b. ʿAlī on his father's side (adding yet another *sayyid* lineage) and a great-grandson of the Manghït Mūsā Bīy, who is well known as a son of Vaqqās Bīy b. Nūr ad-Dīn b. Edigü. Here the details of the relevant intermarriages are given, and are of some interest in tracing the territorial parameters of Noghay/Manghït interaction with Central Asian *sayyids* and Sufis. Sayyid Hāshim Khoja's paternal grandfather, we are told, called Khoja Murtażā, was given in marriage the daughter of "Mūsā Bīy, *pādshāh* of the *Manqït*, who was among the descendants of the Commander of the Faithful Abū Bakr aṣ-Ṣiddīq"; this happened when, "in the time of the Chaghatay rulers," Khoja Murtażā came to Khorezm and settled there.[144] The "Chaghatay" *pādshāhs* mentioned here must refer to the Timurids or their

142. Abū Bakr > Sulṭān Muḥammad > Sulṭān Kaʿb > Sulṭān Valad [vs. Hurmuz elsewhere] > Sulṭān Khāldār [vs. "Khālid"] > Sulṭān Mavlūd [vs. "Valīd"] > Sulṭān Qāydār [vs. "Qāydah;" "Mavlūd" omitted here] > Sulṭān Abū'l-ʿĀṣ > Sulṭān Sālim > Sulṭān Ṣafā [vs. "Ṣadāq;" "Abū'l-Ḥaqq" and "Sulṭān ʿUthmān" omitted here] > Sulṭān Jalāl ad-Dīn *Rūmī* (!) > Tūklās Bābā.

143. MS Berlin, f. 37a.

144. The Shïbānid *Tavārīkh-i guzīdah-i nuṣrat-nāmah* mentions a "Murtażā Khoja" as a descendant of Sayyid Ata (cf. *Materialy po istorii kazakhskikh khanstv*, p. 18; MS British Museum Or. 3222, f. 148b; Akramov, p. 357), noting that Maḥmūd Bahādur Sulṭān, a younger brother of Muḥammad Shïbānī Khan, took a daughter of this Murtażā Khoja in marriage; the girl died, however, and Maḥmūd then married a daughter of Yumnāq Mīrzā, a grandson of Nawrūz Bek b. Edigü Bek. The *Maṭlab aṭ-ṭālibīn* makes no mention of a Sayyid Atāʾī lineage for the Khoja Murtażā named as Khoja Tāj ad-Dīn's great-great grandfather, but if their identity is assumed (as seems reasonable chronologically), we have an interesting set of traditions linking putative descendants of Sayyid Ata and Baba Tükles.

governors in Khorezm, and from chronological considerations the period envisioned here must correspond to the second half of the fifteenth century, but no particulars are given; it is clear, however, that Mūsā Bīy and the Manghïts were understood to have been of considerable prominence in the vicinity of Khorezm still in the latter fifteenth century, as is indeed plausible in view of this Mūsā Bīy's involvement in the rise of Muḥammad Shïbānī Khan. The same Mūsā Bīy was also the common ancestor of several Russified branches of Edigü's descendants, as discussed below.

Finally, the *Maṭlab aṭ-ṭālibīn* adds in this narrative account one interesting detail to the genealogical list recorded for the first link to Edigü. The same Sayyid Hāshim Khoja (Khoja Tāj ad-Dīn's maternal grandfather), the account says, was highly esteemed by the rulers of Khorezm, where his family had evidently lived from the time of his grandfather Khoja Murtażā; when Dīn Muḥammad Khan became ruler of Khorezm and then conquered Marv, Bāghbād [i.e., Bāghābād], Nasā, Bāvard [i.e., Abīvard], and Dirūn in Khurāsān, however, Dīn Muḥammad gave Khorezm to his brother ʿAlī Sulṭān and established himself in Marv, inviting Sayyid Hāshim Khoja to join him there and giving him "his own niece, the daughter of Muḥammad Manṣūr Mīrzā," in marriage. The Khorezmian rulers mentioned in this account, Dīn Muḥammad Khān and his brother ʿAlī Sulṭān, are clearly two sons of Avānish Khān of the Uzbek "ʿArabshāhid" dynasty, which was established in Khorezm c. 921/1516. Avānish Khan was killed during the seizure of Khorezm by forces of the Shïbānid ʿUbaydullāh Khan in 945/1538, and the events referred to in the *Maṭlab aṭ-ṭālibīn* would appear to correspond to the time when Dīn Muḥammad, after defeating ʿUbaydullāh Khan in 946/1539 and restoring Khorezm to ʿArabshāhid control, moved his base to Khurāsān, where he ruled until his death in 960/1553.[145] Dīn Muḥammad was active in Khurāsān well before this time, however, and his assignment of Khorezm to his brother ʿAlī Sulṭān is not explicitly recorded in other sources, leaving uncertain the time of Sayyid Hāshim Khoja's marriage to Mihr Nigār Khānïm and his move to Marv; the date of 946/1539 is not unreasonable in view of Sayyid Hāshim Khoja's birth- and death-dates.

In any event, according to the account of the *Maṭlab aṭ-ṭālibīn*, Khoja

145. On Avānish and Dīn Muḥammad, see Abū'l-Ghāzī, ed. Desmaisons, pp. 213–230, 237–239 (text), 228–246, 254–256 (tr.); Dīn Muḥammad's conflict with ʿUbaydullāh is also recounted in Ḥasan-Bek Rūmlū's *Aḥsan at-tavārīkh* (completed in 985/1577), cf. *Materialy po istorii turkmen i Turkmenii*, t. II (XVI–XIX vv., Iranskie, Bukharskie i Khivinskie istochniki), ed. V. V. Struve, A. K. Borovkov, A. A. Romaskevich, and P. P. Ivanov (Moscow/Leningrad: Izd-vo AN SSSR, 1938), pp. 59–60.

Tāj ad-Dīn's grandmother, Mihr Nigār Khānïm, was thus a niece to the Chingisid Dīn Muḥammad Khan, indicating, evidently, that the khan's sister was the wife of the Manghït descendant of Edigü, Muḥammad Manṣūr. Such marital connections between the Khorezmian "Uzbeks" and the Manghït chieftains descended from Edigü were in fact quite common; we know from Abū'l-Ghāzī that all three sons of Avānish Khan were born of Manghït women, a slave in the case of Dīn Muḥammad but daughters of *mīrzās* in the other two cases,[146] and his history also attests to the ongoing involvement, both friendly and hostile, of the Manghïts in Khorezmian affairs, and vice versa, through the mid-sixteenth century.

Of greater interest, for our purposes, the *Maṭlab aṭ-ṭālibīn* assigns specific lineages to the Manghït women related by marriage to the Khorezmian Uzbek dynasty (unlike Abū'l-Ghāzī, in most cases), and the lineages go back to Edigü; moreover, the work attests to the maintenance of such close links between Manghït descendants of Edigü and the Khorezmian Uzbek dynasty down to the very time in which Ötemish Ḥājjī compiled his collection of oral tradition from the Jöchid *ulus* for a member of that dynasty. This further confirmation of the intimate and ongoing ties between Edigü's descendants and Khorezm, and specifically with the rulers of Khorezm, is worth keeping in mind in considering the Khorezmian provenance of much of the historical and folkloric material on Edigü and Baba Tükles: not only Ötemish Ḥājjī's work, but the short account of Nūrullāh Khorezmī discussed above, and several versions of the epic treatment of Edigü explored below, stem from Khorezm, with specific elements in both the "historical" and epic accounts (i.e., the town of Qumkent) further indicative of a Khorezmian "localization" of the oral tradition surrounding Edigü and Baba Tükles.

Baba Tükles and the Russianized Noghay Aristocracy: Rulership and Bakrid Lineage among Russian Princes and Industrialists

Perhaps the most curious reflection of Baba Tükles' sacred personage in "historical" and genealogical tradition is the preservation—and rediscovery—of his name and lineage among Russian aristocratic families who claimed descent from Edigü. As noted earlier, both the growing power of

146. Desmaisons, pp. 213 (text), 228–229 (tr.).

the Muscovite state in the sixteenth century, and the hostility of the Noghay hordes and their *bīys* toward the Chingisid rulers of the khanates of Kazan, Astrakhan, and the Crimea, led perhaps inevitably to the cooperation of the Noghay chieftains and the *tsar*'s against Moscow's rivals; this cooperation quickly entailed the nominal and later actual submission of the Noghays to Russian power, with the Noghay *bīys*—virtually all descendants of Edigü—granted titles and ranks in the Russian aristocratic hierarchy and thereby drawn into the circle of Russian nobility and its inducements to conversion and assimilation. The history of the so-called "service Tatars," who maintained aristocratic privileges through service to the Russian state, as well as the far-reaching "Tatar" presence in "Russian" families,[147] is generally known and need not detain us here. We will note, rather, the valuable documentary evidence on Edigü's genealogy that the incorporation of the Noghay nobility into the Russian aristocracy served to preserve, as well as a few instances of Baba Tükles' "memory" among his Russianized "descendants," a memory that led our Inner Asian saint far beyond his homeland, not only to Moscow and Saint Petersburg, but to Paris, New York, Washington, and Saint Louis as well.

In the first place, the evidential requirements of the Russian aristocracy ensured the preservation of genealogies submitted by "Tatar" princes enrolled in its ranks. It is for this reason that we have independent attestation of essentially the same genealogies of Edigü known from the Tatar historiographical tradition, fixed in written form well before the earliest known copies of the Tatar histories; indeed, these genealogies are comparable in antiquity to the Tatar histories, which as we have noted were products of the seventeenth century. It was then, too, that descendants of Edigü presented copies of their genealogical *shajarahs* to the famous "*Razriadnyi Prikaz*" or "Office of Ranks," to be translated into Russian and registered as a basis for authenticating claims to aristocratic status. It seems likely that the archival collections in which this office's documents are preserved hold a still largely untapped body of relatively old information on "Tatar" genealogy and history;[148] research in such material was naturally not encouraged in the Soviet era, but fortunately, early documents relating to families that branched out from great-grandsons

147. Cf. N. A. Baskakov, *Russkie familii tiurkskogo proiskhozhdeniia* (Moscow: Nauka, GRVL, 1979).

148. Cf. the note by M. I. Akhmetzianov, "Èvoliutsiia tatarskikh shedzhere i ikh vidy," in *Materialy IV Konferentsii molodykh nauchnykh rabotnikov* (Kazan: AN SSSR, Kazanskii filial, Institut iazyka, literatury i istorii im. G. Ibragimova, 1976), pp. 130–132.

of Edigü were employed in an important nineteenth-century Russian heraldic compendium, whence they have been cited in genealogical studies among the postrevolutionary Russian émigré community.

The nineteenth-century study is a sumptuous volume, in two parts, on the history of the Iusupov princely family, printed in Saint Petersburg in 1866–1867;[149] it was the basis for the earlier history reconstructed in studies of two other lineages, of the Urusov princely family[150] and of the Ischboldins,[151] produced in the United States. The authors of both of the latter works also utilized Khal'fin's publication of the *Daftar-i Chingīz-nāmah*, and Ischboldin cites also Valikhanov's and Melioranskii's publications on the epic tale of Idige (see Chapter 6), all of which is presented as historical material; the Iusupov history is little more skeptical, but has the advantage of reproducing the Russian text of the two central documents in addition to "reconstructing" the family's history.

These two documents are, first, a genealogical history of Edigü's family down to one of his great-great-great grandsons, written in December 1654 by a certain "Kul'sheev[152] Abdul" and said to have been preserved among the family papers of the Iusupov princes, evidently at least down to the time of the history's compilation;[153] and second, a genealogical list with three additional generations, prepared for the *Razriadnyi Prikaz* and submitted, with signatures of the then-living Iusupov princes, on 19 May 1686.[154] Both documents give a lineage down to Edigü corresponding

149. N. Iusupov, *O rode kniazei iusupovykh: Sobranie zhizneopisanii ikh, gramot i pisem k nim rossiiskikh gosudarei, s XVI do poloviny XIX veka i drugikh famil'nykh bumag, s prisovokupleniem pokolennoi rospisi predkov kniazei iusupovykh s XIV-go veka* (ch. 1, 2; SPb., 1866–1867). The first part presents a family history, while the second contains the documents, letters, and papers; not included in this volume, naturally, is perhaps the most famous "descendant" of Baba Tükles from the Iusupov lineage, Prince Feliks Iusupov, who gained notoriety for the murder of Rasputin in 1916. On the Iusupov family see also Baskakov, *Russkie familii*, p. 114, No. 58.

150. N. D. Pleshko, *Kniaz'ia Urusovy i ikh predki: Istoriko-rodoslovie* (New York: Russkoe Istoriko-Rodoslovnoe Obshchestvo v Amerike, 1955); see further Baskakov, *Russkie familii*, pp. 187–189, No. 156.

151. Cf. Boris Ischboldin, "History of the Ischboldin Al Bakri Family," in his *Essays on Tatar History* (New Delhi: New Book Society of India, 1963), pp. 159–182. The author, an economist, also published what is evidently an earlier version of this chapter, entitled "O rode Izhboldinykh," in the émigré journal *Novik: Istoriko-genealogicheskii zhurnal*, 1945, pp. 29–51 (signed "B. S. Izhboldin"), with considerable attention to other illustrious Muslim dynasties claiming Bakrid descent and thus "related" to the Ischboldins; this article was cited by Vernadsky (*The Mongols and Russia*, p. 282, n. 76), who affirms that "the author of this study, now on the faculty of St. Louis University, is a descendant of Edigey."

152. Or "Kul'teev."

153. Printed in Iusupov, *O rode kniazei Iusupovykh*, ch. 2, pp. 3–5.

154. Printed in Iusupov, *O rode kniazei Iusupovykh*, ch. 2, pp. 343–347.

quite well, allowing for the Russianization of names, with the lineages known from the Tatar histories (and from some epic accounts, as discussed below); not only the genealogy, but the narrative history of the family as well, coincides so completely with the account from Jalāyirī's history that the same tradition must underlie both the Tatar histories and the two Iusupov documents. It seems unlikely, however, that the Iusupov princes actually utilized Jalāyirī's history in preparing the documents of 1654 and 1686. To begin with, we find no indications of links between the Iusupov princes, of Noghay origin, and the Chingisid rulers of the Kasimov khanate, in which Jalāyirī's work was produced; in addition, the Iusupov genealogies were drawn up at a time when the family's representatives had been thoroughly Christianized, distancing them both from the more persistent Muslim traditions of the Kasimov khanate, and from the Islamic tenor of Jalāyirī's work as well. In the latter regard it is worth noting that the 1654 Iusupov document's single significant departure from the account of Edigü's lineage known from Jalāyirī's work is the omission of any mention of Baba Tükles' role in converting Özbek Khan to Islam; this theme is clear, if somewhat muted, in Jalāyirī's account and its derivatives, but the Iusupov document ignores it altogether (though preserving the recitation of ancestors who exercised *rule* in Muslim regions).

After a brief introduction on Abū Bakr as the successor to the Prophet, both documents provide a genealogy down to Baba Tükles' father, with the 1654 document indicating where each figure ruled; the full genealogies down to Edigü are given in Table 5.1, as transcribed from the Russian forms.[155] With "Soltan Dzhalialiaddin," the account turns to the following narrative as taken from the earlier document (with the forms given in the 1686 list included, if different, in square brackets, and the term "emperor" used for the text's "*tsar'*," which probably reflects the term "*pādshāh*" in the "Tatar" original):

> From him were born two sons: the first son was *Adgem* and the other was *Babatiuklias*. *Babatiuklias* was emperor in *Kegai* [*Kekhba*], and Mecca as well. *Babatiuklias*' son *Termes* [*Termia*] was born between the Volga and the Yayïq. From him was born a son, *Karapchi*, between the Volga and the Yayïq. From *Karapchi*

155. The different forms of the names given in the Russian text are in all cases quite understandable as efforts to transcribe names written in Arabic script, i.e., with most vowels not written; the forms clearly signal two copies of the Arabic-script genealogy, since some of the forms reflect typical scribal variants in Arabic-script texts.

> was born a son *Islamkaia* [*Slamkai*], between the Volga and the Yayïq. And from *Islamkaia* was born a son *Kadylkaia* [*Kaddyrkai*], between the Volga and the Yayïq. From *Kydylkaia* was born a son *Kutlukaia* [*Kadlukai*], who seized *Kumkent* [*Kunkent*] and served as ruler in *Kumkent*; and from this *Kutlukaia* was born a son, Prince *Èdigi* [*Iddigei*], and *Èdigii bek* seized the *yurt* from the emperor *Dzhanbek* [*Dzhanibek*] and served as ruler in his place.
>
> From Prince *Èdigi* was born a son *Nuradyk Murza* [*Narodyk-Murza*]. From *Nuradyk Murza* was born a son Prince *Okas* [*Akas*]. From Prince *Okas* was born a son Prince *Musa*. From Prince *Musa* was born a son Prince *Iusuf*, and from Prince *Iusuf* was born a son *Il'-Murza*.
>
> But *Babatiukles* had four sons: the first son was emperor in *Kag*, while the second son is interred beside the *Kagba*. The third son is buried in *Iurgench*. The fourth son is buried in *Krym*. But the emperor of the *Kagba* with *Babatiukles* had three sons [?]:[156] the first, called *Abbas*, is buried at the right side of the *Kagba*, while the second, *Abdurakhman Khozia*, is buried at the *Kagba* as well. The third son was *Termia*, who was between the Yayïq and the Volga.

The 1686 list differs from the 1654 list in inserting the names of Baba Tükles' three sons (as given at the end of the earlier account, but without the burial places mentioned there) in the course of the genealogy and omitting entirely the account of Baba Tükles' *four* sons as given in the earlier list; the 1654 list thus conforms to the history of Jalāyirī in its confusing and apparently self-contradictory accounts of the number of Baba Tükles' sons. The later Iusupov list also gives a more extensive genealogy for the generations after Musa, as noted below.

The genealogy presented in these sources thus attests to the relative stability of the Bakrid genealogy ascribed to Edigü and of the five generations between Baba Tükles and Edigü. They also reflect, more or less accurately, the genealogy of Edigü's descendants as traced through his son and grandson who were most important in the political development of the Noghay horde, Nūr ad-Dīn ("Nuradyk," "Narodyk") and Vaqqāṣ

156. This passage is as unclear in the Russian as it is in the two Tatar versions: "*a u Kagbinskogo tsaria u Babatiuklesia bylo tri syna.*" If, as seems likely, the Iusupov genealogies do not depend directly upon Jalāyirī's work, the close correspondence of the two versions—complete with parallel obscurities—suggests the existence of an earlier, independent written version of the genealogy used both by Jalāyirī and by the compiler of the Iusupov family history.

("Okas," "Akas"). The Iusupov, Urusov, and Ischboldin families share their lineage down to Edigü's great-grandson, Vaqqāṣ' son Mūsā, the same Mūsā whose daughter appears in the Jūybārī lineage. This Mūsā, a contemporary of the "Uzbek" Shïbānī Khan, had several sons by his first wife, including Yūsuf (d. 1556), the ancestor of the Iusupov family, and Ismāʿīl (d. 1563),[157] whose son Urus gave his name to the Urusov princes; both were on good terms with Ivan IV ("the Terrible"), cooperating with him against the Chingisids of Kazan and the Crimea. By another wife a son whose name is given as "Alchagyr" or "Alchegir" was born to Mūsā, and although the 1686 Iusupov genealogy describes this figure as childless,[158] the Ischboldin family history names one of "Alchagyr's" grandsons as the head of that lineage, namely "Ishboldu," whose father is identified only as the son of "Alchagyr" and the daughter of the Crimean khan Mengli Girey.[159] This Ishboldu, by contrast with the pro-Muscovite leanings of the Iusupov and Urusov branches, is said to have participated in the defense of Kazan against Ivan's troops in 1552,[160] and in general the Ischboldin family history reveals both a later Christianization, and more persistent links with branches of the family that remained Muslim, than in the case of the Iusupov and Urusov princes.

The subsequent development of these lineages is outlined, with the attention to personal anecdotes and achievements, and to links with still more prominent historical figures, that one expects of family histories, in the three studies noted above, each of which adds to the typical pride in aristocratic heritage a kind of fascination with the "exotic" origins of the respective families. We need not linger over their later history, except to note the evidence we have on the assimilation of the lineages, and to consider the curiosity of our Islamizing saint's incorporation into the Russian nobility.

In the case of the Iusupov princes, the genealogy of 1686 gives names, as noted, for three generations after "Il-murza" (d. 1611 or 1612), the last prince named in the 1654 document; two of Il-murza's grandsons, out of

157. This Ismāʿīl is the "Great Murse" called "Smille" whom Anthony Jenkinson described as master of the Volga and Yayïq valleys, including "Serachick," in 1558; he is "the greatest prince in all Nagay, who hath slaine and driven away all the rest, not sparing his owne brethren and children, and having peace with this Emperour of Russia he hath what he needeth, and ruleth alone" (*The Principal Navigations, Voyages, Traffiques & Discoveries of the English Nation*, ed. Richard Hakluyt, II (Glasgow: James MacLehose and Sons, 1903), p. 454.

158. Iusupov, *O rode kniazei iusupovykh*, p. 345.

159. Ischboldin, "History," pp. 169–170.

160. Ischboldin, "History," pp. 170–171; the Ischboldin genealogy is quite meagerly documented, compared with the Iusupov and Urusov studies, and the purported links are left unnamed at several generations until the late eighteenth century.

seven named, were baptized, while of his great-grandsons seven out of eight named converted to Christianity. The lineage traced in the 1866–1867 volume runs through Il-murza's son "Seiush Murza" (d. 1656) and his youngest son "Abdul'-Murza" (d. 1694), who received the title "*kniaz'* " ("prince") instead of "*murza*" upon his baptism as Dmitrii Seiushevich.[161] Of this Dmitrii's three sons, all of whom bore Christian names, one was a companion of Peter the Great and participated in his seizure of Azov; and the lineage continues through Dmitrii's great-great-grandson, the author's father. It is thus the second half of the seventeenth century that sees the total Christianization and Russification of the Iusupov lineages reported in our nineteenth-century source; we of course find no information in this work on the branches of Edigü's descendants that remained outside Muscovite service.

With the Urusov princes we find a similar situation. The lineage followed in the émigré study traces the family from Ismāʿīl's son Urus, his son "Satyi murza," and the latter's son "Kasim murza," whose dates are uncertain (he was alive between 1615 and 1640); this "Kasim" was baptized as Andrei Satych Urusov, whom the compiler of the Urusov genealogy is careful to designate as the *Russian* ancestor of the Urusov princes. His descendants in the eleventh generation include the several princes and princesses, born in the 1920s and 1930s to aristocratic refugees from the Bolsheviks, registered as living in Washington and New York at the time the work was compiled.

The Ischboldin family, as noted, is recorded in much less detail. According to the compiler of its history, Boris Sergeevich Ischboldin, the last known representative of the émigré branch of the family, who produced the family history cited above, it was a certain "Ischbulat," a descendant of Abū Bakr in the thirty-first generation, who was the first in the family to be baptized, in 1705; he moved to Sarapul (along the middle Kama), where his family resided for six more generations, until the time of Boris Ischboldin's own father (a seventh-generation descendant of Ischbulat), who evidently lived in Moscow until the revolution and died in Paris in 1936. At the same time, Boris Ischboldin notes that many of Ischbulat's "near relatives" refused to abandon Islam and migrated "northwards into the Finnish woodland or eastwards into the region of Bashkirs who lived near the river Kama and the Ural mountains;"[162] some

161. Cf. Iusupov, *O rode kniazei iusupovykh*, ch. 1, pp. 71–75; ch. 2, p. 349, gives a document on his baptism.

162. Ischboldin, "History," p. 176.

of these later adopted Christianity, forming "the younger Russified branch of the family," but yet another branch of the Ischboldin family, also residing in Sarapul, remained Muslim as late as 1917.[163]

More interesting, perhaps, the Ischboldin family's apparent resistance to Christianization, as well as its participation in the 1705 revolt of Tatars and Bashkirs, led to its exclusion from political and administrative affairs, and for this reason, writes Boris Ischboldin, "both branches of the Ischboldin family turned to commercial activity and founded one of the biggest commercial and industrial dynasties of the region between the Kama and the Ural mountains."[164] It is perhaps only fitting that we find, among descendants of Edigü and Baba Tükles who retained knowledge of their heritage, not only Noghay princes, Bukharan Sufis, and Russian aristocrats, but captains of industry on the frontiers of Russian capitalism as well.

Beyond the interest of following the lives of these "descendants" of our Baba Tükles, however, we may consider the curious response within Russian "high society" in the nineteenth and twentieth centuries to the genealogical traditions about Edigü and Baba Tükles. These responses were shaped, naturally, by pride in the historical prominence of the respective family lineages, but the way in which Baba Tükles, and his quite evidently "unhistorical" genealogy, are dealt with is in itself revealing. Most strikingly, all three family historians accept unflinchingly the historicity of Edigü's descent from Abū Bakr, and for the most part respect even the particular genealogical links from Abū Bakr to Edigü; in doing so, however, they reveal their understanding of what it is in that genealogy that legitimates their families, and that understanding most often has little to do with Baba Tükles.

The Iusupov prince who compiled his family history in 1866–1867 was intent upon showing his lineage's noble origins, based primarily upon descent from Edigü; he is only slightly skeptical of the traditions preserved in the seventeenth-century documents he cites recounting the genealogy from Abū Bakr down to Edigü. But it is clear that this author's interest lies neither in "sacred" descent from Abū Bakr nor in any aura of sacrality surrounding Baba Tükles or Edigü. Rather, it is specifically the tra-

163. Ischboldin, "History," p. 182; he mentions as the head of this branch of the family during World War I a certain "Yasutdin Bahautdin Ischboldin," and says that many Ischboldins were invited to the conference convened in Kazan, to determine the future of the Tatar and Bashkir regions, after the February revolution of 1917.

164. Ischboldin, "History," p. 176.

dition of rulership hereditary in this lineage that is meaningful for the Iusupov family. Edigü, the author writes, was an acknowledged descendant of Muslim *sulṭāns* who ruled in the various cities mentioned in the genealogies; in support of this heritage of rulership he notes that his family's namesake, Yūsuf, was addressed by no less than the Ottoman *sulṭān* Süleyman as "prince of princes," and cites the inscription on the tomb, in Moscow, of his great-great-grandfather, Grigorii Dmitrievich Iusupov (1676–1730), in which he is called a "branch" from the golden stock of princes who "wore the purple."[165] The author devotes attention to Baba Tükles only as one of these ruler-ancestors buried in Mecca, and more so as the father of "Termes," who "moved from Arabia to the shores of the Azov and Caspian seas" and "drew to himself many tribes of Muslims" to form the powerful Noghay horde; he further shows his attachment to the tradition of command and rule, and perhaps his sensitivity to the relatively short genealogy between Abū Bakr and Edigü, by insisting that the Abū Bakr mentioned in his family's history is not the Caliph Abū Bakr, but another Abū Bakr from three centuries later who served the Muslim caliphs as "*Èmir el'-Omra*." This is clearly "history" for the author, to be used to establish his family's tradition of political authority; all the same he felt obliged to conclude,

> The veil of the centuries has hidden much from the eye, and much may seem doubtful, but even with the impossibility of demonstrating with decisive accuracy the generational sequence of the ancestors of the Iusupov family *before Èdigei*, the origin of the family from royal figures [*ot tsarstvennykh lits*] is not subject to doubt. Nonetheless the descendants of Iusuf endeavored to confirm their renown more through personal valor than through lofty origins.[166]

Nearly a century later, and half a world away, the Urusov family history was produced for the Russian émigré community in America. Its author was able to utilize several studies of the epic account of Idige, Khal'fin's publication of the *Daftar-i Chingīz-nāmah*, and accounts of Bashkir legends discussed below, all of which he cited as "confirming" the essentials of Edigü's genealogy as known from the seventeenth-

165. Iusupov, *O rode kniazei iusupovykh*, ch. 1, p. 11.
166. Iusupov, *O rode kniazei iusupovykh*, ch. 1, pp. 13–14.

century Iusupov documents.[167] On this basis he was able to "restore" to the family history the Islamizing role of Baba Tükles, ignored both by the nineteenth-century Iusupov genealogist and by the seventeenth-century Iusupov documents; he even mentioned (without citation) "Tatar legends, recorded by many ethnographers," that tell of the Manghït people's inconstancy in Islam until the khan Özbek summoned "Teria Babatiukliasov" from Mecca to strengthen the people in the faith.[168] His motivation in this appears to have lain more in an aim to bibliographical thoroughness than in heightening thereby the family's noble heritage, however; he begins his genealogy seven generations before Abū Bakr, having learned of them from the *Encyclopedia of Islam*, and includes, on the basis of various secondary historical works, a great many Noghay princes extraneous to his Urusov genealogy. It is only with much later generations that genuine family traditions are cited, and in the case of the Urusovs we cannot be certain of any substantial "memory" within the family of its reputed origins before the time of the Noghay princes' submission to Russia. The effort to search out "confirmatory" material on those earlier genealogical links, however, reflects both a concern for the family's heritage of rulership as in the Iusupov history, and a more even-handed (though uncritical) assessment of Muslim and Russian "sources."

In the case of Boris Ischboldin we reach the furthest extent of the appreciation of, and fascination with, the lineage of Edigü among his Russified descendants. His family history is, like the Urusov genealogy, based largely on research in historical works for the early generations; it is difficult to judge to what extent his work, and his own consciousness of his lineage, were informed by any living family traditions (as seems doubtful) rather than by the "discoveries" of his research. Certainly he depended upon family traditions and papers for the later portions of his family history, but his extensive attention to Abū Bakr, Baba Tükles, and Edigü and his sons may reflect his study of various sources, not the memory of such links within his family. Regardless of its origins, how-

167. The author also mentions the account of the Urusov princes in the eighteenth-century *Gerbovnik Dvorianskikh familii* (i.e., the official heraldic guide to noble families), which mentions the family's descent from Abū Bakr and Noghay princes but names no individuals (not even Edigü) until Mūsā, praised for his loyalty to Russia (Pleshko, *Kniaz'ia urusovy*, p. i); he also criticizes (p. ii) the genealogical guide of Prince Dolgorukov published in 1855 as full of errors on the Urusov lineage, among them the family's ascription to the fourteenth-century Chingisid khan Urus.

168. Pleshko, *Kniaz'ia urusovy*, p. 4; the form of the name recalls Bashkir legends discussed in Chapter 6.

ever, his familiarity with his reputed genealogy clearly led Ischboldin to identify closely with it, and to treat the accounts he found of his "ancestors" as his own genuine heritage. He devotes about a page of his study to Baba Tükles, taking care to make sense out of the traditions he knew from the publications of Khal'fin and others on the Idige epic; Baba Tükles, writes Ischboldin, came to the Golden Horde "as a Mohammedan missionary," converted many Mongols and Turks to Islam, and then "returned to Mecca with his elder sons, where one of them, Abbas, became soon ruler."[169] Ischboldin continues with his synthetic family history, drawn from many of the sources we are considering here, but for clearly different aims; Baba Tükles' younger son, "Termez," he writes, remained with Özbek Khan, who appointed him ruler of the Mongol and Turkic nomads of Bashkiria, and from the further particulars he cites in this regard it is clear that Ischboldin is incorporating the Bashkir legends of Baba Tükles, discussed below, into his "history."

In effect, Ischboldin's family history reflects yet another effort to reconcile and "make sense" out of the divergent traditions about Baba Tükles, an effort undertaken, like others we have noted, by someone for whom this saint bore special significance. In Ischboldin's case this significance was above all genealogical; he appears to have been much more fascinated with his descent from Abū Bakr than with Baba Tükles himself. As with the Urusov genealogist, Ischboldin aimed to assemble all the information he could find on prominent members of "his family"; his excursus on Baba Tükles simply reflects, as it does in the Urusov family history, the abundance of material on this figure, for in both cases it is above all descent from Abū Bakr that captured the imagination of these twentieth-century Russian émigrés. Ischboldin devotes nearly five pages to Abū Bakr's life and family, as part of his own family's history, and indeed often refers to himself in his book as "Boris Ischboldin al Bakri"; acquaintances of his from his years in Saint Louis confirm his pride in his Bakrid descent, which he would reportedly mention to anyone he believed would understand its significance.[170]

What is finally most worthy of note about the preservation of the Baba Tükles story in this Russified environment is the way it highlights the charismatic associations of the figure of Baba Tükles among the "Islamized" peoples who revered his name; in the Russian aristocracy it is the Bakrid

169. Ischboldin, "History," p. 164.

170. I am grateful to Dr. Nelly Grosswasser, a former colleague, and Mr. Tim Finnegan, a former student, both of St. Louis, who spoke with me about Professor Ischboldin.

genealogy and/or the tradition of rulership that was emphasized, which indirectly attests to the powerful pull of Baba Tükles in a specifically Islamic setting. It is indeed Baba Tükles who is most prominent among the Muslim Turks who honor Edigü, while Abū Bakr is incidental—the reverse of the situation with the Russian aristocratic documentation, where the name of Baba Tükles was preserved but Abū Bakr was emphasized (at least until the legends of Baba Tükles were "rediscovered" by his Russian descendants through scholarship on Idige and Edigü). This further suggests not only that Baba Tükles must have been of considerable importance to overshadow Abū Bakr in the memory of the Islamized Turks, but also that Baba Tükles must have meant something for his Muslim "descendants" that he did not signify for his Russified and Christianized progeny.

We may also note, with a view to future studies of Baba Tükles in genealogical tradition, that despite the ravages of the Soviet era in matters of family tradition and religious life, it is not at all unlikely that families claiming descent from Edigü have retained not only the memory of that descent, but earlier written accounts as well; we have had to rely upon prerevolutionary studies and émigré publications, and it appears that little archival research was undertaken in the Soviet era to analyze family histories, but it may be that such material will once again become available, and regardless of whether it is authentically preserved or more recently contrived, it may continue the process of "responding" to the genealogical figure of Baba Tükles after what amounts to, after all, a fairly brief interruption.

Postscript to Chapter 5

A *Nasab-nāmah-i Edigü Bek* appears among several genealogical supplements appended to the *Tārīkh-i Abū'l-Khayr Khānī* of Masʿūd b. ʿUthmān Kūhistānī, completed in 1540 (MS LOIVAN C478 [copied 998/1590; see Miklukho-Maklai, *Opisanie*, III, No. 303], f. 246b; on the work see Storey-Bregel', *PL*, I, pp. 397–399); unlike the work itself and all other supplements, which are in Persian, the brief genealogy of Edigü is written in Chaghatay Turkic. It gives a version of the same Bakrid genealogy, through Baba Tükles, known from the traditions explored in this chapter, beginning thus: Abū Bakr > Muḥammad (ruler in Ḥalab) >

Sulṭān Kaʿb > Sulṭān Valad > Sulṭān Mavlūd > Sulṭān Khālid > Sulṭān Abū'l-ʿĀṣ > Sulṭān Qubād > Sālim > Sulṭān Ṣalā > Sulṭān Jalāl ad-Dīn Rūmī. The latter had two sons, Tūkles Bābā and Darvīsh Adham, and as written the genealogy appears to ascribe the remaining lineage to Darvīsh Adham through his son "Sulṭān Ibrāhīm;" "his son" would then be "T.r.mah Q.r.b-chīn," but no doubt the copyist is to blame for failing to clearly ascribe "Ibrāhīm" and "Terme" to Darvīsh Adham and Tükles Baba, respectively. It is less clear whether this copyist has collapsed two figures, "Terme" and "Qarapchï," into one, or gives an earlier and more accurate version of the name split into two in other genealogical traditions. In any case, the lineage proceeds thus down to Edigü: Terme Qarabchīn > Islām Qïyā > Qādir Qïyā > Īdīgah Bék; Edigü's lineage is then followed briefly through his son "Nūrādīn" and the latter's two sons Waqqāṣ Bīy and ʿAbbās Bīy.

6

Baba Tükles in Epic Tradition and Folklore

Of all the settings in which Baba Tükles appears, he figures perhaps most prominently in oral epic and folklore traditions widely known across western Inner Asia. If his appearance in the historical works discussed so far has remained as little known as the works themselves, Baba Tükles' role in oral tradition has been more widely recognized, insofar as Turkic oral literature has attracted relatively wide scholarly attention. Nevertheless, Baba Tükles' role in epic and folklore has not been properly appreciated, precisely because the earlier history of his "character" has been poorly understood; now that we have considered his role in conversion narratives and historical traditions, however, we are in a position to examine Baba Tükles' appearance in oral tradition, and to reevaluate what this most popular of cultural venues may tell us about his ongoing vitality and flexibility as ancestor, mythic progenitor, culture hero, and saint.

The epic environment is of particular importance for its indications of Baba Tükles' prominent place in popular consciousness. We cannot take up here a more general discussion of the Turkic epics,[1] but it is important to note the vital social context of epic recitations. The oral epic tradition was without question the single most important vehicle for the articula-

1. On the epic traditions of Turkic peoples in general see, in addition to the works cited in subsequent notes, A. T. Hatto, "Ḥamāsa; IV, Central Asia," *EI*², III, pp. 115–119; H. Munro Chadwick and N. K. Chadwick, *The Growth of Literature*, vol. 3 (1940), pt. 1 (pp. 1–226), "The Oral Literature of the Tatars"; Ilhan Başgöz, "The Epic Tradition among Turkic Peoples," in *Heroic Epic and Saga: An Introduction to the World's Great Folk Epics*, ed. Felix J. Oinas (Bloomington: Indiana University Press, 1978), pp. 310–335; G. M. H. Shoolbraid, *The Oral Epic of Siberia and Central Asia* (Bloomington: Indiana University, 1975; Uralic and Altaic Series, vol. 111); Thomas G. Winner, *The Oral Art and Literature of the Kazakhs of Russian Central Asia* (Durham: Duke University Press, 1958).

tion, reinforcement, and redirection of communal values and self-conceptions. It ordinarily provided the "meeting-place" between the community as a whole and the creative and traditional instincts of the individual bard. The bard himself was an essentially sacred figure, responsible for preserving and transmitting the community's *tradition* but constrained by the nature of his craft to reach, in every new performance, a *dynamic* synthesis of "memorized" passages, themes, and formulas that were shaped through his apprenticeship with a master singer of tales, and an internalized understanding of his community's values and worldview, which in effect set the unspoken bounds for potential innovations.

The latter point—that the entire community participates, and not only passively, in the oral epic's production and transmission—deserves emphasis if, in "democratic" fashion, we seek to discover notions of communal self-conception and human and social values current among "the masses," the ordinary members of a community; these we will never discover, quite frankly, in view of the nature of our sources, but the closest we can come is surely in the narratives of these epic singers who served as the purveyors of communally endorsed traditions and whose performance amounted to both a reaffirmation and rehearsal of sacred verities and values, and truly "popular" entertainment. The social context for epic performances,[2] with the invitation of singers to perform in villages or camps, with public competitions among bards, and with communal sanction necessary for new singers after their apprenticeship, should remind us that in finding recurrent themes in a wide range of epic recordings we are finding reflections of values and personages that clearly "spoke to" the widest possible spectrum of Inner Asian communities and served to give meaning to their traditional values and way of life.[3]

2. On the social context of epic recitations, and their performative aspects, see the discussions in Chadwick and Zhirmunsky, *Oral Epics of Central Asia*, pp. 213–233 (Chadwick), 324–339 (Zhirmunsky); Zhirmunsky also provides a concise discussion of this social context of epic performance in his "The Epic Folk-Singers in Central Asia (Tradition and Artistic Improvisation)," *VII Congrès international des sciences anthropologiques et ethnologiques/VII Mezhdunarodnyi kongress antropologicheskikh i ètnograficheskikh nauk*, Moscow, 1964, t. 6 (Moscow: Nauka, GRVL, 1969), pp. 234–241. See further on performance and its social context Karl Reichl, "Oral Tradition and Performance of the Uzbek and Karakalpak Epic Singers," in *Fragen der mongolischen Heldendichtung*, Teil III (Vorträge des 4. Epensymposiums des Sonderforschungsbereiches 12, Bonn 1983), ed. W. Heissig (Wiesbaden: Otto Harrassowitz, 1985; Asiatische Forschungen, Bd. 91/III), pp. 613–643; cf. V. M. Zhirmunskii and Kh. T. Zarifov, *Uzbekskii narodnyi geroicheskii èpos* (Moscow: Ogiz, 1947), pp. 23–58; and see also Slawomira Żerańska-Kominek, "The Classification of Repertoire in Turkmen Traditional Music," *Asian Music*, 21/2 (Spring/Summer 1990), pp. 91–109.

3. Such a "democratic" focus is also an important antidote to the usual fixation, in scholarly literature on Central and Inner Asian "Culture," upon the thin layer of westernized, Russianized,

The Epic Tale of *Idige*

Baba Tükles' chief role in Inner Asian oral tradition appears in the epic tradition that grew around the life of Edigü, and it is here in this widely known tale that his role is curiously and revealingly elaborated. Variants of the tale of "Idige Biy," all based ultimately on the activities of the historical Edigü in the Jöchid *ulus* of the late fourteenth and early fifteenth centuries, are known in the epic traditions of the Qazaqs, Qaraqalpaqs, Uzbeks, Noghays, Bashkirs, and Tatars, as well as those of various Siberian Turkic peoples. The extremely wide distribution of the tale of Idige is generally acknowledged to result from the original development of the epic's content and structure during the time of the more or less united Noghay horde, in the fifteenth and sixteenth centuries; as the Noghay horde splintered in the early seventeenth century, *Idige*, like other tales comprising the so-called Noghay epic complex, accompanied groups formerly part of the Noghay confederation as they regrouped under other communal designations, leaving important Noghay elements among most of the Turkic peoples of western Inner Asia.

The development of the *Idige* epic in the Noghay horde naturally reflects the prominence of the historical Edigü and his descendants in that confederation. The epic's focus on Idige, and its wide dissemination, are the central arguments in assigning its "original" form to the fifteenth and sixteenth centuries, when the Noghay horde enjoyed its most unified state. It is naturally impossible to assign dates to the development of the oral tales focused on the historical Edigü that formed the basis for the epic cycle of Idige; our earliest records of the epic based on actual oral performance date only to the early nineteenth century, although some written versions are preserved in manuscripts copied somewhat earlier, in the late eighteenth century. The nature of oral tradition, however, should caution us against denying the tale's antiquity simply on the basis of its relatively late appearance in written form. And there are in fact some indications that Edigü became the focus of popular narratives quite early, possibly even in his lifetime. In particular, the historian Ibn ʿArabshāh (d. 854/1450) noted that Edigü was the subject of "marvellous stories and

"reformist" intellectuals of the latter nineteenth and early twentieth centuries, who were often characterized by an antagonism toward Islam that colored their attitude toward its role in "their" people's lives; unfortunately, such intellectuals are often regarded as the chief or only spokesmen for the cultural heritage of Central Asian peoples, with negative results for our understanding of traditional patterns.

tales";[4] Ibn ʿArabshāh's extensive travels, to Khorezm, Saray, Astrakhan, and the Crimea, suggest his direct familiarity with narratives of this sort, and indeed his account of Edigü, which bears traces of the structure and style of the Idige tale,[5] was most likely based in part on such tales.

There may well be echoes of the oral tradition surrounding the figure of Edigü in two other fifteenth-century sources. One is the account of Barbaro noted earlier ascribing to Edigü a pivotal role in the Islamization of his realm; as suggested, the early attestation of oral accounts linking Edigü with Islamization, as well as the conflation of the Islamizing roles of Edigü and Özbek Khan, may reflect the emergence of tales linking him with Baba Tükles much earlier than the seventeenth century as reflected in extant written sources.

The other, even earlier, fifteenth-century account echoing oral tradition surrounding the figure of Edigü is the work of Johannes Schiltberger, written after his long captivity in the Ottoman, Timurid, and Jöchid realms.[6] Schiltberger, a young Bavarian soldier, was captured in 1396 upon the Ottoman Sulṭān Bāyazīd I's rout of the European army led by the Hungarian King Sigismund in the "Crusade of Nicopolis," only to fall into Temür's hands following the latter's defeat of Bāyazīd at Ankara in 1402; after Temür's death Schiltberger passed into the service of the Great Amīr's son Mīrānshāh, and, after the latter's death in 1408, stayed with Mīrānshāh's son Abū Bakr. Schiltberger remained for four years in the entourage of Abū Bakr, with whom was also the Jöchid prince ("the

4. Tr. Saunders, p. 87; cf. Tiz I, p. 473; MS Cambridge Add. 3237, f. 29b: "*wa lahu ḥikāyāt ʿajībah wa akhbār wa nawādir gharībah.*"

5. This is more readily apparent in his initial discussion of Edigü's role in the conflict between Temür and Toqtamïsh (cf. Tiz I, pp. 457–458, 466–469, Saunders, pp. 75–76, 82–84), and especially in the subsequent account of Edigü's struggles with Toqtamïsh, complete with fifteen battles, Edigü's flight and wandering, his heroic journey to overcome Toqtamïsh in the sixteenth fight, his supremacy over the khans in the Dasht-i Qïpchaq, and his eventual fall and death (cf. Tiz I, pp. 469–474, Saunders, pp. 85–87); the "epic" style is less evident in Ibn ʿArabshāh's account of Edigü's occupation of Khorezm during the struggles following Temür's death (Saunders, pp. 258–259; Tizengauzen, "in order to observe chronological order," inserted this account in the midst of the earlier discussion of Edigü's career, p. 472), and in view of the divergent tone of the two sections and their wide separation in the text, it seems likely that at least two separate oral or written sources or bodies of sources underlie the two accounts of Edigü, one perhaps stemming from oral tradition accessible to Ibn ʿArabshāh during his travels in the Jöchid *ulus* and reflecting Edigü's activity there, and one based on oral tradition or written records of Timurid and Central Asian provenance and reflecting Edigü's involvement in Khorezm.

6. Cf. Telfer, tr., *The Bondage and Travels of Johann Schiltberger*; and Langmantel's edition referred to in Chapter 2, n. 22.

son of a king of Great Tartary") Chegre, a Chingisid protégé of Edigü;[7] and when Chegre was summoned back to the Jöchid *ulus*, presumably by Edigü, Schiltberger accompanied Chegre, remaining in his service until this puppet khan's death in a battle with Ulugh Muḥammad around 1419.

Schiltberger was thus directly familiar with Edigü, and gives a relatively accurate account of his role in the succession struggles in the Golden Horde during the second decade of the fifteenth century; but his account nevertheless includes material probably drawn not from his own observation, but from popular tales already in circulation. Such is most likely the case—although Schiltberger insists he witnessed the events—with the curious account, in epic style, of a "Tartar woman" who came to Edigü and Chegre, "with four thousand maidens and women," seeking revenge upon the "Tartar king" (i.e., khan) who had slain her husband;[8] and such is certainly the case with his account of the country of "Ibissibur," toward which Edigü and Chegre set off as soon as the latter joined his patron.

Schiltberger's description of "Ibissibur"(i.e., "Siberia," referred to as *Ïbïr-Sïbïr*) reflects standard European conceptions about the desolate lands at the ends of the earth, but in one detail we may find echoes of other influences on his account. In the country of "Ibissibur," he writes, there is an enormous mountain, and "on the same mountain there are savages, who are not like other people, and they live there. They are covered all over the body with hair,[9] except the hands and face, and run about like other wild beasts in the mountain, and also eat leaves

7. Schiltberger aptly describes the relationship between Chingisid khan and the chief *bek* or *amīr*: "it is the custom for the king, in Great Tartary, to have a Chief to rule over him, who can elect or depose a king, and has also power over vassals. Now at that time Idigi was the Chief" (tr. Telfer, pp. 34–35).

8. Tr. Telfer, pp. 37–38.

9. The "hairiness" of the people is specifically affirmed in Telfer's English translation, in G. Siemes's German translation (*Eine wunderbarliche und kurzweilige Historie, wie Schiltberger, einer aus der Stadt München in Bayern, von den Türken gefangen, in die Heidenschaft geführet und wieder ist heim kommen* . . . [Leipzig: Im Insel-Verlag, (1917)]; note on cover, *Schiltbergers Reisebuch (Kriegsgefangen in Vorderasien von 1394–1425)*, p. 42: "und sie sein haarig an dem ganzen Leib"), and in the Russian translation of F. K. Brun (published in Iogann Shil'tberger, *Puteshestvie po Evrope, Azii i Afrike s 1394 goda do 1427 god*, ed. Z. M. Buniiatov [Baku: Èlm, 1984], p. 34: "Vse ikh telo . . . pokryto volosami"); the recent German translation by Ulrich Schlemmer (*Als Sklave im Osmanischen Reich und bei den Tataren, 1394–1427* [Stuttgart: Thienemann, Edition Erdmann, 1983], p. 110) reads "am ganzen Körper rot." One of the earliest (fifteenth-century) manuscript versions reads thus: "Und in dem obgenanten perg, do sein wild leut, die chain wanung haben pei andern menschen und sie sein über rauch an dem leyb, aussgenummen an den henden und unter dem antlütz . . ." (Langmantel, ed., *Hans Schiltbergers Reisebuch*, p. 39); cf. the facsimile reprint of the 1476 Augsburg printing prepared by Elisabeth Geck, *Hans Schiltbergers Reisebuch* (Wiesbaden: Guido Pressler, 1969) [no pagination].

and grass, and any thing they can find. The lord of the country sent to Edigi, a man and a woman from among these savages, that had been taken in the mountain."[10] Such descriptions of wild, and hairy, people are not uncommon in accounts of the "monstrous races" beyond the "civilized" world, but Schiltberger's specific linking of Edigü with a man and woman from among these hairy people recalls the account of Mongol origins given by Ibn ad-Dawādārī, as discussed in Chapter 4, involving a "wild" man who lives like an animal in the wilderness by the sacred mountain of the Turks, the "Qarā Ṭāgh"; that account describes the occasion of his taking a wife, as well, and it seems plausible that Schiltberger's description reflects stories similar to those in circulation a century earlier, in Ibn ad-Dawādārī's time. The passage further suggests the possibility that, already in Edigü's lifetime, Schiltberger had heard tales about the "special" circumstances of his birth, ascribed to the union of a maiden of supernatural origin and a man whose very name affirmed that he was covered with body hair; one relatively old version of the epic tale of Idige, moreover, specifies that Baba Tükles dwelt in the mountains and ate grasses, and despite the frequent and *general* parallels between descriptions of "barbarian" peoples and those of "antinomian" holy men—in themselves quite telling—it is not impossible that we should find in Schiltberger's account an echo of a *specific* feature in a narrative tradition about Edigü's ancestry.

In any event, by the eighteenth century at least, and no doubt much earlier, an extraordinary body of oral tales about Edigü was in circulation, as noted both by Nūrullāh Khorezmī in the account discussed in the previous chapter, and by ʿAbd al-Ghaffār Qïrïmī as well;[11] both tapped some of these tales for their accounts, but our best insight into their structure, content, and focus comes naturally through the more extensive, though more recently recorded, versions of the epic tale of Idige.

The Idige tale is known under various designations depending on the protagonists in the particular portion recorded; most often it is known as "Idige" or "Idige Batïr" or "Idige Biy," but variations on the names "Idige and Nuradin," from the prominent role of the hero's son, or "Tokhtamïsh," from the major antagonist, are quite common. While it was one of the earliest Turkic epics to attract scholarly attention, the Idige cycle was

10. Tr. Telfer, p. 35; in the notes, p. 139, the translator supposes that this story reflects the appearance of people dressed in animal skins due to the extreme cold of Siberia.

11. Najīb ʿĀṣim ed., p. 203.

eclipsed in both scholarly and popular literature during the Soviet era by other epics deemed more amenable to ideologically correct interpretations;[12] some remarks on its study may thus be useful.

The most extensive discussion of the Idige tale as a whole, in its historical and literary contexts, appears in an article by V. M. Zhirmunskii,[13] who

12. The relative lack of scholarly, or even popular literary, attention to the "Idige" epic cycle stems no doubt from its condemnation (in 1944, predating even that of the other Turkic "national" epics in the Soviet Union) as an anti-progressive work glorifying the feudal past and inciting nationalist sentiments and ethnic exclusivism; while other epics were "rehabilitated" relatively soon after the initial repudiation of Stalinism in 1956, the Idige tale remained unpublished until the era of *glasnost'*, appearing in modern Tatar and Bashkir editions only in 1988 and 1989 (see below). These most recent versions, as well as the political background of the scholarly and literary struggles to publish them, are noted by Azade-Ayşe Rorlich, "*Idegey* Joins the Family of Rehabilitated Turkic National Epics," *Radio Liberty: Report on the USSR*, I/39 (29 September 1989), pp. 23–24; essentially the same discussion appears in Rorlich's "The Volga Tatars: Modern Identities of the Golden Horde," in *Rulers from the Steppe: State Formation on the Eurasian Periphery*, ed. Gary Seaman and Daniel Marks (Los Angeles: Ethnographics Press, University of Southern California, 1991; Proceedings of the Soviet-American Academic Symposia in Conjunction with the Museum Exhibitions "Nomads: Masters of the Eurasian Steppe," vol. 2), pp. 274–290 (pp. 284–286 on the Idige epic). More recently, the suppression of the epic was discussed by the Tatar scholar Mirkasym Usmanov in an essay published with a Russian translation of the "Tatar" version of the tale ("O tragedii èposa i tragediiakh liudskikh," in *Idegei: Tatarskii narodnyi èpos*, tr. Semen Lipkin [Kazan: Tatarskoe Knizhnoe Izdatel'stvo, 1990], pp. 247–254). For a survey of the Stalinist attack on the "national" epics of Soviet Turkic peoples, see Alexandre A. Bennigsen, "The Crisis of the Turkic National Epics, 1951–1952: Local Nationalism or Internationalism?" *Canadian Slavonic Papers*, 17/2–3 (Summer and Fall 1975), pp. 463–474, and more recently, with attention to the Tsarist colonial background as well, H. B. Paksoy, *Alpamysh: Central Asian Identity under Russian Rule* (Hartford, Connecticut: Association for the Advancement of Central Asian Research, Monograph Series, 1989). The "forbidden" status of the Idige tale in the Soviet Union was noted already by A. N. Kurat (in his *IV–XVIII. yüzyıllarda Karadeniz kuzeyindeki Türk kavimleri ve devletleri* [Ankara, 1972], p. 141, n. 2), who explained thereby the omission of any discussion of the tale from the collection of Chokan Valikhanov's works published in Alma-Ata in 1958.

13. V. M. Zhirmunskii, "P. M. Melioranskii i izuchenie èpose 'Edigei,' " in *Tiurkologicheskii sbornik 1972* (Moscow, 1973), pp. 141–185; the same article (excluding the introductory section [pp. 141–142] on Melioranskii's contribution) was published with the title "Skazanie ob Idige" in the collection of Zhirmunskii's works on Turkic epics, *Tiurkskii geroicheskii èpos* (Leningrad, 1974), pp. 351–386 [citations in the present study are from this latter publication]. Zhirmunskii also dealt extensively with the Idige tale in other works, especially in "Èpicheskie skazaniia o nogaiskikh bogatyriakh v svete istoricheskikh istochnikov" (*Tiurkskii geroicheskii èpos*, pp. 389–516; see also his *Narodnyi geroicheskii èpos* (Moscow/Leningrad, 1962), pp. 221–231, as well as his discussion of the tale (with bibliography) in Chadwick and Zhirmunsky, *Oral Epics of Central Asia*, pp. 296–300, and, more briefly, in his "On the Comparative Study of the Heroic Epic of the Peoples of Central Asia," in *Trudy dvadtsat' piatogo Mezhdunarodnogo kongressa vostokovedov* (Moscow, 9–16 August 1960), t. 3 (Moscow: Izd-vo Vostochnoi Literatury, 1963), pp. 244–252, esp. pp. 248–249; cf. also his "Nekotorye itogi izucheniia geroicheskogo èposa narodov Srednei Azii," in *Voprosy izucheniia èposa narodov SSSR* (Moscow: Izd-vo AN SSSR, 1958), pp. 24–65 [pp. 49–57]. An earlier, less complete overview of the Idige tale, accompanied by

provides the fullest available listing of the recorded versions, published and unpublished, of the tale. But in fact Zhirmunskii's researches provide only an introduction to the study of this extremely rich body of epic material, which clearly deserves further exploration; the basic task, set already early in this century by P. M. Melioranskii, of comparing and analyzing the available variants of the Idige tale in a thoroughly detailed and exhaustive manner, remains to be undertaken. In the absence of such a study we must have recourse not only to the surveys of Zhirmunskii and others, but to the accessible published versions of texts or translations of the tale. The earliest known recording was a Russian recounting of a Qazaq version, published in 1820 by G. I. Spasskii,[14] followed by an English account of a Noghay version recorded in Astrakhan by A. B. Chodzko in 1830.[15] Several versions of

---

the text of a newly recorded variant, is provided by Saadet Çağatay, "Die Ädigä-Sage," referred to earlier; the tale is also discussed in Köprülü, *Türk edebiyatı tarihi*, pp. 383–386. See also the brief popular account of the Idige tale in A. S. Orlov, *Kazakhskii geroicheskii èpos* (Moscow/ Leningrad, 1945), pp. 128–147. An overview and brief analysis of the available variants, prepared by Melioranskii's student, A. N. Samoilovich, was published along with Zhirmunskii's chief article (Samoilovich, "Variant skazaniia o Edigee i Tokhtamyshe, zapisannyi N. Khakimovym," *Tiurkologicheskii sbornik 1972*, pp. 186–211). The study of the Idige cycle completed by Samoilovich's student P. A. Falev before his death in 1922 appears to have been the most complete analysis of the work yet undertaken (including as well another version of the tale recorded by Falev himself among the Stavropol' Noghays), but it was never published (cf. Bartol'd, "Otets Edigeia," *Sochineniia*, II/1, p. 797, n. 1; on Falev's work see B. V. Lunin, "Zhizn' i trudy vostokoveda-tiurkologa P. A. Faleva (K 45-letiiu so dnia smerti)," *Obshchestvennye nauki v Uzbekistane*, 1967, No. 9, pp. 43–48); the manuscript of Falev's work was briefly described by L. V. Dmitrieva in a *prilozhenie* to the publication of Samoilovich's article ("Rukopis' raboty P. A. Faleva ob èpose 'Edigei' v Arkhive vostokovedov Instituta vostokovedeniia AN SSSR," pp. 213–217), but Dmitrieva suggests that the appearance of Zhirmunskii's study makes the publication of Falev's manuscript unnecessary.

14. "Idige, Kirgizskaia skazka," *Sibirskii vestnik*, ch. 10 (1820), pp. 358–373, published as an appendix to Spasskii's article, "Kirgiz'-Kaisaki bol'shoi, srednei i maloi ordy" (according to the article's separate pagination, the Idige tale appears on pp. 189–204). The Russian paraphrase probably conceals a reference to the "hairy saint," "Baba Tükles Shashlï Aziz," in the original text: near the beginning of the tale Idige says, "My father had hair on his head and a very long beard" (*otets moi imel na golove volosy i ochen' bol'shuiu borodu*).

15. Alexander Chodzko, *Specimens of the Popular Poetry of Persia, as found in the Adventures and Improvisations of Kurroglou, the Bandit-Minstrel of Northern Persia; and in the Songs of the People Inhabiting the Shores of the Caspian Sea* (London: Oriental Translation Fund, 1842), pp. 348–362; this version was, according to Chodzko, "communicated to me by one of my Tatar friends, Aly Beg Sharapow," who, however, explained its meaning in Persian for Chodzko's recording. Chodzko refers to the "Adiga" saga as "the most favourite" of the "Astrakan Tatars." A Russian translation of Chodzko's English rendering was published by N. Semenov in 1895 (see n. 20). For a survey of Chodzko's life and activity, with references to other publications (that might include reference to this recording of the Idige tale), see Jean Calmard in *EIr*, V, pp. 502–504, s.v. "Chodźko."

the text itself are included in Radlov's *Proben*,[16] and texts of additional Noghay versions[17] (to be discussed below) were published by the 1880s; one Qazaq version recorded by Chingis Chokanovich Valikhanov, whose text was published in 1905 by Melioranskii, is not only extremely rich, but also perhaps the most frequently cited.[18] Among later versions published only in translation or paraphrase may be noted a Qaraqalpaq version recorded by I. A. Beliaev in 1903,[19] a Noghay version published by N. Semenov in 1895,[20] and in particular the extensive presentations of the tales appearing in several works of G. N. Potanin (cited below).

In the Soviet period, apart from the detailed treatments by Zhirmunskii and others, relatively few actual texts of the tale have been published; a Qazaq version was published in 1922 in Tashkent by A. A. Divaev,[21] and a handful

16. Radlov, *Proben*, IV (text vol.), pp. 35–56 (versions from among the Baraba and Omsk Tatars and from among the Teleuts of the Altai); VII, pp. 99–122, 146–149, 154–165, 198–201 (Crimean versions).

17. Berezin, Osmanov and Anan'ev, see further below; in addition to these, and the Noghay versions of Chodzko and Semenov (see below) published in translation only, yet another Noghay version, which remains unpublished, was recorded by S. Farfarovskii some time before 1909. Described as an "epic poem on the khan Tokhtamysh," it is clearly a version of the Idige tale, pitting the khan against "Adyge" and "Nuradil," the son and grandson of a "*murza*" named "Kutlubai," whom Tokhtamysh had killed; the brief description makes no mention of Baba Tükles. The recording, said to be made from a manuscript of which many copies were current among the Noghays, is preserved at Kazan University; cf. S. B. Radzievskaia, *Opisanie rukopisei nauchnoi biblioteki im. N. I. Lobachevskogo*, vyp. I, "Fol'klor" (Kazan', 1958), pp. 12–13, No. 2.200.

18. P. M. Melioranskii, ed., "Skazanie ob Edigee i Toktamyshe. Kirgizskii tekst po rukopisi, prinadlezhavshei Ch. Ch. Valikhanovu" (Saint Petersburg, 1905), published as a separately paginated supplement to vol. 29 of the *Zapiski Imperatorskago Russkago Geograficheskago Obshchestva po Otdeleniiu ètnografii*. The version published by Melioranskii was earlier translated into Russian by Valikhanov (*Sochineniia*, pp. 233–264), by whom the text had been recorded in 1841–1842. Other, unpublished, recordings of Qazaq variants are noted by Zhirmunskii, "Skazanie ob Idige," p. 353; some of these may have been discussed by the famous Qazaq scholar and writer Mukhtar Auèzov, to judge from an index of his twenty-volume collected works (E. N. Zhanpeisov, *Ètnokul'turnaia leksika kazakhskogo iazyka (na materialakh proizvedenii M. Auèzova)* [Alma-Ata: "Nauka" KazSSR, 1989], p. 256), citing the appearance of "Babay tükti Shashtï Äziz" in vol. 7, p. 80, and vol. 16, p. 86; these volumes have remained inaccessible to me.

19. "Skazanie ob Edigee i Tokhtamyshe. Kara-kalpakskaia narodnaia poèma," *Protokoly zasedanii i soobshcheniia chlenov Zakaspiiskago Kruzhka liubitelei arkheologii i istorii Vostoka* (Ashkhabad), vyp. 3 (1917), separately paginated, pp. i–ix, 1–39; recorded from Bekimbet jïraw of Chimbay.

20. N. Semenov, *Tuzemtsy severo-vostochnago Kavkaza* (Saint Petersburg, 1895), pp. 413–466, preface, translation, and notes; cf. pp. 469–481 for his Russian translation of Chodzko's version (with further notes pp. 481–487). Semenov's version, recorded near Astrakhan in 1880–1881, is a quite full one, with rich elaboration of the hero's Islamic and Sufi character; it is discussed further below.

21. In a collection entitled *Baturlar*, of which "Mirza Edige" forms part 5; this has not been available to me. Incidentally, the Qazaq version published earlier by the same Divaev ("Murza Èdyge-batyr (Kirgizskaia bylina)," *Sbornik materialov dlia statistiki Syr'-Dar'inskoi oblasti*, 5 (1896), pp. 12–32 (reprinted as part 4 of his collected *Ètnograficheskie materialy* [Tashkent, 1900]) is one of the few versions of the Idige tale not to name Baba Tükles as the hero's father or ancestor.

of other versions appeared down to the early 1940s, before the official condemnation of the Idige epic in 1944. Zhirmunskii notes, however, a substantial number of archival recordings of the tale made in the 1920s, 1930s, and late 1950s; in the present atmosphere it seems likely that these will be published, probably in semipopular editions, with increasing frequency. Such is the case with the recently published "Tatar" version, based on the 1919 recording by N. Khakimov (studied already by Samoilovich) and on that of N. Isenbetov from 1929,[22] and the Bashkir version, based on the Isenbetov text and a recording by M. Burangulov (1888–1966) from the late 1930s[23] (the recently published Bashkir version includes a distinctive episode absent from other versions of the Idige tale, and is therefore considered separately below). In addition, recordings of Qaraqalpaq versions are often cited, and it is clear that the tale of Idige has remained in the repertoire of *baksïs* and *akïns*, especially among the Qaraqalpaqs, down to the present day.[24] Finally, the existence

22. Cf. "Idegäy: Tatar khalïk dastanï," *Kazan utlarï*, 1989, No. 1, pp. 3–66; the text, in modern Tatar transcription, was prepared by Flora Äkhmätova, who also supplied a brief introduction. The same version of the epic was also published in book form: *Idegäy: Tatar khalïk dastanï*, ed. M. G. Gosmanov, M. Z. Zäkiev, Ä. G. Iskhak, R. S. Mökhämmädiev, and I. N. Nadirov (Kazan: Tatarstan Kitap Näshriyatï, 1988). Both publications are cited by Rorlich, "*Idegey* Joins the Family"; and a Russian translation appeared in 1990, as noted above (n. 12).

23. "Idheükäy menän Moradhïm," *Agidhel*, 1989, No. 1, pp. 19–74; the text was prepared by Nur Zaripov, who provided commentary under the general heading "'Idheükäy menän Moradhïm' ëposïna qarata," in the form of an introduction on the history and political fortunes of the epic's study ("Ëpostï öyräneü tarikhïnan," pp. 16–18), a survey of the tale's relation to history ("Ëpostïng tarikhqa mönäsäbäti," *Agidhel*, 1989, No. 2, pp. 126–129), and a discussion of the distinctive features of the Bashkir versions ("Bashqort varianttarïnïng üdhensälege," pp. 129–137). According to Zaripov (as noted also by Zhirmunskii, "Skazanie ob Idige," p. 353), Burangulov's recording was based in part on a text copied from a manuscript dated 1762, the earliest of any known recording of the Idige epic; unfortunately there is no indication in the published Bashkir text (or evidently in Burangulov's text) of material taken from that oldest manuscript, nor is there any critical discussion of the material ascribable to any of the various stages in the "re-editing" of the epic. Burangulov's work is further discussed by Zaripov and M. M. Sagitov in the introduction to *Bashkirskoe narodnoe tvorchestvo*, I, "Èpos" (Ufa: Bashkirskoe Knizhnoe Izd-vo, 1987), pp. 10–11 , where he is said to have given his collection of recordings and verse reworkings of various epic tales, including "Idukai and Muradïm" (many of which are said to have been recorded even before 1917, with several in the 1920s), to the Bashkir *filial* of the Soviet Academy of Sciences. The same authors note (pp. 9, 11) the publication of excerpts of Bashkir versions of the Idige tale in local journals and newspapers of Kazan and Ufa, including two dating from 1897 and 1915; these have remained inaccessible. The existence of Bashkir variants of the tale of "Idukay" and "Muradïm" is noted in M. M. Sagitov, "Otrazhenie konsolidatsii bashkirskoi narodnosti v èpicheskikh skazaniiakh," *Arkheologiia i ètnografiia Bashkirii*, 4 (1971), pp. 278–281, with no references, however, to specific recordings or publications.

24. Variants of the Idige epic not mentioned by Zhirmunskii include Qaraqalpaq versions described in 1977 as having been recorded "recently" from five bards (Oteniyaz jïraw, Qïyas

of original literary versions in manuscript form (as distinct from ethnographic recordings from living bards) may be noted; some of these may prove to be quite old. One, from Tashkent, is discussed separately below, but others are likely to come to light, as are other ethnographic recordings, as largely untapped manuscript repositories and folklore collections in places such as Orenburg, Astrakhan, Ufa, and Kazan are explored.

The available variants of the Idige tale were produced by different bards belonging to various peoples across much of western Inner Asia. It is naturally impossible, then, to establish any single "authoritative" version of the text or even of the tale's structure; the various episodes recurring in most versions often appear in different sequences, and show wide variations not only in language and style, but in content as well. With this in mind, we may consider the essential "story" as given, in a synopsis from one unpublished version, by Samoilovich.[25] Following a more or less

jïraw, Jannazar jïraw, Esemurat jïraw, and Jumabay jïraw), with reference to the manuscript *fond* of the Qaraqalpaq *filial* of the then AN UzSSR, R–137, cited in K. M. Maksetov, ed., *Ocherki po istorii karakalpakskogo fol'klora* (Tashkent: Fan, 1977), p. 87 [pp. 87–89 on the Idige tale]. The last of the five bards mentioned by Maksetov, Jumabay-jïraw Bazarov (b. 1929), was also recorded by Karl Reichl in Nukus on 24–25 June 1981 (cf. Reichl, "Oral Tradition and Performance," p. 633); his repertoire included the Idige epic, as Reichl notes, but it is not clear whether this was among the tales recorded, and in any case Reichl does not describe or synopsize his version. Reichl cites another work of Maksetov (*Qaraqalpaq jïraw baqsïlarï*, Nukus, 1983), which has not been accessible to me, as giving the name of Jumabay-jïraw's teacher, Esemurat-jïraw Nurabullaev of Kungrad, who was in turn apparently a pupil of Nurabulla-jïraw (born 1862); and the same account adds that Jumabay-jïraw then (1983) had two pupils, including one of his sons. As for earlier recordings, Maksetov (*Ocherki*) remarks that the version, noted by Zhirmunskii, recorded from Yerpolat-jïraw by K. Ayïmbetov [Russianized surname, "Aiymbetov"] in 1929 was lost, but that the same bard was again recorded in 1934; the latter was the basis for a published version issued in Moscow in 1939, which has not been available to me. The continued inclusion of the *Idige dastan* in the repertoire of Qaraqalpaq bards (called here *bakhsï* and *zhrau*) is mentioned also in Nazhim Davkaraev, *Ocherki po istorii dorevoliutsionnoi karakalpakskoi literatury* (Tashkent: Izd-vo AN UzSSR, 1959), pp. 25–26; Davkaraev includes the Idige tale among the chief epics recited by the "school" of "Soppaslï Spïra-zhrau" (i.e., the "Supra jïraw" who appears *in* the Idige tale itself, in many versions), meaning the bards who trace their training through a lineage of singers that goes back to "Spïra-zhrau" himself. Davkaraev's work is also noteworthy for its explanation of the enormous popularity of the bards and their art, which the author informs us is due to the total absence, down to the Great October Revolution, of sources of "cultural progress such as cinema, theater, and the press." The currency of the tale of Idige among the Qaraqalpaqs is further acknowledged by L. S. Tolstova, "Istoricheskii fol'klor karakalpakov kak istochnik dlia izucheniia ètnogeneza i ètnokul'turnykh sviazei ètogo naroda," in *Ètnicheskaia istoriia i fol'klor* (Moscow: Nauka, 1977), pp. 141–164 [pp. 160–162]; she ascribes it, along with several other epic tales, to the "Noghay layer" in Qaraqalpaq folklore.

25. Samoilovich, "Variant skazaniia o Edigee i Tokhtamyshe," pp. 197–201. Zhirmunskii has discussed extensively, in his works cited above, the echoes of "actual history" in the Idige tale.

extensive account of Idige's ancestry and birth—and it is here that Baba Tükles appears—we see Idige himself brought up at the court of Tokhtamïsh Khan, who admires the young man and takes him into his service. Idige, however, eventually fears the khan's jealousy (or seeks revenge for his father's execution by Tokhtamïsh, which occasionally displaces the initial account of Idige's ancestry), and flees to "Shah Timur" (echoing the historical Edigü's relations with the two famous rivals). Meanwhile, from an ancient bard who served all the khans of the Golden Horde, Tokhtamïsh also learns of Idige's origins and of his future victory over the khan, and resolves to kill him. Idige persuades Timur to make war on Tokhtamïsh, who is defeated and flees; Idige takes the throne and allows his son, Nuraddin, to pursue the khan, whereupon Nuraddin slays Tokhtamïsh and brings his head to Idige. Idige and Nuraddin quarrel, and Idige is forced to flee; Nuraddin, threatened by Tokhtamïsh's son, Qadir-berdi, is rescued by Idige, who is mortally wounded in the fight. Qadir-berdi soon dies, and Nuraddin is left as ruler.

Baba Tükles' Role in the Tale of *Idige*

Within this larger tale, Baba Tükles appears in most versions under various forms of the designation "Baba Tükles Shashlï ʿAzīz," which has generally been understood as "The Hairy Saint Baba Tükles"; he is nearly always cast as Idige's ancestor, often as his father, but unlike the Tatar histories—which likewise affirm Baba Tükles' role as an ancestor of Edigü/Idige—the epic accounts express the saint's sacralizing and legitimizing power in a striking combination of Inner Asian and Islamic terms. In many versions Baba Tükles figures in Idige's genealogy, as recounted at one or more important junctures in the epic tale; as an ancestor he both serves as a protective patron spirit and links the hero with Abū Bakr, with sacralizing ancestors cast in Inner Asian terms, or with both. Likewise, Baba Tükles is appealed to as a protector in some versions, and rescues the hero from difficulty. Most commonly, however, Baba Tükles appears at one or more of three critical points in the epic narrative, all of which emphasize his status as Idige's ancestor but in each case relate that status, and "use" it, in different ways.

First, many versions include at the beginning a section on Idige's origins, in which the hero's birth (and occasionally that of one or more of his ancestors) is recounted in mythic terms. This section invariably portrays

Idige as a foundling brought up at Tokhtamïsh's court, with his real parents identified as Baba Tükles and a supernatural maiden; as we will see, the common features of the variants, while implicitly reinforcing his "Islamizing" function, more clearly link Baba Tükles with an archaic legend of national/communal origin, here implicitly associated with the emergence of the Noghay horde under the descendants of the historical Edigü.

Second, the occasion for mentioning Baba Tükles' ancestry of Idige most widespread among the various versions comes at the time of Idige's flight from Tokhtamïsh, when the khan seeks to learn of his erstwhile protégé's true origins and summons an aged bard, more than 300 years old,[26] who is usually said to be from "Khīva and Bukhārā"; the bard comes reluctantly and, after being plied with cups of *bāl* (mead), recounts Idige's ancestry. In the bard's account Baba Tükles is a holy man and his sanctity is usually described in Islamic terms; the bard also usually recounts his age and mentions the sequence of khans he has seen and served. In this, and in the mounting tension between Idige and Tokhtamïsh, we are justified in seeing a hint at the use of Islamic symbols in challenging the khan's Chingisid charisma, but it is only a hint: the full development of this theme comes only in the third setting, which does not appear in all versions. The bard, incidentally, usually bears a name reflecting variations on the form "Subrā-jïraw"[27] (var. "Safardau," "Sïpïra-jïraw," "Sïp-

26. The motif of the bard's long life, which allows him to speak with authority about past heroes, appears to have been a common stylistic device occasionally transformed unwittingly into claims of actual 300-year life-spans. Evliya Çelebi reports his meeting with three Qalmïqs aged 300, 270, and 310 years, one of whom proposed to recount the stories of Berke Khan and Chingis Khan; the setting Evliya describes is clearly one of an epic recitation (cf. *Kniga puteshestviia*, vyp. 2, p. 168). A report of 300-year-old Mongols in a late thirteenth-century Armenian history may reflect similar tales of Mongol bards; cf. Robert P. Blake and Richard N. Frye, tr., "The History of the Nation of the Archers (the Mongols) by Grigor of Akanc'," *HJAS*, 12 (1949), pp. 269–399 [pp. 295–297].

27. On Supra Jïraw, see Zhirmunskii, "Skazanie ob Idige," p. 385, as well as his "Ėpicheskie skazanie o nogaiskikh bogatyriakh," p. 395 and "Sredneaziatskie narodnye skaziteli" (in the same collection, *Tiurkskii geroicheskii ėpos*), p. 641 (where Zhirmunskii notes contemporary bards who trace their "professional genealogies" to Supra Jïraw); see also A. Kh. Margulan, "O nositeliakh drevnei poėticheskoi kul'tury kazakhskogo naroda," in *M. O. Auėzovu, Sbornik statei k ego shestidesiatiletiiu* (Alma-Ata: Izd-vo AN KazSSR, 1959), pp. 70–89 (pp. 74–75 on Supra Jïraw, "son of Surghantay"). Zhirmunskii suggests that the "original" form of his name was "Safar Jïraw" (*jïraw* meaning a bard or epic singer), and notes the tradition that he lived 180 years (or more) during the reigns of Toqtamïsh's predecessors in the Golden Horde; Margulan goes further, asserting that he was the creator of the "Noghaylï jïr" and lived in Mangïshlaq and Sarāychïq, and identifies him with a "great singer of the Turks" mentioned by Ibn Baṭṭūṭah as dwelling in the latter city (but in fact Ibn Baṭṭūṭah mentions only a pious old man, called "Aṭā," who maintained a *zāwiyah* in Sarāychïq, cf. *Voyages d'Ibn Battûta*, ed. Defrémery and Sanguinetti, III, pp. 1–2). In the long Crimean variant published by Radlov (*Proben*, VII, p. 105), however, "Sïprā Jïrau" is said to live in "Khiva and Bukhara." The *Tavārīkh-i guzīdah-i nuṣrat-nāmah* names a

bashlï Sïpra," "Soppaslï Sabraw-jïraw," etc.), and the element "Subrā" in particular has defied explanation; this figure is further discussed below, but it may be noted here that he is regarded even today as the "founder" of initiatory lineages of bards among the Qazaqs and Qaraqalpaqs, at least, who often trace their apprenticeship and their inspiration to Subrā-jïraw.

Finally, near the end of the epic narrative, many versions portray Idige himself, or more often his son "Nuradïn," recounting his descent from Baba Tükles, often giving an extended genealogy, in the context of specifically challenging the significance of the Chingisid descent of Tokhtamïsh (or of one of the khan's sons) and asserting his own charisma on the basis of Islamic symbols.

Each of these venues for Baba Tükles' appearance in the Idige tale is discussed below. For now we may note that a comparison of available versions, as given in Table 6.1, reveals a pattern of possible significance: while these three settings for the mention of Baba Tükles occur alone and in different combinations in the various versions, it appears that No. 1 (Idige's origins recounted in mythic terms) and No. 3 (Idige's origins used to counter Chingisid charisma) do not occur together in any version. While the likely existence of many more recordings and manuscripts of variants of the Idige tale should caution us against drawing firm conclusions, it would appear that the mythic development of Baba Tükles' ancestry as expressed in indigenous Inner Asian terms was deemed somehow incompatible with the "political" use of Baba Tükles' ancestry as expressed in Islamic terms.

What this suggests is not that either of these modes of portraying and using Baba Tükles' ancestry necessarily predated the other, since we would argue against the view that the "mythic" and "fantastic" elements must represent later, "corrupted" or "degenerate" versions of the narrative, and that the versions which stress genealogy and Islamic-style sacrality are somehow more "historical." Rather, what the "incompatibility" of

"Sufrah Khoja," from among the people called "Ichki," as an early supporter of Abū'l–Khayr Khan (cf. *Materialy po istorii kazakhskikh khanstv*, p. 16; MS British Museum Or. 3222, f. 119a; cf. Akramov's facsimile, p. 266 and p. 463 for variants: the text of the British Museum manuscript appears to read "*s.f.rah-jī ājah*," but the latter portion is surely an error for "*khwājah*"); this would suggest the currency of such a name as might underlie "Subra," but this figure is certainly identical with the "Ichki" supporter of Abū'l–Khayr Khan whose name appears in Bannā'ī's *Shaybānī-nāmah* (*Materialy*, p. 96) and in the somewhat later *Tārīkh-i Abū'l–Khayr Khānī* (p. 144) in the form "Safar Khoja" (the same form appears in Berezin, *Sheibaniada*, p. liv). On the status of "Soppaslï Sïpïra-zhïraw" as the "ancestor" of bard-lineages among the Bashkirs, Noghays, Qaraqalpaqs, and Qazaqs, cf. K. M. Maksetov, "Vzaimosviazi karakalpakskogo i bashkirskogo geroicheskogo èposa," *Arkheologiia i ètnografiia Bashkirii*, 4 (Ufa, 1971), pp. 268–272 (p. 270).

these two modes suggests is that the mythically enhanced expression of Idige's charisma was consciously suppressed or ignored when political and social circumstances required that Islamic discourse be stressed to counter the attractions of Chingisid charisma; when those political circumstances disappeared, the mythic elements came to the fore, while the articulation of Islamic charisma in contrast to Chingisid legitimacy disappeared or was "fossilized." That this is indeed the case is suggested by the likelihood that the epic tale of Idige developed during the formative period of the Noghay confederation, in which opposition to Chingisid authority was a hallmark of practical action, and, we may presume, of affective discourse, among the Noghay leadership; it is precisely in versions of the Idige tale recorded among those "heirs" of the Noghay confederation who retained an ethnic identity as Noghay that the Islamic counter to Chingisid charisma appears most clearly and persistently.

We must not overemphasize here the contrast between these mythical and Islamic modes of depicting Idige's sacralized origins from Baba Tükles; as we will discuss below, the figure of Baba Tükles retains his strong association with Islam and Islamization even in the most "mythicized" developments of the epic, and far beyond the specific confines of the Idige tale as well. Even versions of the tale including the mythic origins of Idige and/or Baba Tükles may also include the Islamized Bakrid genealogy and surround the hero with Islamic symbolism, while versions recorded among the latter-day Noghays include some of the most mythically well-developed variants; as noted, the Islamic/Chingisid tension is latent in all the versions in which the bard recounts Idige's origins. Likewise, versions that stress Islamic sacrality to counter Chingisid charisma also include clear evocations of indigenous Inner Asian modes of sanctity. What seems to be missing from these versions is the *specific* element of Idige's supernatural origins from the union of Baba Tükles and a "fairy-girl"; and even this element was not *necessarily* incompatible with a depiction of Baba Tükles in thoroughly Islamic terms, stressing his role in conversion, as is evident from the account of Nūrullāh Khorezmī discussed in Chapter 5. The point here is that the Idige tale itself, and the character of Baba Tükles within it, became the focus for a melding of Islamic and Inner Asian mythic styles of articulating sacred origins. The separation of the two modes no doubt reflects merely a continued awareness of the political potential inherent in the latent contrasts between Islamic and Inner Asian paradigms; as noted, the fact of conversion to Islam in itself introduced the potential for "purist" and "reformist" Islamic discourse that might take

Key to Map and Table 6.1: Versions of the Idige Tale Featuring Baba Tükles

Circled numbers on the map indicate variants for which we have more or less specific information on where they were recorded; numbers in square brackets indicate variants that cannot be further localized within the general region to which they are assigned.

1. Q̱azaq: Valikhanov (1841–1842)/Melioranskii, 1905 (text); Kokchetav, Aman Karachay okrug
2. Q̱azaq: Potanin, "Tiurkskaia skazka" (1897); no text; Tarbagatai mountains, Semipalatinsk oblast'
3. Q̱azaq: Potanin, "Tiurkskaia skazka" (1897); no text; recorded from Sultan D. Kh. Sultan-Gazin, who learned it in his childhood in his homeland along the Tokrau river in Semipalatinsk oblast'
4. Q̱azaq: Divaev, 1896; no text (probably southern Kazakhstan) [no Baba Tükles: unnamed saint meets three swans at spring, etc.]
5. Q̱araqalpaq: Beliaev, 1917; no text; from a manuscript obtained in Chimbay (in the Amu Darya delta south of the Aral Sea)
6. Q̱araqalpaq: summarized in Maksetov (1977); no text; recorded in Chimbay in 1929 from Yerpolat-zhïrau Zhirmunskii, *TGÈ*, p. 353)
7. Uzbek: "Tulumbii," versions (probably Khorezmian) in manuscripts at Institute of Manuscripts, Tashkent (text)
8. Noghay: described by Zhirmunskii, *TGÈ*, pp. 354, 383; no text; recorded in Karachay-Cherkes Autonomous Oblast' in 1958 by Ashim Sikaliev
9. Noghay: Radlov, VII, pp. 99–122; from Büyük-Khojalar in the Crimea (text)
10. Noghay: Valikhanov/Potanin, "Otryvki," pp. 162–163; no text
11. Noghay: Çağatay (1957); recorded in Ankara from a man who emigrated to Turkey in his youth, from the Crimea (text) [no Baba Tükles: Q̱utlu Q̱aya takes *albasty* for wife]
12. Noghay: Aleinikov, described in Potanin, "Tiurkskaia skazka," p. 320; no text [apparently no Baba Tükles: Q̱utlu Q̱aya marries *albasty* whose husband he shot in forest]
13. Noghay: Valikhanov/Potanin, "Otryvki," pp. 161–162; no text
14. Noghay: Osmanov, 1883; from Dagestan (text)
15. Noghay: Chodzko, 1842; no text; Astrakhan
16. Noghay: Semenov, 1895; no text; near Astrakhan
17. Noghay: Anan'ev, 1900; no text; North Caucasus
18. Noghay (?): Berezin, 1862 (text); "Turkmen" (Trukhmen from North Caucasus?)
19. Noghay: Radlov, VII, pp. 154–165; from Q̱ara Su Bazar in the Crimea (text)
20. Tatar: 1988–1989 publications, based on Bashkir and Tatar recordings (text)
21. Bashkir: 1989 publication
22. West Siberian Tatar: described in Samoilovich, "Variant;" no text; recorded in 1919 from Syddyk-baba (1857–1927) in his native town, Yïlanlï, in the former Tarsk uezd, in Omsk oblast'
23. Q̱azaq: Spasskii, 1820; no text; Siberia

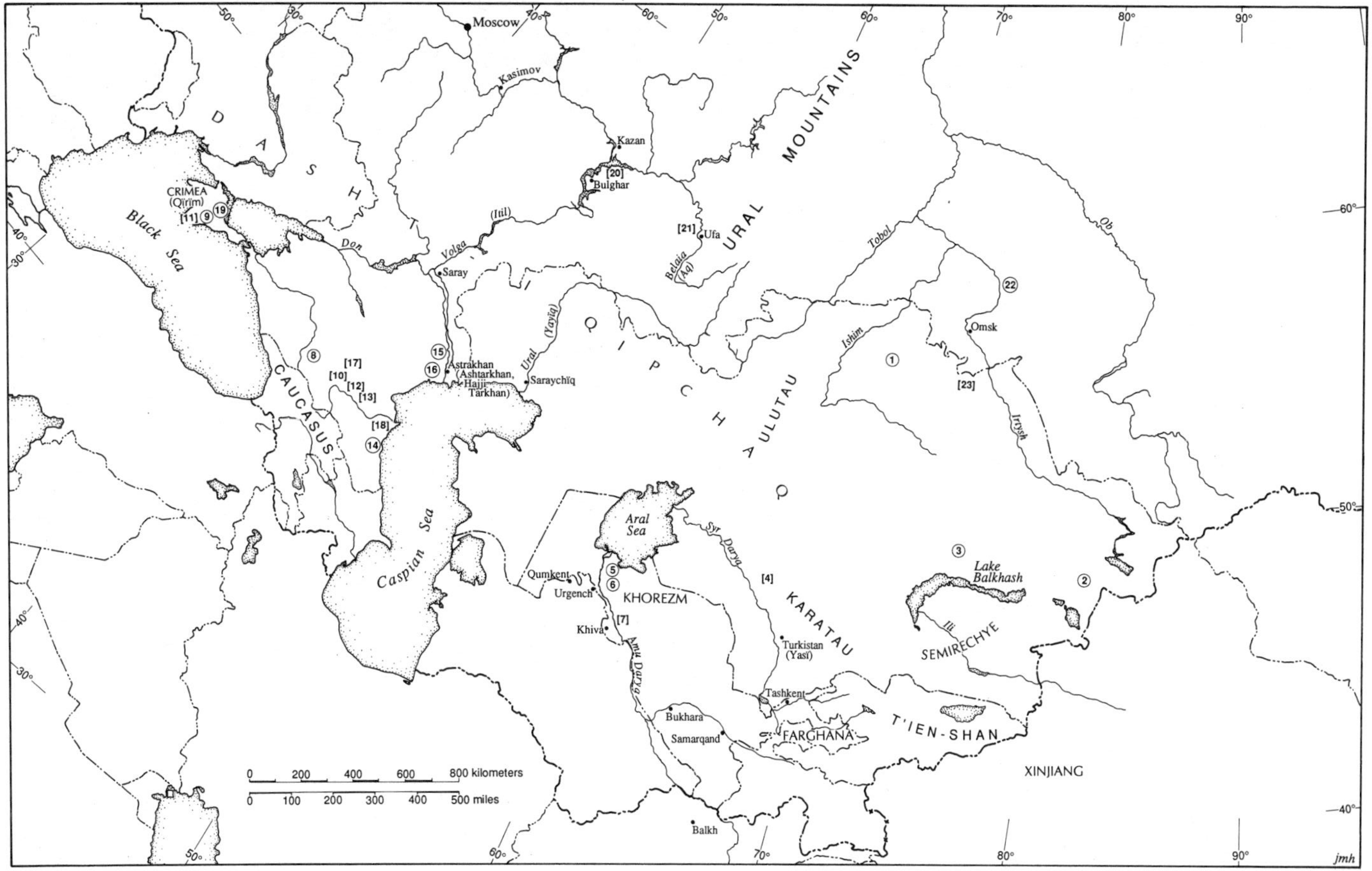

Moscow
Kasimov
Kazan
[20]
Bulghar
DASHT-I QIPCHAQ
URAL MOUNTAINS
CRIMEA
(Qirim)
[11]
9
19
Black Sea
Don
Volga
(Itil)
Saray
[21]
Ufa
Belaia
(Aq)
Tobol
Ob
22
Omsk
Ishim
1
[23]
Irtysh
ULUTAU
8
[17]
[10]
[12]
[13]
[18]
14
15
16
Astrakhan
(Ashtarkhan,
Hajji
Tarkhan)
Ural
(Yayiq)
Saraychiq
CAUCASUS
Caspian Sea
Aral Sea
Syr Darya
[4]
KARATAU
3
Lake Balkhash
2
Ili
SEMIRECHYE
Qumkent
Urgench
5
6
KHOREZM
[7]
Khiva
Amu Darya
Turkistan
(Yasi)
Tashkent
Bukhara
Samarqand
FARGHANA
T'IEN-SHAN
XINJIANG
Balkh
0
200
400
600
800 kilometers
0
100
200
300
400
500 miles
30°
40°
50°
60°
70°
80°
90°
jmh

Table 6.1. Narrative Elements in Versions of the Idige Tale Featuring Baba Tükles

	1 Qazaq	2 Qazaq	3 Qazaq	4 Qazaq	5 Qara-Qalpaq	6 Qara-Qalpaq	7 Uzbek	8 Noghay	9 Noghay	10 Noghay	11 Noghay	12 Noghay	13 Noghay	14 Noghay	15 Noghay	16 Noghay	17 Noghay	18 Noghay	19 Noghay	20 Tatar
Fact of Baba Tükles' ancestry of Idige	X	X	X		X	X	X	X	X	X			X	X	X	X	X	X	X	X [+21,22]
Elements of Name:																				
Baba Tükles	X	X	X		X	X	X	X	X	X			X	X	X	X	X	X	X	X
Chachlï-ʿAzīz	X	X					X		X	X				X		X			X	X
Khoja Aḥmad														X		X	X		X	X
Mythic Elements:																				
Supernatural Wife: *albasty* or *parī* met at pool or spring	X		X		X		X		X		X		X							
Supernatural Wife: Dove/Swan Maiden		X		X		X		X		X			X							
Combing Hair by the Sea	X																			
Three Conditions	X	X					X			X			X							
Son Abandoned	X	X	X	X		X	X						X							
Qumkent	X	X																		
Baba Tükles' father = Baba ʿUmar	X																			
(Baba Tükles' role played by Qutlu Qïya, other ancestor, or unnamed saint)				X				X		X	X	X								
Skull-Dust motif													X							

Table 6.1 continued

Quest for True Ancestry: Guide-Dog, Cave, etc.												[21X]
Baba Tükles Rescues Idige	X		X									
Quest for True Ancestry: Subra Jïraw (Named only)	X	X		X								X
(Involved in revealing ancestry)					X	X	X		X	X		
Genealogy: Bakrid genealogy acknowledged						X	X	X	X			[+22X]
Full line given back to Abū Bakr						X	X		X			
Links between Baba Tükles and Idige only								X		X	X	X
Notable Islamic coloring for Idige or Nūr ad-Dīn	X		X				X	X	X		X	
Anti-Chingisid sentiment in boasts of Nūr ad-Dīn:						X		X	X		X	X

issue with the popular combination of Islamic and Inner Asian values.

Finally, in connection with this apparent incompatibility may be noted the parallel with the case of Ötemish Ḥājjī's conversion narrative. As suggested, that narrative may reflect the splitting of an earlier narrative tradition recounting Özbek Khan's conversion as a key element in his accession to the throne; the conversion, we may suppose, was in effect removed as a legitimizing factor in Özbek Khan's seizure of power when that seizure of power was no longer politically relevant, and was instead employed as the basis for a communal legend of origin. In the case of Baba Tükles' role in the Idige tale, we may likewise suppose that narratives in which the saint provided political legitimation in the face of a specific threat (i.e., Chingisid charisma) gave way to narratives casting the saint as the founder of a community. The fact that Baba Tükles is a central character in both developments is further testimony to his enormous resonance in Islamic Inner Asia; we have yet to add, however, several further aspects of this resonance.

The focus of the tales of Idige is naturally the exploits of the hero himself, with which we will concern ourselves only minimally. Instead we must consider the ancestral and genealogical role of Baba Tükles in connection with the quest for legitimacy in the Noghay horde and with the articulation of sacred communal origins. The mythic elaboration of Baba Tükles in the environment of heroic epic is most richly developed in the latter context, and we will accordingly turn our attention first to several versions of the tale of Idige that offer a fuller account of the "mythic" Baba Tükles and his role in Idige's supernatural background.

In the best-known Qazaq version, recorded originally by Chokan Valikhanov and first published in translation by Potanin,[28] the Idige tale begins thus:

> There once lived a prodigious miracle-working saint named Baba ʿUmar [*Baba Gomar*], whose wife bore him a son named *Baba Tokty Chachty Aziz*; when the son reached the age of 25 he went out into the world to work miracles, and one day he

28. G. N. Potanin, "Otryvki iz kirgizskago skazaniia o Idyge, iz zapisei Ch. Valikhanova," *Zhivaia starina*, 1891, vyp. 4, pp. 156–163 (the portion of the Kazakh version dealing with Baba Tükles is recounted on p. 158); cf. Potanin, "Mar'ia lebed' belaia v bylinakh i skazkakh," *Ètnograficheskoe obozrenie*, 1892, No. 2–3, pp. 1–22 (p. 17 on this account of Baba Tükles). See also Valikhanov, *Sochineniia*, pp. 233–235, for the portion of his translation dealing with Baba Tükles. Essentially the same account is given, with no source cited, in Orlov, *Kazakhskii geroicheskii èpos*, pp. 134–135. For the text itself, cf. Melioranskii, "Skazanie ob Edigee," pp. 2–4.

> came upon a girl sitting by the shore of the sea combing her golden hair with a golden comb. She saw him and jumped into the sea, wherepon the young man thought to himself, "Inasmuch as I am such a one as Baba Tokty Chachty Aziz, I should jump in after her." And so he followed her into the sea. Under the water he saw 60 white nuptial *yurts*, and in one sat the girl, whose beauty was such that Baba Tokty backed away; but the girl caught hold of him and asked, "where are you going, *jigit?*" Baba Tokty said, "I cannot talk to you; if I do I will bring a great sin upon myself." But the girl said, "I have been looking for one like you for a long time, and have finally found you; if you go away and do not marry me you will bring even greater sins upon yourself." Baba Tokty agreed that this was so and decided to stay with her. The girl asked him to promise three things, however: that he would not look at her legs when she took off her boots, that he would not look under her arms when she took off her blouse, and that he would not look at her head as she washed her hair.

Baba Tokty eventually did all of these things, of course, seeing that her legs were like goats' legs, complete with hooves, that her lungs were visible under her arms, and that her brain was visible through her scalp as she washed her hair (all clear indications that she was the daughter of an *albastï*, or demon, as is made explicit in other versions). When the girl discovered that Baba Tokty had broken his word, she announced that she was six months' pregnant, and that when her son was born she would leave him for Baba Tokty to find on the banks of the great river "Nile," under the walls of the city of Qumkent; then she flew away. Baba Tokty eventually found the child where she had said he would be, covered with a silken wrap, and named the boy Idige; he brought the boy to the court of Tokhtamïsh, the ruler of that country, and after raising the boy for three years himself, he left him there to be further trained and educated, and disappeared.

This version then proceeds with the account of Idige himself, his dealings with the khan Tokhtamïsh, and the career of Idige's son "Nuralin" (on whom see below). That the tale of "Baba Tokty" forms an integral part of the Idige tale, and has not simply been added artificially to the account of Idige, is suggested by the words of Idige himself cited later in the narrative; on one occasion he describes how his father, "Baba Chachty Tokty Aziz," found him near Qumkent on the banks of the

Nile and there named him Idige, while elsewhere, in the course of asserting his noble heritage, he affirms that "While still a child I saw my grandfather, Baba ʿUmar, and I often carried Baba Tokty Chachty Aziz upon my shoulders."[29]

The core of this version is thus Baba Tükles' underwater dalliance with a sea-maiden, whom he first spies combing her golden hair on the shore; she becomes his wife upon his agreement to abide by certain conditions, and when he violates them she flies away, first telling Baba Tükles where she will leave their son for him to find. The same story, given so fully in this Qazaq version, is implied in several other versions in which Baba Tükles, or occasionally some other genealogical link between him and Idige, is said to have married a supernatural maiden, usually a *parī* (or a *parī*'s daughter) or an *albastï* or a female *jinn*; such is the case in Beliaev's Qaraqalpaq variant and in a Qazaq version translated by Potanin,[30] while in a version most likely rooted in Noghay tradition from the Crimea it is Qutlu Qaya who lives with an *albastï* on a mountain.[31] Similarly, another Noghay version from the Crimea, published by Radlov, simply reports that Idige's father was a servant of God and his mother the daughter of a *jinn*.[32] An Uzbek version discussed more fully below has Baba Tükles marry a *parīzād*, but here the element of water, which figures so prominently in the Qazaq version, reappears; in this case it is a spring used for ablution, however. And, as noted in the previous chapter, the currency of tales reporting Baba Tükles' marriage with a *parī*-girl at least by the early eighteenth century is established by the brief account of Nūrullāh Khorezmī.

These several variants, however, have only the "supernatural" character of Baba Tükles' wife in common, lacking the imagery of the underwater encounter; indeed, of all known and accessible variants, this Qazaq version originally recorded by Valikhanov is the only one to include this tale of the maid by the sea in its full form. Much more common is a story that in effect echoes the tale of the maid by the sea, but adds a distinctive feature shared by a wide range of variants. This is the motif of the swan-maidens, heavenly birds (usually three, and most often swans, but occasionally

29. Valikhanov's translation, *Sochineniia*, pp. 251–252; Melioranskii's text, pp. 20, 22; cf. Orlov, *Kazakhskii geroicheskii èpos*, pp. 144–145.

30. This is one of four versions given in G. N. Potanin, "Tiurkskaia skazka o Idyge," *Zhivaia starina*, 1897, vyp. 3–4, pp. 294–350 [pp. 301–304].

31. Çağatay, "Die Ädigä-Sage," pp. 244, 248.

32. Radlov, *Proben*, VII, p. 104.

doves) who alight by a lake and take off their swan-suits to become beautiful maidens; Baba Tükles appears in the role of the youth who sees them and succeeds in "capturing" one of them to be his wife, usually by stealing the maidens' swan-suits and bargaining with them, but occasionally just by grabbing one as the others fly away. From this point the story converges with that of the maid by the sea (and of course the element of water is common to both): the girl exacts promises, Baba Tükles breaks them, and the girl flies off to leave their son at a specified place.

In another Qazaq version, for instance, recorded in the Tarbagatai region,[33] Baba Tükles appears as three youths, named *Babai, Tukty*, and *Shash-Tazy*, who chanced upon three swans alighting on a lake; the swans shed their swan-coverings and became beautiful girls, and as the three maidens swam, the boys stole their swan-suits. The boys refused to return them, and the girls had no choice but to marry the boys and live secretly with them, hiding them from their fellow spirits. After several years, the youngest girl, married to Shash-Tazy, became pregnant, and the jealous oldest girl told Shash-Tazy that his "wife" was not the daughter of good spirits, but of demons; she urged him to observe her in secret, and when he did so he saw the same telltale signs of her true origin as appeared in the first version. Shash-Tazy's wife saw that he had seen her and at once donned her swan-suit and flew off, hiding herself for eight days; on the ninth day she returned and addressed him thus:

> "Having paid heed to evil, envious people, you have injured yourself and deprived yourself of your wife and of your future son; you will have to seek him in a foreign land, in the city of "Kumgel," at a place where nine roads cross. I will leave your son there; Azrail will feed him for six days, and Jibrail for seven.[34] On his head there will be a white turban, and "Kydyr Ata" [i.e. Khiḍr] will care for him for forty days; he will be fair-skinned, and will have the seal of Azrail on his shoulder and the seal of Jibrail on his forehead."

Shash-Tazy wept for his loss but resolved to search for his son. Meanwhile, the boy was found by a certain Azhu-Kozha, a caravan leader who happened upon the place where his mother had left him in the

33. Potanin, "Tiurkskaia skazka," pp. 294–297 for this version, with corresponding passages in the second and third variants on pp. 301 and 304.

34. This element is not found in the corresponding place in the first version, but later, when Idige recalls seeing Baba ʿUmar and carrying Baba Tokty Chachty Aziz upon his back, he notes

shade of a great tree; after both Azhu-Kozha and the ruler of the country (who gave the boy his name, Idige) sought to claim the boy, Shash-Tazy arrived and identified the boy by the marks on his shoulder and forehead. But after departing for his native country with the boy, Shash-Tazy stopped at the home of an old childless couple who asked him to leave the boy there with them; he at first was reluctant to do so, but finally agreed to give them the boy in return for a horse on which to return to his homeland. Idige thus remained with them, and no more is heard of the "Baba Tükles" of this version.

Other variants including the swan-maiden story include Noghay versions recorded by Valikhanov and translated by Potanin,[35] in which doves figure rather than swans; in one Baba Tükles marries the dove-maiden, while his son "Kultu-kaya" does so in another. Similarly, an unpublished Noghay version recorded in 1958[36] has Baba Tükles steal the "clothes" of the swan-maiden, who bears him "Qutlï-qaya," who in turn marries the daughter of an *albastï*; here it is Baba Tükles' son who agrees to the three familiar conditions set by this supernatural maiden, and *their* son is Idige. Divaev's Qazaq version, which omits the name of Baba Tükles, nevertheless has an unnamed "saint" come upon a spring where three swans take off their swan-suits, with the narrative then following the familiar pattern.

Somewhat more complete, if less well reported, is an unpublished Qaraqalpaq version recorded in the 1930s,[37] which has the added interest of a possible link to a local shrine: the saint, named Baba Tukli-aziz, is said to live at a grave called "Kubïr," a name that would appear to mask the name of Najm ad-Dīn *Kubrā*, whose tomb in Khorezm was naturally well known among the Qaraqalpaqs of the region. At that shrine, the account goes, there was a spring, and three doves used to fly down to bathe in it; one time Baba Tukli-aziz stole their clothes, demanding that one of them stay with him in return for the others' clothes. They agreed, but set four conditions, which are not described in the available synopsis. In any event, they were broken, prompting the dove/fairy left behind

---

also that he had depended upon *Azrāʾil parista* ("the angel Azrāʾil") for six days, and upon the angel Jibrāʾil for seven (Melioranskii's text, p. 22; the passage was not translated by Valikhanov).

35. Valikhanov, *Sochineniia*, pp. 265–273; Potanin, "Otryvki," pp. 161–163.

36. Discussed by Zhirmunskii, "Skazanie ob Idige," p. 383.

37. Synopsized by Maksetov, *Ocherki*, pp. 87–89; he gives no specific reference to one of the several versions he mentions (see above, n.24), but the version is most likely that of Yerpolat-jïraw. The rest of the narrative follows the familiar pattern, including the appearance of "Sïpïra jïraw"; but Maksetov does not indicate whether the bard recounts Idige's ancestry as in other versions.

to depart, with the promise to leave the son with whom she was pregnant under a tree for Baba Tukli-aziz to find.

Finally, the last variation on the mythic portrayal of Idige's supernatural origins appears also in a Noghay version, recorded by Valikhanov and translated by Potanin.[38] It follows the same outline as the others discussed above, with Baba Tükles witnessing a pigeon, in this case, turn into a maiden by the seashore, and the girl, whom according to the tale some consider the daughter of the sun, and others the daughter of an *albastï*, fleeing into the sea; Baba Tükles jumps in after her, and the narrative follows the same pattern as before. In this version, however, interesting details are added on the origin of Baba Tükles himself, as the ancestor of Idige; and they appear *only* in this version, insofar as this may be judged from the state in which we have access to the various versions.

According to this variant, a man came across a skull that bore an inscription on its forehead claiming, "Alive I killed innumerable people; in death I can kill forty." The man burned the skull, placed its ashes in a pouch, and brought them home to his daughter to keep. The daughter became curious and opened the pouch; seeing the white powder, she touched her finger to it and tasted it, and as a result she became pregnant. The son she bore was Baba Tükles, who, the account affirms, was an extremely intelligent lad. Once the Khan of the country had a dream he wished to understand: he sat in the middle of a bridge over a great river, as dragons jumped out of the river, twenty on each side of the bridge, trying to devour him. The Khan's wise men were confounded, but Baba Tükles said he could interpret the dream if the forty wise men would leave him alone with the Khan. They did, and he told the Khan that the forty dragons were his wise men, who were conspiring against him; the Khan confirmed that this was true and killed the forty wise men, thereby fulfilling the inscription on the skull.[39] This portion of the tale concludes by affirming that Baba Tükles' origin from the white ashes of the skull on the road is the reason that Idige Biy's descendants are called *aq-süyek*, "white-bone," an appellation properly restricted to persons of Chingisid descent.

This Noghay version, then, portrays Baba Tükles himself—and not merely Idige—as of supernatural origin. It completes the mythic image of Baba Tükles, an image central to his transformation into a protective spirit

38. Potanin, "Otryvki," p. 162; cf. Valikhanov, *Sochineniia*, pp. 231–232, 272–273.

39. Another version of the same tale, with a slightly different dream and interpretation and without explicit identification of the magically conceived child as Baba Tükles, was also pub-

and communal founder, as is discussed more fully below. This version also makes Baba Tükles a more distant ancestor of Idige, but the fact of his ancestry, if not the degree, is a nearly universal feature of accounts of the epic "Idige Biy," and it is to these genealogical ties that we must now turn our attention. Even if the supernatural element is not explicitly recounted, Baba Tükles' status as a forebear of Idige is a consistent theme, whether a particular account condenses the genealogy and makes Baba Tükles the father of Idige or multiplies the generations between them; we will consider the details of this genealogical structure as developed most

lished by Potanin; cf. *Kazakhskii fol'klor v sobranii G. N. Potanina (Arkhivnye materialy i publikatsii)* (Alma-Ata: Nauka, 1972), pp. 144–145, 329. Curiously, a virtually identical tale is included in a cycle of oral tradition associated with a putative shrine of Shams ad-Dīn Tabrīzī in Multan, with Shams-i Tabrīz as the son and Jalāl ad-Dīn Rūmī as the finder of the skull; in this version the daughter mistakes the powdered skull for flour, becomes pregnant, and bears Shams-i Tabrīz, while the forty people killed by the skull are slain as they attempt to protect his mother from Shams' rage, prompted by his playmates' taunts that he is the bastard son of his own grandfather. The rest of the cycle deals with Rūmī's search for Shams and the miracles worked by the latter. This version was discussed by W. Ivanow, "Shums Tabrez of Multan," in *Professor Muḥammad Shafiᶜ Presentation Volume / Armaghān-i ᶜilmī*, ed. S. M. Abdullah (Lahore, 1955), pp. 109–118 (p. 110 on this tale), with an appeal for additional references to the theme. The more general theme of the prophesying skull is a common folkloric motif, with reflection in Islamic literary traditions in the Persian *Jumjumah-nāmah* ascribed to ᶜAṭṭār and the Turkic *Dāstān-i Jumjumah Sulṭān* inspired by it (on which see Hofman, *Turkish Literature*, III, pp. 145–149), as well as in the Turkic variants of the *Kesek-bash kitabï*: cf. Ia. S. Akhmetgaleeva, *Issledovanie tiurkoiazychnogo pamiatnika "Kisekbash kitaby"* (Moscow: Nauka, 1979); Jan Ciopiński, "*Késik Báš Kitābý*, Variante de Kazan," *Folia Orientalia*, 11 (1969), pp. 79–88, 12 (1970), pp. 61–68, 13 (1971), pp. 9–13; Fuat Özdemir, "İlk dînî destanlar ve Kesikbaş destanı," *Folklor araştırmaları kurumu yıllığı* (Ankara, 1975), pp. 123–129; and most recently Ahmet Yaşar Ocak, *Türk Folklorunda Kesik Baş (Tarih-Folklor İlişkisinden bir Kesit* (Ankara, 1989). The vitality of the motif in contemporary Central Asia is suggested by its apparent adaptation in at least one example of what would appear to be widespread "oral hagiography," focused on popular saints and healers, as known through the derisive accounts of Soviet antireligious literature; a 1983 article in the Uzbek newspaper *Sovet Ŭzbekistoni* (24 July 1983, p. 4: A. Dilmurodov, "Avliyo emish . . .") scornfully recounted the fame and reputation of a certain Hasanbay Saliev of Samarkand, who tricked gullible people into trusting him as a saint and healer, and who claimed to have gained his saintly powers following an encounter with a skull. Once as he was driving, the story goes, Saliev saw a skull lying by the side of the road; he did not stop, but that night he saw an old man in a dream, telling him that the skull belonged to one of the 1400 saints and that if he would provide the skull with a proper burial, he would gain wondrous powers to cure the sick (see the account in Timur Kocaoglu, "Recent Reports on Activities of Living Muslim "Saints" in USSR," *Radio Liberty Research*, No. 346/83 (15 September 1983), pp. 1–5 [p. 1]; and an abbreviated version in the same writer's "Islam in the Soviet Union: Atheistic Propaganda and "Unofficial" Religious Activities," *Journal, Institute of Muslim Minority Affairs*, 5/1 (1984), pp. 145–152 [pp. 149–150]). Even through the distorting ideological lens we can trace the use of an old hagiographical motif in a new setting, in a way that also implicitly evokes communal concerns about maintaining Muslim burial rites (and most likely about the Soviet-era destruction of Muslim tombs, of saints and ordinary folk, as well).

fully in the Noghay versions of the Idige epic. But we may note here, finally, that the *centrality* of Baba Tükles' ancestry is revealingly stressed in a version of the Idige epic published by Berezin as a "Turkmen" tale of Tokhtamïsh:[40] here Idige first recounts his genealogy, echoing at least a few names known from other traditions (Idige < Nadr Kiyā[41] Biy < Qādir Kiyā Biy < Terme Kiyā Biy < ʿAzīz Kiyā Biy), but then affirms, "If you ask who is my original ancestor (*tüb atam*), it is Baba Tükles Chashlï ʿAzīz."[42]

Baba Tükles and the "Noghay Epic"

The consistent appearance of Baba Tükles in Idige's genealogy suggests a fundamental link between Baba Tükles and the confederation that looked to the historical Edigü—as well as to the epic Idige—and his family as the founders of its strength and even identity: the Noghay horde. We have already touched briefly upon the origins and history of the Noghay steppe confederation, but here we may recall that it included tribal groups that later comprised major elements among the Qazaqs, Qaraqalpaqs, Bashkirs, Tatars, and Uzbeks—thereby accounting for the vast range of the so-called "Noghay" epic cycle of which the Idige tale is a central element—as well as the smaller groups in the Kuban and North Caucasus that have borne the designation "Noghay" down to the present day.

It is not surprising that the versions of the Idige tale recorded among those groups that retained the ethnonym "Noghay" are of considerable importance in evaluating the role of Baba Tükles and the rationale behind the central role he plays. In particular, these versions, while reinforcing the supernatural element in Baba Tükles and thereby adding to his mythic personality, also contain some of the most important clues for correlating the various epic versions with the Tatar historical tradition regarding Edigü, and for understanding the assimilation of Islamic and

40. It cannot be of Turkmen provenance to judge from the content and language (that clearly places it in the Qïpchaq group); Zhirmunskii refers to it in his survey as a Noghay version, without further explanation. Most likely it reflects Noghay influence among the so-called "Trukhmen" of the North Caucasus, who moved there from their earlier homeland in Manghïshlaq, under Qalmïq pressure, in the eighteenth century.

41. *Kiyā*, spelled consistently in this text with *kāf* rather than *qāf*; on this term see chapter 5, n. 129.

42. I. Berezin, ed., *Turetskaia khrestomatiia*, t. II (Kazan', 1862), p. 64.

native Inner Asian conceptions of sacred communal origins.

In the first place, several Noghay versions give Idige's genealogy in a form more closely resembling the ancestry presented in the Tatar histories (see Table 5.1); as indicated, the differences in Baba Tükles' genealogical position vis-à-vis Idige are no doubt less important than the fundamental element of his ancestry, but it seems clear that the more "distant" epic versions have condensed Idige's genealogy in making Baba Tükles his actual father rather than an ancestor; as a rule, intervening ancestors displace the mythic motifs elaborated upon in some epic versions. As noted, however, too many generations are included in both these Noghay versions and the Tatar histories to accord with any sense of historical, genealogical reality. The Noghay variant noted earlier makes Idige a *ninth*-generation descendant of Baba Tükles (rather than his son, as in the Qazaq versions, or a sixth-generation descendant, as in the Tatar histories), while another Noghay version, though presenting the same nine-generation separation, ascribes Baba Tükles' involvement with the bird-maiden by the sea to Idige's father, Qutlu-Qïya,[43] instead.

Neither of these versions names the intervening ancestors, but an important Noghay version of the Idige tale published in 1883 by M. Osmanov[44] twice gives the same genealogy known from the Tatar histories (Idige < Qūtlū-Qïyā < Qādir-Qïyā < Islām-Qïyā < Qïzīčī < Terme < Baba Tükles); the same genealogy is recited once in the Noghay ver-

43. Potanin, "Otryvki," p. 162 (version 3); cf. Potanin, "Tiurkskaia skazka," p. 320, on a Noghay version (recorded by M. Aleinikov) ascribing "Qutluqai's" marriage to an *albastï* to his having killed her demon husband while hunting in the forest: here the bird and water motifs are missing, although the same telltale signs of her true nature appear. Zhirmunskii ("Skazanie ob Idige," p. 383) cites a Noghay version recorded in 1958 in the Karachay-Cherkes Autonomous Oblast, in which Baba Tükles marries the maiden whose swan-suit he stole, and thus fathers Qutlï Qïya, who in turn marries the daughter of an *albastï*; it is this latter supernatural wife who elicits from Qutlï Qïya the promise not to look at her in the three by-now familiar situations, and *their* son, in turn, is Idige. The Crimean variant from "Büyük Khojalar" recorded by Radlov (*Proben*, VII, pp. 99–122; cf. below, n. 60) makes Qutlu Qïya the son of Baba Tükles and the father of Idige; a Noghay version recorded by Falev in the Stavropol' district (but not published) evidently gives the same account (cf. the summary of his report entitled "Zapisi proizvedenii narodnoi slovesnosti u nogaitsev Stavropol'skoi gub. v sviazi s rannee opublikovannym materialam," *ZVOIRAO*, 23 (1916), pp. v–vi). Yet another more recent unpublished Noghay version, recorded in 1978, appears to ascribe the dalliance with a beautiful maiden beneath a tree by a river, who turns out to be an "*albaslï*," to Idige himself; cf. R. Kh. Kereitov, "Mifologicheskie personazhi traditsionnykh verovanii Nogaitsev," *Sovetskaia ètnografiia*, 1980, No. 2, pp. 117–127 (p. 121).

44. M. Osmanov, *Nogaiskie i kumykskie teksty* (Saint Petersburg, 1883), pp. 32–49; the genealogy appears on pp. 35–36 (where it is recounted by the famous Supra Jïraw, on whom see above, n.27), and again on p. 48 (with the generations before Baba Tükles given as well).

sion recorded by Chodzko in 1830,[45] and in a Qara-Noghay account published in 1900 we find essentially the same links, recounted by the bard "Suvra."[46] Of these intervening generations, only Qutlu-Qïya (and to a much lesser extent Terme) are more than mere names, and it seems safe to assume that the supernatural dealings with the bird-maiden were originally attached to the figure of Baba Tükles and only later ascribed to Qutlu-Qïya as the father of the "genealogized" Idige. What is more interesting, the Qara-Noghay account adds an echo of the Tatar histories in the bard "Suvra's" affirmation that Baba Tükles "ruled at the site of our holy Kaᶜbah;" and in an even stronger echo of the Tatar histories, in Osmanov's Noghay version Baba Tükles is likewise said to have ruled at the Kaᶜbah, and his fourteen ancestors going back to Abū Bakr, matching quite well those found in the Tatar histories, are also named.[47] In this case Chodzko's version provides the Bakrid genealogy as well, but with only ten generations between Baba Tükles and Abū Bakr,[48] while the Qara-Noghay variant lists twelve generations between them, again in a list appended to the narrative.[49]

Different names, interspersed with ones familiar from the other variants, are given in the Noghay version recorded in translation by Semenov; here the genealogy is first recited by the bard summoned by Tokhtamïsh to reveal Idige's identity, but is alluded to in speeches of both Idige and

45. Here the same names, recited by the bard "Sobra" as he attempts to dissuade Tokhtamïsh from pursuing Idige, are clearly masked by the transcription (Chodzko, *Specimens*, p. 355): "Baba Túkla, then Túrbay-Kurabchi [collapsing Terme and Qïzïjï/Qarapchï into one link], then Islam-Kaya, then Kaddyr-Kaya, then Kúlly-Kaya."

46. Cf. G. Anan'ev, tr., "Karanogaiskiia narodnyia istoricheskiia predan'ia," *Sbornik materialov dlia opisaniia mestnostei i plemen Kavkaza*, vyp. 27 (Tiflis, 1900), otdel III, pp. 1–38, given in Russian translation only (p. 4 for Suvra's account of "Adige's" ancestry); he says that Adige's "grandfather" (*ded*, but here evidently "ancestor") was "Babi-Tukles," who ruled at the Kaᶜbah; his son was "Turme," his son "Kzyche," and his son "Islan-kaya" [*sic* in this list only], who were all princes. Two additional links, namely "Islam-Kaya's" son "Kadyrkaya" and the latter's son "Kutlukaya," who was Adige's father, are added in the full genealogy back to Abū Bakr appended to the narrative (p. 16).

47. Baba Tükles' genealogy appears thus in Osmanov's Noghay version: Baba Tükles < Sulṭān Jalāl ad-Dīn < Sulṭān ᶜUthmān < Abū'l-Ḥaqq < Sulṭān–Ṣadāq < Sulṭān Salīm < Sulṭān Abū'l-ᶜĀṣ < Sulṭān Mavlūd < Sulṭān Qaydah < Sulṭān Valīd < Sulṭān Khalīd < Sulṭān Hurmuz < Sulṭān Kaᶜb < Muḥammad < Abū Bakr.

48. In Chodzko, *Specimens*, p. 355; again, names and titles have evidently been confused, and several links omitted: Baba Túkla < Salim < Abul-Kalipheh < Jalal-ed-Dyn < Osman < Walid < Khalid < sultan Hamza < sultan Abbas < sultan Ibrahim < sultan Mahmud < Abubekr-Saudyk.

49. Anan'ev, p. 16: Babatukles < Soltan Dzhalal-èddin < Soltan Osman < Abdulkhak < Soltan-Sydak < Soltan-Selim < Soltan-Abul-Az < Soltan Mavlut < Soltan-Kaida < Soltan-Valit < Soltan-Khanit < Soltan-Irmiz < Soltan-Kiab < Ababakiar.

"Nuradil."[50] The bard notes that Idige is a descendant of Abū Bakr, and the lineage evidently runs thus: "Chachly-Aziz"[51] > Batyr-kaya > Bor-kaya > Kadyr-kaya > Kutlu-kaya > Idige; the latter was born, says the bard, through the prayers of "Koja Akhmat, who was called also Yasau-biy." This designation, clearly understood as an allusion to Khoja Aḥmad Yasavī, is discussed further below. In Idige's own speech in this variant, "Chachly-Aziz" is said to be the son of "Jalāl ad-Dīn Khalīfah," reflecting no doubt the traditions incorporating into the lineage a name usually interpreted as that of Jalāl ad-Dīn Rūmī.

What is worth noting in this regard is that despite the occasional differences in the names that figure in the lineage of Idige, it is only the Noghay versions and closely related Tatar versions that pay attention to the genealogy at all, suggesting that these versions are closer to the political environment marked by concern for Edigü's own legitimacy and that of his descendants. Such is the conclusion suggested by the retention of essentially the same genealogical memory among the nineteenth-century Noghays, apparently outside the framework of the Idige tale, as attested in an ethnographic survey of Astrakhan and its environs published in 1852.[52] The author, describing the Noghays of Astrakhan, whom the Russians called "*Iurtovskie Tatary*," records the history and genealogy of these Noghays' chiefs on the basis of accounts related by natives of two small settlements in the region:

> The current Iurtovsk chief from Tsarevo, Abubekr Dzhan-Aliev, and an inhabitant of Kelechi, Iskhaq Diuseev, relate according to the legends of their ancestor, that the forefather of the branch of the Noghays from which the Iurtovsk Tatars originated was a certain *Islam*, by title "Kayá," [meaning] something in between "Ḥājjī" and "Sayyid." *Islam*-Kayá had a son *Karankí*; he had a son *Babá-Tukles*, and his son was *Kydyr*-Kayá. The great-great-grandson of *Kydyr*-Kayá, son of *Terme*-Kayá and grandson of *Kutlu*-Kayá (the son of *Kydyr*-Kayá),[53] named *Èdigei*, proclaimed

50. Cf. Semenov, *Tuzemtsy*, pp. 427–428, 443, 449. The bard, incidentally, is named in this version "Parzdak the son of Shaban," of Khiva, instead of "Supra jïraw."

51. Twice out of the three times his name appears, Semenov gives it as "Chachly-Aliz," without explanation; it is not clear if he transcribed it thus for some reason, or if the error results from a misprint.

52. Pavel Nebol'sin, *Ocherki Volzhskago nizov'ia* (Saint Petersburg: Tipografiia Ministerstva vnutrennikh del, 1852), pp. 54–55.

53. So reads Nebol'sin's text; either a link has been omitted, or, more likely, "great-grandson"

> himself "Biy" over the Noghays. Èdigei had two sons, who received from their father the title "Murza": the elder was *Nur-Adil* and the younger *Mansur*. At the time when Barak-Khan ruled in Khorezm, *Mansur*-Murza made a raid on Khiva, where he died a violent death, being blinded by order of Barak. *Nur-Adil*-Murza had two sons: *Okaz* and *Akas*. The latter died childless, but Okaz's successor to power over the Noghays was his son *Musa*-Biy. Musa-Biy had 30 sons; the ninth of them, *Al'chesmaíl*, having induced all his brothers to quarrel among themselves, deprived them of influence over the people, and became chief over the Noghays himself. Al'chesmail had a son *Urus*, and from him two grandsons, *Aq-Satí* and *Dzhan-Arslan*: the latter died without leaving heirs, but Ak-Satí,[54] through his son *Alí* and grandson *Kazy*, had descendants of whom some branches converted to Christianity and were fully adopted into Russia with the noble dignity befitting their origin, while some remain to this day among the Iurtovtsy.

It is of course likely that the early links in this genealogy were not wholly "independent" of the Idige tale, but rather were recalled from the epic context to serve as part of the Noghays' "history" upon the Russian scholar's request; but this, of course, is precisely the point we are making about the role such epic encodings of communal traditions play in providing historical and popular identity. In this instance the Islamic component is not stressed, and Baba Tükles' role is minimal; we will consider similar accounts, however, in which these elements are much more central to the narrative.

More important, the Noghay versions clearly reveal the social and political motivations for stressing both the supernatural origin of Idige and his descent from Baba Tükles, namely the need for status and legitimacy among the descendants of the non-Chingisid Idige (and indeed within the structure of the Noghay horde itself). A hint of this is found in the Noghay variant cited earlier, where a supernatural justification for considering Idige's descendants "white bone" was provided, but other ver-

should be read instead of "great-great-grandson." The intended genealogy is probably thus: Islam-Kaya > Karanki > Baba Tükles > Kydyr-Kaya > Kutlu-Kaya > Terme > Èdigei. One is tempted to ascribe also the genealogy's sequence, so different from any other recorded, to Nebol'sin rather than to his sources.

54. On "Satyi murza," ancestor of the Russified Urusov princely family, cf. Pleshko, *Kniaz'ia Urusovy*, p. 30.

sions are more explicit in pitting Idige's family against the epic antagonist (and Chingisid) Tokhtamïsh. In Anan'ev's Qara-Noghay account,[55] Idige's son "Nuradil" (i.e., Nūr ad-Dīn[56]) justifies his legitimacy saying, "I accepted the one God from birth, and the same God protected me; the fact that I am not of Chingis Khan's lineage is of little consequence, for I am of the tribe of the glorious Turk hero *Khochakhmat Babatukli.*" In the corresponding passage in Osmanov's chrestomathy, Idige's son "Nūr ʿĀdil" likewise appropriates Islamic symbols as he addresses his people, confirming his superiority over Tokhtamïsh: he notes that he was born on a Friday, the Muslim holy day, and claims that the first sight he saw was the "Night of Power" (*qadr tüni*)[57] and that the first words he spoke were those of the *shahādah*, "There is no God but God"; he affirms that he can read Arabic and has "served" Khiżr and Ilyās, and finally asks of what consequence Tokhtamïsh's Chingisid origin can be, when "I myself am the son of *Qoji Aḥmad Baba Tükli Shashli ʿAzīz Barkhāyah*[58] of blessed Turkistan."[59] A similar passage is found in a Crimean version of the Idige tale recorded by Radlov; here Idige's son "Nuradïn" declares that although he is not of Chingisid origin, he uttered the *shahādah*, "There is no God but God," as soon as he was born, knew Arabic, acknowledged himself a

55. Cf. Anan'ev, "Karanogaiskiia narodnyia istoricheskiia predan'ia," p. 12 for Nuradil's declaration; the same passage is noted in M. G. Safargaliev, *Raspad Zolotoi Ordy* (Saransk, 1960), pp. 228–229, citing K. [*sic*] Anan'ev, "Karanogaitsy i ikh predaniia," *Sbornik svedenii o Severnom Kavkaze*, t. II (Stavropol'-Kavkazskii, 1906), pp. 7–9.

56. On the various forms of the name of Idige's son in the epic tales (*Nuralin, Nuradin, Nūr ʿAlī, Muradim*, etc.), see Melioranskii, "Skazanie," introduction pp. 7–8, and Köprülü, *Türk edebiyatı tarihi*, p. 386; the use of the name in Noghay and Crimean political nomenclature was noted in the preceding chapter.

57. That is, the "*Laylat al-qadr*" on which the Qurʾān was revealed to the Prophet Muḥammad; Chodzko's rendering includes this element, but without the specifically "anti-Chingisid" conclusions drawn from it in other versions.

58. The reading of the latter term is unclear; the text (Osmanov, *Nogaiskie i kumykskie teksty*, p. 43) reads *bārkhāyah-ding*, with the final element seemingly the genitive suffix (though *-ning* would be expected) governing *uuli*, "son of;" but Çağatay ("Die Ädigä-Saga," p. 276) reads this as "*baxayediniñ*," implying that the *laqab* "Bahaʾ ad-Dīn" is intended, while Melioranskii ("Skazanie," introduction, p. 10), evidently understanding the *-ding* as the genitive suffix, reads "*barkhai*," with no further explanation. Zhirmunskii, citing Melioranskii, nevertheless introduces his own interpretation of the word, again without explanation, as *barkan* ("Skazanie ob Idige," p. 383). The form is probably reflected in the appearance of "Bor Kaya," interpreted as a proper name, in some epic genealogies of Idige, but this does not clarify its meaning. A more likely explanation, which requires the assumption that Osmanov's text is inaccurate or "corrupt," is suggested by the shamanic invocation of "Babay Tükti Shashtï Äziz" noted below, n.104, where an appeal for this figure's aid is followed by an invocation of "*bar küday*," which the ethnographer who recorded the shaman interprets as "universal God," i.e., Persian *bār khudāy*.

59. Osmanov, *Nogaiskie i kumykskie teksty*, p. 43.

servant of God, and was descended from *Chashlï Tüklü Qoj Amät.*[60]

Semenov's version, as noted above, has the bard refer to Idige's birth throught the prayers of "Koja Akhmat, known as Yasau-biy," suggesting that this Khoja Aḥmad and "Chachlï-Aziz" are two distinct persons; but the former name is clearly placed in his familial lineage later in the tale, when "Nuradil" declares to Tokhtamïsh's son Kadïr-berdi, "So what if you originate from Chingiz Khan! I myself am the son of the wise man of Turkistan, Khitay, Qïpchaq, Qïrghïz, and Hindustan, Khoja Aḥmad, who was the father of Chachlï-Aziz, who was the father of Bor-kaya."[61] Just prior to this affirmation, Nuradil recites the same litany as given in other versions: he was born on a Friday, repeated God's name ceaselessly since he could speak, reads the Arabic script, and prayed for forty days to Khiżr and Ilyās at a sacred spring. But Semenov's version has Idige himself foreshadow Nuradil's speech to Kadïr-berdi, further cementing the Islamic symbolism evoked for legitimation. Idige tells Nuradil, whom he praises for reading all the books of the four *imāms*, of his life, affirming that he prayed in thirty-two mosques, always journeyed in the footsteps of Khiżr and Ilyās, benefited from the guidance of Chachlï-Aziz, and read the entire Qur'ān seven times, as well as the other three books sent from heaven (the Torah, the Psalms, and the Gospel); he constantly repeats the phrase *ṣubḥānullāh* ("Glory to God!"), he continues, knows the num-

60. *Proben*, VII, pp. 160–162; the passage gives yet another genealogy: Idige < Qutlu Qïya < Temir Qïya < Kär Amät < Är Amät < Chashlï Tüklü Qoj Amät. In another Crimean Tatar version (*Proben*, VII, pp. 99–122, esp. p. 104), Idige is called the son of a "servant of God" who was in turn a son of *Baba Tükli Chashlï ʿAzīz*, and his mother is described as the daughter of a *jinn*. The recently-published Tatar version (*Kazan utlarï*, 1989, No. 1, p. 50; *Idegäy: Tatar khalïk dastanï*, p. 181) has Noradïn scoff at Tuktamïsh's Chingisid origin and recount his own genealogy (Idegäy < Kotlïkïyä < Timerkïyä < Ir Äkhmät < Chächlä-tökle Khuja Äkhmät); here the various evocations of Islam do not appear, although earlier in this version (in the journal, p. 8; in the book, p. 23) the hero's "great ancestor" (*ölkän babasï*) is called "Baba Tökläs Khujakhmät, the master of the saints (*äüliyälar pire*)." The element "Amät" appearing in several of the names in these genealogies, including that of Baba Tükles, recalls the name of the hero of one section of the *Daftar-i Chingīz-nāmah* discussed above, namely the "*dāstān*" of "Amat the son of ʿĪsā" (cf. Usmanov, *Tatarskie istoricheskie istochniki*, pp. 114–116). Here Jānī Bek Khan promises his daughter to this "Amat" but then reneges; Amat steals her away and lives with her on a mountain near the Volga, where she bears him a son, but the son is stolen and taken to Astrakhan, where he grows up in a princely family. The tale's characters are identifiable historical figures, as Usmanov notes; at the same time the tale's similarity with features of the Idige *dāstān* (with the "stolen" bride and son) suggests its conflation with the story of Idige, or, conversely, its common origin with the Idige tale (with "Amat" [= Aḥmad] originally known as the name of both "Baba Tükles" and Sayyid Ata, as reported in several sources), the two subsequently undergoing divergent development in different settings.

61. Semenov, *Tuzemtsy*, p. 449.

ber of Prophets and angels, and is well versed in the laws of Islam.[62] Idige is in fact frequently referred to as "shaykh" in this version, and refers to the many *murīds* he has guided on the *ṭarīqah*; but beyond this clear Sufi coloring, Idige declares that he will be his son's intercessor on the Day of Judgment, and later, while living alone in the steppe subsisting on roots and berries, cures his far-away son by facing Mecca and praying to God.[63]

We thus find repeated intimations of the role Baba Tükles must have played at some early stage in the formation of the Noghay horde, as reflected in the epic tales handed down among many Turkic peoples of western Inner Asia since the era of Noghay unity. He clearly provided a source of political legitimacy for the Noghay leadership that claimed descent from him, in an anti-Chingisid mold that was at the same time "pro-Islamic"; but the pro-Islamic character of Baba Tükles' legitimizing function could also be, and was, carefully wrapped in layers of symbolism evocative of ancestral veneration and mythic ethnogony to appeal to an Inner Asian audience (one that happened to be in the process of Islamization). It is in this careful and altogether striking combination of Islamic and Inner Asian symbolism that the epic figure of Baba Tükles illustrates the potent process of the nativization of Islam; we will return later to some general considerations of how Baba Tükles served as a legitimizer and as a symbol of communal integrity, but for now we will turn to this issue of "nativized" Islam, to consider the *source* of the sacred power he lent to communities in Islamic Inner Asia.

Baba Tükles as a "Nativized" Bringer of Islam

Islamized Natives and Nativized Muslims in Inner Asia

In the Noghay versions of the epic tradition surrounding Idige considered above, it is descent from the figure known elsewhere as "Baba Tükles" that provides, in the epic context, political and social legitimacy for Idige, his son, and the Noghay horde. There is a clear opposition between the steppe tradition of Chingisid legitimacy and the Islamic mode of legitimacy through the spiritual—and genealogical—sanction of the holy Baba Tükles. It is furthermore significant that this opposition places the

62. Semenov, *Tuzemtsy*, pp. 440–444.
63. Semenov, *Tuzemtsy*, p. 445.

Islamic mode of legitimacy squarely on the side of the nonimperial tradition of Inner Asian tribal and political confederation, highlighting the political use of evocations of Islam as a force to unite communities who regarded the Chingisid tradition with hostility or at best indifference.

We will return in Chapter 7 to the significance of the tales about Baba Tükles in communal legitimation; for now, however, we must explore the source of Baba Tükles' legitimizing sanctity. Is it rooted in some preexisting tradition of a figure known as a progenitor or founder who was subsequently identified as a Muslim saint from the holy centers of Islam? Does it simply stem from his reputed descent from the Caliph Abū Bakr, as a means of sanctioning a dynasty's genealogy by linking it with an Islamic one? Or is it based primarily on his role as the bearer of Islam (perhaps reinforced, to be sure, by his sacred Islamic lineage and by numinous associations of a distinctly Inner Asian type), in the memory of the peoples who adopted him as their "political" or mythological ancestor?

In other words, should we assume the existence, among the peoples of the Jöchid *ulus*, of a legend of origin centered upon a personage marked by such numinous features as those surrounding Baba Tükles, who was then assimilated to the figure of "Islamizer" as those peoples sought to explain the process of Islamization, in indigenous terms, through a single "founder"? Should we consider the definitive sacralizing element in Baba Tükles to be his holy ancestry rather than any active role in Islamization, as might be argued from the accounts giving prominence to the genealogies? Or should we suppose that a prominent figure in the process of Islamization came to be surrounded with a variety of stock sacralizing motifs, well known among the peoples of the Jöchid *ulus*, and thereby developed into a "founder," assimilable to "progenitor," as narratives of Islamization and legends of origin merged?

To a large degree, perhaps, the *fact* of this assimilation is remarkable enough, and the specific direction it took may be less important; I would argue, however, that inquiring into the "original" source of Baba Tükles' legitimizing sanctity is not an idle pursuit, since the first two alternatives are fairly common in Inner Asia, while the third is much rarer and would seem to indicate a remarkably strong link between Islam and communal bonds.

The first alternative is perhaps best known as exemplified in Buddhist Mongol tradition of the seventeenth and eighteenth centuries, where the ancestral figure of Börte Chino—the "blue-grey wolf" named as Chingis Khan's first ancestor in the 13th–century *Secret History*—was transformed into a Tibetan prince with links to the sacred centers of Buddhism in India, and implicitly linked with the transmission of Buddhism to the Mongols.[64] Here a "hero," "first king," and "ancestor" of unquestionably Inner Asian origins—Chingis Khan—has been cast in Buddhist guise and fitted into Buddhist sacred history. Less well known but equally well developed are the popular traditions from the Islamic "half" of Inner Asia that transform Chingis Khan into a Muslim. The seventeenth-century *Khān-nāmah*, a little-studied mine of Central Asian popular traditions, describes Chingis Khan's adoption of Islam,[65] while Evliya Çelebi gives an extended account of the dialogue accompanying Chingis' conversion to Islam, an account punctuated by Evliya's repeated affirmations that Chingis did indeed become a Muslim.[66] Similar tales are reflected in oral tradition outside such literary sources, as, for example, in the identification of a particular mosque among the Noghays as the one where Chingis Khan and Jānī Bek prayed.[67]

Such tales are, of course, part of a larger process in which a local community's identity is first "Islamized" and then "universalized," as in

64. Cf. Charles Bawden, ed. and tr., *The Mongol Chronicle Altan Tobči* (Wiesbaden: Otto Harrassowitz, 1955; Göttinger Asiatische Forschungen, Band 5), pp. 112–113, and a more elaborate version in the later *Erdeni-yin tobči*, tr. John R. Krueger, *Sagang Sechen, Prince of the Ordos Mongols: The Bejewelled Summary of the Origin of Khans (Qad-un ündüsün-ü Erdeni-yin Tobči), A History of the Eastern Mongols to 1662*; Part One, Chapters One through Five: From the Creation of the World to the Death of Genghis Khan (1227) (Bloomington, Indiana: Mongolia Society Occasional Papers, No. 2, 1964), p. 41; see also Hans-Reiner Kämpfe, tr., *Das Asaraγči-neretü-yin teüke des Byamba erke daičing alias Šamba jasaγ (Eine mongolische Chronik des 17. Jahrhunderts)* (Wiesbaden: Otto Harrassowitz, 1983; Asiatische Forschungen, Band 81), p. 46. The same account is recorded in an eighteenth-century history of Buddhism written in Tibetan by a Mongol monk; cf. Sh. Soninbaiar, "O sochineniiakh mongol'skikh avtorov na tibetskom iazyke po khronologii buddizma v Tibete i Mongolii," tr. R. E. Pubaev, in *Istochnikovedenie i tekstologiia pamiatnikov srednevekovykh nauk v stranakh Tsentral'noi Azii. Sbornik nauchnykh trudov*, ed. R. E. Pubaev (Novosibirsk: Nauka, 1989), pp. 163–170 (p. 165 for this account). On this theme in general see also Herbert Franke, "From Tribal Chieftain to Universal Emperor and God: The Legitimation of the Yüan Dynasty," *Sitzungsberichte der Bayerischen Akademie der Wissenschaften, Philosophisch-Historische Klasse*, Jahrgang 1978, Heft 2 (Munich, 1978), esp. pp. 64–65; Sh. Bira, "Srednevekovaia mongol'skaia istoriografiia o vzaimosviazi stran Tsentral'noi Azii," *Narody Azii i Afriki*, 1986, No. 6, pp. 34–43 (esp. p. 40); and Tamura Jitsuzō, "The Legend of the Origin of the Mongols and Problems concerning their Migration," *Acta Asiatica*, 24 (1973), pp. 1–19.

65. MS British Museum Or. 14,352 (uncatalogued), pp. 742–743; on the work cf. Zeki Velidi Togan, "Das özbekische Epos Chan-name," *CAJ*, 1 (1955), pp. 144–156, and Orhan Şaik Gökyay, "Hannâme," in *Necati Lugal Armağanı* (Ankara: Türk Tarih Kurumu Basımevi, 1968), pp. 275–329.

66. Text, *Evliyā Çelebī sayāḥat-nāmesi*, vol. 7 (Istanbul: Devlet Maṭbaʿası, 1928; Türk Tārīkh Enjümeni Kulliyātı, No. 11), pp. 627–634; in modern Turkish, *Evliyâ Çelebi seyâhatnâmesi*, ed. Zuhuri Danışman (Istanbul: Kardeş Matbaası, 1970), vol. 11, pp. 220–223.

67. Cf. P. Nebol'sin, "Narody Astrakhanskoi gubernii: zametki o Kundrovskikh Tatarakh,"

Noghay traditions that the first human beings spoke "Tatar," the language taught them by Jibrā'īl;[68] a similar process is at work in Islamized popular etymologies of ethnonyms. An explanation of the ethnonym "Noghay" involving opposition to their Islamization is noted below, and as mentioned earlier the "Uzbek" people were understood as the people who followed Özbek Khan in adopting Islam; a Qïrghïz legend clothing the famous "*qïrq-qïz*" ("Forty Maidens") etymology in remarkable Islamic garb is likewise discussed in Chapter 7. Even more strikingly, a Qazaq legend noted in the late nineteenth century, for instance, mentions alongside the traditional Qazaq hero "Alash" an even more important figure, a wise man called "Qazï-aq" (i.e., "the [pure] white *qāżī*"), to whom the people deferred on all important issues and who was so highly honored that "the newly formed tribe" began to call itself "Qazaq."[69] In each case an important element of indigenous ethnic identity, whether language or self-designation, has been reinterpreted within an Islamic framework.

More to the point, the Islamization of ancestral "founders" well known from pre-Islamic or non-Islamic Inner Asian traditions—such as Oghuz Khan and a number of figures from the Chingisid lineage—is a common process evident as early as the stories of "Turk the son of Yāfīth" in tenth-century Muslim historical and geographical works, and well developed in histories such as those of Rashīd ad-Dīn and Abū'l-Ghāzī. The case of Oghuz Khan is particularly instructive, since a substantial textual fragment illustrating his mythic and legendary development in an entirely non-Islamic environment has survived for comparison with his Islamized legend in the works of Rashīd ad-Dīn and Abū'l-Ghāzī, as discussed further in Chapter 7.

The second alternative, of "discovering" sacred Islamic genealogies for Inner Asian rulers and heroes, is likewise well represented in these same instances as well as others. The process is at work in an Inner Asian context both in the elaboration of genealogical links with the Prophet or some Muslim saint for ruling dynasties, and in the identification of entire tribal communities as sacralized descendants of particular saints. The latter process is particularly well known among the Turkmens, but occured as well among the Uzbeks and other peoples; and the grafting of sacred

---

Vestnik Imperatorskago Russkago Geograficheskago Obshchestva, ch. 2 (1851), otd. V, pp. 28–29; reported also in Nebol'sin's *Ocherki Volzhskago nizov'ia*, p. 108.

68. Cf. Moshkov, "Melodii nogaiskikh i orenburgskikh tatar," p. 22.

69. Cf. A. D. Nesterov, "Proshloe priural'skikh stepei v predaniiakh kirgiz Kazalinskogo uezda," *ZVOIRAO*, 12/4 (1900), pp. 095–0105 [p. 0104].

genealogies onto royal or tribal lineages is hardly limited to Inner Asia, after all. The second alternative is, in short, a quite common response to religious change, and for this reason deserves to be underscored as an element of Islamization in Inner Asia. But for the same reason it is not particularly remarkable or surprising; it still involves the adoption of Islamic discourse to explain and assert the legitimacy of structures and values that grew out of indigenous social and religious traditions.

But the third alternative—the adoption, in effect, of indigenous religious language to incorporate a "foreign" holy man—points to an even more interesting process, which, although actually fairly common in Islamic Inner Asia, has not been recognized or discussed before. This process implies a much deeper assimilation, I would argue, than is evident with the first two alternatives, and the case of Baba Tükles offers perhaps our most vivid illustration of this most revealing process; for it involves the "nativization" of a bearer of an "alien" tradition in the course of constructing a "confederative" legend of origin.

To be sure, elements supportive of all three alternatives as to the origin of Baba Tükles' sanctity may be found in the Noghay versions of the Idige tale (that is, versions circulated among the community most closely linked with Baba Tükles), as well as in many of the other variants. To argue the greater likelihood of the third alternative depends upon showing not only the greater antiquity of Baba Tükles' Islamizing role—confirmed by Ötemish Ḥājjī's account—but the continued association of Baba Tükles with Islamization; and the latter point in particular is suggested by a number of considerations discussed in the remainder of this chapter.

The Traditional Memory of Baba Tükles as Communal Islamizer

THE ANTIQUITY OF THE TRADITION AND ITS TWENTIETH-CENTURY SURVIVALS

To begin with, the earliest known account of Baba Tükles—the account of Özbek Khan's conversion in the work of Ötemish Ḥājjī, recounted earlier—clearly portrays Baba Tükles as an "Islamizer," and his role as a "bearer" of Islam is cast in definitive opposition to native tradition—including, in all probability (as noted above), opposition to the specific element of ancestral royal legitimacy as symbolized by the saints' intrusion into the Khan's *qoruq* or inviolate ancestral burial ground and their disruption of a drinking ceremony signifying both imperial ancestral veneration and imperial regnal legitimacy. In this connection we may note the words ascribed to Idige's son "Nūr ʿĀdil" in the same Noghay version of the Idige tale, published in Osmanov's chrestomathy, in which descent from Baba Tükles was asserted to be superior to Chingisid descent; here Nūr ʿĀdil, who has ignored his father's advice and slain the Chingisid khan Tokhtamïsh, addresses Tokhtamïsh's son Q̱ādir Berdi Sulṭān and scornfully acknowledges the infidel custom of maintaining the sacred burial ground while affirming his victory: "Believing the bones of the khans to be inviolate, they have placed the khans in Sarāychïq; I have taken your father's head and left it there too!"[70] Sarāychïq, as noted earlier, was probably the old *qoruq* of the Jöchid khans, and this mocking challenge to its status as asserted by Nūr ʿĀdil, a descendant of Baba Tükles, is the epic equivalent of Baba Tükles' victory for Islam, achieved symbolically, according to the account of Ötemish Ḥājjī, in the heart of the infidels' sacred "royal reserve."[71]

The antiquity of the tradition linking Baba Tükles with conversion to Islam is thus established by Ötemish Ḥājjī's work, which makes it clear that stories ascribing him the central role in converting Özbek Khan were in circulation at least as early as the first half of the sixteenth century; the fact that this account is also the earliest mention of Baba Tükles recorded anywhere suggests further that this Islamizing function was central to the role for which he was first, and best, known. But it is of equal importance that this Islamizing function remained in popular memory alongside the wide range of mythic motifs (those already discussed and others explored below) attached to Baba Tükles; indeed, we find that among the Noghays, especially, his role as bringer of Islam remained an essential element of stories preserved about Baba Tükles down to the twentieth century.

This retention of Baba Tükles' Islamizing function is attested in nineteenth-century accounts of the Noghays of the North Caucasus. In the survey of I. Bentkovskii, published originally in 1882–1883, "popular legends" are cited concerning the origin of "the Tatars nomadizing in Stavropol' *guberniia*: "they came from Bukhara, were previously idol-worshippers, fol-

70. Osmanov, *Nogaiskie i kumykskie teksty*, p. 47; text: *qan süyäki kiye dep / qan-lardï qoyġan sarāy-jïq / babang-dïng basïn anda äkälip qoyġan-men*. The term translated as "inviolate" is *kiye*, on which see Budagov, II, p. 183 (s.v. *kiyeli*); cf. Bartol'd, "Burial Rites," tr. Rogers, p. 221.

71. Nūr ʿĀdil's boast notwithstanding, the historical Edigü may have been buried there, as discussed in Chapter 3, thereby intruding, from the epic perspective, his non-Chingisid but Islamically sacred origin into the "royal reserve" of the khans.

lowed the religion contained in the Yasa of Chingis Khan, and worshipped God in the form of fire. But when Sultan Babatkul' arrived from Bukhara as a humble and pious pilgrim, and began to preach the Muhammadan religion, many clans of the Uzbek people, such as the Mangit, Kipchak, Noyman [*sic*], Yedishkul, and Yedisan, followed his teachings and became Muhammadans."[72] A similar legend was reported in a study of the same Noghays published in 1909 by S. V. Farfarovskii, who notes that according to their popular legends, the Noghays were originally fire-worshipers until "Sultan Babatkul" became the "preacher of Muhammadanism among them"; Farfarovskii himself collected abundant popular lore and epic tales among the Noghays, but it is not clear whether this report reflects an independent recording of this legend, or merely Bentkovskii's account, which he cites in general.[73] Both Bentkovskii and Farfarovskii attach this story to the well-known popular etymology of the ethnonym "Noghay," said to derive from the derisive words of those who did not adopt Islam, to the effect that those who did become Muslims "will not succeed"—"*ne onggay*"—which Persianized Turkic curse was modified by the newly converted to "Noghay"; here again we find an example of the popular tendency to link communal designation with Islamization. Bentkovskii further notes the political role played by this "Babatkul'," in whom our Baba Tükles is clearly to be recognized, affirming that "the Noghay *murzas* together with the people under their control consider themselves as originating from Babatkul."[74]

Still earlier testimony, with an important reference to the role of Baba Tükles' tomb as a shrine for the Noghays, is found in testimony we may accept as reflecting direct oral communication among the Noghays of Astrakhan (and not merely conclusions based upon a study of the various versions of the Idige tale), provided by Chodzko from the first half of the nineteenth century. In commenting upon a version of the Idige tale (the

72. I. Bentkovskii, *Istoriko-statisticheskoe obozrenie inorodtsev-magometan, kochuiushchikh v Stavropol'skoi gubernii; Nogaitsy*, chast' I (Stavropol': Tipografiia Gubernskago Pravleniia, 1883; Materialy dlia istorii kolonizatsii Severnago Kavkaza, reprinted from *Stavropol'skie Gubernskie Vedomosti* for 1882 and 1883), p. 3.

73. S. V. Farfarovskii, "Nogaitsy Stavropol'skoi gubernii. Istoriko-ètnograficheskii ocherk," *Zapiski Kavkazskago otdela Imperatorskago Russkago Geograficheskago Obshchestva*, kn. 26, vyp. 7 (Tiflis, 1909), pp. 1–34 (p. 3 on this legend); Farfarovskii's article was summarized, with the story of Sultan Babatkul included, by K. v. Hahn, "Die Nogaier im Gouvernement Stawropol (Ziskaukasien)," *Dr. A. Petermanns Mitteilungen aus Justus Perthhes' geographischer Anstalt*, 57 (1911), September issue, pp. 122–126 [p. 122].

74. Bentkovskii, p. 78, speaking in particular of Kalauso-Sablinsk and Beshtovo-Kumsk *pristavstvos* inhabited by Noghays of the Qasay, Yedisan, and Yedishkul tribes.

earliest recorded), Chodzko attests to the continued memory of Baba Tükles' role as a bearer of Islam. Alone among the names included in the genealogy of Idige recited before Tokhtamïsh, "Baba Túkla" is deemed worthy of an explanation: "This man is much renowned among his countrymen, not only as a distinguished warrior, but also as a most zealous and successful propagator of Islamism. He converted many Kalmuks, and was buried with great honours near the *Kazzachi Bughor,* a mile south of Astrakan, where his tomb is still to be seen."[75]

More remarkably, we have some indication that elements of a narrative tradition about Baba Tükles quite similar to that preserved by Ötemish Ḥājjī, and clearly featuring his identity as an Islamic saint, were found among the popular repertoire of tales associated with this "tomb of Baba Tükles" near Astrakhan as late as the 1920s. An early example of Soviet anti-religious literature—a genre often as rich in details about the practices to be battled as in denunciations of religiosity—outlining religious beliefs and practices among the peoples of the Volga valley contains the following testimony to the still-living traditions surrounding Baba Tükles:

> The mud-walled tombs of the "saints" Tukli-baba and Sheikh-Zaman are situated near Astrakhan. Customarily the tombs are visited once a year by pilgrims, with chickens and sheep brought as offerings. Pilgrims from more distant places come constantly. A half-*verst* [approximately 580 yards] from the village of Mashaikovo,[76] where the graves are found, flows the river Baldy, or "honey-laden" [i.e., *baldï,* common Turkic *bal-lï*]. It is so called because the holy Avliia sent from Bukhara, directly by water, a vat of honey for Shaykh-Zaman. How is this any worse than the story of Trifon Viatskii, who made a millstone float on the water? The Muslim and Christian superstitions are worth just the same.
>
> The holy man Tukli-baba (shaggy grandfather) is so called because his body miraculously became covered with protective hair when his enemies cast him into a fire.[77]

Unfortunately no sources are cited for this account, and it is particularly regrettable that we do not have at our disposal in their original language the

75. Chodzko, *Specimens*, p. 355, note.

76. Clearly a Russianized derivation from *mashā'ikh,* "the shaykhs."

77. N. Matorin, *Religiia u narodov Volzhsko-kamskogo kraia prezhde i teper': iazychestvo - islam - pravoslavie - sektantstvo* (Moscow: "Bezbozhnik," 1929), p. 88.

oral or written account from which the author reports these "superstitions." Even without this, however, the signs of the local legend's similarity with Ötemish Ḥājjī's account are plainly evident: the elements of the saint's body hair, his ordeal by fire, and even the vat full of honey,[78] are all present, and their evident "rearrangement" in the stories told about the "two" shaykhs cannot hide the echoes of our earliest account of Baba Tükles.

THE TOMB OF BABA TÜKLES

The information in these accounts on the site of Baba Tükles' shrine is of some interest for the continuing cultic significance of this Islamizing saint. Shrines ascribed to Baba Tükles are known in southern Kazakhstan, where his tomb is presumed in folkore to be located, as are wells and springs regarded as sanctified by Baba Tükles, as noted below; similarly, his tomb is placed in Bashkir territory as well. But without insisting on the "historicity" of traditions about such shrines in various locales—since the veneration of "ahistorical" saints' tombs is a standard feature of the "localization" of sanctity in Islam—we must naturally assume a stronger ritual significance for shrines of Baba Tükles identified by the Noghays with whom he is so closely linked.

The Noghay tradition clearly places Baba Tükles' tomb near Astrakhan, where it must have been a focus of popular pilgrimage at least as late as the 1920s. Unfortunately our knowledge of the "sacred topography" of Muslim Astrakhan is severely limited.[79] On the one hand this is no doubt a result of the long non-Muslim domination of the region; though the environs of Astrakhan were a major center of Noghay habitation and power through the sixteenth century, the Russian conquest and the later Qalmïq inroads left the Noghays only a minor part of the local popu-

78. We may note here that a vat full of honey plays a role of some consequence in Semenov's Noghay version of the Idige tale. In his version, Idige, the son of Qutlu-qaya, serves at the court of Tokhtamïsh, his father's killer, through the ruse of one of his father's servants, who exchanged his own son Kubugul with Idige when the latter was to be killed in his cradle. When Tokhtamïsh came to suspect the identity of the lad "Kubugul," he summoned the bard who had served the khans since Chingis Khan; learning of Idige's true identity and descent from Chachlï-Aziz, as already noted, Tokhtamïsh ordered Idige apprehended, but the youth jumped upon a vat full of honey that stood in the middle of the *yurt*, and from there jumped up through the smoke-hole and down to the ground to make his escape (Semenov, *Tuzemtsy*, p. 428). In several versions of the epic tale, the term used for "vat" in connection with the honey is the same used in Ötemish Ḥājjī, as discussed below in Appendix 2; the same term may underlie Matorin's account.

79. Unfortunately the work of P. I. Rychkov, *Vvedenie k Astrakhanskoi topografii* (Moscow, 1774), sheds no light on shrines in the vicinity.

lation. Muslim holy sites thus fell into neglect, and the stream of western travelers to Astrakhan more often described Qalmïq Buddhist and Russian Christian religious sites than Muslim ones; at the same time, in the absence of a sizable and traditionally educated Muslim "constituency" interested in saints' tombs and traditions surrounding them (interest that if anything *grew* after the Russian conquest among the Tatars and Bashkirs, for instance), local Islamic shrines rarely captured the interest of the local intelligentsia of Astrakhan, and thus remain virtually unknown in descriptions of the city.

We have one possible hint at the existence, in Astrakhan, of an important shrine similar to that of Baba Tükles as described in our nineteenth- and twentieth-century accounts. It appears in the report of Adam Olearius, who visited Astrakhan in 1636 and 1638 and gave an extensive description, complete with a map of the region, in his travel account published in 1656. Describing his departure from the city toward the south along the Volga, Olearius notes that he passed a chapel, called "Ivantzuk," some 30 *versts* (about 20 miles) from Astrakhan, and then reached one of the many islands formed by the river's branches, another 15 *versts* (about 10 miles) downstream, called "Perul":

> On it stands a high wooden building, above which a sheep's head was set up atop a long pole. They told us that a Tartar saint lies buried there, at whose grave the Tartars, as well as some Persians, when they are preparing to travel across the sea or have successfully crossed it, kill a sheep, offer part of it in sacrifice, and consume part in a sacrificial meal, performing their prayers in the process with special ceremonies. The [sheep's] head remains atop the pole until either a new sacrifice is made, or it falls down by itself. Hence this place is called by the Russians "Tatarski molobitza" [i.e., *mol'bishche*, "place of prayer"], that is, "Tartar Sacrifice."[80]

80. Adam Olearius, *Vermehrte Newe Beschreibung der Muscowitischen und Persischen Reyse* (Schleswig, 1656; repr. ed. Dieter Lohmeier, Tübingen: Max Niemeyer Verlag, 1971), p. 385; the woodcut showing the shrine, which is also depicted in miniature in the map of Astrakhan that accompanies the work, appears on p. 386. Cf. the Russian translation, Adam Olearii, *Opisanie puteshestviia v Moskoviiu i cherez Moskoviiu v Persiiu i obratno*, tr. A. M. Loviagin (SPb.: A. S. Suvorin, 1906), pp. 416–417; excerpts in a different translation are published in *Astrakhanskii sbornik, izdavaemyi Petrovskim obshchestvom izsledovatelei Astrakhanskago kraia*, vyp. 1 (Astrakhan: Tipografiia N. L. Rosliakova, 1896), p. 89, and in *Istoricheskie puteshestviia:*

The shrine described is also depicted in a fanciful woodcut, showing a square structure, built of logs, topped by the sheep's head on a pole, standing by the sea; a ship sails in the distance, and pelicans and other sea birds circle in the sky or catch fish at the shore.

We cannot say for certain if this shrine is the same one noted by Chodzko and the Soviet anti-religious tract as the tomb of Baba Tükles. The sheep sacrifice recalls the sheep consumed in Baba Tükles' oven in Ötemish Ḥājjī's account, of course, but offerings of sheep are hardly unique to this saint; and unfortunately Olearius's description does not allow us to correlate the site he describes with the geographical clues offered in the later accounts. Chodzko places Baba Tükles' burial site near a place known as *Kazachii bugor*, that is, "Cossack hill," a reasonably well-known landmark of Astrakhan;[81] this, he says, is a mile south of Astrakhan, apparently much closer than the island of "Perul" described by Olearius, but Astrakhan was a much larger city in 1830 than in 1638. Our other landmarks, provided by the Soviet-era description, are the river "Baldy" and the village of "Mashaikovo"; the river's name associates it with honey,[82] as the legend

---

izvlecheniia iz memuarov i zapisok inostrannykh i russkikh puteshestvennikov po Volge v XV–XVIII vekakh, ed. V. Alekseev (Stalingrad: Kraevoe Knigoizdatel'stvo, 1936), p. 80.

81. The "Kazachii bugor" was mentioned already by Pallas as a landmark of Astrakhan; he does not precisely describe its location, but implies that it lies rather upriver from the center of Astrakhan: going up the Volga, "I passed the convent of Bolda on the little river of that name, which forms an isle near its source; and continued my route in sight of the Kasatshei Bugor" (cf. the English translation, Peter Simon Pallas, *Travels through the Southern Provinces of the Russian Empire in the Years 1793 and 1794*, vol. 1 [London: A. Strahan, 1802], p. 121. Unfortunately Pallas, who frequently devotes attention to tombs and burial places, makes no mention of a specific tomb corresponding either to Olearius' description or to the shrine described specifically as that of Baba Tükles; it may be, however, that either Pallas or Olearius or Chodzko erred in remembering the direction or distance, since both Olearius and Pallas report passing a Christian church or convent. An 1841 description of the city (M. Rybushkin, *Zapiski ob Astrakhani* [Moscow: Tipografiia S. Selivanovskago, 1841]) mentions "Kazachii bugor" as one of the principal hills occupied by "present-day" Astrakhan (p. 14, note), and explains further that it was the site of a cossack settlement in the time of Catherine (p. 140); in the author's time a military office, with its associated establishments, was located there, as well as the "church of the Mother of God of Donsk." Nebol'sin likewise mentions the "Kozache-Bugrovskaia" cossack settlement (*Ocherki*, p. 24). More recently, however, "Kazachii" is given as the name of a Tatar village, in Vladimirovsk *raion*, in the vicinity of Astrakhan; cf. L. Sh. Arslanov, "Ästerkhan ölkäsendäge tatar avïllarï tarikhïna karata," in *Istochnikovedenie i istoriia tiurkskikh iazykov* (Kazan', 1978), pp. 115–124. Undoubtedly a trip to modern-day Astrakhan might clear up the topographical uncertainties from available descriptions and even locate the site of Baba Tükles' shrine.

82. The link between Baba Tükles and honey, both in the conversion tale of Ötemish Ḥājjī and in the legend reported in the Soviet account of 1929, recalls the role of honey in accounts of Kamāl Ata, known from the Sarï Saltïq cycle and from the *Tavārīkh-i Dasht-i*

noted above confirms, and the village's name likewise suggests a link with a Muslim saint. "Mashaik" is listed in a description of Astrakhan from 1841 as one of several villages in the city's environs, along the "Boldy" river, which were inhabited by the *Iurtovskie Tatary*, that is, Noghays;[83] the "Baldy" is in fact one of the major branchings of the Volga, but parts from it at a site (now within the city) well north of the site of "Perul" described by Olearius.[84] In 1852 Nebol'sin likewise identified the village of "Mashaík" or "Mashaék" as a Noghay settlement, having a population of 185 men and 137 women (among a total population for the Noghays of Astrakhan of 5293 men and 4576 women); elsewhere Nebol'sin describes a village near "Mashaík" as located approximately seven *versts* (4.6 miles) from Astrakhan, "beyond Kazachii-Bugor,"[85] while a rural road linking Astrakhan with the village of "Moshaik" is noted in a district guidebook from as late as 1918.[86]

In any event, the reports of Chodzko and the Soviet anti-religious tract provide sufficient evidence both on the continued veneration of a site regarded as Baba Tükles' grave, and on the continued memory of Baba Tükles' role in Islamization, including specific elements of our earliest account of the saint's Islamizing activity.

Qipchāq; a conflation of the two Islamizing figures, or of their tombs, would not be unlikely, and in this connection we may note the testimony of Anthony Jenkinson, the English merchant who traveled through Astrakhan and Sarāychïq to Central Asia in 1558. Jenkinson describes a shrine, evidently much closer to Sarāychïq than to Astrakhan, which may preserve the association of Islamization and honey: eighteen days out of Astrakhan, he writes, his party "fell with a land called Baugleata, being 74 leagues from the mouth of the said Volga, in the latitude of 46 degrees 54 minutes, the coast lying neerest East and by South, and West and by North. At the point of this land lieth buried a holy Prophet, as the Tartars call him, of their law, where great devotion is used of all such Mahometists as doe passe that way" (*The Principal Navigations*, ed. Hakluyt, vol. II, p. 457). The form "Baugleata" would appear to reflect an original "Bāghlï Ata," but "Bāllï Ata" is both equally plausible and more likely as a saint's appellation.

83. Rybushkin, *Zapiski*, p. 70.

84. Pallas mentions this river, as noted above; Olearius mentions the "Baltzik" river, evidently corresponding to the "Baldy." The same river, no doubt, is mentioned under the name "Boulda" in a short tract, purportedly written by an Irishman who had spent time in Astrakhan as a captive, published in 1677 to accompany the English translation of Tavernier's travels (*A Short Description of all the Kingdoms which encompass the Euxine and Caspian Seas*, printed following *The Six Voyages of John Baptista Tavernier*, London, 1677), p. 112; cf. Nebol'sin, *Ocherki*, p. 6 (calling it "Baldu"), and the accounts of the Dutch traveler Cornelius de Bruijn from the early eighteenth century (*Istoricheskie puteshestviia*, p. 168, "Balda"), and of the German Gmelin from c. 1772 (p. 293, "Bolda").

85. Nebol'sin, *Ocherki*, pp. 53, 59. Mashaik also appears, as a village with one mosque, two "religious figures," and 430 inhabitants, in *Al'favitnye spiski armiano-grigorianskikh tserkvei i magometanskikh mechetei v Imperii* (Saint Petersburg: Ministerstvo vnutrennykh del, 1883), pp. 218–219.

86. *Vsia Astrakhan i ves' Astrakhanskii krai: Pamiatnaia knizhka na 1918 g.* (Astrakhan, 1918), under "Zheleznodorozhnye i morskie puti soobshcheniia, pochtovyia, zemskiia i prosalechnyia [*sic*] dorogi," p. 10, *marshrut* No. 10 under "Zemskiia i proselochnyia dorogi" in Astrakhan *uezd*.

Baba Tükles as Patron Saint and Ancestral Protector

Baba Tükles' "Islamizing" function is echoed in folklore tradition outside the context of the Idige tales in his role as a typical ancestral protective spirit who intercedes with God to grant children, aids the hero-offspring in fighting his enemies, and foretells the fate of the hero's descendants; in each case we see the holy man adopted as an ancestral figure by an entire community. Qazaq folklore, in particular, preserves the name of Baba Tükles in other settings quite apart from his role in the tale of Idige Biy, as a Muslim saint and miracle-worker besought by pilgrims who visit his *mazār*; it is his "Islamizing" role that seems to form the common thread in these otherwise anomalous appearances of Baba Tükles. In the Qazaq epic of "Qosy Körpösh," for instance, he appears as a holy, white-turbaned figure called "Babay Tükti Shashty Aziz,"[87] while in the tale of "Shora Batyr," the hero is born after his parents spend the night at the tomb of the saint "Babai Tukty Chach," who names the boy after he is born.[88] Of special interest is the version of "Shora Batyr" published in Russian translation by Divaev,[89] in which the hero's parents, in order to spend the night at the ruined tomb of "Babai-tukty-chach," trek through Central Asia's sacred topography to reach the saint's grave, here situated in a setting reminiscent of the mythic complex of Mountain, Tree, and Water. They follow a path from near Samarqand north across the Syr-Darya, passing Chimkent, Sayram, and Turkistan to the Karatau mountains, and their arduous journey bears fruit when they arrive at the holy grave, located at the foot of a mountain where a great tree grows near a warm spring; there the saint, with his forty companions, appears in a dream and promises a son.

The latter motif of a hero's birth to childless parents, in which the saint often appears in a dream to the hero's mother or father and promises a son, is quite common, with various Muslim saints appearing as the "protective" patron spirit at the beginning of the hero's career; Baba Tükles is the saint in the tale of "Shora Batyr" as well as in one of the versions of "Alpamïsh" (in which the saint's role is most commonly assigned to ʿAlī), while in the Qazaq tale of "Sain Batyr" the role of the saint is assigned to

87. Cf. the text given in Valikhanov, *Sobranie sochinenii*, III, pp. 97–98; Budagov (I, p. 611, s.v. *sach*) cites the name of "Shāshtū Azīz," the "legendary holy man" of the Qazaqs, from the same epic.

88. Cf. Orlov, *Kazakhskii geroicheskii èpos*, pp. 89, 97–98; Orlov notes that the father also visits the tombs of Zangī Ata and a certain Muḥammad Darvīsh Ata on his way to that of "Babai Tukty Chach."

89. A. A. Divaev, *Ètnograficheskie materialy*, pt. 1, "Shurá-Batyr," pp. 1–88.

"Baba Omar," the name of Baba Tükles' father in one Qazaq version of the Idige tale.[90] "Baba Tukty Shashty Aziz" also appears as the saint instrumental in the hero's birth in one "Noghaylï Qaraqïpchaq" version of the epic of "Koblandy Batyr."[91]

The latter theme appears fully developed, with Baba Tükles playing an especially curious role, in the legend of "Aleuko Batyr" recorded by Potanin.[92] In this tale "Baba Tokty Shash Tazy" first appears as a white-turbaned saint who succeeds in interceding with God on the hero's behalf to gain for him a son and a daughter; he reappears, after the twins' birth, as a "Sart *duana*" (i.e., a Central Asian *divānah* or "intoxicated" dervish), astride a grey ass, who comes to name the children, and then repeatedly intervenes in various guises to save the son's[93] life as he fights

90. Cf. Zhirmunskii, "Skazanie ob Alpamyshe i bogatyrskaia skazka," *Tiurkskii geroicheskii èpos*, pp. 139, 229, 240–241; in this version of "Alpamysh" (p. 139), Baba Tükles appears only as "Shashty Aziz," whose tomb is found near a holy lake in the Karatau mountains. Paksoy (*Alpamysh*, p. 128) notes the appeal to "Shashty Aziza" [*sic*] at a lake near the Karatau mountains, both in the early printed version of Alpamysh (Kazan, 1899) and in the Qazaq version (Alma-Ata, 1957). Orlov notes the appearance of the holy "Baba Aziz the Hairy" in a version of "Alpamysh" (*Kazakhskii geroicheskii èpos*, p. 10). On Baba Omar in "Sain Batyr," cf. the text in Radlov, *Proben*, III (tr.), pp. 210–211; cf. Orlov, p. 56. Zhirmunskii (pp. 150, 229) cites this theme as evidence of growing "Islamic influence" on the Turkic epics. Baba Tükles' role in the Alpamysh epic is also noted, following Zhirmunskii, by Riza Mollov, who notes that the Oghuz and Qonghrat versions of Alpamysh cast as the heroes' protector either Dede Qorqut, "Shāh-i mardān," "the forty saints," or "Šaštı Aziz"; cf. his "Parallel entre Alpamıš et Ašık Garib (Quelques observations sur l'évolution du sujet et de l'image d'Ašık Garib)," *Acta Orientalia* 32 (1970, = PIAC XI), pp. 167–189 [p. 177].

91. Cf. O. Nurmagambetova, *Kazakhskii geroicheskii èpos Koblandy batyr* (Alma-Ata: "Nauka," 1988), pp. 29, 132; for a discussion of the motif of saintly intercession in the hero's birth to a childless couple, see pp. 26–33 and 74–83. As further illustration of the interchangeable nature of the more- and less-Islamized accounts of the hero's origins (without pointing, however, to any clear or necessarily unidirectional development), it is worth noting that of the versions of "Koblandy Batyr" surveyed by Nurmagambetova, all but one ascribe the pregnancy of the hero's mother to such saintly intercession (with various names assigned to the saint); the one that does not (see p. 75) ascribes it to a swan-maiden who appears to the mother in a dream and bids her to drink from a cup in which are mixed the "water of the sunbeams" and the water of the Syr Darya.

92. Cf. Potanin, "Kazakh-kirgizskie i altaiskie predaniia, legendy i skazki," *Zhivaia starina*, 1916, vyp. 2–3, pp. 47–198 (cf. pp. 99–104 on Aleuko Batyr, reprinted in *Kazakhskii fol'klor v sobranii G. N. Potanina*, pp. 116–122); the narrative is recounted by Zhirmunskii, "Skazanie ob Alpamyshe," pp. 185–186, 240–241. The role of protective spirit who rescues his "protégé" but scolds him for neglecting his patron is assigned to "Baba Omar" in the version of "Sain Batyr" described by Orlov (pp. 57–58, 60, 68).

93. The son's name is given in Potanin's transcription as "Orak"; this name may echo the "Örek," called *chura*, named in the Tatar histories as the person sent by Özbek Khan to bring Baba Tükles and his companions from Medina. "Orak" is himself, however, the hero of a cycle of tales in which he is paired with Mamay. Orak's twin sister, incidentally, bears the same name

the heathen Qalmïqs. At one point the Qalmïq khan warns his own people against battling Aleuko Batyr's son, because "the holy Baba Tokty Shash Tazy is with him, and he will destroy you all"; in another of these interventions, Baba Tokty Shash Tazy appears in the form of an eagle who first scolds the young man for not remembering who had helped him so often in the past, and then again delivers him, this time flying him on his back to the top of the mountain on which Aleuko Batyr convened his advisory councils (*kenges-töbe*).[94] The motif of the hero flying on the back of a supernatural bird is a well-known mythic theme, occurring also in Beliaev's Qaraqalpaq version of *Idige* when Baba Tükles turns into a swan to carry his son Idige to safety and then fly off to Madīnah; but this and the other fantastic elements in the tale, as well as his role in the miraculous conception of Aleuko Batyr's children, are perhaps less noteworthy than the identification of Baba Tokty Shash Tazy as a holy man of foreign origin who comes to the aid of "believers" (i.e., a sanctified community) in their struggle against the infidels. This, in fact, together with the theme of conversion, is the focus of the final intervention: in the midst of a protracted and inconclusive battle with the Qalmïq champion, the hero mentions the name of Baba Tokty Shash Tazy and at once overcomes his opponent, who thereupon accepts Islam and builds a mosque.

At the level of folklore, then, Baba Tükles became an ancestral protector and "founder" even outside the confines of the Noghay horde and the legacy of Edigü, where his "ethnogonic" role is affirmed in both "historical" works and epic tradition. Now the very fact that the figure of Baba Tükles has often been the subject of either genealogical or, especially, mythic "ethnogonic" elaborations (or both) suggests the displacement by these themes of the comparably "religious" but culturally alien function of bringing the new religion of Islam; the displacement itself testifies to the nature of the original role performed by Baba Tükles. As will be discussed below, the role assigned to Baba Tükles in the less consciously Islamic versions of his story suggests assimilation of the function of "Islamizer" to that of "nation-former." A vivid illustration of the assimilation of Islamic and Inner Asian modes of communal sanctification is in fact found in an

as the twin sister of Alpamysh in the version of the latter's tale in which his parents visit the tomb of "Shashty Aziz".

94. This theme is echoed in the Qaraqalpaq version of the Idige tale recounted by Beliaev, in which the hero's father, "Baba Tukli Shashli Azis," appears, when Idige is endangered, in the form of a yellow-headed swan, lifts him into the air, and carries him off to safety in an open field (Beliaev, "Skazanie," p. 2).

episode from a Noghay version of the Idige tale, where Idige travels to the grave of "Baba Tukty" and appeals to his "father." Baba Tukty answers him, saying "My son, I have appealed to God on behalf of all your descendants"; but in a "prediction" of the calamities to befall the Noghays at the hands of the Qalmïqs, he announces that although Idige himself will be fortunate and powerful, "the last of your successors will fall under the power of the infidels."[95] Here the Muslim saint is cast in the guise of an ancestral, protective spirit invoked by the hero at his burial site for the sake of the "community" of which he is the mythic founder; fittingly enough, the founder here embraces the whole sacred history of his people, for he is present not only at the origin of the community, but symbolically at its end as well, in his apocalyptic prophecy of the imposition of infidel rule and the implicit disappearance of communal integrity.[96]

Baba Tükles' role as a communal protector and patron spirit extends far from the Noghay environment and even beyond the Qazaq folkloric setting. It appears that he was incorporated into Uzbek tribal identity as well, although his presence there is much more attenuated than in the case of his strong profile in Noghay epic and genealogy. First, at the end of a nineteenth-century manuscript found in Tashkent containing a copy of a little-known Turkic work of Yasavī provenance, a list is appended giving the supposed tribal affiliations of a variety of illustrious Sufi shaykhs, as well as of lesser-known figures;[97] here we find "Bābā Tüklük ʿAzīz" listed as belonging to a tribe called "*M.ż.rāt*," a name not traced among Uzbek tribal designations in any form approximating this spelling.[98] This assignment of Sufi

95. Tr. Valikhanov, *Sochineniia*, p. 268.

96. The apocalyptic motifs are of particular interest with regard to notions of communal integrity and their dependence upon ancestral patron spirits; implicitly the end of a community is in the care of its "founder" or ancestor, or simply of one of its protectors. Noghay hero-tales include the story of one "Tova Batïr," who fought the Russians rather than submit, finally drowning in the Volga; he was said to be buried in Astrakhan, and the Noghays believed that he would rise to fight "Tajal" (i.e., *Dajjāl*, the Antichrist) when this apocalyptic figure "broke through the mountains" (cf. Moshkov, "Melodii nogaiskikh i orenburgskikh tatar," p. 65). The cyclical mythic theme of the end contained in the beginning is at work here in the context of a community's life span; it is likewise evident in the ancestral invocations ascribed to epic heroes as they die, in the parallel theme of individuals (saints in particular) aware of their life span, and in the theme (not uncommon in Inner Asian tradition, and characteristically combining individual and communal focuses) of the ruler required at his accession to declare the length of his reign. The development of clan ancestor into protective patron spirit is explored, with interesting parallels in a non-Islamic context, in the case of Yakut epics, in N. V. Emel'ianov, *Siuzhety olonkho o rodonachal'nikakh plemeni* (Moscow: Nauka, 1990), pp. 169–179.

97. MS Tashkent, IVANUz, Inv. No. 12870 (uncatalogued), f. 88b.

98. It is possible (if still unconvincing) that this "*M.ż.rāt*" might mask a metathesized version of the designation *mīrzā* associated with the descendants of Edigü and, hence, of Baba Tükles.

shaykhs to Uzbek tribal groups appears to reflect the "adoption" of particular saints as tribal patron ancestors, and parallels similar processes known among the Turkmens; the appearance of Baba Tükles among them suggests that further information on his memory among Uzbek tribes may come to light through research in oral tradition or in the "popular" manuscript tradition of the late nineteenth and early twentieth centuries.

Of still greater interest, Baba Tükles also appears in the preface to a listing of the well-known "ninety-two Uzbek tribes" found in two manuscripts in Tashkent. Lists of the ninety-two tribes are known from a number of sources and have drawn some scholarly attention;[99] but what has not been noted in earlier studies is the *context* for the listing of the ninety-two tribes: a legend of origin for the Uzbeks.

Baba Tükles appears in these two accounts as "Tūlāsh Bābā," a form distinct enough to raise suspicions about its identity with "Baba Tükles" were it not for the correspondences between the genealogies cited in these manuscripts and those appearing in the historical and epic traditions surrounding Edigü/Idige. The accounts portray the Uzbeks as descended from "Quḥāfah," regarded as Abū Bakr's father or ancestor (evidently echoing Abū Bakr's designation as "Ibn Abī Quḥāfah"), through ninety-nine or ninety-two men who came to the Prophet's aid in a battle with the infidels. In one manuscript,[100] bearing various dates as late as 1321/1903–1904, the account is in Persian; here the ninety-nine Uzbek tribes are said to be descended from a single ancestor, the Caliph Abū Bakr's father Quḥāfah, with the following lineage: Quḥāfah > Abū Bakr > Abū'l-ʿĀṣ > Sulṭān

99. The lists of the ninety-two Uzbek tribes found in more "conventional" sources, namely the sixteenth-century *Majmūʿ at-tavārīkh*, the nineteenth-century *Tuḥfat at–tavārīkh-i khānī*, in MS IVANUz Inv. No. 4330 (cf. *SVR*, VI, p. 38, No. 4188], and in several published lists based on oral/ethnographic collection, are discussed in T. I. Sultanov, *Kochevye plemena Priaral'ia v XV–XVII vv. (Voprosy ètnicheskoi i sotsial'noi istorii)* (Moscow: Nauka, GRVL, 1982), pp. 26–51, cf. especially pp. 45–47 on the sources of the lists; see also the same author's earlier article, "Opyt analiza traditsionnykh spiskov 92 'plemen ilatiia,' " in *Sredniaia Aziia v drevnosti i srednevekov'e (Istoriia i kul'tura)* (Moscow: Nauka, GRVL, 1977), pp. 165–176. Of these versions, apparently only the *Tuḥfat at tavārīkh-i khānī* (see Storey-Bregel', *PL*, II, pp. 1193–1195) includes the genealogy with "Tūlāsh" (cf. MS C440 of the St. Petersburg Branch of the Institute of Oriental Studies of the Russian Academy of Sciences, f. 266a), although most are accompanied by a legend of origin; one of the two manuscripts I examined that do include both these elements (MS IVANUz Inv. No. 3386) was discussed (along with MS IVANUz Inv. No. 4330) in B. A. Akhmedov, "O roli pis'mennykh pamiatnikov v izuchenii ètnogeneza uzbekskogo naroda," *Obshchestvennye nauki v Uzbekistane*, 1981, No. 12, pp. 44–50 [pp. 49–50 on MSS 3386 and 4330], but Akhmedov gives no information about the "fabulous introduction on the origin of the Uzbeks" that precedes the list of tribes in MS 3386. Sultanov does not mention MS 3386, and neither he nor Akhmedov mentions the legend and list as given in MS IVANUz Inv. No. 12870 (see n. 102).

100. MS IVANUz, Inv. No. 3386, ff. 182b–183b, bearing the title "*Nasab-nāmah–i Ūzbīk.*"

Qubūr Sulṭān Ḥākīm > Sulṭān Ṣafā > Sulṭān Jalāl ad-Dīn Rūmī > Tūlāsh Bābā > Salāy Qabāy. In the last-named figure's time, the "realm" was peaceful, and the ninety-nine men had become ninety-nine tribes (*urugh*), each of which selected a "brand" (*dāgh*) "so that worldly and religious affairs might not be undone." In the other manuscript, undated but evidently somewhat earlier, a Turkic version describes a band of people who do not know Arabic or Persian rescuing the Prophet and defeating the infidels; the Prophet asks Abū Bakr who they are, and he answers that they are Turks from Turkistān and are kinsmen of "Imām Quḥāfah," with the following genealogy: Quḥāfah > Abū Bakr > Muḥammad > Sulṭān Dildār > Sulṭān Jā'iz > Sulṭān Abū'l-Fā'iz [*sic*] > Quyūz > Khakīm > Sulṭān Ṣafā > Sulṭān Jalāl ad-Dīn > Tūlāsh Bābā > Salāy Qabāy.[101] And again, in the latter's time the realm was peaceful, and the ninety-two persons became ninety-two tribes and created their *tamghas*.

The accounts are not altogether clear, and it appears that the genealogy given in each is intended as that of the chief of the ninety-nine or ninety-two tribes in existence by the time of Salāy Qabāy; in any event they thus install a figure identifiable with Baba Tükles in the genealogy of the Uzbek tribes, making him the father of the figure in whose era the tribal structure of the Uzbeks was in effect codified. In this case, even more so than in the appearance of "Bābā Tüklük ʿAzīz" as a tribal patron saint, we find echoes of Baba Tükles' association with Islamization, through descent from Abū Bakr and, especially, through his kinsmen's struggle against the infidels on the Prophet's behalf.

Baba Tükles' status as a "patron saint" of Central Asian Muslims is also reflected in his appearance in a Turkic account of the Russian conquest of Central Asia published in 1894.[102] The account, in effect commissioned by the Russian scholar who published it, was written by "Mulla Khali-bai Mambetov" (born ca. 1856), a Qazaq educated in Tashkent but clearly familiar with Qazaq oral tradition as well. He based the work on the recollections of his father, who had served among the Qoqandian troops fighting the Russians down to the time of Tashkent's fall in June of 1865. Baba Tükles appears in a prayer ascribed in the work to the Qoqandian comman-

101. MS IVANUz, Inv. No. 12870, ff. 89b–91b, bearing the heading "*Naṣīb-nāmah-i Ūzbīk*" [*sic*]; this section follows the list of saints and their tribal affiliation noted above. Orthographic similarities suggest that Salāy Qabāy reflects the "Islām Qïyā" named in the Noghay genealogies as a genealogical link between Baba Tükles and Edigü/Idige.

102. N. Veselovskii, ed. and trans., *Kirgizskii razskaz o russkikh zavoevaniiakh v Turkestanskom krae. Tekst, perevod i prilozheniia* (Saint Petersburg: Parovaia Skoropechatnia P. O. Iablonskago, 1894), pp. 13 [translation], 22 [text].

der ʿĀlim-qul, who is portrayed as seeking aid from God and the Prophet, as well as from Ibrāhīm, ʿĪsā, Ādam, the first four Caliphs, Idrīs, "Bābāy Tūktī Sāchtï ʿAzīz," and finally a "Baba Murād" (identified as a saint buried in a local shrine); it is odd to find Khoja Aḥmad Yasavī omitted from such a list (the site of his shrine had already been conquered by the Russians), but the omission seems indeed to heighten the importance of Baba Tükles. In a curious echo of the title associated with Baba Tükles' putative descendants, he is addressed here as the "*mīrzā* of the saints;" to him the commander pledges to fight bravely and sacrifice his life for the sake of religion. The "prayer" is, of course, in all likelihood the author's own invention, but this in itself signals the special, protective character of the saint, whose evocation in a time of communal crisis is thus included in a work designed to reflect native sentiments about the Russian conquest.

Finally, in connection with the continued "ancestral" and "protective" role ascribed to Baba Tükles even down to the present day may be noted his invocation by Qazaq shamans (*baksï*) during the course of their ecstatic performances. The incorporation of Muslim saints, and Islamic religious formulas, into shamanic ceremonies is well attested in Central Asia, where saints such as Khoja Aḥmad Yasavī, Zangī Ata, and other figures usually associated with the Yasavī Sufi tradition are named among the spirits appealed to for assistance, protection, and guidance during the shaman's journey.[103] Baba Tükles appears among them even in quite recent times, evidencing his sustained resonance in Qazaq popular religion.

In material recorded between 1978 and 1983 from the Qazaq shamaness Kenzhegïz Musaeva, born in 1898 and a resident of Sarïsu *raion* of Dzhambul *oblast* in southern Kazakhstan, the *baksï* appealed first to the saints of Turkistan, addressing "Sulayman" (i.e., Ḥakīm Ata) and "Arïstan Bap" (i.e., Arslan Baba, Aḥmad Yasavī's master) by name along with the "Khojas" in general; she invoked again the saints (*äulie*) of Turkistan and Samarqand, and again all saints in general (*äulie bolsang qolday kör*, "If you are a saint, support [me]!"), while her performance was repeatedly puncuated with the Muslim *shahādah* or testament of faith, in a quite corrupted but nevertheless recognizable pronunciation, according to the ethnographer's transcription, "*Laylaukha lillaukha, Mukhambetten rasulla*." Special attention was reserved for the figure of Baba Tükles, as she invoked the "spirits" (*aruaq*, i.e., *arwāḥ*): "O my holy father, my ancestor, Babay-Tükti-Shashtï-Äziz, O my ancestor, support me, support my work!"[104]

103. See for example the texts published and translated by Joseph Castagné, "Magie et exorcisme chez les Kazak-Kirghizes et autres peuples turks orientaux," *REI*, 4 (1930), pp. 53–156.

104. *äulie atam babam-ay, Babay-Tükti-Shashtï-Äziz babam-ay, qolday kör meni demep-ay, qolday kör menin isimdi*; from material collected by K. Baibosynov and published in K. Baibosynov

Similarly, in a shamanic performance by Bala-baksï, a resident of the village of Karaotkel in Samarskii *raion* of Vostochno-Kazakhstan *oblast'*,[105] recorded in August 1982, the *baksï* invoked the same figure with the words, "*Tükti Babay Äziz Shash, siynamyn özinge*," that is, "Tükti Babay Äziz Shash, I venerate [only] you!"[106]

The continued invocation of Baba Tükles as a protective spirit of shamans is perhaps the most vivid reminder of the continued meaning he conveys to Islamized peoples of Inner Asia. On the one hand his appearance in shamanic ceremonies might be taken as a distinctly un-Islamic feature of religious "survivals" in Central Asia, belonging wholly to the pre-Islamic substrate; but such a neat delineation of what is "Islamic" and what is not belies the integration of these elements in actual life and practice and worldview. The point is not only that Baba Tükles is surrounded by Islamic symbols and language in these invocations; most important is the way he serves as a focal point for integrating those elements of popular religious life that specialists are wont to assign "historically" to different traditions, but that are fused seamlessly, and meaningfully, in the ordinary life of communities that regard themselves as Muslim. And the continued resonance of Baba Tükles in melding Islamic and pre-Islamic traditions—of sainthood and protective ancestry—even after seventy years of anti-religious campaigns and social transformations is particularly noteworthy.

The Epic Baba Tükles as Sufi and Patron Saint

As noted earlier, the question of what to make of Baba Tükles was quite often important to address in setting the tone of accounts, both for his "Islamizing" role, and for his "ancestral" role, and one of the most frequent resolutions of the question was to portray him as a Sufi. Elements of this appear already in Ötemish Ḥājjī's account, and the likelihood of an

and R. Mustafina, "Novye svedeniia o kazakhskikh shamankakh," *Novoe v ètnografii: polevye issledovaniia*, vyp. 1 (Moscow: Nauka, 1989), pp. 70–79; interestingly, without further explanation Baibosynov renders the saint's name as simply "Baba-Tuklas" in his translation (p. 74).

105. This locale, incidentally, near Gorno-Altaisk not far from the border with China and Mongolia, marks the easternmost site in which I have found the memory of Baba Tükles recorded.

106. S. N. Akataev, "K perezhitkam kul'ta Tengri u kazakhov," *Izvestiia Akademii nauk Kazakhskoi SSR*, seriia obshchestvennykh nauk, 1984, No. 2, pp. 40–48. Akataev (p. 44) cites only this passage from the "text" of the shamanic performance, but further describes the spirit in question as "the hairy old man Babay," seeking to associate "Tükti Babay" with the Scythian deity "Papaeus" mentioned by Herodotus[!]. More to the point, but without expressly indicating that such a representation is found in his "text," Akataev notes that this "Tükti Babay Äziz Shash" is "portrayed as an armed warrior and protector of shamans."

actual role played by Sufis in the spread of Islam in the Golden Horde has already been discussed. In the case of Baba Tükles, as noted, his Sufi character was much more clearly drawn by ʿAbd al-Ghaffār Qïrïmī, and he was also made into a Central Asian Sufi shaykh by our eighteenth-century Khorezmian writer. His Sufi character is evident also in epic treatments, both in his popular identification as a "Sart *dīvānah*" as noted above, and in his designation as "Khoja." More explicit identification with Sufism is evident in the Noghay version of the Idige tale recorded by Semenov, discussed above, in which Baba Tükles and even Idige and "Nuradil" are described as "*shaykhs*" and repeatedly affirm their association with Sufism by referring to their *murīds* and their guidance in the *ṭarīqah*.

The Sufi identification of Baba Tükles, however, appears to have gained an independent resonance of its own, beyond the specific context of the Noghay "memory" of Edigü's ancestry and "sanctity." This is best illustrated by a previously unknown literary version of the Idige tale, in mixed prose and verse, preserved in manuscript form in Tashkent.[107] Here Baba Tükles[108] retains his mythical features, most prominently his dalliance with a *parī*, but is specifically identified not only with Sufism, but with a

107. Institute of Manuscripts of the Academy of Sciences of the Republic of Uzbekistan, Inventory Nos. 109 (77ff.) and 110 (106ff.); the two volumes are bound together, and the two versions differ somewhat, although both are incomplete. I examined both copies in May, 1991; my attention was drawn to them by their description in the recently published first volume of the catalogue of the Institute's manuscript collection (*Katalog fonda Instituta rukopisei* [Tashkent: Fan, 1989], vol. I, pp. 279–280, Cat. Nos. 911 [Inv. No. 109, judged to be an early nineteenth-century copy] and 912 [Inv. No. 110, early twentieth-century copy]). There they are described as copies of a long "*dāstān* of Tokhtāmïsh Khān and Īdägä Bātïr" said to attribute the hero's birth to the pious "Sagly [read "Sachlï": the letter *jīm* is frequently transcribed as "g" in this catalogue] aziz" and a fairy/*parī* named "Parizad"; the son is then adopted by a certain Tulumbay, who appears in another manuscript labeled *Qiṣṣah-i Tokhtāmïsh Khān* (not described as referring to either Idige or "Sachlï ʿAzīz" [p. 279, Cat. No. 910]) as the ruler's *vazīr*. Unfortunately the provenance of the manuscripts is not indicated, and the dating given in the catalogue appears conjectural at best. Unless otherwise noted subsequent references are to MS No. 109. From the appearance of "Ṭūlūm Khoja" in this version, it would appear to be much the same as the tale of "Tulumbiy" mentioned by Zhirmunsky as an Uzbek variant of the Idige tale in which "the fable element . . . attains its furthest development" ("On the Comparative Study of the Heroic Epic of the Peoples of Central Asia," in IOC XXV, vol. 3 (Moscow, 1963), pp. 244–252 [p. 248]); Zhirmunsky indicates that a version of "Tulumbiy" was included in the chrestomathy of Uzbek folklore published by Hadi Zarif (*Özbek folklori; khrestomatiyä* [Tashkent, 1939], pp. 29–42), but this published version has not been available to me.

108. In MS 109 his name is spelled "*t.w.k.l*," i.e., "Tükel," at the beginning of the tale (down to f. 45b); at ff. 50b–52a, it is spelled "*t.w.k.l.w*," i.e. "Tüklü," and in his final appearance in the tale, at ff. 64a–65b, as "*t.w.k.y.l.w*," i.e., "Tükilü"; in MS 110 his name is written consistently as "*t.w.k.l.w*." For convenience I have adopted the reading "Tüklü" in all references to these two manuscripts, except for direct transcriptions of the text.

particular type of Sufism. Moreover, Idige[109] is not only *not* a Noghay or Manghït in this version; he is cast, rather, as a Qonghrat of Khorezm, which is evidently where this manuscript recording of the tale was produced. In this version Tokhtamïsh is the khan, and it is his *vazīr*, Ṭūlūm Khoja, who raises the foundling Idige; the hero is actually the son of Baba Tükles, who retains his status as a protective spirit in Idige's battles. Here, however, the hero's destiny is not cast in terms of anti-Chingisid polemic, or even the personal struggle with Tokhtamïsh; rather, on the instructions of Baba Tükles, and with his aid at crucial junctures, Idige battles the Russians and Qalmïqs (*ūrūs qālmāq*), who are linked as the common enemy of the Qonghrat and Uzbek people.

In this version the scene is set with this beginning: "Now the tellers of tales relate thus, that in olden times, in bygone days, there was a ruler, a very great ruler, in the town of Qonghrat in the province of Khorezm . . ."[110] The ruler held sway over Bukhārā, Chīn, Māchīn, Khiṭā, and Khūtan, and his name was Tokhtamïsh; we next have the catalogue of his subjects on a more local scale, for we learn that during this ruler's time "in the city of Khorezm" there were 40,000 Qonghrat households, 40,000 Qïfchāq, 40,000 Mangqït, 40,000 Qazāq, 40,000 "Qarāqalfāq," 10,000 "Ūyshūn, 10,000 Uyghūr, 10,000 Nāymān, 10,000 Nūküs, 10,000 Qanglī, 40,000 Khiṭāy, 40,000 Yomut, and 40,000 Chawdur. After introducing the character of Ṭūlūm Khoja, however, the narrative switches to the origins of Idige.[111]

In the *vilāyat* of Khorezm, the story goes, there were two saints (*ʿazīz*), who were elder and younger brothers. One was called Tüklü ʿAzīz and was a *darvīsh* who lived in the mountains, while the other one was called Sāchlï ʿAzīz and was a *khānqāh-nishīn*, that is, a dweller in a Sufi hostel; the other manuscript specifies that the first lived as a dervish eating grass, while the second was an *īshān*.[112] Here we find not only the clear identification of both these figures as Sufis, but a fine distinction between two types of Sufi life-styles; and the figure of Baba Tükles is explicitly tied to the more "unorthodox" and antinomian of the two, a characterization that

109. His name is spelled in both manuscripts "*a.y.d.h-kāh*," as two words (with a final *hā* in both cases), i.e., "Īdä-gāh"; in this case I have continued to use the form "Idige" adopted for the epic hero.

110. *ammā rāvīlär andagh rivāyat qïlurlar ke qadīm al-ayyāmda ötgän zamānda Khwārazm vilāyatida Qongrāt qalʿasida bir fādshāh bar erdi ziyādah ulugh fādshāh erdi.*

111. This initial episode: MS 109, ff. 11b–19b; MS 110, ff. 13a–23a.

112. MS 109, f. 11b; cf. MS 110, f. 13a: *ammā Khwārazm vilāyatide iki ʿazīz bar érdi, birining ātïga Tüklü ʿAzīz derler, ol taġlarda kök kiyāh yeb darvīshlik qïlur érdi, yana birigä Sachli ʿAzīz derler, ol khānqāh-nishīn īshān érdi.*

fits the somewhat "wild" description given in Ötemish Ḥājjī's narrative and implied also by his name.

One day, the account continues, Tüklü ʿAzīz was walking in the mountains and came upon the spring, used for ablutions (*bulaq-ḥawż*), of Shaykh Jalīl Ata;[113] but after reporting that this saint went to perform his ablutions there and took off his clothes, the narrator stops and says, "hear another tale." The new story, giving the familiar pattern, but in Islamized form, known from other versions, runs as follows: On the fabled Kūh-i Qāf lived a *parīzād* (i.e., fairy-born) named Sāchlï Parī, who traveled the world and returned to her mountain and decided to perform her ablutions; and when Tüklü ʿAzīz came to do his ablutions, and saw the *parīzād* washing her body, her radiance lit up the entire *ḥawż*, and "ardor for Sachïl ʿAzīz settled in the chest of Tüklü's bosom, and his heart became distracted."[114] After a long exchange, Tüklü ʿAzīz brought her clothes to her, and the fairy laid down the conditions by which she would consent to marry him: he must not look at her body when she performed her ablutions; he must not look at her heels as she walked; and he must not look at her head when she combed her hair. He agreed to the conditions, and they performed the *nikāh*(marriage ceremony); but inevitably he broke his promise, and the fairy turned into a white dove (*āq-kabūtar*) and flew away.[115]

After a long lament by Tüklü ʿAzīz, the story returns to the fairy-girl. Covering a three-month journey in three days, she reached a plane-tree near the Caspian Sea: "Beside the sea of Hashtūrkhān [i.e., Astrakhan] there was a *chïnār*; she came and alighted on this plane-tree, and by the command of God she experienced a labor pain there[116] and at once fell from the plane-tree to the ground, where the pain of her labor became more intense." She began reciting a lament that somewhat eased her pain, but she soon collapsed in a swoon. When she awoke she saw a boy (*baččah*) standing before her; she took him in her arms, kissed him, and nursed him, telling him, "Tüklü ʿAzīz is this baby's father."[117] She aban-

113. This Khorezmian locale is mentioned by Abū'l-Ghāzī, in connection with a Qalmïq raid on Khorezm early in the seventeenth century (Desmaisons, p. 275 [text], p. 296 [tr.], and by the ninteenth-century Khivan historian Muʾnis, once in connection with a Russian campaign against Khiva by way of "Shaykh Jalīl Tāghï" (which Muʾnis identifies as the site of a gold and silver mine), and as the site of Shaykh Jalīl Ata's tomb (cf. *Firdaws al-Iqbāl*, ed. Bregel, pp. 155, 568, and *Materialy po istorii kazakhskikh khanstv*, pp.460, 469).

114. *Sachïl ʿAzīz-ning ʿishqï Tükel ʿAzīz-ning sīnah-i ṣandūqïnda jāy boldï va köngli bī-qarār bolup* . . .

115. MS 109, ff. 14b–16b; MS 110, ff. 16b–18a.

116. *shol yerde tōlgāqï tutdï.*

117. *Tükel ʿAzīz bu gūdak-ning atasï.*

doned him to God's protection, however, blessing him as she nursed him, and then again turned into a dove and flew away.[118]

The story then turns to Ṭūlūm Khoja, who finds the boy Idige; when he is grown, his adoptive father sends him to "the Russian-Qalmaq country" (*barġïl balam ūrūs qālmāq yurtïna*[119]) to make war. On his way, however, Idige has his first encounter with his true father.[120] He goes atop a high mountain and there sees a *bābā* with a radiant face; he approaches him and greets him, and the *bābā* raises his head, returns the greeting, and says, "O my son, tell me of yourself, what garden's flower are you, what grove's nightingale are you, from what garden have you flown and in what rosebed will you alight?"[121] His interrogation continues, in verse, until Idige speaks in reply:

I am a servant of the one God, *bābā*
  My people, *bābā*, is Qonghrat.
My origin, *bābā*, is as a son of the Uzbek,
  My place is [among] the Qonghrat . . .[122]

Dissatisfied with this answer, the Bābā responds, "O my son, I too have seen much of the Qonghrat people, and they say that name in Uzbekistan; but now tell me your true name: whose son are you, my son, what is your name?"[123] Idige persists, saying his original name was Raḥīm Berdi (i.e., "God-given," in view of the way he was found), but affirming that he is now called Idige; and the Bābā then relents somewhat to tell him of his true origins: your name is indeed Idige, he tells the young man, and your father is Ṭūlūm Khoja; but now these words, he says, are also true: "Your father is a

118. *ay balām allāh yārïng bolsun āl imdi men ketdim dep kabūtar bolup uchup*, "She said, as she nursed him, 'Take, and may God be a friend to you; now I am off'; and becoming a dove she flew off."

119. Eg. ff. 31b, 32b, 33a.

120. MS 109, ff. 39a–41b.

121. *khabaringni berip ketgil, qāysï bāgh-nïng guli-sen va qāysï chaman-ning bulbuli-sen, qāysï bagh-dïn uchup va qāysï guldhār-ġa qonar-sen?* Such formulaic challenge and response regarding the "hero's" ancestry are characteristic features of shamanic performances, both when summoning protective spirits and when encountering spirits on the journey; cf. the exchange noted in Diószegi, "Pre-Islamic Shamanism of the Baraba Turks," p. 146.

122. MS 109, f. 40a: *men bir bābā ḥaqq-ning qulï / élim bābā qōngrāt bolur / āṣlïm bābā özbek oghlï / mening jāyïm qōngrāt bolur / āṣlïm özbek ḥaqq–ġa banda / umīdim köp jānūtïnda [sic] / safar qïldïm ushbu künde / bābā jāyïm qōngrāt bolur / élim qōngrāt ʿajab jāydūr / sagïnġanïm bir khudāy dūr / ātām ādï Ṭūlūm Bek dūr / mening jāyïm qōngrāt bolur / kündin künge miḥnat tartïp / jafā tïgï bagrïm tarïp / men kélür-men naqīb tartïp / Īde-gāh dūr bābā ādïm . . .*

123. *men-ham qōngrāt élin köp körüp-men ūzbak-īstānda laqab ādïn āytūrlar; ammā imdi seni rāst ādïng-nï ayt . . . kim-ning oġlï kim seni özing / oġlïm ādïng kim boladur . . .*

different person. . . . by God's decree your father and mother were separated."[124] Your mother departed, continues the Bābā, and left you atop a plane-tree in a bird's nest;[125] Tulum Khoja found you and named you Raḥīm Berdi.

Hearing all of this, Idige continued on his way without realizing who the Bābā was; but the narrator affirms that "this *bābā* was Idige's father, Tüklü ʿAzīz."[126] Another encounter follows, with Idige again affirming, "I myself am an Uzbek, my essence is truly Qonghrat; I am a rose of the Uzbeks' garden, I am a servant of the creator God; I am the son of Tulum Biy Khoja, I am assuredly an Uzbek."[127] Finally, in their third encounter,[128] the Bābā—who is now identified as Tüklü ʿAzīz—tells Idige the whole truth, winning his apology; and the next we hear of Tüklü ʿAzīz is in the midst of the hero's battle with the infidel Qalmïqs:[129] as Idige went into battle with them, "Idige's blessed father Tüklü ʿAzīz appeared, reciting (the *dhikr*), and stood in the midst of the field, looking at Idige."[130] Tüklü ʿAzīz addressed his son, declaring that "your father has come to take vengeance on the infidels,"[131] but as Idige listened the infidels opened fire with shots from various types of firearms;[132] with the reappearance of Tüklü ʿAzīz, however, the infidels fled in disarray, and in the end the enemy all became Muslims.

The narrative continues, but this is the climax; in any event "Tüklü ʿAzīz" makes no more appearances. What is perhaps most remarkable about this version is not merely the thoroughly developed Sufi coloring attached to Baba Tükles, nor even the striking imagery of his appearance in battle as Idige's protective spirit, but the transformation of the struggle in which this saintly patron must assist Idige: traces of Chingisid/non-Chingisid tensions are detectable, but they are not at all developed here. The Manghït identity of Idige has entirely disappeared, and nothing remains of the Idige tale's links with the Noghay horde; replacing these

124. *ammā sening ātāng özgä kishī tūrūr . . . taqdīr allāh birlän atāng birlän anāng-nïng ārāsïġa firāq tüshdi.*

125. *qush-nïng ūyāsïnda.*

126. *ammā bu bābā Īde-gāh-ning atalarï Tük.l ʿAzīz érdi.*

127. MS 109, f. 45b: *men özim özbek bolur-men . . . aṣlī dhātïm qōngrāt-dūr, özbeklär bāġï guli-men / yarātqan tengri qulï men / Tulum Biy Khoja oġlï men / men özim özbek bolur-men.*

128. MS 109, ff. 50b–52a.

129. MS 109, ff. 64a-65b; MS 110, ff. 83a–84a.

130. MS 109, f. 64a: *Īde-gāh-ning karāmatli Tūkīlū ʿAzīz dādah-läri huwa yāmin huwa lā ilāha illā huwa dép ḥāżir boldïlar maydān-nïng orta yeride turup Īde-gāh-ġa qarāb . . .*

131. MS 109, f. 64b: *Tūkīlū ʿAzīz sening dād.ng kélip-dūr / kāfirlärning ongïn ālïp turup-dur.*

132. They shoot balls from *zanburāks* and *shamkhāls* and *miltūqs*.

identities are those of the Qonghrat tribe, dominant in Khorezm, and of the "Uzbek" people, but in fact Idige's fixation upon these is nothing more than a component of his general ignorance regarding his true origins; and even the Qalmïq enemy has been linked with the Russians to highlight their common status as infidels rather than the tribal conflicts between Qalmïqs and Noghays. In short, even with the thoroughly non-Islamic imagery of the fairy-girl, the birth-nest, and the patron spirit, this version of the Idige tale is among the most insistent upon Islamic verities. Idige is as wrong about his Qonghrat and Uzbek origins as he is about his father; much of the drama here has to do with Idige's discovery that he is not "merely" Uzbek or Qonghrat, but the sacred offspring of a Muslim saint, and his discovery paves the way for his victory over the infidels who in threatening his "communal" faith threaten his true identity and integrity.

Here Baba Tükles is a Sufi saint and patron spirit, roles he fulfills in Qazaq folklore as well as in the Bashkir tales discussed below; other figures regularly appear as Sufi saints and patron spirits for tribal groups throughout Islamic Inner Asia. What is distinctive about this literary version of the Idige tale is that the saint's Sufi character appears to be emphasized not as a means of sanctifying a particular tribe's origins, nor as a counter to claims, e.g. Chingisid, of political and social legitimacy, but as a sign of affiliation with the universal Islamic *ummah* and as a counter to narrower loyalties such as "Qonghrat" and even "Uzbek." As we continue to trace the different directions taken by the character of Baba Tükles, we may observe here that these literary accounts of the Idige tale from Khorezm take his "Islamizing" function as far in the direction of sanctioning a universal *Islamic* identity as we will find.

Baba Tükles in Bashkir Tradition: Hero, King, Ancestor, and Preceptor

Baba Tükles appears in several interesting roles in oral and written tales preserved among the Bashkirs. This is hardly the place to discuss the complexities of Bashkir ethnogenesis and the long history of the ethnonym that underlies our designation "Bashkir" and its various forms; suffice it to say the the people known as Bashkirs comprise a number of tribal groups of quite diverse origins, including several with close connections to the Qaraqalpaqs and groups belonging for some time to the

Noghay confederation.[133] It is surely these "Noghay" elements that have ensured the preservation of Baba Tükles' epic and ancestral roles in Bashkir folklore, but the richness of the Bashkir developments lends them particular interest for us.

As noted earlier, the Idige tale has been preserved among the Bashkirs, under the general designation "Idukay and Muradym"; a particularly distinctive episode from the Bashkir version is discussed below. Baba Tükles (in Bashkir pronunciation *Tökläs* or *Tökläth*) also appears, however, in several other contexts as a heroic and ancestral figure in Bashkir folklore. To begin with, he is named among the "heroes" (*batyrs*) of the Yayïq (Ural) valley, a likely allusion to his Noghay associations, in the epic tale of "*Aqbuzat*,"[134] a continuation of perhaps the best-known Bashkir epic, that of "*Ural-batyr*"; only his name is preserved in this context, but much more of his Noghay connections, as well as his link with Idige, are preserved in a story of "The Forty Noghay Heroes" recorded near Orenburg.[135] The transmitter of the tale ascribes the legend to local elders of Buransy *aul* in Beliaev *raion* of Orenburg *oblast'*, of whom he names "Abdel'gali Uzbekov," born in 1892. The tale itself tells of the forty Noghay *batyrs* who lived in the past, whose heroic status was transmitted from father to son as an inheritance; the names of the heroes are evidently drawn both from the Noghay tradition and from other epic tales. True to form, communal defense against infidels is invoked, and a communal designation is derived from one of these heroes, with the entire story combining elements proper to popular history, hero-tales, and hagiography:

> One of the first forefathers was Tükläs-baba, after him was Idukay, his son Muradïm, Muradïm's son Musa-khan, his son Mamay-khan, Sura-batïr, Yamgïrsï, Agish-batïr . . . and so it went from generation to generation. Last of all, the youngest hero in that family was Koblandï . . .
>
> Mamay-khan drove the Kalmïks from these places. The name of our *aul*, Buransï, was left by a Noghay hero named Buransï. They say that he was a contemporary and intimate of Idukay

133. For a brief survey and further references see Z. V. Togan in *EI*², I, pp. 1075–1077, s.v. "Bashdjirt."

134. Cf. the Russian translation in *Bashkirskoe narodnoe tvorchestvo*, tom 1, *Èpos*, ed. M. M. Sagitov (Ufa: Bashkirskoe Knizhnoe Izdatel'stvo, 1987), pp. 170, 172 (cf. p. 503, n. 9).

135. Given in Russian translation in *Bashkirskoe narodnoe tvorchestvo*, tom 2, *Predaniia i legendy*, ed. F. A. Nadrshina (Ufa: Bashkirskoe Knizhnoe Izdatel'stvo, 1987), pp. 187–188, No. 199; cf. p. 510.

> [whose name is given also in the form "Izhukay"]. Izhukay came forth from the common people; they say that he was originally a commander of a *tümen* [ten-thousand]. As monuments to him were left two gravestones. Along the left side of the road which leads to Beliaevka, in a Muslim cemetery, are found two inscribed stones. During a summer tourist outing we saw those stones with our own eyes, and photographed them. The inscription is very, very old, and it was difficult to understand anything. In the time of Izhukay lived Habrau-yïrau.
>
> After Idukay, Bayal-khan became khan. By origin Bayal was a Qazaq, from simple, poor folk. He was an orphan. Persistence and heroic nature helped him to raise himself. His sons, the heroes Kunsu, Kuku, and Yesem, drove out the Kalmïks from those parts; a great many battles took place in those days. . . .

Of interest, beyond the mention of Baba Tükles as the ancestor of these Noghay heroes and the appropriation of other epic heroes into his lineage, are the implicit links with Islam in the mention of driving out the Qalmïqs; the sacred aura surrounding "Idukay" as suggested by the gravestones; the emphasis upon the origin of Idukay and Bayal among the "common" (i.e., *qara*) people; and the mention, though without further identification, of "Habrau," who figures prominently in the Bashkir version of the Idige tale, and who appears (as Supra-jïraw, etc., in other versions, as noted above), as a contemporary of Idukay.

The heroes in this account are remembered as Noghays, and the Bashkirs provide further evidence of the continued association of Baba Tükles with the Noghays even when the link of Idige himself disappeared. In particular, such a memory of Baba Tükles among the Bashkirs is attested in the eighteenth and nineteenth centuries in traditions recorded about the city of Ufa; these traditions were noted in connection with the Idige tale already by Potanin,[136] who cited an article on Ufa's history by P. L. Iudin.[137] Iudin mentions Bashkir legends relating that before the Russian conquest of the mid-sixteenth century, the last "Noghay" ruler of the town on the site of Ufa belonged to the family of "Baba-tu-Klius" or "Babatu-Kulias"; he notes the existence of a version of these legends in the

136. Cf. Potanin, "Tiurkskaia skazka," p. 320.

137. P. L. Iudin, "Razvaliny drevniago goroda v Ufimskoi gubernii," *Istoricheskii vestnik*, t. 61 (1895), p.151.

Orenburg Central Archives, and refers to the description of the province of Orenburg published by Petr I. Rychkov in 1762.[138] Iudin's account is quite brief; but Rychkov's full account shows the richness of these traditions:

> The eminent Bashkir elder Kedrias Mullakaev[139], of the Noghay *doroga* in Karatabynsk[140] district (*volost'*), stated in his account that, as it were, long before the subjugation of the Kazan kingdom and the Bashkirs to the Russian scepter, on the very site where is now the city of Ufa, there was a great city, which extended upstream along the Belaia river [White, i.e. Aq Idel] to the mouth of the Ufa river and to the Ufinsk rivers, that is, to the mountains located by the river, so that its inhabitants were spread out along a distance of ten *versts* [approximately six and a half miles]. The last ruler of the city was a Noghay Khan by the

138. Petr Rychkov, *Topografiia Orenburgskaia, to est': obstoiatel'noe opisanie Orenburgskoi gubernii* (Saint Petersburg: Imperatorskaia Akademiia nauk, 1762), ch. 2, pp. 195–196; cf. the German translation, Peter Rytschkov, *Orenburgische Topographie, oder umständliche Beschreibung des Orenburgischen Gouvernements*, tr. Jacob Rodde (Riga: Johann Friedrich Hartknoch, 1772), Teil 2, pp. 152–153. Elements of the same legend, involving "Tiuria Babatu Kliussov" as the last "Noghay khan" of Ufa, who departed to the south as the Russians advanced, are recounted without reference to Rychkov's book in M.V. Lossievskii, "Byloe Bashkirii i bashkir po legendam, predaniiam i khronikam (Istoriko-ètnograficheeskii ocherk)," in *Spravochnaia knizhka Ufimskoi gubernii*, ed. N. A. Gurvich (Ufa: N. Vlokhin, 1883), pp.368–389 [pp.373, 384]. It is not clear whether an independent transmission of the tale is reflected here, but in a series of archeological profiles of sites near Ufa published in 1870, R. G. Ignat'ev cites Rychkov's account and notes also the existence of an apparently independent version of the legend (one that does not give the name of the "Noghay khan," however) focused on another site near the town of Birsk ("Turakhana dvorets," "Chortovo gorodishche" [Ufa], Chortovo gorodishche" [Birsk], and "Khusein Beka (Nogaiskago imama) grobnitsa," in *Drevnosti: Trudy Moskovskago Arkheologicheskago Obshchestva*, 2 [1870], pp.45–56); it may be that Lossievskii simply conflated these accounts. On the similiarity of legends surrounding the two sites near Birsk and Ufa, see also Ignat'ev's "Pamiatniki doistoricheskikh drevnostei Ufimskoi gubernii," in *Spravochnaia knizhka Ufimskoi gubernii* (1883), pp. 328–355 [p.337]. The mouth of the Ufa river is named as the *yūrṭ* of "Tīrah Khān" (whose lineage is not given, however) in the *Daftar-i Chingīz-nāmah* from the late seventeenth century (MS Edinburgh, f. 66a); the site of his "palace" is said to be a great hill (*ūbah*) above Ṣarāṭāv (i.e., Saratov). The same figure, "Tiräy Khan," is named in a *shajarah* of the Ayle Bashkirs as the ruler of the city of Ufa and the area at the mouth of the Dim (i.e., Dema) river; see M. Idhelbaev, "Ay häm Yürüdhän buyï bashqorttarnïng shäzhäräläre," in *Bashkirskie shezhere* (Ufa: Institut Istorii, Iazyka i Literatury Bashkirskogo Filiala AN SSSR, 1985), pp. 61–73 [p.67].

139. In the German translation the first name is given as "Kerdräs." "Kadrias Mullakaev" of Karatabynsk *volost'* is named, in a document from 1735, among Bashkir elders who aided the "Orenburg Expedition" of that year, which was charged with suppressing Bashkir resistance to Russian rule; see I. G. Akmanov, "Novyi dokument o nachale bashkirskogo vosstaniia 1735–1740 gg.," in *Iuzhnoural'skii arkheograficheskii sbornik*, vyp. 2 (Ufa, 1976), pp. 343–351.

140. In the German translation, "Karabatin."

name of Tiria[141] Babatu Kliusov, who dwelt in it only during the wintertime; in summer he lived along the Dema river, around 50 *versts* [approximately thirty-three miles] from the city of Ufa, at two sites, namely, near the great lake *Azirat*, and on the stream *Islak*, where there were quite a few dwellings. And indeed until now there is a mosque at that lake, and on the stream *Islak* are a mosque and a building, both of stone; but only recently they have fallen into ruins.[142] Subject to Khan Tiria were the Noghays and twelve Minsk *volost*'s [German: families] of Bashkirs, and they paid tribute to this Khan with martens and honey. But somewhat further down, at the Ufinsk site, which was then called *Turatav* [Turatap],[143] a great serpent appeared, which, coming to the city, poisoned many people with its venom and killed them. And so [the Khan] with all his Noghays went out to the Dema river, where he dwelled for some time; he learned of the seizure of the city of *Kasimov* by the Russians, and of their intentions against *Kazan*, and for this reason, in fear of them, he left for the Kuban. And at the

141. In the German version, "Tirä." According to Iudin, the archival material he saw refers to the figure of "Tiria" as, instead, "Iskur-Babatu-Kuliasov," implying another version of the same basic tale.

142. These sites are further described in the works of Ignat'ev cited in note 138, above. The two buildings along the stream Rychkov calls "Islak" are clearly the ruins that, according to local legend, had been a mosque, and the well-preserved "palace" (actually a mausoleum, says Ignat'ev) ascribed by local legend to "Turakhan" (cf. *Drevnosti*, 2, pp. 46–47; "Pamiatniki," pp. 333–334), both located along the "Slak" river, fifty *versts* from Ufa; Ignat'ev (*Drevnosti*, 2, p. 50) indeed equates this "Turakhan" with the "Tiria-Bebatu Kliussov" known from Rychkov's account, since the local legend surrounding "Turakhan" (though making him a Chingisid formerly in the service of the Siberian khan Kuchum who quarreled with Kuchum and came to Bashkiria as a conqueror) also describes his flight with the Noghays to the south due to Russian encroachment. The "mosque" at the lake that Rychkov calls "Azirat" (suggesting perhaps an original "*Ḥażrat*") must be identified with the "tomb of Ḥusayn Bek" at the lake Ignat'ev calls "Akzirat", a name he explains as meaning "white tomb" (*Drevnosti*, 2, pp. 54–56; "Pamiatniki," p. 334; cf. G. Ignatovich, "O drevnikh pamiatnikakh v Ufimskom uezde," in *Sbornik statisticheskikh, istoricheskikh i arkheologicheskikh svedenii po byvshei Orenburgskoi i nyneshnei Ufimskoi guberniiam, sobrannykh i razrabotannykh v techenii 1866 i 67 gg.* [Ufa: Tipografiia Ufimskago Gubernskago Pravleniia, 1868], pp. 29–30, where the lake is called "Akziarat", and "Ak-Ziiarat," *Protokoly zasedanii i soobshcheniia chlenov Turkestanskago Kruzhka liubitelei arkheologii* (Tashkent), 5 (1900), pp. 93–95); according to local legends noted by Ignat'ev, this Ḥusayn Bek b. ʿUmar Bek, still renowned as an important Islamizer of Bashkiria, was sent by Khoja Aḥmad Yasavī to strengthen Islam among the Noghays (of whose corrupted morals and lawlessness the shaykh had heard), and, after making the pilgrimage to Mecca, settled at the site where his tomb now stands. Iudin ("Razvaliny," p. 149) reproduces a fine drawing, which he found in the Central Archives of Orenburg, of the stone "mausoleum" by the river Islak. Both the "mosque" and the "palace" are discussed in *Arkhitekturnye pamiatniki Bashkirii*, I (Ufa, 1956), p. 24.

143. Rychkov notes that this was called *Kazan'tap* in his time.

very same time, supposedly, that venomous serpent hid itself in the mountain which is located near the Ufa river, and disappeared, so that no harm came from it any longer.

It is not clear whether we should find in "Tiria" a deformation of the name "Terme" widely given as that of Baba Tükles' son. What is clear from this account is (1) the assertion of implicitly hereditary rule of Baba Tükles' descendants in a "city" of the Bashkirs; (2) the simultaneous association of this family with a "holy" lake and with mosque-building (i.e., Islamizing) activity; (3) parallel mythic and historicizing explanations for the dynasty's departure from the region, through the stories of the serpent's ravages and the Russians' advance; (4) the survival of specific echoes of other stories about Baba Tükles, most notably the element of *honey* (cf. Ötemish Ḥājjī, Idige's leap from a vat of honey in some epic accounts, the honey mentioned in the twentieth-century legend of Baba Tükles' tomb), and the implied struggle with the serpent (cf. the dragon in the khan's dream, and the serpent in yet another Bashkir tale discussed below); and (5) the essential attestation of the continued currency of traditions about Baba Tükles and his descendants' status as *biys* ruling both the Noghays and particular Bashkir groups. The threat from the serpent is of particular interest also in connection with legends of origin discussed in Chapter 7 since a serpent figures in several echoes of the mythic complex also invoked in the "ethnogonic" developments of Baba Tükles' persona; and it is especially prominent in the Bashkir tale to which we now turn.

Yet another echo of the figure of "Bābā Tükles Shāshlï ʿAzīz," and one that again reinforces his links to both Islamization and pre-Islamic legends of origin, is probably to be found in the *shajarah* or tribal genealogical legend of one of the major Bashkir tribes, the Yurmatï, published in the collection of *shajarahs* edited and translated into Russian by the Bashkir historian R. G. Kuzeev.[144] This account is quite clearly a legend

144. R. G. Kuzeev, *Bashkirskie shezhere* (Ufa: Bashkirskoe Knizhnoe Izdatel'stvo, 1960), pp. 27–31 (modern Bashkir transcription), 31–35 (Russian translation), 177–183 (notes and commentary), 233–243 (facsimile of the manuscript). The text is obscure in places, and Kuzeev's notes unfortunately do not address a number of textual problems; the summary and translation provided here reflects consideration of all forms in which he has made the text accessible. What is clearly an independent, but very similar, version of the same *shajarah* was summarized in Lossievskii, "Byloe Bashkirii," pp. 381–383; yet another quite similar version is recounted, on the basis of an 1885 publication (unavailable to me) of a Bashkir "chronicle," in D. Sokolov, "Opyt razbora odnoi bashkorskoi [*sic*] letopisi," in *Trudy Orenburgskoi Uchenoi Arkhivnoi Kommissii*, vyp. 4 (1898), pp. 45–65 [pp. 50–51]. On the Bashkir *shajarahs*, see further Kuzeev's *Proiskhozhdenie bashkirskogo naroda: ètnicheskii sostav, istoriia rasseleniia* (Moscow: Nauka, 1974), esp.

of origin with striking structural and thematic parallels to the Kimek legend as related by Gardīzī, discussed in Chapter 7; but it is also quite evidently focused around "Noghay" elements in which *two* figures with names recalling the epithets of Baba Tükles appear. It includes, at the same time, an emphasis upon the status of *biy*, as well as an element strikingly reminiscent of both the earliest account of Baba Tükles and of an older legend of origin reported by Juvaynī for the Uyghurs; this is the image of the holy man inside a tomb-pit who in effect sanctifies and "creates" a community, and its depiction in this Bashkir tale recalls also the Sufi theme of "seeing into" graves.

The account of the Yurmatï *shajarah* begins by promising an account of the khans since the time of "Chïngghïz Khan," but immediately turns to the origins of the Yurmatï, among whom was a certain "Tūkhāl [Tükhäl?] Shaghālī Bīy"; this figure was called "Bīy" by the people because his clan was large, according to the account, but what follows is evidently another explanation of the status of *biy* accorded to Shaghālī and his descendants. In former times, the account goes, the country of the Yurmatï, specifically the region of the Zai and Sheshma rivers [tributaries of the Kama, in western Bashkiria], was inhabited by the Noghays. Suddenly an enormous dragon (*azhdaha yïlan*) appeared in that region,[145] and the people fought with it for many years; many people died, but finally the dragon "disappeared," and the people were left in peace and security. At that time, the account continues, the people were under the rule of a khan called "Ämät Khämät";[146] after a while, however, there

pp. 33–37 (and pp. 118–122 on the Yurmatï *shajarah*), as well as A. I. Kharisov, *Literaturnoe nasledie bashkirskogo naroda (XVIII–XIX veka)* (Ufa: Bashkirskoe Knizhnoe Izdatel'stvo, 1973), pp. 217–220, and especially R. Kh. Khalikova, *Iazyk bashkirskikh shezhere i aktovykh dokumentov XVIII–XIX vv.* (Moscow: Nauka, 1990); for discussions of comparable *shajarahs* among the Volga Tatars, see Usmanov, *Tatarskie istoricheskie istochniki*, pp. 167–195, and further M. I. Akhmetzianov, "Obshchinnye shedzhere," in *Istochnikovedenie i istoriia tiurkskikh iazykov*, ed. È. R. Tenishev, I. A. Abdullin, and F. S. Khakimzianov (Kazan', 1978), pp.45–50.

145. This element in the *shajarah* immediately reminds us of the story about the "Babatu Kliusov" rulers of Ufa reported by Rychkov, as cited above, and recalls also a legend and folk etymology linked to the Noghay center of Astrakhan reported by Evliya Çelebi in the seventeenth century (see the Russian translation, *Kniga puteshestviia*, vyp. 2 (1979), p. 132), and most probably reflecting traditions among the Bashkir tribes of the region (Evliya's "Hashdaks"): a dragon, he says, had despoiled the region where the city now stands, killing many people until a heroic khan slew it and rendered the place peaceful and prosperous; the city was thus called "Azhdarkhān," after the dragon (*azhdahā*, popularly *azhdarkhā*). This account of the origin of Astrakhan's name is not mentioned in I. G. Dobrodomov, "Proiskhozhdenie nazvaniia *Astrakhan'*," in *Onomastika Povolzh'ia*, 3 (Ufa, 1973), pp. 216–227.

146. This name recalls the "Ḥażrat Khamet" who ordered a young boy buried during the construction of Astrakhan's mosque in a Noghay story discussed in Chapter 4.

came a time of intense quarrels and struggles among various khans, and the account specifies that this was the time of "Jänbäk Khan" and "Aqsaq Timer Khan," which was a time of discord, when the "homeland" (*yort*) was beset by enemies on all sides. Ämät Khämät's realm collapsed, and he fled, "with a few people," across a great river, coming to a site where they *dug* a place for their homes (*yort urïnï qazïdïlar*) and settled. There the khan announced that he had experienced a dream or vision (*bir ḥāl boldï*) that indicated to him that they had come to a certain people's burial place: "There must be the bodies of some tribe here," the khan said, and "among these bodies there will be a saint (*ʿazīz*)." The account continues thus:

> When he told them to look at the grave, they saw it at once; they saw a tombstone (*ziyārat tashï*), and on the stone was written "Chülkä Ata." The khan said, "Clearly this must be the saint." At that time the date was 811. The khan ordered them to open the grave to look, and when they looked, [they saw that] the grave was covered over with bricks; but, wondrously, a dark-headed, red-faced youth (*yeget*) was lying there as if alive. The khan said, "O Shaghālī Bīy, there is no one wiser than you among the people. Let this land and water be yours; you care for this saint [*bu ʿazīzni sen tarbīyah eyle*]." Shaghālī Bīy was pleased, and established his *yort* along the river called Shādlïq ["joy"].[147] He made a fenced enclosure (*iḥāṭah*) over this saint, and each year they would gather there and recite the Qurʾān.

After some time, the narrative continues, Shaghālī Bīy died and was buried beside Chülkä Ata[148]; his son[149] ʿAlī Shaykh Darvīsh succeeded him as *bīy* and under him the people returned to their fathers' land of former times, the region of the Zai and Sheshma rivers.[150] When Shaykh Darvīsh died, his son *Chāchlï Darvish* (in one version "Chasli-Dervish")

147. This may echo the name "Shad" in Gardīzī's account of the Kimek legend of origin, discussed in Chapter 7.

148. His name is here evidently written "Chāchīlkā," further suggestive of a conflation of names.

149. Kuzeev understands the text to mean someone else's son, thus breaking the genealogical link between Shaghālī Bīy and the later *bīys*; this is surely not the intent of the text.

150. This pattern of flight, establishment in a safe realm, and return to a previous homeland reflects a common ethnogonic motif, and quite precisely matches the specific pattern in the Kimek legend of origin discussed in Chapter 7.

became *bīy*, and his era is portrayed in glowing terms as a time of joy and prosperity for the Noghays.

Herein is emphasized both the original brotherhood, and then the long-standing hostility, between the Noghays and Bashkirs, however, for at this point the account mentions the "Noghay custom" of referring to *bīys* as *mīrzās* (spelled *m.r.żah*), setting the stage for the division of Bashkir *bīy* from Noghay *mīrzā*. This Chāchlï Darvīsh Bīy had no sons, according to the narrative; he had only a daughter, whom he had given in marriage to a Noghay, and when this Noghay died young, Chāchlï Darvīsh himself raised his daughter's two sons, Burnaq and Yādkār.[151] When Chāchlï Darvish died, the account says, the elder grandson Burnaq became *bīy*, while Yādkār became *mīrzā*, and when several bad years came, with long and harsh winters leaving the herds and people hungry and impoverished, the ensuing stress brought about the division of Noghays and Bashkirs. The Noghays, says the account, assembled and took counsel together, considering that "our ancestors had come from the Kuban" seeking pastures and a cooler climate; but the intense cold had proven more unbearable than the heat, and yet another affliction, more troublesome than even the cold, had come from the north: the Russian infidels (*urïṣ kuffār*), who, it seemed, would become even more numerous. The Noghays thus resolved that "this land is not suitable for us," and set off, under the *mīrzā* Yādkār, in the year 953/1546–1547, to return to the Kuban; a group of the poorest appealed to the *bīy* Burnaq,[152] however, and he changed his mind and agreed to stay in the region of the Aq Idel (i.e., the river Belaia, in Bashkiria).

The rest of the *shajarah* follows the history of the Yurmatï *bīys* in Bashkiria and their submission to the Russians. At the end of the text appears a summary account in which the opening line of the *shajarah* is echoed; this time, however, the first two figures in the lineage of Yurmatï *bīys* are made khans, in the following sequence of "the khans since Chïnghïz Khan": Ämät Khämät became khan in 811/1408–1409,

151. See the discussion of this section in T. Kh. Kusimova, "Antroponimy v bashkirskikh shezhere," in *Onomastika Povolzh'ia*, 3 (Ufa, 1973), pp. 66–71 [p. 67].

152. The *shajarah* is presented as the recollections of the Yurmatï *bīy* who succeeded Burnaq Bīy and eventually submitted to the Russians; he speaks in the first person frequently, and toward the end of the text notes that he has recounted what he knew of "the ancestors" (*babalar*) and the past for a certain Mullā Bāqī to write down, and has entrusted what he wrote to several elders. The extant text includes a note adding that this *bīy* who narrated the *shajarah*'s account died on 8 Ramażān 972/9 April 1565, thus allowing us to date the composition of the original *shajarah* to the latter sixteenth century, as its editor affirms (Kuzeev, p. 177).

then Jänbäk Khan, then Aqsāq Timir Khan[!], then Shaghālī Khan, then Shaykh T.r.w.sh [i.e., Darvish]; then Chāchlï Dar[v]ish became *bīy*, then Purnāq became *bīy*, and Yādkār became *mīrzā*.

Such is the account of the Yurmatï *shajarah*. It recounts the role of the tribal chiefs, the *bīys*, as the decisive figures in the tribe's history, from the beginnings of the chiefly lineage and its dual sanction by a Chingisid khan and by a Muslim saint (whose tomb both determines and sanctifies the place where the tribe takes shape as a community), through a succession of *bīys* and the division of the people in a time of troubles, down to the submission of the Yurmatï to the Russians. The latter point is of importance, for the *shajarah* is a notably "submissive," even despairing, document, and no doubt stands as an example of "traditional" oral histories, composed soon after colonial conquest, intended to justify the subjugated people's (or more properly its rulers') integrity as a community and its rights in a particular territory;[153] as such it was compiled out of traditional oral materials, no doubt, that in some cases—the appearance of the dragon, the prominence of the rivers, the saint's tomb-pit—reflect quite archaic mythic themes, but it bears evidence of being intended both to acquaint the tribe's new imperial masters with the political structures accepted among the Bashkirs (respecting which the Russians might expect minimal organized resistance) *and* to justify the necessity and benefits of submission for a Bashkir audience.[154]

In any event, for our purposes it is important that in the *shajarah*, compiled and transmitted for these likely purposes, we find hints of traditions surrounding our Baba Tükles; these are clearest in the name of Chāchlï Darvish, but may appear also in the name of the saint, "Chülkä"/"Chāchīlkā" Ata, and in the single reference to Shaghālī Bīy as "Tükhāl Shaghālī Bīy."[155] Beyond reflections of the name, beyond the general mythic com-

153. Cf. similar examples in Henige, *The Chronology of Oral Tradition*, pp. 103–105.

154. The latter point is explicitly raised when the putative author of the *shajarah*—the *bīy* who submitted—stresses that he had no choice but to submit.

155. We may note here, finally, the slight possibility that the available manuscripts of the Yurmatï *shajarah* may mask an even clearer link with the figure of Baba Tükles. The name of the "author" appears frequently in the text, in a form transcribed by Kuzeev as "Tatigach Baba" or "Tatigach Bi," and Kuzeev "modernizes" the name in his notes to "Tatigas"; in the manuscript copy reproduced in facsimile, however, the name is consistently written "*t.t.kāč*" or "*t.t.kāčah*," and in view of the long history of the text's transmission and the successive recopying we must assume—since the copy Kuzeev publishes most likely dates from the beginning of the twentieth century—it does not seem altogether implausible that this form may reflect an original "*t.k.lās*" (or perhaps "*t.k.lāč*"). Against this may be noted (1) a reference to a manuscript copy of a "*shajarah* of Tatigas-biy of the Yurmatï tribe," in A. Fattakhutdinov, "Bashkirskie shezhere (kratkoe

plex of the serpent and rivers as evoked in some epic versions of Baba Tükles' role in the Idige tales, and beyond the general elements of a legend of origin in an originally small community's flight to safety in troubled times, we may see specific parallels to other "uses" of Baba Tükles, in the account of "Chāchlï Darvish" raising sons left to him by a girl (in this case his daughter, *qïzï*, instead of a *parī-qïzï* or the like) who here also "disappears," at least from the narrative, and in the attention to linking the ranks of *bīy* and *mīrzā* among the Bashkirs and Noghays, respectively, to descendants (and, practically, sons) of Chachlï Darvish; if we are correct in assuming a Bashkir appropriation of a Noghay tale focused on Baba Tükles, it would be entirely fitting for "Chāchlï Darvish" to be assigned *two* sons, since, as noted above, Baba Tükles' ancestry of the Noghay rulers appears to have been widely recognized among the Bashkirs.

More interesting, in the curious account of the community "digging" to establish homes in the midst of another community's burial ground, inside which a clearly Islamic saint—his grave is, after all, a place for pious visitation (*ziyārat*)—is found enclosed in a grave-pit, but miraculously untouched by corruption (rather than by fire), we may see striking parallels with the narrative of Ötemish Ḥājjī itself, with its elements of digging the oven-pits, the *qoruq*, and the saint's emergence from the pit unharmed. The saint's emergence, or uncovering, is the decisive moment in founding a new community, in one case the "Özbek *ṭāʾifa-sï*" with its Muslim khan, in the other the Yurmatï with its lineage of tribal chiefs who make the grave, properly fenced off as inviolate, the focus of the newly formed people's territory, and oversee the communal recitation of the Qurʾān at the saint's grave.[156]

---

arkheograficheskoe opisanie)," in *Bashkirskie shezhere (Filologicheskie issledovaniia i publikatsii)* (Ufa, 1985), pp. 88–128 [p. 99, No. 25] (the *shajarah*, belonging to one Sabit Tatigasov in the village of Tabyldy in Sterlibashevskii *raion*, "begins with Tatigas-bī and continues to our days, with multiple genealogical branches"; it was compiled by one Akhtiam Karagulov, director of a cement factory in the city of Sterlitamak), suggesting that this form of the name is found in other sources—unless of course all copies derive from a single original in which the name had already been corrupted; and (2) more strongly, the existence of "Tatigasov" as a surname, although this as well may reflect a late adoption based upon written records.

156. The account of the uncovering of this saint's grave recalls the story of the discovery of the putative tomb of ʿAlī in Balkh, reported by the twelfth-century traveler Abū Ḥāmid al-Gharnāṭī; the latter tale involves a dream (comparable to the khan's *ḥāl* in the Bashkir tale), the digging and uncovering of the grave, and the discovery of ʿAlī's uncorrupted state. See in addition to Ferrand's edition, cited in Chapter 2, the translation in McChesney, *Waqf in Central Asia*, pp. 27–28.

We may note here that Baba Tükles also figures in tribal legends and genealogies of another major Bashkir tribe, the Ming. This tribe is said to recall the names of "Töklö Ata" and "Säsle Ata" (i.e., Chachlï Ata) as distant ancestors,[157] but in an unpublised *shajarah*, preserved in Ufa and most likely compiled in the mid-nineteenth century, we find an even more explicit genealogical evocation of Baba Tükles' lineage. In this *shajarah* we find the full genealogy, from Abū Bakr to Idige, as known from the historical and epic accounts discussed earlier (see Table 5.1), in a form that suggests its dependence upon a written text, probably Jalāyirī's work or the *Daftar-i Chingīz-nāmah*. Idige, however, is here ascribed a single son, called "Chalpāq Khān," who is said to have ruled as khan in Sarāychïq during the sixth century A.H.; more important, this Chalpāq Khān is cast as the father of "Ming Ḥadāqlī Ūrādach Bīy," who is clearly to be identified with the "Uradas Biy" or "Ming Hadhaqlï Uradach Biy" widely acknowledged in tribal tradition as the common ancestor of the Ming Bashkirs.[158] The *shajarah* follows his lineage for another twelve or thirteen generations, along lines separate from those known through other Ming *shajarahs*, but what is significant for our purposes is the grafting of Idige's lineage through Baba Tükles onto the Ming tribal genealogy: the *shajarah* also follows a number of other prominent lineages from Islamic and Inner Asian traditions, including those of ancient Iranian kings, pre-Islamic prophets, Chingisids, and Ottomans, but it is clearly the lineage of Baba Tükles that is used to "extend" the ancestry of the most hallowed Ming hero and progenitor.

Finally, a distinctive episode from the recently published, and extremely rich, Bashkir version of the Idige tale appears to reinforce the Islamic origin of Baba Tükles' role while at the same time setting Idige's sacred genealogy squarely within the narrative tradition of native legends

157. Cf. Kuzeev, *Proiskhozhdenie*, p. 305.

158. On this figure, and on the Ming Bashkirs in general, see Kuzeev, *Proiskhozhdenie*, pp. 299–315, and his *Bashkirskie shezhere*, pp. 50–70 (with notes, pp. 186–194). The *shajarah* discussed here is the first part (ff. 1a–28b) of MS 1a–69 from the Collection of Manuscripts and Old Printed Books of the Institute of History, Language and Literature of the Academy of Sciences of Bashkortostan in Ufa; the lineage of Baba Tükles appears on ff. 5a–b (a folio misplaced in binding) and 17a–22b, with subsequent generations through f. 28b. I am indebted for this reference to Allen Frank, who filmed this manuscript during a research trip to Ufa in 1992. In this text, the epithet of the Ming ancestor Ūradāch Bīy might be read "Ming Khudā-qulï (i.e., the Ming "servant of God"), but evidently the form "Ming Hadhaqlï Uradach Bīy" (i.e., Uradach Bīy "of the thousand quivers") is supported by legends about him transmitted orally. Chalpāq Khan is named, without reference to his lineage, in the *Daftar-i Chingīz-nāmah* (MS Edinburgh, f. 66a), where his realm (*yūrt*) is identified as Sarāychïq.

of origin. The passage in question occurs during the hero's flight from Tokhtamïsh as he makes his way toward "Satmïr" (i.e., "Shāh Temür"). Now the episode of Idige's flight from Tokhtamïsh to Shah Timur is well known from virtually all of the recorded versions of the tale, and includes a section in which Tokhtamïsh, learning of Idige's flight, seeks advice on what he ought to do in response; after several "invitations" he has the aged singer of tales, Supra Jïraw, who can foretell the future, brought to his court. Provided with kumiss or other offerings, Supra Jïraw names the khans he has survived in his long life (often beginning with Chingis Khan), and predicts that he will outlive Tokhtamïsh as well, for Idige will defeat him and seize his throne, property, and women; in several variants it is here, in the course of this bard's prophetic recitation, that we learn of Idige's descent from Baba Tükles.[159] As a result of this prediction the khan either tries unsuccessfully to appease Idige, as in some versions, or resolves to kill him, as in others; in both cases he sends Idige's friend Janbay to bring him back, but Idige refuses and continues on his way.

The Bashkir version includes this section, but inserts an otherwise unknown episode[160] in which "Idheükäy" finds an old man guarding a chest (*sandïq*) containing the hero's genealogy; the old man reveals that he, Baba Tükles, and Supra Jïraw[161] had once been companions in the fight against the infidels. Here Idheükäy is guided in his journey by a blue hound (*kük burdhay*), who leads the hero into a cave inside a mountain; there after crossing a lake they reach a high place where the road divides, marked by a sign indicating that the road to the right leads to wealth, the one to the left to warfare, and the one in the middle to the "secret" the hero is seeking to uncover. Following the dog down the middle path, Idheükäy meets the white-bearded old man, who addresses him thus:

> "Both Tökläth and I were together at the Kaʿbah; together we battled the infidels who came into our homeland. Both Habrau and I

159. In the Noghay version translated by Potanin and Valikhanov, a hostile "Sabra Jirau" responds to Tokhtamïsh's specific question about Idige's origin by affirming that "Baba-Tukti-Chachli-azi" was his ancestor (Valikhanov, *Sochineniia*, pp. 266–267); Berezin's version (pp. 63–64) has "Ḥūbir" (or "Ḥūbrā") Jïrāw ask Idige to confirm his descent from Baba Tükles. In Osmanov's text (pp. 35–36) it is "Ṣubrā" (or "Sūbrā") Jïrāw who in reciting his *jïr* for Tokhtamïsh gives Idige's genealogy from Baba Tükles, who he says ruled at the Kaʿbah (cf. note 27 above); and Chodzko's version (p. 355) likewise has "Sobra" recount Idige's ancestry, from Abū Bakr through Baba Tükles, when summoned after Idige's flight.

160. "Idheükäy menän Moradhïm," *Agidhel*, 1989, No. 1, pp. 45–48; cf. Nur Zaripov's discussion of the episode in his supplement to the text (noted above) pp. 132–134.

161. In Bashkir, "Baba Tökläth" and "Habrau."

> became companions of Tökläth; and for a long time the three of us were the closest of friends. The holy Baba Tökläth shared his secret with God: until a hero who would save the country was born in Ural, until a hero who could wield the sword of Ural Batïr arose, he told no one the place where it lay . . . and he summoned me to safeguard the secret beneath the earth. To the old man Habrau he assigned such a task: to go among the people in Ural, close his left eye, pay heed to the saints, and make *beys* of all men who say they are men. I obeyed Tökläth: from that day, making me deaf and dumb, giving me the chest which bore the secret, and seating me on that rock, he turned me into a poor wretch. I had a wife; he had me leave her and made her a widow. I had a single son; he turned him into an immortal dog—that very companion of yours."[162]

The old man then notes that Habrau did not comply with Baba Tökläth's words; as a result, Baba Tökläth angrily laid a curse on Habrau, condemning him to live forever but in sorrow and misery.[163] The old man then speaks again:

> "Now, young man, you have come, now you have learned the secret. With your own hand take the key from around my neck, and inside that chest you will find a great book; when you have read that book, you will understand what has been."
>
> Idheükäy opened the chest and took out a great book written on deerskin. He opened it to the first page and looked at the book, and when he saw his genealogy laid out inside, and his own name written in blood, he was amazed and astonished. As he stared intently, he read these words:

162. Text: *Tökläth menän ikäüläp / Qäghbälä lä buldïq bedh, / Ilgä kilgän gäüergä / Bergä hadhaq yundïq bedh. / Habrau menän ikäüläp / Tökläthkä yuldash buldïq bedh. / Küp saqtardha ösäüläp, / Bergä serdhäsh buldïq bedh. / Baba Tökläth äüliä / Alla menän serläshte; / Uralda tïughan ber batïr / Il haqlardhay bulmaghas, / Ural batïr qïlïsïn / Totor batïr tïumaghas, / Qaydha yatqan urïnïn / His beräügä äytmäne / . . . Mingä erdheng athtïnda / Ser haqlargha öndäshte. / Habrau qartça Uralda / Il aralap yörörgä, / Hul küdhene yommorgha, / Äüliäne tïnglargha, / Irmen tigän irdhärdhä-- / Barïhïn bey qïlïrgha, — / Ugha shunday ësh qushtï. / Min buy birdhem Töklâthkä; / Shul köndän ük ul mine / Telhedh-qolaqhïdh itep, / Serle handïghïn birep, / Osho tashqa ultïrtïp, / Äyländerdhe bayghoshqa. / Ber qatïnïm bar ine, / Unï ayïrtïp, tol qïldï, / Yangghïdh balam bar ine, / Bïna osho yuldashïng — / Ülmäy torghan ët qïldï.*

163. From this, Zaripov (p. 133–134) interprets Habrau as a "popular" and "democratic" character!

> "From my grandson a man called Qotlo will be born who will become a *bey*; the youngest of my children, the most beloved son, the *bey batïr* named Tora, will destroy the *beylek* of my great-grandson Qotlo for not adhering to my ways; he will make him and his clan—all of them, without a single one left out—slaves.[164] From Qotlo will be born my bastard son, and he will call him Idheükäy; his heart will be stern, and he will go about the country, seeking revenge; the son born from him will be called Moradhïm; he will shed blood relentlessly throughout the whole of Ural."[165]

The book, then, is Baba Tökläth's prophecy concerning his descendants; it ends with the revelation that someone from among his descendants, guided by a dog, will come upon this prophetic book, and promises power and success to that person if he will "grasp the sword left to me by Ümer Batïr" (recalling the tradition that Baba Tükles' father was "Baba ʿUmar"), and if he will seek out the grave of Ural Batïr, don the latter's helmet, and mount a special steed that emerges from a sacred lake.

This unique episode from the Bashkir variant[166] illustrates as well as any the rich interweaving of Inner Asian mythic motifs with the still

164. The destruction of the *beylik* of Idheükäy's father by Baba Tökläth's youngest son is recounted (as history, not prophecy) to Idheükäy earlier in this Bashkir version, by none other than Habrau himself (p. 24). The tension reflected here between figures portrayed as descendants of Baba Tökläth suggests the combining of two distinct traditions evoking his sacred ancestry, one a specifically Bashkir tradition involving Baba Tökläth and "Tora" (as echoed in the legends about Ufa discussed above), and one a more general Noghay tradition involving Baba Tükles, "Qotlo" (i.e., Qutlïqïyā), and Idige.

165. Text: *Inde, yeget, kilgänheng / Serdhe khädher belgänheng; / Muyïnïmdaghï asqïstï / Üdh qulïng man alïrhïng; / Osho handïq ësenän / Ber dhur kitap tabïrhïng. / Shul kitaptï uqïghas, / Ni bulghanïn anglarhïng. / Idheükäy handïqtï asqan, / Bolan tiregä yadhïlghan / Ber dhur kitaptï alghan. / Täüge bitte asqas ta, / Kitapqa küdh halghas ta, / Ësenä ïrïuï tedhelep, / Qangha mansïp yadhïlghan / Üdh isemene kürgäs tä / Aptïraghan, tang qalghan. / Küdhen tekläp qaraghas, / Osho hüdhdhe uqïghan: / "Yeyänemdän bey bulïp, / Qotlo tigän ir tïuïr; / Baldarïmdïng kinyähe, / Ing doghamdïng irkähe / Tora tigän bey batïr / Qotlo tigän bülämdeng, / Totmaghangha yolamdï, / Beylegene yuq qïlïr; / Üdhen, ïrïuïn,–barïhïn / Beren quymay qol qïlïr. / Tïumam tïuïr Qotlonan, / Idheükäy tigän at quyïr; / Yauïz bulïr yöräge, / Ildä yöröp, qon qïuïr, / Unan tïughan yete yat / Moradhïm tigän at quyïr, / Bötä Ural buyïnda / His ayamay qan qoyor.*

166. In dealing with Soviet publications of a given "national" epic, even with those based on recordings from the 1920s or 1930s, one inevitably fears "contamination" and outright manipulation in the text for ideological and/or nationalistic purposes, as less egregious but potentially more insidious manifestations of the environment that encouraged, for example, "epic" panegyrics to Stalin; this fear is compounded by the publication of linguistically modernized "popular" texts without critical apparatus, facsimiles, or any indication of the principles used in creating the new text from several variants. On the whole the published Bashkir version does not

essentially Islamic character of the central figure, Baba Tükles. Among the Inner Asian elements, the dog who guides the hero in his quest is strikingly reminiscent of the blue wolf that goes before the hero in the famous Uyghur-script version of the legend of Oghuz Qaghan;[167] the mountain/cave/water complex is extremely widespread in Inner Asian legends of origin and ancestral birth (as will be discussed in Chapter 7), and in this connection we may note that later in the same Bashkir variant Idheükäy first speaks to Satmïr of his longing to return to his own country, to "the mountain of Baba Tökläth," the "mountain where his mother bore him," and then on his return makes a pilgrimage to the site, evidently located at the junction of two streams: "He crossed the Yayïq, and sought refuge at the grave of Baba Tökläth along the rivers called Bäläkäy and Töyäläth."[168] The "secret" locked up in a chest is likewise a recurrent motif also linked with legends of origin: here the link is implicit, with the "secret" consisting of a genealogy cast as prophecy (since a "founder" must predict his community's fate), but occasionally the "secret" is the ancestor himself.[169]

---

appear to exhibit elements that are clearly ideologically motivated. More problematical is the issue of "literary" or "creative" additions or changes in the variants underlying the published text, some of which (e.g., the versions prepared by the writers Burangulov and Isenbetov in the late 1930s) were already literary reworkings of folkloric recordings; here the possible "contaminants" include not only the ideological currents in vogue at the time and the drive to distinguish a standardized "national" (in this case Bashkir) form of the epic, but the scholarly, literary, and folkloric knowledge and education of the editors themselves. In any case, without a thorough study of the full range of variants and edited versions it is impossible to argue for or against the notion that the recently published Bashkir text faithfully reflects the form and content of the epic among traditional bards; that it does is merely assumed here, with the additional assurance that at least in the case of the figure of Baba "Tökläth" (whose role seems hardly amenable to Soviet-era ideological tampering) there seems no good reason to doubt its faithfulness.

167. Other parallels with this early "mythic epic" will be noted in Chapter 7; on the theme of the wolf as guide see most recently R. S. Lipets, " 'Litso volka blagoslovenno . . .' (Stadial'nye izmeneniia obraza volka v tiurko-mongol'skom èpose i genealogicheskikh skazaniiakh)," *Sovetskaia ètnografiia*, 1981, No. 1, pp. 120–133; cf. L. P. Potapov, "Volk v starinnykh narodnykh pover'iakh i primetakh Uzbekov," in *Kratkie soobshcheniia Instituta Ètnografii AN SSSR*, vyp. 30 (1958), pp. 135–142. Ethnogenetic legends involving a wolf's guidance (or occasionally that of some other animal) are particularly widespread among the Bashkirs, as noted (with historicist interpretation) by R. G. Kuzeev, "Uralo-aral'skie ètnicheskie sviazi v kontse I tysiacheletiia N. È. i istoriia formirovaniia bashkirskoi narodnosti," in *Arkheologiia i ètnografiia Bashkirii*, 4 (Ufa, 1971), pp. 17–29 [cf. p. 20], and in the same volume A. N. Kireev, "Ètnogeneticheskie legendy i predaniia bashkirskogo naroda" (pp. 60–63); see also in the same volume F. F. Ilimbetov, "Kul't volka u Bashkir (k ètimologizatsii ètnonima "*bashqort*")" (pp. 224–228), where popular etymologies for the ethnonym involving the word *qurt*, "wolf," are addressed.

168. Cf. pp. 63, 65; in keeping with the cyclical theme of linking origins with endings, Idheükäy recalls his descent from Baba Tökläth just before he dies (p. 73).

169. This theme appears in the Mongol tradition, noted above, identifying Chingis Khan's ancestor Börte Chino as a Tibetan prince; the latter's lineage is in turn traced to an Indian prince, who was locked into a copper box and thrown into the Ganges to be discovered by an

At the same time, however, the originally Islamic flavor of Baba Tökläth's role is unmistakable: he is linked with Mecca, he fights the infidels who threaten the nation *(il)*, and he laments his descendants' departure from the customs he established. Moreover, he is again portrayed as a figure instrumental in *bringing* Islam to a people; his role as "founder" is clearly the product of his active contribution to establishing Islam, and not merely the result of any genealogical links sacred in an Islamic context (e.g., descent from Abū Bakr), which are not even mentioned in this Bashkir version. In short, this newly available account reinforces the conclusion that the figure of Baba Tükles was above all a bearer of Islam—*not* merely a vehicle for grafting an Islamic genealogy onto an Inner Asian one, and *not* a figure already known to Inner Asian tradition who was subsequently cloaked in Islamic garb—and that it was *in his capacity as a bearer of Islam*, and thus a founder of a religiously defined community, that he was susceptible to the "nativizing" narrative transformations that in some accounts merely surrounded him with the trappings of traditional legends of origin, and in others recast him entirely as a mythic ancestor.

We may note, finally, that the role of "Islamizer" is clearly assigned to the figure with whom it may be possible to identify Baba Tükles; and it is with this issue that we conclude this chapter.

Baba Tükles and Sayyid Ata

The Noghay and Crimean accounts of Nūr ad-Dīn's claims to legitimacy based on descent from the Turkistānī saint "Qoji Aḥmad Baba Tükli Shashli ʿAzīz" add an important element to Baba Tükles' designation,

old man of Tibet (cf. Bawden, *The Mongol Chronicle Altan Tobči*, p. 112). In a Qazaq legend recorded by Divaev, Chingis Khan himself was placed in a chest by his mother, ashamed that the boy's father was not her lawful husband, and thrown in a river, where he was discovered and raised by a *parī* (A. Divaev, "Kirgizskii razskaz o Chingiz-khane," *ZVOIRAO*, 11 (1899), pp. 290–292, reprinted in his *Ètnograficheskie materialy* (Tashkent, 1900), part 7), while a Qaraqalpaq legend has Chingis Khan's mother shut up in a *sandïq* and cast into the sea (I. A. Beliaev, "Iz predanii o Chingiz-khane," *Protokoly zasedanii i soobshcheniia chlenov Zakaspiiskago kruzhka liubitelei arkheologii i istorii Vostoka* (Ashkhabad), 3 (1917), pp. 10–12); see further on this theme Kh. Esbergenov and Zh. Khoshniiazov, *Ètnograficheskie motivy v karakalpakskom fol'klore* (Tashkent: Fan, 1988), pp. 22–26. Even closer to the use of the motif in this Bashkir version of Idige is the case of Abū'l-Ghāzī's account of Oghuz Khan in the *Shajarah-i tarākimah*, in which the wise sayings of his son, Kün Khan, are written down on paper, signed by the notables and stamped with their seals, and placed in the khan's "treasury" for posterity (cf. Kononov, *Rodoslovnaia*, pp. 54 [tr.], 38 [text]).

namely the appellation "Khoja Aḥmad." On this basis some researchers[170] have assumed that these accounts assert a genealogical link with Khoja Aḥmad Yasavī himself, whose association with the town of Turkistan is well known; indeed, the Noghay version of the tale published by Semenov makes this identification explicit, but it is the only epic version to do so explicitly, and it is not impossible that the translator himself supplied this "explanation." Now it is undoubtedly true that we should look for Yasavī connections in considering the possible "identity" of Baba Tükles; the activity of Yasavī shaykhs among the Turkic tribes of the Jöchid *ulus* is attested in a number of historical and hagiographical sources, and it is most likely not without significance that the rest of the Tashkent manuscript that contains the text of Ötemish Ḥājjī's work on the Jöchid *ulus* (together with Abū'l-Ghāzī's *Shajarah-i tarākimah*) consists of hagiological legends about Aḥmad Yasavī and his successors, as noted earlier. Yet the appearance of Baba Tükles in Ötemish Ḥājjī's work as the person responsible for the conversion of Özbek Khan implies that we should consider a Yasavī[171] contemporary of Özbek Khan, and it is suggested, accordingly, that in looking to the Yasavī order we need not go back to the "founder" himself; rather, Baba Tükles may well be identi-

170. Cf. Melioranskii, "Skazanie," introduction, p. 10; Safargaliev, *Raspad*, p. 229; Zhirmunskii, "Skazanie ob Idige," p. 383; Usmanov (*Tatarskie istoricheskie istochniki*, p. 84), evidently accepting Melioranskii's interpretation, also cites Safargaliev's mention of the Qara Noghay account of "Khochakhmat Baba Tulik" as evidence of Khoja Aḥmad Yasavī's appearance in the legend of Idige, and feels obliged to explain the absence of Yasavī in the Tatar histories as the result of Yasavī's supposedly greater esteem among the Qazaqs and Noghays than among the Tatars.

171. According to Togan, the important (but regrettably now lost) nineteenth-century hagiographical work by Sayyid Aḥmad Nāṣir ad-Dīn Marghinānī devoted primarily to Yasavī shaykhs, entitled *Manāqib-i mashā'ikh at-turk*, specifies that "Baba Tüktü Şaştı Aziz" [Togan's transcription] was a Yasavī shaykh (cf. *Bugünkü Türkili*, p. 197, n. 210, referring to ff. 26a and 156b of the apparently unique manuscript preserved in Bayazıt Umumî Kütüphanesi, Hâlis Efendi No. 199; Togan here refers also to Osmanov's chrestomathy and to the *ʿUmdat at-tavārīkh* [i.e., ʿAbd al-Ghaffār's *ʿUmdat al-akhbār*] on Baba Tükles). Elsewhere ("Yesevîliğe dair bazı yeni malûmat," in *60 doğum yılı münasebetiyle Fuad Köprülü Armağanı* [Istanbul: Osman Yalçın Matbaası, 1953], p. 525), Togan mentions that the same work (which he calls here *Tārīkh-i mashā'ikh at–turk*) identifies "Baba Tükles" as a son of Jalāl ad-Dīn Rūmī (interesting in itself in light of the association of the "prophetic skull" theme with both Baba Tükles and with Rūmī's "son" Shams–i Tabrīz, and in light of the genealogies found in the Tatar histories and in various Noghay versions of the Idige tale naming Baba Tükles' father "Jalāl ad-Dīn"—who is in fact specified as *Sulṭān* Jalāl ad-Dīn *Rūmī* in the Central Asian *Maṭlab aṭ-ṭālibīn*, and appears also in Nūrullāh Khorezmī's account), but makes no mention of the work's information on his Yasavī affiliation. It is unfortunately not clear from these two brief notices by Togan what specific information on Baba Tükles is provided by this hagiography, and only its rediscovery, or perhaps access to Togan's notes, would allow a proper evaluation of this potentially important source.

fiable with the Yasavī order's "other" *Aḥmad*—Sayyid Aḥmad, known as Sayyid Ata.

In support of this identification, beyond the shared function of converting Özbek Khan to Islam (and the specific element of the drinking ceremony disrupted, at least implicitly, by both figures, as discussed in Chapter 3), we should first stress the name Aḥmad, well attested in Central Asian sources as Sayyid Ata's personal name; the honorific *khoja*, more closely associated with the Naqshbandīyah than with the Yasavīyah, was nevertheless often used in Central Asia as an equivalent of the term *sayyid*, implying descent from the Prophet Muḥammad. Sayyid Ata was from the region of Turkistan, if not from the town by that name, but in fact his place of origin is probably concealed in the designation by which our Baba Tükles is most widely known in the epic accounts: the *Shashlï/Chashlï/Chachtï ʿAzīz* is surely not the "hairy saint," but the "saint of *Chāch*," or Tashkent,[172] and Sayyid Ata's association with Tashkent, where he served Zangī Ata and from where he was sent to the Dasht-i Qïpchāq, is also well attested in the Central Asian hagiographical tradition.

In addition, the appearance of the town of Qumkent in both the Tatar histories (as the dwelling place of Edigü's father) and in the epic tales (as the place where Idige is left by his spirit-mother and found by Baba Tükles) may support the link with Sayyid Ata. Qumkent, as noted above, is known from Abū'l-Ghāzī[173] as the name of a town not far to the east of

172. Abdülkadir İnan must have reached the same conclusion, judging from Çağatay's comment ("Die Ädigä-Sage," p. 276, n. 4), but oddly enough Çağatay suggests instead that "Chashlï Aziz" means "the aged saint" (p. 264); Melioranskii also noted the possibility of interpreting "Shashlï 'Aziz" as "the saint of Shash" ("Skazanie," introduction, p. 10, n. 2), and suggested that interpretation as "the hairy saint" was a later, derivative understanding. Zhirmunskii ("Skazanie ob Idige," p. 383) doubts the interpretation of "Shashlï" as "Tashkentian," but offers no basis for his reservations. Despite the clear distinction between *sach*, "hair of the head," and *tük*, "body hair," the appellation "Tükles" might have encouraged the popular interpretation of "Chachlï ʿAzīz."

173. Abū'l-Ghāzī, ed. Desmaisons, II (text), pp. 220–222; cf. Bartol'd, "Svedeniia ob Aral'skom more," *Sochineniia*, III, pp. 63, 67, 88. Zhirmunskii ("Skazanie ob Idige," p. 383) maintains, without citing his source, that the Qumkent of the Idige tales is to be found in the "ancient city of Kumkent on the northern slopes of the Karatau [that is, in southern Kazakhstan], where also is found the legendary spring of this saint"; he notes that the Qazaq "cult" of Baba Tükles is associated with this region, although "his *mazar* is also mentioned as a cult center in the environs of Astrakhan." Zhirmunskii makes no mention of the more famous Khorezmian Qumkent. On the Qumkent in the Karatau, cf. E. I. Ageeva and G. I. Patsevich, "Iz istorii osedlykh poselenii i gorodov iuzhnogo Kazakhstana," *Trudy Instituta istorii, arkheologii, i ètnografii AN KazSSR*, t. 5 (Arkheologiia) (1958), pp. 112–113, where it is noted that this Qumkent is not described in any written sources. The greater likelihood that it is the Khorezmian Qumkent that

Vazīr in Khorezm, near the Amu Darya rather than the "Nile" of the epics; Sayyid Ata himself is said to have settled in Khorezm following his "missionary" activity in the Dasht-i Qïpchāq, and in fact we also know from Abū'l-Ghāzī that Sayyid Ata's descendants continued to live in the region of Vazīr at least as late as the sixteenth century.[174]

Moreover, a key feature in the "mythologized" tale of Idige Biy is echoed in the life of Sayyid Ata: the epic account of Baba Tükles' loss of his son, explained as his spirit-wife's revenge for his violation of his vow, is paralleled by a well-known story about Sayyid Ata, in which Sayyid Ata's son is stolen by a band of "Turks from the Dasht-i Qïpchāq" in divinely ordained punishment for Sayyid Ata's hostility toward the Khojagānī shaykh ʿAlī ʿAzīzān Rāmitanī (d. 1321).[175]

Finally, Central Asian legendary cycles surrounding Sayyid Ata include two curious elements familiar from Ötemish Ḥājjī's account of Baba Tükles. In Turkic accounts preserved in at least two manuscripts in Tashkent, the process of converting Özbek Khan involves a similar ordeal by fire (though here only one oven is heated up for both the *kāfir* and the Muslim saint),[176] while in other accounts even the *tük* for which Baba Tükles was named is associated also with Sayyid Ata: we learn in one passage[177] that Sayyid Ata was an extremely intense and zealous person, and "when he got angry all of his body hair would stand straight up and come out of his garment." The description so closely parallels the account of Baba Tükles in Ötemish Ḥājjī's work that it may be taken as a convincing indication that one and the same figure inspired both narratives.

---

figures in the Idige/Edigü legends is suggested also by its mention in the early fifteenth-century work of Muʿīn ad-Dīn Naṭanzī, as noted in Chapter 5.

174. Ed. Desmaisons, II (text), pp. 196–197, I (transl.), pp. 211–212. The prominence, in a nearby town, of another descendant of Sayyid Ata, Sayyid Nāṣir Khoja, is attested for the era of Muḥammad Shïbānī Khan's conquest of Khorezm in 1505 in the *Tavārīkh-i guzīdah-i nuṣrat-nāmah* (cf. *Materialy po istorii kazakhskikh khanstv*, p. 23; Akramov facs., p. 278) and in Bannāʾī's *Shaybānī-nāmah* (*Materialy*, p. 114).

175. The story is recorded in the *Rashaḥāt-i ʿayn al-ḥayāt* at the very beginning of the sixteenth century; cf. the edition of Muʿīnīyān, I, pp. 68–69. Stories of "foundling" ancestors are especially common in legends of dynastic origins, presumably because of a wish (for purposes of legitimation or panegyric or both) to assert an underlying noble stock for "founders" (and patrons) of more humble origins; such stories might easily take shape even in the case of figures better represented as historical personages, as, for instance, in the widely known legend casting the Ming tribal dynasty of the Qoqand khanate as descendants of "Altun Beshik" ("Golden Cradle"), an infant son whom Bābur was forced to abandon as he fled the Farghānah valley (see the synopsis in T.K. Beisembiev, *"Taʾrikh-i Shakhrukhi" kak istoricheskii istochnik* [Alma-Ata: Nauka, 1987], pp. 83–84).

176. MS IVANUz, Inv. No. 5738, f. 64b; Inv. No. 5398, ff. 53b–54a.

177. MS IVANUz, Inv. No. 185, f. 13b; Inv. No. 5398, f. 60b (here using Persian *mūy* in place of *tük*).

There are problems with the identification, most notably in the genealogies ascribed to the two figures. The lack of correspondence between the actual names in the genealogies of Sayyid Ata and Baba Tükles is perhaps less troublesome than the ascription of two wholly separate lineages to the two: Sayyid Ata is, naturally, of ʿAlid descent, while Idige and Baba Tükles are ascribed descent from Abū Bakr. This may be explained by the growing disfavor toward specifically ʿAlid genealogies in the Sunnī world from the sixteenth century, or more simply, by the tradition preserved in Central Asian sources naming Sayyid Ata's father "Abū Bakr."[178] In any event, this discrepancy should most likely not weigh heavily against the proposed identification of the figures of Sayyid Ata and Baba Tükles.

Against this identification may also be cited, naturally, the eighteenth-century Khorezmian account identifying Baba Tükles not with Sayyid Ata, but with his companion Ṣadr Ata. If we accept the unique text asserting this identification as an authentic reflection of oral tradition current in Khorezm, the case for seeing in Baba Tükles and Sayyid Ata the same figure would be considerably weakened by this independent testimony. It is more likely, however, as argued above, that the text in question reflects a learned attempt by someone aware of both the oral traditions about Baba Tükles—and here he seems clearly to transmit elements of his legend derived from oral sources not reflected elsewhere—*and* of the literary tradition in Central Asian hagiography that ascribed the Islamization of the Dasht-i Qïpchāq to Sayyid Ata and his companions. An identification with the ʿAlid Sayyid Ata would then be out of the question for this learned "historicizer," since the connection of Baba Tükles and Edigü with Abū Bakr was too strong to allow any confusion of their lineages.

It is thus tempting to see in the figures of Sayyid Ata and Baba Tükles, both "saints of Tashkent," two legendary presentations of the activities of one individual. The version focused on "Sayyid Ata" would represent the account that became established in the Central Asian literary tradition already in the fifteenth or sixteenth century, as reflected in the *Shajarat al-atrāk*, and that connected the establishment of Islam by Sayyid Ata with the formative period of the Uzbek "nation"; it may have originated among the Qonghrat tribes near Khorezm, but the memory of Sayyid Ata's activity in converting the peoples of the Dasht-i Qïpchāq to

178. *Maqāmāt-i Sayyid Atāʾī*, MS India Office Ethé 644, f. 15b; *Shajarat al-atrāk*, MS India Office Ethé 172, f. 153b.

Islam was preserved among his natural and spiritual descendants in Khorezm and Bukhara.[179] The version focused on "Baba Tükles" would then represent the oral tradition widespread among all the peoples of the Jöchid *ulus*, who recalled Baba Tükles as a Muslim saint and made of him a protective, patron spirit, but particularly strong among the Noghays/Manghïts, who conceived of the figure responsible for establishing Islam among them as the "founder" of the Noghay "nation" in natural as well as spiritual terms. The appearance of Baba Tükles in our sixteenth-century Khorezmian literary source is no doubt to be credited to Ötemish Ḥājjī's extensive use of oral tradition and to his own travels in the western regions of the former Golden Horde, including Astrakhan.[180]

If Baba Tükles and Sayyid Ata indeed reflect, at least, the same legendary figure, the core of the tradition that grew around this figure's activity is fairly clear: he came from Tashkent with three companions, and after a confrontation and contest with the representatives of the native Mongol tradition at the court of Özbek Khan, succeeded in demonstrating the greater power of Islam and thereby converted the khan and his people. The special place he holds in Noghay tradition may stem from his links with Khorezm, with which the career of the historical Edigü was closely bound; it may even be conjectured that the story of Sayyid Ata's loss of his son, and its possible refraction in the tales of Baba Tükles' foundling son, allowed partisans of Edigü to claim sacred parentage for him as the saint's "lost son."

It is considerably more risky, however, to attempt to reconstruct from the genealogical, legendary, and mythic accounts the "actual" events and figures instrumental in the Islamization of the Golden Horde. Certainly no such attempt is reasonable before a more complete study of the legendary cycles surrounding the figure suggested as the Central Asian version of Baba Tükles, namely Sayyid Ata. Beyond this reservation, however, based

179. Cf. *Maqāmat-i Sayyid Atā'ī*, ff. 16a–b, and the legendary cycles preserved in the Tashkent manuscripts cited above.

180. While Ötemish Ḥājjī cites no specific source of information for his account of Özbek Khan's conversion, the origin of the sources he cites elsewhere in his work illustrate the strong "western" orientation of the oral material he presents. He names as sources of oral information (1) a certain Ḥājjī Niyāz, a wealthy man of Ḥājjī Tarkhān (Astrakhan), (2) Shaykh Aḥmad Khan of Ḥājjī Tarkhān, (3) Khiṭāy Baba ʿAlī, also of Ḥājjī Tarkhān and an official of ʿAbd al-Karīm Khan, and finally (4) Ilbars Khan, the founder of the Khorezmian Uzbek dynasty (cf. Bartol'd, *Sochineniia*, VIII, pp. 166–167); of these even the "Khorezmian" Ilbars Khan grew up in the Noghay/Manghït-dominated regions of the Jöchid *ulus*. Of later "native" Khorezmians he cites only Dūst Sulṭān himself, who provided information, however, not from his memory, but from his *daftar*.

in the inadequate analysis of the full body of material bearing on the figure of Sayyid Ata, the basic soundness of such an approach must be questioned due to the prevalence of religious, symbolic, and literary conventions (both written and oral) in the type of material available. To infer from the agreement of some accounts that indeed four Muslims went to convert Özbek Khan, including Sayyid Ata and perhaps his son, ascribes historicity to what is most likely an Islamic (and also Inner Asian) convention of four companions (the four Caliphs, the four "martyred imams" of East Turkistan, the four companions of Er Töshtük, etc.); to suppose that the recurrent theme of the saint's body hair indicates not merely a symbolic aura of sacred power,[181] but a "historical" Sayyid Ata so marked by this feature that he became known in the Dasht-i Qïpchāq as "Baba Tükles," or that the account of the disputation and fiery "competition" reflects an actual religious "contest" rather than the implicit link of an Islamic paradigm (conversion as conquest) with an Inner Asian one (religion as power), is not only to ascribe historical reality to narrative conventions: *it is to miss the point and misconstrue the sources*. We are dealing here not with any *ordinary* "history," but with *sacred* history, and likewise not with any ordinary "legends" or bits of folklore, but with accounts focused on the profoundly sacred matter of communal (=human) origins. It is the specifically *religious* character of the "legends" that must be kept in mind here, for as fundamentally religious narratives recounting "sacred ethnogony," these accounts inevitably participate in the *assertive* character of religious language, which is intended as much to *make* a reality as to report it. In sacred history the "truth" of a narrative lies immediately in its telling, and such accounts must be appreciated as vehicles for evoking, reinforcing, and "mobilizing"—and thereby re-creating—the affective bonds of social identity and cohesion that may rightly define and constitute a human community.

In short, these accounts are not so much "sources" yielding clues on "real history" as examples of an ongoing process of articulating and adapting the traditional stock of sacred narratives—not only as *reflections* of changing social and communal groupings, but as active and conscious assertions of "history" designed in effect to *create* new social groupings by reifying latent communal loyalties. What seems most significant in all these accounts, then, is not the reworking of "history" into legend or myth, but the reworking of one narrative (admittedly multivalent in its

181. See Chapter 5 on the numinous associations of *tük*.

original form), focused on Islamization, into narratives of sacred communal origins that often appear on the surface to be of distinctly non-Islamic character, but that in effect signal the nativization and indigenous appropriation of Islam.

7

Baba Tükles and the Uses of Sacred Origins

The multiple roles played by Baba Tükles in the epic and folkloric material examined in the preceding chapter—Tribal Ancestor, Mythic Progenitor, Communal Legitimizer, Islamizer, Patron Saint, Shamanic Protector, Sufi Preceptor, etc.—have in common a focus on familial or communal or confessional *origins* and an accompanying sense of the ongoing relationship between the particular collectivity at issue and its originator. We will conclude our exploration of Baba Tükles' religious meaning in Islamic Inner Asia with more general considerations about his status as a focus for articulating notions of sacred origins, in particular the notions of sacred *communal* origins that typically provide the basis for assertions of communal integrity and legitimacy. We will first consider the specific thematic and structural parallels that reinforce the equivalence, posited above, of ethnogonic tales and conversion narratives, and thereby highlight the enormous resonance of Baba Tükles as the hero of both; we will then suggest the directions his mythic and narrative development took, and finally consider the implications of the narrative patterns underlying tales of ethnogony and conversion for broader questions of religion and communal identity in Islamic Inner Asia.

Baba Tükles and Legends of Origin: Parallel Structures and Themes

As noted above, in the oral tradition surrounding the role of Baba Tükles in the formation of the Noghay horde, his "Islamizing" function is acknowledged at times explicitly, and at times only obliquely; indeed, there is not even an echo, in the tales of Idige, of the actual narrative account of Baba Tükles' activities as given by Ötemish Ḥājjī, with the possible exception of the Noghay version which recounts something of a "contest" between Baba Tükles and an unnamed khan's "wise men." To be sure, Baba Tükles' initial prestige and sacred role as a national or ethnic "founder" clearly stem from his "Islamizing" function, which is in a sense implicitly present even in those developments of his character most removed from a decidedly Islamic conceptual milieu. Even when his role as originator of an *Islamic* community is only dimly preserved, however, his status as a communal originator is almost never in doubt; if he is not *always* cast in popular memory explicitly as a bringer of Islam, he is nearly always cast as the founder/ancestor of a particular community (or of a hero who serves as a focus for communal identity). This is so because Baba Tükles was incorporated, probably quite early but in any case quite seamlessly, into the traditional, pre-Islamic Inner Asian conception of how a people is formed, and indeed of how history begins.

While in Islamic terms a people's history (or at least its significant, sacred history) begins with its entry into the *Dār al-Islām*, in Inner Asian terms sacred history begins with the "First Man," understood as the "Ancestor" and/or First Ruler of a particular tribe, clan, or confederation; in both cases the focus is on the formation and/or organization of human community, and while Sayyid Ata, for instance, serves as the "Islamic originator" for the Uzbek confederation, Baba Tükles fulfills, for the peoples of the Jöchid *ulus* in general, both the "Islamic" and "Inner Asian" expectations for the "founder" or "establisher" of a people or community. We may conceptualize the process whereby Baba Tükles came to fit both patterns as occuring in three stages, as the "Islamizer" is first identified (and venerated) as the founder of a religious community, then equated with the founder/ancestor of a more broadly defined human group (i.e., a "tribe" or "people," whose origins are no less prone to be understood as being of a "sacred" character for being defined in less narrowly "religious" terms), and finally "universalized" into the mythic First Man. This conceptualization suggests a sequential development from a hypothetical Baba Tükles as founder of a religiously-defined subgroup (i.e., of the Muslims, say, of Özbek Khan's entourage, or of the Golden Horde at large), to Baba Tükles as "founder" of the Noghay confederation and ancestor of its aristocracy, to Baba Tükles as mythic protector and First Man; but it is probably wiser not to ascribe a neat chronological sequence for the persona of Baba Tükles, however convenient such a model may be, since in all "stages" what is at work is a fundamentally *religious* discourse able to operate and convey meaning at multiple levels simultaneously.

In any event, the final "stage," a tendency to "universalize" the origins of a particular community, is a common process facilitated by the evocation of universal, sacred symbols and patterns as noted earlier, and seems to occur naturally, without necessary connection to the first two; that is, the widespread communal, human inclination to understand "us" as the true human beings, "our origins" as the beginning of (meaningful) time, "our ancestors" as the First People, and "our destruction" as the end of the world, would assert itself regardless of Islamization or other transformation.The key step, then, is that initial equation, of Islamizer as communal founder. It is this crucial equation that informs the wealth of Inner Asian "popular ethnogonies" making Islamization the central event in communal origins (to be explored in a later setting); and it is this equation that sets the stage for the full range of mythic elaboration we find for Baba Tükles, as he is identified as the *founder* of a (sacral) community and surrounded with mythic symbols and a discursive pattern proper to that role.

We thus find elements of legends of communal origin well known in Inner Asian tradition attached to Baba Tükles, involving a number of themes recurrently evoked in ethnogonic tales; specifically, in the epic and folkloric context the most striking parallels appear in three major developments of the figure of Baba Tükles, namely his "marriage" to a maiden found in or by the sea, his dalliance with the "swan-maidens," and his origin from the ashes of a skull. Beyond these themes, we find additional structural and thematic parallels with legends of origin in the further development of the Idige tale with which Baba Tükles is so closely associated (e.g., in the abandonment of Idige beneath a tree), while, as discussed earlier, themes and narrative structures typically employed in recounting communal origins and communally significant shamanic quests (e.g., the themes of enclosure and emergence) are attached to Baba Tükles already in the work of Ötemish Ḥājjī. Here we will highlight the parallels with legends of origin found in the epic and folkloric material, as the most "popular" and meaningful venue for the developments of Baba Tükles' character.

Potanin long ago noted the similarity between the accounts of Baba Tükles' involvement with the bird-maiden combing her hair by the sea[1] and the episode in the Kimek legend of origin as reported by Gardīzī in the eleventh century;[2] in this account,[3] the first ruler (and "founder") of the Kimek, called Shad, one day heard a voice coming from the water as he stood on the banks of the Irtysh; the voice said, "Shad, give me your hand in the water." Shad, seeing only some hair floating on the surface of the water, tethered his horse and entered the water; he grasped the hair, which turned out to belong to his wife-to-be, called Khatun, and upon inquiring, he learned that she had been seized from the riverbank by a water dragon. Gardīzī's story ends affirming the sacredness of the Irtysh to the Kimek, but in fact the account includes a longer narrative on the origins of the Kimek marked by several mythic motifs characteristic of Inner Asian founder myths and legends of origin; it is, indeed, curious that the close parallels between the account of Kimek origins (in its entirety, and not merely the water-maiden motif) given by Gardīzī and other Inner Asian legends of origin have apparently never been noted, for the parallels highlight a mythic complex associated with sacred origins that is strikingly common throughout Inner Asia.

In its entirety this ethnogonic mythic complex links the sacred mythic symbols, discussed in Chapter 1, of a Mountain, a Tree, a Cave, a body of

1. From an Islamic perspective, Baba Tükles' involvement with "sea spirits" echoes the mythical transformation of Khiḍr, who indeed figures in some of the epic accounts of Baba Tükles, and who was often closely associated in Islamic lore with the sea and sea spirits; cf. I. Friedlaender, *Die Chadhirlegende und der Alexanderroman: Eine sagengeschichtliche und literarhistorische Untersuchung* (Leipzig/Berlin: B.G. Teubner, 1913), esp. pp. 107–123. On the shamanic symbolism of the feminine helping-spirit, cf. Eliade, *Shamanism*, pp. 75–81.

2. G. N. Potanin, *Vostochnye motivy v srednevekovom evropeiskom èpose* (Moscow, 1899), p. 179; cf. his "Doch' moria v stepnom èpose," *Ètnograficheskoe obozrenie*, 1892, No. 1, pp. 38–69.

3. For Gardīzī's account, see Bartol'd, "Izvlechenie iz Zain al-Akhbar," *Sochineniia*, VIII, pp. 27 (text), 44 (transl.), J. Marquart's "Über das Volkstum der Komanen" (in W. Bang and J. Marquart, *Osttürkische Dialektstudien* [Berlin, 1914; Abhandlungen der Königlichen Gesellschaft der Wissenschaften zu Göttingen, Phil.-hist. Klasse, n. F., Bd. XIII], pp. 89–91, and especially the English translation (signaling important emendations to the text from ʿAbd al-Ḥayy Ḥabībī's edition, *Tārīkh-i Gardīzī* [Tehran, 1347/1968; repr. Tehran: Chāpkhānah-i Armaghān, 1363/1984; pp. 549–554 on the Kimek], as well) by A. P. Martinez, upon which I have relied: "Gardīzī's Two Chapters on the Turks," *AEMA*, 2 (1982), pp. 109–175, pp. 120–121 on the Kimek. In particular, Ḥabībī's reading, in which the voice says to Shad "Give me your hand," is obviously preferable to the reading of both Bartol'd and Marquart, wherein the voice asks "Did you see me in the water?"

Water, and a Feminine Spirit, with the birth of the "first man" (or of the ancestor of a particular people, or of the ancestor of that people's rulers, mythically and symbolically equivalent), a threat to the ancestor (usually in his infancy) or to the "people" as a whole, and the flight, concealment, "protective abandonment," and/or "enclosure" of the ancestor (or, already, of his people); it is a familiar archaic cosmogonic theme widely encountered in Inner Asia, recurring (in its entirety or in varying combinations of the elements) in an impressive number of legends of origin among Inner Asian peoples,[4] as well as in the birth stories (and tales of rebirth) among epic and shamanic heroes. The mythic complex that provides the "setting" for these stories was outlined earlier, and we have considered several examples of legends of origin reported for "historical" peoples in the course of examining specific elements evoked also in tales of Baba Tükles. It may be useful here, however, to summarize the major "historical" Inner Asian legends of origin, recalling those discussed in part above and introducing others.

The Mythic Complex

To begin with, the association of the first man, the "tree of all seeds," the lake Vourukasha, the river spirit Harahvaiti, and the world mountain is familiar from the ancient Iranian cosmogony;[5] this complex was no doubt known widely among the ancient Iranian population of Inner Asia, and has the advantage of being "preserved," through echoes in the Avesta and Zoroastrian writings, in what amount to "indigenous" sources.

The same complex seems to be reflected in both of the famous Scythian legends of origin recounted by Herodotus: in one, the ancestor of the Scythians is the son of Zeus and the daughter of the river Borysthenes, while the second makes him the son of Heracles and a "viper-maiden" encountered in a cave in a forest.[6]

4. Roux (*Faune et flore*, pp. 281–380) has assembled a wide-ranging collection of Inner Asian legends of origin, without, however, highlighting the common elements of the mythic association under consideration here.

5. Cf. Mary Boyce, *A History of Zoroastrianism*, vol. I, "The Early Period" (Leiden: E. J. Brill, 1975; Handbuch der Orientalistik I.8.1.2.2A), pp. 131–141.

6. Cf. Herodotus, *The Histories*, tr. Aubrey de Sélincourt (Penguin edition, 1972), pp. 273–274. For analyses of the legends (which make no reference, however, to legends of origin among later Inner Asian peoples), cf. A. A. Neikhardt, *Skifskii rasskaz Gerodota v otechestvennoi istoriografii* (Leningrad: Nauka, 1982), pp. 203–206, and D. S. Raevskii, *Ocherki ideologii skifo-sakskikh plemen: opyt rekonstruktsii skifskoi mifologii* (Moscow: Nauka, GRVL, 1977); a portion of the latter

A Hun legend of origin reflected, imperfectly, in Jordanes' *Gothic History* of the sixth century, probably masks a similar tale. Here we find a preliminary passage of uncertain origin followed by an account ascribed to the Byzantine historian Priscus, who traveled among the Huns of Attila's day.[7] Jordanes first cites "old traditions" in characterizing the Huns as the descendants of "witches" expelled from among the Goths and "unclean spirits" in the "wilderness"; their offspring lived first in the "swamps," and specific mention is made of their barely human language. In the supernatural origin itself, as in the elements of feminine "witch" spirits, early habitation of "swamps" (paralleling the description of the Türk ancestor's initial refuge), and a possible echo of the mention of the people's murmuring inside their enclosure, we may find traces of the same complex. Jordanes next cites Priscus in again mentioning the Huns' dwelling in swamps, and in recounting a clear parallel to the themes of enclosure and emergence, and of guidance by an animal spirit: hunters from among the Huns saw a doe appear to them that, "now advancing and again standing still,"[8] guided them into and out of the swamp to their new abode ("Scythia"); "as they were quick of mind, they believed that this path, utterly unknown to any age of the past, had been divinely revealed to them," and therefore "returned to their tribe" and persuaded them to move to the newfound land.

With the Türks of eastern Inner Asia in the sixth century, we find three legends of origin that are likewise known exclusively from external,

---

work is available in English translation as "The Scythian Genealogical Legend," tr. Michel Vale, *SAA*, 21/1–2 (Summer-Fall 1982), pp. 33–66, 21/3 (Winter 1982–1983), pp. 80–122.

7. *The Gothic History of Jordanes*, tr. Charles Christopher Mierow (Princeton: Princeton University Press, 1915), pp. 85–86; cf. C. D. Gordon, *The Age of Attila: Fifth-Century Byzantium and the Barbarians* (Ann Arbor: University of Michigan Press, 1960), pp. 57–58, giving only the section cited by Priscus. Jordanes's account of the Huns was based on the lost Gothic history of Cassiodorus (487–583), who in turn extensively quoted from Priscus's account; cf. Maenchen-Helfen, *World of the Huns*, pp. 15–17.

8. This echoes a specific narrative feature of accounts of the mythic animal guide in Juvaynī 's account of the Uyghurs and Michael the Syrian's description of the Oghuz. In general the theme of ancestral enclosure in and emergence from a mountain-ringed plain or cavern, discussed in Chapter 4, is often linked with the ancestors' protection and/or guidance by a protective animal; when its gender is indicated, this animal is invariable female, and this immediately recalls the protective female spirit of the Mountain/Tree/Water complex. The most reasonable understanding of the doe that leads the Huns, the she-wolf/dog who leads the Turks, etc., is that it reflects the same mother/mate female spirit reflected otherwise in the maiden by the sea, in the swan-maiden, in the maidens who visit the Uyghur ancestor and the Türk ancestor, in the mythical pairs (wolf and doe, horse and bull) that meet at the juncture of two rivers (cf. the Qïtan legend noted below) or together cross a river to establish themselves at a sacred mountain (as in the Mongol *Secret History*).

in this case Chinese, sources.[9] One begins with the near-extermination of the Türks' ancestors; a single boy survived, in a marsh, and was nourished by a she-wolf, who eventually fled with the boy to a cavern inside a distant mountain by a sea. Inside the cavern was a broad and well-watered plain enclosed by mountains, which became the refuge for the boy and the wolf, his "mother"-turned-wife; she bore the boy ten sons who became the ancestors of the Türks, and several generations later their descendants were led out from the cavern.

A second involves one ancestral ruler of the Türks who was born from a wolf and had power over the wind and rain; he married the daughters of the Spirit of the Summer and of the Spirit of the Winter, one of whom bore him four sons: one turned into a swan, while the other three are said to have established their realms at particular sites marked by specific rivers or mountains. The eldest of these sons gave the Türks the gift of fire, and the legend concludes by noting that this figure's sons chose his successor by gathering beneath a great tree and selecting the one among them who could jump the highest up the tree.

The third is perhaps most reminiscent of elements of the tales of Baba Tükles, and also bears striking parallels to the Uyghur legend reported by Juvaynī, as well as to the Hun legend. This tale involves the ancestor of the Türks, who was brought each night into a lake by a white deer sent by the daughter of the lake spirit to fetch him. These underwater trysts continued for many years, until, on the eve of a great hunt, the lake spirit told the man the conditions under which their meetings could continue: he would see, the next day, a white deer with golden horns emerging from the cavern where his ancestors were born, and he should make sure that his arrow struck the deer. The next day the deer indeed came out of the ancestral cavern; but a man from another tribe shot it, whereupon the Türks' ancestor beheaded the man and instituted the rite of sacrificing a man from the same tribe. The lake spirit then informed the man that their encounters were over—not, evidently, because he had failed to meet her conditions, but because he had shed the blood of another man.

The ethnogonic complex is most clearly evident in the third of these legends, in which the cavern, the lake spirit, and a guiding/protecting creature (here a white deer, recalling the Hun legend) appear alongside

9. Cf. Sinor, "Legendary Origin of the Türks," pp. 223–257; see also the presentation of the accounts by Nobuo Yamada, "The Original Turkish Homeland," in *Journal of Turkish Studies*, 9 (1985), pp. 243–246, and the discussion of Hilda Ecsedy, "Tribe and Tribal Society in the 6th Century Turk Empire," *AOH*, 25 (1972), pp. 245–262 [pp. 250–252].

the supernatural maiden beneath the sea. If we may assume that the Chinese accounts are rather garbled versions of Turkic legends, however, traces of the same complex are probably present in the second version (where the ancestress is the daughter of a spirit, either of the summer or of the winter, someone turns into a swan, and we learn of "states" established between or along particular rivers and mountains) as well as in the first (in which elements of threat and flight, the animal guide/protector, and protective enclosure in a cavern are combined).

The narrative kernel in this first Türk legend—the destruction of the ancestor's people, leaving him virtually alone, the flight of the ancestor with his "mistress" to a verdant valley, and the growth and spread among the mountains of the people who made the ancestor their chief—appears, with the order of elements rearranged, in Gardīzī's full version of the Kimek legend of origin. Here, before "Shad" finds his future wife in the water, he had come to the future Kimek land along the Irtysh as a refugee from his elder brother, whose succession to their father's rank he had opposed; accompanied only by a slave-girl, Shad came to a land with a great river, many trees, and good hunting, where they pitched their tent and lived, dressed in animal skins. Soon seven men from among their people joined them, seeking pasturelands; Shad was hospitable to them, and they stayed through the winter. When one of them returned to their homeland in the spring, however, he found that their enemies had destroyed the country and killed most of the people; the survivors listened to the man's account of Shad, and gladly joined him, soon multiplying and forming the seven tribes of the Kimeks.

The same structure, of threat and flight, appears also at the beginning of the genealogical "history" of the Yurmatï Bashkir tribe discussed in Chapter 6, which also includes the motif of the enclosed ancestor/saint; it also appears in the Indian versions of the Mongol legend of origin, known from Rashīd ad-Dīn, in which the specific element of "tree-birth," as echoed in accounts of Uyghur origins, appears as well (see Chapter 4).

We find other echoes of the same mythic complex in Islamic geographical literature dealing with the Turkic peoples of Inner Asia. The tenth-century *al-Āthār al-bāqīyah* of al-Bīrūnī and, no doubt based on it for this passage, the eleventh-century *Ākām al-marjān* most likely written in Spain by one Isḥāq b. Ḥusayn, record an account we may suppose to be based on travelers' tales ultimately reflecting local popular tradition. It appears in the midst of geographical descriptions, but its mythic tone stands out clearly, and the account may reflect either the Islamic writers' concretization of originally mythic tales accessible to them, or the not unusual tendency to create or imagine a concrete cultic reflection of a mythic complex. In the *Ākām al-marjān*, in the discussion of the land of the Turks, we find descriptions paralleling accounts of the Kimeks known from other sources, and then the following passage: "In their country there is a mighty mountain with a tree on it. On the tree are the marks of two hands, two feet, and a knee, as if (some one had been) worshipping there. And everyone of them who notices those traces worships them."[10] Bīrūnī's account paralleling this passage omits the tree, but adds a spring and more details on what may be seen at this sacred site. Bīrūnī's description appears in the account of a lake near Ṭūs in Khurāsān, which he then compares to a "spring of fresh water in the land of the Kīmāk in a mountain called M.nkūr"; and perhaps reflecting narrative traditions asserting this spring's miraculous qualities as an inexhaustible source, he continues: "The level of the water in it is up to the brim, and sometimes an army drinks from it and it does not dwindle a finger's breadth. Near this spring, there is a trace of a man's foot, of his palms with their five fingers and of his knees, as if he had been worshipping; and also traces of the steps of a child and of the hooves of a donkey. And whenever the Ghuzz Turks see (that place) they worship it."[11] We are no doubt justified in seeing in these accounts a description of the sacred association of mountain, tree, and water, with echoes of a specific ritual function; the "child" most likely reflects an ancestor's birth there in the "original" of the narrative, and the donkey's hooves probably signal the presence of a protective/guiding animal spirit as well.[12]

From eastern Inner Asia, a Qïtan legend of origin is reflected in Chinese sources from the twelfth century.[13] It reports the origin of the eight tribes of the Qïtan from eight sons of a "divine man" on a white horse and

10. Tr. V. Minorsky in his "The Khazars and the Turks in the *Ākām al-Marjān*," *BSOS*, 9 (1937), pp. 141–150 [p. 147, from Sachau's text (Leipzig, 1878), p. 264]; see also the translation, from a more recently discovered manuscript of the text, by Richard N. Frye, "A New Arabic Geographical Manuscript," *Journal of Near Eastern Studies*, 8 (1949), pp. 90–97 [p. 92].

11. Tr. Minorsky, "The Khazars and the Turks," p. 147, from Sachau's text, p. 264.

12. A specific *ritual* implicitly connected with this mythic complex is suggested in the *Ākām al-marjān* in a further description of the same "Turks": "The people are idol-worshipers. They have one holiday in the year on which the people of every village go out with their idols to a place (where there is) a spring and trees. Then they set up (the idols) and cast lots. Thereupon one of (the people), who is *kāhin* [i.e., a "sorcerer," = shaman], approaches them and walks around them for a time. Then he approaches them (i.e., the people) and informs them what will transpire, (both) good and evil, during the year. This *kāhin* comes from a well-known family" (tr. Frye, "A New Arabic Geographical Manuscript," p. 92; the passage is not translated or discussed by Minorsky).

13. See the translation in Karl A. Wittfogel and Fêng Chia-shêng, *History of Chinese Society:*

a "heavenly maiden riding a cart drawn by a gray ox"; each traveled down a river to the point, near a mountain, where the rivers joined, and there these two ancestral figures met and mated to produce the Qïtan people, and Qïtan ancestral veneration continued to entail the sacrifice of a white horse and gray ox, suggesting these creatures' roles as "guiding" animal spirits.

As noted in Chapter 4, the twelfth-century chronicler Michael the Syrian records Oghuz legends of their origins among mountains called "the breasts of the earth," from which they emerged through the guidance of a supernatural creature paralleling the guiding animal spirit of the Huns and sixth-century Turks. Hints of the same mythic complex are likewise evident in the legend of origin of the Uyghurs, as reported by Juvaynī in the thirteenth century and by a fourteenth-century Chinese account; elements of these tales were discussed in Chapter 4, but we may recall here the setting of the hero/ancestor's birth from the light-impregnated mounds located beneath two trees at the juncture of two rivers, the hero's visitation by a supernatural maiden (recalling one of the Türk legends), and a migration of the Uyghurs, led by the cries of animals (recalling Michael the Syrian's account of the Oghuz). The conception and protection of the Uyghur ancestors within the subterranean chambers likewise echoes the themes of enclosure and emergence found both in a Türk legend of origin and in the tale of Ergene Qun, involving a similar enclosure in a setting marked by the complex of Mountain/Tree/Cave/Water; as noted earlier, in the case of the Uyghur hero/ancestors, the people outside the enclosed chambers hear singing from within, providing an additional parallel to the sounds of Baba Tükles' voice heard from inside the oven-pit. Juvaynī's account of the Uyghurs in fact combines several motifs of interest for us, and suggests an important developmental sequence; we will return to its larger significance shortly.

From the same era as our records of the Uyghur tale, the beginning of the *Secret History* of the Mongols, with the ancestral animals crossing the sea and settling at the headwaters of a river by a sacred mountain, un-

---

Liao (907–1125) (Philadelphia: American Philosophical Society, 1949; Transactions, n.s., vol. 36), p. 272; cf. the translations in Rolf Stein, "Leao- tche," *T'oung Pao,* 35 (1940), pp. 1–154 [pp. 10–12], and in Herbert Franke, "The Forest Peoples of Manchuria: Kitans and Jurchens," in Sinor, ed., *Cambridge History of Early Inner Asia,* pp. 400–423 [p. 405]. The ritual counterpart to the Qïtan origin myth, and its later reverberations, are explored in Françoise Aubin, "Cheval céleste et bovin chtonien," in *Quand le crible était dans la paille . . . Hommage à Pertev Naili Boratav,* ed. Rémy Dor and Michèle Nicolas (Paris: G.-P. Maisonneuve et Larose, 1978), pp. 37–63.

doubtedly reflects the same structure.[14] The Indian version of Mongol origins, recorded by Rashīd ad-Dīn, was mentioned earlier; it resembles the Uyghur legend of origin as reported by Juvaynī, with the Mongols' ancestress bearing children inside a hollow tree.

Finally, among "historical" legends of origin may be noted the account, discussed in Chapter 4, from the fourteenth-century history of Ibn ad-Dawādārī, combining the Mountain/Water/Cave complex with specific assertions of the ritual implications of the Turks' origin myth. This account is of additional interest insofar as it illustrates the transition from legends of origin reported for specific historical peoples to more generic or abstracted stories preserved in literary accounts with less clearly "historical" referents. Ibn ad-Dawādārī's account purports to recount the origins of the Turks and Mongols together, rather than of specific Turkic or Mongol groups at a given time, and in this regard mirrors the account of Oghuz origins known from the versions of the story of Oghuz Khan.

The epic-style Uyghur-script version of the legend of Oghuz Qaghan, reflecting similar tales in a literary context, describes the hero's encounter with two beautiful maidens who bear his six sons, the first appearing in a blue ray of light shining down from heaven, and the other found in the hollow of a tree in the middle of a lake.[15] Some of these legendary elements appear also in the "Islamized" version of the story of Oghuz Khan as preserved in Rashīd ad-Dīn, Abū'l-Ghāzī, and other historical works, in which the hero's Islamic character is introduced as well:[16] as an infant Oghuz

14. Cf. De Rachewiltz, tr., "Secret History," *Papers on Far Eastern History*, 4 (1971), p. 118, §1; the junction of two rivers figures in Juvaynī's account of Uyghur origins and in the Chinese record of Qïtan origins, as noted.

15. Cf. the edition of Bang and Rachmati, pp. 688–691; Shcherbak ed., pp. 27–31. The elements of this mythic complex are evoked with extraordinary frequency, as noted earlier, in epic literature, hero-tales, and shamanic narratives, where an encounter with a feminine ancestral spirit at the base of a great tree, or inside a cave, is a virtually obligatory feature.

16. For Rashīd ad-Dīn's version, see Karl Jahn, tr., *Die Geschichte der Oġuzen des Rašīd ad-Dīn* (Vienna: Österreichische Akademie der Wissenschaften/Hermann Böhlaus Nachf., 1969); cf. Fazlallakh Rashid ad-Din, *Oguz-name*, tr. R. M. Shukiurova (Baku: Èlm, 1987); see also A. N. Bernshtam, "Istoricheskaia pravda v legende ob Oguz-kagane," *Sovetskaia ètnografiia*, 1935, No. 6, pp. 33–43, discussing the "pagan" version and the versions of Rashīd ad-Dīn and Abū'l-Ghāzī. For the latter's two versions, which differ considerably in detail, see Desmaisons' ed., pp. 13–25 (text and tr. volumes), and Kononov, *Rodoslovnaia*, pp. 40–54 (tr.), 13–38 (text). The versions of Rashīd ad-Dīn and Abū'l-Ghāzī were compared in the dissertation of Penrose, "The Politics of Genealogy," pp. 70–132, but there were in fact several other versions (both Persian and Turkic) of the Oghuz Khan legend produced in Central Asia before Abū'l-Ghāzī's time that would bear closer study and comparison; cf. Z. B. Mukhamedova, "Neskol 'ko slov ob antroponimakh v Oguz-Name iz sochineniia Salar Baba," in *Onomastika Srednei Azii* (Moscow: Nauka, GRVL, 1978), pp. 169–171; and for example the accounts in the Turkic *Tavārīkh-i*

refuses his mother's breast until she becomes a Muslim and repeats the name of God as a child, and when older he rejects several brides who would not convert to Islam; then after defeating his infidel kinsmen and becoming khan, Oghuz forces his entire people to accept Islam, and, with Oghuz Khan thus established as ruler and "bearer" of Islam, the narratives turn to a catalogue of his conquests and, above all, accounts of his "forming" peoples by assigning them names (usually explained through folk etymologies).

Oghuz Khan is thus both nation-former and bringer of Islam, like Baba Tükles, and it is worth noting that the Islamization of the legends of Oghuz Khan must date to approximately the same time as the conversion of Özbek Khan. We unfortunately know little, with any certainty, about the environment in which the "pagan" Uyghur-script version of the legend was produced; but in view of (1)the differences between Abū'l-Ghāzī's account and the earliest version, of Rashīd ad-Dīn, (2)the frequent evocation of the Oghuz Khan legend in Shïbanid historiography from Central Asia, and (3)the wide variety of late popular versions of the tale, bearing the title *Oghuz-nāmah*, preserved in (unpublished) Central Asian manuscripts but evidently reflecting oral tradition at least in part, it seems reasonable to suppose that Islamized accounts of Oghuz Khan, and the general processes, which such tales reflect, of assimilating Inner Asian heroes and ancestors to Islamic norms, were well known in the Jöchid *ulus* and most likely developed there independently of Rashīd ad-Dīn's literary account.

The tale of Oghuz Khan thus provides a good example of the assimilation of the role of indigenous culture-hero, ancestor, and nation-former with the role of "first convert," as reflected in oral tradition; we find elements of the familiar mythic complex used to mark such indigenous figures, and elements of narrative structures employed in connection with them (i.e., the catalogue of world conquest as in Juvaynī's legend of the Uyghurs, and the naming of tribes), applied to Oghuz Khan, who is likewise identified as the ruler responsible for establishing Islam. As noted above, however, the case of Baba Tükles is of particular note because his character's development in oral tradition, though parallel to that of Oghuz Khan, runs in the opposite direction: Oghuz Khan begins as an Inner Asian hero and becomes an Islamizer, while Baba Tükles is distinctive, as discussed, as a "nativized" Islamizer.

---

guzīdah-i nuṣrat-nāmah from the early sixteenth century (MS British Museum, Or. 3222, ff. 5a–9a, and the facsimile publication of Akramov, pp. 77ff.) and in the Persian history of ʿAbdullāh Khān from late in the same century (tr. Salakhetdinova, ch. 1, pp. 48–65).

Special Ethnogonic Motifs within the Mythic Complex: Swan Maidens and Skulls

A pattern quite similar to the general motif of the hero's dalliance with a supernatural maiden by or under the sea underlies the recurrent legend of origin involving the distinctive "swan-maiden" motif,[17] in which precisely the same elements known from several versions of the Idige cycle appear. This motif is especially prominent in more recently recorded ethnogonic tales, but appears in "historical" recordings as well; it may be echoed in the second of the Türk legends outlined above, in the figure who flies off as a swan. The legend of origin of the Khori Buryats, for instance, runs as follows: by the shores of Baikal the ancestor chanced upon three swans, they turned into beautiful maidens, he stole one of their swan-suits and married the hapless girl who was thus unable to fly away, she bore him sons who became the ancestors of the eleven tribes of the Khori Buryats, and finally flew off after successfully pleading that her husband return her swan-suit.[18] The ancestor of the Ölöt tribe of the

17. On the swan-maiden motif see A. T. Hatto, "The Swan Maiden: A Folk-Tale of North Eurasian Origin?" *BSOAS*, 24 (1961), pp. 327–352; Nikolaus Poppe, "Die Schwanenjungfrauen in der epischen Dichtung der Mongolen," *Fragen der mongolischen Heldendichtung*, Teil I: Vorträge des 2. Epensymposiums des Sonderforschungsbereichs 12, Bonn 1979 (Wiesbaden: Otto Harrassowitz, 1981; Asiatische Forschungen, Band 72), pp. 101–108 (Poppe mentions the Idige cycle, citing Zhirmunskii, but does not mention Baba Tükles); and Roux, *Faune et flore*, pp. 348–355. The motif is extraordinarily widespread, appearing also in the Qïrghïz epic tale of the brothers Zhanïsh and Bayïsh, in which the two brothers steal the clothes of two bathing swan-maidens, who become their wives (cf. I. B. Moldobaev, *Èpos "Zhanysh i Baiysh" kak istoriko-ètnograficheskii istochnik* [Frunze: Ilim, 1983], pp. 17, 27–28); it is also echoed in *Dede Qorqut* with the birth of Depe-Göz from a winged *parī*-maiden captured at a spring (cf. Geoffrey Lewis, tr., *The Book of Dede Korkut* [Harmondsworth, Middlesex: Penguin Books, 1974], pp. 140–141, and the translation by Faruk Sümer, Ahmet E. Uysal, and Warren S. Walker, *The Book of Dede Korkut: A Turkish Epic* [Austin: University of Texas Press, 1972], p. 123; cf. *Kniga moego Deda Korkuta: Oguzskii geroicheskii èpos*, ed. V. M. Zhirmunskii and A. N. Kononov [Moscow/Leningrad: Izd-vo Akademii nauk SSSR, 1962], in which Bartol'd's translation was published [p. 77 on Depe-Göz's birth]); cf. Zhirmunskii's discussion, "Oguzskii geroicheskii èpos i "Kniga Korkuta"," pp. 131–258, esp. pp. 226–227, citing other examples of the motif and comparing the Depe-Göz story with the account of Baba Tükles and the swan-maiden in the Idige tale; see also R. P. Matveeva, "Motiv o devushke-lebedi v russkoi i buriatskoi skazochnykh traditsiiakh," in *Russkii fol'klor Sibiri: Issledovaniia i materialy* (Novosibirsk: Nauk, 1981), pp. 25–40.

18. Described briefly by N. N. Poppe, "Opisanie mongol'skikh "shamanskikh" rukopisei Instituta vostokovedeniia," *Zapiski Instituta vostokovedeniia Akademii nauk*, 1 (Leningrad, 1927), pp. 151–200 [pp. 195–196]; cited further by Poppe, "Die Schwanenjungfrauen," p. 104; cf. M. I. Tulokhonov, "Genealogicheskie legendy i predaniia kak istochnik po ètnicheskoi istorii buriat," in *Ètnokul'turnye protsessy v iugo-vostochnoi Sibiri v srednie veka* (Novosibirsk: Nauka, 1989), pp.164–172 [pp. 167–168].

Oyrats is likewise said to have been born from the union of Böö ("Shaman") Khan and a swan-maiden; abandoned by Böö Khan after threats from his wife, the swan-maiden flies off to heaven, leaving her child beneath a tree that sustains him with the water of life.[19] The Manchu legend of origin has the founder/organizer of the Manchu state born from one of three heavenly maidens who came to bathe in a lake at the foot of a mountain. When they left the water to get dressed, the youngest of the girls found a red fruit laid on top of her clothes by a divine magpie, and, inadvertently swallowing it, she became pregnant and was unable to fly to heaven; she gave birth to a divine son, told him of his origin, gave him a boat, told him to go down the river, and then rose into heaven.[20]

Finally, the Noghay version of the Idige tale in which Baba Tükles' mother is impregnated by the ashes of a skull, which curiosity led her to taste from the pouch in which they were preserved, recalls an element from another Qïtan genealogical tradition, recorded in a Chinese source that must have formed part of a legend of origin; it focused on the reigns of three legendary "first rulers" of the Qïtan, the first of whom was a skull covered with felt and kept hidden inside a tent out of the people's sight; the skull emerged in human form upon ceremonial occasions involving the sacrifice of a white horse and gray ox, but eventually disappeared because the people looked at it.[21] More strikingly, the impregnation of Baba Tükles' mother in this way is paralleled in a late and wonderfully Islamized legend of origin recorded among the Qïrghïz of Osh, in the Farghana valley, in the early twentieth century.[22] This story combines

19. Cf. W. Heissig, "Shaman Myth and Clan-Epic," in *Shamanism in Eurasia*, ed. Hoppál, Part II, pp. 319–324 (esp. pp. 320–321). On a similar motif in Darkhat folklore, see Rintchen, "La généalogie des descendants de Djātak de la race des cent cygnes blancs," *UAJ*, 39 (1967), pp. 230–247.

20. Cf. Stephen W. Durrant, "Repetition in the Manchu Origin Myth as a Feature of Oral Narrative," *CAJ*, 22 (1978), pp. 32–43; Durrant's comments on the deletions and alterations in the Chinese version of this tale, as compared with the Manchu version, are worth recalling when considering Inner Asian legends of origin preserved *only* in Chinese or other "outside" accounts, such as those of the Scythians, Huns, Türks, and Uyghurs. On the Manchu legend in the context of other Inner Asian legends of origin, cf. Roux, *Faune et flore*, pp. 293–294. The versions of the Manchu legend are discussed further in Jun Matsumura, "The Ancestral Legend of the Manchu Imperial House," in *Proceedings of the Fourth East Asian Altaistic Conference* (T'ai-pei, 1971), pp. 192–195; Pamela Kyle Crossley, "An Introduction to the Qing Foundation Myth," *Late Imperial China*, 6/2 (1985), pp. 13–24; and Pei Huang, "New Light on the Origins of the Manchus," *HJAS*, 50/1 (1990), pp. 239–282 (esp. pp. 243–246).

21. See Wittfogel and Fêng, *History*, p. 272, n. 180, and Franke, "Forest Peoples," p. 405.

22. Recorded by A. S. Sydykov, "Rodovoe delenie kirgiz," in *ʿIqd al-jumān: V. V. Bartol'du Turkestanskie druz'ia, ucheniki i pochitateli* (Tashkent: Obshchestvo dlia izucheniia Tadzhikistana

the motif of impregnation by ingesting holy ashes with the familiar setting of a mountain and cave, but the central characters are based on popularized tales of the Sufi saint al-Manṣūr al-Ḥallāj (d. 309/922); known for his martyrdom on account of his blasphemous declaration *"anā'l-ḥaqq"* ("I am the Truth"; i.e., "I am God"), al-Ḥallāj appears as "Sha-Mansur" (i.e., "Shāh-Manṣūr") in this tale, with his blasphemous utterance transformed into his *sister* named "Anal."

Sha-Mansur and Anal, the tale goes, were pious believers; one evening Sha-Mansur noticed that his sister was missing, and went to look for her, finding her in a cavern in the nearby mountains, seated in the midst of a group of drunken young men. Anal was drinking some unknown liquor, and the sight of her at first angered her brother; he was offered some of the drink and refused, but eventually gave in, and at once felt the effects of the drink. Everyone left the cave except the brother and sister, and Sha-Mansur, in his intoxication, began to shout, in Qïrghïz, *"Anal haqq, menam haqq"*; i.e., "Anal is the Truth, I too am the Truth." When *mullās* nearby heard the shouts, they declared them blasphemous and condemned the brother and sister to death; the khan to whom they reported their verdict consented, and the two were strangled. Their bodies continued to shout the blasphemous words, however, so they were burned and their ashes cast into a pool (*ḥawḍ*). It happened that the forty daughters of the khan used to play by that pool. One day they saw that the water in the pool was covered with foam, out of which came the words, *"Anal haqq, menam haqq"*; out of curiosity each of them put some of the foam in her mouth, and, thus impregnated, bore forty sons who became the ancestors of the Qïrghïz (here implicitly understood, according to a common popular etymology, as *"qïrq-qïz,"* "Forty Maidens").

Here we find the Sufi martyr transformed into the progenitor of the

---

i iranskikh narodnostei za ego predelami, 1927), pp. 273–300 [p. 275]; it was cited by Louis Massignon in "La légende de Hallace Mansur en pays turcs," *REI*, 1941–1946, pp. 77–78 (repr. in his *Opera Minora* (1963), II, p. 103), and thence by Roux, *Faune*, p. 331. A manuscript *shajarah* of the Qïrghïz evidently containing much the same narrative is discussed in A. M. Mokeev, "Sheikh-Mansur al-Khalladzh i ego mesto v genealogiiakh kirgizskogo naroda," in *Bartol'dovskie chteniia, 1981, god piatyi; tezisy dokladov i soobshchenii* (Moscow: Nauka, GRVL, 1981), pp. 60–61; here "Analhaq" is the name of "Shaykh Manṣūr Ḥallāj" himself. Mokeev suggests that the tale represents a reworking of old Qïrghïz legends by Sufi shaykhs designed to strengthen their position among the Qïrghïz tribes, and dates this reformulation to the fifteenth–sixteenth centuries; the dating is most likely too early, but in general the development of such Islamized legends of origin in Sufi circles (but not quite so artificially as Mokeev implies) accords well with what we find in the case of Baba Tükles, and in other cases to be examined in another setting.

Qïrghïz, in a narrative that appeals to indigenous Inner Asian "ethnogonic" patterns (complete with the elements of the cavern and water) but at the same time retains the central features of the hagiographical life of al-Ḥallāj, i.e., his "blasphemy" and execution; even the specific content of his blasphemous utterance has survived, in the form of the feminine spirit of the tale, here cast as his sister. This process is all the more instructive because al-Ḥallāj is also known, under various designations (often in a form such as "Analaq"), as a *genealogical* ancestor of the Qïrghïz,[23] figuring in tribal *shajarahs* and historical works in which his name remains without the mythic, "ethnogonic" elaboration found in this oral tale; here we find a nice parallel to the genealogical and folkoric developments of the figure of Baba Tükles. The case of al-Ḥallāj and the Qïrghïz is of further interest in connection with the issue of Islamized native figures versus nativized Islamic figures. As we are suggesting with Baba Tükles, al-Ḥallāj is a Muslim saint nativized with mythic accoutrements proper to legends of origin to serve as a progenitor, although unlike Baba Tükles, al-Ḥallāj appears to have no intimate connection specifically with *conversion* or with the Islamization of the Qïrghïz; the latter issue does appear, however, in the Uyghur case considered below.

The Mythic and Narrative Development of Baba Tükles: Reconstructions and Parallels

The point of citing these examples is not to propose historical, ethnic, or even literary continuities on the basis of the common elements, but to suggest that these features form part of a common Inner Asian stock of mythic themes drawn upon when recounting a community's origins; and the sacrality of a community's origins, its adherence to a pattern venerated as universal and essentially holy, is vital to the community's legiti-

23. Cf. Mokeev, "Sheikh-Mansur." The antiquity of the tradition naming "Anā'l-ḥaqq" as the ancestor of the Qïrghïz is suggested by its appearance in the Persian *Majmūʿ at-tavārīkh*, a problematical work evidently produced in the sixteenth century (but preserved in manuscripts dating only from the early nineteenth century); see the facsimile of one copy published by Tagirdzhanov, "*Sobranie istorii:*" *Madzhmūʿ at-tavārīkh*, ff. 21a, 22b, 57a, and the remarks of S. M. Abramzon, "Die Stammesgliederung der Kirgisen und die Frage nach ihrer Herkunft," *AOH*, 14 (1962), pp. 197–206 [p. 200].

macy *as a community*, and not only or even primarily in the eyes of other communities, but above all in the hearts of the potential members of the community so asserted. At the same time it is instructive to note especially the versions of ethnogonic myths drawn from historical sources, rather than those collected by ethnographers in more recent times; these "literary" versions not only reflect an era closer to that in which the legends of Baba Tükles took shape, but also provide useful illustrations, from venues paralleling those in which we find the conversion stories centered on Baba Tükles, of the often garbled and fragmentary form in which the mythic tales were frequently recorded and transmitted.

In each case we find elements and structures known from the various tales of Baba Tükles serving as standard features in stories of communal origins. The parallels are further summarized in Table 7.1; here we must emphasize that the lesson of these parallels is that Baba Tükles too served in a variety of ways as the central figure in communal legends of origin. When we add to these the additional echoes of elements of this mythic complex, and of hero-tales and shamanic narratives, found in accounts of Baba Tükles, including the original conversion story, we find still more evidence for the assimilability of conversion narratives and popular ethnogonies. We may summarize the ways in which Baba Tükles serves as a holy Ancestor/Shaman/Hero in a number of settings that evoke the mythic complex of Mountain/Tree/Cave/Water/Goddess, and the theme of communal formation in general:

- as the shamanic figure who enters the pit and in effect leads his people out as a nation, evoked already in Ötemish Ḥ ājjī's narrative;
- as the shamanic figure forged in the initiatic fires which serve to regenerate and "re-form" his community, also evoked in Ötemish Ḥājjī 's tale;
- as the holy Ancestral figure enclosed inside the earth, his murmurings heard from within, whose birth also marks the origin of a people, evoked in the Bashkir tale of the buried saint and echoed, at least, already in Ötemish Ḥājjī 's account;
- as the Hero who confronts the King and meets the Test, thereby establishing his heroic credentials, as already implicit in Ötemish Ḥājjī's account and paralleled in other epic-style narratives;
- as the Ancestor who traps a swan-maiden, an epic development;
- as the Ancestor born of skull-dust, also an epic development;
- as the Ancestor who dallies with a water-spirit by or beneath the

Table 7.1. Recurrent Motifs in Historical Legends of Origin and Tales of Baba Tükles

Motif	Scythian	Hun	Türk 1	Türk 2	Türk 3	Kimek	Michael the Syrian	Ibn ad-Dawadārī	Uyghur	Mongol, SH	Mongol Indian	Mongol, Ergene Qun	Oghuz Qaghan	Qïtan	Manchu	Khori Buryat	Ölöt	Qïrghïz	Yurmatï Bashkir	Baba Tükles
Mountain			X	X			X	X	X	X		X		X	X			X		X
Enclosure in Earth or behind Mountains			X				X	X	X			X						X	X	X
Voices from Within Enclosure		:							X											X
Cave	X		X		X			X				X						X		X
Tree				X				X	X		X		X				X			X
Tree Birth or Nourishment								X	X		X		X				X			:
Water	X	X	X	X	X	X		X	X	X			X	X	X			X	X	X
Swamps		X	X																	
Junction of Rivers				X					X	X				X					X	
Ancestor's Wife is Daughter of Lake Spirit	X				X	X														X
Ancestor and Spirit Wife meet by or in Stream	X		X		X	X			:				X	X	X					X
Hair in the Water						X														X

Serpent	X					X													X	X
Feminine Spirit	X	X	X	X	X	X			X	X			X	X	X			X		X
Animal Guide		X	X		X		X		X				X							X
Guide Walks and Stops		X					X		X											
Animal Protector			X		X			X												X
Trysts by Night					X				X											
Bird-Wife/ Swan				X											X	X	X			X
Flight/ Refuge		X	X			X		X			X	X							X	
Emergence to New Homeland		X	X				X					X								
Rest of People Join Discoverers		X				X		X											X	
Sanctifying Tomb: Buried Saint, Skull								X						X				X	X	X

sea, an epic development for Baba Tükles but a theme of ancient origins in Inner Asia;
as the Ancestor/*Kulturträger* who assumes his nation-forming role by displacing the "false" ancestral spirits, a displacement achieved ritually by intruding himself into a royal and ancestral burial place and disrupting an ancestrally focused ceremony, themes evident already in Ötemish Ḥājjī's work.

Keeping in mind the attachment of this mythic complex, indicative of ancestral "nation-former" status, to Baba Tükles, we may recall the equally dynamic personality of his Central Asian "counterpart" and suggest a hypothetical sequence for the emergence of his many mythic and historical personae. Whether or not Baba Tükles can be considered the "western," Noghay version of the Central Asian, "Qonghrat" Sayyid Ata, it is clear that his function in legend and myth as the "founder" of his people is reflected not only through his role in establishing Islam among his people, but through his status as his "people's" ancestor, whether conceived in genealogical or mythic terms. If we may assume that Baba Tükles and Sayyid Ata reflect the same figure—and they undeniably *do* in typological terms if perhaps not in narrow historical terms—then what we seem to be able to trace here is the parallel development of traditions regarding the conversion of the Jöchid *ulus* to Islam.

The traditions begin with a focus on Islamization, which is immediately correlated with the process of forming or reshaping a particular human community; in the Central Asian strand, the narratives show the newly converted people adopting the name of Özbek Khan, a name sanctified by Sayyid Ata, while in the western development the tales show the Noghays adopting Baba Tükles as their progenitor, fitting his role as sanctifier of their identity as a people into a genealogical framework. In Central Asia the role of Sayyid Ata was quickly fixed in literary tradition, although it seems to have survived also in oral tradition not written down for several centuries; but in the Noghay horde, the "Islamizing" function was joined by a much stronger emphasis upon the "nation-forming" role, which developed as genealogy in the literary tradition and as mythic cosmogony in oral tradition. The marked development of the nation-forming role was no doubt itself enhanced by the usefulness of evoking the *Islamizing* function in order to provide an alternative basis for political legitimation with which to counter Chingisid charisma; this trend was quite pronounced in the Noghay horde, but is less evident in the Central

Asian tradition, although the emphasis upon *tribal* sanctification and upon the role of Temür and other *amīrs* that we find in the eighteenth-century tales of Sayyid Ata (not discussed at length here) suggests that anti-Chingisid sentiment was carried over into Central Asia as well. At the same time, the specifically Islamic character of Baba Tükles' sanctity was recalled in tales of his supernatural patronage of various heroes in their struggles against the infidels, and we may even see evidence of "re-Islamization" in the nativized narratives that introduce Khiḍr or Azrāʾīl as protectors of the foundling Idige; but here too an Inner Asian "style" of sanctity, linked with archaic mythic themes and a focus upon spiritual ancestry, colored the various narratives.

Narrative and mythic developments quite similar to those suggested in the case of Baba Tükles are evident in the case of the Uyghur "hero" who appears in Juvaynī's extended account of the Uyghur legend of origin; his account confirms for the figure of "Būqū Khan" a narrative and mythical development closer even than in the case of Oghuz Khan, whose "Islamization" appears to have followed, rather than preceded, his mythic elaboration as hero and ancestor. In the case of the Uyghurs, however, we find the figure of Bögü Khan, ruler of the Uyghurs, mentioned in sources dating within a century of his reign, and in these earliest accounts he is credited with the conversion of the Uyghurs to Manichaeanism; and as in our earliest narrative of Baba Tükles, the role he plays is cast as distinctly "oppositional," especially in the Qarabalghasun inscription, where the khan is made to renounce the error of his former inclination to Buddhism, call for the destruction of Buddhist images, and hail the transformation of the Uyghur realm into the peaceful abode of the true religion. By Juvaynī's time, however, some five centuries after the conversion itself, the pivotal role of the khan in adopting a new religion remained in popular memory even though the new religion he adopted was almost entirely forgotten. Moreover, of even greater significance for the parallels with Baba Tükles, the initial heroic bearer of the new faith has become, in Juvaynī's account, a mythic First Ruler and First Man, surrounded with imagery affirming his miraculous birth and his trysts with a supernatural maiden. It is certainly of added importance that he is not surrounded with just any mythic imagery affirming his holiness, but with elements of precisely the same ethnogonic imagery invoked in the case of Baba Tükles, i.e., the birth complex involving trees and streams and enclosures (the impregnated mounds), the latter paralleled already in Baba Tükles' oven-pit, and the relationship with the supernatural maiden.

We have considered elements of the Uyghur legend of origin in Chapter 4; here it may be useful to summarize the sequence of the fullest account, from Juvaynī. It begins noting the sacred center of Uyghur origins, along a river flowing from a great mountain; where two rivers flowed together, beneath two trees, were the light-impregnated mounds in which the Uyghurs' five ancestors were born. The youngest of them, Būqū Khan, was chosen to rule; he received each night for more than seven years a supernatural visitation from a maiden who entered through the smoke-hole and carried him off to a mountain. Their meetings ended with the maiden's charge to rule justly over the world, and the account then proceeds to a catalogue of Būqū Khan's campaigns and conquests; one of these is preceded by another "supernatural" intervention, when the Khan and his *vazīr* both see in a dream an old man dressed in white handing the khan a special stone as a sign of his rule. The account then turns to the story of Būqū Khan's conversion to Buddhism, and concludes with the report of the Uyghurs' migration, led by the cries of animals, to the later Uyghur center of Besh-Balïq.

The First Convert, the Bearer of the new religion, thus became the royal ancestor of the Uyghurs, and in this capacity his memory survived even when the new religion did not. We have clear evidence that gradually, between the ninth century and the thirteenth, he came to be surrounded with the symbolic trappings of the mythic First Man, and his role as sacred ancestor of the Uyghurs was recalled and articulated by invoking the standard symbols well known from the Inner Asian cosmogony: he is born at a sacred center, communes with a female spirit by night, leads his people in conquest and worldwide dominion. In the latter developments Būqū Khan is paralleled by Oghuz Khan; but the nearest parallel for the Uyghur development of First Convert > First Man is precisely the case of Baba Tükles.

Moreover, the example of the Uyghurs and "Būqū Khan" also suggests, for *narratives* about conversion, a developmental sequence similar to that outlined here for the stories of Baba Tükles. In the case of the Uyghurs our sources are somewhat more sparse, but the earliest account reflecting Bögü Khan's conversion is probably the fragmentary Uyghur text that appears to preserve the description of an eyewitness to the events surrounding the official establishment of Manichaeanism at the Uyghur court in 763. In this text the *qaghan*'s religious preceptors offer further instruction in the faith, successfully inducing him to repent for an evident lapse (either actual or didactically appropriate) from the new religion he had adopted somewhat earlier; the *qaghan's* public affirmation of Manichaeanism is then greeted by popular acclaim and celebration. The account has the ring of an "indigenous" eyewitness account, but probably one produced within Manichaean "missionary" circles. It most likely represents an early story circulated not among ordinary subjects of the Uyghur *qaghan*, but among devoted converts and Soghdian court advisers, and was probably aimed at affirming the faith and the importance of the *qaghan's* patronage in primarily Manichaean terms; the account is full of Manichaean religious terminology, most of it in Soghdian garb rather than in Turkic equivalents or explanations,[24] and conveys the impression that what we have in the text is members of the "Manichaean-izing" circle talking to one another.

In this text the only "enemies" of the new faith are the *qaghan's* own internal wavering and, apparently, an unnamed official who is portrayed as having threatened the pro-Manichaean party. In the next narrative account of the conversion we have, however, the rival to Manichaeanism is quite clearly Buddhism. The Qarabalghasun inscription, erected in the early ninth century in the center of the Uyghur state in Mongolia, commemorates the same establishment of Manichaeanism in 763. It recounts the *qaghan's* proclamation that he had formerly "called demons 'Buddhas,'" but could no longer serve those false gods now that he had learned the Manichaean doctrine; the ruler calls for the "sculpted or painted images of the demon" to be burned and utterly destroyed.[25] Curiously, the Chinese text (only this version of the originally trilingual inscription has substantially survived) is full of terminology characteristic of Buddhist teaching; it is not clear whether this results from mere terminological necessity, or reflects a conscious effort to appeal to a constituency familiar with Buddhism and inclined toward it rather than toward the state-supported Manichaean establishment. In any case, the quite pointed hostility toward Buddhist doctrine and practice evident in the inscription is enough to suggest a new purpose for recounting the conversion: if in the "eyewitness" account we find committed Manichaeans congratulating one another to affirm their "mission," in the Qarabalghasun inscription from a half-century later, we find the *qaghan* and the pro-Manichaean party recounting the conversion as a religious, and probably political, message to potential

24. Cf. Asmussen, *Xuāstvānīft*, pp. 147–149.

25. Cf. Chavannes and Pelliot, "Un traité manichéen," pp. 193–194; cf. Hans-J. Klimkeit, "Manichaean Kingship: Gnosis at Home in the World," *Numen*, 29 (1982), pp. 17–32 [pp. 21–23 on the Qarabalghasun inscription and the Uyghur text on Bögü Khan's conversion].

rivals who might invoke Buddhist affinities in opposition to the dominant party. If, as has been argued,[26] Buddhism was virtually unknown among the Uyghur ruling dynasty (though familiar to much of the Uyghur state's population) at the time of the conversion to Manichaeanism, we have a much clearer example of a revisionist narrative, casting the state religion's rival in the early ninth century in the same role in 763; but regardless of the actual historical circumstances of the events reflected in the two accounts, the differences in the narratives themselves are worth noting for the distinct religious environments they seem to reflect.

We may thus suggest an early development of a narrative circulated within pro-Manichaean circles soon after they won royal support, later transformed to emphasize tension with a rival faith, as a strategy in countering the religious and political influence of that rival—influence that may have been entirely absent, or at least quite muted, at the time of the initial winning of royal patronage. We then find no echoes of the conversion narrative for several centuries, during which the nomadic Uyghur state collapsed, and Uyghur kingdoms established themselves in the sedentary oasis cities of the Tarim basin, states increasingly identified with the dominant Buddhist civilization there. By the thirteenth-century account of the Uyghurs' conversion, as reflected in Juvaynī's history, Manichaeanism is at best a dim memory, and a conversion narrative in which the central character is clearly modeled on the Uyghur *qaghan* who converted to Manichaeanism is told to explain the Uyghurs' status as Buddhists; in short, the first version mentions Manichaeanism but not Buddhism, the second version self-consciously makes the *qaghan* abjure Buddhism (but does so in language fraught with Buddhist terminology), while in the last version Manichaeanism is forgotten and the "new" religion is Buddhism itself.

More important, that same central character has been transformed into a mythical hero, surrounded by symbolic evocations of the standard Inner Asian mythic complex so strongly evident in legends of communal origin, evocations that bear striking similarities with those employed in the case of Baba Tükles: his miraculous birth is recounted, as is his dalliance with a supernatural maiden, and his heroic nature is affirmed through his military campaigns and through his status as First Ruler (with his dynastic legacy recalled as well). With Juvaynī's "Būqū

26. Cf. Asmussen, *Xuāstvānīft*, p. 148.

Khan," we find a thirteenth-century echo of an eighth-century figure, whose survival in popular memory and clothing in the mythic garb appropriate to Ancestor, First Ruler, and First Man, can only be based on the strong numinous associations of his conversion to a new religion, and on the popular equation wherein First Convert = Communal Founder.

We may imagine a parallel development in the case of Baba Tükles, with an "original" celebratory narrative circulated within the pro-Muslim party at Özbek Khan's court to recount its success, providing a basis for a later revision, closer to the version reflected in Ötemish Ḥājjī's account, highlighting the tension between the Muslims and the supporters of the native tradition. Such a revision, we might suppose, would have been necessary after opponents of Islamization had had time to regroup and threaten the success of the pro-Muslim party; in the case of Baba Tükles, however, there is clearer evidence of entrenched hostility toward Islam well before Özbek Khan's reign, and in any event we have no firm basis for speculating on the contents of versions of the narrative that must have preceded that of Ötemish Ḥājjī. What is clear, however, is that for Baba Tükles, his inclusion in that originally multivalent and religiously charged story known from Ötemish Ḥājjī's work—a story that was itself an assemblage of allusions to elements of Inner Asian religious life integrally linked to communal self-conception, and of pointed evocations of religious transformation encoded in both Islamic and Inner Asian terminology—establishes him as a pivotal figure in narrative tradition and popular memory, in which he was suitable for the transformations, in "historical" and folkloric accounts, into the wide range of roles tied to sacred origins in which we find him still "alive" in the twentieth century.

This popular equation wherein "Islamizer" equals "nation-founder" equals "ancestor," suggests the need for considerable revision of the standard interpretations of Inner Asian religious history, in which conversion to "missionary" religions from outside Inner Asia is regarded as of little consequence; some ideal notion of "Islam," for instance, is typically said to"sit lightly" on the nominally converted nomads, unequipped as they are presumed to be for fitting a "civilized" religion into any spiritual context that could possibly have profound meaning for them. To be sure, we are not considering here questions of ritual usage or orientation or the impact of conversion on language or the new religion's effects on kinship structures or other equally important consequences of adopting a "foreign faith," all of which bear signs of an equally intimate assimilation and highlight the fact that in successful conversions, foreign religions do not remain foreign; but certainly the incorporation of bearers of Islam into indigenous mythic structures is no less potent a sign of the successful native "appropriation" of Islam. For now we may stop short of examining this larger issue in depth and suggest broader conclusions to be drawn from the *functional* parallels between the tales of Baba Tükles and legends of origin, with regard to political and social organization, and communal and religious identity, in Inner Asia.

Religion and the Articulation of Communal Identity in Islamic Inner Asia

We considered at the outset of this study the central elements of traditional Inner Asian religious practice and worldview, highlighting the mythic complex evoked in ethnogonic narratives, hero-tales, and accounts of shamanic journeys; we have likewise discussed here specific elements of the tales focused on Baba Tükles that illustrate the way his personage was adapted so as to make his story, originally focused on Islamization, fit the structural and thematic patterns of Inner Asian legends of origin. More important than the structural and thematic parallels, however, are the functional parallels, and it is the use of these patterns we will explore briefly, by way of suggesting some broader lessons of relevance to Islamization in Inner Asia that may be drawn from the example of Baba Tükles. For the elements of the ethnogonic mythic complex found in the legends about Baba Tükles—especially the encounter with the maid by the sea (to which the version with the swan-maidens may be assimilated), but including also the element of the abandoned child, the cave and "enclosure" theme represented in the Bashkir version of the Idige tale, and the "shamanic" character of Baba Tükles' ordeal already in Ötemish Ḥājjī's account—clearly indicate the portrayal of a figure originally associated with Islamization as a typical Inner Asian ancestor whose recollection and invocation are vital to the expression of a people's sacred origins and thereby to the evocation of communal solidarity.

The functions of oral tradition not only in "preserving," but above all in "making" communal history and articulating communal norms have been widely discussed;[27] with regard to Inner Asia in particular, the role of (oral) genealogies in articulating communal structures and relationships has begun to be explored,[28] but the "epic idiom" has remained too little appreciated, not to mention the general inattention to sacred history and religio-

27. Among general treatments, the classic work of Jan Vansina (cf. the new edition, *Oral Tradition as History* [Madison: University of Wisconsin Press, 1985]), while less attuned to a specifically religious approach to oral traditions, offers a useful analysis of the functions of oral narratives; the well-known work of Benedict Anderson, *Imagined Communities: Reflections on the Origin and Spread of Nationalism* (London: Verso Editions, 1983), explores related issues but with a distinctive neglect of nonliterate venues of communal self-expression. See also the collection of essays entitled *History and Ethnicity*, ed. Elizabeth Tonkin, Maryon McDonald, and Malcolm Chapman (London: Routledge, 1989; ASA Monographs, No. 27), especially the editors' introduction (pp. 1–21) in which the differential capacities of "nations" and subnational communities to, in effect, field "armies" of definers, memorizers, and transmitters of communal "history" are explored. Western discussions of this issue focused on Inner Asia in particular are remarkably few; cf. Walther Heissig, "Ethnische Gruppenbildung in Zentralasien im Licht mündlicher und schriftlicher Überlieferung," *Studien zur Ethnogenese*, I (= *Abhandlungen der Rheinish-Westfälischen Akademie der Wissenschaften*, Bd. 72, Opladen, 1985), pp. 29–55. While some Soviet specialists have examined the Inner Asian epic traditions, and oral literature in general, as sources on "real" ethnogenesis and ethnic history (cf. S. M. Abramzon and L. P. Potapov, "Narodnaia ètnogoniia kak odin iz istochnikov dlia izucheniia ètnicheskoi i sotsial'noi istorii (na materiale tiurkoiazychnykh kochevnikov)," *Sovetskaia ètnografiia*, 1975, No. 6, pp. 28–41; Esbergenov and Khoshniiazov, *Ètnograficheskie motivy v karakalpakskom fol'klore*; Tulokhonov, "Genealogicheskie legendy"; and the collective volume *Fol'klor i istoricheskaia ètnografiia* (Moscow: Nauka, 1983), especially L. S. Tolstova, "Ispol'zovanie fol'klora pri izuchenii ètnogeneze i ètnokul'turnykh sviazei narodov (na sredneaziatskom materiale)" [pp. 6–22], and G. I. Mikhailov, "Mify v istoricheskikh sochineniiakh XIII–XIV vv. mongol'skikh narodov" [pp. 88–106]), none to my knowledge has considered the creation, refinement, and transmission of such tales *as in themselves significant steps in reifying the "formation" of a "people"*—that is, not as evidence for some "real" process of ethnogenesis, but as an integral part in asserting and forging group identity through the evocation of some recognizable and authoritative (albeit "revised") version of sacred origins. The latter approach (without reference to Inner Asia, naturally) is suggested in the important work of Bruce Lincoln, *Discourse and the Construction of Society: Comparative Studies of Myth, Ritual, and Classification* (New York/Oxford: Oxford University Press, 1989); Lincoln's insights add an invaluable dimension to analyses of oral narratives (such as Vansina's) which tend to underplay the essentially *sacred* character of the narratives. See also Anthony D. Smith, "National Identity and Myths of Ethnic Descent," *Research in Social Movements, Conflict and Change*, 7 (1984), pp. 95–130, with a useful typology of legends of origin, and Mircea Eliade, "Cosmogonic Myth and 'Sacred History,' " in his *The Quest: History and Meaning in Religion* (Chicago: University of Chicago Press, 1969), pp. 72–87. Finally, for a brief discussion of "sacred history" in a Central Asian context see my "Yasavian Legends," pp. 2–3. Yet to be explored, however, are the links between the "assertive" (and self-conscious) religious language employed to articulate such visions of communal identity and notions common among preliterate peoples of the "magical" potency of language (and of the special appeal of "story").

28. Cf. Caroline Humphrey, "The Uses of Genealogy: A Historical Study of the Nomadic and Sedentarised Buryat," in *Pastoral Production and Society* (Cambridge: Cambridge University Press, 1979), pp. 235–260; Rudi Paul Lindner, "What Was a Nomadic Tribe?" *Comparative Studies in Society and History*, 24 (1982), pp. 689–711.

political language in Inner Asia. We cannot take up here an extensive theoretical examination of the ways in which oral tradition of the types in which Baba Tükles' "memory" was kept alive serve the ends of social and political mobilization; rather, we may suggest the likely uses of stories of Baba Tükles and Islamization in general, in the political and social context of traditional Inner Asia.

To begin with, as noted, specialists on the "Noghay cycle" of epics date the formation of the cycle to the time of the historical development of the Noghay horde in the fifteenth and sixteenth centuries, thereby accounting for the widespread appearance of tales from this epic cycle among peoples who were part of, or had close contacts with, the Noghay horde. This rather obvious insight is usually utilized as the starting point for considering the subsequent development of the epic cycle itself, or of probing for a "historical core" in the epic variants, but I would suggest that another perspective is of equal or greater importance: the historical context of the epic's formation may suggest the larger motives (beyond the specific issue of challenging Chingisid legitimacy) behind the central sacralizing role assigned to Baba Tükles.

For although the Noghay epic cycle, in which Baba Tükles and Idige play such crucial roles, far outlived the Noghay confederation itself, the political context in which the epic must have taken shape is clearly worth keeping in mind, especially as we consider Baba Tükles' role. While the Noghay epic clearly displays the full richness of Inner Asian oral tradition with its reflection of stock mythic and heroic themes and structures, it nevertheless developed as a distinctive epic cycle within a steppe confederation that was itself in the throes of a formative process; this fact should in turn suggest that the Idige tale took shape not so much as a "reflection," but as an *assertion*, of that confederation's unity and integrity.

In other words, we may consider that the Noghay horde, like other Inner Asian confederations, depended for its viability on the continuous reassertion and confirmation of both the legitimacy of, and the benefits secured by, the confederation. And we may further consider that such reassertion and confirmation naturally involved discursive and affective aspects in addition to the more obvious (because external) symbolic and practical elements. From this perspective, it seems reasonable to suggest that the Noghay epic cycle was intended to articulate, within the context of traditional Inner Asian values and of a traditional worldview shared by all the elements of the nascent confederation, a vision of the Noghay horde's unity, integrity, and legitimacy, all rooted ultimately in its essential *sacrality* as a properly constituted human community.

That essential sacrality, in turn, was sealed by the figure of Baba Tükles, who in popular memory and in explicit epic portrayal distinctively encapsulated the melding of indigenous values with Islamic identity. In this connection the role of the narratives about Baba Tükles within the Idige tale is of particular significance. As a bringer of Islam transformed into an ancestor—and in *both* capacities serving as legitimizer, patron, and protector—Baba Tükles serves as a key element in the "assertive" religious discourse that we may assume was intended to provide the constructive "myth"[29] of the Noghay confederation, evoking which the bards and their audiences could activate latent or potential social groupings and thereby reify the religious, social, and political bonds of a confederation still in the process of solidification. In other words, the nativization of a bearer of Islam shows not only the native "appropriation" of Islam, but the adoption of that appropriated Islam as the cornerstone of the "sacred history" of a particular collectivity, and thereby as a definitive element within the central social and communal structures of steppe society.

And appropriately enough, as the vehicle for reaffirming this potent sacralizing mixture, the Noghay oral tradition itself developed into an epic cycle so distinctive that its integrity is recognizable in the variants and fragments collected throughout western Inner Asia long after the disappearance of the ever tentative unity and integrity of the political structure we may assume it was designed to affirm. In any event, it is in the end the work of Ötemish Ḥājjī—in a real sense the earliest record of that oral tradition among the peoples of the erstwhile Jöchid *ulus*—that clearly establishes what is only implied or hinted at in certain versions of the Idige tale and in Baba Tükles' legendary persona: that the figure of Baba Tükles first gained his saintly reputation as the person responsible for bringing Islam to the Jöchid *ulus*, and that the subsequent adaptations of Baba Tükles' role amount to "nativizing" interpretations of the process of Islamization.

The direction of this development, as explored above, suggests already one broad conclusion with regard to both "conversion" and conversion

29. The term is used here in Bruce Lincoln's sense of an "*authoritative*" historical narrative; as he writes, "myth is not just a coding device in which important information is conveyed, on the basis of which actors *can then* construct society. It is also a discursive act through which actors evoke the sentiments out of which society is actively constructed" (see *Discourse and the Construction of Society*, pp. 24–25).

narratives to be drawn from the case of Baba Tükles, namely, the argument for a roughly inverse relationship between the degree of tension and hostility toward indigenous traditions *articulated* in accounts of conversion on the one hand, and the degree of genuine appropriation and "nativization" of Islam on the other. That is, we see a general sequence from narratives reflecting the early stages of Islamization, evoking sharp choices and contrasts (usually with much more vehemence than was possible, or desirable, in actual practice, no doubt), followed by narratives, produced when the "old ways" were no longer a threat, that either rely upon stylized and stereotyped symbols for Islam's rival, or in effect ignore pre-Islamic times and assert the veritable "eternity" of a community's Islam. This pattern is inevitably (and naturally) disrupted by the emergence of reformist movements, by colonial pressures, and by a host of other external and homegrown forces, all of which contribute their own dynamics to the articulation of communal identity and its "religious" roots. These are other stories, however; and the initial pattern itself requires further elaboration on the basis of other Inner Asian conversion narratives that I intend to explore in other writings.[30]

More generally, we may suggest here some implications of the case of Baba Tükles for our understanding of the way political and communal identities were structured in traditional Inner Asia, and especially for the potential impact of "conversion" and specifically Islamization on those structures. In the case of Baba Tükles, we see a key element in narratives of Islamization (of which we find the earliest record in the work of Ötemish Ḥājjī) "nativized" and adapted to Inner Asian traditions, retaining enough of Baba Tükles' association with Islam to ensure an Islamic coloring even in the context of popular folklore, but not so much as to prevent his transformation into a mythic ancestral figure or the infusion of archaic mythic motifs into the tales surrounding him. This nativization of a narrative originally focused on *conversion*—and typically stressing outright conflict between Islam and native traditions—is particularly instructive with regard to the significance of Islamization; it points to the essential assimilability, spoken of previously, of conversion narratives to legends of origin. In fact the process of recasting "Islamizers" as "ancestors" or "nation-formers,"

30. These other narratives include accounts of the conversion of the Bulghars, mentioned in Chapter 2; accounts of the conversion of the Qarakhanid ruler Satūq Bughrā Khan; accounts of the spread of Islam in Central Asia circulated in Yasavī Sufi circles; accounts of the conversion of the Chaghatayid khan Tughluq Temür; and the legendary cycle associated with Sayyid Ata's Islamizing activity, frequently alluded to above.

within both the narrative structures and the mythic environment characteristic of communal ancestors or the "first man," is not uncommon in Inner Asia, as studies of other examples will reveal.

For now we may note that the example of Baba Tükles, as a "nativized" bearer of a new religion, suggests further possibilities in understanding the use of *sacred* genealogy and ancestral invocation in "constructing" new collectivities. In particular, it has been suggested that ancestral invocation "can only remobilize groups that existed previously but that have more recently fallen into latency";[31] when "ancestors" are drawn from among representatives of a *new* religious order, however, "ancestral invocation" would appear to become a quite powerful tool for redefining and remaking communal borders.

To explore this issue we may return briefly to the question of political legitimation in Inner Asia. To begin with, we may recall the prevalence, noted in Chapter 1, of approaches to political organization and legitimation in Inner Asia that stress imperial structures and "ideology" rooted in royal charisma.[32] It is as if Western scholarship, perhaps enchanted with imperial models and centralized rule, or with the administrative marvel implicit in vast land empires, has cast the grand steppe empire as the normative goal or ideal against which political and social organization in Inner Asia should be measured; empires decayed, in this view, when khans weaker than their stalwart ancestors lost control of fractious tribes and tribal chieftains blind to the benefits of imperial consolidation. In extreme form this approach posits an "imperial ideology" as a constant in Inner Asian history, a dream revived periodically from the Hsiung-nu to the Turks to the Mongols, with imperial centralization held up as a standard

31. Lincoln, *Discourse*, p. 20.

32. See on the issue of imperial ideology and royal charisma in Inner Asia Peter B. Golden, "Imperial Ideology and the Sources of Political Unity amongst the Pre-Činggisid Nomads of Western Eurasia," *AEMA*, 2 (1982), pp. 37–97; K. Czeglédy, "Das sakrale Königtum bei den Steppenvölkern," *Numen*, 13 (1966), pp. 14–26; Manabu Waida, "Notes on Sacred Kingship in Central Asia," *Numen*, 23 (1976), pp. 179–90; Jean-Paul Roux, "L'Origine céleste de la souveraineté dans les inscriptions paléo-turques," in *The Sacral Kingship* (supplement to *Numen*) (Leiden: E. J. Brill, 1959), pp. 230–241, and his "Sacerdoce et empires universels chez les turco-mongols," *RHR*, 204 (1987), pp. 151–174; Mori Masao, "The T'u-chüeh Concept of Sovereign," *Acta Asiatica*, 41 (1981), pp. 47–75; Eric Voegelin, "The Mongol Orders of Submission to European Powers, 1245–1255," *Byzantion*, 15 (1940–1941), pp. 378–413; Joseph Fletcher, "Turco-Mongolian Monarchical Tradition in the Ottoman Empire," *HUS*, 3–4 (1979–1980), pp. 236–251; Herbert Franke, "From Tribal Chieftain to Universal Emperor and God"; Thomas J. Barfield, "Tribe and State Relations: The Inner Asian Perspective," in *Tribes and State Formation in the Middle East*, ed. Philip S. Khoury and Joseph Kostiner (Berkeley and Los Angeles: University of California Press, 1990), pp. 153–182 (esp. pp. 164ff.); and Iudin, "Ordy: Belaia . . .".

attained in some eras of grandeur, poorly realized but aspired to in other times, and obstructed by tribal rabble in ages of total disarray and decadence.

Without denying the power and occasional longevity of various imperial models, however, we should recognize the assertions of royal charisma and imperial legitimacy not as universally revered and accepted norms in and of themselves, but as politically motivated "platforms" or charters asserted in particular circumstances *on the basis of still deeper universally revered and accepted norms*, with the aim of adding an affective counterpart to the bonds of political loyalty or submission engendered by military power and/or economic advantage. With this in mind we may appreciate the imperial models and their legitimizing symbolism in their proper perspective, seeking those more basic patterns and norms as the genuine constants in Inner Asian political discourse; at the same time, we can better understand both the periods in Inner Asian history not "blessed" by large-scale political formations, and the polities (e.g., the Noghay horde) that survived outside and at times in opposition to the imperial ideal, but that claimed legitimacy through parallel evocations of those more fundamental sacred norms.

To consider those "genuine constants" we may suggest that the keys to communal, and hence political, legitimacy most often detectable in Inner Asian political discourse—which not only underlie the imperial ideals, but also inform the "charters" asserted for nonimperial states (i.e., tribal groups, large but loose tribal confederations, regional "kingdoms")—are to be found in the sacred symbolism evoked by applying the patterns of ethnogonic narrative (involving the now-familiar mythic complex) to specific communal and political circumstances. Evoking that symbolism, moreover, is an essentially "religious" act, for it involves revising a taxonomy of the sacred: asserting a community's legitimacy and sacrality amounts to asserting a symbolic equivalence in terms of the sacred patterns of the mythic complex, involving the type of religious, assertive language that can effectively claim that "this community" is "that (sacred) world." This is indeed why the mythic pattern we have discussed recurs so regularly: it is evoked again and again in the ethnogonic narratives (which are often but the shells of assertive "charters") not only because it reflects conceptions of universal sacred origins and was therefore "popular," but above all because, due to its encapsulation of those conceptions of universal sacred origins, asserting its "magical" and symbolic equivalence with a particular collectivity appears to have been an essential step for any ruling group seeking political legitimation.

Here we may recall the political potential, alluded to earlier, of the mythic assimilation of universal and domestic elements in the symbolic equivalence of the hearth and the sacred cosmic center. As suggested, the centrality of the domestic cult centered upon the individual hearth marks the definitive ritual reflection of cosmological principles in Inner Asia, and in it lies the key to the affective significance of appeals to the mythic complex associated with those cosmogonic or ethnogonic principles. That is, through the mythic identification of the microcosmic household hearth (both ancestrally through the feminine spirits and orientationally through axial symbolism) with the macrocosmic center of the world, a set of universally sacred symbols is particularized and evoked in each Inner Asian dwelling, while the individual ritual center is universalized, allowing the individual household to inhabit and participate in a symbolic cosmos whose essential structures are familiar and popularly endorsed not only within a particular community, but throughout the entire Inner Asian world. The mythic complex itself is thus a meeting place for two fundamentally important features central to an assertive legend of origin aimed at "making" a people: first, a universalizing principle stemming from the fact that this entire mythic complex speaks to cosmogony at the truly universal level and in sacral terms; and second, the particular, localized communal level of ancestral religious ritual and conceptualization.[33]

It is through this mythic evocation that one might appeal to popular religious life at the basic levels of communal organization that constitute the foundational elements out of which larger confederative and/or imperial (and ultimately "ethnic") polities (and hence "peoples") are constructed. It is thus reasonable to understand the recurrent evocation, in ethnogonic narratives and hero-tales, of the mythic complex discussed above as rooted in the capacity of that mythic complex to suggest both the microcosmically sacred cultic focus of domestic life and the macrocosmically sacred conceptual focus of cosmogonic symbolism. The domestic link of the complex appeals to people in the smaller collectivity conceived of as clan or ancestrally based; the universal link appeals to them to consider larger links as legitimate. And with its potency to summon both elements, this mythic complex is naturally evoked in legends of origin that seek to mobilize people for whom domestic rites are sacred

33. As discussed earlier, the meeting place of these two levels within this mythic complex lies in the locus of the feminine ancestral spirits in the hearth and the centrality of offerings to these spirits, and the hearth in general, in the domestic rites of Inner Asian peoples, as well as in the spatial symbolism of the hearth as the center of the world.

and valid into accepting the social, political, and ultimately sacral validity of a larger-scale collectivity.

If the ritual evocation of family ancestral origins is centered at the hearth, however, the ritual evocation of a universalized "people" asserted by a communal legend of origin must await the articulation of a particular assertive legend of origin. When that happens, the ritual evocation of communal bonds may become a celebration of statehood or imperial structure. In such cases the ritual counterpart of the assertive, mythic legend of origin may focus on a de-mythologized "center" of the new "state-community" (as is evident in the second Türk empire's appeal to the Ötüken, and as may also appear in recognition of sacred mountains, or trees, as signaled in some subimperial systems). But more often than not, that ritual counterpart focuses on the sacrality ascribed to the ruling figure or dynasty responsible for forging the political union that required the assertive legend of origin as its affective prop; that is, the ritual evocation of communal/state solidarity as expressed in the legend of origin is focused on the person or family of the ruler, as the embodiment of the community (and as direct heir to the First Man), as we see in the case of the first Türk empire's ritual in the ancestral cave, and more vividly and enduringly in the case of the Chingisid dynasty.

In this case, with ritual expressions of communal sanctity bound up with sacral dynastic ancestry, the "royal" or "imperial" equivalent of the ordinary domestic rites—that is, the ancestral rites of the dynasty itself—take on enormous importance for the state, and thus, for example, the tombs of the imperial dynasty, as well as the ancestral offerings to royal forebears, acquire a double religious significance, participating both in the domestic-style sanctity of any ancestral rite, and in the universal-style sanctity reserved for rites evoking larger communal groupings.

At the domestic level, again, ancestral veneration includes such ritual elements, but also the celebratory and self-affirming "affective" evocation of the living community's bonds to the ancestors; in this connection we may recognize the assertion of tribal and confederational genealogies as the equivalents of such ancestral evocation on a larger scale, subsuming in its essentially political character—that is, in the synthetic innovation of a confederative "charter" aimed at *constructing* a viable collectivity—an essential trust, common to indigenous Inner Asian religious traditions, in the efficacy of religious language to *assert* a reality, and thereby make it so, through its inherently magical power.

If, then, particular groups succeed in asserting power over a particular range of communities, beyond the tribal group, within that Inner Asian world—whether locally or regionally or imperially—they will naturally insert a hierarchy of symbolic centers between the individual family and that universal symbolic cosmos, thereby (1) establishing intermediate "sacred centers" (e.g., the Ötüken, Burkhan Khaldun, the hearth of Chinggis Khan identified as the center of the world, etc.) between the domestic hearth and World Center, as "national" or "imperial" centers; (2) asserting intermediate ancestries, complete with sacred origins marked in various ways that evoke both domestic and cosmic symbols and values, as royal or imperial clans, each potentially (and for political purposes necessarily) assimilable to First Man, etc.; and (3) creating intermediate "charters" for communal integrity at levels ranging from confederation to "kingdom" to "empire," with the charters in each case largely taking the recognizable and value-laden form of legends of origin.

The "imperial" tradition should thus not be regarded as something ongoing and preserved and hoped-for, certainly among the people at large but probably even among specific "imperial" groups; rather, we see not recurrent *ideals*, but recurrent *patterns* of evoking the intimately linked assimilative mythic complex reflecting cosmic and domestic order. This accounts for the remarkable similarity of images and symbols evoked in successive generations of successful or attempted communal and political mobilization; it also accounts for the flexibility repeatedly shown by the smaller communities in temporarily subsuming their identities in a succession of larger political structures while retaining the more localized loyalties that allow them to change larger structures when economic or military vagaries compel or suggest. Such changes would be surprising if we truly accept the existence of a long-standing Imperial Ideal, for if it existed on a large scale we would be constantly puzzled by the remarkable indifference shown by particular groups for that "Ideal's" integrity. Rather, the "ideal" existed only as a tool for mobilization, and the commonalities we find in successive evocations of that ideal by successive power elites *may* in some cases reflect the preservation of traditions (as is clear in the Chingisid case), but most often appear to reflect the recurrent imperative to evoke, in ways naturally adjusted to meet altered circumstances, symbolic patterns whose shared features and durability reside not at the level of transitory (often quite short-lived!) political structures, but at the more stable levels of domestic religion and cosmic myth.

Such evocations were usually most effective, it seems, at the level of tribal confederations, where the "success" of a particular "assertive" formulation of the ethnogonic mythic complex is signaled when that formulation comes to be regarded as a genuine legend of origin for a "people." It is more difficult to jump from this level to that of royal or imperial charters, for here the political circumstances in which the charter emerged were often of minimal longevity (e.g., the Chingisid charter outlived the early Chingisid states), and the transformation of the royal or imperial dynasty's ancestry into universalized form, while asserted by the dynasty, may take hold imperfectly or not at all. In the Old Turkic inscriptions from the second Türk empire we find what would appear to be just such assertions, which to judge from the short life span of the dynasty's rule in the Mongol steppe enjoyed little success; in them we find clear evocations of the domestic and universal mythic symbols needed to induce the dynasty's subjects to "buy into" its legitimacy as an "intermediate" center of sacralized legitimacy[34] (i.e., the sacred center of the Ötüken, transforming mythic images of the World Mountain, etc., into a state center; the ancestral myth, attaching cosmic associations to "my ancestors" Bumïn and Ishtemi, whose activity is situated at that cosmogonic moment "when the blue sky above and the brown earth below were created"; and the sacred charter intermediate between domestic and universal, namely in the assertion of a Türk "nation" with a Türk God and a Türk dynasty ruling from a Türk sacred center and successfully resisting the threat of Chinese domination, while subduing the peoples who, it was hoped, might also buy into the charter because of their common recognition of the universal and domestic levels of the worldview evoked and transformed).

More successful by far was the Chingisid dispensation, although outside Mongolia proper the *practical* success of the ideological charter asserting exclusive Chingisid rights to sovereignty was probably always less thorough than the record left by primarily pro-Chingisid court historians would suggest. The repeated challenges to Chingisid authority by tribal leaders in the Golden Horde (e.g., Mamay, Edigü), Ilkhanid Iran (the Chupanids), and the Chaghatay *ulus* (Temür is only the most obvious example), as well as non-Chingisid formations such as the Noghay horde of the fifteenth–seventeenth centuries and the checks on Chingisid power that emerged in the khanates of Central Asia, would all suggest that the assumption of Chingisid rights was never complete, but was, rather, as often as not a political tool used—with the appropriate

34. It may thus be suggested that the inscriptions provide an indigenous record not so much of "native" religion, but of "nativistic" ideology among the Türk ruling elite; see Chapter 4, n. 87.

evocations of the mythic features— by powerful tribal chieftains as a screen for their own political ends. The Chingisid ideology was not something they *had to* at least pay lip service to, but something convenient to use as a charter, to assert and maintain a political structure from which they benefited. The fact that it was so widely used, of course, attests at least to the *affective* success of the Chingisid myth, if not its practical acceptance; indeed, the Chingisid myth was no doubt the product of an unparalleled range of sacred themes and symbols.[35]

In general we can hardly claim that the Chingisid "ideal" was entirely meaningless; it plainly was not, as its remarkable longevity alone affirms. Rather, we are suggesting only that the Chingisid "ideal," as with the "imperial ideal" of the eighth-century Türks, was not irreducible; it was not itself an absolute "value" that survived through the centuries after (or even before) the career of Chingis Khan as a normative goal accepted by all peoples of Inner Asia, who were just waiting for a "rightful khan" to meet those shared expectations and who automatically gave way when he appeared. It was, instead, a charter built originally of many components, some of which survived while others were discarded, and it is those components—of which the most potent, to judge from their recurrence, were symbols drawn from ethnogonic myths that lent legitimacy and sacrality to communal formations—that should be regarded as the "irreducible" political values for Inner Asian peoples, able to serve them at every level of political organization, from individual tribal units to large-scale confederations to "empires."

In any case, the trappings of the "imperial religion" may be best understood as pointed evocations of certain elements of the values and practices characteristic of the domestic religion that was common to most of the people the imperial system sought to control, carefully packaged (though at certain times more successfully than at others) with a view to maintaining affective loyalties and mobilizing active support for

35. In the century after his career we find evidence of a wide range of sacralizing and legitimizing assertions apparently circulated about Chingis Khan, some of which were apparently discarded (though not before being echoed in Muslim and European sources) while others "stuck" to his persona to form the mythic basis of Chingisid charisma: they include (1) his sacral genealogy (with the holy personages of Alan Qoa and others, known from the *Secret History* and Rashīd ad-Dīn and later sources); (2)his links to sacred cosmogony (in the legend of Börte Chino, likewise known from the *Secret History* and Rashīd ad-Dīn); (3)his personal sacred character, as asserted in stories of his birth holding a blood-clot (*Secret History*), of his numinous status as a blacksmith (reflected in European and Muslim sources), and of his shamanic and/or visionary character (Muslim and European sources); and (4)his sanction as khan by the shaman Teb Tengri (*Secret History* and Muslim and European reports).

the royal or imperial state. What is at issue here is not the frequent dominance of the "imperial" brand of legitimation, or at least of its articulation,[36] but rather the locus of sacred power upon which it rests. What is suggested by the case of Baba Tükles is that appeals to imperial charisma, as well as appeals to Islam, *both* rest upon evocations of traditional mythic conceptions more deeply rooted in the life of ordinary people than either of those ideological superstructures, and that the success or failure of either type of appeal depended upon its effectiveness in fitting in with those conceptions.

Now such a static picture, of course, never endured long, since particular communities were dissolved, joined with others, divided, regrouped, etc. But the *patterns* of reaffirming communal identity proved remarkably stable, as new communities, possibly larger or smaller, were explained and "justified" in genealogical and mythic terms. Moreover, these patterns proved not only stable, but positively dynamic and productive, *even* when a particular community underwent the potentially fundamental challenge to its value system and organizational pattern implicit in religious *conversion*. In traditional, "aboriginal" communities, "religion" is simply "life," with the whole of life infused with, and understood through, elements of mythic and ritual patterns cherished by the community; one's "religion" is the product of membership in a community, and *not* a product of "choice," *not* something that could be "renounced" without that renunciation being understood—by the community as well as by the "renouncer" himself in many cases—as a rejection of communal life, and thus of life itself, since the only conceivable context for life is the communal context. So it is natural that "conversion" *often* occurred, and was nearly *always* understood, in a communal context, with an entire communal group imagined as adopting the new religion *as a group*—and, of certain significance for our concern with conversion narratives, the community would inevitably be understood as adopting the new religion as a group *under the leadership of* a heroic figure, transmutable into an ancestral figure, who for all his boldness in breaking with his community's past

36. The fact that the "sponsors" of the imperial vision were ordinarily more effective in articulating their model and its legitimacy (since they had more material and rhetorical resources at their disposal, the latter often adopted from outlying sedentary societies even when the ideology enunciated through that essentially foreign rhetoric was avowedly hostile to foreign intellectual traditions) should not necessarily convince us that their vision was somehow the "norm" or a universal "ideal" aspired to throughout history by all segments of Inner Asian society. On this issue (again, without Inner Asian referents), see Graeme MacQueen, "*Whose* Sacred History? Reflections on Myth and Dominance," *Studies in Religion*, 17/2 (1988), pp. 143–157.

and adopting the "true religion" nevertheless faces enemies who themselves are portrayed as violating communal norms.

The central figure in the conversion narratives is thus usually a khan or prince, but he becomes much more: he is a culture-hero,[37] a just ruler who organizes a state, a communal shaman who cares for the community's spiritual needs, and eventually an ancestor of one kind or another, for he typically gives his name to his newly converted (and hence newly formed) people, and/or assigns various people under his rule their new ethnonyms; in each case the community's designation is sacralized by the hero/ruler/ancestor's role in assigning it. And in the final analysis, as a function of the typical universalization of the particular community's experience, the hero/ruler/ancestor/bearer of the new religion is the First Man, ancestor of all (relevant) human beings.

When Islam is added to this pattern of symbolic evocations we find a particularly receptive integration of religious values undoubtedly rooted in the paramount emphasis, which Islam shares with indigenous Inner Asian tradition, on *community*. Now it would not be surprising to find instances of the practical appeal to Islamic symbols and values for legitimation in Inner Asian settings, or alliances between representatives of Islamically sacred power and rulers, or would-be rulers, in Inner Asia. Such patterns are well known from other Islamic frontiers and have been noted,[38] at least, in the Inner Asian context; in the latter regard, we have suggested (in Chapter 2) such uses of Islamizing policies in the Golden Horde itself, and it is hoped that further studies of the role of Sufi shaykhs and orders in Central and Inner Asia may illuminate the actual,

37. As such he is also an innovator, although the "edge" of his innovation is often removed, in the Islamic context but no doubt reflective also of Inner Asian communal conservatism, by the device of former apostasy: e.g., the Turks had all been Muslim, but went astray, and so in fact Oghuz Khan, as in the Islamized versions of his tale, or even Özbek Khan as in Ötemish Ḥājjī's work, were restoring the rightful religion to a community gone (temporarily) astray.

38. See, for example, N. Levtzion, "Islam and State Formation in West Africa," in *The Early State in African Perspective: Culture, Power and Division of Labor*, ed. S. N. Eisenstadt, Michel Abitbol, and Naomi Chazan (Leiden: E. J. Brill, 1988), pp. 98–108, and the considerations in Ira M. Lapidus, "Tribes and State Formation in Islamic History," in *Tribes and State Formation in the Middle East*, ed. Khoury and Kostiner (Berkeley and Los Angeles: University of California Press 1990), pp. 25–47. On the question of Sufi shaykhs' support of rulers and *amīrs*, see R. D. McChesney, "The Amirs of Muslim Central Asia in the XVIIth Century," *Journal of the Economic and Social History of the Orient*, 26/1 (1983), pp. 33–70 [pp. 66–69], and more recently Jürgen Paul's *Die politische und soziale Bedeutung der Naqšbandiyya*, as well as his "Scheiche und Herrscher im Khanat Čağatay," *Der Islam*, 67 (1990), pp. 278–321; in the former work in particular, he outlines a system of protection and patronage relationships in the case of Khoja Aḥrār that may serve as models for understanding the roles of other Sufi shaykhs in Inner Asia.

historical links between "religion" and "politics" in Islamic Inner Asia. For now, however, we will limit ourselves to suggesting instead the underlying rationale that made those links plausible, appealing to our examination of Baba Tükles to illustrate why and how Islam was able to serve as a central feature in various strategies of legitimation.

That underlying rationale rests in the oppositional and assimilative potential of conversion legends such as we find in the case of Baba Tükles, and its fruitfulness is confirmed by the narrative development we have sketched above. For at first the conversion narrative affords an assertive vision of tension between old and new ways, suitable for use in legitimizing a politically motivated challenge to an existing regime; this emphasis upon the opposition and distinction between Islam and indigenous traditions remains latent in conversion tales, to be called upon in later generations, by spokesmen for particular visions of Islam's role in the Islamized society, for use in political and social reform or opposition. Yet at the same time the assimilative potential of the conversion narratives provided the rationale for affirming both communal integrity and religious legitimacy, more smoothly integrating indigenous values with the newly introduced *status* entailed by Muslim identity and its consequences. This assimilative vision is what appears most readily and popularly accepted, to judge from the epic and folkloric treatments of Baba Tükles.

What we are suggesting here as the central focus of the assimilation and integration of the two traditions, Inner Asian and Islamic, lies in the "change of status" implicit in Islamization, and in the appropriation of that status, both individually and communally, through the adoption of the self-designation "Muslim" and of communal self-designations linked in some way with the "sacred history" of the group's Islamization. In other words, Islamization was understood as a change of status, especially communal status; but the "new" status was imagined in ways rooted in traditional concepts of communal origin and identity, concepts frequently called upon, outside the context of Islamization, to legitimate the formation of new, large-scale groupings (e.g., tribal confederations) out of smaller and more basic units of social organization. Islamization thus amounted to the "joining" of a new "confederation," which was the Islamic *ummah* in theory, but an Inner Asian community with a new *name* (or a newly [re]-sacralized old name) in practice; there were, in Inner Asian tradition, well-established discursive patterns with which to assert the integrity and legitimacy of such "new" communities.

As a final suggestion as to the "lessons" of Baba Tükles with regard to

Islamization in Inner Asia we may highlight the frequent identification of Baba Tükles as a Sufi. Baba Tükles' Sufi status is implicit in Ötemish Ḥājjī's account, where he is a "saint" and practices the *dhikr*, while his Sufi character is assumed in the Tatar historiographical tradition and in most versions of the Idige epic tale. We may recall here also the reworking of Ötemish Ḥājjī's narrative by the eighteenth-century Crimean historian ʿAbd al-Ghaffār Qïrïmī, who clearly portrays the saints who appear at Özbek Khan's court as Sufis and goes so far as to provide names for Baba Tükles' companions—one of whom is the ancestor of a leading figure in the Khalvatī Sufi *silsilah*. Similarly, the newfound Khorezmian account of Özbek Khan's conversion is especially insistent on Baba Tükles' Sufi character. In the epic tradition, meanwhile, his appelation "*ʿazīz*" identifies him as a Sufi saint; he is a "Sart *dīvānah*" in one Qazaq epic tale, and in the Khorezmian version of the Idige epic he is clearly portrayed as a Sufi shaykh, and one of a particularly "popular" type, well suited for becoming a patron spirit. And as noted, Baba Tükles' Sufi status is strongly and repeatedly underscored in one of the Noghay versions of the Idige tale.

In fact, Baba Tükles is only one among many popular, "mythologized" figures in Central and Inner Asian tradition who are identified as Sufis and ascribed central roles in conversion to Islam and in forming, and sanctifying, particular human communities; this in turn suggests what is confirmed in other contexts, that the transmission and circulation of narratives focused on such "Islamizing" personages was largely the work of figures associated with Sufism, both in urban centers and at the village and tribal level. The role of Central and Inner Asian Sufis, with links primarily to the Yasavī *silsilah*, in formulating and articulating the popular equation of "Islamizer" equals "nation-former" equals "ancestor" adds potentially important dimensions to our understanding of the role of popular Sufism in Central and Inner Asia; in addition to the important political and economic activity associated with the Sufi orders, we must acknowledge also the role of Sufis as creators, transmitters, and revisers of the vision or "myth" instrumental in "constructing" late medieval Islamic society in Central and Inner Asia.

In the end, we may suggest also that the case of Baba Tükles illustrates for us the actual bases for the "political" role of religion in general, and of Islam in particular, in the Inner Asian world. At a time when the political future of the traditionally Islamic peoples of the former Soviet world has entered, with such remarkable speed, a new and decisive period of development, it is worth pausing to recall the level of popular consciousness at which Islam and Islamic-style discourse function. Despite the "successes" of the Soviet era in diminishing "religiosity" and in creating (on purpose or "reactively") a "de-Islamized" intelligentsia, it seems likely that for most ordinary people the virtually indivisible connection between "Islamic" and "communal" (the latter term still more appropriate than "national") identity has remained dormant only out of necessity, and will again become one of the central "givens" shaping their political attitudes and responses. This in turn may help to put in clearer perspective the course of "debate" among claimants to the role of "national spokesmen" in the articulation of those communal Islamic "givens." If the present considerations help to clarify, then, the level at which Islamic discourse may touch the communities in question, and why, then Baba Tükles may remain of some relevance even today, if not for those communities themselves (and here the question remains to be decided), then at least for "outsiders" whose interest in Islamic Inner Asia is still all too often fueled by concerns of "what devils" represent Islam there.

Appendix 1

Ötemish Ḥājjī's Account of the Conversion of Özbek Khan

(Tashkent: Institut vostokovedeniia Akademii nauk Uzbekistana MS No. 1552, ff. 48a–49b)

حضرت خان مذکور علیه الرحمه عظمت اولوغ پادشاه
ایردی بر نیجه یل پادشاه لیق قلغاندین سونك الله تعالی ننك [1]
عنایتی بولوب مسلمان بولدیلار

حکایت سبب اسلام اوزبك خان ** سبب [2] اسلامی اول
ایردی کم اول زمان ننك ولی لاری دین ترور [3] تورت ولی کا
الله تعالی دین الهام بولدی کم سزلار باریب اوزبك نی
اسلام غه دعوت قلنکزلار تقی الله تعالی ننك امری بیلا
اوزبك خان ننك ایشکیکا کلیب قورونك تاشیده اولتوروب

1. The manuscript is quite irregular orthographically, especially with regard to the representation of the genitive suffix - *nïng*, which appears as نك - and ننك - ; the latter form is written, however, with only one point above the two *markaz*es, and might thus be read also as نیك Following Bartol'd, I have transcribed the sequence ننك - as if written with two *nūn*'s, unless otherwise noted.

2. Written سیب .

3. Written thus, and Iudin retains it without comment, but most likely ترور was written by mistake and not crossed out when تورت alone was intended.

متوجه بولدی لار انداغ روایت قلورلار کافرلار [4] ساحرلار
برلا کافر کاهن لار خانغه انداغ کرامت کورساتیب
ایردیلار که خان نك مجلسی غه سبجاقنی [5] کلتوروب
قویار ایردی لار جورغاتی و دوستیغانلارنی [6] طیار قلور
ایردی لار بال اوزی جورغاتیغه قویولور ایردی و دوستغانغه
سوزولور ایردی و دوستیغان اوزی اول کشی کا برور ایردی
برجا [7] بو ساحر کاهن لاری نی خان اوزلاری کا شیخ بلیب
یان لاریده یانه شا [8] اولتورتوب بسیار اعزاز و اکرام قلور
ایردی

اما بر کون که بولار کلیب متوجه بولوب اولتوردیلار
کوندا [کی] تك [9] خان مجلس * اراسنده سنة * [10] قلدی
شیخ لاری [11] برلا کلیب باری اولتوردیلار کونداکی تك
بیمانه سی بیلا بال کلتوردیلار جورغاتی و دوستغانغه [12]

4. Written thus; Iudin emends to کافر , deleting the plural suffix to parallel the phrase that follows.

5. Written سبجاقی بیلا (?), the first reading unclear (سجاقنی ?) and the بیلا perhaps to be crossed out; alternatively, the بیلا may hint that بال was intended, as in the parallel (بیمانه سی بیلا بال) below. Iudin's transcription assumes سبجاقی بیلا , but in his notes he proposes such an emendation, i.e., to read سبجاقی بیلا بال . See note [4] to the translation.

6. Written دوستیغالارنی , as Iudin also notes.

7. Iudin's transcription assumes this reading, but in his notes he emends to delete برجا .

8. Written thus.

9. Iudin emends thus, on the model of the term's subsequent occurrences.

10. Reading uncertain; Iudin suggests emending to اراسته , and transcribes accordingly. See note [10] to the translation.

11. Clearly so in the text; Iudin transcribes without the final ی , without comment.

12. Written thus, but Iudin emends to دوستغاننی ; see note [11] to the translation.

کلتوروب قویدیلار [13] بر خیلی مدت اوتدی کم نه بال
کونداکی تك جورغاتیغه قویولور نه دوستغانغه سوزولور
ایردی خان بو شیخ لارینغه ایدی نه جهتدین بو بال معطل
قالب / 48b / [14] ترور شیخ لاری ایدیلار غالب بو یقین
محمدی کلیب ترور بو اننك علامتی [15] ترور تیدیلار
خان حکم قلدی کم قورو دین [16] یوروب استانکزلار [17] تقی
محمد [18] بولسا الیب کلنکزلار ملازم لار جقیب قورو دین [19]
تفتیش قلدیلار ایرسا کوردیلار قورینك [20] تاشیده [21]
تورت اوزکا صورتلیغ کشی لار باش لارنی قویو سالیب
اولتورا[ور] [22] ایردی ملازم لار ایدیلار کم سزلار نه
کشی لار ترور سز [23] بولار ایدیلار بزلارنی خان [24] قاشیغه

13. Written قویدیلا , as Iudin also notes.

14. قالب repeated, as Iudin also notes.

15. Written علی متی ; Iudin also emends thus.

16. Apparently written قورقوتدین ; Iudin, in his transcription and notes, reads قورقوردین , without comment. See note [1] and [12] to the translation.

17. Written استانکزلار ; cf. note 1 on the sequence -ننك-.

18. Written thus; Iudin emends, appropriately, to محمدی .

19. Apparently written قورقوددین ; Iudin reads قورقوردین . See notes [1] and [12] to the translation.

20. Here perhaps to be read thus, rather than قورننك (cf. note 1 above); Iudin's transcription assumes قورنینك .

21. Or تاشینده , as Iudin transcribes; what may be a dot for a ن is indeed present, but two dots marking the single *markaz* as a ی are clearly visible.

22. Iudin also emends thus.

23. Written ترو سز ; Iudin also emends thus.

24. Written حاخان , the undotted حا no doubt the copyist's error not fully crossed out; Iudin notes also.

الیب برنکز[25] کلدیلار خان ننك کوزی[26] بولارغه توشدی
جون نور هدایت بیلا الله تعالی خان ننك کونکلی نی منور
قلیب ایردی بولارنی که کوردی میل و محبتی کونکلونده
بیدا بولدی سوردیلار که سزلار نی کشی لار ترور نه ایشکا
یورییورسز نه ایشکا برورسز بولار ایدی لار بزلار محمدی
تروربز خدای تعالی ننك * امری برلا *[27] کلیب تروربز کم
سزلارنی مسلمان قلغای مز بو اثناده[28] خان ننك شیخ لاری
فریاد قلیب ایدیلار بولار یمان کشی لار بولور بولارنی
سویلاماك کا[29] اولتورماك کراك تیدیلار خان ایدیلار
نیجون اولتورادرمن پادشاه من سزلارننك هیج قیسی نکزدین[30]
فروایم[31] یوق ترور * قیسی نکزنك دینی نکز *[32] بر حق
بولسه انك برلا بولورمن اکر بولارننك دینی نا حق بولسا
سزلارننك بو کونداکی ایش لارنکز[33] نجوك باطل بولوب

25. An imperative verb has been added in the margin, but the stem is missing due to the trimming of the page; Iudin's facsimile clearly shows the complete برنکز .

26. Written کوزوی ; Iudin also emends thus.

27. Added in margin; only the لا of the برلا remains visible. Iudin's facsimile shows the entire phrase.

28. Written انثاده ; Iudin says the manuscript reads انتاده , but only two dots are visible above the third letter.

29. Only part of the word to be added here is visible in the margin (ending in ماز ?) in my microfilm. Iudin's facsimile shows رکماز, and his emendation, to read سویلاماك کارکماز , is no doubt correct, but see note [15] to the translation.

30. Written قیسی ننکزدین ; cf. note 1 above.

31. Written thus, for Persian پروا .

32. Written قیسی ننکزنك دینی ننکز ; cf. note 1 above.

33. Written ایش لارننکز ; cf. note 1 above.

معطل قالدی و سوزلاشکز قیسنکزننك دینکز حق بولسا انکا
تابع بولورمن تیدی

بو ایکی جماعت بری بریسی برلا بحث کا توشدی لار
کوب غوغا و جدل [34] قلشدیلار عاقبت انکا قرار بردیلار
کم ایکی تنور قازغایلار هر برسنی اون اربا سوکسوك بیلا
قیزدورغایلار بر تنورغا ساحرلاردین بر کشی کیرکای ینه بر
تنورغه بولاردین بر کشی کرکای هر قیسی کویمای جقسا
اننك دینی حق بولغای تیب قرار بردیلار

تانکلاسی ایکی اولوغ [35] تنور .قازدیلار سوکسوك
اوتون لاردین یغیب قیزدوردیلار برسنی ساحرلارغه تعین [36]
قلدیلار ینه برسنی مسلمانلارغه تعین قلدیلار بو عزیزلار
بری بریسی برلا مراعت قلشدیلار قیسمز کیراربز بولارنك
بریسی کا بابا توکلاس دیر ایدیلار / 49a / تمام
اعضالارینی *توك یبیب* [37] ایردی اول ایدی منکا
ایجازت [sic] برینکز [38] من کراین سز منکا همت
توتونکز [39] تیدی بو عزیزلار انك حقی نه فاتیحه [sic]

34. What seems to be a ق appears at the end of this word, perhaps indicating that جدلق (for جدل لیق ?) was intended; or it may simply anticipate the following word. Iudin's transcription assumes جدل alone.

35. Here تنو تنور crossed out.

36. Written thus here and in the following line, for تعیین .

37. Interpretable also as تولك بسیب or تولك بییب (?); see note [17] to the translation. Iudin's notes discuss neither phrase, but his transcription assumes توك بسیب .

38. Written بزینکز .

39. Written توتوننکز ; cf. note 1 above.

اوقوديلار اول بابا ايدى منكا جيبه حاضر قيلنكز جيبه نى
حاضر قلديلار ايرسا جيبه كيدى يلانك اتكا تقى
الله تعالى يادى طلقين بشلاب تنور طرفه غه [40] متوجه
بولدى ايتور باباننك توكلارى اورا قوبوب جيبه ننك
كوزلاريدين جقيب ايردى بو حالات نى بارجا كورار
ايردى لار بولار يوروب تنورغه كيردى بر قوى اتينى [41]
كلتوروب تنورغه اسديلار اغزينى بركتى لار

ايمدى كلدوك كاهن لار قصه سينغه كاهن لار ضرورتدين
برسنى جقاريب تنورغه سلدى همينك [42] توشكاج كولى
كوكلى ياشل لى بولوب يالنى تنورنك اغزيندين * جقار
ايردى * [43] بو حالتنى خان بشليغ بارجا خلايق لار
كورديلار ايرسا كونكول لارى كافر دينى دين اورولوب
مسلمان ليق غه ميل قلديلار

و تقى باباننك تلقين ايتقان اوازى تنوردين متصل كلور
ايردى قوى اتى بشدى تيكان محلده تنورنك اغزين اجديلار

40. Iudin, no doubt correctly, emended to طرفى غه .

41. Iudin, in his transcrition and notes, treats this reading as an emendation, saying that the manuscript reads اتنى ; the photographs, however, clearly show a *markaz* for the ى , and the two dots are quite often omitted in this manuscript.

42. Written حمينك ; the term همينك seems quite appropriate here, but Iudin's transcription assumes همين كه (he does not comment on the spelling with ح). In either case the meaning is the same.

43. To judge from his transcription, Iudin read this phrase as جقارا بردى (he makes no comment in his notes); such a reading is indeed plausible from the photograph, but the context requires an intransitive verb such as *čïq-*, instead of the causative stem *čïqar-*.

بابا مبارك يوزلارينـدين تيرلارينى سورت كاج نا آشوقدنكز [44] اكر بر زمان توقف قلسانكز [45] ايردى ايشم تمام بولوب ايردى تيب تنوردين جقدى كورديلار كه جيبه جوغ [46] بكين [47] قزيل بولوب ايردى اما خداى تعالى ننك قدرتى برلا بابانك بر توكى كويماين جقدى بو حالنى خان بشليغ برجا خلايق لار كورديلار ايرسا فى الحال شيخ لارننك اتاكلارينى توتوب مسلمان بولديلار الحمد لله على دين الاسلام

بسه بركه [48] خان زمانينده اوزبك طائفه سى مسلمان بولوب ايرديلار اولاردين سونك ينه مرتد / 49b / بولوب كافر * بولديلار ايردى * [49] بويوك [50] اوزبك خان مسلمان بولدى اندين بارو اوزبك طائفه سى نك اسلامى تغير تبمادى

ايتورلار اوزبك خان يكرمى يل پادشاه ليق قلدى و بعضى لار ايتورلار اون سكز يل پادشاه ليق قلدى اندين حق رحمتكا واصل بولوب انا لله و انا اليه راجعون

44. Written آشوقدننكز ; cf. note 1 above.

45. Written قلساننكز ; cf. note 1 above.

46. Written جوع .

47. Apparently written بكين or بلين ; see note [21] to the translation.

48. Written برك

49. Written thus; Iudin's transcription assumes this reading, but in his notes he suggests emending to بولورلار ايردى or, as he prefers, to بولوب ايردى .

50. ل added in margin above, as if to be read بو يول ; Iudin combines the elements to read بو يول كه , but see note [22] to the translation.

Appendix 2

Ötemish Ḥājjī's Account: Translation and Commentary (MS IVAN UzSSR Inv. No. 1552, ff. 48a–49b)

Translation

[48a] . . . The aforementioned khan [Özbek Khan], peace be upon him, was a great ruler. When he had ruled for several years, he became a Muslim through the favor of God most high.

The Story of Özbek Khan's Conversion to Islam

The cause of Özbek Khan's [conversion to] Islam was [that] inspiration came from God most high to four saints (*valī*) from among the saints of that age: "Go and summon Özbek to Islam." And by the command of God most high they came to the door (*eshik*) of Özbek Khan and sat outside [his] royal reserve (*qoru* [1]). It is related [that] the infidel sorcerers and diviners [2] of the unbelievers used to display such a wonder (*karāmat*) [3] to the Khan: they would bring a large bowl (*sapchaq* [4]) [full of honey] and place it before the Khan's assembly, and would prepare the kumiss vessel (*chorghatï* [5]) and pitchers (*dostïghan* [6]); a ferment made from honey [7] would be poured into the kumiss vessel and [the product] strained into the pitcher, and they would give the essence [8] from the pitcher to him. The Khan considered all his sorcerers and diviners as his *shaykhs*, and, seating them at his side, [9] he paid them great respect and honor.

But one day, when these [saints] came and seated [themselves], the

Khan as on every day observed the custom in the assembly; [10] he came with his *shaykhs*, and all of them sat down; as on every day they brought his goblet (*paymānah*) and the honey, and placed them before the kumiss vessel and the pitcher. [11] Quite a long time passed during which no honey was poured into the kumiss vessel as usual, nor was it strained into the pitcher. The Khan said to these *shaykhs* of his, "Why has this honey been left in abeyance?" [48b] His *shaykhs* said, "Probably a Muḥammadan has come near, and this is his sign." The Khan commanded, "Go and look beyond the royal reserve, [12] and if there is a Muḥammad[an], bring him." When the servants went out and investigated beyond the royal reserve, they saw [that] outside the royal reserve four persons of a different appearance were seated with their heads cast down [13]. The servants said, "What kind of people are you?" They said, "[Take] us into the Khan's presence;" and they brought them [there]. The Khan's gaze settled upon them; and because God most high illuminated the Khan's heart with the light of guidance, an attraction and affection appeared in his heart toward these whom he saw. He asked, "What kind of people are you, and on what business have you come?" [14] They said, "We are Muḥammadans, and we have come by the command of God most high in order to make you a Muslim."

At this moment the Khan's *shaykhs* cried out saying, "These are bad people; one should kill them rather than speak [with them]" [15]. The Khan said, "Why would I kill them? I am a *pādshāh*; I have no cause for alarm from any of you. Whoever's religion may be true, I will be with him; if their religion is not true, why was your work today confounded and left without effect? [So] debate with one another (*sözläshingiz*); whoever among you has the religion that is true, I will follow him."

These two parties fell into discussion with one another, and together made much turmoil and contention. At last they gave him their decision: they would dig two oven-pits (*tanūr*) and fire up each one with ten cartloads of tamarisk (*süksük* [16]) [wood]; one person from among the sorcerers would enter one oven, and one person from among these [saints] would enter the other oven. "Whoever emerges without being burned, his religion will be true," they resolved.

The next morning they dug two great oven-pits; they gathered *süksük* wood and heated them up. They assigned one to the sorcerers and the other to the Muslims. These saints (*ʿazīzlär*) were solicitous for one another, [saying] "Which of us shall go in?" One of them was called Baba Tükläs, [49a] because all of his limbs were covered with body hair (*tük*) [17]. He said, "Give me permission; let me go in. You fix your attention on me." The [other] saints recited the *fātiḥah* on his behalf. [Then] that Baba said, "Prepare armor (*jība* [18]) for me;" [and] when they had prepared the armor, he put it on over his bare flesh. Then he began to recite the remembrance of God most high, and moved toward the oven. They say [that] the Baba's body hair stood straight up [19] and came out through the eyelets of the armor; everyone saw this phenomenon. He walked [on] and entered the oven. [And] they brought the flesh of a sheep and hung it over the oven, and fastened its opening.

Now we have come to the story of the soothsayers. The soothsayers took out one among them by force and threw him into the oven; as soon as he fell in, the ashes of [his body] turned blue and green [20] and the flames [from his body] came out of the mouth of the oven. When all the people, beginning with the Khan, saw this phenomenon, their hearts turned away from the infidel religion and inclined to the Muslim way (*musulmānlïq*).

And the voice of the Baba uttering [his] recitation came uninterruptedly out of the [other] oven. When it was presumed that the sheep's flesh was fully cooked, they opened the mouth of the oven; [and] the Baba, wiping the sweat from his blessed face, came out of the oven, saying "Why did you hurry? If you had held off for a time, my business would have been finished." They saw that the armor was glowing red hot [21], but by the power of God most high not a hair of the Baba's body was burned. When all the people, beginning with the Khan, saw this situation, they at once grasped hold of the hems of the *shaykhs*' [garments] and became Muslims; praise be to God for the religion of Islam!

Thus, the Özbek nation (*ṭāʾifah*) became Muslim in the time of Berke Khan, [but] after him they apostatized [49b] and became infidels. [But] the great [22] Özbek Khan became a Muslim, and since then the Islam of the Özbek nation has not wavered.

They say [that] Özbek Khan ruled for twenty years, and others say he ruled eighteen years. Then he attained to the mercy of God: "Verily we are God's and unto Him do we return" [23].

Commentary

At the end of several of the following notes (and in three new notes) I have added comments upon the interpretation of the text found in the recently published *Chingiz-name* of V.P. Iudin (see Acknowledgments); his translation of the relevant portion of the text appears on pp. 105–107, with the transcription of the text on pp. 132–134, textological notes on pp. 191–195, and facsimiles on Plates XXVI–XXIX. With regard to the facsimiles it is worth noting that although the reproductions in the publication are not of high quality, they are for the most part legible; what is more important, and disturbing, the facsimile of folio 48b clearly shows more of three marginal additions than what appears in the microfilm I obtained in 1984. When the photographs were made for the publication is not indicated, but (assuming that they have not been "improved" by the editor) the difference suggests additional damage to the manuscript.

[1] *qūrū, qūrī*. The term *qoru* appears here in this form (*qoru-nïng tašïda*) and in the same phrase on f. 48b where it is probably to be read *qorï-nïng tašïda*; it most likely appeared in the form *qoru* (or possibly as *qoruq*) in two other places, as I emend the available text(s), but it was apparently misunderstood by the copyist(s) (see note no. [12]). The range of meanings of the term *qoruq* (and variant forms *qorïġ, qoruġ, qorïq, ġoruq*, etc., with the first vowel always indicated by *wāw* if written at all and the second indicated by either *wāw* or *yā* if written) has been discussed above in Chapter 3 (and in Chapter 2 with regard to the apparent use of the term in Ötemish Ḥājjī's work outside the conversion narrative), as were the arguments for the interpretation adopted here; we may recall that in the present context the term may refer to the khan's private encampment or "royal enclosure," or to an area reserved for private hunting, but it very likely indicates a sacred center as the site of the tombs of the royal clan, the sacred site "reserved" for dynastic burials. If some uncertainty must remain concerning the specific meaning of *qoruq* intended in Ötemish Ḥājjī's account, there can be little doubt that the form here does indeed reflect the term more often found (in the Mongol age, at least) in the form *qoruq* or *qoruġ*, etc. As noted earlier, vowel-final forms of the shape *qorï* and *qoru* are attested, if uncommon, and as suggested below, a final *qāf* may actually have been intended in the manuscript(s) from which the extant copies were transcribed. In any case, no other interpretation makes sense. The only word remotely plausible in

this context is in fact a derivative from the same Turkic root from which *qoruq* itself is derived: this is *qōriyā*, known as a Mongol loanword in Persian and appearing also in the form *qōrah*, meaning a fenced-in or otherwise enclosed place, a courtyard, livestock pen, barracks, or residence of a prince (cf. Doerfer, *TMEN*, I, pp. 432–434); the term is used, for instance, to refer to fenced enclosures constructed for princes and commanders in Timur's army in preparation for winter encampment, and thus appears suitable in the context of a nomadic military retinue. The shape of this word (with final *-ā* or *-ah*) appears less amenable to the form in our manuscript than the term we have understood as *qoruq*, however. Iudin reads this first occurrence of the term in the narrative as *qoru*, but elsewhere transcribes it as *qor* or *qorqor*, translating the term in all cases with the Russian word *kuren'*, a term itself of Mongol orgin (cf. Doerfer, *TMEN*, I, pp. 477–480) meaning an enclosed encampment and used in Russian to refer to cossack settlements. To the extent that the term implies an enclosed space, the translation is perhaps apt, but Iudin provides no commentary on his reading of the term or on his translation. To judge from his reading, he sought to make sense out of the term—which indeed first appears in the text (just before the conversion narrative, in the account of the killing of the usurper Bājir Tūq Būghā by Özbek's supporters, discussed in Chapter 2) in a form resembling *qūrqūr*—as a reduplicated version of the word *qor* (perhaps assuming the preservation of the labial vowel harmony to give the suffixed form *qūrū-n.k* in this occurrence, although we must note that the possessive suffix is not otherwise found in a form *+u/+ü* in this text). However, against this we may note that no such reduplicated form is attested: it is not cited in dictionaries of Chaghatay, nor does the form appear in modern languages. To be sure such a reduplicated form was perhaps necessary for Iudin to account for the peculiar way in which the term is written in three out of its five occurrences (once as discussed in Chapter 2, and twice more discussed below in note [12]), since each of these three occurrences, as well as the form *qūrū* here (if the likelihood of a labialized possessive suffix is dismissed), render the reading "*qor*" by itself implausible. Only in one occurrence, on f. 48b [*qūr.y.n.k/qūr.n.y.k* (?)] is the reading "*qor*" possible, and in this case, in view of the irregular spelling of the genitive suffix throughout the text, interpreting this form as *qorï-nïng* is as plausible as interpreting it as "*qor-nïng*." The latter reading (i.e., one assuming "*qor*," or its hypothetical reduplicated form as implied by Iudin's reading) may be discounted on semantic grounds as well. The meanings suggested for a word with the orthographic shape *qūr* by Budagov (II, pp. 72–73) and A. Pavet de Courteille (*Dictionnaire turc-oriental* [Paris, 1870; repr. Amsterdam: Philo Press, 1972], p. 425) are all either semantically inappropriate in the present context, or derivative (or erroneously interpreted) meanings based on better-known Mongol or Turkic words (for these see Clauson, *ED*, pp. 641–642, and Doerfer, *TMEN*, I, pp. 427–428, the latter discussing Mongol *qor*, "quiver", the basis for well-known terms such as *qorkhānah* ["arsenal"], *qorbashï* ["chief of armaments"], and *qorchï* ["bodyguard," cf. Doerfer, *TMEN*, I, pp. 429–432], and the probable origin of ʿAbd al-Ghaffār Q̣ïrïmī's rendering of the term as "*ʿaskar*," "troops," in one occurrence).

In sum: (1) Iudin's *qorqor* (A) is otherwise unattested, (B) makes no sense (why would *qor* be doubled?), and (C) is preferable to *qor* by itself only because it attempts to account for orthographic peculiarities that argue against the reading *qor*; (2) the reading *qor* by itself is rendered implausible (A) by the attested meanings of a word of that shape, none of which makes sense in the context, and (B) by the ways the term is written, ways that I argue mask a form of the term *qoruq*.

[2] The Arabic terms *sāḥir* (sorcerer) and *kāhin* (soothsayer) are standard equivalents for the Turkic *qam*, "shaman" (cf. Bartol'd, *Sochineniia*, VIII, p. 444).

[3] The exact process described here remains unclear because of its rather condensed presentation in the text and the considerable uncertainties in both the reading and interpretation of the key terms; the range of religious themes that may have been evoked by the description was discussed in Chapter 3. The passage seems clearly to refer to a royal ceremony (involving kumiss or another intoxicating drink) of a type well known from the Golden Horde and other Inner Asian courts; the ritual aspects of such ceremonies were discussed in Chapter 3, but none of our sources describes in sufficient detail the process *and* its products *and* the native terminology. Unfortunately the extensive secondary literature on kumiss-making and on beverages in general in Inner Asia, though helpful, does not offer a clear resolution of the problem; among general surveys the best (though hard to find) is F. A. Fiel'strup, "Molochnye produkty turkov-kochevnikov," in *Kazaki: Sbornik statei antropologicheskogo otriada Kazakstanskoi èkspeditsii Akademii nauk SSSR; Issledovanie 1927 g.*, ed. S. I. Rudenko (Leningrad: AN SSSR, 1930; *Materialy komissii èkspeditsionnykh issledovanii*, vyp. 15;

seriia Kazakstanskaia), pp. 263–301, and see also: G. Montell, "Distilling in Mongolia," *Ethnos*, 2/5 (September 1937), pp. 321–332, with good illustrations; Sławoj Szynkiewicz, "Nahrungsmittel und ihre Zubereitung," in *Die Mongolen*, ed. Walther Heissig and Claudius C. Müller (Innsbruck: Pinguin-Verlag, 1989), pp. 142–149; Gustav Ränk, "Gegorene Milch und Käse bei den Hirtenvölkern Asiens," *Journal de la Société Finno-ougrienne*, 70 (1970), No. 3, pp. 4–21; Ulla Johansen, "Tranken die Alten Türken Milch-Branntwein?" *UAJ*, 33 (1961), pp. 226–234; Pentti Aalto, "Le "lait noir" chez Pline l'ancien," in *Reşid Rahmeti Arat İçin* (Ankara: Türk Kültürünü Araştırma Enstitüsü, 1966), pp. 1–4; and N. L. Zhukovskaia, "Tsentral'n͡aia Aziia," in *Ètnografiia pitaniia narodov stran zarubezhnoi Azii*, ed. S. A. Arutiunov (Moscow: Nauka, GRVL, 1981), pp. 120–139, and Konovalov, *Kazakhi iuzhnogo Altaia*, pp. 80–83, both with further references. See also Doerfer, *TMEN*, III, pp. 512–517, s.v. "*qimīz*," and on Mongol-era food ways see Yan-shuan Lao, "Notes on Non-Chinese Terms in the Yüan Imperial Dietary Compendium Yin-shan chang-yao," *Bulletin of the Institute of History and Philology, Academia Sinica*, 39 (October 1969), pp. 399–416; Herbert Franke, "Additional Notes on Non-Chinese Terms in the Yüan Imperial Dietary Compendium Yin-shan chang-yao," *ZAS*, 4 (1970), pp. 7–16; Paul D. Buell, "*The Yin-shan Cheng-yao*, a Sino-Uighur Dietary: Synopsis, Problems, Prospects," in *Approaches to Traditional Chinese Medical Literature*, ed. Paul U. Unschuld (Dordrecht: Kluwer Academic Publishers, 1989), pp. 109–127; and Buell's "Pleasing the Palate of the *Qan*: Changing Foodways of the Imperial Mongols," *Mongolian Studies*, 13 (1990), pp. 57–81.

The present text presents two primary dilemmas beyond the individual terminological problems discussed below. First, the manipulation of vessels as described in the account seems to reflect in part the kind of ritual libations and/or presentations of drinking cups discussed in Chapter 3 with regard to the ritual intrusion implied by the account; the terminology employed, however, seems rather to reflect a description of the *preparation* of a particular beverage, perhaps through distillation. Second, the nature of the beverage prepared or presented is unclear: the account seems to refer *either* to the preparation of kumiss (or distilled kumiss) to which mead or honey is added, possibly as a fermenting agent, *or* to the preparation of mead or other fermented (or distilled) drink made from honey alone. Before examining the passage itself and its terminology, a number of general considerations affecting the interpretation should be noted.

In the first place, the text itself makes no explicit mention of *qïmïz* or of mare's milk, while the phrase *bal avuzï/bal özi* (discussed below) *is* used and clearly indicates the use of honey in some form; if we suggest nevertheless that the preparation of kumiss is intended here, we must suppose that the use of kumiss in the process would have been assumed by the intended audience either from the setting of the narrative or from the context of the process—i.e., that the vessels mentioned are specifically kumiss vessels and therefore imply the use of kumiss.

Second, there is likewise no explicit mention of fire or heating in the text, again requiring us to assume, if we suggest that a *distilled* drink is intended, that the process or vessels mentioned must imply the use of heating.

Third, as unclear as the terminology may be, it seems certain that it does *not* refer to the standard preparation of simple kumiss by churning mare's milk in large leather sacks; rather, if it reflects the preparation of a beverage rather than its ritual presentation, the account describes a successive decanting of a drink (presumably in the course of purifying it or strengthening its alcoholic content), a process that might properly be interpreted in the context of either distillation or catalyzed fermentation—again offering no decisive resolution.

Fourth, contemporary descriptions of drinks enjoyed at the Mongol courts imply a clear distinction between kumiss and mead or other beverages made from honey, but at the same time attest to the use of both; the descriptions, as brief as they are, of the vessels used for these drinks, might lead us moreover to argue against the rigid association of particular vessels with kumiss. Marco Polo, for instance, does not indicate the process of producing kumiss, but describes its use at court along with other unspecified beverages; he does, however, describe the herd of special horses kept to produce kumiss for the Great Khan and for use in sacred libations (cf. Pelliot, *Notes on Marco Polo*, I, p. 240), as noted earlier. Among other European travelers (cf. *The Mongol Mission*), Plano Carpini notes the use of mare's milk and insists that the Mongols had no mead or wine "unless it is sent or given to them by other nations" (p. 17), and speaks only of "drinks" in gold and silver vessels on a table in Batu's tent; Rubruck, who mentions the use of "cosmos" at Batu's court (p. 127) and in a major "drinking festival" sponsored by Möngke (p. 202), describes a drink made from rice, millet, wheat, and honey used in lieu of kumiss (pp. 96–97) and maintains that four chief drinks are offered at court: wine, "caracosmos" (the "refined milk of mares," whose preparation by churning-induced fermentation he describes, p. 99), mead (which he says is called *bal* or *boal*; on the latter forms cf. Paul Pelliot, *Recherches sur les chrétiens d'Asie Centrale et d'Extrême-Orient* [Paris: Imprimerie Nationale, 1973], p. 149), and a wine, "mead," or "ale" made from rice (pp. 149, 154, 163, 176, in the latter instance referring to the four drinks provided by the famous "silver tree" devised for Möngke by the Parisian master Guillaume Buchier). More relevant to our text, Ibn Baṭṭūṭah's account of his stay at the court of Özbek Khan includes frequent reference to the use of kumiss in ceremony and hospitality; he appears clearly to distinguish it from the drink of *fermented* honey (*nabīdh al-ᶜasal*) whose use he describes in the Muslim context of *ᶜĪd al-fiṭr*, the festival of breaking the fast of Ramaḍān, but his testimony that this *nabīdh al ᶜasal* was the drink most commonly used at court may be tempered by his explanation that the adherence of Özbek's people to the Ḥanafī *madhhab* allowed them to consider fermented liquor to be licit (cf. *Voyages d'Ibn Battûta*, ed. and tr. Defrémery and Sanguinetti, II, pp. 378, 386, 392–393, 408). The account of al-Mufaḍḍal describing the use of a *distilled* honey drink at the Mongol court was mentioned above; he notes that Berke provided the Mamlūk ambassadors with *qïmïz* and "boiled" honey (*al-ᶜasal al-maṭbūkh*; E. Blochet, ed. and tr., *Histoire des sultans mamlouks, Patrologia Orientalis*, 12/3 (Paris, 1919), p. 461). In short, although the contemporary descriptions might seem on balance to support the view that a honey-based drink was the focus of our text, they do not do so decisively.

And finally, as perplexing as the account remains in itself, our author adds to the uncertainties by referring to the process as a *karāmat*. All in all, despite the terminological difficulties and the seeming preponderance of historical evidence, sketchy as it is, supporting the conclusion that a drink of fermented *honey* is implied here, I am inclined, on the basis of the probable interpretation of the apparatus employed, to understand the account as referring to the addition of fermented honey—as a catalyst or perhaps only for taste—to kumiss, in the process of a ritual mixing and presentation of beverages that may also have been accompanied by libations from the same vessels; the specific terminological issues are discussed (with no greater conclusiveness, I fear) in subsequent notes.

In any case, part of the obscurity may stem, indeed, from the likelihood that the extant narrative reflects a conflation of several accounts or an abbreviated, "encoded" account designed to evoke particular religious counterpoints. We may console ourselves by remembering that the point of the narrative—that the process supervised by the khan's "religious specialists" failed on the occasion of the Muslim saints' arrival, undermining the soothsayers' prestige and setting the stage for the subsequent disputation and "test"—is not in itself dependent on a precise understanding of the process in question.

Iudin again offers no discussion of his understanding of this passage, but his transcription and translation would seem to support my interpretation of some of the terminology, though differing on one important point; the key difference is in the final stage of the "wonder," and his interpretation, though not without difficulties, is attractive in several ways. Iudin's Russian translation runs as follows [with his brackets omitted]: "They would bring honey in a jug [*zhban*, for the term Iudin transcribes as *subjaqï*] to Uzbek-khan at the assembly and would set it up. Then they would fit a coil [or "pipe," *zmeevik*, for the term Iudin transcribes as *jorghatï*] to the jug, and would prepare cups [*chashi*, for the text's *dostïghanlar*]. The honey itself would accumulate in the pipe and decant into the cup, and the cup itself would move to that person." Iudin thus reads "*barur erdi*," "would move," where I had read "*berür erdi*," "would give," and while with my reading the account parallels descriptions of the presentation of cups at Mongol-era drinking ceremonies, as discussed in Chapter 3, Iudin's reading provides a remarkable parallel to Marco Polo's description of the *bakhshï*s making cups fly through the air, cited in the same chapter. In favor of Iudin's interpretation is, above all, the clear "wonder" it provides; grammatically, as well, the lack of a plural suffix on "*erdi*" (and of an accusative suffix after "*dostïghan özi*") might support an interpretation making "*dostïghan özi*" ("the vessel itself") the subject of the verb rather than the sorcerers, although the use of both suffixes is too irregular to make much of this. The verb he interprets as "*barur*" is written without an *alif*, i.e., "*b.rūr*," and although this spelling is usually reserved for the verb-stem "*ber-*" ("to give"), with the verb-stem "*bar-*" ("to go") more often written with an *alif*, "*bar-*" is occasionally found without an *alif* in this text (once, even, in the conversion narrative, and in this instance also in the aorist, i.e., "*b.rūr*", cf. note [14] below), leaving no room for objection on orthographic grounds. In addition, ʿAbd al-Ghaffār Qïrïmī's version of the drinking ceremony seems to allow a similar interpretation (his text describes a series of decantings, on which see note [4] below, but what then "comes by itself to the khan's hand [and] to the others" is not necessarily the vessel, and the term "*özi*" [i.e., *a.w.z.y*] in Ötemish Ḥājjī's text is more ambiguous than ʿAbd al-Ghaffār's "*kendüliginden*").

Objections to his interpretation include the remaining uncertainties (ignored by Iudin) surrounding the terminology of the account, as discussed in the following notes; in particular, the term he translates as "coil" or "pipe" should probably be understood, instead, as a vessel *possessing* a "pipe," while the term he translates as "cup" seems more likely to refer not to a vessel from which one drinks (as implied if this vessel "moves" to he recipient), but to a vessel from which one pours. In this connection we may note that Iudin's translation of *süzül-* as "to be decanted" rather than "to be strained" seems off the mark. In addition, the description of the *disrupted* "wonder" goes only so far as the failure of the honey/mead to be strained into the *dostïghan*, suggesting that the particular "wonder" is somehow to be found in the decantings and strainings rather than in the way in which the beverage or cup moved to the khan; to be sure, the entire process was thereby halted, leaving no need to note explicitly the failure of the ensuing steps, but stopping the account of the disrupted "wonder" at that point would seem to undermine the narrative's dramatic impact. Finally, we might object that the verb *bar-*, "to go," seems altogether too dull a word to have used in describing such a "wonder." Compared with Marco Polo's account, for instance, this narrative is both excessively attentive to the "instrumentation" of the wonder, and noticeably understated when it comes to describing the most astonishing moment in the sorcerers' "show," if indeed the cups moving by themselves is what was intended as the climactic wonder. Although we are assuming a great deal of "telescoping" in the account as it has been preserved, these considerations may caution us against adopting Iudin's reading too readily. The text is, I believe, more complex than Iudin's quite reasonable, but somewhat facile, translation suggests, and I am not convinced that we have yet a satisfactory interpretation.

[4] *s.bjāq*. The uncertainty begins with this term, the most likely reading for which is *sapchaq*, a form reported in the early fourteenth-century glossary of Abū Ḥayyān with the meaning of a copper-handled bucket; cf. Caferoğlu, *Kitâb al-Idrâk*, p. 86 (text), p. 56 (tr.); cf. also Radlov, *Opyt*, IV, 410 (*sapchaq*, "bucket," in the Sagai dialect). It may be a descriptive term for a vessel with a handle, since it seems reasonable to consider it to be derived from *sap* ("handle," cf. *ED*, p. 782) plus the denominal suffix *-čaq*, which Clauson (*ED*, p. xli) describes as forming concrete nouns for instruments; the form and apparent function recall the shallow wooden bowl called *saptayak* used among the Qazaqs

in boiling milk with heated pebbles for the preparation of a special mixture of kumiss, whole milk, and boiled milk, as described by Fiel'strup ("Molochnye produkty," p. 281; cf. Radlov, *Opyt*, IV, 408–409). However, a larger vessel is implied in what remains one of the best accounts of the preparation of kumiss and its distillates: A. V. Adrianov, "Airan v zhizni minusinskago inorodtsa," *Zapiski Imperatorskago Russkago Geograficheskago Obshchestva po otdeleniiu ètnografii*, t. 34 (1909; = *Sbornik v chest' semidesiatiletiia Grigoriia Nikolaevicha Potanina*), pp. 489–524; Adrianov cites (pp. 500, 522) the term *sapchak* among the Sagais, meaning the "tub" or "vat" used as the most characteristic part of one variety of the apparatus used in the further distillation of kumiss (i.e., from *ayran* into *araq*), but notes that the word is used also to refer to the entire apparatus. Now Adrianov (pp. 497–501) describes two set-ups for distillation: one involves an iron cauldron, in which the liquid is heated, topped with a wooden "cap" from which a bow-shaped tube (called *sorga* among the Sagais) extends to draw the steam and its condensate into a narrow-necked collecting vessel, while the other consists of a large vat (the *sapchak*) filled with the liquid, in which is set a conical cask topped by an iron bowl (filled with cold water, to condense the steam); from the side of the cask leads a grooved handle attached to a furrowed spade-like paddle, whose grooves catch the condensing liquid and drain it outside the cask into the collecting vessel. The second type of apparatus is also described by Potapov among the Tuvans, who, however, call the grooved paddle *shorga* (cf. L. P. Potapov, *Ocherki narodnogo byta tuvintsev* [Moscow: Nauka, GRVL, 1969], p. 171, and his earlier study, "Materialy po ètnografii tuvintsev raionov Mongun-taigi i Kara-kholia," in *Trudy Tuvinskoi kompleksnoi arkheologo-ètnograficheskoi èkspeditsii*, I [*Materialy po arkheologii i ètnografii zapadnoi Tuvy*] [Moscow/Leningrad: Izd–vo AN SSSR, 1960], pp. 171–237 [p. 178]); similarly, among the Qalmïqs, Pallas described (with fine illustrations) an apparatus resembling Adrianov's first set-up, but assigns the designation *chapchak* to the cover placed over the "cauldron," calling the tube which conveys the condensate *zorgo* (Peter Simon Pallas, *Sammlungen historischer Nachrichten über die mongolischen Völkerschaften*; Erster Theil [Frankfurt and Leipzig, 1779; repr. Graz: Akademische Druck-u. Verlagsanstalt, 1980], pp. 134–135, Pl. III [cf. Montell, "Distilling," pp. 329–330; see the similar apparatus depicted in S. K. Krukovskaia, *Astrakhanskii krai* (Saint Petersburg, 1904), p. 113; and note the similar description, from among the "Tatars" of west Siberia in 1721, by D. G. Messerschmidt, *Forschungsreise durch Sibirien 1720–1727*, ed. E. Winter and N. A. Figurovskij, Teil 1 (Berlin: Akademie Verlag, 1962), pp. 61–62]; Pallas also describes, more briefly, and illustrates a set-up resembling Adrianov's second as in use among the Buryats and eastern Mongols [p. 182, Pl. VII], but in this case does not give the native terms for the parts of the apparatus).

Terms similar to those found in our text are thus applied to different parts of typical Inner Asian distilling set-ups. It is tempting to transpose our text's terminology onto one of these methods and assign the role of the distillery set-up as a whole to the *sapchaq*, and equate the *chūrghātī* with either the tube or the grooved paddle, and the *dostïghan* with the collecting vessel. Such a reading is supported by ʿAbd al-Ghaffār Qïrïmī's version, where the first term was apparently understood as a kind of vessel into which the khan's "sorcerers" placed their "intoxicating drinks" (*muskirāt*); the published text (ed. Najīb ʿĀṣim, p. 36) has the drink placed into "a vessel [*qāb*] called *chapchaq*" (on this form, cf. Budagov, I, p. 467 [*chabchāq*, described as meaning a barrel or cask (in the Crimea), a tub or vat (in his "Tatar"), and a bucket (in the Altay), with the form *shapshaq* attested among other Siberian Tatars], and I, p. 453 [*chāpchïq*, a vat or large tub in the dialect of Kazan]), then poured into another "vessel" [*ẓarf*] called *chughrātī* [*sic* in the published version; see below], and finally poured into "a bowl [*qadaḥ*] called *ṭūstiġān*" [or *ṭūstiʿān*; the latter form is adopted in the published version, while the MS is unclear and could be read either way, but the possible omission of the dot above the *ʿayn* is hardly significant; see below on this term].

However, in our text's *second* description of the apparatus used in this ceremony, noting its *failure*, the place of the *sapchaq* seems to be taken by *paymānah* ("cup" or "goblet"), indicating that some kind of large vessel (probably with handles) is meant; and the parallelism of the phrases (second: *paymāna-si bilä bal keltürdilür*; first: *sapchāq-nï bilä keltürüp qoyar erdi-lär* [here the word *bilä* is inappropriate: it was perhaps to have been crossed out, since it appears to have been awkwardly written, or conversely its presence may indicate that the word *bal* should have followed it as in the second case, or, finally, the phrase should have read *sapchāqï bāl*; see the text] suggests that the *sapchaq*, whatever its size or shape, was a vessel in which the honey or mead was to be brought. This is how I have interpreted it.

Such an interpretation is perhaps supported by the curious echoes of this terminology in several versions of the epic account of Idige; together with the appearance of "honey" in several conversion narratives, and the preservation of the specific element of a *vat* of honey in the twentieth-century tradition about Baba Tükles preserved near Astrakhan, the mention, in the Idige tale, of *bal* specifically linked with two of the apparent names of vessels found in Ötemish Ḥājjī's account (i.e., *sapchaq* and *tostuqan*) may reflect a formulaic echo of the earliest versions of the narrative elements that made their way into the account of Baba Tükles (and into accounts of other Islamizers as well).

The element of the *sapchaq* appears in the recently published "Tatar" version of the Idige tale (p. 16 in the journal version), in which the bard Sobra is plied with drink before consenting to recount Idige's origins: he was given "yellow honey with its *chapchak*" and three *tustagans* of honey (*chapchagi belän sarï bal / öch tustagan bal birde*); the latter element appears in other versions, as noted below. More remarkable is a passage in the "Crimean" version published by Çağatay ("Die Ädigä-Sage," pp. 244 [text], 249 [tr.]) and clearly reflected also in Semenov's Noghay version (given only in translation, *Tuzemtsy*, p. 428), where the "vat" of honey figures in what appears to be a stylized echo of an account of shamanic ascent: when the true origin of Idige (known at court up to that point as "Qubūl," the "Kubugul" of several other versions) is revealed by the aged bard, the hero flees by jumping upon a vat of honey and escaping out the smoke-hole of the yurt (in Çağatay's text, *bal çapçaqtan basıp, şıγaraqtan / çıγıp qaşar boγay qubūl*).

An altogether different, though unlikely, reading is possible from the manuscript, namely *sachaq*, in the meaning of "tablecloth" as reported in the *Sanglākh* (ed. G. Clauson, *Muḥammad Mahdī Xān, Sanglākh: A Persian Guide to the Turkish Language* [London, 1960; Gibb Memorial Series, n.s. 20], facs., f. 229v; cf. Clauson, *ED*, p. 796 [s.v. "saçgak"], A. Pavet de Courteille, *Dictionnaire turc-oriental* [Paris, 1870], p. 333). Yet another reading is suggested by the use of derivatives [e.g., usually of the form "*sačïq*"] of the Turkic verb *sač-*, "to scatter," to refer both to ritual aspersions of kumiss and to "scatterings" of coins at royal audiences as a sign of the sovereign's munificence.

Iudin, again without comment, transcribes the term as *subjaqï*, translating it simply as "*zhban*" (a "can" or "hooped wooden jug"); although his transcribed text (p. 133) reads "*subjaqï billä*" [*sic*], in his notes (p.191) he suggests emending the text to read "*subjaqï bilä bal*" (see above in this note for other alternatives).

[5] *jūrġātī*. This word, written always in this form, is the most problematical of the terms in this passage. To begin with, its basic form is uncertain, since from the context it may be understood as an independent term or as *jūrghāt* plus a possessive suffix. The word is attested in this latter form only in Radlov (*Opyt*, III, 2173), who cites *churghat* in the dialect of Kazan as a "copper vessel for the preparation of beer," unfortunately adding no useful details. However, the form *jurghāt*, explicitly vowelled thus, appears in a nineteenth-century Persian history of Qoqand, in the context of a genealogical legend of origin for the ruling Ming tribal dynasty of the Qoqand khanate (discussed by Beisembiev, *"Ta'rikh-i Shakhrukhi" kak istoricheskii istochnik*, pp. 84, 86; I have checked also a manuscript of the *Tārīkh-i Shāhrukhī*, MS LOIVAN C468 [described in N. D. Miklukho-Maklai, ed. *Opisanie persidskikh i tadzhikskikh rukopisei Instituta vostokovedeniia*, vyp. 3 (Istoricheskie sochineniia) (Moscow: Nauka, GRVL, 1975), pp. 331–332, No. 459], f. 26b). Beisembiev interprets the term as "soured milk," and the context makes it clear that it is a liquid; indeed, it seems reasonable to understand the form given in the nineteenth-century source as a metathesized form of *jughrat*, "soured whole milk, yoghurt," itself a Qazaq or general "Qïpchaq" form of an apparently original Old Turkic form *"yughrut"* (cf. Clauson, *ED*, p. 905, s.v. *"yuğrut"*). Now the use of the possessive suffix seems unusual in our text, but it is not impossible that the basic term here is indeed *jūrghāt*, meaning "soured milk," perhaps for use in the preparation of kumiss; such an interpretation would provide a much clearer basis for assuming the use of kumiss in the ceremony described by Ötemish Ḥājjī. However, the metathesized form *jurghāt* must itself be regarded as unusual (for example, Budagov [I, p. 434] cites only the form *jurgha*, in Tatar and Qazaq, while the modern Qïrghïz *juurat* implies a nonmetathesized form; cf. Budagov, II, p. 377, citing several unmetathesized forms), and despite the attractiveness of finding this "soured milk" in our ceremony (especially in view of its appearance in another legend of origin), the more likely explanation for the form *jūrghātī* appears to lie elsewhere.

From the context the term may also refer to some type of vessel, rather than a substance, into which honey or mead could be poured and from which it could be strained into yet another vessel; as noted above, the Ottoman version treats the term (given inexplicably in the form *č.ġrātī*) as an unfamiliar word for a kind of "vessel" (*ẓarf*). The final *-t* (or *-tï*) is problematical, but it seems likely that the term may be connected with the word *chorgha*, of Mongol origin, which the *Sanglakh* explains as a narrow-necked vessel "in which they beat soured milk" (facs. ed. Clauson, f. 212v [*čūrġā*], and p. 96; cf. Pavet de Courteille, p. 293); Clauson, citing the meaning of "a narrow-necked jug," derives the term from Mongol *chorgho*, for which he cites the meanings "tube," "pump," "spout," "tap," and "gutter." As mentioned in the preceding note, the same term, in the form *sorga*, is noted by Adrianov ("Airan," pp. 498, 522) as referring quite clearly to the distillation *tube* draining the distilled liquor into a collection vessel, while it is used in the form *shorga* among the Tuvans (cf. Potapov) to refer to the grooved paddle performing the same function—suggesting that a more general meaning for the term might be "drain." Radlov (*Opyt*, III, 2020) cites the form *chorgho* in Altai and Teleut with two meanings, (1) tubes used in the distillation of (milk) liquor, and (2) the tap or spigot of a samovar; he cites the form *shorgha* in Shor (IV, 1028) as referring to a "bowed wooden tube used in the distillation of wine from milk," and the form *sorgha* in Sagai and Koibal meaning "funnel." Fiel'strup ("Molochnye produkty," pp. 283–284) reports that the Qïrghïz of Semirechye refer to their apparatus for distilling kumiss or *airan* into *arak* as "*kapka chorgo*," because the two chief components are the iron cauldron (*kapkak*) and one or two bowed tubes (*chorgo*). The meaning "tube" for Mongol *chorgho* was mentioned to me by Professor György Kara, who suggested a suffixed form *chorghotay*, meaning an apparatus *possessing* such a tube or drain, as a possible basis for the form in our text; and in fact the form *tsorghotoi* is cited in this sense in F. D. Lessing's *Mongolian-English Dictionary* (Berkeley and Los Angeles: University of California Press, 1960), p. 198. The Turkic equivalent of this form, *chorghalïgh*, explained as a vessel "possessing" a tube or drain, is attested in a Ming-era Sino-Uyghur glossary (Louis Ligeti, "Glossaire supplémentaire au vocabulaire sino-ouigour du bureau des traducteurs," *AOH*, 22 (1969), p. 23, with references to other Mongol and Turkic forms of *chorgho*), reinforcing my inclination to regard the form in our text as a somewhat corrupted representation of the Mongol term for a type of kumiss vessel familiar to Turks and Mongols alike, one whose designation in both languages was determined by the component (distillation tube or drain?) that was most distinctive in both the form and the function of the vessel; in any case it appears that both suffixed and nonsuffixed forms might refer to a part of the apparatus or to the whole.

Further support for the reading "*chūrghātay*" may be found in the vowelling of the corresponding term's ending in the manuscript of ʿAbd al-Ghaffār Qïrïmī's work (MS, f. 263a [Latin]/261a [Arabic]); the *ḥarakahs* indicating the vowels are omitted in Najīb ʿĀṣim's published version): there the term is clearly written "*chagharātay*"; but in view of the inversion of the *rā* and *ghayn* and the other "incorrect" vowels it is difficult to place too much reliance on the clearly vowelled ending *-tay*.

Without resolving the problem of the ending, I am inclined to suppose that the term in our text refers to a vessel, no doubt fitted with a drain of some sort, forming part of an apparatus used for the further distillation or, more probably, for the accelerated fermentation of kumiss. A similar term (*csorgó*) whose meanings include "tube," "channel," "groove," exists in Hungarian, and was identified by Gyula Németh as attested, in the form *tzerga*, in a tenth-century Greek text of Constantine Porphyrogenitus; there it appears as a "Turk" [meaning Hungarian] word for a portable bathing apparatus (which evidently included a tube), but Németh rejects any relation between this term and several Turkic words, cited from Radlov, including the "*chorgho*" noted above, although he does not cite the Mongol terms (J. Németh, "Ein ungarisches Lehnwort in Byzanz im 10. Jahrhunderts," in *Beiträge zur Sprachwissenschaft, Volkskunde und Literaturforschung: Wolfgang Steinitz zum 60. Geburtstag am 28. Februar 1965 dargebracht* [Berlin: Akademie-Verlag, 1965], pp. 291–294).

Iudin transcribes *jorghatï* and translates as "*zmeevik*" ("coil" or "pipe"); I have not found a word of this form with this meaning, and without any discussion on Iudin's part it is difficult to judge why he chose to render the term thus. The weight of evidence noted in the preceding discussion renders his interpretation unlikely.

[6] *dūstīġān*. Found more commonly with initial "*t-*," as *tostaqan* or *tostughan*, the term is described in the *Sanglākh* [*tūstūġān*] as a narrow-necked vessel with a spout (*kūzah-i lūlah-dār*), or ewer (*ibrīq*); the work cites a verse implying that the *tostughan* may hold wine (*chaghïr*) and is something held by a cupbearer (*ayaghchï*), but also cites a verse referring to a *tostughan* full of *qïmïz*, confirming its role in the sort of ceremony described in the present text, and gives finally another meaning, as simply a "bowl" or "cup" (facs., ed. Clauson, f. 176r). Budagov (I, p. 394), however, gives the form *tūstāġān* from Qazaq and describes it as a ladle or dipper or small bucket for drawing out kumiss, while Radlov (*Opyt*, III, 1211–1212, 1501) explains it as a Qazaq term for a drinking glass (*stakan*) or small wooden bowl; these meanings are maintained in modern

Qazaq and Qaraqalpaq. In the epic tale of Idige, the bard Subrā-jïraw is induced to speak by being offered food and drink, as noted above; in several versions (cf. Osmanov, p. 34, "*üš tūstuqāy bāl berdi*"; the Tatar version published in *Kazan utlarï*, p. 16; Radlov, *Proben*, VII, p. 147) he is given "three *tostaghans* of *bāl*," and upon drinking them he is ready to recount Idige's descent from Baba Tükles, in a curious echo of the saint's association with *bāl* as discussed above. From the present text I am inclined to understand it not as a cup itself, but as a vessel used to convey to the recipients the final product of the process, and I am likewise inclined to cite the term as further evidence, though not decisive in view of the *Sanglākh*'s account, of the implicit presence of kumiss in our text's process. As noted above, it might seem possible to interpret the *dostïghan* as the collection vessel for a distillation apparatus, and the "straining" mentioned in the text might be compatible with such an interpretation, but the evidence seems to argue against a process of distillation. Iudin's interpretation of this term as "cup" is entirely plausible, but the examples cited above suggest a larger vessel.

[7] *bāl a.w.z.ī*. The first of these terms is clear enough, although its precise meaning remains uncertain, while the second may be read in several ways. In the case of *bal*, we may understand either "honey" or "mead," but, again, it is unfortunately not clear from the present text precisely what procedure is described, and there is even less material available on the use of honey in such circumstances than on the use of kumiss; the most thorough treatment (Edward Tryjarski, "Beekeeping Among the Turks," *Acta Orientalia*, 32 (1970; = PIAC XI), pp. 241–277) offers little assistance on this point (Samojlovič, "Beiträge zur Bienenzucht," provides even less). The phrase as a whole is reminiscent, orthographically, of the compound form *bal-avuz* meaning "wax" or "honeycomb," (cf. Tryjarski, "Beekeeping," p. 261, citing the *Codex Cumanicus*, the medieval Qïpchaq language manuals, and modern Qïpchaq languages); while this reading is not entirely ruled out by the context (since the phrase *quyulur erdi* ["was poured"] may also be read *qoyulur erdi* ["was placed"]), it seems unlikely that we should envision wax or a honeycomb being placed into the *chorghatï* and its contents then strained into the *dostïghan*, and in any case the appearance of the phrase *dostïghan a.w.zī* (see below), as unclear as it may be, seems to argue against this reading of the word. As an entirely separate word, the second element in the phrase would appear to be simply *özi*, implying the "self," "essence," or "best part" of honey or mead; the exten-

sive range of meanings attested for *öz* (cf. , È. V. Sevortian, *Ètimologicheskii slovar' tiurkskikh iazykov (obshchetiurkskie i mezhtiurkskie osnovy na glasnye)* [Moscow: Nauka, 1974], pp. 506–508) suggests this reading (which might also apply for the subsequent phrase *dostïghan özi*), by which we might even understand some product of the *distillation* of mead—especially in view of the meaning of *öz* cited by Abū Ḥayyān (cf. Caferoğlu, p. 12), that of the "grease that rises to the top when boiling food." However, the Mamlūk-era manual *Bulghat al-mushtāq fī lughat at-turk wa'l-qifjāq*, dating most probably from the mid-fourteenth century, cites for the form *avuz* two meanings: first the familiar "colostrum," "first milk after parturition" (i.e., the term more commonly found in the form *aghuz*), and the second (possibly misvowelled for *öz*?) "ferment," "rennet," i.e., a substance used to promote the curdling of milk (Ananiasz Zajączkowski, ed., *Vocabulaire arabe-kiptchak de l'époque de l'État Mamelouk* (*1-ère partie, Le nom*) (Warsaw: Państwowe wydawnictwo naukowe, 1958), p. 9, facs. p. 8; cf. Sevortian, pp. 405–407). This latter meaning seems a likely derivative from the basic sense of either *öz* ("essence," "pith") or *avuz* ("colostrum"), and since for the latter term one would expect *aghuz* in this text, I would lean toward adopting the reading *bal özi*. In any case, while the form (*özi* or *avuzï*) remains uncertain, I am inclined to interpret the phrase as referring to a honey- or mead-based fermenting agent, produced perhaps from the "boiled honey" mentioned at Berke's court, added to kumiss to curdle it (the fact that the product in our text is *strained* is perhaps significant here), to hasten the fermentation process (for a mention of the use of honey among the Altai Turks as a component in fermenting agents for kumiss, cf. N. A. Trofimukh, "Sanitarnyi ocherk obsledovaniia vodosnabzheniia, pitaniia, zhilishcha i odezhdy zhitelei Kazakstana," in *Kazaki*, ed. Rudenko, pp. 163–228 [pp. 181–182]), or to enhance the taste (cf. the mention of "honeyed kumiss" in Hatto, *Memorial Feast*, pp. 2 [text], 3 [tr.]).

Finally we may note in this regard the curious recurrence of "honey" as an element in conversion stories connected with the Crimea (from the legends surrounding Sarï Saltïq and from the seventeenth-century *Tavārīkh-i Dasht-i Qipchāq*, both linking honey to "Kamāl Ata"); as noted, Baba Tükles' association with honey was preserved down to the twentieth century. Iudin understands the term simply as "*özi*" in this and the following case, referring to the "honey itself" and "the cup itself"; this is entirely plausible, and reflects the different understanding of the "wonder" described, as discussed above in note [3].

[8] *dostïghan a.w.zī*. The same form as in the phrase *bal özi /avuzï*, here perhaps referring to the essence or "cream" of the honeyed kumiss; it may, of course, mean simply that "the *dostïghan* itself" was given to the people, but as noted above I am more inclined to understand the *dostïghan* as a vessel from which one pours than as one from which one drinks.

[9] *yān-lārïda yāna-šā olturtup*; on *yanaša* ("beside," "next to," from *yanaš-*), cf. Budagov, II, p. 343. In ʿAbd al-Ghaffār Qïrïmī's Ottoman version this is altered to read that the "shaykhs" who directed the Mongols' worship of fire were esteemed by Özbek Khan and "sat knee-to-knee" with him [*zānū ba-zānū oturup*]. The protocol of seating arrangements, and further echoes of such protocol in tales of Islamization, were discussed in Chapter 3.

[10] Iudin emends this passage—which I have read "*khān majlis arasïnda sunnat qïldï*," "the khan observed the custom in the [midst of the] assembly"—to read "*khān majlis ārāstah qïldï*," "the khan arranged the assembly." The word I have interpreted as "*sunnat*" is indeed written pecularily, with *tā marbūṭah*, and Iudin's emendation is attractive for suggesting that the letters "*-sïnda*" were wrongly written instead of "*-stah*" and were to be crossed out, the correct ligature added afterwards. In fact neither interpretation is particularly satisfying: "*sunnat qïl-*" more commonly has a meaning quite inappropriate in this context ("to circumcise"), while the use of "*ārāstah*" (more commonly "adorned" than "arranged") is hardly typical in the context of a *majlis*.

[11] Iudin emends "*dostïġanġa*" to "*dostïġannï*," translating the full passage as "they brought the honey in the vessel; they brought also the pipe and the cup and set them up." The emendation seems imprudent, but would seem to make more sense than the text as it stands if we adopt Iudin's interpretation of the drinking ceremony.

[12] Here the manuscript appears to read *qorqut-dïn yürüp istängizlär*, and in the next line *qorqud-dïn taftīš qïldïlar ersä*, and evidently the inaccessible Togan manuscript reads the same: in his article mentioned above in Chapter 2 ("'Kitab-ı Dede Korkut' hakkında"), İnan interprets this *qorqut* as the proper name of Qorqut Ata, i.e., Dede Korkut, whom he thus casts as a leader of the "sorcerers" from whom the khan's servants are ordered to learn why the procedure failed. While the suggestion is tanta-

lizing, I am inclined rather to emend the text and assume that the copyists in each case "corrected" an unfamiliar form *qoru-dïn* (or possibly *qoruq-dïn*) to read *qorqut-dïn*; even this may have been done hesitatingly, for the first occurrence in the Tashkent manuscript is not at all clearly written (the second *qāf-wāw* ligature, in which the *qāf* bears no dots, appears to have been created out of either a single *rā* or a nearly joined *rā* + *wāw*, with another *rā* supplied above the line, while the *tā* has clearly been inserted clumsily before the *dāl* of the ablative suffix), while the more clearly written second occurrence suggests only that the copyist had already decided how to interpret the unfamiliar form. The emendation is suggested by the context and by the appearance of the term *qoru* in the text, although admittedly the repetition of the term three times in quick succession renders the emendation a less than elegant solution. The reading "Qorqut," however, is surely less desirable, since neither Togan nor Kafalı mentioned it (the former would surely have cited it), since there is no trace of such a reading in ʿAbd al-Ghaffār Qïrïmī's Ottoman version (which evidently renders the term in this instance by *ʿaskar*, i.e., "the troops"), since "Qorqut" is not further identified in the text and does not seem to appear elsewhere in the work (although İnan cites Ötemish Ḥājjī's work, from the Togan manuscript but without a folio reference, as locating Qorqut's grave near Sarāy—or is there instead a passage identifying Sarāy*chïq* as the royal *qoruq?*), and since the passage makes little sense grammatically with "Qorqut." In the latter connection, İnan gives what appears to be a transcription of the passage, differing in some regards from the Tashkent manuscript's reading but, more important, betraying the improbability of his reading by rendering the phrase *qorï-nïng tašïda*, clearly attested twice in our text, as "Korkut'nıng başında." His text is given thus (in the transcription adopted for the 1968 reprint):

> *Han hüküm kıldı kim Korkut'dın yürüp istengizler. . . . Mülâzim çıkıp, Korkut'dan baktı irse, kördiler Korkut'nıng başında özge suratlık kişiler başını koynıga salıp olturur irdiler.*

The corresponding passage in our text (with the proposed emendation) runs thus:

> *Khān ḥukm qïldï kim qoru-dïn yürüp istängizlär. . . . Mulāzim-lar čïqïp, qoru-dïn taftīš qïldïlar érsä, kördilär qorï-nïng tašïda tört özgä ṣūratlïġ kiši-lär baš-larnï qoyu salïp oltur[ur] érdi.*

Iudin's treatment of this term is discussed above in note [1] to the translation.

[13] Or "were seated and bowing their heads down" (*baš-larnï qoyu salïp oltur[ur] érdi*), i.e., presumably performing Muslim prayer; on *qoyu* ("downwards") cf. Clauson, *ED*, p. 596, s.v. "ko<u>d</u>ı:". *qoyu* is written clearly in this text, but İnan's text (see preceding note) reads *koynıga* and has their heads resting on their bosoms; it is not clear if this was İnan's interpretation/emendation or if this form actually appears in the Togan manuscript.

[14] The question is doubled as if from an idiom or from typical epic-style repetition (*ne iškä yüriyür-siz ne iškä b[a]rur-siz*, i.e., "on what business are you traveling, on what work are you journeying"); other possible implications from the repetition are unclear.

[15] The text is unclear here: *söylämäk-kä [ ] öltürmäk keräk*, with an illegible word added in the margin; see note 29 to the edited Turkic text (Appendix 1).

Iudin emends this passage to read, "*söylämäk kärekmäz öltürmäk keräk*," and indeed in the published facsimile of f. 48b a clear, if pecularily written, "*r.k.māz*" is visible; in the microfilm I obtained, the *rā* is missing and only a hint of the *kāf* is visible. The emendation makes sense, but two reservations may be noted: (1) the form *-mäz* would appear to be anomalous in a text of this date, although as a "fossilized" form with *kerek* may be less suspect; (2) the emendation supposes a spelling "*kār.k*" for the word that is spelled "*k.rāk*" in the same line (although orthographic inconsistencies are not uncommon in this text).

[16] The term *süksük* appears to be another name for the shrub or tree known also by the name "*saqsaul*," whence the Russian "*saksaul*," both terms referring to a type of tamarisk; in any case it refers to a light wood known for its intense heat when burned. Cf. Radlov, *Opyt*, IV, 799; Clauson, *ED*, p. 823; Budagov, I, p. 648. Pelliot (*Recherches sur les chrétiens d'Asie Centrale et d'Extrême-Orient*, p. 149) prefers the form *söksök* on the basis of a fourteenth-century Chinese transcription. The Yasavī *silsilah*, incidentally, includes a saint known as "Süksük Ata," known from oral tradition as well as from a number of unpublished Yasavī hagiographies.

[17] The passage is unfortunately unclear; I have read it thus: *birisi-gä baba tükläs dér aydïlar* [or *édilar?*] *tamām aʿżā-larïnï tük yapïp érdi*, i.e., "They used to call one of them "Baba Tükläs, for body hair covered all his limbs" (the "pluperfect" form in *-ip erdi* often suggests a prior condition or cause; cf. the examples cited by János Eckmann, *Chagatay Manual* [Bloomington: Indiana University Uralic and Altaic Series, No. 60, 1966], p. 179, §129). The words read as *tük yapïp*, however, are problematical. The first is written unclearly, but appears to be *tül.k*, interpretable as *tülüg* or *tülük*, the former properly adjectival, i.e., "hairy" (from *tü*, according to Clauson the original form of the word) and therefore inappropriate here, and the latter evidently possible as a substantive in view of the attested form *tülüklüg* (on the forms *tü/tük*, etc., cf. Clauson, *ED*, pp. 433 [s.v. "tü:"] and 498 [s.v. "tü:lüg"], Budagov, I, p. 400, and Radlov, *Opyt*, III, cols. 1530, 1533, as well as the discussion in Chapter 5). However, the latter form as well would seem to violate the clear intention of the passage, which is to explain an epithet derived from the form *tük*, and the form *tük* is clearly written twice later in the text; I have therefore preferred to take the form in the text as an orthographical peculiarity or a simple error (one perhaps suggested by the currency of the other forms) and read "*tük*." The second word is also not clear: it seems to end in *-ib*, and reading it as a gerund is suggested also by the past-tense verb *érdi* that follows it. The stem, however, appears to consist of two letters of which only one is provided with points, as a (-)*b*-; a transitive verb is demanded by the accusative suffix on *aʿżā-larï* (ruling out *biyi-*, "to become large" [cf. Clauson, *ED*, p. 299, s.v. "bed̲ü:-"]), and logical candidates are *bas-* ("to press," used in modern Uzbek, for instance, to mean "to cover" in the sense called for; and the modern Uyghur translation of the "pagan" legend of Oghuz Khan translates the phrase cited in Chapter 5, referring to the hero's body being covered with body hair [*tük tülüklüg*], using the phrase *pütün bädinini quyuq tük basqan edi* [cf. Geng and Ayub, p. 41]) and *yap-* ("to close over," "to cover," "to clothe"; cf. Clauson, *ED*, pp. 870–871, s.v. "yap-"). Since the letter *sīn* is usually indicated in this text by three dots, rarely omitted, below the letter, while the dots for *yā* are routinely left out (although admittedly not so often in initial position), and since the semantic range of the latter verb appears more suitable in the period of this text, I have read *yapïp*. As noted earlier, the form "*tükläs*"—which must be accepted as the original form of the name in view of the antiquity of Ötemish Ḥājjī's work relative to the later epic accounts—has no

evident etymology. Iudin, without comment, opts for "*basïp*," an entirely reasonable interpretation.

[18] *jébä*. A "cuirass" of chain mail; a Mongol term, cf. Doerfer, *TMEN*, I, pp. 284–286.

[19] *örä qopup*. *ör-* ("to rise," "to sprout up;" cf. Clauson, *ED*, p. 195), plus *qop-* ("to rise," "to stand up;" cf. Clauson, *ED*, p. 580, s.v. "kop-").

[20] *küli kökli yāšïl-lï bolup*. Evidently, "his ashes became bluish and greenish"; the use of the *-li* suffix with these adjectives of color is peculiar, and it is not clear whether the phrase is purely descriptive or has some idiomatic or symbolic connotation. Iudin translates, "his ashes sparkled with all colors of the rainbow."

[21] *jībe čoġ begin qïzïl bolup érdi*. Evidently, "the cuirass had turned red as a flame." The term interpreted as *begin* (or *bigin*), a common postposition in Chaghatay meaning "like," "resembling," is not quite clear; it is assumed here to be written as "*b.kīn*," but in fact the *kāf* is unusual, appearing more as a *lām* with a stray mark or overlining crossing it. The form "*b.līn*" would be meaningless, but *bā* seems clearly indicated, instead of *yā*; otherwise we might assume that the word intended was *yalïn*, "flame," understanding the substantive-pair *čoġ yalïn*, "fire-flame" as descriptive of *qïzïl*, "red" (and indeed *čoġ yalïn* is a common hendiaduoin; cf. Clauson, *ED*, pp. 405 [s.v. "ço:ğ"] and 929 [s.v. "yalın"]). The word *yalïn* appears several lines above in the form *yāl.n*, however, and although the text is full of different spellings for particular words, it is most likely *begin* that is intended here. See also note 47 to the edited Turkic text (Appendix 1). On the postposition *begin/bikin*, etc., cf. Budagov, I, p. 303; Clauson, *ED*, p. 686, s.v. "ki:b"; further references in A. K. Borovkov, *Leksika sredneaziatskogo tefsira XII–XIII vv.* (Moscow: Izd-vo Vostochnoi literatury, 1963), p. 100; and citations from fourteenth- and fifteenth-century texts, e.g., A. Bodrogligeti, *A Fourteenth Century Turkic Translation of Saʿdī's Gulistān (Sayf-i Sarāyī's Gulistān bi't-turkī)* [Bloomington: Indiana University/The Hague: Mouton, 1970; Uralic and Altaic Series, vol. 104], vocabulary, p. 229 [*bigi* and *bigin*]; È. I. Fazylov, ed. and tr., *Khodzhandi: Latafat-name, Kniga o krasote* (Tashkent: Fan, 1976), p. 110; V. Rähmanov, *Ozbek klässik ädäbiyati äsärläri uchun*

qisqächä lughät (Tashkent: Oqituvchi, 1983), p. 36, citing Atāʾī. Iudin reads "*čoġ bäkin*."

[22] Iudin reads "*bu yol ke*" (literally "this way, that"), evidently translating the phrase as "from the moment when Özbek Khan became a Muslim," instead of "*büyük*," "great." He asserts (p. 195) that the *lām* of the word "*yol*" is written above the *wāw* of the same word and the word *ke* (i.e., *kāf* + *hā*); the *kāf* in question, however, is quite clearly a final *kāf*, and it appears that the *lām* above the line was added by a different hand. In any case, *büyük* makes sense, and even if the marginal addition were to be adopted, the appropriate emendation would be simply "*bu yol*," "[in] this way."

[23] Qurʾān II.156.

Appendix 3

An Eighteenth–Century Khorezmian Account of the Conversion of Özbek Khan

(Staatsbibliothek zu Berlin - Preussischer Kulturbesitz, Orientabteilung, MS Diez A. Quart. 14, ff. 234b –236a)

ارباب بصارت و فراست و اصحاب فطانت و كياست غه [] [1] و مستور قالماسون اهل تواريخ و نساب نيك كلاملرى اكرجه توهم كذب و افترآ دن خالي ايماسدور لكن شوق كلاملرى بناء على الشهرة در و ثبوت نسب هم بناء [2] على التّسامع اولمق ايله در مؤرّخ و نساب غه لازم اولغان روايت و نقل در و العهده على الرّاوى الاوّل

ايديل و قوبان كنارنده اولتورغان نوغاى و ميرزا لر ارالرنده مشهور بو در كه اديكى بى [3] بابا تكلس اولادى در و اوزبك خان و انكا تابع بولغان ايل اول عزيز دعوتى

1. Word omitted, evidently a synonym of مستور , e.g. مخفى .
2. Written بناو .
3. Or بيى .

برله شرف اسلامه مشرّف بولدیلر ظاهرا الار نیك آدی صدر الدّین احمد اولمق کرك که دیار خوارزم و ماورآءالنّهر دا صدر اتا لقبی ایله مشهور درلر چون الار شعرانی و بدنلری نیك توکی کوب بولمق جهتندن نوغای اراسنده بابا تکلس درلر و بعضی نسب نامه دا [4] الار غه حاجی آخی هم درلر اول وجهدن که حضرت سیّد اتا غه اخ رضاعی ایمشلر

و حضرت سیّد اتا و صدر اتا و بدر اتا و اوزون حسن اتا بو تورت عزیز کچك لیکدن بر یر دا مصٰاحب اولوب ماورآءالنّهر ده تحصیل علوم ظاهری قیلدیلر ایرسه داعیۀ سلوك مشایخ باطنلرینده بیدا اولوب پیر [5] کامل طلب قیلب جمله مشایخ خوارزم و ماورآءالنّهر غا [6] زیارت قیلدقلرنده بارچه مشایخ دن الار غه اشارت بولدی که ترکستان ویلایتیغه [7] باریب مقصودینی اندا طلب اتکایلر بس بو تورت عزیز مشایخ ارشادی ایله ترکستان غه باریب مرادلرین زنکی اتا دن حاصل قیلدیلر و زنکی اتا حکیم [8] اتا دن مرخّص در و حکیم اتا سلطان خواجه احمد یسوی دن مرخّص در رحمة الله علیهم بس زنکی اتا اوّلا

4. Written نسب نامه و

5. Written بر .

6. Unclear; apparently written as ی and then altered to the dative suffix (as was clearly intended), but appears as غا instead of the expected غه .

7. Written thus, for ولایتیغه .

8. Written حکم .

صدر اتا غه رخصت بردی اول جهتدن الار غه باش خلیفه دیرلر بس اول اوش عزیز هم مرخّص اولدیلر بس حضرت زنکی اتا سیّد اتا ایله صدر اتا غه امر قیلدیلر که دشت قبچاق و سرایچق غه باریب انداغی کفّار و خلایق نی اسلامغه دعوت ایده سز

اولزمانده سرایچق ده پادشاه اوزبك خان ایردی که چنکیز خان نیك اولوغ اوغل [9] جوچی خان بشنچی اوغل شبان خان اولادی در أول زمانده چنکیز خان اولادیدن هنوز مسلمان اولغان پادشاه یوق ایردي بس حضرت سیّد اتا و صدر اتا پیر [10] امری ایله سرایچق غه باریب [11] اوزبك خان نی اسلامه / 235a / دعوت ایتدیلر و کوب کرامت و خارق عادات ظاهر قیلدیلر اوزبك خان عاقل و صاحب راي و قصص و تواریخ ملوك ماضیه نی کوب بیلور ایردی بو عزیز لر غه ایتدی کم سزنیك دینکیزنیك حق لوغین بیلور من بر شرط ایلیم شرطم بو دور که اولزمانده که فرعون نیك ساحر لری حضرت موسی علیه السّلام غه مقابل بولوب سحر ایتدیلر موسی علیه السّلام غه تاثیر ایتمای موسی علیه السّلام نیك معجزه سی اول سحر لر ني باطل قلدی جنانجه [12]

9. Written thus, without a possessive suffix, and consistently so in this text.

10. Written پر

11. Written below the line.

12. Written جنابنجه .

عصٰا سي اژدها اولوب بارچه سحر لر ني يوتوب يوق ايتدی اولزمانده ساحر لر بارچه سی موسی عليه السّلام غه ايمان [13] كتورديلر فی الحال اول ساحر لره [14] شرافت ايمان ايله يتی قات يـر و يـتـی قـات كـوك و عـرشـی [15] و كـورسـی [16] الار غه منكشف [17] بولدی اكر من هم مسلمان اولغاچ بو شكل دا منكا هم منكشف [18] اولسه بيلور من كه سز نيك دينكيز حقدر بس حضرت سيّد اتا صدر اتا غه اشارت قيلديلر كه سيز باش خليفه سز بو ايشنك تصرّفی سزكا مفوّضدر بس حضرت صدر اتا اوزبك خانغه كلمهٔ شهادت تلقين ايتديلر و اركان ايمان و شرايط و احكام اسلام و آبدست و نماز تعليم ايتدلر بس [19] وقتی نماز بولدی ايرسه قبله طرفنه متوجّه بولدی بس اوزبك خان ايتدی كعبه ني من كورمسام نچوك نماز ايتار من ديدوكنده صدر اتا قول لارين كوثروب [20] اُول كورنكان كعبه در ديو اشارت قيلديلر ايرسه اوزبك خان و حاضر تورغان بارچه خلايق نيك نظرندن حجابلر / 235b / كوتاريلوب حضرت كعبهٔ مكرّمه

13. Written below the line.

14. Written سحر لره .

15. Written thus, for عرش .

16. Written thus, for كرسی .

17. Written منكتّق ; the form is quite clear, and appears once more below, but منكشف is surely the word intended.

18. Written منكتق .

19. Written بش .

20. Written thus, instead of كوتاروب .

عیان و بیان ظاهر اولدی اوّل کشف که اوزبك خانغه ظاهر اولدی بو ایردی و مشهور در که اوزبك خان ایتور ایردی مدّت حیاتمده نمازغه شروع اتکانمده کعبه نی کورمکونجه [21] تکبیر تحریمه نی ایتمادیم حاصل کلام اول کونده یتمش منك کشی شرف اسلامغه مشرف بولدیلر و الحمد لله الذی هدانا لهذا و ما کنا لنهتدی لولا ان هدانا الله

و صدر اتا نیك نسب لرنده اختلاف دور بعض ایتورلر صدر اتا امام محمد حنفی نسلی در و بعض ایتورلر ابو بکر صدّیق رضی الله عنه نسلی در بو ایکی روایتدا وجه توفیق ممکن در که بر وجه دن اتا [22] طرفندن بولغی و بر وجه دن انا طرفندن بولغی و لکن نوغای اراسنده حضرت صدّیق نسلی اولمق ایله مشهور در و الله اعلم

و صدر اتا نیك اتا سی درویش ادهم در که سلطان ابراهیم بن ادهم نیك کچك اوغل در امّا سلطان ابراهیم بلخ ویلایتنده [23] پادشاه ایردی بر کیجه تخت اوستنده عبادته مشغول ایدی قصر اوستنده بر کمسه یورور ابراهیم سوردی کیم دور بنم قصریم اوستنده جواب کلدی کم بر عرب من

21. Appears to be written کورمکونیجه .

22. Written تا .

23. Written thus, for ولایتنده .

تیوه ایزلاب یوروب من ابراهیم دیدی بو نه عجب سوز در
بو قصر اوستنده تیوه بولمق نه ممکن در جواب کلدی کیم
تخت اوستنده درویش لك ایتب تنکری تعالی نی [24] ایزلمك
نه ممکن در ابراهیم غه بو سوز تاثیر [25] قیلب پادشاه لیغنی
ترك قیلب و درویش [26] کسوتین کیب بلخ دن غایب
اولوب و کعبه طرفنه کتدی خاتونی اوغل ایله ابراهیم طلبنه
ایردی کعبه که باریب اندا مرحم اولدیلر و کیچك اوغل
ادهم بلخ دن درویش لیك اختیار ایتب کتدی و اما سلطان
جلال الدّین رومی سلطان ابراهیم نیك اتاسی ایماسدر بل که
سلطان ابراهیم ایله ابن عم در

و صدر اتا که الحال بابا تکلس لقبی ایله مشهور در
پری قزین الوب دور دیکان سوز مشهور در اکر بو سوز
ثابت بولسه هم ممکن در زیرا که انسان جنیّه نی نکاح اتمك
شریعت ده فی الجمله جدارتی [27] بار در

حاصل الکلام بابا نیك اوش اوغل بار در اولوغ
اوغل نیك آتی اسلام بابا در / 236a / عالم عامل و شیخ و
اتا مندی الار غه قالدی و الار خوارزم [28] ویلایتنه توشدی
و بر اوغل ترکستانغه توشدی و برسی یاش قالدی و آنی

24. Written تعالنی .
25. Written تاثر .
26. Written دریش .
27. Uncertain; appears to be written حدازی .
28. The *alif* appears to have been added by a later hand.

منغت اسرادی انیك مشهور آتی ترمه در که نوغای اراسنده جمیع مرزالر نیك [29] اولوغ اتاسیدر و الله اعلم تحقیق الحال و الیه المرجع و المجال [30]

صدره الحقیر الفقیر الی الله نور الله بن عبید الله الصدّیق الخوارزمی سنه ۱۱۳۱

29. Written thus, for میرزالر نیك .

30. Written المحال .

Bibliography

Aalto, Pentti. "Le 'lait noir' chez Pline l'ancien." In *Reşid Rahmeti Arat İçin* (Ankara: Türk Kültürünü Araştırma Enstitüsü, 1966), pp. 1–4.

ʿAbdullāh b. Riżvān. *La chronique des steppes kiptchak, Tevārīḫ-i Dešt-i Qipčaq du XVIIe siècle.* Ed. Ananiasz Zajączkowski. Warsaw: Państwowe wydawnictwo naukowe, 1966; Prace orientalistyczne, tom XVI.

Abramzon, S. M. "Die Stammesgliederung der Kirgisen und die Frage nach ihrer Herkunft." *AOH,* 14 (1962), pp. 197–206.

Abramzon, S. M., and L. P. Potapov. "Narodnaia ètnogoniia kak odin iz istochnikov dlia izucheniia ètnicheskoi i sotsial'noi istorii (na materiale tiurkoiazychnykh kochevnikov)." *Sovetskaia ètnografiia,* 1975, No. 6, pp. 28–41.

Abū'l-Ghāzī. *Histoire des Mongols et des Tatares par Aboul-Ghâzî Béhâdour Khan.* Ed. and tr. P. I. Desmaisons. Saint Petersburg, 1871–72; repr. Amsterdam: Philo Press, 1970. 2 vols.

_____. *Rodoslovnaia turkmen: sochinenie Abu-l-Gazi khana khivinskogo,* ed. and tr. A. N. Kononov. Moscow/Leningrad: Izd-vo AN SSSR, 1958.

Adam, William [Guillelmus Adae]. "De modo sarracenos extirpandi." Ed. Ch. Kohler. In *Recueil des historiens des Croisades, Documents Arméniens,* t. II (Paris: Imprimerie Nationale, 1906), pp. 521–555.

Adrianov, A. V. "Airan v zhizni minusinskago inorodtsa." *Zapiski Imperatorskago Russkago Geograficheskago Obshchestva po otdeleniiu ètnografii,* t. 34 (1909; = *Sbornik v chest' semidesiatiletiia Grigoriia Nikolaevicha Potanina*), pp. 489–524.

Ageeva, E. I., and G. I. Patsevich. "Iz istorii osedlykh poselenii i gorodov iuzhnogo Kazakhstana." *Trudy Instituta istorii, arkheologii, i ètnografii AN KazSSR,* t. 5 (Arkheologiia) (1958), pp. 3–215.

al-Aharī, Abū Bakr al-Quṭbī. *Taʾrīkh-i Shaikh Uwais (History of Shaikh Uwais), An Important Source for the History of Ādharbaijān in the Fourteenth Century.* Ed. J. B. Van Loon. 's-Gravenhage, 1954.

Ahlwardt, W., ed. *Verzeichniss der arabischen Handschriften der königlichen Bibliothek zu Berlin,* 10 vols. Berlin: A.W. Schade/A. Asher, 1887–1899.

Aitmatov, Chingiz. *The Day Lasts More than a Hundred Years,* tr. John French. Bloomington: Indiana University Press, 1983.

Akataev, S. N. "K perezhitkam kul'ta Tengri u kazakhov." *Izvestiia Akademii nauk Kazakhskoi SSR,* seriia obshchestvennykh nauk, 1984, No. 2, pp. 40–48.

_____. "Kul't predkov u kazakhov v proshlom i Zoroastrizm." *Izvestiia AN KazSSR,* seriia obshchestvennaia, 1973, No. 2, pp. 43–49.

Äkhmätova, Flora, ed. "Idegäy: Tatar khalïk dastanï." *Kazan utlarï,* 1989, No. 1, pp. 3–66.

Akhmedov, B. A. *Gosudarstvo kochevykh uzbekov*. Moscow: Nauka, GRVL, 1965.

_____. *Istoriia Balkha*. Tashkent: Fan, 1982.

_____. "O roli pis'mennykh pamiatnikov v izuchenii ètnogeneza uzbekskogo naroda." *Obshchestvennye nauki v Uzbekistane*, 1981, No. 12, pp. 44–50.

_____. "Rol' dzhuibarskikh khodzhei v obshchestvenno-politicheskoi zhizni Srednei Azii XVI-XVII vekov." In *Dukhovenstvo i politicheskaia zhizn' na Blizhnem i Srednem Vostoke v period feodalizma* (Moscow: Nauka, GRVL, 1985 = Bartol'dovskie chteniia, 1982), pp. 16–31.

_____. "Ulugbek i ego istoricheskii trud 'Tarikh-i Arba'ulus.' " In *Iz istorii nauki èpokhi Ulugbeka* (Tashkent: Fan, 1979), pp. 29–36.

Akhmetgaleeva, Ia. S. *Issledovanie tiurkoiazychnogo pamiatnika "Kisekbash kitaby."* Moscow: Nauka, 1979.

Akhmet'ianov, R. G. *Obshchaia leksika dukhovnoi kul'tury narodov Srednego Povolzh'ia*. Moscow: Nauka, 1981.

Akhmetzianov, M. I. "Èvoliutsiia tatarskikh shedzhere i ikh vidy." In *Materialy IV Konferentsii molodykh nauchnykh rabotnikov* (Kazan: AN SSSR, Kazanskii filial, Institut iazyka, literatury i istorii im. G. Ibragimova, 1976), pp. 130–132.

_____. "Obshchinnye shedzhere." In *Istochnikovedenie i istoriia tiurkskikh iazykov,* ed. È. R. Tenishev, I. A. Abdullin, and F. S. Khakimzianov (Kazan, 1978), pp. 45–50.

Akhsīkandī, Sayf ad-Dīn. *Majmūᶜ at-tavārīkh*. MS: Saint Petersburg Branch of the Institute of Oriental Studies of the Russian Academy of Sciencs, MS B667.

_____. *"Sobranie istorii:" Madzhmūᶜ at tavārīkh*. Facs. ed. A.T. Tagirdzhanov. Leningrad: Izd-vo Leningradskogo Universiteta, 1960.

Akmanov, I. G. "Novyi dokument o nachale bashkirskogo vosstaniia 1735–1740 gg." In *Iuzhnoural'skii arkheograficheskii sbornik*, vyp. 2 (Ufa, 1976), pp. 343–351.

"Ak-Ziiarat." *Protokoly zasedanii i soobshcheniia chlenov Turkestanskago Kruzhka liubitelei arkheologii*. (Tashkent), 5 (1900), pp. 93–95.

Alekseev, N. A. *Rannie formy religii tiurkoiazychnykh narodov Sibiri*. Novosibirsk: Nauka, Sibirskoe otdelenie, 1980.

_____. *Shamanizm tiurkoiazychnykh narodov Sibiri*. Novosibirsk: Nauka, Sibirskoe otdelenie, 1984; German translation: *Schamanismus der Türken Sibiriens: Versuch einer vergleichenden arealen Untersuchung*, tr. Reinhold Schletzer (Hamburg: Reinhold Schletzer, 1987; Studia Eurasia: Monographienreihe zur Anthropologie und Archäologie der Völker Eurasiens, 1); partial English translation: "Shamanism among the Turkic peoples of Siberia." *SAA*, 28/1 (Summer 1989), pp. 56–107.

Alekseev, V., ed. *Istoricheskie puteshestviia: izvlecheniia iz memuarov i zapisok inostrannykh i russkikh puteshestvennikov po Volge v XV–XVIII vekakh*. Stalingrad: Kraevoe Knigoizdatel'stvo, 1936.

Alektorov, A. E. *Ukazatel' knig, zhurnal'nykh i gazetnykh statei i zametok o kirgizakh*. Kazan: Tipo-litografiia Imperatorskago Universiteta, 1900.

Al'favitnye spiski armiano-grigorianskikh tserkvei i magometanskikh mechetei v Imperii. Saint Petersburg: Ministerstvo vnutrennykh del, 1883.

Algar, Hamid. "Shaykh Zaynullah Rasulev, the Last Great Naqshbandi Shaykh of the Volga-Urals Region." In *Muslims in Central Asia: Expressions of Identity and Change*, ed. Jo-Ann Gross (Durham: Duke University Press, 1992), pp. 112–133.

Alishanina, L. I., and F. B. Inoiatova. "Toponim Uzbekistan." In *Onomastika Srednei Azii*, 2 (Frunze: Ilim, 1980), pp.226–230.

Allsen, Th. T. "The Princes of the Left Hand: An Introduction to the History of the *Ulus* of Orda in the Thirteenth and Early Fourteenth Centuries." *AEMA*, 5 (1985 [1987]), pp. 5–40.

Amitai-Preiss, Reuven. "Evidence for the Early Use of the Title *īlkhān* among the Mongols." *JRAS*, 1991, pp. 353–361.
Anan'ev, G., tr. "Karanogaiskiia narodnyia istoricheskiia predan'ia." *Sbornik materialov dlia opisaniia mestnostei i plemen Kavkaza*, vyp. 27 (Tiflis, 1900), otdel III, pp. 1–38.
Anderson, Benedict. *Imagined Communities: Reflections on the Origin and Spread of Nationalism*. London: Verso Editions, 1983.
Anisimov, A. F. *Kosmologicheskie predstavleniia narodov Severa*. Moscow/Leningrad: Izd-vo AN SSSR, 1959; English translation: "Cosmological Concepts of the Peoples of the North." In *Studies in Siberian Shamanism*, ed. Henry N. Michael (Toronto: Arctic Institute of North America, 1963; Anthropology of the North: Translations from Russian Sources; vol. 4), pp. 157–229.
Arkheologicheskaia karta Tatarskoi ASSR; Predkam'e. Moscow: Nauka, 1981.
Arkhipov, A. "Ètnograficheskii ocherk Nogaitsev i Turkmen." *Kavkazskii kalendar' 1859* (Tiflis, 1858, year 14), pp. 347–355.
Arkhitekturnye pamiatniki Bashkirii, I. Ufa: Bashkirskoe knizhnoe izdatel'stvo, 1956.
Arnold, T. W. *The Preaching of Islam: A History of the Propagation of the Muslim Faith*. Aligarh, 1896; repr. Lahore: Shirkat-i-Qualam, 1956.
Arslanov, L. Sh. "Ästerkhan ölkäsendäge tatar avïllarï tarikhïna karata." In *Istochnikovedenie i istoriia tiurkskikh iazykov* (Kazan, 1978), pp. 115–124.
Ashmarin, N. I. "Bolgary i chuvashi." *IOAIÈ*, 18/1–3 (1902), pp. 1–132.
Ashtor, E. "Some Unpublished Sources for the Baḥrī Period." In *Studies in Islamic History and Civilization*, ed. Uriel Heyd (Jerusalem: Hebrew University, 1961; "Scripta Hierosolymitana," vol. 9), pp. 11–30.
Ashurbeili, S. B. "Khanaka na reke Pirsagat i Shirvanshakhi." In *Dukhovenstvo i politicheskaia zhizn' na Blizhnem i Srednem Vostoke v period feodalizma* (Moscow: Nauka, GRVL, 1985; = Bartol'dovskie chteniia, 1982), pp. 32–36.
Asmussen, Jes P. *Xᵘāstvānīft: Studies in Manichaeism*. Copenhagen: Munksgaard, 1965.
Astrakhanskii sbornik, izdavaemyi Petrovskim obshchestvom izsledovatelei Astrakhanskago kraia. Vyp. 1. Astrakhan: Tipografiia N. L. Rosliakova, 1896.
Aubin, Françoise. "Cheval céleste et bovin chtonien." In *Quand le crible était dans la paille . . . Hommage à Pertev Naili Boratav*, ed. Rémy Dor and Michèle Nicolas (Paris: G.-P. Maisonneuve et Larose, 1978), pp. 37–63.
Aubin, Jean. "Un santon quhistani de l'époque timouride." *REI*, 35 (1967), pp. 185–216.
ʿAvaż Muḥammad ʿAṭṭār. *Tuḥfat at-tavārīkh-i khānī*. MS: Saint Petersburg Branch of the Institute of Oriental Studies of the Russian Academy of Sciences, MS C440 (described in Miklukho-Maklai, ed., *Opisanie*, vyp. 3, pp. 329–330, No. 458.
Ayākūzī (Qārī Qurbān-ʿAlī b. Khālid Ḥājjī Ayākūzī). *Tārīkh-i jarīdah-i jadīdah*. MS LOIV C578 (described in Dmitrieva et al., *Opisanie tiurkskikh rukopisei Instituta narodov Azii*, I, p. 143, No. 137).
Ayalon, D. "The European-Asiatic Steppe: A Major Reservoir of Power for the Islamic World." In *Trudy XXV Mezhdunarodnogo Kongressa Vostokovedov* (Moscow, 1960), t. II (Moscow: Izd-vo Vostochnoi Literatury, 1963), pp. 47–52.
Babinger, F. *Die Geschichtsschreiber der Osmanen und ihre Werke*. Leipzig: Otto Harrassowitz, 1927; Turkish ed.: *Osmanlı tarih yazarları ve eserleri*, tr. Coşkun Üçok. Ankara: Kültür ve Turizm Bakanlığı, 1982.
Bābur. *The Bābur-nāma in English*, tr. A. S. Beveridge. London: Luzac & Co., 1922, repr. 1969.
Bagrov, L. S. *Materialy k istoricheskomu obzoru kart Kaspiiskago moria*. SPb.: Tipografiia Morskago Ministerstva, v Glavnom Admiralteistve, 1912.

Baibosynov, K., and R. Mustafina. "Novye svedeniia o kazakhskikh shamankakh." *Novoe v ètnografii: polevye issledovaniia*, vyp. 1 (Moscow: Nauka, 1989), pp. 70–79.

Banākatī. *Tārīkh-i Banākatī, Rawżat ūlī'l-albāb fī maʿrifat at-tavārīkh va'l-ansāb*. Ed. Jaʿfar Shiʿār. Tehran, 1348/1969; Silsilah-i Intishārāt-i Anjuman-i Āthār-i Millī, 66.

Bang, W., & A. von Gabain, eds. and trs. "Türkische Turfan-Texte: II, Manichaica." Repr. in *Sprachwissenschaftliche Ergebnisse der deutschen Turfan-Forschung*, Bd. 2 (Leipzig: Zentralantiquariat der Deutschen Demokratischen Republik, 1972), pp. 31–50.

Bang, W., and G. R. Rachmati, eds. and trs. "Die Legende von Oγuz Qaγan." *Sitzungsberichte der Preussischen Akademie der Wissenschaften* (Berlin), Phil.-Hist. Klasse, XXV, 1932, pp. 683–724.

Barbaro, Iosaphath. *Barbaro i Kontarini o Rossii: K istorii italo-russkikh sviazei v XV v.*, ed. and tr. E. Ch. Skrzhinskaia. Leningrad: Nauka, 1971.

______. *Travels to Tana and Persia by Barbaro and Contarini*. Tr. William Thomas. London: Hakluyt Society, Series I, No. 49, 1873.

Barfield, Thomas J. "Tribe and State Relations: The Inner Asian Perspective." In *Tribes and State Formation in the Middle East*, ed. Philip S. Khoury and Joseph Kostiner (Berkeley and Los Angeles: University of California Press, 1990), pp. 153–182.

Bartholomaeo de Pisa. *De conformitate vitae beati Francisci vitam Domini Iesu. Analecta Franciscana*, IV-V. Quaracchi: Ex Typographia Collegii S. Bonaventurae, 1906.

Bartol'd, V. V. "Berke." *EI*[1], I, pp. 737–739; reworked by J. A. Boyle in *EI*[2], I, pp. 1187–1188; in Russian, "Berkai," in his *Sochineniia*, II/1, pp. 503–507.

______. "Bolgary." In *Sochineniia*, II/1, pp. 509–520; from *EI*[1], I, pp. 819–825.

______. [M. [*sic*] Barthold]. "The Bughra Khan Mentioned in the Qudatqu Bilik." *BSOS*, 3 (1923), pp. 151–158.

______. "K voprosu o pogrebal'nykh obriadakh turkov i mongolov." In *Sochineniia*, IV, pp. 377–396; English translation: "The Burial Rites of the Turks and Mongols," tr. J. M. Rogers. *CAJ*, 14/2–3 (1970; = "*Rashid al-Din Commemoration Volume (1318–1968)*"), pp. 195–227; Turkish translation: "Türklerde ve Moğollarda defin merasimi meselesine dair," tr. Abdülkadir İnan. *Belleten*, No. 43 (1947), reprinted in İnan's *Makaleler ve İncelemeler* (Ankara: Türk Tarih Kurumu Basımevi, 1968), pp. 362–386.

______. "Otchet o komandirovke v Turkestan." *ZVOIRAO*, 15 (1904), pp. 173–280; repr. in his *Sochineniia*, VIII, pp. 119–210.

______. "Otets Edigeia." *Sochineniia*, II/1, pp. 792–804.

______. *Sochineniia*. 9 vols. Moscow: Izd-vo Vostochnoi Literatury (vols. I–II/1) /Nauka, GRVL (vols. II/2–IX), 1963–1977.

______. "Svedeniia ob Aral'skom more." *Sochineniia*, III, pp. 13–94.

______. "Toktamysh." *Sochineniia*, V, pp. 564–567, from *EI*[1], IV, pp. 874–876.

______. "Tseremonial pri dvore uzbetskikh khanov v XVII veke." *Sbornik v chest' . . . Potanina* (= *Zapiski Imperatorskago Russkago Geograficheskago Obshchestva po otdeleniiu Ètnografii*, 34 [1909]), pp. 293–308; repr. *Sochineniia*, II/2, pp. 388–399.

______. (W. Barthold). *Turkestan Down to the Mongol Invasion*. 4th ed. Tr. V. and T. Minorsky, ed. C. E. Bosworth. London: Luzac & Co., 1977; E. J. W. Gibb Memorial Series, 5.

______. "Ulugbek i ego vremia." *Sochineniia*, II/2, pp. 23–196; English translation by V. and T. Minorsky, *Four Studies on the History of Central Asia*; vol. II, "Ulugh-Beg." Leiden: E. J. Brill, 1958.

Başgöz, Ilhan. "The Epic Tradition among Turkic Peoples." In *Heroic Epic and Saga: An Introduction to the World's Great Folk Epics*, ed. Felix J. Oinas (Bloomington: Indiana University Press, 1978), pp. 310–335.

Bashkirskoe narodnoe tvorchestvo. Tom 1, *Èpos*, ed. M. M. Sagitov. Ufa: Bashkirskoe Knizhnoe Izdatel'stvo, 1987.

Bashkirskoe narodnoe tvorchestvo. Tom 2, *Predaniia i legendy*, ed. F. A. Nadrshina. Ufa: Bashkirskoe Knizhnoe Izdatel'stvo, 1987.

Baskakov, N. A. *Russkie familii tiurkskogo proiskhozhdeniia*. Moscow: Nauka, GRVL, 1979.

Bawden, Charles, ed. and tr. *The Mongol Chronicle Altan Tobči*. Wiesbaden: Otto Harrassowitz, 1955; Göttinger Asiatische Forschungen, Band 5.

Bazarova, D. Kh. "K ètimologii nekotorykh drevnetiurkskikh nazvanii ptits." *Sovetskaia tiurkologiia*, 1975, No. 4, pp. 11–22.

Bazin, Louis. "Turcs et sogdiens: les enseignements de l'inscription de Bugut (Mongolie)." In *Mélanges linguistiques offerts à Emile Benveniste* (Louvain: Éditions Peeters/Société de linguistique de Paris, 1975), pp. 37–45.

Beckwith, Christopher I. *The Tibetan Empire in Central Asia: A History of the Struggle for Great Power among Tibetans, Turks, Arabs, and Chinese during the Early Middle Ages*. Princeton: Princeton University Press, 1987.

Beisembiev, T. K. *"Ta'rikh-i Shakhrukhi" kak istoricheskii istochnik*. Alma-Ata: Nauka, 1987.

Beliaev, I. A. "Iz predanii o Chingiz-khane." *Protokoly zasedanii i soobshcheniia chlenov Zakaspiiskogo kruzhka liubitelei arkheologii i istorii Vostoka* (Ashkhabad), vyp. 3 (1917), pp. 10–12.

_____. tr. "Skazanie ob Edigee i Tokhtamyshe. Kara-kalpakskaia narodnaia poèma." *Protokoly zasedanii i soobshcheniia chlenov Zakaspiiskago Kruzhka liubitelei arkheologii i istorii Vostoka* (Ashkhabad), vyp. 3 (1917), separate pagination, pp. i-ix, 1–39.

Bennigsen, Alexandre. "The Crisis of the Turkic National Epics, 1951–1952: Local Nationalism or Internationalism?" *Canadian Slavonic Papers*, 17/2–3 (Summer–Fall, 1975), pp. 463–474.

_____. "L'Expédition turque contre Astrakhan en 1569 d'après les Registres des "Affaires importantes" des Archives ottomanes." *Cahiers du monde russe et soviétique*, 8 (1967), pp. 427–446.

Bennigsen, Alexandre, and Mihnea Berindei. "Astrakhan et la politique des steppes nord pontiques (1587–1588)." *HUS*, 3–4/1 (1979–80), pp. 71–91.

Bennigsen, Alexandre, Pertev Naili Boratav, et al. *Le khanat de Crimée dans les Archives du Musée du Palais de Topkapı*. Paris: Mouton Éditeur/École des Hautes Études en Sciences Sociales, 1978.

Bennigsen, Alexandre, and Fanny E. Bryan. "Islam in the Caucasus and the Middle Volga," and "Islam in Central Asia." *Encyclopedia of Religion*, ed. Mircea Eliade (New York: Macmillan, 1987), vol. 7, pp. 357–377.

Bennigsen, Alexandre, and Chantal Lemercier-Quelquejay. "La Grande Horde Nogay et le problème des communications entre l'Empire Ottoman et l'Asie Centrale en 1552–1556." *Turcica*, 8/2 (1976), pp. 203–236.

Bennigsen, Alexandre, and Chantal Lemercier-Quelquejay. "La Moscovie, l'Empire Ottoman et la crise successorale de 1577–1588 dans le Khanat de Crimée: La tradition nomade contre le modèle des monarchies sédentaires." *Cahiers du monde russe et soviétique*, 14 (1973), pp. 453–487.

Bennigsen, Alexandre, and S. Enders Wimbush. *Muslims of the Soviet Empire: A Guide*. Bloomington: Indiana University Press, 1986.

Bennigsen, Élisabeth. "Contribution a l'étude du commerce des fourrures russes: La route de la Volga avant l'invasion mongole et le royaume des Bulghars." *Cahiers du monde russe et soviétique*, 19 (1978), pp. 385–399.

Bentkovskii, I. *Istoriko-statisticheskoe obozrenie inorodtsev-magometan, kochuiushchikh v Stavropol'skoi gubernii; Nogaitsy*. Chast' I. Stavropol': Tipografiia Gubernskago Pravleniia, 1883; Materialy dlia istorii kolonizatsii Severnago Kavkaza, reprinted from *Stavropol'skie Gubernskie Vedomosti* for 1882 and 1883.

Berezin, I. "Bulgar na Volge." *Uchenye zapiski Kazanskago universiteta*, vyp. 3 (1852), pp. 74–160.

_____. *Khanskie iarlyki. II: Tarkhannye iarlyki Tokhtamysha, Timur-Kutluka i Saadet-Gireia*. Kazan: Tipografiia Universiteta, 1851.

_____. "Ocherk vnutrenniago ustroistva ulusa Dzhuchieva." *TVOIRAO*, 8 (1864).

_____, tr. *Sheibaniada, istoriia mongolo-tiurkov*. Kazan, 1849; Biblioteka vostochnykh istorikov, t. I.

_____. *Turetskaia khrestomatiia*, t. II. Kazan, 1862.

Bernshtam, A. N. "Istoricheskaia pravda v legende ob Oguz-kagane." *Sovetskaia ètnografiia*, 1935, No. 6, pp. 33–43.

Bihl, M., and A. C. Moule, eds. "De duabus epistolis Fratrum Minorum Tartariae Aquilonaris an. 1323." *Archivum franciscanum historicum*, 16 (1923), pp. 9–112.

Bihl, M., and A. C. Moule, eds. "Tria nova documenta de missionibus Fr. Min. Tartariae Aquilonaris annorum 1314–1322." *Archivum franciscanum historicum*, 17 (1924), pp. 55–71.

Bira, Sh. "Srednevekovaia mongol'skaia istoriografiia o vzaimosviazi stran Tsentral'noi Azii." *Narody Azii i Afriki*, 1986, No. 6, pp. 34–43.

Bleichsteiner, Robert. "Zeremonielle Trinksitten und Raumordnung bei den turko-mongolischen Nomaden."*Archiv für Völkerkunde*, 6–7 (1952), pp. 181–208.

Blochet, E., ed. *Catalogue des manuscrits turcs*. 2 vols. Paris: Bibliothèque Nationale, 1932–1933.

Bodrogligeti, A. J. E., ed. *A Fourteenth Century Turkic Translation of Saʿdī's Gulistān (Sayf-i Sarāyī's Gulistān bi't-turkī)*. Bloomington: Indiana University / The Hague: Mouton, 1970; Uralic and Altaic Series, vol. 104.

_____, ed. and tr. *Ḫāliṣ's Story of Ibrāhīm: A Central Asian Islamic Work in Late Chagatay Turkic*. Leiden: E. J. Brill, 1975.

Bombaci, Alessio. "'Qutluɣ bolzun!' A Contribution to the History of the Concept of 'Fortune' among the Turks." *UAJ*, 36 (1964), pp. 284–291; 38 (1966), pp. 13–43;

Boratav, Pertev Naili. "Le myth turc du Premier Homme d'après Abū Bekr b. ʿAbd-Allah (XIVᵉ siècle)." In *Proceedings of the Twenty-Third International Congress of Orientalists* (Cambridge, 1954), ed. Denis Sinor (London: Royal Asiatic Society, 1954), pp. 198–199.

Boratav, Pertev, and Louis Bazin, ed. and tr. *Aventures merveilleuses sous terre et ailleurs de Er-Töshtük le géant des steppes*. Paris: Gallimard/Unesco, 1965.

Borïngï Tatar Ädäbiyatï. Kazan: Tatarstan Kitap Näshriyatï, 1963.

Borovkov, A. K. *Leksika sredneaziatskogo tefsira XII–XIII vv.*. Moscow: Izd-vo Vostochnoi literatury, 1963.

_____. "Opyt filologicheskogo analiza tarkhannykh iarlykov, vydannykh khanami Zolotoi Ordy russkim mitropolitam." *Izvestiia Akademii nauk SSSR*, seriia literatury i iazyka, t. 25 (1966), vyp. 1, pp. 13–24.

Bosworth, Clifford Edmund. "Barbarian Incursions: The Coming of the Turks into the Islamic World." *In Islamic Civilisation 950–1150*, ed. D. S. Richards (Oxford: Oxford University Press, 1973), pp. 1–16.

______. "Islamic frontiers in Africa and Asia: (B) Central Asia." In *The Legacy of Islam*, ed. Joseph Schacht and C. E. Bosworth (2nd ed., Oxford: Oxford University Press, 1974), pp. 116–130.

______. [Remarks on Khadr and Cahen, "Deux actes de *waqf*"]. *JA*, 256 (1968), pp. 449–453.

Boyce, Mary. *A History of Zoroastrianism*. Vol. I, *The Early Period*. Leiden: E. J. Brill, 1975; Handbuch der Orientalistik I.8.1.2.2A.

Boyle, John Andrew. "The Alexander Legend in Central Asia." *Folklore*, 85 (Winter, 1974), pp. 217–228.

______. "The Alexander Romance in Central Asia." *ZAS*, 9 (1975), pp. 265–273.

______. "The Burial Place of the Great Khan Ögedei." *Acta Orientalia*, 32 (1970, = PIAC XI), pp. 45–50.

______. "A Form of Horse Sacrifice amongst the 13th- and 14th-Century Mongols." *CAJ*, 10 (1965), pp. 145–150.

______. "Kirakos of Ganjak on the Mongols." *CAJ*, 8 (1963), pp. 199–214.

______. "Some Thoughts on the Sources for the Il-Khanid Period of Persian History." *Iran*, 12 (1974), pp.185–188.

______. "The Thirteenth-Century Mongols' Conception of the After Life: The Evidence of their Funerary Practices." *Mongolian Studies*, 1 (1974), pp. 5–14.

______. "Turkish and Mongol Shamanism in the Middle Ages." *Folklore*, 83 (1972), pp. 177–193.

Bregel, Yuri. "Mangit," *EI*², VI, pp. 417–419.

______. "The Role of Central Asia in the History of the Muslim East." New York: Afghanistan Council Occasional Paper #20, February 1980.

______. "Tribal Tradition and Dynastic History: The Early Rulers of the Qongrats according to Munis." *Asian and African Studies (Journal of the Israel Oriental Society)*, 16 (1982), pp. 357–398.

Bretschneider, E. *Mediaeval Researches from Eastern Asiatic Sources*. 2 vols. London: Kegan Paul, Trench, Trübner & Co., 1910.

Browne, E. G. *A Handlist of the Muḥammadan Manuscripts . . . in the Library of the University of Cambridge*. Cambridge: Cambridge University Press, 1900.

______. *A Literary History of Persia*. Vol. 4, *Modern Times (1500–1924)*. Cambridge: Cambridge University Press, 1930.

Browne, L. E. *The Eclipse of Christianity in Asia*. Cambridge: Cambridge University Press, 1933.

Budagov, L. *Sravnitel'nyi slovar' turetsko-tatarskikh narechii*. SPb., 1869; repr. Moscow, 1960.

Buddrus, Georg. "Spiegelungen der Islamisierung Kafiristans in der mündlichen Überlieferung." In *Ethnologie und Geschichte: Festschrift für Karl Jettmar*, ed. Peter Snoy (Wiesbaden: Franz Steiner Verlag, 1983; Beiträge zur Südasienforschung, Südasien-Institut, Universität Heidelberg, Band 86), pp. 73–88.

Buell, Paul D. "Pleasing the Palate of the *Qan*: Changing Foodways of the Imperial Mongols." *Mongolian Studies*, 13 (1990), pp. 57–81.

______. "The *Yin-shan Cheng-yao*, a Sino-Uighur Dietary: Synopsis, Problems, Prospects." In *Approaches to Traditional Chinese Medical Literature*, ed. Paul U. Unschuld (Dordrecht: Kluwer Academic Publishers, 1989), pp. 109–127.

Bulliet, Richard. "Conversion Stories in Early Islam." In *Conversion and Continuity: Indigenous Christian Communities in Islamic Lands Eighth to Eighteenth Centuries*, ed. Michael Gervers and Ramzi Jibran Bikhazi (Toronto: Pontifical

Institute of Mediaeval Studies, 1990; Papers in Mediaeval Studies, 9), pp. 123–133.
_____. *Conversion to Islam in the Medieval Period: An Essay in Quantitative History*. Cambridge: Harvard University Press, 1979.
_____. "Process and Status in Conversion and Continuity." In *Conversion and Continuity: Indigenous Christian Communities in Islamic Lands Eighth to Eighteenth Centuries*, ed. Michael Gervers and Ramzi Jibran Bikhazi (Toronto: Pontifical Institute of Mediaeval Studies, 1990; Papers in Mediaeval Studies, 9), pp. 1–12.
Bursalı Mehmed Tâhir Bey. *Osmanlı müellifleri*. Ed. İsmail Özen. Istanbul: Yaylacık Matbaası, 1975.
Butterworth, E. A. S. *The Tree at the Navel of the Earth*. Berlin: De Gruyter, 1970.
Caferoğlu, A., ed. *Abû-Hayyân, Kitâb al-Idrâk li-lisân al-Atrâk*. Istanbul: Evkaf Matbaası, 1931.
Çağatay, Saadet. "Die Ädigä-Sage." *UAJ*, 25/3-4 (1953), pp. 243–282.
Calmard, Jean. "Chodźko." *EIr*, V, pp. 502-504.
Castagné, Joseph. "Magie et exorcisme chez les Kazak-Kirghizes et autres peuples turks orientaux." *REI*, 4 (1930), pp. 53–156.
Chadwick, Hector Munro, and N. K. Chadwick. *The Growth of Literature*. 3 vols. Cambridge: Cambridge University Press, 1932–1940; vol. 3, pt. 1 (pp. 1–226), "The Oral Literature of the Tatars."
Chadwick, Nora K., and Victor Zhirmunsky. *Oral Epics of Central Asia*. Cambridge: Cambridge University Press, 1969.
Chavannes, Édouard, tr. *Documents sur les Tou-kiue (Turcs) Occidentaux*. St. Petersburg, 1903; repr. with additional notes, Paris: Librairie d'Amérique et d'Orient, 1941; repr. Taipei: Ch'eng Wen Publishing, 1969.
_____. "Inscriptions et pièces de chancellerie chinoises de l'époque mongole." *T'oung pao*, série II, 5 (1904), pp. 357–447.
Chavannes, Éd., and Paul Pelliot. "Un traité manichéen retrouvé en Chine." Pt. 2, *JA*, sér. 11, 1 (January–June, 1913), pp. 99–199, 261–394.
Chichlo, B. "L'ours chamane." *Études mongoles . . . et sibériennes*, 12 (1981), pp. 35–112.
Chiodo, Elisabetta. "'The Book of the Offerings to the Holy Činggis Qaγan': A Mongolian Ritual Text." *ZAS*, 22 (1989-1991), pp. 190–220.
Chodzko, Alexander. *Specimens of the Popular Poetry of Persia, as found in the Adventures and Improvisations of Kurroglou, the Bandit-Minstrel of Northern Persia; and in the Songs of the People Inhabiting the Shores of the Caspian Sea*. London: Oriental Translation Fund, 1842.
Chronica XXIV Generalium Ordinis Minorum. *Analecta Franciscana*, III. Quaracchi: Tipographia Collegii S. Bonaventurae, 1897.
Ciopiński, Jan. "*Késik Báš Kitābý*, Variante de Kazan." *Folia Orientalia*, 11 (1969), pp. 79–88; 12 (1970), pp. 61–68; 13 (1971), pp. 9–13.
Clark, Larry V. "The Theme of Revenge in the *Secret History of the Mongols*." In *Aspects of Altaic Civilization II* (= PIAC XVIII; Bloomington: Research Institute for Inner Asian Studies, 1978; Indiana University Uralic and Altaic Series, vol. 134), pp. 33–57.
Clauson, Sir Gerard. *An Etymological Dictionary of Pre-Thirteenth-Century Turkish*. Oxford: Oxford University Press, 1972.
_____. "Turks and Wolves." *Studia Orientalia*, 28/2 (1964), pp. 16–20.
Cleaves, Francis Woodman, tr. *The Secret History of the Mongols*. Cambridge: Harvard University Press, 1982.

Crossley, Pamela Kyle. "An Introduction to the Qing Foundation Myth." *Late Imperial China*, 6/2 (1985), pp. 13–24.
Czeglédy, K. "Monographs on Syriac and Muhammadan Sources in the Literary Remains of M. Kmoskó." *AOH*, 4 (1955), pp. 19–90.
_____. "Das sakrale Königtum bei den Steppenvölkern." *Numen*, 13 (1966), pp. 14–26.
Daftar-i Chingīz-nāmah. MS Edinburgh University Library, No. Or. (Turk) 7.
Dankoff, Robert. "Baraq and Burāq." *CAJ*, 15 (1971), pp. 102–117.
_____. "Kashgari on the Beliefs and Superstitions of the Turks." *JAOS*, 95 (1975), pp. 68–80.
_____. "Three Turkic Verse Cycles Relating to Inner Asian Warfare." *HUS*, 3–4/1 (1979–1980), pp. 151–165.
_____, tr. *Wisdom of Royal Glory (Kutadgu Bilig), a Turko-Islamic Mirror for Princes*. Chicago: University of Chicago Press, 1983; Publications of the Center for Middle Eastern Studies, 16.
Dāstān-i Amīr Timūr [ascr. Sayyid Muḥammad Khoja b. Jaᶜfar Khoja]: MSS. MS Tashkent, IVAN Uz, Inv. No. 5738 (*SVR*, V, No. 3503); Inv. No. 185, ff. 1b–19a (*SVR*, I, No. 206); Inv. No. 5398 (*SVR*,VII, No. 5016; "*Tīmūr-nāmah*").
Davkaraev, Nazhim. *Ocherki po istorii dorevoliutsionnoi karakalpakskoi literatury*. Tashkent: Izd-vo AN UzSSR, 1959.
Davletshin, G. M. "O kosmogonicheskikh vozzreniiakh Volzhskikh bulgar domongol'skogo perioda." In *Iz istorii tatarskoi obshchestvennoi mysli* (Kazan, 1979), pp. 44–55
Dawson, Christopher, ed. *The Mongol Mission*. Translated by a nun of Stanbrook Abbey. London: Sheed and Ward, 1955.
Defrémery, C., tr. "Fragments de géographes et d'historiens arabes et persans inédits, relatifs aux anciens peuples du Caucase et de la Russie méridionale." *JA*, ser. 4, 13 (1849), pp. 457–522.
De La Harpe, Jean-François. *Istoriia o stranstviiakh voobshche po vsem kraiam zemnago kruga*. Moscow, 1782-1787.
De Rachewiltz, Igor, tr. "The Secret History of the Mongols." *Papers on Far Eastern History* (Canberra), 4 (September 1971), pp. 115–163 (chapters 1 & 2); 5 (March 1972), pp. 149–175 (ch. 3); 10 (September 1974), pp. 55–82 (ch. 4); 13 (March 1976), pp. 41–75 (ch. 5); 16 (September 1977), pp. 27–65 (ch. 6); 18 (September 1978), pp. 43–80 (ch. 7); 21 (March 1980), pp. 17–57 (ch. 8); 23 (March 1981), pp. 111–146 (ch. 9); 26 (September 1982), pp. 39–84 (ch. 10); 30 (September 1984), pp. 81–160 (ch. 11); 31 (March 1985), pp. 21–93 (ch. 12); 33 (March 1986), pp. 129–137 (Additions and Corrections).
DeWeese, Devin. "Atāʾīya Order." *EIr*, II, pp. 904–905.
_____. "Bābā Kamāl Jandī and the Kubravī Tradition among the Turks of Central Asia." *Der Islam*, (forthcoming).
_____. "The Descendants of Sayyid Ata and the Rank of *Naqīb* in Central Asia." *JAOS* (forthcoming).
_____. "The Eclipse of the Kubravīyah in Central Asia." *Iranian Studies*, 21/1–2 (1988), pp. 45–83.
_____. "The Influence of the Mongols on the Religious Consciousness of Thirteenth Century Europe." *Mongolian Studies*, 5 (1978–79), pp. 41–78.
_____. "A Neglected Source on Central Asian History: the 17th-Century Yasavī Hagiography *Manāqib al-akhyār*." In *Essays on Uzbek History, Culture, and Language*, ed. Denis Sinor and Bakhtiyar A. Nazarov (Bloomington: Indiana University, 1993; Uralic and Altaic Series, vol. 156) pp. 38–50.
_____. "Sayyid ᶜAlī Hamadānī and Kubrawī Hagiographical Traditions." In *The*

Legacy of Mediaeval Persian Sufism, ed. Leonard Lewisohn (London: Khaniqahi Nimatullahi Publications / SOAS Centre of Near and Middle Eastern Studies, 1992), pp. 121–158.

———. "An 'Uvaysī' Sufi in Timurid Mawarannahr: Notes on Hagiography and the Taxonomy of Sanctity in the Religious History of Central Asia." *PIA*, No. 22 (1993), 36 pp.

———. "Yasavian Legends on the Islamization of Turkistan." In *Aspects of Altaic Civilization III* (= PIAC XXX), ed. Denis Sinor (Bloomington: Research Institute for Inner Asian Studies, 1990; Indiana University Uralic and Altaic Series, vol. 145), pp. 1–19.

Dhahabī, Shams ad-Dīn. *Min dhuyūl al-ʿIbar li'dh-Dhahabī wa'l-Ḥusaynī.* Ed. Muḥammad Rashād ʿAbd al-Muṭṭalib, Kuwait: Maṭbaʿah Ḥukūmat al-Kuwayt, n.d.

Diószegi, Vilmos. "Libation Songs of the Altaic Turks." *AEH*, 19 (1970), pp. 95–106.

———. "Pre-Islamic Shamanism of the Baraba Turks and some Ethnogenetic Conclusions." In *Shamanism in Siberia*, ed. V. Diószegi and M. Hoppál (Budapest: Akadémiai Kiadó, 1978; Bibliotheca Uralica, 1), pp. 83–167.

———. "The Problem of the Ethnic Homogeneity of Tofa (Karagas) Shamanism." In *Popular Beliefs and Folklore Tradition in Siberia*, ed. V. Diószegi (Bloomington: Indiana University / The Hague: Mouton, 1968; Indiana University Uralic and Altaic Series, vol. 57), pp. 239–329.

Divaev, A. A. *Ètnograficheskie materialy*. Tashkent, 1900.

———. "Kirgizskii razskaz o Chingiz-khane." *ZVOIRAO*, 11 (1899), pp. 290–292; repr. in his *Ètnograficheskie materialy*, pt. 7.

———. "Murza Èdyge-batyr (Kirgizskaia bylina)." *Sbornik materialov dlia statistiki Syr'-Dar'inskoi oblasti*, 5 (1896), pp. 12–32; repr. in his *Ètnograficheskie materialy*, pt. 4.

———. "Shurá-Batyr." In his *Ètnograficheskie materialy*, pt. 1.

Dmitrieva, L. V. "Rukopis' raboty P. A. Faleva ob èpose "Edigei" v Arkhive vostokovedov Instituta vostokovedeniia AN SSSR." *Tiurkologicheskii sbornik 1972*, pp. 213–217.

Dmitrieva, L. V., A. M. Muginov, and S. N. Muratov, eds. *Opisanie tiurkskikh rukopisei Instituta narodov Azii*, I. Moscow: Nauka, GRVL, 1965.

Dmytryshyn, Basil. *Medieval Russia: A Source Book, 900–1700*. 2nd ed. Hinsdale, Ill.: Dryden Press, 1973.

Dobrodomov, I. G. "Proiskhozhdenie nazvaniia '*Astrakhan*'." In *Onomastika Povolzh'ia*, 3 (Ufa, 1973), pp. 216–227.

Doerfer, G. *Türkische und mongolische Elemente im Neupersischen*. 4 vols. Wiesbaden: Franz Steiner Verlag, 1963–1975.

Donnelly, Alton S. *The Russian Conquest of Bashkiria 1552–1740: A Case Study in Imperialism*. New Haven and London: Yale University Press, 1968.

Dunlop, D. M. *The History of the Jewish Khazars*. Princeton: Princeton University Press, 1954.

———. "The Karaits of Eastern Asia." *BSOAS*, 11 (1943–46), pp. 276–289.

Durrant, Stephen W. "Repetition in the Manchu Origin Myth as a Feature of Oral Narrative." *CAJ*, 22 (1978), pp. 32–43.

Dyer, Svetlana Rimsky-Korsakoff. "T'ang T'ai-tsung's Dream: A Soviet Dungan Version of a Legend on the Origin of the Chinese Muslims." *Monumenta Serica*, 35 (1981-83), pp. 545–570.

Dylykov, S. D. "Èdzhen-khoro." In *Filologiia i istoriia mongol'skikh narodov: Pamiati Akademika Borisa Iakovlevicha Vladimirtsova* (Moscow: Izd-vo Vostochnoi Literatury, 1958), pp. 228–234 (with *prilozhenie*, pp. 235–274).

Dyrenkova, N. P. "Kul't ognia u altaitsev i teleut." *Sbornik Muzeia antropologii i ètnografii*, t. 6 (Leningrad, 1927), pp. 63–78.
Eaton, Richard M. "Approaches to the Study of Conversion to Islam in India." In *Approaches to Islam in Religious Studies*, ed. Richard C. Martin (Tucson: University of Arizona Press, 1985), pp. 106–123.
_____. "Sufi Folk Literature and the Expansion of Indian Islam." *History of Religions*, 14/2 (November 1974), pp. 117–127.
Eckmann, János. *Chagatay Manual*. Bloomington: Indiana University Uralic and Altaic Series, No. 60, 1966.
_____. "Die kiptschakische Literatur." In *Philologiae Turcicae Fundamenta*, II (Wiesbaden: Otto Harrassowitz, 1964), pp. 275–304.
Ecsedy, Ildikó. "Ancient Turk (T'u-chüeh) Burial Customs." *AOH*, 38 (1984), pp. 263–287.
_____. "A Note on 'Slavery' in the Turk Rulers' Burial Customs (Around 649 A.D.)." *AOH*, 42 (1988), pp. 3–16.
_____. [Hilda]. "Tribe and Tribal Society in the 6th Century Turk Empire." *AOH*, 25 (1972), pp. 245–262.
Edsman, Carl-Martin. "Fire." In *Encyclopedia of Religion*, ed. Mircea Eliade (New York: Macmillan, 1987), vol. 5, pp. 340–346.
Egorov, V. L. *Istoricheskaia geografiia Zolotoi Ordy v XIII–XIV vv.*. Moscow: Nauka, 1985.
Eliade, Mircea. "Cosmogonic Myth and 'Sacred History.'" In his *The Quest: History and Meaning in Religion* (Chicago: University of Chicago Press, 1969), pp. 72–87.
_____. *The Forge and the Crucible*. 2nd ed. Tr. Stephen Corrin. Chicago: University of Chicago Press, 1978.
_____. *Shamanism: Archaic Techniques of Ecstasy*. Tr. Willard R. Trask. Princeton: Princeton University Press, 1972; Bollingen Series, v. 76.
Emel'ianov, N. V. *Siuzhety olonkho o rodonachal'nikakh plemeni*. Moscow: Nauka, 1990.
Èrdzhiliasun, Akhmed B. [Ahmet B. Ercilasun]. "Nekotorye soobrazheniia o dastane 'Oguz Kagan,'" tr. Iu. V. Sheki. *Sovetskaia tiurkologiia*, 1987, No. 6, pp. 28–31.
Erdal, Marcel. "Early Turkish Names for the Muslim God, and the Title Çelebi." *Asian and African Studies* (Jerusalem), 16 (1982, = PIAC XXIV), pp. 407–416.
_____. "The Turkish Yārkand Documents." *BSOAS*, 47 (1984), pp. 260–301.
Èrgis, G. U. *Istoricheskie predaniia i rasskazy iakutov*, Ch. 1. Moscow/Leningrad: Izd-vo Akademii nauk SSSR, 1960.
Ernst, Carl W. *Eternal Garden: Mysticism, History, and Politics at a South Asian Sufi Center*. Albany: State University of New York Press, 1992.
_____. *Words of Ecstasy in Sufism*. Albany: State University of New York Press, 1985.
Esbergenov, Kh., and Zh. Khoshniiazov. *Ètnograficheskie motivy v karakalpakskom fol'klore*. Tashkent: Fan, 1988.
Ethé, Hermann. *Catalogue of the Persian Manuscripts in the Library of the India Office*. Vol. I. Oxford: Oxford University Press, for the India Office, 1903.
Evgen'eva, A. P., and V. N. Putilov, eds. *Drevnie rossiiskie stikhotvoreniia sobrannye Kirsheiu Danilovym*. Moscow/Leningrad: Izd-vo AN SSSR, 1958.
Evliya Çelebi. *Evliyā Chelebī sayāḥat-nāmesi*. Vol. 7. Istanbul: Devlet Maṭbaʿası, 1928; Türk Tārīkh Enjümeni Kulliyāti, No. 11 (in Arabic script).
_____. Èvliia Chelebi: *Kniga puteshestviia (Izvlecheniia iz sochineniia turetskogo puteshestvennika XVII veka)*. Vyp. 2, Zemli Severnogo Kavkaza, Povolzh'ia i Podon'ia, tr. and comm. A. D. Zheltiakov and A. P. Grigor'ev. Moscow: Nauka, GRVL, 1979.

_____. *Evliyâ Çelebi seyâhatnâmesi*. Vol. 11. Ed. Zuhuri Danışman. Istanbul: Kardeş Matbaası, 1970 (in modern Turkish).

Falev, P. A. "Zapisi proizvedenii narodnoi slovesnosti u nogaitsev Stavropol'skoi gub. v sviazi s rannee opublikovannym materialam." *ZVOIRAO*, 23 (1916), pp. v–vi.

Farfarovskii, S. V. "Narodnoe obrazovanie u nogaitsev Severnago Kavkaza v sviazi s ikh sovremennym bytom." *Zhurnal Ministerstva narodnago prosveshcheniia*, 1909, ch. 24, No. 12, pp. 179–212.

_____. "Nogaitsy Stavropol'skoi gubernii. Istoriko-ètnograficheskii ocherk." *Zapiski Kavkazskago otdela Imperatorskago Russkago Geograficheskago Obshchestva*, kn. 26, vyp. 7 (Tiflis, 1909), pp. 1–34.

Faṣīḥ Khwāfī. *Mudzhmal-i Fasikhi (Fasikhov svod)*. Tr. D. Iu. Iusupova. Tashkent: Fan, 1980.

_____. *Mujmal-i Faṣīḥī*. 3 vols. Ed. Maḥmūd Farrukh. Mashhad, 1339–1341/1960–1962.

Fattakhutdinov, A. "Bashkirskie shezhere (kratkoe arkheograficheskoe opisanie)." In *Bashkirskie shezhere (Filologicheskie issledovaniia i publikatsii)* (Ufa, 1985), pp. 88–128.

Fazylov, È. I. *Fragmenty neizvestnogo starotiurkskogo pamiatnika*. Tashkent: Fan, 1970.

_____, ed. and tr. *Khodzhandi: Latafat-name, Kniga o krasote*. Tashkent: Fan, 1976.

_____. "Un texte inédit en proto-Çagatay." *Turcica*, 4 (1972), pp. 43–77.

Fedorov, Ia. A., and G. S. Fedorov. *Rannie tiurki na Severnom Kavkaze (Istoriko-ètnograficheskie ocherki)*. Moscow: Izd-vo Moskovskogo Universiteta, 1978.

Fedorov-Davydov, G. A. *Obshchestvennyi stroi Zolotoi Ordy*. Moscow: Izd-vo Moskovskogo Universiteta, 1973.

Fiel'strup, F. A. "Molochnye produkty turkov-kochevnikov." In *Kazaki: Sbornik statei antropologicheskogo otriada Kazakstanskoi èkspeditsii Akademii nauk SSSR; Issledovanie 1927 g.*, ed. S. I. Rudenko (Leningrad: AN SSSR, 1930; *Materialy komissii èkspeditsionnykh issledovanii*, vyp. 15; seriia Kazakstanskaia), pp. 263–301.

Fierman, William. "Cultural Nationalism in Soviet Uzbekistan: A Case Study of *The Immortal Cliffs*." *Soviet Union / Union soviétique*, 12/1 (1985), pp. 1–41.

Firdawsī: Abu'l-Qasem Ferdowsi. *The Shahnameh (The Book of Kings)*. Vol. 2. Ed. Djalal Khaleghi-Motlagh. Costa Mesa, California: Mazda Publishers, 1990.

Fischer, Theobald. *Sammlung mittelalterlicher Welt- und Seekarten italienischen Ursprungs*. Venice: F. Ongania, 1886; repr. Amsterdam: Meridian Publishing, 1961.

Fisher, Humphrey J. "Dreams and Conversion in Black Africa." In *Conversion to Islam*, ed. Nehemia Levtzion (New York/London: Holmes & Meier, 1979), pp. 217–235.

Fletcher, Giles. *Russia at the Close of the Sixteenth Century, comprising The Treatise "Of the Russe Common Wealth," by Dr. Giles Fletcher; and The Travels of Sir Jerome Horsey*. Ed. Edward A. Bond. London: Hakluyt Society, Series I, No. 20, 1856.

_____. *Of the Rus Commonwealth*. Ed. Albert J. Schmidt. Ithaca: Cornell University Press / Folger Shakespeare Library, 1966.

Fletcher, Joseph. "Confrontations between Muslim Missionaries and Nomad Unbelievers in the Late Sixteenth Century: Notes on Four Passages from the 'Ḍīya' [*sic*] al-Qulūb.' " In *Tractata Altaica: Denis Sinor sexagenario optime de rebus altaicis merito dedicata* (Wiesbaden: Otto Harrassowitz, 1976), pp. 167–174.

_____. "The Mongols: Ecological and Social Perspectives." *HJAS*, 46 (1986), pp. 11–50.

_____. "Turco-Mongolian Monarchical Tradition in the Ottoman Empire." *HUS*, 3–4 (1979–80), pp. 236–251.

Fodor, A. "The Rod of Moses in Arabic Magic." *AOH*, 32/1 (1978), pp. 1–21.

Formaleoni, Vincenzio. *Saggio sulla nautica antica de' Veneziani, con una illustrazione d'alcune carte idrografiche antiche della Biblioteca di S. Marco*. Venice: Presso l'Autore, 1783.

Franke, Herbert. "Additional Notes on Non-Chinese Terms in the Yüan Imperial Dietary Compendium Yin-shan chang-yao." *ZAS*, 4 (1970), pp. 7–16.

_____. "The Forest Peoples of Manchuria: Kitans and Jurchens." In *The Cambridge History of Early Inner Asia*, ed. Denis Sinor (Cambridge: Cambridge University Press, 1990), pp. 400–423.

_____. "From Tribal Chieftain to Universal Emperor and God: The Legitimation of the Yüan Dynasty." *Sitzungsberichte der Bayerischen Akademie der Wissenschaften, Philosophisch-Historische Klasse*, Jahrgang 1978, Heft 2 (Munich, 1978), 84 pp.

Frazer, J. G. "The Killing of the Khazar Kings." *Folklore*, 28 (1917), pp. 382–407.

Fren, Kh. D. (C. Fraehn). *De numorum bulgaricorum forte antiquissimo*, libri duo. Casani [Kazan], 1816.

Friedlaender, I. *Die Chadhirlegende und der Alexanderroman: Eine sagengeschichtliche und literarhistorische Untersuchung*. Leipzig/Berlin: B. G. Teubner, 1913.

Friedman, Lionel J. "Joinville's Tartar Visionary." *Medium Aevum*, 27/1 (1958), pp. 1–7.

Froianov, I. Ia., A. Iu. Dvornichenko, and Iu. V. Krivosheev. "Vvedenie khristianstva na Rusi i iazycheskie traditsii." *Sovetskaia ètnografiia*, 1988, No. 6, pp. 25–34; English translation: "The Introduction of Christianity in Russia and the Pagan Traditions." *SAA*, 29/3 (Winter 1990–91), pp. 12–24.

Frye, R. N. "Comparative Observations on Conversion to Islam in Iran and Central Asia." *Jerusalem Studies in Arabic and Islam*, 4 (1984), pp. 81–88.

_____. "A New Arabic Geographical Manuscript." *Journal of Near Eastern Studies*, 8 (1949), pp. 90–97.

Gabain, Annemarie von. "Buddhistische Türkenmission." In *Asiatica: Festschrift Friedrich Weller*, ed. Johannes Schubert and Ulrich Schneider (Leipzig: Otto Harrassowitz, 1954), pp. 161–173.

_____. "Inhalt und magische Bedeutung der alttürkischen Inschriften." *Anthropos*, 48 (1953), pp. 537–556.

_____. "Die komanische Literatur." In *Philologiae Turcicae Fundamenta*, II (Wiesbaden: Otto Harrassowitz, 1964), pp. 243–251.

Gadzhieva, S. Sh. *Material'naia kul'tura nogaitsev v XIX-nachale XX v*. Moscow: Nauka, 1976.

Galiautdinov, I. G. "Paleograficheskie osobennosti spiskov pamiatnika 'Daftar-i Chingiz-name.' " In *Bartol'dovskie chteniia 1981 (god piatyi): Tezisy dokladov i soobshchenii* (Moscow: Nauka, GRVL, 1981), pp. 27–28.

Gardīzī. "Gardīzī's Two Chapters on the Turks." Tr. A. P. Martinez. *AEMA*, 2 (1982), pp. 109–175.

_____. "Izvlechenie iz Zain al-Akhbar." Ed. and tr. V. V. Bartol'd; in his *Sochineniia*, VIII, pp. 23–62.

_____. *Tārīkh-i Gardīzī*. Ed. ʿAbd al-Ḥayy Ḥabībī. Tehran, 1347/1968; repr. Tehran: Chāpkhānah-i Armaghān, 1363/1984.

Garipov, T. M. *Bashkirskoe imennoe slovoobrazovanie*. Ufa: AN SSSR, Bashkirskii Filial, 1959.

Geng Shimin and Tursun Ayup, eds. *Qadïmqï uyghurlarnïng tarikhiy dastanï Oghuznama*. Beijing: Millatlar Nashriyati, 1980.

Gening, V. F., and A. Kh. Khalikov. *Rannie bolgary na Volge*. Moscow, 1964.
al-Gharnāṭī. *Abū Ḥāmid el Granadino y su relación de viaje por tierras eurasiáticas*. Tr. and comm. César E. Dubler. Madrid: Imprenta y Editorial Maestre, 1953.
______. "Le *Tuḥfat al-albāb* de Abū Ḥāmid al-Andalusī al-Ġarnāṭī édité d'après les Mss. 2167, 2168, 2170 de la Bibliothèque Nationale et le Ms. d'Alger." Ed. Gabriel Ferrand. *JA*, 207 (July–December 1925), pp. 1–148, 193–303.
______. "La *Tuḥfa al-Albāb* d' Abū Ḥāmid al-Andalusī al-Ġarnāṭī, traduction annotée." Tr. Guy Ducatez. *Revue des études islamiques*, 53/2 (1985), pp. 141–241.
al-Ghazālī. *The Remembrance of Death and the Afterlife, Kitāb dhikr al-mawt wa-mā baʿdahu; Book XL of The Revival of the Religious Sciences, Iḥyāʾ ʿulūm al-dīn*. Tr. T. J. Winter. Cambridge: Islamic Texts Society, 1989.
Gil'ferding, A. F. *Onezhskie byliny*. III. Moscow/Leningrad: Izd-vo AN SSSR, 1951.
Gilson, Étienne. *Les métamorphoses de la Cité de Dieu*. Paris: Librairie Philosophique J. Vrin, 1952.
Giuzal'ian, L. T. "Chetyre dvustishiia na iranskom izraztse XIII v." In *Kul'turnoe nasledie Vostoka: Problemy, poiski, suzhdeniia* (Leningrad: Nauka, 1985), pp. 297–306.
Gökyay, Orhan Şaik. "Hannâme." In *Necati Lugal Armağanı* (Ankara: Türk Tarih Kurumu Basımevi, 1968), pp. 275–329.
Golb, N. "Who Were the Maġārīyah?" *JAOS*, 80 (1960), pp. 347–359.
Golb, Norman, and Omeljan Pritsak. *Khazarian Hebrew Documents of the Tenth Century*. Ithaca: Cornell University Press, 1982.
Golden, Peter B. "The *Codex Cumanicus*." In *Central Asian Monuments*, ed. Hasan B. Paksoy (Istanbul: Isis Press, 1992), pp. 33–63.
______. "Imperial Ideology and the Sources of Political Unity amongst the Pre-Čing-gisid Nomads of Western Eurasia." *AEMA*, 2 (1982), pp. 37–97.
______. "The Karakhanids and Early Islam." In *The Cambridge History of Early Inner Asia*, ed. Denis Sinor (Cambridge: Cambridge University Press, 1990), pp. 343–370.
______. *Khazar Studies: An Historico-Philological Inquiry into the Origins of the Khazars*. Budapest: Akadémiai Kiadó, 1980.
______. "Khazaria and Judaism." *AEMA*, 3 (1983), pp. 127–156.
______. "The Peoples of the Russian Forest Belt." In *The Cambridge History of Early Inner Asia*, ed. Denis Sinor (Cambridge: Cambridge University Press, 1990), pp. 229–255.
Goldziher, Ignaz. *Introduction to Islamic Theology and Law*. Tr. Andras and Ruth Hamori. Princeton: Princeton University Press, 1981.
Golubovich, Girolamo. *Biblioteca Bio-bibliografica della Terra Santa e dell'Oriente Francescano*. II–III. Florence: Collegio de S. Bonaventura, 1913, 1919.
Golzio, Karl-Heinz. [Review of ash-Shujāʿī, ed. and tr. Schäfer]. *CAJ*, 31 (1987), pp.150–152.
Gordon, C. D. *The Age of Attila: Fifth-Century Byzantium and the Barbarians*. Ann Arbor: University of Michigan Press, 1960.
Graham, William A. *Beyond the Written Word: Oral Aspects of Scripture in the History of Religion*. Cambridge: Cambridge University Press, 1987.
Grammatika sovremennogo bashkirskogo literaturnogo iazyka. Moscow: Nauka, 1981.
Grekov, B. D. "Volzhskie Bolgary v IX-X vekakh: predvaritel'nye zamechaniia." *Istoricheskie zapiski*, 14 (1945), pp. 3–37; repr. in his *Izbrannye trudy* (Moscow, 1959), vol. 2, pp. 519–553.
Grekov, B. D., and A. Iu. Iakubovskii. *Zolotaia Orda i ee padenie*. Moscow/Leningrad: Izd-vo AN SSSR, 1950.

Grigor of Akanc'. "The History of the Nation of the Archers (the Mongols) by Grigor of Akanc'." Tr. Robert P. Blake and Richard N. Frye. *HJAS*, 12 (1949), pp. 269–399.
Grigor'ev, A. P. " 'Iarlyk Edigeia' ": analiz teksta i rekonstruktsiia soderzhaniia." *Istoriografiia i istochnikovedenie istorii stran Azii i Afriki*, vyp. 11 (Leningrad: Izd-vo Leningradskogo Universiteta, 1988), pp. 55–93.
______. "Zolotoordynskie khany 60-70-kh godov XIV v.: khronologiia pravlenii." *Istoriografiia i istochnikovedenie istorii stran Azii i Afriki*, vyp. 7 (Leningrad: Izd-vo Leningradskogo Universiteta, 1983), pp. 9–54.
Grigor'ev, A. P., and V. P. Grigor'ev. "Iarlyk Uzbeka venetsianskim kuptsam Azova: Rekonstruktsiia soderzhaniia." *Istoriografiia i istochnikovedenie istorii stran Azii i Afriki*, vyp. 13 (Leningrad: Izd-vo Leningradskogo universiteta, 1990), pp. 74–107.
Grigor'ev, V. *O dostovernosti iarlykov, dannykh khanami Zolotoi Ordy russkomu dukhovenstvu*. Moscow, 1842.
Grønbech, K., ed. *Komanisches Wörterbuch: Türkischer Wortindex zu Codex Cumanicus*. Copenhagen: Einar Munksgaard, 1942.
Gronke, Monika. "The Arabic Yārkand Documents." *BSOAS*, 49 (1986), pp. 454–507.
Grousset, René. *The Empire of the Steppes: A History of Central Asia*. Tr. Naomi Walford. New Brunswick, Rutgers University Press, 1970.
Haarmann, Ulrich. "Alṭun Ḫān und Čingiz Ḫān bei den ägyptischen Mamluken." *Der Islam*, 51 (1974), pp. 1–36.
______. *Quellenstudien zur frühen Mamlukenzeit*. Freiburg im Breisgau: K. Schwarz, 1970; Islamkundliche Untersuchungen, Bd. 1.
Ḥāfiẓ Tanïsh Bukhārī. Khafiz-i Tanysh ibn Mir Mukhammad Bukhari, *Sharaf-nama-ii Shakhi (Kniga shakshkoi slavy)*. Facs. ed. and tr. M. A. Salakhetdinova, ch. 1. Moscow: Nauka, GRVL, 1983.
Hahn, K. v. "Die Nogaier im Gouvernement Stawropol (Ziskaukasien)." *Dr. A. Petermanns Mitteilungen aus Justus Perthhes' geographischer Anstalt*, 57 (1911), September issue, pp. 122–126.
Ḥājjī Khalīfa. *Jahān-numā*. Printed ed., Istanbul: Müteferrika, 1145/1732; MS, Paris, Bibliothèque Nationale, Suppl. Turc 215 (Blochet, Turc, I, p. 265).
Halevi, Judah. *The Book of Kuzari by Judah Hallevi*. Tr. Hartwig Hirschfeld. New York: Pardes Publishing House, 1946.
______. *The Kuzari (Kitab al-Khazari) of Judah Halevi (12th Century)*. Tr. Henry Slonimsky. New York: Schocken Books, 1964.
Halperin, Charles J. *Russia and the Golden Horde*. Bloomington: Indiana University Press, 1985.
______."Russia in the Mongol Empire in Comparative Perspective." *HJAS*, 43 (1983), pp. 239–261.
______. *The Tatar Yoke*. Columbus, Ohio: Slavica Publishers, 1986.
Hammer-Purgstall, Joseph von. *Geschichte der Goldenen Horde in Kiptschak*. Pesth, 1840.
______. [review of literature on the Black Sea littoral]. *Jahrbücher der Literatur* (Vienna), 65 (January–March, 1834), pp. 1–31.
Die Handschriften in Göttingen. Berlin: A. Bath, 1984; *Verzeichnis der Handschriften im Preussischen Staate*, I, Hannover, 3: Göttingen.
Haneda Akira. "Introduction: Problems of the Turkicization, Problems of the Islamization." *Acta Asiatica*, 34 (1978) [Special Issue: Historical Studies on Central Asia in Japan], pp. 1–21.
Hardy, P. "Modern European and Muslim Explanations of Conversion to Islam in South Asia: A Preliminary Survey of the Literature." In *Conversion to Islam*, ed.

Nehemia Levtzion (New York/London: Holmes & Meier, 1979), pp. 68–99.
Hartmann, Richard. "Ergeneqon." In *Festschrift Georg Jacob*, ed. Theodor Menzel (Leipzig: Otto Harrassowitz, 1932), pp. 68–79.
Harva [né Holmberg], Uno. *Finno-Ugric, Siberian*. Vol. 4 of *The Mythology of all Races*. New York: Cooper Square, 1964; originally published 1927.
______. *Die religiösen Vorstellungen der altaischen Völker*. Helsinki: Werner Söderström Osakeyhtiö, 1938; Folklore Fellows Communications, vol. 125.
______. "The shaman costume and its significance." *Annales Universitatis Fennicae Aboensis*, ser. B, 1 (2) (1923), pp. 1–36.
Hasluck, F. W. *Christianity and Islam under the Sultans*. 2 vols. Oxford, 1929; repr. New York: Octagon Books, 1973.
______. "Studies in Turkish History and Folk-Legend." *Annual of the British School at Athens*, No. 19 (1912–1913), pp. 198–220 (II, "The Story of Sari Saltik," pp. 203–208).
Hatto, Arthur T. "Ḥamāsa; IV, Central Asia." *EI*², III, pp. 115–119.
______. "Kirghiz, Mid-Nineteenth Century." In *Traditions of Heroic and Epic Poetry*, vol. I, *The Traditions*, ed. A. T. Hatto (London: Modern Humanities Research Association, 1980), pp. 300–327.
______, ed. and tr. *The Manas of Wilhelm Radloff*. Wiesbaden: Otto Harrassowitz, 1990; Asiatische Forschungen, Band 110.
______, ed. and tr. *The Memorial Feast for Kökötöy-Khan (Kökötöydün Aši): A Kirghiz Epic Poem*. Oxford: Oxford University Press, 1977; London Oriental Series, vol. 33.
______. "Mongols in Mid-Nineteenth-Century Kirghiz Epic." In *Gedanke und Wirkung: Festschrift zum 90. Geburtstag von Nikolaus Poppe*, ed. Walther Heissig and Klaus Sagaster (Wiesbaden: Otto Harrassowitz, 1989; Asiatische Forschungen, Band 108), pp. 139–145.
______. "Shamanism and Epic Poetry in Northern Asia." In his *Essays on Medieval German and Other Poetry* (Cambridge: Cambridge University Press, 1980), pp. 117–138.
______. "The Swan Maiden: A Folk-Tale of North Eurasian Origin?" *BSOAS*, 24 (1961), pp. 327–352.
Hayton. *La Flor des estoires de la Terre d'Orient*. In *Recueil des historiens des Croisades, Documents arméniens*, t. 2 (Paris: Imprimerie Nationale, 1906), pp. 111–363.
Heissig, Walther. "Ethnische Gruppenbildung in Zentralasien im Licht mündlicher und schriftlicher Überlieferung." In *Studien zur Ethnogenese*, I (= *Abhandlungen der Rheinish-Westfälischen Akademie der Wissenschaften*, Bd. 72, Opladen, 1985), pp. 29–55.
______. *The Religions of Mongolia*. Tr. Geoffrey Samuel. London: Routledge & Kegan Paul, 1980.
______. "Shaman Myth and Clan-Epic." In *Shamanism in Eurasia*, ed. Mihály Hoppál (Göttingen: Edition Herodot, 1984), Pt. II, pp. 319–324.
Henige, David P. *The Chronology of Oral Tradition: Quest for a Chimera*. Oxford: Clarendon Press, 1974.
Herodotus. *The Histories*. Tr. Aubrey de Sélincourt. Harmondsworth, Middlesex: Penguin Books, 1972.
Heyd, W. *Histoire du commerce du Levant au Moyen-Âge*. Tr. and ed. F. Raynaud. Leipzig, 1885; repr. Amsterdam: A. M. Hakkert, 1959.
Hodgson, Marshall. *The Venture of Islam*. Vol. 2, *The Expansion of Islam in the Middle Periods*. Chicago: University of Chicago Press, 1974.

Hofman, H. F. *Turkish Literature: A Bio-Bibliographical Survey*, Section III (Chaghatai), Part I (Authors); 6 vols. in 2. Utrecht, 1969.

Hommaire de Hell, Xavier. *Travels in the Steppes of the Caspian Sea, the Crimea, the Caucasus, & c.*. London: Chapman and Hall, 1847.

Hoppál, Mihály. "Shamanism: An Archaic and/or Recent System of Beliefs." *UAJ* [Bloomington], 57 (1985), pp. 121–140.

Howorth, Henry H. *History of the Mongols from the 9th to the 19th Century*. Part II, "The So-Called Tartars of Russia and Central Asia," Division 1. London: Longmans, Green, 1880.

Hrbek, Ivan. "Bulghār." *EI*², I, pp. 1304–1308.

_____. "The Chronology of Ibn Baṭṭūṭa's Travels." *Archiv Orientální*, 30 (1962), pp. 409–486.

Huang Pei. "New Light on the Origins of the Manchus." *HJAS*, 50/1 (1990), pp. 239–282.

Huart, Cl. "Trois actes notariés de Yārkend." *JA*, 1914, No. 4, pp. 607–627.

Ḥudūd al-ʿĀlam, "The Regions of the World," A Persian Geography 372 A.H.*–982* A.D. Tr. V. Minorsky; 2nd ed., ed. C. E. Bosworth. London: Luzac & Co., 1970; E. J. W. Gibb Memorial Series, n.s., XI.

Humphrey, Caroline. "The Uses of Genealogy: A Historical Study of the Nomadic and Sedentarised Buryat." In *Pastoral Production and Society* (Cambridge: Cambridge University Press, 1979), pp. 235–260.

Humphreys, R. Stephen. *Islamic History: A Framework for Inquiry*. Rev. ed. Princeton: Princeton University Press, 1991.

Hunter, Erica C. D. "The Conversion of the Kerait to Christianity in A.D. 1007." *ZAS*, 22 (1989–1991), pp. 143–163.

Husseinov, Rauf. "Les sources syriaques sur les croyances et les moeurs des Oghuz du VIIᵉ au XIIᵉ siècle." *Turcica*, 8/1 (1976), pp. 21–27.

Iakobson, A. L. *Srednevekovyi Krym: Ocherki istorii i istorii material'noi kul'tury*. Moscow/Leningrad: Izd-vo "Nauka," 1964.

Iakubovskii, A. Iu. "K voprosu o proiskhozhdenii remeslennnoi promyshlennosti Saraia Berke." *Izvestiia Gosudarstvennoi Akademii istorii material'noi kultury*, 8/2–3 (1931), pp.1–48.

_____. "K voprosu ob istoricheskoi topografii Itilia i Bolgar v IX i X vekakh." *Sovetskaia arkheologiia*, 10 (1948), pp. 255–270.

Ibn ʿArabshāh. *ʿAjāʾib al-maqdūr*. MS Cambridge University Library, MS Add. 3237 (Browne, *Handlist*, 1900, No. 679).

_____. *Tamerlane, or Timur the Great Amir*. Tr. J. H. Sanders. London: Luzac & Co., 1936.

Ibn Baṭṭūṭah. *The Travels of Ibn Baṭṭūṭa,* A.D. *1325–1354*. Vol. 2. Tr. H. A. R. Gibb. Cambridge: Cambridge University Press, 1962; Hakluyt Society, 2nd series, No. 117.

_____. *Voyages d'Ibn Battûta*. 4 Vols. Ed. and tr. C. Defrémery and B. R. Sanguinetti. Paris, 1854; repr. Éditions Anthropos Paris, 1969.

Ibn ad-Dawādārī. *Die Chronik des Ibn ad-Dawādārī*. Siebter Teil, *Der Bericht über die Ayyubiden*. Ed. Saʿīd ʿAbd al-Fattāḥ ʿĀšūr. Cairo: Deutsches Archäologisches Institut Kairo, 1972; Quellen zur Geschichte des Islamischen Ägyptens, Band 1g; In Kommission bei Schwarz Freiburg/Br.

_____. *Die Chronik des Ibn ad-Dawādārī*. Neunter Teil, *Der Bericht über den Sultan al-Malik an-Nāṣir Muḥammad ibn Qalaʾun*. Ed. H. R. Roemer. Cairo: Deutsches Archäologisches Institut Kairo, 1960; In Kommission bei Sami al-Khandji.

Ibn Faḍlān. *Ibn Faḍlān's Reisebericht*. Ed. and tr. A. Zeki Validi Togan. Leipzig, 1939; Abhandlungen für die Kunde des Morgenlandes, XXIV/3.

______. *Kniga Akhmeda Ibn Fadlana o ego puteshestvii na Volgu v 921–922 gg*. Tr. A. P. Kovalevskii. Khar'kov, 1956.

______. "The Risālah of Ibn Faḍlān: An Annotated Translation with Introduction." Tr. James E. McKeithen. Ph.D. dissertation, Indiana University, 1979.

Ibn al-Fuwaṭī: *Talkhīṣ Majmaᶜ al-adab*. Vol. 5; serialized in *Oriental College Magazine* (Lahore) from 1939 to 1947.

Ibn Ḥajar al-ᶜAsqalānī. *ad-Duraru'l-kāmina fī aᶜyāni'l-miʾatith-thāmina*. Vol. 6. Hyderabad: Daʾiratu'l-maᶜarifi'l-Osmania, 1396/1976.

Ibn Karbalāʾī: Ḥāfiẓ Ḥusayn Karbalāʾī Tabrīzī. *Rawżāt al-jinān va jannāt al-janān*. Ed. Jaᶜfar Sulṭān al-Qurrāʾī. 2 vols. Tehran: Bungāh-i Tarjimah va Nashr-i Kitāb, 1344–1349/1965–1970.

Ibn Kathīr. *al-Bidāyah wa'n-nihāyah fi't-tārīkh*. 14 vols. Cairo, 1932–1939.

Ibn Khurdādhbih: *Kitâb al-masâlik wa'l-mamâlik (Liber viarum et regnorum) auctore Abu'l-Kâsim Obaidallah ibn Abdallah Ibn Khordâdhbeh et excerpta e Kitâb al-Kharâdj auctore Kodâma ibn Djaᶜfar*. 2nd ed. Ed. M. J. de Goeje. Leiden: E. J. Brill, 1967; Bibliotheca Geographorum Arabicorum, VI.

______. "Le Livre des Routes et des Provinces par Ibn Khordadbeh." Tr. C. Barbier de Meynard. *JA*, ser. 6, no. 5 (1865), pp. 5–127, 227–280, 446–527.

Ibn an-Nafīs: *ar-Risālat al-kāmilīyah fī's-sīrat an-nabawīyah taʾlīf al-faqīh al-mutaṭabbib ᶜAlī ᶜAlāʾ ad-Dīn b. Abī'l-Ḥazm al-Qurashī al-maᶜrūf bi-Ibn an-Nafīs*. Ed. ᶜAbd al-Munᶜim Muḥammad ᶜUmar. Cairo, 1985.

______. *The Theologus Autodidactus of Ibn al-Nafīs*. Tr. Max Meyerhof and Joseph Schacht. Oxford: Clarendon Press, 1968.

Ibn Rustah. *Les atours précieux*. Tr. Gaston Wiet. Cairo: Publications de la Société de Géographie d'Egypte, 1955.

______. *Kitâb al-aᶜlâk an-nafîsa*. Ed. M. J. de Goeje. Leiden: E. J. Brill, 1892; Bibliotheca Geographorum Arabicorum, VII.

Ibn Shaddād, ᶜIzz ad-Dīn Muḥammad b. ᶜAlī b. Shaddād al-Ḥalabī. *al-Aᶜlāq al-khaṭīrah fī dhikr umaraʾ ash-shām wa'l-jazīrah*. Ed. Yaḥyā ᶜAbbārah. Damascus, 1978.

Ibn Taghrībirdī. *an-Nujūm az-zāhirah fī mulūk Miṣr wa'l-Qāhirah*. Vol. 9. Cairo: Maṭbaᶜah Dār al-Kutub al-Miṣrīyah, 1361/1942; repr. 1963–1972.

Ibn al-Wardī: *Tatimmat al-mukhtaṣar fī akhbār al-bashar (Tārīkh Ibn al-Wardī)*. Ed. Aḥmad Rifᶜat al-Badrāwī. Beirut, 1389/1970.

Idhelbaev, M. "Ay häm Yürüdhän buyï bashqorttarnïng shäzhäräläre." In *Bashkirskie shezhere* (Ufa: Institut Istorii, Iazyka i Literatury Bashkirskogo Filiala AN SSSR, 1985), pp. 61–73.

Idige tale. MSS, Institute of Manuscripts of the Academy of Sciences of the Republic of Uzbekistan, Inventory Nos. 109 (77 ff.) and 110 (106 ff.).

al-Idrīsī: *La Géographie d'Édrisi*. Tr. Pierre-Amédée Jaubert. Paris: Imprimerie Royale, 1836–40; repr., 2 vols. in one, Amsterdam: Philo Press, 1975.

______. *Opus geographicum*. Ed. A. Bombaci, U. Rizzitano, E. Cerulli, et al. Leiden: E. J. Brill/Naples-Rome: Istituto Universitario Orientale de Napoli-Istituto Italiano per il Medio ed Estremo Oriente, 1970–1984.

Ignat'ev, R.G. "Pamiatniki doistoricheskikh drevnostei Ufimskoi gubernii." In *Spravochnaia knizhka Ufimskoi gubernii*, ed. N.A. Gurvich (Ufa: N. Vlokhin, 1883), pp. 328–355.

______. "Turakhana dvorets," "Chortovo gorodishche" [Ufa], "Chortovo gorodishche" [Birsk], and "Khusein Beka (Nogaiskago imama) grobnitsa." *Drevnosti: Trudy*

Moskovskago Arkheologicheskago Obshchestva, 2 (1870), pp. 46–56.
Ignatovich, G. "O drevnikh pamiatnikakh v Ufimskom uezde." In *Sbornik statisticheskikh, istoricheskikh i arkheologicheskikh svedenii po byvshei Orenburgskoi i nyneshnei Ufimskoi guberniiam, sobrannykh i razrabotannykh v techenii 1866 i 67 gg.* (Ufa: Tipografiia Ufimskago Gubernskago Pravleniia, 1868), pp. 29–30.
Ilimbetov, F. F. "Kul't volka u Bashkir (k ètimologizatsii ètnonima "*bashqort*")." In *Arkheologiia i ètnografiia Bashkirii*, 4 (Ufa, 1971), pp. 224–228.
Imāmī. *Khān-nāmah.* MS British Museum, Or. 14,352 (uncatalogued).
Imart, Guy. "The Islamic Impact on Traditional Kirghiz Ethnicity." *Nationalities Papers*, 14/1–2 (Spring–Fall 1986), pp. 65–88.
İnalcık, Halil. "The Khan and the Tribal Aristocracy: The Crimean Khanate under Sahib Giray I." *HUS*, 3–4/1 (1979–80), pp. 445–466.
_____. "Power Relationships between Russia, the Crimea and the Ottoman Empire as Reflected in Titulature." In *Passé turco-tatar, présent soviétique: Études offertes à Alexandre Bennigsen*, ed. Ch. Lemercier-Quelquejay, G. Veinstein, and S. E. Wimbush (Louvain/Paris: Éditions Peeters/Éditions de l'École des Hautes Études en Sciences Sociales, 1986), pp. 175–211.
İnan, Abdülkadir. "Destân-i nesl-i Çengiz Han kitabı hakkında." *Azerbaycan Yurt Bilgisi*, 3 (1934), pp. 9–14, 131–135; repr. in his *Makaleler ve İncelemeler* (Ankara: Türk Tarih Kurumu Basımevi, 1968), pp. 198–206.
_____. " 'Kitab-ı Dede Korkut' hakkında," *Türkiyat Mecmuası*, 1 (1925), pp. 213–219; repr. in his *Makaleler ve İncelemeler*, pp. 165–172.
_____. "Sibirya'da İslâmiyetin yayılışı." In *Necati Lugal Armağanı* (Ankara: Türk Tarih Kurumu Basımevi, 1968), pp. 331–338.
_____. *Tarihte ve bugün şamanizm: materyaller ve araştırmalar.* 3rd ed. Ankara: Türk Tarih Kurumu Basımevi, 1986.
İpşiroğlu, M. Ş. *Saray-Alben: Diez'sche Klebebände aus den Berliner Sammlungen.* Wiesbaden: Franz Steiner Verlag, 1964; *Verzeichnis der orientalischen Handschriften in Deutschland*, Bd. VIII.
Ischboldin, Boris. *Essays on Tatar History.* New Delhi: New Book Society of India, 1963.
_____ ["B. S. Izhboldin"]. "O rode Izhboldinykh." *Novik: Istoriko-genealogicheskii zhurnal*, 1945, pp. 29–51.
İstanbul kütüpaneleri tarih-coğrafya yazmaları katalogları. I: *Türkçe tarih yazmaları*; 1 fasikül, *Umumi tarihler.* Istanbul: Maarif Matbaası, 1943.
Iudin, P. L. "Razvaliny drevniago goroda v Ufimskoi gubernii." *Istoricheskii vestnik*, 61 (1895), pp. 147–151.
Iudin, V. P. "Ordy: Belaia, siniaia, seraia, zolotaia . . ." In *Kazakhstan, Sredniaia i Tsentral'naia Aziia v XVI-XVIII vv.* (Alma-Ata, 1983), pp. 106–165.
Iusupov, G. V. "Tatarskie èpigraficheskie pamiatniki XV v. (K voprosu o proiskhozhdenii kazanskikh tatar)." *Èpigrafika Vostoka*, 5 (1951), pp. 78–94.
_____. *Vvedenie v bulgaro-tatarskuiu èpigrafiku.* Moscow/Leningrad: Izd-vo AN SSSR, 1960.
Iusupov, N. *O rode kniazei iusupovykh: Sobranie zhizneopisanii ikh, gramot i pisem k nim rossiiskikh gosudarei, s XVI do poloviny XIX veka i drugikh famil'nykh bumag, s prisovokupleniem pokolennoi rospisi predkov kniazei iusupovykh s XIV-go veka.* Ch. 1, 2. SPb., 1866–1867.
Ivanov, P. P. *Khoziaistvo dzhuibarskikh sheikhov; k istorii feodal'nogo zemlevladeniia v Srednei Azii v XVI-XVII vv.* Moscow/Lenigrad: Izd-vo Akademii Nauk SSSR, 1954.

_____. "Ocherk istorii karakalpakov." In *Materialy po istorii karakalpakov; sbornik* (Moscow/Leningrad: Izd-vo Akademii Nauk SSSR, 1935; *Trudy Instituta vostokovedeniia*, t. 7), pp. 9–89.

Ivanov, S. V. *Skul'ptura altaitsev, khakasov i Sibirskikh tatar, XVIII-pervaia chetvert' XX v.*. Leningrad: Nauka, 1979.

Ivanow, W. "Shums Tabrez of Multan." In *Professor Muḥammad Shafiᶜ Presentation Volume / Armaghān-i ᶜilmī*, ed. S. M. Abdullah (Lahore, 1955), pp. 109–118.

Jackson, P. "The Dissolution of the Mongol Empire." *CAJ*, 22 (1978), pp. 186–244.

Jacobson, Esther. "The Stag with Bird-Headed Antler Tines: A Study in Image Transformation and Meaning." *Bulletin of the Museum of Far Eastern Antiquities*, 56 (1984), pp. 113–180.

Jahn, Karl. "An Indian Legend on the Descent of the Mongols." In *Charisteria Orientalia praecipue ad Persiam pertinentia*, ed. Felix Tauer, Věra Kubíčková, and Ivan Hrbek (Prague: Československé Akademie Věd, 1956), pp. 120–127.

Jāmī, Nūr ad-Dīn ᶜAbd ar-Raḥmān. *Nafaḥāt al-uns*. Ed. Mahdī Tawḥīdīpūr. Tehran: Kitābfurūshī-i Maḥmūdī, 1337/1958.

Jarring, Gunnar. *Materials to the Knowledge of Eastern Turki: Tales, Poetry, Proverbs, Riddles, Ethnological and Historical Texts from the Southern Parts of Eastern Turkestan*, I, *Texts from Khotan and Yarkand*. Lund: C. W. K. Gleerup, 1946; *Lunds Universitets Årsskrift*, N.F., Avd. 1, Bd. 43, No. 4.

Jaworski, J. "Quelques remarques sur les coutumes funéraires turques d'après les sources chinoises." *Rocznik Orientalistyczny*, 4 (1926), pp. 255–261.

Jenkinson, Anthony. [Travels]. In *The Principal Navigations, Voyages, Traffiques & Discoveries of the English Nation*, ed. Richard Hakluyt, vol. 2 (Glasgow: James MacLehose and Sons, 1903), pp. 449–479.

Jeziorska, Irena. "Religious Themes in the Novels of Chingiz Aitmatov." In *Cultural Change and Continuity in Central Asia*, ed. Shirin Akiner (London: Kegan Paul International / Central Asian Research Forum, SOAS, 1991), pp. 45–70.

Jochelson, W. "Kumiss Festivals of the Yakut and the Decoration of Kumiss Vessels." In *Boas Anniversary Volume* (New York: G. E. Stechert, 1906), pp. 257–271.

Johansen, Ulla. "Tranken die Alten Türken Milch-Branntwein?" *UAJ*, 33 (1961), pp. 226–234.

Johnson, H. J. T. "Sweat, Sweat-House." *ERE*, vol. 12, pp. 127–129.

Jones, Russell. "Ten Conversion Myths from Indonesia." In *Conversion to Islam*, ed. Nehemia Levtzion (New York/London: Holmes & Meier, 1979), pp. 129–158.

Jordanes. *The Gothic History of Jordanes*. Tr. Charles Christopher Mierow. Princeton: Princeton University Press, 1915.

Jordanus Catalani. *Mirabilia Descripta. The Wonders of the East, by Friar Jordanus, of the Order of Preachers and Bishop of Columbum in India the Greater (circa 1330)*. Tr. Col. Henry Yule. London: Hakluyt Series No. 31, 1863.

Jūybārī, Khoja ᶜAbd ar-Raḥīm b. Khoja Tāj ad-Dīn Ḥasan. *Maṭlab aṭ-ṭālibīn*. MS Staatsbibliothek zu Berlin-Preussischer Kulturbesitz, Orientabteilung MS Or. oct. 1540 (*Verzeichnis der orientalischen Handschriften in Deutschland*, XIV/1, No. 158).

Jūzjānī, Minhāj ad-Dīn ᶜUthmān b. Sirāj ad-Dīn. *Ṭabaḳāt-i-Nāṣirī: A General History of the Muhammadan Dynasties of Asia . . . by Maulānā, Minhāj-ud-Dīn, Abū-ᶜUmar-i-ᶜUsmān*. 2 vols. Tr. H. G. Raverty. Calcutta, 1881; repr. New Delhi: Oriental Books Reprint Corporation, 1970.

_____. *Ṭabaqāt-i Nāṣirī*. 2 vols. Ed. ᶜAbd al-Ḥayy Ḥabībī. Lahore: Maṭbaᶜah-i Kūh-i Nūr, 1949–1954; 2nd ed., Kabul, 1342–43/1963–64; repr. Tehran, 1363/1984–85.

Kafalı, Mustafa. *Altın Orda hanlığının kuruluş ve yükseliş devirleri*. Istanbul: Edebiyat Fakültesi Matbaası, 1976.
_____. "Cuci sülâlesi ve şu'beleri." Tarih Enstitüsü Dergisi, 1 (1970), pp. 103–120.
Kal', E. *Persidskiia, arabskiia i tiurkskiia rukopisi Turkestanskoi Publichnoi Biblioteki*. Tashkent: Tipografiia Okruzhnago Shtaba, 1889.
Kämpfe, Hans-Reiner, tr. *Das Asaraγči-neretü-yin teüke des Byamba erke daičing alias Šamba jasaγ (Eine mongolische Chronik des 17. Jahrhunderts)*. Wiesbaden: Otto Harrassowitz, 1983; Asiatische Forschungen, Bd. 81.
Karamzin, N. M. *Istoriia gosudarstva rossiiskago*. SPb.: Izdanie Evg. Evdokimova, 1892.
Katalog fonda Instituta rukopisei, t. 1. Tashkent: Fan, 1989.
Katanov, N. F. "O pogrebal'nykh obriadakh u tiurkskikh plemen s drevneishikh vremen do nashikh dnei." *IOAIÈ*, t. 12, vyp. 2 (1894), pp. 109–142; German translation: "Ueber die Bestattungsgebräuche bei den Türkstämmen Central - und Ostasiens," *Keleti Szemle / Revue orientale* [Budapest], 1 (1900), pp. 100–113, 225–233, 277–286.
_____. "O religioznykh voinakh uchenikov sheikha Bagauddina protiv inorodtsev Zapadnoi Sibiri." *Ezhegodnik Tobol'skago Gubernskago Muzeia*, 14 (1904), pp. 3–28.
_____. "Predaniia Tobol'skikh Tatar o pribytii v 1572 g. mukhammedanskikh propovednikov v g. Isker." *Ezhegodnik Tobol'skago Gubernskago Muzeia*, 7 (1897), pp. 51–61.
Kellner-Heinkele, Barbara. *Aus den Aufzeichnungen des Saʿīd Giray Sulṭān: eine zeitgenössische Quelle zur Geschichte des Chanats der Krim um die Mitte des 18. Jahrhunderts*. Freiburg im Breisgau: Klaus Schwarz Verlag, 1975; Islamkundliche Untersuchungen, Bd. 28.
Kereitov, R. Kh. "Mifologicheskie personazhi traditsionnykh verovanii Nogaitsev." *Sovetskaia ètnografiia*, 1980, No. 2, pp. 117–127.
Khadr, Mohamed, and Claude Cahen. "Deux actes de *waqf* d'un Qaraḫānide d'Asie Centrale." *JA*, 255 (1967), pp. 305–334.
Khairullin, A. N. "O novom spiske 'Tavarikhe Bulgariia' Muslimi." In *Istoriko-lingvisticheskii analiz staropis'mennykh pamiatnikov* (Kazan, 1983), pp. 132–139.
_____. [Änver Khäyrullin]. "Galimneng kul'yazma mirasï." *Kazan utlarï*, 1984, No. 1, pp. 157–164.
Khakimzianov, F. S. "Èpigraficheskie pamiatniki g. Bulgara." In *Istochnikovedenie i istoriia tiurkskikh iazykov* (Kazan, 1978), pp. 21–36.
_____. *Èpigraficheskie pamiatniki Volzhskoi Bulgarii i ikh iazyk*. Moscow: Nauka, 1987.
_____. *Iazyk èpitafii Volzhskikh Bulgar*. Moscow: Nauka, 1978.
_____. "New Volga Bulgarian Inscriptions." *AOH*, 40/1 (1986), pp. 173–177.
Khalikov, A. Kh. "Kul'tura narodov Srednego Povolzh'ia v X-XIII vekakh." *Voprosy istorii*, 1976, No. 4, pp. 102–119; English translation, *SAA*, 16/1 (Summer 1977), pp. 49–86.
Khalikova, E. A. *Musul'manskie nekropoli Volzhskoi Bulgarii X–nachala XIII v*. Kazan: Izd-vo Kazanskogo universiteta, 1986.
Khalikova, R. Kh. *Iazyk bashkirskikh shezhere i aktovykh dokumentov XVIII–XIX vv.*. Moscow: Nauka, 1990.
Kharisov, A. I. *Literaturnoe nasledie bashkirskogo naroda (XVIII–XIX veka)*. Ufa: Bashkirskoe Knizhnoe Izdatel'stvo, 1973.
Khisamieva, Z. A. "Nekotorye tekstologicheskie problemy dastanov Kadyir-Gali Bika." In *Istochnikovedenie i istoriia tiurkskikh iazykov* (Kazan, 1978), pp. 63–69.
Khorezmī, Nūrullāh. [Untitled account of the conversion of Özbek Khan]. MS:

Staatsbibliothek zu Berlin-Preussischer Kulturbesitz, Orientabteilung, MS Diez A. Quart. 14, ff. 234b–236a.
Khorezmī, Sharīf ad-Dīn Ḥusayn. *Jāddat al-ʿāshiqīn*. MSS: MS Aligarh Subhanullah No. 297.71/1 (uncatalogued); MS India Office, Ethé 1877; MS Hyderabad, Andhra Pradesh Government Oriental Manuscripts Library, Persian MSS, *Tadhkirah* No. 168.
Kireev, A. N. "Ètnogeneticheskie legendy i predaniia bashkirskogo naroda." In *Arkheologiia i ètnografiia Bashkirii*, 4 (Ufa, 1971), pp. 60–63.
al-Kisāʾī. *The Tales of the Prophets of al-Kisāʾī*. Tr. W. M. Thackston, Jr. Boston: Twayne Publishers, G. K. Hall, 1978.
Kissling, Hans Joachim. "Aus der Geschichte des Chalvetijje-Ordens." *ZDMG*, 103 (1953), pp. 233–289.
Klaproth, J. "Notice et explication des inscriptions de Bolghari." *JA*, ser. 2, 8 (1831), pp. 483–503.
Klimkeit, Hans-Joachim. "Manichaean Kingship: Gnosis at Home in the World." *Numen*, 29 (1982), pp. 17–32.
______. "Qut: Ein Grundbegriff in der zentralasiatischen Religionsbegegnung." In *Humanitas Religiosa: Festschrift für Haralds Biezais* (Stockholm, 1979), pp. 252–260.
Kljaštornyj, Sergej G. [*sic*], and Vladimir A. Livšic [*sic*]. "The Sogdian Inscription of Bugut Revised." *AOH*, 26/1 (1972), pp. 69–102.
Kocaoglu, Timur. "Islam in the Soviet Union: Atheistic Propaganda and 'Unofficial' Religious Activities." *Journal, Institute of Muslim Minority Affairs*, 5/1 (1984), pp. 145–152.
______. "Recent Reports on Activities of Living Muslim 'Saints' in USSR." *Radio Liberty Research*, No. 346/83 (15 September 1983), pp. 1–5.
Kochekaev, B.-A. B. *Nogaisko-russkie otnosheniia v XV–XVIII vv*. Alma-Ata: Nauka, 1988.
______. *Sotsial'no-èkonomicheskoe i politicheskoe razvitie nogaiskogo obshchestva v XIX-nachale XX veka*. Alma-Ata: Karachaevo-Cherkesskoe Otdelenie Stavropol'skogo Knizhnogo Izdatel'stva, 1973.
Konovalov, A. V. *Kazakhi iuzhnogo Altaia (Problemy formirovaniia ètnicheskoi gruppy)*. Alma-Ata: Nauka, 1986.
Köprülü, M. F. *L'Influence du chamanisme turco-mongole sur les ordres mystiques musulmans*. Istanbul, 1929.
______. ["Keuprulu Zadé Mehmed Fuad Bey"]. "Une institution magique chez les anciens Turcs: Yat." In *Actes du Congrès International d'Histoire des Religions* (Paris, 1923), t. 2 (Paris: Librairie ancienne Honoré Champion, 1925), pp. 440–451.
______. *Türk edebiyatı tarihi*. Istanbul, 1926.
Kornilov, I. "Zametki ob Astrakhanskoi gubernii." *Vestnik Imperatorskago Russkago Geograficheskago Obshchestva*, ch. 27 (1859), otd. 2, pp. 1–48.
Kortepeter, Carl Max. *Ottoman Imperialism during the Reformation: Europe and the Caucasus*. New York: New York University Press, 1972.
Kortt, I. R. "The Shaman as Social Representative in the World Beyond." In *Shamanism in Eurasia*, ed. M. Hoppál (Göttingen: Edition Herodot, 1984), vol. 2, pp. 289–306.
Kotwicz, W. "Remarques complémentaires" [to J. Jaworski, "Quelques remarques"]. *Rocznik Orientalistyczny*, 4 (1926), pp. 261–266.
Krachkovskaia, V. A. *Izraztsy mavzoleia Pir-Khuseina*. Tbilisi: Izd-vo AN Gruzinskoi SSR, 1946.

"Kratkii obzor polozheniia nogaiskikh tatar, vodvorennykh v Melitopol'skom uezde Tavricheskoi gubernii." *Teleskop*, 1833, ch. 33, pp. 3–23, 210–230, 269–297.
Kretschmer, Konrad. "Die Katalanische Weltkarte der Biblioteca Estense zu Modena." *Zeitschrift der Gesellschaft für Erdkunde zu Berlin*, 32 (1897), pp. 65–111, 191–218.
Krukovskaia, Sof'ia Karlovna. *Astrakhanskii krai*. SPb.: Izdanie Peterburgskago Uchebnago Magazina, 1904.
Kurat, A. N. *IV–XVIII. yüzyıllarda Karadeniz kuzeyindeki Türk kavimleri ve devletleri*. Ankara: Türk Tarih Kurumu Basımevi, 1972.
Kusimova, T. Kh. "Antroponimy v bashkirskikh shezhere." In *Onomastika Povolzh'ia*, 3 (Ufa, 1973), pp. 66–71.
Kuzeev, R. G. *Bashkirskie shezhere*. Ufa: Bashkirskoe knizhnoe izdatel'stvo, 1960.
______. *Proiskhozhdenie bashkirskogo naroda: ètnicheskii sostav, istoriia rasseleniia*. Moscow: Nauka, 1974.
______. "Uralo-aral'skie ètnicheskie sviazi v kontse I tysiacheletiia N. È. i istoriia formirovaniia bashkirskoi narodnosti." In *Arkheologiia i ètnografiia Bashkirii*, 4 (Ufa, 1971), pp. 17–29.
Lao, Yan-shuan. "Notes on Non-Chinese Terms in the Yüan Imperial Dietary Compendium Yin-shan chang-yao." *Bulletin of the Institute of History and Philology, Academia Sinica*, 39 (October, 1969), pp. 399–416.
Lapidus, Ira M. *A History of Islamic Societies*. Cambridge: Cambridge University Press, 1988.
______. "Tribes and State Formation in Islamic History." In *Tribes and State Formation in the Middle East*, ed. Philip S. Khoury and Joseph Kostiner (Berkeley and Los Angeles: University of California Press, 1990), pp. 25–47.
Laurent, J. C. M., ed. *Peregrinatores Medii Aevi Quatuor*. Leipzig: J. C. Hinrichs, 1864.
Lawrence, Bruce B. "Early Indo-Muslim Saints and Conversion." In *Islam in Asia*, vol. I, *South Asia*, ed. Yohanan Friedmann (Boulder, Colo.: Westview Press, 1984), pp. 109–145.
______. "Islam in India: The Function of Institutional Sufism in the Islamization of Rajasthan, Gujarat and Kashmir." In *Islam in Local Contexts*, ed. Richard C. Martin (Leiden: E. J. Brill, 1982; Contributions to Asian Studies, vol. 17), pp. 27–43.
Lazzerini, Edward. "The Revival of Islamic Culture in Pre-Revolutionary Russia: Or, Why a Prosopography of the Tatar *Ulema*?" In *Passé turco-tatar, présent soviétique: Études offertes à Alexandre Bennigsen*, ed. Ch. Lemercier-Quelquejay, G. Veinstein, and S. E. Wimbush (Louvain: Éditions Peeters / Éditions de l'École des Hautes Études, 1986), pp. 367–372.
Lessing, F. D. *Mongolian-English Dictionary*. Berkeley and Los Angeles: University of California Press, 1960.
Levtzion, Nehemia. "Conversion under Muslim Domination: A Comparative Study." In *Religious Change and Cultural Domination*, ed. D. N. Lorenzen (Mexico City: El Colegio de México, 1981; 30th International Congress of Human Sciences in Asia and North Africa, 1976), pp. 19–38.
______, ed. *Conversion to Islam*. New York/London: Holmes & Meier, 1979.
______. "Islam and State Formation in West Africa." In *The Early State in African Perspective: Culture, Power and Division of Labor*, ed. S. N. Eisenstadt, Michel Abitbol, and Naomi Chazan (Leiden: E. J. Brill, 1988), pp. 98–108.
______. "Patterns of Islamization in West Africa." In Levtzion, ed., *Conversion to Islam*, pp. 207–216.

_____. "Toward a Comparative Study of Islamization." In Levtzion, ed., *Conversion to Islam*, pp. 1–23.

Lewis, Bernard. "The Mongols, the Turks and the Muslim Polity." *Transactions of the Royal Historical Society*, 5th series, 18 (1968), pp. 49–68.

Lewis, Geoffrey, tr. *The Book of Dede Korkut*. Harmondsworth, Middlesex: Penguin Books, 1974.

Ligeti, Louis. "Glossaire supplémentaire au vocabulaire sino-ouigour du Bureau des Traducteurs." *AOH*, 22 (1969), pp. 1–49, 191–243.

_____. "Prolegomena to the Codex Cumanicus." *AOH*, 35/1 (1981), pp. 1–54.

_____. "Un vocabulaire sino-ouigour des Ming." *AOH*, 19 (1966), pp. 117–199, 257–316.

Lincoln, Bruce. *Discourse and the Construction of Society: Comparative Studies of Myth, Ritual, and Classification*. New York/Oxford: Oxford University Press, 1989.

Lindner, Rudi Paul. "What Was a Nomadic Tribe?" *Comparative Studies in Society and History*, 24 (1982), pp. 689–711.

Lipets, R. S. " 'Litso volka blagoslovenno . . .' (Stadial'nye izmeneniia obraza volka v tiurko-mongol'skom èpose i genealogicheskikh skazaniiakh)." *Sovetskaia ètnografiia*, 1981, No. 1, pp. 120–133.

Lipkin, Semen, tr. *Idegei: Tatarskii narodnyi èpos*. Kazan: Tatarskoe knizhnoe izdatel'stvo, 1990.

Little, Donald Presgrave. *An Introduction to Mamlūk Historiography: An Analysis of Arabic Annalistic and Biographical Sources for the Reign of al-Malik an-Nāṣir Muḥammad ibn Qalāʾūn*. Wiesbaden: Franz Steiner Verlag, 1970; Freiburger Islamstudien, Bd. II.

_____. "Notes on Aitamiš, a Mongol Mamlūk." In *Die islamische Welt zwischen Mittelalter und Neuzeit: Festschrift für Hans Robert Roemer zum 65. Geburtstag*, ed. Ulrich Haarmann and Peter Bachmann (Beirut: In Kommission bei Franz Steiner Verlag, Wiesbaden, 1979), pp. 387–401.

_____. "The Recovery of a Lost Source for Baḥrī Mamlūk History: al-Yūsufī's *Nuzhat al-naẓir fī sīrat al-Malik al-Nāṣir*." *JAOS*, 94 (1974), pp. 42–54.

Liu Mau-tsai, tr. *Die chinesischen Nachrichten zur Geschichte der Ost-Türken*; 2 vols. Wiesbaden: Otto Harrassowitz, 1958.

Lopatin, Ivan A. *The Cult of the Dead among the Natives of the Amur Basin*. 's-Gravenhage: Mouton, 1960; Central Asiatic Studies, vol. 6.

Lossievskii, M.V. "Byloe Bashkirii i bashkir po legendam, predaniiam i khronikam (Istoriko-ètnograficheskii ocherk)." In *Spravochnaia knizhka Ufimskoi gubernii*, ed. N. A. Gurvich (Ufa: N. Vlokhin, 1883), pp. 368–389.

Lot-Falck, E. "A propos d'Ätügän, Déesse mongole de la terre." *RHR*, 149 (1956), pp. 157–196.

Lunin, B. V. "Zhizn' i trudy vostokoveda-tiurkologa P. A. Faleva (K 45-letiiu so dnia smerti)." *Obshchestvennye nauki v Uzbekistane*, 1967, No. 9, pp. 43–48.

L'vova, E. L., I. V. Oktiabr'skaia, A. M. Sagalaev, and M. S. Usmanova. *Traditsionnoe mirovozzrenie tiurkov Iuzhnoi Sibiri*. Novosibirsk: Nauka, Sibirskoe otdelenie; 3 vols. bearing subtitles: *Prostranstvo i vremia; veshchnyi mir* (1988); *Chelovek; obshchestvo* (1989); and *Znak i ritual* (1990).

McChesney, R. D. "The Amirs of Muslim Central Asia in the XVIIth Century." *Journal of the Economic and Social History of the Orient*, 26/1 (1983), pp. 33–70.

_____. *Waqf in Central Asia: Four Hundred Years in the History of a Muslim Shrine, 1480–1889*. Princeton: Princeton University Press, 1991.

MacQueen, Graeme. "*Whose* Sacred History? Reflections on Myth and Dominance." *Studies in Religion*, 17/2 (1988), pp. 143–157.

Madelung, Wilferd. "Borhān-al-Dīn Nasafī." *EIr*, IV, p. 371.

———. "The spread of Māturidism and the Turks." *Actas do IV Congresso des Estudos Arabes et Islâmicos, Coimbra-Lisboa* (Leiden: E. J. Brill, 1971), pp. 109–168; repr. in his *Religious Schools and Sects in Medieval Islam* (London: Variorum Reprints, 1985), No. II.

Maenchen-Helfen, J. *The World of the Huns: Studies in their History and Culture*. Ed. Max Knight. Berkeley and Los Angeles: University of California Press, 1973.

Maḥmūd b. Amīr Valī. *Baḥr al-asrār*. MSS: MS Tashkent, IVAN Uz, Inv. No. 1385 (*SVR*, V, No. 3564); MS India Office, Ethé 575.

Maksetov, K. M., ed. *Ocherki po istorii karakalpakskogo fol'klora*. Tashkent: Fan, 1977.

———. "Vzaimosviazi karakalpakskogo i bashkirskogo geroicheskogo èposa." *Arkheologiia i ètnografiia Bashkirii*, 4 (Ufa, 1971), pp. 268–272.

Maliavkin, G. "Karanogaitsy." *Terskii sbornik*, vyp. 3, kn. 2 (1893), pp. 133–173.

Mälläev, N. M. *Ŭzbek ädäbiyati tärikhi*. Vol. I. Tashkent: "Ŭqituvchi" Näshriyati, 1965.

Malov, S. E. "Shamanskii kamen' "iada" u tiurkov zapadnogo Kitaia." *Sovetskaia ètnografiia*, 1947, No. 1, pp. 151–160.

Malyshev, V. I. *Povest' o Sukhane: Iz istorii russkoi povesti XVII veka*. Moscow/Leningrad: Izd-vo AN SSSR, 1956.

Manas: kirgizskii geroicheskii èpos. Ed. A. S. Sadykov, S. M. Musaev, and A. S. Mirbadaleva. Kn. 1–3. Moscow: Nauka, GRVL, 1984, 1988, 1990.

Mandeville, John. *Mandeville's Travels: Texts and Translations*. Ed. & tr. Malcolm Letts; I. London: Hakluyt Society, 2nd Series, No. 101, 1953.

Mano Eiji. "Moghūlistān." *Acta Asiatica*, 34 (1978) [Special Issue: Historical Studies on Central Asia in Japan], pp. 46–60.

Marazzi, Ugo, tr. *Māday Qara: An Altay Epic Poem*. Naples: Istituto Universitario Orientale, 1986; Series Minor, XXV.

Margulan, A. Kh. "*O nositeliakh drevnei poèticheskoi kul'tury kazakhskogo naroda*." In *M. O. Auèzovu, Sbornik statei k ego shestidesiatiletiiu* (Alma-Ata: Izd-vo AN KazSSR, 1959), pp. 70–89.

Marjānī, Shihāb ad-Dīn. *Mustafād al-akhbār fī aḥvāl Qazān va Bulghār*. Vol 1, 2nd ed. Kazan: Tipografiia B.L. Dombrovskago, 1897.

———. [Shihabetdin Märjani]. *Möstäfadel-äkhbar fi äkhvali Kazan vä Bolgar*. Ed. A. N. Khäyrullin (in Cyrillic-script Tatar). Kazan: Tatarstan Kitap Näshriyatï, 1989.

Marquart, J. "Čuwainī's Bericht über die Bekehrung der Uiguren." *Sitzungsberichte der Königlich Preussischen Akademie der Wissenschaften* (Berlin), 1912, XXVII, pp. 486–502.

———. "Über das Volkstum der Komanen." In W. Bang and J. Marquart, *Osttürkische Dialektstudien* (Abhandlungen der Königlichen Gesellschaft der Wissenschaften zu Göttingen, Phil.-hist. Klasse, n. F., Bd. XIII; Berlin, 1914), pp. 25–238.

Martin, B. G. "A Short History of the Khalwati Order of Dervishes." In *Scholars, Saints, and Sufis: Muslim Religious Institutions since 1500*, ed. Nikki R. Keddie (Berkeley and Los Angeles: University of California Press, 1972), pp. 275–305.

Martynov, Anatoly I. *The Ancient Art of Northern Asia*. Tr. Demitri B. Shimkin and Edith M. Shimkin. Urbana: University of Illinois Press, 1991.

Massignon, Louis. "Le culte liturgique et populaire des VII Dormants Martyrs d'Ephese (Ahl al-Kahf): Trait d'union orient-occident entre l'Islam et la Chrétienté." In his *Opera minora*, ed. Y. Moubarac (Beirut: Dar al-Maarif Liban, 1963), vol. 3, pp. 119–180.

______. "La légende de Hallace Mansur en pays turcs." *REI*, 1941–1946, pp. 77–78; repr. in his *Opera Minora*, vol. 2, p. 103.

______. "Les 'Sept Dormants' apocalypse de l'Islam." In his *Opera minora*, vol. 3, pp. 104–118.

Materialy po istorii kazakhskikh khanstv XV–XVIII vekov (Izvlecheniia iz persidskikh i tiurkskikh sochinenii). Ed. S. K. Ibragimov, N. N. Mingulov, K. A. Pishchulina, and V. P. Iudin. Alma-Ata: Nauka, 1969.

Materialy po istorii turkmen i Turkmenii. T. II (XVI–XIX vv., iranskie, bukharskie i khivinskie istochniki), ed. V. V. Struve, A. K. Borovkov, A. A. Romaskevich, and P. P. Ivanov. Moscow/Leningrad: Izd-vo AN SSSR, 1938.

Matorin, N. *Religiia u narodov Volzhsko-kamskogo kraia prezhde i teper': iazychestvo—islam—pravoslavie—sektantstvo*. Moscow: "Bezbozhnik," 1929.

Matsumura, Jun. "The Ancestral Legend of the Manchu Imperial House." In *Proceedings of the Fourth East Asian Altaistic Conference* (T'ai-pei, 1971), pp. 192–195.

Matthias of Miechow [Matvei Mekhovskii]. *Traktat o dvukh Sarmatiiakh*. Ed. & tr. S. A. Anninskii. Moscow/Leningrad: Izd-vo Akademii nauk SSSR, 1936.

Matveeva, R. P. "Motiv o devushke-lebedi v russkoi i buriatskoi skazochnykh traditsiiakh." In *Russkii fol'klor Sibiri: Issledovaniia i materialy* (Novosibirsk: Nauka, 1981), pp. 25–40.

Melioranskii, P. M., ed. "Skazanie ob Edigee i Toktamyshe. Kirgizskii tekst po rukopisi, prinadlezhavshei Ch. Ch. Valikhanovu." Saint Petersburg., 1905 (separately paginated supplement to *Zapiski Imperatorskago Russkago Geograficheskago Obshchestva po otdeleniiu ètnografii*, vol. 29).

Melville, Charles. "The Itineraries of Sultan Öljeitü, 1304–16." *Iran*, 28 (1990), pp. 55–70.

Meserve, Ruth. "The *Yüan Shih* and Middle Mongolian." *Mongolian Studies*, 13 (1990), pp. 117–131.

Messerschmidt, D. G. *Forschungsreise durch Sibirien 1720–1727*. Ed. E. Winter and N. A. Figurovskij. Teil 1. Berlin: Akademie-Verlag, 1962.

Michael the Syrian. *Chronique de Michel le Syrien, Patriarche Jacobite d'Antioche (1166–1199)*. Ed. and tr. J.-B. Chabot. 4 vols. Paris: Ernest Leroux, Éditeur, 1899–1910.

Michell, Robert, and Nevill Forbes, trs. *The Chronicle of Novgorod, 1016–1471*. London: Camden Society, 3rd series, vol. 25, 1914.

Mikhailov, G. I. "Mify v istoricheskikh sochineniiakh XIII–XIV vv. mongol'skikh narodov." In *Fol'klor i istoricheskaia ètnografiia* (Moscow: Nauka, 1983), pp. 88–106.

Mikhailov, T. M. *Buriatskii shamanizm: istoriia, struktura i sotsial'nye funktsii*. Novosibirsk: Nauka, Sibirskoe Otdelenie, 1987.

Miklukho-Maklai, N. D., ed. *Opisanie persidskikh i tadzhikskikh rukopisei Instituta vostokovedeniia*. Vyp. 3 (Istoricheskie sochineniia). Moscow: Nauka, GRVL, 1975.

Mingana, A. "The Early Spread of Christianity in Central Asia and the Far East: A New Document." *Bulletin of the John Rylands Library*, 9 (1925), pp. 297–371.

Minorsky, V. "The Khazars and the Turks in the *Ākām al-Marjān*." *BSOS*, 9 (1937), 141–150.

Mirbadaleva, A. S., N. V. Kidaish-Pokrovskaia, and S. M. Musaev. "Obzor zapisei variantov èposa 'Manas.' " In *Manas: Kirgizskii geroicheskii èpos*, kn. 1 (Moscow: GRVL, 1984), pp. 443–491.

Mīrkhwānd. *Tārīkh-i Rawżat aṣ-ṣafā.* Vol. 5. Tehran: Khayyām, 1339/1960.
Mirzhanova, S. F. *Iuzhnyi dialekt bashkirskogo iazyka.* Moscow: Nauka, 1979.
Mokeev, A. M. "Sheikh-Mansur al-Khalladzh i ego mesto v genealogiiakh kirgizskogo naroda." In *Bartol'dovskie chteniia, 1981, god piatyi; tezisy dokladov i soobshchenii* (Moscow: Nauka, GRVL, 1981), pp. 60–61.
Moldobaev, I. B. *Èpos "Zhanysh i Baiysh" kak istoriko-ètnograficheskii istochnik.* Frunze: Ilim, 1983.
Mollov, Riza. "Parallel entre Alpamıš et Ašık Garib (Quelques observations sur l'évolution du sujet et de l'image d'Ašık Garib)." *Acta Orientalia* 32 (1970, = PIAC XI), pp. 167–189.
Mollova, Mefküre. "Traces des querelles religieuses dans le Codex Cumanicus." *AOH*, 39 (1985), pp. 339–351.
Molnár, Adam. "Qām, Yātčï and Bügü: Notes on Old Turkic Shamanism." In *Beşinci Milletler Arası Türkoloji Kongresi* (Istanbul, 1985), *Tebliğler*, I. Türk Dili, cilt 1 (Istanbul: Edebiyat Fakültesi Basımevi, 1985), pp. 197–204.
Montell, G. "Distilling in Mongolia." *Ethnos*, 2/5 (September 1937), pp. 321–332.
Morgan, David. *The Mongols.* Oxford: Basil Blackwell, 1986.
Mori Masao. "The T'u-chüeh Concept of Sovereign." *Acta Asiatica*, 41 (1981), pp. 47–75.
Mostaert, Antoine. "Sur quelques passages de l'*Histoire Secrète des Mongols.*" *HJAS*, 13 (1950), pp. 285–361.
Mote, Frederick W. "Yüan and Ming." In *Food in Chinese Culture: Anthropological and Historical Perspectives*, ed. K. C. Chang (New Haven: Yale University Press, 1977), pp. 195–257.
Movsēs Dasχuranci. *The History of the Caucasian Albanians by Movsēs Dasχuranci.* Tr. C. J. F. Dowsett. London: Oxford University Press, 1961.
al-Mufaḍḍal. *Ägypten und Syrien zwischen 1317 und 1341 in der Chronik des Mufaḍḍal b. Abī l-Faḍāʾil.* Tr. Samira Kortantamer. Freiburg im Breisgau: Klaus Schwarz Verlag, 1973; Islamkundliche Untersuchungen, Bd. 23.
______. [Moufazzal ibn Abil-Fazaïl]. *Histoire des sultans mamlouks.* Ed. and tr. E. Blochet. *Patrologia Orientalis*, t. 12, fasc. 3; t. 14, fasc. 3; t. 20, fasc. 1 (Paris, 1919–1928).
Muḥammad Ḥaydar Dūghlāt. *A History of the Moghuls of Central Asia, being the Tarikh-i-Rashidi of Mirza Muhammad Haidar, Dughlát.* 2nd ed. Ed. and tr. N. Elias and E. Denison Ross. London, 1898; repr. London: Curzon Press / New York: Barnes and Noble, 1972.
Muḥammad Mahdī Khān. *Sanglāx: A Persian Guide to the Turkish Language by Muḥammad Mahdī Xān.* Facs. ed. G. Clauson. London: Luzac & Co., 1960; Gibb Memorial Series, n.s., No. 20.
Muḥammad Qāżī. *Silsilat al-ʿārifīn.* MSS: MS Tashkent, IVAN Uz, Inv. No. 4452 (uncatalogued); MS Aligarh, Maulana Azad Library, Subhanullah Collection, No. 297.7/72.
Muḥammad-Yaʿqūb b. Muḥammad Dāniyāl-bīy. *Gulshan al-mulūk.* MS: MS IVAN Uz, Inv. No. 1507 (*SVR*, I, p. 83, No. 208).
Mukhamadiev, A. G. *Bulgaro-tatarskaia monetnaia sistema XII–XV vv.* Moscow: Nauka, 1983.
Mukhamedova, Z. B. "Neskol'ko slov ob antroponimakh v 'Oguz-Name' iz sochineniia Salar Baba." In *Onomastika Srednei Azii* (Moscow: Nauka, GRVL, 1978), pp. 169–171.
Muʾnis: Shīr Muḥammad Mīrāb Mūnis and Muḥammad Rizā Mīrāb Āgahī. *Firdaws al-Iqbāl: History of Khorezm.* Ed. Yuri Bregel. Leiden: E. J. Brill, 1988.

Nabiev, R. N. *Iz istorii Kokandskogo khanstva (feodal'noe khoziaistvo Khudoiar-khana)*. Tashkent: Fan, 1973.

Nasab-nāmah-i Ūzbīk. MSS: MS Tashkent, IVAN Uz, Inv. No. 3386, ff. 182b–183b; MS IVAN Uz, Inv. No. 12870, ff. 89b–91b ("*Naṣīb-nāmah-i* "*Ūzbīk*").

Naṭanzī, Muʿīn ad-Dīn. *Muntakhab at-tavārīkh-i Muʿīnī*. Ed. Jean Aubin. Tehran: Kitābfurūshī-i Khayyām, 1336/1957.

Navāʾī, ʿAbd al-Ḥusayn, ed. *Asnād va mukātabat-i tārīkhī-i Īrān az Tīmūr tā Shāh Ismāʿīl*. Tehran: Bungāh-i Tarjimah va Nashr-i Kitāb, 1341/1962.

Navāʾī, Mīr ʿAlī-shīr. *Mäjalisun Näfais: ilmiy-tänqidiy tekst*. Ed. Suyimä Ghänieva. Tashkent: Fan, 1961.

Nebol'sin, Pavel. "Narody Astrakhanskoi gubernii: zametki o Kundrovskikh Tatarakh." *Vestnik Imperatorskago Russkago Geograficheskago Obshchestva*, ch. 2 (1851), otd. V, 30 pp.

_____. *Ocherki Volzhskago nizov'ia*. SPb.: Tipografiia Ministerstva vnutrennikh del, 1852.

Neikhardt, A. A. *Skifskii rasskaz gerodota v otechestvennoi istoriografii*. Leningrad: Nauka, 1982.

Neimatova, M. S. "Nadpisi kak istochnik dlia izucheniia istoriia khanaki Pir Khusaina." In *Vostochnoe istoricheskoe istochnikovedenie i spetsial'nye istoricheskie distsipliny*, vyp. 1 (Moscow: Nauka, GRVL, 1989; "Bartol'dovskie chteniia," 1984), pp. 292–298.

Németh, J. "Ein ungarisches Lehnwort in Byzanz im 10. Jahrhunderts." In *Beiträge zur Sprachwissenschaft, Volkskunde und Literaturforschung: Wolfgang Steinitz zum 60. Geburtstag am 28. Februar 1965 dargebracht* (Berlin: Akademie-Verlag, 1965), pp. 291–294.

Nesterov, A. D. "Proshloe priural'skikh stepei v predaniiakh kirgiz Kazalinskago uezda." *ZVOIRAO*, 12/4 (1900), pp. 095–0105.

Nīshābūrī, Mīr ʿAbd al-Avval. *Masmūʿāt*. MSS: MS Tashkent, IVAN Uz, Inv. No. 3735 (*SVR*, VIII, No. 5977); MS India Office, Delhi Pers. 890; MS Lucknow, Shiblī Nuʿmānī Library, Nadwat al-ʿUlamā Madrasah, Taṣavvuf Fārsī 172/2457.

Nithārī Bukhārī, Khoja Bahāʾ ad-Dīn Ḥasan. *Mudhakkir-i-Aḥbāb ("Remembrancer of Friends") of Khwāja Bahā al-Dīn Ḥasan Nithārī Bukhārī*. Ed. Syed Muhammad Fazlullah. Hyderabad: Osmania University, Da'iratu'l-Maʿarif Press, 1969.

Nöldeke, Th., tr. "Die von Guidi herausgegebene syrische Chronik, übersetzt und kommentiert." *Sitzungsberichte der Wiener Akademie der Wissenschaften*, 128 (1893), No. 9, pp. 1–48.

Noonan, Thomas S. "Suzdalia's Eastern Trade in the Century before the Mongol Conquest." *Cahiers du monde russe et soviétique*, 19 (1978), pp. 371–384.

Nordenskiöld, A. E. *Periplus: An Essay on the Early History of Charts and Sailing Directions*. Tr. Frances A. Bather. Stockholm: P. A. Norstedt & Söner, 1897.

Novik, E. S. *Obriad i fol'klor v sibirskom shamanizme: opyt sopostavleniia struktur*. Moscow: Nauka, GRVL, 1984; partial English translation: "Ritual and Folklore in Siberian Shamanism: Experiment in a Comparison of Structures." *SAA*, 28/2 (Fall 1989), pp. 20–84.

Nurmagambetova, O. *Kazakhskii geroicheskii èpos Koblandy batyr*. Alma-Ata: Nauka, 1988.

Nuwayrī. *Nihāyat al-arab fī funūn al-adab*. Ed. Saʿīd ʿĀshūr, M. Muṣṭafā Ziyādah, Fuʾād ʿAbd al-Muʿṭī aṣ-Ṣayyād; vol. 27. Cairo: Dār al-Kutub al-Miṣrīyah, 1405/1985.

Ocak, Ahmet Yaşar. *Türk Folklorunda Kesik Baş (Tarih-Folklor İlişkisinden bir Kesit.*

Ankara: Türk Kültürünü Araştırma Enstitüsü (Yayınları, 25), 1989.
Oda Juten. "Uighuristan." *Acta Asiatica*, 34 (1978) [Special Issue: Historical Studies on Central Asia in Japan], pp. 22–45.
Öhrig, Bruno. *Bestattungsriten alttürkischer Aristokratie im Lichte der Inschriften.* Munich: Minerva, 1988; Münchner Ethnologische Abhanddlungen, Band 8.
Olbricht, Peter, and Elisabeth Pinks, trs. *Meng-ta Pei-lu und Hei-ta Shih-lüeh: Chinesische Gesandtenberichte über die frühen Mongolen 1221 und 1237; nach Vorarbeiten von Erich Haenisch und Yao Ts'ung-wu übersetzt und kommentiert.* Wiesbaden: Otto Harrassowitz, 1980; Asiatische Forschungen, Bd. 56.
Olearius, Adam. *Opisanie puteshestviia v Moskoviiu i cherez Moskoviiu v Persiiu i obratno.* Tr. A. M. Loviagin. SPb.: A. S. Suvorin, 1906.
______. *Vermehrte Newe Beschreibung der Muscowitischen und Persischen Reyse.* Schleswig, 1656; repr. ed. Dieter Lohmeier, Tübingen: Max Niemeyer Verlag, 1971.
Olschki, Leonardo. *Guillaume Boucher, A French Artist at the Court of the Khans.* Baltimore: Johns Hopkins University Press, 1946.
______. *Marco Polo's Asia: An Introduction to his "Description of the World" called "Il Milione".* Berkeley and Los Angeles: University of California Press, 1960.
Orlov, A. S. *Kazakhskii geroicheskii èpos.* Moscow/Leningrad, 1945.
Osmanov, M. *Nogaiskie i kumykskie teksty* (in Arabic script). Saint Petersburg: Tipografiia Imperatorskoi Akademiia nauk, 1883.
Ötemish Ḥājjī. *Tārīkh-i Dūst Sulṭān.* MS Tashkent, IVAN Uz, Inv. No. 1552/III (*SVR*, I, No. 148).
Owusu-Ansah, David. "Islamization Reconsidered: An Examination of Asante Responses to Muslim Influence in the Nineteenth Century." *Asian and African Studies* (Jerusalem), 21 (1987), pp. 145–163.
Özdemir, Fuat. "İlk dînî destanlar ve Kesikbaş destanı." *Folklor araştırmaları kurumu yıllığı* (Ankara, 1975), pp. 123–129.
Paksoy, H. B. *Alpamysh: Central Asian Identity under Russian Rule.* Hartford, Conn.: Association for the Advancement of Central Asian Research, Monograph Series, 1989.
Pallas, Peter Simon. *Sammlungen historischer Nachrichten über die mongolischen Völkerschaften*; Erster Theil. Frankfurt and Leipzig, 1779; repr. Graz: Akademische Druck-u. Verlagsanstalt, 1980.
______. *Travels through the Southern Provinces of the Russian Empire in the Years 1793 and 1794.* Vol. 1. London: A. Strahan, 1802.
Pantusov, N. N. "Gorod Almalyk i Mazar Tugluk-Timur-khana," and "Legenda o Tugluk-Timur-khane." In *Kaufmanskii sbornik, izdannyi v pamiat' 25 let, istekshikh so dnia smerti pokoritelia i ustroitelia Turkestanskogo kraia, general-ad'iutanta K. P. fon-Kaufmana* (Moscow, 1910), pp. 161–202.
Paul, Jürgen. *Die politische und soziale Bedeutung der Naqšbandiyya in Mittelasien im 15. Jahrhundert.* Berlin/New York: Walter de Gruyter, 1991; Studien zur Sprache, Geschichte und Kultur des islamischen Orients, Neue Folge, Bd. 13.
______. "Scheiche und Herrscher im Khanat Čaġatay." *Der Islam*, 67 (1990), pp. 278–321.
Paulson, Ivar. *Die primitiven Seelenvorstellungen der nordeurasischen Völker: eine religionsethnographische und religionsphänomenologische Untersuchung.* Stockholm: The Ethnographical Museum of Sweden, 1958; Ethnographical Museum of Sweden, Monograph Series, v. 5.
Pavet de Courteille, A. *Dictionnaire turc-oriental.* Paris, 1870; repr. Amsterdam: Philo Press, 1972.

Peers, E. Allison. *Ramon Lull: A Biography*. London: Society for Promoting Christian Knowledge, 1929.
Pelliot, Paul. "Neuf notes sur des questions d'Asie Centrale." *T'oung Pao*, 26 (1929), pp. 201–266.
______. *Notes on Marco Polo*. 2 vols. Paris, 1959 & 1963.
______. *Notes sur l'histoire de la Horde d'Or*. Paris: Librairie d'Amérique et d'Orient Adrien-Maisonneuve, 1949.
______. *Recherches sur les chrétiens d'Asie Centrale et d'Extrême-Orient*. Paris: Imprimerie Nationale, 1973.
______. "Sur la légende d'Uγuz-khan en écriture ouigoure." *T'oung Pao*, 27 (1930), pp. 247–358.
Pelliot, Paul, and Louis Hambis, trs. *Histoire des campagnes de Gengis Khan: Cheng-wou ts'in-tcheng lou*. Leiden: E. J. Brill, 1951.
Penrose, George Larry. "The Politics of Genealogy: An Historical Analysis of Abu'l-Gazi's *Shejere-i Terakima*." Ph.D. dissertation, Indiana University, 1975.
Peretiatkovich, G. I. *Povolzh'e v XV i XVI vekakh (ocherki iz istorii kraia i ego kolonizatsii)*. Moscow, 1877.
Pertsch, W. *Verzeichniss der türkische Handschriften der Königlichen Bibliothek zu Berlin*. Bd. VI, *Die Handschriften-Verzeichnisse der Königlichen Bibliothek zu Berlin*. Berlin, 1889.
Piacentini, Valeria Fiorani. *Turchizzazione ed islamizzazione dell'Asia Centrale (VI–XVI secolo d. Cr.)*. Milan: Società Editrice Dante Alighieri, 1974; Biblioteca della "Nuova Rivista Storica," No. 33.
Pimenov, N. N., tr. "Opisanie Chernago moria i Tatarii, sostavil dominikanets Èmiddio Dortelli d'Askoli, prefekt Kaffy, Tatarii i proch. 1634." *Zapiski Odesskago Obshchestva istorii i drevnostei*, 24 (1902), pp. 89–180.
Pleshko, N. D. *Kniaz'ia Urusovy i ikh predki: Istoriko-rodoslovie*. New York: Russkoe Istoriko-Rodoslovnoe Obshchestvo v Amerike, 1955.
Polo, Marco. *The Description of the World*. 2 vols. Ed. and tr. A. C. Moule and Paul Pelliot. London: George Routledge & Sons, 1938.
______. *Le livre de Marco Polo, citoyen de Venise, conseiller privé et commissaire impériale de Khoubilaï-Khaân*. Tr. M. G. Pauthier. Paris: Librairie de Firmin Didot Frères, Fils, 1865.
______. *The Travels of Marco Polo*. Tr. Ronald Latham. Harmondsworth, Middlesex: Penguin Books, 1958.
Popov, A. "Consecration Ritual for a Blacksmith Novice among the Yakuts." *Journal of American Folklore*, 46 (1933), pp. 257–271.
Poppe, N. N. "Das mongolische Sprachmaterial einer Leidener Handschrift." *Izvestiia AN SSSR*, 1927, Nos. 12–14, pp. 1009–1040; Nos. 15–17, pp. 1251–1274; 1928, pp. 55–80; repr. in his *Mongolica* (Westmead, Farnborough: Gregg International, 1972), No. 1.
______. "Opisanie mongol'skikh "shamanskikh" rukopisei Instituta vostokovedeniia." *Zapiski Instituta vostokovedeniia Akademii nauk*, 1 (Leningrad, 1927), pp. 151–200; repr. in his *Mongolica*, No. 2.
______. "Die Schwanenjungfrauen in der epischen Dichtung der Mongolen." In *Fragen der mongolischen Heldendichtung*, Teil I: Vorträge des 2. Epensymposiums des Sonderforschungsbereichs 12, Bonn 1979 (Wiesbaden: Otto Harrassowitz, 1981; Asiatische Forschungen, Bd. 72), pp. 101–108.
______. "Zolotoordynskaia rukopis' na bereste." *Sovetskoe vostokovedenie*, 2 (1941), pp. 81–134 + XXIV Pl.; repr. in his *Mongolica*, No. 3.
______. "Zum Feuerkultus bei den Mongolen." *Asia Major*, 2 (1925), pp. 130–145.

Potanin, G. N. "Doch' moria v stepnom èpose." *Ètnograficheskoe obozrenie*, 1892, No. 1, pp. 38–69.

_____. *Kazakhskii fol'klor v sobranii G. N. Potanina (Arkhivnye materialy i publikatsii)*. Alma-Ata: Nauka, 1972.

_____. "Kazakh-kirgizskie i altaiskie predaniia, legendy i skazki." *Zhivaia starina*, 1916, vyp. 2–3, pp. 47–198.

_____. "Mar'ia lebed' belaia v bylinakh i skazkakh." *Ètnograficheskoe obozrenie*, 1892, No. 2–3, pp. 1–22.

_____. "Otryvki iz kirgizskago skazaniia o Idyge, iz zapisei Ch. Valikhanova." *Zhivaia starina*, 1891, vyp. 4, pp. 156–163.

_____. "Tiurkskaia skazka o Idyge." *Zhivaia starina*, 1897, vyp. 3–4, pp. 294–350.

_____. *Vostochnye motivy v srednevekovom evropeiskom èpose*. Moscow, 1899.

Potapov, L. P. "Drevnii obychai otrazhaiushchii pervobytno-obshchinnyi byt kochevnikov." *Tiurkologicheskii sbornik*, 1 (1951) (= *Sbornik S. E. Malovu*), pp. 164–175.

_____. "Materialy po ètnografii tuvintsev raionov Mongun-taigi i Kara-kholia." In *Trudy Tuvinskoi kompleksnoi arkheologo-ètnograficheskoi èkspeditsii*, I (*Materialy po arkheologii i ètnografii zapadnoi Tuvy*) (Moscow/Leningrad: Izd-vo AN SSSR, 1960), pp. 171–237.

_____. *Ocherki narodnogo byta tuvintsev*. Moscow: Nauka, GRVL, 1969.

_____. "Umai—bozhestvo drevnikh tiurkov v svete ètnograficheskikh dannykh." *Tiurkologicheskii sbornik 1972* (Moscow: Nauka, GRVL, 1973), pp. 265–286.

_____. "Volk v starinnykh narodnykh pover'iakh i primetakh Uzbekov." In *Kratkie soobshcheniia Instituta Ètnografii AN SSSR*, vyp. 30 (1958), pp. 135–142.

Povest' vremennykh let. Ed. D. S. Likhachev. 2 vols. Moscow-Leningrad: Izd-vo Akademii nauk SSSR, 1950.

Priselkov, M. D. *Khanskie iarlyki russkim mitropolitam*. Petrograd, 1916.

Pritsak, Omeljan. "Bolgaro-Tschuwaschica." *UAJ*, 31 (1959), pp. 274–314.

_____. "Die Karachaniden." *Der Islam*, 31 (1953-54), pp. 17–68.

_____. "Karachanidische Streitfragen, 1–4." *Oriens*, 3 (1950), pp. 209–228.

_____. "The Khazar Kingdom's Conversion to Judaism." *HUS*, 2–3 (1978), pp. 261–281.

_____. "The Pečenegs: A Case of Social and Economic Transformation." *AEMA*, 1 (1975), pp. 211–235.

_____. "Von den Karluk zu den Karachaniden." *ZDMG*, 101 (1951), pp. 270–300.

Putilov, V. N. "Pesnia o Shchelkane." In *Russkii fol'klor: Materialy i issledovaniia*, t. 3 (Moscow/Leningrad: Izd-vo AN SSSR, 1958), pp. 46–68.

Qādir ʿAlī Bek Jalāyirī. *Sbornik letopisei. Tatarskii tekst*. Ed. I. Berezin. Kazan, 1854; Biblioteka vostochnykh istorikov, t. II, ch. 1.

al-Qalqashandī. *Ṣubḥ al-aʿshā fī ṣināʿat al-inshā*. 14 vols. Cairo: al-Maṭbaʿah al-Amīrīyah, 1913–1919.

Qāshānī, Abū'l-Qāsim ʿAbdullāh b. Muḥammad. *Tārīkh-i Ūljāytū*. Ed. Mahīn Hambly. Tehran: Bungāh-i Tarjimah va Nashr-i Kitāb, 1348/1969; Persian Texts Series, No. 40.

Qazvīnī, Ḥamdullāh Mustawfī. *Tārīkh-i guzīdah*. Ed. ʿAbd al-Ḥusayn Navāʾī. Tehran, 1339/1960; repr. Tehran: Amīr-i Kabīr, 1362/1983.

_____. *The Geographical Part of the Nuzhat-al-Qulūb composed by Ḥamd-allāh Mustawfī of Qazwīn in 740 (1340)*. Ed. and tr. G. Le Strange. London: Luzac & Co., 1915 (part 1, text), 1919 (part 2, tr.); E. J. W. Gibb Memorial Series, vol. 23, pt. 1 & 2.

Qïrïmī, ʿAbd al-Ghaffār. *ʿUmdat al-akhbār*. Ed. Najīb ʿĀṣim. Separately paginated supplement to *Türk Tarih Encümeni Mecmuası*, 15–16 (1925–1926).

_____. *ʿUmdat al-akhbār*. MS Istanbul, Sülemaniye Library, Esad Efendi No. 2331.

Quatremère, Étienne. [Notes and commentary in Rashīd ad-Dīn, *Histoire des Mongols de la Perse*].

_____, tr. "Notice de l'ouvrage persan qui a pour titre: Matla-assaadeïn ou-Madjma-albahreïn et qui contient l'histoire des deux sultans Schah-Rokh et Abou-Saïd." *Notices et extraits des manuscrits de la Bibliothèque du Roi et autres bibliothèques*, 14/1 (1843), pp. 1–514.

Radlov, V. V. *Opyt slovaria tiurkskikh narechii*. SPb., 1893–1911; repr. Moscow: Izd-vo Vostochnoi Literatury, 1963, 4 vols. in 8.

_____. *Proben der Volkslitteratur der nördlichen türkischen Stämme* (Russian title: *Obraztsy narodnoi literatury severnykh tiurkskikh plemen*). SPb., 1866-1907.

Radzievskaia, S. B. *Opisanie rukopisei nauchnoi biblioteki im. N. I. Lobachevskogo*. Vyp. I, "Fol'klor." Kazan, 1958.

Raevskii, D. S. *Ocherki ideologii skifo-sakskikh plemen: opyt rekonstruktsii skifskoi mifologii*. Moscow: Nauka, GRVL, 1977; partial English translation: "The Scythian Genealogical Legend," tr. Michel Vale. *SAA*, 21/1–2 (Summer–Fall 1982), pp. 33–66, 21/3 (Winter 1982–1983), pp. 80–122.

Rähmanov, V. *Ozbek klässik ädäbiyati äsärläri uchun qisqächä lughät*. Tashkent: Oqituvchi, 1983.

Ränk, Gustav. "Gegorene Milch und Käse bei den Hirtenvölkern Asiens." *Journal de la Société Finno-ougrienne*, 70 (1970), No. 3, pp. 4–21.

Rashīd ad-Dīn. *Dzhāmiʿ at-tavārīkh*. T. I, ch. 1. Ed. A. A. Romaskevich, L. A. Khetagurov, and A. A. Ali-zade. Moscow: Nauka, GRVL, 1965.

_____. *Die Geschichte der Oġuzen des Rašīd ad-Dīn*. Tr. Karl Jahn. Vienna: Hermann Böhlaus Nachf., 1969; Österreichische Akademie der Wissenschaften, Philosophisch-Historische Klasse, Denkschriften, Bd. 100; Forschungen zur islamischen Philologie und Kulturgeschichte, Bd. IV.

_____. *Histoire des Mongols de la Perse écrite en persan par Raschid-eldin*. Ed. and tr. Étienne Quatremère. Paris, 1836; repr. Amsterdam: Oriental Press, 1968.

_____. [Fazlallakh Rashid ad-Din]. *Oguz-name*. Tr. R. M. Shukiurova. Baku: Èlm, 1987.

_____. *Sbornik letopisei*. T. 1, kn. 1, tr. L. A. Khetagurov, ed. A. A. Semenov. Moscow/Leningrad: Izd-vo AN SSSR, 1952; t. 1, kn. 2, tr. O. I. Smirnova. Moscow, 1952; t. II, tr. Iu. P. Verkhovskii. Moscow/Leningrad: Izd-vo AN SSSR, 1960.

_____. *Shuʿab-i panjgānah*. MS Istanbul, Topkapı Sarayı Müzesi, MS Ahmet III, No. 2937.

_____. *The Successors of Genghis Khan*. Tr. John Andrew Boyle. New York: Columbia University Press, 1971.

Ratchnevsky, Paul. *Genghis Khan: His Life and Legacy*. Ed. and tr. Thomas Nivison Haining. Oxford: Basil Blackwell, 1991.

_____. "Über den mongolischen Kult am Hofe der Grosskhane in China." In *Mongolian Studies*, ed. Louis Ligeti (Amsterdam: Verlag B. R. Grüner, 1970), pp. 417–443.

Redhouse, Sir James W. *A Turkish and English Lexicon*. Constantinople, 1890; repr. Istanbul: Çağrı Yayınları, 1978.

Reichl, Karl. "Oral Tradition and Performance of the Uzbek and Karakalpak Epic Singers." In *Fragen der mongolischen Heldendichtung*, Teil III (Vorträge des 4. Epensymposiums des Sonderforschungsbereiches 12, Bonn 1983), ed. W. Heissig (Wiesbaden: Otto Harrassowitz, 1985; Asiatische Forschungen, Bd. 91/III), pp. 613–643.

Richard, Jean. "Le christianisme dans l'Asie centrale." *Journal of Asian History*, 16 (1982), pp. 101–124.

______. "La conversion de Berke et les débuts de l'islamisation de la Horde d'Or." *REI*, 35 (1967), pp. 173–184.

______. "Les missions chez les Mongols aux XIIIe et XIVe siècles." In *Histoire universelle des missions catholiques*, I: "Les missions des origines au XVIe siècle" (Paris, 1956), pp. 173–195.

______. *La papauté et les missions d'Orient au Moyen Age (XIIIe–XVe siècles)*. Rome: École Française de Rome, 1977.

Richter-Bernburg, Lutz. "Bokhtīšūʿ." *EIr*, IV, pp. 333–336.

Rieu, Charles. *Catalogue of the Turkish Manuscripts in the British Museum*. London: British Museum, 1888.

Rintchen. "La généalogie des descendants de Djātak de la race des cent cygnes blancs." *UAJ*, 39 (1967), pp. 230–247.

Róna-Tas, András, and S. Fodor. *Epigraphica Bulgarica: A volgai bolgár-török feliratok*. Szeged, 1973; Studia uralo-altaica, 1.

Rorlich, Azade-Ayşe. "*Idegey* Joins the Family of Rehabilitated Turkic National Epics." *Radio Liberty: Report on the USSR*, I/39 (29 September 1989), pp. 23–24.

______. "The Volga Tatars: Modern Identities of the Golden Horde." In *Rulers from the Steppe: State Formation on the Eurasian Periphery*, ed. Gary Seaman and Daniel Marks (Los Angeles: Ethnographics Press, University of Southern California, 1991; Proceedings of the Soviet-American Academic Symposia in Conjunction with the Museum Exhibitions "Nomads: Masters of the Eurasian Steppe," vol. 2), pp. 274–290.

Rossabi, Morris. *Khubilai Khan: His Life and Times*. Berkeley and Los Angeles: University of California Press, 1988.

Roux, Jean-Paul. "Le chaman gengiskhanide." *Anthropos*, 54 (1959), pp. 401–432.

______. *Faune et flore sacrées dans les sociétés altaïques*. Paris: Librairie d'Amérique et d'Orient Adrien-Maisonneuve, 1966.

______. "Fonctions chamaniques et valeurs du feu chez les peuples altaïques." *RHR*, 189 (1976), pp. 67–101.

______. *La mort chez les peuples altaïques anciens et médiévaux d'après les documents écrits*. Paris: Librairie d'Amérique et d'Orient Adrien-Maisonneuve, 1963.

______. "Le nom du chaman dans les textes turco-mongols." *Anthropos*, 53 (1958), pp. 133–142.

______. "L'Origine céleste de la souveraineté dans les inscriptions paléo-turques." In *The Sacral Kingship* (supplement to *Numen*) (Leiden: E. J. Brill, 1959), pp. 230–241.

______. "La religion des Turcs de l'Orkhon des VIIe et VIIIe siècles." *RHR*, 161 (1962), pp. 1–24.

______. *La religion des Turcs et des Mongols*. Paris: Payot, 1984.

______. "Les religions dans les sociétés turco-mongoles." *RHR*, 201 (1984), pp. 393–420.

______. "Sacerdoce et empires universels chez les turco-mongols." *RHR*, 204 (1987), pp. 151–174.

Rubruck, William of. *The Mission of Friar William of Rubruck: His Journey to the Court of the Great Khan Möngke, 1253–1255*. Tr. Peter Jackson. London: The Hakluyt Society, 1990; Series 2, No. 173. [See also Dawson, *The Mongol Mission*].

Rūmī, Abū'l-Khayr. *Ṣaltuḳ-nāme. Ebū'l-Ḫayr Rūmī'nin sözlü rivayetlerden topladığı Ṣarı Ṣaltuḳ menakibi*. 7 parts. Ed. Fahir İz. Cambridge: Harvard University,

1974–1984; Sources of Oriental Languages and Literatures, ed. Şinasi Tekin and Gönül Alpay Tekin, Turkic Sources, 4.

______. [Ebü'l-Hayr-ı Rumî]. *Saltuk-nâme*. Ed. Şükrü Halûk Akalın. Vol. 1. Ankara: Kültür ve Turizm Bakanlığı, 1987.

Rūmī, Jalāl ad-Dīn. *The Mathnawí of Jalálu'ddín Rúmí*. Tr. R. A. Nicholson. London: Luzac & Co., 1926–1934, repr. 1977; E. J. W. Gibb Memorial Series, n. s. IV.2, 4, 6.

Rybushkin, M. *Zapiski ob Astrakhani*. Moscow: Tipografiia S. Selivanovskago, 1841.

Rychkov, Petr. *Topografiia Orenburgskaia, to est': obstoiatel'noe opisanie Orenburgskoi gubernii*. SPb.: Imperatorskaia Akademiia nauk, 1762; German translation: [Peter Rytschkov], *Orenburgische Topographie, oder umständliche Beschreibung des Orenburgischen Gouvernements*, tr. Jacob Rodde. Riga: Johann Friedrich Hartknoch, 1772.

______. *Vvedenie k Astrakhanskoi topografii*. Moscow: Imperatorskii Moskovskii Universitet, 1774.

Sablukov, G. S. "Ocherk vnutrenniago sostoianiia kipchakskago tsarstva," *IOAIÈ*, t. 13, vyp. 2 (1896), pp. 89–146.

Safargaliev, M. G. *Raspad Zolotoi Ordy*. Saransk: Mordovskoe Knizhnoe Izd-vo, 1960.

"Ṣafī," Fakhr ad-Dīn ʿAlī b. Ḥusayn. *Rashaḥāt-i ʿayn al-ḥayāt*. Ed. ʿAlī Aṣghar Muʿīnīyān; 2 vols. Tehran, 2536/1356/1977.

Sagang Sechen. *Sagang Sechen, Prince of the Ordos Mongols: The Bejewelled Summary of the Origin of Khans (Qad-un ündüsün-ü Erdeni-yin Tobči), A History of the Eastern Mongols to 1662*; Part One, *Chapters One through Five: From the Creation of the World to the Death of Genghis Khan (1227)*. Tr. John R. Krueger. Bloomington, Indiana: Mongolia Society Occasional Papers, No. 2, 1964.

Sagaster, Klaus. "Die Verehrung Činggis Khans bei den Mongolen." In *XXIV. Deutscher Orientalistentag, vom 26. bis 30. September 1988 in Köln, ausgewählte Vorträge*, ed. Werner Diem and Abdoldjavad Falaturi (Stuttgart: Franz Steiner Verlag, 1990; *ZDMG*, Supplement VIII), pp. 365–371.

______. *Die Weisse Geschichte: Eine mongolische Quelle zur Lehre von den beiden Ordnungen und Staat in Tibet und der Mongolie*. Wiesbaden: Otto Harrassowitz, 1976.

Sagitov, M. M. "Otrazhenie konsolidatsii bashkirskoi narodnosti v èpicheskikh skazaniiakh." *Arkheologiia i ètnografiia Bashkirii*, 4 (1971), pp. 278–281.

Samoilovich, A. N. "Neskol'ko popravok k iarlyku Timur-Kutluga." *Izvestiia Rossiiskoi Akademii Nauk*, 1918, pp. 1109–1124.

______. "Variant skazaniia o Edigee i Tokhtamyshe, zapisannyi N. Khakimovym." *Tiurkologicheskii sbornik 1972* (Moscow: Nauka, GRVL, 1973), pp. 186–211.

______. [A. Samojlovič]. "Beiträge zur Bienenzucht in der Krim im 14.–17. Jahrhundert." In *Festschrift Georg Jacob*, ed. Theodor Menzel (Leipzig: Otto Harrassowitz, 1932), pp. 270–275.

Samolin, William. *East Turkistan to the Twelfth Century: A Brief Political Survey*. The Hague: Mouton, 1964; Central Asiatic Studies, ed. Karl Jahn and John R. Krueger, IX.

Santarem, Visconde de [Manuel Francisco de Barros]. *Estudos de Cartographia Antiga*; vol. I. Lisbon, 1919.

Savory, R. M. "A 15th Century Ṣafavid Propagandist at Harāt." In *American Oriental Society, Middle West Branch: Semi-Centennial Volume*, ed. Denis Sinor (Bloomington: Indiana University Press, 1969), pp. 189–197.

Schamiloglu, Uli. "The Formation of a Tatar Historical Consciousness: Şihabäddin

Märcani and the Image of the Golden Horde." *Central Asian Survey*, 9/2 (1990), pp. 39–49.
______. "The *Qaraçı* Beys of the Later Golden Horde: Notes on the Organization of the Mongol World Empire." *AEMA*, 4 (1984), pp. 283–297.
______."The *Umdet ül-Ahbar* and the Turkic Narrative Sources for the Golden Horde and the Later Golden Horde." In *Central Asian Monuments*, ed. Hasan B. Paksoy (Istanbul: Isis Press, 1992), pp. 81–93.
Schiefner, Anton. *Heldensagen der minusinskischen Tataren*. SPb., 1859.
Schiltberger, Johannes. *Als Sklave im Osmanischen Reich und bei den Tataren, 1394–1427*. Tr. Ulrich Schlemmer. Stuttgart: Thienemann, Edition Erdmann, 1983.
______. *The Bondage and Travels of Johann Schiltberger, a native of Bavaria, in Europe, Asia and Africa, 1396-1427*. Tr. John Buchan Telfer. London: Hakluyt Society, Series I, No. 58, 1879.
______. *Hans Schiltbergers Reisebuch* [facsimile reprint of the 1476 Augsburg edition]. Ed. Elisabeth Geck. Wiesbaden: Guido Pressler, 1969.
______. *Hans Schiltbergers Reisebuch nach der nürnberger Handschrift herausgegeben*. Ed. Valentin Langmantel. Tübingen, 1885; Bibliothek des Litterarischen Vereins in Stuttgart, No. 172.
______. *Puteshestvie po Evrope, Azii i Afrike c 1394 goda do 1427 god*. Tr. F. K. Brun. Ed. Z. M. Buniiatov. Baku: Èlm 1984.
______. *Eine wunderbarliche und kurzweilige Historie, wie Schiltberger, einer aus der Stadt München in Bayern, von den Türken gefangen, in die Heidenschaft geführet und wieder ist heim kommen . . .* [on cover: *Schiltbergers Reisebuch (Kriegsgefangen in Vorderasien von 1394–1425)*]. Tr. G. Siemes. Leipzig: Im Insel-Verlag, [1917].
Schmidt, Wilhelm. *Der Ursprung der Gottesidee*. Vols. 9–12. Münster: Aschendorff; 1949–1955.
Schubert, J. "Zum Begriff und zur Lage des 'Ötükän.' " *UAJ*, 35 (1963), pp. 213–218.
Seid-zadè, A. A. "Pir-Khusein Shirvani (Shirvanan)." *Doklady Akademii nauk Azerbaidzhanskoi SSR*, 16/12 (1960), pp. 1265–1268.
Semenov, A. A. "K voprosu o proiskhozhdenii i sostave uzbekov Sheibani-khana." In *Materialy po istorii tadzhikov i uzbekov Srednei Azii*, I (Trudy Instituta istorii, arkheologii i ètnografii AN TadzhSSR, t. XII, Stalinabad, 1954), pp. 3–37.
Semenov, N. *Tuzemtsy severo-vostochnago Kavkaza*. Saint Petersburg, 1895.
Serruys, Henry. "The Cult of Činggis-Qan: A Mongol Manuscript from Ordos." *ZAS*, 17 (1984), pp. 82–117.
______, tr. *Kumiss Ceremonies and Horse Races: Three Mongolian Texts*. Wiesbaden: Otto Harrassowitz, 1970; Asiatische Forschungen, Bd. 37.
______. "Mongol 'Qoriγ:' Reservation." *Mongolian Studies*, 1 (1974), pp. 76–91.
Sevortian, È. V. *Ètimologicheskii slovar' tiurkskikh iazykov (obshchetiurkskie i mezhtiurkskie osnovy na glasnye)*. Moscow: Nauka, 1974.
Shahrani, M. Nazif. "Local Knowledge of Islam and Social Discourse in Afghanistan and Turkistan in the Modern Period." In *Turko-Persia in Historical Perspective*, ed. Robert L. Canfield (Cambridge: Cambridge University Press, 1991), pp. 161–188.
Shajarah of the Ming Bashkir tribe. MS 1a–69/I (ff. 1a–28b), Collection of Manuscripts and Old Printed Books of the Institute of History, Language and Literature of the Academy of Sciences of Bashkortostan, Ufa.
Shajarat al-atrāk: MS India Office, Ethé 172.
______. *The Shajrat ul Atrak, or Genealogical Tree of the Turks and Tatars*. Tr. Col. Miles. London, 1838.

Shāmī, Niẓām ad-Dīn. *Ẓafar-nāmah*. Ed. Felix Tauer, *Histoire des conquêtes de Tamerlan*. Vol. 1, *Texte*. Prague: Orientalní ústav, 1937.

Shastina, N. P. "Mongol and Turkic Ethnonyms in the Secret History of the Mongols." In *Researches in Altaic Languages*, ed. Louis Ligeti (Budapest: Akadémiai Kiadó, 1975; Bibliotheca Orientalis Hungarica, 20 = PIAC XIV), pp. 231–244.

Shaw, M. R. B., tr. *Joinville and Villehardouin, Chronicles of the Crusades*. Harmondsworth, Middlesex: Penguin Books, 1963.

Shcheglov, I. L. *Trukhmeny i Nogaitsy Stavropol'skoi gubernii: Svedeniia o khoziaistve osedlykh i kochuiushchikh inorodtsev, russkikh krest'ian i khutorian-ovtsevodov v Trukhmenskoi i Achikulakskoi stepi Stavropol'skoi gubernii*. Stavropol': Tipografiia Gubernskago Pravleniia, 1910.

Shcherbak, A. M., ed. *Oguz-nāme. Muḥabbat-nāme. Pamiatniki drevneuigurskoi i starouzbekskoi pis'mennosti*. Moscow: Izd-vo Vostochnoi Literatury, 1959.

Shīrāzī, Rukn ad-Dīn Masʿūd b. ʿAbdullāh. *Nuṣūṣ al-khuṣūṣ fī tarjamat al-fuṣūṣ, sharḥ-i Fuṣūṣ al-ḥikam-i Muḥyī 'd-Dīn Ibn ʿArabī*. Ed. Rajab-ʿAlī Maẓlūmī. Tehran: McGill University / Tehran University, Institute of Islamic Studies, 1359/1980.

Shirokogoroff, S. M. *The Psychomental Complex of the Tungus*. London: Kegan Paul, Trench, Trubner, 1935.

Shoolbraid, G. M. H. *The Oral Epic of Siberia and Central Asia*. Bloomington: Indiana University, 1975; Uralic and Altaic Series, vol. 111.

A Short Description of all the Kingdoms which encompass the Euxine and Caspian Seas. Printed with *The Six Voyages of John Baptista Tavernier*. London, 1677.

ash-Shujāʿī, Shams ad-Dīn. *Die Chronik aš-Šuǧāʿīs*. Erster Teil, arabischer Text. Ed. Barbara Schäfer. Wiesbaden: Franz Steiner, 1977; Deutsches Archäologisches Institut Kairo, Quellen zur Geschichte des islamischen Ägyptens, Bd. 2a.

_____. *Tārīḫ al-Malik an-Nāṣir Muḥammad b. Qalāwūn aṣ-Ṣāliḥī wa-aulādihī* [*sic*]. Zweiter Teil, Übersetzung, tr. Barbara Schäfer. Wiesbaden: Franz Steiner, 1985; Deutsches Archäologisches Institut Kairo, Quellen zur Geschichte des islamischen Ägyptens, Bd. 2b.

Siikala, Anna-Leena. *The Rite Technique of the Siberian Shaman*. Helsinki: Suomalainen Tiedeakatemia, 1978; Folklore Fellows Communications, v. 220.

Sinor, Denis. "A propos de la biographie ouigoure de Hiuan-tsang." *JA*, 231 (1939), pp. 543–590.

_____. "The Legendary Origin of the Türks." In *Folklorica: Festschrift for Felix J. Oinas*, ed. Egle Victoria Žygas and Peter Voorheis (Bloomington: Research Institute for Inner Asian Studies, 1982), pp. 223–257.

_____. "Oğuz Kağan destanı üzerinde bazı mülâhazalar." Tr. Ahmed Ateş. *Türk Dili ve Edebiyatı Dergisi*, 4/1–2 (1950), pp. 1–14.

_____. "Some Latin Sources on the Khanate of Uzbek." In *Essays on Uzbek History, Culture, and Language*, ed. Denis Sinor and Bakhtiyar A. Nazarov (Bloomington: Indiana University, 1993; Uralic and Altaic Series, vol. 156) pp. 110–119.

_____. " 'Umay', a Mongol Spirit Honored by the Türks." In *Proceedings of the International Conference on China Border Area Studies* (Taipei: National Chengchi University, 1984), pp. 1771–1781.

Smirnov, A. P. *Volzhskie bulgary*. Moscow, 1951; Trudy Gosudarstvennogo istoricheskogo muzeia, vyp. 19.

Smith, Anthony D. "National Identity and Myths of Ethnic Descent." *Research in Social Movements, Conflict and Change*, 7 (1984), pp. 95–130.

Smith, Grace M. "Some *Türbes/Maqāms* of Sarı Saltuq, an Early Anatolian Turkish Ġāzī-Saint." *Turcica*, 14 (1982), pp. 216–225.

Smith, John. *The Complete Works of Captain John Smith (1580–1631)*. Ed. Philip L. Barbour. Vol. 3. Chapel Hill: University of North Carolina Press/ Williamsburg, Virginia: Institute of Early American History and Culture, 1986.

Sokolov, D. "Opyt razbora odnoi bashkorskoi [*sic*] letopisi." *Trudy Orenburgskoi uchenoi arkhivnoi kommissii*, vyp. 4 (1898), pp. 45–65.

Sokolov, Pl. "Podlozhnyi iarlyk Uzbeka mitropolitu Petru." *Russkii istoricheskii zhurnal*, kn. 5 (Petrograd, 1918), pp. 70–85.

Soninbaiar, Sh. "O sochineniiakh mongol'skikh avtorov na tibetskom iazyke po khronologii buddizma v Tibete i Mongolii." Tr. R. E. Pubaev. In *Istochnikovedenie i tekstologiia pamiatnikov srednevekovykh nauk v stranakh Tsentral'noi Azii. Sbornik nauchnykh trudov*, ed. R. E. Pubaev (Novosibirsk: Nauka, 1989), pp. 163–170.

Sourdel, D. "Bukhtīshūᶜ." *EI*², I, p. 1298.

Spasskii, G. I. "Idige, Kirgizskaia skazka." *Sibirskii vestnik*, ch. 10 (1820), pp. 358–373 [according to separate pagination, pp. 189–204].

Spuler, Bertold. *Die Goldene Horde: Die Mongolen in Russland 1223-1502*. 1st ed., Leipzig, 1943; 2nd ed., Wiesbaden: Otto Harrassowitz, 1965.

Stebleva, I. V. "Poèticheskaia struktura 'Oguz-name'." *Pis'mennye pamiatniki Vostoka*, 1969, pp. 289–309.

Stein, Rolf, tr. "Leao-tche." *T'oung Pao*, 35 (1940), pp. 1–154.

Stevenson, Edward Luther. *Genoese World Map, 1457: Facsimile and Critical Text Incorporating in Free Translation the Studies of Professor Theobald Fischer revised with the Addition of Copious Notes*. New York: American Geographical Society / Hispanic Society of America, 1912.

Sultanov, T. I. *Kochevye plemena Priaral'ia v XV–XVII vv. (Voprosy ètnicheskoi i sotsial'noi istorii)*. Moscow: Nauka, GRVL, 1982.

_____. "Opyt analiza traditsionnykh spiskov 92 'plemen ilatiia.' " In *Sredniaia Aziia v drevnosti i srednevekov'e (istoriia i kul'tura)* (Moscow: Nauka, GRVL, 1977), pp. 165–176.

Sultanov, I., and A. Hayitmetov, eds. *Ozbek näsri tärikhidän*. Tashkent: Fan, 1982.

Sümer, Faruk, Ahmet E. Uysal, and Warren S. Walker, trs. *The Book of Dede Korkut: A Turkish Epic*. Austin: University of Texas Press, 1972.

Surazakov, S. S., ed. and tr. *Maadai-Kara. Altaiskii geroicheskii èpos*. Moscow: Nauka, 1973.

Sushanlo, M. *Dungane (istoriko-ètnograficheskii ocherk)*. Frunze: Ilim, 1971.

Sydykov, A. S. "Rodovoe delenie kirgiz." In *ᶜIqd al-jumān: V. V. Bartol'du Turkestanskie druz'ia, ucheniki i pochitateli* (Tashkent: Obshchestvo dlia izucheniia Tadzhikistana i iranskikh narodnostei za ego predelami, 1927), pp. 273–300.

Syzdykova, R. G. *Iazyk "Zhami'at-tauārikh" Zhalairi*. Alma-Ata: Nauka, 1989.

Szynkiewicz, Sławoj. "Nahrungsmittel und ihre Zubereitung." In *Die Mongolen*, ed. Walther Heissig and Claudius C. Müller (Innsbruck: Pinguin-Verlag, 1989), pp. 142–149.

aṭ-Ṭabarī. *The History of al-Ṭabarī*. Vol. 2, *Prophets and Patriarchs*, tr. William M. Brinner. Albany: State University of New York Press, 1987.

Tahir, Mahmud. "Rizaeddin Fahreddin." *Central Asian Survey*, 8/1 (1989), pp. 111–115.

Tamura Jitsuzō. "The Legend of the Origin of the Mongols and Problems concerning their Migration." *Acta Asiatica*, 24 (1973), pp. 1–19.

Tatár, Magdalena. "Tragic and Stranger Ongons among the Altaic Peoples." In *Altaistic Studies* (PIAC XXV, 1982), ed. Gunnar Jarring and Staffan Rosén (Stockholm: Almqvist & Wiksell International, 1985), pp. 165–171.

______. "Two Mongol Texts Concerning the Cult of the Mountains." *AOH*, 30 (1976), pp. 1–58.

Tatar tele grammatikasï (morfologiia häm sintaksis). Kazan: Tatarstan Kitap Näshriyatï, 1959.

Taube, Erika. "South Siberian and Central Asian Hero Tales and Shamanistic Rituals." In *Shamanism in Eurasia*, ed. M. Hoppál, vol. 2, pp. 344–352.

______. "Die Widerspiegelung religiöser Vorstellungen im Alltagsbrauchtum der Tuwiner der Westmongolei." In *Traditions religieuses et para-religieuses des peuples altaïques* (Paris: Presses universitaires de France, 1972; PIAC XIII, Strasbourg, 1970), pp. 119–138.

Tavārīkh-i guzīdah-i nuṣrat-nāmah. MS British Museum, Or. 3222 (Rieu, *Turkish Manuscripts*, pp. 276–280); facs. ed. A. M. Akramov, *Tavarikh-i guzīda-Nuṣrat-nāme* [*sic*]. Tashkent: Fan, 1967.

Tekin, Şinasi. "A Qaraḫānid Document of A.D. 1121 (A.H. 515) from Yarkand." *HUS*, 3–4 (1979–1980), pp. 868–883.

Tekin, Talât. *Volga Bulgar kitabeleri ve Volga Bulgarcası*. Ankara: Türk Tarih Kurumu Basımevi, 1988.

Temir, Ahmet. "Die alten Quellen der Kazan- und nord-turkischen Literatur (bis zum XIX. Jahrundert)." In *Studies in General and Oriental Linguistics presented to Shirô Hattori on the Occasion of his Sixtieth Birthday*, ed. Roman Jakobson and Shigeo Kawamoto (Tokyo: TEC Company, 1970), pp. 612–626.

Teufel, J. K. *Eine Lebensbeschreibung des Scheichs ᶜAlī-i Hamadānī (gestorben 1385): Die Xulāṣat ul-Manāqib des Maulānā Nūr ud-Dīn Caᶜfar Badaxšī*. Leiden: E. J. Brill, 1962.

Thomas, George Martin, ed. *Diplomatarium Veneto-Levantinum*. Venice, 1880; repr. New York: Burt Franklin, n.d.

Tizengauzen V., ed. and tr. *Sbornik materialov, otnosiashchikhsia k istorii Zolotoi Ordy*; t. 1, *Izvlecheniia iz sochinenii arabskikh*. SPb., 1884 [Turkish translation: *Altınordu devleti tarihine ait metinler*, tr. İsmail Hakkı İzmirli. Istanbul: Maarif Matbaası, 1941]; t. 2, *Izvlecheniia iz persidskikh sochinenii sobrannye V. G. Tizengauzenom i obrabotannye A. A. Romaskevichem i S. L. Volinym*. Moscow/Leningrad: Izd-vo AN SSSR, 1941.

Togan, A. Zeki Velidi. "Bashdjirt." *EI*², I, pp. 1075–1077.

______. *Bugünkü Türkili (Türkistan) ve yakın tarihi*, Cilt I, *Batı ve kuzey Türkistan*. Istanbul: Arkadaş, İbrahim Horoz ve Güven Basımevleri, 1942–1947.

______. [Zeki Velidi Togan]. "Kazan Hanlığında İslâm Türk Kültürü (Kanunî zamanında 1550 de Kazandan gönderilen bir rapor)." *İslâm Tetkikleri Enstitüsü Dergisi*, 3/3–4 (1959–1960), pp. 179–204.

______. [Zeki Velidi Togan]. "Das özbekische Epos Chan-name." *CAJ*, 1 (1955), pp. 144–156.

______. [Zeki Velidi Togan]. "Timur's Campaign of 1395 in the Ukraine and North Caucasus." *Annals of the Ukrainian Academy of Arts and Sciences in the U.S.*, 6 (1958), pp. 1358–1371.

______. *Tarihde usûl*. Istanbul: İbrahim Horoz Basımevi, 1950.

______. [Ahmet Zeki Validov]. "Vostochnyia rukopisi v Ferganskoi oblasti." *ZVOIRAO*, 22 (1915), pp. 303–320.

______. [Zeki Velidi Togan]. "Yesevîliğe dair bazı yeni malûmat." In *60 doğum yılı*

münasebetiyle Fuad Köprülü Armağanı (Istanbul: Osman Yalçın Matbaası, 1953), pp. 523–529.
Togan, Nazmiye, İsenbike Arıcanlı, and Tuncer Baykara. "A. Zeki Velidi Togan'in Kendi Tasnifine Göre Mesai Evrakı." In *Fen-Edebiyat Fakültesi Araştırma Dergisi; Ord. Prof. Dr. Ahmed Zeki Velidi Togan Özel Sayısı*, fasükül 1, sayı 13 (Erzurum: Atatürk Üniversitesi Basımevi, 1985), pp. 33–58.
Tolstova, L. S. "Ispol'zovanie fol'klora pri izuchenii ètnogeneze i ètnokul'turnykh sviazei narodov (na sredneaziatskom materiale)." In *Fol'klor i istoricheskaia ètnografiia* (Moscow: Nauka, 1983), pp. 6–22.
_____. "Istoricheskii fol'klor karakalpakov kak istochnik dlia izucheniia ètnogeneza i ètnokul'turnykh sviazei ètogo naroda." In *Ètnicheskaia istoriia i fol'klor* (Moscow: Nauka, 1977), pp. 141–164.
Tonkin, Elizabeth, Maryon McDonald, and Malcolm Chapman, eds. *History and Ethnicity*. London: Routledge, 1989; ASA Monographs, No. 27.
Tott, Baron de. *Mémoires du Baron de Tott sur les Turcs et les Tartares*. Vol. 2. Maestricht: J. E. Dufour & Ph. Roux, 1785.
Trofimukh, N. A. "Sanitarnyi ocherk obsledovaniia vodosnabzheniia, pitaniia, zhilishcha i odezhdy zhitelei Kazakstana." In *Kazaki: Sbornik statei antropologicheskogo otriada Kazakstanskoi èkspeditsii Akademii nauk SSSR; Issledovanie 1927 g.*, ed. S. I. Rudenko (Leningrad: AN SSSR, 1930; *Materialy komissii èkspeditsionnykh issledovanii*, vyp. 15; seriia Kazakstanskaia), pp. 163–228.
Troiakov, P. A. "Promyslovaia i magicheskaia funktsiia skazyvaniia skazok u khakasov." *SÈ*, 1969, No. 2, pp. 24–34; English translation: "Economic and Magical Functions of Taletelling among the Khakasy." *SAA*, 14/1–2 (Summer–Fall 1975), pp. 146–67.
Troitskaia, A. L. *Katalog arkhiva Kokandskikh khanov XIX veka*. Moscow: Nauka, GRVL, 1968.
_____. "Zapovedniki kuruk kokandskogo khana Khudaiara." In *Sbornik Gosudarstvennoi Publichnoi Biblioteki im. M.E. Saltykova-Shchedrina* (Leningrad), vyp. 3 (1955), pp. 122–156.
Tryjarski, Edward. "Beekeeping Among the Turks." *Acta Orientalia*, 32 (1970 = PIAC XI), pp. 241–277.
_____. "Les religions des petchenègues." In *Traditions religieuses et para-religieuses des peuples altaïques* (PIAC XIII, 1970) (Paris: Presses Universitaires de France, 1972), pp. 139–148.
Tulokhonov, M. I. "Genealogicheskie legendy i predaniia kak istochnik po ètnicheskoi istorii buriat." In *Ètnokul'turnye protsessy v iugo-vostochnoi Sibiri v srednie veka* (Novosibirsk: Nauka, 1989), pp. 164–172.
Turnerelli, Edward Tracy. *Russia on the Borders of Asia: Kazan, the Ancient Capital of the Tartar Khans*. London: Richard Bentley, 1854.
Ṭūsī, Naṣīr ad-Dīn. *Tansūkh-nāmah-i Īlkhānī*. Ed. Sayyid Muḥammad Taqī Mudarris Riżavī. 2nd ed. Tehran: Intishārāt-i Iṭṭilāʿāt, 1363/1984.
Uluçay, Çağatay, and Martin B. Dickson. "Unpublished Works of Prof. Z. V. Togan." In *Zeki Velidi Togan'a Armağan* (Istanbul, 1950–1955), pp. xlvii–l.
al-ʿUmarī. *Das mongolische Weltreiche: Al-ʿUmarī's Darstellung der mongolischen Reiche in seinem Werk Masālik al-abṣār fī mamālik al-amṣār*. Ed. and tr. Klaus Lech. Wiesbaden: Otto Harrassowitz, 1968; Asiatische Forschungen, Bd. 22.
Usmanov, M[irkasym] A. "Ètapy islamizatsii dzhuchieva ulusa i musul'manskoe dukhovenstvo v tatarskhikh khanstvakh XIII–XVI vekov." In *Dukhovenstvo i politicheskaia zhizn' na Blizhnem i Srednem Vostoke v period feodalizma* (Moscow: Nauka, GRVL, 1985; Bartol'dovskie chteniia, 1982), pp. 177–185.

_____. [Mirkasïym Gosmanov]. "Katlaulï chornïng karshïlïklï väkile." *Kazan utlarï*, 1984, No. 1, pp. 142–157.

_____. "O tragedii èposa i tragediiakh liudskikh." In *Idegei: Tatarskii narodnyi èpos*, tr. Semen Lipkin (Kazan: Tatarskoe Knizhnoe Izdatel'stvo, 1990), pp. 247–254.

_____. [Mirkasïym Gosmanov]. "Rizaetdin Fäkhretdinev mirasï." In his *Utkännänkilächäkkä* (Kazan: Tatarstan Kitap Näshriyatï, 1990), pp. 51–70.

_____. *Tatarskie istoricheskie istochniki XVII–XVIII vv*. Kazan: Izd-vo Kazanskogo Universiteta, 1972.

_____. *Zhalovannye akty Dzhuchieva ulusa XIV–XVI vv*. Kazan: Izd-vo Kazanskogo Universiteta, 1979.

Usmanov, M. A. [M. G. Gosmanov], M. Z. Zäkiev, Ä. G. Iskhak, R. S. Mökhämmädiev, and I. N. Nadirov, eds. *Idegäy: Tatar khalïk dastanï*. Kazan: Tatarstan Kitap Näshriyatï, 1988.

Usmanov, M. A. "Rasprostranenie islama i ego rol' v istorii Srednei Azii." In *Iz istorii obshchestvenno-filosofskoi mysli i vol'nodumiia v Srednei Azii*, ed. M. M. Khairullaev (Tashkent: Fan, 1991), pp. 10–26.

Valikhanov, Chokan Chingisovich. "O musul'manstve v stepi." *Sobranie sochinenii v piati tomakh*, I (Alma-Ata: Izd-vo AN KazSSR, 1961), pp. 524–529.

_____. *Sobranie sochinenii v piati tomakh*. Alma-Ata, 1961.

_____. "Idige (dzhir). Vstuplenie" and "Èdigei" (tr.). In *Sochineniia Chokana Chingisovicha Valikhanova*, ed. N. I. Veselovskii; = *Zapiski Imperatorskago Russkago Geograficheskago Obshchestva po Otdeleniiu Ètnografii*, t. 29 (SPb., 1904), pp. 223–264, 265–273.

Vámbéry, Hermann. *Das Türkenvolk in seinen ethnologischen und ethnographischen Beziehungen*. Leipzig, 1885; repr. Osnabrück: Biblio Verlag, 1970.

Van den Wyngaert, Anastasius, ed. *Sinica Franciscana*. I: *Itinera et relationes fratrum minorum saeculi XIII et XIV*. Quaracchi-Florence, 1929.

Vansina, Jan. *Oral Tradition as History*. Madison: University of Wisconsin Press, 1985.

Vásáry, István. "Bemerkungen zum uigurischen Schrifttum in der Goldenen Horde und bei den Timuriden." *UAJ*, Neue Folge, 7 (1987), pp. 115–126; published also in *Beşinci Milletler Arası Türkoloji Kongresi, İstanbul, 23–28 Eylül 1985; Tebliğler*, I, Türk dili, cilt 2 (Istanbul: Edebiyat Fakültesi Basımevi, 1987), pp. 235–247.

_____. " 'History and Legend' in Berke Khan's Conversion to Islam." In *Aspects of Altaic Civilization III* (= PIAC XXX), ed. Denis Sinor (Bloomington: Indiana University, Research Institute for Inner Asian Studies, 1990), pp. 230–252.

_____. "Orthodox Christian Qumans and Tatars of the Crimea in the 13th–14th Centuries." *CAJ*, 32 (1988), pp. 260–271.

Vaṣṣāf. *Taḥrīr-i Tārīkh-i Vaṣṣāf*. Ed. ʿAbd al-Muḥammad Āyatī. Tehran: Intishārāt-i Bunyād-i Farhang-i Irān, 1346/1967.

Vel'iaminov-Zernov, V. V. *Izsledovanie o kasimovskikh tsariakh i tsarevichakh*. II. *TVOIRAO*, 10 (SPb., 1864).

Vernadsky, George. *The Mongols and Russia*. New Haven: Yale University Press, 1953.

Veselovskii, N., ed. and tr. *Kirgizskii razskaz o russkikh zavoevaniiakh v Turkestanskom krae. Tekst, perevod i prilozheniia*. Saint Petersburg: Parovaia Skoropechatnia P. O. Iablonskago, 1894.

Vladimirtsov, B. *Le régime social des Mongols*. Tr. Michel Carsow. Paris, 1948.

Voegelin, Eric. "The Mongol Orders of Submission to European Powers, 1245–1255." *Byzantion*, 15 (1940–1941), pp. 378–413.

Voigt, Vilmos. "Shamanism in Siberia (A Sketch and a Bibliography)." *Acta Ethnographica Academiae Scientiarum Hungaricae*, 26 (1977), pp. 385–395.

Vsia Astrakhan i ves' Astrakhanskii krai: Pamiatnaia knizhka na 1918 g. Astrakhan, 1918.

Waida, Manabu. "Notes on Sacred Kingship in Central Asia." *Numen*, 23 (1976), pp. 179–190.

Walsh, John R. "The Turkish Manuscripts in New College, Edinburgh." *Oriens*, 12 (1959), pp. 171–189.

Wansbrough, John. *The Sectarian Milieu: Content and Composition of Islamic Salvation History*. Oxford: Oxford University Press, 1978.

Wensinck, A. J. "Yādjūdj wa-Mādjūdj." *EI*[1], IV, p. 1142.

Winner, Thomas G. *The Oral Art and Literature of the Kazakhs of Russian Central Asia*. Durham: Duke University Press, 1958.

Wittek, Paul. "Yazijioghlu ʿAlī on the Christian Turks of the Dobruja." *BSOAS*, 14 (1952), pp. 639–668.

Wittfogel, Karl A., and Fêng Chia-shêng. *History of Chinese Society: Liao (907–1125)*. Philadelphia: American Philosophical Society, 1949; Transactions, N.S., vol. 36.

Woods, John E. "The Timurid Dynasty." *Papers on Inner Asia*, No. 14; Bloomington: Research Institute for Inner Asian Studies, 1990.

Yamada, Nobuo. "The Original Turkish Homeland." *Journal of Turkish Studies*, 9 (1985; = *Niġuča Bičig/Pi Wên Shu, An Anniversary Volume in Honor of Francis Woodman Cleaves*), pp. 243–246.

Yazdī, Sharaf ad-Dīn ʿAlī. *Shäräfuddin Äli Yäzdiy, Zäfärnamä*. Facs. ed. A. Urunbaev. Tashkent: Fan, 1972.

Yüce, Kemal. *Saltuk-nâme'de Tarihî, Dinî ve Efsanevî Unsurlar*. Ankara: Kültür ve Turizm Bakanlığı, 1987.

Yule, Henry. *Cathay and the Way Thither, Being a Collection of Medieval Notices on China*. 4 vols. New ed., revised . . . by Henri Cordier. London: Hakluyt Society, 2nd series, Nos. 38, 33, 37, 41, 1913–1916.

Zajączkowski, Ananiasz, ed. *Vocabulaire arabe-kiptchak de l'époque de l'État Mamelouk (1-ère partie, Le nom)*. Warsaw: Państwowe wydawnictwo naukowe, 1958.

Zaidi, Zawwar Hussain. "Conversion to Islam in South Asia: Problems in Analysis." *American Journal of Islamic Social Sciences*, 6/1 (1989), pp. 93–117.

Zaripov, Nur, ed. "Idheükäy menän Moradhïm." *Agidhel*, 1989, No. 1, pp. 19–74.

_____. " 'Idheükäy menän Moradhïm' ëposïna qarata." *Agidhel*, 1989, No. 1, pp. 16–18; No. 2, pp. 126–137.

Zelenin, D. K. "Religiozno-magicheskaia funktsiia fol'klornykh skazok." In *Sergeiu Fedorovichu Ol'denburgu k piatidesiatiletiiu nauchno-obshchestvennoi deiatel'nosti 1882–1932: Sbornik statei* (Leningrad: Izd-vo AN SSSR, 1934), pp. 215–240.

Zenkovsky, Serge A., ed. and tr. *Medieval Russia's Epics, Chronicles, and Tales*. 2nd ed. New York: E. P. Dutton, 1974.

Zenkovsky, Serge A., and Betty Jean Zenkovsky, trs. *The Nikonian Chronicle*; vol. 3 (1241–1381). Princeton: Kingston Press, 1986.

Żerańska-Kominek, Slawomira. "The Classification of Repertoire in Turkmen Traditional Music." *Asian Music*, 21/2 (Spring/Summer 1990), pp. 91–109.

Zhakhanova, N. Zh. "Pishcha v pogrebal'no-pominal'nom komplekse kazakhov (XIX–nachalo XX v.)." In *Kratkoe soderzhanie dokladov sredneaziatsko-kavkazskikh chtenii: Voprosy ètnosotsial'noi i kul'turnoi istorii Srednei Azii i Kavkaza* (Leningrad: Nauka, November 1983), pp. 21–22.

Zhamtsarano, Tsyben. "Kul't Chingisa v Ordose: Iz puteshestviia v iuzhnuiu Mongoliiu v 1910 g." *CAJ*, 6 (1961), pp. 194–234.

Zhanpeisov, E. N. *Ètnokul'turnaia leksika kazakhskogo iazyka (na materialakh proizvedenii M. Auèzova)*. Alma-Ata: Nauka, 1989.

Zhirmunskii, V. M. "The Epic Folk-Singers in Central Asia (Tradition and Artistic Improvisation)." In *VII Congrès international des sciences anthropologiques et ethnologiques/VII Mezhdunarodnyi kongress antropologicheskikh i ètnograficheskikh nauk*, Moscow, 1964, t. 6 (Moscow: Nauka, GRVL, 1969), pp. 234–241.

______. "Èpicheskie skazaniia o nogaiskikh bogatyriakh v svete istoricheskikh istochnikov." In his *Tiurkskii geroicheskii èpos*, pp. 389–516.

______. *Narodnyi geroicheskii èpos*. Moscow/Leningrad, 1962.

______. "Nekotorye itogi izucheniia geroicheskogo èposa narodov Srednei Azii." In *Voprosy izucheniia èposa narodov SSSR* (Moscow: Izd-vo AN SSSR, 1958), pp. 24–65.

______. "Oguzskii geroicheskii èpos i 'Kniga Korkuta.' " In Zhirmunskii and Kononov, eds., *Kniga moego Deda Korkuta*, pp. 131–258.

______. "On the Comparative Study of the Heroic Epic of the Peoples of Central Asia." In *Trudy dvadtsat' piatogo Mezhdunarodnogo kongressa vostokovedov* (Moscow, 9–16 August 1960), t. 3 (Moscow: Izd-vo Vostochnoi Literatury, 1963), pp. 244–252.

______. "P. M. Melioranskii i izuchenie èpose 'Edigei.' " In *Tiurkologicheskii sbornik 1972* (Moscow, 1973), pp. 141–185.

______. "Skazanie ob Idige." In his *Tiurkskii geroicheskii èpos*, pp. 351–386.

______. *Tiurkskii geroicheskii èpos*. Leningrad: Nauka, 1974.

Zhirmunskii, V. M., and A. N. Kononov, eds. *Kniga moego Deda Korkuta: Oguzskii geroicheskii èpos*. Moscow/Leningrad: Izd-vo AN SSSR, 1962.

Zhirmunskii, V. M., and Kh. T. Zarifov. *Uzbekskii narodnyi geroicheskii èpos*. Moscow: Ogiz, 1947.

Zhukovskaia, N. L. "Tsentral'naia Aziia." In *Ètnografiia pitaniia narodov stran zarubezhnoi Azii*, ed. S. A. Arutiunov (Moscow: Nauka, GRVL, 1981), pp. 120–139.

Zichy, Étienne. "Le voyage de Sallâm, l'interprète, à la muraille de Gog et de Magog." *KCsA*, 1 (1921–1925), pp. 190–204.

Zirke, Heidi, ed. and tr. *Ein hagiographisches Zeugnis zur persischen Geschichte aus der Mitte des 14. Jahrhunderts: Das achte Kapitel des Ṣafwat aṣ-ṣafā in kritischer Bearbeitung*. Berlin: Klaus Schwarz Verlag, 1987; Islamkundliche Untersuchungen, Bd. 120.

[Untitled list of shaykhs and tribal affiliations in uncatalogued MS containing work of Isḥāq Khoja b. Ismāʿīl Ata: MS Tashkent, IVAN Uz, Inv. No. 12870, f. 88b.]

Index

Abaqa (Ilkhanid), 191
ʿAbbās, 385, 393
ʿAbbāsid, 279
ʿAbd al-Ghaffār Q̈ïrïmī, xiv, 107, 145, 148, 151 nn. 191–92, 153 n. 200, 154, 167 n. 1, 180, 194 n. 84, 236, 249, 291, 322, 330, 352–66, 370, 379, 381–83, 384 n. 128, 392, 414, 462, 484 n. 171, 531, 546, 550, 553, 557, 560–61
ʿAbd al-Karīm Khan (Jöchid), 488 n. 180
ʿAbd ar-Raḥmān Khoja, 385
ʿAbdullāh (Jöchid), 334
ʿAbdullāh b. Riżvān, 207
ʿAbdullāh Khān (Shïbanid), 193 n. 79, 502 n. 16
ʿAbdullāh-nāmah, 273 n. 79
Abdul'-Murza, 402
Abīvard, 395
Abū Bakr (Caliph), 287, 358–59, 374, 380–84, 389–90, 392–94, 399, 402–7, 412, 420, 437, 438, 443, 458–59, 478, 479 n. 159, 483, 487
Abū Bakr b. Mīrānshāh, 412
Abū Bakr Qalandar, 123
Abū'l-Fidā, 85 n. 29
Abū Ḥanīfah, 26
Abū Ḥayyān, 551, 559
Abū'l-Ghāzī, 85, 103, 143–44, 146, 147 nn. 181–82, 148, 193–94, 198–99, 275, 280 n. 95, 323, 366–69, 371, 390–91, 396, 445, 483 n. 169, 484–86, 501–2
Abū'l-Khayr Khan (Uzbek), 345–48, 390, 422 n. 27
Abū Muslim, 279
Abū Saʿīd (Ilkhanid), 92, 123, 129, 191, 196 n. 92
Abūlak, 144 n. 170
Abuscan, 98
Āb.šqah, 98 n. 65
Abusta, 98
ač-, "to open," 23
Ādam (prophet), 460
adhān, 260
Adhkash, 80
ʿĀdites, 25
Africa, sub-Saharan, 18, 30
Agish-batïr, 468
Agnani, Lorenzo, 198 n. 99
al-Aharī, Abū Bakr al-Quṭbī, 115–16
ahl al-kahf, 288
Aḥmad, Sayyid, 379
Aḥmad, Shaykh, 358, 359
Aḥrār, Khoja, 249–50, 253, 529 n. 38
Aitmatov, Chingiz, 220 n. 140
Akā Bekī/ Öge Beki, 102 n. 75
Ākām al-marjān of Isḥāq b. Ḥusayn, 498–99
Akhbār ad-duwal wa āthār al-awwal (al-Qaramānī), 121 n. 127
akhī, 136
Akhī Bichaqchī, 131
akïn, 418
ʿĀlam-Murtażā Sayyid, 385
Alan Qoʾa, 326 n. 7, 390 n. 134, 527 n. 35
Alans, 80
al-Aʿlāq al-khaṭīrah fī dhikr umarāʾ ash-shām wa'l-jazīrah, 259
Alash, 445
Ālāṭāy, Alatay, 151, 154, 155 n. 203
albastï, 429–30, 432–33, 436 n. 43 (*albaslï*)
Alchagyr, 401
Al'chesmail, 439
Aleuko Batyr, 455, 456
Alexander, 288
Alexander romance, 274 n. 79
Alghūy, 110 n. 97
ʿAlī (Caliph), 358, 369 n. 106, 374 n. 118, 393, 454, 477 n. 156
ʿAlī-Bek b. ʿĪsā b. Tülük Temür, 132 n. 153
ʿAlī Shaykh Darvīsh, 474

ʿAlī Sulṭān, 395
ʿAlids, ʿAlid descent, 228, 487
ʿĀlim-qul, 460
Almalïq, 96 n. 58
Almambet, 60–66
Almish ibn Shilkī Yilṭawār, 75 n. 10
Almush, 74 n. 10
Alp' Ilit'uēr, 292–94
Alpamïsh, Alpamysh, 454, 455 n. 90
Altai-kizhi, 44
Altay, 15, 240
Altay (people), 30, 42, 44, 239, 241, 553
Altun Beshik, 486 n. 175
Alṭun Khān, 281
Aly Beg Sharapow, 416 n. 15
Amat, son of ʿĪsā, 441 n. 60
Ämät Khämät, 473–75
Amīnak, 144 n. 170
amīr, 84, 108, 139, 224, 260, 334, 337, 339–40
Amu Darya, 486
An Lu-shan rebellion, 178 n. 31
Anal, 505
anā 'l-ḥaqq, 505
Anatolia, 131, 142, 254, 278, 337
angels (*berishtä*), 63
"animal-style" art, 45
"animism," 27
Ankara, 412
Anna Ivanovna, Tsarina, 367
Antioch, 384
Aq Buqa Qïyat, 151 n. 194
Aq Idel, 470, 475
Aq Manghït, 384 n. 130
Aq-Noghay, 351
Aq Orda, 335
Aq-Satí, 439
Aq Ṣūfī Qonghrat, 102
aq-süyek, 433
Aq-Tagh, 172
Aqbuzat, 468
Aqsāq Timir Khan, Aqsaq Timer Khan, 474, 476
Är Amät, 441 n. 60
Arab, 15, 24, 73, 108, 131, 177–78, 254, 278, 315
Arabia, 404
ʿArabshāhid dynasty, 144, 395
Aral Sea, 153 n. 198
Ardabīl, 142
Arghun, 173, 191–92, 203, 259
arghuvānī, 108
Arïstan Bap, 460. *See also* Arslan Baba
ark of the covenant, 303 n. 137
Armenian Christianity, 292
Armenians, 80
Arnold, T. W., vi, 18
Arrān, 106
Arslan Baba, 460. *See also* Arïstan Bap
arvāḥ, *arbak* (ancestral spirits), 63–64
aṣḥāb al-jaḥīm, 247 n. 30
aṣḥāb al-kahf, 288
Ashtarkhanid, 185
al-Aṣī, ʿAlāʾ ad-Dīn, faqīh, 131
aslama, "submitted," 23
Astāy, 151, 153–54, 155 n. 203
Astrakhan, 6, 251–52, 269–70, 347, 350–51, 397, 412, 416, 417 n. 20, 419, 438, 441 n. 60, 448–53, 457 n. 96, 464, 473 nn. 145–46, 485 n. 173, 488, 554
ata, 323, 378
Āṭā, Aṭā, 132–33, 421 n. 27
atalïq, 151
al-Āthār al-bāqīyah (al-Bīrūnī), 498
ʿAṭṭār, Farīd ad-Dīn, 123, 434 n. 39
Attila, 186 n. 55, 496
Avānish Khān, 395–96
Avesta, 495
awliyā, 60
Ay Aṭam, 280
Ayākūzī, Qārī Qurbān-ʿAlī b. Khālid Ḥājjī, 178 n. 32
Ayle Bashkirs, 470 n. 138
al-ʿAynī, 84 n. 28, 86, 116 n. 110, 119, 120, 123–24, 128–29
ayran, 552
azan, 63. *See also adhān*
Azāq, Āzāq, 131–32, 201, 341. *See also* Azov
Āżāw, 201
Azerbaijan, 92
al-Azhar, 58
Azhu-Kozha, 431–32
Azirat, 471
ʿazīz, 157, 323, 371, 463, 474, 531
ʿAzīz Shaykh (Jöchid khan), 333–35
Azov, 131, 341, 402, 404. *See also* Āzāq, Āżāw
Azrāʾīl, 431, 432 n. 34, 511

baba, 323

Baba Faraj, 330 n. 24
Baba Murād, 460
Baba Oghul, 151 n. 194
Baba Omar, 455. *See also* Baba ʿUmar
Bābā Saltūq, 251
Baba Tükles, 5–6, 11, 13, 15–16, 75, 105–6, 122, 129, 134, 144, 145 n. 174 and 176, 148, 155, 157–60, 164–66, 173, 176, 178 n. 29, 179–80, 186, 193–94, 199, 202–7, 226, 230–39, 241–48, 253–56, 258, 262, 265, 267–70, 272–73, 275, 277, 282, 285–87, 289–92, 298, 307–9, 311, 317–19, 321–25, 327–28, 330–31, 335–37, 340, 342–43, 345, 348, 352, 355–56, 358–60, 362–66, 370–72, 375–85, 389–94, 396–97, 399–400, 403–7, 409, 411–12, 414, 417, 420–23, 428, 430–39, 441 n. 60, 442–43, 446–63, 466–69, 472–73, 476–79, 481–89, 491–95, 497, 500, 502, 503 n. 17, 504, 505 n. 22, 506–7, 510–12, 514–16, 518–21, 528, 530–32, 542, 554, 558–59
  Baba Tokty Chachty Aziz, 428, 430, 431 n. 34
  Baba Tokty Shash Tazy, 455–56
  Bābā Tükläs Shaykh Najīb ad-Dīn, 358
  Baba Tükles Chashlï ʿAzīz, 435
  Bābā Tükles Shāshlï ʿAzīz, 416, 420, 472
  Baba Tukli-aziz, 432–33
  Baba Tukli Shashli Azis, 456 n. 94
  Bābā Tüklük ʿAzīz, 457, 459
  Baba Tukty, 457
  Baba Tukty Shashty Aziz, 455
  Babai, Tukty, and Shash-Tazy, 431
  Babai Tukty Chach, 454
  Baba-tu-Klius, 469
  Babatu Kliusov, 473 n. 145
  Babatu-Kulias, 469 (Iskur-Babatu-Kuliasov, 471 n. 141)
  Bābāy Tūktī Sāchtï ʿAzīz, 460
  Babay Tükti Shashtï Aziz, 417 n. 18, 440 n. 58, 454, 460
  Chächlä-tökle Khuja Äkhmät, 441 n. 60
  Chachlï-Aziz, Chachly-Aziz, 438, 441, 450 n. 78
  Chāchlï Darvīsh, 474–75, 477
  Chachty ʿAzīz, 485
  Chashlï ʿAzīz, 485
  Chashlï Tüklü Qoj Amät, 441
  Chasli-Dervish, 474
  Khochakhmat Babatukli, 440
  Qoji Aḥmad Baba Tükli Shashli ʿAzīz Barkhāyah, 440
  Sachïl ʿAzīz, Sāchlï ʿAzīz, Sāchlï Parī, 463–64
  Säsle Ata, 478
  Shashlï ʿAzīz, 485
  Sultan Babatkul', 448
  Töklö Ata, 478
  Tökläth, 468, 479, 480–83
  Tükläs-baba, 468
  Tukli-baba, 449
  Tüklü ʿAzīz, 463–64, 466
  Tükti Babay Äziz Shash, 461
  Tūlāsh Bābā, 458
Baba ʿUmar, 428, 430, 481. *See also* Baba Omar
Babuch, 329 n. 22
Badr Ata, 101, 372, 376
Bāghābād, 395
Baghdād, 84, 249 n. 32, 259
Bahāʾ ad-Dīn ʿAlī b. Muḥammad b. as-Sāʿātī, 362 n. 93
Bahāʾ ad-Dīn Naqshband, 227. *See also* Naqshband, Bahāʾ ad-Dīn
Baḥr al-asrār, 143, 191, 193, 222 n. 141, 226–28
Baikal, 503
Bājïr Tūq Būghā, 151–54, 155 n. 203, 200, 545
Bākharzī, Sayf ad-Dīn, 83, 86, 101, 357–58
bakhshï, bakhshī, 82 n. 22, 83, 96, 112–13, 209, 225 n. 150, 260
Bakhtī Bī Khātūn, 102 n. 75
al-Bakrī, 79, 171 n. 11, 172, 301 n. 132
Bakrid lineage, 370, 400, 406
baksï, 418, 460
bāl, bal, 206–8, 421, 548–49, 553–54, 558–60
bāl avuzï, 548, 558–60
Bala-baksï, 461
Bäläkäy, 482
Baldy, river, 449, 452–53
Balkh, 226–27, 374–75, 477 n. 156
Banākatī, 89 n. 45, 106, 108 n. 91, 116, 149, 191
Bar Hebraeus, 268 n. 74, 309 n. 141
Baraba, Baraba Tatars, 41 n. 24, 200 n. 104, 417 n. 16

barakah, 89
Baraq (Chaghatayid), 189 n. 61
Barbaro, Iosaphath, 341–42, 412
al-Barchïnlïqī, Rażī ad-Dīn Yaḥyā b. Fakhr ad-Dīn al-Qaṣṣārī, 130 n. 149
Barchuq Art Tegin, 285
Barlas, 326
Bartol'd, V. V., 147, 181–82, 184, 189–90, 192, 194–95, 227
Bascardia, Baschardia, 140
Bashkir(s), 6, 140, 252, 270, 282, 327–28, 351, 363–64, 380, 402–4, 406, 411, 418, 422 n. 27, 435, 450, 467–79, 481–83, 498, 516
Bashkiria, 6, 147 n. 181, 471 n. 142, 473, 475
"Basjirt," 80
Batu, 3, 81, 82 n. 21, 148–49, 189–90, 199, 223 n. 144, 261–62, 265, 345, 376, 548
Baugleata, 453 n. 82
bavurchï, 224 n. 149
Bāy-Būqā, 108
Bay Terek, 44, 45 n. 31, 237
Bay-Timür, 120
Bayal-khan, 469
Bayalïn, Bayalun, Bayālūn, 119–21, 123, 150–52
Bāyān, 108
Bāyazīd I, Ottoman Sulṭān, 412
Baybars al-Manṣūrī, Rukn ad-Dīn, 84, 86, 87 n. 39, 88, 89 n. 44, 112 n. 99, 116 n. 110, 118 n. 120, 119 n. 122, 259
al-Baykandī, ʿAlī b. Muhammad b. Dihqān [ʿAlī an-Nasafī], 124 n. 134
Bāynāl, 108
Bayżāvī, 354 n. 80
Bazarov, Jumabay jïraw, 419 n. 24
bek, 148, 151, 154, 275, 339, 363, 366, 392. *See also bīy*
Bek Toro, 61 n. 44
Bektashi, 251–52
Belaia river, 470, 475. *See also* Aq Idel
Beliaevka, 469
Berdi Bek, 135 n. 158, 193, 332–33
Berke, 3, 61, 83–86, 88–90, 101, 111–12, 122, 125, 149, 158, 175 n. 23, 199, 206, 248 n. 30, 315, 358, 421 n. 26, 543, 549, 559
Berke [or "Bürge"] Sulṭān b. Yādgār, 144 n. 170, 346
Besh-Baligh, Besh-Balïq, 278 n. 88, 512
Beshdagh, 130–31
Beshtovo-Kumsk, 448 n. 74
Bethlehem, 278
Bianco, Andrea, 197 n. 93
bidʿah, 52
Birsk, 470 n. 138
Bīrūs, 108 n. 91
al-Bīrūnī, 498–99
al-Birzālī, 112–13, 114 n. 104, 116 n. 110, 121, 125–26, 128, 149
bīy, 104 n. 79, 345, 397, 472–73, 475–77. See also *bek*
Black Sea, 72, 92, 195–96, 251, 371
blacksmith, 275
body hair. See *tük*
Bögü Qaghan, Bügü Khan (Uyghur), 169, 172 n. 14, 285, 314, 511–12. *See also* Būqū Khan
bökävül, 224 n. 149
Bolsheviks, 402
Böö Khan, 504
Boratav, Pertev, 236
Boris Godunov, 383
Bor Kaya, 440 n. 58, 441
Borysthenes, 495
Börte Chino, 443, 482, 527 n. 35. *See also* Būrtah Chīnah
Buchier, Guillaume, 209, 549
Buchugha Khan, 144 n. 170
Būdānjār Bek, 151 n. 194
Buddhism, Buddhists, 8, 27–28, 30, 33, 41, 82, 83 n. 22, 96, 152, 168–69, 172–73, 178, 217, 251, 282 n. 101, 286, 330 n. 25, 363, 443–44, 451, 511–14
Bügü Khan, Bögü Qaghan (Uyghur), 169, 172 n. 14, 285, 314, 511–12. *See also* Būqū Khan
Bukhārā, 6, 15, 185, 322, 347 n. 69, 393, 421, 447–49, 463, 488
Bukharan khanate, 185
al-Bukhārī, Ḥusām ad-Dīn, *imām*, 131–32
Būlād Timūr, 332–35
būlaq-ḥawż, 464
Bulghār, 76–78, 97, 130 n. 149, 334–35, 362, 369 n. 107
Bulghar(s), 4, 20, 69, 72–75, 78–79, 81–82, 169, 175, 520 n. 30
Bulghat al-mushtāq fī lughat at-turk wa'l-qifjāq, 559
Bumïn, 526
Būqū Khan, 172, 278 n. 88, 282 n. 101,

283–85, 511–12, 514. *See also* Bügü/Bögü Khan
Buqu Tegin, 284
Burangulov, M., 418, 482 n. 166
Buransï, 468
Burhān ad-Dīn, Shaykh, 118, 124, 129
Burkhan Khaldun, Burqan Qaldun, 184, 525
Burnāq, 475–76
Būrtah Chīnah, 275. *See also* Börte Chino
buydah, 154 n. 201
Büyük Khojalar, 436 n. 43
būzah, 132
Buzurjmihr, 279, 353 n. 77
Byzantine, 91, 315

Cairo, 125
Cambridge document, 171 n. 10, 303, 305
Caspian Sea, 72, 196–97, 201, 361, 404, 464
Cassiodorus, 496 n. 7
Cathogonti, 98–99
Caucasus, Caucasian, 72–73, 83–84, 92, 130–31, 269, 292, 325, 351
Cem Sulṭān, 252
Central Asia, 7–10, 18–20, 26, 68, 82, 130, 143, 148, 150, 178 n. 32, 182, 185, 226, 228–29, 280, 309, 322, 337, 340, 343, 347, 352, 363, 376, 379, 392, 411 n. 3, 434 n. 39, 453 n. 82, 454, 459–61, 485, 502, 510–11, 520 n. 30, 531
Central Asian Archives, 148
Chāch, 485
Chächlä-tökle Khuja Äkhmät, 441 n. 60. *See also* Baba Tükles
Chachlï-Aziz, Chachly-Aziz, 438, 441, 450 n. 78. *See also* Baba Tükles
Chāchlï Darvīsh, 474–75, 477. *See also* Baba Tükles
Chachty ʿAzīz, 485. *See also* Baba Tükles
Chaghatay Turkic (language), 15, 327, 367, 369
Chaghatayids, 92, 101, 134 n. 156, 151 n. 192, 174, 189 n. 61, 337, 394
Chaghatayid *ulus*, 92, 184, 349 n. 72, 357, 526
Chalpāq Khān, 478
Chashlï ʿAzīz, 485. *See also* Baba Tükles
Chashlï Tüklü Qoj Amät, 441. *See also* Baba Tükles
Chasli-Dervish, 474. *See also* Baba Tükles
Chegre, 83 n. 22, 413
Cherkes, 131, 151, 368
Chimkent, 454
Chīn, 463
China, 111, 163, 172, 178, 223, 280
Chinese, 36, 55, 65, 169, 186, 187, 204, 223, 258, 276, 300, 364 n. 98
Chïngghïz Khan, 473, 475
Chingis Khan, 67, 81, 108, 143 n. 169, 148, 183, 185–88, 191, 197 n. 93, 211, 214–15, 217–18, 222, 235, 257, 260, 264, 275, 279 n. 91, 281–82, 284–85, 323, 353, 368, 372, 390 n. 134, 393, 421 n. 26, 440, 443–44, 448, 450 n. 78, 479, 482 n. 169, 525, 527 n. 35
Chingisid(s), Chingisid principle, 39, 60, 63, 70, 83, 148, 152, 183, 189, 194 n. 82, 200–203, 205, 224, 292, 318, 334–35, 337–40, 344–45, 348, 350–51, 353, 366, 382–83, 392, 397, 399, 401, 413, 421–23, 428, 433, 439–40, 442–43, 445, 447, 463, 466–67, 476, 478, 510–11, 518, 524–27
Choctaws, 21 n. 11
Chodzko, A. B., 416, 448–49, 452–53
chorghatï, 541, 558
Christian, Christianity, 25–28, 30, 41, 57, 67 n. 1, 74, 82, 96–97, 99, 131, 135, 140–41, 168–71, 173, 175–76, 198, 211, 246, 253, 258, 261–62, 292–94, 296–99, 308–11, 313, 316, 401–3, 439, 449, 451
Chūbān, 123
Chülkä Ata, "Chülkä"/"Chāchīlkā" Ata, 474, 476
Chupanids, 526
Clavijo, 209 n. 115
Codex Cumanicus, 97, 325
Coktoganus, 98–100
Comans, 188 n. 60, 263. *See also* Qumans
Constantine Porphyrogenitus, 557
Constantinople, 79, 98, 132, 251, 384
čop'ay, 297 n. 128
Cosogan, 98
Cossacks, 194, 351
Cotogan, 98
Creeks, 21 n. 11
Crimea, Crimean Khanate, 9, 15, 41 n. 24, 88, 93, 97, 123–24, 130–31, 132

n. 153, 140, 145 n. 173, 201, 206–7, 250 n. 35, 252–54, 329 n. 21, 334, 341, 347–48, 350, 352, 354 n. 80, 356, 365, 368–69, 380, 385, 389, 392, 397, 400–401, 412, 430, 483, 553, 559
Curamas, 98

Daftar-i Chingīz-nāmah, 194 n. 83, 383, 385 n. 131, 392, 398, 404, 441 n. 60, 470 n. 138, 478
dāgh, 459
dāʿī, 22, 137
Dajjāl, 457 n. 96
dakhala ("to enter"), 23
Damascus, 125, 341 n. 47
Daniel, 246
Danube, 251
Dār al-Ḥarb, 24
Dār al-Islām, 24, 67, 136, 164, 492
Darkhat, 504 n. 19
Darvīsh Adham, 374
"Dasht-i Berke," 89
Dasht-i Qïpchaq, 58, 82, 85 n. 29, 89, 101–2, 104, 109, 114 n. 104, 116, 117 n. 113, 125, 153 n. 198, 202, 227–29, 250 n. 36, 338, 341 n. 47, 354 n. 80, 372, 376–77, 379, 412 n. 5, 485–87, 489
daʿwah, the "summons" to adopt Islam, 22–23, 79
"Dāy Ming," *pādshāh* of China, 117 n. 113
Day of Judgment, 245, 248 n. 30, 442
De La Harpe, Jean-François, 174 n. 21
De modo sarracenos extirpandi (William Adam), 140
De Pace Fidei, Nicholas of Cusa, 174 n. 20
dede, 323
Dede Qorqut, 455 n. 90, 503 n. 17
Dema river, 471
Depe-Göz, 503 n. 17
adh-Dhahabī, 84 n. 25, 114 n. 104
dharma, 172
dhikr, 157, 239, 311, 466, 531
Dhū'l-Qarnayn, 275 n. 82, 288
Dīn Muḥammad Khan, 395–96
Dirūn, 395
Diuseev, Iskhaq, 438
Divaev, A. A., 238, 417, 432, 454, 483 n. 169
dīvānah, 455, 462, 531
Dobrudja, 251–53
Dolossa, 98 n. 64
Dominican, 135, 142, 246
Don, 341
dostïghan, 541, 550–51, 553, 558–60
dual kingship, 300 n. 130
Dūghlāt, Mīrzā Muḥammad Ḥaydar, 174
Dungans, 61, 177–78, 364 n. 98
ad-Durar al-kāminah (Ibn Ḥajar al-ʿAsqalānī), 128
Dūst (Muḥammad) Khān, Dūst Sulṭān, 144, 488 n. 180
Duva (Chaghatayid), 141 n. 166
Dzhambul *oblast*, 460
Dzhan-Aliev, Abubekr, 438
Dzhan-Arslan, 439

East Turkistan, 8–9, 20, 65, 178 n. 32, 489
ečige, 323
Edigü (Manghït *amīr*), 13, 83 n. 22, 95, 105, 148, 194, 202, 321–22, 336–50, 352, 356, 359, 363, 365–66, 371, 377–84, 389–98, 400–405, 407, 411–14, 420–21, 435, 438, 456, 458, 462, 485, 486 n. 173, 487, 488, 526. *See also* Idige
Egypt, 72, 339, 361, 384
Ejen Qoruġ-a, 185
Eliade, Mircea, 33 n. 18, 233–35, 269
Elijah, Nestorian metropolitan, 176
elteber, 75 n. 10
emegender, 47
Er Töshtük, 61 n. 44, 236–42, 275, 489
Ergene Qūn, 235, 273–75, 280 n. 95, 288, 500
Esen Bugha (Chaghatayid), 126 n. 138
Estokis, lord of Baschardia, 98 n. 64
Eucharist, 297, 308–9, 311
Europe, European, 28–29, 140, 169, 204
Europe, pre-Christian, 30
Evenki, 45
Evliya Çelebi, 251–53, 343, 421 n. 26, 444, 473 n. 145

facarii, 141
Fakhruddinov, Rizauddin, 146
Falev, P. A., 416 n. 13, 436 n. 43
falsarios/falcharios, 140 n. 164
faqīh, 76–77, 79, 85, 224
faqīr, 131, 140–42, 340
farajah, farajīyah, 95 n. 57, 229
Farghānah, 65, 486 n. 175, 504

Faṣīḥ Khwāfī, 123 n. 133
fataḥa ("to open"), 22
fātiḥah, 157, 318, 543
Fedor, *Voyevoda*, 262
Finnegan, Tim, 406 n. 170
Finno-Ugric, 8, 73, 325, 327 n. 13
Firdaws al-iqbāl, 371
fiṭrah, 62 n. 45
Fletcher, Giles, 41 n. 24
four "martyred imams," 489
Fra Mauro, 196 n. 93
Franciscan, 82 n. 21, 88, 96 n. 58, 97–100, 135, 140, 142, 183, 198, 199 n. 101, 211, 246
Fuṣūṣ al-ḥikam (Ibn ʿArabī), 127
futuwwah, 131, 136, 228

Gaddiano, Laurenziano, 196 n. 93
Ganges, 482 n. 169
Gardīzī, 473, 474 n. 147, 494, 498
Gassur, 98 n. 64
Gazaria, 141 n. 166
Genoese, 91, 141, 252
George of Hungary/George von Mühlenbach, 254 n. 48
Georgia, 129
Georgio, 98
Germans, 169
al-Gharnāṭī, Abū Ḥāmid, 75–77, 79, 477 n. 156
al-Ghazālī, 202 n. 107, 245
Ghāzān Khan (Ilkhanid), 101, 115, 123, 173, 190–92, 222 n. 141, 357
ghāzī, 207 n. 113
Ghuzz, 499
Gīlān, 142
Girey Khan b. Qaplān Girey, 353
glasnost', 170
Gog and Magog, 275 n. 82, 287–88
"Golden Tombs' Mare-Milking" rite, 217
Gorno-Altaisk, 461 n. 105
Gospel, 441
Goths, 496
"grandmothers," 43, 47, 200
Great Khan, 195, 214, 216–17, 223
"Great *Qoruq*," 183–84
Greeks, 131, 169
Grosswasser, Nelly, 406 n. 170
Grousset, René, 91 n. 47
Gulistān, 334
Gulshan al-mulūk, 185
Gulzār (Pādshāh Khoja), 377 n. 122
güregän, 361
Gurgān, 361
Gūrgānī/Kūrkānī, Shaykh Ḥasan, 359, 361

Habrau, 479–80
Habrau-yïrau, 469
Ḥāfiẓ-i Abrū, 107, 108 n. 92, 109–10, 151 n. 194
ḥajj, 201, 341 n. 47
Ḥājjī Ākhī, 372
Ḥājjī Bektash, 251
Ḥājjī Khalīfah, 197
Ḥājjī Niyāz, 488 n. 180
Ḥājjī Tarkhān, 130, 201, 251, 488 n. 180. *See also* Astrakhan, Hashtūrkhān
Ḥakīm Ata, 101, 147 n. 180, 323, 372, 460
ḥāl, 378
Halevi, Judah, 301 n. 132, 302–3
al-Ḥallāj, 505, 506
Hamadānī, Sayyid ʿAlī, 127 n. 142
ḥammām, 250, 356
Ḥammūyī, Ṣadr ad-Dīn Ibrāhīm, 173, 357
Ḥanafī, 132, 133 n. 155, 206, 260, 549
ḥaram, 199
Hārūn ar-Rashīd, 279 n. 92
Ḥasdai b. Shaprut, 171 n. 10, 304
Hashdak, 252
Hāshim Khoja, Sayyid, 394–95
Hashtūrkhān, 464
Ḥaydar Rāzī, 107, 109 n. 93
Hayton, 274
Ḥażrat Khamat, 269–70
hearth, 36, 40–43, 46–47, 62, 200, 237, 243–44, 271, 523–25
Hell, 245
Henry the German, 98 n. 64
Herodotus, 41–42, 61 n. 44, 200, 495
hijrah, 287
ḥimā, 199 n. 103
Hindustan, 252, 441. *See also* India
Ḥirā, 287
Hö'elün, 256–57
holy war, 136, 245
honey, 206–7, 450, 452, 453 n. 82, 471–72, 541–42, 547–51, 553–55, 558–60
Hsiung-nu, 521
Ḥudūd al-ʿĀlam, 75 n.10
Hülegü, 84, 248 n. 30, 264
Hun(s), 181, 496–97, 500, 504 n. 20

"Huns" (North Caucasus), 170, 175, 291–94, 297–99, 306, 311, 314, 316–17
Hungarian, 254
Hungary, 195
Ḥusayn b. ʿAlī, 394
Ḥusayn Bek, 471 n. 142
Ḥusayn Ṣūfī Qonghrat, 102 n. 75

al-ʿIbar fī khabar man ghabar (adh-Dhahabi), 114 n. 104
Ïbir-Sïbïr, 345, 413. *See also* Siberia
Ibn ʿAbd al-Ḥamīd, Sayyid, 133–34, 224
Ibn ʿAbd aẓ-Ẓāhir, 85 n. 30, 86
Ibn ʿArabī, 127
Ibn ʿArabshāh, 194, 340, 344, 411–12
Ibn Baṭṭūṭah, 102 n. 75, 103, 106, 116, 124, 126, 129–34, 206, 217–18, 222 n. 141, 223–25, 229, 251, 264, 329 n. 21, 374 n. 116, 421 n. 27, 549
Ibn ad-Dawādārī, 112, 124, 274, 279–80, 282, 286, 300, 330, 414, 501
Ibn Duqmāq, 117–20, 123–24, 129, 149
Ibn Faḍlān, 73–75, 186 n. 55, 193 n. 78, 214
Ibn al-Furāt, 87
Ibn al-Fuwaṭī, 362
Ibn Ḥajar al-ʿAsqalānī, 128
Ibn Kathīr, 114 n. 104
Ibn Khaldūn, 86, 119–20, 123, 149
Ibn Khurdādhbih, 80
Ibn an-Nafīs, vi, 136 n. 159, 281 n. 96
Ibn Rustah, 73, 74 n. 10, 75, 80 n. 17
Ibn Shaddād, ʿIzz ad-Dīn Muḥammad b. ʿAlī b. Shaddād al-Ḥalabī, 259
Ibn Shuhbah al-Asadī, 118 n. 119
Ibn Taghrībirdī, 121–22
Ibn al-Wardī, 114 n. 104
Ibrāhīm (prophet), 24, 243–44, 247–48, 255, 258, 287, 290, 318, 460
Ibrāhīm b. Adham, 374, 375, 377, 378, 379
Ibrāhīm Zāhid, Shaykh, 362 n. 92
Ichen, 148
Ichki, 422 n. 27
ʿĪd al-fiṭr, 206
Idheükäy, 479–82. *See also* Idige
Idige (epic hero), 13, 411–12, 414–16, 418–23, 428–30, 432–42, 447, 454, 456–58, 462–63, 465–67, 478–79, 483 n. 169, 486, 492–93, 503–4, 511, 516, 518–19, 531, 553–54, 558. *See also* Edigü
Idige epic, Idige tale, 200–201, 329, 380, 383 n. 124, 389, 398, 406, 414–19, 435, 441, 448, 450 n. 78, 457, 462, 467, 484 n. 171, 485 n. 173, 486, 503 n. 17, 504, 518, 531
Īdīl (Volga), 371
"Idil-Jayïq," 384–85, 389
idiqut, 285 n. 105
"idols," 40–41, 212, 214
Idrīs (prophet), 460
al-Idrīsī, 80
Idukay, 468. *See also* Idige
Idukay and Muradym, 468
iḥāṭah, 474
Īkīrās, 326 n. 7
Ilbars Khan, 488 n. 180
Il-Basar, Īl-baṣār, 108 n. 91, 115 n. 108, 116, 119, 149, 151
Īlbāṣmīsh, 115
Il-murza, 401–2
Ilkhanid, Ilkhanids, 82, 84, 92, 94, 101, 110, 123, 140–41, 143, 150, 162, 173, 181, 184, 190, 191, 196 n. 92, 216, 259, 337, 357, 526
Ilyās, 131, 440–41
ʿImād ad-Dīn [b.] al-Maskīrī, 118–19
ʿimāmah, 95 n. 57
īmān, 23
India, Indian, 36, 55, 234, 337, 376, 444, 482 n. 169. *See also* Hindustan
Indiana University, 148
Inner Mongolia, 185
Institute of Oriental Studies, Tashkent, 146
Iohanca (Franciscan friar), 140–41
Iohannes, 98, 99 n. 69
ʿIqd al-jumān fī tārīkh ahl az-zamān (al-ʿAynī), 120
Iran, Iranian, 28–29, 82, 117 n. 113, 142, 143, 162–63, 280, 325, 337
ʿIrāq, 130
Iroquois, 21 n. 11
irshād, 363
Irtysh, 153 n. 198, 494, 498
ʿĪsā (prophet), 460
ʿĪsā Güregän, *amīr*, 109, 133
Ischboldin, Boris Sergeevich, 402–3, 405–6
Ischboldin (family), 398, 401–3
Ischboldin, "Yasutdin Bahautdin," 403 n. 163
Ischbulat, 402
Isenbetov, N., 418, 482 n. 166

Iṣfahān, 127
īshān, 463
Isḥāq b. Ḥusayn, author of *Ākām al-marjān*, 498
Isḥāq, Khoja, Naqshbandī shaykh, 251
Ishboldu, 401
ʿIshqī, 138 n. 161
Ishtemi, 258, 526
Iskur-Babatu-Kuliasov, 471 n. 141
Islak, 471
islām, 23
Islām Bābā, 375, 380
Islām-Qïyā (Bīy), 384, 393, 436, 459 n. 101
Ismāʿīl, 258
Ismāʿīl, Manghït, 401
Israyēl (Bishop), 292–94, 298 n. 129, 299, 300 n. 130, 311, 316
Istak, 252
Iṣṭakhrī, 73, 300 n. 130
Istanbul, 201, 369 n. 106
It Küchük, 133
Itil, 343. *See also* Idil, Volga
Iudin, V. P., xii–xiv, 147
Iurtovskie Tatary, 438, 453
Iusupov (family), 398–405
Iusupov, Dmitrii Seiushevich, 402
Iusupov, Feliks, 398 n. 149
Iusupov, Grigorii Dmitrievich, 404
Ivan IV ("the Terrible"), 401
Ivantzuk, 451
Izhukay, 469. *See also* Idige
ʿIzz ad-Dīn, *wāʿiẓ*, 131

Jāddat al-ʿāshiqīn, 201, 203, 347
Jagello, 336 n. 39
Jaghātū, 191 n. 70
Jahāngīr b. Temür, 102 n. 75
Jahān-numā, 197
Jalāl ad-Dīn (b. Muḥammad Khorezmshāh), 85 n. 32
Jalīl Ata, 464
Jalāyirī. *See* Qādir ʿAlī Bek
Jamāl ad-Dīn, Sayyid, "Khoja Dīvānah Sayyid Atāʾī," 227
Jamāl Qarshī, 84 n. 24
Jambuyluq, 352
Jāmī, 127 n. 141
Jāmiʿat-tavārīkh (Rashīd ad-Dīn), 98 n. 65
Jāmiʿat-tavārīkh (Qādir ʿAlī Bek), 382
Jänbäk Khan, 474, 476
Janbay, 479
Jānī Bek, 91, 95, 96 n. 57, 117 n. 113 (Jānī Khān), 123, 124 n. 134, 133–34, 148–49, 193–94, 198, 224, 229, 332, 334–35, 339 n. 44, 342, 444
Jand, 130 n. 149
Jandī, Bābā Kamāl, 249 n. 35, 357–58
al-Jannābī, 85 n. 29
Jannazar jïraw, 419 n. 24
Jenkinson, Anthony, 401 n. 157, 453 n. 82
Jeremiah, 303 n. 137
Jerusalem, 125, 129
Jesus, 168
jība, 157, 232 n. 2, 543
Jibrāʾīl, 247 n. 30, 431, 432 n. 34, 445
Jibrīl b. Bukhtīshūʿ, 279
Jijak-khātūn, 84
jinn, 375, 430
Jöchi, 67, 143 n. 169, 148, 153 n. 198, 154, 190, 193 n. 79, 329 n. 22, 345, 372
Jöchid *ulus*, 13, 32, 67–69, 72–73, 81–82, 88, 91–93, 97, 104–5, 107, 117, 122, 130, 141 n. 166, 142–45, 147–48, 150, 152, 155, 159–60, 162, 165, 191, 195–96, 197 n. 93, 203, 216, 229, 242, 246, 279, 331–32, 334–39, 342, 345, 347–48, 353–54, 356, 377, 396, 411, 412 n. 5, 413, 443, 484, 488, 492, 502, 510, 519
Joinville, 214, 263, 268 n. 74
Jordanes, 496
Jordanus of Sévérac, 189, 264
"Joseph," king of the Khazars, 171 n. 10, 304
Judah Halevi, 171
Judaism, 28, 73, 169–71, 246, 292, 298, 300–308, 310–11, 313–17
julagh, 211
Jumaduq, 345
Jumjumah-nāmah, 434 n. 3
Junghar, 363
Jungharia, 8
jūrghāt, 555
Juvaynī, ʿAlāʾ ad-Dīn, 172, 179, 221, 259, 264, 278 n. 88, 282–86, 473, 496 n. 8, 497, 500–502, 511–12, 514
al-Juwaynī, Abū'l-Maʿālī, 76
Jūybārī khojas, 393, 401
Jūzjānī, 85, 189–90, 259, 265, 267, 273, 275 n. 82

Kaʿbah, 203, 373–75, 385, 479

Käbäk, Kebek (*khatun* of Özbek Khan), 102 n. 75, 134
Kafalı, Mustafa, xiv, 145 n. 176
Kaffa, 99, 207 n. 113, 252–53
al-Kaffawī, 122
kāfir, 60, 207–8
kāhin, 499 n. 12, 546
Kalauso-Sablinsk, 448 n. 74
kalimah-i shahādat, 373
Kalmat bin Valī (?), 368 n. 104
Kama river, 140, 402–3, 473
Kamāl Ata, 207–8, 250 n. 35, 253, 358, 559
Kamalashri, 286
Kan Kojo, 65
Kanz ad-durar wa jāmiʿ al-ghurar, 279
Kao ch'ang, 285
Karamzin, 194 n. 85
Karaotkel, 461
Karatabynsk, 470
Karatau mountains, 454, 455 n. 90, 485 n. 173
Kardar, 130 n. 149
Karkaralinsk uezd, 220
karāmat, 205, 209, 549
Kasim murza, 402
Kasimov, 382, 399, 471
Kāshgharī, Maḥmūd, 80 n. 17, 199 n. 103, 328 nn. 18–19
Kātib Chelebī, 197. *See also* Ḥājjī Khalīfah
Kazachii Bugor, 449, 452–53
Kazakhstan, 6, 8, 153 n. 198, 221, 450, 460
Kazan, 9, 104 n. 83, 347, 349 n. 73, 350, 397, 401, 403 n. 163, 419, 471, 553, 555
Kazan Tatar, 327
Kebek, Käbäk (*khatun* of Özbek Khan), 102 n. 75, 134
Kelechi, 438
kengesh, 63, 108, 228
kenges-töbe, 456
Kereyt, 183 n. 44, 267 n. 74, 292, 316
Kerley, 98
Kesek-bash kitābï, 434 n. 39
Khakimov, N., 418
Khal'fin, I., 398, 406
Khalvatī, 138 n. 161, 249 n. 32, 361–62, 531
Khanbalïq, 96 n. 58, 264
Khān-nāmah, 444
khānkāh [*sic*], 125
khānqāh-nishīn, 463
khāqān, 73, 80, 171 n. 8. See also *qaghan*
kharāj, 208
khaṭīb, 224
khatun, *khawātīn*, 131, 207, 224
Khazars, 73–76, 78, 80, 170–71, 181, 186 n. 55, 193 n. 78, 246, 292–93, 298, 300–308, 311, 314–17
Khazar correspondence, 304–5
Khiḍr, 131, 431, 494 n. 1, 511. *See also* Khiżr
Khitāy, Khiṭāy, 151 n. 191, 338, 463
Khiṭāy Baba ʿAlī of Ḥājjī Tarkhān, 488 n. 180
Khīva, 421
Khiżr, 440, 441. *See also* Khiḍr
Khiżr Bek, 95 n. 57, 134 n. 156
Khochakhmat Babatukli, 440. *See also* Baba Tükles
khoja, 485
Khojagān, 101
Khorezm, 9, 72, 83, 88, 92–93, 102 n. 75, 103, 109, 115–16, 119–20, 123, 124 n. 134, 125, 130–32, 135, 144, 148, 150, 151 n. 194, 201, 338, 345–48, 357, 366, 369–72, 375–78, 380–81, 389–91, 394–96, 412, 432, 439, 463, 467, 486–88
Khorezmī (author of *Muḥabbat-nāmah*), 89 n. 44
Khorezmī, Mawlānā Ḥusayn, 346
Khorezmī, Nūrullāh. *See* Nūrullāh Khorezmī
Khorezmī, Shaykh Kamāl ad-Dīn Ḥusayn, 201–2
Khorezmshāh, 82
Khori Buryats, 503
Khūtan, 463
Khujandī, Kamāl, 249, 250, 253
Khurāsān, 92, 130 n. 149, 131, 265–66, 395, 499
khuṭbah, 75 n. 10
Khwāndamīr, 390 n. 135
Kichik Muḥammad Khan, 341, 342 n. 53
Kiev, 195
Kimek(s), 282, 473, 474 n. 147 and 150, 494, 498–99
kir-, "to enter," 23
Kirakos of Ganjak, 264
Kisāʾī, 248 n. 31
Kitāb al-aʿlāq an-nafīsah (Ibn Rustah), 75 n. 10

Kitāb al-ʿibar (Ibn Khaldūn), 119
Kitāb al-Khazarī (Judah Halevi), 171
Kitāb al-masālik wa'l-mamālik (Ibn Khurdādhbih), 80 n. 17
Kitāb al-mijdāl, 267 n. 74, 308
kiye, 447 n. 70
Koblandï, Koblandy Batyr, 455, 468
Kögüdey Mergen, 45, 239–42
Koibal, 556
Kökchö, 62, 64
Kököchü, 323
Kök Orda, 335
Kök-Timūr Güregän, 107
Koshoy, 63
Köz-kaman, 64 n. 52
K'uar, 293
Kuban, 300, 351, 371 (Qūbān), 435, 471, 475
Kubrā, Najm ad-Dīn, 249 n. 35, 356–58, 432
Kubravī, 101, 138 n. 161, 201, 346, 376
Kubugul, 450 n. 78, 554
Kuchum, 471 n. 142
Kūh-i Qāf, 464
kük burdhay, 479
Kuku, 469
Kul'sheev Abdul, 398
Kumgel, 431. *See also* Qumkent
kumiss, 40, 206–7, 210–15, 217–23, 257, 308–9, 479, 541–42, 546–49, 552, 554–60. See also *qïmïz*
Kün Khan, 483 n. 169
Kūnchāk, 110 n. 97
Kundrov Tatars, 269
Kungrad, 419 n. 24
Kunh al-akhbār, 354 n. 80
Kūnkīz/Kūrkīz, 98 n. 65
Kunsu, 469
Kunūz al-aʿẓam, 228 n. 155
Kūrkānī/Gūrgānī, Shaykh Ḥasan, 359, 361
Kurmanov, Jamanbala, 220
Kūr.mās, 98 n. 65
Kydyr Ata, 431. *See also* Khiḍr

al-Lakzī, Ṣadr ad-Dīn Sulaymān, 131
lama 178
Land of Darkness, 126 n. 138
laylat al-qadr, 440 n. 57
Lezgī, 131
Life of St. Louis (Joinville), 263
Louis IX, 3
Lull, Ramón, 173

Maccabees, 303 n. 137
Māchīn, 463
Māday Qara, 44, 239
Madāʾin, 384
Madelung, Wilferd, 19 n. 7, 26
Madīnah, 85, 125, 384, 456
Magi, 278
"Magian," 79
Māh Sulṭānïm, 393–94
Maḥmūd b. Amīr Valī, 191, 226
Maḥmūd Bahādur Sulṭān, 394 n. 144
Mahmudov, Mamadali (*Ölmäs qayälär*), 45 n. 31
Mājar, 131
Majd ad-Dīn Aṭā (envoy of Töde Mengü), 87
Majmūʿ at-tavārīkh, 364 n. 98, 458 n. 99, 506 n. 23
al-Malik an-Nāṣir, Sulṭān, 86, 111, 128, 131
al-Malik aẓ-Ẓāhir, Sulṭān, 88
Malik-Temür, 125
Mālikī, 131
Mamay, 334–35, 455 n. 93, 526
"Mamay-khan," 468
Mambetov, Mulla Khali-bai, 459
Mamïts, four, 238
mamlūk, 264, 279
Mamlūks, Mamlūk Egypt, 84–85, 91–92, 94, 98, 111–12, 122, 129, 141, 150, 225 n. 150
Manāqib al-akhyār, 104 n. 80, 227
Manāqib-i mashāʾikh at-turk, 484 n. 171
Manas, 59–69, 64–65, 236
Manchu, 504
Manchuria, 8
Mandeville, John, 274 n. 79
Manghïshlaq, 146 n. 179, 201, 421 n. 27, 435 n. 40
Manghït(s), 104–5, 145 n. 174, 148, 185, 227, 343–47, 375, 379–80, 394–96, 405, 448, 463, 466, 488. *See also* Noghays
"Manghït Uzbeks," 202, 347
Mani, 168
Manichaeanism, 28, 169, 314, 511–14
Mankūr, 499
Manqïshlāqī, Shaykh Artūq, 201, 202
Mansur (Noghay tribe), 352
Mansur, Manghït, 439

al-Maqrīzī, 85 n. 30, 88 n. 43, 114 n. 104, 339
Mar ʿAbd Īshūʿ, 308
Mar Sergius, 267 n. 74, 311
Marghinānī, Sayyid Aḥmad Nāṣir ad-Dīn, 484 n. 171
Mārī b. Sulaymān, 267 n. 74, 308–9
Marignolli, John de, 96 n. 58
Marjānī, Shihāb ad-Dīn, 90 n. 46
Marv, 308–9, 395
Marxism, Marxism-Leninism, 30–31, 52, 170 n. 7
Masālik al-abṣār (al-ʿUmarī), 125
Mashaik, Mashaikovo, 449, 452–53
Masmūʿāt, 249–50
al-Masʿūdī, 73, 171 n. 11
Mathnavī (Rūmī), 378
Maṭlab aṭ-ṭālibīn, 393–96, 484 n. 171
Matthias of Miechow, 348–49
Mawarannahr, 65, 347 n. 69, 348, 372
Mawlavī, 138 n. 161
Mayyāfāriqīn, 259
mazār, 454
Mecca, 65, 85, 87, 125, 199 n. 103, 203, 271, 369 n. 106, 380, 404–6, 442, 471 n. 142, 483
Melioranskii, P. M., 398, 416–17
Menander Protector, 258
Mengli Girey, 401
Mesopotamian religion, 36
metallurgy, 235, 275
Michael the Syrian, 278, 496 n. 8, 500
Miftāḥ al-ʿadl (Pādshāh Khoja), 377 n. 122
Miftāḥ al-ʿulūm (as-Sakkākī), 124 n. 134
Mihr Nigār Khānïm, 393, 395–96
Mikhail, Prince of Kiev, 261–62
Mikhail, Prince of Tver', 94 n. 55
millah, 23, 112
Ming Ḥadāqlī Ūrādach Bīy, 478
Ming Bashkirs, 478
Ming dynasty (Qoqand), 486 n. 175, 555
Minusinsk, 44
miʿrāj, 25
Mīrānshāh, 412
Mīrkhwānd, 95 n. 57
mīrzā, 104 n. 79, 145 n. 174, 322, 350, 368, 371, 375, 379–81, 396, 475–77
al-Miṣrī, Shams ad-Dīn, 131
Möngke, 3, 173, 188, 209, 223 n. 144, 548–49
Möngke Temür, 97, 110 n. 97, 149
Mönglik, 323
Mongolia, 7–8, 513
Moradhïm, 481
Moscow, 7, 93, 252, 338, 350, 397, 402, 404
Mountain/Tree/Cave/Water, etc. (mythic complex), 43–44, 46–48, 172, 200, 273, 276, 280, 303–4, 482, 500, 507
Movsēs Dasχuranci, 293
muʾadhdhin, 84
al-Mufaḍḍal, 84, 112, 114 n. 104, 122, 124, 549
Mughān steppe, 369 n. 105
Muḥabbat-nāmah (Khorezmī), 89 n. 44, 124 n. 134
Muḥammad, 178, 248 n. 30, 287. *See also* Prophet
Muḥammad b. Abū Bakr aṣ-Ṣiddīq, 358
Muḥammad b. al-Ḥanafīyah, 358–59, 374, 379–80
"Muḥammad al-Yasavī," Sayyid, 336
Muḥammad Ḥusayn b. Ḥājjī Aqā-yi Ṣūfī T.r.k.kī, 367
Muḥammad Islām, Khoja, 393
Muḥammad Jūkī, 338 n. 41
Muḥammad Khoja Bek b. Yaylagh Qutlugh (Qonghrat), 89 n. 44
Muḥammad-Khwājā, 120
Muḥammad Manṣūr Mīrzā, 393, 395–96
Muḥammad Qāżī, Mawlānā, 249–50
Muḥammad Shïbānī Khan, 151 n. 194, 345–47, 390 n. 135, 394 n. 144, 395, 401, 486 n. 174
Muḥammad Ṭāhir Bīy, 393
Muḥammad-Yaʿqūb b. Muḥammad Dāniyāl-bīy, 185
mujāhid, 137, 318
mujāvur, 125
muʿjizah, 373
Mujmal-i Faṣīḥī (Faṣīḥ Khwāfī), 123 n. 133
Mukhtār b. Maḥmūd az-Zāhidī (d. 658/1260), 85 n. 29
Mullā Bāqī, 475 n. 152
Mullakaev, Kedrias, 470
Mūm.k.qiyāy, 108
Münjükī, 120
Muʾnis, 103, 104 n. 79, 135, 151 n. 193, 346 n. 65, 371, 374 n. 116
Muntakhab at-tavārīkh (Naṭanzī), 116, 144

Muqaddimah fī'l-jadal wa'l-khilāf wa'n-naẓar (Burhān ad-Dīn Nasafī), 126 n. 140
Muqtadir (Caliph), 74 n. 9
al-Muqtafā li-tārīkh ash-Shaykh Shihāb ad-Dīn Abī Shāmah (al-Birzālī), 112
Muradi̇̄m, 468
al-Muʿrib ʿan baʿḍ ʿajāʾib al-buldān al-maghrib (al-Gharnāṭī), 76 n. 11
murīd, 377, 462
Murīd (Jöchid khan), 334–35
Murtażā, Khoja, 394–95
Mūsā (prophet), 373
Mūsā Bīy (Manghït, son of Vaqqāṣ Bīy), 346, 349, 394–95, 401, 439
Musa-khan, 468
Musaeva, Kenzhegïz, 460
Muslim Religious Board, Ufa, 146
Muṣṭafā, Shïbānid, 390
Mustafād al-akhbār fī aḥvāl Qazān va Bulghār (Marjānī), 90 n. 46
al-Mutawakkil, 279 n. 92
Muẓaffar ad-Dīn, Shaykh, 131
M.ż..rāt, 457

nabīdh, 132
nabīdh al-ʿasal, 206, 549
nadhr, 208
Nādir Shāh, 369 n. 105
Nadr Muḥammad Khan, 227
Nāghādāy, Naghdāy, 102 n. 75, 103, 104 n. 79, 134, 151 n. 193, 346 n. 65, 374 n. 116. *See also* Nanghïday
an-Nahrmalikī, Rajab, 131
Najīb ʿĀṣim, 145
namāz, 374
Nanghïday, 102 n. 75, 135. *See also* Nāghādāy
naqīb, 226–28
naqīb ash-shurafā, 133
Naqshbandī, Naqshbandīyah, 138 n. 161, 175, 185, 228, 249, 251, 393, 485
Naqshband, Khoja Bahāʾ ad-Dīn, 185, 227, 238 n. 14
Nasā, 395
Nasab-nāmah-i Ūzbīk, 458 n. 100
Nasafī, Burhān ad-Dīn, 126
an-Nasawī, 85 n. 32
Naṣīb-nāmah-i Ūzbīk, 459 n. 101
"*an-Nāṣirīyah*" (Mukhtār b. Maḥmūd az-Zāhidī), 85 n. 29
Natanzī, Muʿīn ad-Dīn, 93 n. 54, 95 n. 57, 102 n. 75, 116–17, 144, 152 n. 197, 199 n. 101, 332, 335, 346, 384 n. 128, 390, 486 n. 173
"national epics," 415 n. 12
Navāʾī, Mīr ʿAlī-shīr, 346
Nawrūz, *amīr* of Ghāzān Khan, 123
Nawrūz, son of Edigü, 341–42, 394 n. 144
Nāymān, 463
Nāymtāy, 98 n. 65
ne onggay, 448
Near East, 28–29, 72, 83
Nestorian Christianity, 173, 176, 267 n. 74, 292, 299, 308, 316
New York, 397, 402
Nicholas of Cusa, 174 n. 20
Nicopolis, 412
Nïghday, 102 n. 75. *See also* Nāghādāy, Nanghïday
Nihāyat al-arab fī funūn al-adab (an-Nuwayrī), 111
nikāh, 464
niqābat, 229
Nīshābūrī, Mīr ʿAbd al-Avval, 249
Nithārī Bukhārī, Ḥasan, 376–77
Niẓām ad-Dīn, *ḥājjī*, of Sarāy Berke, 132
Nizhnii Novgorod, 333, 335
Nogaiskie dela, 195 n. 85
Noghay (Mongol commander in the Golden Horde), 88–89, 91, 111, 118 n. 120, 152 n. 197, 153 n. 200, 343 n. 57. *See also* Nūqāy
Noghay(s), 6, 42 n. 27, 60 n. 41, 64 n. 52, 66, 90, 195, 197, 203, 270, 322, 342, 349–51, 363–66, 368, 370–72, 374–75, 377, 379–81, 394, 397, 399, 405, 411, 416–17, 422 n. 27, 423, 430, 433, 435–39, 442, 444–45, 447–48, 450, 453, 457, 459 n. 101, 462, 467–69, 471–73, 475, 477, 479 n. 159, 483, 484 n. 170, 488, 493, 504, 510, 518–19
Noghay horde, 6, 13, 16, 194, 198 n. 99, 201, 269, 336–37, 343–44, 347–48, 350, 400, 404, 411, 421, 428, 435, 439, 442, 456, 466, 492, 510, 518, 522, 526
nöker, 151, 154, 368
nom, 172
North America, 30

North Caucasian Huns, 291, 316–17. *See also* Huns
North Caucasus, 21, 74, 131, 170, 175, 298, 311, 351, 435, 447
Novgorod chronicle, 261
noyon, 104 n. 79, 108
an-Nujūm az-zāhirah fī mulūk Miṣr wa'l-Qāhirah (Ibn Taghrībirdī), 121
Nūküs, 463
Nukus, 419 n. 24
Nüküz, 274
Nuʿmān Khorezmī (Nuʿmān ad-Dīn al-Khwārazmī, an-Nuʿmān b. Dawlatshāh b. ʿAlī al-Khwārazmī al-Ḥanafī, ʿAlāʾ ad-Dīn), 125–30, 132
Nūqāy, 110 n. 97. *See also* Noghay, Mongol *amīr*
Nūr ad-Dīn (envoy of Töde Mengü), 87
Nūr ad-Dīn (son of Edigü), 194, 348, 393, 400, 440, 483. *See also* Nūr ʿĀdil, Nuradin
Nūr ad-Dīn, *qāzī*, Shaykh, 124, 129
Nūr ʿĀdil, 440, 447
Nurabullaev, Esemurat jïraw, 419 n. 24
Nuraddin, Nuradïn, Nuradil, Nuralin, 417 n. 17, 420, 422, 429, 439–41, 462
nuradin (title), 348 n. 70
Nūrullāh Khorezmī (Nūrullāh b. ʿUbaydallāh aṣ-Ṣiddīq al-Khwārazmī), 371, 375–81, 394, 396, 414, 423, 430, 484 n. 171
an-Nuwayrī, 84 n. 25 and 28, 87, 89 n. 44, 111–12, 113, 116 n. 110, 118 n. 120
Nuzhat al-anām fī tārīkh al-islām (Ibn Duqmāq), 117
Nuzhat al-qulūb (Qazvīnī), 192, 203

ochoq, 42
Öge Beki/Akā Bekī, 102
oghlān, 368
Oghuz, 50, 73, 78, 177 n. 26, 214, 275, 278, 496 n. 8, 500–501
Oghuz Khan, Oghuz Qaghan, 61, 85, 146 n. 179, 284, 330–31, 445, 483 n. 169, 501–502, 511–12, 529 n. 37, 563
Oghuz-nāmah, 85
Ögödey, 183, 221, 264
Olearius, Adam, 451–53
Öljey Khatun, 192
Öljeytü (Ilkhanid), 92, 107, 123, 151 n. 194, 173, 190, 191, 216, 259–61
Ölöt, 503
Omsk, 417 n. 16
Ongin inscription, 182
Or Tegin, 284
Orak/Örek, 455 n. 93
Örek-chura/Üzek-chura, 385
Orda, 148, 153
Ordos, 185–86, 218, 257
Orenburg, 146, 419, 468, 470
Orenburg Expedition, 470 n. 139
Orkhon, Orqon, 283
orun-i niqābat, orun-i nuqabā, 227
Osh, 504
Ötemish Ḥājjī, xi–xiv, 5, 13, 60, 85–86, 89, 102 n. 75, 105, 107, 110–11, 116 n. 110, 117, 118 n. 118, 120–21, 142–52, 158–70, 172, 174, 179–80, 184–86, 189 n. 61, 190, 192–93, 199–200, 203–6, 208–10, 213 n. 122, 215–16, 218–19, 221–23, 226, 229–32, 236–38, 240–49, 253–54, 256, 260, 267–69, 272–73, 286–87, 290–92, 297, 304, 307–8, 310, 317, 322, 324, 326, 328–31, 340, 352–62, 365–66, 369–71, 375, 378–79, 381–83, 390, 396, 428, 446–47, 449–50, 452, 461, 464, 472, 477, 484, 486, 488, 492–93, 507, 510, 515–16, 519–20, 529 n. 37, 531, 541, 544, 550, 554–55, 561, 563
Oteniyaz jïraw, 418 n. 24
Otrar, 338
Ottoman(s), 251, 254, 347, 350–51, 361, 368, 369, 404, 412, 478
Ötükän, 276–7, 301, 524–26
oven-pit, 232, 234–35, 241–44, 255, 271, 290, 477, 500, 511
Oyrat(s), 60, 64, 251, 347, 363, 504
ozan, 104
Özbek Khan, xiii, 5, 12 n. 5, 13, 15, 83, 88–91, 93–96, 98, 100–102, 105–9, 111–35, 140–44, 147, 149–55, 158, 160–67, 175 n. 23, 179, 193, 196 n. 92, 198–99, 201–2, 206, 208, 215 n. 128, 216–17, 224, 226, 229–30, 232, 243, 251, 279, 315–16, 318, 322, 329 n. 21, 332, 335, 342–43, 346 n. 65, 356–65, 370–73, 377, 379–81, 383, 385, 389, 392, 399, 405–6, 412, 428, 445–47, 455 n. 93, 484–86, 488–89, 493, 502, 510, 515, 529 n. 37, 531, 541, 543, 549, 560, 565

Özek-chura/Örek-chura/Üzek-chura, 385

Pādshāh Khoja, 377 n. 122
Pallas, Peter Simon, 452 n. 81, 552
parī, 430, 462, 483 n. 169, 503 n. 17
parī-qïzï, 477
parīzād, 430, 464
Paris, 397, 402
Pascal of Vittoria, 96 n. 58
Pazyryk, 47 n. 36
Pechenegs, 73, 78–79
Pelliot, 181, 183–84, 187, 189–90, 192, 195, 275
People's Republic of China, 7
Perekop Tatars, 349 n. 72
perestroika, 170
perezhitki, religious "survivals," 54 n. 39
Persians, 131
Perul, 451–53
Peter the Great, 402
Petr, Russian metropolitan, 111 n. 97
Petra, son of Caramus, 98 n. 64
Pharaoh, 373, 379
Philippe de Toucy, 263
Pīr Ḥusayn, 106
Pizzigani, Francesco and Marco, 196
Plano Carpini, John of, 183, 187, 193 n. 78, 195, 214, 259, 264–65, 548
Poland, 252
Polo, Marco, 40, 181, 188, 209, 212, 215, 217, 220, 222 n. 141, 223, 282, 285, 548, 550, 551
Pontic steppe, 79, 300
Potanin, G. N., 238–39, 417, 428, 430, 432–33, 455, 469, 494
Prévost d'Exiles, Antoine François, 175 n. 21
"primitive religion," 27
Priscus, 186 n. 55, 496
Prophet (Muḥammad), 25–26, 76, 78, 133, 228, 253, 256, 374, 385, 445, 458, 459, 460, 485. *See also* Muḥammad
Psalms, 441
Purusha-hymn, 38 n. 20

Qādir ʿAlī Bek (Jalāyirī), 151 nn. 194–95, 155 n. 203, 349 n. 73, 382–83, 389, 391–92, 394, 399–400, 478
Qādir Berdi, 339, 420, 441, 447
Qādir-Qïyā, 384, 394, 436
qaghan, 74, 169, 276, 293, 300, 314 n. 143, 512–14
Qalandar-nāmah, 123
Qalāwun, Mamlūk Sulṭān, 86
Qalmāq (ancestor), 364 n. 98
Qalmïqs, "Qalmaqs," 6, 60, 62, 64 n. 52, 65, 153, 251, 322, 347, 350–51, 362–64, 365–66, 421 n. 26, 435 n. 40, 449, 450–51, 456–57, 463, 464 n. 113, 465–67, 552
al-Qalqashandī, 114 n. 104
qam, 172, 259, 284, 301, 546
Qāmīnāzār, 197
Qamlanchu, 283
Qanglī, 463
Qaplān Girey I, 368
qara kishi, 152
Qarabalghasun, 169, 511, 513
Qarakhanid(s), 8, 19, 20 nn. 8–9, 284, 520 n. 30
al-Qaramānī, Abū'l-ʿAbbās Aḥmad, 121 n. 127
Qara-Noghay, 351, 437, 440, 484 n. 170
Qarapchï, Qïzïjï or "Qarïjï," 384, 394, 399
Qaraqalpaq(s), 6, 351, 370–71, 377, 411, 417–18, 419 n. 24, 422, 430, 432, 435, 456, 463 (Qarāqalfāq), 483 n. 169, 558
Qara-Qorum, 265, 267 (Qarā-Quram), 283
Qarā Ṭāgh, 280–82, 414
Qasay, 448 n. 74
Qaṣāy Bek, 368
Qāshānī, Jamāl ad-Dīn ʿAbdullāh b. ʿAlī, 107–11, 115, 117, 119, 149, 190 n. 68, 259–60
Qashqa Darya, 347 n. 69
Qāsim al-Anvār, 250 n. 36
Qāsim, Sayyid, 250
Qaydu, 141 n. 166
qaymaq, 207
Qazanchi Bahādur, 384 n. 128
Qazaq(s), 6, 21 n. 11, 66, 200 n. 104, 220, 236–39, 241, 347, 349 n. 72, 351, 363, 369, 377, 411, 416–17, 422, 428, 430–32, 435–36, 445, 454–55, 457, 459–60, 463, 467, 469, 483 n. 169, 484 n. 170, 485 n. 173, 531, 555, 557–58
qāżī, 224
qāżī Nūr, 112, 124. *See also* Nūr ad-Dīn, *qāżī*
Qazï-aq, 445

Qazvīn, 142
Qazvīnī, Ḥamdullāh Mustawfī, 123 n. 133, 192–93, 198
al-Qazvīnī, Zakariyā, 76 n. 11, 77 n. 14
qiblah, 266
qïmïz, 206, 224, 547, 549, 557. *See also* kumiss
Qïpchaq(s), 97, 131, 181 n. 40, 242, 279, 325, 339, 369, 435 n. 40, 441, 463 (Qïfchāq), 555
Qïrghïz, 21, 59, 62, 65–66, 175, 236, 238, 241, 363, 369, 441, 445, 503 n. 17, 504–6, 555–56
Qïrïm, 114 n. 104, 117 n. 113, 132, 133 n. 155, 207–8, 252
qïrq-qïz, 445, 505
Qiṣṣah-i Tokhtāmïsh Khān, 462 n. 107
Qïtan, 496 n. 8, 499–500, 504
Qivāmī, Badr ad-Dīn, *imām*, 132
qïya, 384 n. 129
Qïyan, 274–75
Qïyas jïraw, 418 n. 24
Qïyāt, 151, 153–54, 155 n. 203
Qïzīčī, 436
Qoduqai, 99
Qoduqan, 99
Qoji Aḥmad Baba Tükli Shashli ʿAzīz Barkhāyah, 440. *See also* Baba Tükles
Qonghrat, 88–89, 103, 152 n. 197, 344 n. 59, 346 n. 65, 455 n. 90, 463, 465–67, 487, 510
"Qonghrat Sufi" dynasty, 102 n. 75, 135
Qongrāt (town), 463. *See also* Kungrad
Qoqand, 459, 555
Qoqand khanate, 486 n. 175
qorqut, 560–61
qoruğčï, *qoruqčï*, 183, 217 n. 132
qoruq, 154, 165, 179–86, 189–95, 196 n. 90, 197 n. 93, 198–204, 210, 215–21, 229–30, 243, 257, 264–65, 267, 270–71, 290–91, 307, 311, 318, 447, 477, 544–46, 561
qoruq-i Arghūn, 191
Qosy Körpösh, 454
Qotlo, 481. *See also* Qutlu Qïya
Qotur Tegin, 284
Qubilay, 91, 173, 209, 212
Questions of King Milinda, 168
Quḥāfah, 458–59
Qumans, 73, 78, 181, 197, 214, 263. *See also* Comans
Qumkent, 384, 389–91, 396, 400, 429, 485
Qur'ān, 24, 26, 52, 56, 62, 79, 80, 112, 131, 244–45, 247, 288, 340, 440 n. 57, 441, 474, 477
qurïltay, 191
Qūrlās, 326
qut, 46
"Quṭb" (poet), 124 n. 134
Qūtlū-Qïyā, Qutlu Qaya, 384, 389–90, 430, 432, 436–37, 450 n. 78
Qutlugh Temür, Quṭluq-timür, etc., 93, 108–10, 115–16, 118–21, 123, 133, 150
Qūtmūq [*sic*] Qïyā Bīy, 393. *See also* Qutlu Qïya

rābiṭah ("hospice"), 131
Radlov, V. V., 236, 417, 430, 440
rāhib, 253
Raḥīm Berdi, 465–66
rain-stone, 175–76
Rāmitanī, Shaykh ʿAlī ʿAzīzān, 101, 486
Rashaḥāt-i ʿayn al-ḥayāt, 101, 376, 379, 486 n. 175
Rashīd ad-Dīn, 85, 88–89, 98 n. 65, 99, 108 n. 91, 110 n. 97, 152 n. 197, 153 n. 200, 173, 183, 189 n. 61, 190–91, 217 n. 132, 259, 273, 275 n. 81, 280 n. 95, 282, 285, 326, 329 n. 22, 383, 445, 498, 501, 502, 527
Rashīd ad-Dīn, Khoja, of Balkh, 265
Rasputin, 398 n. 149
Razriadnyi Prikaz, 397–98
Richard, Jean, 67 n. 1, 82 n. 21
Ricoldo of Monte Croce, 264
ar-Rifāʿī, Aḥmad, Shaykh, 131
"Rižvān," Muḥammad Qāsim, 227
Roger II of Sicily, 80
Roux, Jean-Paul, 31 n. 21, 38, 39 n. 21, 67 n. 1
Rubruck, William of, vi, 3–4, 40–41, 84, 100 n. 73, 173, 187, 188 n. 60, 193 n. 78, 209, 211, 213, 223, 259, 548
Rukn ad-Dīn Baybars al-Manṣūrī. *See* Baybars al-Manṣūrī
Rūm, 130–31
Rūmī, Abū'l-Khayr, 251–52
Rūmī, Jalāl ad-Dīn, 123, 374 n. 119, 375, 377–78, 394, 434 n. 39, 438, 459, 484 n. 171
Rus', 169

Russia, Russian(s), 65, 81, 131, 140, 170, 195, 207 n. 113, 252–53, 261, 270, 309–10, 322, 332, 338, 347, 350–52, 364, 397, 450, 460, 463, 465, 467, 472, 475–76
Russian Federation, 7
Russian Orthodox church, 97
Russian Primary Chronicle, 170
Ruthenian, 140

Sachïl ʿAzīz, Sāchlï ʿAzīz, Sāchlï Parī, 463–64. *See also* Baba Tükles
Saʿd b. Waqqāṣ, 177
ṣadaqah, 131
Ṣadr Ata, 101, 371–79, 487
Safardau, 421. *See also* Supra Jïraw
Ṣafavī, Ṣafavīyah, 138 n. 161, 362 n. 92
Ṣafwat aṣ-ṣafā, 329
Sagai, 556
sāḥir, 253, 373
as-Sāʾilī, Shihāb ad-Dīn, *qāżī'l-qużāt*, 133
Sain Batyr, 454, 455 n. 90, n. 92
Ṣāʾin Khān, 376. *See also* Sayïn Khan
Saint Louis, Missouri, 397, 406
St. Louis University, 398 n. 151
Saint Petersburg, 367, 397
Sajās, Sujās, 142, 191–92
as-Sakkākī, Sirāj ad-Dīn Yūsuf, 124 n. 134
saksavïl, 239
ṣalāt, 260
salāṭīn-i Chaghatāy, 151 n. 192
Salāy Qabāy, 459. *See also* Islām Qïyā
Saliev, Hasanbay, 434 n. 39
Saljïday Güregen, Qonghrat tribal chief, 88–89
Saljūq, 8, 280
Sallām the Interpreter, 80–81, 287–89,
Ṣaltūq-nāmah, 207, 251–53
Samarqand, 130 n. 149, 209 n. 115, 454, 460
Samarskii *raion*, 461
Samoilovich, A. N., 418–19
sandïq, 479
Sānggsūn, 153 n. 200
sangha, 169
sapchaq, 541, 551, 553–54
Saqsīn, 76
Saracen, 140–42
Sarapul, 402–3
sarāqūj, *sarūqūj*, 121–22
Saratov, 470 n. 138
Sarāy, 96 n. 58, 97–98, 108, 111, 117 n. 58, 130, 140, 196, 198, 249, 358, 412, 561
Sarāy Batu, 92
Sarāy Berke, 92, 126–27, 130–32
Sarāy al-Jadīd, 92, 130 n. 149, 334
Ṣarāy-timür, 120
Sarāychïq, 96 n. 57, 130, 132, 134 n. 156, 193–201, 351, 372, 379, 421 n. 27, 447, 453 n. 82, 478, 561
Sarï Saltïq, 86 n. 35, 207–8, 250 n. 35, 251–55, 355, 559
Sarï Su, 193 n. 79
Sarïsu *raion* 460
Sart, 455, 462, 531
Sartaq, 82 n. 21, 100 n. 73
Sarytav volost', 220
Sasanid, 279
Säsle Ata, 478. *See also* Baba Tükles
Satmïr, 479, 482
Satūq Bughrā Khan, 520 n. 30
Satyi murza, 402, 439 n. 54
Ṣāyïn Khan, 148, 345, 376 (*ūlūs* of Ṣāʾin Khān)
Sayram, 454
sayyid(s), 228, 485
Sayyid Aḥmad Khan, 341 n. 50
Sayyid Ata, 101–6, 129, 134–35, 144, 147 n. 180, 160, 175 n. 23, 178 n. 32, 224, 226–29, 250 n. 36, 322–23, 335–36, 345–46, 348, 356, 359–60, 364–65, 372–74, 376–77, 391, 394 n. 144, 441 n. 60, 483, 485–89, 492, 510–11, 520 n. 30
Sayyid Atāʾī, 228
Sayyid Nāqib [*sic*], 385
Sayyid Nāṣir Khoja Sayyid Atāʾī, 486 n. 174
Schechter text, 171 n. 10, 303, 305
Schiltberger, Johannes, 83 n. 22, 412–14
Scythian(s), 42, 47 n. 36, 61 n. 44, 200, 461 n. 106, 495, 504 n. 20
Scytho-Siberian civilization, 45
Second Türk empire, 301
Secret History of the Mongols, 257, 275, 325–26, 443, 496 n. 8, 500, 527 n. 35
Seid al-Vakhas, 177
Seiush Murza, 402
Selenge, 283
Seljüks. *See* Saljūqs
Semirechye, 556
"service Tatars," 397
Seven Sleepers of Ephesus, 288

Sevin Beg, 102 n. 75
Shad, 474 n. 147, 494, 498
Shādī Bek Khan (Jöchid), 341 n. 50
Shādlïq, 474
Shāfiʿī, 131, 260
Shaghālī Bīy, Shaghālī Khan, 474, 476
"Shah Timur," 420, 479
shahādah, 440, 460
Shāhanshāh-nāmah, 274 n. 79
Shāhnāmah, 247
Shāhrukh, 117 n. 113, 338
Shāhrukhīyah, 376
shajarah, 370, 397, 470 n. 138, 472–73, 475–76, 478, 506
Shajarah-i tarākimah, 146, 147 n. 182, 483 n. 169, 484
Shajarah-i Turk va Moghūl, 103, 147 n. 181, 323, 366–67, 371
Shajarat al-atrāk, 85, 101–3, 111, 117, 273 n. 79, 364 n. 98, 376, 487
Sha-Mansur, 505
shaman, "shamanism," 6, 33–38, 44, 156, 175, 204, 209–10, 214, 230, 232–35, 238, 242, 244, 255–57, 259, 268, 289, 318, 323, 328, 330, 460–61, 493, 499, 504, 516, 529, 546
Shāmī, Niẓām ad-Dīn, 117, 344, 390
Shāmil, 21 n. 11
Shang-tu, 214
Sharaf-nāmah-i shāhī, 193 n. 79
sharīʿah, 108, 340
Shashlï ʿAzīz, 485. *See also* Baba Tükles
Shaṭṭārī, 138 n. 161
Shaybānī-nāmah (Bannāʾī), 422 n. 27, 486 n. 174
Shaykh Aḥmad Khan of Ḥājjī Tarkhān, 488 n. 180
Shaykh Jalīl Tāghï, 464 n. 113
Shaykh T.r.w.sh [i.e. Darvish], 476
Shchelkan, Shelkan, 94 n. 56
Sheikh-Zaman, 449
Sheshma river, 473–74
Shïban b. Jöchi, 148, 339, 345, 372, 379, 393
Shïbanid, 143, 148, 340
Shīʿism, Shīʿites, 260–61
Shīrāzī, Rukn ad-Dīn, 127
Shirvānī, Sayyid Yaḥyā, 361
Shirvānī, Shaykh Majd ad-Dīn, 358, 361–62
Shirwān, 362
Shora Batyr, 454
Shuʿab-i panjgānah (Rashīd ad-Dīn), 98 n. 65, 110 n. 97
ash-Shujāʿī, 95 n. 57, 134 n. 156
Siberia, 7–9, 20, 21 n. 10, 44, 83 n. 22, 140, 147 n. 181, 236, 339, 345, 413, 414 n. 10
Siberian Tatars, 238–39, 553
Sībīr, Sibur, 140, 197. *See also* Ïbïr-Sïbïr
Sigismund, Hungarian King, 412
Sījūt, 151, 154, 155 n. 203
Silk Road, 72
silsilah, 139, 531, 562
Silsilat al-ʿārifīn, 249–50
Simnānī, ʿAlāʾ ad-Dawlah, 173
aṣ-Ṣīn, 280
Sïp-bashlï Sïpra, 421. *See also* Soppaslï Sabraw-jïraw
Sïpïra-jïraw, 421, 432 n. 37. *See also* Supra Jïraw
Siyāvush, 246–47
Slavic, 325
Smith, Captain John, 41 n. 24
smithing, 235
Soghdian, 169, 513
Solkhat, 88, 93 n. 52
Sonqur Tegin, 284
Soppaslï Sabraw-jïraw, 422. *See also* Supra Jïraw
Soppaslï Spïra-zhrau, 419 n. 24
sorcerer(s), 205, 221, 223, 253, 290–91, 294–96, 299, 318, 355, 373, 379, 499 n. 12
South Asia, 18
Soviet Union, 5, 7, 10, 14, 30–31, 68
Stavropol', 436 n. 43, 447
Stephen of Hungary, Franciscan friar, 96 n. 58, 246 n. 26
Sterlitamak, 477 n. 155
Subḥān-Qulī Khan, 185
Subrā-jïraw, 421–22. *See also* Supra Jïraw
Sufi, Sufi shaykhs, 6, 65, 135–38, 168, 174–75, 179, 185, 201, 203, 322, 379, 529, 531
Sufrah Khoja, 422 n. 27
Suhravard, 142, 192
Suhravardī, 138 n. 161
Sui dynasty, 300
Sujās, Sajās, 142, 191–92
Sukhan, 94 n. 56
süksük, 157, 542, 562

Süksük Ata, 562
Süleyman, Ottoman sulṭān, 404
Sulṭānīyah, 140, 142, 191, 209 n. 115
Sultan Babatkul', 448. *See also* Baba Tükles
Supra Jïraw, 419 n. 24, 436 n. 44, 438 n. 50, 469, 479. *See also* Soppaslï Sabraw jïraw, Subra-jïraw
Supraw-zhïraw, 469
Sura-batïr, 468. *See also* Shora Batyr
sūrat al-kahf, 288
Suvra, 437. *See also* Supra Jïraw
swan-maiden(s), 430–32, 455 n. 91, 493, 496 n. 8, 503–4, 516
Syr-Darya, 357, 454, 455 n. 91
Syria, 337, 339, 384
Syriac, 175

*ta*ᶜ*aṣṣub*, 249
Ṭabaqāt-i Nāṣirī, 85, 189
aṭ-Ṭabarī, 248 n. 31, 354 n. 80
Tabrīz, 190, 192, 249 n. 35, 362
Tabrīzī, Aḥmad, 274 n. 79
Tabrīzī, Ṣhams ad-Dīn, 434 n. 39
Tabyldy, 477 n. 155
Tadhkirah-i Ṭāhir Īshān, 371
T'ai-tsung, 177
Tāj ad-Dīn Ḥasan, Khoja, 393–96
Tāj ad-Dīn b. Yalchïghul, 194 n. 83
Tamīmī, Shaykh Muḥammad, 127 n. 142
Tan Ṣūfī, 346
Tana, 201, 341, 342 n. 53
T'ang dynasty, 177, 178 n. 31
T'angri Khan, 293. *See also* Tengri
tanūr, 156, 250, 542
Taoist, 168, 173
Ṭaqṭaqāy, 114 n. 104. *See also* Toqtogha
Tarbagatai, 431
Tārīkh-i Abū'l-Khayr Khānī, 407
Tārīkh-i Āpūshqā-yi Chingīzī, 354 n. 80
*Tārīkh-i arba*ᶜ*ah ulūs*, 102 n. 75
Tarīkh Bulghār, 76
Tārīkh-i Dūst Sulṭān (Ötemish Ḥājjī), 5, 144, 354
Tārīkh-i guzīdah (Ḥamdullāh Qazvīnī), 123 n. 133
Tārīkh-i Ḥaydarī, 109
Tārīkh-i jarīdah-i jadīdah (Qārī Qurbān-ᶜAlī b. Khālid Ḥājjī Ayākūzī), 178 n. 32
Tārīkh-i Rashīdī, 174, 176
Tārīkh-i Shaykh Uvays, 114, 116, 149
Tārīkh-i Ūljāytū Sulṭān (Qāshānī), 107, 109, 116, 119, 260
Tarim, 285
ṭarīqah, 138–39, 228, 442, 462
"Tartar(s)," 136, 140–41, 188–89, 264, 341
Tashkent, 101–2, 376, 419, 459, 485
*Tashrīf al-ayyām wa'l-*ᶜ*uṣur fī sīrat al-Malik al-Manṣūr* (Ibn ᶜAbd aẓ-Ẓāhir), 86
Tatar(s), 6, 13, 41 n. 24, 68, 78, 227, 252, 328, 339, 349, 363–64, 368, 397, 403, 418, 420, 435–38, 445, 484 n. 170, 485, 553–55, 558
Tatār Khān, 282
"Tatarski molobitza," 451
Tātārstān, 329, 363
Tatigach Bīy, Tatigas Bīy, 476 n. 155
Tatigasov, Sabit, 477 n. 155
Tavārīkh-i Bulghārīyah, 77 n. 15, 147 n. 181
Tavārīkh-i Dasht-i Qipchāq, 207–8, 253, 452 n. 82, 559
Tavārīkh-i guzīdah-i nuṣrat-nāmah, 144, 151, 155, 273 n. 79, 345, 394, 421 n. 27, 486 n. 174, 501 n. 16
tawakkul, 329
tawbah, "repentance," 22
Ṭayfūr, Ṭunghūr, Ṭunghūz, 120 n. 125
Ṭāz (b. Münjük), 118, 120
Teb Tengri, 268 n. 74, 323, 527 n. 35
telbe, 344 n. 58
Teleuts, 42, 417 n. 16, 556
Temür, 117 n. 113, 209 n. 115, 326, 329, 336–38, 340, 343–44, 361, 412, 511, 526
Temür Bek Khan (Jöchid), 384 n. 128
Temür Qutlugh (Jöchid), 336 n. 39, 338, 349 n. 72
Tengri, 294
Terme, 375, 379–80, 384–85, 389–90, 399, 404, 435–36
Tharmagar, 98 n. 64
Thodothelia, 98
Tholethemur, 98 n. 64
Tibet, Tibetan, 7–8, 31, 281, 286, 363, 444, 482 n. 169
Timurid, 20, 101, 116, 143–44, 148, 191
Tïnï Bek, Tinī Bek, 96 n. 57, 124 n. 134, 134, 224
Tīrah Khān, Tiräy Khan, 470 n. 138. *See also* Turakhan
Tiria Babatu Kliusov, 471

Tirmidh, 266, 267
Tiumen', 236, 345
Tizengauzen, V., 81 n. 20
Tö'äläs, 326
Tobolsk, 147 n. 181
Tödeken, 99
Töde Mengü, Töde Möngke, 86, 87, 110 n. 97 (Tūdā Mūnkkā), 149
Togan, Zeki Velidi, 145–46
Tögeles, 326
Toghrulcha (father of Özbek Khan), 95 n. 56. *See also* Ṭūghrīlchah
Tokhtamïsh (epic figure) 414, 420–22, 429, 435, 437, 440–41, 447, 449, 450 n. 78, 463, 479. *See also* Toqtamïsh
Tokhtay, 125. *See also* Toqtogha
Töklö Ata, 478. *See also* Baba Tükles
Tökläth, 468, 479, 480–83. *See also* Baba Tükles
Töläsh, 326
Toqay Temür, 148
Toqtaghu, 193. *See also* Toqtogha
Toqtamïsh, 147, 149, 249 n. 35, 336–39, 343–44, 384 n. 128, 391 n. 136, 412 n. 5, 421 n. 27
Toqtogha, 83 n. 22, 88, 91, 98–100, 108, 110–13, 116, 119, 121, 123, 126 n. 138, 149–53, 189 n. 61, 198, 199 n. 101, 216. *See also* Toqtaghu, Ṭūghtā', Ṭūqtā
Tora, 481
Torah, 303, 441
töre, 227
Torghuts, 364–65. *See also* Ṭūrghā'ūt
Tova Batïr, 457 n. 96
Tovlubii, 332
toy, 228. See also *ṭūy*
Töyäläth, 482
Tractatus de moribus condictionibus et nequicia Turcorum, 254
Trans-Volga Tatars, 348, 349 n. 72
Trifon Viatskii, 449
Trukhmen, 435 n. 40
Tsarevo, 438
Tū'ālās, 326
Tuḥfat al-albāb (al-Gharnāṭī), 76 n. 11
Tuḥfat at-tavārīkh-i khānī, 458 n. 99
Tughla, 283
Ṭughlū Bāy, 332
Tughluq Temür Khan (Chaghatayid), 101, 174, 520 n. 30
Ṭūghrīlchah, Ṭughrīljā, Ṭughrïljāy, Tūghrūl (father of Özbek Khan), 110 n. 97, 118–19, 151. *See also* Toghrulcha
Ṭūghtā', Ṭughṭāy Khān, 114 n. 104, 115. *See also* Toqtogha
tük ("body hair"), 157, 318, 324–25, 329–31, 372, 485 n. 172, 486, 489 n. 181, 543, 563
Tükäl (governor of Kāt and Khīva), 329 n. 22
Tūkālās, 326
Tükel, 329
Tükel Būqā, 108 n. 91, 329 n. 22
Tükel Qutlugh Senggün Bay, 329 n. 22
Tükel Tegin, 284
Tūkhāl Shaghālī Bī, 473, 476
Tükläs-baba, 468. *See also* Baba Tükles
Tukli-baba, 449. *See also* Baba Tükles
Tüklü ʿAzīz, 463–64, 466. *See also* Baba Tükles
Tükti Babay Äziz Shash, 461. *See also* Baba Tükles
Tula, 283
Tūlā Būqā, 110 n. 97
Tūlās, 326
Tūlāsh Bābā, 458. *See also* Baba Tükles
Tülük Temür, Amīr, 132, 329 n. 21
Ṭūlūm Khoja, 463, 465–66
Tulumbiy, 462 n. 107
Ṭunghūr, Ṭunghūz, Ṭayfūr, 118, 120 n. 125
Tungus, 45
Tūqtā, Ṭuqṭāy, 108, 110 n. 97, 118–20, 128–29, 193. *See also* Toqtogha
Tura, Ṭūrā, 194 n. 84, 345
Turakhan, 471 n. 142. *See also* Tīrah Khān
Tūrān, 114 n. 104
Turatav, 471
Ṭūrghā'ūt, 362. *See also* Torghut
Türk(s), 56, 169, 173 n. 17, 176, 181, 235, 275, 277, 284 n. 104, 300, 496–98, 500, 503, 504 n. 20, 524, 526–27
Turk b. Yāfīth, 25, 445
Turkistān, 102, 252, 365, 372, 375, 380, 440–41, 454, 459–60, 484–85
Turkmens, 363, 445, 458
Ṭūs, 499
Tuvans, 30, 552, 556
ṭūy, 108. See also *toy*
Tver', 93, 94 n. 56
T.w.k.l b. Mawlā Sayyid Aḥmad, 329

ʿUbaydullāh Khan, 395
Üch-Ütlük, 385
Ufa, 419, 469–72, 473 n. 145, 478, 481 n. 164
Ulū Khān Aṭā Bitigi, 279
Ulugh Beg, 101, 117
Ulugh Muḥammad Khan (Jöchid), 341, 413
Ulugh Tagh, 153, 193 n. 79
ulus-i ūzbakī, 346
ūlūs of Ṣāʾin Khān, 376
ulus of Shïban, 345
Ulutau, 193 n. 79. *See also* Ulugh Tagh
al-ʿUmarī, Ibn Faḍlullāh, 96 n. 57, 125
Umay, 47 n. 35
ʿUmdat al-akhbār, 145, 194 n. 84, 352, 356, 391
Ümer Batïr, 481
ummah, 23–24, 136, 247 n. 30, 288–89, 530
ünde-, "to summon," 22
United States, 21 n. 11
ʿUqba b. ʿĀmir, 245 n. 21
Uradach Biy, Uradas Biy, 478
Ural (mountains, river, region), 193, 194 n. 83, 196–97, 343, 402–3, 468, 480–81. *See also* Volga-Ural region, Yayïq
Ural Batïr, Ural-batyr, 468, 480–81
Urgench, 119, 120, 380, 385, 389, 391 n. 136, 400
urugh, 459
Urus b. Ismāʿīl (Manghït), 401–2
Urus Khan, 343–44, 384, 405 n. 167
Urusov (family), 398, 401–2, 404–6, 439 n. 54
Urusov, Andrei Satych, 402
"Uvaysī" Sufis, 25
Uyghur(s), 82, 83 n. 22, 88, 113, 152, 169, 172, 179, 275–76, 278 n. 88, 282, 283, 284 n. 104, 285–86, 314, 326, 330 n. 25, 336 n. 39, 463, 473, 496 n. 8, 497–98, 500–2, 504 n. 20, 506, 511–14
Uyghūrīyah, 112
Ūyshūn, 463
"Ūzbakistān," 201, 347
Uzbek(s), 6, 30, 68, 143–44, 227–28, 322, 345–46, 348, 363–66, 396, 411, 430, 435, 445, 448, 457–59, 466–67, 487
Uzbek confederation, 346
Uzbekov, Abdel'gali, 468
Ūzūn Ḥasan Ata, 101, 372, 376

Valikhanov, Chingis Chokanovich, 21 n. 11, 398, 417, 428, 430, 433
Vankhas, 177–78
Vaqqāṣ Bīy (Manghït), 345–46, 348–50, 390 n. 135, 394, 400
Varačan, 295
Vaṣṣāf, 106, 120 n. 124, 133, 264
Vazīr, 390–91, 486
Vedic religion, 38 n. 20
Venetian, Venice, 92, 96 n. 57, 195–96, 341
Vishtaspa, 168
Vitovt, 338
Vladimir, 169–70, 175 n. 23
Volga, 92, 130 n. 149, 140, 195, 252, 333–35, 342–43, 348, 351, 369, 392, 399, 441 n. 60, 449, 451, 452 n. 81, 453, 457 n. 96
Volga-Ural region, 8–9, 15, 45 n. 31, 72, 76–77, 197 n. 93, 327 n. 13, 328, 380, 384, 389
von Hammer-Purgstall, Joseph, 195, 197
Vorskla river, 338
Vourukasha, 495

wāʿiẓ, 131
Wall of Gog and Magog, 80, 287, 289
Wang-khan, 183 n. 44
Washington, 397, 402
al-Wāthiq (Caliph), 80
weather sorcery, 295
Western Türk, 258
William Adam, 96 n. 58, 140–42

Xinjiang, 7

yadachï, 175
Yādgār (Jöchid), 144 n. 170
Yādkār, 475–76
al-Yāfiʿī, 127 n. 141
yāğ, 208
Yājūj and Mājūj, 288. *See also* Gog and Magog
Yakuts, 211 n. 118, 457 n. 96
Yamgïrsï, 468
Yaʿqūb b. an-Nuʿmān, *qāḍī*, 76
yasa, yāsāq, 108, 143 n. 169, 151 n. 195, 226, 260, 448

Yasavī, Yasavīyah, 101, 138 n. 161, 145 n. 174, 147, 359–60, 374, 380, 438, 457, 460, 484–85, 520 n. 30, 531, 562
Yasavī, Khoja Aḥmad, 147 n. 180, 251, 372, 460, 471 n. 142, 484
Yayïq, 193, 194 n. 83, 196–97, 343, 399, 468, 482. *See also* Ural
Yaylaq, 88
Yaylaq Khatun, 88 n. 44
Yāyqū, 197
yayuchï, "birth spirit," 46
Yazdī, Sharaf ad-Dīn ʿAlī, 102 n. 75, 192, 336, 338, 344, 354 n. 80
Yazıcıoğlu ʿAlī, 251
Yedisan, 352, 448
Yedishkul, 352, 448
yeke qoruq, 183
Yerpolat jïraw, 419 n. 24, 432 n. 37
Yesem, 469
yiltavar, 75 n. 10
yoġ, yogh, 181 n. 40, 182
Yomut, 463
yosun, 108, 143 n. 169, 151 n. 194, 226, 260
ysyakh, 211 n. 118
Yüan-shih, 214–15, 217, 223, 256–58, 285
Yūghra, 126 n. 138
Yumnāq Mīrzā, 394 n. 144
Yurmatï, 472–73, 475–77, 498
Yūsuf (Manghït), 401, 404
Yūsuf Ṣūfī Qonghrat, 102 n. 75

Zai river, 473–74
zakāt, 207
Zangī Ata, 101–2, 104, 372, 375–76, 377 n. 122, 460, 485
zāwiyah, 131, 208, 421 n. 27
Zemarchus, 258
Zeus, 495
Zhanïsh and Bayïsh, 503 n. 17
Zhirmunskii, V. M., 415–18
Żiyāʾ al-qulūb, 175, 250
ziyārat, 477
Zoroaster, 168
Zoroastrian(ism), 28, 495
Zubdat al-āthār, 273 n. 79
Zubdat al-fikrah fī tārīkh al-hijrah (Rukn ad-Dīn Baybars al-Manṣūrī), 86, 88 n. 43, 112 n. 99